EXPLORING CIVICS
& ECONOMICS

Richard G. Boehm, Ph.D.

Gary E. Clayton, Ph.D.

Nafees M. Khan, Ph.D.

Peter Levine, Ph.D.

Emily M. Schell, Ed.D.

Mc
Graw
Hill

About the Cover

The U.S. Capitol Building in Washington, D.C., is the meeting place for members of the U.S. Senate and the U.S. House of Representatives.

This stamp commemorates the passage of the 19th Amendment which gave women the right to vote in the United States.

The Great Seal of the United States depicts an eagle clutching an olive branch in one talon and 13 arrows in the other. The motto "E pluribus unum," meaning "out of many, one," is written on a banner held in the eagle's beak. Thirteen stars above the eagle's head represent the 13 original states.

A gavel is used to get the attention of people in a court of law. Tapping a gavel is also a signal that the judge's decision is final.

The United States flag has 50 stars to represent the 50 states in the country. The 13 alternating red and white stripes represent the original 13 states which joined to form the union.

Containers in a shipyard await transport on a cargo ship.

mheducation.com/prek-12

Mc Graw Hill

Thurgood Marshall served as U.S. Supreme Court justice from 1967–1991. This photo was taken in 1957.

Copyright © 2024 McGraw Hill

Send all inquiries to:
McGraw Hill
8787 Orion Place
Columbus, OH 43240

ISBN: 978-0-07-902054-3
MHID: 0-07-902054-2

Printed in the United States of America.

1 2 3 4 5 6 7 8 9 LKV 28 27 26 25 24 23 22

Authors

Richard G. Boehm, Ph.D., is one of the original authors of the *Guidelines for Geographic Education*, in which the Five Themes of Geography were first articulated. Dr. Boehm has received many honors, including "Distinguished Geography Educator" by the National Geographic Society (1990), the "George J. Miller Award" from the National Council for Geographic Education (NCGE) for distinguished service to geographic education (1991), "Gilbert Grosvenor Honors" in geographic education from the American Association of Geographers (2002), and the NCGE's "Distinguished Mentor Award" (2010). In 2020 he was named a "Fellow" of the American Association of Geographers. He served as president of the NCGE and also received the NCGE's "Distinguished Teaching Achievement" award. Presently, Dr. Boehm holds the Jesse H. Jones Distinguished Chair in Geographic Education at Texas State University in San Marcos, Texas, where he serves as Director of The Gilbert M. Grosvenor Center for Geographic Education. His most current project includes the development of "Powerful Geography," a new method of teaching and learning that acknowledges the diverse classroom and how geography can prepare students to fulfill their career goals in life.

Gary E. Clayton, Ph.D., is Professor and Chair of the Economics and Finance Department at Northern Kentucky University. He received his Ph.D. in economics from the University of Utah and an honorary doctorate from the People's Friendship University of Russia in Moscow. Dr. Clayton has authored several best-selling textbooks and a number of articles, has appeared on numerous radio and television programs, and was a guest commentator for economic statistics on NPR's Marketplace. Dr. Clayton won the Freedoms Foundation Leavey Award for Excellence in Private Enterprise Education in 2000. Other awards include a national teaching award from the National Council on Economic Education (NCEE), NKU's 2005 Frank Sinton Milburn Outstanding Professor Award, and the Excellence in Financial Literacy Education Award from the National Institute for Financial Literacy® in 2009. Dr. Clayton has taught international business and economics to students in England, Austria, and Australia. In 2006 he helped organize a microloan development project in Uganda.

Nafees M. Khan, Ph.D., is Assistant Professor of Social Foundations at Clemson University. Nafees holds a Ph.D. in Educational Studies from Emory University and a B.A. in Sociology with a minor in History from Tufts University. His doctoral work was on how the history of slavery was presented in secondary U.S. and Brazilian history textbooks. He serves on the Operational Committee for the *Slave Voyages Consortium* (www.slavevoyages.org) and has led numerous presentations on this digital humanities resource at conferences and workshops for teachers around the country. In addition, he is on the planning and advisory committee of the African Diaspora Consortium (www.adcexchange.org), wherein he is one of the developers of a new Advanced Placement (AP) Seminar course with African Diaspora Content with the College Board. His current research interests incorporate the legacies of slavery as related to education and the experiences of Afro-Brazilians, African Americans, and other diaspora communities.

Peter Levine, Ph.D., is the Associate Dean of Academic Affairs and Lincoln Filene Professor of Citizenship & Public Affairs in Tufts University's Jonathan Tisch College of Civic Life. He is also a full professor of Political Science at Tufts. In the domain of civic education, Levine was a co-organizer and co-author of *The Civic Mission of Schools* (2003), *The College, Career & Citizenship Framework for State Social Studies Standards* (2013), and *The Educating for American Democracy Roadmap* (2021). He has published eleven books, including *What Should We Do? A Theory of Civic Life* (Oxford University Press, 2022). He formerly directed CIRCLE (The Center for Information & Research on Civic Learning & Engagement) and has served on the boards of such civic organizations as AmericaSpeaks, Street Law Inc., the Newspaper Association of America Foundation, the Campaign for the Civic Mission of Schools, Discovering Justice, the Charles F. Kettering Foundation, the American Bar Association Committee's for Public Education, and Everyday Democracy.

Emily M. Schell, Ed.D., is Executive Director of the California Global Education Project in the School of Leadership and Education Sciences at the University of San Diego. She received her Ed.D. in Education Leadership at the University of San Diego, M.S. in Journalism from Northwestern University, and B.A. in Diversified Liberal Arts at the University of San Diego. Emily was a teacher, district Social Studies Resource Teacher, and school principal in San Diego Unified, K-12 History-Social Science Coordinator at the San Diego County Office of Education, and liaison for the National Geographic Society Education Foundation. She was Teacher Education faculty at San Diego State University teaching Social Studies Methods for 20 years. She has authored numerous articles and two books, *Teaching Social Studies: A Literacy-based Approach* and *Social Studies Matters: Teaching and Learning with Authenticity.* She serves in statewide leadership roles to promote History-Social Science, Geography and Global Education, and Environmental Literacy in California schools. Her research and current work is based in professional learning for TK-12 teachers.

Contributing Author

Douglas Fisher, Ph.D., is Professor and Chair of Educational Leadership at San Diego State University and a leader at Health Sciences High & Middle College having been an early intervention teacher and elementary school educator. He is the recipient of an International Reading Association William S. Grey citation of merit, an Exemplary Leader award from the Conference on English Leadership of NCTE, as well as a Christa McAuliffe award for excellence in teacher education. He has published numerous articles on reading and literacy, differentiated instruction, and curriculum design as well as books, such as *The Distance Learning Playbook, PLC+: Better Decisions and Greater Impact by Design,* and *Visible Learning for Social Studies.*

Program Consultants

Timothy M. Dove, M.A.
Secondary Social Studies Educator
Founding staff member of Phoenix Middle School
Worthington, Ohio

Linda Keane, M.Ed.
Special Education Resource Teacher
Merrimack Middle School
Merrimack, New Hampshire

Nicole Law, Ph.D.
Professional Learning Author/Consultant
Culturally Responsive and Fortifying Practices
Corwin Professional Learning
Indianapolis, Indiana

Meena Srinivasan, MA, NBCT
Executive Director
Transformative Educational Leadership, (TEL)

Dinah Zike, M.Ed.
Creator of Foldables™
Dinah Zike Academy
Author, Speaker, Educator

Academic Consultants

Pedro Amaral, Ph.D.
Associate Professor of Economics
California State University
Fullerton, California

David Berger, Ph.D.
Ruth and I. Lewis Gordon Professor of Jewish History
Dean, Bernard Revel Graduate School
Yeshiva University
New York, New York

Kimberly P. Code, Ph.D.
Director, Institute for Talent Development and Gifted
  Studies
Northern Kentucky University
Highland Heights, Kentucky

Seife Dendir, Ph.D.
Professor of Economics
Radford University
Radford, Virginia

Jamie Wagner, Ph.D.
Assistant Professor of Economics, Director of UNO
  Center for Economic Education
University of Nebraska
Omaha, Nebraska

Table of Contents

TOPIC 2
The Constitution

TOPIC 3
The Legislative Branch

TOPIC 6
Citizenship

TOPIC 7
Civic Participation

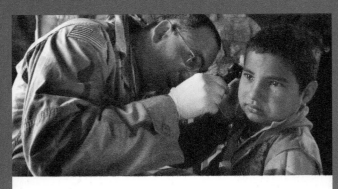

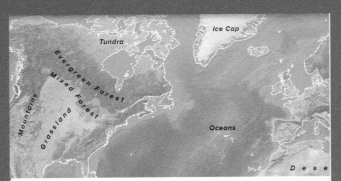

TOPIC 14
The Global Economy

Appendix

Primary and Secondary Sources

Analyzing Supreme Court Cases

Maps

Charts, Graphs, Diagrams, and Time Lines

Topic Activities

Writing an Argument

Writing an Argumentative Essay

Writing an Informative Essay

Writing an Informative Paragraph

Writing an Informative Report

Writing a Persuasive Argument

Scavenger Hunt

This book contains a wealth of information. The trick is to know where to look to access all the information.

ACTIVITY Complete this scavenger hunt exercise with your teachers or parents. You will see how the textbook is organized and how to get the most out of your reading and studying time. Let's get started!

1. How many lessons are in Topic 8?

2. What is the title of Topic 12?

3. How many Inquiry Activity Lessons are in Topic 2?

4. What is the Compelling Question for Topic 7, Lesson 5?

5. Which Supreme Court case is discussed in Topic 6, Lesson 4?

6. You want to quickly find a map in the book about the world. Where do you look?

7. In which two places can you find the contents and page numbers for a topic?

8. Where can you find information on what you will learn in a particular topic?

9. If you needed to know the definition for *civil liberty,* where would you look?

10. Where in the back of the book can you find page numbers for information about Gross Domestic Product?

PeopleImages/E+/Getty Images

This 1899 painting by Jean Leon Ferris shows the signing of the Mayflower Compact in 1620.

The Origins of American Government

Types of Governments

Various types of governments exist today. Many countries have been ruled under different forms of governments throughout history. Each country has their own way of choosing leaders, making laws, and engaging with their people. Ideas of government from Ancient Greece to the Enlightenment period influenced the development of the United States and continue to shape the views of Americans. The thirteen colonies, starting with the first representative government in Virginia, grew under various leaders and laws. Colonists would later declare their independence from Great Britain and establish their own representative government that is still in use to this day in the United States.

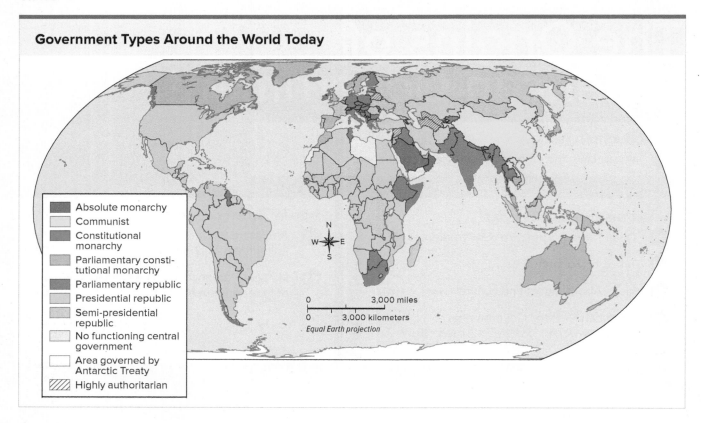

Government Types Around the World Today

Legend:
- Absolute monarchy
- Communist
- Constitutional monarchy
- Parliamentary constitutional monarchy
- Parliamentary republic
- Presidential republic
- Semi-presidential republic
- No functioning central government
- Area governed by Antarctic Treaty
- Highly authoritarian

0 — 3,000 miles
0 — 3,000 kilometers
Equal Earth projection

> 66 The Second Day of July 1776, will be the most memorable Epocha, in the History of America. I am apt to believe that it will be celebrated, by succeeding Generations, as the great anniversary Festival. . . . It ought to be solemnized with Pomp and Parade, with Shews, Games, Sports, Guns, Bells, Bonfires and Illuminations from one End of this Continent to the other from this Time forward forever more. 99

—letter from John Adams to Abigail Adams, July 3, 1776

TEXT: Adams, J., Letter from John Adams to Abigail Adams, 3 July 1776, Massachusetts Historical Society

Jamestown: The Statehouse

In 1619, the colony of Virginia established the House of Burgesses, one of the earliest representative assemblies in the colonies. The Burgesses met in Jamestown in a building named the Statehouse, which burned down and was rebuilt on three separate occasions. One fire is believed to have been an act of arson committed by a prisoner awaiting execution.

Laws of the First General Assembly of Virginia, August 1619

- No idleness, gaming, or excess of apparel.
- Every household must keep a year's supply of corn.
- Every man must plant 6 mulberry trees and 10 vines for a vineyard.
- Do not sell or give English dogs, including greyhounds, blood hounds, land or water spaniels, to the Native Americans.
- No one may travel more than 20 miles from home without informing the Governor.
- Every Sunday, all must attend religious services and sermons in the mornings and afternoons.

Source: Online Library of Liberty

Note: These are examples from the full set of laws.

» Tarring and feathering was a common way for colonists to show disapproval of the British monarchy. Pine tar from local shipyards would be poured on victims, who were usually Loyalists or tax collectors. Then feathers were dumped over them to humiliate the individuals.

Getting Ready to Learn About . . .
The Origins of American Government

Why Government Is Necessary

Societies need government to keep order so that people can live together peacefully. Governments make and enforce laws, which provide the rules of conduct for communities. Without laws, conflicts between people can lead to violence and disorder. People would feel unsafe and be unable to live productive, satisfying lives.

Governments can do more than just make and enforce laws. They can provide essential services, such as schools and fire protection. Governments may use their power to solve problems in the community, such as protecting people from unsafe products. They also manage the relationships with outside communities and countries. They sometimes work with other governments to promote trade and travel. Governments also create and maintain military forces to protect their people from attack by outsiders.

Government Before the Colonists

Before European colonists arrived in North America, Native Americans had already developed systems of government for their communities. In the area that eventually became the colony of New York, a group of Native American nations formed an alliance called the Iroquois League. It consisted of the Cayuga, Seneca, Onondaga, Mohawk, and Oneida Nations. These nations agreed to an unwritten constitution called the Great Law of Peace, which organized a government to keep relations peaceful between the different groups.

The Iroquois League created a Grand Council that was in charge of settling disputes among the member nations. Each nation was represented by men who were chosen as council members. No decisions could be made unless all members of the council agreed. This government worked to keep peace among its five nations for an extended period of time.

This image, created in 1724, shows a meeting of Iroquois leaders.

One of the main functions of the national government is to make laws for all Americans. Lawmakers meet here in the United States Capitol Building in Washington, D.C.

Early Government in the English Colonies

The first English colonists who landed on the shores of North America were starting new lives. Even though they were building new communities, they brought with them the traditions and beliefs that had shaped England's government. These early colonists believed strongly in their rights and the need for new governments.

The new colonial governments made decisions for the people who lived under their rule. Decisions reflected the values and beliefs of the people they governed. For example, the Massachusetts Bay Colony required its people to worship as the Puritans did or be forced to leave the colony. Other colonies, such as Rhode Island and Connecticut, offered more freedom and tolerance.

The governments of the colonies had one thing in common. They all provided men a voice in their government. For example, the colonists elected the men who served in the colonial legislatures. At that time, women were not elected. These legislatures made the laws. Although the governors of the colonies were appointed by the king, the colonists deeply valued the right to govern themselves.

Government Today

Today, government in the United States is far more complex than were the governments in the original colonies. For instance, the United States has elected governments at more than one level. At the highest level, our national government is led by elected leaders instead of appointed governors. The national government handles issues that affect everyone, such as national defense and rules of citizenship.

In addition, we now have state governments, which perform functions such as building roads and overseeing the educational system. State governments also have the power to set up local governments. Local governments manage services such as hiring firefighters and police officers and providing emergency medical services.

As in colonial times, these state and local officials are elected by the people. Much has changed since the colonists established governments in North America. However, one thing has stayed the same—the people's belief in the right to govern themselves.

Looking Ahead

You will learn about the Origins of American Government. You will examine Compelling Questions and develop your own questions about the Origins of American Government in the Inquiry Activities. You can preview some of the key concepts that you will learn about by reviewing the infographic.

What Will You Learn?

In these lessons about the Origins of American Government, you will learn:

- the purpose of government.
- the major types of government, including autocracy, democracy, monarchy, oligarchy, republic, and theocracy.
- the important documents, such as the Magna Carta and the English Bill of Rights, that influenced the development of American government.

- how the Enlightenment thinkers, including Montesquieu and John Locke, influenced the Founders.
- how early colonial governments developed.

 COMPELLING QUESTIONS IN THE INQUIRY ACTIVITY LESSONS

- **Why might Enlightenment ideas have been used as a foundation for democratic government?**
- **How did people view American independence differently?**

Some Functions of Government

Governments provide functions for the people they govern. These functions are too large or expensive for people to provide on their own. Below are five examples of government functions.

Protecting Society	Ensuring Order	Providing Services	Promoting Commerce	Making Laws
Armed forces protect the nation from outside threats.	Police keep residents in their communities safe.	Public schools provide a free education to every student.	Governments make agreements that encourage free and fair trade.	Governments make laws for how people interact with each other.

Origins and Purposes of Government

READING STRATEGY

Analyzing Key Ideas and Details As you read, use a graphic organizer like the one shown to take notes about the functions of government.

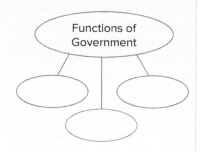

Functions of Government

GUIDING QUESTION

What is government, and what is its purpose?

Think about your classroom. There are certain rules you need to follow, such as staying in your seat and not talking when your teacher is speaking. Without rules like these, your classroom could become out of control. Similarly, if there were no government to make and enforce rules of conduct, or laws, people would live in disorder. Communities would experience confusion, violence, and fear. Government makes it possible for people to live together peacefully and productively.

The government manages the community. It makes sure that people follow the laws that are designed to help everyone live together. The government makes decisions on behalf of its people to make a community stronger.

Keep Order and Provide Security

People who live in a community will not always agree with one another. This often leads to conflicts. The government creates laws for people to follow so that conflicts are less likely to happen. Sometimes people will disagree so strongly with someone that an encounter could become physical. Laws help protect people's safety by making it a crime to attack another person. Other laws help protect personal property by making it a crime to steal things. Laws also protect people's right to speak out about things that are important to them.

Police officers help maintain order in many ways, such as being present at community events.

In addition to making the laws, governments have the power to enforce them. For example, if a driver breaks a traffic law, a police officer can issue that person a ticket. Governments also establish courts that decide whether people accused of crimes are guilty. Courts decide the punishment for someone found guilty. By making sure people follow the law, governments help to keep order.

People who live in a society want to feel secure. Governments help provide security by protecting people from attacks by other groups or countries. They do this by setting up armed forces to fight enemies that pose a threat. Without government, people would not have stability in their lives. An effective government allows citizens to get an education, raise a family, live orderly lives, and plan for the future.

Provide Services

Governments are responsible for providing services that people might not be able to get otherwise. Governments run public schools, libraries, and parks. They build and repair **infrastructure** such as roads, bridges, and railroad tracks. Governments collect people's garbage and deliver the mail. Private organizations also help with these types of services.

Governments work to keep the public safe and healthy. Local governments establish fire and police departments to protect public safety. They require vehicle inspections and issue drivers' licenses to ensure safety on the roads. Licenses are also required for workers, such as doctors and nurses, who do jobs that affect people's health and safety. Governments work to stop harmful products, food, and medicine from being sold.

If a disease threatens large numbers of people, the government could take steps to try to slow its spread. For example, during the COVID-19 pandemic, many governments required people to wear masks in indoor places. However, some governments, citing the personal freedoms of their citizens, banned orders to wear masks.

Governments also offer help when people are in need. They provide food, housing, and health care to people who struggle to make enough money. Those who are out of work can sometimes receive money from the government while they look for another job. Some governments are more

infrastructure the physical systems that allow a country, state, or region to function

Road maintenance is one of the services provided by local governments.
Drawing Conclusions How do people benefit when governments provide roads?

In 2018, the leaders of Mexico (left), the United States (center), and Canada (right) signed an agreement to promote trade among all three countries.

Inferring How does this scene indicate the importance with which these leaders viewed the trade agreement?

determined to economically help their citizens. Governments of countries with successful economies are often better able to provide aid to citizens. However, no country gives its citizens everything they need or want.

Guide the Community

Communities work to solve problems and make life better for their citizens. Government takes a leading role in making this happen by setting public policy. **Public policy** refers to the decisions and actions a government takes to solve problems in the community and guide it forward. Providing funds for building affordable housing in a community is an example of a public policy goal. Other examples of policy goals might include reducing hunger or helping small businesses succeed. Governments that pass and implement laws to reach their goals are making public policy.

Governments also guide the community by working with other governments or countries. For example, countries might work together to make agreements on how to trade with one another. Governments sometimes make agreements to help each other if one of them is attacked. They might also agree to reduce the number of weapons they have, which protects the people of all countries involved. Local governments might work with neighboring communities on a plan for how to improve traffic congestion.

✓ **CHECK FOR UNDERSTANDING**

1. **Explaining** What are the three basic functions of government?
2. **Understanding Supporting Details** Why does the government sometimes provide money to people who are out of work?

public policy the decisions and actions a government takes to solve problems in the community

The United States flag flies above the state flag of Florida atop the dome of Florida's capitol building in Tallahassee.

Nation, State, and Country

GUIDING QUESTION

What is the difference between a nation and a state or country?

People often use the words *nation* and *country* to mean the same thing, but there is a difference. A **nation** is a group of people who are united by their common bonds, such as race, language, customs, beliefs, or religion. A **country** is a political community that has a defined geographic area and an organized government. Some countries are also nations. Some groups that see themselves as nations do not have their own country. For example, the Kurds consider themselves a nation, but they do not have their own country. They are an ethnic group who share the same culture and language. The Kurds are mostly spread across five countries in the Middle East.

In the United States, people usually think of a state, such as Florida, as one of the fifty parts of the country. However, a **state** is also another word for a country. When speaking of a country, its government is sovereign, or independent. A sovereign country is free to make decisions about itself without approval from other countries.

The federal government is the highest level of government in the United States. It makes and enforces laws that affect everyone who lives inside its borders. State and local governments are not allowed to make laws that **violate**, or go against, the laws of the federal government. For example, in 2009, the federal government required businesses in every state to pay workers a minimum wage of at least $7.25 per hour. State and local governments have the option to require a higher minimum wage. California had one of the highest minimum wages of any state in the country in 2022 at $14.00 per hour for medium and large businesses.

In the United States, the level of government below the federal government is state government. Each of the 50 states has its own government. States set policy and write laws for matters that the national government is not responsible for. Examples include rules for education, marriage, and elections. States also have the power to set up local governments.

Local governments include county, city, and town governments. At this level, government has the most direct impact on people's lives. Local governments provide schools, police and fire departments, emergency medical services, libraries, and local courts. They are responsible for providing public services such as outdoor lighting, trash pickup, and snow removal. They must make sure their laws do not violate the laws of the state or the national government.

✓ CHECK FOR UNDERSTANDING

Explaining When is a nation not a country?

LESSON ACTIVITIES

1. **Informative/Explanatory Writing** In an essay, explain how the government impacts your community, state, or country. Explore how your life might be different if your community, state, or country did not have a government.

2. **Collaborating** Work with a partner to create a short graphic novel that shows how the government has an impact on your daily life. Include illustrations that show examples of how you interact with the government during your day.

nation a group of people united by common bonds of race, language, custom, or religion

country a political community with a defined geographic area and organized government

state another word for *country*, or a smaller political unit, such as the fifty states of the United States, that is part of a larger country

violate to go against

Types of Government

READING STRATEGY

Analyzing Key Ideas and Details As you read, use a graphic organizer like the one shown to take notes about the different systems of government.

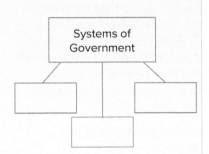

Systems of Government

Systems of Government

GUIDING QUESTION

What are the systems of government?

When a government forms, it must decide how to distribute power. Some governments allow citizens a great deal of power. Other governments keep most power among their leaders and allow their citizens to have very little.

Societies also must decide on how to distribute power within the government itself. They must decide how much power to allow the central, national government and how much power should be given to other, lower levels of government, such as state, county, and city governments. There are three main systems of government that distribute power in different ways: the unitary, confederal, and federal systems of government. Each form has advantages and disadvantages.

Unitary System

In a **unitary system** (YOO•nuh•tehr•ee SIS•tuhm) of government, the most important powers are held by the central government. This does not mean there is only one level of government. However, it does mean that state or local governments have only those powers that the central government gives them. In a unitary system, the central government may create smaller administrative units to carry out certain functions. However, the central government can dissolve those units or divide up their powers as it chooses. This can happen because the smaller units are not protected by a constitution.

A unitary government has certain advantages, but giving less power to lower levels of government can createa number of problems.

unitary system a government in which the most important powers are held by the central or national government

The Palace of Westminster is the meeting place of the United Kingdom's Parliament, its lawmaking body.

Inferring What does the grand style of architecture suggest about the role of this building in the United Kingdom's government?

This lack of power can make it difficult to serve the people. The central government may not understand the needs of residents in specific parts or regions of a country. Japan, France, and the United Kingdom have unitary governments.

Confederal System

A **confederal system** (kuhn•FED•uh•ruhl SIS•tuhm) is a loose union of sovereign, or independent, states. They form a central government to carry out certain limited functions, but the member states keep their power.

After independence from Great Britain, the United States adopted a confederal system under the Articles of Confederation, the nation's first constitution. Under the Articles of Confederation, the states held most of the power and the central government was weak. This caused a number of problems for the new nation. For example, the central government could not collect taxes, and each state was allowed to print its own money. The Articles' weaknesses led the

early leaders of the United States to create a new government under a different system that gave more power to the central government.

Today, few countries have a confederal system of government. One example is the Federated States of Micronesia in Asia. It has a very weak central government and four independent states. The states hold most of the power, especially over their own budgets.

Federal System

A **federal system** (FED•uh•ruhl SIS•tuhm) of government shares powers between national and state governments. Each level is free to make its own decisions in some areas. When the United States adopted the Constitution in place of the Articles of Confederation, it created a federal system of government. Many other nations operate under a federal system, such as Mexico, Germany, and Brazil.

The federal system of government has several advantages. It prevents the central

confederal system a loose union of independent and sovereign states that give only a few powers to a central government

federal system a government that shares powers between national and state governments

---

Power Sharing in Different Systems of Government

The three systems of government share power in different ways between the national government and other, lower levels of government within the country.

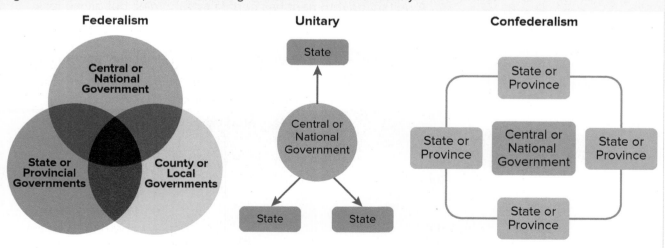

EXAMINE THE CHART

1. **Analyzing Visuals** What do federal, unitary, and confederal systems of government have in common?

2. **Identifying** In which system of government do the national and state governments share power?

government from becoming too powerful because different levels of government share power. Another advantage of federalism is that it allows state and local governments to meet the needs of their residents more easily. These needs may be different from the needs of people in other parts of the country. For example, people in a heavily populated area might expect their government to spend more money on public transportation, such as trains, buses, or subways. However, people in a lightly populated area might prefer that more money be spent on roads.

However, federalism does have some drawbacks. State and local governments can make many of their own laws, so what is legal in one place may be illegal in another place. This can lead to confusion.

The federal system in the United States allows each state to decide its own structure of government. Some state governments are unitary and make almost all important decisions for the entire state. In other states, power is shared with city, county, or other local governments. For example, Maryland gives its counties much more authority to make their own decisions than most states.

✓ CHECK FOR UNDERSTANDING

1. **Explaining** Why did the United States replace its confederal system of government in its early years?

2. **Understanding Supporting Details** What are some advantages of the federal system of government?

Constitutional Governments

GUIDING QUESTION

How is a constitutional government different from a country without a constitution?

A **constitution** (kahn•stuh•TOO•shuhn) is a plan that establishes the rules for government. A constitution presents the ideals or values that the people who live under the constitution believe in and share. It defines the basic structure of government and outlines its powers and duties. It serves as the supreme law for the country. Constitutions provide the rules that shape the

The Constitution of the United States was written in 1787 and is located at the National Archives in Washington, D.C.

actions of government, much as the rules of soccer define the action in a soccer match.

A constitution is not necessarily a written document. Some countries are ruled by unwritten constitutions, but most modern countries have written constitutions. The United States Constitution, which went into effect in 1789, is the oldest written constitution still serving a nation. Other nations with written constitutions include France, Kenya, India, and Italy. Great Britain, on the other hand, has an unwritten constitution which, unlike others, includes customs.

Constitutions place clear limits on the powers of those who govern. Leaders may want to take certain actions, but they will be unable to do so if the constitution says they are not allowed. A country that is ruled this way is called a **constitutional government** (kahn•stuh•TOO•shnuhl). Just because a country has a written constitution does not mean that it would be called a constitutional government. It must also actually follow that constitution.

---

constitution a plan that establishes the rules for government

constitutional government a government in which a constitution has authority to place clearly recognized limits on the powers of those who govern

Constitutions are important, but they cannot provide a complete guide to how a country is actually governed. For one thing, no written constitution can possibly spell out all the laws, customs, and ideas that the document has inspired. For example, until Franklin D. Roosevelt was elected president four times, all U.S. presidents had followed the custom of serving a maximum of two terms of office. The Constitution provided no limit on the number of terms that a president could serve. The Twenty-second Amendment was added to the Constitution to limit the president to two elected terms.

The United States Constitution can be printed in a dozen or fewer pages, but the federal laws in place today take up more than 2,000 pages of text. They deal with many topics that the authors of the Constitution could not even have imagined, such as nuclear power or the Internet.

Secondly, a constitution does not always reflect actual government practice. For example, the written constitution of the People's Republic of China discusses the basic rights, freedoms, and duties of citizens. Yet, the Chinese government does not uphold many of those rights and freedoms. The Chinese government has violated those rights by spying on its citizens. It sometimes punishes citizens whose ideas it finds unacceptable. The Chinese government blocks its citizens from using websites that are popular and available to people around the world. Twitter, Facebook, and YouTube are blocked, as are sites that report news or

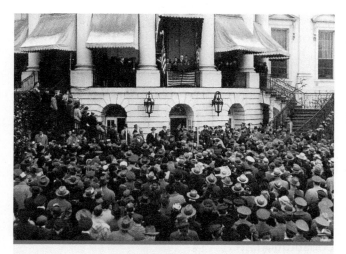

Franklin D. Roosevelt, shown here on the balcony at his last inauguration, was the only president to be elected to four terms of office.

information related to political activism. The government also prevents people from searching for politically sensitive terms and blocks embarrassing news stories.

✓ CHECK FOR UNDERSTANDING

Predicting How might citizens of a country respond to a decision to suspend, or discontinue use of, its constitution?

Major Types of Government

GUIDING QUESTION

What are the differences between authoritarian and democratic governments?

People have organized their governments in many different ways. In Saudi Arabia, the ruling royal family chooses the king and controls the government and its resources. In Sweden, the people elect the *Riksdag*, the national legislature, which selects the prime minister to carry out the laws. In the Netherlands, the government consists of a king or queen and a cabinet of ministers. The House of Representatives is elected by the people to make laws. The king or queen reviews new laws and helps select cabinet ministers.

Governments distribute power in different ways. The decisions about how to distribute power are guided by each society's **political philosophy**. A political philosophy involves ideas about how society should be governed and how people should act within that society.

Imagine a line with one end labeled "democratic" and the other labeled "authoritarian." Democratic governments give people economic, social, and political freedoms. Democracies rely on input from their citizens to govern. Authoritarian governments, at the opposite end of the range, control all aspects of citizens' economic, political, and social lives. All governments fall somewhere between those two forms.

Democratic Governments

The concept of democracy has been expanding and changing for more than 3,500 years. Some scholars believe that ancient indigenous societies practiced elements of democracy. Democracy as we recognize it began in the ancient Greek city

political philosophy the study of how to distribute or limit public power to maintain human survival and improve quality of life

Principles of American Democracy

The principles forming the foundation of American democracy reflect American values.

RULE OF LAW	All people, including those who govern, are bound by the law.
LIMITED GOVERNMENT	Government is not all-powerful. It may do only those things that the people have given it the power to do.
CONSENT OF THE GOVERNED	American citizens are the source of all government power.
INDIVIDUAL RIGHTS	In American democracy, individual rights are protected by government.
REPRESENTATIVE GOVERNMENT	People elect government leaders to make the laws and govern on their behalf.
FREE, FAIR, AND COMPETITIVE ELECTIONS	Every citizen's vote has equal value. They choose between candidates and parties. They vote by secret ballot free from government interference.
MAJORITY RULE	A majority of the members of a community has the power to make laws binding upon all the people.

EXAMINE THE CHART

1. **Explaining** In your own words, explain what is meant by "consent of the governed."
2. **Making Connections** How are the rule of law and limited government similar?

of Athens around 2,500 years ago. Athens had a direct, or pure, democracy. All male citizens 18 years or older met to discuss government matters and voted to decide what to do. Today, nations are too large for direct democracy to be practical. Instead, many countries choose to have a **representative democracy** (reh•pree•ZEHN•tuh•tihv dih•MAH•kruh•see). In this kind of democracy, citizens choose a group of people to represent them, make laws, and govern on their behalf. The United States is the world's oldest representative democracy.

One kind of representative democracy is a republic. Under **republicanism**, the head of the government or the head of state work for the people. In the United States and in many other republics, that leader is called the president.

When democracies work well, all people are bound by the rule of law. Under the rule of law, everyone must follow the same laws. Citizens understand what they can and cannot

do, and leaders cannot **arbitrarily** (ahr•buh•TREHR•uh•lee) tell people how to live.

Democracy works on the principle of majority rule. This means that a majority, or more than half, of the community has the power to make laws, often through elected officials, that everyone must follow. Citizens agree to follow the laws put in place by the majority, but members of the minority keep their basic rights as citizens. In a democracy, ruling majorities are determined through free and fair elections in which candidates from two or more political parties compete for the voters' approval.

Monarchies

In a **monarchy** (MAHN•uhr•kee), one person—a king, queen, or emperor—has great power. Monarchs inherit their power from the previous monarch, usually a family member. In ancient times, rulers were considered sacred, or approved by the gods of the society's religion.

representative democracy a government in which citizens choose a smaller group to govern on their behalf

republicanism commitment to a republican form of government in which citizens choose their lawmakers

arbitrarily randomly, unreasonably

monarchy form of government in which one person has great power

Later, some monarchs used force or fear tactics to maintain their power. In czarist Russia, for example, nobles or church leaders were unable to prevent the czar from increasing his powers. In some cases, a monarch's power became limited by tradition or law. In medieval France, a group of noble judges was supposed to review the king's laws to formally approve them.

Today, most European monarchies are constitutional monarchies, in which the monarch has a limited ceremonial role. The government is led by a prime minister, who is chosen by elected legislators. Some modern constitutional monarchies include the European countries of Sweden and the Netherlands, and Japan in Asia.

A few absolute monarchies still exist, although they are rare. In absolute monarchies, political parties are banned, and the monarch retains nearly all the power. Saudi Arabia has an absolute monarchy.

Authoritarian Governments

In **authoritarian regimes** (aw•THAHR•uh•TEHR•ee•uhn ray•ZHEEMZ), one person or group holds great power and is not accountable to the people. There are different kinds of authoritarian regimes.

Dictatorships In a **dictatorship** (dik•TAY•tuhr•ship), a leader or group of leaders exercises complete control over the state. Dictators often come to power by overthrowing an existing government and seizing power. Sometimes, when a serious situation demands a strong leader, government officials and even some citizens may welcome rule by a dictator.

Once in power, dictators rarely give it up. Most rely on the police and the military to stay in power. They often refuse to hold elections, but if they do, they usually take steps to make sure the outcome is the one they desire.

Dictatorships often turn into totalitarianism, in which the government controls almost all aspects of people's lives. Totalitarian leaders ban all efforts to oppose them and take away individual freedoms. They force people to follow their

ideology (EYE•dee•AH•luh•jee) by controlling the media and using scare tactics and violence. People can be jailed, or even killed, for criticizing the government or gathering in public places.

Three infamous totalitarian regimes arose in the 1920s and 1930s. They were Nazi Germany under Adolf Hitler, Fascist Italy under Benito Mussolini, and the Soviet Union under Joseph Stalin. Today, the nations of Cuba, North Korea, and Chinaa are thought to be totalitarian states.

Oligarchies and Theocracies Other forms of authoritarian governments include oligarchies and theocracies. In an **oligarchy**, (AH•luh•gahr•kee), a small group of people holds power. Such power is often based on wealth, and most oligarchies have been considered authoritarian. A **theocracy** (thee•AH•kruh•see) is a government ruled by religious leaders. In a theocracy, religious law is the basis of all of society's laws. Often, religious law is absolute and forced upon a nation's citizens.

ideology a strict idea about life and society

oligarchy a form of government in which a small group of people holds power

theocracy a form of government in which religious leaders rule the people

---

✓ **CHECK FOR UNDERSTANDING**

1. **Describing** Under the principle of majority rule, what is the agreement that the people make with one another?

2. **Understanding Supporting Details** What is one difference between authoritarian and democratic forms of government?

LESSON ACTIVITIES

1. **Argumentative Writing** Do you believe that democracy is the best form of government? Write an essay in which you clearly state your view and defend it with evidence.

2. **Identifying Arguments** Suppose you were forming a new country and had to decide whether to set up a unitary, confederal, or federal government. With two classmates, stage a debate in which each student argues in favor of one of the systems. Prepare for your debate by researching countries that have used or currently use these systems.

---

authoritarian regime form of government in which one leader or group holds great power and is not accountable to the people

dictatorship form of government in which a leader or group of leaders exercises complete control over the state

Ideas About Rights and Natural Law

Analyzing Key Ideas and Details As you read, make a chart about the documents, laws or acts, and people who influenced the development of democracy in the United States.

Influence	Description

The Foundations of Democracy

GUIDING QUESTION

What ancient principles, traditions, and events have shaped the system of government we have today?

The rights, freedoms, and form of government that Americans enjoy did not begin with the adoption of the Constitution in 1788. Nor did they begin with our Declaration of Independence from Great Britain in 1776. In fact, the origins of the American political system can be traced to ancient times.

The growth of **democracy**, or rule by the people, has not occurred at a steady pace over those thousands of years. There have been long periods of time when little democracy existed. During some of these periods, people were governed by monarchs. At other times, however, the ideas and practices of democracy have developed, spread, and grown strong.

Early Democracies

One of the earliest foundations for democracy can be found in the Jewish religion. Since ancient times, Judaism has taught (and teaches today) that every person has worth and that the law treats every man equally. This belief is a basic principle of democracy.

democracy a government in which citizens hold the power to rule

In this scene painted in the mid-1800s, a leader of Athens gives a speech celebrating the city's democracy.

In this modern painting of a scene in the Roman Senate, the government official Cicero (standing, left) accuses Catiline (extreme right) of being a traitor.

Speculating Why do you think the artist showed all the other senators on one side of the room and Catiline on the other?

Centuries later, in the 400s B.C.E., the Greek city-state, or *polis* (PAH•luhs), of Athens created the world's first democracy. All free men older than 18 were considered citizens. They could take part in the Athens assembly and vote on issues. This system, in which the people govern themselves, is called **direct democracy**.

A council of 500 members governed Athens and carried out the decisions of the assembly. Citizens took turns serving on the council. Since this required taking time off from work, council members were paid for their service.

The political system was later described by the philosopher Aristotle or one of his students in a text called the Constitution of Athens. Direct democracy was possible in Athens because the city-state was small. In places with large populations, direct democracy is not practical and can make getting things done difficult. In such places, people choose leaders to govern for them and make decisions on their behalf. This form of democracy is called representative democracy. A government based on representative democracy is called a **republic**. The United States is a republic.

The ancient Romans invented the word *republic* to refer to a government they formed. The word *republic* means that a society belongs to the whole public, not to a king or any other individual or small group. In 509 B.C.E. the Romans overthrew their king. Government was put in the hands of a senate. Members of this body were chosen from among Rome's wealthy upper class, called *patricians*. The senators elected two members, called *consuls*, to lead the government. Both consuls had to agree on government decisions. Each consul had the power to block the actions of the other by saying *veto*, meaning "I forbid!" Power was divided between the senate and consuls so that no one person or group had too much. This idea is called the separation of powers.

Rome's common citizens, called *plebeians*, soon grew tired of the rule of the patricians. A long struggle followed. The plebeians finally gained political power in 287 B.C.E.

The Roman Republic created a set of laws called the Twelve Tables in 451 B.C.E. They were a collection of written laws that were displayed in a public place. Plebeians could read the laws and protect themselves against the abuse of power by patricians.

In both Rome and Greece, male citizens had the ability to participate in civic life. Any man who was not enslaved could vote and speak out on issues affecting the community. Greek and Roman men also served for a time in the armies that defended the state. Generally, women were not allowed to take part in civic or military life.

Another example of a democracy existed in North America before the arrival of Europeans. Five Native American nations in the area that includes present-day New York formed the Iroquois Confederacy in the 1100s. After years of conflict, the groups banded together under a document called the Great Law of Peace. It included concepts that are similar to those found

---

direct democracy a form of government in which the people vote firsthand

republic a representative democracy in which citizens choose their lawmakers

later in the Constitution of the United States. For example, the Great Law of Peace explains how to make laws and who has the power to declare war.

Early Systems of Law

Law is the set of rules and standards by which a society governs itself. In democratic societies, law resolves conflict between and among individuals and groups and protects individuals against government power. It defines criminal acts and determines the punishments for them.

One of the earliest known sets of written laws are called the Laws of Hammurabi. These laws were collected by Hammurabi, king of the Babylonian Empire from 1792 to 1750 B.C.E. This set of laws put crimes in categories and provided 282 examples and their punishments. Today we would say these categories were criminal law, property law, and family law, to name a few examples.

The Ten Commandments were a source of law for the ancient Israelites. According to the Hebrew Bible, Moses received these commandments from

---

law the set of rules and standards by which a society governs itself

God on Mount Sinai. They are about individual responsibility and responsibility to the community. They are an important influence on lawmaking. These ideals have been adopted in the United States and much of the world.

Roman law is another early source of law. As the Roman Empire spread, laws were often added to the Twelve Tables. As a result, the body of law became very complex and difficult to follow. Emperor Justinian had scholars simplify and organize the laws. They became the Justinian Code, a final Roman legal code that was completed in 534 C.E.

Early English Influences

After the collapse of the Roman Empire around 476 C.E., kings and nobles ruled most of Europe for hundreds of years. Eventually the kings gained greater control of their kingdoms. Many nobles resisted this change. In England they rose up against King John in 1215. They forced him to sign a document called the Magna Carta (Latin for "Great Charter").

The Magna Carta limited the king's power. It forbade him from placing certain taxes on the nobles without their consent. It gave rights to free men, such as the rights to equal treatment under the law and to trial by one's peers.

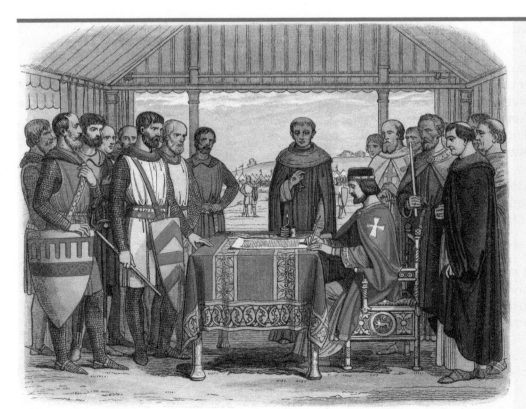

An artist from the 1800s made this illustration of King John, surrounded by rebellious nobles and other officials, signing the Magna Carta in 1215 C.E.

Analyzing Why do you think the artist shows all of the nobles facing the king instead of standing behind him?

The Magna Carta reestablished the principle of limited government. This is the idea that a ruler or a government is not all-powerful. At first, the Magna Carta protected only the rights of nobles. Over time, however, those rights came to apply to all English people.

Later kings sought advice from nobles and church officials. Gradually this group grew to include representatives of the common people as well. By the late 1300s, the advisers had become a **legislature**, or lawmaking body, called Parliament.

In the mid-1600s, a power struggle developed between England's monarch and Parliament. In 1625 King Charles I dismissed Parliament and ruled alone. When he recalled the members in 1628, they forced him to sign the Petition of Right. This document limited the king's power, further supporting the principle of limited government set out in the Magna Carta. When Charles failed to uphold the terms of the agreement, a civil war broke out. Eventually, Parliament removed the king and ruled without a monarch for about 20 years.

The English people were required to support the Church of England. That changed in 1689, when the Toleration Act allowed most Protestants to practice their own form of religion. Catholicism and certain forms of Protestantism were still outlawed, but the idea of religious toleration and liberty was beginning to spread. The idea of religious liberty would become very significant in the English colonies and later in the United States.

The English system of common law also became a major influence on our modern system of laws. It developed over centuries and expanded as judges resolved individual cases. The decisions made by these judges set **precedent**, which is a ruling that is used as the basis for a decision in a later, similar case. These rulings became part of the country's laws. Centuries of these court decisions, customs, and parliamentary laws have become known as England's unwritten constitution.

The English Bill of Rights

In 1688 Parliament forced King James II, the son of Charles I, from the throne. It asked James's daughter Mary and her husband, William, to rule instead. This transfer of power is known as the Glorious Revolution.

legislature a group of people that makes laws
precedent a judge's ruling that is used as the basis for a judicial decision in a later, similar case

But first William and Mary had to agree to new rules set by Parliament. They agreed that English citizens had rights that no king could violate. Citizens had the right to a fair trial. Monarchs could not levy taxes or suspend laws without Parliament's approval. The rights set out by Parliament became known as the English Bill of Rights.

The signing of the English Bill of Rights signaled the end of the struggle between Parliament and the monarch. Parliament had won. It was now the leading force in English government. These events weakened the monarchy—and received much notice in the English colonies in North America.

✓ CHECK FOR UNDERSTANDING

1. **Contrasting** Why did the people of Rome establish a republic instead of a direct democracy like the Athenians?

2. **Identifying Cause and Effect** What was the long-term effect of the signing of the Magna Carta?

When William III and Mary II signed the English Bill of Rights, shown in this illustration, England became a constitutional monarchy.

FALKENSTEINFOTO/Alamy Stock Photo

Enlightenment Thinkers

Although Enlightenment thinkers had different ideas about how people should be governed, they also shared some basic beliefs.

NAME	YEARS LIVED	BELIEFS
Thomas Hobbes	1588–1679	People agree to be ruled because their ruler pledges to protect their rights.
John Locke	1632–1704	People have rights to life, liberty, and property that the government must protect for the common good.
Baron de Montesquieu	1689–1755	Separate the parts of government so no one part can become too powerful.
Voltaire	1694–1778	People have the right to speak freely, and this right should be defended by everyone.
Jean-Jacques Rousseau	1712–1778	The legislative power belongs to the people.

HISTORY CONNECTION

1. **Making Connections** What did the Enlightenment thinkers believe the relationship between the government and the people should be?
2. **Identifying** Which thinker believed separating powers would prevent one part of government from growing too powerful?

Influence of the Enlightenment

GUIDING QUESTION

How did Europe's Enlightenment influence ideas about government in what became the United States?

The conflict between England's monarch and Parliament produced new ideas about government. These new ideas were part of a larger cultural movement in Europe known as the Enlightenment.

During the 1600s, scientific discoveries reinforced a belief that God had created a universe that ran according to regular laws of nature. Some people thought that its laws could be discovered through human reason.

These thinkers wanted to apply the laws that ruled nature to people and society. These new ideas had a great effect on political thinking in Europe and the Americas.

Enlightenment thinker Thomas Hobbes (1588–1679) argued that people create a society by entering into a **social contract**. This is an agreement between the people and their government. He wrote that people need government to resolve conflicts. They give up their control over their own lives to the government. In exchange, the government provides peace and order. Hobbes thought that people needed a strong leader because they were too selfish to be able to rule themselves.

John Locke (1632–1704), another English thinker, was influenced by the events of the Glorious Revolution. He reasoned that people have **natural rights** simply because they are human beings. These rights include the right to life, liberty, and property. Locke said people make a contract among themselves to create a government that protects their natural rights.

social contract an agreement among people in a society with their government

natural rights freedoms people have because they are human beings, including the rights to life, liberty, and property

Jean-Jacques Rousseau was a Swiss-born thinker who produced many of his writings while living in France.

freedom of speech and religion, came from people living together in a community. By working cooperatively, people created a social contract that allowed them to preserve their rights while at the same time creating law and government.

The French thinker Baron de Montesquieu (1689–1755) supported the idea that the power of government should be divided into branches, or different parts with different responsibilities. Montesquieu believed that dividing powers among branches would stop any one of them from becoming too strong and threatening people's rights. Montesquieu called this idea the separation of powers.

Educated colonists in America were familiar with the ideas of Hobbes, Locke, and other Enlightenment thinkers. The Declaration of Independence and the Constitution reflected these ideas.

✓ **CHECK FOR UNDERSTANDING**

1. **Determining Central Ideas** Why did Enlightenment thinkers believe that people would be willing to give up some rights?

2. **Predicting** What did Montesquieu think might happen if power is concentrated in one branch of government?

LESSON ACTIVITIES

1. **Informative/Explanatory Writing** Write a paragraph explaining how the idea of limited government developed over time from the Magna Carta to the English Bill of Rights.

2. **Identifying Arguments** In small groups, hold a roundtable discussion in which each of your classmates plays the role of one of the Enlightenment thinkers. Each thinker should discuss his beliefs. Record the roundtable as a podcast.

He argued a government that does not protect these rights has broken the social contract. In that case, the people should be able to choose new leaders. For Locke, a government was acceptable only if the people agreed to be governed by it.

French writer Francois-Marie Arouet (1694–1778), who wrote under the name Voltaire, also believed people should have liberty. He supported freedom of religion and freedom of trade.

Jean-Jacques Rousseau (1712–1778) believed that property rights and other basic rights, such as

05

Analyzing Sources: The Influence of Enlightenment Thinkers

? COMPELLING QUESTION

Why might Enlightenment ideas have been used as a foundation for democratic government?

Plan Your Inquiry

DEVELOPING QUESTIONS

Democratic government is based on such ideas as the rule of law, the consent of the governed, and individual rights. The rule of law means that all people, including those who govern, must follow the law. Consent of the governed means that the citizens are the source of government power. Individual rights are basic rights that all citizens have. Thinkers in the 1600s and 1700s wrote much about these ideas. American leaders in the North American colonies read their works and thought deeply about them. Think about what you know about American democracy. Then read the Compelling Question for this lesson. What questions can you ask to help you answer this Compelling Question? Create a graphic organizer like the one below. Write these Supporting Questions in your graphic organizer.

Supporting Questions	Primary Source	What the source tells me about the influence of Enlightenment principles on democratic government	Questions the source leaves unanswered
	A		
	B		
	C		

ANALYZING SOURCES

Next, examine the sources in this lesson. Analyze each source by answering the questions that follow it. How does each source help you answer each Supporting Question you created? What questions do you still have? Write these in your graphic organizer.

After you analyze the sources, you will:
- use the evidence from the sources,
- communicate your conclusions,
- and take informed action.

Background Information

In the 1600s, European thinkers began to focus on reason to consider solutions to problems they saw in society. This period, which lasted into the late 1700s, became known as the Enlightenment.

Many Enlightenment thinkers developed ideas about how countries should be governed. Three of these thinkers were John Locke, Baron de Montesquieu, and Jean-Jacques Rousseau. Their ideas influenced Europeans, as well as English colonists in North America. Enlightenment ideas were essential to the Declaration of Independence and the U.S. Constitution, two of the founding documents of the United States.

In this lesson, you will examine primary source excerpts from three Enlightenment thinkers. You will also learn about the role of Enlightenment ideas in the design of U.S. democracy.

American colonists who sought independence from British rule drew on Enlightenment ideas about the role of government and individual rights when writing the Declaration of Independence.

Locke on Natural Rights

In 1688, the bloodless Glorious Revolution replaced one English monarch, James II, with two others, William and Mary. To take the throne, William and Mary had to accept the English Bill of Rights. That document specified rules that protected individual liberties and recognized the power of Parliament. John Locke wrote his *Two Treatises on Civil Government*, in part, to defend this change in government. His argument centered on the idea that people consent, or agree, to be governed. In exchange, governments make laws to protect citizens' natural rights. Locke did not include people of African descent as free and even helped to write the constitution of the colony of Carolina, which legalized slavery.

PRIMARY SOURCE: BOOK

❝ The state of nature has a law of Nature to govern it. ... that being all equal and independent, no one ought to harm another in his life, health, liberty, or possessions. ❞

— John Locke, *Second Treatise on Civil Government,* Chapter 2, Section 6, 1689

❝ Men being, as has been said, by nature, all free, equal, and independent, no one can be put out of this **estate**, and subjected [exposed] to the political power of another, without his own consent. ❞

— John Locke, *Second Treatise on Civil Government*, Chapter 8, Section 119, 1689

❝ The end [purpose] of law is not to **abolish** or restrain, but to preserve and enlarge freedom: for in all the states of created beings capable of laws, where there is no law there is no freedom. ❞

— John Locke, *Second Treatise on Civil Government*, Chapter 6, Section 57, 1689

estate condition or state of being

abolish to get rid of

EXAMINE THE SOURCE

1. **Explaining** How does Locke describe the "state of nature" in the first excerpt?
2. **Inferring** If people must consent in order to be governed, as Locke says in the second passage, what does that suggest about the power of government?
3. **Analyzing Perspectives** According to the third excerpt, why do people agree to be ruled?

Montesquieu on the Separation of Powers

French writer Baron de Montesquieu wrote his book, *The Spirit of the Laws*, in the 1730s and 1740s. Montesquieu used the term "separation of powers" to refer to the idea that government power should be divided among different branches. He argued against having too much power in one branch. He felt this would prevent abuse of power.

PRIMARY SOURCE: BOOK

  " When the **legislative** and **executive** powers are united in the same person, or in the same body of **magistrates**, there can be no liberty; because apprehensions [fears] may arise, lest the same monarch or senate should enact tyrannical [oppressive] laws, to execute them in a tyrannical manner.

Again, there is no liberty if the **judiciary** power be not separated from the legislative and executive. Were it joined with the legislative, the life and liberty of the subject would be exposed to arbitrary [random] control; for the judge would be then the legislator. Were it joined to the executive power, the judge might behave with violence and **oppression**.

There would be an end of every thing, were the same man, or the same body, whether of the nobles or of the people, to exercise those three powers, that of enacting laws, that of executing the public **resolutions**, and of trying the causes of individuals. "

— Baron de Montesquieu, *The Spirit of the Laws,* Book XI, Ch. VI, 1748

legislative relating to the making of laws

executive relating to the carrying out or enforcing of laws

magistrate a public official charged with upholding laws

judiciary the branch of government that decides questions of the law

oppression the unjust or cruel use of power

resolution will or intent

EXAMINE THE SOURCE

1. **Identifying** What does Montesquieu say will likely happen if one person or body holds the combined powers of making, enforcing, and deciding questions of the law?

2. **Making Connections** How does the principle of separation of powers support Locke's ideas of how government can protect natural rights?

3. **Predicting** Think of the United States' government. What might happen if Congress not only made laws but also had judicial power to decide if they were legal?

PHOTO: Paris Musées / Musée Carnavalet. TEXT: de Secondat de Montesquieu, Baron Charles-Louis, The Spirit of Laws. Edited by Thomas Nugent. Vol. 1. New York, NY: The Colonial Press, 1899.

Rousseau on the Social Contract

In *The Social Contract*, French philosopher Jean-Jacques Rousseau wrote that when people form a society, they give up some of their freedoms in exchange for a government that will protect their rights. Rousseau called this agreement a social contract. He defined two kinds of liberty. Natural liberty is the freedom someone has in nature. Civil liberty is the rights protected in a society by law.

PRIMARY SOURCE: BOOK

> The passage from the state of nature to the civil state produces a very remarkable change in man. . . . Then only, when the voice of duty takes the place of physical impulses [whims]. . . does man. . . find that he is forced to act on different principles [rules], and to consult his reason [intelligence] before listening to his inclinations [feelings or desires]. . . .
>
> What man loses by the social contract is his natural liberty and an unlimited right to everything he tries to get and succeeds in getting; what he gains is civil liberty and the proprietorship [ownership] of all he possesses. . . .
>
> We might. . . add, . . . what man acquires in the civil state, moral [righteous] liberty, which alone makes him truly master of himself; . . . obedience to a law which we prescribe [impose on] to ourselves is liberty.

— Jean-Jacques Rousseau, *Of the Social Contract, Or Principles of Political Right,* I, Ch. 8, 1762

EXAMINE THE SOURCE

1. **Summarizing** According to Rousseau, what are the advantages and disadvantages for an individual in a society that follows the rule of law?
2. **Contrasting** According to Rousseau, how does civil liberty differ from natural liberty?
3. **Speculating** How do laws protect a right or freedom that you have, and what might happen to your freedom without those laws?

Complete Your Inquiry

EVALUATE SOURCES AND USE EVIDENCE

Refer back to the Compelling Question and the Supporting Questions you developed at the beginning of the lesson.

1. **Drawing Conclusions** How does Rousseau's social contract relate to Locke's ideas about natural rights and consent of the governed?
2. **Making Connections** Think about a situation in which you agree to join a group or a team to accomplish something. What might you gain and lose from joining the group?
3. **Gathering Sources** Which sources helped you answer the Supporting Questions and the Compelling Question? Which sources, if any, challenged what you thought you knew when you first created your Supporting Questions? What information do you still need in order to answer your questions? What other viewpoints would you like to investigate? Where would you find that information?
4. **Evaluating Sources** Identify the sources that helped answer your Supporting Questions. How reliable are those sources? How would you verify their reliability?

COMMUNICATE CONCLUSIONS

5. **Collaborating** In a small group, write "Enlightenment ideas" on a piece of paper. Each student should write two details he or she learned from the sources in a web around that phrase. Use those details to write a group response to the Compelling Question. Then, share your web and your response with the class.

TAKE INFORMED ACTION

Creating Social Media Pages for Enlightenment Thinkers Working in groups of three, use online or print sources to learn more about the views Locke, Montesquieu, and Rousseau had about government. With each member of your group writing for one of the thinkers, create profiles for a social media site on paper or poster board. Write a post on your thinker's page explaining his beliefs on government. Then leave thoughtful responses to posts on the other thinkers' pages. Use your research to respond as your thinker might have responded. Present your pages to the class.

Rousseau, J-J., "The Social Contract and Discources" E. P. Dutton & Co, New York, 1920

American Colonial Governments

READING STRATEGY

Analyzing Key Ideas and Details As you read, complete the graphic organizer with details about the first colonial governments.

First Colonial Governments	
Jamestown	Plymouth

The First Colonial Governments

GUIDING QUESTION

How were the first English colonies in America shaped by earlier ideas about democracy and government?

England founded colonies in North America throughout the 1600s. A colony is an area of settlement in one place that is controlled by a country in another place. Most of the early colonists came from England and brought to America the traditions, beliefs, and structures that had shaped England's government. These included a strong belief in their rights and representative government.

Jamestown

The first permanent English settlement in North America was Jamestown. It was located in what is now Virginia on land where Native Americans had been living for thousands of years. Jamestown was founded in 1607 by the Virginia Company. The Virginia Company was a business owned by a group of London merchants. The company provided the supplies and settlers for the colony. The owners hoped the colony would make money for the company.

At first, the Virginia Company appointed a governor and a council to govern Jamestown. In 1619, the company realized it needed to attract more settlers. It decided to allow the colony to make its own laws. The colonists living in Jamestown elected leaders to represent them in an assembly, or a group of people who make decisions.

The first lasting English settlement in what is now the United States was established at Jamestown.

Analyzing Visuals What natural features might have given advantages to the settlement at Jamestown?

These leaders were called burgesses. The assembly was named the House of Burgesses. This legislature marked the beginning of self-government and representative democracy in colonial America. That same year, 20 or more enslaved Africans were brought to Jamestown against their will and sold to wealthy English planters. This was the beginning of more than 200 years of slavery in the colonies and the United States.

The Mayflower Compact

In 1620, another group of English colonists set sail for Virginia. They were seeking religious freedom and called themselves Pilgrims. A storm in the Atlantic blew the Pilgrims' small ship, the *Mayflower*, off course. They anchored off the coast of what is now Massachusetts.

The Pilgrims knew they had reached a land that had no English government. They understood that to survive they needed to form their own government, so they drew up a compact, or written agreement. All the Pilgrim men aboard the ship signed. They agreed to choose leaders and work together to make their own laws for the colony. They also agreed to obey the laws that were made:

> 66 [We] combine ourselves together into a Civil Body Politic, . . . to enact, constitute, and frame such just and equal laws . . . unto which we promise all due Submission and Obedience. 99
>
> —The Mayflower Compact, 1620

The signers of the Mayflower Compact **established**, or founded, a direct democracy in colonial America. The people of Plymouth held town meetings to discuss problems and make decisions. Anyone in the town could attend and express his or her views. However, only some male members of the colony could vote. The tradition of the town meeting continues in much of New England today.

✓ **CHECK FOR UNDERSTANDING**

Making Connections Why was the Jamestown colony a representative democracy?

establish to found; to start something

In a modern town meeting, such as this one, citizens gather to discuss important issues.

This reconstruction of the Plymouth Colony shows what the settlement might have looked like for the early Pilgrim settlers.

Making Generalizations How might the layout of this settlement benefit the settlers?

Settling the English Colonies

GUIDING QUESTION

Why did people settle in England's colonies in America?

Where did the colonists who settled in England's American colonies come from? Most were from England. Others came from Scotland, Ireland, and Wales. Settlers also arrived from other parts of Europe, such as Germany. Over time, many thousands of enslaved Africans were brought to the colonies against their will. They were forced to work without pay in the fields, shops, and homes of the European settlers.

Settlers from other countries also founded colonies along the Atlantic Coast. The Dutch founded New Amsterdam. England later took it over and renamed it New York. Sweden founded a colony that became part of the English colonies of Delaware and New Jersey.

Economic Opportunity

People came to America for several reasons. For many settlers, the chance to earn a living was the main one. America offered land for farming and other jobs too.

Those too poor to pay for their trip to America came as **indentured servants**. These workers agreed to work for American colonists in exchange for paid passage to America and food and shelter. The servants worked from four to seven years, until their debt was paid. Then the workers were free to make better lives for themselves.

Religious Freedom

Other people wanted religious freedom. At this time, there was religious unrest in Europe, especially in England. Some groups were treated harshly by the government because of their religious beliefs. To find a place where they could worship in their own way, some people from these groups decided to come to the English colonies.

The Puritans founded Massachusetts for this reason. They were religious **dissenters** because they opposed official or commonly held views. The Puritans wanted to purify, or reform, the church in England. Some Puritans sought to leave the church altogether. They were called the Pilgrims. It was a group of Pilgrims who founded Plymouth Colony in 1620. Another group of Puritans started the much larger Massachusetts Bay Colony nearby.

Although they wanted religious freedom for themselves, the Puritans did not support religious freedom for others. Those who did not worship as the Puritans did were forced to leave the colony. Some Massachusetts settlers left to establish the colonies of Rhode Island and Connecticut. Rhode Island became known for the religious freedom its colonists enjoyed. Connecticut developed America's first written constitution in 1639. It was called the Fundamental Orders of Connecticut. This document gave the people the right to elect a governor, judges, and representatives to make laws.

Other colonies were more accepting of religious freedom. In Maryland, the Toleration Act allowed most Christians to practice their religion as they liked.

✓   **CHECK FOR UNDERSTANDING**

Analyzing How did the Puritans view religious freedom?

---

indentured servant a worker who contracted with American colonists for paid passage, food, and shelter in return for labor

dissenter a person who opposes official or commonly held views

Colonial Life

GUIDING QUESTION

How was life in the colonies shaped by where people lived?

The colonists came to America from many places and for a variety of reasons. They lived in different ways depending on where they settled. By 1733 Great Britain had thirteen colonies along the Atlantic Coast of North America. For each colony, the features of its geography influenced its **economy**, or the way people used and distributed scarce resources to meet people's needs and wants. These factors shaped how people lived. Over time, three economic regions developed. Each had its own way of life.

The New England Colonies

The New England Colonies were located farthest north. They were Massachusetts Bay, New Hampshire, Connecticut, and Rhode Island. Most people in this region lived in towns. The cold climate and rocky soil made large-scale farming difficult. Most farms were small and located near towns.

Many colonists in New England were Puritans. The Puritan religion stressed the values of thrift and hard work. Some New Englanders worked as shopkeepers or in other small businesses. Others were employed in shipbuilding or fishing. Some colonists worked in the fur trade by trapping fur-bearing animals or by trading for them with Native Americans. They shipped the furs to Europe, where they were made into coats and hats.

The Middle Colonies

New York, Pennsylvania, New Jersey, and Delaware were English colonies located south of New England. These colonies were known as the Middle Colonies. The climate and soil were better for agriculture, so farmers raised wheat and other cash crops. **Cash crops** are grown in large quantities to be sold rather than to feed the farmer's family. Farmers often sent cash crops overseas for sale. This trade helped turn New York City and Philadelphia into busy ports.

The Middle Colonies were also rich in natural resources. Sawmills, mines, ironworks, and other businesses grew in the region. The colonists here depended upon resources such as lumber, metals, and natural harbors.

The Southern Colonies

The English colonies farthest south along the Atlantic Coast were Maryland, Virginia, North Carolina, South Carolina, and Georgia. A warm climate, a long growing season, and rich soil

economy system for making choices about how to use scarce resources and distribute them to meet people's needs and wants

cash crop a crop produced mainly for sale

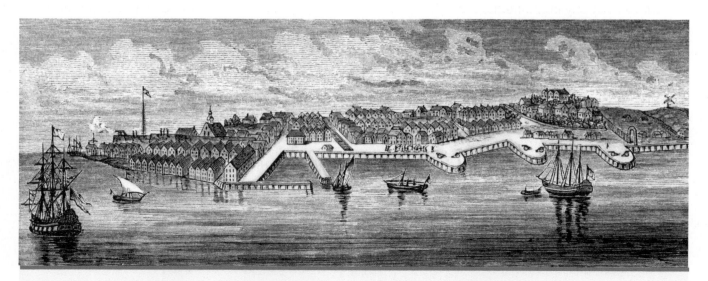

New York City grew to be a bustling port city due to its location on the Atlantic Ocean.

North Wind Picture Archives/Alamy Stock Photo

Colonial Economy, c. 1750

Geography influenced the types of goods that the colonists living in different regions produced.

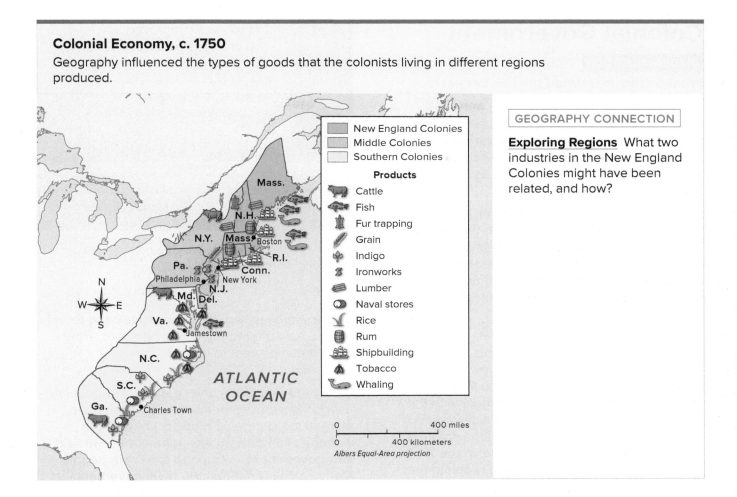

Products
- Cattle
- Fish
- Fur trapping
- Grain
- Indigo
- Ironworks
- Lumber
- Naval stores
- Rice
- Rum
- Shipbuilding
- Tobacco
- Whaling

New England Colonies
Middle Colonies
Southern Colonies

0 / 400 miles
0 / 400 kilometers
Albers Equal-Area projection

GEOGRAPHY CONNECTION

Exploring Regions What two industries in the New England Colonies might have been related, and how?

made large-scale agriculture successful in the Southern Colonies. Tobacco became the main cash crop in some of these colonies. Other colonies grew rice. Both crops grew best on the low, flat coastal plains of the region.

Large farms called plantations developed on the coastal plains. **Plantations** are large agricultural estates usually worked by people who live on the estate. Many laborers were needed to plant, tend, and harvest the large fields of crops. At first, indentured servants did much of this work. Over time, however, plantation owners found it more profitable to use the forced labor of unpaid, enslaved Africans.

Farther inland, away from the coast, the soil was not as rich, and farms were smaller. Farmers here mainly grew only what they needed to feed their families. Some of these small farmers also used enslaved laborers, although fewer than on plantations.

There were far more small farmers than plantation owners, but the plantation owners had greater wealth and power. As a result, plantation owners had more influence over the decisions of the representative assemblies. They also controlled the region's economy. Due in part to the influence of plantation owners, few large towns and little industry developed in the Southern Colonies.

✓ **CHECK FOR UNDERSTANDING**

1. **Identifying Cause and Effect** Why was there no large-scale farming in the New England colonies?

2. **Understanding Supporting Details** Who had most of the influence in the Southern representative assemblies?

---

plantation a large agricultural estate usually worked by people who live on the estate

Colonial Government

What factors weakened the ties between England and its colonies?

The colonies developed different economies and ways of life. One thing they shared was their English heritage. Most colonists were loyal to England. They valued their rights as English subjects.

England was far away, however. Messages took weeks to arrive by ship. Over the years, the colonists began to depend on their own governments—and their elected legislatures—for leadership. They began to see themselves as Americans rather than English subjects.

Governing the Colonies

England's government did not focus much attention on the colonies when they were first founded. Political unrest distracted Parliament, as its members were in a power struggle with the king. Nevertheless, English leaders always believed that the main purpose of the colonies was to **benefit** England. Therefore, in the 1650s, Parliament began passing laws to regulate the colonies' trade.

These laws were hard to enforce. In the colonies south of New England, few people lived along the coast. Colonists' ships could secretly load or unload goods without being seen. In this way, colonial traders ignored English trade laws intended to control their actions.

In time, most colonies had a royal governor, appointed by the king. The governor took his orders from the English king and Parliament. His job was to enforce England's laws in his colony. Local laws were usually passed by the colony's elected assembly, however.

A Time of Change

As time passed, the colonists' elected assemblies grew stronger. They sometimes competed with governors for control of the colonies.

The Governor's Palace was the home of the royal governors of Virginia.

The assemblies had the power to tax and to decide how the money would be spent. They used these powers to weaken the royal governors.

By the mid 1700s, the colonies had become used to governing themselves through their elected legislatures. Colonists knew of the writings of English thinker John Locke. He said that governments existed to serve the people. Many colonists felt that the royal governors put British interests ahead of their own. They began to resent the fact that they had fewer rights than people living in Great Britain.

✓ CHECK FOR UNDERSTANDING

Explaining How did the writings of John Locke influence the colonists' feelings toward their governor?

LESSON ACTIVITIES

1. **Informative/Explanatory Writing** Write a short essay that explains why different groups of people came to the English colonies.

2. **Analyzing Information** With a partner, create a graphic novel that tells the story of how the colonists at either Jamestown or Plymouth formed their governments.

---

benefit to be useful or profitable to

The Causes of the American Revolution

READING STRATEGY

Integrating Knowledge and Ideas As you read, use a series of graphic organizers like the one shown to take notes about events that led to the American Revolution.

British Action	→	Colonists' Response

Social and Political Changes in the Colonies

GUIDING QUESTION

What events and movements affected colonial attitudes?

From the 1740s through the 1760s, colonists became involved in a religious movement called the Great Awakening. They listened to fiery preachers who challenged the direction of the church at the time. These preachers stressed the value of personal religious experience. They urged people to build a direct relationship with God.

Colonists began to question traditional religious **authority**, or power, during the Great Awakening. At the same time, Enlightenment leaders urged people to question accepted political authority. American colonists became influenced by these social and political movements, and they began to develop a strong spirit of **liberty**, or personal freedom. This spirit strengthened the colonists' belief that they should have the same rights as people in Great Britain.

Colonists believed that Parliament should protect the rights of British people from abuses by the king. Yet the king and Parliament made laws for the colonists. Also, America was far away, so the colonists had little voice in what happened in Great Britain. In addition, the king's governors ruled many of the colonies. Colonists did not have a voice in choosing these leaders. Their policies often favored British interests over the colonists' needs. These concerns, combined with a series of events in the 1760s, contributed to a growing resentment against British rule.

authority power or influence over other people

liberty quality or state of being free

Colonists in the English colonies grew resentful of King George III, shown here in a portrait from the 1760s. They accused him of abusing their rights.

The French and Indian War

As the colonies grew, some colonists moved westward into areas claimed by France. Native American groups lived on this land, as they had for many years. The movement of British colonists into these areas increased tensions that soon led to war. In 1754, French forces joined with some Native American groups who were angered by British settlements on their lands. They drove British colonists from land west of the Appalachian Mountains. This began the conflict called the French and Indian War.

Britain sent troops to the colonies. Finally, the British army won the war in 1763. Britain took control of lands claimed by France all the way to the Mississippi River, most of which were inhabited by Native Americans. However, the victory would lead to new conflicts between colonists and Great Britain.

New Laws and Taxes

The long, costly French and Indian War had left Britain in debt. King George III believed the colonists had caused the war by moving west. He decided they should be the ones to pay for it. He also wanted to end the fighting between the colonists and the Native Americans areas that had been claimed by France. He issued a **proclamation**, or an official statement. It forbade the colonists from settling in the lands won from France. He placed more than 10,000 British troops in the colonies to keep order.

These actions angered the colonists. Many felt that they had lost their only hope of owning land. Others felt that the king was punishing the colonies by limiting their economic growth.

Next, King George asked Parliament to tax the colonies. The money would help pay off Great Britain's war debts. In 1765 Parliament passed the Stamp Act. The law required colonists to buy and place tax stamps on many kinds of documents, such as legal papers and newspapers.

The tax greatly upset the colonists. They decided to take civic action. Colonial leaders called on the colonists to **boycott**, or refuse to buy, British goods. They claimed that only their elected representatives had the right to tax them. Leaders based the claim on the English Bill of Rights and on political traditions. For more than

proclamation an official, formal public announcement
boycott to refuse to purchase certain goods

100 years, only their own legislatures had taxed the colonists.

Colonial leaders organized a meeting in New York called the Stamp Act Congress. Representatives from nine colonies met to write a united protest to Parliament and the king. In 1766 Parliament **repealed**, or canceled, the Stamp Act. The same day, however, it passed the Declaratory Act. This law stated that Parliament had the right to tax the colonies and make decisions for them "in all cases whatsoever."

✓ **CHECK FOR UNDERSTANDING**

Describing What did the Stamp Act require colonists to do?

Colonial Dissatisfaction Grows

GUIDING QUESTION

What events increased colonists' anger toward British rule?

A year after repealing the Stamp Act, Parliament levied a new set of taxes. The Townshend Acts placed **duties** on a wide range of goods that the colonies imported from overseas. The colonists resisted with boycotts and protests. In 1770 Parliament repealed all the duties except for a tax on tea.

repeal to cancel a law
duty tax on an imported good

Colonial protests against the Stamp Act took many forms. Teapots such as this one were made in Britain and shipped to the colonies for sale.

Speculating Why might British companies sell teapots that protested British policies to colonists in America?

The Metropolitan Museum of Art, Rogers Fund, 1927

Taxing the Colonies

Tensions increased as Great Britain passed a series of laws to tax the colonies.

1764

Sugar Act (1764)
The Sugar Act put a three-cent tax on foreign refined sugar and increased taxes on coffee, indigo, and certain kinds of wine.

1765

Stamp Act (1765)
The Stamp Act imposed the first direct British tax on the American colonists. It required them to pay a tax on every piece of printed paper they used. Ships' papers, legal documents, licenses, newspapers, and other publications were all included.

1766

1767

Declaratory Act (1766)
Stated that Great Britain had full rights to tax and govern the colonies as it saw fit.

Townshend Acts (1767)
Named for Charles Townshend, British Treasurer, the Townshend Acts placed new taxes on glass, lead, paints, paper, and tea.

Coercive Acts (Intolerable Acts) (1774)

- **The Boston Port Act** closed Boston's harbor until the tea that was used in the Boston Tea Party was fully paid for.
- **The Massachusetts Government Act** made town meetings illegal except by the written consent of the colony's British governor.
- **The Quartering Act** required the colonists to provide housing for British soldiers.
- **The Impartial Administration of Justice Act** allowed trials of British officials from Massachusetts to be held in other colonies or in Great Britain.
- **The Quebec Act** extended the Canadian border southward to the Ohio River, eliminating the colonies' claim to the land.

1773

Tea Act (1773)
The Tea Act required American colonists to buy tea only from the British East India Company. While taxes on some goods had been lifted, the tax on tea was still in place.

1774

1776

Declaration of Independence

HISTORY CONNECTION

1. **Identifying** Which act stated that Great Britain could tax and govern the colonies as it wished?

2. **Contrasting** How were the Coercive Acts different from the other acts that Parliament had passed?

One of the Townshend Acts allowed general search warrants. British officials used these to combat smuggling—illegally moving goods in or out of a country. These warrants were called *writs of assistance*. They made it lawful for officers to enter any business or home to look for goods on which the import duty had not been paid. These searches greatly angered the colonists. Nearly 20 years later, Americans remembered writs of assistance. They demanded that a protection against "unreasonable searches and seizures" be added to the United States Constitution.

In 1773 Parliament passed the Tea Act. It allowed a British company that grew tea in India to import its tea into the colonies without paying the existing tea tax. This made the British company's tea cheaper than other tea sold in the colonies. Though it was not a tax, the new law angered the colonists.

In December 1773, some angry colonists boarded several ships in Boston Harbor. The British company's tea was on these ships, waiting to be unloaded. The protesters had disguised themselves as Native Americans. Urged on by a large crowd onshore, they dumped 342 chests of the company's tea into the water. This protest became known as the Boston Tea Party.

In response to the Boston Tea Party, Parliament passed a set of laws called the Coercive Acts. These laws were meant to punish Massachusetts—and especially Boston. The Coercive Acts were so harsh that the colonists called them the Intolerable Acts. Some of the laws violated the English Bill of Rights, which the colonists highly valued.

During the 1770s, leaders from different colonies organized by sending letters to one another. They shared ideas, debated, and made decisions on how to best resist the British. After the Coercive Acts were passed, leaders in Boston reached out to other colonies to spread the news and ask for help.

✓ **CHECK FOR UNDERSTANDING**

Analyzing Why were the colonists so angry with Parliament's actions after the repeal of the Stamp Act?

Steps Toward Independence

GUIDING QUESTION

What ideas about government influenced the Declaration of Independence?

Parliament thought the Coercive Acts would frighten the colonists into respecting British rule. Instead, the reverse occurred. The other colonies banded together to help Massachusetts and challenge British authority.

The First Continental Congress

In September 1774, **delegates**, or representatives, from 12 colonies met in Philadelphia to plan a united response to the Coercive Acts. Although the group was called the Continental Congress, it did not pass laws like Congress does today. Instead, the delegates discussed what to do about the colonies' issues with Great Britain.

delegate representative to a meeting

This print from the 1800s shows the Boston Tea Party.

Analyzing Perspectives How does the creator of the print depict the reaction of Boston residents to the Tea Party?

They decided to send a letter to the king asking him to respect the colonists' rights as British citizens. They also organized a total boycott of British goods and a ban on all trade with Britain. They agreed to meet again in the spring if British policies had not improved.

King George responded by calling for even stronger measures. "The New England governments are in a state of rebellion," he declared. "Blows [a fight] must decide whether they are subject to this country or independent."

The Second Continental Congress

The first "blows" already had been struck when the delegates met again in May 1775 in the Second Continental Congress. In April, British troops and colonial militiamen had fought at Lexington and Concord in Massachusetts. Militia are citizen-soldiers. Congress had to decide whether to continue working toward peace or to split with Great Britain.

This time the Congress acted as a governing body for the colonies. The Congress debated whether the colonies should split from Great Britain entirely. Some delegates remained loyal to Britain and the king. Others feared that the colonies could not defeat Great Britain in a war. Even so, the Congress organized an army and navy, made plans to issue money, and appointed George Washington as commander of the Continental Army.

Meanwhile, support for independence grew in the colonies. In January 1776, Thomas Paine published a pamphlet titled *Common Sense*. Paine used the ideas of John Locke to make the case for independence. He argued that "common sense" called for the colonists to rebel against the king's "violent abuse of power." Paine continued,

66 The cause of America is in a great measure the cause of all mankind. . . . We have it in our power to begin the world over again. 99

More than 500,000 copies of *Common Sense* were sold in 1776. By the spring of that year, more than half the delegates of the Second Continental Congress favored independence.

The Declaration of Independence

The Congress chose a committee to draft a document to explain to the world why the colonies should be free. The committee consisted of John Adams, Benjamin Franklin, Thomas Jefferson,

In this print from the late 1800s, members of the Second Continental Congress appoint George Washington (standing near center) as the commander of the Continental Army.

Robert Livingston, and Roger Sherman. The committee chose Jefferson to write what became the Declaration of Independence.

Jefferson's words show that his thinking was greatly influenced by John Locke. In fact, a passage in the second paragraph of the Declaration clearly was inspired by Locke's ideas about natural rights:

66 We hold these truths to be self-evident, that all men are created equal, that they are endowed by their Creator with certain unalienable Rights, that among these are Life, Liberty, and the pursuit of Happiness. 99

Then, drawing on Locke's views about the social contract, Jefferson wrote:

66 [T]o secure these rights, Governments are instituted among Men, deriving [getting] their just powers from the consent of the governed, That whenever any form of government becomes destructive of these ends, it is the Right of the People to alter or abolish it, and to institute [create] new Government. 99

Later in the Declaration, Jefferson offered proof that the social contract had been broken. He put together a long list of ways in which King George had abused his power.

PHOTO: Pictorial Press Ltd./Alamy Stock Photo; TEXT:(t) King George III, GEORGE III'S OFFICIAL CORRESPONDENCE JULY 1772-1783, Royal Collection Trust, Royal Archives, © Her Majesty Queen Elizabeth II 2020, (bcl) Paine, Thomas. Common Sense; Addressed to the Inhabitants of America, On the following interesting Subjects (2008), Urbana, Illinois: Project Gutenberg. Retrieved January 1, 2017, from http://www.gutenberg.org/files/147/147-h/147-h.htm, (bcr) U.S. Declaration of Independence, July 4, 1776, transcript, The Charters of Freedom, National Archives and Records Administration [http://www.archives.gov/exhibits/charters/declaration_transcript.html].

This painting showing the presentation of the Declaration of Independence to the Second Continental Congress was painted in the early 1800s and hangs in the U.S. Capitol.

Jefferson was clearly influenced by the political thoughts of Locke. He also drew ideas from other times in history. For example, he drew inspiration about democracy from the ancient Greeks. In addition, Jefferson was inspired by the writings of Enlightenment thinkers other than Locke. For instance, Jean-Jacques Rousseau wrote that if a government did not protect its people's freedom, it should not exist. Voltaire also believed that people had a right to liberty. The Declaration of Independence reflects many of these old and new beliefs.

The Second Continental Congress approved the Declaration of Independence on July 4, 1776. John Hancock, the president of the Congress, was first to sign it.

The Declaration of Independence was a revolutionary document. Few other nations at that time were based on the principle of government by consent of the governed. Over the years, many other nations have used the Declaration of Independence as a model in their own efforts to gain freedom. Still, the Declaration's statements on rights and equality were not meant to apply to all people living in the colonies. The men who wrote the Declaration did not belive that women, Native Americans, and enslaved Africans had the same rights and freedoms.

✓ CHECK FOR UNDERSTANDING

1. **Understanding Supporting Details** What did Thomas Paine argue in *Common Sense*?

2. **Making Connections** How did the Enlightenment influence Thomas Jefferson?

LESSON ACTIVITIES

1. **Narrative Writing** Write a fictional story based on the perspective of a colonist living in Boston during the Boston Tea Party. In your story, explain your character's thoughts about the Boston Tea Party, and provide the reasons behind your character's views.

2. **Analyzing Main Ideas** With a partner, hold a debate in which each person takes different sides in the argument about whether to declare independence from Britain. One person should argue that the colonies should remain loyal to Britain. The other should argue for independence.

08

Multiple Perspectives: Views on American Independence

? COMPELLING QUESTION

How did people view American independence differently?

Plan Your Inquiry

DEVELOPING QUESTIONS

Think about events leading up to the Second Continental Congress and the writing of the Declaration of Independence. What reasons did American colonists have for opposing British rule? How did colonists' lives differ across regions and classes? Then read the Compelling Question for this lesson. What questions can you ask to help you answer this Compelling Question? Create a graphic organizer like the one below. Write these Supporting Questions in your graphic organizer.

Supporting Questions	Primary or Secondary Source	What the source tells me about how different people viewed American independence	Questions the source leaves unanswered
	A		
	B		
	C		
	D		
	E		
	F		
	G		

ANALYZING SOURCES

Next, examine the sources in this lesson. Analyze each source by answering the questions that follow it. How does each source help you answer each Supporting Question you created? What questions do you still have? Write these in your graphic organizer.

After you analyze the sources, you will:
- use the evidence from the sources,
- communicate your conclusions,
- and take informed action.

Background Information

Different groups from England began founding colonies in North America in the 1600s. They were officially under English rule, but the colonies developed their own local governments.

For many years, Great Britain largely permitted the colonies to rule themselves. This policy led the colonies to get used to a degree of self-rule. In the 1760s, though, Britain needed money to cover the costs rising from the French and Indian War. It moved to tighten its control on the colonies by raising taxes and passing other laws. Many colonists resisted. Some opposed the way these laws hurt trade and business. Others resented limits the British placed on westward settlement. Soon, some colonists began talking about declaring independence. However, not everyone agreed that independence was a good idea.

⌃ After the signing of the Declaration of Independence, copies were distributed throughout the colonies for public readings of the document.

Samuel Seabury: Loyalist View

In 1774, the British passed a set of laws that angered many colonists. Colonists called the laws the Intolerable Acts. Soon after, leaders from several colonies met in Philadelphia. The meeting came to be called the First Continental Congress. This group proposed a boycott on British goods in response to the Intolerable Acts. Some colonists were ready to join this movement. Others were not. Samuel Seabury was a Loyalist, an American who was loyal to Britain. He disapproved of the actions of the Continental Congress. Seabury wrote this pamphlet in New York.

PRIMARY SOURCE: PAMPHLET

66 [M]y Friends, . . . have nothing to do with these men. . . . Peace and quietness suit *you* best. Confusion, and Discord [conflict], and Violence, and War, are sure destruction to the *farmer*. Without peace he cannot till his lands; unless protected by the laws, he cannot carry his produce to market. . . . **Renounce** all dependence on Congresses, and Committees. They have neglected, or betrayed your interests. Turn then your eyes to your *constitutional* representatives. They are the true, and legal, and have been **hitherto**, the faithful defenders of your rights, and liberties; . . . They are the proper persons to obtain redress [remedy] of any grievances [wrongs] that you can justly complain of. . . . [T]hey will use the most reasonable, constitutional, and **effectual** methods of restoring that peace and harmony. 99

— Samuel Seabury, "Free Thoughts on the Proceedings of the Continental Congress," 1774

renounce to give up
hitherto up to this time

effectual producing a desired outcome

EXAMINE THE SOURCE

1. **Identifying Themes** What does Seabury believe will happen as a result of the actions of the Continental Congress?

2. **Analyzing Perspectives** What does Seabury try to persuade his readers to do?

Alexander Hamilton's Response to Seabury

In the early 1770s, Alexander Hamilton opposed the new British policies and favored the protests against them. These protesters argued that since colonists had not elected any members of the British Parliament, it had no right to pass laws taxing them.

Samuel Seabury's pamphlet moved Hamilton to write a response. The two men continued to debate issues through pamphlets.

PRIMARY SOURCE: PAMPHLET

66 Pray who can tell me why a farmer in America, is not as honest and good a man, as a farmer in England? or why has not the one as good a right to what he has earned by his labour [labor], as the other? I can't, for my life, see any distinction between them. And yet it seems the English farmers are to be governed and taxed by their own Assembly, or Parliament; and the American farmers are not. The former are to choose their own Representatives from among themselves. . . . The latter are to be loaded with taxes by men three thousand miles off. . . . How do you like this **doctrine** my friends? . . . Are you willing to acknowledge [the English farmer's] right to take your property from you, and when they please? I know you scorn [reject] the thought. You had rather die, than submit to it. 99

— Alexander Hamilton, "A Full Vindication of the Measures of the Congress, from the Calumnies of Their Enemies," 1774

doctrine a statement of principle or policy

EXAMINE THE SOURCE

1. **Analyzing** What does Hamilton say is the major difference between English and American farmers?

2. **Interpreting** How does Hamilton appeal to the emotions of his readers to encourage support for the Continental Congress?

(t) Farmer, A.W., "Free Thoughts on the Proceedings of the Continental Congress" 1774, Project Canterbury. (b) Hamilton, A., "A full Vindication of the Measures of Congress, from the Calumnies of Their Enemies" James Riverton, New York, 1774

C

A Changing Viewpoint from Britain

James Boswell, a Scottish lawyer and author shown in the image, exchanged hundreds of letters with Reverend William Temple, his friend and fellow author. Both men were British, living in Great Britian. In these letters, Boswell explains his shifting views on the cause of the American colonists. *Tory* refers to a political group within Great Britain that supported the power of the king over that of the Parliament. In the colonies, the word *Tory* described someone loyal to Britain during the American Revolution.

PHOTO: Archivart/Alamy Stock Photo; TEXT:Boswell, J., Tinker, C. B., "Letters of James Boswell Volume 1", The University of California,1924, Clarendon Press, 2008.

PRIMARY SOURCES: LETTERS

❝ As to American affairs, I have really not studied the subject. It is too much for me perhaps. . . . From the **smattering** which newspapers have given me, I have been of different minds several times. That I am a Tory, a lover of power in monarchy, and a discourager of much liberty in the people I avow [declare]. But it is not clear to me that our colonies are compleately [completely] our **subjects**. I am puzzled with **charters**. At any rate, the measures of **Administration** seem to have been **ill digested** and violent. I should hope that things may now take a good turn. I can figure Britain and the colonies in a most agreable [agreeable] state, like a father and son who are both sensible and spirited [forceful] men, who can make **mutual** allowances, and who, having a kindness for each other, study to promote a common interest. But selfishness and narrowness of comprehension [understanding] destroys men and nations. ❞

— James Boswell, letter to the Reverend William Temple, March 18, 1775

❝ I am growing more and more American. I see the unreasonableness of taxing them without the consent of their Assemblies. I think our ministry [government leaders] are mad in undertaking this desperate war. ❞

— James Boswell, letter to the Reverend William Temple, August 12, 1775

smattering little bit of knowledge

subject a person under the rule of a monarch

charter a document that gave certain people the right to establish a colony

Administration action by the British government

ill digested objected to

mutual directed toward each other

EXAMINE THE SOURCE

1. **Analyzing Perspectives** How does Boswell describe his general political viewpoint at the beginning of the first letter?
2. **Drawing Conclusions** How does the British practice of taxing the colonies change Boswell's view?

American Laborers

This excerpt, written 200 years following the Revolution, explores the role of workers at the time. Many colonists wanted more land and control over trade. Those who favored independence called themselves Whigs, after a group of British nobles and businesspeople who wanted to limit the power of the king. Those who remained loyal to the king called themselves Tories.

SECONDARY SOURCE: BOOK

66 Although the American Revolution was not fought for the explicit [stated] purpose of improving the lot [fate] of workers, labor was indeed a principal **beneficiary** of that contest. The war offered the free white male a fabulous opportunity for upward **social mobility**. First, he had a chance to pick up confiscated [seized] Tory lands. While those in urban areas went . . . to Whig **speculators**, a good part of the rural estates of Tories was divided up according to laws recognizing tenant [renter] **preemption** rights. Second, there were the vast new lands [gained] at the peace table, which provided veterans of the Revolution with an opportunity to secure homesteads [farms]. 99

—"The Emergence of American Labor," *The U.S. Department of Labor: Bicentennial History of the American Worker,* 1976

beneficiary one who benefits
social mobility improving one's position in society
speculator an investor in a risky business plan
preemption the right to purchase something before others

EXAMINE THE SOURCE

1. **Identifying** What is meant by "labor" in the first sentence?
2. **Drawing Conclusions** Based on this excerpt, why might many free white male laborers and their families have supported independence in the colonies?

Against the Declaration

Thomas Hutchinson served in several public offices in Massachusetts. As the colony's royal governor from 1771 to 1774, his role was to enforce Parliament's laws. He wrote this letter as a response to some of the points made in the Declaration of Independence.

PRIMARY SOURCE: LETTER

66 I should therefore be impertinent [rude] if I attempted to show in what case a *whole people* may be justified in rising up in oppugnation [opposition] to the powers of government . . . ; or in what sense all men are created equal, or how far life, liberty, and the *pursuit* of happiness may be said to be **unalienable**. Only I could wish to ask the Delegates of Maryland, Virginia, and the Carolinas how their **Constituents** justify the depriving [of] more than an hundred thousand Africans of their rights to liberty and the *pursuit of happiness*, and in some degree to their lives, if these rights are so absolutely unalienable; nor shall I attempt to confute [disprove] the absurd notions of government . . . contained in this Declaration; but rather to show the false representation made of the facts which are **alleged** to be . . . the special motives to Rebellion. 99

—Thomas Hutchinson, *Strictures Upon the Declaration of the Congress at Philadelphia,* October 15, 1776

unalienable impossible to take away
constituent a citizen who elects a representative
alleged stated to be true but not proven

EXAMINE THE SOURCE

1. **Interpreting** What point does Hutchinson make about unalienable rights when he mentions Maryland, Virginia, and the Carolinas?
2. **Analyzing Perspectives** How does Hutchinson's choice of words illustrate his view of the Declaration of Independence?

TEXT:(t) Morris, R.B., "Bicentennial History of the American Worker" U.S. Department of Labor, 1976; (b) Hutchinson, T., "A Loyalist's Rebuttal to the Declaration of Independence" U.S. Government Printing Office

"Liberty Further Extended"

Born to a white mother and a black father in New England, Lemuel Haynes served in the local militia and the Continental Army during the American Revolution. Even as he supported independence, he wrote and spoke strongly against slavery. Haynes went on to serve as a minister. He begins this essay with a quote from the Declaration of Independence.

PRIMARY SOURCES: ESSAY

66 'We hold these truths to be self-Evident, that all men are created Equal, that they are Endowed [provided] By their Creator with Certain unalienable rights, that among these are Life, Liberty, and the pursuit of happiness.'

— Congress.

. . . Liberty, & freedom, is an **innate** principle, which is unmovably placed in the human Species. . . .

Liberty is a Jewel which was handed Down to man from the cabinet of heaven, and is **Coeval** with his Existence. . . .

I know that those that are concerned in the Slave-trade, Do pretend to Bring arguments in vindication [defense] of their practice; yet if we give them a **candid** Examination, we shall find them (Even those of the most cogent [convincing] kind) to be Essentially Deficient [lacking]. . . .

And the main proposition, which I intend for some Brief illustration is this, Namely, That an *African . . . may Justly Challenge, and has an undeniable right to his Liberty: Consequently, the practice of Slave-keeping, which so much abounds in this Land is illicit* [unlawful]. 99

— Lemuel Haynes, "Liberty Further Extended: Or Free Thoughts on the Illegality of Slave Keeping," 1776

innate existing from birth

coeval of the same age or duration

candid honest or blunt

EXAMINE THE SOURCE

1. **Explaining** What does Haynes believe about liberty and freedom?
2. **Analyzing Perspectives** What is Haynes's viewpoint on slavery?

"To His Excellency, General Washington"

Born in Africa in 1753, Phillis Wheatley was captured, enslaved, and sent to the Massachusetts colony as a child. There, she was sold to a family in Boston, who taught her to read and write. Wheatley was freed from slavery sometime in 1773 or after. She became the first published African American poet in the colonies in 1773. In this poem, she personifies the United States as Columbia, a symbol that became even more popular after the Revolution.

PRIMARY SOURCE: POEM

❝ Celestial [heavenly] choir! **enthron'd** in realms of light, Columbia's scenes of glorious **toils** I write. While freedom's cause her anxious breast alarms, She flashes **dreadful** in refulgent [radiant] arms. See mother earth her offspring's fate **bemoan**, And nations gaze at scenes before unknown! See the bright beams of heaven's revolving light Involved in sorrows and veil of night!

The goddess comes, she moves divinely fair, **Olive and laurel** bind her golden hair: Wherever shines this native of the skies, Unnumber'd charms and recent graces rise. ❞

—Phillis Wheatley, from "To His Excellency, General Washington," 1776

---

enthron'd enthroned; seated in a place of authority or assigned great value

toil hard work

dreadful provoking fear

bemoan to express grief or sadness about

olive and laurel symbols of peace and victory

EXAMINE THE SOURCE

1. **Identifying** Which lines of the poem show Wheatley's optimism about the future of the United States? How?

2. **Analyzing Perspectives** Why might Wheatley personify the spirit of the revolution as a female named Columbia?

Complete Your Inquiry

EVALUATE SOURCES AND USE EVIDENCE

Refer back to the Compelling Question and the Supporting Questions you developed at the beginning of the lesson.

1. **Comparing and Contrasting** Think about the sentiments in Sources E, F, and G. How are they alike and different?

2. **Synthesizing** According to the sources, how does economics relate to ideals of personal liberty?

3. **Gathering Sources** Which sources helped you answer the Supporting Questions and the Compelling Question? Which sources, if any, challenged what you thought you knew when you first created your Supporting Questions? What information do you still need in order to answer your questions? What other viewpoints would you like to investigate? Where would you find that information?

4. **Evaluating Sources** Identify the sources that helped answer your Supporting Questions. How reliable are the sources? How would you verify the reliability of the sources?

COMMUNICATE CONCLUSIONS

5. **Collaborating** In a small group, make a T-chart for the arguments in the sources both supporting and opposing independence. As you take turns sharing your Supporting Questions and responses, record details in the appropriate column. Then, share your completed chart with the class. Summarize reasons why people held different opinions on independence.

TAKE INFORMED ACTION

Creating a Presentation Showing Different Perspectives Just as colonists felt differently about American independence, people today have diverse viewpoints about current issues. With a partner, investigate a local, state, or national public policy issue. Identify at least two different perspectives on the issue, and learn more about the ideas of the people who support those positions. Consider economic and political influences. Create a presentation that clearly summarizes the issue, and explain the different perspectives on it. Present your completed work.

Wheatley, P., "To His Excellency, General Washington" 1775, Founders Online, National Archives

09

Reviewing The Origins of American Government

Summary

Functions and Types of Governments

- Governments provide services and keep order.
- Governments are organized in several ways.
- Democracies, monarchies, and authoritarianism are types of government.
- Ancient Greece and Rome developed ideas that influenced democracies.
- The Iroquois Confederacy was an early form of democracy in North America.

Ideas about Rights and Natural Laws

- English influences on the United States include the Magna Carta and English Bill of Rights.
- Enlightenment thinkers believed in a social contract.

Origins of American Government

The First American Governments

- The first colonial governments were in Jamestown and Plymouth.
- Colonists came looking for economic opportunity and religious freedom.
- Colonial governments strengthened over time.

Causes of the American Revolution

- Laws and taxes passed by the British government angered colonists.
- Colonists staged protests, like the Boston Tea Party, against taxes.
- In 1776, the United States declared independence.

Ian.CuiYi/Getty Images

Checking For Understanding

Answer the questions to see if you understood the topic content.

1. Identify each of the following terms and explain its significance to the origins of American government.

    A. public policy **E.** social contract

    B. federal system **F.** dissenter

    C. constitutional government **G.** liberty

    D. republic **H.** boycott

REVIEWING KEY FACTS

2. **Explaining** How do laws help communities maintain order and protect the health, safety, and property of citizens?

3. **Summarizing** How is power divided among different levels of government in the United States?

4. **Analyzing** How does a constitutional government help to ensure that a country's leaders cannot become too powerful?

5. **Explaining** What is the rule of law?

6. **Identifying Cause and Effect** How did English nobles change the power of the king after their uprising in 1215?

7. **Explaining** What ideas held by John Locke later became important to the government in the United States?

8. **Explaining** Why was the House of Burgesses important in the development of government in colonial America?

9. **Making Connections** How did the Greek city-state, or *polis*, of Athens influence the development of democracy?

10. **Identifying** What was the Mayflower Compact?

11. **Identifying Cause and Effect** How did colonial leaders respond to the Stamp Act?

12. **Interpreting** How did Thomas Jefferson argue in the Declaration of Independence that the social contract between the British government and the colonists had been broken?

CRITICAL THINKING

13. **Speculating** What is likely to happen if government did not exist to make and enforce laws?

14. **Comparing and Contrasting** How are a direct democracy and representative democracy alike and different?

15. **Explaining** Why did Montesquieu believe in the separation of powers?

16. **Making Connections** How did Thomas Paine use John Locke's ideas in his pamphlet *Common Sense*?

17. **Analyzing** What was so unusual about the Puritan practice of expelling from their colony people who would not worship as they did?

18. **Contrasting** How did the authority of the royal governors differ from that of the colonies' elected assemblies?

19. **Identifying Cause and Effect** How did the colonies respond to the Coercive Acts?

20. **Analyzing** The principle of "consent of the governed" greatly influenced Jefferson's writing of the Declaration of Independence. Why was that principle considered so significant?

NEED EXTRA HELP?

If You've Missed Question	1	2	3	4	5	6	7	8	9	10
Review Lesson	2, 3, 4, 6, 7	2	3	3	3	4	4	6	6	6

If You've Missed Question	11	12	13	14	15	16	17	18	19	20
Review Lesson	7	7	2	3	4	4, 6, 7	6	6	7	7

Apply What You Have Learned

A Understanding Multiple Perspectives

The founders of the United States were influenced by Enlightenment thinkers in Europe. Their ideas about government's duty to serve the people contributed to the colonists declaring independence. The writings of Enlightenment thinkers explain their ideas about government.

ACTIVITY **Writing a Comparison Essay** In their writings about government, Thomas Hobbes and John Locke both wrote about society before government existed. They called this the state of nature. Read the excerpts below. Consider how each thinker imagined society operated before government. Then write a brief essay comparing the two.

- Analyze the arguments both writers make to support their perspectives.
- Evaluate which argument is stronger, citing both thinkers.

> If any two men desire the same thing, which neverthelesse they cannot both enjoy, they become enemies; and in the way to their End, . . . endeavour [seek] to destroy, or subdue one another. . . . .
>
> Hereby it is manifest, that during the time men live without a common Power to keep them all in awe, they are in that condition which is called Warre [war]. . . .
>
> In such condition, there is no place for Industry [work]; because the fruit [profit] thereof is uncertain; and consequently no Culture of the Earth; . . . no Knowledge of the face of the Earth; no account of Time; no Arts; no Letters; no Society; and which is worst of all, continuall feare [continual fear], and danger of violent death; And the life of man, [is] solitary, poore [poor], nasty, brutish, and short.

— Thomas Hobbes, from *Leviathan* (1651)

> To understand political power . . . we must consider what estate [condition] all men are naturally in, and that is, a state of perfect freedom to order their actions, and dispose of their possessions and persons as they think fit, within the bounds of the law of Nature, without asking leave [permission] or depending upon the will of any other man. . . .
>
> Men being, as has been said, by nature all free, equal, and independent, no one can be put out of this estate and subjected to the political power of another without his own consent, which is done by agreeing with other men, to join and unite a community for their comfortable, safe, and peaceable living, one amongst another, in a secure enjoyment of their properties, and a greater security against any that are not of it.

— John Locke, from *The Second Treatise of Civil Government* (1689)

(t) Hobbes, Thomas. Leviathan. London: Andrew Crooke, 1651., (b) Locke, John. Two Treatises of Government. London: Whitmore and Fenn, 1821.

B Understanding Chronology

More than 150 years passed between the time the first English colonists reached the shores of North America and the Declaration of Independence. During that time, many Enlightenment thinkers wrote their thoughts on government. These ideas had an important impact on the colonists living in North America.

ACTIVITY Creating an Enlightenment Time Line Research and list major Enlightenment thinkers of the 1600s and 1700s. Look up the books they wrote, beginning with *Leviathan* by Thomas Hobbes and ending with *The Social Contract* by Jean-Jacques Rousseau. Create a time line that shows six to eight books written by Enlightenment thinkers. Include a brief explanation of why each book is significant.

 ## C Informative/Explanatory Writing

In this topic, you studied the development of the democratic form of government over the ages, and how those developments influenced the American colonists' views of government. Greece and Rome developed early forms of democracy that involved portions of their populations in the government. In North America, the Iroquois Confederacy also included elements of democracy. Later the writings of the Enlightenment thinkers helped frame how government and citizens should interact, advancing democratic thinking even further.

ACTIVITY Writing About Democracy and Colonial America Write an informative essay describing the development of democracy from ancient times through the American revolutionary era and the Declaration of Independence. Explain the history of democracy up to the revolutionary period, including the early forms of democracy around the world. Note English influences in the colonists' beliefs about self-government Also explain how Enlightenment ideas about government related to democracy. Finally, describe how the American colonists' struggles with Great Britain and the Declaration of Independence reflected a desire for a true democratic government.

D Making Connections to Today

Today, when Americans want to persuade government to change, they often do some of the same things that colonists did to challenge the British government. These civic actions include boycotts, petitions, and protests.

ACTIVITY Creating a Presentation on Civic Actions
Search recent news articles to find two examples of these activities. In your presentation, be sure to explain what the issues were, how they affected the community, and what effects these civic actions had. Give your presentation to your class. After you finish, answer any questions your classmates have.

The writers of the Declaration of Independence included Benjamin Franklin, John Adams, and Thomas Jefferson.

The Declaration of Independence

When the Declaration of Independence was written in 1776, most of the people of the world were governed by monarchs, emperors, or absolute rulers. Since Roman times, few political ideas had focused on the rights of citizens or the relationship between individual citizens and the government. By the time of the Enlightenment in the 1700s, however, many new ideas had emerged. Those ideas came together in the American Declaration of Independence.

The entire text of the Declaration of Independence follows. The printed text of the document shows the spelling and punctuation of the parchment original.

GO ONLINE Explore the Student Edition eBook and find interactive maps, charts, graphs, and tools.

JULY 4, 1776.

PRIMARY SOURCE : THE DECLARATION OF INDEPENDENCE

In Congress, July 4, 1776.

The unanimous Declaration of the thirteen united States of America,

[Preamble]

When in the Course of human events, it becomes necessary for one people to dissolve the political bands which have connected them with another, and to assume among the powers of the earth, the separate and equal station to which the Laws of Nature and of Nature's God entitle them, a decent respect to the opinions of mankind requires that they should declare the causes which **impel** them to the separation.

[Declaration of Natural Rights]

We hold these truths to be self-evident, that all men are created equal, that they are **endowed** by their Creator with certain unalienable Rights, that among these are Life, Liberty and the pursuit of Happiness.

That to secure these rights, Governments are instituted among Men, deriving their just powers from the consent of the governed,

That whenever any Form of Government becomes destructive of these ends, it is the Right of the People to alter or to abolish it, and to institute new Government, laying its foundation on such principles and organizing its powers in such form, as to them shall seem most likely to effect their Safety and Happiness. Prudence, indeed, will dictate that Governments long established should not be changed for light and transient causes; and accordingly all experience hath shewn, that mankind are more disposed to suffer, while evils are sufferable, than to right themselves by abolishing the forms to which they are accustomed. But when a long train of abuses and **usurpations**, pursuing invariably the same Object evinces a design to reduce them under absolute **Despotism**, it is their right, it is their duty, to throw off such Government, and to provide new Guards for their future security.

PREAMBLE

The Declaration of Independence has four parts. The Preamble explains why the Continental Congress drew up the Declaration.

DECLARATION OF NATURAL RIGHTS

The second part, the Declaration of Natural Rights, states that people have certain basic rights and that government should protect those rights. John Locke's ideas strongly influenced this part. In 1690, Locke wrote that government was based on the consent of the people and that people had the right to rebel if the government did not uphold their right to life, liberty, and property.

impel force
endowed provided

usurpations unjust uses of power
despotism a government in which a ruler has unlimited power

Engrossed copy of the Declaration of Independence, August 2, 1776; Miscellaneous Papers of the Continental Congress, 1774–1789; Records of the Continental and Confederation Congresses and the Constitutional Convention, 1774–1789, Record Group 360; National Archives.

[List of Grievances]

Such has been the patient sufferance of these Colonies; and such is now the necessity which constrains them to alter their former Systems of Government. The history of the present King of Great Britain is a history of repeated injuries and usurpations, all having in direct object the establishment of an absolute Tyranny over these States. To prove this, let Facts be submitted to a candid world.

He has refused his Assent to Laws, the most wholesome and necessary for the public good.

He has forbidden his Governors to pass Laws of immediate and pressing importance, unless suspended in their operation till his Assent should be obtained; and when so suspended, he has utterly neglected to attend to them.

He has refused to pass other Laws for the accommodation of large districts of people, unless those people would **relinquish** the right of Representation in the Legislature, a right **inestimable** to them and formidable to tyrants only.

He has called together legislative bodies at places unusual, uncomfortable, and distant from the depository of their public Records, for the sole purpose of fatiguing them into compliance with his measures.

relinquish give up   **inestimable** priceless

LIST OF GRIEVANCES

The third part of the Declaration is a list of the colonists' complaints against the British government. Notice that King George III is singled out for blame.

The painting *Declaration of Independence* by John Trumbull depicts the presentation of the Declaration of Independence to John Hancock (seated right), president of the Continental Congress.

Ian Dagnall/Alamy Stock Photo

He has dissolved Representative Houses repeatedly, for opposing with manly firmness his invasions on the rights of the people.

He has refused for a long time, after such dissolutions, to cause others to be elected; whereby the Legislative powers, incapable of **Annihilation**, have returned to the People at large for their exercise; the State remaining in the mean time exposed to all the dangers of invasion from without, and **convulsions** within.

He has endeavoured to prevent the population of these States; for that purpose obstructing the Laws for **Naturalization of Foreigners**; refusing to pass others to encourage their migrations hither, and raising the conditions of new Appropriations of Lands.

He has obstructed the Administration of Justice, by refusing his Assent to Laws for establishing Judiciary powers.

He has made Judges dependent on his Will alone, for the **tenure** of their offices, and the amount and payment of their salaries.

He has erected a multitude of New Offices, and sent hither swarms of Officers to harrass our people, and eat out their substance.

He has kept among us, in times of peace, Standing Armies without the Consent of our legislatures.

He has affected to render the Military independent of and superior to the Civil power.

He has combined with others to subject us to a jurisdiction foreign to our constitution, and unacknowledged by our laws; giving his Assent to their Acts of pretended Legislation:

For **Quartering** large bodies of armed troops among us:

For protecting them, by a mock Trial, from punishment for any Murders which they should commit on the Inhabitants of these States:

For cutting off our Trade with all parts of the world:

For imposing Taxes on us without our Consent:

For depriving us in many cases, of the benefits of Trial by Jury:

For transporting us beyond Seas to be tried for pretended offences

For abolishing the free System of English Laws in a neighbouring Province, establishing therein an Arbitrary government, and enlarging its Boundaries so as to **render** it at once an example and fit instrument for introducing the same absolute rule into these Colonies:

For taking away our Charters, abolishing our most valuable Laws, and altering fundamentally the Forms of our Governments:

---

annihilation destruction

convulsions violent disturbances

naturalization of foreigners the process by which foreign-born persons become citizens

tenure term

quartering lodging

render to make

For suspending our own Legislatures, and declaring themselves invested with power to legislate for us in all cases whatsoever.

He has **abdicated** Government here, by declaring us out of his Protection and waging War against us.

He has plundered our seas, ravaged our Coasts, burnt our towns, and destroyed the lives of our people.

He is at this time transporting large Armies of foreign Mercenaries to compleat the works of death, desolation and tyranny, already begun with circumstances of Cruelty & **perfidy** scarcely paralleled in the most barbarous ages, and totally unworthy the Head of a civilized nation.

He has constrained our fellow Citizens taken Captive on the high Seas to bear Arms against their Country, to become the executioners of their friends and Brethren, or to fall themselves by their Hands.

He has excited domestic **insurrections** amongst us, and has endeavoured to bring on the inhabitants of our frontiers, the merciless Indian Savages, whose known rule of warfare, is an undistinguished destruction of all ages, sexes and conditions.

In every stage of these Oppressions We have **Petitioned for Redress** in the most humble terms: Our repeated Petitions have been answered only by repeated injury. A Prince whose character is thus marked by every act which may define a Tyrant, is unfit to be the ruler of a free People.

Nor have We been wanting in attentions to our Brittish brethren. We have warned them from time to time of attempts by their legislature to extend an **unwarrantable** jurisdiction over us. We have reminded them of the circumstances of our emigration and settlement here. We have appealed to their native justice and magnanimity, and we have conjured them by the ties of our common kindred to disavow these usurpations, which, would inevitably interrupt our connections and correspondence. They too have been deaf to the voice of justice and of **consanguinity**. We must, therefore, acquiesce in the necessity, which denounces our Separation, and hold them, as we hold the rest of mankind, Enemies in War, in Peace Friends.

---

abdicated given up

perfidy violation of trust

insurrections rebellions

petitioned for redress asked formally for a correction of wrongs

unwarrantable unjustified; inexcusable

consanguinity originating from the same ancestor

John Hancock's signature on the Declaration of Independence

[Resolution of Independence by the United States]

We, therefore, the Representatives of the united States of America, in General Congress, Assembled, appealing to the Supreme Judge of the world for the **rectitude** of our intentions, do, in the Name, and by Authority of the good People of these Colonies, solemnly publish and declare, That these United Colonies are, and of Right ought to be Free and Independent States; that they are Absolved from all Allegiance to the British Crown, and that all political connection between them and the State of Great Britain, is and ought to be totally dissolved; and that as Free and Independent States, they have full Power to levy War, conclude Peace, contract Alliances, establish Commerce, and to do all other Acts and Things which Independent States may of right do.

And for the support of this Declaration, with a firm reliance on the protection of divine Providence, we mutually pledge to each other our Lives, our Fortunes and our sacred Honor.

John Hancock
President from Massachusetts

Georgia
Button Gwinnett
Lyman Hall
George Walton

North Carolina
William Hooper
Joseph Hewes
John Penn

South Carolina
Edward Rutledge
Thomas Heyward, Jr.
Thomas Lynch, Jr.
Arthur Middleton

Maryland
Samuel Chase
William Paca
Thomas Stone
Charles Carroll of
* Carrollton*

Virginia
George Wythe
Richard Henry Lee
Thomas Jefferson
Benjamin Harrison
Thomas Nelson, Jr.
Francis Lightfoot Lee
Carter Braxton

Pennsylvania
Robert Morris
Benjamin Rush
Benjamin Franklin
John Morton
George Clymer
James Smith
George Taylor
James Wilson
George Ross

Delaware
Caesar Rodney
George Read
Thomas McKean

New York
William Floyd
Philip Livingston
Francis Lewis
Lewis Morris

New Jersey
Richard Stockton
John Witherspoon
Francis Hopkinson
John Hart
Abraham Clark

New Hampshire
Josiah Bartlett
William Whipple
Matthew Thornton

Massachusetts
Samuel Adams
John Adams
Robert Treat Paine
Elbridge Gerry

Rhode Island
Stephen Hopkins
William Ellery

Connecticut
Roger Sherman
Samuel Huntington
William Williams
Oliver Wolcott

rectitude rightness

DNY59/E+/Getty Images

WDC Photos/Alamy Stock Photo

The Constitution

In this painting from 1940, members of the Constitutional Convention prepare to sign the U.S. Constitution as George Washington (standing at right) presides.

Creating the Constitution

Though written more than 235 years ago, the U.S. Constitution is a document of enduring importance. It still structures our government today.

The Preamble, or introduction, explains why the Constitution was written. It spells out the purposes of the government. The Constitution was written in 1787 and became the law of the land in 1789.

The Preamble

66 We the People of the United States, in Order to form a more perfect Union, establish Justice, insure domestic Tranquillity, provide for the common defence, promote the general Welfare, and secure the Blessings of Liberty to ourselves and our Posterity, do ordain and establish this Constitution for the United States of America. 99

—Preamble to the U.S. Constitution, 1787

While students do not lose their constitutional righs when they enter a school, their First Amendment right of freedom of speech can be limited. As seen in the cartoon, freedom of speech in U.S. schoools can be limited to prohibit disrespectful, inappropriate, or distruptive speech.

"SORRY, YOUR TALKING IN CLASS IS NOT PROTECTED BY THE 1ST AMENDMENT."

Ending Slavery and Gaining the Right to Vote

In 1865 the Thirteenth Amendment outlawed slavery. Five years later, the Fifteenth Amendment stated the right to vote could not be denied to citizens based on their race. But women could still not vote. It took the Nineteenth Amendment, ratified in 1920, to give all women the right to vote.

» Around 1910, these African American suffragists, or active supporters of women's right to vote, marched in support of the cause.

» On January 20, 2021, Vice President Kamala Harris was sworn in by Supreme Court Justice Sonia Sotomayor, the first Latina on the Supreme Court. Vice President Harris was the first African American, South Asian, and woman elected to the office.

> 66 As legendary orator Lucy Stone, one of America's first advocates for women's rights, asked in 1853: '"We the People"? Which "We the People"? The women were not included.' Neither were white males who did not own property, American Indians, or African Americans—slave or free. Yet, one by one, these groups were eventually brought within the Constitution's definition of 'We the People' through civic movements dedicated to that purpose. 99
>
> —Linda R. Monk, "Why We the People? Citizens as Agents of Constitutional Change." *History Now*, Fall 2007

Getting Ready to Learn About . . .
The Constitution

Foundations of Democracy

In a democracy, the people rule. They make the laws, as they did in ancient Greece around 400 B.C.E. The Greeks created a direct democracy in which the people governed themselves. The ancient Romans created the first republic, a form of government in which the people choose leaders to govern them. The United States is the world's oldest representative democracy. It is also a republic. How did we develop that form of government?

English Political Tradition

The development of government in England greatly influenced the government we have today. Over many centuries, England went from having a king with complete power to the people having power. The English also deeply valued their individual rights and took steps to protect them.

One English principle that later influenced the U.S. government was the concept of limited government. This is the idea that a ruler or a government is not all-powerful. In other words, all people, even the king, are subject to the laws. This principle first took form in 1215. That year, English nobles forced King John to sign the Magna Carta. This document declared that nobles had certain rights the king had to recognize. They included the right to agree to any taxes, to have a fair trial judged by their peers, and to not have their property taken from them except by law. Later these rights were extended to all free people in England.

In the 1600s, the English put more limits on the ruler's power. Parliament—the body of people who meet and make laws in England—led this effort. In 1628 Parliament forced King Charles I to sign the Petition of Right. This document said that the king could not impose taxes without the consent of Parliament. He also could not put people in prison without having a reason. And he could not force people to house soldiers in their homes.

In 1688 Parliament went further. It required the English rulers to agree to protect certain individual rights. These rights were named in the English Bill of Rights. The English Bill of Rights protected people's rights from the government and guaranteed those rights to people.

From Colonies to Nation

During the 1600s, thousands of people left England to settle in North America. They founded 13 colonies and began to thrive. They were governed by the king and Parliament. They also had local governments in which the colonists chose representatives who made laws for the town or colony. These colonists were well aware of the dangers of harsh government and of the importance of individual rights. When they set up their own governments, they put limits on government power to protect their freedoms.

In the 1760s, disagreements developed between the colonists and their home country, now called Great Britain. These differences led to a war that resulted in American independence. They formed a new country, the United States of America. The colonies—now called *states*—formed their own governments with their own constitutions.

A New Constitution

A body called the Second Continental Congress wrote a constitution for the United States. It was called the Articles of Confederation. At the time, many states included a bill of rights as part of their state constitutions.

This building in Williamsburg was home to the legislature of the colony of Virginia.

Weaknesses of the Articles of Confederation

The Articles of Confederation were aimed at setting up a new government but had some serious weaknesses.

Lack of Power and Money	• Congress had no power to collect taxes. • Congress had no power to regulate trade. • Congress had no power to enforce its laws.
Lack of Central Power	• No single leader or group directed governmental policy. • No national court system existed.
Rules too Rigid	• Congress could not pass laws without the approval of 9 states. • The Articles could not be changed without the agreement of all 13 states.

HISTORY CONNECTION

1. **Inferring** Based on the diagram, what was the only national governmental body under the Articles of Confederation?
2. **Analyzing** Why was it a serious problem that the Articles were almost impossible to change?

The Founders wanted to avoid a powerful central government. As a result, they formed a central government with little authority or power. They intended to make sure this government would not become oppressive. However, in 1787, this new government was too weak to function well. The states sent delegates to a meeting to change the Articles of Confederation. Instead, they ended up writing a new Constitution. This is the Constitution that still governs the country today.

When the new Constitution was proposed in 1787, many people feared it would not protect the liberties for which they had fought so hard in the American Revolution. They feared the power of the national government would overwhelm the power of the states. In particular, they said that the people needed a bill of rights to protect individual freedoms. Several states refused to ratify the Constitution without a bill of rights. To convince them to adopt the new Constitution, the Framers agreed to create the Bill of Rights.

Structure and Principles of the Constitution

The Constitution is based on several principles: popular sovereignty, limited government and the rule of law, separation of powers, checks and balances, and federalism. Under federalism, the Constitution divides power between the federal government and the states. However, the Constitution's supremacy clause makes it the "supreme law of the land."

The Constitution has three parts. Its Preamble names six purposes of government. Its opening words make it clear that the government's power comes from the people. Three of its seven articles set up the three branches of government—the legislative branch, the executive branch, and the judicial branch. There are also twenty-seven amendments to the Constitution. The first ten are the Bill of Rights. The process for changing the Constitution was purposefully made difficult to preserve the delicate balance of power among the three branches of government and between the federal and state governments.

Looking Ahead

You will learn about the Constitution of the United States. You will examine Compelling Questions and develop your own questions about the Constitution in the Inquiry Activities. You can preview some of the key concepts that you will learn about by reviewing the infographic.

What Will You Learn?

In these lessons about the Constitution, you will learn:

- how the weaknesses of the Articles of Confederation led to the formation of a new plan of federal government, the Constitution.
- the distinct viewpoints of the Federalists and the Anti-Federalists.
- the debates and compromises that happened during the Constitutional Convention.
- how the federal government is organized.
- the structure and principles of the Constitution.
- the three branches of government and the amendment process.
- which civil liberties are protected by the First Amendment of the Bill of Rights.
- the reasons for limits on individual rights.
- which civil liberties are protected by the Bill of Rights, particularly by the Second through the Tenth Amendments to the U.S. Constitution.

- how the Bill of Rights places limits on the power of government.
- the reasons for the Thirteenth, Fourteenth, and Fifteenth Amendments to the Constitution.
- how several amendments added in the 1900s extended voting rights and changed the election process.
- why the civil rights movement occurred and what impact it had on society and the law.

 COMPELLING QUESTIONS IN THE INQUIRY ACTIVITY LESSONS

- **How does the form of government shape the society it governs?**
- **How does the First Amendment apply to students?**
- **How can people change government policy?**

The Five Basic Principles of the U.S. Constitution
The Constitution is based upon five principles.

Popular Sovereignty

Limited Government and Rule of Law

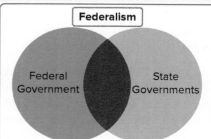
Federalism

Federal Government | State Governments

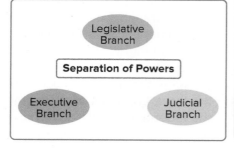
Separation of Powers

Legislative Branch

Executive Branch | Judicial Branch

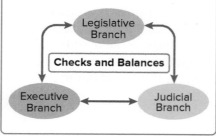
Checks and Balances

Legislative Branch

Executive Branch | Judicial Branch

02

The Country's First Governments

PHOTO: David R. Frazier Photolibrary, Inc./Alamy Stock Photo; TEXT: "[Fryday May 10. 1776.]," Founders Online, National Archives, https://founders.archives.gov/documents/Adams/01-03-02-0016-0116. [Original source: The Adams Papers, Diary and Autobiography of John Adams, vol. 3, Diary, 1782–1804; Autobiography, Part One to October 1776, ed. L. H. Butterfield. Cambridge, MA: Harvard University Press, 1961, pp. 382–384.]

READING STRATEGY

Analyzing Key Ideas and Details As you read about the Articles of Confederation, complete a graphic organizer like the one shown here to analyze that document and the government it established.

Achievements of the Confederation Congress	Weaknesses of the Articles of Confederation

State Constitutions

GUIDING QUESTION

How did citizens set up governments as they transitioned from colonies to states?

Native peoples who lived in the territories that became British colonies had governments of their own. When British colonists arrived, they had colonial charters that set out the conditions of British rule. Independence created a need for new plans for governing the former colonies, now called *states*. The Second Continental Congress urged the colonists to form state governments "as shall . . . best conduce [contribute] to the happiness and safety of their constituents [people]." In January 1776, New Hampshire became the first colony to discard its charter and adopt a constitution. A **constitution** is a detailed, written plan for government. Within a few years, the other 12 colonies had all done the same.

State Governments

The constitutions of the new states established three-branch governments. An official called a governor was appointed as the state's central authority. The governor's job was to **implement**, or enforce, state laws. The citizens of each state chose their governor, either by direct election or through elected representatives.

Lawmaking was assigned to an elected legislature. Most legislatures were **bicameral**, meaning that they consisted of two separate bodies called *houses*. Members of each house were chosen by different methods, giving different groups in the state more influence. Both houses would have to agree to pass laws.

Finally, each state had a judicial system consisting of courts. Judges presided over those courts, making decisions that applied and interpreted the laws.

implement to apply or enforce

New Hampshire was the first of the thirteen colonies to replace its colonial charter with a state constitution.

▶ GO ONLINE Explore the Student Edition eBook and find interactive maps, charts, graphs, and tools.

C61

Bills of Rights

States wrote their new constitutions with the Declaration of Independence in mind, particularly its claim that all people had "unalienable rights" to "life, liberty, and the pursuit of happiness." Constitutions also drew upon important ideas from documents of the past. Both the Magna Carta and the English Bill of Rights, for example, had protected the rights to trial by jury and of ownership of private property. State constitutions included these rights and others. These bills of rights guaranteed specific freedoms and legal protections to a state's people. No state government could ignore those listed rights or take them away.

✓ **CHECK FOR UNDERSTANDING**

Explaining Why did the colonies create new governments for themselves when they became states?

The Articles of Confederation

GUIDING QUESTION

What problems were created by the Articles of Confederation for governing the United States?

By 1780, each state had a new constitution. However, members of the Congress knew that they needed some central government to lead all the states. After all, they had a war to win. That would take a large army, something no state could raise and support on its own.

To meet that need, the Second Continental Congress wrote a document in 1777 that established a confederation of states. A **confederation** is a group of individual state governments that unite for a common purpose. The document, called the **Articles of Confederation**, became the first constitution of the United States of America.

By 1781, all 13 states had approved the Articles. The result was a "league of friendship" among 13 independent states.

The Articles created the Confederation Congress, which would organize and control a national army. The Congress was also empowered to represent the United States in its dealings with foreign countries. Under this arrangement, each state was given a single vote in this Congress, with the agreement of nine states needed to pass a law.

The Northwest Ordinances

The peace that settled the American Revolution gave the new United States control of land west of the Appalachian Mountains. The Confederation Congress took steps to organize this area, called the Old Northwest. It included present-day Ohio, Michigan, Indiana, Illinois, Wisconsin, and part of Minnesota. The Congress's decisions would come to have a major effect on the development of the United States. The Congress passed two **ordinances**, or laws, affecting these lands. The first of the two, known as the **Ordinance of 1785**, set up a plan for surveying, or measuring, land. It also established rules that regulated how that land would be sold or awarded to settlers. It divided the Old Northwest into townships that were 6 miles square, or 36 square miles. Each was further divided into 36 sections of one square mile each. This approach to surveying is still used today.

The second ordinance, called the **Northwest Ordinance**, was passed in 1787. It renamed the Old Northwest area the Northwest Territory and established a legislative body to govern it. This law included a procedure for admitting new states into the Union. As the United States later added more territories, this ordinance became the model for organizing them.

This ordinance had another clause, or section, that would later have a significant **impact** on U.S. history. It read:

66 There shall be neither slavery nor involuntary servitude in said territory. 99

—the Northwest Ordinance

---

confederation a group of individual state governments that unite for a common purpose

Articles of Confederation the first constitution of the United States

ordinance a law, usually of a city or country

Ordinance of 1785 a law that set up a plan for surveying western lands

Northwest Ordinance a 1787 law that set up a government for the Northwest Territory and a plan for admitting new states into the Union

impact an effect

The Northwest Territory

The Ordinance of 1785 established a system for measuring and dividing up government-owned land for sale. It reserved every sixteenth section for public schools.

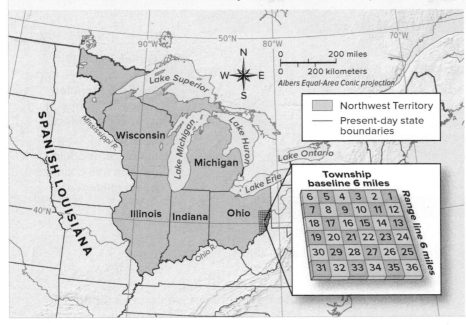

United States Continental Congress. "An Ordinance for the Government of the Territory of the United States, North-west of the River Ohio." Library of Congress. https://www.loc.gov/item/90898154/.

GEOGRAPHY CONNECTION

1. **Exploring Regions** What present-day states were created out of the Northwest Territory?

2. **Spatial Thinking** Which compass directions did the township baselines and range lines follow?

The Ordinance of 1785 and the Northwest Ordinance guided the orderly settlement of the Northwest Territory. During the American Revolution, only a few thousand settlers had lived there. By the 1790s, about 120,000 people had settled in this area.

Weaknesses of the Articles

The Confederation Congress had three major successes. It oversaw the war that gained American independence, which the British recognized in 1783 by signing the Treaty of Paris. It also passed the two Northwest Territory ordinances. At the same time, however, the Confederation Congress struggled to govern the country. The reasons for these struggles and the failure of the Articles were written into the Articles themselves. First, Congress could not pass a law unless nine states voted for it. That meant five states could join together to block any action. Second, Congress also could not amend, or change, the Articles without the agreement of all 13 states. This meant that one state alone could prevent any change to the Articles. These rules made it hard for the Congress to accomplish anything.

The Articles had other weaknesses, too. Congress could not tax people to raise money.

It could not regulate, or make rules about, trade between the states. Instead, each state set its own rules. The Articles had no one to carry out the laws Congress did pass. The Articles also had no national courts. If two states disagreed on something, such as the boundaries between them, there was no way to settle the dispute. Finally, the Articles did not provide for a permanent army. If someone attacked the United States, Congress had to ask the states to supply troops. Even if the states did so, the delay could be dangerous.

The limits placed on Congress had been intentional. Colonists had only recently thrown off Britain's strict rule. They did not want their new government to misuse its power and violate people's rights, as they thought the British had done. For this reason, the 13 states gave the Confederation Congress little power. However, this decision made the failure of the Congress very likely. If a state ignored a law, Congress could do nothing about it.

Perhaps the Articles' biggest oversight was that the Confederation Congress could do no more than ask states for money. It had no authority to demand funds or to directly tax Americans. This created problems because the Confederation Congress had gone into debt to pay for the American Revolution.

Weaknesses of the Articles of Confederation

The Articles of Confederation set up a new national government that had several serious weaknesses.

LACK OF POWER AND MONEY

- Congress had no power to collect taxes.
- Congress had no power to regulate trade.
- Congress had no power to enforce its laws.

LACK OF CENTRAL POWER

- No single leader or group directed government policy.
- No national court system existed.
- No standing army was created to protect the country.

RULES TOO RIGID

- Congress could not pass laws without the approval of 9 states.
- The Articles could not be changed without the agreement of all 13 states.

HISTORY CONNECTION

1. **Explaining** Which weakness prevented the Confederation Congress from putting its laws into effect?

2. **Calculating** How many states could prevent any changes being made to the Articles?

Shays's Rebellion

Meanwhile, the new nation was struggling. Several states had fallen deeply into debt. They raised taxes to try to pay off that debt, but this decision caused more problems. High taxes hurt merchants and businesspeople. Many people lost their jobs. Farmers could not sell their crops. They had to borrow money, but without income from selling crops they could not repay the loans. Some farmers lost their land. It was becoming clear that the Confederation Congress fell far short of what the country needed.

During 1786 and 1787, riots broke out in several states. The worst occurred in Massachusetts. A farmer in that state named Daniel Shays owed money due to high taxes. State courts threatened to take his farm and sell it to pay for his debts. Shays believed that his problems were the state's fault, not his own. He was not alone—other farmers were in the same situation and felt the same way. About 1,200 of them, including some free African Americans, joined together under Shays's leadership. They attacked an arsenal. Although the uprising, known as **Shays's Rebellion**, was quickly subdued, it worried many Americans. Political leaders, businesspeople, and ordinary citizens began calling for a stronger national government.

> 66 I do not conceive we can exist long as a nation, without having lodged somewhere a power which will pervade the whole Union. 99

—Letter from George Washington to John Jay, 1786

✓ CHECK FOR UNDERSTANDING

1. **Understanding Supporting Details** List three weaknesses of the Articles of Confederation.

2. **Making Connections** How did the colonists' experience with Britain's government lead to a major weakness of the Articles of Confederation?

LESSON ACTIVITIES

1. **Informative/Explanatory Writing** Suppose you were a reporter who interviewed Daniel Shays before he and others attacked the arsenal. Write a news story that reports on the complaints that Shays and other farmers had.

2. **Using Multimedia** Work with a partner to create a media presentation analyzing how three flaws in the Articles of Confederation made it difficult for Congress to govern the country. Include images that support your analysis. Share your presentation with your class.

Shays's Rebellion an uprising of Massachusetts farmers who did not want to lose their farms because of debt caused by heavy state taxes after the American Revolution

"From George Washington to John Jay, 15 August 1786," Founders Online, National Archives, https://founders.archives.gov/documents/Washington/04-04-02-0199. [Original source: The Papers of George Washington, Confederation Series, vol. 4, 2 April 1786 –31 January 1787, ed. W. W. Abbot. Charlottesville: University Press of Virginia, 1995, pp. 212–213.]

03

Creating a New Constitution

READING STRATEGY

Analyzing Key Ideas and Details As you read about the drafting of the United States Constitution, complete a graphic organizer like the one shown here to list and describe important compromises made by the delegates.

Name of the Compromise	What the Compromise Did

The Constitutional Convention

GUIDING QUESTION

Why did American leaders decide to create a new plan of government?

In the spring of 1787, delegates from 12 of the then 13 United States met in Philadelphia. The Confederation Congress had governed the nation for 10 years. During that time, it had become clear that the Articles of Confederation prevented that Congress from governing effectively.

The delegates were instructed to fix the Articles. They intended to do this by creating a stronger central government. Rhode Island did not participate because its leaders opposed changing the document.

The Delegates

Fifty-five people attended the convention, or conference. It was held in a building known today as Independence Hall. All of these delegates were white, male, and well-educated. No Native Americans, African Americans, or women were invited to participate.

The delegates included merchants, lawyers, college presidents, physicians, governors, and military leaders. All of them had political experience. Eight had signed the Declaration of Independence. Seven had been state governors. Forty-one had either been members of the Continental Congress, were currently members of the Confederation Congress, or both.

The oldest delegate was 81-year-old Benjamin Franklin. He was a respected diplomat, writer, scientist, and inventor. Most delegates, however, were in their thirties or forties.

Many delegates went on to serve in the new national government that was created by the gathering. Two—George Washington and James Madison—would later become U.S. presidents. Nineteen others would serve as U.S. senators, and thirteen would be elected to the House of Representatives. Four would become Supreme Court justices. Another four would become federal judges.

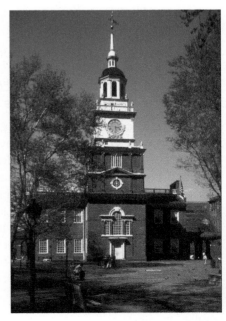

» The Constitutional Convention met at Independence Hall in Philadelphia, Pennsylvania.

NPS Photo

Not all of the Founders of the United States attended, however. Thomas Jefferson and John Adams were serving the Confederation Congress by representing the nation to countries in Europe. Patrick Henry, a Virginian and a leader during the Revolution, was also absent. Although he had been elected as a delegate, Henry opposed the idea of making the central government stronger. As a result, he refused to attend.

The First Decisions

The first thing the delegates needed to do was choose someone to lead the meeting. They picked George Washington out of respect for his leadership during the American Revolution. Washington ran the meetings in an orderly way, often reminding the delegates how important their mission was. He warned that if they did not come up with an acceptable plan of government, "perhaps another dreadful conflict is to be sustained [suffered]."

Next, the delegates set the rules for their discussions. It was agreed that each state would get one vote, regardless of how many delegates it had sent. This was the same way that states voted in the Confederation Congress. In a change from the rules in Congress, though, the delegates agreed that a simple majority—7 votes out of 12—would settle any issue.

Finally, the delegates decided to keep their work secret so they could talk freely. Doors were guarded. Windows were shut **despite**, or in spite of, the summer heat. No one from the public was allowed in, and the delegates did not discuss the progress of the Convention with anyone outside the group.

Because of the secrecy surrounding the proceedings, we have few written records of the convention. The most detailed account comes from a notebook kept by Virginia's James Madison.

We do know that the original aim of the gathering was to **revise**, or improve, the Articles of Confederation. However, the delegates soon realized that making a few changes would not be enough. What was needed was a new government altogether. They decided to scrap the Articles completely and write a new constitution. This development led to the meeting in Philadelphia becoming known as the

despite in spite of

revise to improve

Constitutional Convention. Today, we call the convention's delegates the *Framers* because they created the frame of government that Americans have used since the Constitution was adopted.

✓ CHECK FOR UNDERSTANDING

Explaining Why did the meeting to revise the Articles of Confederation come to be called the Constitutional Convention?

Compromising for a Constitution

GUIDING QUESTION

Why were compromises made at the Constitutional Convention?

The delegates wanted to create a constitution that all states would accept. The situation was critical, and failure might mean disaster. The Framers were dedicated to their task, however. According to James Madison's notes, George Mason of Virginia said the following:

Constitutional Convention meeting of delegates in 1787 that led to the writing of the U.S. Constitution

Virginia's James Madison is known as the "Father of the Constitution." He is remembered for his role in writing the Constitution and working for its approval by the states.

PHOTO: Granger, NYC – All rights reserved.; TEXT: Washington, George. Quoted in Morris, G. An Oration Upon the Death of General Washington, December 31, 1799. In The Records of the Federal Convention of 1787, Volume 3. Edited by Max Farrand. 1911. New Haven, Conn.: Yale University Press, 1911.

> 66 [I] would bury [my] bones in this city rather than [leave] . . . the Convention without any thing being done. 99

Early in the Convention, James Madison presented the delegates with a blueprint for a strong national government. Today his plan is known as the Virginia Plan.

The Virginia Plan

The Virginia Plan laid out a federal government that had features similar to the one that was eventually created. It called for a president, courts, and a congress with two houses. The makeup of those two houses differed from what we have now, however. Madison suggested a state's population would determine how many representatives the state would have in each house. This meant that larger states would have more representatives—and more votes—than smaller states.

Delegates from states with large populations —Massachusetts, Pennsylvania, Virginia, and New York—liked this plan. Delegates from smaller states did not. They were afraid that the larger states would ignore their interests.

The New Jersey Plan

After two weeks of heated debate, William Paterson of New Jersey offered a different idea, which is called the New Jersey Plan. It had much in common with the Articles of Confederation. For one thing, it kept the Confederation's one-house congress. It also gave each state one vote. At the same time, Paterson's plan differed from the Articles. He did want to make Congress stronger.

As a result, he gave it authority to regulate, or control, trade and to impose taxes. Paterson rejected Madison's idea of having a president, but he did want to have an executive branch. His version took the form of a committee named by Congress to enforce laws.

Support for Paterson's plan was the opposite of support for Madison's. The delegates from Delaware, Maryland, and New Jersey—all smaller states—liked it. It gave them the same power as larger states. Those from the larger states opposed it. They believed that states with larger populations should have more influence on the government.

The Great Compromise

Finally, a committee headed by Roger Sherman of Connecticut combined features of the two plans and created a third **alternative**, or option. The committee proposed a Congress with two houses—a Senate and a House of Representatives. In the Senate, each state would have two members. This pleased the smaller states. In the House, the number of seats for each state would reflect the state's population. This pleased the larger states. Both houses would have to agree to a proposal for it to become law.

Although neither the large states nor the small states were fully satisfied, both groups accepted the committee's plan. Historians call Sherman's plan the Connecticut Compromise, or the **Great Compromise**. A compromise is an agreement among two or more sides. Each side gives up something it wants in exchange for something else.

Great Compromise an agreement providing a dual system of congressional representation

Mason, George. Quoted in "Proceedings of Convention, June 9-July 13." In The Records of the Federal Convention of 1787, Volume 1. Edited by Max Farrand. 1911. New Haven, Conn.: Yale University Press, 1911.

The Great Compromise

The Great Compromise settled the disagreement between states with large populations and those with small populations over the form that the federal legislature should take.

VIRGINIA PLAN	CONNECTICUT COMPROMISE
Two-house legislature	Two-house legislature
Number of legislators varies according to state population	Representation in House of Representatives based on state population
NEW JERSEY PLAN	
One-house legislature	Equal representation in Senate, with two members from each state
Each state gets one vote regardless of population	

HISTORY CONNECTION

Analyzing Points of View Why would those who favored either the Virginia Plan or the New Jersey Plan agree to the Great Compromise?

Southern states wanted enslaved people, such as the three men in this illustration, counted for purposes of representation. In some Southern states, enslaved African Americans made up as much as 45 percent of the population.

The Three-Fifths Compromise

That settled one dispute, but others remained. One of them concerned slavery and representation in Congress. In 1787 more than 550,000 African Americans were enslaved. Most were in Southern states. Nobody proposed giving enslaved persons a voice in the new government. Nonetheless, delegates from slaveholding states wanted to count enslaved people in a state's populations. That would mean more seats—and votes—in the House of Representatives.

The North, on the other hand, had few enslaved persons. Delegates from those states said that enslaved persons were property under the law. Since enslaved persons could not vote or take part in government, Northern delegates said it was wrong to count them for the purpose of representation.

The Southern delegates got most of what they wanted. The delegates agreed to a plan that became known as the **Three-Fifths Compromise**. In it, every five enslaved persons counted as three free persons. Thus, three-fifths of the enslaved population in each state would count for representation in Congress. The Southern delegates had to accept that the same guideline would be used by the federal government when calculating taxes on states.

Other Compromises

More compromises were made to settle other disagreements. One significant issue involved the method for choosing the president. Some delegates thought that Congress should elect the president. Others believed that the voters should elect this leader. The solution was to establish an **Electoral College** to select both presidents and vice presidents. As originally written, each state's electors would be named by the state legislature, and those electors would choose the president and vice president. The Electoral College still exists today, but now voters instead of legislators choose electors. Each state's number of electors is based on the total number of representatives and senators it sends to Congress.

Delegates made compromises on trade matters, too. Northern states wanted to give Congress the power to regulate trade among the states and with other countries. Southern states feared that Congress might tax their exports—goods sold to other countries. This would hurt the Southern economy since the South exported large amounts of tobacco, rice, and other products.

Southerners also worried that Congress's power to regulate trade would result in a law that prevented them from bringing in more enslaved people from Africa. They thought that such a law

Three-Fifths Compromise agreement providing that enslaved persons would count as three-fifths of other persons in determining representation in Congress

Electoral College a group of people originally named by each state legislature, but now chosen by voters, to select the president and vice president

would harm the region's ability to produce farm-based products.

Yet another compromise settled these issues. The Southern delegates agreed to let Congress regulate trade among the states and with other countries. In return, the North supported denying Congress the authority to tax exports. In addition, it was agreed that Congress could not ban the slave trade until 1808—about 20 years in the future.

✓ CHECK FOR UNDERSTANDING

1. **Making Connections** How did the Framers settle the disagreement between large and small states over the structure of the federal government?

2. **Explaining** What disagreement was settled by the Three-Fifths Compromise?

Federalists and Anti-Federalists

GUIDING QUESTION

How did Federalist and Anti-Federalist viewpoints differ?

The delegates discussed, argued, and compromised for four months. As their task neared its end, some delegates headed home. On September 17, 1787, 42 met for the final time. All but three of them signed their names at the bottom of the document. The Constitution was now ready to be submitted to each state for approval.

The delegates called for the states to hold conventions to consider the Constitution. When at least 9 of the 13 states voted to ratify, or approve, it, the Constitution would become law.

Who Were the Federalists?

Americans held different views about the proposed Constitution. Those who supported it called themselves **Federalists**. They chose this name because they believed the Constitution would create a system of **federalism**, that is, a form of government in which power is divided between the federal, or national, government and the states. They believed that federal law should have more weight than state law.

To win support, the Federalists wrote essays and made speeches. They pointed out the weaknesses in the Articles of Confederation. They argued that the United States had to have a stronger national government to protect property rights and to solve the country's problems at home and defend its interests abroad. Alexander Hamilton, James Madison, and John Jay were among the Federalists. They wrote a series of essays called **the Federalist Papers**, or *The Federalist*. They used these essays to explain the advantages of the Constitution and to answer criticisms of it. Madison wrote this in one of these essays:

❝ [a] Republic, by which I mean a Government in which the scheme of representation takes place . . . promises the cure for which we are seeking. ❞

—James Madison, *The Federalist*, No. 10

Who Were the Anti-Federalists?

Anti-Federalists took an opposing view. They argued that the new Constitution would strengthen the national government but weaken the states. Some also feared that such a government would act in ways that would benefit wealthy people and not everyone else. They wanted to limit the power of the national government to only what was necessary to preserve the union.

The Anti-Federalists had one other important objection. They complained that the new Constitution did not include a bill of rights to protect individual freedoms. The conventions in several states insisted on adding one. If a bill of rights was not added, they would not ratify the Constitution.

Launching a New Nation

At first, the Federalists did not believe a bill of rights was necessary. They thought that individual rights were guaranteed by the Constitution as it was. In order to gain ratification, however, they promised that the new government would quickly add a bill of rights if the Constitution was adopted.

That promise helped win public support for the proposed Constitution. Voters in each state

---

Federalist a supporter of the Constitution

federalism a form of government in which power is divided between the federal, or national, government and the states

the Federalist Papers a series of essays written to defend the Constitution

Anti-Federalist a person who opposed ratification of the Constitution

Federalist No. 10: The Same Subject Continued: The Union as a Safeguard Against Domestic Faction and Insurrection, from the New York Packet, from The Federalist Papers, by James Madison, 1787. Library of Congress, Manuscript Division.

Ratification of the Constitution

Nine of the 13 states were needed to ratify the Constitution for it to take effect.

New Hampshire
June 1788

New York
July 1788

Massachusetts
February 1788

Rhode Island
May 1790

Pennsylvania
December 1787

Connecticut
January 1788

Northwest
Territory

New Jersey
December 1787

Maryland
April 1788

Delaware
December 1787

Virginia
June 1788

ATLANTIC OCEAN

North Carolina
November 1789*

South
Carolina
May 1788

Georgia
January 1788

0   300 miles
0   300 kilometers
Albers Equal-Area Conic projection

Unanimously ratified

Strongly supported ratification

Opposed ratification until
Bill of Rights agreed upon

Ratified after the Constitution
became fully effective in
March 1789

*Ratification was originally defeated;
date represents second vote.

GEOGRAPHY CONNECTION

1. **Exploring Place** Which state held two votes before ratifying the Constitution?

2. **Patterns and Movement** Which three states ratified the Constitution in 1787?

elected delegates to attend a special convention to ratify the Constitution or vote it down. Several of these conventions had already voted for ratification before the question of the bill of rights came up. With the promise of a bill of rights, the Massachusetts convention voted to ratify. New Hampshire became the ninth state to do so. The Constitution took effect in June 1788. In time, the remaining four states also ratified it. The last to do so was Rhode Island, in May 1790. The 13 independent states were no longer a loose confederation. Under the new government, the states became even more united as they faced the future.

✔ **CHECK FOR UNDERSTANDING**

1. **Comparing and Contrasting** How did the viewpoint of the Federalists differ from that of the Anti-Federalists?

2. **Identifying Cause and Effect** What promise helped convince enough people to ratify the Constitution?

LESSON ACTIVITIES

1. **Informative/Explanatory Writing** Write an essay on the topic of Federalism and Anti-Federalism. Explain the main points of Federalism and the arguments made to support it. Then, do the same for Anti-Federalism. Conclude your essay by stating an example of how each viewpoint was represented in the final governing document.

2. **Collaborating** In a small group, examine the compromises made to resolve disputes during the Constitutional Convention. Discuss the democratic ideals behind each compromise, but also consider how each compromise did or did not affect groups in the United States that were not allowed to participate in the framing of the government, such as Native Americans, enslaved or free African Americans, women, or working-class whites. Discuss whether the compromises were fair to everyone in the country. Collect your findings in a chart or a short report.

The Structure of the Constitution

The Parts of the Constitution

GUIDING QUESTION

How does the U.S. Constitution organize the government?

The United States Constitution is the framework of our nation's government. It is our highest authority and the foundation of all laws in the United States. It describes the functions of the three branches of the federal government and their relationships to one another. It also establishes our basic ideals of democracy, freedom, and personal liberty. Apart from that, like the American flag, it is a symbol of our nation.

The Constitution is fairly brief, at just under 7,000 words. It is also less detailed than the constitutions of many other nations. This leaves room for interpretation, which has proven to be both a benefit and a challenge over the years.

There are three parts to the Constitution. The first is called the **Preamble** (PREE·AM·buhl). The preamble is an introduction that declares our government's ideals, goals, and purposes. This is followed by three **articles** that describe the structure, organization, and powers of the federal government and four more articles that address other important matters. Finally, there are 27 formal additions and changes to the Constitution. Those are called **amendments**.

Preamble the opening section of the Constitution

article one of seven main parts of the Constitution

amendment any change to the Constitution

READING STRATEGY

Analyzing Key Ideas and Details As you read, use a table like this one to help you describe the content of the United States Constitution's articles.

Articles of the Constitution	
Article	**Description**
Article I	
Article II	
Article III	
Article IV	
Article V	
Article VI	
Article VII	

When they enter the U.S. Army, new recruits take an oath to support and defend the U.S. Constitution.

The U.S. Constitution was not the first ever written. It was, however, the first complete and comprehensive plan for a national government. Its adoption inspired people in Poland, France, and other countries to craft constitutions of their own. Most of those documents have not been as successful as our own, but people around the world have seen the U.S. Constitution as a model to follow.

The Preamble

The Preamble consists of a single, powerful sentence. It begins and ends as follows:

> 66 We the People of the United States . . . do ordain and establish this Constitution for the United States of America. 99

—Preamble of the U.S. Constitution

These carefully chosen words make clear that the power of government comes from the people. The middle part of the Preamble sets forth six purposes of the federal government:

1. To "form a more perfect Union" means to unite the states more firmly than they were united under the Articles of Confederation.

2. To "establish Justice" means to make sure that all citizens are treated equally and fairly under the law.

3. To "insure domestic Tranquility" means to ensure peace and order and to keep citizens and their property safe.

4. To "provide for the common [defense]" means to be able to protect the country and its people from attack.

5. To "promote the general Welfare" means to provide conditions that make it possible for citizens to live healthy, happy, and prosperous lives.

6. To "secure the Blessings of Liberty to ourselves and our Posterity" means to protect freedoms

Comparing the Constitutions of the United States and India
The preamble of the Indian constitution is similar to that of the United States.

Purpose	Preamble to the U.S. Constitution (1787)	Preamble to India's Constitution (1949)
Group acting	"We the People of the United States,	"We, the people of India,
Purpose	in Order to form a more perfect Union, establish Justice, insure domestic Tranquility [peace], provide for the common defence, promote the general Welfare, and secure the Blessings of Liberty to ourselves and our Posterity [people that come later],	having solemnly [seriously] resolved [decided] to constitute [form] India into a sovereign [independent] . . . secular [non-religious] democratic republic and to secure to all its citizens: justice, social, economic and political; liberty of thought, expression, belief, faith and worship; equality of status and of opportunity; and to promote among them all fraternity [fellowship] assuring the dignity of the individual and the unity and integrity [wholeness] of the nation;
Action taken	do ordain [proclaim] and establish this Constitution for the United States of America."	having solemnly resolved to constitute in our constituent [representative] assembly this twenty-sixth day of November, 1949, do hereby adopt, enact and give to ourselves this constitution."

HISTORY CONNECTION

1. **Summarize** What are the goals of the Indian Constitution, according to its Preamble?
2. **Comparing** Which of these goals is similar to goals of the U.S. Constitution?

Constitution of the United States, 1787, National Archives and Records Administration.

Comparing the National Government Under the Articles and the Constitution

The Constitution corrected several weaknesses in the Articles of Confederation.

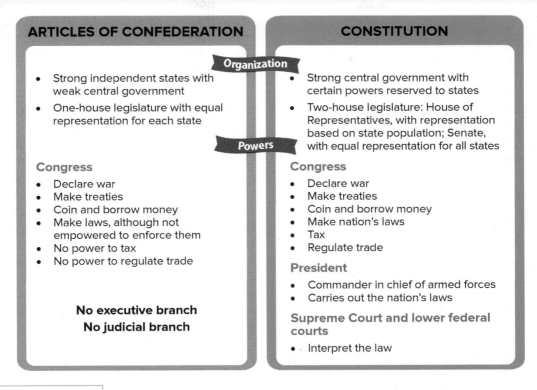

ARTICLES OF CONFEDERATION

Organization

- Strong independent states with weak central government
- One-house legislature with equal representation for each state

Powers

Congress
- Declare war
- Make treaties
- Coin and borrow money
- Make laws, although not empowered to enforce them
- No power to tax
- No power to regulate trade

No executive branch
No judicial branch

CONSTITUTION

- Strong central government with certain powers reserved to states
- Two-house legislature: House of Representatives, with representation based on state population; Senate, with equal representation for all states

Congress
- Declare war
- Make treaties
- Coin and borrow money
- Make nation's laws
- Tax
- Regulate trade

President
- Commander in chief of armed forces
- Carries out the nation's laws

Supreme Court and lower federal courts
- Interpret the law

HISTORY CONNECTION

1. **Analyzing** How did the Constitution increase the power of the central government over the economy?
2. **Comparing** What new parts of the government did the Constitution establish?

and maintain the basic rights of all Americans, including those who will come in the future.

The Seven Articles

The seven articles that follow the Preamble make up most of the Constitution. Each is assigned a Roman numeral, and each has a specific focus.

Articles I, II, and III describe the powers and responsibilities of each of the three branches of the federal government. Article I addresses the lawmaking powers of the **legislative branch**, or Congress. It outlines the structure of Congress's two houses—the Senate and the House of Representatives—and gives those houses the authority to make laws for the entire country. It also describes how members of each house are elected and what qualifications a person must

meet to serve in either house. Finally, it identifies specific areas where Congress can and cannot make laws.

Article II establishes an **executive branch**, which is the part of the government that carries out the laws. It is headed by a president and vice president. This article sets forth how these leaders are elected and describes how they can be removed from office if necessary. This article also describes the president's powers. Those include leading the armed forces and making treaties with other nations.

Article III establishes the **judicial branch**. This branch interprets the laws and sees that they are fairly applied.

legislative branch the lawmaking branch of government

executive branch the branch of government that carries out laws

judicial branch the branch of government that interprets laws

The article calls for "one supreme Court," along with lower courts that Congress can create as needed. The article explains how people become federal judges and says that judges of the federal court are to hold office for life.

Article IV describes the relationship between the states and the national government and their relationship to each other. Article V explains how the Constitution can be amended, or formally changed. Article VI declares the Constitution to be the "supreme Law of the Land." Article VII describes how the Constitution was to be ratified, or formally approved.

The Amendments

Constitutional amendments form the final part of the Constitution. So far, there are 27 of them. The first 10 Constitutional amendments are known as the Bill of Rights. They were added to the Constitution in 1791, shortly after its ratification.

The Bill of Rights is the clearest declaration of individual freedoms to be found in the Constitution. The First Amendment prohibits Congress from interfering with the people's rights to free speech, free religious expression, and a free press. Other amendments prohibit the government from making unreasonable searches and seizures of property and guarantee a person accused of a crime a fair and speedy trial.

✓ CHECK FOR UNDERSTANDING

1. **Identifying** Which part of the Constitution do you think is the most significant, and why?
2. **Speculating** Why might the Framers have decided that a three-branch federal government was better than a one-branch federal government?

Amending and Interpreting the Constitution

GUIDING QUESTION

In what ways can the Constitution be changed?

You might be surprised to learn that thousands of Constitutional amendments have been considered over the years, yet only 27 have ever been ratified. Few proposed amendments make it into the Constitution because the Framers deliberately made the process difficult. A lot of work went into drafting the Constitution. After much debate and compromise, the final product

was a document that delicately balanced the interests of different parts of the country and people with different views. The Framers understood that changing even one small detail might produce unexpected and unwelcome results. Realizing this, they made sure the Constitution could not be amended without a great deal of thought and effort.

At the same time, they knew that being able to change the Constitution was necessary. Remember that every single state had to agree to even the smallest change in the Articles of Confederation. The Framers had seen how the opposition of only one state made it impossible to make important changes to the government when those changes were needed. They also knew that societies change, and they wanted a constitution that could adapt to those changes. At the time of ratification, for example, most African Americans were enslaved and women did not have the right to vote. If the Constitution could not have been changed when society demanded it, its authority—and that of our government—would probably not have lasted.

Formal and Informal Amendments

Amending the Constitution, as outlined in Article V, is a two-step process—proposal and ratification. An amendment may be proposed in either of two ways. The first method—the only one used so far—is by a two-thirds vote of both houses of Congress. The second, never-used

When the Constitution was written, U.S. senators were chosen by the state legislatures. The Seventeenth Amendment changed that to a system in which senators are elected by a state's voters. Here, Senator Mitch McConnell of Kentucky campaigns to win reelection to another term.

Amending the Constitution

The Constitution provides two ways for proposing amendments and two ways for ratifying amendments.

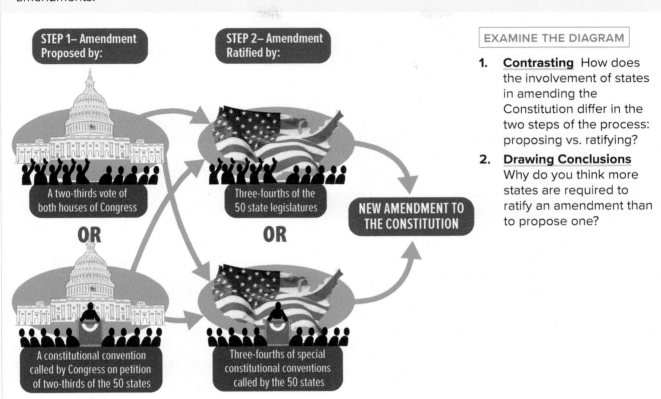

STEP 1– Amendment Proposed by:

A two-thirds vote of both houses of Congress

OR

A constitutional convention called by Congress on petition of two-thirds of the 50 states

STEP 2– Amendment Ratified by:

Three-fourths of the 50 state legislatures

OR

Three-fourths of special constitutional conventions called by the 50 states

NEW AMENDMENT TO THE CONSTITUTION

EXAMINE THE DIAGRAM

1. **Contrasting** How does the involvement of states in amending the Constitution differ in the two steps of the process: proposing vs. ratifying?

2. **Drawing Conclusions** Why do you think more states are required to ratify an amendment than to propose one?

method is through a national convention called by two-thirds of all state legislatures.

Once an amendment has been proposed and passed by Congress, three-fourths of the states must ratify it by either a vote of the state legislature or through special state conventions. The Twenty-first Amendment is the only one that has ever been ratified by the second method. That amendment repealed, or nullified, the Eighteenth Amendment, which had prohibited the sale of alcohol in the country. That is the only amendment to have been cancelled.

While 27 official, or formal, amendments have been added to the Constitution, some situations have led to informal, or unofficial, changes as well. These changes can be as influential as the formal ones. In 1841, for instance, William Henry Harrison became the first president to die in office. Vice President John Tyler took the presidential oath of office and assumed, or took up, the powers of the president. That action is clearly proper under the Constitution. However, it was unclear whether a vice president actually *became* president in this

circumstance or for how long that should be the case. Tyler assumed that he did, and nobody stopped him from doing so. On seven later occasions when presidents died in office, the vice president took the office, citing what Tyler had done. It was not until 1967, when the Twenty-fifth Amendment was ratified, that Tyler's action was formally permitted by the Constitution.

Interpreting the Constitution

The Framers went into great detail about some aspects of government. However, they left others open for interpretation. For example, Article I gives Congress the power to "make all Laws which shall be necessary and proper" to carry out its duties. This is called *the necessary and proper clause*. It has also been interpreted to grant Congress powers not directly stated in the Constitution, which are called *implied powers*. Much of what the federal government does today—from licensing broadcast television stations to regulating air pollution—is not spelled out in the Constitution but based on the idea of implied powers.

Visitors to the National Archives Building in Washington, D.C., can view a carefully preserved early copy of the Constitution.

Of course, not everyone agrees on which laws are "necessary and proper." Some people think Congress should be allowed to make any laws the Constitution does not directly forbid. These people believe in a loose interpretation of the Constitution. Others maintain that Congress should make only the kinds of laws directly stated in the Constitution. They reject the idea of implied powers, favoring a *strict* interpretation of the Constitution.

The final authority for interpreting the Constitution is the Supreme Court. At different points in our history, the Supreme Court has interpreted the Constitution in different ways—sometimes strictly, sometimes loosely. Whichever direction the Court takes, it changes how the government can function until a new Court states the meaning of the Constitution in a different way. Of course, the Supreme Court's power to strike down laws is not directly stated in the Constitution. It, too, is an informal amendment.

Congress and the president also take actions not mentioned in the Constitution. For example, nowhere in the Constitution does it state that the president should propose bills to Congress. Yet since the presidency of George Washington, each president has done so hundreds of times.

The actual processes of government also involve institutions that are not mentioned in the Constitution. For example, the Constitution does not mention political parties. Yet they have existed since our earliest days as a nation. Though they have never been an official part of our government, parties are central to elections and to the actions of Congress.

It is fair to say that today's government is quite different from the government created by the Constitution written in 1787. It will certainly change even more as time passes. However, the basic ideals and principles of our government remain in place to guide those changes.

✓ **CHECK FOR UNDERSTANDING**

Speculating Why might the concept of implied powers be a useful and necessary one?

LESSON ACTIVITIES

1. **Argumentative Writing** Those who believe in a loose interpretation of the Constitution say that it is necessary to view it this way because society changes and people's attitudes change. Those who believe in a strict interpretation say that the Framers created a strong system that protects people's freedoms, and it should not be tampered with. Write a brief argumentative essay explaining which view of the Constitution you think is best and give reasons for your position.

2. **Analyzing Main Ideas** Work with a partner to create an oral presentation on one of the following topics:
   - the basic structure of the Constitution
   - how the federal government is organized
   - how the Constitution is amended

   Partners should take turns presenting the prepared text and respond to any questions from the class on their part. Use at least two visual images in your presentation.

The Principles of the Constitution

Analyzing Key Ideas and Details As you read, use a graphic organizer like this one to name and describe the principles expressed in the Constitution.

Constitutional Principles	
Principle	**What It Means**
1.	
2.	
3.	
4.	
5.	
6.	

Major Principles of Government

GUIDING QUESTION

What are the principles of United States government?

A **principle** is a fundamental idea on which something is based. Principles guide beliefs, customs, and behavior. They also guide governments. Governments use principles to determine the rules by which their citizens are governed. They set forth these rules in a document called a constitution.

There are many written constitutions in use throughout the world, but ours has been in effect the longest. That did not just happen. The U.S. Constitution contains some of the most important and influential ideas in human history.

When the Framers drafted our Constitution, they studied the governments of past nations. They tried to take the best principles of those governments and combine them with the ideas of the greatest thinkers of the time. The result was a document that aims to preserve Americans' rights and liberties more than 200 years later.

As complicated as our Constitution may seem, it is based upon five principles:

- popular sovereignty
- limited government and the rule of law
- separation of powers
- checks and balances
- federalism

principle a fundamental idea

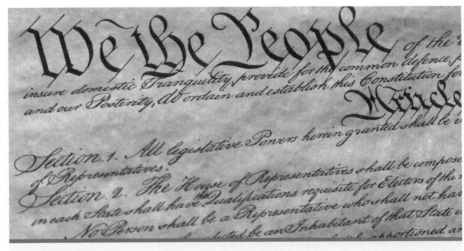

This image shows a copy of the final version of the U.S. Constitution.

Analyzing Visuals How do the position and style of the words "We the People" give them special importance?

The power of voters, such as these in Coral Gables, Florida, to choose their representatives demonstrates the constitutional principle of popular sovereignty.

While our Constitution is certainly remarkable, it is not perfect. The United States we know today is not the one created by the Framers. In its original form, the Constitution permitted slavery and took little thought of the rights of Native Americans, women, and other groups. Despite its strengths, the Constitution could not prevent a devastating civil war when states disagreed over its interpretation.

The Constitution endures because the means to bring it closer to its ideals were written into the document itself. Throughout our history, this fact has gradually brought our nation nearer to its stated principles. That process continues today, although controversy around the document's meaning and intent also continue.

Popular Sovereignty

Article IV of the Constitution guarantees the American people "a *Republican* Form of Government." A *republic* is a form of *representative government*. In a representative government, the people elect representatives to make decisions on their behalf. A republic is a form of democracy because the people are the source of the government's power. Great Britain's government contained democratic elements, but it was ruled by a monarch. The British people did not choose their rulers. The kings and queens who ruled Britain inherited their positions and authority.

The idea that the power of government lies with the people is called **popular sovereignty** (SAH•vuhrn•tee). *Sovereignty* means "the right to rule." The Declaration of Independence is based on this idea. That document proclaims that governments draw their powers "from the consent of the governed."

The Constitution puts the consent of the governed into action in its rules for electing members of Congress. Presidents and vice presidents are selected by the Electoral College, and the votes of those electors reflect the choices of the people in their states. When those officials run for reelection, voters can replace representatives who they think have served them poorly.

Limited Government and the Rule of Law

The Framers firmly believed that the government should be strong but not too strong. They built into the Constitution the principle of **limited government**. This means that government can do only what the Constitution allows it to do. The government must follow the rules set forth in the Constitution when it makes decisions. James Madison expressed the importance of limiting the power of government in this way:

> 66 In framing a government which is to be administered [run] by men over men, the great difficulty lies in this: you must first enable the government to control the governed; and in the next place oblige [require] it to control itself. 99

—James Madison, *The Federalist*, No. 51

The Constitution limits the power of both the federal and state governments. This reflects the Framers' idea that people had the right of resistance to tyrannical government. A tyrannical government is one that abuses its power and violates the natural rights of the people. The Framers believed that all people possessed natural rights. One of those rights was the right to rebel against an abusive government. The American Revolution occurred because the colonists felt that the British government had become tyrannical and that they had the right to

popular sovereignty the idea that power lies with the people

limited government the principle that a government can do only what the Constitution allows it to do

PHOTO: ROBERTO SCHMIDT/AFP/Getty Images; TEXT: (l) US Constitution, Article IV, §4, (r) "The Federalist No. 51, [6 February 1788]," Founders Online, National Archives, https://founders.archives.gov/documents/Hamilton/01-04-02-0199. [Original source: The Papers of Alexander Hamilton, vol. 4, January 1787–May 1788, ed. Harold C. Syrett. New York: Columbia University Press, 1962, pp. 497–502.]

rebel. By limiting the powers of government, the Framers hoped to prevent anyone from using the powers of government in a tyrannical way.

Placing limits on the government is one of the basic purposes of a written constitution. By writing a constitution, the Framers wanted to make clear what the government did not have the power to do. Then all actions taken by the government could be compared to that standard.

Under the Constitution, the U.S. government is also limited by the **rule of law**. This means that no one, not even those who govern, may break the law. This principle is carried out in the Constitution's requirement that accused people are given due process of law. Due process means that everyone is entitled to fair treatment in a court of law.

Separation of Powers

The Framers intended to protect Americans against the abuse, or misuse, of power. They also took steps to keep any one person or group from gaining too much power.

They were influenced by French thinker Baron de Montesquieu. Montesquieu stressed the importance of dividing the legislative, executive, and judicial functions of government into separate branches. He believed this would prevent the concentration of too much governmental power in one place. This division of authority among the legislative, executive, and judicial branches is called **separation of powers**. The idea relies on human nature. It assumes that people in each branch of government will protect their own authority from being taken by the other branches.

The Framers also established separation of powers between the federal and state governments. They gave some powers to the federal government and others to the state governments.

---

rule of law the principle that the law applies to everyone, even those who govern

separation of powers the division of authority among the legislative, executive, and judicial branches

---

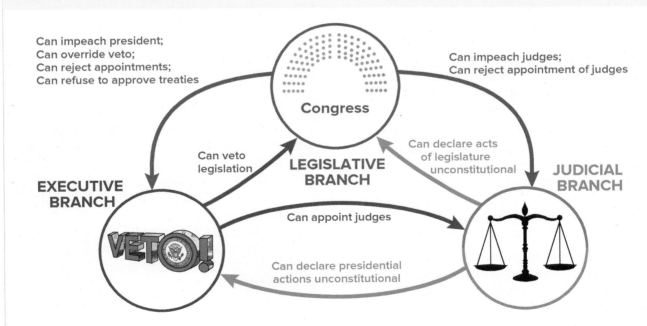

A System of Checks and Balances

The Constitution provides a complex system of checks and balances among the three branches of the federal government.

Can impeach president;
Can override veto;
Can reject appointments;
Can refuse to approve treaties

Can impeach judges;
Can reject appointment of judges

Congress

Can veto legislation

LEGISLATIVE BRANCH

Can declare acts of legislature unconstitutional

JUDICIAL BRANCH

EXECUTIVE BRANCH

Can appoint judges

Can declare presidential actions unconstitutional

EXAMINE THE DIAGRAM

1. **Comparing** How are the checks of the judicial branch similar to the other two branches?
2. **Contrasting** Which branch has the most checks on the other branches?

Checks and Balances

The Framers added an additional safeguard to the separation of powers. They devised a system of **checks and balances**. Each branch of government can check, or restrain, the power of the others. As the diagram shows, each branch has powers that limit each of the other two branches.

✓ CHECK FOR UNDERSTANDING

1. **Identifying** Which principle of the U.S. Constitution shows that the Framers intended the power of the government to reside with the people?

2. **Making Connections** How do the separation of powers and checks and balances contribute to limited government?

Federalism

GUIDING QUESTION

How is power distributed under federalism?

The Framers gave the new government a federal system, which placed more limits on government. In writing the Constitution, the Framers faced a problem. They wanted a strong central government: How could they create one nation out of 13 independent states in a way that would protect citizens' liberties from an all-powerful central government? Their solution was an approach called federalism. In our federal system the central, or national, government has certain powers over all citizens. The states have other powers that the federal government does not have, and the two share some powers.

Before the Constitution could become the law of the land, it had to be approved by the states. That was somewhat difficult because many state leaders were uneasy about having a strong national government. They were concerned that the national government might ignore the states' sovereignty and take too much power for itself.

Supporters of federalism, such as Alexander Hamilton, James Madison, and John Jay, had to convince state leaders that their rights would be preserved under the new Constitution. Hamilton wrote these words to try to reassure state leaders:

checks and balances a system in which each branch of government can check, or limit, the power of the other two branches

66 The proposed Constitution, so far from implying an abolition [elimination] of the State governments, makes them constituent [basic] parts of the national sovereignty, by allowing them a direct representation in the Senate, and leaves in their possession certain exclusive and very important portions of sovereign power. 99

—Alexander Hamilton, *The Federalist* No. 9, 1787

In the end, the Constitution was ratified. A government was established based on a federal model for dividing and sharing power among different levels of government. Even today, however, Americans still disagree about how much power the federal government has and what issues should be left to the states.

Types of Power

The roles of state and national government officials in our federal system have developed over more than 200 years. They have done this within the Constitution's framework.

Powers that the Constitution grants to the federal government are known as **delegated powers**. There are two types. The first, called *enumerated powers*, are those powers directly assigned by the Constitution. The word *enumerated* means "listed" or "spelled out." Most of these powers are named in the first three articles of the Constitution. In Article I, Section 8,

delegated powers powers that the Constitution grants to the federal government

The nation's highways demonstrate federalism at work. The red and blue shield signs indicate interstate highways, which are part of a national system. The green sign for business route 40 is maintained by the state.

PHOTO: Henk Meijer/Alamy Stock Photo; TEXT: "The Federalist No. 9, [21 November 1787]," Founders Online, National Archives, https://founders.archives.gov/documents/Hamilton/01-04-02-0162. [Original source: The Papers of Alexander Hamilton, vol. 4, January 1787– May 1788, ed. Harold C. Syrett. New York: Columbia University Press, 1962. pp. 333–339.]

National and State Powers Under Federalism

Under the Constitution, some powers are shared by both the national and state governments. Other powers are delegated to the national government or set aside for the states.

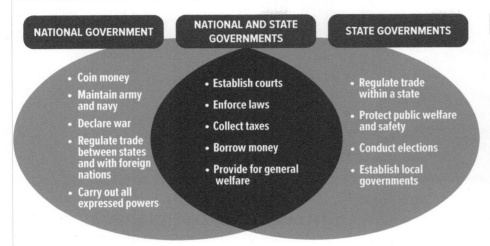

NATIONAL GOVERNMENT

- Coin money
- Maintain army and navy
- Declare war
- Regulate trade between states and with foreign nations
- Carry out all expressed powers

NATIONAL AND STATE GOVERNMENTS

- Establish courts
- Enforce laws
- Collect taxes
- Borrow money
- Provide for general welfare

STATE GOVERNMENTS

- Regulate trade within a state
- Protect public welfare and safety
- Conduct elections
- Establish local governments

EXAMINE THE DIAGRAM

1. **Identifying** What are examples of powers reserved for the states?
2. **Speculating** Why do you think the Framers gave the power to coin money to the national government and not to the states?

US Constitution, Amendment X

the Framers listed the specific powers given to Congress. These powers include the power to levy and collect taxes, to coin money, to declare war, to raise an army and navy, and to regulate commerce, or trade, among the states. The enumerated powers are also called the *expressed powers.*

Some of the national government's powers are not stated specifically in the Constitution. They are called *implied powers.* Even though, for example, the Constitution does not specifically mention building and maintaining nuclear weapons, it does state that the national government has the power to "provide for the common Defence." The authority of the federal government to make weapons is interpreted from that specific text in the Constitution.

While the national government has many powers under federalism, the states have powers as well. There are certain powers that the Constitution does not give to the national government. These are called **reserved powers** because they are set aside, or reserved, for states. The Constitution does not list these powers specifically. It suggests the states have powers in Article IV, where it promises that each state will have a republican form of government.

reserved powers powers that the Constitution does not give to the federal government; powers set aside for the states

Since the states have a government, those governments must have powers. The Constitution directly says that the states have powers in the Tenth Amendment:

> 66 The powers not delegated to the United States by the Constitution, nor prohibited by it to the states, are reserved to the states respectively, or to the people. 99
>
> —Tenth Amendment, United States Constitution

Traditionally, the states' reserved powers have included the powers to conduct elections, set up schools, and regulate business and trade within the state.

The federal government and the states also have certain powers that they share. These are called **concurrent powers**. Each level of government exercises these powers independently. Examples of concurrent powers are the power to tax, to maintain courts and define crimes, and to take private property for public use. States may exercise any power not reserved for the federal government, as long as it does not conflict with any national laws.

The Supremacy Clause

No state law or state constitution may conflict with any national law. For instance, the Twenty-sixth Amendment to the U.S. Constitution makes 18-year-olds eligible to vote in all national, state, and local elections.

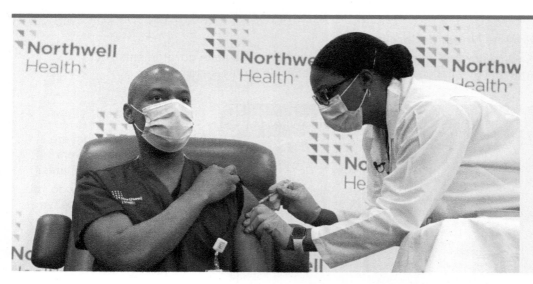

During the COVID-19 pandemic, states set public health rules regarding masking and social distancing, but the federal government approved the vaccines used to fight the disease.

If a state passed a law requiring voters to be 21 years of age, that law would not be valid. According to Article VI of the Constitution, all federal laws, acts, and treaties of the United States are "supreme."

> 66 This Constitution, and the Laws of the United States which shall be made in Pursuance thereof; and all Treaties made . . . under the Authority of the United States, shall be the supreme Law of the Land; and the Judges in every State shall be bound thereby. 99
>
> —Article VI, U.S. Constitution

This **supremacy clause** means that a state cannot pass a voting law that keeps citizens from voting if their right to vote is granted by the Constitution. A state could, however, pass a law allowing 16-year-olds to vote since that would not conflict with the national law.

Similarly, because states create and give power to local governments, cities and counties are bound by the supremacy of their state constitutions as well as that of the U.S. Constitution.

The Constitution Today

The entire system of government in the United States rests on a single document: the Constitution. Thomas Jefferson was proud of what the Framers had accomplished. He wrote:

---

supremacy clause a clause stating that the Constitution and other laws and treaties made by the national government are "the supreme Law of the Land"

> 66 I am persuaded no constitution was ever before so well calculated [thought out] as ours for . . . self-government. 99

More than two hundred years of history have proved Jefferson right. The Constitution has shown itself to be both durable and adaptable. The five principles that support it—popular sovereignty, limited government and the rule of law, separation of powers, checks and balances, and federalism—have led to a strong and responsible government. The Constitution gives our elected representatives enough power to defend our country's freedom and to keep order. At the same time, it sets limits that protect Americans from tyranny. The U.S. Constitution is more than just a framework of government. It stands as a powerful symbol of American values, pride, and unity.

✓ CHECK FOR UNDERSTANDING

1. **Explaining** Describe the federal system that the U.S. Constitution creates.

2. **Determining Central Ideas** According to Article VI of the Constitution, what is the supreme law of the land? Why is this important?

LESSON ACTIVITIES

1. **Informative/Explanatory Writing** Write a paragraph explaining any one principle of the Constitution. Give an example of how it is applied to the U.S. government.

2. **Interpreting Information** Work with a partner to prepare a presentation. Explain how two or three of the principles of the Constitution work to ensure limited government in the United States. Provide examples of how each principle limits government power.

PHOTO: Storms Media Group/Alamy Stock Photo; TEXT: (l) U.S. Constitution, Art VI., (r) "Thomas Jefferson to James Madison, 27 April 1809," Founders Online, National Archives, https://founders.archives.gov/documents/Jefferson/03-01-02-0140. [Original source: The Papers of Thomas Jefferson, Retirement Series, vol. 1, 4 March 1809 to 15 November 1809, ed. J. Jefferson Looney. Princeton: Princeton University Press, 2004, pp. 168–170.]

06

Analyzing Sources: Different Forms of Government

? COMPELLING QUESTION

How does the form of government shape the society it governs?

Plan Your Inquiry

DEVELOPING QUESTIONS

Think about how the form of government shapes the society it governs. Then read the Compelling Question for this lesson. What questions can you ask to help you answer this Compelling Question? Create a graphic organizer like the one below. Write these Supporting Questions in your graphic organizer.

Supporting Questions	Primary or Secondary Source	What the source tells me about how the form of government shapes the society it governs	Questions the source leaves unanswered
	A		
	B		
	C		
	D		
	E		

ANALYZING SOURCES

Next, examine the sources in this lesson. Analyze each source by answering the questions that follow it. How does each source help you answer each Supporting Question you created? What questions do you still have? Write these in your graphic organizer.

After you analyze the sources, you will:
- use the evidence from the sources,
- communicate your conclusions,
- and take informed action.

Background Information

Forms of government have different structures and give power to different groups of people. Power can be held by just a few people or groups, or it can be widely shared. Government power can be limited by law, based on tradition, or simply be the will of the ruler. Governments differ in other ways too. They can be involved in many areas of people's lives or give people a great deal of freedom. They can take care of people in need or leave them on their own.

A country's form of government sets how the people and the government interact. It affects whether people have ways to bring about changes in the law or have no opportunity to do so. It affects whether officials pursue the public interest or work to make themselves and their friends rich. It affects whether people can criticize the government or are punished for doing so.

The form of government also sets how individuals relate to each other. Can people trust strangers, or must they worry that some are government spies? Can people take action against businesses that treat workers poorly, or does the government protect those businesses?

» In the ancient world, powerful rulers led many civilizations. These rulers expected their people to follow their commands. The Egyptian pharaoh Ramses II, whose statues still stand today, was one such powerful ruler.

Anton_Ivanov/Shutterstock

Direct Democracy

In a direct democracy, each citizen shares responsibility for making decisions. Much of New England has practiced direct democracy in local government since colonial times. Many towns there were governed by town meetings. All eligible citizens of these towns could come to the meetings, voice their opinions, and vote directly to make laws and other decisions for the town. Some towns in all six New England states still hold town meetings today. The photograph shows an outdoor town meeting held during the COVID-19 pandemic.

SECONDARY SOURCE: NEWS ARTICLE

❞ The town meeting, for centuries, was a staple of New England life—but the coronavirus [COVID-19] pandemic could accelerate [speed] the departure from the tradition where people gather to debate everything from the purchase of local road equipment to multimillion-dollar budgets to pressing social issues. . . .

Some communities are delaying meetings this year until the virus will, hopefully, be more under control. Others are using pre-printed ballots to decide issues, forgoing [skipping] the daylong debate altogether. . . .

'I'd be very disappointed if people think that this is a new model because that would move us away completely from the essence [spirit] of town meeting, which is the opportunity to assemble with our fellow voters, to hear from our elected officials directly, to question, to challenge them, to debate a budget and public questions in an assembled meeting,' said former Vermont Gov. Jim Douglas, who served for 33 years as **moderator** in his hometown of Middlebury. . . .

A lot of people can't attend traditional town meetings, which can last all day.

'They may live in one town and work in another town and it's hard to get time off,' [Vermont Secretary of State Jim] Condos said. 'They may have kids, school, whatever it is that interferes with their lives. It's not like it was 100 years ago.' . . .

Eric Conrad of the Maine Municipal Association said that more people cast secret ballots [in 2020 in Maine during the pandemic] than took part in previous traditional town meetings.

'That democratic give-and-take is lost. But participation is better,' he said. ❟

— "Could Pandemic Further Erode the New England Town Meeting?" by Wilson Ring, Associated Press, Feb. 26, 2021

---

moderator the town official who conducts a town meeting

EXAMINE THE SOURCE

1. **Identifying Cause and Effect** How did towns respond to the problems created by the COVID-19 pandemic?
2. **Identifying Themes** Besides voting, why are town meetings thought to be important?

Representative Democracy

The United States is a representative democracy. In this form of government, citizens vote to elect representatives who make laws for them. The article discusses two ideas about how representatives are meant to serve the people they represent.

SECONDARY SOURCE: ARTICLE

66 The U.S. system is based on a delegate model of representation, as advocated by Founding Father James Madison. This view holds that our elected representatives act as a stand-in for their **constituents**, adhering to [supporting] the specific preferences of the voters. If they don't, We, the People, get to throw them out in biannual elections for the House of Representatives, as provided in Article I, Section 2, of the U.S. Constitution.

Edmund Burke, the 18th century Irish political philosopher, is associated with the trustee model of representation. . . . Burke [stated] in a 1774 speech, a member of Parliament should consider the wishes of his constituents, but he is duty bound to put the interests of the nation above his own and his constituents'. . . .

A representative should listen to and consider the opinions of constituents, Burke said. But blind obedience to instructions or mandates (common in Burke's day) that run counter to a representative's judgment and conscience are "utterly unknown to the laws of this land" and "arise from a fundamental mistake of the whole order and tenor of our constitution," Burke said.

The U.S. system may have been based on a delegate model, but it evolved into something more individualistic, closer to a trustee relationship. 99

— "Opinion: You can blame James Madison for our bloated tax code," Caroline Baum, *Market Watch*, Oct. 4, 2017

---

constituent a person whom a member of Congress represents

EXAMINE THE SOURCE

1. **Contrasting** What is the main difference between the two models of representation—the trustee and the delegate models?
2. **Inferring** How might representatives learn the views of their constituents?

Totalitarian Regime

A *totalitarian* government controls nearly all aspects of life. Under totalitarian rule, personal freedoms are extremely limited.

This text is from the first-hand account written by a woman who lived in the Soviet Union, or USSR, as a child. The USSR was a totalitarian state founded by Communists led by Vladimir Lenin in 1917. Communists ruled using fear and propaganda until they lost power and the country broke up in 1991.

PRIMARY SOURCE: MEMOIR

❝ [S]chool children all over the country, in their identical uniforms . . . studied a school curriculum and participated in youth programs designed to instill [encourage] appreciation for communism and reverence for its leader, our dear Vladimir Ilyich Lenin—*dedushka* (grandfather) Lenin, as we were taught to refer to him. . . .

As part of our early education, we absorbed the Soviet **propaganda** . . . . Our nursery school teachers talked to us about 'them.' 'They' were the people in the **West**. . . .

For many of us far behind the **iron curtain**, communism and its rituals—salutes, slogans, flag ceremonies—in some ways replaced religion. . . .

[W]e participated in patriotic marches and frequent **ideological** ceremonies, which replaced regular school classes. Numbering in the hundreds, we marched to a small plaza, sang hymns, and chanted slogans. . . .

Instead of Mickey Mouse, we were raised on stories about politically active children—little Soviet heroes. A major role model for Soviet kids was Pavlik Morozov, a **martyr** of the 1930s. At the tender age of thirteen, he turned his father in to authorities for not sharing Pavlik's belief in communism. . . .

I didn't have a bedroom. The entire family of five—my parents, my aunt, my grandmother, and I—shared a small two-room apartment . . .

Though party leaders and those close to the administration enjoyed immense privileges, millions of people had a very low quality of life. The state provided them with homes, healthcare, cheap consumer goods and basic food. . . .

We were not allowed contact with the western world, and very few Soviet citizens were permitted to go abroad. . . .

I and most other children in the empire were tiny fish swimming through a sea of propaganda. . . .❞

— Katya Soldak, "This is How Propaganda Works: A Look Inside a Soviet Childhood," *Forbes*, December 20, 2017

---

propaganda messages that aim to influence popular opinion

West the United States and its allies

iron curtain the political barrier between Communist countries and those that opposed them

ideological based on a certain set of ideas

martyr someone who suffers for a cause

EXAMINE THE SOURCE

1. **Identifying Themes** What does the writer mean by the final sentence?
2. **Making Generalizations** What does the writer suggest was most important to the government of the USSR?

Soldak, Katya. "This is How Propaganda Works: A Look Inside a Soviet Childhood." Forbes, December 20, 2017. https://www.forbes.com/sites/katyasoldak/2017/12/20/this-is-how-propaganda-works-a-look-inside-a-soviet-childhood/?sh=6785S8613566.

Monarchy

A *monarchy* is a government headed by royalty—members of a family that is seen as having the right to rule. Monarchs, such as kings or queens, rule for life. A monarchy used to be a common form of government. Since the American and the French Revolutions in the late 1700s, people have increasingly come to believe that they have the right to choose their leaders. Since then, many countries have changed to give power to elected leaders instead of a monarch. Monarchs today may continue to act as the head of state, playing a symbolic role for the country. Most do not have real power. In the United Kingdom, for instance, Queen Elizabeth II has formal duties and an advisory role, but an elected parliament governs. In this photograph, Queen Elizabeth II and her late husband, Prince Philip, take part in opening a new session of Parliament.

PRIMARY SOURCE: PHOTOGRAPH

REUTERS/Alamy Stock Photo

EXAMINE THE SOURCE

1. **Analyzing** Where are the queen and her husband positioned in relation to most of the people in the photograph?

2. **Interpreting** Keeping in mind that the role of British royalty today is mostly ceremonial, what can you infer about British society based on this photograph?

Theocracy

A *theocracy* is a government in which laws are based upon the teachings of a religion. All members of the society are required to follow these laws. Religious freedom is rare in a theocracy. All must follow the religion of the leaders. People who choose to practice a different religion, or no religion, are often treated harshly.

A group called the Taliban ruled Afghanistan in the late 1990s and early 2000s. They created a government based on their ideas about the teachings of Islam. Islam requires men and women to dress modestly. Based on that teaching, the Taliban had strict laws for women. They required women to wear burqas. A *burqa*, shown in the photograph, is a full body covering with a mesh screen across the eye area for seeing out. Women who did not wear them were beaten in punishment. The Taliban was removed from power in 2001 but regained it in 2021. When that happened, many Afghan women feared the government would return to those harsh policies.

PRIMARY SOURCE: PHOTOGRAPH

Horizons WWP/Alamy Stock Photo

EXAMINE THE SOURCE

1. **Contrasting** How does the clothing of the man and boy differ from the woman's clothing in the photograph?

2. **Analyzing** How does a theocracy differ from a representative democracy?

Complete Your Inquiry

EVALUATE SOURCES AND USE EVIDENCE

Refer back to the Compelling Question and the Supporting Questions you developed at the beginning of the lesson.

1. **Analyzing** In what ways do the sources show how the form of government affects the society it governs?

2. **Speculating** Which forms of government do you think result in the most and least closely knit societies? Explain your answer.

3. **Gathering Sources** Which sources helped you answer the Supporting Questions and the Compelling Question? Which sources, if any, challenged what you thought you knew when you first created your Supporting Questions? What information do you still need in order to answer your questions? What other viewpoints would you like to investigate? Where would you find that information?

4. **Evaluating Sources** Identify the sources that helped answer your Supporting Questions. How reliable are the sources? How would you verify the reliability of the sources?

COMMUNICATE CONCLUSIONS

5. **Collaborating** Work with a partner to discuss how particular forms of government shape their societies. Use the graphic organizer you created at the beginning of the lesson to help you. Share your conclusions with the class.

TAKE INFORMED ACTION

Blogging About Our Form of Government
Work with a partner. Review what you have learned about how the form of a government can shape a society. Think about the differences between life in the United States and life in societies with other types of governments. Work with your partner to write a series of blog posts about how our society is shaped by our form of government. Include images to support your writing.

The First Amendment

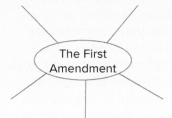

The First Amendment

Guaranteeing Civil Liberties

GUIDING QUESTION

Which individual rights are protected by the First Amendment?

When the Constitutional Convention proposed the new Constitution in 1787, many Americans objected that the document did not include a list of guaranteed individual rights. Massachusetts refused to ratify the Constitution until the Constitution's supporters promised to add a bill of rights.

In 1791, the Bill of Rights was added to the Constitution as the first 10 amendments. The Bill of Rights protects many of the civil liberties that are an essential part of a democracy. **Civil liberties** are the freedoms we have to participate in society without unfair interference from the government. They include the freedom to think and to act without fear of being punished. They are the cornerstone of our way of life.

The most basic civil liberties, freedom of thought and expression, are protected by the First Amendment. The amendment reads:

66 Congress shall make no law respecting an establishment of religion, or prohibiting the free exercise thereof; or abridging the freedom of speech, or of the press; or the right of the people peaceably to assemble, and to petition the Government for a redress of grievances. 99

civil liberty the freedom to participate in society and act without unfair interference from the government

James Madison introduced the Bill of Rights, shown here, on June 8, 1789. By December 15, 1791, ten amendments were ratified by the states.

The First Amendment does not tell individuals what they must or may do. It tells the United States Congress that it may not pass laws that would prevent people from exercising certain rights. If Congress does pass such laws, a court may strike them down to preserve people's rights. Thus the First Amendment gives courts power to protect rights. Since it was written, the First Amendment has been interpreted to cover the president and state and local governments as well as Congress.

Freedom of speech is one of five freedoms protected by the First Amendment. The others are freedom of religion, freedom of the press, freedom of assembly, and freedom to petition the government.

Freedom of Religion

The desire for freedom of religion was central to the founding of the colonies that eventually became the United States. Many of the English and European settlers who came to America in the 1600s had left their homes because they did not have the freedom to worship as they wished. The Plymouth and Massachusetts Bay colonies were founded by people who had fled religious persecution in England. Connecticut and Rhode Island were founded by people who left Massachusetts because they sought greater religious freedom than was allowed in the Massachusetts colony. Maryland was founded to provide Catholics with religious freedom. When William Penn founded Pennsylvania, he made freedom of religion a basic right.

The First Amendment has two clauses that protect religious freedom. The **establishment clause** does not allow Congress to make a religion the official religion of the country. The protection is very broad. In 1802 President Thomas Jefferson called this clause a "wall of separation between church and state." The establishment clause has been interpreted to mean that any government action that favors any religion or religions over others is prohibited.

The **free exercise clause** of the First Amendment protects people's freedom to observe and express their faith as they wish. Conflicts can arise, however, when religious groups take certain actions that go against the law. For example, some church-based organizations have claimed their right to religious freedom permits them to discriminate against people. In the 1970s, Bob Jones University had an admissions policy that discriminated against African Americans. The university claimed this policy was based on religious beliefs. In 1983 the Supreme Court ruled against the university. The Court ruled that the benefit of prohibiting racial discrimination outweighed the university's First Amendment rights.

establishment clause a part of the First Amendment that does not allow Congress to establish an official state religion

free exercise clause a part of the First Amendment that protects the freedom of individuals to observe and express their faith as they wish

The desire for religious freedom was a factor in the settling of some of the first English colonies in North America. Here, American Muslims (left) and Christians (right) take part in religious services today.

Making Connections How do these scenes demonstrate the protections of the First Amendment?

PHOTO/(l)) Yasin Ozturk/Anadolu Agency/Getty Images, (r) LHB Photo/Alamy Stock Photo; TEXT: "V. To the Danbury Baptist Association, 1 January 1802," Founders Online, National Archives, https://founders.archives.gov/documents/Jefferson/01-36-02-0152-0006. [Original source: The Papers of Thomas Jefferson, vol. 36, 1 December 1801–3 March 1802, ed. Barbara B. Oberg. Princeton: Princeton University Press, 2009, p. 258.],

The First Amendment requires that the government not favor any religion, but it does not require complete government neutrality regarding religion. Government hearings and other events sometimes begin with a prayer. These prayers reflect beliefs or ideas shared by many faiths. In that way, they avoid favoring one religion over another. Some people, such as many atheists, or people who do not believe in God, feel that this practice violates the First Amendment. Courts have permitted such prayers, however.

Freedom of Speech

The right to **free speech** is essential to democratic government. For most people, making one's opinions known is one of the main ways of influencing the government. Freedom of speech enables public debate about what the government should do. It allows people to criticize the government and individual officials without fear of being punished.

Freedom of speech is guaranteed by the First Amendment. It protects what people say in meetings, conversations, speeches, and lectures. It protects words spoken in radio and television broadcasts. The Supreme Court has judged many cases that are connected to this freedom. Its decisions have shown that speech includes more than just spoken words. Internet messages, art, music, and even clothing are protected. The right to express one's views through actions is also protected by the First Amendment. This includes actions such as burning the U.S. flag as a protest.

Courts have said that freedom of speech protects not only the speakers but also listeners. People have the right to hear, to see, to read, and in general to be exposed to different messages and points of view. People in the United States have the right to hear opposing views and to form their own opinions.

Originally, the First Amendment only protected people's speech from punishment by the federal government. Over time, courts have ruled that state and local governments also may not pass laws that restrict people's freedom of speech.

Freedom of the Press

In 1733 when the American colonies were still ruled by Great Britain, publisher John Peter

Student activists gathered outside the Democratic Presidential Debate in Detroit, Michigan, to express their views in 2019.

Explaining How does the First Amendment protect these students' actions?

Zenger criticized the governor of New York in his newspaper. As a result, Zenger was arrested. Zenger's lawyer, Andrew Hamilton, argued that only a press that was free to criticize the government can keep that government from misusing its power. The jury agreed, and Zenger was found not guilty. The Zenger case is seen as a major step in the rise of a free press in the United States.

The First Amendment's protections regarding freedom of the press limit the government's power to restrict the actions of the press. When the Framers wrote the Bill of Rights, "the press" referred to printed materials such as books, newspapers, and magazines. They could not have foreseen the growth of technology and mass communication. Today the press includes many other media sources, such as radio, television, and the Internet. Freedom of the press allows Americans access to a range of views on public issues.

The First Amendment protects the press from the government, and it protects the public's right to have information.

free speech the right to say our opinions, in public or in private, without fear of being stopped or punished by the government for those ideas

Censorship is the banning of printed materials or films because of the ideas they express. In some countries, the government reviews the content of news stories before they are published, and the government can prevent their publication. This form of censorship is called *prior restraint*, from the words *prior* meaning "before" and ***restrain*** meaning "to hold back." In the United States, the First Amendment prohibits the practice of prior restraint. U.S. news organizations do not need to seek government approval in order to report what they think is newsworthy.

The Supreme Court decision *Near* v. *Minnesota* (1931) illustrates the principle of prior restraint. A Minnesota state law required newspapers to get governmental approval before publishing. One newspaper wanted to publish a

censorship the banning of printed materials or films due to alarming or offensive ideas

restrain to hold back

story referring to local government officials as "gangsters" and "grafters." *Grafters* are public officials who illegally take public money for themselves. The public officials then obtained a court order to prevent the newspaper from being published. The Supreme Court ruled that this use of prior restraint was an unconstitutional restriction of the freedom of the press.

Freedom of Assembly

The First Amendment protects people's right to gather in groups for any reason, as long as the groups are peaceful. People can attend meetings, rallies, celebrations, and parades. The government has the power to make rules about the time and the place where these activities are held. It cannot ban them, though.

Freedom of assembly also includes the freedom of association. That is, the First Amendment protects people's rights to form and join clubs, political parties, labor unions, and other groups.

These activists assembled together to show support for local teachers.

Making Connections What factors might government officials need to consider when approving a time and place for large demonstrations such as this one?

This man is gathering signatures on a petition to the government. A petition is a request for the government to solve a problem.

Freedom to Petition

The First Amendment gives people the right to send petitions to the government. A **petition** is a formal request for the government to act. Often the word *petition* is used to mean a written statement that many people sign, such as a proposed ballot measure. This is a request from citizens to have a suggested law or question put to the voters to decide. Even a simple letter or e-mail from one person is a petition, though. The right to petition is the right for people to express themselves to the government and to request it to solve a problem. Like the rights to freedom of speech, a free press, and assembly, the right to petition the government is essential if government is to be responsive to the people.

Suppose you are not happy about overcrowded schools. You have the right to send a complaint to members of the school board. If enough people express similar views, the board may act.

✓ CHECK FOR UNDERSTANDING

1. **Analyzing** How are Americans' rights to express themselves protected by the First Amendment?

2. **Summarizing** How does the First Amendment help us protect our form of government?

petition formal request for the government to act

Limits on Civil Liberty

GUIDING QUESTION

Why are limits placed on individual rights?

The First Amendment provides very broad rights to all Americans. Sometimes these rights conflict. The rights of one individual must be balanced against the rights of others. Individual rights must also be balanced against the rights of the community. When there is a conflict, the rights of the community often come first. If that were not the case, society would break apart.

To live peaceably in a community, citizens should use their civil liberties responsibly. In exercising their individual rights, they should not interfere with the rights of others. For example, you are free to campaign for causes, but you may not disturb your neighbors with blaring loudspeaker broadcasts. However, the responsible exercise of individual rights is not always acceptable to everyone. In the past, governments have tried to prohibit flag-burning, marriage between two people from different races, and other acts because these acts offended some people. The Supreme Court has repeatedly protected these and other actions as exercises of individual liberty.

As you read earlier, the government has the power to set some limits on the right of assembly. If an organization wants to stage a parade, the government can limit when and where the parade can be held.

This cartoon focuses on the danger of a news report slandering someone.
Analyzing Visuals How will this news organization's approach protect it from slander?

But it cannot ban an assembly just because it disagrees with the viewpoints of the people who gather.

Just as the exercise of First Amendment rights can be limited in order to prevent harm to others, content can be restricted as well. For instance, the First Amendment protects your right to criticize public officials. However, you do not have the right to spread lies that will harm a person's reputation. Spreading such lies in speech is called **slander**. It is the crime of **libel** if the lies are published in a more lasting form—for example, a book, an article, a movie, an audio recording, or a blog. The First Amendment does not protect speech that is slanderous or libelous. Someone who commits slander or libel may be sued by the person harmed by the false statements.

Free speech is limited in other ways as well. No person, for example, has the right to speak or write in a way that directly leads to criminal acts.

---

slander spoken untruths that are harmful to someone's reputation

libel written untruths that are harmful to someone's reputation

Also, people do not have the right to make a speech that will lead to efforts to overthrow the government by force. These kinds of speech are illegal.

✓ **CHECK FOR UNDERSTANDING**

Analyzing How can individuals' First Amendment rights be limited, and why?

LESSON ACTIVITIES

1. **Argumentative Writing** Write a brief essay in which you name the First Amendment right that you believe is most important to protecting democracy. Explain why you think so in your essay.

2. **Analyzing Information** Conduct research to learn about religious, speech, press, or assembly rights in another country. Then work in a group with two or three other students and share your findings. Have a spokesperson from your group explain to the class how individuals' rights in the countries researched were similar to or different from the rights protected by the First Amendment.

08

Analyzing Supreme Court Cases: Student Speech

 COMPELLING QUESTION

How does the First Amendment apply to students?

Plan Your Inquiry

DEVELOPING QUESTIONS

Think about how the First Amendment applies to you in school. Then read the Compelling Question for this lesson. What questions can you ask to help you answer this Compelling Question? Create a graphic organizer like the one below. Write these Supporting Questions in your graphic organizer.

Supporting Questions	Primary or Secondary Source	What the source tells me about how the First Amendment applies to students	Questions the source leaves unanswered
	A		
	B		
	C		
	D		
	E		
	F		

ANALYZING SOURCES

Next, examine the sources in this lesson. Analyze each source by answering the questions that follow it. How does each source help you answer each Supporting Question you created? What questions do you still have? Write these in your graphic organizer.

After you analyze the sources, you will:

- use the evidence from the sources,
- communicate your conclusions,
- and take informed action.

Case Summaries

This lesson focuses on two Supreme Court cases involving students and the First Amendment.

Tinker* v. *Des Moines In December 1965, a few public school students in Des Moines, Iowa, began wearing black armbands. They were protesting the involvement of the United States in the Vietnam War. School officials decided that the armbands were "disturbing influences" and banned them. When students, including brother and sister John and Mary Beth Tinker, continued to wear the armbands, they were suspended. Their parents sued in federal court. They argued that the students' First Amendment rights had been violated.

Hazelwood* v. *Kuhlmeier About 20 years after *Tinker*, Kathy Kuhlmeier was a student at Hazelwood East High School, near St. Louis, Missouri. Her journalism class published the school newspaper. The principal, Robert Reynolds, always reviewed the paper before it was published. One issue of the paper was to include an article about three pregnant students and an article about the experiences of one student whose parents were divorcing. Before the issue was published, Reynolds removed the two pages on which those articles appeared. Reynolds believed readers could identify who the students were, though they were not named in the article. Kuhlmeier and two other students sued the school claiming that their First Amendment rights had been violated.

» Mary Tinker was in eighth grade and John Tinker was in tenth grade when they were suspended for wearing armbands to school to protest the Vietnam War.

Majority Opinion: *Tinker* v. *Des Moines*

In *Tinker* v. *Des Moines*, the Supreme Court ruled that the suspensions violated the students' First Amendment rights. Justice Abe Fortas wrote the opinion for the 7-2 majority.

PRIMARY SOURCE: SUPREME COURT OPINION

❝ First Amendment rights . . . are available to teachers and students. It can hardly be argued that either students or teachers shed their constitutional rights to freedom of speech or expression at the schoolhouse gate. . . .

The school officials banned and sought to punish **petitioners** for a silent, passive expression of opinion, unaccompanied by any disorder or disturbance on the part of petitioners. . . . [T]his case does not concern speech or action that intrudes upon [interrupts] the work of the schools or the rights of other students. . . .

Students in school as well as out of school are 'persons' under our Constitution. They are possessed of fundamental [basic] rights which the State must respect. . . . They [students] may not be confined to the expression of those sentiments [feelings] that are officially approved. In the absence of a specific showing of constitutionally valid [suitable] reasons to regulate their speech, students are entitled to [have a right to] freedom of expression of their views. ❞

— Justice Abraham Fortas, Opinion of the Court, *Tinker* v. *Des Moines*, 393 U.S. 503 (1969)

petitioner party that appeals a case to an appeals court

EXAMINE THE SOURCE

1. **Drawing Conclusions** What guidance does the final sentence of the excerpt give to schools as to how they should think about students' speech rights?

2. **Explaining** Why is it important that the Tinkers' speech was silent and passive?

Dissenting Opinion: *Tinker* v. *Des Moines*

Justice Hugo Black and Justice John Marshall Harlan II disagreed with the majority in *Tinker* and wrote dissenting opinions. A dissent is a written statement disagreeing with the majority decision. The text here is from Justice Black's dissent.

PRIMARY SOURCE: SUPREME COURT OPINION

❝ In Cox v. Louisiana . . . the Court clearly stated that the rights of free speech and assembly 'do not mean that everyone with opinions or beliefs to express may address a group at any public place and at any time.' . . .

[C]ertainly a teacher is not paid to go into school and teach subjects the State does not hire him to teach as a part of its selected curriculum. Nor are public school students sent to the schools at public expense to broadcast political or any other views to educate and inform the public. . . .

School discipline, like parental discipline, is an integral [essential] and important part of training our children to be citizens—to be better citizens. Here a very small number of students have . . . refused to obey a school order designed to give pupils who want to learn the opportunity to do so. . . . [A]fter the Court's holding today some students in . . . schools will be ready, able, and willing to defy their teachers on practically all orders. ❞

— Justice Hugo Black, Dissenting Opinion, *Tinker* v. *Des Moines*, 393 U.S. 503 (1969)

EXAMINE THE SOURCE

1. **Inferring** Why do you think Justice Black quotes from the Court's decision in *Cox* v. *Louisiana*?

2. **Identifying** What danger does Justice Black say the Court's ruling poses for schools?

Interview with Mary Tinker

More than 50 years after the *Tinker* case was decided, a reporter interviewed Mary Tinker about her case and about students' rights regarding off-campus speech today.

Keierleber, Mark and Mary Beth Tinker. "74 Interview: Mary Beth Tinker on Her Landmark Student Speech Victory Central in New SCOTUS Case — And Why Today's Youth Activism is as Vital as Ever."

PRIMARY SOURCE: INTERVIEW

❝ [Interviewer:] Was that rule [prohibiting armbands] made because school officials disagreed with your political stance?

[Tinker:] Yes, it seemed that the school administrators were willing to allow students' speech, but they just wanted it to be speech that they agreed with. So that was part of the problem because in our democracy, the government is not allowed to prefer one viewpoint over the other. That's called viewpoint discrimination. . . .

[Interviewer:] The landmark opinion in *Tinker* protected the free speech rights of public school students on campus unless it caused a substantial disruption to the learning environment. Do you believe that's the right standard today?

[Tinker:] Well, that standard was very interesting because it initially came from a case in Mississippi where African-American high school students wore buttons to school in the fall of 1964. The button said "One man, one vote SNCC," which is the Student Nonviolent Coordinating Committee. They wore those buttons to school because they were protesting murders by the Ku Klux Klan and white supremacists. Some students wore the buttons to school to protest and they were told they could not do that. So that case started working its way through the court. When it was decided in 1966 after we wore the armbands, the appeals court in Mississippi . . . said that they should have been allowed to wear those buttons. Why? Because they did not substantially disrupt school. That case and that standard was then later cited in the *Tinker* ruling. [I]t's a reasonable standard but it's open to interpretation. . . .

[Interviewer:] Your speech with the black armbands was clearly political in nature, but [some student speech] . . . is not. Do you believe that both forms of speech deserve the same level of free speech protections?

[Tinker:] Yes, I do because I think that it's important for students to be able to express themselves.

[Interviewer:] Education groups argue that schools need authority to punish off-campus speech to protect other students from cyberbullying and threats of violence. What is your response to that argument . . . ?

[Tinker:] Of course there's a line to be drawn when it comes to truly threatening speech or bullying, but schools have other ways of dealing with that besides trampling on students' speech rights. They don't need to weaken the overall rights of students and to expand the reach of administration. . . . ❞

— 74 Interview: Mary Beth Tinker on Her Landmark Student Speech Victory Central in New SCOTUS Case," *The 74*, April 27, 2021

EXAMINE THE SOURCE

1. **Making Connections** Why is Tinker's argument that her school was specifically trying to censor political speech important?

2. **Explaining** Explain Mary Tinker's view on a school's authority to regulate out-of-school speech.

Opinion of the Court: *Hazelwood* v. *Kuhlmeier*

Nearly 20 years after *Tinker*, the Supreme Court made another significant decision about the First Amendment rights of students. In that decision, the Court ruled 5-3 to uphold the principal's actions regarding administrative control over content in a school newspaper. In writing the majority opinion in *Hazelwood*, Justice Byron White drew a sharp distinction between individual expression and a school-sponsored publication.

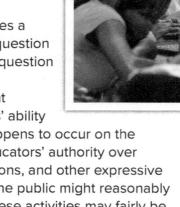

PRIMARY SOURCE: SUPREME COURT OPINION

66 The question whether the First Amendment requires a school to tolerate particular student speech—the question that we addressed in *Tinker*—is different from the question whether the First Amendment requires a school affirmatively [actively] to promote particular student speech. The former question addresses educators' ability to silence a student's personal expression that happens to occur on the school premises. The latter question concerns educators' authority over school-sponsored publications, theatrical productions, and other expressive activities that students, parents, and members of the public might reasonably perceive to bear the **imprimatur** of the school. These activities may fairly be characterized as part of the school curriculum. . . .

Educators are entitled to exercise greater control over this second form of student expression to assure that participants learn whatever lessons the activity is designed to teach, that readers or listeners are not exposed to material that may be inappropriate for their level of maturity, and that the views of the individual speaker are not erroneously [wrongly] attributed [connected] to the school. . . .

Accordingly, we conclude that . . . educators do not offend the First Amendment by exercising editorial control over the style and content of student speech in school-sponsored expressive activities so long as their actions are reasonably related to legitimate [rightful] **pedagogical** concerns. 99

— Justice Byron White, Opinion of the Court, *Hazelwood* v. *Kuhlmeier*, 484 U.S. 260 (1988)

imprimatur official approval

pedagogical related to education

EXAMINE THE SOURCE

1. **Explaining** Why does Justice White say that school authorities have different rights and responsibilities when dealing with individual expression than when dealing with school-sponsored activities?

2. **Drawing Conclusions** Do you think the *Hazelwood* decision is consistent with the decision in *Tinker*? Explain.

Dissenting Opinion: *Hazelwood* v. *Kuhlmeier*

Justice William Brennan disagreed with the majority in *Hazelwood* and wrote a dissenting opinion.

PRIMARY SOURCE: SUPREME COURT OPINION

66 This case arose when the Hazelwood East administration breached [broke] its own promise, dashing its students' expectations. The school principal . . . **excised** six articles . . . of the May 13, 1983, issue of Spectrum. He did so not because any of the articles would "materially and substantially interfere with the requirements of appropriate discipline," but simply because he considered two of the six "inappropriate, personal, sensitive, and unsuitable" for student consumption. . . .

In my view the principal broke more than just a promise. He violated the First Amendment's prohibitions against censorship of any student expression that neither disrupts classwork nor invades the rights of others. . . .

[P]ublic educators must accommodate some student expression even if it offends them or offers views or values that contradict those the school wishes to inculcate [teach or impress]. . . .

I fully agree with the Court that the First Amendment should afford an educator the **prerogative** not to sponsor the publication of a newspaper article that is "ungrammatical, poorly written, inadequately researched, biased or prejudiced," or that falls short of the "high standards for . . . student speech that is disseminated under [the school's] auspices [guidence]. . . ." . . . But we need not abandon Tinker to reach that conclusion; we need only apply it. . . . The educator may, under Tinker, constitutionally "censor" poor grammar, writing, or research because to reward such expression would "materially disrup[t]" the newspaper's curricular purpose.

The same cannot be said of official censorship designed to shield the audience or dissociate the sponsor from the expression. . . . [U]nless one believes that the purpose of the school newspaper is to teach students that the press ought never report bad news, express unpopular views, or print a thought that might upset its sponsors. Unsurprisingly, Hazelwood East claims no such pedagogical purpose. . . .

The young men and women of Hazelwood East expected a civics lesson, but not the one the Court teaches them today. 99

— Justice William Brennan, Dissenting Opinion, *Hazelwood* v. *Kuhlmeier*, 484 U.S. 260 (1988)

excise to cut out or remove
prerogative a privilege

EXAMINE THE SOURCE

1. **Explaining** What type of journalism does Justice Brennan imply would be disruptive to a student newspaper's curricular purpose?

2. **Analyzing** What civics lesson is Justice Brennan referring to in the last sentence here?

Cartoon: First Amendment Rights in and out of School

As students' use of social media has grown, so has the need to understand what legal authority school officials might have to regulate student speech on social media platforms.

PRINCIPAL
←

Campbell.

"Who would've thought Ms. Kent was following our tweets?"

EXAMINE THE SOURCE

1. **Interpreting** Where are the students going, and why do you think they are going there?

2. **Evaluating** What is your attitude about the students' situation?

Complete Your Inquiry

Refer back to the Compelling Question and the Supporting Questions you developed at the beginning of the lesson.

1. **Evaluating** Which sources do you find most convincing regarding what First Amendment rights students have?

2. **Contrasting** What differences do the sources describe between adults' First Amendment rights and the First Amendment rights of students in school?

3. **Gathering Sources** Which sources helped you answer the Supporting Questions and the Compelling Question? Which sources, if any, challenged what you thought you knew when you first created your Supporting Questions? What information do you still need in order to answer your questions? What other viewpoints would you like to investigate? Where would you find that information?

4. **Evaluating Sources** Identify the sources that helped answer your Supporting Questions. How reliable are the sources? How would you verify the reliability of the sources?

5. **Collaborating** Work with a partner to discuss how the First Amendment applies in school. Using these sources, think about differences between adults' and youths' rights and the rights of youth in school versus outside of school. Share your conclusions with the class.

Analyzing School Rules on Clothing Messages Some people wear clothing, such as T-shirts or hats, bearing messages. What rules for such printed messages can a school or school district make? In a small group, brainstorm a list of guidelines that align with how the First Amendment applies to student clothing choices in schools. Compare your list to your school's rules. Are there rules that conflict with what you have learned about First Amendment rights? If so, request a meeting with your school officials or school board to begin a discussion about a change.

Other Bill of Rights Protections

Analyzing Key Ideas and Details As you read, use a diagram to note the amendments in the Bill of Rights that relate to the rights of the accused and the convicted in criminal cases.

Amend-ment	Whom it protects	What government actions it bars or requires
Fourth		
Fifth		
Sixth		
Eighth		

Rights of the Accused

GUIDING QUESTION

How does the Bill of Rights protect the rights of people accused of crimes?

Several amendments in the Bill of Rights help ensure that the legal system is fair and just. Some protect the rights of people who authorities think may have committed a crime. Others protect the **accused**—people officially charged with crimes. Some give protections to those who have been found guilty of crimes.

Every government has a duty to protect society against criminal activity. When the government investigates and prosecutes crimes, however, it is not allowed to deny individuals their fundamental rights. Being charged with a crime is very serious. Being convicted of a crime may result in a person losing his or her freedom for a time or even losing his or her life. Because the stakes are so high, it is crucial that the criminal justice system operates fairly, and that innocent people are not punished.

Before the American Revolution, the British government used the legal system to punish its critics. The Framers wanted to prevent such abuses of power in the newly formed United States.

accused a person officially charged with a crime

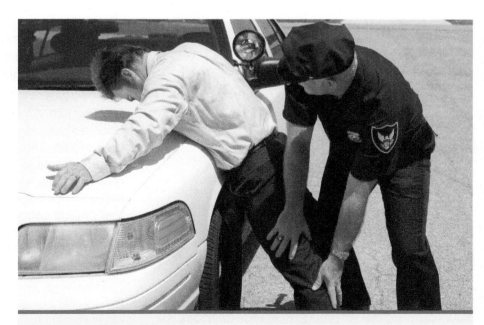

A person who is believed to have committed a crime, such as the one here being checked by a police officer for weapons, has certain rights.

Explaining Why is it important to protect peoples' rights as they are investigated by police?

Therefore, they included a number of amendments in the Bill of Rights to protect the rights of people involved in the criminal justice system.

The Fourth, Fifth, Sixth, and Eighth Amendments placed significant limits on the government's power. These checks are designed to help ensure that people suspected or accused of crimes are treated fairly in the legal system.

The Fourth Amendment

The Fourth Amendment protects us against "unreasonable searches and seizures." No officer of the government can search people's property or take their possessions at will. The officer must have **probable cause**, or strong reasons based on evidence to think that a person or property was involved in a crime.

When law enforcement officers want to do a search for evidence, they must first get approval. They must ask a judge to issue a **search warrant**. This court order allows police to search a person's property and seize evidence. Only items listed in the warrant can be taken. Judges do not give out search warrants automatically. They must be convinced that a search is likely to yield evidence.

Law enforcement officers are expected to follow the law to protect suspects' Fourth

probable cause a strong reason to think that a person or property was involved in a crime

search warrant a court order allowing police to search property and seize evidence

Law enforcement officers need probable cause before they may search private property such as an automobile or luggage. Here a specially trained police dog is in service at an airport.

Amendment rights. What happens when they do not? If a court decides that evidence was gained through an illegal search, then the evidence cannot be used at trial. This principle is called the *exclusionary rule* because the court must exclude the illegally obtained evidence during a trial.

The Fifth Amendment

The Fifth Amendment protects several rights of accused persons. First, it states that no one can be tried for a serious crime without an indictment. An **indictment** (ihn•DITE•muhnt) is a document that formally charges someone with a crime. Indictments are issued by a body called a **grand jury**. This body is made up of ordinary citizens who are randomly selected to participate for a limited amount of time. Members of the grand jury review the evidence of a possible crime. They look only at the evidence presented by the prosecution to determine if it is reasonable to charge a person with committing a crime. If they believe that it is, the person is indicted. Someone who is indicted is not necessarily guilty. An indictment simply states the grand jury's belief that the accused may have carried out a crime. A trial will decide if the accused is guilty or innocent.

The Fifth Amendment prevents charging someone more than once for the same crime. If a person is found not guilty, the government is not allowed to try to convict that person a second time. Putting someone on trial again for a crime of which they were already found not guilty is called *double jeopardy*. The Fifth Amendment blocks the government from that action.

The Fifth Amendment protects the right of accused people not to be witnesses against themselves. Throughout history, governments have forced people to confess to crimes they did not really commit. To prevent this, the Fifth Amendment protects against self-incrimination. This term means that people cannot be forced to testify against themselves. This right is often stated as the right to remain silent. This right applies in criminal trials but also in criminal investigations.

The Fifth Amendment states that no one may be denied life, liberty, or property "without due

indictment document issued by a body called a grand jury that formally charges someone with a crime

grand jury a group that hears evidence and decides whether to issue an indictment

PHOTO:Monika Wisniewska/Shutterstock; TEXT: U.S. Constitution, Amendment IV

The Sixth Amendment provides persons accused of crimes the right to a jury trial.

Analyzing How will these jury members help ensure a fair trial for the accused?

process of law." **Due process** means following set and fair legal procedures. It includes the idea that the laws to be followed must be reasonable. The idea of due process also applies to rules at school. If a student causes disruptions at a public school, the school must follow certain procedures before expelling the student. The school or district cannot take away the student's right to an education without following due process.

Finally, the Fifth Amendment protects property rights. It limits the government's power of eminent domain. **Eminent domain** (EH•mih•nehnt doh•MAYN) is the government's right to take private property—usually land—for public use. For example, if your home lies in the path of a proposed highway, the government can take your land and tear down the home to make way for the highway. The Fifth Amendment limits this power. It requires the government to pay a fair price for the property.

The Sixth Amendment

The Sixth Amendment guarantees other rights to the accused. First, it requires that accused persons be clearly told what the charges against them are. This is simple fairness. You cannot know how to defend yourself if you do not know what you are accused of.

---

due process following established and fair legal procedures

eminent domain the right of government to take private property—usually land—for public use

The Sixth Amendment also covers criminal trials. It grants the right to a trial by jury. As with other rights, individuals have the choice to exercise this right or not. An accused person can choose to be tried by a judge without a jury.

The lawyers for both sides of the case choose the jury. Members of the jury must be selected from the community, and they must be impartial. That means they must be able to focus on the facts of the case and on the law and not have any personal interest in the outcome. The lawyers question potential jurors, and they may eliminate those who seem biased. However, the lawyers may not exclude jurors simply on the basis of their race, gender, or national origin.

The Sixth Amendment also grants the right to a trial that is speedy and held in public. This requirement prevents secret proceedings that cannot be watched to make sure they are fair. If possible, the trial should be held in the community where the crime took place.

People who are accused have the right to hear and question all witnesses against them. They must be allowed to call witnesses in their defense. They also have the right to obtain a court order to force witnesses to appear and testify. Finally, the accused has the right to a lawyer. The Supreme Court has said that when an accused person cannot afford to pay a lawyer, the government must provide and pay for one. This right is basic to the idea of a fair trial.

In a criminal trial, the state is represented by a prosecutor who is a lawyer and who prepares the case against the accused. The accused also needs a skillful lawyer to ensure a fair trial.

The Eighth Amendment

Even though accused people have the right to a speedy trial, sometimes weeks or months can pass before a trial can be held. During that time, accused people may have the choice to remain free by paying bail. **Bail** is a sum of money used as a security deposit. In exchange for being let out of jail, an accused person pays the sum and promises to appear at the trial. When the person comes to court for the trial, the bail is returned. If the person fails to appear, the bail is not returned.

A judge decides how much bail a person must pay. The Eighth Amendment, however, forbids "excessive" bail—that is, an amount that is much too high.

Excessive does not just refer to what a person is able to pay. In setting bail, a judge must weigh several other factors. These include the type of crime committed, the accused person's history of criminal behavior, and the likelihood that the person will appear in court. Judges may deny bail if they think the accused person will try to flee, or escape, rather than show up for the trial.

When a person is found guilty of a crime, the Eighth Amendment protects that person from punishment that is too harsh. It also prevents fines from being set too high. This amendment forbids "cruel and unusual punishments." Americans have long debated what punishments are cruel and unusual. Many agree that punishment should be in proportion to, or fit, the crime committed. That is, the more serious the crime, the more serious the punishment. For example, a sentence of life imprisonment for stealing a loaf of bread would be too harsh. People disagree strongly about whether the death penalty is cruel and unusual punishment.

✓ **CHECK FOR UNDERSTANDING**

1. **Analyzing** Which of the Fourth, Fifth, Sixth, and Eighth Amendments apply to the police? Which apply to the courts?

2. **Speculating** Why do you think there are so many amendments directed specifically to the rights of the accused?

Additional Protections

GUIDING QUESTION

Which other protections does the Bill of Rights offer?

When the Framers wrote the Bill of Rights, they remembered the events that led to the American Revolution. They felt that certain actions taken by the British government were abuses of power.

bail a sum of money used as a security deposit to ensure that an accused person returns for the trial

Over the years, there has been intense debate over whether the death penalty is constitutional. Here, protesters against the death penalty march and carry signs in front of the U.S. Supreme Court in Washington, D.C.

Many Americans disagree about the meaning of the Second Amendment. Gun advocates argue for the responsible use of guns. Opponents link guns to violence.

The Framers wanted to prevent the American government from taking such actions, so they included additional protections in the Bill of Rights.

The Second Amendment

The Second Amendment says this: "A well regulated Militia being necessary to the security of a free State, the right of the people to keep and bear Arms shall not be infringed." To infringe a right is to limit it.

When the Second Amendment was written, each state had its own militia. Members of the militia were people who served as soldiers when needed.

People have long debated what rights, exactly, this amendment protects. In 2008 the U.S. Supreme Court commented on the Second Amendment. The Court stated that the Second Amendment means that individuals have a constitutional right to keep firearms in their homes for personal safety.

Two years later, the Court ruled that this right extends to state laws as well as federal law. In *McDonald* v. *Chicago*, the Court said that the Second Amendment protects the right to lawful self-defense. Because of that, the ruling prohibits states or cities from banning handguns.

But the right to bear arms is not absolute. Courts have generally ruled that the government can pass laws to control gun ownership. For example, federal and state governments can spell out who can have a license to own firearms.

The Third Amendment

Before the American Revolution, the British Parliament passed the Quartering Act, which required the colonies to provide food and shelter for British soldiers. The intention was for soldiers to stay in barracks, inns, stables, or other buildings. Many colonists feared they would have to allow soldiers to live in their own homes. The Third Amendment was a reaction to this act, and it bans this practice. It says that, when there is no war, the military may not require civilians to house soldiers without permission of the homeowner.

The Seventh Amendment

The Seventh Amendment concerns civil cases. These cases usually involve disputes between private individuals or organizations. Civil cases can arise when people's rights are in conflict or when a person harms or wrongs another person. Contract disputes and property damage are examples of issues that can lead to civil disputes.

The Seventh Amendment guarantees the right to a jury trial in most civil disputes heard in the federal courts. This guarantee specifically applies to disputes about property worth more than $20. Today, however, nearly all disputes involve sums larger than $20. As a result, this requirement of the amendment is almost always met.

The Ninth Amendment

The Ninth Amendment states that all other rights not spelled out in the Constitution are **retained** by the people. This amendment prevents the government from claiming that the only rights people have are those listed in the Bill of Rights.

retain to keep

Passage of the Quartering Act in 1774 made many colonists fearful that British soldiers would soon be stationed in their homes. The Third Amendment was intended to prevent this practice. This illustration from the 1800s depicts what colonists might have experienced.

Analyzing Visuals Describe the situation shown in the illustration. How are the colonists reacting?

The Ninth Amendment makes it clear that citizens have other rights beyond those listed in the Constitution, and they may not be taken away.

The Tenth Amendment

The last amendment in the Bill of Rights did not add anything to the ratified Constitution. Instead, the Tenth Amendment **confirms** that the power of the federal government is limited.

The Tenth Amendment states that the federal government has only the powers that the Constitution specifically gives it. Any other powers belong to the states or the people. In this way, the amendment is intended to prevent Congress and the president from becoming too strong. The government of the United States can have only the powers the people give it.

confirm to verify

✓ CHECK FOR UNDERSTANDING

1. **Comparing** In what ways do the Ninth and Tenth Amendments protect individuals?

2. **Speculating** Why do you think the Framers chose not to list all the rights of the people in the Bill of Rights?

LESSON ACTIVITIES

1. **Argumentative Writing** Which of the amendments dealing with the rights of the accused do you believe is the most important in creating a fair legal system in our country? Explain why you think so in a short essay.

2. **Interpreting Information** With a partner, create a poster that could be used to remind accused persons of their rights as guaranteed in the Constitution.

10

Furthering Civil Liberties

The Civil War Amendments

GUIDING QUESTION

How were civil rights extended following the Civil War?

Before 1865, most African Americans were enslaved, and the issue of slavery greatly divided the nation. While Southern states used large numbers of enslaved people to improve profits on the region's plantations, Northern states had mostly done away with the practice. In the mid-1800s, serious conflicts arose between North and South over slavery and related issues. These sectional differences and conflicts led to the Civil War. The North won that war and reunited the country. The war resulted in the end of slavery.

Three constitutional amendments were passed after the Civil War. These were the Thirteenth, Fourteenth, and Fifteenth Amendments. All three amendments were intended to make African Americans full, equal citizens. However, the Southern states found ways to prevent that from happening. Many states kept African Americans separated from whites. New laws, in the South especially, continued to deny African Americans their basic rights.

Although the original reason for passing these amendments was to protect African Americans, who had been enslaved and then denied rights, the authors did not limit the amendments to African Americans. The Fourteenth Amendment does not even mention race but declares rights for "all persons born or naturalized in the United States."

In an illustration from 1865, members of the House of Representatives celebrate the enactment of the Thirteenth Amendment.

North Wind Picture Archives/Alamy Stock Photo

This image from 1867 shows white and African American election officials supervising the first African American voters in Washington, D.C.

Analyzing Visuals
Why would it have been important to have both white and African American election officials?

Since these amendments were passed, they have frequently been used to protect other groups and individuals.

The Thirteenth Amendment

The Thirteenth Amendment was the first of the Civil War amendments. Approved in 1865, the Thirteenth Amendment outlawed slavery. It freed hundreds of thousands of enslaved African Americans.

The Thirteenth Amendment also banned forced labor, which means forcing someone to work. The only legal forced labor was as punishment for committing a crime. Because of this exception, prisoners can be made to work in prison workshops. The exception for prisoners also makes it possible for judges to order some people who break the law to do community service work.

The Fourteenth Amendment

Although the Thirteenth Amendment ended slavery, it did not extend full rights for African Americans. Southern states soon passed laws known as **black codes**. These laws kept African Americans from holding certain jobs, restricted their right to own property, and limited their rights in other ways.

The Fourteenth Amendment was ratified in 1868 to try to protect African Americans from these laws. It defined an American citizen as anyone "born or naturalized in the United States." This definition included most African Americans. It also made African Americans citizens of the state in which they lived.

black codes laws from after the Civil War that kept African Americans from holding certain jobs, restricted their right to own property, and limited their rights in other ways

PHOTO: North Wind Picture Archives/Alamy Stock Photo; TEXT: U.S. Constitution, Amendment XIV, Section 1

Besides making everyone who was born in the United States a citizen, the Fourteenth Amendment said that every state must give all citizens "equal protection of the laws." The purpose was to force states to end unfair laws that discriminated against African Americans. This "equal protection clause" has also been used to help other groups who have been treated unequally. Those groups include women and people with disabilities.

Third, the amendment forbade state governments from unreasonable action or interference with U.S. citizens. Finally, the amendment said that no state can take a person's "life, liberty, or property" unless it follows due process. Due process means fair procedures set by law.

Soon after ratification, the Fourteenth Amendment was used to overturn many laws that discriminated against African Americans. One example was a ban on African Americans serving on juries. However, this shift toward equality did not last long.

By the late 1800s, about half of the states had passed laws requiring racial segregation, or separation by race. In these states, segregation applied to schools, hotels, theaters, public transportation, and other public places or services. In 1896 the Supreme Court ruled in *Plessy* v. *Ferguson* that states were allowed to segregate by race, as long as the state provided equal facilities to all. The justices said that this practice did not violate the Fourteenth Amendment's equal protection clause.

Over several decades, Americans' ideas about discrimination began to change. By 1954, the Supreme Court ruled in *Brown* v. *Board of Education* that having separate facilities for African Americans and whites was unequal by its very nature. The Court ruled that this practice violated the Fourteenth Amendment.

The "due process" clause proved very important over time, as the courts have used it to redefine the reach of the Bill of Rights. As written, the Bill of Rights only limited the power of the federal government. When the Fourteenth Amendment was ratified in 1868, many thought that it would extend all of the Bill of Rights protections to the states. That did not begin to happen until 1925. That year, the Court decided *Gitlow* v. *New York*. In its decision, the Court ruled that the Fourteenth Amendment required states to protect freedom of speech and freedom of the press. The Fourteenth Amendment promised that no one could be deprived of liberty without due process of law. In *Gitlow*, the justices said that free speech was one of those protected liberties.

This was the first in a number of cases in which the Supreme Court has ruled that the due process clause requires state and local governments to uphold people's First Amendment rights. Eventually, the Court used several other cases to apply almost all of the Bill of Rights to the states.

In 1954 the Supreme Court ruled that separate schools for African American and white students violated the equal protection clause of the Fourteenth Amendment. This photo, taken after the Court's decision, shows a classroom that includes both African American and white students.

The Fifteenth Amendment

The Fifteenth Amendment, ratified in 1870, was the last of the Civil War amendments. It says that no state may deny a person the right to vote because of "race, color, or previous condition of servitude." The amendment was meant to guarantee **suffrage**—the right to vote—for African Americans.

However, the Fifteenth Amendment does not establish a right to vote, it only limits the rules that states can make about voting. It says states cannot deny the right to vote on the basis of race. They can deny it for other reasons. States found other ways to keep African Americans from voting. They also continued to deny suffrage to women.

✓ **CHECK FOR UNDERSTANDING**

1. **Summarizing** What was the purpose of the Civil War amendments?

2. **Determining Central Ideas** Why is the due process clause of the Fourteenth Amendment so significant?

suffrage the right to vote

Constitutional Amendments

Since the addition of the Bill of Rights, 17 amendments have been added to the Constitution.

Eleventh Amendment (1795)	Places limits on lawsuits against states
Twelfth Amendment (1804)	Revises procedure for electing the president and vice president
Thirteenth Amendment (1865)	Abolishes slavery
Fourteenth Amendment (1868)	Defines U.S. citizenship; guarantees all citizens "equal protection of the laws"
Fifteenth Amendment (1870)	Prohibits restrictions on the right to vote based on race and color
Sixteenth Amendment (1913)	Gives Congress the power to levy an income tax
Seventeenth Amendment (1913)	Enables voters to elect senators directly
Eighteenth Amendment (1917)	Prohibits making, transporting, selling, importing, and exporting alcoholic beverages; repealed by Twenty-first Amendment
Nineteenth Amendment (1920)	Prohibits denying women the right to vote on the basis of sex
Twentieth Amendment (1933)	Changes the dates of congressional and presidential terms
Twenty-first Amendment (1933)	Repeals Prohibition (Eighteenth Amendment)
Twenty-second Amendment (1951)	Limits presidents to two terms in office except for some vice presidents who succeed to the presidency
Twenty-third Amendment (1961)	Gives residents of the District of Columbia the right to vote
Twenty-fourth Amendment (1961)	Abolishes poll taxes in federal elections
Twenty-fifth Amendment (1967)	Establishes procedures for succession to the presidency
Twenty-sixth Amendment (1971)	Prohibits denying the right to vote to those 18 or older on the basis of age
Twenty-seventh Amendment (1992)	Delays congressional pay raises until the term following their passage

HISTORY CONNECTION

1. **Identifying** Which amendments affected the office of the president? What did they do?

2. **Speculating** Why do you think women won the right to vote before 18-year-olds?

This 1913 parade demanding woman suffrage was one event in a long struggle for women's rights.

Speculating How might a parade like this one help the cause of gaining voting rights for women?

Electoral Process and Voting Rights

GUIDING QUESTION

In what ways have several amendments added in the 1900s affected voting rights and changed elections?

During the 1900s, new amendments made important changes in voting and elections. Some made clear who had the right to vote in every state. Others changed the way elections were **conducted**. Together, these new amendments put more power in the hands of the people.

The Seventeenth Amendment

Article I of the Constitution says that members of the House of Representatives shall be elected by the people. However, it calls for members of the Senate to be chosen by the state legislatures. The Seventeenth Amendment, ratified in 1913, changed that. It required that voters elect their senators directly. This change made legislators more accountable to the people and gave Americans a greater voice in their government.

conduct to carry out

The Nineteenth Amendment

The Constitution does not give the federal government power to create voting rights. Under the Tenth Amendment, this power falls to the states. As early as the 1840s, Elizabeth Cady Stanton and Susan B. Anthony led campaigns for woman suffrage. The first women's rights convention was held in 1848. The most controversial issue to come out of the convention was the demand for the right to vote. At that time, many Americans did not think women should have the same rights as men.

That began to change by the end of the 1800s. Women in Wyoming, Colorado, Idaho, and Utah gained the right to vote. Elsewhere, women, and the men who supported their cause, marched, petitioned, and even picketed the White House. They staged hunger strikes and were arrested to draw attention and support to their cause.

Finally, in 1920, the Nineteenth Amendment was approved. It prohibited states from denying women the right to vote in all national and state elections. However, this still did not protect the right to vote for African American women in all states. The states that limited the voting rights of African American men also limited the voting rights of African American women.

In 1969 a young woman rests during a demonstration in support of the Twenty-sixth Amendment.

Analyzing Visuals What cause is she supporting?

The Twenty-third Amendment

Another group that was denied full voting rights was citizens living in our nation's capital, Washington, D.C. For many years, they could not vote for president or vice president. "D.C." stands for the District of Columbia, an area between Maryland and Virginia. Since the District is not a state, people there had no representation in Congress and could not vote in national elections.

The Twenty-third Amendment changed that situation in 1961. It said that people in the District may vote for president and vice president. It gave the District the same number of electoral votes as the smallest state—three.

The Twenty-fourth Amendment

The Fifteenth Amendment gave African American men the right to vote. However, Southern states used various methods to prevent them from voting. One such method was the **poll tax**.

---

poll tax a sum of money required of voters before they are permitted to cast a ballot

This was a sum of money voters were required to pay before they were permitted to cast a ballot. This money had to be paid not only for the current year but for previous unpaid years as well. That made it a great financial burden. Many African Americans were denied the vote because they could not afford to pay the tax.

The Twenty-fourth Amendment, passed in 1964, made poll taxes illegal in national elections. Two years later, the Supreme Court banned poll taxes in state elections, too. As a result, many African Americans were able to vote for the first time.

The Twenty-sixth Amendment

Throughout our nation's history, many teens have bravely fought for our country. By law, however, they were unable to vote for the leaders who sent them into battle. Most states set the minimum age for voting at 21. That changed in 1971, at a time when many young Americans were being drafted to fight in the Vietnam War. The Twenty-sixth Amendment says that the right to vote cannot be denied because of age to anyone 18 years of age or older. As a result, you can register, or sign up, to vote once you turn 18.

✓ **CHECK FOR UNDERSTANDING**

1. **Identifying Cause and Effect** How did the Twenty-fourth Amendment affect voting rights?
2. **Explaining** Why has Congress used constitutional amendments to expand voting rights instead of passing federal laws?

LESSON ACTIVITIES

1. **Informative/Explanatory Writing** The expansion of voting rights in the United States has mostly been achieved through constitutional amendments. Write an informative essay describing the role of constitutional amendments in changing voting rights in America.

2. **Using Multimedia** Work with a small group to create a documentary video to report on how the Fourteenth Amendment has changed and improved Americans' lives. Each person in the group should describe how the Fourteenth Amendment affected the lives of people from a specific group. Then work together with your group to record each member's report and assemble the documentary. Present your video documentary for the class.

11

The Civil Rights Movement

READING STRATEGY

Analyzing Key Ideas and Details As you read, use a diagram to note the forms of discrimination the civil rights movement addressed and the actions that the movement took.

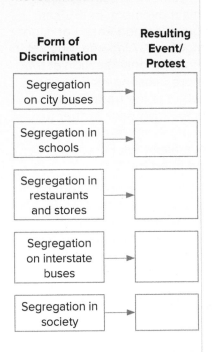

Form of Discrimination	Resulting Event/ Protest
Segregation on city buses	→
Segregation in schools	→
Segregation in restaurants and stores	→
Segregation on interstate buses	→
Segregation in society	→

Origins of the Civil Rights Movement

GUIDING QUESTION

Why did the civil rights movement occur?

The Fourteenth Amendment says that all Americans have the right to equal protection of the laws. The Fourteenth Amendment was intended in part to eliminate the black codes imposed after the Civil War. But African Americans still faced **discrimination**, or unfair treatment based on prejudice, every day. Southern states passed laws to separate African Americans and whites in most public places. This practice is called **segregation**. These segregation laws were known as **"Jim Crow" laws**. The name came from a well-known stage character who presented a negative image of African Americans.

Segregation Laws

Segregation persisted for decades. African Americans were forced to ride in the back of buses. They were sent to separate schools. They had to drink from separate drinking fountains. Even in the North, prejudice put limits on the opportunities African Americans had in life.

discrimination unfair treatment based on prejudice against a certain group

segregation the social separation of the races

"Jim Crow" law a Southern segregation law

In the first half of the 1900s, drinking fountains were among the many public facilities that remained segregated by race.

The campaign for African Americans' **civil rights**—the rights of full citizenship and equality under the law—has been a long and difficult one. They gained some of their rights in part because they started a movement to win them. That movement continues today, however, as full equality has not yet been achieved.

For many years the courts let segregation laws stand. In 1896 the Supreme Court declared in *Plessy* v. *Ferguson* that segregation was legal if the facilities offered to each group were "separate, but equal." In fact, the services and facilities for African Americans were far from equal to those for white people. For example, states in the South spent far more money on schools for white people than they did on schools for African Americans.

In many places, African Americans faced unprovoked violence. White people launched race riots, violently attacking people and property in African American neighborhoods. White lynch mobs tortured and murdered African Americans. Lynching is publicly and unlawfully killing someone without a trial.

Fighting Segregation

African Americans fought discrimination on many fronts. The National Association for the Advancement of Colored People (NAACP) organized marches and worked for anti-lynching legislation. News reporter Ida B. Wells wrote movingly about the injustice of lynching.

The NAACP also worked within the legal system. Led by attorney Thurgood Marshall, the NAACP fought in court against *Plessy* v. *Ferguson*, arguing that racially divided facilities were not in fact equal. One by one, African Americans won victories against segregated buses, juries, political parties, and law schools.

A signal that America was changing was Jackie Robinson's entry in 1947 as the first African American baseball player in the Major Leagues. Another sign of progress occurred when President Truman ordered the end of segregation in the U.S. military in 1948.

A major victory over segregation came in 1954 in a case involving a young African American girl named Linda Brown. Lawyers led by Thurgood Marshall argued on behalf of Brown

that the education being given to African American students was not equal to the one given to white students. The problem, they said, was not just unequal spending and unequal facilities. The problem was segregation itself.

Linda Brown's case went all the way to the U.S. Supreme Court. The Court agreed with Marshall's argument. The Court said that separating children in school by race violated the promise of equal protection found in the Fourteenth Amendment. *Brown* v. *Board of Education of Topeka, Kansas* (1954) was a great victory for civil rights.

Soon after Brown came another important event in the civil rights movement. In 1955 an African American woman named Rosa Parks got on a city bus in Montgomery, Alabama. She sat in the first row of the "colored only" section at the rear of the bus. As more passengers boarded, the "whites only" section at the front filled. The driver ordered Parks to move back farther to make room for white passengers. She refused. At the next bus stop, police took Parks off the bus, arrested her, and fined her $10.

Rosa Parks, who had trained and prepared for this kind of situation, was a respected leader and activist in Montgomery's African American community. Her arrest sparked a mass protest by African Americans, led by a young preacher named Martin Luther King, Jr. For a year, African Americans boycotted Montgomery's buses. A boycott is a refusal to deal with a group as a protest of the group's actions.

The arrest of Rosa Parks in 1955, shown here being fingerprinted by the police, sparked the Montgomery bus boycott.

---

civil rights the rights of full citizenship and equality under law

Brown v. Board of Education of Topeka, Kansas (1954)

BACKGROUND OF THE CASE In the 1950s, the public schools of Topeka, Kansas, were racially segregated by law—as were schools in 16 other states. The Supreme Court's ruling in *Plessy* v. *Ferguson* had declared that segregated schools were legal, as long as they were equal. In reality, however, the schools for African American children were not at all equal to those for white children.

Linda Brown was a young African American girl who lived in Topeka. She was assigned to attend a school for African American children far from her home. Her parents tried to enroll her in a school for white children that was closer, but the school refused to accept her. In response, Linda's parents joined with the National Association for the Advancement of Colored People (NAACP) to sue the Topeka Board of Education. Their argument was that separate schools violated the equal protection clause of the Fourteenth Amendment. Thurgood Marshall, the head lawyer for the NAACP, represented them in court. When the case reached the Supreme Court, it was combined with four similar cases from other states. The five cases together became known as *Brown* v. *Board of Education of Topeka, Kansas*.

» The parents of the children shown here, led by the NAACP Legal Defense Fund and Thurgood Marshall, sued their local boards of education to end segregated schooling. Linda Brown, of Topeka, Kansas, is third from the left.

THE DECISION OF THE COURT In 1954 the Court unanimously ruled that laws requiring segregated schools were unconstitutional, even if they met equal standards. In explaining the Court's decision, Chief Justice Earl Warren wrote:

> To separate [children in grade and high schools] from others of similar age and qualifications solely because of their race generates a feeling of inferiority as to their status in the community that may affect their hearts and minds in a way unlikely ever to be undone. . . . We conclude that, in the field of public education, the doctrine of 'separate but equal' has no place. Separate educational facilities are inherently unequal.

—Chief Justice Earl Warren, *Brown* v. *Board of Education of Topeka*, 1954

The Court ruled that because separate schools could never be equal, the state laws requiring segregation violated the equal protection clause of the Fourteenth Amendment. In doing so, the Court overturned the "separate but equal" doctrine from the *Plessy* case and set a precedent, or model, that guided many later court decisions.

1. **Analyzing** How did 17 states justify their laws that required segregated schools before the *Brown* decision?
2. **Citing Text Evidence** What reason did Chief Justice Warren give to support the Court's decision that segregated schools were a violation of the equal protection clause?

MARTIN LUTHER KING, JR. (1929–1968)

» Martin Luther King, Jr., speaks at the March on Washington in August 1963.

Martin Luther King, Jr., pulled at the nation's conscience. He urged people to work to make the American ideal of justice and equality for all citizens come true. His words and efforts supported African Americans in their struggle, and they challenged those who tried to ignore discrimination. King was one of many talented and dedicated leaders of the civil rights movement. He is the best-known civil rights figure today, but he relied on many partnerships and worked alongside other respected leaders.

King was born in Atlanta, Georgia, in 1929. The son of a Baptist minister, he decided when he was 18 years old to become a minister also. King's ideals came from his Christian belief that all people were children of God. Before King became influential, African American civil rights leaders had already learned about and begun to use the methods of Mohandas Gandhi. Gandhi had used nonviolent resistance to win India's freedom from British colonial rule.

Soon after King moved to Montgomery, Alabama, Rosa Parks was arrested, and many African American residents began a nonviolent campaign against segregation. King became the most prominent voice of that campaign and learned more about Gandhi and his methods.

As a founder of the Southern Christian Leadership Conference, he helped organize civil rights protests throughout the South. King's efforts to end "Jim Crow" laws and to gain voting rights for African Americans won him the Nobel Peace Prize in 1964.

Though King always preached nonviolence, he was often the target of violent attacks. The last of those came in April 1968, when he was shot and killed. Though millions were saddened by his death, King's message of inspiration and hope lives on.

Making Connections How did Martin Luther King, Jr., draw inspiration from the independence movement in India?

The bus boycott ended when the Supreme Court ruled that segregation in public transportation, such as city buses, was against the Constitution.

Peaceful Protests

Martin Luther King Jr. was a young minister and a stirring speaker. He believed in confronting injustice through **nonviolent resistance**—peaceful protest against laws believed to be unfair. For several years of the civil rights movement, King led marches, boycotts, and demonstrations.

nonviolent resistance peaceful protest against laws believed to be unfair

Many others also pushed for civil rights. African American students held sit-ins, sitting at lunch counters that served only white people and refusing to leave until they were served. Their actions forced businesses to change. In 1961 white activists joined African American activists and traveled through the South on interstate buses. These "Freedom Rides" protested segregation on the buses and in the bus stations that served them. At several stops in the South, the Freedom Riders met violent opposition.

In 1963 more than 200,000 people marched in Washington, D.C., to show support for a new civil rights law. At this gathering, King gave his famous "I Have a Dream" speech, full of hope for racial equality.

Over time, these protests drew growing support. One reason was the violent police response to the peaceful protests. News coverage of police violence helped convince many Americans to support the struggle for civil rights. However, the movement was always controversial and had many critics.

Civil Rights Act of 1964

The movement led to a growing public demand for government action. As a result, Congress passed the Civil Rights Act of 1964. This law banned segregation in public businesses—stores, restaurants, hotels, and theaters. It also prohibited employers from discriminating in hiring workers. The law did not protect just African Americans. It also outlawed discrimination based on gender, religion, and national origin.

Voting Rights Act of 1965

Despite this advance, African Americans faced another problem—many Southern states denied them the right to vote. Most African Americans in the South were prevented from voting by unfair laws.

One of those laws required voters to pay a poll tax before they were permitted to cast a ballot. Many African Americans had been denied the vote because they could not afford to pay the tax. In 1964 Congress passed the Twenty-fourth Amendment to outlaw poll taxes for national elections.

Other state laws required voters to pass a literacy, or reading, test. White officials made it very difficult for African Americans to pass these tests. The Voting Rights Act of 1965 banned the unfair use of literacy tests. Many people see the Voting Rights Act of 1965 as one of the most effective civil rights laws. After it passed, the number of African American voters in the South rose dramatically.

The Voting Rights Act was strengthened several times after 1965. However, a 2013 U.S. Supreme Court decision weakened how the act could be enforced. Another decision in 2021 weakened the act further by limiting the reasons why people could challenge voting laws.

✓ **CHECK FOR UNDERSTANDING**

1. **Identifying** What were two methods that were used by the civil rights movement?

2. **Explaining** How was nonviolent resistance an effective strategy for gaining civil rights?

Martin Luther King, Jr., (front row, fifth from right) witnessed President Lyndon B. Johnson signing the Voting Rights Act of 1965 into law.

Speculating Why do you think it was important that Martin Luther King Jr. was among the guests invited to witness the signing?

PF-(usna)/Alamy Stock Photo

The Struggle Continues

GUIDING QUESTION

What other groups of citizens have struggled to win civil rights?

The civil rights gains of the 1960s helped other groups, too. The Civil Rights Act of 1964 sought to protect many groups from discrimination. The success of the civil rights movement also convinced other groups to work for their own rights. Women, Latinos and Latinas, Native Americans, and disabled people all called for equal treatment.

Even today the struggle for equal rights goes on. About 80,000 people per year report that they have been harmed by discrimination where they work. Each year some people are subjected to unfair treatment by police. One practice is called **racial profiling**. This occurs when police single out certain people as suspects because of their racial appearance. Each year, some people are the victims of **hate crimes**. These are violent acts against people because of a group that they belong to.

Affirmative Action

In 1961 President John F. Kennedy sought to improve the opportunities for African Americans in the workforce and in higher education. He urged companies to take what he called *affirmative action* to make that happen. The term refers to a policy meant to increase the number of underrepresented groups and women at work and in colleges. The purpose of affirmative action is to make up for past actions that harmed people in these groups. Colleges use affirmative action to help underrepresented students and women enter college in larger numbers than before. Companies use these programs to hire and promote members of underrepresented groups and women.

From the start, critics objected to affirmative action. They called the idea "reverse discrimination." They said that affirmative action gave special treatment to people from underrepresented groups or to women. They argued that affirmative action policies treated white people and men unfairly.

The U.S. Supreme Court has narrowed the way colleges and universities can use race as a factor in making decisions about admitting students to their schools. In two cases in the early 2000s, the Court said that race could be considered in these decisions. However, these schools could not automatically give favorable treatment to members of underrepresented groups.

Other Civil Rights Gains

Other groups observed the successes of the civil rights movement. They began to raise their voices in hopes of gaining rights long denied to them.

Native American Rights In 1968 several Native Americans came together to form the American Indian Movement (AIM). Its goal was to improve

Demonstrators marched to the Michigan State Capitol in 2006 to protest a law that would limit affirmative action.

racial profiling unfair treatment that occurs when police single out certain people as suspects because of their racial appearance

hate crime a violent act against a person because of a group they belong to

A large crowd of women cheers a speaker during a 1981 rally for passage of the Equal Rights Amendment.

the lives of Native Americans, many of whom were poor. It worked to protect the rights granted to Native American peoples by treaties. AIM has also tried to keep native culture alive.

Chicano Rights The Chicano Movement was formed by Mexican Americans. It tried to fight segregation and discrimination in the Southwest. Other Mexican American leaders worked for fair treatment of farm workers, most of whom were from this group. Seasonal and migrant farm workers were commonly **exploited**, or treated unfairly, by the companies they worked for. César Chávez and Dolores Huerta led Mexican Americans in strikes and boycotts to gain better working conditions and pay for farm workers. They used the same methods of nonviolent protest used by Martin Luther King, Jr.

Women's Rights The movement for women's rights gained new energy in 1966 when the National Organization for Women was formed.

The group dealt with many issues important to women, such as discrimination on the job and domestic violence.

Progress has not been smooth, however. The Equal Pay Act of 1963 prohibits wage discrimination. Despite this and other laws, women continue to earn less money than men. The pay gap is generally even larger for African American women and Latina women. The women's movement continues to fight for equal pay for equal work.

Many people worked hard to get an Equal Rights Amendment, or ERA, added to the Constitution. An ERA had first been proposed in 1923. It said that no state could deny any person equal rights because of gender. In 1972 Congress approved the ERA, but it was never ratified by enough states to become an amendment.

Women gained more equality in education with the passage of Title IX of the Education Amendments Act of 1972. Title IX prohibits discrimination against women and girls in federally funded schools and universities.

exploit to treat unfairly for someone else's gain

The Americans with Disabilities Act requires accessible public transportation for everyone.

Analyzing Visuals How has this bus been made accessible to this woman who uses a wheelchair?

By banning discrimination in college admissions, Title IX resulted in more women attending college. It also opened up greater opportunities for women in school and college-level sports. Title IX prohibits discrimination against pregnant students and students who have children.

Rights of Persons with Disabilities People who have disabilities have also won rights. In 1990 Congress passed the Americans with Disabilities Act. This important law protects the rights of people with disabilities in the workplace, in housing, and in public places such as shopping malls and restaurants. It requires employers to make accommodations for people who have disabilities that do not affect their ability to do their jobs.

LGBTQ Rights The effort to end violence and discrimination based on sexual orientation and gender identity started before the 1960s. However, during the 1960s, in part because of the civil rights movement, this effort gained momentum, media attention, and influence.

Throughout the 1970s and 1980s, additional groups formed to advocate for change around this issue. This movement involves people who identify themselves in different ways and who face discrimination based on their sexual orientation or gender identify. As a result, people in this movement adopted the term **LGBTQ**, which stands for lesbian, gay, bisexual, transgender, and queer or questioning.

The 1969 Stonewall riots were a pivotal event that helped bring the issue of LGBTQ equality into broader focus. In the 1960s, discriminatory laws in New York City and many other places made actions such as dancing together, holding hands, and kissing illegal for same-sex couples. These laws gave police a reason to break up gatherings of LGBTQ people. New York City police often raided a business named the Stonewall Inn. During one raid in June 1969, some customers and neighborhood residents refused police orders to leave the area. As police tried to force the crowd to leave, onlookers began throwing objects at the officers. Soon rioting erupted. Though that incident ended, protests continued for many days. Stonewall inspired LGBTQ activists to demand equal rights more vocally and publicly.

✓ **CHECK FOR UNDERSTANDING**

1. **Describing** What did President John F. Kennedy hope to achieve with affirmative action?
2. **Identifying** What other groups were inspired by the civil rights movement to work for equality for themselves?

LESSON ACTIVITIES

1. **Informative/Explanatory Writing** Write a brief essay that describes the various tactics of the civil rights movement and other rights movements of the 1960s and 1970s.
2. **Collaborating** With a group, present a panel discussion to describe the conditions that led to the civil rights movement, and evaluate how well they have been addressed. To plan for the discussion, assign each group member an area to focus on, such as education, employment, or criminal justice.

LGBTQ lesbian, gay, bisexual, transgender, and queer or questioning

12

Analyzing Sources: Civil Rights for All

 COMPELLING QUESTION

How can people change government policy?

Plan Your Inquiry

DEVELOPING QUESTIONS

Think about how Americans have made their voices heard regarding civil rights. Then read the Compelling Question for this lesson. What questions can you ask to help you answer this Compelling Question? Create a graphic organizer like the one below. Write these Supporting Questions in your graphic organizer.

Supporting Questions	Primary or Secondary Source	What the source tells me about how people can change government policy	Questions the source leaves unanswered
	A		
	B		
	C		
	D		
	E		

ANALYZING SOURCES

Next, examine the sources in this lesson. Analyze each source by answering the questions that follow it. How does each source help you answer each Supporting Question you created? What questions do you still have? Write these in your graphic organizer.

After you analyze the sources, you will:
- use the evidence from the sources,
- communicate your conclusions,
- and take informed action.

Background Information

The Constitution and the Bill of Rights were designed with the intent that Americans' rights would be protected. At times, the federal or state governments have denied groups of people their rights. African Americans, Latinos, Asian Americans, Native Americans, and women have sometimes been denied their rights. Throughout U.S. history, discrimination has affected these groups. Unequal access to voting and other civil rights have been an issue.

Many Americans have worked to end unfair treatment and secure their rights. They have joined in groups to monitor the government and hold it accountable. They have worked to influence the government by attending meetings, staging protests, and sending messages to government agencies and officials. Citizens have voted and have chosen to run for office to create change. Some have filed lawsuits to make policy makers obey and enforce the Bill of Rights and to overturn unjust laws. In some cases, people have convinced fellow American citizens and lawmakers to amend the Constitution in order to ensure equal treatment and correct abuses of power.

» This statue in New York City's Central Park honors important women's rights leaders including (from left) Sojourner Truth, Susan B. Anthony, and Elizabeth Cady Stanton.

Civil Rights and Interracial Marriage

Mildred Jeter and Richard Loving got married in the District of Columbia. They settled in Virginia, where they were arrested, tried, and convicted for violating Virginia law against interracial marriage. Jeter was African American and Loving was white. Virginia was one of 16 states at the time that banned marriage between people of different races. The Lovings sued to have the state laws overturned but lost in Virginia courts. They appealed their case to the U.S. Supreme Court. In a unanimous decision in *Loving* v. *Virginia*, the Court ruled that the law violated the Fourteenth Amendment.

PRIMARY SOURCE: SUPREME COURT OPINION

❝ This case presents a constitutional question never addressed by this Court: whether a **statutory scheme** [law] adopted by the State of Virginia to prevent marriages between persons solely on the basis of racial classifications violates the Equal Protection and Due Process Clauses of the Fourteenth Amendment. For reasons which seem to us to reflect the central meaning of those constitutional commands, we conclude that these statutes cannot stand consistently with the Fourteenth Amendment. . . .

The freedom to marry has long been recognized as one of the vital personal rights essential to the orderly pursuit of happiness by free men.

Marriage is one of the 'basic civil rights of man,' fundamental to our very existence and survival. . . . To deny this fundamental freedom on so **unsupportable** a basis as the racial classifications embodied [found] in these statutes, classifications so directly **subversive** of the principle of equality at the heart of the Fourteenth Amendment, is surely to deprive all the State's citizens of liberty without due process of law. The Fourteenth Amendment requires that the freedom of choice to marry not be restricted by **invidious** racial discriminations. Under our Constitution, the freedom to marry, or not marry, a person of another race resides with the individual and cannot be infringed [broken] by the State. ❞

— Chief Justice Earl Warren, Opinion of the Court, *Loving* v. *Virginia* (1967)

statutory scheme laws
unsupportable unable to defend or excuse

subversive tending to upset or weaken the government
invidious hateful

EXAMINE THE SOURCE

1. **Explaining** According to Chief Justice Warren, why is freedom to marry an important civil liberty?
2. **Drawing Conclusions** What do you think happened to the laws similar to Virginia's law in other states?

B

Equal Rights for Women

The Equal Rights Amendment (ERA) reads: "Equality of rights under the law shall not be denied or abridged by the United States or by any state on account of sex." This amendment was introduced to Congress in 1923 and in every session of Congress thereafter. In 1972, it finally passed and was sent to the states for ratification. It was not ratified by enough states to be added to the Constitution before the deadline.

Representative Shirley Chisholm was the first African American woman to serve in Congress. This text is from a 1970 speech that she gave in support of the ERA.

PHOTO: Bob Peterson/Getty Images; TEXT: "For the Equal Rights Amendment," Shirley Chisholm to the U.S. House of Representatives, August 10, 1970, Congressional Record, 91st congress, 2nd session. Copyright © U.S. Government Printing Office.

PRIMARY SOURCE: SPEECH

❝ Mr. Speaker,

House Joint Resolution 264, before us today, which provides for equality under the law for both men and women, represents one of the most clear-cut opportunities we are likely to have to declare our faith in the principles that shaped our Constitution. It provides a legal basis for attack on the most subtle, most pervasive, and most institutionalized form of prejudice [bias] that exists. . . . It is time we act to assure full equality of opportunity to those citizens who, although in a majority, suffer the restrictions that are commonly imposed [forced] on minorities, to women.

The argument that this amendment will not solve the problem of sex discrimination is not relevant. If the argument were used against a civil rights bill, as it has been used in the past, the prejudice that lies behind it would be embarrassing. Of course laws will not eliminate prejudice from the hearts of human beings. But that is no reason to allow prejudice to continue to be enshrined [written] in our laws—to **perpetuate** injustice through inaction.

. . . [T]he Constitution guarantees due process of law, in the Fifth and 14th amendments. But the **applicability** of due process to sex distinctions is not clear. Women are excluded from some State colleges and universities. In some States, restrictions are placed on a married woman who engages in an independent business. Women may not be chosen for some juries. Women even receive heavier criminal penalties than men who commit the same crime. . . .

The Constitution they [the Founders] wrote was designed to protect the rights of white, male citizens. As there were no black Founding Fathers, there were no founding mothers—a great pity, on both counts. It is not too late to complete the work they left undone. Today, here, we should start to do so. ❞

— Rep. Shirley Chisholm, "For the Equal Rights Amendment," Speech in Congress, August 10, 1970

perpetuate to continue   **applicability** ability to apply a principle or rule

---

EXAMINE THE SOURCE

1. **Identifying** What specific changes does Chisholm say the ERA would bring about?
2. **Explaining** Why does Chisholm say that an amendment to the Constitution is necessary?

Protecting LGBTQ Individuals in the Workplace

The Civil Rights Act of 1964 aimed to end discrimination, or unfair treatment, based on race. Title VII, a part of that law, makes it illegal for employers to discriminate on the basis of sex. LGBTQ citizens filed lawsuits in the 2010s based on the law and had their cases appealed to the Supreme Court. They said that they were unfairly fired because of their sexual orientation or transgender status. In *Bostock* v. *Clayton County, Georgia*, the Court combined the three cases.

Justice Neil Gorsuch wrote the Court's decision. The photograph shows activists gathered outside the Supreme Court when the Court heard arguments in this case.

PRIMARY SOURCE: SUPREME COURT OPINION

❝ In our time, few pieces of federal legislation rank in significance with the Civil Rights Act of 1964. There, in Title VII, Congress outlawed discrimination in the workplace on the basis of race, color, religion, sex, or national origin. Today, we must decide whether an employer can fire someone simply for being homosexual or transgender. The answer is clear. An employer who fires an individual for being homosexual or transgender fires that person for **traits** or actions it would not have questioned in members of a different sex. Sex plays a necessary and undisguisable role in the decision, exactly what Title VII forbids.

Those who adopted the Civil Rights Act might not have anticipated their work would lead to this particular result....But the limits of the drafters' imagination supply no reason to ignore the law's demands....

Each of the three cases before us started the same way: An employer fired a long-time employee shortly after the employee revealed that he or she is homosexual or transgender—and allegedly for no reason other than the employee's homosexuality or transgender status....

In Title VII, Congress adopted broad language making it illegal for an employer to rely on an employee's sex when deciding to fire that employee. We do not hesitate to recognize today a necessary consequence of that legislative choice: An employer who fires an individual merely for being gay or transgender **defies** the law. ❞

— Justice Neil Gorsuch, Opinion of the Court, *Bostock* v. *Clayton County, GA* (2020)

trait special quality   **defy** disobey

EXAMINE THE SOURCE

1. **Explaining** Why does Gorsuch believe that the Civil Rights Act applies to LGBTQ people in the workplace?

2. **Analyzing Points of View** Why does Gorsuch make the point that "the limits of the drafters' imagination supply no reason to ignore the law's demands"?

PHOTO:UPI/Alamy Stock Photo; TEXT: Bostock v. Clayton County, Georgia, 590 U.S. ___ (2020)

D

Native American Voting Rights Act

In August 2021, members of Congress introduced the Native American Voting Rights Act of 2021 (NAVRA) in the House and Senate. They did so hoping to protect Native American voting rights. They introduced the law around the time that the U.S. Supreme Court issued a ruling in a case involving a new Arizona voting law. Many Native Americans thought the law would make it harder for their people to vote. The Court upheld the law. This passage is from a report published by a Native American news organization. It covers remarks made by John Echohawk about the proposed law. Echohawk leads a group named the Native American Rights Fund (NARF).

❝ From Alaska, Montana and North Dakota, we have fought and won cases against discrimination[,] cases that tried to suppress [hold down] the Native vote,' [John] Echohawk said.

'Particularly up in North Dakota—it was very obvious. They knew most of our **reservation residents** did not have street addresses so they passed a law that said you cannot vote unless you have an **ID** with a street address, not a post office box number on it. Of course, that **disqualified** our people. That discrimination was very obvious. It was a violation of our rights under the Constitution,' Echohawk said.

Echohawk referenced NARF's Native American Voting Rights Coalition that held nine public hearings among Native voters during 2017 and 2018. The group produced a 176-page . . . report last June prior to the 2020 presidential election.

'Regardless of whether they live in urban or rural areas, members of the 574 federally recognized tribes face many contemporary barriers to political participation. Although many other American voters share some of these obstacles, no other racial or ethnic group faces the combined weight of these barriers to the same degree as Native voters in Indian Country,' the report says. . . .

'We really need the Native American Voting Rights Act,' Echohawk said. 'We all have to get involved in the political process in Washington, D.C. This is our only hope. Congress needs to fix what the Supreme Court did. We need to get Congress to act on this now,' Echohawk said. ❞

— Levi Rickert, "Congress Needs to Pass the Native American Voting Rights Act" Native News Online, August 10, 2021

reservation resident a person living on a reservation, a special area set aside for Native Americans

ID identification card

disqualified made a person not eligible to do something

EXAMINE THE SOURCE

1. **Explaining** Why does Echohawk say the North Dakota law was obviously unfair to Native Americans?

2. **Summarizing** What approaches have Native Americans used to fight attempts at suppressing the Native vote?

Rights for People With Disabilities

The Medicaid Community Attendant Services and Supports Act (MiCASSA) was first introduced in 1997. MiCASSA aimed to give people with disabilities who are on Medicaid the chance to obtain care and nursing services they needed at home so they would not be forced to live in nursing facilities. In 2003, Congress still had not passed MiCASSA. That year, activists organized the Free Our People March. Over 14 days, marchers walked 144 miles from Philadelphia to Washington, D.C. Many of them had serious disabilities, and some made the trip by wheelchair. The marchers, shown here in Washington, D.C., appealed directly to Congress, again without success. In 2010 a new version of the bill was reintroduced under another name. Congress approved that version as part of the Affordable Care Act.

The community remained active. In 2017, Congress considered cuts to Medicaid, which pays for the medical care of disabled people. Dozens of activists protested near the office of the senate majority leader, Senator Mitch McConnell. Several were arrested.

PRIMARY SOURCE: PHOTOGRAPH

EXAMINE THE SOURCE

1. **Evaluating** Describe the marchers shown in the photo. What was significant about their march?

2. **Interpreting** Explain the phrases and slogans displayed by the protestors. What civil rights issues do these suggest?

Complete Your Inquiry

EVALUATE SOURCES AND USE EVIDENCE

Refer back to the Compelling Question and the Supporting Questions you developed at the beginning of the lesson.

1. **Analyzing** In what ways do the sources show how people can make their voices heard?

2. **Evaluating** Which sources did you find particularly powerful? Explain your answer.

3. **Gathering Sources** Which sources helped you answer the Supporting Questions and the Compelling Question? Which sources, if any, challenged what you thought you knew when you first created your Supporting Questions? What information do you still need in order to answer your questions? What other viewpoints would you like to investigate? Where would you find that information?

4. **Evaluating Sources** Identify the sources that helped answer your Supporting Questions. How reliable is the source? How would you verify the reliability of the source?

COMMUNICATE CONCLUSIONS

5. **Collaborating** Work with a partner to discuss how people work to change government policy. What insights do these sources provide about effective ways of speaking, demonstrating, or otherwise taking action? What ways of making your voice heard do you think you yourself could use effectively? Use the graphic organizer you created at the beginning of the lesson to help you. Share your conclusions with the class.

TAKE INFORMED ACTION

Creating a Presentation on Methods of Changing Public Policy Work in a small group to prepare a presentation on ways of working to change government policy. Have group members each choose an approach to changing policy to research. Examples include using the courts, asking Congress to act, staging peaceful protests, supporting a candidate, and using social media. Each group member should explain the actions required for their approach, how the approach has been used in the past, and why the method was successful. Create a video of the presentation that can be shared with interested community groups.

13

Reviewing The Constitution

Summary

Articles of Confederation

The Articles of Confederation formed the first government of the United States but the government was too weak. The Framers met in Philadelphia in 1787 to replace the Articles.

The Constitutional Convention

The Framers drafted the U.S. Constitution to create a stronger central government and protect individual rights. Federalists won ratification by promising to add a bill of rights to the Constitution.

The Bill of Rights

The Bill of Rights protects individuals' liberties from the government. The Supreme Court has said that many of these rights also apply to the state governments.

The Struggle for Rights

Later amendments to the Constitution ended slavery, extended due process rights to all people, and protected the right to vote for more groups of Americans. Some groups had to campaign for their rights.

The Framers based the Constitution on five principles:

- **popular sovereignty:** the people as the source of power

- **limited government and the rule of law:** government power is limited, laws apply to all

- **separation of powers:** government with three branches

- **checks and balances:** each branch can check the others

- **federalism:** national and state governments both have powers

James Madison

Checking For Understanding

Answer the questions to see if you understood the topic content.

IDENTIFY AND EXPLAIN

1. Identify each of the following terms and explain its significance to the Constitution.

   A. confederation
   B. Constitutional Convention
   C. Great Compromise
   D. federalism
   E. popular sovereignty
   F. limited government
   G. rule of law
   H. supremacy clause
   I. establishment clause
   J. probable cause
   K. due process

REVIEWING KEY FACTS

2. **Identifying** What were three weaknesses of the government established by the Articles of Confederation?

3. **Comparing and Contrasting** How did the Anti-Federalists' objections to the U.S. Constitution result in changes to it?

4. **Identifying** What were three goals that the Framers set for the Constitution in the Preamble that introduces the document?

5. **Explaining** What are the two steps in the process of formally amending the Constitution?

6. **Contrasting** How are the principles of separation of power and checks and balances different?

7. **Identifying** What is the Bill of Rights?

8. **Explaining** Under what circumstances can individuals' right to freedom of speech be limited?

9. **Summarizing** What rights of the accused are protected by the Bill of Rights?

10. **Identifying Cause and Effect** How did the Civil War Amendments affect African Americans' rights?

11. **Identifying** What other groups besides African Americans began to work to secure their own civil rights during or after the 1960s?

CRITICAL THINKING

12. **Drawing Conclusions** Why did the Framers of the Constitution create an amendment process that intentionally made amending the Constitution difficult?

13. **Synthesizing** What constitutional principle underlies the Constitution's opening words "We the People"? Explain.

14. **Making Connections** How did French thinker Baron de Montesquieu influence the government formed under the U.S. Constitution?

15. **Synthesizing** How does the federal system established by the Constitution limit government power?

16. **Explaining** Why is it so important that the First Amendment protects religious liberty?

17. **Interpreting** Describe a scenario in which a local government action violates a group's First Amendment freedom of assembly.

18. **Drawing Conclusions** Why is it important that the Fifth Amendment protects a person accused of a crime from self-incrimination?

19. **Explaining** How did the decision in *Gitlow* v. *New York* use the due process clause of the Fourteenth Amendment to change the way the Bill of Rights was applied?

20. **Summarizing** Why was the decision in *Brown* v. *Board of Education of Topeka, Kansas* a great victory for civil rights?

NEED EXTRA HELP?

If You've Missed Question	1	2	3	4	5	6	7	8	9	10
Review Lesson	2, 3, 5, 7, 9	2	3	4	4	5	7	7	9	10

If You've Missed Question	11	12	13	14	15	16	17	18	19	20
Review Lesson	11	4	5	5	5	7	7	9	10	11

Apply What You Have Learned

 ## A Understanding Multiple Perspectives

Federalism is a central principle of the U.S. Constitution that state and national leaders accept, but they sometimes disagree on where the line between state and federal power should be drawn.

ACTIVITY **Stating and Evaluating Arguments** Conduct research online to find three or four different perspectives on the limits to state and to national power. Focus your research on one of these areas: public education, setting a minimum wage for workers, making rules for elections, or ensuring health and safety. Find at least two conflicting points of view on your chosen issue reflecting a perspective that favors either leaving the matter to each state or supporting the involvement of the federal government. Then create a presentation that summarizes all the perspectives you found and analyzes the strengths and weaknesses of each argument.

 ## B Making Connections to Today

The U.S. Constitution is based on five principles. Some Americans may not be aware of the reasons the Framers favored those principles and how they put them into practice.

ACTIVITY **Creating an Informative Video** With a partner, prepare a short, informative video that details the reason behind each of the five principles and gives an example of how each one is supported in the Constitution. To connect the principles to the United States today, give an example of how that principle is involved in modern American government.

 ## C Understanding Chronology

The Constitution rests on the principle of popular sovereignty, yet the majority of Americans were not given a voice in choosing their leaders when it was written and ratified. At that time, most African Americans in the United States were enslaved. Native Americans could not vote, nor could women. Over the years, people began to understand that the Constitution's promise of sovereignty was for everyone. Gradually, the United States began to work toward that goal.

ACTIVITY **Understanding the Expansion of Rights and Freedoms** Work with a partner to create a time line of at least six events that expanded recognition of rights and freedoms in the United States for a historically oppressed group. Include a sentence for each event, noting its relation to the principles of the Constitution.

D Writing an Argumentative Essay

One of the principal arguments that the Anti-Federalists made against the U.S. Constitution was that the new plan of government lacked a bill of rights. Anti-Federalists such as Patrick Henry, Samuel Adams, George Mason, and Elbridge Gerry said that the freedoms fought for in the American Revolution needed to be protected from the proposed federal government. Federalists such as James Madison and Alexander Hamilton said that the protections provided in the U.S. Constitution and in the state constitutions would be enough.

ACTIVITY **Writing About the Bill of Rights** Find and read at least three short versions of the essays written by Anti-Federalists and Federalists on the issue of adding a bill of rights. Consider the arguments of both sides. Then write an argumentative essay in which you say which side you think had the correct position. Quote from the arguments offered by both sides. Evaluate their claims. Were the Anti-Federalists worried unnecessarily? Were the Federalists wrong to dismiss their concerns? Give reasons for your opinion of their arguments in your conclusion.

E Understanding Chronology

The civil rights movement has been called "the greatest mass movement in modern American history." U.S. presidents, Congress, the courts, and prominent individuals all played important parts, but the greatest, sustained action came from countless African Americans and their supporters who showed up to demand justice and that the country live up to its promises.

» Marchers at the 1965 Voting Rights March in Alabama were honored in 2016 with the Congressional Gold Medal.

ACTIVITY **Creating a Media Presentation** Create a media presentation summarizing the milestones of the civil rights movement of the 1950s and 1960s. After reviewing the information in the topic, conduct research using the Internet to identify the events you think were most significant in changing African Americans' social and legal status. Include at least 10 events in your presentation and present them in the order in which they occurred. Explain what you think was important about each event.

▶ This painting shows delegates at the Constitutional Convention in Philadelphia in 1787.

The Constitution of the United States

The Constitution of the United States is a truly remarkable document. It was one of the first written constitutions in modern history.

The entire text of the Constitution and its amendments follow. The printed text of the document shows the spelling and punctuation of the parchment original. For easier study, those passages that have been set aside or changed by the adoption of amendments are printed in blue. Also included are explanatory notes that will help clarify the meaning of important ideas presented in the Constitution.

PREAMBLE

The Preamble introduces the Constitution and sets forth the general purposes for which the government was established. The Preamble also declares that the power of the government comes from the people. The Constitution contains seven parts, called articles. Articles I, II, and III create the three branches of the national government.

ARTICLE I

THE LEGISLATIVE BRANCH

Article I is the longest part of the Constitution, describing the structure and powers of the legislative branch.

SECTION 2, CLAUSE 3

Representation The number of representatives from each state is based on the size of the state's population. Each state is entitled to at least one representative. *What are the qualifications for members of the House of Representatives?*

PRIMARY SOURCE : THE CONSTITUTION OF THE UNITED STATES

[Preamble]

We the People of the United States, in Order to form a more perfect Union, establish Justice, insure domestic Tranquility, provide for the common defence, promote the general Welfare, and secure the Blessings of Liberty to ourselves and our Posterity, do ordain and establish this **Constitution** for the United States of America.

Article. I.

Section. 1.

All legislative Powers herein granted shall be vested in a Congress of the United States, which shall consist of a Senate and House of Representatives.

Section. 2.

[1.] The House of Representatives shall be composed of Members chosen every second Year by the People of the several States, and the Electors in each State shall have the Qualifications requisite for Electors of the most numerous Branch of the State Legislature.

[2.] No person shall be a Representative who shall not have attained to the Age of twenty five Years, and been seven Years a Citizen of the United States, and who shall not, when elected, be an Inhabitant of that State in which he shall be chosen.

[3.] Representatives and direct Taxes shall be apportioned among the several States which may be included within this Union, according to their respective Numbers, which shall be determined by adding to the whole Number of free Persons, including those bound to Service for a Term of Years, and excluding Indians not taxed, three fifths of all other Persons. The actual **Enumeration** shall be made within three Years after the first Meeting of the Congress of the United States, and within every subsequent Term of ten Years, in such Manner as they shall by Law direct. The Number of Representatives shall not exceed one for every thirty Thousand, but each State shall have at Least one Representative; and until such enumeration shall be made, the State of New Hampshire shall be entitled to chuse three; Massachusetts eight, Rhode-Island and Providence Plantations one, Connecticut five, New-York six, New Jersey four, Pennsylvania eight, Delaware one, Maryland six, Virginia ten, North Carolina five, South Carolina five, and Georgia three.

preamble introduction

constitution principles and laws of a nation

enumeration census or population count

United States Constitution, 1787.

[4.] When vacancies happen in the Representation from any State, the Executive Authority thereof shall issue Writs of Election to fill such Vacancies.

[5.] The House of Representatives shall chuse their Speaker and other Officers; and shall have the sole Power of **Impeachment.**

Section. 3.

[1.] The Senate of the United States shall be composed of two Senators from each State, chosen by the Legislature thereof, for six Years; and each Senator shall have one Vote.

[2.] Immediately after they shall be assembled in Consequence of the first Election, they shall be divided as equally as may be into three Classes. The Seats of the Senators of the first Class shall be vacated at the Expiration of the second Year, of the second Class at the Expiration of the fourth Year, and of the third Class at the Expiration of the sixth Year, so that one third may be chosen every second Year; and if Vacancies happen by Resignation, or otherwise, during the Recess of the Legislature of any State, the Executive thereof may make temporary Appointments until the next Meeting of the Legislature, which shall then fill such Vacancies.

[3.] No Person shall be a Senator who shall not have attained to the Age of thirty Years, and been nine Years a Citizen of the United States, and who shall not, when elected, be an Inhabitant of that State for which he shall be chosen.

[4.] The Vice President of the United States shall be President of the Senate, but shall have no Vote, unless they be equally divided.

[5.] The Senate shall chuse their other Officers, and also a **President pro tempore,** in the Absence of the Vice President, or when he shall exercise the Office of President of the United States.

[6.] The Senate shall have the sole Power to try all Impeachments. When sitting for that Purpose, they shall be on Oath or Affirmation. When the President of the United States is tried, the Chief Justice shall preside: And no Person shall be convicted without the Concurrence of two thirds of the Members present.

[7.] Judgment in Cases of Impeachment shall not extend further than to removal from Office, and disqualification to hold and enjoy any Office of honor, Trust or Profit under the United States: but the Party convicted shall nevertheless be liable and subject to **Indictment**, Trial, Judgment and Punishment, according to Law.

Section. 4.

[1.] The Times, Places and Manner of holding Elections for Senators and Representatives, shall be prescribed in each State by the Legislature thereof; but the Congress may at any time by Law make or alter such Regulations, except as to the Places of chusing Senators.

---

impeachment bringing charges against an official

president pro tempore the presiding officer of the Senate who serves when the vice president is absent

indictment charging a person with an offense

SECTION 3, CLAUSE 1

Electing Senators Originally, senators were chosen by each state's legislature. The Seventeenth Amendment changed this, and senators are now elected directly by the state's people. There are 100 senators, 2 from each state.

SECTION 3, CLAUSE 6

Impeachment Trials One power of Congress is the power to impeach government officials—or accuse them of wrongdoing—put them on trial, and, if found guilty, remove them from office. The House decides if an official should be impeached. The Senate acts as a jury in the trial, and when the president is impeached, the Chief Justice of the Supreme Court serves as the judge. A two-thirds vote of the members present is needed to convict impeached officials. *What punishment can the Senate give if an impeached official is convicted?*

[2.] The Congress shall assemble at least once in every Year, and such Meeting shall be on the first Monday in December, unless they shall by Law appoint a different Day.

Section. 5.

[1.] Each House shall be the Judge of the Elections, Returns and Qualifications of its own Members, and a Majority of each shall constitute a **Quorum** to do Business; but a smaller Number may **adjourn** from day to day, and may be authorized to compel the Attendance of absent Members, in such Manner, and under such Penalties as each House may provide.

[2.] Each House may determine the Rules of its Proceedings, punish its Members for disorderly Behaviour, and, with the **Concurrence** of two thirds, expel a Member.

[3.] Each House shall keep a Journal of its Proceedings, and from time to time publish the same, excepting such Parts as may in their Judgment require Secrecy; and the Yeas and Nays of the Members of either House on any question shall, at the Desire of one fifth of those Present, be entered on the Journal.

[4.] Neither House, during the Session of Congress, shall, without the Consent of the other, adjourn for more than three days, nor to any other Place than that in which the two Houses shall be sitting.

Section. 6.

[1.] The Senators and Representatives shall receive a Compensation for their Services, to be ascertained by Law, and paid out of the Treasury of the United States. They shall in all Cases, except Treason, Felony and Breach of the Peace, be privileged from Arrest during their Attendance at the Session of their respective Houses, and in going to and returning from the same; and for any Speech or Debate in either House, they shall not be questioned in any other Place.

[2.] No Senator or Representative shall, during the Time for which he was elected, be appointed to any civil Office under the Authority of the United States, which shall have been created, or the **Emoluments** whereof shall have been encreased during such time; and no Person holding any Office under the United States, shall be a Member of either House during his Continuance in Office.

Section. 7.

[1.] All Bills for raising **Revenue** shall originate in the House of Representatives; but the Senate may propose or concur with Amendments as on other **Bills**.

SECTION 6, CLAUSE 1

Congressional Pay To strengthen the federal government, the Founders set congressional salaries to be paid by the United States Treasury rather than by members' respective states. Originally, members were paid $6 per day. Since 2009, all members of Congress have received a base salary of $174,000.

SECTION 7, CLAUSE 1

Where Tax Laws Begin All tax laws must originate in the House of Representatives. This ensures that the house of Congress that is elected by the people every two years has the major role in determining taxes.

---

quorum the minimum number of members that must be present to conduct sessions

adjourn to suspend a session

concurrence agreement

emoluments salaries; payments

revenue income raised by the government

bill a draft of a proposed law

[2.] Every Bill which shall have passed the House of Representatives and the Senate, shall, before it become a Law, be presented to the President of the United States; If he approve he shall sign it, but if not he shall return it, with his Objections to that House in which it shall have originated, who shall enter the Objections at large on their Journal, and proceed to reconsider it. If after such Reconsideration two thirds of that House shall agree to pass the Bill, it shall be sent, together with the Objections, to the other House, by which it shall likewise be reconsidered, and if approved by two thirds of that House, it shall become a Law. But in all such Cases the Votes of both Houses shall be determined by yeas and Nays, and the Names of the Persons voting for and against the Bill shall be entered on the Journal of each House respectively. If any Bill shall not be returned by the President within ten Days (Sundays excepted) after it shall have been presented to him, the Same shall be a Law, in like Manner as if he had signed it, unless the Congress by their Adjournment prevent its Return, in which Case it shall not be a Law.

[3.] Every Order, **Resolution,** or Vote to which the Concurrence of the Senate and House of Representatives may be necessary (except on a question of Adjournment) shall be presented to the President of the United States; and before the Same shall take Effect, shall be approved by him, or being disapproved by him, shall be repassed by two thirds of the Senate and House of Representatives, according to the Rules and Limitations prescribed in the Case of a Bill.

Section. 8.

[1.] The Congress shall have Power To lay and collect Taxes, Duties, Imposts and Excises, to pay the Debts and provide for the common Defence and general Welfare of the United States; but all Duties, Imposts and Excises shall be uniform throughout the United States;

[2.] To borrow Money on the credit of the United States;

[3.] To regulate Commerce with foreign Nations, and among the several States, and with the Indian Tribes;

[4.] To establish an uniform Rule of **Naturalization,** and uniform Laws on the subject of Bankruptcies throughout the United States;

[5.] To coin Money, regulate the Value thereof, and of foreign Coin, and fix the Standard of Weights and Measures;

[6.] To provide for the Punishment of counterfeiting the Securities and current Coin of the United States;

[7.] To establish Post Offices and post Roads;

[8.] To promote the Progress of Science and useful Arts, by securing for limited Times to Authors and Inventors the exclusive Right to their respective Writings and Discoveries;

SECTION 7, CLAUSE 2

How a Bill Becomes a Law A bill becomes a law after it is passed by both houses of Congress and the president signs it. The president can check the power of Congress by rejecting—or vetoing—its bills. *How can Congress override a president's veto?*

SECTION 8

Powers of Congress Enumerated powers are those powers specifically given to Congress in the Constitution. Most of the enumerated powers are listed in Article I, Section 8. The enumerated powers are sometimes called the expressed powers. *Which clause gives Congress the power to coin money?*

resolution a legislature's formal expression of opinion

naturalization process by which a citizen of a foreign nation becomes a citizen of the United States

[9.] To constitute **Tribunals** inferior to the supreme Court;

[10.] To define and punish Piracies and Felonies committed on the high Seas, and Offences against the Law of Nations;

[11.] To declare War, grant Letters of Marque and Reprisal, and make Rules concerning Captures on Land and Water;

[12.] To raise and support Armies, but no Appropriation of Money to that Use shall be for a longer Term than two Years;

[13.] To provide and maintain a Navy;

[14.] To make Rules for the Government and Regulation of the land and naval Forces;

[15.] To provide for calling forth the Militia to execute the Laws of the Union, suppress **Insurrections** and repel Invasions;

[16.] To provide for organizing, arming, and disciplining, the Militia, and for governing such Part of them as may be employed in the Service of the United States, reserving to the States respectively, the Appointment of the Officers, and the Authority of training the Militia according to the discipline prescribed by Congress;

[17.] To exercise exclusive Legislation in all Cases whatsoever, over such District (not exceeding ten Miles square) as may, by Cession of particular States, and the Acceptance of Congress, become the Seat of the Government of the United States, and to exercise like Authority over all Places purchased by the Consent of the Legislature of the State in which the Same shall be, for the Erection of Forts, Magazines, Arsenals, dock-Yards, and other needful Buildings;—And

[18.] To make all Laws which shall be necessary and proper for carrying into Execution the foregoing Powers, and all other Powers vested by this Constitution in the Government of the United States, or in any Department or Officer thereof.

Section. 9.

[1.] The Migration or Importation of such Persons as any of the States now existing shall think proper to admit, shall not be prohibited by the Congress prior to the Year one thousand eight hundred and eight, but a Tax or duty may be imposed on such Importation, not exceeding ten dollars for each Person.

[2.] The Privilege of the Writ of Habeas Corpus shall not be suspended, unless when in Cases of Rebellion or Invasion the public Safety may require it.

[3.] No Bill of Attainder or ex post facto Law shall be passed.

[4.] No Capitation, or other direct, Tax shall be laid, unless in Proportion to the Census or Enumeration herein before directed to be taken.

[5.] No Tax or Duty shall be laid on Articles exported from any State.

[6.] No Preference shall be given by any Regulation of Commerce or Revenue to the Ports of one State over those of another: nor shall Vessels bound to, or from, one State, be obliged to enter, clear, or pay Duties in another.

---

tribunal a court   **insurrection** rebellion

SECTION 8, CLAUSE 18

Elastic Clause Clause 18 is often called the "elastic clause." It allows Congress to "make all laws which shall be necessary and proper" to carry out its enumerated powers listed in the Constitution. It is called the elastic clause because it lets Congress "stretch" its powers to meet future unknown situations.

SECTION 9

Powers Denied to Congress A writ of habeas corpus issued by a judge requires a law official to bring a prisoner to court and show cause for holding the prisoner. A bill of attainder is a bill that punishes a person without a jury trial. An ex post facto law is one that makes an act a crime after the act has been committed. *What does the Constitution say about bills of attainder?*

[7.] No Money shall be drawn from the Treasury, but in Consequence of Appropriations made by Law; and a regular Statement and Account of the Receipts and Expenditures of all public Money shall be published from time to time.

[8.] No Title of Nobility shall be granted by the United States: And no Person holding any Office of Profit or Trust under them, shall, without the Consent of the Congress, accept of any present, Emolument, Office, or Title, of any kind whatever, from any King, Prince, or foreign State.

Section. 10.

[1.] No State shall enter into any Treaty, Alliance, or Confederation; grant Letters of Marque and Reprisal; coin Money; emit Bills of Credit; make any Thing but gold and silver Coin a Tender in Payment of Debts; pass any Bill of Attainder, ex post facto Law, or Law impairing the Obligation of Contracts, or grant any Title of Nobility.

[2.] No State shall, without the Consent of the Congress, lay any Imposts or Duties on Imports or Exports, except what may be absolutely necessary for executing its inspection Laws: and the net Produce of all Duties and Imposts, laid by any State on Imports or Exports, shall be for the Use of the Treasury of the United States; and all such Laws shall be subject to the Revision and Controul of the Congress.

[3.] No State shall, without the Consent of Congress, lay any Duty of Tonnage, keep Troops, or Ships of War in time of Peace, enter into any Agreement or Compact with another State, or with a foreign Power, or engage in War, unless actually invaded, or in such imminent Danger as will not admit of delay.

Article. II.

Section. 1.

[1.] The executive Power shall be vested in a President of the United States of America. He shall hold his Office during the Term of four Years, and, together with the Vice President, chosen for the same Term, be elected, as follows

[2.] Each State shall appoint, in such Manner as the Legislature thereof may direct, a Number of Electors, equal to the whole Number of Senators and Representatives to which the State may be entitled in the Congress: but no Senator or Representative, or Person holding an Office of Trust or Profit under the United States, shall be appointed an Elector.

[3.] The Electors shall meet in their respective States, and vote by Ballot for two Persons, of whom one at least shall not be an Inhabitant of the same State with themselves. And they shall make a List of all the Persons voted for, and of the Number of Votes for each; which List they shall sign and certify, and transmit sealed to the Seat of the Government of the United States, directed to the President of the Senate. The President of the Senate shall, in the Presence of the Senate and House of Representatives, open all the Certificates, and the Votes shall then be counted. The Person having the greatest Number of Votes shall be the President, if such Number be a Majority of the whole Number of Electors appointed;

SECTION 10

Limits on State Powers
Section 10 lists powers denied to the states. These restrictions were designed, in part, to prevent an overlapping in functions and authority with the federal government.

ARTICLE II
THE EXECUTIVE BRANCH
Article II creates an executive branch to carry out the laws passed by Congress. Article II lists the powers and duties of the president, describes the qualifications for office and the procedures for electing the president, and provides for a vice president.

SECTION 1, CLAUSE 3

Former Method of Election In the election of 1800, the top two candidates received the same number of electoral votes, making it necessary for the House of Representatives to decide the election. To eliminate this problem, the Twelfth Amendment changed the method of electing the president, requiring that the electors cast separate ballots for president and vice president.

and if there be more than one who have such Majority, and have an equal Number of Votes, then the House of Representatives shall immediately chuse by Ballot one of them for President; and if no person have a Majority, then from the five highest on the List the said House shall in like Manner chuse the President. But in chusing the President, the Votes shall be taken by States, the Representation from each State having one Vote; A quorum for this Purpose shall consist of a Member or Members from two thirds of the States, and a Majority of all the States shall be necessary to a Choice. In every Case, after the Choice of the President, the Person having the greatest Number of Votes of the Electors shall be the Vice President. But if there should remain two or more who have equal Votes, the Senate shall chuse from them by Ballot the Vice President.

[4.] The Congress may determine the Time of chusing the Electors, and the Day on which they shall give their Votes; which Day shall be the same throughout the United States.

[5.] No Person except a natural born Citizen, or a Citizen of the United States, at the time of the Adoption of this Constitution, shall be eligible to the Office of President; neither shall any Person be eligible to that Office who shall not have attained to the Age of thirty five Years, and been fourteen Years a Resident within the United States.

[6.] In Case of the Removal of the President from Office, or of his Death, Resignation, or Inability to discharge the Powers and Duties of the said Office, the Same shall devolve on the Vice President, and the Congress may by Law provide for the Case of Removal, Death, Resignation or Inability, both of the President and Vice President, declaring what Officer shall then act as President, and such Officer shall act accordingly, until the Disability be removed, or a President shall be elected.

[7.] The President shall, at stated Times, receive for his Services, a Compensation, which shall neither be encreased nor diminished during the Period for which he shall have been elected, and he shall not receive within that Period any other Emolument from the United States, or any of them.

[8.] Before he enter on the Execution of his Office, he shall take the following Oath or Affirmation:—"I do solemnly swear (or affirm) that I will faithfully execute the Office of President of the United States, and will to the best of my Ability, preserve, protect and defend the Constitution of the United States."

Section. 2.

[1.] The President shall be Commander in Chief of the Army and Navy of the United States, and of the Militia of the several States, when called into the actual Service of the United States; he may require the Opinion, in writing, of the principal Officer in each of the executive Departments, upon any Subject relating to the Duties of their respective Offices, and he shall have Power to grant Reprieves and Pardons for Offences against the United States, except in Cases of Impeachment.

SECTION 1, CLAUSE 5

Presidential Qualifications The president must be a citizen of the United States by birth, at least 35 years of age, and a resident of the United States for 14 years.

SECTION 1, CLAUSE 6

Vacancies If the president dies, resigns, is removed from office by impeachment, or is unable to carry out the duties of the office, the vice president becomes president (see Amendment XXV).

SECTION 1, CLAUSE 7

Presidential Salary Originally, the president's salary was $25,000 per year. The president's current salary is $400,000 plus a $50,000 nontaxable expense account per year. The president also receives living accommodations in two residences—the White House and Camp David.

SECTION 2, CLAUSE 1

The Cabinet Mention of "the principal Officer in each of the executive departments" is the only suggestion of the president's cabinet to be found in the Constitution. The cabinet is an advisory body, and its power depends on the president. Section 2, Clause 1 also makes the president the head of the armed forces. This established the principle of civilian control of the military.

[2.] He shall have Power, by and with the Advice and Consent of the Senate, to make Treaties, provided two thirds of the Senators present concur; and he shall nominate, and by and with the Advice and Consent of the Senate, shall appoint Ambassadors, other public Ministers and Consuls, Judges of the supreme Court, and all other Officers of the United States, whose Appointments are not herein otherwise provided for, and which shall be established by Law: but the Congress may by Law vest the Appointment of such inferior Officers, as they think proper, in the President alone, in the Courts of Law, or in the Heads of Departments.

[3.] The President shall have Power to fill up all Vacancies that may happen during the Recess of the Senate, by granting Commissions which shall expire at the End of their next Session.

Section. 3.

He shall from time to time give to the Congress Information of the State of the Union, and recommend to their Consideration such Measures as he shall judge necessary and expedient; he may, on extraordinary Occasions, convene both Houses, or either of them, and in Case of Disagreement between them, with Respect to the Time of Adjournment, he may adjourn them to such Time as he shall think proper; he shall receive Ambassadors and other public Ministers; he shall take Care that the Laws be faithfully executed, and shall Commission all the Officers of the United States.

Section. 4.

The President, Vice President and all civil Officers of the United States, shall be removed from Office on Impeachment for, and Conviction of, Treason, Bribery, or other high Crimes and Misdemeanors.

Article. III.

Section. 1.

The judicial Power of the United States, shall be vested in one supreme Court, and in such inferior Courts as the Congress may from time to time ordain and establish. The Judges, both of the supreme and inferior Courts, shall hold their Offices during good Behaviour, and shall, at stated Times, receive for their Services, a Compensation, which shall not be diminished during their Continuance in Office.

Section. 2.

[1.] The judicial Power shall extend to all Cases, in Law and Equity, arising under this Constitution, the Laws of the United States, and Treaties made, or which shall be made, under their Authority;—to all Cases affecting Ambassadors, other public Ministers and Consuls;—to all Cases of admiralty and maritime Jurisdiction;—to Controversies to which the United States shall be a Party;—to Controversies between two or more States;—between a State and Citizens of another State,—between Citizens of different States,—between Citizens of the same State claiming Lands under Grants of different States, and between a State, or the Citizens thereof, and foreign States, Citizens or Subjects.

SECTION 2, CLAUSE 2

Treaties The president is responsible for the conduct of relations with foreign countries. *What role does the Senate have in making treaties?*

SECTION 3

Executive Orders An executive order is a rule or command the president issues that has the force of law. Only Congress can make laws, but executive orders are considered part of the president's duty to "take Care that the Laws be faithfully executed." This power is often used during emergencies. Over time, the scope of executive orders has expanded. Decisions by federal agencies and departments are also considered to be executive orders.

ARTICLE III
THE JUDICIAL BRANCH

The Constitution establishes the Supreme Court and gives Congress power to create other federal courts. The judiciary of the United States has two systems of courts. One consists of the federal courts, whose powers derive from the Constitution and federal laws. The other includes the courts of each of the 50 states, whose powers derive from state constitutions and laws.

SECTION 2, CLAUSE 1

General Jurisdiction Federal courts deal mostly with "statute law," or laws passed by Congress, treaties, and cases involving the Constitution itself.

[2.] In all Cases affecting Ambassadors, other public Ministers and Consuls, and those in which a State shall be Party, the supreme Court shall have **original Jurisdiction.** In all the other Cases before mentioned, the supreme Court shall have **appellate Jurisdiction,** both as to Law and Fact, with such Exceptions, and under such Regulations as the Congress shall make.

[3.] The Trial of all Crimes, except in Cases of Impeachment, shall be by Jury; and such Trial shall be held in the State where the said Crimes shall have been committed; but when not committed within any State, the Trial shall be at such Place or Places as the Congress may by Law have directed.

Section. 3.

[1.] **Treason** against the United States, shall consist only in levying War against them, or in adhering to their Enemies, giving them Aid and Comfort. No Person shall be convicted of Treason unless on the Testimony of two Witnesses to the same overt Act, or on Confession in open Court.

[2.] The Congress shall have Power to declare the Punishment of Treason, but no Attainder of Treason shall work Corruption of Blood, or Forfeiture except during the Life of the Person attainted.

Article. IV.

Section. 1.

Full Faith and Credit shall be given in each State to the public Acts, Records, and judicial Proceedings of every other State. And the Congress may by general Laws prescribe the Manner in which such Acts, Records and Proceedings shall be proved, and the Effect thereof.

Section. 2.

[1.] The Citizens of each State shall be entitled to all Privileges and Immunities of Citizens in the several States.

[2.] A Person charged in any State with Treason, Felony, or other Crime, who shall flee from Justice, and be found in another State, shall on Demand of the executive Authority of the State from which he fled, be delivered up, to be removed to the State having Jurisdiction of the Crime.

[3.] No Person held to Service or Labour in one State, under the Laws thereof, escaping into another, shall, in Consequence of any Law or Regulation therein, be discharged from such Service or Labour, but shall be delivered up on Claim of the Party to whom such Service or Labour may be due.

original jurisdiction the authority to be the first court to hear a case

appellate jurisdiction the authority to hear cases appealed from lower courts

treason a violation of the allegiance owed by a person to his or her own country, for example, by aiding an enemy

Section. 3.

[1.] New States may be admitted by the Congress into this Union; but no new State shall be formed or erected within the Jurisdiction of any other State; nor any State be formed by the Junction of two or more States, or Parts of States, without the Consent of the Legislatures of the States concerned as well as of the Congress.

[2.] The Congress shall have Power to dispose of and make all needful Rules and Regulations respecting the Territory or other Property belonging to the United States; and nothing in this Constitution shall be so construed as to Prejudice any Claims of the United States, or of any particular State.

Section. 4.

The United States shall guarantee to every State in this Union a Republican Form of Government, and shall protect each of them against Invasion; and on Application of the Legislature, or of the Executive (when the Legislature cannot be convened) against domestic Violence.

Article. V.

The Congress, whenever two thirds of both Houses shall deem it necessary, shall propose **Amendments** to this Constitution, or, on the Application of the Legislatures of two thirds of the several States, shall call a Convention for proposing Amendments, which, in either Case, shall be valid to all Intents and Purposes, as Part of this Constitution, when ratified by the Legislatures of three fourths of the several States, or by Conventions in three fourths thereof, as the one or the other Mode of **Ratification** may be proposed by the Congress; Provided that no Amendment which may be made prior to the Year One thousand eight hundred and eight shall in any Manner affect the first and fourth Clauses in the Ninth Section of the first Article; and that no State, without its Consent, shall be deprived of its equal Suffrage in the Senate.

Article. VI.

[1.] All Debts contracted and Engagements entered into, before the Adoption of this Constitution, shall be as valid against the United States under this Constitution, as under the Confederation.

[2.] This Constitution, and the Laws of the United States which shall be made in Pursuance thereof; and all Treaties made, or which shall be made, under the Authority of the United States, shall be the supreme Law of the Land; and the Judges in every State shall be bound thereby, any Thing in the Constitution or Laws of any State to the Contrary notwithstanding.

[3.] The Senators and Representatives before mentioned, and the Members of the several State Legislatures, and all executive and judicial Officers, both of the United States and of the several States, shall be bound by Oath or Affirmation, to support this Constitution; but no religious Test shall ever be required as a Qualification to any Office or public Trust under the United States.

---

amendment a change to the Constitution

ratification the process by which an amendment is approved

SECTION 3, CLAUSE 1

New States Congress determines the basic guidelines for applying for statehood. Maine and West Virginia were created within the boundaries of another state. President Lincoln recognized the West Virginia government as the legal government of Virginia during the Civil War. This allowed West Virginia to secede from Virginia without obtaining approval from the Virginia legislature.

ARTICLE V

THE AMENDMENT PROCESS

Article V explains how the Constitution can be changed. All 27 amendments were proposed by a two-thirds vote of both houses of Congress. Only the Twenty-first Amendment was ratified by constitutional conventions of the states. The other amendments were ratified by state legislatures. *What is an amendment?*

ARTICLE VI

CONSTITUTIONAL SUPREMACY

Article VI contains the "supremacy clause." This clause establishes that the Constitution, laws passed by Congress, and treaties of the United States "shall be the supreme Law of the Land." The supremacy clause recognizes the Constitution and federal laws as supreme when in conflict with those of the states.

ARTICLE VII
RATIFICATION

Article VII addresses ratification and provides that, unlike the Articles of Confederation, which required the approval of all thirteen states for adoption, the Constitution would take effect after it was ratified by nine states.

Article. VII.

The Ratification of the Conventions of nine States, shall be sufficient for the Establishment of this Constitution between the States so ratifying the Same.

done in Convention by the Unanimous Consent of the States present the Seventeenth Day of September in the Year of our Lord one thousand seven hundred and Eighty seven and of the Independance of the United States of America the Twelfth. In witness whereof We have hereunto subscribed our Names,

Signers

George Washington,
President and Deputy
from Virginia

New Hampshire
John Langdon
Nicholas Gilman

Massachusetts
Nathaniel Gorham
Rufus King

Connecticut
William Samuel Johnson
Roger Sherman

New York
Alexander Hamilton

New Jersey
William Livingston
David Brearley
William Paterson
Jonathan Dayton

Pennsylvania
Benjamin Franklin
Thomas Mifflin
Robert Morris
George Clymer
Thomas FitzSimons
Jared Ingersoll
James Wilson
Gouverneur Morris

Delaware
George Read
Gunning Bedford, Jr.
John Dickinson
Richard Bassett
Jacob Broom

Maryland
James McHenry
Daniel of St. Thomas Jenifer
Daniel Carroll

Virginia
John Blair
James Madison, Jr.

North Carolina
William Blount
Richard Dobbs Spaight
Hugh Williamson

South Carolina
John Rutledge
Charles Cotesworth Pinckney
Charles Pinckney
Pierce Butler

Georgia
William Few
Abraham Baldwin

Attest: *William Jackson, Secretary*

THE AMENDMENTS

This part of the Constitution consists of changes and additions. The Constitution has been amended 27 times throughout the nation's history.

THE BILL OF RIGHTS

The first 10 amendments are known as the Bill of Rights (1791). These amendments limit the powers of the federal government. The First Amendment protects the civil liberties of individuals in the United States. Yet the amendment's freedoms are not absolute. They are limited by the rights of other individuals. *What freedoms does the First Amendment protect?*

Amendment I

Congress shall make no law respecting an establishment of religion, or prohibiting the free exercise thereof; or abridging the freedom of speech, or of the press; or the right of the people peaceably to assemble, and to petition the Government for a redress of grievances.

Amendment II

A well regulated Militia, being necessary to the security of a free State, the right of the people to keep and bear Arms, shall not be infringed.

Amendment III

No Soldier shall, in time of peace be **quartered** in any house, without the consent of the Owner, nor in time of war, but in a manner to be prescribed by law.

quarter to provide living accommodations

Amendment IV

The right of the people to be secure in their persons, houses, papers, and effects, against unreasonable searches and seizures, shall not be violated, and no **Warrants** shall issue, but upon **probable cause**, supported by Oath or affirmation, and particularly describing the place to be searched, and the persons or things to be seized.

Amendment V

No person shall be held to answer for a capital, or otherwise infamous crime, unless on a presentment or indictment of a Grand Jury, except in cases arising in the land or naval forces, or in the Militia, when in actual service in time of War or public danger; nor shall any person be subject for the same offence to be twice put in jeopardy of life or limb; nor shall be compelled in any criminal case to be a witness against himself, nor be deprived of life, liberty, or property, without due process of law; nor shall private property be taken for public use, without just compensation.

Amendment VI

In all criminal prosecutions, the accused shall enjoy the right to a speedy and public trial, by an impartial jury of the State and district wherein the crime shall have been committed, which district shall have been previously ascertained by law, and to be informed of the nature and cause of the accusation; to be confronted with the witnesses against him; to have compulsory process for obtaining witnesses in his favor, and to have the Assistance of Counsel for his defence.

Amendment VII

In Suits at common law, where the value in controversy shall exceed twenty dollars, the right of trial by jury shall be preserved, and no fact tried by a jury, shall be otherwise re-examined in any Court of the United States, than according to the rules of **common law.**

Amendment VIII

Excessive **bail** shall not be required, nor excessive fines imposed, nor cruel and unusual punishments inflicted.

Amendment IX

The enumeration in the Constitution, of certain rights, shall not be construed to deny or disparage others retained by the people.

AMENDMENT 5

Rights of the Accused This amendment contains protections for people accused of crimes. One of the protections is that government may not deprive any person of life, liberty, or property without due process of law. This means that the government must follow proper constitutional procedures in trials and in other actions it takes against individuals. *According to Amendment V, what is the function of a grand jury?*

AMENDMENT 6

Right to a Speedy and Fair Trial A basic protection is the right to a speedy, public trial. The jury must hear witnesses and evidence on both sides before deciding the guilt or innocence of a person charged with a crime. This amendment also provides that legal counsel must be provided to a defendant. In 1963, in *Gideon v. Wainwright*, the Supreme Court ruled that if a defendant cannot afford a lawyer, the government must provide one to defend him or her. *Why is the right to a "speedy" trial important?*

AMENDMENT 9

Powers Reserved to the People This amendment prevents the government from claiming that the only rights people have are those listed in the Bill of Rights.

warrant a document that gives police particular rights or powers

probable cause a reasonable basis to believe a person is linked to a crime

common law law established by previous court decisions

bail money that an accused person provides to the court as a guarantee that he or she will be present for a trial

Amendment X

The powers not delegated to the United States by the Constitution, nor prohibited by it to the States, are reserved to the States respectively, or to the people.

Amendment XI

The Judicial power of the United States shall not be construed to extend to any suit in law or equity, commenced or prosecuted against one of the United States by Citizens of another State, or by Citizens or Subjects of any Foreign State.

Amendment XII

The Electors shall meet in their respective states and vote by ballot for President and Vice-President, one of whom, at least, shall not be an inhabitant of the same state with themselves; they shall name in their ballots the person voted for as President, and in distinct ballots the person voted for as Vice-President, and they shall make distinct lists of all persons voted for as President, and of all persons voted for as Vice-President, and of the number of votes for each, which lists they shall sign and certify, and transmit sealed to the seat of the government of the United States, directed to the President of the Senate; —The President of the Senate shall, in the presence of the Senate and House of Representatives, open all the certificates and the votes shall then be counted; —The person having the greatest number of votes for President, shall be the President, if such number be a **majority** of the whole number of Electors appointed; and if no person have such majority, then from the persons having the highest numbers not exceeding three on the list of those voted for as President, the House of Representatives shall choose immediately, by ballot, the President. But in choosing the President, the votes shall be taken by states, the representation from each state having one vote; a quorum for this purpose shall consist of a member or members from two-thirds of the states, and a majority of all the states shall be necessary to a choice. And if the House of Representatives shall not choose a President whenever the right of choice shall devolve upon them, before the fourth day of March next following, then the Vice-President shall act as President, as in the case of the death or other constitutional disability of the President. —The person having the greatest number of votes as Vice-President, shall be the Vice-President, if such number be a majority of the whole number of Electors appointed, and if no person have a majority, then from the two highest numbers on the list, the Senate shall choose the Vice-President; a quorum for the purpose shall consist of two-thirds of the whole number of Senators, and a majority of the whole number shall be necessary to a choice. But no person constitutionally ineligible to the office of President shall be eligible to that of Vice-President of the United States.

Amendment XIII

Section 1.

Neither slavery nor involuntary servitude, except as a punishment for crime whereof the party shall have been duly convicted, shall exist within the United States, or any place subject to their jurisdiction.

majority more than half

Section 2.

Congress shall have power to enforce this article by appropriate legislation.

Amendment XIV

Section 1.

All persons born or naturalized in the United States, and subject to the jurisdiction thereof, are citizens of the United States and of the State wherein they reside. No State shall make or enforce any law which shall **abridge** the privileges or immunities of citizens of the United States; nor shall any State deprive any person of life, liberty, or property, without due process of law; nor deny to any person within its jurisdiction the equal protection of the laws.

Section 2.

Representatives shall be apportioned among the several States according to their respective numbers, counting the whole number of persons in each State, excluding Indians not taxed. But when the right to vote at any election for the choice of electors for President and Vice-President of the United States, Representatives in Congress, the Executive and Judicial officers of a State, or the members of the Legislature thereof, is denied to any of the male inhabitants of such State, being twenty-one years of age, and citizens of the United States, or in any way abridged, except for participation in rebellion, or other crime, the basis of representation therein shall be reduced in the proportion which the number of such male citizens shall bear to the whole number of male citizens twenty-one years of age in such State.

Section 3.

No person shall be a Senator or Representative in Congress, or elector of President and Vice-President, or hold any office, civil or military, under the United States, or under any State, who, having previously taken an oath, as a member of Congress, or as an officer of the United States, or as a member of any State legislature, or as an executive or judicial officer of any State, to support the Constitution of the United States, shall have engaged in insurrection or rebellion against the same, or given aid or comfort to the enemies thereof. But Congress may by a vote of two-thirds of each House, remove such disability.

Section 4.

The validity of the public debt of the United States, authorized by law, including debts incurred for payment of pensions and bounties for services in suppressing insurrection or rebellion, shall not be questioned. But neither the United States nor any State shall assume or pay any debt or obligation incurred in aid of insurrection or rebellion against the United States, or any claim for the loss or emancipation of any slave; but all such debts, obligations and claims shall be held illegal and void.

abridge to reduce

AMENDMENT 14

Rights of Citizens The Fourteenth Amendment (1868) was originally intended to protect the legal rights of formerly enslaved people, although there have been periods when it was not enforced. Its interpretation has been extended to protect the rights of citizenship in general by prohibiting a state from depriving any person of life, liberty, or property without "due process of law." It also states that all citizens have the right to equal protection of the laws.

AMENDMENT 14, SECTION 2

Representation in Congress This section reduced the number of members a state had in the House of Representatives if it denied its citizens the right to vote. Later civil rights laws and the Twenty-fourth Amendment supported African Americans' right to vote.

AMENDMENT 14, SECTION 3

Penalty for Engaging in Insurrection Confederate leaders were barred from holding state or federal offices unless Congress allowed it. By the end of Reconstruction, all but a few Confederate leaders had returned to public service.

AMENDMENT 14, SECTION 4

Public Debt The public debt acquired by the federal government during the Civil War was valid and could not be questioned by the South. The debts of the Confederacy, however, were declared to be illegal.

Section 5.

The Congress shall have the power to enforce, by appropriate legislation, the provisions of this article.

Amendment XV

Section 1.

The right of citizens of the United States to vote shall not be denied or abridged by the United States or by any State on account of race, color, or previous condition of servitude.

Section 2.

The Congress shall have the power to enforce this article by appropriate legislation.

Amendment XVI

The Congress shall have power to lay and collect taxes on incomes, from whatever source derived, without **apportionment** among the several States, and without regard to any census or enumeration.

Amendment XVII

Section 1.

The Senate of the United States shall be composed of two Senators from each State, elected by the people thereof, for six years; and each Senator shall have one vote. The electors in each State shall have the qualifications requisite for electors of the most numerous branch of the State legislatures.

Section 2.

When **vacancies** happen in the representation of any State in the Senate, the executive authority of such State shall issue writs of election to fill such vacancies: Provided, That the legislature of any State may empower the executive thereof to make temporary appointments until the people fill the vacancies by election as the legislature may direct.

Section 3.

This amendment shall not be so construed as to affect the election or term of any Senator chosen before it becomes valid as part of the Constitution.

Amendment XVIII

Section 1.

After one year from the ratification of this article the manufacture, sale, or transportation of intoxicating liquors within, the importation thereof

---

apportionment the distribution of House seats or taxes based on population

vacancy an office or position that is unfilled or unoccupied

into, or the exportation thereof from the United States and all territory subject to the jurisdiction thereof for beverage purposes is hereby prohibited.

Section 2.

The Congress and the several States shall have concurrent power to enforce this article by appropriate legislation.

Section 3.

This article shall be inoperative unless it shall have been ratified as an amendment to the Constitution by the legislatures of the several States, as provided in the Constitution, within seven years from the date of the submission hereof to the States by the Congress.

Amendment XIX

Section 1.

The right of citizens of the United States to vote shall not be denied or abridged by the United States or by any State on account of sex.

Section 2.

Congress shall have power to enforce this article by appropriate legislation.

Amendment XX

Section 1.

The terms of the President and Vice President shall end at noon on the 20th day of January, and the terms of Senators and Representatives at noon on the 3d day of January, of the years in which such terms would have ended if this article had not been ratified; and the terms of their successors shall then begin.

Section 2.

The Congress shall assemble at least once in every year, and such meeting shall begin at noon on the 3d day of January, unless they shall by law appoint a different day.

Section 3.

If, at the time fixed for the beginning of the term of the President, the **President elect** shall have died, the Vice President elect shall become President. If a President shall not have been chosen before the time fixed for the beginning of his term, or if the President elect shall have failed to qualify, then the Vice President elect shall act as President until a President shall have qualified; and the Congress may by law provide for the case wherein neither a President elect nor a Vice President elect shall have qualified, declaring who shall then act as President, or the manner in which one who is to act shall be selected, and such person shall act accordingly until a President or Vice President shall have qualified.

---

president elect the person who is elected president but has not yet begun serving his or her term

---

AMENDMENT 19

Woman Suffrage The Nineteenth Amendment (1920) guaranteed women the right to vote. By then, women had already won the right to vote in many states, but the amendment guaranteed women in all the states the right to vote.

AMENDMENT 20

"Lame-Duck Amendment" The Twentieth Amendment (1933) sets new dates for Congress to begin its term and for the inauguration of the president and the vice president. Under the original Constitution, elected officials who had been defeated remained in office for several months. For the outgoing president, this period ran from November until March. Such outgoing officials, referred to as "lame ducks," could accomplish little. *What date was chosen as Inauguration Day?*

AMENDMENT 20, SECTION 3

Succession of President and Vice President This section provides that if the president elect dies before taking office, the vice president elect becomes president.

Section 4.

The Congress may by law provide for the case of the death of any of the persons from whom the House of Representatives may choose a President whenever the right of choice shall have devolved upon them, and for the case of the death of any of the persons from whom the Senate may choose a Vice President whenever the right of choice shall have devolved upon them.

Section 5.

Sections 1 and 2 shall take effect on the 15th day of October following the ratification of this article.

Section 6.

This article shall be inoperative unless it shall have been ratified as an amendment to the Constitution by the legislatures of three-fourths of the several States within seven years from the date of its submission.

Amendment XXI

Section 1.

The eighteenth article of amendment to the Constitution of the United States is hereby repealed.

Section 2.

The transportation or importation into any State, Territory, or possession of the United States for delivery or use therein of intoxicating liquors, in violation of the laws thereof, is hereby prohibited.

Section 3.

This article shall be inoperative unless it shall have been ratified as an amendment to the Constitution by conventions in the several States, as provided in the Constitution, within seven years from the date of the submission hereof to the States by the Congress.

Amendment XXII

Section 1.

No person shall be elected to the office of the President more than twice, and no person who has held the office of President, or acted as President, for more than two years of a term to which some other person was elected President shall be elected to the office of the President more than once. But this Article shall not apply to any person holding the office of President when this Article was proposed by the Congress, and shall not prevent any person who may be holding the office of President, or acting as President, during the term within which this Article becomes operative from holding the office of President or acting as President during the remainder of such term.

Section 2.

This article shall be inoperative unless it shall have been ratified as an amendment to the Constitution by the legislatures of three-fourths of the

---

AMENDMENT 21

Repeal of Prohibition The Twenty-first Amendment (1933) repealed the Eighteenth Amendment. It is the only amendment ever passed to overturn an earlier amendment. It is also the only amendment ratified by special state conventions instead of state legislatures.

AMENDMENT 22

Presidential Term Limit The Twenty-second Amendment (1951) limits presidents to a maximum of two elected terms. The amendment wrote into the Constitution a custom started by George Washington. It was passed largely as a reaction to Franklin D. Roosevelt's election to four terms between 1933 and 1945.

several States within seven years from the date of its submission to the States by the Congress.

Amendment XXIII

Section 1.
The District constituting the seat of Government of the United States shall appoint in such manner as the Congress may direct:

A number of electors of President and Vice President equal to the whole number of Senators and Representatives in Congress to which the District would be entitled if it were a State, but in no event more than the least populous State; they shall be in addition to those appointed by the States, but they shall be considered, for the purposes of the election of President and Vice President, to be electors appointed by a State; and they shall meet in the District and perform such duties as provided by the twelfth article of amendment.

Section 2.
The Congress shall have power to enforce this article by appropriate legislation.

Amendment XXIV

Section 1.
The right of citizens of the United States to vote in any primary or other election for President or Vice President, for electors for President or Vice President, or for Senator or Representative in Congress, shall not be denied or abridged by the United States or any State by reason of failure to pay any poll tax or other tax.

Section 2.
The Congress shall have power to enforce this article by appropriate legislation.

Amendment XXV

Section 1.
In case of the removal of the President from office or of his death or resignation, the Vice President shall become President.

Section 2.
Whenever there is a vacancy in the office of the Vice President, the President shall nominate a Vice President who shall take office upon confirmation by a majority vote of both Houses of Congress.

Section 3.
Whenever the President transmits to the President pro tempore of the Senate and the Speaker of the House of Representatives his written declaration that he is unable to discharge the powers and duties of his office, and until he transmits to them a written declaration to the contrary, such powers and duties shall be discharged by the Vice President as Acting President.

AMENDMENT 23

D.C. Electors The Twenty-third Amendment (1961) allows citizens living in Washington, D.C., to vote for president and vice president, a right previously denied residents of the nation's capital. The District of Columbia now has three presidential electors, the number to which it would be entitled if it were a state.

AMENDMENT 24

Abolition of the Poll Tax The Twenty-fourth Amendment (1964) prohibits poll taxes in federal elections. Some states had used such taxes to keep low-income African Americans from voting. In 1966, the Supreme Court banned poll taxes in state elections, as well.

AMENDMENT 25

Presidential Disability and Succession The Twenty-fifth Amendment (1967) established a process for the vice president to take over leadership of the nation when a president is disabled. It also set procedures for filling a vacancy in the office of vice president. This amendment was used in 1973, when Vice President Spiro Agnew resigned after being charged with accepting bribes. President Nixon appointed Gerald R. Ford as vice president. A year later, Nixon resigned and Ford became president. President Ford then filled the vice presidential vacancy with Nelson A. Rockefeller.

Section 4.

Whenever the Vice President and a majority of either the principal officers of the executive departments or of such other body as Congress may by law provide, transmit to the President pro tempore of the Senate and the Speaker of the House of Representatives their written declaration that the President is unable to discharge the powers and duties of his office, the Vice President shall immediately assume the powers and duties of the office as Acting President.

Thereafter, when the President transmits to the President pro tempore of the Senate and the Speaker of the House of Representatives his written declaration that no inability exists, he shall resume the powers and duties of his office unless the Vice President and a majority of either the principal officers of the executive department or of such other body as Congress may by law provide, transmit within four days to the President pro tempore of the Senate and the Speaker of the House of Representatives their written declaration that the President is unable to discharge the powers and duties of his office. Thereupon Congress shall decide the issue, assembling within forty-eight hours for that purpose if not in session. If the Congress, within twenty-one days after receipt of the latter written declaration, or, if Congress is not in session, within twenty-one days after Congress is required to assemble, determines by two-thirds vote of both Houses that the President is unable to discharge the powers and duties of his office, the Vice President shall continue to discharge the same as Acting President; otherwise, the President shall resume the powers and duties of his office.

Amendment XXVI

Section 1.

The right of citizens of the United States, who are eighteen years of age or older, to vote shall not be denied or abridged by the United States or by any State on account of age.

Section 2.

The Congress shall have power to enforce this article by appropriate legislation.

Amendment XXVII

No law, varying the compensation for the services of Senators and Representatives, shall take effect, until an election of Representatives shall have intervened.

AMENDMENT 26

Voting Age of 18 The Twenty-sixth Amendment (1971) lowered the voting age in both federal and state elections to 18.

AMENDMENT 27

Congressional Salary Restraints The Twenty-seventh Amendment (1992) was initially proposed by James Madison in 1789, but it was never adopted. In 1982, Gregory Watson, then a student at the University of Texas, discovered the amendment while doing research for a class paper. Watson made the amendment's passage his goal.

The Legislative Branch

Speaker of the House Nancy Pelosi stands in front of the flag and gives the oath of office to members of the House of Representatives at the beginning of the 117th Congress.

Introducing The Legislative Branch

Congress

As representatives of American citizens, members of Congress have an important role in U.S. democracy. They are elected to either the Senate or the House of Representatives to become the country's lawmakers. While the structure of those two houses has remained the same since 1789, much about the make up of Congress has changed over time.

While Congress consisted of only white men for many years, it is more diverse and representative of all Americans today. Congress members' jobs, however, remain the same today as 1789: to create and pass laws that represent the interests of the people who elected them.

1932 POLITICAL WORLD SERIES

Democrats
— VS —
Republicans

OF THE HOUSE OF REPRESENTATIVES

Benefit of D. C. Unemployed

G.O.P.

(1932)

AS THE GAME GOES SO GOES THE ELECTION

Congressional Baseball Game

Each year since 1909, members of Congress enjoy a friendly rivalry as participants in an annual Democrats versus Republicans baseball game. The Congressional Baseball Game raises money for charities, such as the Boys and Girls Club of Greater Washington and The Washington Literacy Center.

» Here, in the 2018 game, Representative Tim Ryan (Ohio) slides to steal third base as Representative Trent Kelly (Michigan) prepares to field the ball.

Party Symbols

» The iconic symbols of the Republican and Democratic parties were inspired by political cartoonist Thomas Nast in the late 1800s. Nast initially used the elephant for Republicans and the donkey for Democrats to insult the politicians of the time, but both parties have since embraced the animals as representations of their respective parties.

Senate "Candy Desk"

In 1968 California Senator George Murphy filled his Senate desk with candy and allowed his fellow Senators to take pieces as they entered the chamber. Ever since, each Senator assigned to that specific desk keeps it stocked with their favorite candy or candy made in the state they represent.

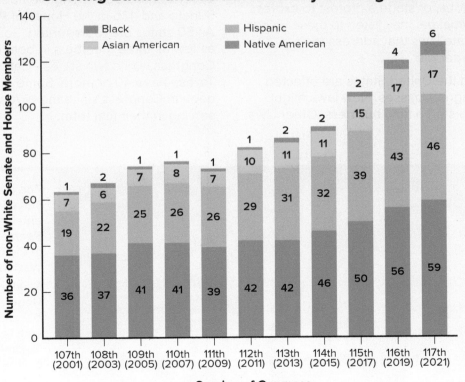

Growing Ethnic and Racial Diversity in Congress

Number of non-White Senate and House Members

Legend: Black, Asian American, Hispanic, Native American

Session of Congress	Black	Hispanic	Asian American	Native American
107th (2001)	36	19	7	1
108th (2003)	37	22	6	2
109th (2005)	41	25	7	1
110th (2007)	41	26	8	1
111th (2009)	39	26	7	1
112th (2011)	42	29	10	1
113th (2013)	42	31	11	2
114th (2015)	46	32	11	2
115th (2017)	50	39	15	2
116th (2019)	56	43	17	4
117th (2021)	59	46	17	6

Session of Congress

Note: Nonvoting delegates and commissioners are excluded. Figures for the 117th Congress are as of Jan. 26, 2021. Asian Americans include Pacific Islanders, and Hispanics are of any race. Members who have more than one racial or ethnic identity for the above groups are counted in each applicable group.

Source: Congressional Research Service, CQ Roll Call, Brookings Institution.

Getting Ready to Learn About . . . The Legislative Branch

Your Voice in Government

Americans rely on the people who work in government to serve them and understand their needs. The United States has too many people for everyone to participate directly in every matter involving the governing of the nation. Instead, Americans elect people to represent them in the nation's capital of Washington, D.C. These representatives make decisions on behalf of the people.

The United States Constitution gives elected officials the power to make these decisions. The power to make laws belongs to Congress.

The way members of Congress represent the will of the people who elect them is by passing laws. For example, suppose some Americans believe that there should be better laws to promote job growth. They may talk to their elected representatives, join a group with other people who believe the government should do more to create jobs, or stage a protest to express their views. Lawmakers may listen to these voices and work to create laws that address the concerns of the people.

All people in the United States are affected by the laws Congress passes. New laws might make it easier to start a new business. Other laws affect what levels of pollution are allowed in water and air or what benefits military veterans can receive. Americans often have differing opinions about laws. For example, in 2020 during the COVID-19 pandemic, Congress passed the CARES Act. This law provided assistance to individuals and businesses that suffered financial harm because of the pandemic. Some Americans believed that the act would help people manage during the pandemic. Others argued that the act did not offer enough help to people.

In a democracy, disagreements such as these are common. When writing legislation, lawmakers consider different viewpoints, and sometimes they make compromises to pass laws that people can accept. Lawmakers are supposed to recognize that everyone's interests and needs are important.

Who Serves in Congress?

Congress has 535 voting members—100 in the Senate and 435 in the House of Representatives. All 50 states are represented. Some states have as few as three members in both houses of Congress, while two states—California and Texas—have 40 or more. Some members have been in Congress since the 1970s. Others are serving in their first term.

The people who serve in the Senate and House of Representatives meet in the Capitol in Washington, D.C.

Making Generalizations Describe the architecture of the Capitol building. Why do you think the Capitol was built in such a style?

Jon Bilous/Shutterstock

In 2018 new members of the 116th Congress posed for a "class photo" in front of the Capitol. This Congress made history when more than 100 women were elected to the House of Representatives, the most up to that time.

Members of Congress vary in age. In the 117th Congress, the oldest member was 87 years old when the congressional term opened in January 2021. The youngest was 25, just making the minimum age for members of the House. The average ages were 58 years for House members and 64 years for senators.

Those who served in that Congress came from a variety of backgrounds and occupations. The vast majority had a college degree. About two dozen worked as physicians of some kind before joining Congress, and a few were ministers. The most common occupation for members of that Congress, though, was public service and politics. This was the case for about two-thirds of both senators and representatives. Members often begin their careers by serving in local and state office before winning election to Congress. The other most common careers were business and law. More than 90 members of the 117th Congress had served in the nation's military, and 14 were still in the reserve forces or the National Guard.

Congress has become a much more diverse place in the last 35 years, with more women and members from underrepresented groups. In the 100th Congress, which lasted from 1987 to 1988, only 26 members were women. In the 117th Congress, which began in 2021, that number had risen to 147 women. Even that record number amounted to only about 27 percent of members.

The number of members from underrepresented ethnic groups has increased as well. Sixty African Americans served in the 117th Congress, which was more than three times as many as had served in the 99th. These 60 seats were a record number for African Americans. Latino members totaled a record 54 in the 117th Congress, up from 14 in the 99th Congress. Twenty-one Asian Americans served in the 117th Congress, four times the number in the 99th Congress. The 117th Congress also had five members who were Native American or Native Hawaiian, which was also a record.

Most members of Congress were born in the United States, but 28 came here from another country. Many members are Christian, but Congress also has members who are Jewish, Muslim, Buddhist, Hindu, Mormon, and of other faiths.

These differences of background and experience reflect the diversity of the United States. Members of Congress serve the American people by bringing different points of view to discussions about public issues. They give voice to the concerns of the people who sent them to Congress.

Looking Ahead

You will learn about the legislative branch of government. You will examine a Compelling Question and develop your own questions about the legislative branch in the Inquiry Activity. You can preview some of the key concepts that you will learn about by reviewing the infographic.

What Will You Learn?

In these lessons about the legislative branch, you will learn:

- that Congress is the lawmaking branch of the federal government.
- that Congress's expressed and implied powers are set by the Constitution.
- the qualifications for becoming a member of Congress.
- how members of Congress make decisions that affect all Americans.
- the steps for a bill to become a law.
- why it is difficult for a bill to become a law.

 COMPELLING QUESTION IN THE INQUIRY ACTIVITY LESSON

- **Does the legislative branch today represent the people as was intended by the Framers?**

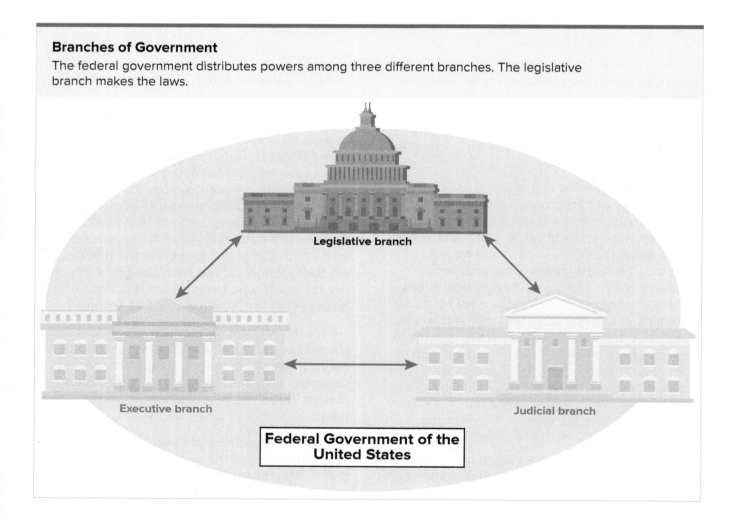

Branches of Government
The federal government distributes powers among three different branches. The legislative branch makes the laws.

Legislative branch

Executive branch

Judicial branch

Federal Government of the United States

Structure of Congress

READING STRATEGY

Analyzing Key Ideas and Details As you study the lesson, use a chart like this one to describe the differences between the House of Representatives and the Senate.

	House	Senate
Number of Members		
Term of Office		
Leadership		

The Two Houses of Congress

GUIDING QUESTION

Why does Congress include two chambers, a House of Representatives and a Senate?

Congress writes our nation's laws. It is divided into two houses: the Senate and the House of Representatives. Each has its own rules and procedures. The decision to divide Congress this way was made when the Framers wrote the Constitution in 1787.

The Framers debated how to organize the new government of the United States. They agreed it should have a Congress that could pass laws. Each state would be represented in Congress, but the Framers did not agree on how to do this. Delegates from the larger states wanted the number of representatives to be based on population. Those from the smaller states wanted each state to have the same number of representatives. They feared that if representation was based on population, they would have a lesser voice in making laws.

In the end, the Framers reached a compromise, called the Great Compromise. They made Congress a two-part, or *bicameral*, body. In the **Senate**, each state would have an equal number of representatives—two. The population of a state would not have an impact on its number of senators.

Senate the upper house of Congress, consisting of two representatives from each state

The Capitol Rotunda is a circular room beneath the dome of the U.S. Capitol. Visitors to the rotunda can view paintings that show scenes from the nation's history.

Congressional Apportionment

Every 10 years, the population of each state is counted as part of the census. Then, each state's number of seats in the House of Representatives is adjusted due to population changes.

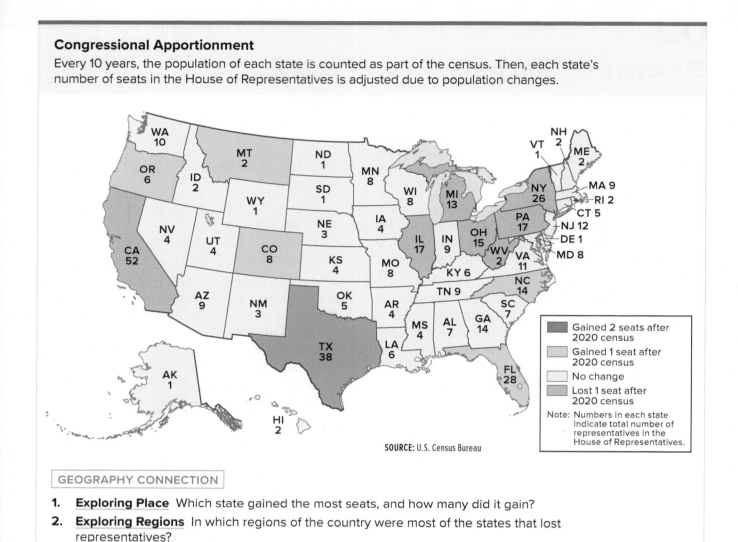

SOURCE: U.S. Census Bureau

GEOGRAPHY CONNECTION

1. **Exploring Place** Which state gained the most seats, and how many did it gain?
2. **Exploring Regions** In which regions of the country were most of the states that lost representatives?

In the **House of Representatives**, the number of members for each state would be based on its population.

James Madison called Congress "the First Branch of this Government." This statement reflected the belief of some Founders that the legislative branch of government should be the most powerful of the three. Not surprisingly, the first part of the Constitution, Article I, is devoted to describing Congress and its new powers. It takes up nearly half the text of the Constitution.

Every year, 535 elected members of Congress gather inside the Capitol in Washington, D.C. There, they discuss the many issues facing our country and write, debate, and pass laws to address them.

House of Representatives the lower house of Congress with representatives from each state, depending on population

Terms and Sessions

Every two years, a new Congress is seated. It usually begins meeting on January 3 the year after a national election and meets on and off for a two-year term. Each Congress has a number to identify it. Those numbers go in sequence starting with the first Congress, which met in 1789. The term of the 117th Congress lasted from January 2021 to January 2023.

The Constitution requires Congress to assemble at least once a year in meetings, which are called *sessions*. A session of Congress usually lasts from January until November or December of the same year. Congress may also meet during special sessions or in times of crisis. A joint session occurs when the House and Senate meet together. They do so when they must conduct business as a unit or hear a presidential speech.

The House of Representatives

The House of Representatives has 435 voting members, each of whom serves a two-year term. It is the larger of the two houses of Congress.

The number of seats assigned to states depends on their population. Every 10 years, the Census Bureau takes a **census**, or population count. The census results are used to **adjust**, or change, the number of representatives given to each state. States might get one or two more House members than before if they have gained enough residents since the last census. Those that lose enough residents might lose one or more seats. Each state, even those with the smallest populations, has at least one seat.

Each state is divided into one or more congressional districts. The voters in each district elect one representative, or House member. For states with only one House member, the single district is the entire state. States with two or more members are divided into two or more districts. By law, the districts must include roughly the same number of **constituents** (kuhn•STIHCH•wuhnts), or persons represented by a government official. In most states, the state legislature draws the district lines. In some states, a separate commission does the work.

The Constitution allows for states with more than one representative to choose all their representatives in a single statewide election. States are not required to use districts, but all of them do today.

Sometimes lawmakers draw these lines to favor their political party over the other party. This practice is called *gerrymandering*. A **gerrymander** is an oddly shaped district designed to increase the voting strength of a particular group. Many voters consider this to be an abuse of power by the people who draw the district lines.

Suppose that one party has a strong majority in the state legislature. In that case, party members could draw the lines so that voters from their party outnumber those from other parties in as many districts as possible. Sometimes, lawmakers from one party draw one district to include a very large number of voters from the other party. This nearly guarantees the other party will win that district. The party will have difficulty winning others because so many of their voters are packed into that one district. Laws have tried to limit gerrymandering, but the practice has not been stopped. Groups can file a lawsuit in state court if they believe that district lines have been drawn unfairly. Sometimes the court strikes down the redistricting plan, and a new one must be drawn.

Six nonvoting members also serve in the House of Representatives. They come from areas that are part of the United States but are not states. One represents the people of the District of Columbia. The other five represent the people of Puerto Rico and four island territories in the Pacific Ocean—American Samoa, Guam, Northern Mariana Islands, and the U.S. Virgin Islands. These six members do not vote on bills being considered in the House, but they can serve on committees, speak about issues, introduce bills, and offer amendments.

The origin of the term *gerrymandering* dates back to 1812 when Massachusetts's Governor Elbridge Gerry approved a district that opponents thought looked like a salamander, leading to the cartoon shown here.

Drawing Conclusions How does the cartoon portray the practice of gerrymandering? Is the portrayal positive or negative? Explain.

---

census a population count taken by the U.S. Census Bureau

constituent a person represented by a government official

gerrymander an oddly shaped election district designed to increase the voting strength of a particular group

If a House member dies or resigns during the first session of Congress, the state must hold a special election to fill the vacancy. States differ on how they handle vacancies that occur during the second session.

The Senate

Unlike the House of Representatives, members of the Senate represent their entire state rather than a particular district. Two senators serve each state, giving the Senate 100 members. Senators serve six-year terms, but their elections are staggered. No more than one-third of Senate seats are up for election every two years. Having two-thirds of the senators hold their seats after each election ensures that the Senate remains stable and helps shield the Senate from sudden shifts in public opinion.

A senator may die or resign before the end of the term. How that senator is replaced depends on state law. In most states, the governor chooses a temporary replacement who serves until there is an election. Most states wait until the next regular election to choose a permanent new senator. Some states hold a special election sooner.

Congressional Leadership

Every member of the House of Representatives and the Senate decides how to vote on laws. Every vote counts the same. However, both the House and Senate are large, and it would be hard for those bodies to make decisions if all their members acted as individuals. Instead, most members of the House and the Senate identify as

In 2020 then Senate Majority Leader Mitch McConnell, a Republican, and Speaker of the House Nancy Pelosi, a Democrat, joined together for the presentation of an award.

either Democrats or Republicans—just a few choose to be Independents. There are disagreements within each party about many issues. Nevertheless, the members of each party choose a few of their own group to lead them. The party with the most members also decides who leads the whole House and the whole Senate.

In both the House and the Senate, one political party usually has the most members. It is known as the **majority party**. At times, the Senate's 100 members can be divided evenly between the two parties. The party that controls the Senate in that case is the party of the vice president because that official can cast a deciding vote when the Senate is tied. The party that does not control the chamber is called the **minority party**.

At the beginning of each new Congress, the Democrats and Republicans in each house choose the party's leaders. The leader of the party with the most seats is called the *majority leader*. The leader of the party with fewer seats is called the *minority leader*. Both leaders speak for their party on important issues. They create legislative strategies and plans for their party. They try to advance bills supported by their party, and they try to convince members to vote for those bills.

Each party leader has an assistant leader called a *whip*. The whip helps each party leader in a variety of ways. For example, the whip makes sure legislators are present for key votes and will support the position of the party leadership.

Leadership in the House In addition to these party leaders, each house of Congress has one presiding officer. A presiding officer is the person who presides over, or runs, a meeting. In the House of Representatives, this leader is called the Speaker of the House. Members of the majority party choose the Speaker at a caucus, or closed meeting, at the start of each session of Congress. The rest of the House then votes on whether to approve the choice of Speaker. This vote simply confirms what the majority party already decided in their caucus.

As both the presiding officer of the House and the leader of the majority party, the Speaker of the House has great power. The Speaker

majority party in Congress, the political party whose members control each chamber

minority party in Congress, the political party that does not control either chamber

YEA 69   NAY 30

H.R. 3684, the INVEST in America Act

This photograph from August 2021 shows Vice President Kamala Harris serving in her role as the presiding officer over the Senate.

REUTERS/Alamy Stock Photo

presides over the House, guides legislation through the House, and leads floor debates. The Speaker can influence proceedings by deciding which members to recognize, or call on to speak, first. The Speaker can appoint members to certain committees, schedule bills for action, and refer bills to a particular House committee. If both the president and vice president become unable to serve, the Speaker is next in line to become president, as long as all legal qualifications are met.

The Constitution mentions the office of the Speaker, but it gives no other details about the office or its powers. The duties of the office have developed over time, shaped by the actions of the people who have served as Speaker.

The Speaker has a busy and demanding job. A typical day includes talking with dozens of members of Congress. These members often request the Speaker's help with certain matters because the position of Speaker holds so much power. The Speaker expects the representatives' support on important issues in return for meeting such requests. Speakers are skilled at using persuasion, and their powerful position, to influence other House members.

Leadership in the Senate Like the House, the Senate needs a presiding officer to keep order. The vice president fulfills this duty and runs the sessions of the Senate. The vice president differs from the Speaker of the House in two ways. The Speaker can take part in House debates and vote on any matter before the House. The vice president cannot take part in Senate debates and can vote only when there is a tie.

The vice president often has other work to do and cannot always be present when the Senate is in session. The Senate chooses a temporary officer to preside over the Senate when the vice president is absent. That officer is called the *president pro tempore* (proh TEHM•puh•ree)—meaning "for the time being." This officer is a member of the majority party and is usually its most senior member. The president pro tempore is third in the line of succession for the presidency, after the Speaker of the House.

✓ **CHECK FOR UNDERSTANDING**

1. **Contrasting** How does a senator differ from a member of the House of Representatives?

2. **Comparing and Contrasting** How are the roles of the Speaker of the House and the vice president within Congress alike and different?

The Committee System

GUIDING QUESTION

Why are members of Congress assigned to work on committees?

In each session that it meets, each house of Congress handles thousands of bills, or proposed laws. It would be impossible for every member of each chamber to read and study all those bills. To make this workload manageable, each house does much of the work of lawmaking through smaller bodies called *committees*. Many committees focus on a particular area of government activity. They carefully consider the bills in that area and decide what steps to take next.

Types of Committees

Congress has different types of committees. There are standing committees, select committees, and joint committees. Standing committees are permanent, meaning they are formed each term. They are the committees that focus on specific areas of government work. For example, both the Senate and the House have standing committees to deal with the budget, education and labor, and the armed forces. Committees can also be split into smaller groups called *subcommittees* that focus on a particular part of the main committee's work.

The second type of committee is the select committee. These are temporary committees formed to address a special issue. These committees meet only until they complete their assigned task. The House formed a select committee in 2019 to address climate change.

Occasionally, the Senate and the House form joint committees. A joint committee includes both senators and representatives. Like a special committee, a joint committee is formed to consider a specific issue. For example, Senate and House members of the Joint Economic Committee review economic conditions and make recommendations regarding economic policy.

Serving on Committees

Party leaders decide which committees each member will serve on. In doing so, they consider members' experience, loyalty to their party, and interests. For example, a member interested in improving rail service might want to serve on the Transportation and Infrastructure Committee. Seniority, or years of service, can also play a role in committee assignments. The senators and representatives who have been in Congress longest usually get to serve on the most powerful committees.

Newly elected senators and representatives serve their districts by trying to get on committees that address matters important to the people in their home districts. For example, members of Congress from a state that produces oil or natural gas will want to serve on the committee that handles energy. Representatives with many members of the military in their districts might be interested in serving on the House Armed Services Committee.

The chair, or leader, of a committee is usually the committee member who is part of the

U.S. Supreme Court nominee Amy Coney Barrett (center front, facing away from camera) attended her confirmation hearing before the Senate Judiciary Committee in October 2020. One job of this committee is to make its recommendations on the nominee to the full Senate.

majority party and has served the longest. Chairs have a great deal of power. They decide when and if a committee will meet. They also decide who will serve on each subcommittee. Most importantly, they decide which bills the committee will consider and which will not be addressed. If a committee does not take up a bill, that bill will not become law. The minority party members of the committee are led by a member called the *ranking member*. The ranking member is the longest-serving committee member from the minority party.

✓ CHECK FOR UNDERSTANDING

Contrasting How do standing committees differ from select and joint committees?

LESSON ACTIVITIES

1. **Informative/Explanatory Writing** Take the role of a senator or member of the House of Representatives from your state. Write an explanation of why you chose to serve on a particular committee in Congress and how it will benefit your district or state.

2. **Collaborating** With a partner, research the U.S. senators from your state and the member of the House who represents your district. Create a profile of each person that includes when they were first elected to Congress, how long they have served, and what committees they are on. Identify three key issues and where the Congressional members stand on those issues.

READING STRATEGY

Analyzing Key Ideas and Details As you read, use a chart like this one to identify the powers of Congress.

Expressed powers	
Implied powers	
Lawmaking powers	
Nonlegislative powers	

Legislative Powers

GUIDING QUESTION

What kinds of lawmaking powers were given to Congress by the Constitution?

Have you noticed the nutrition labels on food packaging? That information is required by law. Congress passed that law so consumers would know more about the food they buy.

Congress influences the lives of every American in significant ways. Its laws affect our nation's society and economy. For example, Congress uses government funds to pay for many of the highways that trucks use to carry goods from ports to stores. Congress ensures that you can receive mail. Actions taken by Congress can even affect people living in other countries. Every year, Congress sends money to foreign countries to help them in areas such as security and health. It is important for every American citizen to understand what powers Congress has—and how those powers are limited.

Expressed Powers

Article I, Section 8 of the Constitution outlines most of the powers of Congress. Its 18 clauses list the **expressed powers**, or powers specifically granted to Congress. These are also known as enumerated powers. No other branch of government has these powers. Clause 5, for example, says, "The Congress shall have the Power . . . To coin Money." Clause 12 gives Congress the power to "raise and support Armies."

The expressed powers are the powers that the Framers specifically wanted Congress to have. Some of these powers were not granted to the national government under the Articles of Confederation. For example, the Constitution gives Congress the power to make laws regarding the regulation of business between the states. The Articles did not grant this power.

expressed power power of the U.S. Congress that is specifically listed in the Constitution

The Framers of the Constitution granted Congress the power "to coin Money" as one of its expressed powers. That power is extended to paper money as well as coins.

Implied Powers

Congress has additional powers that are not directly stated in the Constitution. These powers come from Article I, Section 8, Clause 18. This clause says that Congress has the power to "make all Laws which shall be necessary and proper" to carry out its expressed powers. The powers that Clause 18 grants to Congress are called **implied powers**. These powers are assumed to be granted, even though they are not stated specifically in the Constitution. Sometimes Americans disagree on and debate whether Congress actually has an implied power that it claims.

Clause 18 allows Congress to stretch its powers to meet new and changing needs. For this reason, some people call Clause 18 the **elastic clause**. An example of the elastic clause in action is the post office. Article I of the Constitution gives Congress the expressed power to "establish Post Offices and post Roads." The Constitution does not state that Congress has the power to hire hundreds of thousands of postal workers. Under the elastic clause, however, Congress has done just that.

Lawmaking Powers

The majority of congressional power involves making laws. Many of these powers fall into three major groups. They are powers involving money and government finance, those having to do with commerce, and those related to military matters and foreign policy. Still, Congress has other kinds of powers as well, such as the power to create courts below the U.S. Supreme Court.

implied power power of the U.S. Congress that is not specifically stated in the Constitution

elastic clause clause in Article I, Section 8 of the Constitution that gives Congress the right to make laws "necessary and proper" to carry out its expressed powers

Expressed and Implied Powers of Congress

The expressed powers of Congress imply certain other powers under the "necessary and proper" clause.

Selected Expressed Powers Powers clearly stated in the text of the Constitution	Related Implied Powers Powers that Congress assumes, although these powers may be questioned by the public
Money Powers • To lay and collect taxes to provide for the general welfare (Clause 1) • To borrow money (Clause 2)	• To support public schools, welfare programs, public housing, and similar programs • To pay interest on federal bonds
Commerce Powers • To regulate foreign and interstate commerce (Clause 3)	• To prohibit discrimination in restaurants, hotels, and other public accommodations
Military and Foreign Policy Powers • To raise, support, and regulate an army and navy and make rules about state militias (Clauses 12, 13, 14, 15, and 16)	• To draft people into the armed services and to form the U.S. Air Force
Other Legislative Powers • To establish laws of naturalization (Clause 4) • To create courts below the Supreme Court (Clause 9)	• To limit the number of immigrants into the United States • To establish the types of legal matters these courts will handle

EXAMINE THE CHART

1. **Identifying** Which three expressed powers have a clear impact on the nation's economy?
2. **Explaining** Why is the power to limit the number of immigrants considered an example of an implied power of Congress?

U.S. Constitution, Article I, Section 8

Congress has the power to raise and spend money. To raise money, it can require people to pay taxes. It also has the power to borrow money, which it does by selling bonds. The bonds are agreements in which the government receives money with the promise to repay it with interest in the future. Congress can also **regulate**, or manage, commerce that takes place across state lines. *Commerce* is the business of buying and selling goods and services. For example, Congress has the power to set rules for trucks that carry goods across state lines.

Congress makes laws about defense and foreign policy issues. It has the power to form an army and navy and to provide the weapons, supplies, and ships they need to be effective. Congress has the sole power to declare war. It also has the power to set rules for the militia. Militia are groups of citizen-soldiers formed by the state government. Today, that militia consists of National Guard units. Congress can set the rules for training these forces and call them into national service if they are needed.

Some of Congress's lawmaking powers fall outside of these categories. For example, Congress has the power to set up the government of Washington, D.C., and to create a postal service.

✓ CHECK FOR UNDERSTANDING

1. **Identifying** What is the difference between expressed powers and implied powers?
2. **Explaining** Why is Clause 18 often called the "elastic clause"?

Other Powers and Limits

GUIDING QUESTION

What powers does Congress have to check the powers of the other branches of government?

Congress does more than make laws. It has a number of other duties and responsibilities. These powers are called **nonlegislative powers**.

Nonlegislative Powers

One nonlegislative power of Congress is the authority to propose amendments to the Constitution. Congress also has the power to determine the president and vice president if no candidate wins a majority in the Electoral College. In that case, the House chooses the president from among the three candidates with the most electoral votes. The Senate selects the vice president from among the top two vote-getters. Congress has decided two elections—in 1800 and 1824.

One of the most important nonlegislative powers is the ability to check the other branches of government. For example, the Senate can check the executive branch by using its power to approve or reject the president's nominees for various offices. The offices include Supreme Court justices, federal judges, and the heads of executive agencies. Senators approve the majority of choices made by the president, but they can vote down any nominee.

Congress can remove from office federal officials involved in serious wrongdoing. This power is a check on both the judicial and executive branches. Congress exercises this power through a two-step process called *impeachment*. In step one, the House votes to **impeach**, or formally accuse an official of misconduct in office. The House can impeach with a simple majority vote.

In step two, the Senate holds a trial to determine if the official is guilty of the charges made by the House. Two-thirds of the senators— 67 of the full 100 members—must vote to convict an official. If found guilty, the official is removed from office and can never hold office again.

Congress has rarely used its right to impeach. Most of these cases have involved federal judges.

impeach to formally accuse a government official of misconduct in office

In February 2020, the Senate acquitted President Donald Trump in his first impeachment trial.

regulate to manage or control
nonlegislative power duty and responsibility Congress holds besides lawmaking

PHOTO: Maurice Savage/Alamy Stock Photo; TEXT: US Const, Art I, § 8. https://www.archives.gov/founding-docs/constitution-transcript

Only three presidents have been impeached: Andrew Johnson in 1868, Bill Clinton in 1998, and Donald Trump in 2019 and 2021.

In all four cases, the presidents stood trial in the Senate and were **acquitted**, or found not guilty. The acquittals of Johnson, Clinton, and Trump (in his first impeachment trial) allowed them to remain in office. Trump's second trial took place when he was no longer in office, but he was acquitted then as well.

Another important nonlegislative power of Congress is its oversight authority. **Oversight** is the power to oversee the actions of another branch or agency. Congress can hold hearings, or fact-finding investigations, to examine the actions of members of the executive branch. It can do so to try to learn the causes of problems or to see if any officials acted wrongly.

Limits on Congress

The Framers of the Constitution wanted to ensure that Congress could not abuse its power. For that reason, they also identified powers that Congress did not have. For example, Article I, Section 9 says that Congress may not set taxes on commerce between states, tax exports, or favor one state over another.

The Framers put some limits on the powers of Congress to protect the rights of individuals. Article I, Section 9 forbids Congress from passing laws that would take away the legal rights of individuals. For example, judges can require police and other law enforcement officials to bring prisoners into court and explain why they are holding them. This rule is called **habeas corpus** (HAY•bee•uhs KAWR•puhs), and it is meant to protect individuals from being arrested without a good reason or in secret. Section 9 states that Congress cannot block the writ of habeas corpus except to protect public safety in times of rebellion or invasion.

The Constitution prevents Congress from passing **ex post facto laws**. These laws make an act a crime after the act has been committed, even though it was legal at the time. Congress also cannot pass **bills of attainder**. These are laws that make a person guilty without a trial.

These restrictions on the powers of Congress are written in the main text of the Constitution. When the Bill of Rights was passed, it placed more limits on the powers of Congress as well. The First Amendment is part of the Bill of Rights. It says that Congress may not pass laws that restrict the freedom of the press or the right of people to assemble peacefully.

The powers of Congress are also limited by the system of checks and balances. The president can veto, or reject, bills that Congress passes. The Supreme Court can declare laws or parts of laws passed by Congress to be unconstitutional. If it does so, the law is no longer legal and cannot be enforced. In each of these cases, though, Congress has its own check. It can override the president's veto if two-thirds of both the Senate and the House of Representatives vote to do so. Congress can also rewrite a law to correct any problems identified by the Supreme Court in the original law.

Further limits on the powers of Congress result from the fact that the Constitution sets aside many powers for the state governments. Those powers are denied to the federal government. For example, Congress cannot regulate business that takes place only within a state.

✓ **CHECK FOR UNDERSTANDING**

Explaining What steps must Congress follow to remove federal officials from office?

LESSON ACTIVITIES

1. **Informative/Explanatory Writing** Explain the differences between expressed and implied powers and how creation of the U.S. Air Force demonstrates them both.

2. **Presenting** Research the outcomes of a recent president's appointments. Did any nominees face major opposition in the Senate, or were they all easily approved? What do these nominations tell you about this check that Congress has on presidential power? Present your findings to the class.

---

acquit to find a defendant not guilty

oversight the power to oversee the actions of another branch or agency

writ of habeas corpus a court order that requires police to bring a prisoner to court to explain why they are holding the person

ex post facto law a law that allows a person to be punished for an action that was not against the law when it was committed

bill of attainder a law that punishes a person accused of a crime without a trial or a fair hearing in court

Qualifications and Staffing

Making Laws	
Helping the District or State	
Doing Casework	

GUIDING QUESTION

What are the qualifications for becoming a member of Congress?

Why might a person want to become a member of Congress? There are many reasons. Members of Congress make the laws for our country. They have opportunities to improve the lives of their neighbors in their states or districts. Congresspeople try to solve important problems by working with officials from our government and the governments of other nations. Sometimes they can meet and work closely with the president. The job also offers a good salary and health insurance. Members of Congress often are honored as important people in their communities. Finally, representatives and senators generally find their work exciting and meaningful.

On the other hand, working in Congress can also be difficult and demanding. Members of Congress are responsible for serving their constituents—the people of their district or state—and the nation as a whole. Citizens and the media constantly observe them and their work. One mistake or misstatement can lead to criticism. Members of Congress are busy almost all the time and need to make hard decisions. Their vote on a bill can bring complaints by some citizens. In contrast, voting the other way can result in criticism from those on the other side of the issue. Meanwhile, party leaders in Congress urge members to support the party position. Finally, congresspeople must keep reelection in mind. They might be voted out of office in two or six years. These parts of the job can be stressful and challenging.

Chuck Grassley, a senator from Iowa, listens to a constituent speak at a town hall meeting.

Rachel Mummey/The Washington Post/Getty Images

Requirements and Benefits

Members of Congress must meet certain qualifications to hold office. The Constitution states that senators must be at least 30 years old by the time they take office. When elected, they must live in the state they represent, and they must have been a U.S. citizen for at least nine years. Members of the House of Representatives have different qualifications. They must be at least 25 years old and, when elected, live in the state they represent. In addition, they need to have been a U.S. citizen for at least seven years before taking office.

Members of Congress come from different occupations. In the 117th Congress, 230 senators and House members—more than 40 percent—were lawyers. Some other members of Congress were farmers, doctors, or former members of the armed forces. Even a few former professional athletes served in Congress.

Members of Congress tend to be older than the average American. In the 117th Congress, the average age of a senator was 64 years old, and the average age of representatives was 58. Only about 30 House members and senators were younger than 40.

The positions of senator and representative come with many benefits. In 2021 both senators and representatives received salaries of $174,000 a year. All members are entitled to an income tax deduction so they can afford to have two residences, one in their home state and one in the Washington, D.C., area. They receive life

Profile of Congress

The 117th Congress, shown here, had a record number of women serving.

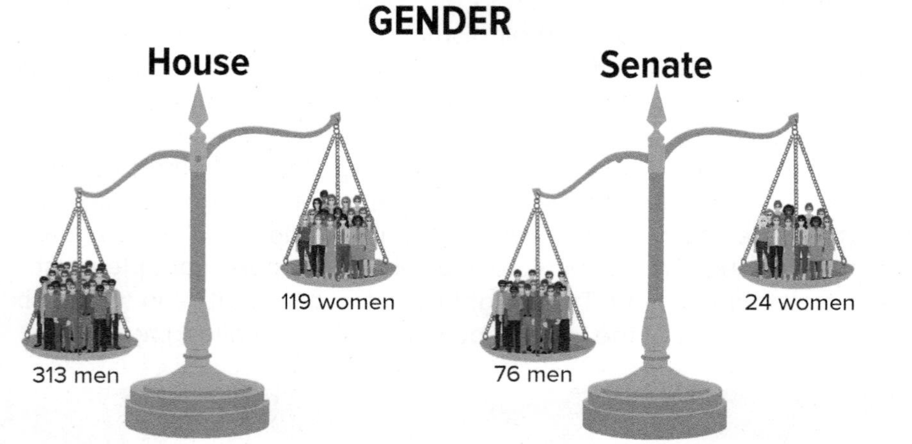

GENDER

House

119 women

313 men

Senate

24 women

76 men

EXAMINE THE DIAGRAM

1. **Comparing** In which house of Congress is there a greater percentage of women?

2. **Analyzing** How strong was the Democratic majority in the House in the 117th Congress?

PARTY AFFILIATION

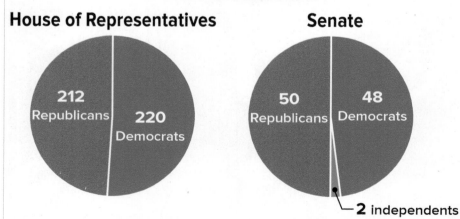

House of Representatives

212 Republicans

220 Democrats

Senate

50 Republicans

48 Democrats

2 independents

Note: The House had three vacant seats when this data was collected. The two independents in the Senate meet with the Democrats, giving them 50 members in effect.

Source: House.gov; Senate.gov; Accessed September 17, 2021

and health insurance. They also have the use of a gymnasium, special restaurants, and a medical clinic. Members of Congress may be eligible for pensions of up to 80 percent of their final salaries. A pension is a regular payment made to people after they retire.

Another benefit is that senators and representatives have **immunity**, or legal protection, in certain situations. This allows them to speak their minds freely in debates and other official communications without fear of lawsuits or criminal arrest. Of course, this protection does not give them the right to break the law.

Other benefits help members of Congress carry out their duties. For example, members' office space, parking, and travel between Washington, D.C., and their home states are paid for by the government. Another job-related benefit is the ability to send job-related mail without paying postage. This is called the **franking privilege**. Members can send messages to constituents to inform them of the work they are doing.

Congressional Staffs

To help them carry out their work, members of Congress can hire a staff. Each senator and representative may hire clerks, secretaries, and special assistants to aid them with daily tasks.

Members of Congress have at least two offices. They each have an office in or near the Capitol in Washington, D.C. They also have one or more offices in their home district or state. Congresspeople have staffs in both locations to run these offices. The offices in the district or state make it easier for constituents to meet with staff members in person if they have a problem. Representatives and senators can also use these offices to meet with individuals or groups when they visit their home district or state.

Staff members do a lot of work to support their legislator. They research information about issues to help with drafting new bills. They handle communications with constituents, including phone calls, emails, and letters. They respond to questions from news reporters on behalf of the Congressperson. They may meet with lobbyists.

This protest shows constituents concerned about the ties of congresspeople to lobbyists.

Lobbyists are people who represent interest groups that work for certain causes or policies. Lobbyists try to influence policy. Staff members often support their legislators by working on their reelection campaigns. They must be careful to do this work on their own time. Since the staff members are government employees, it is illegal for them to work on campaigns during their regular working hours.

Congressional committees also need staffs to help with their workload. Committee staff members do many of the day-to-day tasks that are necessary to make laws. They conduct research on issues the committee considers. They organize committee hearings and make sure that all members of the committee have copies of any documents they need. Some committee staff members are experts in a particular policy area. This expertise helps them **draft**, or write a rough version of, bills. Sometimes they work with lobbyists who have an interest in the legislation. For example, lobbyists from banks might be involved with writing a bill regulating the financial industry.

In addition, many members of Congress bring in high school or college students from their districts to work for them on a volunteer or paid basis. The students serve as interns and pages. Interns help with research and office duties. Pages deliver messages and documents within the Capitol. This experience gives young people a firsthand look at the political process.

immunity legal protection
franking privilege the right of congresspeople to send job-related mail without paying postage

lobbyist representative of an interest group who contacts government officials to influence policy
draft to write a rough version

Agencies of Congress

Congress has also created agencies to support its work. The Library of Congress is the largest library in the world, with nearly 172 million books and other items in its collection. The Library of Congress is an important source of information for members of Congress and their staffs. Private citizens researching the history, society, or culture of the United States may also use the library.

Congress relies on the Congressional Budget Office (CBO) as it develops the yearly budget of the U.S. government. The budget is a plan that details how much money the government will receive from taxes and other sources and how much it plans to spend on different activities. Budgeting takes place every year and is one of the most important activities of Congress. After the budget is approved, the CBO continues to help Congress. It explains the possible costs and benefits of different actions Congress is considering. The CBO does not suggest policies but evaluates proposals in Congress. For example, the CBO estimates, or tries to identify, how much a program will cost and how it will benefit a community or the economy as a whole.

Congress formed the Government Accountability Office (GAO) to help ensure that government officials spend funds wisely. It reviews spending by federal agencies to make sure they are using funds as intended and that money is not being wasted or spent on the wrong things. It studies federal programs to see if they are working as intended. It also suggests ways to improve how the government spends money. When Congress is considering new laws, the GAO analyzes different actions that Congress can take to address an issue. The GAO does not work only with Congress. It also advises executive departments.

The Government Publishing Office (GPO) produces and distributes official federal government publications. These include the *Congressional Record*, House and Senate bills, and reports. The GPO began in the era of printing presses, but today it makes its publications available on the Internet.

✓ **CHECK FOR UNDERSTANDING**

1. **Speculating** Why is it important for members of Congress to have their travel to their home states paid for?

2. **Identifying** What does the Government Accountability Office do?

Congress at Work

GUIDING QUESTION

How do members of Congress meet their responsibilities?

More than 330 million people live in the United States today. They are represented by fewer than 550 members of Congress. That includes the 535 members who can vote on laws and the 6 nonvoting members of the House.

These senators and representatives are responsible for representing the people of their states and districts. They are supposed to understand the interests and concerns of their constituents and work to address them. Members of Congress do three main kinds of work. Their main tasks are making laws, helping individual constituents with problems, and working to acquire funding for their district or state.

Making Laws

Members of Congress are also known as *lawmakers*. This is because making laws is one of their major responsibilities. Each year, Congress considers thousands of bills. Bills are drafts of proposed laws presented to the House and Senate.

As lawmakers, members of Congress fill various roles. First, they work as investigators. They study issues to understand them and how they affect their constituents. Lawmakers then

In 1800, President John Adams signed a bill to create the Library of Congress, now housed in this building in Washington, D.C. The Library of Congress was intended to support the work of the Senate and House.

In 2021 Speaker of the House Nancy Pelosi signed the final version of the bill to make Juneteenth a federal holiday. The bill was sent to President Biden for his approval.

PHOTO: SOPA Images Limited/Alamy Stock Photo; TEXT: Pontius, J. S., "Congressional Member Office Operations" Congressional Research Service & The Library of Congress, December 29, 2003

plan and develop legislation to address the issues under consideration. If they write a law, they often take on the role of salesperson, trying to persuade others to support their law. A bill that does not win support will not have a chance to become law. Members of Congress are also evaluators. They examine bills proposed by other members. They consider how those bills would affect their communities and the nation if they became law.

Doing Casework

People sometimes encounter problems when dealing with the federal government. They may turn to their representatives to ask for help. This part of a congressperson's job is called **casework**. Some members receive as many as 10,000 requests a year for this help. These requests cover many types of issues.

> 66 The casework requests are as diverse as the federal government: a lost Social Security check; a veteran's widow requesting burial assistance for her deceased spouse; . . . immigration; farmers' loans; Medicare claims; railroad retirement; and federal rental housing. 99
>
> —Anonymous congressional staff member, quoted in Congressional Research Service, Congressional Member Office Operations, 2003

Lawmakers take casework very seriously. They can support their constituents by helping them with difficult processes, such as applying for U.S. citizenship. Providing help to constituents helps those people, but it also helps the lawmaker. Citizens who are grateful to the lawmaker for this help are more likely to vote for the congressperson in the next election. They are also likely to encourage friends and family members to vote for the lawmaker. Casework also helps lawmakers see how well the executive branch is handling programs that affect their constituents, such as Social Security or veterans' benefits.

Helping the District or State

Casework is not the only way members of Congress serve their constituents. They try to help citizens back home by securing federal government projects for their districts and states. People who are critical of these kinds of projects sometimes call them **pork-barrel projects**. To understand this term, think of a member of Congress dipping into the "pork barrel" (the federal treasury) and pulling out a piece of "fat" (funding for a federal project for the district or state). Some critics say that this spending is a waste of taxpayers' money.

casework the work that a lawmaker does to help constituents solve a problem with a federal agency

pork-barrel project government project grant that primarily benefits a congressperson's home district or state

Many lawmakers disagree with this view. They argue that it is one of their jobs to make sure that the people they represent get their fair share of spending by the federal government. They see this practice as a way to help people or groups they serve who have a need.

Every year, Congress passes public works bills. These bills set aside billions of dollars for local projects. The money can be used to build dams, widen highways, build a new post office or veterans' hospital, or meet some other need. Other projects are intended to improve the health of the community, such as replacing old water pipes that contain lead. These projects bring jobs and money into a community that the member serves. If the project involves building a new federal office or other facility, it can generate jobs for years to come. However, the money must come from taxes that Americans across the country pay. In some instances, lawmakers must work hard to win projects for their district or state. They do not have the power to grant the money directly. Instead, executive branch agencies, such as the Department of Transportation or the Department of Veterans Affairs, have control over grants and contracts.

Lawmakers can, however, try to influence agency decisions. They can meet with agency officials and try to convince them of the importance of placing the project in their state or community. They can emphasize the jobs that it will create and how the economic gains will help the community. Members of Congress may also encourage key leaders from their community to talk to agency officials and set up important meetings between the two groups.

In some situations, members of Congress have another way to promote projects they favor. They can add wording to bills to provide funds for their projects. These additions are called *earmarks*. Inserting the project in a bill is not the end of the members' work. They still need to gain the support of other legislators because the funding only goes through if both chambers pass the bill. The process of earmarking has been controversial, and, for a time, fell out of use. New rules for earmarking were put in place to help keep the process in check.

The extension of the metropolitan Boston subway system is one example of a pork-barrel project, partially paid for with federal funding.

Drawing Conclusions Based on this photograph, what category of projects do members of Congress try to get approved for funding?

✓ CHECK FOR UNDERSTANDING

1. **Describing** What is the basic job of members of Congress?

2. **Identifying Cause and Effect** How might lawmakers win a project for their states or districts?

LESSON ACTIVITIES

1. **Argumentative Writing** You believe your district needs to have a new highway built. Write a letter to your senator or representative asking for support of a highway project in your district. To help persuade the lawmaker, provide reasons that this project would help people in your district, and cite examples of other similar successful projects.

2. **Using Multimedia** With a partner, conduct research to find out how members of Congress help their constituents. Examine the official websites of your senator or representative. Read local news reports to find five or six people, groups, or businesses that your senator or representative has helped. Then, create a slide presentation to show different ways that your congresspeople support their constituents.

05
How a Bill Becomes a Law

READING STRATEGY

Analyzing Key Ideas and Details As you read, use a diagram like the one below to describe the major steps to turn a bill into a law.

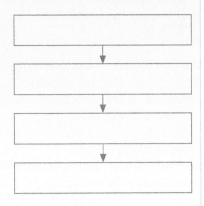

Types of Bills

GUIDING QUESTION

What kinds of bills come before Congress?

Congress is a legislature, which means that passing laws is its major job. More than 10,000 bills—proposals for new laws—are introduced each session. Only a small percentage—just a few hundred—are signed into law. A long and complicated process helps to make sure lawmakers consider the bills carefully. Some bills can take more than a year to become law.

There are two types of bills: private and public bills. Private bills concern individuals or a single organization or place. For instance, a private bill might grant an individual person U.S. citizenship. The vast majority of bills are public bills, which apply to whole groups of people or even the entire nation. Public bills are often controversial because it is difficult to shape policies that satisfy all Americans. Public bills might address tax rates, law enforcement, access to the Internet, or highways among other issues. They may be debated for months before going to a vote. Not all bills become law.

Along with bills, Congress also considers resolutions. Resolutions are formal statements by one or both houses of Congress that express the majority's opinions on a matter the chamber believes is important or explain a decision the chamber has taken. For example, resolutions can be used to offer sympathy to the family of a member of Congress who has died or to make the views of Congress known on an important issue.

Each year, Congress votes on bills that appropriate, or set aside, money for different purposes. One such purpose is to maintain national parks, such as Yosemite in California.

Many resolutions do not have the power of law. **Joint resolutions**—those passed by both houses of Congress—do become law if they are signed by the president. Congress uses joint resolutions to propose amendments to the Constitution or to set aside money for a special purpose.

> ✓ **CHECK FOR UNDERSTANDING**
>
> **Explaining** What is the purpose of public bills?

From Bill to Law

GUIDING QUESTION

How does a bill become a law?

Just as an essay you write begins with an idea, so does every bill. Members of Congress get their ideas for new bills from a number of different sources. Private citizens who care about a particular issue may suggest bills. Presidents can discuss ideas they want to see made into law. Special-interest groups can also offer proposals for bills. **Special-interest groups** are organizations of people that share common interests and try to influence government decisions. For example, special-interest groups could campaign for aid for farmers or for stronger laws to protect the environment.

---

joint resolution a resolution that is passed by both houses of Congress

special-interest group an organization of people with some common interest that tries to influence government decisions

---

Although ideas for bills can come from outside Congress, only a member of the House or Senate can **submit**, or offer for consideration, a bill. The member who introduces a bill is known as its sponsor, but other members can agree to cosponsor the bill. A bill can have any number of cosponsors.

Every bill submitted to either chamber is given a title and a number. The first bill introduced after a new Congress begins is numbered S.1 in the Senate and H.R.1 in the House. The bills that follow are numbered in sequence. The title of a bill is meant to inform the public what the bill intends to accomplish. Often sponsors seek a title for a bill that sounds appealing or is easy to remember.

Committee Action

After the sponsor introduces the bill in Congress, it is sent to the standing committee that handles the subject of the bill. For example, a bill introduced in the House to protect wetlands would go to the Natural Resources Committee. Sometimes, complex issues are divided among several committees that handle matters from different parts of the bill. Standing committees vote to decide whether a bill can continue through the process of becoming a law. If the committee approves a bill, it can continue by going to the floor of the full House or Senate for a vote. If the committee does not approve the bill, the bill dies. The vast majority of bills never make it out of committee.

Most Senate committees have fewer than 25 members. Most House committees have

---

submit to offer a bill for consideration

In addition to reviewing pending legislation, the Senate Judiciary Committee, made up of around 22 senators, oversees the Department of Justice and considers judicial nominees.

Drawing Conclusions How does the size of a committee, such as the one shown here, make it a good place to consider the details of a bill?

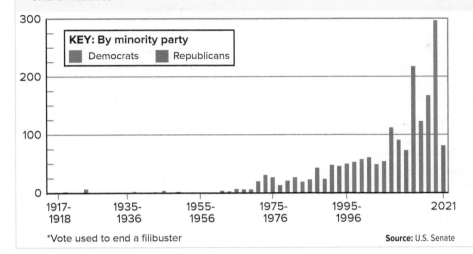

Number of Cloture Votes in Each Session of Congress, 1917–2021

Cloture votes are cast to end a filibuster in the Senate. It takes 60 votes in favor of cloture to end a filibuster.

KEY: By minority party
- Democrats
- Republicans

*Vote used to end a filibuster

Source: U.S. Senate

HISTORY CONNECTION

1. **Analyzing Visuals** In which Senate session were the most cloture votes taken?

2. **Explaining** What trend does this graph show?

fewer than 50 members. If the committee is large, the committee chair may assign the bill to a subcommittee first. That group will be the first to consider the bill in detail.

Committee members may hold hearings on a bill if they think it is worth considering. These hearings allow experts on the bill's subject matter to share their knowledge with the committee. Generally, committees will listen to witnesses with different points of view on the bill. A hearing also gives members an opportunity to question the witnesses. Committee members try to more fully understand the issue the bill addresses, as well as how effective the bill may. After the hearings, committee members discuss the bill.

The committee can then take one of five actions on a bill:

- pass the bill as written, which sends it to the full chamber
- make changes to the bill, pass it, and send it to the full chamber
- replace the original bill with a new bill on the same subject
- "pigeonhole" the bill, which means to let the bill die in committee by ignoring it
- kill the bill outright by having a majority vote against it

Debating a Bill

Once a committee approves a bill, it goes to the full House or Senate for consideration. This stage of the process is called the *floor debate*. Usually only a few lawmakers take part in floor debates. The pros and cons of the bill will already have been argued in committee hearings and are known to those with a strong interest in the bill.

Members explain why they support or oppose the bill during the debate. They also discuss possible amendments, or changes, to it. The House accepts only amendments that are related to the bill, but the Senate allows **riders**— completely unrelated amendments—to be added.

The two chambers have different rules for debating bills. In the House, the Rules Committee sets the terms for debate. Typically, the Rules Committee sets an overall limit on the time that the House will debate the bill. A leading member of each party divides the time among party members who wish to speak on the bill.

Debate in the Senate is much different. Senate rules put no limits on debate. Neither the overall time of the debate nor the time used by any one senator is limited. Sometimes one or more senators who oppose a bill use a tactic called the **filibuster** to block debate and try to force the bill's sponsor to withdraw the bill. Traditionally, senators used the filibuster by holding the floor and talking for hours. That is no longer the case, however.

rider a completely unrelated amendment added to a bill in the Senate

filibuster a tactic for defeating a bill in the Senate by talking or using other procedures until the bill's sponsor withdraws it

How a Bill Becomes a Law

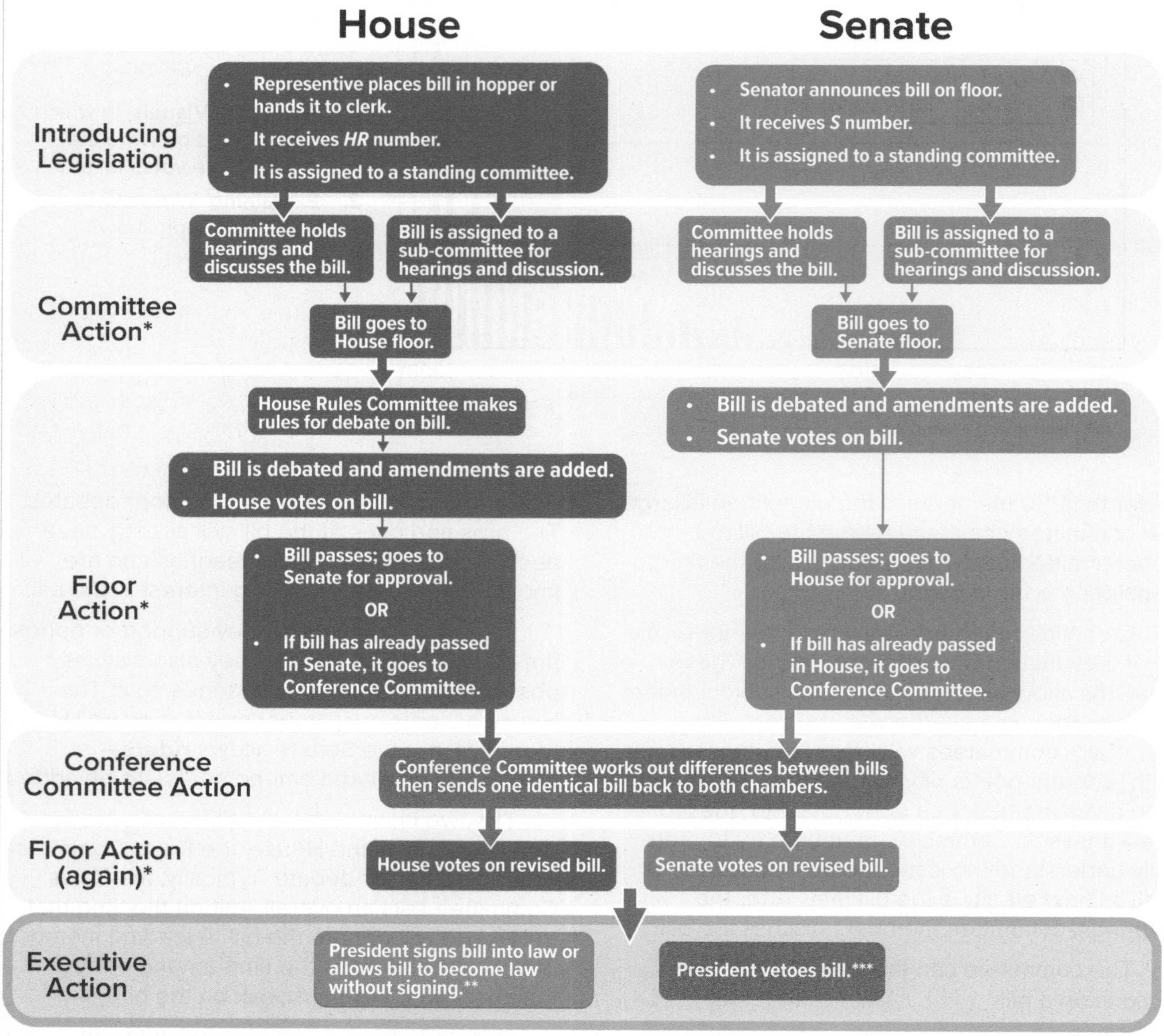

House | Senate

Introducing Legislation

House:
- Representative places bill in hopper or hands it to clerk.
- It receives *HR* number.
- It is assigned to a standing committee.

Senate:
- Senator announces bill on floor.
- It receives *S* number.
- It is assigned to a standing committee.

Committee Action*

House:
- Committee holds hearings and discusses the bill.
- Bill is assigned to a sub-committee for hearings and discussion.
- Bill goes to House floor.

Senate:
- Committee holds hearings and discusses the bill.
- Bill is assigned to a sub-committee for hearings and discussion.
- Bill goes to Senate floor.

Floor Action*

House:
- House Rules Committee makes rules for debate on bill.
- Bill is debated and amendments are added.
- House votes on bill.
- Bill passes; goes to Senate for approval.
  OR
- If bill has already passed in Senate, it goes to Conference Committee.

Senate:
- Bill is debated and amendments are added.
- Senate votes on bill.
- Bill passes; goes to House for approval.
  OR
- If bill has already passed in House, it goes to Conference Committee.

Conference Committee Action

Conference Committee works out differences between bills then sends one identical bill back to both chambers.

Floor Action (again)*

House votes on revised bill.

Senate votes on revised bill.

Executive Action

President signs bill into law or allows bill to become law without signing.**

President vetoes bill.***

*At this step, legislators can stop a bill from moving forward.

**President can keep bill for 10 days and bill becomes law. If Congress adjourns before the 10 days, the bill does not become law.

***Congress can override a veto by a 2/3 majority in both chambers. If either fails to override, the bill dies.

Source: Vote Smart, https://votesmart.org/education/how-a-bill-becomes-law#.YXa39RrMJaR; Accessed 10/25/2021.

EXAMINE THE DIAGRAM

1. **Comparing and Contrasting** What are the differences and similarities in how bills are introduced in the two chambers of Congress?

2. **Explaining** What is the purpose of a conference committee?

The Senate can end a filibuster if three-fifths of the members vote for cloture. **Cloture** (KLOH•chuhr) is a procedure that limits debate on a bill and prevents or ends a filibuster. If 60 senators vote in favor of cloture, no senator may speak for more than one hour, which brings an end to a filibuster.

The record for the longest filibuster came during the Senate debate on the Civil Rights Act of 1964. Senators opposed to the bill staged a filibuster that lasted for 60 days of the Senate's session. Finally, senators who supported the bill convinced enough senators to vote for cloture to end the debate. Just nine days later, the Senate passed the bill. Soon after, President Lyndon Johnson signed the Civil Rights Act into law.

Today senators rarely need to talk for hours to filibuster. Instead, they only have to find a total of 41 senators willing to vote against cloture. Today just the threat of a filibuster is often enough to stop action on bills. As a result, bills effectively cannot pass the Senate with fewer than 60 votes in most situations. This makes it very difficult for the Senate to pass bills without at least some support from both parties. It can be particularly difficult if the majority party has a small majority of just a few seats.

Voting on the Bill

After a bill is debated in the House, it is brought to a final vote. A majority of the members must be present for the vote to take place. In the Senate, members must vote for cloture if a bill has been filibustered before it can come up for a vote.

Members of the House vote in one of three ways. The simplest is a **voice vote**. All representatives who favor the bill say "Aye" aloud and then all opponents say "No." The Speaker then determines which side has the most votes. A second method is by **standing vote**, during which those in favor of a bill stand to be counted.

cloture a procedure used in the Senate to limit debate on a bill and end or prevent a filibuster

voice vote a voting method in which those in favor say "Aye" and those against say "No"

standing vote in Congress, when members stand to be counted for a vote on a bill

The electronic tally board at the top of the photograph displays the vote cast by each member of the House on the bill that is being considered.

Then, those who are against it stand to be counted. Neither voice votes nor standing votes result in a record of the exact final count or show how each member voted. The third method is a recorded vote, in which votes are made electronically. Each member's vote is shown on a large screen at the front of the House chamber. Each vote is also written in the House records.

Senators can also cast their votes using a voice vote or a standing vote. They also have a third option, which is the **roll-call vote**. In a roll-call vote, senators respond "Aye" or "No" one by one as their names are called. As with a recorded vote in the House, roll-call votes leave a clear record of where each senator stands on a given bill.

A bill passes when a simple majority of all members votes in favor of it. When a bill passes, it goes to the other house for debate and a vote. If a bill is rejected by either house, the bill dies.

The Senate and House must pass the exact same form of a bill before it can go to the president. Sometimes each chamber passes a different version of the same bill. When that happens, the bill is sent to a type of joint committee called a *conference committee*. The committee has members from each house who resolve the differences and make changes to the bill. That version of the bill then goes back to both chambers for a vote. At this point, both House and Senate must vote for the bill exactly as agreed to by the conference committee. No more changes are allowed.

Action by the President

Bills approved by both houses go to the president, who has three possible actions. The president may sign the bill into law. The president may veto, or refuse to sign, the bill. It is then returned to Congress, along with an explanation of the president's objections. The president may also do nothing. If Congress is in session, the bill becomes law after 10 days without the president's signature. If Congress is not in session, the bill dies after 10 days. Killing legislation in this indirect way is called a **pocket veto**.

If the president vetoes a bill, Congress has one last chance to make it law. If two-thirds of the

President George H. W. Bush held an outdoor signing ceremony when he signed the Americans with Disabilities Act into law in 1990.

members of each chamber vote in favor of overriding the veto, the bill becomes law. This is a difficult task. From 1789 through September 2021, Congress overturned only 112 out of 2,584 vetoes.

✓ CHECK FOR UNDERSTANDING

1. **Describing** What happens to a bill if it is approved in committee?
2. **Explaining** What are two ways that a president can prevent a bill from becoming law?

LESSON ACTIVITIES

1. **Informative/Explanatory Writing** Write a brief explanation of how a bill can *fail* to become a law. Note all the points during the lawmaking process in which the bill can be rejected. Consider numbering all the steps to help readers more easily understand the process.

2. **Collaborating** In a small group, research a bill that became law and prepare a presentation documenting the process of passing that bill. Discuss the actions that senators and representatives took as they considered the bill. Include the votes cast by the congresspeople from your district and state, and explain their reasons for those votes. Look for the record of their votes on the websites for the House and Senate.

roll-call vote a voting method in the Senate in which members voice their votes in turn
pocket veto president's power to kill a bill, if Congress is not in session, by not signing it for 10 days

06

Analyzing Sources: Representing the People

? COMPELLING QUESTION

Does the legislative branch today represent the people as was intended by the Framers?

Plan Your Inquiry

DEVELOPING QUESTIONS

Think about the debates that took place during the Constitutional Convention of 1787 and the role of the legislative branch today. Then read the Compelling Question for this lesson. What questions can you ask to help you answer this Compelling Question? Create a graphic organizer like the one below. Write these Supporting Questions in your graphic organizer.

Supporting Questions	Primary or Secondary Source	What this source tells me about the ways in which the legislative branch works and the Framers' intentions	Questions the source leaves unanswered
	A		
	B		
	C		
	D		
	E		
	F		

ANALYZING SOURCES

Next, examine the sources in this lesson. Analyze each source by answering the questions that follow it. How does each source help you answer each Supporting Question you created? What questions do you still have? Write these in your graphic organizer.

After you analyze the sources, you will:
- use the evidence from the sources,
- communicate your conclusions,
- and take informed action.

Background Information

The U.S. Constitution grants Congress the power to make laws. Congress is part of a government structure in which power is divided among three branches. The Framers included the concept of separation of powers in the new government to make sure that one institution or person did not hold too much power.

The Framers also provided ways for each branch to check the power of the other two. For example, the president, as head of the executive branch, can veto laws passed by Congress. However, the Framers believed that Congress, as the most representative body, should hold more power to govern than the others. Therefore they gave Congress a process to override a veto.

The Framers of the Constitution had to make compromises to produce this new framework for government. Over time, additional debates and compromises led to changes that exist today.

Senators meet in the Senate chamber, which is located inside the Capitol in Washington, D.C.

James Madison: The Role of the Senate

James Madison took detailed notes of the debates at the Constitutional Convention. The convention's delegates debated the format for the legislative body, finally agreeing to a plan with a bicameral Congress. Congress would have a House of Representatives, in which larger states would have more members, and a Senate, in which every state would have the same number of members. This compromise was designed to earn the support of both large and small states. In this excerpt, Madison records his response during a debate on the length of term for senators.

PRIMARY SOURCE: SPEECH

66 In order to judge of the form to be given to this institution, it will be proper to take a view of the ends to be served by it. These were first to protect the people agst. [against] their rulers: secondly to protect the people agst. the **transient** impressions into which they themselves might be led. A people deliberating . . . on the plan of Govt. most likely to secure their happiness, would first be aware, that those chargd. [charged] with the public happiness, might betray their trust. An obvious precaution agst. this danger wd. [would] be to divide the trust between different bodies of men, who might watch & check each other. . . . It wd. next occur to such a people . . . that men chosen for a short term, & employed but a small portion of that in public affairs, might err. . . . This reflection wd. naturally suggest that the Govt. be so constituted [created], as that one of its branches might have an oppy. [opportunity] of acquiring a competent knowledge of the public interests. Another reflection equally becoming a people on such an occasion, wd. be that they themselves, as well as a numerous body of Representatives, were liable [likely] to **err** also, from **fickleness** and passion. A necessary fence agst. this danger would be to select a portion of enlightened [informed] citizens, whose limited number, and firmness might seasonably **interpose** agst. **impetuous** councils. 99

— James Madison, Debates in Convention, June 26, 1787

transient short-term, brief

err to make a mistake

fickleness given to sudden change; unreliable

interpose to put oneself between

impetuous marked by rash, or sudden, behavior

EXAMINE THE SOURCE

1. **Analyzing Perspectives** Why does Madison argue for a Congress made up of two bodies? Why does he suggest a longer term for members of the Senate?

2. **Drawing Conclusions** In his speech, Madison refers to a part of Congress as a "necessary fence." To which part is he referring? How do you know? Why might he use that term?

PHOTO: WDC Photos/Alamy Stock Photo; TEXT: Madison, J., Madison Debates, Tuesday June 26, 1787, Yale Law School

B

Bob Dole on Leadership

From 1998 to 2002, the Senate hosted a series of lectures in which lawmakers discussed the institution's history and practices. Senator Bob Dole of Kansas, who served in the Senate from 1969 to 1996, took part. Previously, he had served four terms in the U.S. House of Representatives.

PRIMARY SOURCE: SPEECH

❝ Unfettered [unrestrained] by ancient hatreds, the founders raised a lofty [high] standard—admittedly too high for their own generation to obtain, yet a continuing source of inspiration to their descendants—for whom America is nothing if not a **work in progress**. . . .

It is precisely because I have experienced so much of our past that I have no fears—no fears—for our future, not so long as this institution continues to attract men and women who are patriots as well as **partisans**, legislators who combine **idealism** and **realism**, and who answer to posterity [future generations] rather than polltakers. Anyone can take a poll; only a true leader can move a nation. ❞

— Senator Bob Dole, Address to the U.S. Senate, March 28, 2000

work in progress unfinished project

partisan someone loyal to a political party

idealism a way of thinking based on a belief that one can reach high goals

realism a way of thinking that focuses on practical solutions to problems

EXAMINE THE SOURCE

1. **Explaining** What did Dole mean when he said that America is "a work in progress"?
2. **Analyzing Perspectives** Why does Dole have confidence in the Congress?

C

Partisan Interests and Aid

By March 2020 in the United States, the outbreak of COVID-19 had become a pandemic, or a disease affecting a large part of the population. To slow its spread, some state governments required businesses to close. Millions of people lost their jobs. Congress passed the CARES Act to provide financial relief, but the funds ran out. Americans looked to Congress for help. For months, lawmakers debated the type and amount of aid to offer. In December 2020, Congress passed another relief bill. Representative Jared Golden of Maine spoke about partisanship in the passing of the CARES Act.

PRIMARY SOURCE: PRESS RELEASE

❝ The unwillingness of so many members of Congress to accept compromise throughout the fall has been deeply frustrating for so many people who are facing economic uncertainty and concerns about their health and well-being. This legislation will provide much-needed aid to small businesses and hospitals, the unemployed, and families struggling to put food on the table. It will also provide funds to speed the availability of the COVID-19 vaccine. . . .

We shouldn't let the fact that Congress is finally taking action distract from its failure to act sooner. This relief legislation could have and should have happened months ago, and it's sad that congressional leaders let partisan interests get in the way of agreeing to an earlier deal. ❞

— Representative Jared Golden, "Golden Statement on Passage of COVID-19 Relief Package, Government Funding Bill," December 21, 2020

EXAMINE THE SOURCE

1. **Explaining** Why does Golden say it took so long for Congress to pass the relief bill?
2. **Analyzing Perspectives** What is Golden's opinion of how well Congress did its job to help Americans during the COVID-19 pandemic? Can you imagine a different opinion about the same topic?

Partisanship and Cooperation in Congress

Citizens and politicians alike generally agree that extreme partisanship is not good for the government and the country. In this article, Dr. Molly Reynolds, a political researcher, examines the history of partisanship in Congress and how it affects the work of the legislative branch. The photograph shows Senators Mitch McConnell, a Republican (left), and Chuck Schumer, a Democrat (right).

SECONDARY SOURCE: ARTICLE

❝ Increasing **partisanship** has also made it more difficult for members of Congress to assert [use] its authority as the first branch. The **electoral fate** of individual legislators is now more closely tied to national political forces than in previous eras [time periods]. Voters **split their tickets** at much lower rates; in 2016, for example, no state elected a senator from one party while awarding its Electoral College votes to a presidential candidate of a different party. . . . These electoral circumstances reduce the **incentive** of many legislators to **work across the aisle**. . . .

The increased competition for partisan control of the House and Senate has also made working with members from the opposite party less attractive. Between the early 1950s and the early 1980s, Democrats held a virtual lock on the congressional majority, and Republicans did not reasonably expect to regain the majority after each **successive** election. Since roughly 1980, however, both parties have seen achieving a majority in the next cycle [election] as an at least somewhat achievable goal. Because of this heightened [greater] competition, members of the minority party have fewer reasons to work with their majority party **counterparts** to make them seem like **capable** legislators. ❞

— Molly Reynolds, "Improving Congressional Capacity to Address Problems and Oversee the Executive Branch," *Policy 2020*, December 4, 2019

partisanship a strong commitment to one political party

electoral fate outcome of political elections

split their ticket to vote for candidates from more than one political party for different positions

incentive something that moves a person to take a certain action

work across the aisle to work on legislation with members of the opposite political party

successive following in order without interruption

counterpart someone in a similar position

capable able to get work done or achieve a goal

EXAMINE THE SOURCE

1. **Identifying Cause and Effect** According to Reynolds, why has partisanship in Congress increased since the early 1980s?

2. **Analyzing Perspectives** Why might members of the minority party choose not to work with members of the majority party on legislation?

PHOTO: Drew Angerer/Getty Images; TEXT: Reynolds, M.E., "Improving congressional capacity to address problems and oversee the executive branch" December 4, 2019, Brookings

The Work of Lobbyists

Special interest groups work to influence voters, lawmakers, and other officials. They bring together people who share a goal and want to achieve change through public policy. Many represent specific groups of people, such as farmers, small business owners, veterans, or senior citizens. They might also represent businesses, such as insurance companies, or causes, such as protecting the environment. Special interest groups employ lobbyists to work with and influence government officials on legislation that affects the group's members.

SECONDARY SOURCE: BOOK

> 66 The most active companies now have upwards of 100 lobbyists representing them who are active on a similar number of different bills in a given [particular] session of Congress. They serve as **de facto** adjunct [temporary] staff for congressional offices, drafting bills, providing testimony, and generally helping to move legislation forward. They provide policy expertise, helping **stretched-too-thin** staffers to get up to speed [become informed] on a wide range of subjects and assisting administrative agencies in writing complex rules. They provide generous funding for **think tanks** and fill the intellectual environment of Washington with panel discussions and **op-eds** and subway advertisements. They build large coalitions, mobilize [organize] **grassroots constituencies**, and **discredit** opponents. They host fundraising events and donate to charities. They hire former congressional staffers and former members of Congress and former agency **bureaucrats** and former agency heads by the dozens to make sure they have a connection to every person who matters, as well as an insider's understanding on how the process works and how to work the process. They heed [follow] the old Washington adage [saying], 'if you are not at the table, you are probably on the menu,' by showing up at every table. 99

— Lee Drutman, *The Business of America is Lobbying: How Corporations Became Politicized and Politics Became More Corporate*, 2015

de facto in effect

stretched-too-thin not having enough time to do all the work

think tank an institution formed to study and share information about a particular subject

op-ed an opinion essay in a news outlet

coalition a temporary alliance of people or groups to work toward a shared goal

grassroots constituency a group of people that agrees on a policy or action and makes their views known

discredit to portray in a negative way

bureaucrat a government worker who is not elected

EXAMINE THE SOURCE

1. **Explaining** How does the author show the influence of lobbyists on members of Congress?

2. **Interpreting** What does the phrase "If you are not at the table, you are probably on the menu," mean? How does it guide lobbyists?

"Government Can Be a Force for Good"

Many Americans believe that Congress is too partisan and accomplishes little valuable work. Senator Elizabeth Warren of Massachusetts spoke about her hopes of regaining the country's faith in the government.

PRIMARY SOURCE: SPEECH

" There are millions of good people working in government. People who show up to do a hard day's work in federal, state and local government. . . .

They are Members of Congress on both sides of the aisle, their staffs, **interns** and volunteers. . . .

They are unified by a belief in the greater good of government. . . .

Only 18% of Americans believe our government is doing right most of the time. But I'm not throwing my hands up [quitting] and walking away. I'm not giving in to the **cynicism**. I still believe . . . government can be a force for good to bring us back together. . . .

Americans know that they have a government that isn't working for them. But instead of giving up, more and more people are demanding a government that is run by the people for the people. "

— Senator Elizabeth Warren, at the National Press Club in Washington, D.C., on August 18, 2018

intern a person who works in an organization to gain experience

cynicism belief that people are not driven by good motives

EXAMINE THE SOURCE

1. **Analyzing Perspectives** Does Warren believe that American government is fundamentally bad? Explain.

2. **Explaining** How does Warren think Americans are reacting to the problems they see in government?

Complete Your Inquiry

EVALUATE SOURCES AND USE EVIDENCE

Refer back to the Compelling Question and the Supporting Questions you developed at the beginning of the lesson.

1. **Comparing and Contrasting** Think about the views expressed in Sources B and F. How does Dole's view of the future of Congress compare and contrast with Warren's?

2. **Synthesizing** How do the authors of Sources C and D view the dangers of partisanship?

3. **Gathering Sources** Which sources helped you answer the Supporting Questions and the Compelling Question? Which sources, if any, challenged what you thought you knew when you first created your Supporting Questions? What information do you still need in order to answer your questions? What other viewpoints would you like to investigate? Where would you find that information?

4. **Evaluating Sources** Identify the sources that helped answer your Supporting Questions. How reliable are the sources? How would you verify the reliability of the sources?

COMMUNICATE CONCLUSIONS

5. **Collaborating** With a partner, make a two-column chart. In the first column, list evidence from the sources showing how Congress should work for the people. In the second column, list evidence from the sources showing how Congress has failed to do so. Share your chart with another pair and discuss any differences.

TAKE INFORMED ACTION

Encouraging Cooperation Learn about your senators' positions on policy issues. Visit their official websites and review their positions on past legislation. Look for evidence showing whether they worked with members of the opposite party or voted the same as their own party most of the time. Then write a letter to each senator thanking them for their cooperation or encouraging them to work more closely with members of the other party.

PHOTO:Sara Stathas/Alamy Stock Photo; TEXT: Warren, E., Remarks at National Press Club, Washington, DC, August, 21, 2018, U.S. Senate

07
Reviewing The Legislative Branch

Summary

Congress's Structure
Congress has two houses: the House of Representatives and the Senate. The Senate has two members from each state. The number of House members from each state depends on the state's population.

Congress's Powers
Congress uses its expressed and implied powers to make laws. It also has nonlegislative powers that give it checks on the executive and judicial branches. The Constitution puts some limits on what Congress can do.

How Congress Works
Members of the House and Senate must meet certain requirements. Leaders guide the work in each chamber. Members of Congress receive help from their staff and agencies. They pass laws and help constituents.

How a Bill Becomes a Law
After a bill is introduced, it is discussed in a committee. If the committee passes a bill, it is considered by the full House or Senate. A bill becomes a law if both houses pass it and the president signs it.

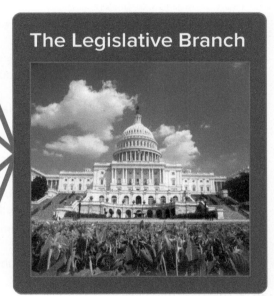

The Legislative Branch

Checking For Understanding

Answer the questions to see if you understood the topic content.

IDENTIFY AND EXPLAIN

1. Identify each of the following terms and explain its significance to the legislative branch.

   A. Senate
   B. House of Representatives
   C. expressed power
   D. impeach
   E. writ of habeas corpus
   F. casework
   G. filibuster
   H. roll-call vote

REVIEWING KEY FACTS

2. **Explaining** How did the Framers of the Constitution compromise so that both large and small states were satisfied that they were well-represented in Congress?

3. **Contrasting** How are the presiding officers of the House and Senate different?

4. **Explaining** How does Congress address the large workload of reviewing thousands of proposed laws in a single session?

5. **Evaluating** Why is Article I, Section 8, Clause 18 also known as the elastic clause?

6. **Making Connections** What part of the Constitution prevents Congress from passing laws that limit freedom of the press?

7. **Identifying** What are the qualifications for members of the House of Representatives?

8. **Explaining** Why do lawmakers devote time and resources to casework?

9. **Contrasting** How do private bills and public bills differ?

10. **Explaining** What happens to a bill after it is introduced by a member of Congress and given a title and number?

CRITICAL THINKING

11. **Identifying Cause and Effect** What effect does gerrymandering often have on congressional districts?

12. **Analyzing** What is the benefit of having a line of succession for the presidency that includes the Speaker of the House and the president pro tempore of the Senate?

13. **Drawing Conclusions** Why does the Constitution forbid Congress to pass bills of attainder and ex post facto laws and to block the writ of habeas corpus except in special circumstances?

14. **Drawing Conclusions** The powers to collect taxes, borrow money, regulate commerce, and raise an army are expressed powers given to Congress. Why were these powers considered so important that they were included in the Constitution?

15. **Identifying** What power does the judicial branch have to check the power of Congress to pass laws?

16. **Analyzing** How does the Congressional Budget Office (CBO) aid members of Congress in the creation of a bill?

17. **Speculating** Why do you think members of Congress should be especially careful when dealing with lobbyists who promote interest groups?

18. **Identifying Cause and Effect** Why do members of Congress work hard to bring pork-barrel projects to their home district or state?

19. **Evaluating** Why is the work of the standing committees so critical in the lawmaking process?

20. **Explaining** What actions can the president take on a bill after both houses of Congress approve it?

NEED EXTRA HELP?

If You've Missed Question	1	2	3	4	5	6	7	8	9	10
Review Lesson	2–5	2	2	2	3	3	4	4	5	5

If You've Missed Question	11	12	13	14	15	16	17	18	19	20
Review Lesson	2	2	3	3	3	4	4	4	5	5

Apply What You Have Learned

A Understanding Multiple Perspectives

Over the past several decades, the filibuster has been increasingly used to stop legislation from coming to a vote. In the past, a senator using the filibuster needed to speak on the floor of the Senate. However, this is no longer how the filibuster works. Senators can now use what is called the *silent filibuster* to stop legislation. This allows the Senate majority leader to refuse to call a vote on legislation if at least 41 senators simply threaten a filibuster.

ACTIVITY **Writing an Argumentative Essay About the Filibuster** Write a blog post that argues either for or against keeping the filibuster as an option to delay or prevent a vote in the Senate. Conduct research to learn more about the arguments in favor of and against the filibuster. Then decide which side of the argument you are on, and take a stand. When writing your blog post, explain the opposing viewpoint, and present your reasons to oppose those arguments. Address the arguments in these two passages when writing your blog post.

❝ The framers designed the Senate to require deliberation [careful thought] . . . to force cooperation . . . and to ensure that federal laws in our big, diverse country earn broad enough buy-in [acceptance] to receive the lasting consent of the governed.

James Madison said the Senate should be a 'complicated check' against 'improper acts of legislation.' Thomas Jefferson said 'great innovations should not be forced on slender [small] majorities.' ❞

— Senator Mitch McConnell, March 2021

❝ The Founders considered requiring House or Senate supermajorities [large majorities] to pass bills. But they said no—a simple majority in the House, a simple majority in the Senate, & a presidential sign-off [approval] should be enough. It was good enough for them. It's good enough for me. ❞

— Senator Elizabeth Warren, June 2021

B Understanding Chronology

In November 1916, Jeannette Rankin of Montana became the first woman elected to the U.S. House of Representatives—four years before the Nineteenth Amendment gave all women the right to vote in national elections. Over time, more women were elected to Congress. Today, an increasing, but still low, number of women serve in Congress.

ACTIVITY **Creating a Time Line of Women in Congress** Research the history of women in the Senate and the House of Representatives. Then create a time line that shows six to eight key events demonstrating the growing gender diversity of Congress. Include events such as when the first African American woman was elected to the House of Representatives and when the first woman was elected to the Senate. Place the entries on your time line in chronological order. Provide short explanations of the significance of each event.

Jeannette Rankin

PHOTO: Library of Congress, Prints & Photographs Division [LC-DIG-ggbain-23837]; TEXT:(t) McConnell, M. "Democrats Hypocritically Killing the Filibuster Would Break the Senate" Washington, D.C., March 16 2021, U.S. Senate, (b) Warren, E., End the Filibuster, June 3, 2021, Twitter

C Building Citizenship

In this lesson you have learned how a bill becomes a law. It starts with an idea. A bill is drafted and then submitted by a member of Congress. Each bill must have a title. The body of the legislation includes the main effect of the legislation, any limits or restrictions, and the cost of the legislation.

ACTIVITY **Drafting a Bill for a Community Problem** Think about a problem in your community and how it might be addressed. Are there ways a new law might help solve this problem? Learn about bills that have been written to address similar problems. Then draft a bill to help solve the problem in your community. Summarize the proposed law and include a title, the main effect of the legislation, and any limits or costs. Share your draft of the bill with your classmates. Discuss the values and potential drawbacks of the bill. Then take a vote on whether or not the bill will help solve the community problem.

D Making Connections to Today

The Constitution requires the federal government to conduct a census every 10 years to count the number of people who live in the United States. The purpose of the census is to determine how many representatives each state may send to the House of Representatives. After each census, states may lose or gain one or more seats because of the change in their population. Usually, most states do not experience a change. Districts might also be redrawn after a census, so some people may have a different representative serving them. This process of redistributing representatives is called *reapportionment*.

ACTIVITY **Creating a Presentation on Reapportionment** Working in a small group, go online and research if and how districts in your state changed after the censuses of 2000, 2010, and 2020. Determine the number of congressional districts assigned to your state after each census. Did the number of districts increase, decrease, or stay the same? Determine if and how your district was redrawn because of each census. Then create a presentation that shows your state's districts after each census, placing a border around your own district. In addition to maps, include statistics that explain how your district may have changed. Include information about the party affiliations of the people who live in the district. If you do not live in a state with multiple districts, choose another state to research.

TOPIC

4

From the White House, President Joe Biden addresses the nation about the COVID-19 vaccine in 2021.

The Executive Branch

Introducing The Executive Branch

Office of the President

Since 1789, forty-five individuals have served as president of the United States. The president is the head of the executive branch. The president enforces laws and serves as commander in chief of the military. Many agencies and individuals, including the vice president and the president's cabinet, work within the executive branch.

Presidential Inauguration: Then and Now

The Framers of the Constitution originally set the date for presidential inauguration as March 4. In the earlier years of the United States, it took a lot of time to communicate information. With election day in November, transitioning power on March 4 gave plenty of time to do this. Eventually, as communication became faster, four months was too long to wait to inaugurate a newly elected president. In 1933, just after Franklin D. Roosevelt was sworn into office, Congress ratified the Twentieth Amendment to move inauguration day to January 20.

» Inauguration of President Franklin D. Roosevelt, March 4, 1933

» Inauguration of President George W. Bush, January 20, 2005

> 66 I do solemnly swear (or affirm) that I will faithfully execute the Office of President of the United States, and will to the best of my Ability, preserve, protect and defend the Constitution of the United States. 99
>
> —*U.S. presidential oath of office*

» On a chilly and cloudy March 4, 1841, William Henry Harrison was inaugurated as the ninth President of the United States. Harrison refused to wear a coat for the two-hour ceremony, where he gave the longest inaugural address in history. Soon after, he developed pneumonia. He died a month later, becoming the shortest-serving president and first president to die in office.

Birth States of the Presidents

Twenty-one states have been the birthplace of U.S. presidents. Virginia and Ohio are the most common, with 15 out of 46 presidents being born in those two states.

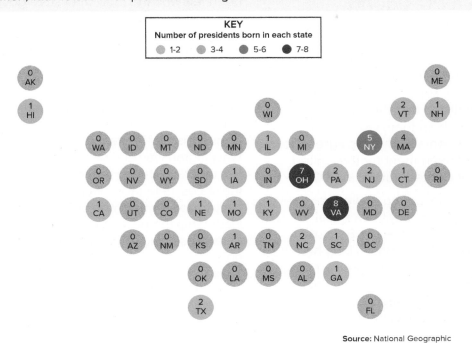

KEY
Number of presidents born in each state
● 1-2 ● 3-4 ● 5-6 ● 7-8

0 AK	0 ME
1 HI	2 VT 1 NH

0 WA | 0 ID | 0 MT | 0 ND | 0 MN | 1 IL | 0 MI | 5 NY | 4 MA

0 OR | 0 NV | 0 WY | 0 SD | 1 IA | 0 IN | 7 OH | 2 PA | 2 NJ | 1 CT | 0 RI

1 CA | 0 UT | 0 CO | 1 NE | 1 MO | 1 KY | 0 WV | 8 VA | 0 MD | 0 DE

0 AZ | 0 NM | 0 KS | 1 AR | 0 TN | 2 NC | 1 SC | 0 DC

0 OK | 0 LA | 0 MS | 0 AL | 1 GA

2 TX | 0 FL

Source: National Geographic

Presidents' Political Parties, 1789–2021

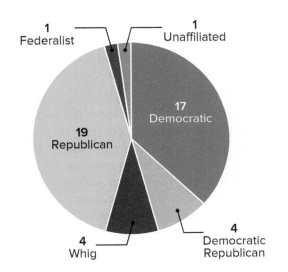

- 1 Federalist
- 1 Unaffiliated
- 17 Democratic
- 19 Republican
- 4 Whig
- 4 Democratic Republican

Today, the two main political parties are the Democratic and Republican parties. As the graph shows, other political parties have existed throughout American history. The only president not affiliated with a political party was the first president, George Washington.

Presidential Pets

Most presidents have pets during their time in the White House. They range from exotic to the most common of house pets, like dogs and cats. Exotic or uncommon pets, such as a hyena, were typically gifts from foreign leaders to the president.

- Most common presidential pet: Dog
- Hyena—T. Roosevelt
- Bears—T. Roosevelt, Coolidge, Jefferson
- Alligators—J.C. Adams, Hoover
- Bald Eagles—Buchanan

» Rebecca the Raccoon and First Lady Grace Coolidge, 1927

Getting Ready to Learn About . . .
The Executive Branch

Why Is There a President?

Today, the president of the United States is often considered the most powerful person in the country, or even the world. But that was not always the case. As the Revolutionary War raged, leaders in the 13 former British colonies fighting for independence realized that they needed a central government to help them work together. Members of the Continental Congress agreed to the very first plan of government for the United States, the Articles of Confederation, in 1777.

Under the Articles, governing power was placed entirely in a legislature with an equal number of members from each state. Because American leaders believed the British king had abused his authority, they remained concerned about placing a large amount of power in the hands of a single person. The Articles, therefore, did not call for a chief executive, or president. The Confederation Congress did, however, choose a leader with the title "President of the United States, in Congress assembled." This president's power was limited to overseeing the work of Congress. The powerful position of president that exists today was created several years later when the U.S. Constitution was adopted.

Weaknesses in the Articles of Confederation hindered the new country both during and after the Revolutionary War. Too much power had been left with the individual state governments. The new national government faced economic crisis, but it had little power to overrule the individual states and collect taxes. The lack of a chief executive with national powers also made it difficult to govern the country.

The Founders knew that a change needed to occur, so they held the 1787 Constitutional Convention in Philadelphia, Pennsylvania. George Washington was elected to preside over, or lead, this meeting. During the four-month convention, the states' delegates decided to create a stronger central government and debated what type of leadership the new country should possess. The delegates decided on three equal branches of government: the legislative, judicial, and executive. They did not want a leader with limitless powers, as in the British monarchy they had fought. Instead, they desired a single executive leader who had clearly defined powers under a constitution. George Washington would continue to lead by becoming the first president of the United States in April 1789.

What Does the President Do?

On most days, the media reports on the actions of the president of the United States. What does a president do that deserves so much attention? And what makes a great president? Why have a number of presidents come to be considered some of history's greatest leaders?

Presidents have diverse backgrounds and experiences prior to being elected. George Washington was a farmer and a military leader. Many presidents have been lawyers and politicians. Donald Trump, the 45th president, was a businessperson with no previous political or military experience when he won the presidency.

Presidents can reflect the values and culture of American society during a particular time in history. They can also influence through their executive role and distinct leadership position. For example, while ensuring that legislation is carried out once it is passed, presidents can suggest new laws they believe would benefit the country. At the same time, the president serves as the leader of U.S. foreign policy and spends time meeting and negotiating with other world leaders.

» George Washington, first U.S. president

Stand Out Leaders

Each president faces unique challenges while they hold office. As the first president, George Washington was tasked with determining exactly what the role of the president should be and what actions a president should take.

Washington's meetings with trusted advisers created the presidential cabinet. Washington was always mindful, and aware, that his actions would have future consequences. He wanted Americans to never forget that the United States does not have a monarchy with lifetime appointments, but rather a leader who is elected by the people, for the people. So he stepped down after two terms. This set a precedent, or example, for all future presidents with the exception of Franklin D. Roosevelt who was elected to four terms during an especially difficult time in the country's history.

Many presidents served the country during times of crisis. One role of the president is leader of the country's armed forces. While presidents do not lead troops in battle, they are responsible for major decisions regarding the military. Abraham Lincoln, the 16th president, led the country during the Civil War and eventually brought about a military victory. During those years, dealing with the questions of slavery and rebellion, Lincoln proved to be a wise and understanding leader of the American people.

Some presidents are remembered because they took the nation to new frontiers. John F. Kennedy, the 35th president, brought a fresh perspective to the office with actions like permanent creation of the U.S. Peace Corps, in an effort to "promote world peace and friendship." JFK urged Americans to be community-focused, which he proclaimed by saying, *"Ask not what your country can do for you – ask what you can do for your country."* He also drastically expanded the space program and sent U.S. astronauts to outer space.

More recently, presidents have dealt with changing world politics and unexpected attacks from new groups. George W. Bush, 43rd president, led the country during the September 11, 2001 terrorist attacks. He continued to lead as military actions and war followed in the Middle East.

Enduring Legacy

While many presidents have not faced crises that allowed them to perform extraordinary acts of leadership, they all have worked to better the lives of Americans. Presidents address the details of American society, the economy, and foreign policy on a daily basis. The only constant for the President of the United States is that their role, duties, and challenges will never be entirely the same as for those who came before them. As American society and global issues change, so too will the position of the U.S. president.

A few challenges to the executive branch will endure regardless of the year, as President George Washington knew. When he delivered his Farewell Address, in 1796, he stressed the importance of the country remaining united and cautioned against three things: cultural division, allowing political parties to create division, and involvement within foreign wars.

In modern politics, there is an echo of Washington's warning from over 200 years ago. However, Washington had hope for the new nation, declaring, *"Liberty itself will find in such a government, with powers properly distributed and adjusted, its surest guardian."* When Washington delivered this statement, he set the most enduring legacy for this position, the idea that America will always work toward a better future, despite the challenges.

In February 1962, President John F. Kennedy and astronaut Lieutenant Colonel John Glenn, Jr., peer into the Mercury *Friendship 7* spacecraft. This space capsule helped John Glenn, Jr., become the first American to orbit the Earth.

Looking Ahead

You will learn about the executive branch of the federal government. You will examine a Compelling Question and develop your own questions about the executive branch in the Inquiry Activity. You can preview some of the key concepts that you will learn about by reviewing the infographic.

What Will You Learn?

In these lessons focused on the executive branch, you will learn:

- the requirements for becoming president and vice president.
- how the president is selected.
- the importance of the position of vice president.
- the roles of the president and the functions performed with each role.

- the powers granted to the president by the Constitution.
- the duties and responsibilities of the executive branch.
- that the president has a lot of help to carry out major duties.
- that the work of the executive branch affects the lives of all Americans.

 COMPELLING QUESTION IN THE INQUIRY ACTIVITY LESSON

- **How much power should the president have?**

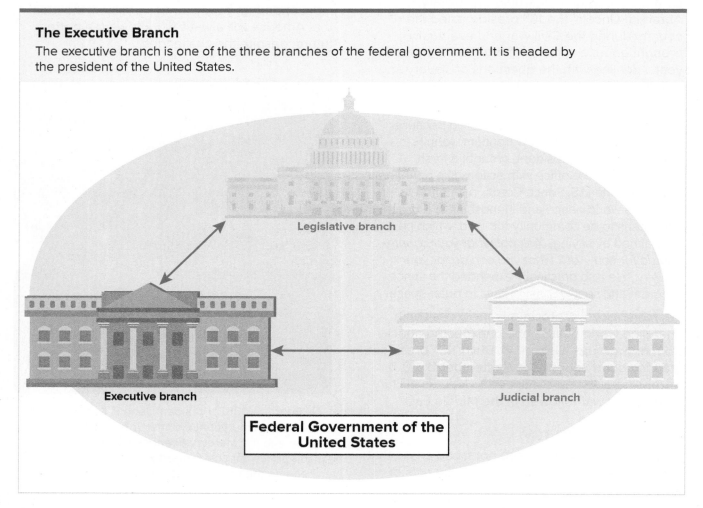

The Executive Branch

The executive branch is one of the three branches of the federal government. It is headed by the president of the United States.

Legislative branch

Executive branch

Judicial branch

Federal Government of the United States

The President and Vice President

READING STRATEGY

Integrating Knowledge and Ideas As you read, complete a graphic organizer such as this one to record key facts about the offices of president and vice president of the United States.

	Key Facts
President	
• Requirements: • Election: • Benefits: • Succession:	
• Characteristics of past officeholders	
Vice President	
• Requirements: • Election: • Benefits: • Succession:	
• Characteristics of past officeholders	

Office of the President

GUIDING QUESTION

How does a citizen become president?

What would you write in a job description for potential applicants for the position of president of the United States? You might ask for someone who is honest, strong, and responsible. The U.S. Constitution sets three requirements for someone to be eligible to become president:

- The candidate must be at least 35 years old.
- The candidate must be a native-born American citizen.
- The candidate must have lived in the United States for at least 14 years.

Even though there are only three requirements to be eligible to run for president, you might include other characteristics in the job description. The president of the United States is often said to be the most powerful person in the world. The job is challenging. It takes a lot of skill, talent, and appropriate experience to be responsible for running a nation of more than 330 million people. To do this job well, a person should have good communication skills, excellent organization skills, political skill, and a clear sense of policy goals.

Some people would also list experience in government in a job description. Nearly every U.S. president has previously been a vice president, a member of Congress, a state governor, or a general in the U.S. Army. One exception was Donald Trump, a businessperson who was elected as president in 2016 with no previous government experience.

In addition, you would probably want to make sure that the president shared some of your most important opinions about issues. Choosing a president who shares your opinions is one way to exercise your power in a democracy.

Characteristics of Presidents

More than 40 people have held the office of president of the United States. They have been as different as the energetic Theodore Roosevelt and the reserved Calvin Coolidge. One—William Henry Harrison—served only a month before dying in office.

» Before he was elected president, Joe Biden served as vice president from 2009 to 2017, under Barack Obama.

Franklin Delano Roosevelt, on the other hand, won four elections to the presidency and served more than 12 years.

Despite their differences, past U.S. presidents share several traits. To start, they all have been men. All but one of the presidents have been white. Barack Obama became the first African American president when he took office in 2009.

Most presidents have been college educated. Since it is helpful in the role of president to have some understanding of law, it is not surprising that many presidents have been lawyers.

Most presidents have held moderate political positions. Candidates who have extreme views have little chance of being elected. For that reason, the major parties usually choose candidates who are moderate. Exceptions, such as the very conservative Barry Goldwater and the very liberal George McGovern, can win a party's nomination. Both lost by wide margins in the general election, however.

Presidents—and candidates for president—have been more diverse in recent years. Before 1960, all presidents had been Protestant Christians. That year, John F. Kennedy, a Roman Catholic, won election as president. He remained unique until Joe Biden, another Catholic, was elected in 2020. In 2000 Joseph Lieberman was the first Jewish vice presidential candidate. Twelve years later, Republican Mitt Romney became the first Mormon to win a major party's nomination for president. Both Lieberman and Romney were defeated.

Women have been more active in presidential races in recent years also. In 2016 Democrat Hillary Clinton was the first woman to win a major party's nomination for president. Two women—Democrat Geraldine Ferraro and Republican Sarah Palin—ran for vice president but lost.

Most vice presidents have been white males. There have been two exceptions. In 2021 Kamala Harris took office as the first female, the first Asian American, and the first African American to be vice president. Charles Curtis, who was vice president from 1929 to 1933, was part Native American.

Electing the President and Vice President

Every four years, in years that can be divided by the number four, the nation elects a president. For example, 2012, 2016, and 2020 were all presidential election years.

While voters cast votes for president and vice president on Election Day, those votes do not directly choose the winners. Instead, the president and vice president are elected by a group called the Electoral College. The Electoral College is made up of 538 members called **electors**. Each state has as many electors as they have people serving in Congress. Wyoming, with two senators and one member of the House, has three electors. Georgia, with 2 senators and 14 members of the House, has 16 electoral votes. In addition, the District of Columbia has three electors. Political parties choose who they want to serve as electors. Those people promise to vote for their party's candidates. On Election Day in November, voters are really voting for the electors from the party of the two candidates whose names they mark. The electors cast their votes in December, and Congress officially counts them the next month. That is when the winners of the election are officially declared.

Most states award their electoral votes on a "winner-take-all" basis. Whichever presidential and vice presidential pair wins the state's popular vote—the most votes by regular voters—receives all the state's electoral votes. For example, in 2020, President Donald Trump and Vice President Mike Pence won about 51% of the vote in Florida and were awarded all of Florida's 29 electoral votes. As a result, an election can end with the popular vote close, but one candidate having a large electoral vote majority.

elector person appointed by their party to vote in presidential elections for president and vice president

On January 20, 2021, Kamala Harris made history by becoming the first woman to serve as vice president.

Presidential Election of 2020

Democrat Joe Biden won the 2020 presidential election with a total of 306 electoral votes.

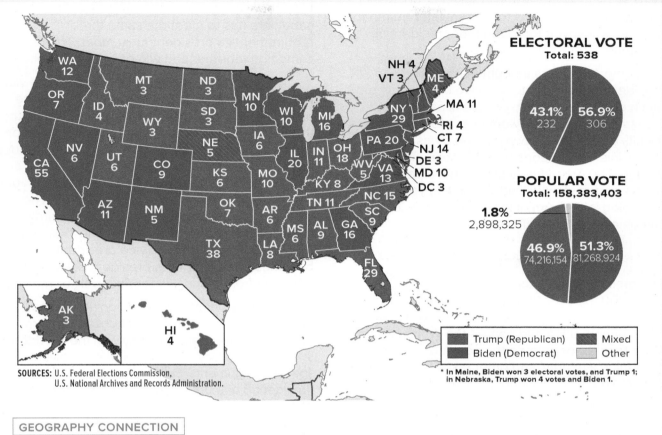

ELECTORAL VOTE
Total: 538

43.1% 232
56.9% 306

POPULAR VOTE
Total: 158,383,403

1.8% 2,898,325

46.9% 74,216,154
51.3% 81,268,924

Trump (Republican)
Biden (Democrat)
Mixed
Other

SOURCES: U.S. Federal Elections Commission,
U.S. National Archives and Records Administration.

* In Maine, Biden won 3 electoral votes, and Trump 1;
in Nebraska, Trump won 4 votes and Biden 1.

GEOGRAPHY CONNECTION

1. **Exploring Place** Who won the state of Minnesota, and how many electoral votes did that victory represent?
2. **Exploring Regions** Which parts of the country most favored Biden, and which most favored Trump?

That happened in 2020. An election can also end with the loser of the popular vote winning a majority of the electoral vote. That happened in 2016.

The winning pair must gain at least 270 electoral votes—more than half of the 538 total electoral votes. What happens if no one gains that majority? The election goes to Congress. The House of Representatives then elects the president, which happened in 1800 and 1824. The Senate decides who will be vice president.

Less than 20 years after the Constitution was adopted and the electoral system was put in place, it was changed to fix unforeseen problems. Under the original system, each elector simply cast two votes. The person with the most votes became president and the one with the second most became vice president. In the 1796 election, John Adams won as president and Thomas

Jefferson won as vice president. They came from two different political parties, though, and did not work well together. Four years later, two candidates—Thomas Jefferson and Aaron Burr—received the same number of electoral votes. The tie had to be settled in the House of Representatives, which elected Jefferson as president and Burr as vice president.

To prevent these problems from ever happening again, Congress passed the Twelfth Amendment, which the states ratified in 1804. This amendment required presidential electors to vote separately for president and vice president.

Term of Office

Presidents serve four-year terms, and they can only be elected twice. Originally, the Constitution placed no limit on the number of terms a president could serve.

It became a tradition to serve only two terms following the example set by George Washington, the first president. The tradition ended in 1940. In 1940, early in World War II, Franklin D. Roosevelt ran for a third term, and four years later he ran for another. Roosevelt thus won four presidential elections.

Some Americans thought that electing a president for so many terms gave one person too much power. As a result, Congress passed, and the states ratified, the Twenty-second Amendment. It limits a president to two elected terms in office. It is possible for someone to serve nearly 10 years, though. The Amendment allows that a person who becomes president with less than two years remaining in the term of the previous president can be elected to two full terms.

Salary and Benefits

The president receives a yearly salary of $400,000, plus an allowance for living costs and travel expenses. The president is provided with a combination office and home—the White House. More than 90 people do the cooking, cleaning, gardening, security, and other tasks to care for the president's family and the White House.

Presidents have a few other benefits. When they want a break from the White House, they can visit Camp David, an estate about 60 miles northwest of Washington, D.C. When they travel, presidents ride in special cars, helicopters, and airplanes, and they are accompanied by many aides and advisers. Some of the 3,200 Secret Service agents are on duty at all times to protect the president, vice president, and their families.

Air Force One is the presidential jet. It has office space for the president, a medical area with an operating room, and two kitchens. There is also space for aides, press members, and guests.

The Vice President

Political parties choose a person as their party's candidate for vice president at the same time they choose a presidential candidate. The candidate has to meet the same three requirements a president must meet. The two campaign together and win or lose together.

The Constitution gives little power to the vice president. Most of what it states about the vice president is found in Article I and has to do with the Senate. The vice president presides over, or oversees, the Senate, but the vice president does not vote on bills in the Senate unless there is a tie. A tie vote is most likely to occur if the number of senators from each party is exactly 50. The main job of vice presidents is one they hardly ever have the opportunity to do: The Twenty-fifth Amendment says that the vice president becomes president if the president dies, is removed from office, falls seriously ill, or resigns.

A vice president's work and power can be much greater if the president chooses. Modern vice presidents have met frequently with the president, taken part in policy meetings, and been given special assignments. For example, in 2021, President Biden put Vice President Harris in charge of the effort to reduce the number of people illegally entering the country along the southern border.

The vice president's salary is more than $250,000. Since the late 1970s, vice presidents and their families have lived in a home on the grounds of the U.S. Naval Observatory in Washington, D.C. Vice presidents have an office in the West Wing of the White House. Vice presidents also have use of a special plane, which is called *Air Force Two* when they fly on it.

✓ **CHECK FOR UNDERSTANDING**

1. **Summarizing** What are the three requirements stated in the Constitution for serving as president or vice president?

2. **Explaining** How did the Twelfth Amendment change the way presidents are elected?

Presidential Succession

GUIDING QUESTION

What happens if the president leaves office or cannot perform the duties of the office?

At the Constitutional Convention, the Framers discussed what should happen if the president

Presidential Succession

The Presidential Succession Act sets the order in which officials become president if the office becomes vacant.

PRESIDENTIAL SUCCESSION	
1 Vice President	10 Secretary of Commerce
2 Speaker of the House	11 Secretary of Labor
3 President *pro tempore* of the Senate	12 Secretary of Health and Human Services
4 Secretary of State	13 Secretary of Housing and Urban Development
5 Secretary of the Treasury	14 Secretary of Transportation
6 Secretary of Defense	15 Secretary of Energy
7 Attorney General	16 Secretary of Education
8 Secretary of the Interior	17 Secretary of Veterans Affairs
9 Secretary of Agriculture	18 Secretary of Homeland Security

EXAMINE THE CHART

1. **Identifying** Which two officials in the line of succession come from the legislative branch?
2. **Speculating** Why is it important to have the order of succession clearly set?

Source: Nelson, Ed. *The Presidency A to Z*, 3rd ed, (Washington, D.C.: CQ Press, 2003)

dies, is removed, or becomes unable to do the job. From notes on their debates, we know they intended the vice president to *act* as president, but not to actually *become* president.

In 1841 the issue became a real question when William Henry Harrison died just a month after being sworn in as president. Vice President John Tyler acted boldly. He took the presidential oath and acted as though he had, indeed, become president. Congress, after some debate, treated him as the official president. That set a tradition that was followed eight other times. The Twenty-fifth Amendment, ratified in 1967, placed the tradition started by Tyler in the Constitution. It states that if the president dies or leaves office, "the Vice President shall become President." In seven of those cases, a vice president succeeded a president who had died. One assumed office after a president resigned.

The Presidential Succession Act

In 1792 Congress passed a law to set forth who would take on the president's duties if something happened to prevent the vice president from becoming president. It named the president *pro tempore* of the Senate and the Speaker of the House as next in line for the job. In 1947 Congress passed the law that still governs the matter. Called the Presidential Succession Act, it lists the full line of succession after the vice president. A **line of succession** is the order in which officials are expected to succeed, or come next, to an office if something happens to the people ahead of them in line.

According to this law, the Speaker of the House, followed by the president *pro tempore* of the Senate, remain next in line after the vice president. These two come before any cabinet members because they are elected by the people, which means they have the approval of the people. The members of the president's cabinet come after those two elected officials. First comes the Secretary of State, who is followed by the other department heads in the order in which Congress created the departments. The cabinet is a group of special advisers chosen by the president.

The Twenty-fifth Amendment

This law solved the problem of presidential succession, but left other matters unsettled. One question was, what happens if both the offices of the president and vice president become vacant at the same time?

line of succession the order in which officials are expected to succeed, or come next, to an office

The Twenty-fifth Amendment, adopted in 1967, also answered this question. Before this amendment, the vice president's office was vacant if the vice president became president, left office, or died. This amendment provided a way of filling the office. It says that the president should choose a new vice president, who must be approved by votes in both the Senate and the House of Representatives.

Soon after approval of the Twenty-fifth Amendment, this provision was put to use. In 1973 Vice President Spiro Agnew resigned. President Richard Nixon named Gerald Ford, a member of the House, to replace Agnew, and both houses of Congress approved the choice. The next year, Nixon resigned from office, and Ford—the first appointed vice president—became president. Once again, there was no vice president. Ford named Nelson A. Rockefeller as vice president, and the House and the Senate once again voted to approve the choice. For more than two years, then, the United States was led by a president and vice president who had both been appointed rather than elected.

The Twenty-fifth Amendment addressed another important question. That is, what happens if a president becomes unable to fulfill the duties of the office? Several presidents had become unable to fulfill their duties for a time due to illness. For example, President Dwight D. Eisenhower had a heart attack in 1955. While he recovered, he was disabled for several days and had little energy for several months. During that time, his aides ran the executive branch.

The Twenty-fifth Amendment addressed this problem with an important change. It gives the vice president and Congress a role in deciding whether a president is unable to do the job. According to the amendment, the process works in this way. The vice president and a majority of the cabinet officers, or some other body specified by Congress, must inform the president *pro tempore* of the Senate and the Speaker of the House that the president is unable to fulfill the duties of the office. Then, the vice president serves as acting president until the president informs Congress that he or she can return to work. Of course, the president and vice president may disagree on the president's ability to fulfill

After the assassination of President John F. Kennedy on November 22, 1963, Vice President Lyndon B. Johnson was sworn in as president aboard Air Force One.

Inferring What can you infer from the fact that Johnson was sworn in while aboard the presidential plane?

the duties of the office. The president must formally claim to be capable of acting as president. Then, Congress decides the issue by a two-thirds vote in each chamber.

✓ CHECK FOR UNDERSTANDING

Summarizing What three problems was the Twenty-fifth Amendment meant to solve?

LESSON ACTIVITIES

1. **Argumentative Writing** The United States Constitution sets only three requirements for a person to serve as president or vice president. Do you think those rules are enough, or should there be others? In an essay, explain why you support specific changes or why you believe the current rules are adequate.

2. **Presenting** In a small group, research a vice president who became president. Determine how long the vice president served as president, the person's accomplishments in both offices, and whether the person carried out the priorities of the preceding president. As a group, give a presentation to the class.

The President's Powers and Roles

PHOTO:The Granger Collection, New York; TEXT: US Constitution, Article II, § 1.

Analyzing Key Ideas and Details As you read, organize details about the roles of the president by completing a graphic organizer such as the one shown.

Role	Details
Chief executive	
Chief diplomat	
Head of state	
Commander in chief	
Legislative leader	
Economic leader	
Party leader	

Presidential Powers

GUIDING QUESTION

What are the duties of the president?

The president is an important public figure not only in the United States, but also around the world. As chief executive of the U.S. government, the president is the single most powerful public official in the United States. In addition, the president is one of only two officials, the other being the vice president, elected to hold nationwide office. As a result, the president is a symbol of both the federal government and the entire nation.

As with Congress, the president's powers come from the U.S. Constitution. Article II says that "executive Power shall be vested [placed] in a President," making the president the leader of the executive branch. The Constitution also says that the president "shall take Care that the Laws be faithfully executed", meaning the president ensures that the laws passed by Congress are carried out. Congress cannot provide enough details in every law to explain exactly how the law should be **implemented**. The president must decide how the law is put into effect, working within the boundaries provided in the law. That is, the law must be executed in a way that is faithful to the language and intent of the law.

implement to put into practice

In 1789 George Washington became the first president to be inaugurated and take the oath to "preserve, protect and defend the Constitution of the United States."

The Constitution is vague about some of the powers given to the three branches of government. Still, in Article II, it grants the president several specific powers:

- The president can sign bills passed by Congress into law or veto them. To veto a bill is to reject it, which means it does not become law.

- The president can call Congress into special session, which means it must meet at a time not part of its regular schedule.

- The president leads the armed forces as commander in chief.

- The president receives leaders and other officials of foreign countries.

- The president can make **treaties** with other countries, although this power is limited by the Senate's power to approve or reject those treaties.

- The president names the heads of executive agencies, federal judges, **ambassadors**, and other top government officials. As with treaties, this power is checked by the Senate's power to approve or reject these appointments.

- The president can **pardon** people accused or convicted of federal crimes, though presidents have no pardoning power over those convicted of state crimes.

With power also comes responsibility. One responsibility outlined in the Constitution is that the president must tell Congress about the "state of the union," meaning the most important issues facing the nation. To meet that need, the president gives a State of the Union address each year.

This speech was originally called the "Annual Message." It was mostly full of details about the work of the executive branch. Since 1913, presidents have used the speech as an opportunity to promote their policies. In this speech, presidents discuss their successes to that point and their plans to address the country's problems.

✓ **CHECK FOR UNDERSTANDING**

Identifying Name three powers the Constitution gives to the president.

treaty a formal agreement between the governments of two or more countries

ambassador an official representative of a country's government

pardon a declaration of forgiveness and freedom from punishment

Presidential Roles

GUIDING QUESTION
What roles does the president have?

The powers given under the Constitution determine some of the roles that the president has. Other roles have developed over time as the executive branch has grown and more demands have been placed on the president.

Chief Executive

The first U.S. government, under the Articles of Confederation, did not have an official charged with carrying out the laws passed by Congress. The Framers created the presidency in part to fix that problem. The president's main role is the role of chief executive. As chief executive, the president is in charge of 15 executive departments and many government agencies staffed by about 2.1 million workers.

In December 2017, President Donald Trump signed an executive order intended to increase American activities in space. The rocket shown here is part of the program called for by that order.

NASA/Kennedy Space Center

One tool presidents use to give directions to these workers is the executive order. An **executive order** is a rule or command the president issues that has the force of law. Presidents use executive orders to spell out details of the policies set by Congress. Presidents cannot issue any executive orders they want. These orders must be connected in some way to powers given to the president in the Constitution or laws passed by Congress. These orders can take effect immediately. That gives the president the opportunity to shape government actions quickly.

Many executive orders concern the everyday work of the executive branch. Some have had great effect, though. In 1948 President Harry S. Truman used an executive order to end segregation in the armed forces. Until then, African Americans had been assigned to separate military units, often with white officers. Truman's order meant people of all races could serve in the same unit in the military. President Franklin D. Roosevelt issued the most executive orders of any president thus far, with his record of 3,721.

Executive orders are a common way for a new president to quickly change the previous administration's policies. President Biden signed nine executive orders on his first day in office and eight more the next day.

Critics of executive orders argue that some orders violate the separation of powers called for by the Constitution. Those critics believe that only Congress should make laws.

Presidents exercise the role of chief executive when they nominate people to serve as judges in the federal courts, including the Supreme Court. Federal judges serve for life. As a result, these nominations extend a president's influence over the government long after they have left office.

Presidents also take the role of chief executive when they use their pardon power. They usually issue pardons to single individuals, but they can also grant an amnesty. An **amnesty** is a pardon for a group of people who are all accused or have been found guilty of the same crime. The president may also issue a **reprieve**, which is an order that delays punishing a person until a higher court can hear an appeal on the case.

Chief Diplomat

A major role of the president is to represent the United States to other countries as its foreign policy leader. As chief diplomat, the president directs how our country interacts with other countries, both allies and foes. An important part of this role is naming people to serve as ambassadors. These officials represent the United States government in other nations.

The president also meets and negotiates with leaders of other countries. To **negotiate** is to work with other parties to come to an agreement. Sometimes those agreements take the form of formal treaties that the leaders from all of the countries involved sign.

The president may also enter into executive agreements with other countries. These agreements have the same legal status as treaties, but they do not require Senate approval. Most involve routine matters, but some have greater impact. During World War II, President Roosevelt used an executive order to lend American ships to the British, a friendly ally. Some Americans protested the order because they felt it brought the United States closer to a war in which many did not want to take part.

Head of State

Presidents also fill the role of head of state, a figure that represents the nation to other leaders and to the American people. This role involves greeting world leaders when they visit the United States.

The president also represents the country at important ceremonies. For example, the president awards medals to members of the armed forces who have shown bravery and to civilians who have contributed to American society and culture.

Commander in Chief

Under the Constitution, the president is commander in chief of the nation's armed forces. Some foreign policy decisions are supported by military force. This role gives presidents the ability to provide such force.

Presidents cannot declare war on another country. That is a power of Congress.

---

executive order a rule or command the president issues that has the force of law

amnesty a pardon for a group of people

reprieve an order to delay a person's punishment until a higher court can hear an appeal on the case

negotiate to work with other parties to come to an agreement on something

As commander in chief, President Donald Trump (left) met with service members at Joint Base Elmendorf-Richardson in Anchorage, Alaska.

At the same time, only the president can order troops into battle, and this can be done without a formal declaration of war by Congress. The commanders of the army, navy, air force, marines, coast guard, and space force all follow orders of the president.

Congress has declared war just five times. Presidents, however, have sent troops into action more than 150 times. For example, Congress never officially declared war on Iraq, a country in the Middle East that was thought to be stockpiling dangerous weapons. Congress did vote in 2002 to authorize the use of force against Iraq. The following year, President George W. Bush sent American troops into Iraq with the aim of overthrowing the dictator who ruled it and setting up a new democratic government.

In 1973 after the Vietnam War, a controversial conflict opposed by many Americans, Congress passed the War Powers Resolution. It requires the president to inform Congress within 48 hours of sending troops into battle. It also requires the troops to be brought home after 60 days unless Congress approves their use or declares war. The law was meant to prevent presidents from getting the country involved in war without a declaration of war. It has not quite worked, though, as Congress has never forced a president to recall troops.

Legislative Leader

Only members of Congress can introduce bills, but every president wants Congress to pass certain new laws. Presidents can send the text of these bills to supporters in Congress who will introduce the president's bills. They can make speeches to generate public support for the bill. They also meet with members of Congress to work out details of the bills.

These talks do not always go smoothly. That is often the case when the president comes from one political party and the other party controls one or both houses of Congress. That situation can result in little new legislation being passed.

Economic Leader

Presidents try to take actions that will help the country's economy. Voters expect the president to deal with such problems as a lack of jobs, rising prices for consumers, and high taxes. The reality is that presidents cannot solve all these problems. First, Congress has a role. Second, the economy is so large that it takes a long time for new policies to have an effect. Still presidents often get the blame for economic troubles.

Each year the president sends Congress a budget plan for the coming year. That plan is based on many discussions with the heads of executive departments and agencies. These officials advise on what programs to support and what programs to cut back. The budget that the president submits to Congress is a starting point for the final budget. Congress typically makes many changes to that initial plan.

Party Leader

Presidents are also seen as the leaders of their political party. The president gives speeches to help fellow party members running for different offices. The president also helps the party to raise money.

✓ **CHECK FOR UNDERSTANDING**

1. **Understanding Supporting Details** What checks and balances does Congress have that limit the president's role as commander in chief?

2. **Describing** What influence does the president have over Congress?

LESSON ACTIVITIES

1. **Argumentative Writing** Explain what you think is the president's most important role. Defend your position by providing examples of situations presidents must face in that role. Explain why the role you chose is more important than at least two other roles.

2. **Collaborating** With a partner, create a short graphic novel illustrating the president's roles.

Trump White House Archived/Official White House Photo by Shealah Craighead

04

Analyzing Sources: Presidential Power

? COMPELLING QUESTION

How much power should the president have?

Plan Your Inquiry

DEVELOPING QUESTIONS

Think about the powers granted to the president under the Constitution and the system of checks and balances that the Framers put in place. Then read the Compelling Question for this lesson. What questions can you ask to help you answer this Compelling Question? Create a graphic organizer like the one below. Write these Supporting Questions in your graphic organizer.

Supporting Questions	Primary Source or Secondary Source	What this source tells me about how much power the president should have	Questions the source leaves unanswered
	A		
	B		
	C		
	D		
	E		
	F		
	G		

ANALYZING SOURCES

Next, examine the sources in this lesson. Analyze each source by answering the questions that follow it. How does each source help you answer each Supporting Question you created? What questions do you still have? Write these in your graphic organizer.

After you analyze the sources, you will:
- use the evidence from the sources,
- communicate your conclusions,
- and take informed action.

Background Information

When the Framers established the presidency, some feared that a chief executive would have too much power. The Federalists who supported the Constitution dismissed these fears. The nation needed a strong executive, they said. Two hundred years later, some critics and historians spoke of "the imperial presidency." They believed the president had taken on more power over the years and become as strong as a king or emperor.

What powers does the Constitution give to the president? What powers have presidents claimed? How successful have they been in using those powers? Are those claims allowed by the Constitution, or do they go beyond what it permits? Does the role of the United States in the modern world give presidents a good reason to claim more power? Americans have been debating questions like these for many years.

President Obama established Bears Ears National Monument in Utah by executive order in 2016 to protect lands important to Native American peoples. The next year, President Trump used an executive order to reduce its size dramatically. In 2021 President Biden issued an executive order to reverse Trump's action and protect the land again.

Don Grall/Photodisc/Getty Images

Hamilton on the Power of the President

The Articles of Confederation formed the first national government for the United States. That government had only one branch—the legislative body, Congress. There was no executive power to make sure the laws passed by Congress were enforced. In 1787, 55 delegates wrote a new framework for the government: the United States Constitution. Hoping to fix the problems created by the Articles of Confederation, they created the executive branch with the president as its head. One of the delegates, Alexander Hamilton of New York, believed that a strong executive was necessary. He, James Madison, and John Jay wrote a series of essays in support of the new Constitution. Those essays became known as the Federalist Papers, or *The Federalist*. This passage is from one of Hamilton's essays about the presidency.

PRIMARY SOURCE: ESSAY

❝ Energy [forcefulness] in the Executive is a leading character in the definition of good government. It is essential to the protection of the community against foreign attacks; it is not less essential to the steady administration [carrying out] of the laws; to the protection of property . . . to the security [safety] of liberty against the enterprises [plans] and assaults [attacks] of ambition, of **faction**, and of **anarchy**. . . .

A feeble [weak] Executive implies a feeble execution of the government. A feeble execution is but another phrase for a bad execution; and a government ill [poorly] executed, whatever it may be in theory, must be, in practice, a bad government. ❞

— Alexander Hamilton, *The Federalist*, No. 70, March 15, 1788

faction party or group working only for itself
anarchy lawlessness; lack of government

EXAMINE THE SOURCE

1. **Summarizing** Why does Hamilton argue that the nation needs a strong executive?
2. **Interpreting** What does Hamilton mean when he writes of "assaults of ambition, of faction, and of anarchy"?

Jefferson on His Legacy

Thomas Jefferson of Virginia wrote the first draft of the Declaration of Independence. He then worked to revise Virginia's colonial laws to better fit those of an independent state. Among the laws adopted was the Virginia Statute for Religious Freedom. Jefferson went on to hold many offices, serving as secretary of state, vice president, and president for two terms. Yet he expressed distrust of the presidency and federal power. In 1798 he was angered by a law passed by Congress. He wrote the Kentucky Resolutions to argue that a state could refuse to enforce a federal law it opposed. On the other hand, Jefferson claimed he had power as president to purchase the Louisiana Territory from France. Late in life, Jefferson founded the University of Virginia. Before his death, Jefferson left instructions on how to mark his burial site. The photograph shows how the monument at his grave looks today.

PRIMARY SOURCE: DOCUMENTS

❝ [I]n questions of power then, let no more be heard of confidence [trust] in man, but bind him down from mischief [bad actions] by the chains of the constitution. ❞

— Thomas Jefferson, Jefferson's Copy of the Kentucky Resolutions of 1798

❝ On the faces of the **Obelisk** the following **inscription**, & not a word more

Here was buried

Thomas Jefferson

Author of the Declaration of American Independance [Independence]

of the **Statute** of Virginia for religious freedom

& Father of the University of Virginia.

because by these, as **testimonials** that I have lived, I wish most to be remembered. ❞

— Thomas Jefferson, from notes on his epitaph and design of his headstone, c. March 1826

---

obelisk a pillar with four sides that usually taper as it rises and ends in a pyramid
inscription words written, printed, or carved onto a surface
statute a law
testimonial a statement in honor of someone

EXAMINE THE SOURCE

1. **Inferring** In the first excerpt, what concern can you infer from Jefferson's statement regarding the Constitution?
2. **Analyzing Perspectives** Why do you think Jefferson wanted those three achievements on his tombstone and not the fact that he was president?

Andrew Jackson as King

Andrew Jackson won the presidency in 1828 and served two terms. He believed in a strong presidency—one so strong that it could determine whether a law passed by Congress was constitutional. In 1832 members of Congress passed a bill renewing the charter of the Bank of the United States. Opposed to the bank, Jackson vetoed the law, claiming that the Constitution did not give Congress the authority to create a national bank. The Supreme Court, using its power of judicial review, had already deemed the creation of the bank a valid exercise of Congress's powers under the Constitution. This political cartoon appeared in 1833.

PRIMARY SOURCE: POLITICAL CARTOON

BORN TO COMMAND.

OF VETO MEMORY.

HAD I BEEN CONSULTED.

KING ANDREW THE FIRST.

EXAMINE THE SOURCE

1. **Analyzing Points of View** What do the details in the cartoon suggest about Jackson's use of his power as president?
2. **Drawing Conclusions** What message is the cartoon projecting about the separation of powers and checks and balances?

D

Eisenhower's Use of Executive Privilege

Executive privilege refers to the president's right not to reveal communications to Congress. The Constitution says nothing about such a right, however, many presidents have claimed it. In 1954 President Dwight D. Eisenhower sought to protect his staff from testifying in hearings led by Senator Joseph McCarthy. McCarthy claimed communists were in the federal government.

SECONDARY SOURCE: BOOK

❝ Eisenhower [said], 'Congress has absolutely no right to ask [White House staff] to testify in any way, shape, or form about the advice that they were giving to me at any time on any subject.'

Three days later, on May 17, the President told the Republican leaders [in Congress] that 'any man who testifies as to the advice he gave me won't be working for me that night. I will not allow people around me to be **subpoenaed** and you might just as well know it now.' . . .

[Eisenhower] gave the orders the next day. The key sentence read, 'It is not in the public interest that *any* of their [employees of the executive branch] conversations or communications, or *any* document or reproductions, concerning such advice be disclosed [made public].' This was the most sweeping assertion [claim] of executive privilege ever uttered, . . . ❞

— Stephen E. Ambrose, *Nixon: The Education of a Politician, 1913-1962*, 1988

---

subpoena to order a person to appear before a court or committee, such as Congress

---

EXAMINE THE SOURCE

1. **Explaining** Why does Eisenhower suggest that executive privilege should be protected?
2. **Drawing Conclusions** How does the situation in this excerpt relate to separation of powers and checks and balances?

E

The Supreme Court on Executive Privilege

In May 1973, people working for the reelection campaign of President Richard Nixon broke into the Democratic Party headquarters at the Watergate Hotel. They were arrested and put on trial. Further investigations led to charges against aides close to Nixon. The federal prosecutor requested tapes of the president's private conversations in the Oval Office with these aides. Nixon, claiming executive privilege, refused to turn them over. The debate went to the U.S. Supreme Court, which issued a decision that set some rules for executive privilege.

PRIMARY SOURCE: SUPREME COURT DECISION

66 The President's need for complete candor [honesty] and **objectivity** from advisers calls for great **deference** from the courts. However, when the privilege depends solely on the broad, **undifferentiated** claim of public interest in the confidentiality [privacy] of such conversations, a confrontation [conflict] with other values arises. Absent [without] a claim of need to protect military, diplomatic, or **sensitive** national security secrets, we find it difficult to accept the argument that even the very important interest in confidentiality of Presidential communications is significantly diminished . . . 99

— Chief Justice Warren E. Berger, Majority Opinion in *U.S.* v. *Nixon*, July 24, 1974

objectivity freedom from bias
deference respect
undifferentiated not specific
sensitive requiring careful handling

EXAMINE THE SOURCE

1. **Interpreting** What does the Chief Justice mean by "a confrontation with other values arises"?

2. **Explaining** What reasons does the opinion suggest are acceptable for claiming executive privilege?

F

Franklin Roosevelt's Executive Order on Japanese Internment

On December 7, 1941, Japanese forces attacked Pearl Harbor, a U.S. naval base in Hawaii. Congress quickly issued a declaration of war. Some people in the government raised concerns that some Japanese Americans might work to help Japan. In response, President Franklin D. Roosevelt issued an executive order. This order was used to relocate more than 100,000 Japanese Americans and force them to live in camps under guard. Most of them were U.S. citizens. The order was challenged in court but upheld by the Supreme Court. In 1988 Congress issued an apology for this action and gave each survivor $20,000.

PRIMARY SOURCE: DOCUMENT

66 I hereby authorize and direct the Secretary of War, and the Military Commanders . . . to **prescribe** military areas in such places and of such extent . . . from which any or all persons may be excluded, and with respect to which, the right of any person to enter, remain in, or leave shall be subject to whatever restrictions the Secretary of War or the **appropriate** Military Commander may impose [require] in his **discretion.** 99

— Franklin D. Roosevelt, Executive Order No. 9066, Resulting in the Relocation of Japanese, February 19, 1942

prescribe to identify something in an official way
appropriate proper or right
discretion good or sound judgment

EXAMINE THE SOURCE

1. **Interpreting** How does this order give the executive branch and the military broad powers over people in the United States?

2. **Speculating** What does the Supreme Court's decision about this order suggest about the use of presidential powers during a national emergency like a war?

Truman's Executive Order Desegregating the Armed Forces

About one million African American soldiers served in the armed forces during World War II. They served in all branches of the military. However, they served in units that were segregated, or separated, by race. In 1948, three years after that war, President Harry Truman issued an executive order ending the practice of segregation in the armed forces. The photograph shows present-day soldiers marching in a Veterans Day parade.

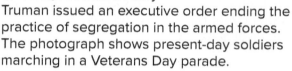

PRIMARY SOURCE: DOCUMENT

66 It is hereby declared to be the policy of the President that there shall be equality of treatment and opportunity for all persons in the armed services without regard to race, color, religion or national origin. This policy shall be put into effect as rapidly as possible, having due regard to the time required to effectuate [bring about] any necessary changes without impairing [harming] **efficiency** or **morale**. 99

— Harry S. Truman, Executive Order No. 9981, Desegregation of the Armed Forces, July 26, 1948

efficiency the ability to do something without wasting resources

morale the level of mental well-being or enthusiasm for a task

EXAMINE THE SOURCE

1. **Contrasting** How does Truman's executive order differ from Roosevelt's with regard to civil rights?

2. **Contrasting** Consider the people affected by both Roosevelt's and Truman's orders. How might Truman's order pose less of a constitutional issue than Roosevelt's?

Complete Your Inquiry

EVALUATE SOURCES AND USE EVIDENCE

Refer back to the Compelling Question and the Supporting Questions you developed at the beginning of the lesson.

1. **Comparing and Contrasting** How are the debates over executive privilege and executive orders reflected in these sources similar and different?

2. **Synthesizing** Hamilton and Jackson favored a strong executive branch. Jefferson, however, distrusted the power of that branch. How do you think Hamilton, Jackson, and Jefferson would view executive privilege and executive orders?

3. **Gathering Sources** Which sources helped you answer the Supporting Questions and the Compelling Question? Which sources, if any, challenged what you thought you knew when you first created your Supporting Questions? What information do you still need in order to answer your questions? What other viewpoints would you like to investigate? Where would you find that information?

4. **Evaluating Sources** Identify the sources that helped answer your Supporting Questions. How reliable are the sources? How would you verify the reliability of the sources?

COMMUNICATE CONCLUSIONS

5. **Collaborating** In small groups, take turns identifying what you consider the main idea expressed in each source. Then, categorize them according to whether they offer evidence supporting a more powerful or a more restrained presidency. Present your results to the class.

TAKE INFORMED ACTION

Making a Podcast About Presidential Powers Work in a small group to research the use of executive orders, executive privilege, or the veto power by several presidents. Find out why they took the actions they did, how Congress and the courts responded, and what happened afterward. Use your research as the basis of a brief podcast about the use of presidential power and limits on that power.

How the Executive Branch Works

READING STRATEGY

Analyzing Key Ideas and Details As you read, complete a chart like the one shown to summarize the functions of the federal agencies.

Group	Function
Executive Office agencies	
Department heads	
Independent agencies	
Government corporations	
Regulatory commissions	

Executive Office Agencies

GUIDING QUESTION

What offices make up the Executive Office of the President?

As chief executive of the United States, the president is responsible for about 2.7 million civilians who work for the federal government and about 1.4 million military personnel. They hold a huge range of jobs and roles, from park ranger to FBI agent, from Army general to accountant. They are divided among many large agencies, such as the National Weather Service, the Air Force, and numerous others. The executive branch has grown enormously and would probably amaze the authors of the Constitution.

To coordinate and manage all of those employees, the president needs a staff to work closely with him or her. Some of them work in the Executive Office of the President (EOP). The EOP forms the president's closest group of advisers. Members of this staff gather information, advise the president, and help in shaping policy. For instance, when the president travels to make a speech, dozens of people go along.

The Constitution charges the president with carrying out the nation's laws. To do so, the president needs help. In the 1930s, President Franklin D. Roosevelt faced the worst economic crisis in the nation's history. To meet these challenges, Roosevelt established the EOP in 1939. Today the EOP has nearly 1,900 employees. Its budget is more than $400 million. This is still a small portion of the executive branch as a whole.

The president works in this room of the White House, called the *Oval Office*. It has been the main work space of the president since the expansion of the West Wing in 1909. Presidents usually decorate the Oval Office the way they like.

The White House Office

An important part of the EOP is the White House Office. It is a central part of the president's administration. The White House Office employs more than 550 people who work directly for the president. They help the president develop policy and communicate with Congress and the public.

The president's chief of staff heads both the White House Office and the EOP. The chief of staff is unofficially called the White House gatekeeper because this aide may control who has access to the president and how much time they have. The chief of staff, along with the deputy chiefs of staff and senior advisers, serve as the president's closest advisers.

Office of Management and Budget

The Office of Management and Budget (OMB) is one of the largest units in the Executive Office of the President. It has two jobs—to prepare the federal budget for the coming year and to **monitor**, or oversee, each executive agency's spending. The director of the OMB works closely with the president.

Each year all executive departments and agencies send OMB a request for a certain

budget. OMB officials review those requests and suggest changes, increasing the funding for some programs and cutting it for others. The president reviews these plans and makes the final decision on spending. This system gives the OMB significant influence over executive agencies. The OMB combines all the agency budgets to make an overall budget proposal for the president to submit to Congress.

National Security Council

The National Security Council (NSC) advises the president on matters of national security. **National security** means protection of the country and its people. Members of the NSC meet to discuss foreign policy and defense issues.

Some officials are part of the NSC by law. They include the vice president and the secretaries of state, defense, energy, treasury, and homeland security. Presidents can add other officials, such as the chairperson of the Joint Chiefs of Staff among others. The Joint Chiefs of Staff are the top commanders from the six branches of the armed services. The chairperson serves as the NSC's military adviser. The Director of National Intelligence advises the NSC based

monitor to oversee

national security involved with the protection of the nation and its people

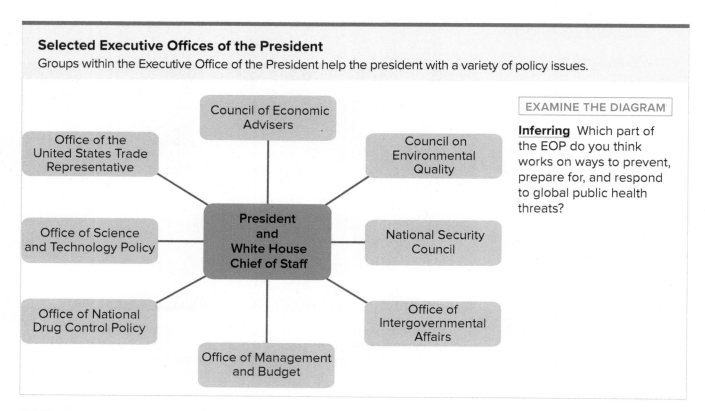

Selected Executive Offices of the President

Groups within the Executive Office of the President help the president with a variety of policy issues.

- Council of Economic Advisers
- Office of the United States Trade Representative
- Council on Environmental Quality
- Office of Science and Technology Policy
- President and White House Chief of Staff
- National Security Council
- Office of National Drug Control Policy
- Office of Intergovernmental Affairs
- Office of Management and Budget

EXAMINE THE DIAGRAM

Inferring Which part of the EOP do you think works on ways to prevent, prepare for, and respond to global public health threats?

Rising prices and unemployment often force consumers to make choices on how they spend their money. The Council of Economic Advisers makes recommendations to the president on programs and policies to address economic problems that could hurt the U.S. economy.

on the latest intelligence. Intelligence is information about the actions and plans of other governments or international groups.

The president's national security adviser also attends NSC meetings. This official meets regularly with the president to discuss security issues.

Council of Economic Advisers

Presidents work to influence the nation's economy. The Council of Economic Advisers (CEA) helps in this work. The council has three members appointed by the president. The head of the council, called the chair, must be approved by the Senate.

The council studies how well the nation's economy is doing. It tries to predict what the economy will be like in the coming months and years. It also proposes solutions to **specific**, or definite, problems, such as rising unemployment or rising prices. In addition, the council prepares

an annual report that the president gives Congress on the state of the economy.

✓ **CHECK FOR UNDERSTANDING**

1. **Contrasting** How does the White House staff differ from the rest of the Executive Office of the President?

2. **Explaining** What are the steps in preparing the president's annual budget?

The Executive Departments

GUIDING QUESTION

What are the functions of the executive departments and their heads?

Article II, Section 2, of the Constitution states that the president may require the opinion of the heads of "each of the executive Departments." The Framers said nothing more about how many departments there should be or what issues they should address.

specific definite

The Executive Departments

Each of the 15 executive branch departments has a broad range of responsibilities.

Department	Role
Department of State (1789)	Plans and carries out the nation's foreign policy
Department of the Treasury (1789)	Collects, borrows, spends, and prints money
Department of Defense (1789 as War Department; renamed in 1949)	Manages the armed forces
Department of Justice (1870)	Responsible for all aspects of law enforcement
Department of the Interior (1849)	Manages and protects nation's public lands and natural resources
Department of Agriculture (1889)	Assists farmers and consumers of farm products
Department of Commerce (1903)	Supervises trade, promotes U.S. business, tourism
Department of Labor (1913)	Deals with working conditions, wages of U.S. workers
Department of Health and Human Services (1953)	Works for the well-being and health of all Americans
Department of Housing and Urban Development (1965)	Deals with the special needs and problems of cities
Department of Transportation (1966)	Manages nation's highways, railroads, airlines, and sea traffic
Department of Energy (1977)	Directs overall energy plan for the nation
Department of Education (1979)	Provides advice and funding for schools
Department of Veterans Affairs (1989)	Directs services for armed forces veterans
Department of Homeland Security (2002)	Oversees America's defenses against terrorist attacks

EXAMINE THE CHART

1. **Calculating** How many years passed before the number of departments expanded beyond the first three?
2. **Identifying** Which departments would be involved in addressing threats to the nation's security?

In 1789 President George Washington formed the first departments. These were the Department of State, Department of War, and Department of the Treasury. Washington also appointed officials named secretaries to head each department. He named an attorney general to advise him on legal matters, though the Department of Justice, which the attorney general leads, was not created for another 100 years. These four officials formed the first presidential **cabinet**.

Over time Congress has decided the government should focus on new issues and has added more executive departments. For example, after World War II, the Department of War was renamed the Department of Defense. Today, the executive branch has grown to include 15 departments. The most recent addition was the Department of Homeland Security, added in 2002. This department has the job of protecting the nation from attacks by terrorists.

Today, the president's cabinet includes more officials than just the heads of the executive departments. The vice president is a member of the cabinet. So are the heads of several agencies in the Executive Office of the President. All advise the president both in their individual roles and when taking part in group meetings of the cabinet.

Article II of the Constitution also gives the Senate the power to confirm or reject "Officers of the United States." Those officers include the heads of the executive departments. Generally, the Senate approves the people the president names to these positions. Many senators believe that presidents should have the advisers they want. Sometimes, though, senators reject a nominee. Unlike appointments, the Constitution

cabinet group of presidential advisers that includes the heads of the executive departments

does not require the president to get approval from Congress to fire these officials.

The department heads advise the president on matters that their departments oversee. The secretary of education, for example, gathers data on the nation's public schools and distributes federal education money to school systems. Presidents also expect the department heads to carry out their plans within their departments. Executive departments generally follow the president's direction. However, they must also abide by the law and can be subject to review by Congress and the courts.

George Washington began the practice of regularly meeting with the department heads. Later presidents have carried on that tradition. The president decides when they meet as a group and how often. Different presidents have relied more heavily on these advisers than others. Presidents tend to pay more attention to department heads involved in national security issues.

Two things limit how much a president relies on the department heads. First, those officials may not be completely loyal to the president. They have to take care of the people and mission of their department as well. Those desires might go against the president's policies. Second, presidents tend to rely on those closest to them. Recent presidents have relied much more on the Executive Office of the President and the White House staff than on department heads.

✓ CHECK FOR UNDERSTANDING

Making Connections How is the appointment of the heads of the executive departments an example of checks and balances?

Secretary of Defense Lloyd Austin, appointed by President Biden, is shown at a press briefing.

Alex Wong/Getty Images

The Federal Bureaucracy

GUIDING QUESTION
What is the federal bureaucracy?

Often natural disasters, such as hurricanes, tornadoes, or severe storms, strike certain parts of the country. These events can destroy or damage homes, shut down businesses, and cut essential services such as electric power, communications, and heat to millions of people. When these disasters happen, the president may order the federal government into action. Employees of the Federal Emergency Management Agency (FEMA) arrive on the scene and provide shelter, medical supplies, and other aid to help people recover and rebuild.

FEMA is one of hundreds of agencies that carry out the work of the federal government. These agencies deal with everything from exploring space to managing our national parks to deciding what medicines are safe for doctors to prescribe.

Together, these agencies and their employees make up the **federal bureaucracy** (byu•RAH•kruh•see). More than 2.7 million **civilians**, or people not in the armed forces, work in the executive branch. Another 1.4 million or so serve in the armed forces.

What the Bureaucracy Does

Workers in the federal bureaucracy do three basic kinds of tasks. First, agencies write rules that turn the general language of laws passed by Congress into specific directions. That way, people and businesses can know what to do to follow the law. For instance, any appliance you can buy in a store must meet federal regulations for safety and use of energy. Workers in the federal bureaucracy have written those regulations to implement laws passed by Congress.

The process of rule-making is long and complex. The agency writes draft rules that the public can comment on for a period of time. Based on those comments, the agency might revise the rule. If a person, business, or group thinks the final rule is unfair or wrong, they can file a lawsuit and ask the courts to overturn it.

federal bureaucracy the agencies and employees of the federal government

civilian person who is not serving in the armed forces

The goal is to make rule-making a fair procedure that follows the intent of the guiding legislation.

Second, workers in the bureaucracy provide services to the public. Postal service workers deliver the mail. Agents of the Federal Bureau of Investigation try to solve crimes. National Park Service rangers guide people who visit the national parks.

Third, federal agencies oversee certain activities. For example, some workers review the activities of banks to make sure that they obey the rules about banking. Others make sure companies that make products have met all standards for the safety of those goods. Agencies cannot simply take this work on for themselves. Congress must pass a law to give them the power to do their work. This limit on executive branch power shows the rule of law at work.

Agencies Outside the Departments

Most executive agencies are formed within an executive department. For example, FEMA is part of the Department of Homeland Security.

However, the executive branch also has more than a hundred organizations that are not part of any executive department. These agencies can be grouped into three types: independent agencies, government corporations, and regulatory commissions. They, too, are part of the federal bureaucracy.

Independent agencies carry out certain specific activities. The National Aeronautics and Space Administration (NASA), for example, runs the space program. The Office of the Special Counsel (OSC) works to protect federal employees from illegal practices in the workplace.

Government corporations are businesses owned and operated by the government. Like a business, they provide goods or services for

independent agency an executive agency that carries out certain activities and is not part of an executive department

government corporation a business owned and operated by the federal government to provide specific services

NASA has sent several rovers to explore the surface of Mars. This photo is a "selfie" taken by the rover *Curiosity*.

which they charge people. The United States Postal Service (USPS) collects and delivers mail and packages to people and businesses across the country. The National Railroad Passenger Corporation—known as Amtrak—provides train service to people. Unlike most government corporations, Amtrak is supposed to earn a profit.

Regulatory commissions make rules that an industry or group must follow and can also punish those that do not follow the rules. Congress established regulatory commissions to help ensure large industries and businesses do not adopt practices that might harm the public. For instance, the Consumer Product Safety Commission (CPSC) writes safety guidelines for consumer goods such as toys, power tools, and cleaning products. It informs the public about possible hazards and can issue recalls of dangerous products.

Unlike the other two types of independent organizations, regulatory commissions do not report to the president. The president also has limited control over these bodies. The president names the people who head the commissions, but the Senate must approve them. The terms the commission members serve are long, and no president has the opportunity to name all the members. In addition, the president cannot fire them. Only Congress can remove them.

Government Workers

Political appointees hold many of the top jobs in executive departments and agencies. They are chosen by the president but may need to be confirmed by the Senate. The president appoints some individuals because they are knowledgeable about the department's or agency's work. Choosing people to lead departments is one way for a president to influence the direction of the country. Presidents are generally considered to have a right to choose people who agree with them on important issues. Officials may also be named as a reward for supporting the president during the election. Appointees generally lose their

NATIONAL CONSUMER PROTECTION WEEK
March 3–9, 2019

Day 1 **Your Safety Is Our Business!**

Day 2 Go to **SaferProducts**.gov to Report. Search. Protect.

Consumers can report their experiences with unsafe products to the Consumer Product Safety Commission.

positions when a new president is elected and appoints new people to those offices.

Before 1883, the government filled many federal jobs following a practice called the **spoils system**. Under this system, officials filled government jobs by hiring people who were political supporters. It was based on the idea that "to the victor belong the spoils." Spoils means something valuable taken through a battle or contest. In elections, the spoils were government jobs.

Under the spoils system, many workers did not have the skills and experience needed to do their jobs. Their loyalty was to the official who appointed them rather than to the duties of their office. In 1883, Congress passed the Civil Service Reform Act to change this system. This law created the civil service system. It also limited the number of jobs a new president could fill through appointments.

Most government workers today are civil service workers. They are hired through the **civil service system**. This is the organized system the federal government uses to hire workers. To be hired, these workers must pass tests and demonstrate that they have the knowledge and skills needed for the job. These workers keep their jobs from one president to the next.

---

regulatory commission independent agency created by Congress that can make rules concerning certain activities and punish organizations that break those rules

political appointee a person appointed to a federal position by the president

spoils system practice of filling government jobs by rewarding people for their political support

civil service system the processes used to hire government workers on the basis of open, competitive examinations and merit

This political cartoon shows President Chester Arthur as a magician on stage pulling presidential appointments out of a hat.

Analyzing Visuals Does the cartoon appear to present a positive or negative view of President Arthur and his choices for presidential appointments? Explain.

The Office of Personnel Management (OPM) oversees the civil service system. It sets specific standards of knowledge and skills that people holding each federal job must meet. It also runs the testing system for people who want to qualify for government jobs. These tests create a **merit system** for hiring. In a merit system, people get jobs based on their qualifications. Only people who pass tests or have other specific job skills and education can get civil service jobs. This system is meant to ensure that civil service workers are fully able to do their jobs.

Government jobs offer many benefits. Salaries, or yearly pay, for most federal workers are similar to those paid by businesses. Benefits include paid vacation days, days off for illness and injury, health insurance, and a retirement plan. Government workers also have the satisfaction of knowing that they contribute to the public good.

merit system hiring people into government jobs on the basis of their qualifications

✓ **CHECK FOR UNDERSTANDING**

1. **Summarizing** What steps are followed to make sure that the process used to make federal rules is fair?

2. **Comparing and Contrasting** How are civil service jobs similar to and different from jobs of political appointees?

LESSON ACTIVITIES

1. **Informative/Explanatory Writing** Write a brief paragraph explaining the differences between independent agencies, government corporations, and regulatory agencies. Be sure to point out how they are different in their relationship to the president and in the work that they do.

2. **Presenting** Choose one of the 15 executive departments or another executive agency and research what work that department or agency does and what services it provides. Include interesting information about the department or agency. Present your findings to your class.

06

Reviewing The Executive Branch

Summary

The Executive Branch

President

Powers:

- signs and vetoes bills
- calls special sessions
- commands armed forces
- makes treaties
- nominates judges and executive officials
- grants pardons, reprieves, amnesty

Roles:

- chief executive
- chief diplomat
- head of state
- commander in chief
- legislative leader
- economic leader
- party leader

Vice President

Powers:

- votes in Senate if there is a tie

Roles:

- presides over Senate
- serves in cabinet and advises president
- performs tasks assigned by president
- becomes president if the president dies, resigns, is removed, or is unable to fulfill the duties of the office

Federal Bureaucracy

Makeup:

- Executive Office of the President (EOP)
- 15 executive departments
- hundreds of agencies outside departments (independent agencies, government corporations, regulatory commissions)
- 2.7 million civilian workers

Roles:

- EOP, department and agency heads: advise the president
- Departments and agencies: write rules to implement laws, provide services to public, oversee certain activities

Checking For Understanding

Answer the questions to see if you understood the topic content.

IDENTIFY AND EXPLAIN

1. Identify each of the following terms and explain its significance to the executive branch.

   A. elector
   B. pardon
   C. executive order
   D. reprieve
   E. cabinet
   F. independent agency
   G. government corporation
   H. regulatory commission
   I. spoils system
   J. merit system

REVIEWING KEY FACTS

2. **Explaining** What three requirements must a person meet to become president or vice president of the United States?

3. **Summarizing** How did the Twelfth Amendment solve the problems raised by the 1796 and 1800 elections?

4. **Identifying** How did the Twenty-second Amendment change rules for becoming president?

5. **Speculating** For what reasons might the Twenty-fifth Amendment be used to replace a president?

6. **Identifying** As head of the executive branch, what is the president's main job?

7. **Summarizing** What is the president's role as commander in chief?

8. **Identifying** What are two examples of checks that Congress has on a president's power?

9. **Interpreting** Which power given to the president by the Constitution enables the president to act as a check on legislation from Congress?

10. **Summarizing** How would you summarize the responsibilities of cabinet members?

11. **Explaining** What are the three tasks of the federal agencies that are part of the executive branch?

CRITICAL THINKING

12. **Analyzing** If the state of Florida has 29 electoral votes, how many representatives does Florida have in the House of Representatives? Explain your answer.

13. **Evaluating** Why can a small margin of victory in a presidential election in one state result in the winning candidate getting a large number of electoral votes?

14. **Making Connections** How would being given an expanded role while serving as vice president help a vice president if he or she had to take the office of the presidency?

15. **Drawing Conclusions** Why might a president issue an executive order instead of waiting for the members of Congress to approve legislation?

16. **Identifying Cause and Effect** Why has the number of departments making up the president's cabinet increased over time?

17. **Evaluating** Why is the position of White House chief of staff a key role in the modern presidency?

18. **Inferring** What are some advantages of having a team to help the president make decisions about national security?

19. **Comparing and Contrasting** How is a merit system a fairer and more open way of filling government jobs than a spoils system?

20. **Explaining** How do the rules for filling the positions of the leaders of regulatory commissions help these bodies remain independent of the president?

NEED EXTRA HELP?

If You've Missed Question	1	2	3	4	5	6	7	8	9	10
Review Lesson	2, 3, 5	2	2	2	2	3	3	3	3	5

If You've Missed Question	11	12	13	14	15	16	17	18	19	20
Review Lesson	5	2	2	2, 3	5	5	5	5	5	5

Apply What You Have Learned

A Understanding Multiple Perspectives

Recent presidents have been sharply criticized for the number of executive orders they issued. Critics have also attacked the content of some of those orders. Presidents from George Washington to Joe Biden have issued these orders. Yet they remain a hotly debated tool of the president.

ACTIVITY Comparing and Contrasting Perspectives on Executive Orders Read the two passages discussing executive orders. Then write a short essay that compares and contrasts the two views. Are executive orders an attempt by presidents to make law? Are they an abuse of power? Are they against the Constitution? Are they used too often? Use ideas and statements from the two sources in your writing.

66 Federal power has been gravitating [shifting] toward the president . . . for decades. That reflects the growth of the federal government itself as well as the polarization [deep divisions along party lines] of Congress. Government initiatives [policies] enacted through legislation are generally more durable [lasting] because they have attracted broader political support and are less susceptible [at risk] to unfavorable court judgments. But because of political gridlock [inability to pass laws because parties disagree], presidents have increasingly chosen the regulatory route [using regulations].

Defenders of this strategy say presidents are appropriately [rightly] implementing their electoral mandate [popular support]. Critics say it subverts [undercuts] the fundamental constitutional role of a Congress elected to pass laws. 99

— New Civil Liberties Alliance

66 [P]residents have relied less on executive orders over time. Indeed, modern presidents used drastically fewer orders per year—an average of 59—than their pre-World War II counterparts [presidents before 1941], who averaged 314. . . .

Why don't presidents always issue executive orders, a seemingly powerful policy device? Because they come with serious constraints [limits].

First, executive orders may not be as unilateral [independent] as they seem. Drafting an order involves a time-consuming bargaining process with various agencies negotiating [working out] its content.

Second, if they are issued without proper legal authority, executive orders can be overturned by the courts—although that happens infrequently. . . .

Finally, executive orders are not the last word in policy. They can be easily revoked [cancelled]. 99

— Sharece Thrower, "What Is an Executive Order?," The Conversation

B Building Citizenship

The White House, the cabinet departments, and executive agencies all maintain websites with information on their structure, staffing, mission, and activities. Some of these websites have a lot of information, but that information can sometimes be difficult to find.

ACTIVITY **Explaining an Executive Department Website and Its Use** Visit an executive department website. Look at the site's menus to learn how the site is structured. Look at some of the individual pages and read the content. Consider whether the site's content is clearly and effectively presented. Think about how useful the site's content would be to someone looking for information about this department. Use the site's search function to find specific information on a topic. How useful are the search results? Check the website's page that allows people to contact the agency. How easy is that to use? Use the information that you gather to prepare a guide or handbook for anyone who wants to use the site. Describe its structure and content. Include advice on how to navigate the site. Combine your findings with those of your classmates to form a guide to accessing information about the executive branch of the federal government.

C Writing an Informative Essay

As of 2021, seventeen state governors have become president. Sixteen people who had been U.S. senators have become president. Which of those positions includes roles or has responsibilities that are most closely related to the roles and duties of the president?

ACTIVITY **Comparing Roles of Governors, U.S. Senators, and the President** Do some research to learn about the roles and responsibilities of the governor of your state. Learn about the roles and responsibilities of a U.S. senator. Then write a brief essay that compares roles and responsibilities of those two offices to those of the president. Which office is closest to the president in activities performed? Which is closest to the president in awareness of issues facing the country?

D Making Connections to Today

Presidents lead the entire country, and at times, like to speak to all of the country's people. In the past, presidents spoke to reporters or used press releases to have their messages published in newspapers. They then used radio, and later television, to speak directly to Americans. More recently, presidents have come to use a variety of online social media sites to communicate with the public.

ACTIVITY **Reporting on Presidents and Social Media** Examine the social media use of recent presidents. How and why have presidents used social media sites in recent years? What sites have they used and what types of announcements have presidents made on the sites? Have they used them for announcing actual policies, or for sharing personal messages with the public, or both? Prepare a short report commenting on the effectiveness of social media use by one or more presidents. Include screenshots or descriptions of posts by the president that you believe show an effective, or ineffective, use of the media. Share your findings in a class discussion.

U.S. Department of Defense. "Homepage." October 7, 2021. https://www.defense.gov/.

A lawyer makes oral arguments to the justices of the U.S. Supreme Court.

The Judicial Branch

Introducing The Judicial Branch

The Federal Court System

The Judicial Branch is made up of federal courts. This includes the Supreme Court, district courts, and appeals courts. The Supreme Court has roles and responsibilities that help balance the powers of the federal government. For example, the Court uses the power of judicial review to ensure that laws passed by Congress follow the Constitution. The Supreme Court is also responsible for hearing and making decisions for cases that have been reviewed by lower courts. The rulings in these cases can set national precedents, or examples used for similar cases, and can directly impact citizens' rights.

66 I think the important thing about my appointment is not that I will decide cases as a woman, but that I am a woman who will get to decide cases. 99

—Sandra Day O'Connor, March 1982

In the 1800s, the Supreme Court would provide white quill pens and ink to each counsel's table for note taking. This tradition continues today. It is very rare for any attorney to have the opportunity to argue a case in front of the Supreme Court. If an attorney does argue before the Supreme Court, they are gifted a white quill pen to take as a souvenir.

As a boy, Thurgood Marshall learned about the U.S. Constitution from his parents, a railroad porter and a schoolteacher. When he misbehaved in school, one of his teachers sent him to the basement to study the Constitution. He said he made his way "through every paragraph." He became an attorney and successfully argued before the Supreme Court that racial segregation in schools was unequal. In 1967 Thurgood Marshall became the first African American Supreme Court justice.

PHOTO:(t)World History Archive/Alamy Stock Photo, (cr) R'images/Alamy Stock Photo, (b) Stock Montage/Archive Photos/Getty Images; TEXT: O'Connor, Sandra Day. Quoted in Gutgold, Nichola D. The Rhetoric of Supreme Court Women: From Obstacles to Options. Lanham, MD: Lexington Books, 2012.

The Highest Court in the Land

On the top floor of the Supreme Court building is a basketball court nicknamed the "highest court in the land." Before 1940, the room was used as storage but was later transformed into a gym and basketball court.

Select Federal Judges Appointed by Each President

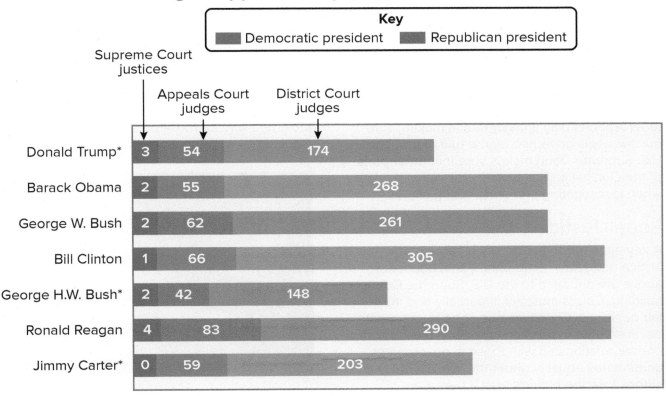

Key
- Democratic president
- Republican president

Supreme Court justices → | Appeals Court judges → | District Court judges →

President	Supreme Court justices	Appeals Court judges	District Court judges
Donald Trump*	3	54	174
Barack Obama	2	55	268
George W. Bush	2	62	261
Bill Clinton	1	66	305
George H.W. Bush*	2	42	148
Ronald Reagan	4	83	290
Jimmy Carter*	0	59	203

*Served one term.

Source: Pew Research Center analysis of Federal Judicial Center data.

©Arthur Lien

Getting Ready to Learn About . . .
The Judicial Branch

The judicial branch is the name for the U.S. court system. It consists of judges and the staff who support them. Like the other two branches of the government, it is much larger today than when the Constitution initially took effect. The country has grown since 1787, from fewer than 4 million people in 13 states to more than 330 million people in 50 states. Yet the principles on which the judicial branch is based and the ideals it is meant to defend have not changed since the Constitution was ratified.

The Rule of Law

One of the basic principles of the U.S. Constitution is the rule of law. The rule of law means that no one is above the law. The laws apply to everyone equally, including government officials. If someone breaks the law or if officials abuse their power, they must be held accountable. As John Adams said, we should have "a government of laws, and not of men." Laws must be clear and known to all. Laws must be equally, fairly, and consistently enforced.

To ensure the rule of law, the Framers built safeguards into the U.S. Constitution. The Fifth Amendment calls for "due process of law." That means that government officials must use proper procedures. The courts are subject to due process—there are rules they must follow. They are also the guardians of due process. The federal courts play a major role in making sure our society is governed by the rule of law. The U.S. Supreme Court makes sure that other parts of the criminal justice system stay within the law when investigating and prosecuting crimes.

Equal Justice

A key element of democracy is that of "equal justice under law"—the phrase that appears above the entrance to the U.S. Supreme Court building. Courts must act impartially and make fair decisions. Giving anyone special treatment because of their position in society, their wealth, or their relationship with those in government undermines equality under the law. Courts and judges lose the public's trust if they are influenced or controlled by special interests or other outside forces. The Constitution demands equal justice. The Fourteenth Amendment requires "equal protection of the laws" for all citizens. Judges play a major role in ensuring that other parts of the government meet that goal.

Independence of Judges

Judges must be free of political pressure. The Constitution provides that federal judges "hold their Offices during good Behaviour." That means that they can serve for life, until they retire, resign, or die. This provision helps keep the judicial branch free from the influence of political leaders in the executive and legislative branches. It also protects them from being pressured by voters and campaign donors rather than following the law.

Ensuring Safety

As the Preamble of the Constitution states, one goal of the Constitution is to "insure domestic Tranquility." *Tranquility* means peace and calm. The courts help achieve this goal by providing an orderly way to settle disputes. Disputes are common occurrences of everyday life. Individuals come into conflict with one another for many different reasons. Neighbors sometimes clash over property disputes. Employers and workers may disagree on the terms of employment, such as working conditions or pay. Two state governments might disagree about how to share a common resource, such as water. The courts provide a way for these parties to resolve disputes fairly and peacefully. If people trust the

Judges preside over trials to ensure that the accused are treated fairly and justly.

PHOTO:Paul Sakuma-Pool/Getty Images News/Getty Images; TEXT: (t) Adams, John. Massachusetts Constitution. The General Court of the Commonwealth of Massachusetts. https://malegislature.gov/laws/constitution., (b) U.S. Constitution, Amendment V

The Federal and State Court Systems

The dual court system allows for both state and federal courts to operate, though they handle different kinds of cases.

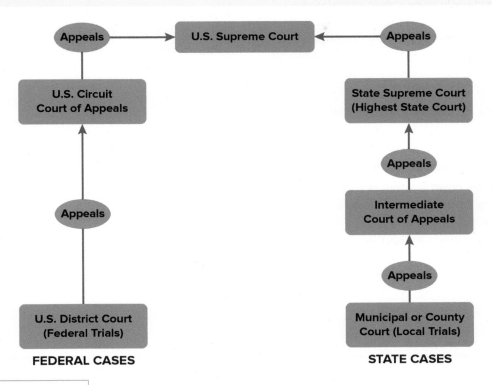

FEDERAL CASES

STATE CASES

EXAMINE THE DIAGRAM

1. **Analyzing Visuals** What kinds of cases do state courts hear?
2. **Drawing Conclusions** Which federal court can hear appeals from decisions of a state court?

court system, the law helps people resolve conflicts without resorting to violence.

A Dual Court System

The United States has a dual court system. Each state has its own courts, including trial courts and courts that hear appeals. The federal government also has a court system, which handles federal law.

People accused of a crime have their cases decided in trial courts by a jury or judge. People who claim that another person harmed them can sue that person in a civil court. A judge or jury decides the outcome of those trials as well.

Sometimes the party that lost a case believes that due process was not followed or that justice was not provided equally. This party can appeal the decision of the trial court to an appeals court. The highest appeals court in the country is the U.S. Supreme Court.

The judicial branch is different from the other two branches of the federal government. Congress and the president reflect our democratic values, as they are chosen by the people through elections. However, judges on the federal courts are appointed by the president and confirmed by the Senate. Congress and the president are accountable to the voters since they must be reelected to keep their jobs. But, federal judges serve for life. Congress and the president try to meet the public's desire for open discussion of public issues. The judges on the courts debate their positions in private and publish only their final decisions. Even though they are not accountable through elections, federal judges are like Congress and the president in that they are a vital part of the American republic. They protect people's liberties and make decisions that directly impact people's lives.

Looking Ahead

You will learn about the judicial branch of government. You will examine Compelling Questions and develop your own questions about the judicial branch in the Inquiry Activity. You can preview some of the key concepts that you will learn about by reviewing the infographic.

What Will You Learn?

In these lessons focused on the judicial branch you will learn:

- that the federal courts make up the judicial branch of the U.S. government.
- that the federal court system is made up of district courts, appeals courts, and the Supreme Court.
- the powers and limits placed on the Supreme Court.
- the jurisdictional limits and organization of the federal and state courts.
- the role of the Supreme Court and its impact on society.
- that judicial review acts as a check on other branches of government.
- that very few cases are heard by the Supreme Court.

 COMPELLING QUESTION IN THE INQUIRY ACTIVITY LESSON

- **How has judicial review shaped American government?**

The Judicial Branch

The judicial branch is one of the three branches of the federal government. It contains the federal court system. The U.S. Supreme Court is the highest court in this branch.

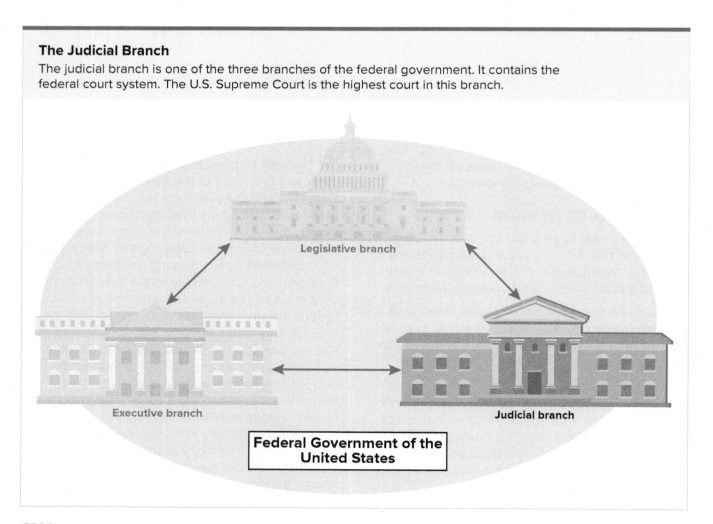

Legislative branch

Executive branch

Judicial branch

Federal Government of the United States

David R. Frazier Photolibrary, Inc./Alamy Stock Photo

Analyzing Key Ideas and Details As you read, use a graphic organizer such as the one shown to describe four main features of the U.S. federal court system.

Federal Court System	
Jobs	
Levels	
Goal	
Jurisdiction	

Role of the Federal Courts

GUIDING QUESTION

What is the role of the federal courts?

What is a court? A court is a room where people come to resolve disputes. One or more judges oversee the proceedings. Lawyers usually represent each side in the dispute. They argue the position of the person or organization they represent, trying to show that this side is right. They ask questions of witnesses, who have some knowledge of the matter in dispute. In some trials, a jury sits in the room, watching and listening, and then votes to decide which side is right. The judge's job is to make sure everyone taking part in the proceedings follows the rules and the law.

Courts are essential parts of safe and orderly societies. Imagine what life would be like if people settled all their disagreements by bullying or fighting one another. Instead, we have courts to provide a way for people to settle disputes in a fair, orderly, and peaceful manner.

We also need courts to keep us safe in a just and fair way. Imagine if the government just picked up people off the streets and put them in jail without explanation. That does happen in places that have authoritarian governments. However, in a society that believes in the rule of law, the government must formally accuse someone of committing a crime. Then it has to provide evidence to convince a jury that the charges against the accused are true. Only then can the government punish the person.

The judicial branch of government consists of courts. This branch has two main jobs. First, it makes sure that laws are fairly enforced.

An attorney presents her side of a case to the jury, which will decide the matter.

Analyzing Images How are the members of the jury acting? Why do you think they are acting that way?

GO ONLINE Explore the Student Edition eBook and find interactive maps, charts, graphs, and tools.

C229

Public officials must follow the laws and apply the law equally to all citizens. Second, the courts **interpret**, or explain the meaning of, the laws. When questions arise about how the law applies to a particular case or whether a law conflicts with the Constitution, the courts make that decision.

Courts hear criminal cases and civil cases. In a **criminal case**, the government brings the case. It tries to prove that someone is guilty of committing a crime. During the trial, the government calls on witnesses to present their view of the case. The accused may present witnesses in their defense. Then a jury or a judge decides whether the accused is guilty or not. An accused person found guilty is punished. One found not guilty is set free.

Civil cases arise from disputes between two parties. A *party* is any person, organization, or entity such as a company or a government. In a civil case, one party sues another party, claiming that the other party injured them in some way. Civil disputes can be between two private parties, such as two neighbors, between a private party and a government, or between two governments.

---

interpret to explain the meaning of

criminal case legal matter concerning whether someone committed a crime

civil case legal matter in which one party in a dispute claims to have been harmed by the other

In a civil dispute, each side presents its position to the court. A jury or judge decides whether the party was wronged by the other party in a way that violates the law. If so, the court decides how to remedy the matter. The remedy may be in the form of a monetary payment to the wronged party.

Origin of the Federal Court System

The first national government of the United States was under the Articles of Confederation. The Articles provided no national court system. There was no way to enforce a law across all the states or to ensure equal justice across the nation.

The Framers of the U.S. Constitution aimed to fix those problems. In Article III of the Constitution, they created a national Supreme Court. They also gave Congress the power to create lower federal courts if they were needed.

The First Congress acted quickly, passing the Judiciary Act of 1789. This law established two types of lower federal courts, called *district courts* and *circuit courts*. The district courts served as trial courts for minor cases. The circuit courts took more serious cases and also heard appeals from the district courts. In 1891 Congress removed trials from the circuit courts. As a result, all federal trials take place in district courts, and circuit courts function only as courts of appeal.

Dual Court System

Each state has its own court system separate from the federal system and those of other states.

Federal Courts	State Courts
• Three levels of courts: trial, appeals, Supreme	• Three levels of courts: trial, appeals, supreme*
• Derives powers from U.S. Constitution and federal laws	• Derives powers from state constitution and state laws
• Hears cases involving federal law	• Hears cases involving state law
• Most judges appointed for life	• Most judges elected or appointed for set terms
• U.S. Supreme Court can hear appeals from state supreme courts.	• State appeals courts never hear cases that originate in federal courts.

*structure and names of courts vary by state

> EXAMINE THE CHART

1. **Comparing** How are federal and state court systems similar?
2. **Comparing and Contrasting** How are the sources of powers of federal and state courts similar and different?

In 2020 the Supreme Court settled a case between Texas and New Mexico about their contract to share water from the Pecos River, which begins in New Mexico and runs through west Texas.

Dual Court System

In addition to the federal courts, each state has its own courts. For this reason, we say that the United States has a **dual court system**. The dual court system is an example of federalism.

Each court system receives power from a different source. State courts get their powers from state constitutions and laws. Federal courts get their powers from the Constitution and laws passed by Congress.

The Goal of the Court System

Carved above the entrance to the United States Supreme Court are the words "Equal Justice Under Law." This principle is the foundation, or basis, of the American legal system. The law aims to treat every person the same.

The Constitution gives every person accused of a crime the right to due process of law and a fair public trial. *Due process* means that the government must follow specific rules of justice in making its case. Each person is **presumed**, or assumed to be, innocent until proven guilty. If a person convicted of a crime believes the law has not been applied correctly and fairly, they have the right to ask the appeals courts to review the case.

The ideal of equal justice is difficult to achieve. Judges and juries have prejudices that

can affect their decisions. Poor people do not have the money to hire lawyers, as wealthy people and large companies do. Poor people also have other disadvantages in the legal system, such as not being able to post bail.

✓ CHECK FOR UNDERSTANDING

1. **Explaining** Why did the Framers create a federal court system?
2. **Contrast** Contrast the roles of the district and circuit courts.

Federal Court Jurisdiction

GUIDING QUESTION

What kinds of cases are heard in federal courts?

Federal courts do not hear every type of case. The Constitution gives federal courts limited **jurisdiction**—the authority to hear and decide a case. In Article III, the Constitution identifies the types of cases that are within the federal courts' jurisdiction. Putting limits on the jurisdiction of federal courts prevents them from interfering with state courts. It is an example of federalism at work.

State courts have jurisdiction in disputes that involve the laws of their state and events that are contained within a single state. Federal courts have jurisdiction in cases that involve the Constitution or federal law. They also hear cases involving disputes between parties from different states.

The Constitution and Federal Law

Cases that involve the Constitution, federal law, or the federal government are heard in federal courts. This includes cases concerning violations of constitutional rights, such as First Amendment or Fourteenth Amendment rights. It also includes cases involving actions that Congress has defined as federal crimes. Examples are kidnapping, tax evasion, and counterfeiting. Federal courts also hear civil cases that involve federal laws. An example would be if a person sued a business or local government for discrimination that violated the Civil Rights Act. Federal courts also handle certain financial matters, such as the regulation of the sale of stocks or banking matters.

---

dual court system a court system made up of both state and federal courts
presume to assume

jurisdiction authority to hear and decide a case

The U.S. Army has its own court system, where it tries soldiers accused of breaking laws under the Uniform Code of Military Justice.

Disputes Between States or Their Residents

Sometimes two state governments have a dispute with one another. Those cases are resolved in federal court. States sue one another for a variety of reasons. Cases have involved arguments over borders, water rights, and sewage from one state polluting the water of another.

Federal courts also hear disputes between parties in different states. Suppose someone in Maryland is hurt while properly using a product made by a Michigan company. The person could sue the company in federal court.

Admiralty and Maritime Laws

Federal courts have jurisdiction over cases involving admiralty and maritime laws. These laws concern crimes, accidents, and property at sea. For example, a company that operates a fishing fleet might believe that an oil spill has damaged the fishing waters. It can sue the oil company in federal court.

The Federal Government

Federal courts have jurisdiction over all cases in which the U.S. government is a party. For example, the United States might sue a computer manufacturer in federal court for failing to deliver computers as promised in a contract. If the computers were delivered but the government did not pay as promised in a contract, the manufacturer would sue the government in federal court.

Cases Involving Other Countries

Federal courts have jurisdiction over international cases. This includes disputes between foreign governments and the U.S. government, and disputes between foreign governments and American companies or citizens. Suppose a U.S. government official working in another nation, such as an ambassador, is accused of a crime. That would be a federal case.

Types of Jurisdiction

For most of these cases, federal courts have **exclusive jurisdiction**. That is, they have the sole authority to hear the cases. Most court cases in the United States are not federal cases. Most involve state law, where state courts have exclusive jurisdiction.

Sometimes, jurisdiction overlaps. This happens when either a federal court or a state court could hear a case. In this type of situation, the two courts are said to have **concurrent jurisdiction**. Concurrent jurisdiction can apply to criminal and to civil cases. Someone can be accused of murder in either state court or federal court. When citizens of different states have a dispute with a value of at least $75,000, the person who brings the suit can choose to have the case heard by either a federal court or a state court.

✓ **CHECK FOR UNDERSTANDING**

1. **Identifying** Name three types of cases that fall under the jurisdiction of federal courts.
2. **Contrasting** What is the difference between concurrent jurisdiction and exclusive jurisdiction?

LESSON ACTIVITIES

1. **Informative/Explanatory Writing** Write a brief essay that explains how both the Constitution and Congress define and limit the power of the federal courts.

2. **Identifying Arguments** The U.S. Constitution is based on five principles: popular sovereignty, limited government and rule of law, separation of powers, checks and balances, and federalism. With a partner, write and present a podcast that explains how the court systems in the United States show at least three of those principles at work.

---

exclusive jurisdiction sole authority to hear and decide a case

concurrent jurisdiction authority of both state and federal courts to hear a case

The Federal Court System

Analyzing Key Ideas and Details As you read, use a graphic organizer, such as the one shown, to record details about the two types of lower federal courts. Identify each court's jurisdiction, the types of cases it hears, the number of judges it has, and the number of courts of each type in the federal system.

District Courts	Circuit Courts

The Lower Courts

How are the federal courts organized?

The federal court system includes the district courts, the courts of appeals, also known as circuit courts, and the Supreme Court. The Constitution created the Supreme Court—the highest court in the federal system. Congress created district courts and the courts of appeals. Together these two courts are known as the lower federal courts. Each of the three types of courts has its own purpose and structure.

District Courts

The lowest level of the federal court system contains the district courts. There are 94 district courts throughout the country. Each state has at least one of them. The states with the largest populations have more than one. For example, California, New York, and Texas each have four district courts. District courts have also been established in Washington D.C., Puerto Rico, Guam, the Northern Marinara Islands, and the U.S. Virgin Islands.

District courts are trial courts. A trial court is where a case first comes before a judge and perhaps a jury. Because of this, district courts are also called courts of original jurisdiction. **Original jurisdiction** means these courts have the authority to hear a case for the first time.

original jurisdiction the authority of a court to hear cases for the first time

Built in 1858, the Lewis F. Powell, Jr., Courthouse in Richmond, Virginia, is home to the U.S. Court of Appeals for the Fourth Circuit. It is the oldest federal courthouse still in use.

Federal Judicial Circuits

Appeals in the federal court system are heard in 13 circuits and the Supreme Court.

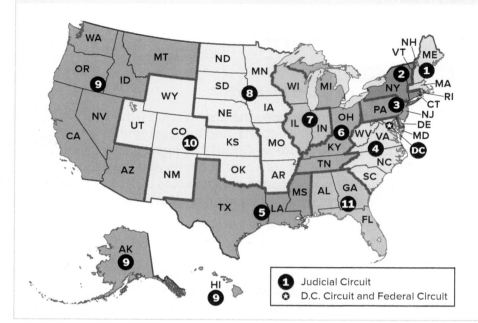

GEOGRAPHY CONNECTION

1. **Contrasting** Which circuit has the largest area?

2. **Inferring** In which circuit court would someone file an appeal on a decision made in the district court in Miami?

Legend:
- **1** Judicial Circuit
- **✪** D.C. Circuit and Federal Circuit

District courts hear both criminal and civil cases. In a criminal case, an attorney representing the government brings charges and argues the case against a person accused of a crime. This is called a *prosecution*. In a civil case, one party brings a complaint that someone else has injured them. The party that brings the complaint is the *plaintiff*. The party accused of doing the harm in a civil or criminal case is the *defendant*.

As trial courts, district courts are responsible for determining the facts of a case. In a criminal case, the jury or the judge will listen to evidence and decide if the accused person is guilty or not. In a civil case, the jury or judge will decide if the plaintiff has been wronged and if they deserve to be compensated. District courts are the only federal courts in which witnesses testify and juries hear cases and reach verdicts.

District courts hear only cases that are authorized by the U.S. Constitution or federal laws. Because they hear only certain kinds of cases, these courts are said to have *limited jurisdiction*.

Circuit Courts of Appeals

What if you lose a trial in district court and are sentenced to a punishment or required to pay money to someone who has sued you? If you believe that the process followed in the trial was unfair, you can appeal to a higher court.

The second level of the federal court system makes up the circuit courts. They are also called circuit courts of appeals, courts of appeals, federal appeals courts, or appellate (uh•PEH•luht) courts.

Appeals courts differ from trial courts. They do not conduct trials, consider evidence, or call witnesses. They do not decide guilt or innocence in criminal cases or which party wins in civil cases. Instead, they decide whether the judge in the district court made the case decision properly and followed the rules. They have **appellate jurisdiction**, which means the authority to hear appeals from a lower court.

An appeal is a request for a judge to review how the decision in a case was made. Who can appeal? In a civil case, the losing side can appeal. In a criminal case, only a defendant who has been found guilty can appeal. The prosecution cannot appeal if it loses. The U.S. courts of appeal are required to accept the cases appealed to them. They cannot refuse to hear an appeal.

Lawyers appeal a case when they believe that the district court made a mistake. For

---

appellate jurisdiction the authority of a court to hear a case appealed from a lower court

example, they might claim that the judge made a procedural error such as allowing testimony or evidence that should have been **excluded**, or kept out of, the trial. They might appeal because they believe that the judge made an error in interpreting or applying the law. They can also appeal on the grounds that the law at the center of the trial is unconstitutional.

Appeals courts may also review the decisions of federal agencies that regulate an industry or activity. Such cases can arise if a party claims that the agency acted unfairly or implemented a law incorrectly.

There are twelve United States courts of appeals that serve a geographic area. One of these circuit courts is based in the District of Columbia. Most of the others serve one or more states or territories. These areas vary in size. The First Circuit includes four New England states. In contrast, the Ninth Circuit consists of nine states, including California. Each appellate court hears cases from district courts within its area.

There is also a thirteenth appeals court called the Court of Appeals for the Federal Circuit. This court hears cases involving patent law, international trade, or other civil cases brought against the United States. Although it is based in Washington, D.C., it can hear cases from all parts of the country.

Rulings

The process for appeals courts differs from the trials carried out in district courts. Lawyers for the two sides write formal arguments presenting their view of the disputed issue. These documents are called *briefs*. This is followed some time later by a stage called *oral arguments*. In this step, a panel of three or more judges listens to the arguments made by lawyers for both sides. The judges also review the record of the case from the trial court. The panel rules only on whether the original trial was a fair one. It does not rule on the verdict in the case. It does not determine the guilt or innocence of the accused, only whether laws and procedures were followed correctly.

The panel makes its decision by majority vote. The decision is known as a **ruling**—an official decision that settles a case and helps establish the meaning of the law. Appellate court judges can decide a case in one of three ways:

- They can *uphold*, or agree with, the result of the original trial. This leaves the verdict in that trial unchanged.

ruling an official decision by a judge or a court that settles a case and may also establish the meaning of a law

exclude to keep out

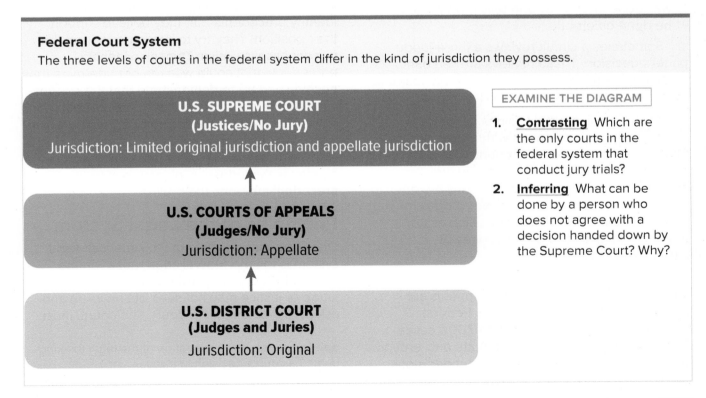

Federal Court System
The three levels of courts in the federal system differ in the kind of jurisdiction they possess.

U.S. SUPREME COURT
(Justices/No Jury)
Jurisdiction: Limited original jurisdiction and appellate jurisdiction

U.S. COURTS OF APPEALS
(Judges/No Jury)
Jurisdiction: Appellate

U.S. DISTRICT COURT
(Judges and Juries)
Jurisdiction: Original

EXAMINE THE DIAGRAM

1. **Contrasting** Which are the only courts in the federal system that conduct jury trials?

2. **Inferring** What can be done by a person who does not agree with a decision handed down by the Supreme Court? Why?

In special circumstances an appellate court may sit en banc, with more judges hearing a case than the usual panel of three judges.

Identifying What is the role of appellate courts?

- They can *overturn*, or reverse, the result of the trial. For instance, they may take this action if they think the trial judge made an error in procedure that can no longer be fixed.
- They can *remand* the case. This means sending the case back to the lower court to be tried again. The judges do this if they think the original trial was not fair in some way. When an appellate court remands a case, it gives instructions to the lower court that detail what was done incorrectly and tells it what should be done differently.

Sometimes a circuit reviews a three-judge panel's decision. These reviews are "en banc," meaning that all the judges in the circuit hear and judge the case.

These circuit court decisions become binding rulings on all courts within their circuits. That means that the district courts within the circuit must apply the law in the way the circuit court decided. These decisions are not binding on other circuits. However, judges in another circuit could use the decision as an argument in favor of a particular way of interpreting the law.

Decisions of the courts of appeals can themselves be appealed. Those appeals are heard by the U.S. Supreme Court. Federal appeals courts decide more than 7,000 cases each year. The Supreme Court hears only around 100 cases a year. Most appeals court decisions stand.

Opinions

When an appeals court makes a ruling, one judge writes an opinion for the court. The **opinion** states the ruling and explains the legal thinking behind the court's decision.

The opinion sets a precedent for all courts and agencies within the court's jurisdiction. A precedent is a judge's ruling that can be used as the basis for a decision in similar cases that come later. When lawyers argue their cases, they identify precedents that they believe support their position. They try to demonstrate that the current case is similar. They also identify precedents that could weaken or undermine their position and try to demonstrate that the current case is different enough that those precedents do not apply. A precedent is not a law, but it is a very powerful legal argument. Judges and courts follow precedents. A major part of any judicial opinion is the judges' explanation of how precedent supports their ruling.

Principles of the Legal System

One important principle in the American legal system is that no federal court, not even the Supreme Court, may **initiate** action. That is, a judge or justice may not seek out an issue and ask parties to bring it to court. The courts must

opinion a detailed explanation of the legal thinking behind a court's decision in a case

initiate to begin

wait for **litigants**, or parties to a lawsuit, to come before them.

Another important principle is respect for precedent. The importance of precedent comes from a principle of British law. This principle states that lower courts must abide by the decisions of the highest court in a jurisdiction. As a result, federal district courts in a circuit must follow the precedents of the circuit court. Because the United States Supreme Court is the highest court in the land, all courts in the country must follow the precedents it establishes.

However, there are countless issues on which the Supreme Court has not established a clear precedent. This makes it possible that two different circuit courts could establish different, conflicting precedents. When this happens, rulings in the two circuits will remain inconsistent until the Supreme Court accepts a relevant case and establishes a precedent that all courts must follow.

✓ **CHECK FOR UNDERSTANDING**

1. **Comparing and Contrasting** Compare and contrast trial and appellate courts.
2. **Determining Central Ideas** What force or weight does precedent have?

Federal Judges

GUIDING QUESTION

What is the selection process for federal judges?

Congress sets the number of judges on any federal court, including the Supreme Court. Each district court has at least two judges. District courts in high-population areas may have more because there are more cases to hear. In total, more than 670 judges serve on district courts in the United States.

Circuit appeals courts have from 6 to 29 judges. The number of judges on the U.S. Supreme Court has been as low as five and as high as ten. Since 1869, it has been fixed at nine. Supreme Court judges use the title *justice*.

Appointing Federal Judges

At the state level, judges can be elected, appointed, or a combination of the two. That is not the case at the federal level. Under Article II of the U.S. Constitution, the president nominates all federal judges. The nominees are then confirmed or rejected by the Senate. Confirmation takes a simple majority of senators voting yes.

In general, presidents want to appoint judges who share their ideas about justice and the law. The Constitution does not state any qualifications for judgeship, such as age, citizenship, or education.

Presidents often practice senatorial courtesy when selecting candidates for district and circuit court judgeships. Before making the nomination, the president discusses the potential candidate with the senators from the candidate's state. If one of the senators objects, the president usually chooses another candidate. Senatorial courtesy does not apply to nominees for the Supreme Court.

Presidents choose candidates whom they think are likely to be approved by the Senate. Many individuals and groups offer their opinions on nominees. For example, interest groups and the American Bar Association, an organization of lawyers, offer their views on nominees. Sometimes the Senate rejects a nominee based on concerns about the person's qualifications or legal philosophy. In recent years, Senate action on presidential appointments to federal courts has become more sharply divided along political party lines.

The tow trucks labeled right and left refer to conservative (right) and liberal (left) political positions.

Analyzing Visuals What does the cartoon suggest is the influence of the executive branch on the federal courts?

Keefe, The Denver Post

litigant a party to a lawsuit

The U.S. Marshals Service protects federal courts and those who work in them or visit them.

Term of Office

Once appointed, federal judges have their jobs for life or until they retire or resign. They can be removed from office only through the process of impeachment. The Framers gave federal judges this right to hold their office, or **tenure**, so they can be free from public and political pressures when they hear cases. They wanted federal judges to be independent.

Other Court Officials

The federal court system includes workers who are not judges. Other employees include law clerks, administrative assistants, and court reporters. Each district court also has three key officials.

Magistrate (MA-juh-strate) **judges** do much of a judge's routine work. They issue court orders, such as search warrants. At preliminary hearings, they consider evidence and decide if a case should be brought to trial. They decide whether people under arrest should be held in jail or released on bail. Magistrates may also serve as judges in less serious, or misdemeanor (mis-duh-MEE-nur), cases. Magistrates do not serve for life. They have eight-year terms.

They are not appointed by the president but named by a majority vote of the judges in a district.

Each district has a U.S. attorney and at least one deputy attorney. These lawyers investigate and prosecute people accused of breaking federal law. In civil cases, they represent the government. The president nominates U.S. attorneys and the Senate confirms them. They are appointed to four-year terms. While the U.S. attorneys are part of the legal system, they are employees of the executive branch. They work under the Attorney General, the head of the Department of Justice.

A U.S. Marshal serves in each district as well. The Marshals Service is part of the Department of Justice, which is in the executive branch, but also serves as the law enforcement arm of the federal courts. Marshals protect judges, jurors, and other court personnel. They keep accused persons in custody and escort convicted persons to prison. They work to apprehend fugitives who flee from justice. They also deliver subpoenas. A **subpoena** (suh•PEE•nuh) is a court order that requires a person to appear in court to testify as a witness or to provide documents as evidence.

✓ CHECK FOR UNDERSTANDING

1. **Summarizing** How do people become federal district and circuit court judges?

2. **Explaining** What services do U.S. Marshals provide?

LESSON ACTIVITIES

1. **Informative/Explanatory Writing** Describe how the procedures in district and circuit courts differ.

2. **Analyzing Information** With a partner, prepare a presentation in question-and-answer format that explains the structure and functions of the federal court system. In your presentation, one of you will take the part of an interviewer and the other a federal judge. Present your interview to the class.

tenure the right to hold an office once a person is confirmed
magistrate judge a federal judge who does much of a district court judge's routine work
subpoena court order to appear in court or to produce evidence

The Supreme Court

READING STRATEGY

Integrating Knowledge and Ideas As you read, complete a graphic organizer such as the one shown by citing key facts about the U.S. Supreme Court in each category.

Category	Key Facts
Jurisdiction	
Duties	
Powers	
Limits on Power	

Jurisdiction and Duties

GUIDING QUESTION

What is the jurisdiction of the Supreme Court?

The U.S. Supreme Court has the final word on the meaning of the U.S. Constitution and federal laws. Its justices hear cases and determine how the law applies to specific issues. For example, could a school principal suspend a student for wearing clothing with a political message, or would that violate the First Amendment? Must a state enforce federal immigration laws, or would that violate the division of powers between federal and state governments? Supreme Court justices decide issues such as these.

Jurisdiction

Congress defines the jurisdiction and responsibilities of judges who sit on federal district and appeals courts. The Constitution sets the jurisdiction and responsibilities of the Supreme Court. Article III, Section 2, identifies the types of cases for which the Supreme Court has original jurisdiction and the types of cases for which it has appellate jurisdiction.

Most of the Supreme Court's work involves its appellate jurisdiction. It mainly hears cases that have been appealed from the lower courts. The Supreme Court has original jurisdiction in only two types of cases. One type is cases that involve disputes between two or more states. The other type is cases that involve diplomats from foreign countries.

The Supreme Court building faces the U.S. Capitol.

GO ONLINE Explore the Student Edition eBook and find interactive maps, charts, graphs, and tools.

C239

Because the Supreme Court is the highest federal court, it has final authority in cases involving the Constitution, acts of Congress, and treaties with other nations. The Court's decisions are binding on all lower courts, including state courts.

Duties of Justices

The main duty of the justices is to hear and rule on cases. Yet the justices do not rule on every case presented to them. U.S. Courts of Appeals are required to hear all appeals filed with them. The Supreme Court is not. The justices can choose whether or not to take a case. They choose to hear only a fraction of the cases they receive—fewer than 150 cases out of more than 7,000 filed each year. When the Supreme Court refuses to hear a case, the decision of the lower court stands, that is, remains in effect.

The Supreme Court has nine justices. The number of justices is not fixed but is set by Congress. The number has remained nine since 1869. The **chief justice** is the Supreme Court's leader. Eight associate justices complete the panel.

Chief Justice William Howard Taft is the only person to serve as both president—from 1909 to 1913—and Chief Justice of the Supreme Court, from 1921 to 1930.

The chief justice has some additional duties besides hearing and judging cases. The chief justice is responsible for the operation of the Supreme Court and for overseeing the whole federal judicial system.

Qualifications of Justices

The Constitution does not name any qualifications to become a Supreme Court justice. There is no requirement that they must be lawyers, although, so far, all justices have had legal training. Before being named to the Court, many have practiced or taught law. More than three dozen had never been judges before joining the Court. Eight of the nine current members of the Court served as judges in a U.S. Court of Appeals.

The U.S. Supreme Court has become more diverse in recent years. For more than 126 years, every member of the Court was a white male. In 1967 Thurgood Marshall became the first African American to join the Court. He was replaced in 1991 by Clarence Thomas, who is also African American. The first woman to become a justice was Sandra Day O'Connor in 1981. There are now three women on the Court. In 2009 Sonia Sotomayor became the first Hispanic person to join the Court. Louis Brandeis became the first Jewish person to serve on the Court when he was confirmed in 1916. Eight out of 113 justices have been Jewish. Six of the current justices are Catholic.

Senate Action

The men and women who sit on the Court, like all federal judges, have their jobs for life. That means that any person named to the Court will likely have influence for a long time. For this reason, nominees are investigated thoroughly. Presidents study a candidate's record carefully to ensure that a nominee shares their general outlook on the law. Presidents also try to choose a nominee whom they believe will win the Senate's approval.

Once the president nominates someone for the Supreme Court, the Senate Judiciary Committee holds a **confirmation hearing** to consider the nominee. For several days, senators

chief justice the leader of the U.S. Supreme Court who is also responsible for overseeing the whole federal judicial system

confirmation hearing set of meetings by the Senate Judiciary Committee to consider and vote on people nominated to be federal judges

Justices of the U.S. Supreme Court

Associate Justice Clarence Thomas is the longest serving current member of the U.S. Supreme Court.

Justice	Year Confirmed	Appointing President	Confirmation Vote in Senate
Clarence Thomas	1991	George H. W. Bush	52-48
Stephen G. Breyer	1994	Bill Clinton	87-9
John G. Roberts, Jr. (chief justice)	2005	George W. Bush	78-22
Samuel A. Alito, Jr.	2006	George W. Bush	58-42
Sonia Sotomayor	2009	Barack Obama	68-31
Elena Kagan	2010	Barack Obama	63-37
Neil M. Gorsuch	2017	Donald Trump	54-45
Brett Kavanaugh	2018	Donald Trump	50-48
Amy Coney Barrett	2020	Donald Trump	52-48

Source: United States Senate

HISTORY CONNECTION

1. **Identifying** How many justices have each of the last three presidents appointed to the Court?
2. **Analyzing Visuals** What trends can you see over time in the size of the majority in the Senate's confirmation votes?

question the nominee. They ask about the person's background, character, experience, and view of the law. The committee then votes on whether or not to approve the nominee. If approved, the nomination goes to the full Senate for a vote.

In addition to examination of their professional experience, some nominees may face questions about their judgment and character. Senators also try to learn the nominee's thinking on different issues. Nominees typically refuse to answer questions on issues that may come before the Court in a case. They say that doing so could raise questions about whether they would have an open mind if the issue came before them.

The Senate does not always approve nominees. In a dozen cases, nominations have been withdrawn before they were voted on. The Senate has rejected 12 nominees, most recently in 1987.

The Senate has refused to act on 10 nominations. The most recent example occurred in 2016. In March of that election year, President Barack Obama nominated Merrick Garland to the Court. Republicans held a majority in the Senate and refused to consider the nomination made by the Democratic president. They said that the American people should have the chance to elect the president who would choose someone to fill the vacant seat on the Court. Republican Donald Trump won the presidential election in November and nominated Neil Gorsuch, who was confirmed.

Four years later, a similar situation arose. Justice Ruth Bader Ginsburg died in September of 2020. Trump nominated Amy Coney Barrett to fill the seat. Democrats complained about the move since a presidential election was just weeks away. Republicans again had a majority in the Senate and confirmed Barrett in late October.

✓ CHECK FOR UNDERSTANDING

1. **Identifying Cause and Effect** What happens when the Supreme Court refuses to hear an appeal?
2. **Making Connections** How does the appointment of justices to the U.S. Supreme Court show the principle of checks and balances?

The Supreme Court at the opening of a new term in October 2021: *(front row from left)* Samuel A. Alito, Jr., Clarence Thomas, Chief Justice John G. Roberts, Jr., Stephen G. Breyer, Sonia Sotomayor. *(back row from left)* Brett Kavanaugh, Elena Kagan, Neil M. Gorsuch, and Amy Coney Barrett.

Analyzing Visuals
What diversity can you see from this photograph of the current U.S. Supreme Court?

Powers and Limits

GUIDING QUESTION
What powers are given to the Supreme Court?

Article III of the Constitution creates the judicial branch but does not include much detail about it. Over the years, Congress has established rules that govern the powers and the organization of the Supreme Court. In addition, the Court has a role in the Constitution's system of checks and balances, which limit the power of each of the three branches of government.

Judicial Review

One of the most important powers of the Supreme Court is the power of **judicial review**. Judicial review is analysis of whether an action by the legislative or executive branches or by a state goes against the Constitution. A law that is not allowed under the Constitution is not a valid law. If the Court decides that a law is not constitutional, it will **nullify**, or legally cancel, that law. In *Reed* v. *Reed*, for example, the Court ruled that a state law that discriminated against women was unconstitutional because it violated the Fourteenth Amendment.

judicial review the power of the Supreme Court to say whether any federal, state, or local law or government action goes against the Constitution

nullify to cancel legally

Every federal or state law must be acceptable under the rules set by the Constitution. If not, the law cannot stand. This position is based on the supremacy clause found in Article IV of the U.S. Constitution. It says that the Constitution

66 shall be the supreme Law of the Land; and the Judges in every State shall be bound thereby, any Thing in the Constitution or Laws of any State to the Contrary notwithstanding. 99

Congress passes laws that are complex and have many **provisions**, or specific statements. The cases that reach the Supreme Court may not challenge an entire law but only one or a few of those provisions. The Court's decision can determine that one section of a law is unconstitutional but let the rest of the law stand. For example, Congress passed the Dodd-Frank Act to increase government's ability to oversee activities of banks. One part of the law limited the president's power to fire the head of a new federal agency that the law created. In 2019 the Supreme Court ruled that part of the law unconstitutional. The rest of the law remained in force.

The Court can also nullify actions of the executive branch if they violate the Constitution. In 1974 the Court ruled that President Richard Nixon had to give some tape recordings of his

provision specific part of a law

PHOTO: Sipa USA/Alamy Stock Photo; TEXT: US Constitution, Article VI

conversations with aides to a government prosecutor. Nixon had refused to do so. After the Court issued its decision, he handed over the tapes.

John Marshall, the first chief justice of the United States, described the great power of judicial review when he said,

> 66 It is emphatically [absolutely] the province [realm] and duty of the judicial department to say what the law is. Those who apply the rule to particular cases, must of necessity expound [have to explain] and interpret that rule. If two laws conflict with each other, the courts must decide on the operation [working] of each. 99
>
> —Chief Justice John Marshall, *Marbury* v. *Madison* (1803)

The power of judicial review is an important check on the legislative and executive branches of government. To fulfill their functions, they must make and implement laws, but their actions are subject to oversight by the Supreme Court.

The idea of judicial review has influenced constitutions in other countries. Many countries have created a special constitutional court. It has the power to review and nullify laws.

Marbury v. *Madison*

The Constitution does not explicitly give the power of judicial review to the Supreme Court. It was something the Framers had in mind for the Court, however. Alexander Hamilton explained the idea in one of the Federalist Papers. He said that judges should ensure that the will of the people—as shown in the Constitution—was protected against the will of Congress—as shown in laws passed.

Congress gave the power of judicial review to the Court in part in the Judiciary Act of 1789. That law said the Court had the power to review the acts of state governments. In 1803 the Court used the case of *Marbury* v. *Madison* to apply this power to acts of Congress as well. In his opinion, Chief Justice Marshall set forth three principles of judicial review:

- The Constitution is the supreme law of the land.
- If there is a conflict between the Constitution and any other law, the Constitution rules.
- The judicial branch has a duty to uphold the Constitution. Thus, it must be able to determine when a law conflicts with the Constitution and to nullify such laws.

Limits on the Supreme Court

The Constitution's checks and balances limit the power of federal courts, including the Supreme Court. First, the Court can hear and make rulings only on the cases that are **submitted** to it. The Court may not open cases on its own.

Second, all cases the Court takes up must be actual legal disputes. Individuals cannot ask the Court to decide whether a law is constitutional without claiming that his or her constitutional rights have been personally violated by the law. Third, the Court can hear only cases that involve a federal question. That is, it has to involve federal law or the U.S. Constitution.

Tradition limits the Supreme Court in another way. Traditionally, the Court does not deal with political matters. Those matters are left to be resolved by the executive or legislative branch. Why does the Court avoid political issues? Americans disagree about many topics. The justices do not wish their decisions to be seen as reflecting the interests or ideas of any political party. They want the public to view the Court as independent and focused on justice. In that way, they hope to maintain the trust of the people.

The Court broke from this tradition during the 2000 presidential election when it heard two cases concerning the recounting of votes in Florida. In 2020 many lawsuits challenged state court rulings about emergency measures related to voting during the COVID-19 pandemic.

---

submit to put forward

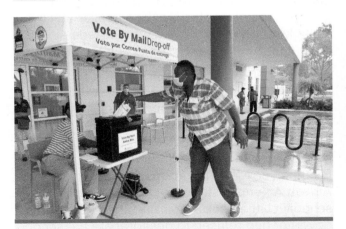

In 2020 executive officials and judges in some states ordered emergency measures to make it easier for people to vote during the COVID-19 pandemic. The Supreme Court generally allowed those state actions to stand.

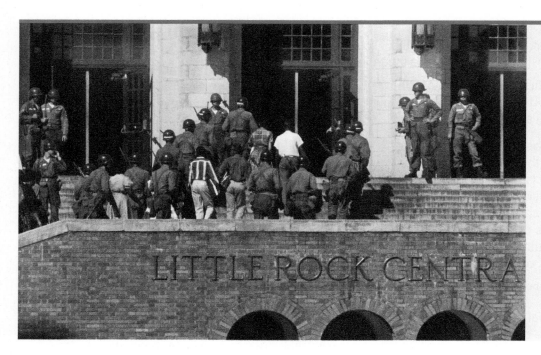

Soldiers from the U.S. Army stand by as African American students enter a Little Rock, Arkansas, high school in 1957. President Dwight Eisenhower sent army troops to the city to enforce a U.S. Supreme Court decision to end segregation in schools. The state's governor had prevented the students from entering the school.

The Supreme Court did not take most of these cases. It let policies set by state officials or courts stand.

Another check on the Court is that it has no power to enforce its rulings. That is, it cannot ensure that its orders are carried out. In some cases, it must depend on the executive branch and on state and local officials to obey and enforce its decisions.

The executive branch usually accepts and follows the Supreme Court's decisions, but not always. For instance, President Andrew Jackson refused to obey the Court's ruling in *Worcester* v. *Georgia*. In this 1832 case, the Supreme Court ordered Georgia to stop breaking treaties that the Cherokee Nation had signed with the federal government. Jackson refused to enforce the Court's order, and Georgia continued to break the treaties.

In contrast, President Dwight Eisenhower enforced Supreme Court decisions with the full power of the federal government. In 1953 the Supreme Court ruled that segregated public schools were unconstitutional. In 1957 Eisenhower sent army troops to escort nine African American students into an all-white school in Little Rock, Arkansas, after the state's governor had refused to desegregate the school.

If the Court rules a law unconstitutional, Congress and state legislatures have options. They can repeal the law. They can change the law so it is no longer unconstitutional. They can try to undo Court rulings by changing the Constitution with an amendment. That approach requires the approval of three-quarters of the states. In the years before the Civil War, the Supreme Court ruled in *Dred Scott* v. *Sandford* that African Americans could not be U.S. citizens. After the war, Congress adopted the Fourteenth Amendment, which made anyone born in the United States a citizen.

✓ **CHECK FOR UNDERSTANDING**

1. **Explaining** How can the U.S. Supreme Court claim to have the power to nullify a state law or element of a state constitution?

2. **Summarizing** What was Chief Justice John Marshall's basis for claiming the power of judicial review for the U.S. Supreme Court in *Marbury* v. *Madison*?

LESSON ACTIVITIES

1. **Argumentative Writing** Write two paragraphs in which you explain what characteristics you think a Supreme Court justice should have. Think about background, personal character, professional experience, education, legal training, and any other factor you think matters. Give reasons explaining why each characteristic you list is important.

2. **Analyzing Information** With a partner, prepare a diagram that shows the checks and balances between the U.S. Supreme Court and both Congress and the executive branch. Include specific examples of ways the Court can check those two branches and the checks that they have on the Court's power.

05

Analyzing Supreme Court Cases: Judicial Review

? COMPELLING QUESTION

How has judicial review shaped American government?

Plan Your Inquiry

DEVELOPING QUESTIONS

Think about the separation of powers and the system of checks and balances in the United States. What powers do the courts have? How does the judicial branch check and balance the other branches? Then read the Compelling Question for this lesson. What questions can you ask to help you answer this Compelling Question? Create a graphic organizer like the one below. Write these Supporting Questions in your graphic organizer.

Supporting Questions	Primary or Secondary Source	What the source tells me about how judicial review has shaped American government	Questions the source leaves unanswered
	A		
	B		
	C		

ANALYZING SOURCES

Next, examine the sources in this lesson. Analyze each source by answering the questions that follow it. How does each source help you answer each Supporting Question you created? What questions do you still have? Write these in your graphic organizer.

After you analyze the sources, you will:
- use the evidence from the sources,
- communicate your conclusions,
- and take informed action.

Case Summary

This lesson focuses on the Supreme Court case which established judicial review.

Marbury v. Madison In 1801 as President John Adams's term was ending, he nominated 42 federal judges. The Senate confirmed these appointments. However, all of these individuals did not receive their official paperwork before Thomas Jefferson took office as president. Jefferson ordered Secretary of State James Madison not to deliver the papers to the remaining appointees. William Marbury was one of them. Marbury sued Madison. He asked the Supreme Court to force Madison to give him his official paperwork.

Chief Justice John Marshall knew that if the Court took this action, Madison would probably refuse. Since Marshall could not force Madison to act, that ruling would weaken the Court. Marshall found a way to solve the problem. Marbury's right to sue Madison in the Supreme Court came from the Judiciary Act passed by Congress in 1789. Marshall said that the law conflicted with the Constitution. So, in his majority opinion, he declared that portion of the law unconstitutional. In doing so, Marshall claimed for the U.S. Supreme Court the power of judicial review over acts of Congress.

» From 1810 to 1860, the U.S. Supreme Court met in this chamber inside the U.S. Capitol.

VW Pics/Universal Images Group/Getty Images

Opinion of the Court in *Marbury v. Madison*

In Article III of the U.S. Constitution, the Framers established the judicial branch and created the U.S. Supreme Court. They did so in part to check the power of the other branches. However, in the Constitution itself, they did not specify what power the Court had in order to check the other branches. Some of the Framers thought the Supreme Court could nullify, or cancel, laws that conflict with the Constitution. In 1789 Congress enacted the Judiciary Act. It gave the Supreme Court the power to declare state laws unconstitutional. Did that power extend to federal laws? In 1803 John Marshall decided that it did. This passage from *Marbury* v. *Madison* shows Marshall's reasoning.

» Chief Justice John Marshall

PRIMARY SOURCE: SUPREME COURT OPINION

66 It is emphatically [strongly] the **province** and duty of the judicial department to say what the law is. Those who apply the rule to particular cases, must of necessity expound [state] and interpret that rule. If two laws conflict with each other, the courts must decide on the operation of each.

So if a law be in opposition to the constitution: if both the law and the constitution apply to a particular case, so that the court must either decide that case **conformably** to the law, disregarding the constitution; or conformably to the constitution, disregarding the law: the court must determine which of these conflicting rules governs the case. This is of the very **essence** of judicial duty.

If then the courts are to regard the constitution; and [t]he constitution is superior to any ordinary act of the legislature; the constitution, and not such ordinary act, must govern the case to which they both apply. 99

— Chief Justice John Marshall, Opinion of the Court, *Marbury v. Madison*, 1803

province a proper function or area of activity

conformably done in a way that is consistent with the law

essence the basic nature or qualities of something

EXAMINE THE SOURCE

1. **Summarizing** What powers does Marshall say the courts have in the first paragraph?
2. **Explaining** How does Marshall develop his reasoning in the other two paragraphs?
3. **Analyzing Perspectives** How does this line of reasoning justify the power of judicial review?

Is the Court Nonpartisan?

Under the U.S. Constitution, federal judgeships are life appointments. The purpose is to create an independent judiciary that is free from the influence of politics. In recent years, however, Supreme Court justices have come under increasing criticism for seeming to base their decisions on political considerations. In addition, senators have increasingly seemed to take party-based positions on nominees to the Court. This article was published in 2021, about a year after heated debate over President Donald Trump's appointment of Amy Coney Barrett to the Court.

» U.S. Supreme Court Building

SECONDARY SOURCE: ARTICLE

66 Justice Amy Coney Barrett is offended by those questioning the **impartiality** of the Supreme Court.

'This Court is not comprised of a bunch of **partisan hacks**,' she announced at a recent event. . . . 'Judicial philosophies are not the same as political parties.' . . .

This insistence—that justices are simply following the law—is a common **rhetorical** tool in the partisan conflict over the Court. . . .

Justice Stephen Breyer . . . recently wrote that 'it is a judge's sworn duty to be impartial, and all of us take that oath seriously.' I have little doubt that the justices are so full of self-regard [self-importance] as to *believe* that they are impartial [fair], but the public is under no obligation to take this seriously. The justices' actual behavior is the obvious rebuttal [argument against]. Furthermore, the shape of the Court today is the direct result of decades of partisan politics. . . .

The day [Justice] Thurgood Marshall retired, he issued a furious dissent to a decision that strengthened the death penalty. 'Power, not reason, is the new currency of this Court's decisionmaking,' Marshall wrote . . . 'Neither the law nor the facts . . . underwent any change in the last four years, only the personnel of this court did.' . . .

Make no mistake, I am not criticizing the justices or the conservative legal movement for pursuing their political project with zeal [eagerness]. . . . This is how democracy works—people with a common goal work together to realize it. . . .

What I take exception to is the demand from judges and justices that the public acquiesce to [accept] their self-delusion [false beliefs] that they are wise **sages** who hold themselves above the vulgarities [nastiness] of partisan politics. 99

— Adam Serwer, "The Lie About the Supreme Court Everyone Pretends to Believe," The Atlantic, 2021

impartiality equal treatment, fairness

partisan hack someone who carries out party beliefs regardless of what is right

rhetorical concerned with speaking or writing in order to influence people

sage scholarly person

EXAMINE THE SOURCE

1. **Explaining** What did Justice Marshall say had become the basis of the Court's decisions?
2. **Analyzing Perspectives** What is the author's main criticism of the Court?

PHOTO: Win Wiskerke/Alamy Stock Photo; TEXT: Serwer, Adam. "The Lie About the Supreme Court Everyone Pretends to Believe." The Atlantic. September 28, 2021. https://www.theatlantic.com/ideas/archive/2021/09/lie-about-supreme-court-everyone-pretends-believe/620198/.

The Proper Role of Courts

Republican Sam Brownback of Kansas served in the U.S. Senate from 1996 until 2011. He prepared this statement for the confirmation hearing of Supreme Court nominee Samuel Alito. He offers his view of the role of the courts.

PRIMARY SOURCE: SPEECH

66 [T]he role of judiciary in our society . . . has become an ever-expanding and important discussion because of the expanding role of the courts in recent years. . . . When the courts, improperly, . . . assume the power to decide more political than legal issues in nature, the people naturally focus less on the law and more on the lawyers . . . Most Americans want judges who will stick to interpreting the law rather than making it. It is beyond dispute [argument] that the Constitution and its Framers intended this to be the role of judges. . . .

Chief Justice Marshall later explained in *Marbury* v. *Madison* that the Constitution permitted Federal courts neither to write nor execute the laws but, rather, to say what the law is. That narrow **scope** of judicial power was the reason the people accepted the idea that the Federal courts could have the power of judicial review. . . .

It may seem **ironic**, but the judicial branch preserves its **legitimacy** through **refraining** from action on political questions. 99

— Senator Sam Brownback, "Brownback's opening statement on Alito," January 9, 2006

scope the range or extent of something

ironic expressing something opposite from the literal, or actual, meaning

legitimacy lawfulness

refrain to keep oneself from doing something

EXAMINE THE SOURCE

1. **Analyzing Perspectives** What criticism of the courts is made in the first paragraph?

2. **Explaining** What narrow role does Brownback think the courts should fill?

Complete Your Inquiry

EVALUATE SOURCES AND USE EVIDENCE

Refer back to the Compelling Question and the Supporting Questions you developed at the beginning of the lesson.

1. **Explaining** How does Chief Justice Marshall see the power of judicial review?

2. **Making Connections** What criticisms do the authors of Sources B and C make of the courts?

3. **Gathering Sources** Which sources helped you answer the Supporting Questions and the Compelling Question? Which sources, if any, challenged what you thought you knew when you first created your Supporting Questions? What information do you still need in order to answer your questions? What other viewpoints would you like to investigate? Where would you find that information?

4. **Evaluating Sources** Identify the sources that helped answer your Supporting Questions. How reliable are the sources? How would you verify the reliability of the sources?

COMMUNICATE CONCLUSIONS

5. **Collaborating** Write down one of your Supporting Questions. In a group, pass your papers to the right, and take turns writing responses to the other students' questions. Then discuss your responses as a group and work together to write a group response to the Compelling Question. Also note any questions you still have about judicial review. When you are done, share your responses and questions with the class and discuss how you might find answers to the remaining questions.

TAKE INFORMED ACTION

Making a Podcast on Judicial Review In a small group, prepare 5-6 interview questions about the judicial review process. Interview a judge, court official, lawyer, or history teacher in your local community or a nearby city. Email your questions to your interviewee ahead of time so that the person can prepare. Set up a time for a call to conduct the interview. If possible, record it for your podcast. After the interview, be sure to send a thank you note to the official. Share your podcast with the class.

United States Congress. Confirmation Hearing on the Nomination of Samuel A. Alito, Jr. To Be An Associate Justice of the Supreme Court of the United States: Hearing Before the Committee on the Judiciary. United States Senate. 109th Congress, 2nd Session, January 9-13, 2006. Serial No. J-109-56. Washington, DC: Government Printing Office, 2006.

Key Ideas and Details As you read, complete a flowchart to show the steps a case moves through from the appeal to the Supreme Court to the final decision.

Steps in a Supreme Court Case
1.
2.
3.
4.
5.
6.
7.
8.
9.

Court Procedures

GUIDING QUESTION

What kinds of cases does the Supreme Court decide to hear?

Supreme Court procedures follow longstanding traditions. Since 1800, the justices have always worn black robes when in session. Since the late 1800s, every official meeting of the Court has begun with each justice shaking each other justice's hand—this adds up to 36 handshakes for a nine-member Court. The justices sit in a set order, with the chief justice in the center, the most senior associate justice on the right, the next most senior associate on the left, and so on, with the newest justice on the far left.

How Cases Reach the Court

The Supreme Court receives cases appealed to it by everyone from prisoners to the president of the United States. Nearly all cases come to the Supreme Court as appeals of a lower-court decision. In most cases, a party that lost in a case petitions the Supreme Court to hear its appeal. If it accepts the case, the Supreme Court issues a *writ of certiorari* (ser•shee•oh•RARE•ee). A *writ* is a judicial order. A **writ of certiorari** is a judicial order that tells a lower court to send its records on a case to a higher court for review. The party requesting a writ of certiorari must explain why he or she thinks the lower court made an error.

Sometimes a lower court will ask the Supreme Court to hear one of its cases. This is done when the court is not sure how to apply the law to the case. The Supreme Court does not accept all cases presented to it.

writ of certiorari an order a higher court issues to a lower court to obtain the records of a particular case

The justices of the U.S. Supreme Court sit in the nine chairs at the front of this room when in public session.

The Court receives around 7,000 appeals each year. It hears no more than 150 of them.

Selecting Cases

The Supreme Court meets each year for a nine-month term. Each term begins the first Monday in October. Terms are named for the year in which they begin. For instance, the 2021 term ran from October 2021 to June 2022. Additional special sessions may be called to deal with urgent matters.

During the term, the justices select which cases they will hear. Some cases are selected because they involve a key constitutional question, such as freedom of speech or fair trials.

The Supreme Court also looks for cases that involve legal issues that have been decided differently by courts in different circuits. The Court can settle the issue involved in those cases. By doing so, it ensures that lower courts can apply the law consistently across the country.

Requests are filed throughout the year, and the justices meet regularly to consider them and decide which ones to accept. The Supreme Court accepts a case when at least four of the nine justices agree to hear it. These cases go on the Court's calendar of cases, or **docket**.

The justices usually select cases that involve legal issues, rather than political ones. They also try to choose cases that affect the entire country rather than individuals or particular groups. Some of the Court's most significant decisions arise from cases involving civil liberties, such as those that deal with First Amendment issues and those that concern the rights of the accused, as well as those that help define the powers of the federal government. These cases involve issues related to determining the limits of government power and protecting the rights of the individual.

The justices' workload of cases in a term is its **caseload**. The Court's decisions in these cases set out principles that apply not only to the parties involved but to the entire nation. Through these cases, the Court interprets the law.

✓ CHECK FOR UNDERSTANDING

1. **Determining Meaning** What is a writ of certiorari, and what does it signal?
2. **Summarizing** How do the justices decide whether to hear a case?

How the Court Makes Its Rulings

GUIDING QUESTION

What factors affect the Court's decisions?

What happens once the Supreme Court accepts a case? What process do they follow in hearing the case? How do they make decisions and inform the public?

Arguments and Conference

Once the Court takes a case, the lawyers for each party file initial legal briefs. A **brief** is a written document that explains one party's position on the case.

The two parties also have a chance to review each other's briefs. Each then submits a second brief to answer the other party's arguments. The second briefs are shorter than the first ones.

The Court may also agree to accept briefs from parties that are not part of the dispute but have an interest in the case. These might include public interest groups such as the American Civil Liberties Union (ACLU), the NAACP Legal Defense Fund, or the Cato Institute. These briefs are called *amicus curiae*, or "friend of the court," briefs. In some cases, the solicitor general files a brief. This official works in the Justice Department. This brief states the view of the executive branch on the case. These additional briefs are meant to explain to the justices an aspect of the case or a point of law they might otherwise overlook, but justices can ignore them.

After all the briefs have been filed, the justices study them. They may develop questions about the arguments as they read.

Sometimes the justices decide a case at this point and do not go further into the process. When that occurs, they issue an unsigned opinion that states the decision, sometimes called a *per curiam*, or "by the court," opinion.

docket a court's calendar, showing the schedule of cases it is to hear

caseload a judge's or court's workload of cases in a period of time

brief a written document explaining the position of one side or the other in a case

Landmark Supreme Court Decisions

Some Supreme Court decisions mark a turning point for legal history and American society.

CIVIL LIBERTIES

- **Brown v. Board of Education (1954)** overturned **Plessy v. Ferguson (1896)**, which said African Americans could be provided with "separate but equal" public facilities; began school integration
- **Reed v. Reed (1971)** held that a state law that discriminated against women was unconstitutional
- **Roe v. Wade (1973)** legalized a woman's right to an abortion under certain circumstances
- **Obergefell v. Hodges (2015)** ruled that marriage is a fundamental right guaranteed to same-sex couples by the Fourteenth Amendment

FIRST AMENDMENT RIGHTS

- **Near v. Minnesota (1931)** ruled against censorship of information, defining "prior restraint" of written material as unconstitutional
- **DeJonge v. Oregon (1937)** reinforced peaceable assembly and association protection of the First Amendment
- **Engel v. Vitale (1962)** held that a public school district's practice of starting the day with prayer violates the establishment clause
- **Hazelwood v. Kuhlmeier (1988)** upheld a principal's decision to remove articles from a student-produced school newspaper as not violating the First Amendment
- **United States v. Eichman (1990)** struck down Federal Flag Protection Act; held that flag burning is expressive speech

FEDERAL POWER

- **Marbury v. Madison (1803)** established the Supreme Court's power of judicial review
- **McCulloch v. Maryland (1819)** ruled that in a conflict between national and state power, the national government is supreme
- **Gibbons v. Ogden (1824)** established that Congress has sole authority to regulate interstate commerce
- **Bush v. Gore (2000)** ruled that Florida recount of presidential votes violated Fourteenth Amendment; recount stopped and Bush became president

RIGHTS OF THE ACCUSED

- **Gideon v. Wainwright (1963)** declared that a person accused of a major crime had the right to legal counsel during a trial
- **Miranda v. Arizona (1966)** ruled that at the time of arrest suspects cannot be questioned until informed of their rights
- **In re Gault (1967)** held that procedures in a Juvenile Court had to meet the due process standards set by the Fourteenth Amendment

---

HISTORY CONNECTION

1. **Identifying** Which case showed the power of the Court to strike down a state law that discriminated against women?
2. **Identifying** Which case upheld a power of Congress?

If not, the justices next schedule a session of open discussion of the issues, called **oral arguments**. In the oral arguments, the attorneys for the two sides speak for 30 minutes each. The party making the appeal speaks first, followed by the other party. Justices can interrupt the speaker to ask questions. Later in the week, the Court releases audio recordings of the arguments. This is one of the few parts of the Court's consideration of a case that is made public.

About every two weeks during the term, Supreme Court justices meet in conference to have their first discussion of the cases they have been studying. These meetings are private. No onlookers are present, and no notes are kept.

oral argument public session of the U.S. Supreme Court in which lawyers for each party discuss their view of the law and answer the justices' questions

The chief justice presides over the meeting and presents his or her views on the case. The other justices follow in order of seniority, from the longest-serving justice to the newest. Each states his or her views on the case.

After each justice has spoken, they vote. At least six justices must be present for a vote to take place. A majority vote decides a case. If all justices are present, a vote of five to four decides the issue. Sometimes an even number of justices votes on a particular case. If the vote is a tie, the decision made in the lower appeals court stands.

Rarely, the justices ask for the case to be reargued. That means the sides must file briefs again. A few important cases, such as *Brown* v. *Board of Education*, were reargued. The justices may do this if there was a vacancy on the Court when the case was first argued and they want the full nine-member panel to make the decision. They may also do this to ask the lawyers for both parties to consider a specific new issue that arose during oral arguments.

Factors Influencing Decisions

Supreme Court decisions are based on the facts of a case and the law that applies to it. Yet many factors can influence these decisions, including precedents, the nation's social atmosphere, and the justices' individual perspectives.

A guiding principle for all judges is **stare decisis** (STEHR•ee dih•SY•suhs). This Latin term means "let the decision stand." It refers to the practice of using earlier court decisions as the basis for deciding cases. These earlier decisions are called *precedents*. By following precedent, courts make the law predictable. This is an important consideration, as it helps people and organizations know what to expect from the law. Although precedent is important, the makeup of the Court changes, and current justices might see a case differently than did those in the past. The Supreme Court is free to ignore precedent and interpret the law in a different way that fits with their personal views and society as it exists today. For instance, look at the Court's rulings on segregation, which is the practice of keeping races separate. The Court's decisions in the mid-1900s showed how it was responding to changes in society.

The Court considers several factors in deciding whether to follow precedent. First is the quality of the legal reasoning in the decision that set the precedent. A second factor is whether the precedent fits well with related Court decisions. A third is whether new information has become known that makes the thinking behind the earlier

stare decisis Latin for "let the thing stand"; the legal principle of using earlier judicial rulings as a basis for deciding cases

---

Key U.S. Supreme Court Rulings on Segregation

Segregation is the policy of keeping racial groups separate. Over the years, the Supreme Court's rulings changed from supporting segregation to supporting integration.

Segregation

1896—*PLESSY* v. *FERGUSON*
established "separate but equal" doctrine

1927— *GONG LUM* v. *RICE*
applied "separate but equal" to public schools

1938—*STATE OF MISSOURI EX REL. GAINES* v. *CANADA*
set precedent for states to "equalize" African American schools

1948—*SIPUEL* v. *BOARD OF REGENTS OF UNIVERSITY OF OKLAHOMA* ruled race-based denial of entrance to state law school unconstitutional

1950—*SWEATT* v. *PAINTER* and *MCLAURIN* v. *OKLAHOMA STATE REGENTS FOR HIGHER EDUCATION* set precedent that segregation in higher education was unconstitutional

1954—*BROWN* v. *BOARD OF EDUCATION*
overturned *Plessy* v. *Ferguson*, declaring segregation in public schools unconstitutional

Integration

HISTORY CONNECTION

1. **Making Connections** How did the cases from 1948 and 1950 build a basis for the *Brown* decision?

2. **Identifying** Which two precedents did the *Brown* decision overturn?

Steps to a U.S. Supreme Court Decision

The Supreme Court goes through several steps in making its decisions.

Filing of Party Briefs
Lawyers for the two parties file briefs.

Oral Arguments
Lawyers for the two parties meet with justices to present case and answer questions.

Conference
Justices meet to discuss the case and vote on a decision.

Filing of Other Briefs
• Other parties may file briefs.
• A brief reflecting the executive branch's view of the case may be filed.

Writing the Majority Opinion
One justice writes the majority opinion and shares it with the other justices.

Finalizing Opinions
The author of the majority opinion revises it. Other justices write concurring (agreeing) opinions and dissenting (disagreeing) opinions.

The Decision
The Court announces its decision.

EXAMINE THE DIAGRAM

1. **Identifying** At which step does the executive branch try to influence the justices' decision?

2. **Inferring** At which steps do the justices try to influence each other?

decision less reasonable. A fourth factor is the issue of people's reliance on precedent. Overturning precedent can disrupt the lives and behavior of people and organizations. The longer society has relied on a precedent, the less likely the Court is to overturn it.

Each justice has a unique view of the law and the role of the courts in society. Ultimately, each justice sees the world through his or her own life experiences. Those views affect the Court's decisions.

Writing Opinions

A **majority opinion** is the Court's statement of its decision in a case. A written opinion explains the legal reasoning for the decision. An opinion also sets a precedent for courts to follow in the future.

After the vote to decide the case, one justice is assigned the task of writing the majority opinion. If the chief justice is in the majority, he or she chooses which justice in the majority will write that opinion. Sometimes the chief justice

decides to write it. If the chief justice is not in the majority, the longest-serving member of the majority assigns the task.

When the justice writes the majority opinion, he or she not only gives the Court's ruling, but also states the facts of the case. The opinion also explains how the Court reached its decision, including its legal reasoning and any precedents that were involved.

After **drafting** the opinion, the justice shares it with the other justices—including those who voted against the decision. They provide comments, which are addressed when the justice who is writing the opinion revises it. That justice continues passing it around and making more revisions.

The Court issues a *unanimous* opinion when all the justices agree. These decisions have special force.

Sometimes a justice agrees with the majority decision but has different reasons for reaching that decision. In that case, the justice may write a **concurring opinion**.

majority opinion the Court's statement of its decision in a case

draft to write an early version of something

concurring opinion a statement written by a justice who votes with the majority but reaches the same conclusion based on different legal reasoning

The late justices Antonin Scalia and Ruth Bader Ginsburg were known for their sharp dissenting opinions.

A concurring opinion is a separate statement that lays out the justice's reasons for the decision that are not shared by others in the majority. Some concurring opinions offer different reasons for only a part of the majority opinion.

Often one or more justices oppose the majority decision. One or more of those justices may write a **dissenting opinion**. In it, the justice explains why he or she disagrees with the majority's decision and lays out the precedents and views that form the basis of their opinion. Some dissents have become celebrated for their forceful statements and legal reasoning. Sometimes dissents are adopted into majority decisions issued years later.

The justices who write concurring opinions and dissents also share their opinions with the other justices on the Court. The process of editing opinions continues until they are all finalized and every justice has agreed to the final language and has joined, or written, at least one opinion.

The process of writing and sharing opinions can affect the vote. The majority opinion might be written in such a way as to convince a justice who had been in the minority to change sides. The reverse can also happen. A justice may write a dissenting opinion that is so forceful it convinces one or more justices in the majority to change their mind. It can even cause a minority of the

justices to become a new majority, which changes the Court's final ruling in the case.

Finally, the Court announces its ruling in a public session. The author of the majority opinion presents a summary of the decision. All the opinions from the term are usually handed down before the Court's summer recess. The published majority opinion will guide judges in future cases before the Supreme Court and lower courts around the country.

✓ CHECK FOR UNDERSTANDING

1. **Contrasting** What is the difference between briefs and oral arguments?
2. **Determining Meaning** What are majority opinions, concurring opinions, and dissenting opinions?

LESSON ACTIVITIES

1. **Informative/Explanatory Writing** Write a brief essay in which you describe the process that Supreme Court justices follow in writing opinions.

2. **Analyzing Information** With a group, choose one of the cases decided by the Supreme Court in a recent term. Find three reliable sources that describe the issues involved in the case, the justices' decision, and the legal reasoning. Learn about any concurring or dissenting opinions as well. In your research, identify ideas about the way the decision could affect American society. Prepare a group presentation that explains these features of the case to your classmates.

dissenting opinion a statement written by a justice who disagrees with the majority opinion, and presents his or her opinion and legal reasoning

Reviewing The Judicial Branch

Summary

U.S. District Courts

- Courts of original jurisdiction for most federal cases
- Trial courts for both civil and criminal cases
- 94 federal districts, each within a federal circuit
- Created by Congress
- Justices nominated for life by the president and confirmed by the Senate
- Criminal trials prosecuted by a U.S. attorney

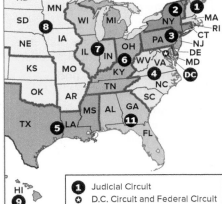

1 Judicial Circuit
✪ D.C. Circuit and Federal Circuit

U.S. Circuit Courts

- Courts of appellate jurisdiction from district courts
- Appeals courts for both civil and criminal cases
- Must accept appeals
- 13 federal circuits, each with 6 to 29 judges
- Created by Congress
- Justices nominated for life by the president and confirmed by the Senate
- Decisions by three-judge panels or en banc
- Decisions set precedent within the circuit

U.S. Supreme Court

- Court of appellate and original jurisdiction
- Hears both civil and criminal appeals
- Chooses which cases to hear
- Created by the U.S. Constitution, Article III
- Power of judicial review
- Chief Justice and eight associate justices
- Justices nominated for life by the president and confirmed by the Senate
- Highest court in the land
- Sets precedents for whole country

Checking For Understanding

Answer the questions to see if you understood the topic content.

1. Identify each of the following terms and explain its significance to the judicial branch.

   A. jurisdiction
   B. concurrent jurisdiction
   C. original jurisdiction
   D. ruling
   E. opinion
   F. subpoena
   G. chief justice
   H. confirmation hearing
   I. judicial review
   J. nullify
   K. writ of certiorari
   L. stare decisis

REVIEWING KEY FACTS

2. **Identifying** What are the two main jobs of the judicial branch of government?

3. **Comparing and Contrasting** What are two ways federal district courts and circuit courts are alike and two ways they are different?

4. **Identifying** What are the three different actions an appeals court can take in their rulings?

5. **Making Connections** How does the selection of federal judges demonstrate the constitutional system of checks and balances?

6. **Identifying** What are the two types of cases over which the Supreme Court has original jurisdiction?

7. **Analyzing** Why is the Supreme Court's decision in *Marbury* v. *Madison* so important?

8. **Contrasting** How many Supreme Court justices must agree to take a case compared to how many are required to decide a case?

9. **Explaining** What are the four factors that Supreme Court justices are supposed to consider when evaluating a precedent?

10. **Contrasting** What is the difference between a Supreme Court majority opinion and a concurring opinion?

CRITICAL THINKING

11. **Explaining** Why do we have both state court systems and a federal court system?

12. **Comparing and Contrasting** How are federal courts and state courts alike and different?

13. **Explaining** Why does a decision by the First Circuit Court of Appeals apply only within the area of its circuit, not to the entire country?

14. **Drawing Conclusions** Why is it considered important that federal judges hold their jobs for life?

15. **Evaluating** Is it important for the members of the U.S. Supreme Court to come from diverse backgrounds? Explain your response.

16. **Making Connections** How did the ruling in *Marbury* v. *Madison* expand the Supreme Court's power of judicial review?

17. **Identifying Cause and Effect** How do the actions of President Andrew Jackson in the 1830s demonstrate a limit to the power of the U.S. Supreme Court?

18. **Inferring** What can Congress do if the Supreme Court rules that a law it passed is unconstitutional?

19. **Analyzing** What are the advantages and disadvantages of following precedent?

20. **Inferring** Why do you think the Supreme Court justices go through a process of sharing their opinions with each other and revising them more than once?

NEED EXTRA HELP?

If You've Missed Question	1	2	3	4	5	6	7	8	9	10
Review Lesson	2, 3, 4, 6	2	2	3	3	4	4	6	6	6

If You've Missed Question	11	12	13	14	15	16	17	18	19	20
Review Lesson	2	2	3	3	4	4	4	6	6	6

Apply What You Have Learned

Understanding Multiple Perspectives

In many decisions, the Supreme Court has taken steps to bring the United States closer to the ideal stated above the entrance to its building: "equal justice under law." For example, in *Gideon* v. *Wainwright*, the Court enlarged its interpretation of the Sixth Amendment. The Sixth Amendment promises any accused person the right to "the assistance of counsel for his defence." The Supreme Court ruled in Gideon that the Sixth Amendment applies to state governments as well as the federal government. The Court required state governments to pay for a defense attorney if the accused is unable to. In his written opinion, Justice Hugo Black noted that the government depends on lawyers to prosecute criminal cases and that defendants who have the money can hire lawyers to defend them. According to Black, the criminal justice system contains "safeguards designed to assure fair trials." Requiring the state to pay for an attorney, he wrote, helps meet the goal of having every defendant stand "equal before the law."

Gideon has helped defendants who could not afford a lawyer. Still, many critics say the criminal justice system has not fulfilled its goal of providing "equal justice under the law."

ACTIVITY **Presenting a Dialogue About Equal Justice** Research to find at least three sources that argue that the United States has not achieved equal justice under the law. Identify the specific criticisms made. With a partner, prepare and present a dialogue that represents at least two perspectives on the ideal of equal justice.

Evaluating

The Preamble of the U.S. Constitution states the Constitution's purposes:

66 to form a more perfect Union, establish Justice, insure domestic Tranquility, provide for the common defense, promote the general Welfare, and secure the Blessings of Liberty to ourselves and our Posterity. 99

Each branch of the federal government has a role in achieving these goals. What is the role of the federal courts in achieving these aims?

ACTIVITY **Creating a Visual Presentation on the Role of Federal Courts** Create a visual presentation that illustrates the role of the federal courts in achieving the purposes set forth in the Preamble. Include examples of the court systems working to achieve at least four of the goals stated in the Preamble. Use text and images to illustrate your examples.

C Making Connections

Examine the political cartoon shown here. "Lady Justice" is meant to be a symbol of the independence of judges. Some Americans think that in recent years political concerns have become too important in the selection of justices of the U.S. Supreme Court. How have political questions impacted the outcome of recent nominations?

ACTIVITY **Writing About a Nominee to the U.S. Supreme Court** Research the confirmation process of a recent nominee to the U.S. Supreme Court. Read three or four news reports from the time the president nominated the person and during or after Senate consideration of the nomination. Look in the reports for evidence of the degree to which political considerations affected senators' and public views of the nominee. Then write an essay explaining whether you think partisanship was a significant factor in the nomination and the Senate action. Give evidence from your reading, including quotations from people for and against confirmation of the nominee, to support your position.

D Informative/Explanatory Writing

The dual court system of the United States can be confusing. Which courts are trial courts and which courts are used for appeals? Which legal issues are handled in state courts and which ones appear in federal courts?

ACTIVITY **Writing About State and Federal Courts** Write a short paper that explains the structure of the state and federal court systems and identifies the different types of jurisdiction possessed by courts at each level of each system. For each court, explain the source of its authority, whether it is a trial or appellate court, and whether it handles civil or criminal matters or both. Include an explanation of how and why a case might move from the state system to the federal courts. Add a diagram to your written explanation if you wish.

E Building Citizenship

Some Americans may have vague ideas about the role, makeup, and processes of the U.S. Supreme Court. Yet the Court is an important part of the federal government, and its decisions can affect Americans in many ways.

ACTIVITY **Creating a Resource About the Supreme Court** Work with one or two partners to create a teaching resource about the U.S. Supreme Court. Include the following information:

- the role of the Court in the federal government
- the Court's jurisdiction over federal and state cases
- the importance of the power of judicial review
- how the Court works
- examples of landmark decisions
- brief explanations of how at least two of those decisions affected Americans' lives

You can prepare your handbook in print or digital format.

TOPIC

6

The National Museum of Immigration at Ellis Island, between New York and New Jersey, is home to this flag made of photographs of Americans that show the nation's diversity.

Citizenship

Introducing Citizenship

Responsibilities of Citizens

There are different ways someone can become a citizen of the United States, including being born in the United States or through a legal process called naturalization. All citizens can make a positive impact on their community. Citizens have various duties and responsibilities to perform in their homes, schools, communities, and country. These responsibilities can change as someone gets older. For instance, a U.S. citizen becomes able to vote at the age of 18.

Citizenship Class

Immigrants wishing to become U.S. citizens must pass an oral civics test. The test covers American government, history, geography, symbols, and holidays. Citizenship classes, like this one in Las Vegas, Nevada, help people prepare for the test.

U.S. Immigrants by Region, 1820-2010

Each circle graph shows the number of legal immigrants who arrived in the United States in a 50-year period.

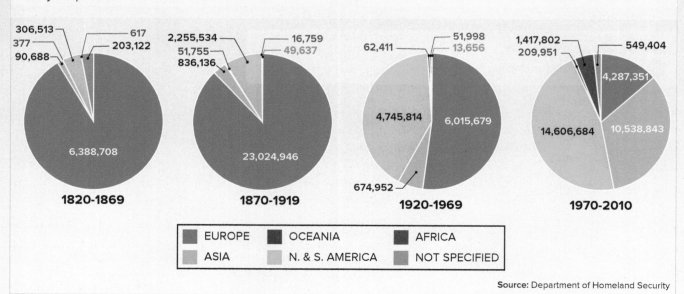

1820-1869
306,513
377
90,688
617
203,122
6,388,708

1870-1919
2,255,534
51,755
836,136
16,759
49,637
23,024,946

1920-1969
62,411
51,998
13,656
4,745,814
6,015,679
674,952

1970-2010
1,417,802
209,951
549,404
4,287,351
14,606,684
10,538,843

EUROPE   OCEANIA   AFRICA
ASIA   N. & S. AMERICA   NOT SPECIFIED

Source: Department of Homeland Security

Jim West/Alamy Stock Photo

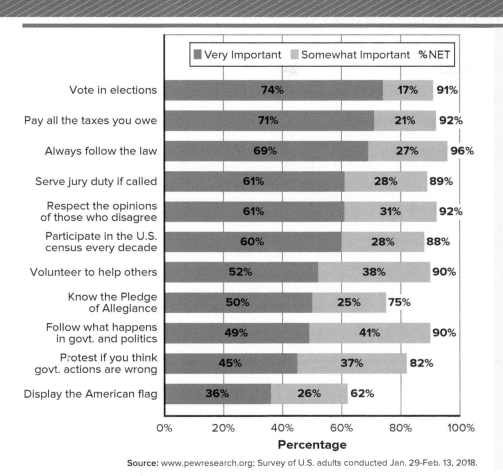

Very Important ■ **Somewhat Important** ■ **%NET**

Trait	Very Important	Somewhat Important	%NET
Vote in elections	74%	17%	91%
Pay all the taxes you owe	71%	21%	92%
Always follow the law	69%	27%	96%
Serve jury duty if called	61%	28%	89%
Respect the opinions of those who disagree	61%	31%	92%
Participate in the U.S. census every decade	60%	28%	88%
Volunteer to help others	52%	38%	90%
Know the Pledge of Allegiance	50%	25%	75%
Follow what happens in govt. and politics	49%	41%	90%
Protest if you think govt. actions are wrong	45%	37%	82%
Display the American flag	36%	26%	62%

Percentage (0% 20% 40% 60% 80% 100%)

Source: www.pewresearch.org; Survey of U.S. adults conducted Jan. 29-Feb. 13, 2018.

U.S. Adults' Opinions on Citizenship Traits

More than 4,600 U.S. adults were surveyed about the qualities of what makes a good citizen.

❝ The average citizen must be a good citizen if our republics are to succeed. . . . [T]he main source of national power and national greatness is found in the average citizenship of the nation. ❞

—Theodore Roosevelt, speech "Citizenship in a Republic," April 23, 1910

Volunteering

Volunteering in your community is an easy and important activity that citizens of all ages can participate in. Organizations such as school groups, scouting troops, and church groups frequently volunteer to clean up locations around their community.

Getting Ready to Learn About . . .
Citizenship

Citizens and Citizenship

Sometimes the word *citizen* means a responsible member of any community, as in this sentence, "She is a great citizen of this school." That means that this person makes choices that benefit the whole school community.

A different meaning of the word *citizen* is a person who has specific rights and responsibilities in a country. For instance, citizens of the United States have certain rights, responsibilities, and obligations, or duties. Who are citizens of the United States? They are either people born in the United States or people who came to the United

States from another country and followed the process to become citizens. The rights and responsibilities of all U.S. citizens are the same no matter how someone became a citizen.

Everyone who lives in the United States has certain duties, such as obeying the law and paying taxes. U.S. citizens have additional rights—for example, the right to vote—and additional duties. They must serve on a jury if asked. New citizens promise to be loyal to the nation.

Citizens are expected to take care of themselves and accept personal responsibility for their lives. They are also expected to act in a

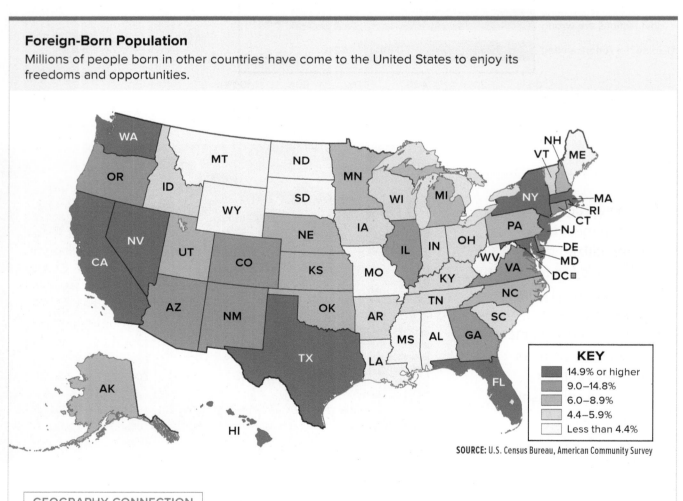

Foreign-Born Population

Millions of people born in other countries have come to the United States to enjoy its freedoms and opportunities.

KEY

- 14.9% or higher
- 9.0–14.8%
- 6.0–8.9%
- 4.4–5.9%
- Less than 4.4%

SOURCE: U.S. Census Bureau, American Community Survey

GEOGRAPHY CONNECTION

Exploring Regions Which parts of the country have the highest percentage of foreign-born people?

kind, fair, and respectful way toward others. The United States is a large country with people from many different backgrounds. Americans have different points of view and different ways of looking at and thinking about the world. Each person has the obligation to try to understand the views of others and to respect and protect everyone's right to express their opinions.

The government in a democracy should reflect the values of its citizens. People form opinions by expressing their own views and listening to others. Opinions are generally wiser when each citizen tries to listen to and learn from people who have diverse perspectives and ideas.

When the U.S. Constitution was written, Benjamin Franklin was asked what sort of government he and the other Framers had given to the United States. He replied, "A republic—if you can keep it." Franklin's words carry an important truth. All American citizens share in the responsibility of keeping the republic.

Voting is one way to help keep the republic. Along with the right to vote, citizens have the responsibility to be informed about the candidates and issues that are on the ballot. Keeping the republic also requires Americans to observe and evaluate the actions of public officials. Voters can let those officials know what they think about their actions by voting for or against those officials. Sometimes, Americans are obliged to protest policies that they believe are wrong.

Good Citizenship

What does being a good citizen mean? One view is that good citizens contribute to their community. Why? A good citizen knows that everyone benefits from having a strong, healthy community. People live better lives if everyone contributes to the common good.

The common good is the things that benefit everyone in the society. All Americans have the opportunity every day to work for the common good. Shoveling the snow off the sidewalk contributes to the common good. The cleared sidewalk is easier and less dangerous for everyone else in the neighborhood to walk on. Stopping to pick up litter off the street and throwing it in a trash can, or recycling it when possible, contribute to the common good. These actions make the neighborhood a more pleasant place to live.

Americans disagree about whether some things serve the common good. For instance, would

Good citizens support the common good. Community gardens are places where neighbors work together to grow food to share with their families. Working in a community garden is one of many ways to support the common good.

requiring people to pay less money in taxes be good for everyone, or would it be good for everyone to pay more taxes so that the government could provide more services? People who care equally about the common good may disagree about this issue, and disagreement is a part of democracy. Citizens have a responsibility to listen to the ideas of others and think for themselves.

There are many ways for citizens to do more than what is legally required of them. Following are several examples of how many Americans give to the country.

Every year thousands of Americans join the armed forces. They add to the hundreds of thousands already in service. These Americans receive benefits for doing this job. They are paid and they receive food, housing, and health care. They may also receive education and healthcare benefits when they leave the service. While they serve, their work for the military can put their lives at risk. That is why some Americans honor them for their service.

Some Americans serve in another way—they run for political office or work for those who do. Political involvement can include everything from running for a local school board or city council to mounting a campaign for U.S. president. Working for a political party or cause can also mean doing such work as fundraising or answering the phone at a candidate's office.

Millions of Americans work for the common good by volunteering. Volunteering is not restricted to people over the age of 18. Teens can form their own local groups of volunteers to pick up litter, maintain the area around a local monument, or visit people in nursing homes. Even small acts such as these can help keep American society strong.

Looking Ahead

You will learn about citizenship. You will examine Compelling Questions and develop your own questions about citizenship in the Inquiry Activities. You can preview some of the key concepts that you will learn about by reviewing the infographic.

What Will You Learn?

In these lessons about citizenship, you will learn:

- the diversity of Americans.
- the countries of origin of many immigrants.
- what Americans value.
- what a citizen is.
- how a person becomes a citizen of the United States.
- the responsibilities, duties, and obligations of citizenship.

- how not fulfilling citizenship responsibilities, duties, and obligations affects society.
- how to take part in civil discourse.

 COMPELLING QUESTIONS IN THE INQUIRY ACTIVITY LESSONS

- **How has citizenship been defined for African Americans?**
- **How can citizens disagree with each other in a civil manner?**

The Process of Becoming a U.S. Citizen

Under the U.S. Constitution, Congress has set the rules and requirements for someone born in another country to become naturalized, which means to become a U.S. citizen.

Becoming a Naturalized United States Citizen	
Meeting the Qualifications	Immigrants who want to become U.S. citizens must be at least 18 years of age and have lived legally in the United States for at least 5 years, among other qualifications.
Completing an Application	Candidates for citizenship must complete an application and send it to the U.S. Citizenship and Immigration Services (USCIS).
Being Interviewed	A USCIS official interviews the applicant to make sure that the person meets all the requirements to become a citizen.
Taking the Exam	The applicant takes an examination to test his or her knowledge of United States history and civics.
Taking the Oath of Citizenship	After passing the exam, the applicant takes the Oath of Citizenship and becomes a citizen of the United States.

Being an American

Analyzing Key Ideas and Details As you read about American values, complete a graphic organizer like this one to list institutions that shape the lives of Americans.

American Institutions
1.
2.
3.
4.
5.

A Diverse Population

GUIDING QUESTION

From what areas did early American immigrants come?

Think for a moment about some of the holidays that are celebrated in the United States. Many people across the country celebrate American Independence Day, known as the Fourth of July, Cinco de Mayo, St. Patrick's Day, and Juneteenth, among other holidays. Some of these holidays celebrate America's history and some honor the backgrounds of people who live in the United States. Many people also practice traditions related to their own background with their family and friends.

More than 13 percent of people living in the United States today were born in another country. These inhabitants are **immigrants** (IH•muh•gruhnts), or people who have moved here permanently from other countries. Almost all Americans—98 percent—are descendants of immigrants. People of all nations have come to the United States, making their own unique contributions to its history and culture.

A History of Immigration

Most scholars believe that the very first people to live in what is now the United States came from Asia. They arrived about 20,000 years ago and spread out over time across North America. As they did, they developed many different cultures and hundreds of different languages. These people as a whole are called Native Americans, although they consist of many **distinct**, or separate and different, groups.

immigrant an individual who moves permanently to a new country

distinct separate and different

Americans of all backgrounds come together to celebrate special occasions and holidays, such as the Fourth of July.

Many Latino families follow tradition by holding a *quinceañera* (keen·say·ahn·YAYR·ah), a party celebrating a girl's fifteenth birthday.

Spanish people began settling in parts of the present-day United States during the 1500s. Some Spanish settlers founded St. Augustine, in what is today northern Florida, in 1565. It is the oldest city permanently settled by Europeans in what is now the United States.

Beginning in the 1600s, people from England, France, and the Netherlands began settling in North America. Later, more immigrants arrived from Germany, Sweden, Ireland, and Scotland. These early immigrants lived in the thirteen colonies that became the United States.

Some people who came to the Americas in these early years were forced to make the journey. They were taken from their homes in western and central Africa, brought by ship across the Atlantic Ocean, and sold into slavery in the Americas. By the early 1800s, about 500,000 enslaved Africans had been forcibly brought to what is now the United States.

From the 1830s to the 1860s, about 5 million immigrants came to the United States. Most came from Ireland and Germany. The discovery of gold in California in 1848 drew thousands more people from around the world who hoped to become rich.

The second half of the 1800s and most of the 1900s saw high levels of immigration. The countries of origin of these new Americans, however, shifted over time. From 1890 to 1924, most came from southern and eastern Europe. By the late 1900s, a much larger proportion of immigrants were from Asia and Latin America.

Today, Latin Americans account for about half of all foreign-born people in the United States. Asian Americans make up about a third.

American Diversity

Between 1830 and 1930, the nation's population grew from about 12 million people to nearly 120 million. About 40 million immigrants contributed to that population growth. They brought many different beliefs and ways of life with them. Their arrival added to the diversity that distinguishes the United States today.

Over time the American population changed in other ways, too. During the mid-1800s, business owners in cities built new businesses and whole new industries. They needed workers, and they paid higher wages than people could earn working on a farm. This drew millions of people from rural areas to cities. Toward the end of the 1800s, after the Civil War and Reconstruction, many African Americans began leaving the South to find work and build new lives in Northern cities. By 1920, more than half of all Americans lived in towns and cities.

Many of these new city-dwellers worked in factories. Other people living in cities found jobs in schools, offices, and stores. Many of the workers in these jobs became part of a growing middle class.

The working world has changed a great deal since then. Women and minorities have made progress in overcoming unfair treatment in the labor force. The number of factory jobs has decreased while the number of jobs in service industries has grown. Service jobs involve performing a service rather than making a product. For example, a service job is the work of a physical therapist as opposed to the work of assembling automobiles. The number of people who work from their homes has risen in recent years as well.

The American population continues to be diverse. People belong to a variety of racial and ethnic groups. Racial groups include people who identify themselves as being white, African American, Asian American, or Native American, for example. An increasing share of American people identify as having more than one race.

Members of an **ethnic** (EHTH•nihk) **group** share a common national, cultural, or racial background. For example, about 18 percent of Americans identify ethnically as Latinos. Their heritage traces back to Latin America and southern Europe. Latinos and other groups, such as African Americans and Asian Americans, are said to be members of ethnic and racial minority groups. By the 2040s, minority groups, taken together, will be more than half of the whole population of the United States.

Americans are also quite diverse when it comes to religion. About two-thirds of Americans identify as Christians. Around four percent follow Judaism, Islam, Buddhism, or Hinduism. More than 20 percent of Americans claim no religion at all.

✓ **CHECK FOR UNDERSTANDING**

Describing Name and describe three types of diversity that help define the people of the United States.

Values and Institutions

GUIDING QUESTION

What do Americans value?

Suppose you must make a difficult decision. You probably make your choice based on what is important to you and on what you believe to be right and wrong. The general principles, or beliefs, you use to make decisions and judgments are your **values**. Values are broad ideas about what is good or desirable and what is bad or not desirable. People's values influence how they act.

People with many different beliefs and backgrounds have made lives for themselves in the United States. These people have made the nation a land of much diversity. At the same time, certain shared values **unite**, or bring together, all of us. Examples of these values are freedom, equality, opportunity, justice, and democracy. Knowing these values and making thoughtful decisions based on them allows Americans of diverse backgrounds to share a common identity as Americans.

---

ethnic group a group of people who share a common national, cultural, or racial background

values the general principles or beliefs people use to make judgments and decisions

unite to bring together

Racial and Ethnic Diversity in the United States

The American people identify themselves as belonging to different racial or ethnic groups.

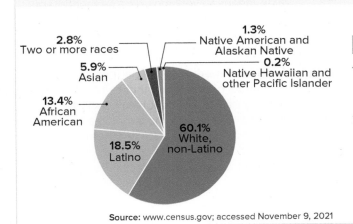

- 2.8% Two or more races
- 5.9% Asian
- 13.4% African American
- 18.5% Latino
- 60.1% White, non-Latino
- 1.3% Native American and Alaskan Native
- 0.2% Native Hawaiian and other Pacific Islander

Source: www.census.gov; accessed November 9, 2021

EXAMINE THE GRAPH

1. **Identifying** What percentage of the American people identify themselves as Native American and Alaskan Native?

2. **Analyzing Visuals** Other than white, non-Latino, which are the two largest groups represented in the graph?

Students in the United States represent diverse ethnic, racial, cultural, and religious backgrounds.

People also disagree about exactly what these words mean. Disagreement should be expected and valued. It comes with being a diverse and free people.

Many of these values are stated in the country's founding documents. For example, the Declaration of Independence says that all people are equal. This statement means that all people have the same basic rights. Those rights include the rights to "life, liberty, and the pursuit of happiness." *Liberty* is another word for freedom, a right that all Americans value highly. However, Americans disagree about exactly what freedoms everyone should have. One benefit of a democracy is the right to debate such matters and then make decisions about them together.

Social Institutions

Americans' values are reflected in its institutions. **Institutions** are the key practices, relationships, and organizations in a society. Starting in childhood, Americans also learn values from these institutions.

One important institution in American life is the family. The family is the center of social life. In families, parents and adult caregivers teach children values. They teach the values that are important to their families and to society as a whole.

Religious institutions include churches, temples, and mosques. In these settings, members can gain a sense of meaning and belonging as well as guidance on how to behave based on different belief systems.

Schools do more than teach students facts. They can reflect society's culture, history, and knowledge, helping students develop a shared sense of being American.

People who have similar values or interests or support the same causes come together in social institutions such as clubs and volunteer groups. In those settings, they learn about teamwork and working toward goals.

Government Institutions

Government institutions reflect how strongly Americans value freedom. Freedom is the right to make one's own choices in life without **arbitrary**, or random and unfair, interference from the government. American government is based on the idea that the government receives its power from the people. This idea is called *popular sovereignty*. The people choose the nation's leaders. If they do not like the job those leaders are doing, they can vote them out of office.

The Constitution reflects another key principle: putting limits on government power. It forms a government of three branches and makes sure that no single branch can have too much power. In addition, the Bill of Rights makes sure that the government cannot violate the rights of individuals.

✓ **CHECK FOR UNDERSTANDING**

Explaining What are some institutions that help preserve and pass along society's values?

LESSON ACTIVITIES

1. **Informative/Explanatory Writing** Prepare a brief essay explaining what one American value means to you. Include a description of how an institution such as a family, religious institution, school, or social group influenced how you see that value.

2. **Using Multimedia** With a partner, create a multimedia presentation that celebrates the diversity of the U.S. population. Include images and text showing examples of different foods, music, art, or other features of culture that show the different backgrounds of people across the country.

institution a key practice, relationship, or organization in a society

arbitrary random and unfair

03

Becoming a Citizen

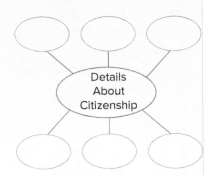

READING STRATEGY

Analyzing Key Ideas and Details As you read, complete a web diagram like the one shown here to note details about the idea of citizenship. Add more ovals if you need to.

Details About Citizenship

What Is Civics?

GUIDING QUESTION

How does a person become a citizen of the United States?

Citizens of the United States have both duties and rights. **Citizens** of a nation owe loyalty to the government of that nation and are entitled to its protection. **Civics** is the study of how the government works, including the rights and duties of citizens.

The Founders of the United States believed that citizens should be educated about their government, its workings, and its actions. Thomas Jefferson wrote, "Wherever the people are well-informed, they can be trusted with their own government." He meant that for government to work effectively, citizens must keep a watchful eye on government officials and what they do. They must also hold officials accountable. To be accountable is to be answerable for your actions. Citizens should also participate in the government and become informed on issues. Informed citizens have the knowledge to make good decisions about public issues. Being informed also prepares citizens to make good choices about who will hold public office.

citizen a member of a community of people who owe loyalty to a government and are entitled to its protection

civics the study of how government works, and the rights and duties of citizens

The National Constitution Center in Philadelphia has life-size bronze statues of the Framers of the U.S. Constitution, including this group of statues with Benjamin Franklin seated on the right.

GO ONLINE Explore the Student Edition eBook and find interactive maps, charts, graphs, and tools.

C269

Roots of Citizenship

Citizenship (SIH•tuh•zuhn•ship) refers to the legal status of being a citizen. Early ideas about citizenship developed among the people in ancient Greece and Rome. Some thought citizenship should give people legal rights and allow them to take part in government. In some Greek and Roman communities, citizens could vote and hold political office. Sometimes, citizenship was limited to men who owned property or who had served in the military. Citizens' duties to the government included paying taxes.

Over the centuries, other ideas about citizenship developed. In the 1700s, thinkers in America and France developed a new idea of citizenship. It was influenced by ancient Greek and Roman ideas but included new concepts as well. These thinkers were part of a movement called the Enlightenment. They said that all people, not just property owners, were citizens. They believed that governments were formed when people agreed to give up some of their rights. They did so in order to enjoy the protection that government provided. Part of this arrangement was that the people also had the right to replace those who made the laws.

America's Founders adopted this idea of citizenship, but they did not apply it to all Americans at first. For many years, U.S. citizenship was limited to white men who owned property. As a result of much struggle over a long time, others gained citizenship. African Americans won citizenship rights when the Fourteenth Amendment was ratified in 1868. Women fought for the right to vote, which they gained when the Nineteenth Amendment was passed in 1920. In 1924 Congress passed a law that made all Native Americans citizens. Asian immigrants were finally allowed to become citizens in 1952. Even as laws granted citizenship to these groups, true equality was not guaranteed, and the struggle for that goal continued for many years.

Today individuals become American citizens in one of two ways. They can be born in the United States, or they can go through a special process called naturalization.

citizenship the legal status of being a citizen, or official member of a nation, with certain rights and duties

Citizenship by Birth

The Constitution and federal law set the rules for citizenship. According to the Fourteenth Amendment, anyone born in the United States is a citizen. That means any person born in any of the 50 states or the District of Columbia is an American citizen at birth. The same is true for someone born in an American territory, such as Puerto Rico or Guam, or on a U.S. military base outside the country. This rule also applies to children born in the United States of parents who are not citizens.

Some people born in another country can claim American citizenship, too. Such a person can claim citizenship if both parents are U.S. citizens or if one parent is a citizen who has lived in the United States for a certain number of years.

Someone who is born in another country may choose to hold dual citizenship. A person can be a citizen of both the United States and the country where they, or their ancestors, were born, if the other country allows it.

Citizenship by Naturalization

Naturalization (na•chuh•ruh•luh•ZAY•shuhn) is a legal process to obtain citizenship by someone

naturalization a legal process to obtain citizenship

After signing the bill that gave citizenship to all Native Americans, President Calvin Coolidge (center) posed with four members of the Osage Nation.

Inferring How are the members of the Osage Nation dressed in the photograph? Why do you think they chose to dress in that manner at the event depicted?

Children under 18 who are born in another country and adopted by U.S. citizens can also become U.S. citizens under certain rules.

born in another country. More than 50 percent of the foreign-born people who live in the United States are naturalized citizens. Many of these people have made tremendous contributions to American society. For example, Rosemary Barkett was born in Mexico. Her parents were Syrian immigrants. They moved to Florida when she was six. Barkett became a naturalized citizen and then a judge. Later she served as the first female chief justice of the Florida Supreme Court, the highest court in the state.

The Constitution allows Congress to set the rules and requirements for citizenship. Today, the law says that immigrants who want to become United States citizens must meet these conditions:

- They must be 18 years old or older.
- They must have been a lawful permanent resident for at least five years (with some exceptions).
- They must have been physically present in the United States for at least 30 months.
- They must be able to read, write, and speak English. This requirement is not enforced if the applicant is age 50 or older and has lived legally in the United States for a certain number of years.
- They must be of good moral character.
- They must show an understanding of the history and government of the United States by passing a citizenship test.

- They must demonstrate that they believe in the principles of the U.S. Constitution and wish to promote the well-being and order of the country.
- They must be willing to swear allegiance to the U.S. Constitution and loyalty to the United States.

Someone who is married to a citizen may usually apply for citizenship after having permanent residence in the United States for three years. A child automatically becomes a citizen if a parent is naturalized before the child is 18.

The first step in this process is to complete an application and send it to the U.S. Citizenship and Immigration Services (USCIS). Next, a USCIS official interviews the applicant to make sure that the person meets all the requirements to become a citizen. If so, they are allowed to take the citizenship exam.

Even after passing the exam, however, the applicant does not become a U.S. citizen until they take the Oath of Allegiance at a naturalization ceremony. That oath reads in part:

"I hereby declare, on oath, . . . that I will support and defend the Constitution and laws of the United States of America against all enemies, foreign and domestic; that I will bear true faith and allegiance to the same; . . . and that I take this obligation freely, without any mental reservation or purpose of evasion."

Foreign-born individuals who serve in the armed forces can become naturalized citizens without meeting the residency requirement. These service members are taking the Oath of Allegiance on the deck of the U.S.S. *Midway*, a naval museum in San Diego, California.

More than 840,000 people took the Oath of Allegiance and became naturalized citizens in 2019.

Losing Citizenship

American citizens can lose their citizenship in one of three ways:

- *Expatriation.* Someone who swears loyalty to a foreign country is expatriated. Becoming an officer in the armed forces of another country has the same effect. Serving in the government of another country may result in expatriation as well.

- *Denaturalization.* Naturalized citizens who are found to have lied or not revealed facts on their citizenship application can be denaturalized. That is, they lose their naturalization. For this to take place, they had to lie or hide the information knowingly and willfully. Also, the information had to be important and part of the reason they were allowed to become naturalized. They may then be deported, or sent out of the country.

- *Being convicted of certain crimes.* Those guilty of committing some very serious crimes can lose citizenship. One of these crimes is treason, or helping an enemy of the United States. The others are rebelling against the government or trying to overthrow it by violent means.

Only the federal government can grant citizenship or take it away. States, however, can **deny**, or take away, some privileges of citizenship. For instance, a state can take away the right to vote as a punishment for some crimes. Someone who receives this punishment remains a citizen, however.

✓ **CHECK FOR UNDERSTANDING**

1. **Making Connections** How did ancient Greece and Rome influence the idea of citizenship?

2. **Explaining** Explain the process of becoming a naturalized citizen.

Residents Born in Another Country

GUIDING QUESTION

In what ways can a person born in another country live in the United States?

Not everyone who lives and works in the United States is a citizen. Many are **aliens** (AY·lee·uhnz),

---

deny to take away

alien a foreign-born resident of the United States who has not been naturalized

PHOTO: PJF Military Collection/Alamy Stock Photo ; TEXT: Office of the Federal Register. Electronic Code of Federal Regulations (e-CFR), Title 8 CFR § 337.1 Oath of Allegiance. Washington, D.C. Government Publishing Office, 1991.

or foreign-born residents of the United States who have not been naturalized. There are two kinds of aliens. The first is referred to as **documented immigrants**. They are in the country legally. The second group is referred to as **undocumented immigrants.** They are in the country illegally.

Documented Immigrants

There are two types of documented immigrants. A *resident alien* is a legal immigrant who permanently lives in the United States. Resident aliens are allowed to stay in the country as long as they wish. A *nonresident alien* is someone who has permission to stay in the United States for a short, agreed-upon period of time. People who come to the United States from another country as students and study at a U.S. college are nonresident aliens.

Like citizens, legal aliens may have jobs, own property, go to public schools, and receive other government services. They pay taxes to the government, and they are protected by U.S. law. They do not have all the rights of citizens, however. They cannot vote in elections or run for office. Nor may they serve on juries or occupy most government jobs. Resident aliens must carry identification cards, called *green cards*, at all times to prove their status as legal aliens.

Refugees

The United States accepts some foreign-born people as refugees. A **refugee** (reh•fyoo•JEE) is a person who has left their country to escape danger. People being persecuted by their governments are one example. These *political refugees* come to our country for protection. Other refugees come here to escape natural disasters, such as earthquakes, or violent social disturbances, such as war. The government grants refugee status only to people who can prove that they would be in danger if they returned to their homeland.

Some 25,000 refugees are resettled in Florida each year. The majority come from Cuba, but others come from a wide variety of countries, such as Haiti, Afghanistan, Ukraine, and Burma. Florida's refugee program is the largest of its kind in the United States.

Refugees must apply to become permanent residents of the United States one year after being admitted into the country. After five years, they can apply to become naturalized citizens.

---

documented immigrant a foreign-born resident of the United States who is in the country legally

undocumented immigrant a foreign-born resident of the United States who is not in the country legally

refugee someone who has left their home to escape danger, such as persecution by the government, war, or natural disaster

Resident aliens have many of the rights of citizens, such as the right to own a business.

Estimated Number of Undocumented Immigrants Living in the United States, 2010–2019

The number of undocumented immigrants living in the United States declined during the 2010s.

2010	2011	2012	2013	2014	2015	2016	2017	2018	2019
11.7 million	11.3 million	11.1 million	11.0 million	11.0 million	11.0 million	10.8 million	10.64 million	10.6 million	10.4 million

Source: The Center for Migration Studies, www.cmsny.org.

EXAMINE THE CHART

Calculating How much did the number of undocumented immigrants go down from 2010 to 2019?

Undocumented Immigrants

The United States currently limits the number of legal immigrants to about 1 million people each year. Relatives of U.S. citizens receive the highest **priority**, or ranking, and are placed first on the list for acceptance. Those with job skills needed by employers in the United States are also given high priority. In addition, the law allows for increased numbers of immigrants from certain countries.

Still, there are many more people who want to immigrate here than the law allows. Some undocumented immigrants enter the country illegally each year. In 2018 about 250,000 people are believed to have entered by crossing the border illegally. In recent years, most undocumented immigrants are people who are granted entry into the country for a period of time but stay beyond that limit. No matter how they arrived in the United States, undocumented immigrants can be arrested and sent back to their home countries if they are discovered.

In the early 2020s, about 10.3 million undocumented immigrants lived in the United States. That number declined from 2010 to 2019. Although most came here looking for work and a better life, they face many difficulties. Many have jobs, although it is against the law to hire undocumented workers. Those who work are often paid poorly and receive no benefits. In addition, undocumented immigrants may live daily with the fear that government officials will discover them and send them back to their home countries. In some cases, this may mean being separated from their families.

✓ CHECK FOR UNDERSTANDING

1. **Comparing and Contrasting** What are the two types of documented immigrants, and how do they differ?
2. **Describing** How do undocumented immigrants enter the United States?

LESSON ACTIVITIES

1. **Argumentative Writing** Read the words of the Oath of Allegiance that foreign-born individuals take to become naturalized citizens. Write a paragraph or two explaining what you think that oath means. Then explain why you think it is or is not important.
2. **Collaborating** Work with a partner to make an informational brochure, poster, or podcast that explains the steps in becoming a naturalized citizen. Include information on what requirements must be met for someone to be qualified for naturalization.

priority ranking

04

Analyzing Supreme Court Cases: The *Dred Scott* Decision

? COMPELLING QUESTION

How has citizenship been defined for African Americans?

Plan Your Inquiry

DEVELOPING QUESTIONS

Think about what it means to be an American citizen today. How do people become citizens? What does citizenship entail? How might those details have changed over time? Then read the Compelling Question for this lesson. What questions can you ask to help you answer this Compelling Question? Create a graphic organizer like the one below. Write these Supporting Questions in your graphic organizer.

Supporting Questions	Primary Source	What the source tells me about how citizenship has been defined for African Americans	Questions the source leaves unanswered
	A		
	B		
	C		
	D		
	E		

ANALYZING SOURCES

Next, examine the sources in this lesson. Analyze each source by answering the questions that follow it. How does each source help you answer each Supporting Question you created? What questions do you still have? Write these in your graphic organizer.

After you analyze the sources, you will:
- use the evidence from the sources,
- communicate your conclusions,
- and take informed action.

Background Information

In 1787 the U.S. Constitution did not define who was a citizen. It gave Congress the power to make laws setting rules for naturalization. That is the process of a person born in another country becoming a citizen. It also required that the president be a "natural born Citizen." A natural-born citizen is someone who is a citizen from birth, not someone who has become a citizen through naturalization. The Constitution left the task of defining who was a citizen to the states.

In 1790 Congress passed the country's first naturalization law. It said that only "free white persons" could be naturalized. Despite this law, five states had already recognized free African Americans as citizens. One of them was North Carolina, a slave state.

The question of whether African Americans were citizens remained a state matter until the mid-1800s. Then an African American man filed a lawsuit asking that the courts declare him to be a free man. His action set off a series of events that affected the lives of millions of people.

» Dred Scott filed a lawsuit asking to be declared free. His case had a lasting impact.

The Missouri Compromise

In 1819 Congress debated the terms of admission of two new states. At the time, the nation had 22 states. Eleven outlawed slavery, and 11 allowed it. Senators in the states with slavery wanted to preserve the balance. They feared that the free states would end slavery if they had a majority in Congress. Long negotiations ended with the Missouri Compromise of 1821, which admitted Maine as a free state and Missouri as a slave state. The compromise included another act as well. Under it, Congress banned slavery from any area that had been part of the Louisiana Purchase north of a line made by Missouri's southern border. Although Congress achieved a compromise, it made a choice to allow slavery to expand into new areas. About 1.5 million people were enslaved in the United States in 1820. They had no representation in Congress, which consisted entirely of white men, including many who had enslaved workers. The map shows the country as it looked after the states were admitted.

The Missouri Compromise, 1820

Legend:
- Free state/territory
- Closed to slavery by the Missouri Compromise
- Slave state/territory
- Territory opened to slavery by the Missouri Compromise

400 miles / 400 kilometers
Albers Equal-Area projection

PRIMARY SOURCE: ACT OF CONGRESS

❝ SEC. 8. And be it further enacted. That in all that territory **ceded** by France to the United States, under the name of Louisiana, which lies north of thirty-six degrees and thirty minutes north **latitude**, not included within the limits of the state [Missouri], contemplated [considered] by this act, slavery and **involuntary servitude**, . . . shall be, and is hereby, forever prohibited [forbidden]: Provided always, That any person escaping into the same [area], from whom labour [labor] or service is lawfully claimed, in any state or territory of the United States, such **fugitive** may be lawfully reclaimed [seized] and conveyed [taken] to the person claiming his or her labour or service. ❞

— Missouri Compromise, March 6, 1820

cede to yield or give up

latitude distance north or south of the equator, measured in degrees

involuntary servitude forced work or service

fugitive a person who flees or tries to escape something

EXAMINE THE SOURCE

1. **Explaining** What does the law establish for areas north of latitude 36° north?
2. **Analyzing** What exception does the law provide? How does that exception reflect a compromise?

Conference Committee Report on the Missouri Compromise, March 1, 1820, Joint Committee of Conference on the Missouri Bill, 03/01/1820-03/06/1820; Record Group 128; Records of Joint Committees of Congress, 1789-1989; National Archives.

Opinion of the Court: *Dred Scott* v. *Sandford*

In the 1830s Dr. John Emerson brought an enslaved man named Dred Scott with him to live in the free state of Illinois and later in the free territory of Wisconsin. In the 1840s, Emerson returned with Scott and his family to the slave state of Missouri. Following Emerson's death, Scott won his freedom in a state court on the grounds that he had become free by living on free soil. Mrs. Emerson's brother, John F. A. Sanford, took the case to the U.S. Supreme Court. (*Sanford* was misspelled *Sandford* in court documents.) In 1852 Chief Justice Roger Taney issued the Court's majority opinion, which denied Scott and his family their freedom. The opinion flatly states that African Americans were "inferior" and denied that they could be citizens. It also said that the Missouri Compromise ban on slavery in parts of the country was unconstitutional because it violated the Fifth Amendment protection against seizure of property without due process. In the Court's opinion, enslaved people were property, not human beings with rights protected by law. The ruling is considered one of the worst in the Court's history. The image from an illustrated magazine of the 1850s shows Dred Scott, his wife Harriet, and their two children.

PRIMARY SOURCE: SUPREME COURT OPINION

❝ The words 'people of the United States' and 'citizens' . . . mean the same thing. They both describe the **political body** who . . . form the **sovereignty**, and who hold the power and conduct the Government through their representatives. They are what we familiarly call the 'sovereign people,' and every citizen is one of this people. . . . The question before us is, whether the class of persons described [referring to African Americans] . . . compose a portion of this people, and are **constituent members** of this sovereignty? We think they are not, and that they are not included, and were not intended to be included, under the word 'citizens' in the Constitution, and can therefore claim none of the rights and privileges which that instrument [document] provides for and secures to citizens of the United States. On the contrary, they were at that time considered as a **subordinate** and inferior [lesser] class of beings, who had been **subjugated** by the dominant race, and, whether emancipated [freed] or not, yet remained subject to their authority, and had no rights or privileges but such as those who held the power and the government might choose to grant them. ❞

— Chief Justice Roger Taney, Majority Opinion, *Dred Scott* v. *Sandford*, March 6, 1857

political body the people of a nation or state
sovereignty freedom from control by others

constituent member someone belonging to a greater whole, such as a group of citizens
subordinate of a lower class or rank
subjugate to bring under control, to rule

EXAMINE THE SOURCE

1. **Identifying** How does Chief Justice Taney define *citizens* and *sovereign people*?
2. **Analyzing Perspectives** Why does Taney say that African Americans are not citizens?

Frederick Douglass on the *Dred Scott* Decision

Born into slavery in Maryland in 1818, Frederick Douglass escaped to freedom in 1838. He went on to become a leader of the anti-slavery movement. He gained fame from his powerful anti-slavery speeches, which he delivered across the United States as well as in the United Kingdom and Ireland. In 1857 in response to the *Dred Scott* decision, he gave a speech to the American Anti-Slavery Society in New York. Part of the speech appears here.

PRIMARY SOURCE: SPEECH

❝ The argument here is, that the Constitution comes down to us from a slaveholding period and a slaveholding people; and that, therefore, we are bound [sure] to suppose that the Constitution recognizes [Black] persons of African descent [parentage], the victims of slavery at that time, as debarred [prevented] forever from all participation in the benefit of the Constitution and the Declaration of Independence, although the plain reading of both includes them in their **beneficent range**.

As a man, an American, a citizen, a [Black] man of both Anglo-Saxon [English] and African descent, I **denounce** this representation as a most **scandalous** and devilish [evil] **perversion** of the Constitution, and a brazen [shamelessly bold] misstatement of the facts of history.

But I will not content myself [be happy] with mere **denunciation**; I invite attention to the facts.

It is a fact, a great historic fact, that at the time of the adoption of the Constitution, the leading religious denominations [groups] in this land were anti-slavery, and were laboring [working] for the emancipation [freeing] of the [Black] people of African descent. ❞

— Frederick Douglass, to the American Anti-Slavery Society, May 14, 1857

beneficent range within a group permitted to claim certain benefits
denounce to publicly declare something to be wrong
scandalous offensive or shocking; causing displeasure
perversion twisting or distorting something
denunciation the act of publicly declaring something to be wrong

---

EXAMINE THE SOURCE

1. **Identifying** What are the founding documents that Douglass uses to make his arguments?
2. **Analyzing Perspectives** What point does Douglass make in the final paragraph?

Abraham Lincoln on the *Dred Scott* Decision

Abraham Lincoln lived in the free state of Illinois. He served several terms in its state legislature and one term in the U.S. House of Representatives. He opposed slavery but did not push for abolition, or the ending of slavery. In the 1850s, the spread of slavery to western territories became a focus of debate. Lincoln joined the Republican Party, which formed in 1856 in opposition to the spread of slavery. The *Dred Scott* decision of 1857, however, declared that Congress could not ban slavery from any territory. Lincoln presented his thoughts about the *Dred Scott* decision and its discussion of the citizenship of African Americans in a speech at Springfield, Illinois. In this excerpt, Lincoln shares his opinion about the meaning of equality in the Declaration of Independence, an opinion with which many Americans at the time would not have agreed.

PRIMARY SOURCE: SPEECH

“ They [the Founders] defined with tolerable [acceptable] **distinctness**, in what respects they did consider all men created equal— equal in 'certain **inalienable** rights, among which are life, liberty, and the pursuit of happiness.' This they said, and this meant. They did not mean to assert [state] the obvious untruth, that all were then actually enjoying that equality, nor . . . that they were about to confer [bestow] it immediately upon them. In fact they had no power to confer [award] such a **boon**. They meant simply to declare the right, so that the enforcement of it might follow as fast as circumstances [conditions] should permit [allow]. They meant to set up a standard **maxim** for free society, which should be familiar to all, and revered [honored] by all; constantly looked to, constantly labored for, and even though never perfectly attained [achieved], constantly **approximated**, and thereby constantly spreading and deepening its influence, and **augmenting** the happiness and value of life to all people of all colors everywhere. The assertion that 'all men are created equal' was of no practical use in effecting [bringing about] our separation from Great Britain; and it was placed in the Declaration, nor for that, but for future use. ”

— Abraham Lincoln, speech, June 26, 1857

distinctness quality of being clear in meaning

inalienable incapable of being taken away or given up

boon a benefit or favor

maxim a general truth or guiding principle

approximate to come near or close to

augment to make greater

EXAMINE THE SOURCE

1. **Explaining** What does Lincoln believe the Founders meant in saying "all men are created equal" in the Declaration of Independence?

2. **Interpreting** According to Lincoln in 1857, why did the Founders include this language, which he says was not necessary to achieve independence from Great Britain?

PHOTO: ART Collection/Alamy Stock Photo; TEXT: Lincoln, Abraham. "Speech in Springfield, Illinois. June 26, 1857." In Complete Works of Abraham Lincoln, Volume 1. Edited by John G. Nicolay and John Hay. New York: The Century Co., 1922.

The Fourteenth Amendment

Prior to the end of the Civil War in April 1865, Congress passed the Thirteenth Amendment making slavery illegal. It was ratified late that year. However, the *Dred Scott* ruling had left the status of freed African Americans in question. In 1866 Congress passed the Fourteenth Amendment. It overturned the Dred Scott decision and established the citizenship of African Americans born in the United States. It was ratified in 1868.

PRIMARY SOURCE: AMENDMENT TO THE CONSTITUTION

66 Section 1

All persons born or naturalized in the United States, and subject to the **jurisdiction** thereof, are citizens of the United States and of the State wherein they reside [live]. No State shall make or enforce any law which shall **abridge** the **privileges** or **immunities** of citizens of the United States; nor shall any State deprive any person of life, liberty, or property, without **due process of law**; nor deny to any person within its jurisdiction the equal protection of the laws. **99**

— Fourteenth Amendment to the U.S. Constitution, passed June 13, 1868, and ratified July 9, 1868

jurisdiction an area in which the law applies

abridge to reduce; to lessen

privilege a special right or benefit

immunity a special protection under the law

due process of the law formal processes carried out in accordance with rules and principles

EXAMINE THE SOURCE

1. **Identifying** How does the first sentence define citizenship?
2. **Drawing Conclusions** How does the Fourteenth Amendment represent a response to the *Dred Scott* decision?

Complete Your Inquiry

EVALUATE SOURCES AND USE EVIDENCE

Refer back to the Compelling Question and the Supporting Questions you developed at the beginning of the lesson.

1. **Contrasting** How are Sources B and E related to the others?
2. **Comparing and Contrasting** How are the arguments by Douglass and Lincoln (Sources C and D) similar and different?
3. **Gathering Sources** Which sources helped you answer the Supporting Questions and the Compelling Question? Which sources, if any, challenged what you thought you knew when you first created your Supporting Questions? What information do you still need in order to answer your questions? What other viewpoints would you like to investigate? Where would you find that information?
4. **Evaluating Sources** Identify the sources that helped answer your Supporting Questions. How reliable are the sources? How would you verify the reliability of the sources?

COMMUNICATE CONCLUSIONS

5. **Collaborating** With one or two partners, take turns sharing your Supporting Questions and answers. Together, write down the main idea of the *Dred Scott* decision, and respond to the Compelling Question. Then, explain why the ruling led members of Congress to view the Fourteenth Amendment as a necessary action to take. Share your ideas with the class.

TAKE INFORMED ACTION

Teaching About the Impact of the Fourteenth Amendment Work in a small group to identify cases in which the U.S. Supreme Court applied the Fourteenth Amendment to a situation. Each member of the group should choose one case to research. Write a short lesson explaining the background of the case, how the Court applied the Fourteenth Amendment, how the decision affected Americans' lives, and the ongoing importance of the Fourteenth Amendment. Share the lessons with civic groups in the community.

US Const, Amend XIV, § 1., https://www.archives.gov/founding-docs/amendments-11-27

Duties and Responsibilities of American Citizens

READING STRATEGY

Analyzing Key Ideas and Details As you read, use a graphic organizer like the one shown here to list the duties and responsibilities of citizens.

Duties (Obligations)

Responsibilities

Obligations or Duties of Citizens

GUIDING QUESTION

What are the duties of American citizens?

What comes to mind when you hear the word *community*? Do you think of neighborhood? Your town? Each of us belongs to many communities, including our school or workplace, our state, and our nation as a whole. We are also members of the worldwide community of all people.

We are all expected to help make our communities safe and successful. All Americans have certain duties that we must carry out. **Duties** are actions that we are legally required to perform.

National, state, and local governments all expect us to do certain things and observe certain rules. Noncitizens living in our country must also meet some of these duties. Some duties, however, are connected directly to citizenship.

Obey Laws

An American's most important duty is to obey the law. Obeying the law allows people to live together in a society. Laws keep order in society by letting people know which actions are acceptable and which are not. What would life be like if everyone did not obey the law? Communities would not be able to maintain order or protect people's health, safety, and property.

duty an action we are legally required to perform

Obeying traffic laws is a duty of all people and helps promote safety.

Pay Taxes

Governments need money to get things done. Most of that money comes from the taxes that individuals and businesses pay to the government. Governments at all levels—local, state, and federal—collect taxes of different types. They use that money to pay their employees, protect people, provide schools, build roads, and provide other services. Paying taxes is an obligation. People who try to avoid doing so face large fines and other penalties.

Defend the Nation

U.S. law requires male citizens aged 18 to 25 to register with the Selective Service System (SSS). In the event of war or other emergency, the government may decide to **draft**, or call for required military service, men from this list.

Registering with the SSS does not mean that a person will be drafted. The government has not drafted a single person since 1973. Since then, the needs of the armed forces have been met entirely by volunteers. Around 80,000 people a year volunteer to join the U.S. Army and the Army Reserve. Thousands more volunteer each year for the Navy, Marine Corps, Air Force, Space Force, and Coast Guard.

Serve on a Jury

The U.S. Constitution guarantees anyone accused of a crime the right to a trial by jury.

A jury is a group of citizens who hear evidence in a trial and determine if the accused person is guilty. Every adult citizen must serve on a jury if called to do so. Federal law requires employers to give their workers time off for jury duty. It does not require them to pay the workers for that time off. Some states require that workers be paid.

Citizens also have the duty to serve as witnesses at a trial if they are called to do so. Witnesses take an oath to tell the truth. Violating that oath by lying is a crime that can be punished.

Attend School

The government provides free public elementary and secondary education. All states require children to attend school, although exceptions can be made for homeschooling. The age range for mandatory attendance is also set, but varies by state. Students who miss too many days of school without an excuse are considered truant. In some states, such as Florida, teens who are found to be truant can have their driver's license taken away or be prevented from getting a license.

In school, students are supposed to learn the knowledge and skills they need to become good citizens. They should learn to **resolve** problems in constructive ways, to form reasoned opinions, and to express their views clearly.

Public school and higher education have another benefit. They can prepare students to

draft to call for required military service

resolve to settle a disagreement

Serving on a jury is a duty that citizens must fulfill when they are called. Doing so helps protect the right all Americans have to a trial by jury if they are accused of a crime.

Citizens' Duties and Responsibilities

Citizenship involves duties and responsibilities.

Duties	Responsibilities
Obey the law	Be informed and vote
Pay taxes	Participate in your community and government
Defend the nation	Respect the rights and property of others
Serve in court	Tolerate different opinions and ways of life
Attend school	Contribute to the common good

EXAMINE THE CHART

1. **Evaluating** Which responsibilities are owed by all residents of the United States, and which are owed only by citizens?
2. **Comparing** How are duties and responsibilities alike?

earn a living as adults. In school, students may gain skills that will enable them to be productive adults who can support themselves and help keep the economy strong. That benefits them and their communities.

✓ CHECK FOR UNDERSTANDING

1. **Speculating** What would society be like without reasonable laws and ways to enforce those laws?
2. **Describing** Describe a situation in which someone meets a duty of citizenship.

Responsibilities of Citizens

GUIDING QUESTION

What are American citizens' responsibilities?

Have you ever been part of a team? If so, you know that each person on the team is responsible for their job. To succeed, all team members must work together.

As Americans, each of us has certain responsibilities to fulfill. **Responsibilities** (rih•spahn•suh•BIH•luh•teez) are actions or tasks that we are expected to meet of our own free will. Being a citizen sets expectations for meeting several responsibilities. Everyone needs to participate—and work together—to meet the shared goal of having a society that works well.

responsibility an obligation that we meet of our own free will

influence to have an effect on

Be an Informed and Active Citizen

Government decisions **influence**, or have an effect on, all people's lives—including yours. Your city council might pass a law closing a nearby park where you like to meet up with friends. The state legislature might pass a law requiring students in your grade to take a skills test. Since these things affect you, you should know about them so that you can form and express an informed opinion. You also have a responsibility to understand decisions and issues that affect other people.

Citizens are also responsible for making sure that the government is working properly. If you expect public officials to act in your interest, or treat other people fairly, you must pay attention to what they are doing. You can make your voice heard by supporting a cause that you care about and by contacting elected officials to let them know what you think. Above all, eligible citizens make their voices heard by voting.

Voting is one of American citizens' most important responsibilities. By electing leaders and voting on proposed laws, Americans shape the government that makes decisions for them and writes the laws they must follow.

The U.S. Constitution gives all citizens 18 years of age and older the right to vote. This gives the people the means to shape the governments at all levels—local, state, and federal. Responsible voters study the candidates and issues carefully before casting their votes. They get information they need from reliable sources—sources that publish material that is truthful and accurate.

Responsible citizens work to stay aware of what their elected leaders are doing. How can they do that? They can visit the websites of those officials to see what they say about issues. They can visit news sources that have stories on proposed new laws. People can also look at the information provided by groups that pay attention to particular issues. These groups often have useful information, although it may reflect some bias based on the groups' points of view.

If officials perform poorly, it is up to the voters to replace them in the next election. It is through voting that our nation's leadership can be kept or changed as citizens see fit. Citizens also have a duty to accept the results of elections, even if they do not like the outcome.

Respect the Rights of Others

Society runs more smoothly when individuals respect one another's rights. The United States has a very diverse population, made up of people with many different viewpoints.

Respecting the rights of others means recognizing other peoples' right to have ideas or ways of life that are different from yours. Everyone has the right to their opinions and beliefs. Accepting others, regardless of their beliefs, practices, or differences is called **tolerance**. It is a central value to any free society. Tolerating others also means respecting their

tolerance respecting and accepting others, regardless of their beliefs, practices, or differences

Voting—going to the polls—is a responsibility of citizens in our representative democracy.

Inferring Why do you think this polling place sign is written in different languages?

property rights. We all need to show others the tolerance we want them to give us.

Contribute to the Common Good

By meeting our responsibilities and duties, we all contribute to the **common good**. The common good is the things that benefit all members of the community. Obeying the law contributes to the common good by bringing order to society. Treating others with tolerance contributes to the common good by making interactions with others go more smoothly.

Contributing to the common good often means working with others. That can require you to compromise. A **compromise** is an agreement in which disagreeing parties each get something they want but also give up something they want.

Responsible citizens show compassion, or concern for others who are facing difficulties. They also make thoughtful decisions, thinking through problems carefully and not letting themselves be ruled by emotion.

✓ **CHECK FOR UNDERSTANDING**

1. **Determining Central Ideas** Why is tolerance of others' differences so important to a free society?
2. **Determining Meaning** Explain what the common good means in your own words.

Being Involved

GUIDING QUESTION

How can citizens make their community a better place to live?

Have you ever volunteered to help at school or in your community? Volunteering makes our communities better places to live. We can also learn valuable skills, such as how to lead and how to be a good team member, in the process.

Good citizens share responsibility with the government and with one another for meeting community needs. They care about the **welfare**—the health, prosperity, and happiness—of everyone

common good the things that benefit all members of the community

compromise an agreement in which disagreeing parties each get something they want but also give up something they want

welfare the health, prosperity, and happiness of the members of a community

Volunteering in America

Millions of Americans of all ages do many kinds of volunteer work in their communities.

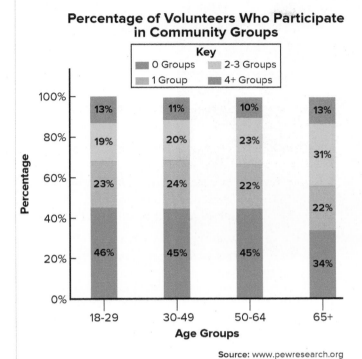

Percentage of Volunteers Who Participate in Community Groups

Key
- 0 Groups
- 1 Group
- 2-3 Groups
- 4+ Groups

Age Group	0 Groups	1 Group	2-3 Groups	4+ Groups
18-29	46%	23%	19%	13%
30-49	45%	24%	20%	11%
50-64	45%	22%	23%	10%
65+	34%	22%	31%	13%

Percentage / Age Groups

Source: www.pewresearch.org

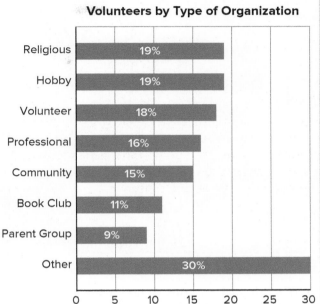

Volunteers by Type of Organization

Type	Percentage
Religious	19%
Hobby	19%
Volunteer	18%
Professional	16%
Community	15%
Book Club	11%
Parent Group	9%
Other	30%

Percentage

Note: People may volunteer with more than one.
Source: www.pewresearch.org

EXAMINE THE GRAPHS

1. **Analyzing** What general trend do you see in the graph for volunteering among different age groups?
2. **Analyzing Visuals** Which types of organizations share the same percentage of volunteers?

in their community. They give back to improve the quality of life for those in their community.

Donating Time and Money

Volunteerism (vah·luhn·TIHR·ih·zuhm) is the practice of giving time and services to others without receiving payment. More than 60 million Americans aged 16 and older do volunteer work. Younger children also volunteer in their schools and communities. Without the efforts of so many citizens, many important needs would not be met.

There are many kinds of volunteer work. Neighbors can gather on a Saturday to clean up a park. Church groups can make holiday baskets for needy families. Retirees can tutor schoolchildren or record themselves reading books so that blind

volunteerism the practice of giving time and services to others without receiving payment

people can hear the recordings. You and your fellow students might visit nursing homes or collect canned goods for a local food pantry.

People can also support causes by donating money. Americans gave around $471 billion to charity in 2020.

The Spirit of Volunteerism

Americans have a long history of volunteerism. In the 1700s, people living in Boston and Philadelphia formed volunteer companies to put out fires. During the Civil War of the 1860s, women volunteered to make clothing and blankets for men serving in the army. Many women also became volunteer nurses who cared for sick and wounded soldiers.

Today, the United States has more than 1 million charities. Many are small and local, such as animal shelters and food pantries.

Many Americans contribute to their community by volunteering time to work at food pantries that help people who are in need.

Some are local branches of national organizations, such as Boys and Girls Clubs. Other groups serve many people across the country—or even around the world. The Red Cross provides blood to hospitals, relief help to people who have suffered a natural disaster, and assistance to families in the armed forces. Habitat for Humanity, for example, has built more than 600,000 homes for people in many countries who needed housing.

National Service Programs

The government has a long history of supporting volunteerism. Today, AmeriCorps provides money, training, and other help for volunteer groups. This government agency also manages several national volunteer organizations, including the Senior Corps.

AmeriCorps members work in the fields of education, public safety, health, and the environment. They do work that helps meet the needs of a community, such as aiding victims of a natural disaster, cleaning polluted waterways, and assisting people with disabilities. In exchange for a year of service, AmeriCorps volunteers receive money to support themselves and to pay for college. Americans aged 55 and older can help their communities by serving in Senior Corps. Some Senior Corps members act as foster grandparents, helping children with special needs. Others provide needed assistance to other seniors in their homes.

Some volunteers work in other countries. The Peace Corps recruits people for international work. Peace Corps volunteers do such work as advising farmers, teaching children, helping people start small businesses, and working to fight disease.

✓ **CHECK FOR UNDERSTANDING**

1. **Analyzing** What is volunteerism, and what purpose does it serve?

2. **Identifying** What is an example of a national service program run by the federal government?

LESSON ACTIVITIES

1. **Informative/Explanatory Writing** Write two or three paragraphs describing a situation that involves one of the following topics: the obligations or duties of citizens, the responsibilities of citizens, or community involvement. Explain how the actions related to the situation benefit both the individual and the common good.

2. **Collaborating** Work with a partner to research a local community group. Find out what their mission is, what kinds of activities they do, and what impact they have had on the community. Include contact information and facts on how people can contribute to the group's work. Combine your findings with those of the class to make a database of local groups that support the community.

Participating in Civil Discourse

What Is Civil Discourse?

READING STRATEGY

Analyzing Key Ideas and Details As you read, create a graphic organizer showing five important characteristics of civil discourse.

Characteristics of Civil Discourse
1.
2.
3.
4.
5.

GUIDING QUESTION

How do people exchange ideas and opinions in a productive manner?

Suppose your town's school board is considering changing your school's mascot. You have a strong opinion on the idea. You want your voice to be heard. Of course, other people—students and adults—have strong opinions too. Not all of them agree with you. How can everyone talk about this issue without it becoming a shouting match in which no one is listening to anyone else?

Civil discourse is a way to discuss matters of public importance. *Discourse* means conversation or discussion. *Civil* has many different meanings, but two are relevant. First, *civil* refers to matters affecting the public. *Civil* also describes behavior that allows groups to discuss topics in a positive and constructive manner. Examples of such behaviors are taking turns to speak, addressing the issue rather than attacking the other speaker, and demonstrating a willingness to listen. **Civil discourse**, then, is reasoned conversation people use to discuss public issues.

You may have seen what happens when one or two people in a disagreement fail to act in a civil way but try to talk over each other or deny each other's right to speak. Acting that way delays reasonable discussion of the matter. It also can ruin, or at least delay, any chance to resolve the disagreement. Sometimes it can be more useful to set aside the anger or frustration you feel and focus on acting calmly. That can help resolve a situation.

civil discourse reasoned conversation people use to discuss public issues

These students are learning how to debate ideas using civil discourse.

Analyzing Visuals Based on the photograph, what do you think civil discourse involves?

When people get together to **debate**, or discuss, public issues, it is effective to use civil discourse. Civil discourse makes it possible for people who disagree to find ways to cooperate.

We live in a democratic society in which power rests with the people. Involving many people in a decision means debating different ideas about what to do. For democracy to work, people must work together to make decisions when they disagree.

Civil Disagreement

Civil discourse does not require people to agree with each other. In fact, it is disagreement that makes civil discourse necessary.

Talking is one way that we can try to work through disagreements. Talking about an issue may lead to compromise. A compromise is an agreement in which disagreeing parties each get something they want but also give up something they want. Suppose a town council is debating whether to build two new skate parks or repair several old playgrounds. The council members might compromise by deciding to build one new skate park and repair some of the old playgrounds. However, compromise is not always the right thing to do. Early in our country's history, government leaders agreed to compromises that preserved slavery, which was deeply unjust.

Sometimes people feel that a compromise ignores their needs. They may stage a public rally or demonstration to express their views. People typically participate in demonstrations when they feel they are not being listened to. Demonstrations are one way for people to make their views known to public officials.

Civic Friendship

Civil discourse also helps build bonds, or ties, among the people of a community. According to the ancient Greek philosopher Aristotle (AR•uh•stah•tuhl), no one can be happy without living a virtuous, or good, life. He also believed that this good life must take place within a community. Aristotle argued that all members of a community should practice civic friendship. **Civic friendship** is a relationship among people who do not know each other very well. They are not

---

debate to discuss

civic friendship a relationship based on appreciating others in the community and wishing them well

People who help others that they do not know in the community after a natural disaster, such as a flood, are acting out of civic friendship.

friends by the common meaning of the word. However, they appreciate, or care about, each other enough that they are willing to listen to and work with each other. People practice civic friendship because they believe that all people should support the community and wish to promote the common good.

In Aristotle's view, civic friendship forms the basis of other virtues. It encourages people to be generous toward others and help others when they are in need. It promotes justice because people will wish to behave justly to others. Civic friendship leads people to take part in institutions. They do so because they know that everyone in the community benefits from those institutions.

For example, when a rainstorm is forecast to cause flooding, residents who live in a neighborhood that is on higher ground and not in danger of flooding may volunteer their time to fill sandbags to help prevent water from flooding houses and businesses in lower-lying areas of town. This is an example of civic friendship.

Civil Discourse in the Digital Age

Today, much public discussion occurs online. The Internet provides access to many varied sources of information. People can easily choose to read many different points of view online. However, people tend to interact with others who share similar interests and opinions. They also prefer to read news from sources that reflect their own point of view. As a result, social media users typically communicate with others who share their opinions and outlook.

In fact, social media sites reinforce that tendency. Some platforms provide a personalized newsfeed that keeps people connected to friends and to the sites they and their friends visit most frequently. Those platforms also show advertising tailored to individuals' interests. Since people often see the world as their friends do, they may have contact with only one view of issues. Many people, for example, tend to watch cable news networks that often share information that is slanted in a way that favors the viewers' own opinions. In that way, these social media and news sites put people in an information bubble that closes off other points of view.

Researchers have identified some worrying effects of these trends. Social media has increased polarization. **Polarization** is the division of the public into groups with hardened and opposing political views. It has become harder for Americans with liberal and conservative political views to find areas of agreement. At the same time, hostility and distrust between these two groups—and between members of the Democratic and Republican Parties—is increasing. Since 1994, the number of Americans who see the opposing political party as a threat to "the nation's well-being" has doubled.

Dividing audiences by their likes and opinions is good for advertisers on social media sites. This practice does not promote civil discourse, however. Although it increases the number and variety of places where people can discuss and debate questions of public policy and the public good, increasing hostility and distrust of people with different opinions make it difficult to carry out civil discourse.

Remember that tone may not be clear in writing, especially if the text is short. That makes it easier to misunderstand what someone is saying. You might be speaking less than seriously in a particular statement, but other people might not understand that just from reading your words. Try to imagine you are another person reading your message. Is there any way it could be misinterpreted? Could someone see it as unintentionally insulting? If so, consider rephrasing your statement.

polarization the division of the public into groups with hardened and opposing political views

Think carefully before you post something. Remember that what you say may be on the Internet for a long time. You may not always have the same opinion of an issue for your whole life. Could someone use your words against you, such as your school or a future employer? Finally, be careful what you share or re-post from someone else. It is easy to pass along information that may not be true, so fact-check any information that you share.

✓ **CHECK FOR UNDERSTANDING**

1. **Explaining** Why is civil discourse important to addressing public issues?
2. **Identifying** Why is increased polarization a barrier to civil discourse?

Building Civil Discourse

GUIDING QUESTION

What skills do you need to engage in civil discourse?

Think about a time when you have changed your mind. Was it because someone insulted you or called you an unkind name? More likely, you listened to someone who treated you like a reasonable person. They gave you information you felt you could trust. They recognized that you had the right to believe whatever made sense to you. They also recognized that people need good reasons to change their minds.

In a democratic society, we use civil discourse to discuss public matters. Democracy calls for civil discourse because in a democracy, every person has a right to think for themselves.

Civil discourse is strengthened if people use social media wisely.

Students will benefit from using civil discourse when they make and respond to presentations in class.

As a citizen of a democracy, you have an obligation to others to treat them as equals. Civil discourse involves showing respect for others, listening carefully, speaking effectively, evaluating arguments, and being ready to reach an agreement. These are attitudes and skills that you can practice and improve throughout your life.

Showing Respect

Showing respect is the most basic requirement of civil discourse. To respect others is to regard them as human and, as a result, of equal human worth. That means we must regard others as equal persons with equal rights and treat them in the way that equals deserve to be treated. This includes listening and speaking to them as reasonable people. Remember that you can treat others with respect even though you do not agree with them. You can also set an example for others by showing respect for people with whom you disagree. If people see you showing respect for others, they may be more likely to act that way as well.

Listening

There are at least three reasons to listen carefully to people who disagree with you. One is civic friendship. Your fellow citizens have a right to their own opinions.

Second, if you think another person is wrong, you may want to get them to change their mind. To do so, you must first know what they think. If a person has reasons for their opinions, you need to address those reasons. Opinions must be based on facts. Be sure that both you and the other person are forming your opinions based on

accurate information. You cannot engage in reasoned discussion or debate with someone unless you hear what and why they believe what they do.

Third, no one is always right. It can be worth listening to someone with a different opinion explain their views and their reasons. You might find their arguments convincing.

It can be difficult to listen to people with whom you disagree. It also can be hard to listen to opinions based on misinformation or poor logic. When a speaker resorts to name-calling or insults, one must try to listen calmly. Still, it is the responsibility of everyone in a democracy to try to engage in civil discourse.

To listen effectively, you need to engage in active listening. **Active listening** is a way of listening that makes sure that you are paying full attention to what another person is saying. Some of the rules of active listening are simple, including concentrating on what is being said and showing respect for the person who is speaking. You would appreciate the same respect when people are listening to you.

Speaking

Civil discourse calls on you to speak in an effective way. Effective speaking helps others understand and take seriously what you say. Keep your tone moderate so you do not sound angry or mean. Carefully select your words and deliver them in a way that will allow your audience to hear your ideas.

Civil discourse means trying to convince someone to recognize your point of view. To do so, you need to offer valid reasons that support your opinion. In civil discourse, you need to make an argument. An **argument** is a statement of someone's position on an issue that is supported by reasoning and evidence.

An argument has three parts. The first part is a statement of an opinion or position. The other two parts provide support for that statement. They are reasoning and evidence. Reasoning is logical thinking that explains why you believe

active listening a way of listening that makes sure you are paying full attention to what another person is saying

argument a statement of someone's position on an issue that is supported by reasoning and evidence

what you believe. For example, someone might say, "I think we need to clean up the playground because it is messy and dangerous." Evidence is facts that support your reasoning. In the playground example, a person could give examples of how much trash is found on the playground and point out why some of it is dangerous, such as broken glass.

You may want to explain why you disagree with what someone else has said. Start by showing that you understand what the person said. You can use phrases such as, "I understand what you said," or "I hear you," or repeat back to them what they said in your own words. Then respond to the *content* of the other person's ideas. You might provide evidence from an expert that counters the other person's argument. You might provide facts the person did not know about. You might give reasons in favor of your point of view that the person had not thought of. However you respond, make sure you focus on the other person's ideas and evidence.

Evaluating Arguments

As you take part in civil discourse, you need to evaluate arguments to see if they make sense. You must evaluate your own argument to make sure it holds up. If not, you may need to revise your position. You evaluate others' arguments to see if you can learn from them, have come to agree with them, or want to argue against them.

You must evaluate all three parts of an argument—the evidence, the reasoning, and the statement. To evaluate the evidence, use these questions:

- Is the evidence opinions or facts? Facts provide stronger support than opinions.
- Does the evidence agree with what you know about the issue being discussed? If not, how reliable are the sources of the evidence?
- Does the person offer expert evidence? If so, how reliable is the expert?

You should also consider how the person applies reasoning to the evidence:

- Does the evidence actually support the person's position?
- Is there enough evidence to convince you of that position?

Finally, think about the person's position. Based on the evidence and the reasoning, ask:

- Is the person's position the only way to interpret the evidence?
- Is there other evidence that has not been considered?
- Does the person make logical connections between the evidence and their position?

Reaching Consensus

The purpose of civil discourse is to discuss an issue and try to come to a decision about it.

Rules for Active Listening

Active listening involves several practices that can easily be learned.

Practice	Meaning
Wait your turn.	Avoid interrupting the other person.
Listen carefully.	Put your full attention on what the other person is saying. Avoid making comments about the speaker to others while the person is speaking.
Focus on the content.	Think about what the person is saying. Does it make sense? Do the facts sound correct?
Watch your facial expressions.	Look at the person in an engaged way. Avoid making faces or gestures that show you disagree.
Ask questions.	If you are not sure what the other person means, calmly ask them to clarify the point.
Find common ground.	Listen for points with which you agree. You can use them to bridge differences.

EXAMINE THE CHART

1. **Identifying** Which of these practices are about the listener's attitude?
2. **Identifying** Which of these practices are about the content of the person's argument?

Fans of the winning team and the losing team will have a different reaction to the result, but both should accept the final score.

A **unanimous** decision is one in which everyone in a group agrees. A **consensus** exists when everyone in the group accepts a decision. In other words, in a consensus, nobody insists on disagreeing. Some small groups require a unanimous decision to act. For instance, a jury must reach a unanimous decision in order to convict someone of a serious crime. For the most part, large groups do not require a unanimous decision or consensus to act because those are too hard to achieve.

Yet even when there is deep disagreement, we can sometimes find common ground and resolve conflicts. Elections show how this works. Elections are an example of how agreement on a *procedure* can produce consensus. Before an election, people agree to be bound by the results, win or lose. When the losers of an election and their voters accept the decision, a consensus exists. Without such consensus, society would fall apart. Agreeing to accept an election result even if your side lost is a good example of civic friendship.

Civil Discourse on a Global Scale

The importance of civil discourse and reaching consensus on issues is obvious within a community, and within our country. The rules for civic engagement apply internationally as well. Many issues affect people across international borders, even around the world.

Global pandemics, worldwide trade, and environmental issues are examples of global issues that affect all societies. Civil wars, ethnic conflict, and natural disasters can strike one country but have effects on neighboring countries—or even some that are far away.

National governments often work together to address international issues. The United Nations (UN) was created in the 1940s as an organization encouraging cooperation among the world's nations. With nearly 200 member nations, the UN provides a place where representatives of each country can engage in civil discourse. Working together, members of the UN have supplied food and resources following natural disasters and sent international troops to keep the peace when local conflicts arise.

✓ **CHECK FOR UNDERSTANDING**

1. **Determining Central Ideas** What sorts of speaking and listening behaviors support civil discourse?

2. **Explaining** How does majority rule lead to consensus?

LESSON ACTIVITIES

1. **Informative/Explanatory Writing** Write a list of listening and speaking rules that you and your classmates could follow to promote civil discourse.

2. **Collaborating** Look at three or four news stories about a recent election in at least two different online news sources. Identify examples of comments from the candidates that reflect civil discourse and some that do not. Compare findings with three or four classmates. Do you all agree on how you categorized the comments? Discuss any differences.

---

unanimous describing a decision with which everyone in a group agrees

consensus the situation that exists when everyone in a group accepts a decision

Bruce Leighty - Sports Images/Alamy Stock Photo

07

Multiple Perspectives: Civil Discourse

? COMPELLING QUESTION

How can citizens disagree with each other in a civil manner?

Plan Your Inquiry

DEVELOPING QUESTIONS

Think about the ways in which citizens can participate in government in the United States. What are some ways they can influence policy other than voting? How do members of different political parties work together to govern? What might happen when they fail to work together? Then read the Compelling Question for this lesson. What questions can you ask to help you answer this Compelling Question? Create a graphic organizer like the one below. Write these Supporting Questions in your graphic organizer.

Supporting Questions	Primary or Secondary Source	What this source tells me about the ways in which citizens can disagree civilly	Questions the source leaves unanswered
	A		
	B		
	C		
	D		
	E		
	F		

ANALYZING SOURCES

Next, examine the sources in this lesson. Analyze each source by answering the questions that follow it. How does each source help you answer each Supporting Question you created? What questions do you still have? Write these in your graphic organizer.

After you analyze the sources, you will:
- use the evidence from the sources,
- communicate your conclusions,
- and take informed action.

Background Information

Democratic societies such as the United States rely on the participation of their citizens. Societies also depend on citizens clearly expressing their views on public issues. That means citizens must be able to gather, share opinions and ideas, debate policies, and agree on actions. People on the various sides of a debate can have strong views on the issue being debated. To get anything accomplished, they will have to find a way to work together on a solution to the issue. A solution with broad support is more likely to find acceptance across American society than a solution favored only by those with one point of view. Also, such a solution is more likely to get people to make an effort to put the solution into action. In addition, working together to solve one problem makes people more willing to work together to solve another problem.

Civil discourse refers to reasoned conversation on public issues. Civil discourse is not just about talking but also about trying to understand others' points of view. In this lesson, you will examine primary and secondary sources to learn more about how people engage in civil discourse and how they can avoid conflict when they disagree.

People use civil discourse when they speak at public meetings such as those of town councils or school boards.

Lincoln's First Inaugural Address

In November 1860, Republican Abraham Lincoln was elected president. Lincoln opposed the spread of slavery into new territories. Many Southerners worried that he and Congress would act to end slavery. A month after his election, South Carolina became the first Southern state to secede, or withdraw, from the United States. Six more states seceded by February of 1861. When Lincoln gave his inaugural address soon after, the nation faced the threat of civil war. In his speech, Lincoln tried to appeal to Southerners' sense of being united as Americans.

PRIMARY SOURCE: SPEECH

    66 We are not enemies, but friends. We must not be enemies. Though passion may have strained, it must not break our bonds of affection. The **mystic chords** of memory, stretching from every battlefield and patriot grave to every living heart and **hearthstone** all over this broad land, will yet swell the chorus of the **Union**, when again touched, as surely they will be, by the **better angels** of our **nature**. 99

— President Abraham Lincoln, First Inaugural Address, March 4, 1861

mystic mysterious or spiritual

chords emotional response to something

hearthstone stone forming a hearth, or fireplace

Union the United States

better angels positive aspects of one's character

nature the way a person behaves, personality

EXAMINE THE SOURCE

1. **Interpreting** What message is Lincoln trying to send by referring to "the chorus of the Union"?
2. **Analyzing** What is Lincoln's main point in this passage?

Civility at the Supreme Court

Justice Neil Gorsuch joined the U.S. Supreme Court in 2017. He is one of nine justices serving on the nation's highest court. The practice he describes here is known as the judicial handshake. It began in the late 1800s with Chief Justice Melville Fuller. He asked justices to shake hands before each session to emphasize that they had a common purpose even if they held different opinions.

PRIMARY SOURCE: BOOK

    66 At the Supreme Court . . . [w]e eat lunch together regularly and share experiences and laughs along the way. . . . [W]henever we gather for work, no matter how stressful the moment, each justice shakes the hand of every other justice. That practice dates back to the late nineteenth century [late 1800s] and may seem a small **gesture**, but those thirty-six handshakes can **break the ice** and lead to kind words or a personal story. . . . My worry is that in our country today we sometimes overlook the importance of these kinds of bonds and traditions, and of the appreciation for **civility** and civics they **instill**. 99

— U.S. Supreme Court Justice Neil Gorsuch, *A Republic, If You Can Keep It*, 2020

gesture a movement that expresses something

break the ice to end a period of silence and start a conversation

civility courteous or polite behavior

instill to encourage

EXAMINE THE SOURCE

1. **Explaining** What actions does Gorsuch suggest encourage a sense of civility among Supreme Court justices?
2. **Speculating** How might these activities encourage civility among people who hold differences in opinion?

The Importance of Respect

One of the most basic features of civil discourse is respect for others—including those we disagree with. The authors of this opinion piece argue that respect has been missing in recent years in the behavior of political leaders and ordinary Americans.

Reeves, Richard V. and Isabel V. Sawhill. A New Contract With the Middle Class. Washington, DC: The Brookings Institution, 2020.

PRIMARY SOURCE: BOOK

❝ Respect is shown in very direct and personal ways. But it is also **modeled** for us—or not—by public figures. . . . [M]ost Americans see our political discourse [discussions] **deteriorating** into disrespect. Rather than debating ideas, politics too often consists of demeaning [shaming] individuals. The danger is that this trickles down into general attitudes.

Both political **ethos** and electoral procedures matter here. We need politicians, teachers, and preachers who **embody** and express the value of respect—and institutional **norms** that support respectful exchange. To be clear, we are not arguing for a **conformist** politeness. Disagreements will often be uncomfortable. The point is simply that all of us, and above all those in positions of authority or high visibility [recognition], or both, must have the discipline and skills to disagree with each other without **disparaging** each other. . . .

Respect is expressed and created in the way our leaders treat each other, especially their opponents, and in the language and tone they use about people, especially those who are different from them. But respect won't just trickle down from the top. It is created and expressed in the way we treat each other '**in the thick of daily life**.' Respect is one of the foundational [basic] values of the American middle class—and it needs **renewal**. We need a society where every one of us is willing and able to look each other squarely in the eye. ❞

— "Respect: A New Contract With the Middle Class," Richard V. Reeves and Isabel V. Sawhill, September 2020

model to serve as an example

deteriorate to become worse

ethos shared attitudes or characteristics

embody to be an example of

norm standard of behavior

conformist acting according to the rules

disparage to criticize harshly

in the thick of daily life in the middle of everyday activities

renewal to be revived or restored

EXAMINE THE SOURCE

1. **Analyzing** What do the authors say is the responsibility of political and other leaders in promoting discussion based on respect?
2. **Interpreting** What responsibility do the authors say all Americans have in this matter?

Seeking Common Ground

Cory Booker has served in the U.S. Senate since 2013. Before that, he served on the city council of Newark, New Jersey, and then as the city's mayor. In 2020 Booker ran for the Democratic Party nomination for president but withdrew from the race. In the book quoted here, and during his campaign, he urged Americans to practice "civic grace." That meant bringing people together to accomplish tasks. Booker begins this passage with the phrase *E pluribus unum*, which appears on the great seal of the United States and on the country's coins and some paper money. The Latin words mean "out of many, one."

PRIMARY SOURCE: BOOK

❝ *E pluribus unum*—out of many, one. I am proud of this **virtue**, so **evident** in the people I've met in my life, and find myself returning to it as one of our most consequential [important] values. Our nation speaks of individual rights and freedoms, personal responsibility, and **self-reliance**, and yet we have consistently [regularly] demonstrated, in spirit and sacrifice, the idea that we are better together—that while our differences matter, our nation matters more. . . .

When too many are despairing [losing hope] over a nation that seems mired [stuck] in **partisanship**, divisions, and **petty grievances**, and a society that still struggles to address enduring **injustices**, it is imperative [necessary] that we recognize the power we have to transform [change] the reality we criticize or condemn. ❞

— Senator Cory Booker, *United: Thoughts on Finding Common Ground and Advancing the Common Good*, 2017

virtue moral goodness

evident easy to see

self-reliance depending on one's own efforts and abilities

partisanship strong loyalty to a political party

petty grievance a minor complaint

injustice unfairness, the violation of another's rights

EXAMINE THE SOURCE

1. **Analyzing Perspectives** What behaviors does Booker encourage and what behaviors and attitudes does he want to reduce?
2. **Interpreting** How do Senator Booker's remarks relate to the concept of "civic grace"?

What Should Politicians *Not* Say?

The Pew Research Center is a nonpartisan group that researches and reports on current issues and events. *Nonpartisan* means that some thing or some one is not connected with a specific political party and tries to share information without bias. In the 2019 survey here, the Pew Research Center asked a group of Americans "what's out of bounds for elected officials" to say? The group was then given several different statements to rate. *Out of bounds* means unacceptable or wrong behavior.

SECONDARY SOURCE: SURVEY RESULTS

Americans' Views on Elected Officials' Statements

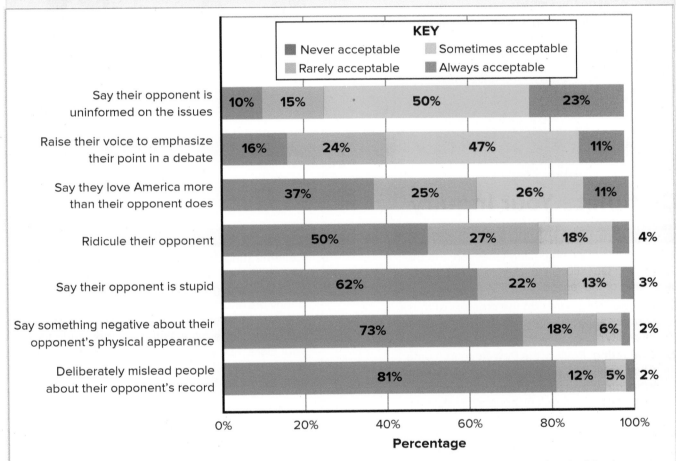

Note: Some responses do not equal 100% because some participants did not answer.

Source: www.pewresearch.org; Survey of U.S. adults conducted April 29-May 13, 2019.

EXAMINE THE SOURCE

1. **Evaluating** What three behaviors do more than 50 percent of those polled consider largely unacceptable?

2. **Inferring** How might a majority of those polled describe civil behaviors in public discourse?

Civility and Civil Discourse

In this cartoon, one of the characters refers to a "slogan." A *slogan* is a memorable word or phrase used to express a person's or group's goal or way of thinking. Groups often use slogans to rally support for their cause and to unify group members.

CartoonStock.com

EXAMINE THE SOURCE

1. **Explaining** What do the two signs say? What do they mean?

2. **Analyzing Perspectives** How do you know that the two pairs disagree with one another in some way even though their signs are the same?

Complete Your Inquiry

EVALUATE SOURCES AND USE EVIDENCE

Refer back to the Compelling Question and the Supporting Questions you developed at the beginning of the lesson.

1. **Synthesizing** What do the creators of these sources suggest might happen in the absence of civility?

2. **Evaluating** Review the Pew Research data. What behaviors do you consider civil or uncivil? What other behaviors might you consider unacceptable in civil discourse? Explain your reasoning.

3. **Gathering Sources** Which sources helped you answer the Supporting Questions and the Compelling Question? Which sources, if any, challenged what you thought you knew when you first created your Supporting Questions? What information do you still need in order to answer your questions? What other viewpoints would you like to investigate? Where would you find that information?

4. **Evaluating Sources** Identify the sources that helped answer your Supporting Questions. How reliable are the sources? How would you verify the reliability of the sources?

COMMUNICATE CONCLUSIONS

5. **Collaborating** With one or two partners, make a T-chart labeled "civil" and "uncivil." As you share your Supporting Questions and answers, add behaviors and qualities that support civil discourse in one column and those that work against civil discourse in the other. With the other students in your class, use your charts to make a classroom poster highlighting ways citizens can engage in civil discourse.

TAKE INFORMED ACTION

Finding a Solution to an Issue Using Civil Discourse As a class, agree on a current public issue to debate. Then, in smaller groups, research the issue. Develop a solution to it with which all members of the group agree. Use civil discourse within your group to arrive at this solution. Then present your solution to the rest of the class. Explain your solution's benefits and any possible drawbacks and answer questions from other groups. As a class, respectfully discuss the different suggestions. Then hold a vote to determine which idea the class supports. When the activity is complete, write a paragraph evaluating how the use of civil discourse worked.

www.CartoonStock.com

Summary

The American People

- The population is diverse. Over time people have come to the United States from countries throughout the world.
- Americans have specific values that support and are supported by institutions.

Civics and Citizenship

- Civics is the study of the duties and rights of citizens.
- Citizens are born in the United States or naturalized.
- Some foreign-born residents of the United States are not citizens.

Citizenship

Roles of Citizens

- Citizens have responsibilities they *should* fulfill.
- Citizens have duties they *must* fulfill.
- Volunteerism is one way to meet civic responsibilities.

Civil Discourse

- Civil discourse is respectful conversation about public matters.
- It is marked by respectful speaking and listening.
- It is a rational means of achieving consensus, or agreement.

PHOTO: John Lund/Blend Images

GO ONLINE Explore the Student Edition eBook and find interactive maps, charts, graphs, and tools.

C299

Checking For Understanding

Answer the questions to see if you understood the topic content.

IDENTIFY AND EXPLAIN

1. Identify each of the following terms and explain its significance to civic participation.

   A. immigrant
   B. ethnic group
   C. citizen
   D. civics
   E. naturalization
   F. duty
   G. responsibility
   H. tolerance
   I. civil discourse
   J. polarization

REVIEWING KEY FACTS

2. **Explaining** What are some values that most Americans share?

3. **Identifying** What two groups have made up most of the immigrants to the United States since the late 1900s?

4. **Identifying** How does the Fourteenth Amendment define citizenship?

5. **Summarizing** What are the steps in the naturalization process?

6. **Contrasting** Describe the differences between resident and nonresident aliens.

7. **Identifying** What are some duties of a citizen?

8. **Identifying** What are some responsibilities of a citizen?

9. **Explaining** How does the term *civil discourse* reflect two meanings of the word *civil*?

10. **Contrasting** What is the difference between a unanimous decision and a consensus?

CRITICAL THINKING

11. **Analyzing** How is the American population growing more diverse?

12. **Making Connections** What is the relationship between American institutions and American values?

13. **Comparing and Contrasting** How are resident aliens and refugees alike and how do both differ from nonresident aliens?

14. **Making Generalizations** How might naturalization positively affect American society and government?

15. **Contrasting** What is the difference between a duty or obligation of being a citizen and a responsibility of being a citizen?

16. **Explaining** Describe a situation in which someone meets a duty of being a citizen.

17. **Making Connections** How does meeting our duties and responsibilities contribute to the common good?

18. **Making Connections** What will most likely happen if citizens in a democracy do not take action to prevent or stop abuses of, or threats to, the system?

19. **Explaining** How does the election process help to resolve disagreements on public issues in an orderly manner?

20. **Making Connections** Why is civil discourse a good way to discuss public issues?

NEED EXTRA HELP?

If You've Missed Question	1	2	3	4	5	6	7	8	9	10
Review Lesson	2, 3, 5, 6	2	2	3	3	3	5	5	6	6

If You've Missed Question	11	12	13	14	15	16	17	18	19	20
Review Lesson	2	2	2	3	5	5	5	6	6	6

Apply What You Have Learned

A Understanding Multiple Perspectives

Many of our ideas about citizenship have been passed down from the Founders and the concepts that were put forth in the U.S. Constitution. However, Americans' understanding of how to be a citizen, and our rights and responsibilities as citizens, has changed over time. Today, Americans have connections with places outside of their local community, even outside of the United States, and our definition of citizenship has developed and changed.

ACTIVITY **Creating a Chart on the Rights and Responsibilities of a Citizen** Create a chart to show some rights and responsibilities that people have in these different roles: (1) as students in a school, (2) as residents of a town, (3) as citizens of the United States, and (4) as human beings.

B Argumentative Writing

Our constitutional republic was created to protect the rights of the individual. At the same time, citizens are sometimes expected to put aside their own wants and concerns for the sake of the common good.

ACTIVITY **Writing a Speech About Personal Concerns vs. the Common Good** Think for a few moments about the sentence "Citizenship means that personal concerns are not as important as the common good." Do you agree or disagree with that statement? Perhaps you think it is true in some situations but not in others. Write an argumentative speech in which you state your position and support it with reasoning and evidence. Conclude your speech with a statement that will prompt your audience to continue to consider your position. Present your speech to the class and be prepared to answer classmates' questions using the principles of civil discourse.

C Building Citizenship

People of all ages help improve their communities by getting involved in community service. They can volunteer to help individual people or work with established groups that have identified a need in their area.

ACTIVITY **Identifying Community Service Projects** Investigate a nonprofit, nongovernmental group that is active in your community. For example, the group could provide food banks, help older people, tutor students, or promote environmentally responsible choices. There are many possibilities. Gather basic information about the group, including what it does and the people it serves. Find out if the group has any volunteer work that could be carried out by middle school students. Prepare a fact sheet about the group and contribute it to a class binder of community service possibilities.

D Making Connections

With modern means of transportation, people can travel around the world much more quickly than our ancestors could. We can communicate instantly with people in distant lands. We are also aware that events in one country or region can have an impact on other areas. In addition, some developments, such as climate change, have effects on people across the world. As a result, your rights, duties, and responsibilities as a citizen extend to the world community.

ACTIVITY **Creating a Slideshow on Citizenship and Our Role in the World** What obligations, if any, do we have to the people in the world outside of our own country? Go online to find images that illustrate your view. Use the images to create a multimedia slideshow presentation. Add text to explain how each image relates to your personal view of the concept of our obligations to the world. Share your presentation with your class and use civil discourse to develop a shared explanation of the concept.

E Informative Writing

In this topic, you learned that there are many ways to make a difference in your community. Now you will explore a practical example of that idea.

ACTIVITY **Writing a Plan for Civic Action** Using sources such as newspapers, newsletters, and the Internet, identify and list three or four issues or problems in your school, neighborhood, or town. Work with a small group to brainstorm practical ways to address one of these problems. Work together to create a plan of action, consisting of numbered steps, to address the issue. Include ideas for steps the government can take and ideas for steps that individuals or groups can take. Include a summary document that explains how the plan will address the issue.

Civic Participation

President Barack Obama joins marchers celebrating the fiftieth anniversary of a march in Selma, Alabama. The original protest march helped lead to passage of the 1965 Voting Rights Act.

REUTERS/Alamy Stock Photo

Introducing Civic Participation

Being an Active Citizen

Civic participation can take on many forms. While voting is a right for citizens 18 and older, younger people can still be active citizens. By volunteering, staying informed, and sharing your voice about local and national issues, you can make an impact on your community and country.

» **Voting Then** This 1852 painting titled *The County Election* shows eligible voters gathered at their town's polling place in Missouri to cast their votes in a local election. At this time, only white men with property were eligible to vote.

» **Voting Now** Over time, voting rights expanded to allow more individuals to cast their votes on candidates and issues important to them. Voters still line up at their assigned polling place to take part in elections. With improvements in technology, voters can use touch screens to cast their votes instead of using paper ballots.

Americans' News Sources

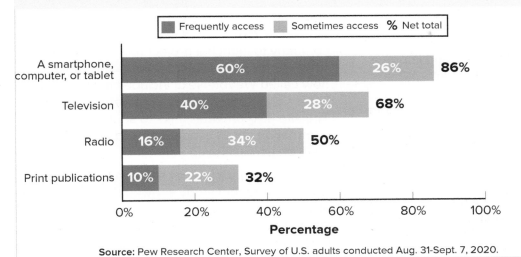

Legend: ■ Frequently access ■ Sometimes access **%** Net total

- A smartphone, computer, or tablet: 60% | 26% | **86%**
- Television: 40% | 28% | **68%**
- Radio: 16% | 34% | **50%**
- Print publications: 10% | 22% | **32%**

X-axis: 0% 20% 40% 60% 80% 100%
Percentage

Source: Pew Research Center, Survey of U.S. adults conducted Aug. 31-Sept. 7, 2020.

» Reliable news can be found in several forms. To stay an informed and engaged citizen, it is important to know what is happening in your town, state, and country, as well as around the world.

> ❝ Today, every citizen, regardless of his interest in politics, "holds office"; every one of us is in a position of responsibility and . . . the kind of government we get depends upon how we fulfill those responsibilities. We, the people, are the boss, and we will get the kind of political leadership, be it good or bad, that we demand and deserve. ❞
>
> —Senator John F. Kennedy, Feb. 19, 1957, "The Education of an American Politician"

Youth Speak Out

In 2016, 8-year-old Mari Copeny wrote a letter to President Barack Obama telling him about the water crisis in her hometown of Flint, Michigan. The water was contaminated with lead. It lacked enough chlorine to disinfect the water, which caused an outbreak of disease. Mari's letter inspired President Obama to visit Flint and led to him approving $100 million in relief money to the city. Since then, Mari continues to empower young people to have their voices heard.

Getting Ready to Learn About . . .
Civic Participation

What Is Civic Participation?

The phrase *civic participation* refers to the range of actions citizens can take to influence and improve life in their community and in their country. What does civic participation look like in action? It can include simply voting in an election or running for a political office. But even students not yet old enough to vote can also be civically active.

When she was only eight years old, Mari Copeny saw that people in her city of Flint, Michigan, were suffering and thought that she could help. The city was providing dangerous water to its residents, including Mari and her family. Mari wrote to then-president Barack Obama about the problem. He came to the city and talked with her and others. Spurred to action, the president began an effort that resulted in money and resources being sent to Flint. Mari did not stop there, though. She started an online funding effort to raise money to help the city's people. She raised enough to provide 700,000 bottles of clean water to Flint families. Helping others, as Mari did, is an important form of civic participation.

Sometimes, young people inform others and encourage them to take part in civic life. American teen actor Yara Shahidi recognized the importance of voting. After turning 18 in 2018, Yara was eager to vote in that year's elections.

A poll worker checks voter sign-in sheets during an election. Many poll workers are volunteers who spend some of their time helping an election run smoothly.

However, she wanted to do more than just cast her ballot. Yara teamed with a social media company to launch a project that encouraged 18-year-olds to register and vote. The project, now called WeVoteNext, includes a website that helps young people register to vote in their state. The site also provides links to sources of information about candidates and issues in every election across the country.

Mari and Yara are not alone in being youth activists. A recent study showed that a quarter of all American teens were working as volunteers in some way. These millions of teens were contributing to their communities.

Participation in Our Democracy

Civic participation is a vital part of a democracy. In a dictatorship or monarchy, people are subjects who must obey the leader. In a democracy, the people are the source of government power. In the United States, we govern ourselves by electing the people who represent us in the different levels of government.

The Declaration of Independence and the U.S. Constitution state that this is a country of equal rights, but equality has not always been practiced or achieved. Voting rights are still being fought for today. However, throughout U.S. history, many people have worked to ensure that Americans have an equal right to vote. Elections give people a very important way to participate in self-government. When the people vote, they express their will.

In the United States, civic participation involves many rights and activities beyond voting. We have the right of free speech, which means we can criticize government leaders. We can share information and debate public issues on social media. We enjoy a free press, which means we can obtain information about what the government is doing and decide whether its actions help or harm people. We have the right to assemble in public spaces and protest—or applaud— government actions. We can join a political party or an interest group. Finally, we have the right to "petition the government for a redress of grievances." This means we can ask the government to do something to solve a problem.

PHOTO:Alamy Stock Photo; TEXT: The U.S. Bill of Rights, Amendment I. 1789. National Archives and Records Administration. https://www.archives.gov/founding-docs/bill-of-rights-transcript.

Vote!

Go to public meetings

Join a group

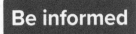

Be informed

Join a political party

Message elected officials

Join a rally

Civic Participation

There are many actions that Americans can take to participate in public life and to influence government decisions.

Exercising these rights is not just a matter of freedom. These activities are all important ways to build a strong community.

Participation in a Community

As you have already seen, civic participation does not need to involve politics or the government. Volunteers work in many different types of organizations to help make their communities better places to live. Here are some examples of volunteer work that are not related to government:

- walking dogs that are awaiting adoption at the animal shelter
- volunteering to care for young children while their parents attend religious services or community-group meetings
- visiting with or reading to residents of nursing homes
- joining or planning a clean-up along public roads or local rivers

Civic participation also includes more than volunteering. Many people have jobs working directly for the public good. These include people who work for government at the federal, state, and local levels. They serve their communities as law officers, 911 call-center workers, and people who maintain our parks. Others do work for local nonprofit groups that help homeless families, teach adults who need more schooling, or coach youth sports teams.

Our freedoms make it possible for Americans to participate in our communities and in our government in many ways.

Looking Ahead

You will learn about Civic Participation. You will examine Compelling Questions and develop your own questions about Civic Participation in the Inquiry Activities. You can preview some of the key concepts that you will learn about by reviewing the infographic.

What Will You Learn?

In these lessons focused on Civic Participation, you will learn:

- why it is important to vote.
- how U.S. voting rights have been expanded since 1870.
- how political campaigns are conducted and financed.
- the role of electors and the Electoral College in selecting the president of the United States.
- how the media and interest groups affect government.

 COMPELLING QUESTIONS IN THE INQUIRY ACTIVITY LESSONS

- **How do laws shape political participation?**
- **Why should the public evaluate the media and its influence?**

Political Participation and Influence

Citizens participate in politics by working through institutions and organizations, such as the ones shown on this diagram. These groups try to influence each other and are influenced by each of the other groups in turn.

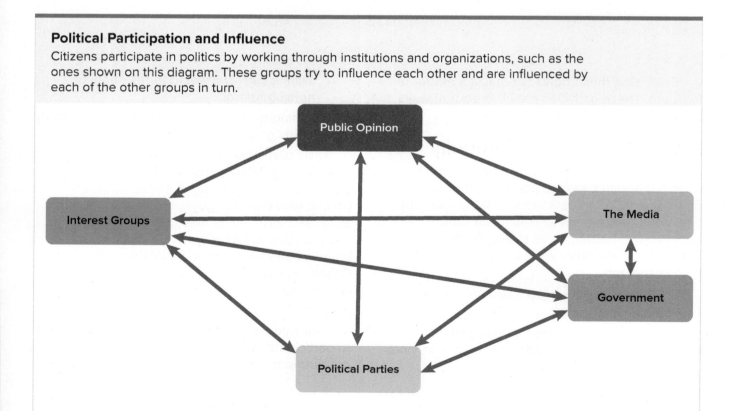

History of Political Parties

READING STRATEGY

Analyzing Key Ideas and Details As you read, complete a graphic organizer like the one shown here to identify the two major U.S. political parties today and their positions on several issues.

Major U.S. Political Parties Today	
Party	Positions on Issues

Growth of American Parties

GUIDING QUESTION

Why did political parties develop in the United States?

A **political party** is a group of voters with broad, shared interests and ideas about government. They aim to influence or control government decision making by electing the party's candidates to public offices. All members of a party do not agree on every issue. People join the party that has basic positions on government that they agree with.

You can participate in American politics without joining a party. When you register to vote, you have the choice of naming a party or registering as independent.

Two major parties have competed for power during most of the nation's history. For this reason, the United States is said to have a **two-party system**. The names and the makeup of the main parties have changed over time. For most of U.S. history, though, two parties have dominated politics.

political party an organized group of voters with broad common interests and ideas about government who want to influence or control government decision making by electing the party's candidates to public offices

two-party system a system of government in which two major political parties compete for power

The Republican Party named Dwight Eisenhower and Richard Nixon as their candidates for president and vice president in 1952. Choosing candidates is an important function of any party.

Today, those two parties are the Republican Party and the Democratic Party. Still, about a third of Americans do not identify with either major party.

The First Parties

Many of the Founders did not like parties, or *factions*, as they called them. They feared that factions would divide people and weaken the country. In his Farewell Address in 1796, President George Washington warned against the "baneful [very harmful] effects of the spirit of party." Despite his concerns, two parties had emerged by the end of Washington's presidency. Different political leaders had different ideas about the role the government should play. These different ideas led to the formation of the Federalist Party and the Democratic-Republican Party.

The leader of the Federalist Party, Alexander Hamilton, believed that if the federal government was too weak, individuals' rights would be in danger. For example, he argued that a strong government could ensure people's safety by being able to protect them from a revolt. Hamilton and other Federalists favored a strong national government. Hamilton also believed that a healthy economy could only be achieved under strong central government.

Thomas Jefferson led the Democratic-Republican Party, which opposed the Federalists. Jefferson disagreed with Hamilton. He believed in limiting the power of the national government in order to protect people's rights. The Democratic-Republicans wanted a system in which most power belonged to the states, not the central government. They thought that state governments, being more local, would be closer to their citizens.

Under Presidents Washington and Adams, the new central government grew, and its power expanded. These changes reflected Federalist goals. However, that changed starting in 1800. Jefferson won the presidential election that year, His party, the Democratic-Republicans then grew stronger, and the Federalists lost support. Over the next few years, the Federalist Party faded away.

Evolution of American Political Parties

For most of its existence, the United States has had a two-party system.

PARTY	DATES OF EXISTENCE	DESCRIPTION
Federalist	1790s–1820	Favored a strong central government
Democratic-Republican	1790s–1828	Formed to oppose Federalists; favored state over national government
National Republican	1825–1834	Split from Democratic-Republicans to oppose Andrew Jackson and work for strong central government
Democratic	1825–Present	Formed from Democratic-Republicans; supported Andrew Jackson; said it supported common people
Whig	1834–1854	Formed from National Republicans and others; favored internal improvements
Republican	1854–Present	Formed from Whigs and other groups; opposed spread of slavery to new territories and favored internal improvements

HISTORY CONNECTION

1. **Making Connections**
   Why did the National Republican Party form?

2. **Analyzing Visuals**
   Which two parties grew out of the Democratic-Republicans?

In 1856 John C. Frémont was the first presidential candidate of the newly formed Republican Party.

Analyzing Visuals Which symbols used in this campaign poster might appear in a modern campaign ad?

Formation of Today's Major Parties

After John Adams's presidency, the Democratic-Republican Party became **dominant**. All four presidents who served from 1800 to 1828 came from that party. The last Democratic-Republican president was John Quincy Adams, who defeated Andrew Jackson in 1824. That election came after a heated campaign, however, and Jackson's supporters were bitter about his loss. Soon after, the Democratic-Republicans split. Jackson and his followers called themselves the Democratic Party and claimed to represent the common people. Adams and others who opposed Jackson called themselves National Republicans.

dominant in control

The Democrats proved more popular and won three presidential elections under Jackson and Martin Van Buren.

The National Republican Party quickly lost support. They were replaced by the Whig Party. The Whigs tried to win broad support by proposing to build roads and canals. They believed these improvements would help the country's economy grow. They also tried to avoid the controversial issue of slavery.

The practice and expansion of slavery gradually became a very divisive issue. As that happened, the Whig Party broke apart. In 1854 people who opposed slavery joined together to form a new party. They called themselves the Republican Party and had very little support in the South. Some Republicans thought slavery should be ended completely. Others thought that slavery should be limited and not be allowed in the western territories of the country. Leading Democrats, however, wanted to allow the voters in each territory, generally white men, to decide whether to permit slavery. Since the late 1850s, the Republicans and the Democrats have remained the major parties in the United States.

When Republican Abraham Lincoln was elected president in 1860, several Southern states seceded from, or left, the Union. They feared that Republicans would end slavery. The Southern states formed a new government, the Confederate States of America. The Civil War followed. During the war years, from 1861 to 1865, Republicans controlled the U.S. government. The Union defeated the Confederate states, and the Republicans dominated the government for more than 70 years. A Democrat served as president for only four terms between the years of 1860 and 1932.

That changed when the Great Depression struck in 1929. Many Americans blamed Republican President Herbert Hoover for not doing more to overcome this economic collapse. They elected Democrat Franklin Delano Roosevelt as president in 1932. A Democrat was president for 28 of the next 36 years. Since 1968, the two parties have often split control of the presidency and Congress.

✓ **CHECK FOR UNDERSTANDING**

Explaining Why is the United States said to have a two-party system?

Third Parties

GUIDING QUESTION

What is the importance of third parties in American politics?

The Democrats and Republicans, although dominant, have not been the only American political parties. Smaller political parties have challenged the two main parties for power throughout the country's history. These smaller parties are known as **third parties**.

Importance of Third Parties

In our two-party system, third parties have not had widespread support from voters. Nevertheless, they have had an important influence on American politics. For example, third parties have often promoted ideas that were unpopular at first but gained support over time. Some of these ideas have even become law. For example, the Populist Party of the 1890s called for senators to be elected directly by voters, instead of being chosen by state legislatures. It also wanted the workday to last only eight hours. Both of these ideas were later put into effect. Woman suffrage, child labor laws, and the 40-hour workweek were proposed by third parties before the Democrats took up these ideas.

third party a political party that challenges the two main parties

Supporters of Green Party presidential candidate Jill Stein protest the fact that she was not allowed to take part in a televised presidential debate during the 2016 election.

Analyzing Visuals What do the voters' signs suggest that they think of the decision to prevent Stein from debating?

THE MAN HUNT.

Oppel Project, The Ohio State University Cartoon Research Library

— Westerman in Ohio State Journal

This cartoon from the 1912 election uses animals to represent the three candidates. The Bull Moose stands for third-party candidate Teddy Roosevelt, the elephant is Republican William Howard Taft, and the donkey is Democrat Woodrow Wilson.

Analyzing Visuals Who does the figure running in front of them represent?

Third parties have sometimes influenced the outcome of national elections. Former President Theodore Roosevelt thought one-time ally William Howard Taft was too supportive of business interests, rather than the interests of the workers. When Taft ran for reelection in 1912, Roosevelt refused to support Taft. He and other Progressives split off from the Republican Party and started the Bull Moose Party. Roosevelt drew so many Republican votes that Democratic candidate Woodrow Wilson was elected. In 2000 Green Party candidate Ralph Nader earned almost 3 million votes. Some analysts believe that if Nader had not been a candidate, those who voted for him would have voted for Democrat Al Gore. Instead, Gore lost to Republican George W. Bush in one of the nation's closest elections.

Types of Third Parties

Third parties form for many different reasons. Some are based on working for a particular cause. These are known as single-issue political

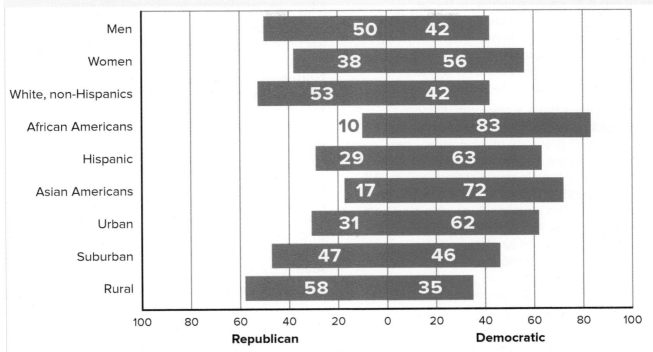

Group	Republican	Democratic
Men	50	42
Women	38	56
White, non-Hispanics	53	42
African Americans	10	83
Hispanic	29	63
Asian Americans	17	72
Urban	31	62
Suburban	47	46
Rural	58	35

SOURCE: Pew Research Center, https://docs.google.com/spreadsheets/d/1v58Nt6SW832ZUq7xLI6N8qdDs3qN4qWoDU-2EyEOGZg/edit#gid=2104546316; Accessed 8/4/2021

EXAMINE THE GRAPH

This chart allows you to compare different groups' support for each of the two major parties.

1. **Contrasting** How does the party identification of men and women differ?
2. **Identifying** Which party do African Americans tend to support? Hispanic Americans?

parties. For example, the Prohibition Party was formed in 1872. Its main purpose was to ban the sale of alcohol. Single-issue parties usually fade away. Sometimes the issue loses importance. Sometimes one of the major parties adopts the issue, and the third party loses its reason to exist.

Other third parties are formed by people with a certain ideology, or set of beliefs, about government. One example is the Communist Party USA. Its members believe that the government or workers should own all productive resources and businesses. Third parties united by an ideology can last for a long time.

A splinter party is a party that breaks off from a major party. Splinter parties generally arise from a conflict within the major party. Splinter parties are often united around an independent leader with a strong personality—such as Theodore Roosevelt, the leader of the Bull Moose Party. Such parties often do not last beyond the defeat of that candidate.

In the United States, third parties have a difficult time competing against the two major parties. There are several reasons for this. The names of Republican and Democratic candidates are always placed on the ballot in many states. Third parties have to gather the signatures of a large number of voters in order to appear on the ballot. That effort requires time and money. Also, third parties find it difficult to raise as much money as the major parties. Without money, they cannot campaign across the country.

Other Party Systems

Most countries have political parties, but few have a two-party system like the American system. As a result, political parties in other countries generally play different roles than American parties play.

Many democracies have multiparty systems, which means they have three or more major parties competing for power.

For example, Canada has four parties with wide support, and France has nine parties with many seats in the national legislature. In these countries, voters have a wide **range**, or variety, of choices on Election Day. In addition, one party rarely wins enough support to control the government in these countries. As a result, several parties must work together.

Some nations have a one-party system. In this system, one political party controls the government and prevents other parties from challenging it. In the People's Republic of China, for instance, only the Communist Party exists. All government positions are filled by Communist Party members. The party decides who may be a candidate for office. No rival candidates are allowed to run. Elections are held, so the government appears democratic. Those elections mean little, however, since the people do not have freedom to choose their leaders.

Russia officially has many parties, but the system is not truly democratic. President Vladimir Putin and his party control the government. Opposition parties are allowed, but the government prevents them from competing fairly. As a result, they have no real chance of winning. Opposition leaders and journalists who question the ruling party are often harassed. As in China, elections are mainly for show.

✓ **CHECK FOR UNDERSTANDING**

1. **Identifying** Name three types of third parties and explain why they form.
2. **Understanding Supporting Details** Why do parties have to work together to govern a country with a multiparty system?

Party Differences

GUIDING QUESTION

How do America's major modern political parties differ?

Today, the two major political parties have distinct positions on many issues. The Republican Party tends to be more conservative. Conservatives want the government to be small and have a generally limited role in people's personal lives and in the economy. The Democratic Party tends

to be more liberal. Liberals support a government that is more actively involved in the economy and provides help to people who are struggling.

Each party tends to do better in some sections of the country than in others. The Democrats are particularly strong in the Northeast and on the West Coast. Republican support is very strong in the South and in the mountainous areas of the West. Democrats have strong support in urban areas. Republicans are strong in rural areas.

On some issues there may be little or no difference between the two major parties. First, both parties hold some moderate views. They hope this will help them appeal to as many voters as possible. Second, the parties seem similar because there are many issues on which most Americans generally agree.

You can identify the differences between the parties by reading each party's platform. The **platform** is a series of statements expressing the party's principles, beliefs, and positions on issues. Each party writes a platform when it nominates a presidential candidate every four years.

✓ **CHECK FOR UNDERSTANDING**

Contrasting How do the two major parties differ geographically?

LESSON ACTIVITIES

1. **Argumentative Writing** Do you think the two-party system is a benefit to the country, or would it be better if third parties had more influence? Write two paragraphs answering this question and explaining your opinion of America's two-party system.

2. **Using Multimedia** Work with a partner to create a media presentation comparing the Democratic and Republican parties. Choose three to five issues that are important to you and your partner. Look for information in sources such as party websites and news sources. Beware of potential bias in your sources. In your presentation, clearly state each party's view on each issue. Share your slide show with the class.

---

range variety

platform a series of statements expressing a party's principles, beliefs, and positions on issues

03
Political Parties Today

READING STRATEGY

Analyzing Key Ideas and Details As you read, use a graphic organizer like this one to identify the roles of political parties.

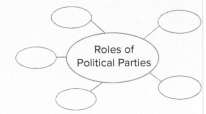

Roles of Political Parties

Organization of Political Parties

GUIDING QUESTION

How are political parties organized?

Political parties want their party members to win elections. Parties compete in elections at the local, state, and national levels, so they have local, state, and national organizations. While these organizations are separate, party members at all levels share similar political beliefs. Therefore, they have a **fundamental**, or basic, goal in common. They want to help their party win election to as many offices as possible.

Parties have less influence with the general voting public than they once did. They still play a role in organizing the processes for choosing candidates for office. They may advise candidates on running for office, especially if those candidates are new to politics. They also contact voters registered with the party to make sure they vote for the party's candidates. They tend to have less influence over candidates, however. Citizens more often volunteer to campaign for a particular candidate rather than a political party.

fundamental basic

Barack Obama was an Illinois state senator who was not well known at the national level until he was chosen to give a key speech at the 2004 Democratic National Convention. That speech skyrocketed Obama into national notice, leading to his winning the party's nomination for president four years later.

ROBYN BECK/AFP/Getty Images

Organization of Political Parties

Political parties are organized from the national to the local level.

NATIONAL CHAIRPERSON

NATIONAL CONVENTION → NATIONAL COMMITTEE

CONGRESSIONAL CAMPAIGN COMMITTEE

SENATORIAL CAMPAIGN COMMITTEE

STATE CHAIRPERSON

STATE COMMITTEE

LOCAL CHAIRPERSON

CITY, TOWN, OR COUNTY COMMITTEE

PRECINCT CAPTAIN PRECINCT WORKERS

EXAMINE THE DIAGRAM

1. **Identifiying** Who directs each of the following levels of the party: national committee, state committee, and local (city, town, or county) committee?

2. **Analyzing Visuals** Based on the chart, which groups work to put party candidates into the U.S. Congress?

National Organization and Convention

The Democratic Party and the Republican Party, each has a **national committee** that includes members from every state. The party's national chairperson heads this committee. The national committee organizes the party's national convention. It also raises money for the party's presidential candidate.

The state level party organizations have similar functions. They organize the state convention and support candidates. Party organizations at the local level select delegates to the state organizations and support candidates in local elections.

The party chooses its candidates for president and vice president at the national convention. National conventions are held in presidential election years. Delegates to the national convention are chosen in one of two ways. In most states, the delegates are chosen through presidential primary elections. In a handful of states, they are chosen in a **caucus** (KAW•kuhs), a special meeting of party members held to conduct party business.

national committee representatives from the 50 state-party organizations who run a political party
caucus a meeting of political party members to conduct party business

In the past, the national conventions were full of suspense since the candidate who would be nominated was not known beforehand. Today, however, the suspense is mostly gone. The identity of the candidate is already known when the convention begins. Still, the convention is an important time for building party unity. The parties use their national conventions to educate the public on the party's ideology, its positions on issues, and to publicize key members of the party. Delegates at the convention decide on the party platform. The convention also officially launches the election campaign.

The major parties also form committees to support their candidates running for the House and Senate. These committees raise money for the candidates and give them advice.

State and Local Organizations

The 50 state committees work to elect party candidates to state offices. These include the offices of governor, members of the state legislature, and others. The committees also help to elect their parties' candidates to national offices.

At the local level, parties have thousands of city, town, and county committees. These local party committees tend to be less active between elections.

During primary season, activity grows. Local committees may organize events where voters can meet and listen to candidates. They try to make voters aware of candidates' experience and ideas. Local committees may have volunteers go door to door, call, or text voters to discuss a candidate and urge them to vote.

Local parties are much weaker than in the past. From the 1800s to the mid-1900s, many city governments were firmly controlled by one party. Those party organizations were so tightly run that they were called *machines*.

Becoming Involved in a Political Party

In the United States, you do not have to join a political party in order to vote. However, parties offer citizens a way to participate in politics and to work for goals they believe in. Party members can do volunteer work for the party, such as calling on potential voters to urge them to vote for the party candidates. They also can register people so they can vote. Party organizations hold training sessions to teach volunteers how to carry out these tasks. Very active members can help shape the party's position on issues. Recently, more people have begun to volunteer for individual candidates than for parties.

✓ **CHECK FOR UNDERSTANDING**

1. **Determining Central Ideas** Who participates in the national convention? What is its main purpose?
2. **Explaining** What kind of work can party members do?

Selecting Party Candidates

GUIDING QUESTION

How do political parties nominate candidates?

Any American citizen over the age of 18 can run for almost any public office in the community where he or she lives. Yet at election time, voters find they often have only two candidates to choose from. Why is that the case? How are candidates chosen to run in an election?

The answer involves political parties. Political parties choose, or nominate, candidates to run for office. They do so in order to win as many offices as possible so they can shape government policy. To choose candidates,

parties often use a type of election called a **direct primary**. When they vote in a direct primary, voters choose a party's candidates who will run in the general election.

Types of Primary Elections

There are two main forms of the direct primary: closed and open. They differ in terms of which voters can take part.

Some states have an **open primary.** In this primary, voters do not need to declare their party preference in order to vote in the election.

---

direct primary an election in which voters choose candidates to represent a political party in a general election

open primary an election in which voters do not need to declare their party preference to vote

Party volunteers often take part in efforts to register voters.

Speculating Where do you think a political party might hold a voter registration event or set up a voter registration table like the one shown in this image? Explain.

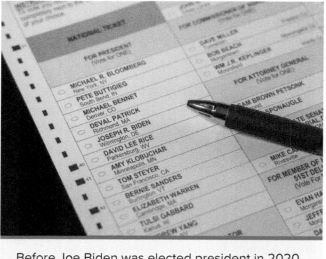

Before Joe Biden was elected president in 2020, he had to compete with several other candidates in state primaries. This primary ballot is from West Virginia.

Analyzing Visuals What information is presented to the voter on the primary ballot?

Most states hold a **closed primary**. Only the party's registered members may vote in a closed primary. It is closed to everyone else. For example, only Republicans can vote in the Republican Party's primary. In some states, primaries are not completely closed to those outside the parties. They allow voters who are not listed as members of any party to vote in the primary of either party.

Parties favor the closed primary because it prevents members of the other party from interfering with the voting party's choice. For example, crossover voters might vote for candidates who do not support the party's core ideas. Also, voters in one party could vote in the other party's primary in order to vote for a weak candidate. These weak candidates would then be easy to defeat in the general election.

Some people oppose the closed primary. They say that it prevents independent voters from taking part in primaries. Of course, people can change their party registration before a primary in order to vote for, or against, a specific candidate.

Winning a Primary

Primaries may have many candidates running for the same office. For this reason, the candidate who wins the primary is typically the one who gets a plurality. A **plurality** is the most votes among those running for an office, though it might not be more than half of all the votes. This means that some candidates are chosen even though most voters voted against them.

In a few states, a candidate must receive a **majority** of the votes cast, or more than half of the total, to win the election. If no candidate receives a majority, the party holds a second primary, called a runoff, between the two candidates with the most votes. The winner of the runoff becomes the party's candidate in the general election.

Third-Party Nominees

Major political party candidates are always listed on the general election ballot. In most states, third-party candidates can also get on that ballot through the power of petition. A nomination petition is a paper that officially asks that a person be placed on the ballot as a candidate. To appear on the ballot, the candidate must get enough qualified voters to sign his or her nomination petition.

✓ **CHECK FOR UNDERSTANDING**

1. **Contrasting** What is the difference between an open and a closed primary?

2. **Summarizing** What are the three ways to decide the winner of a primary?

Other Political Party Functions

GUIDING QUESTION

What other roles do political parties play?

While the main purpose of political parties in the United States is to elect candidates to office, parties also play another important role. They help the people of the United States practice self-government. Political parties enable citizens to

---

closed primary an election in which only the declared members of a political party are allowed to vote for that party's nominees

plurality the most votes among those running for an office, though it might not be more than half of all the votes

majority a number that is more than 50 percent of the total

communicate with their government leaders and help ensure that the government remains responsive to the needs of the people. Political parties do this by:

- supporting candidates.
- communicating with the people.
- running the government.
- linking different parts of the government.
- acting as a watchdog over the government.

Supporting Candidates

After a political party selects its candidates, it helps them try to win the general election. Parties can help candidates by paying for campaign appearances, purchasing ads, and paying workers. In the past, parties provided candidates with much of the money they needed to run. Today, candidates generally raise their own money, though parties still help to some extent. Party workers and volunteers register citizens to vote. On Election Day, party workers try to make sure that supporters of their party go to the polls.

Providing support can be as simple as choosing someone as the party's candidate. A voter can decide to support a candidate just because he or she belongs to the party the voter supports. Knowing that a candidate is a Democrat or a Republican tells voters generally how that candidate stands on key issues. In this way, the party label helps voters assess which candidate will be more acceptable to them.

Communicating With the People

Parties help citizens and candidates talk to each other. This helps government work in two ways. First, through speeches, printed material, and ads, parties tell voters where candidates stand on issues. Parties' websites and social network sites provide information about the parties' candidates and seek to engage supporters. They also have information on upcoming events.

Second, parties arrange opportunities for candidates to hear what citizens have to say on the issues. Sometimes people feel strongly about an issue. They may oppose some government policy or want new laws on a particular issue. A political movement that begins with the people is known as a **grassroots movement**. When a

grassroots movement a political movement that begins with the people

grassroots movement becomes strong enough, a political party often adopts its ideas. If no major party responds quickly and effectively enough, a grassroots movement can gain enough strength to become a third party.

Parties also get information about people's views from social media sites that voters, citizen groups, or people with influence maintain. Posts that have many "likes" or high numbers of re-posts show what voters think. Parties use this information to tailor their messages and their advertising.

Running the Government

Political parties play a key role in running the government. Congress and most state legislatures are organized based on party membership. Leaders within the legislature work hard to make sure that all the lawmakers in their party support the party's position on any bills being discussed.

Parties play a role in the executive branch as well. The president, governors, and some mayors work with members of their party in the legislature to pass laws that the party prefers. These leaders also have the power to appoint individuals to fill certain high-level jobs. These public officials usually name people who believe in their party's ideas and who supported their campaign by working on it or by donating money. In this way, leaders can count on their top aides to carry out policies they support.

Business executives or special interest groups give money to parties and candidates with the hope of influencing public policy.

Senator Marco Rubio of Florida talks to voters at a town hall event.

Inferring Based on the photograph, what can you infer is the purpose of a town hall event?

In this image, members of a Senate committee question members of the president's Cabinet, including the Secretaries of State and Defense. During such proceedings, questions from members of the party that is not in power are often critical of the president and administration policies.

Those who contribute heavily to a political party may expect party leaders and elected officials to meet with them and listen to their concerns.

Linking Parts of Government

Political parties also help officials at different levels or branches of government work together. Suppose the mayor of Tampa, Florida, and the governor of Florida are from the same party. Being members of the same party means they most likely have similar goals and ideas on many issues. They might even have worked together on campaigns or party business in the past. These connections can make it easier for them to join forces to address problems that affect both the city and the state.

Remember that new laws are passed by the legislature and approved or vetoed by the chief executive. If the chief executive and the majority of lawmakers belong to the same party, laws that the party prefers are more likely to be passed. Legislative leaders from each party work to secure the votes of their party members for the bills that the party favors.

Acting as a Watchdog

Between elections, one political party is out of power. This is the party that lost the elections for president or governor or that has a minority of seats in the legislature. The party out of power is often called the opposition party.

The opposition gives voice to people who disagree with the policies of the party in power. In this way, the opposition party hopes to attract voters. This role also forces the party in power to pay greater attention to the views of a wider range of people.

The opposition also acts as a watchdog over the party in power. It tries to make sure that members of that party do not misuse or abuse their power. Members of the opposition observe the party that is in power, criticize it, and offer their party's solutions to public issues. If the opposition party does this successfully, public opinion might swing in its favor and return it to power in a future election. Additionally, when a new party comes into power, it may exercise the watchdog role by investigating the actions of the previous majority party.

✓ **CHECK FOR UNDERSTANDING**

1. **Analyzing** How do political parties help the American people practice self-government?
2. **Explaining** How does the opposition party help keep the government in check?

LESSON ACTIVITIES

1. **Argumentative Writing** Write a paragraph explaining why you think primaries should be either open or closed.
2. **Collaborating** With a partner, conduct online research to learn about the local organization of a political party. Together, create a short presentation describing the local organization, its goals, members, and any events the organization sponsors, including the purpose of those events.

READING STRATEGY

Integrating Knowledge and Ideas As you read, create a chart like the one shown to list the steps in the voting process.

The Voting Process	
1.	
2.	
3.	

Qualifying to Vote

GUIDING QUESTION

What are the requirements to vote?

For much of the history of human civilization, voting by the public was not a common idea. Around the world, most people lived under kings, queens, and other rulers. These rulers often inherited their position, so no matter how cruel or unworthy of power the ruler was, the people had to suffer in silence. Regular people had no voice in government.

Today, in the United States it is different. Americans have the right to vote for the people who lead them. It is both a responsibility and a right—one denied to many until just the last 100 years.

Expanding Suffrage

At the time of the founding of the United States, it was generally accepted that only educated, wealthy white males should be involved in government. As a result, women, African Americans, Native Americans, Asian Americans, and people who did not own property were not allowed to vote or otherwise participate in government.

In 1872 Susan B. Anthony voted in the presidential election in her hometown of Rochester, New York. She was arrested, tried, and convicted of voting illegally. Women were not allowed to vote. Anthony was just one of thousands of people who have fought to have **suffrage**, or the right to vote, expanded. Their efforts convinced leaders to overturn the laws that banned people from voting.

In the years leading up to and after the American Civil War, African Americans fought for the right to vote. Following the war, the people in some states were unhappy with the rights given to the newly freed enslaved people. In these states, political leaders developed new ways to limit voting by African Americans.

suffrage the right to vote

Many polling places hand out stickers that read "I voted!" Wearing the sticker is an outward display that you have fulfilled a civic responsibility. It can also remind others to vote.

It took many years to remove those barriers, and the struggle for full voting rights continues for some groups of Americans today.

Voting Rights for African Americans The first effort to expand voting rights for African Americans came soon after the Civil War. Following the war, three amendments were added to the U.S. Constitution. They attempted to bring African Americans as equals into American society.

- The Thirteenth Amendment ended slavery.
- The Fourteenth Amendment states that all people born in the United States are citizens and promises equal protection under the laws.
- The Fifteenth Amendment states that no citizen can be denied the right to vote because of race or color.

The Fifteenth Amendment was meant to extend suffrage to African Americans who were recently freed from slavery. However, it was unable to achieve that goal due to the efforts of white political leaders in the South. They came up with ways to prevent or make it difficult for African Americans to cast their votes. They hoped these roadblocks would discourage people from even trying to vote.

One method used to block African Americans from voting was to require voters to pass a literacy test before they could vote. Officials made these tests difficult for African American voters. For example, a voter had to explain a complicated part of the state or national constitution.

Another obstacle was the poll tax. This tax was a fee that citizens had to pay in order to vote. The tax blocked thousands of poor African Americans from going to the polls. Southern states found ways to protect white people from the poll tax. An exception to the tax, called the grandfather clause, stated that voters whose grandfathers had voted before 1867 were automatically eligible to vote. This rule applied only to white voters because African Americans had been enslaved and not allowed to vote. The Supreme Court, however, declared grandfather clauses unconstitutional in 1915.

In 1964 the Twenty-fourth Amendment outlawed the poll tax in national elections. Even then, states continued to use it in state elections. In 1966, the Supreme Court ruled that this practice was not allowed by the Constitution.

In the early 1900s, the Democratic Party in many states prevented African Americans from having a voice in elections by barring them from the party. As a result, African Americans could not vote in the party's primary elections. In a primary, party voters choose the party's candidate for an office in the later general election. Only white people could choose Democratic candidates. Those candidates nearly always won the general election. This practice had the effect of taking away African Americans' voting power. The Supreme Court ruled that white primaries were illegal in 1944.

In the 1960s, the voting rights of African Americans were still very limited in Southern states. The federal Voting Rights Act of 1965 tried to address that unfair treatment. The act allowed the federal government to register voters and to send poll watchers on Election Day. Voting rights laws of 1970, 1975, and 1982 broadened the federal role in elections. They outlawed literacy tests and required that ballots be provided in Spanish or in other languages. These laws resulted in large increases in the number of

This 1955 document is a poll tax receipt from a county in Texas.

Analyzing Visuals What three categories of information about voters are recorded in the center of the document?

Milestones in Expanding Voting Rights

By the early 1800s, most adult white males could vote, but it took other groups longer to gain voting rights.

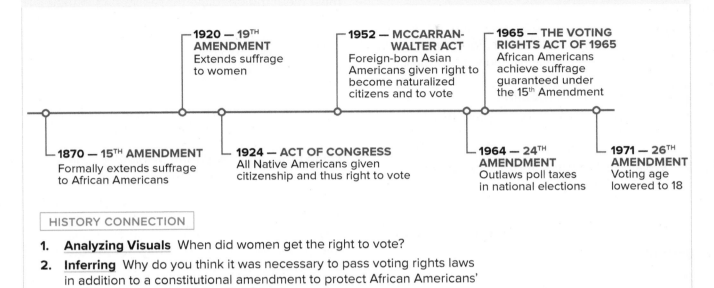

1920 — 19TH AMENDMENT
Extends suffrage to women

1952 — MCCARRAN-WALTER ACT
Foreign-born Asian Americans given right to become naturalized citizens and to vote

1965 — THE VOTING RIGHTS ACT OF 1965
African Americans achieve suffrage guaranteed under the 15th Amendment

1870 — 15TH AMENDMENT
Formally extends suffrage to African Americans

1924 — ACT OF CONGRESS
All Native Americans given citizenship and thus right to vote

1964 — 24TH AMENDMENT
Outlaws poll taxes in national elections

1971 — 26TH AMENDMENT
Voting age lowered to 18

> HISTORY CONNECTION
>
> 1. **Analyzing Visuals** When did women get the right to vote?
> 2. **Inferring** Why do you think it was necessary to pass voting rights laws in addition to a constitutional amendment to protect African Americans' voting rights but not those of women?

African Americans who registered to vote. The number of African Americans who won political office rose as well.

In 2006 Congress determined that racial discrimination in voting **persisted** in many places. It renewed the Voting Rights Act of 1965 for another 25 years.

Voting Rights for Women Women began fighting for suffrage starting in the mid-1800s. Groups of women suffragists marched, lectured, lobbied, and wrote articles and pamphlets demanding the right to vote. They wanted a constitutional amendment that would provide them suffrage. By 1914 they had won the right to vote in 11 states—all of them west of the Mississippi River. They finally achieved their goal in 1920, when the Nineteenth Amendment guaranteeing women the right to vote was ratified.

Voting Rights for those 18 and Older In the 1960s, citizens had to be at least 21 years old in most states to vote. At the time, many Americans as young as 18 were being drafted into the armed forces to fight in the Vietnam War. Many people felt that Americans who were old enough to be drafted and fight for their country were also old enough to vote. The Twenty-sixth Amendment, ratified in 1971, lowered the voting age to 18.

Voting Requirements Today

Each state can set its own rules about who can vote. That authority comes from the Constitution. However, state rules must meet basic standards set by several constitutional amendments and federal laws. States cannot exclude U.S. citizens from voting based on gender, religious beliefs, income, race, ethnicity, or age. Every state requires voters to be U.S. citizens and to live in the same state for a certain period of time before they are eligible to vote.

However, some groups of people do not have the right to vote. In most states, people in prison for serious crimes cannot vote while they are in prison. Also, people with certain mental illnesses may lose their eligibility. Immigrants cannot vote until they become citizens. Other than these exceptions, most adult American citizens are eligible to vote.

After the 2020 election, voting laws became an issue in many states. That year, Donald Trump lost his attempt to win reelection as president.

persist to continue

Many Trump supporters claimed that illegally cast votes were responsible for his loss, though no court found these claims to be true. **Subsequently**, lawmakers in 49 states introduced bills that would restrict some people's ability to vote. Many states passed these laws. These changes limited reforms made over the previous 25 years. During that time, many states made voting easier. For example, they allowed people to vote early and vote by mail.

✓ CHECK FOR UNDERSTANDING

1. **Understanding Supporting Details** Which constitutional amendments expanded voting rights? Whom did they enable to vote?
2. **Explaining** What was the significance of the Voting Rights Act?

Steps in the Voting Process

GUIDING QUESTION

What are the steps that must be followed to vote?

There is more to voting than completing a ballot. Voting is a process that involves three steps. These steps are registering, preparing, and casting a ballot.

Registering to Vote

Except for North Dakota, all states require citizens who are at least 18 years old to register

subsequently later, following that

Following the 2020 elections, some states passed legislation limiting or banning remote ballot drop boxes like the one shown here. Such laws may make it more difficult for some people to vote.

before they can vote. To **register** means to officially sign up to vote. Registering puts a person's name on the list of eligible voters.

How do people register to vote? First, they must meet the deadline for registering in their state. Though some states let voters register on Election Day, most states require voters to register at least 25 days before an election. Check state rules by contacting the state board of elections or the state's chief election official.

To register, people must fill out a form. They provide their name, address, and age. They need to show a driver's license, a birth certificate, or some other approved form of identification to prove citizenship and age.

In many states, people can register online or download the form, fill it out, and mail it in. Some government offices and public libraries also have the forms. People can even register to vote when they renew their driver's licenses.

Political parties and campaign workers are eager to help people register to vote, especially if they think those people will support their candidates. Many nonpartisan groups such as the League of Women Voters and Rock the Vote help people register as well.

Preparing to Vote

After registering, a person is able to vote in the next election. First, the voter must take an important step in the voting process: preparing to vote.

Each vote helps decide the outcome of an election. This means it will affect the lives of many people. Because votes have serious effects, responsible voters prepare to vote by becoming informed about public issues and current events. They learn about each candidate's abilities and knowledge as well as their positions on issues.

Some elections also contain special items on the ballot that ask voters to approve laws or even change the state constitution. Before voting, voters need to learn about such proposals so they can make an informed choice when they vote.

To learn about candidates and questions, voters can access many good websites, television

register to officially sign up to vote

These U.S. soldiers serving overseas are taking part in a voter registration drive.

news programs, radio talk shows, newspapers, and magazines that will provide trustworthy information. Other sources include candidates' speeches, debates, and campaign literature.

Anyone using campaign literature, websites, and social media as sources of information needs to watch for bias. Bias is an unfair preference for or against something. Bias can affect how people present information. Biased presentations often try to give opinions as facts, and the facts they do provide are often misleading. They may misstate what the facts describe. They can leave out key facts that go against their point of view.

Information on issues and candidates can answer questions such as these:

- What does the candidate believe in?
- Is the candidate reliable and honest?
- Does the candidate have relevant experience?
- Will the candidate be effective in office?

Casting Your Vote

Many Americans vote in person on Election Day. In-person voting occurs at a **polling place**. Each city or county is usually divided into precincts, or voting districts. Each precinct has certain locations chosen as polling places. They are often set up in

schools, community centers, fire stations, or other public buildings. Voters can find the location of their polling place by contacting the state board of elections or a local election official, such as the town clerk, or checking the state website.

At the polling place, officials check each voter's name against the list of registered voters. In some states, voters need to show identification or sign in. Next, an official hands the voter a **ballot**, which is the official form that voters use to cast their votes. If the polling place uses electronic voting machines, there is no paper ballot. The voter is then directed to a voting booth. The booth has barriers, such as curtains or dividers, so no one else can see the choices the voter is making. This keeps each person's vote secret.

States decide what kind of ballot to use. A state may provide a piece of paper with check boxes that you mark with a special pen. For many years, most votes were cast using a punch card system, in which voters punch a hole next to the name of their chosen candidates. Technical problems with punch cards in Florida caused problems in the 2000 presidential election. After that election, many states switched to voting machines with touch screens. However, problems can occur with those machines as well. In recent years, some states have chosen to use paper ballots again or at least make sure there is a paper record of each person's vote.

Not everyone chooses to vote in person on Election Day. In most states voters can cast a ballot in person during a period prior to Election Day in a process called **early voting**. Anyone can vote early without giving an excuse or reason.

Many states allow people to vote by using an **absentee ballot**. This type of ballot allows voters to cast their votes without going to a polling place. All 50 states permit absentee voting for people who will be out of town, in the hospital, observing a religious holiday, or working on Election Day. This includes military personnel and their family members who are stationed outside their home cities and states. Most states do not require voters to provide a reason for requesting an absentee ballot, though some do.

---

polling place official place where people can vote in person on or before Election Day

ballot the official form provided to voters that they use to cast their votes

early voting the process of casting a ballot in person during the allowed period prior to Election Day

absentee ballot a type of ballot that allows voters to cast their votes without going to a polling place

Bush v. *Gore*, 2000

BACKGROUND OF THE CASE The 2000 presidential election between Democratic candidate Vice President Al Gore and Republican Governor George W. Bush of Texas was a tight race. Victory came down to a single state: Florida. Whoever won Florida would have the 270 electoral votes needed to win. The race was so close that only a few hundred votes separated the two candidates in the state. Unfortunately, many of the paper ballots were damaged or not marked properly.

The candidates asked the Florida courts to decide how the disputed votes should be counted. The Florida Supreme Court said that each ballot that showed a "clear indication of the intent of the voter" should be counted. The court ordered a recount, where all votes were to be counted again. Lawyers for Bush appealed the case to the U.S. Supreme Court. They argued that it would be impossible to tell a voter's intent on a ballot that was unclearly marked.

» Florida election officials carefully view ballots during the recount after the 2000 election.

THE DECISION OF THE COURT On December 12, the U.S. Supreme Court ruled for Bush in a 5-4 decision. It said that the votes could not be counted the same way across Florida because counties used different methods. As a result, not every ballot would be treated equally.

> [W]e are presented with a situation where a state court . . . has ordered a statewide recount with minimal [few] procedural safeguards. . . . [T]here must be at least some assurance that the . . . requirements of equal treatment and fundamental fairness are satisfied.
>
> —*Bush* v. *Gore* (2000)

The Supreme Court ordered the recount to stop. As a result, Bush won Florida by 537 votes. Winning Florida gave him enough electoral votes to win in the Electoral College. Bush received 271 electoral votes to Gore's 266. George W. Bush became the 43rd president of the United States.

1. **Explaining** What reason did the U.S. Supreme Court give for its decision?
2. **Analyzing** Do you agree with the Court's decision in this case? Why or why not?

The office that runs elections—it may be a town clerk or a local board of elections—provides absentee ballots to those who request them. Voters may request an absentee ballot in person, by mail, or online. Rules vary by state, as do the deadlines for requesting an absentee ballot and for returning them. If an absentee ballot is returned late, the vote will not count.

A few states carry out all their elections by mail. In these states, ballots are mailed to all registered voters, who must mark and return their ballots before a deadline.

✓ **CHECK FOR UNDERSTANDING**

1. **Determining Central Ideas** What is voter registration?

2. **Understanding Supporting Details** Name three types of information you should know before voting.

Why Your Vote Counts

GUIDING QUESTION

Why is it important to vote?

Have you ever heard the phrase "every vote counts"? It is true. The United States is pledged to the ideal of equality in voting. When you vote, your vote will be counted exactly the same way, and be given the same value, as everyone else's vote.

Reasons to Vote

Some people think their vote is not important. In reality, it is vital. Your vote is your voice in the government. The people who are elected will make the laws and set public policy that will affect you and your family. It may also affect the more than 330 million other people across the nation. If you do not vote, you let other people decide who will lead our communities and country. Without voters voting, we lose our democracy.

Voting is a right and a responsibility of citizenship. Once you are eligible to vote, there are important reasons why you should vote in every election. Voting gives you a chance to choose your government leaders. It also allows you to show whether you are satisfied or upset with the performance of those who already hold office and want to be reelected. It gives you a voice in how your town, state, and country are run. As President Franklin Roosevelt said,

❝ The ultimate [final] rulers of our democracy are not a president and senators and congressmen and government officials, but the voters of this country. ❞

—Franklin Roosevelt, speech at Marietta, Ohio, July 8, 1938

Voters at a polling place in Ferguson, Missouri, cast their ballots.

Analyzing Visuals Do you think the arrangement of voting stations shown here is effective in protecting the secrecy of each ballot? Explain your answer.

PHOTO: ASSOCIATED PRESS; TEXT: Roosevelt, Franklin D. "Annual Message to Congress, January 3, 1938." The Public Papers and Addresses of Franklin D. Roosevelt. 1938 Volume, The Continuing Struggle for Liberalism: With a Special Introduction and Explanatory Notes by President Roosevelt [Book 1]. New York: Macmillan, 1941.

Turnout was high in the 2020 election despite the threat posed by the COVID-19 pandemic.

Analyzing Visuals What does this photograph suggest voters might face when turnout is high?

Citizens who do vote share some characteristics. Many believe that they have a right—and a duty—to make their voice heard.

Understanding Voter Participation

Still, some Americans choose not to vote. The **voter turnout rate** is the percentage of eligible voters who actually do vote. For example, if 100 people are eligible to vote and only 60 people vote, the voter turnout rate is 60 percent. Although it varies by election, the voter turnout rate in American elections is often well below 50 percent. Overall, this rate in the United States is quite low compared to other democracies.

The percentage of Americans voting in presidential elections declined to 55 percent in 2016. Then the 2020 election reversed that trend. Nearly 67 percent of eligible voters cast a ballot in 2020. That was the highest turnout rate since 1900. Even fewer Americans vote for Congress or state and local offices. Turnout in the 2018 midterm elections—a national election when people do not vote for president—was 53 percent. This was the highest turnout for a midterm election in 40 years.

---

voter turnout rate the percentage of eligible voters who actually vote

Why is turnout low? One reason is apathy, or lack of interest. Many people feel they are too busy to vote. Some people may have decided that no candidate deserves their vote or that they cannot decide among the candidates. Some people think their vote will not make a difference or change the results of the election. Some people fail to register to vote. When people move to a new address—which millions of Americans do every year—they need to register again in their new location. Many simply do not. People who are registered are likely to take the time to vote.

✓ **CHECK FOR UNDERSTANDING**

Summarizing What does the saying "every vote counts" mean?

LESSON ACTIVITIES

1. **Informative/Explanatory Writing** Create an infographic describing the steps in the voting process. Include the steps in the process and simple illustrations to describe each step.

2. **Analyzing Information** With a group, prepare a time line describing how Americans' voting rights have changed since the Civil War.

05

Analyzing Sources: Voting Rights Amendments

? COMPELLING QUESTION

How do laws shape political participation?

Plan Your Inquiry

DEVELOPING QUESTIONS

Think about how laws have changed to expand the number of people eligible to vote in the United States. Then read the Compelling Question for this lesson. What questions can you ask to help you answer this Compelling Question? Create a graphic organizer like the one below. Write these Supporting Questions in your graphic organizer.

Supporting Questions	Primary or Secondary Source	What the source tells me about the effect of laws on voter participation	Questions the source leaves unanswered
	A		
	B		
	C		
	D		
	E		
	F		

ANALYZING SOURCES

Next, examine the sources in this lesson. Analyze each source by answering the questions that follow it. How does each source help you answer each Supporting Question you created? What questions do you still have? Write these in your graphic organizer.

After you analyze the sources, you will:
- use the evidence from the sources,
- communicate your conclusions,
- and take informed action.

Background Information

In 1787 delegates from the states met in Philadelphia to discuss their concerns about the national government under the Articles of Confederation. They wrote a new plan for government, the U.S. Constitution. Approved in 1788, it established a republic in which citizens directly or indirectly elected their leaders. However, the Framers of the Constitution left the method and qualifications for voting to the states. At the time, most states allowed only white men over the age of 21 who owned property and paid taxes to vote. Women, African Americans, and Native Americans did not have the right to vote. In addition, white males without enough money to own property usually could not vote.

In time, that changed. State laws, and a few key constitutional amendments, expanded who could vote. In this lesson, you will explore primary and secondary sources to help you understand how and why voting rights expanded. You will also consider the impact of voting laws on civic participation.

Over time, more Americans gained the right to vote. In 1971 the voting age was lowered to 18.

An African American Senator Appeals for Justice

In 1870 Hiram Revels of Mississippi became the first African American to serve in the U.S. Senate. In his first speech to the Senate, he talked about events in Georgia. There, voters, including African Americans who had recently received the right to vote, had elected more than 30 African Americans to the state legislature. However, white state lawmakers refused to seat them. In this image, Revels (seated on the far left) is shown with several African American men who served in the U.S. Congress in the 1870s.

THE FIRST COLORED SENATOR AND REPRESENTATIVES.
In the 41ˢᵗ and 42ⁿᵈ Congress of the United States.

PRIMARY SOURCE: SPEECH

❝ Mr. President, I maintain that the past record of my race is a true index of [guide to] the feelings which today animate [move] them. They bear toward their former masters [slaveholders] no revengeful thoughts, no hatreds, no **animosities**. They aim not to elevate [raise] themselves by sacrificing one single interest of their white fellow-citizens. They ask but the rights which are theirs by God's universal law, and which are the natural outgrowth, the logical sequence of the condition in which the **legislative enactments** of this nation have placed them. They appeal to you and to me to see that they receive that protection which alone will enable them to pursue their daily **avocations** with success and enjoy the liberties of citizenship on the same footing with their white neighbors and friends. I do not desire simply to defend my own race from unjust and unmerited [undeserved] charges, but I also desire to place upon record an expression of my full and entire confidence in the integrity of purpose with which I believe the president, Congress, and the Republican party will meet these questions so **prolific** of **weal or woe**, not only to my own people, but to the whole South. . . .

. . . Mr. President, . . . I rose to plead for protection for the defenseless race who now send their delegation to the seat of government to sue for that which this Congress alone can secure to them. ❞

— Hiram Revels, "The State of Georgia," March 16, 1870

animosity a strong feeling of dislike
legislative enactment law
avocation job or occupation
prolific productive
weal or woe good times or bad times

EXAMINE THE SOURCE

1. **Summarizing** What does Revels say that African American citizens want?
2. **Analyzing** Why was the decision by the Georgia legislature not to seat African American lawmakers a violation of African American rights?

Women and the Vote

In June 1919 Congress passed the Nineteenth Amendment. Ratified in August 1920, it granted women the right to vote across the nation. Less than three months later, millions of women took part for the first time in federal elections. The number of votes cast in that election increased by more than 40 percent from the 1916 election. The photograph shows some women in New York voting for the first time in the 1920 election. This excerpt is from a book about the history of women voting.

SECONDARY SOURCE: BOOK

66 The first women voters **lagged** considerably behind men in their tendency to enter polling places, although the extent to which women and men turned out (and the size of the turnout **gender gap**) varied from state to state depending on the political context. By 1964, women's increasingly high turnout combined with women's greater numbers in the eligible **electorate** translated into more women than men casting ballots for president. Since 1980 women have been more likely than men to turn out in presidential elections. . . .

The national woman suffrage amendment was the culmination [end] of a long-term process of expanding, and sometimes constricting [limiting], voting rights for women in the United States. . . .

There were short-term delays for women; four Southern states [Arkansas, Georgia, Mississippi, and South Carolina] refused to let women vote in 1920 due to their failure to meet registration deadlines that occurred months before the Nineteenth Amendment was ratified. (Other states with similar deadlines adjusted their rules to accommodate [allow for] new women voters.) Women in those states were unable to vote in a presidential election until 1924.

In the longer term, **Jim Crow** practices in the South meant most black women continued to be **disenfranchised** on the basis of their race for decades following the presidential election of 1920. . . .

The impact of Jim Crow on access to the vote for black women was enormous. Nationwide, women of color comprised [made up] only about 5% of the total female electorate in any election before 1964, despite black women being 11% of the population. . . . 99

— Christina Wolbrecht and J. Kevin Corder, *A Century of Votes for Women*, 2020

lag to come behind
gender gap difference in voting patterns between men and women
electorate all the people entitled to vote

Jim Crow Southern segregation laws that discriminated against African Americans and denied them equal rights
disenfranchise to deny someone the legal right to vote

EXAMINE THE SOURCE

1. **Contrasting** How did voter participation among women and men change from 1920 onward?
2. **Making Connections** How did race affect voter participation among women, and why?

Poll Taxes

Though the Fifteenth Amendment was meant to ensure the voting rights of African Americans, many Southern states enacted laws to prevent African Americans from voting. Laws requiring the payment of poll taxes, or fees paid per person in order to vote, were difficult for poor African Americans to pay. In August 1962, Congress passed the Twenty-fourth Amendment. This addition to the Constitution barred the use of poll taxes as a requirement for voting. States ratified the amendment in January 1964. This passage is from an article written to celebrate the fiftieth anniversary of that amendment. The photograph shows a sign posted in Mineola, Texas, in 1939 reminding people to pay their poll taxes.

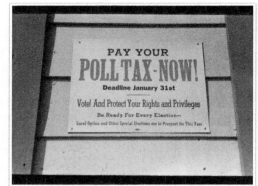

SECONDARY SOURCE: ARTICLE

66 Fifty years ago today, the 24th Amendment, prohibiting the use of poll taxes as voting qualifications in federal elections, became part of the U.S. Constitution. Poll taxes were among the devices [techniques] used by Southern states to restrict African Americans (as well as poor whites, Native Americans and other **marginalized** populations) from voting. The taxes had been ubiquitous [widespread] across the old **Confederacy** earlier in the 20th century [1900s], but by 1964 only five states—Alabama, Arkansas, Mississippi, Texas and Virginia—retained them.

The **nominal** amount of the taxes wasn't very much, then or now. Alabama, Texas and Virginia set theirs at $1.50 per year, or $11.27 in today's dollars; Arkansas had the lowest tax, $1 (or $7.51 today), while Mississippi's was highest at $2 ($15.03 today). But the taxes were more onerous [burdensome] than they might appear. In Virginia, Alabama and Mississippi the taxes were **cumulative**, meaning a person seeking to vote had to pay the taxes for two or three years before they were eligible to register. Often only property owners were billed for the taxes, and the due dates were several months before the election. Virginia, Mississippi and Texas allowed cities and counties to impose local poll taxes on top of the state charge. And in some **jurisdictions** taxes had to be paid in person at the sheriff's office, an **intimidating** prospect for many. 99

— Drew DeSilver, "Anti-poll tax amendment is 50 years old today," *Pew Research Center,* January 23, 2014

---

marginalized treated unfairly or as less important

Confederacy the Confederate States of America, the government formed by eleven Southern states that seceded from the Union in 1860 and 1861

nominal in name or in form only

cumulative increasing over time or through additions

jurisdiction an area in which laws apply

intimidating causing fear

EXAMINE THE SOURCE

1. **Analyzing** How did the Twenty-fourth Amendment seek to expand voter participation?
2. **Explaining** What made poll taxes so "onerous" or burdensome for many people?

PHOTO: Library of Congress Prints & Photographs Division, FSA/OWI Collection, [LC-USF3301-011961-M2]; TEXT: DeSilver, Drew. "Anti-poll Tax Amendment is 50 Years Old Today," Pew Research Center, January 23, 2014. https://www.pewresearch.org/fact-tank/2014/01/23/anti-poll-tax-amendment-is-50-years-old-today/.

Lowering the Voting Age

For most of the country's history, states required voters to be at least 21 years old. Debate over the voting age grew during the Vietnam War of the 1960s and 1970s. Many people argued that if 18-year-old men were required to serve in the armed forces, they should be allowed to vote. In March 1971, Congress passed the Twenty-sixth Amendment, lowering the voting age to 18. Senator Edward Kennedy of Massachusetts offered his support before Congress approved the amendment.

PRIMARY SOURCE: TESTIMONY

" I believe the time has come to lower the voting age in the United States, and thereby to bring American youth into the mainstream of our political process. . . .

First, our young people today are far better equipped—intellectually, physically, and emotionally—to make the type of choices involved in voting than were past generations of youth. . . .

The contrast is clear in the case of education. . . . [O]ur youth are extremely well informed on all the crucial [important] issues of our time, foreign and domestic, national and local, urban and rural. . . .

Indeed, in many cases, 18 to 21 year-olds already possess a better education than a large proportion of adults among our general electorate. And, they also possess a far better education than the vast majority of the electorate in all previous periods of our history. . . .

Second, by lowering the voting age to 18, we will encourage civic responsibility at an earlier age, and thereby promote lasting social involvement and political participation for our youth.

We know that there is already a high incidence [rate] of political activity today on campuses and among young people generally, even though they do not have the **franchise**. . . . By granting them the right to vote, we will demonstrate our recognition of their ability and our faith in their capacity for future growth within our political system. . . .

Third, 18 year-olds already have many rights and responsibilities in our society comparable to voting. It does not automatically follow of course—simply because an 18 year-old goes to war, or works, or marries, or makes a contract, or pays taxes, or drives a car, or owns a gun, or is held criminally responsible, like an adult—that he should thereby be entitled to vote. Each right or responsibility in our society presents unique questions dependent on the particular issue at stake. "

— Senator Edward Kennedy, to Senate Subcommittee on Constitutional Amendments, March 9, 1970

franchise the right to vote

EXAMINE THE SOURCE

1. **Identifying** What role does education play in Kennedy's reasoning?
2. **Explaining** What effect does Kennedy say lowering the voting age will have on young Americans? What does it say about the nation?

Kennedy, E., "Voting Age to 18 Testimony Before the Senate Subcommittee on Constitutional Amendments" March 9, 1970, Senate Subcommittee on Constitutional Amendments

Voting Rates by Age

The U.S. Census Bureau asks Americans whether they voted. Then it compares voting rates by different age groups in presidential election years.

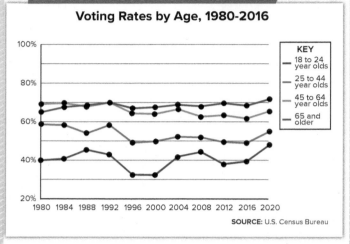

Voting Rates by Age, 1980–2016

KEY
— 18 to 24 year olds
— 25 to 44 year olds
— 45 to 64 year olds
— 65 and older

SOURCE: U.S. Census Bureau

EXAMINE THE SOURCE

1. **Analyzing** Which two age groups consistently show the highest rates of voter participation?

2. **Summarizing** How has the trend in the youth vote (ages 18 to 24) changed over time?

Complete Your Inquiry

EVALUATE SOURCES AND USE EVIDENCE

Refer back to the Compelling Question and the Supporting Questions you developed at the beginning of the lesson.

1. **Synthesizing** In what ways do the sources support the conclusion that voting rights have generally expanded over time?

2. **Analyzing** What evidence from the sources suggests that voting rights did not continuously expand?

3. **Gathering Sources** Which sources helped you answer the Supporting Questions and the Compelling Question? Which sources, if any, challenged what you thought you knew when you first created your Supporting Questions? What information do you still need in order to answer your questions? What other viewpoints would you like to investigate? Where would you find that information?

4. **Evaluating Sources** Identify the sources that helped answer your Supporting Questions. How reliable is the source? How would you verify the reliability of the source?

COMMUNICATE CONCLUSIONS

5. **Collaborating** Work with a partner to think about ways to boost the share of younger people who vote. You might use social media messages, public service announcements, voter registration drives, or other approaches. Develop a plan that you think will work, and share your ideas with the class.

TAKE INFORMED ACTION

Developing a Voters' Guide With one or two partners, research voting requirements in your community and the national, state, or local offices that will appear on the ballot in the next election. Use what you learn to develop a print brochure or a website in which you inform citizens about how to be ready to vote in the next election. Present your complete guide to the class.

Analyzing Key Ideas and Details As you read, make a list of tasks that a candidate must complete. Add items to your list as needed.

Tasks for a Candidate
-
-
-

Types of Elections

GUIDING QUESTION

Why are there different types of elections in the American political system?

How many people do you think hold elected office in the United States? The answer is: enough to fill a city. In all levels of government, from federal down to local governments, the country has more than half a million (500,000) elected officials. It is not surprising that elections are a large part of American life.

Primary and General Elections

Most states have two kinds of elections. The first is called a *primary*. A **primary election** is an election to choose a party's candidates for each office. States usually schedule primaries in the spring or summer. The candidates who win their party's primary for an office then run for that office in the general election in the fall.

The national general election is held throughout the country on the first Tuesday after the first Monday in November in even-numbered years. Every two years, voters elect all members of the House of Representatives and about one-third of the members of the Senate. Presidential elections are held every four years. State and local elections often do not take place on the same days as these national elections.

Initiatives and Referendums

Many states allow citizens to vote on certain ballot questions. A ballot question is a proposal that voters are asked to approve or reject. Sometimes they are suggested laws. Sometimes voters are asked to approve a proposal to borrow money for a particular purpose. These measures are examples of direct democracy. They give voters a direct say in the laws that govern them.

primary election election to choose a party's candidates for each office in the general election

The numerous campaign signs suggest that voters will be selecting people to fill many political offices in this election.

An **initiative** lets voters propose new laws or amendments to state constitutions. People in favor of the proposal must first get voters to sign a petition, a formal written request. If they gather the number of signatures set by state law, their measure will be placed on the ballot for all voters to approve or reject. The proposed law is called a *proposition*.

Voters can also petition to reject a law passed by a state or local legislature through a **referendum**. Often, a referendum involves new taxes or tax increases. Some states require voters to approve all changes to the state constitution by referendum.

Special Elections

Some states allow recall elections. In a **recall**, people can choose to remove an official from office before the term of office ends. First, as with an initiative, enough citizens must sign a petition asking for a recall. If they do, a special election is held. If a majority votes in favor of the recall in that election, the official must give up the office.

Sometimes an official dies in office or resigns before the end of the term of office. In those cases, the government may call a special election to fill the vacant office. These elections are called *special* because they do not take place at a regularly scheduled time.

✓ CHECK FOR UNDERSTANDING

1. **Identifying** What is the result of a primary election?
2. **Analyzing** How does the initiative process make the political system more democratic?

Presidential Elections

GUIDING QUESTION

How are presidents elected?

In a presidential election, people across the country vote for the person they want to fill that office. However, presidents are not elected directly by the people. The rules for choosing a president are different from those for filling most offices.

---

initiative process that lets voters propose new laws or amendments to the state constitution

referendum a procedure by which citizens vote on state or local laws

recall a special election in which citizens can vote to remove an official from office before the term ends

Understanding the Electoral College

The **popular vote** is the count of votes cast for president directly by the people. When voters cast their ballots in a presidential race, they are actually electing special representatives called *electors*. Each party chooses a group of presidential electors before the election. Those electors pledge to vote for the party's candidate. Together, all the electors are called the Electoral College. A person voting for a Republican presidential candidate is really voting for a Republican elector to vote for that candidate in the Electoral College.

---

popular vote the votes cast by individual voters in a presidential election, as opposed to the electoral vote

---

The Electoral College Process

The election and inauguration of the president and vice president take place over several months.

TUESDAY AFTER FIRST MONDAY IN NOVEMBER
- On Election Day, voters cast ballots for a slate of electors pledged to a particular presidential candidate.

MONDAY AFTER SECOND WEDNESDAY IN DECEMBER
- Winning electors in each state meet in their state capitals to cast their votes for president and vice president.
- A statement of the vote is sent to Washington, D.C.

JANUARY 6
- Congress counts electoral votes. A majority of electoral votes is needed to win (270 out of 538).

JANUARY 20
- The candidates receiving the majority of electoral votes for each office are sworn in as president and vice president in Washington, D.C.

EXAMINE THE DIAGRAM

1. **Calculating** About how much time passes between the day voters cast their votes and the day the president and vice president are inaugurated?
2. **Interpreting** Which steps take place across the country, and which take place in Washington, D.C.?

Presidential Election Results, 1984–2020

Because most states give all their electoral votes to the candidate who wins the popular vote in the state, candidates can win a higher percentage of electoral votes than popular votes.

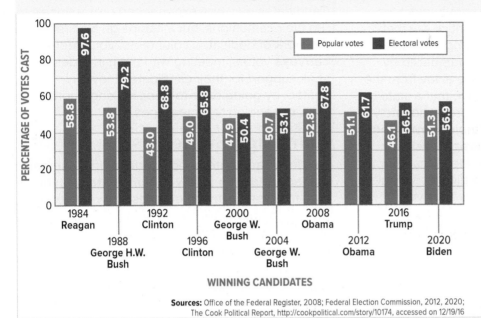

PERCENTAGE OF VOTES CAST

Popular votes · Electoral votes

1984 Reagan	58.8	97.6
1988 George H.W. Bush	53.8	79.2
1992 Clinton	43.0	68.8
1996 Clinton	49.0	65.8
2000 George W. Bush	47.9	50.4
2004 George W. Bush	50.7	53.1
2008 Obama	52.8	67.8
2012 Obama	51.1	61.7
2016 Trump	46.1	56.5
2020 Biden	51.3	56.9

WINNING CANDIDATES

Sources: Office of the Federal Register, 2008; Federal Election Commission, 2012, 2020; The Cook Political Report, http://cookpolitical.com/story/10174, accessed on 12/19/16

HISTORY CONNECTION

1. **Identifying** In which four elections shown here did the candidate win the electoral vote without receiving a majority of the popular vote?

2. **Calculating** In which election were the popular and electoral vote percentages the closest to each other? In which were they farthest apart?

Each state has the same number of electors as it has members of Congress. New Jersey, for instance, has 12 representatives in the House and 2 senators, so it has 14 electors. Wyoming, with one representative and two senators, has three electors. In addition, the District of Columbia has three electors. There are 538 electors in all.

A few weeks after the election, the electors of the candidate who won the popular vote in their state meet in their state capital. They cast their electoral votes and send them to the U.S. Senate. In January, the House and Senate meet to count each state's vote. The candidates for president and vice president with a majority of the electoral votes—at least 270—win the election.

Why do we have an Electoral College? When the Framers discussed how to choose the president, several different views arose. Some wanted the American people to vote for the president. Others worried that the people would not have enough information to choose among candidates from other parts of the country. Some Framers wanted Congress to choose the president. Others argued that such a system would weaken the president. The Framers compromised. Citizens show who they prefer with their votes. Electors cast the deciding votes.

What if no one wins the Electoral College? If the vote for president ends in an electoral tie, or if no candidate receives a majority of the electoral votes, the House of Representatives chooses the president. The U.S. Senate elects the vice president in the event of an electoral tie for that office.

Criticisms of the Electoral College

In most states, the winner of the popular vote wins all of that state's electors in a **winner-take-all** system. For instance, in 2020, Joe Biden won slightly more votes than Donald Trump in Wisconsin. Biden won 49.5 percent of the total to Trump's 48.8 percent. As a result, Biden received all 10 of Wisconsin's electoral votes. Some people say this process is undemocratic—that it ignores the will of the people. They argue that a candidate can lose the national popular vote but still win the electoral vote and gain the presidency. This is not just a possibility—it has happened five times, most recently in 2016.

Only Maine and Nebraska do not use the winner-take-all system. They give two electoral votes to the winner of the state's popular votes. The other electoral votes are given to the winner of the popular vote in each congressional district. In these two states, then, both presidential candidates may win some electoral votes.

winner-take-all a system in which the candidate who wins the popular vote in a state receives all of the state's electoral votes

The winner-take-all system supports the two-party system. This system makes it extremely difficult for third-party candidates to win any electoral votes.

Many Americans believe we should elect the president by direct popular vote. Critics say that this might lead to candidates ignoring rural areas because rural voters would be outnumbered by those in cities. Others want to move away from the winner-take-all system. They believe that a state's electoral votes should be divided proportionately among candidates according to their share of the state's popular vote. Critics of this approach say this change would produce more elections without anyone winning a majority. These elections would be decided by the House of Representatives. Of course, no change to the Electoral College can happen without amending the Constitution.

✓ **CHECK FOR UNDERSTANDING**

Summarizing Explain why the Framers decided to have the Electoral College choose the president.

Running for Office

GUIDING QUESTION

How do candidates run for political office?

An election campaign is a candidate's effort to win an election. Conducting a campaign is serious business. It is also expensive—even for local offices. For a national election, the cost is staggering. In 2020 total spending in the presidential campaign was more than $6 billion.

Running a Campaign

A person running for town council faces different challenges than one running for president. Yet all campaigns have some things in common.

First, a candidate must meet the legal qualifications for office. For example, people must be a certain age to be eligible to serve as a state legislator. Candidates for state and local offices commonly must be residents of the place they will serve.

Candidates have to divide their time among several types of activities. They appear at community events and make speeches and give interviews to the press. They attend meetings to listen to voters' concerns and answer their questions. Candidates talk to possible donors to raise the money they need to fund their campaign. They try to boost their image by getting

endorsements, or public support, from important people and groups. They release statements giving their positions on policy issues.

Most candidates have staffs to help them. Candidates may hire experienced professionals to run their campaigns, but a campaign also relies on the work of dedicated volunteers. Volunteers **canvass** voters, meeting with them in order to seek support for their candidate. They make contact by going door-to-door, making phone calls, or sending text messages.

Campaign Strategies

To win, a candidate needs to develop a campaign strategy and then follow it. That strategy is the plan for what issues to emphasize, what voting groups to appeal to, and how to use their time and money. This requires strong organization as well as a clear message.

Advertising is a major campaign expense. Candidates use advertising to tell voters about their position on issues, to present themselves in an appealing way, and to criticize their opponents. Political parties and interest groups also buy ads supporting the candidate they favor or criticizing the opponent.

Many ads could be considered propaganda. **Propaganda** involves using biased or misleading ideas, information, or rumors to influence opinion. There are many propaganda techniques. Most propaganda relies on emotion. Ads can also tell partial truths that can be misleading. For instance, candidates tend to quote statistics that support their position and ignore statistics that call it into doubt.

Campaigns often use propaganda to attack their candidate's opponent. Attack ads and name-calling can draw attention away from the important issues of a campaign. Propaganda often uses **symbolism**, which is the use of sounds or images that have strong positive or negative appeal. A key to identifying propaganda is to know who produced a message. This can help you to identify the speaker's **bias**, a person's

canvass meeting with voters to seek support for a candidate

propaganda messages that use biased or misleading ideas, information, or rumors to influence opinion

symbolism the use of sounds or images that have strong positive or negative appeal

bias a person's beliefs about another person or group that may not be based on facts and may affect the person's judgment

Propaganda Techniques

Political campaigns and companies advertising products use similar propaganda techniques.

CANDIDATE "A" IS A WINNER!

"Polls show our candidate is pulling ahead, and we expect to win in a landslide."

NAME-CALLING

"Candidate A is a dangerous extremist."

ENDORSEMENT

Popular beauty queen says, "I'm voting for Candidate B and so should you."

SYMBOLISM

Associating a patriotic symbol with a candidate

GLITTERING GENERALITY

"Candidate B is the one who will bring us peace and prosperity."

JUST PLAIN FOLKS

"My parents were ordinary, hardworking people, and they taught me those values."

STACKED CARDS

"Candidate C has the best record on the environment."

EXAMINE THE DIAGRAM

1. **Identifying Bias** Which of these methods would be used by a group to attack the opposing candidate?

2. **Analyzing Points of View** Which of these methods promises hope for the future?

---

beliefs about another person or group that may not be based on facts and may affect the holder's judgment. Any ad produced by a campaign must include the statement that the candidate approves of the message. This is required by a law Congress passed in 2002.

This rule does not apply to political commercials known as *issue ads*. These ads are paid for by groups that are not part of a candidate's campaign. They are supposed to focus on an issue rather than to support a candidate.

Television is a very important communication tool for candidates. Watching television is one of the ways that many citizens find out about candidates and their position on issues. Televised debates, often occurring late in a campaign, can have an impact on undecided voters. In the weeks just before an election, campaigns and special interest groups air an increasing number of ads.

In recent years, newer media have become important to campaigns. Candidates have websites that provide information—and give supporters a place to donate money. Social

media is important to campaigns too. Campaigns use social media sites to reach voters. Targeted advertising uses personal information about users of the Internet and social media. This practice guides the media user **specifically** to certain sites or messages. Campaigns take advantage of this practice to get their message to people likely to support their candidate.

Supporters of a candidate use social media too. They spread messages they like to their friends. These messages can reach voters the campaign had not reached. Supporters' messages can be difficult for a campaign to control, however.

Some groups use the Internet and social media with bad intent. The Internet Research Agency, a group directed by the Russian government, used the Internet to try to sway the 2016 U.S. presidential election. It created hundreds of fake social media accounts and used them to post misleading messages to influence American voters.

---

specifically for a particular purpose

Thirteen Russians and three Russia-based organizations were charged with crimes for interfering with U.S. elections.

Users can manipulate content on social media because many platforms have limited programs for fact-checking posts. Critics say those programs are not fully effective. For this reason, it is difficult to identify reliable information on these platforms. Professional news organizations work to meet higher standards. Such organizations include television network news, news services such as Associated Press and Reuters, and news and current affairs publications such as *Time* and *The New York Times*. These organizations invest in research to develop news stories of public interest. They pursue stories that government officials may not want made public. These organizations generally fact-check their stories to make sure that factual claims are accurate.

Trusted news sources that employ careful fact-checking and have the public interest in mind make it possible for citizens to be informed. This is why a free press is essential to the preservation of democracy. The First Amendment right to freedom of the press allows news organizations to monitor the government. They can help hold officials accountable. In doing so, they serve the public interest.

Campaign Finance

Political campaigns are expensive. Congressional campaigns can cost tens of millions of dollars. How do candidates raise the money they need?

Most campaign funding comes from donations. Individuals, corporations, industry groups, labor unions, and various private groups give money to the campaigns of candidates whom they believe will work for policies that benefit them. Corporations and interest groups form **political action committees (PACs)** to support candidates by contributing money to their campaigns.

---

political action committee (PAC) an organization set up by a corporation, labor union, or other special-interest group to support candidates by contributing money to their campaigns

Money has become an essential element of political campaigns.

Analyzing What does the cartoon say about the role of money? Why do you think so?

The Federal Election Commission (FEC) regulates campaigns and how they raise and use money. Many Americans worry that campaigns have gotten too expensive. They worry that elected officials spend more time and energy seeking contributions and running for reelection than they do making public policy. They believe that politicians want to help the people who donate money more than they want to serve the public.

✓ CHECK FOR UNDERSTANDING

1. **Describing** Describe the role of propaganda in elections.

2. **Explaining** Why is money important to political campaigns?

LESSON ACTIVITIES

1. **Argumentative Writing** Review the criticisms of the Electoral College and the ideas for changing it. Write a brief argumentative essay in which you explain at least one of the ideas. Give reasons why you support or oppose it.

2. **Using Multimedia** Work with a partner to create a campaign advertisement for a fictional candidate. Decide which policies you want your candidate to favor and be known for. Create a 30-second TV spot to persuade people to vote for your candidate.

READING STRATEGY

Integrating Knowledge and Ideas As you read, complete a graphic organizer like this one by identifying main ideas about public opinion.

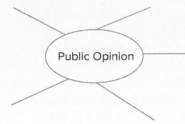

Public Opinion

Public Opinion

GUIDING QUESTION

What is public opinion?

Public opinion refers to the ideas and attitudes that people hold about elected officials, candidates, government, and public issues. In a democracy, the people are the source of political power. They can exercise that power by voting. The people's votes tell public officials what they think of their decisions. Of course, people also want to express their views before laws are passed or policies are formed. If government is to be responsive to the people, the people need ways to make their views known before officials make policy.

The Role of Public Opinion in a Democracy

Public opinion plays two important roles in a democracy. First, it helps shape the decisions that officials make. Members of Congress and state legislators often travel back to their home districts to meet with voters and talk about bills that are being considered or issues that are on people's minds. They try to judge public opinion. Some lawmakers believe that if they are to represent the people, their votes should reflect the views of the people. Others want to take a position that reflects public opinion because they think it will help them get reelected.

public opinion the ideas and attitudes that people hold about elected officials, candidates, government, and public issues

Citizens can communicate how they feel about an issue when a member of Congress comes back to the state or district to meet with the people.

Analyzing Visuals Why might a politician find it helpful to hold a local meeting like the one shown in the image?

People often take part in marches or demonstrations when they feel strongly that the government is not addressing an issue or is doing so in a way they think is wrong.

Presidents are guided by public opinion in this way too. Public opinion helps shape the ideas put forth by the president as well as the ultimate success of the president's plans. Presidents need the support of Congress to carry out their programs. A president is more likely to have that support if the public approves of those plans. The same is true of state governors and city mayors. Public opinion affects the success of the executive in another way. Suppose the majority of the public says they do not approve of the job a president or governor is doing. Those leaders will then have a difficult time convincing legislators to agree to their plans.

Of course, public opinion is a complicated thing. One reason for this is the country's size. The United States has more than 330 million people. Also, America's population is highly diverse. Americans live in different parts of the country with different concerns. They have different backgrounds that shape the way they see the world and issues. As a result, Americans have a wide range of opinions on public issues. When enough people hold a similar opinion, however, government officials listen.

Features of Public Opinion

Public opinion is often described in terms of three factors: direction, intensity, and stability. Each measures a different aspect of public opinion.

Direction refers to whether public opinion about someone or something is mainly positive or negative. That is, do people like an idea or not? For example, do people want to have a new school built or not? Do people trust this candidate or not? On some topics, the public is evenly split. Still, a majority of the public may favor one side over the other.

Intensity refers to how strongly people hold their opinions on issues. In other words, how much do they care? People generally have the strongest opinions about issues that directly affect them. For example, store owners care more about sales tax rates than doctors do. When people hold a strong opinion on an issue, they pay more attention to it. They may also decide to become active on that issue.

Stability refers to how firmly people hold to their views over time. That is, how likely are they to change their minds? People generally maintain opinions that are based on strong beliefs. They are more likely to change their minds on other matters. For example, most people's opinions about civil rights are more stable than their opinions about rules for trading with other countries.

✓ CHECK FOR UNDERSTANDING

Determining Central Ideas What are two ways that public opinion influences government decisions?

Sources of Public Opinion

GUIDING QUESTION

How is public opinion formed?

How do people develop their opinions? What factors affect their views? The key influences are people's backgrounds, the mass media, and interest groups.

Personal Background

People's opinions often reflect their experiences and their situation in life. Age, race, religion, social class, culture, and **gender** can all help shape a person's opinions. A person's job, income, and where he or she lives may affect opinions too. These personal factors can shape how we think. They also shape how others treat us, which can affect how we see the world.

However, you can never tell just from someone's identity and background what that person will think about a specific issue. All groups

gender being male or female

within a society include many people who disagree with each other. For instance, think about the issue of education. You might expect parents to support spending on public education and people without children to have less interest in it. However, some parents homeschool their children or send them to private schools. They might have less interest in public education. Some people without children support public education because they think it reduces crime. Some people think the government should provide public education to help prepare children to become working adults.

Mass Media

The mass media can be an important factor that shapes opinion. *Media* is the plural of *medium*, which refers to any method or means of communication. Cell phone text messages are a medium of communication. The **mass media** are the methods of communication that reach large numbers of people. These include television, radio, Internet websites, newspapers, magazines, books, and movies.

Mass media influence public opinion in many different ways. Television news shows and newspapers shape public opinion with the stories they air and publish. First, the choice of stories they cover can have an influence. When mass media carry a story about a particular topic, such as crime, the coverage suggests that crime is important. Similarly, if an issue is not covered, people may assume that it is not important.

Second, how the news is reported can influence the opinions of news consumers. Placing an item as the top story on a website or the first item on a television newscast signals that the story is more important than others. However, this placement may give a distorted view of a story's importance. The mass media often focus on news that has visual appeal or shock value. The stories covered are not necessarily the most important or relevant stories, though.

Third, the media influence opinion with what they say about a story. News stories provide information, but they can also include opinions. Opinion pieces may be clearly labeled as *opinion* or *commentary*. This signals to media consumers that they are hearing or reading someone's point of view. However, stories that are not labeled in that way can contain opinions too. In fact, opinions can be transmitted in news stories in subtle ways. For instance, when reporting on an issue, is it called an *issue*, a *problem*, or a *crisis*? The word choice sends a particular message about what is being described.

Deciding when news reporting is biased or more balanced can be difficult. One way to detect bias is to read more than one source on the same story or event.

mass media methods of communication that reach large numbers of people

News media often focus on stories that have strong visuals and drama, such as the hurricane damage in Louisiana shown here.

Mario Tama/Getty Images

Thousands of protestors joined Black Lives Matter marches across the country in 2020, hoping to bring about changes in how the police treat African Americans.

Drawing Conclusions How might a crowd of this size influence public officials?

Compare what the different sources say by asking questions such as these:

- Are the same facts presented in all the accounts? What facts are omitted?
- Are about the same number of people with different perspectives on the event quoted, or do most of the quotes reflect only one perspective?
- Does the writer use biased language that conveys a particular point of view?

Interest Groups

Another source of public opinion is **interest groups**. These are organizations of people who share a point of view about an issue and unite to promote their beliefs. Interest groups want to build public support for the policies they favor. They also work to convince public officials to support their positions.

Interest groups try to influence public opinion in many ways. They may present their views in advertisements in a variety of media. They post information on their websites and social media accounts. They take part in public meetings, where members of interest groups speak on

issues that matter to them. Interest group members can send messages to public officials and take part in public events that call attention to their cause.

✓ **CHECK FOR UNDERSTANDING**

1. **Identifying Cause and Effect** What factors influence public opinion?
2. **Understanding Supporting Details** In what ways do mass news media influence public opinion?

Public Opinion Polls

GUIDING QUESTION

How is public opinion measured?

How do public officials know what opinions the public has? Of course, they hear from the people they represent through letters or emails. They can also hold town hall meetings that allow the public a chance to speak out to them directly. Those methods may only tell them about the views of a few people, though. Public officials have two important ways to learn the opinions of large numbers of people. Those are election results and polls.

Election Results

Election results clearly say whether voters approve one candidate or another. They may suggest that

---

interest group organization of people who share a point of view about an issue and unite to promote their beliefs

the voters agree with the winning candidate's policy ideas and views on public issues.

Election results are not a sure way to measure public opinion, however. People vote for candidates for many reasons. They may like how a candidate looks or speaks. They may not strongly favor one candidate but strongly oppose the other one. They may strongly support the candidate on one or two issues but agree with them less on others. They may back a candidate because of his or her party. For these reasons, election results give only a very rough sense of public opinion.

Another problem with using elections as measures of public opinion is that they happen every few years. If leaders had to wait for elections to know what the public believes, they might have to wait several years. Also, the public needs to make its views known when immediate decisions are needed. Action cannot always wait until the next election.

Polls Measure Public Opinion

To keep in touch with public opinion more regularly, public officials generally rely on polls. A **public opinion poll** is a survey that asks individuals' opinions about public issues or individuals who are holding or seeking office. People's answers are collected and combined to produce **statistical**, or numerical, measures of public opinion. Today hundreds of groups conduct such polls. Members of the media and public officials refer to poll results to help them understand people's attitudes.

Some public officials or political parties hire a **pollster**, a specialist whose job is to conduct polls. The pollster can measure how the public views the official and his or her policies. Regular reports can show if public opinion is moving in one direction or another.

Pollsters have different ways of selecting the people they survey. One way is by picking a group of people at **random**, or by chance.

Pollsters may talk to about 1,500 people from all over the nation. A good sample is a representation of the entire population. That means it should include both men and women, people of varied races and ages, and people from different income categories and different occupations. Each of these groups should be represented in the poll in proportion to their share of the population. If they are, the poll can present a reasonably accurate picture of public opinion as a whole. Polls conducted using random sampling are known as *scientific polls*. They tend to be more reliable than polls that are not scientific.

To find out how people really feel about an issue, pollsters must word questions carefully. The wording of questions can influence the way people answer. Compare these versions of a question intended to find out people's opinions on tax cuts:

- Do you like paying high taxes?
- Do you want lower taxes?
- Do you agree or disagree with this statement: Taxes should be reduced?

These questions could produce different answers even from the same person.

Some polling organizations word their questions in a way to get a specific response. These are called *push polls* because the questions are designed to push the person being polled to answer in a certain way.

Pollsters usually conduct opinion surveys by phone, but they may ask questions in person as well.

Analyzing Visuals What difficulties might this pollster face in trying to select a scientific sample?

DigitalVues/Digital Vision/Alamy Stock Photo

public opinion poll a survey that asks individuals' opinions about public issues or individuals who are holding or seeking office

statistical numerical

pollster a specialist whose job is to conduct polls

random by chance

Newspapers and public opinion polls each have their own role in shaping public opinion.

Analyzing Points of View
What attitude does the cartoon express toward polling? Why do you think so?

The companies and individuals who carry out scientific polls strongly criticize push polls. Scientific polling companies often publish their questions along with their results so that readers can decide whether they think the questions were fair and unbiased.

Pros and Cons of Polls

Polls have many uses. They indicate what citizens think about issues. They show officials whether people approve or disapprove of the way they are doing their jobs. Officials do not have to wait for the next election to find out what is important to voters.

In addition, scientific pollsters break down responses to show the answers given by people from particular groups. They can show how men and women or people earning different amounts of money respond to the same question. Knowing what specific groups think about an issue can help guide officials' decisions.

Critics see problems with polls. They argue that polling makes elected officials focus on pleasing the public. They think officials should focus on making wise decisions for the common good rather than trying to be popular.

Many people also worry that polls influence how people vote. The media cite polls constantly during election campaigns, reporting who is ahead in the race. Critics argue that focusing on polls regarding election results ignores the

candidates' views on important issues. In addition, some say that polls can discourage voting because people believe they already know how the election will turn out and their vote does not matter.

✓ CHECK FOR UNDERSTANDING

1. **Identifying** Besides elections, what is another way to measure public opinion?

2. **Explaining** Why do scientific polls use random sampling?

LESSON ACTIVITIES

1. **Informative/Explanatory Writing** Read two articles on the same event on news websites or in newspapers. Use the questions for detecting bias at the end of the section "Mass Media" to compare how the two sources covered the event. Decide whether each source is biased. If a source is biased, identify the details or words in the story that show bias. Write an analysis in which you explain why you decided that each source is or is not biased.

2. **Collaborating** With a partner, plan and conduct a public opinion poll that will gather opinions on a political issue of your choice. Conduct your poll. Then, report to the class on how you chose the wording for your questions and how well you think your poll captured the opinions of the people you polled.

Print and Digital Media

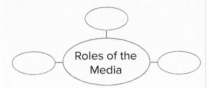

READING STRATEGY

Analyzing Key Ideas and Details As you read, create a graphic organizer like this one to record the roles of the media.

Roles of the Media

The Influence of the Media

GUIDING QUESTION

How do the media influence public opinion and government?

If you are like most Americans, you rely on mass media to provide you with information about news and current events in the United States and the world. In fact, the mass media play several important civic roles.

Mass media sources can be either print or digital. Print media include newspapers, magazines, newsletters, and books. Digital media include radio, television, and the Internet.

In using media information, you must remember an important fact. Most American media outlets are private businesses. Their purpose is to make a profit. The larger the audience, the more the media company can charge advertisers. The more money a company takes in, the higher its profits. The job of a news producer, then, is to attract—and keep—readers and viewers. This fact shapes what the media cover and what news they make available to you.

Influencing the Public Agenda

The government deals with many problems and issues. It cannot resolve all of them. Those issues that receive the most time, money, and attention make up the public agenda. An agenda is a set of items that a person or group wants to address. The **public agenda** is the issues that government officials believe are most important.

public agenda the issues that government officials believe are most important

In this image, members of the media are shown covering the launch of a private spacecraft from the Kennedy Space Center in Florida.

Analyzing Visuals Why do you think the media would choose to cover an event like the one described in the caption?

Americans' Use of Media for News

Americans of different ages get their news from different media.

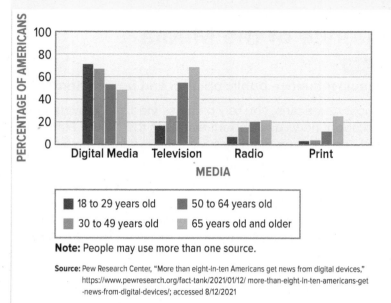

Note: People may use more than one source.

Source: Pew Research Center, "More than eight-in-ten Americans get news from digital devices," https://www.pewresearch.org/fact-tank/2021/01/12/ more-than-eight-in-ten-americans-get -news-from-digital-devices/; accessed 8/12/2021

EXAMINE THE GRAPH

1. **Comparing** Which source is used the most by the two age groups under 50 years old?

2. **Identifying** Which two sources do those 65 years old and older rely on the most?

The media can influence which problems make it onto the public agenda. Greater media focus on a problem can lead more people to care about that problem. This results in people wanting the government to take action. The media also influence the public agenda by publicizing calls for action and campaign promises made by people running for public office.

Digital Media and Citizens

Think about all the things you use the Internet for. How would you do these things if you did not have the ability to go online? Since the 1990s, the ways that Americans participate in civic life have shifted. People used to take part in activities in person or by telephone. Now they often take part online. People can use the Internet to sign petitions, contact government officials, comment on news and on news reporting, organize events, attend online meetings, and more.

In many ways, the Internet has made participating in civic life easier. It takes less time and effort to "like" content on social media than to write to a government official or attend a rally about an issue. Does the use of social media add a new dimension to civic participation—or does it replace personal involvement? According to one study, nearly one-fifth of people who used social media report that it has motivated them to take

action. This study also found that people who use social media for political purposes are also more involved politically in other ways.

Government officials in the United States and other countries have grown increasingly concerned about dangers posed by social media. They say that people with **radical** views can easily attract new followers online. Some of these followers have committed acts of violence toward members of groups that they dislike. Since they often develop their plans and act alone, it can be very difficult to prevent these attacks. Cyberbullying—attacking or harassing people on websites or in social media—is also an issue. Social media companies have taken some steps to try to limit hate speech on their platforms. With around 4 billion social media users worldwide, they face a huge task.

Covering Candidates and Officials

The mass media can also influence election campaigns. Some candidates are experienced politicians. They spend years working in their political parties and gaining recognition with the public. Some candidates, though, are people who were famous in another field. For instance, Donald Trump was a real estate developer and television

radical extreme

personality before he was elected president in 2016. The amount of media coverage that candidates receive affects their chances of being elected. More media coverage of a candidate brings public attention to that candidate.

Coverage is particularly important for people who are new to politics or who do not have a long record of public service. Media coverage helps increase voter recognition of these candidates and their political beliefs.

Reporters and politicians have a complex relationship. They depend on each other. Reporters need information from politicians to write informative articles. Politicians need media coverage to get their message out to voters. At the same time, the two groups often clash. The reason for this is that they have different goals and interests.

Reporters want to inform the public. They view this goal as more important than simply telling what a political figure said. They often provide background information or fact-checking on politicians' statements. As a result, media attention is not always flattering or supportive. Reporters can present news in ways that show an official or candidates in a bad light. They may investigate politicians' professional and personal lives. Reporters can ask officials or candidates tough questions about their positions. Politicians may try to avoid answering difficult questions, but that can reflect badly on them.

At the same time, politicians try to use the media to their advantage. They grant interviews, hoping to receive positive coverage. Another way officials use reporters is by leaking, or secretly passing on, information. They may do this to test the public's response to a proposal without **acknowledging**, or admitting publicly, that they are considering it. If the public likes the idea, officials can openly back it. If the public objects to the idea, officials can drop it—or campaign against it. Politicians also use leaks to shape public opinion on an issue or to gain favor with a reporter.

Watchdog Role

The mass media also play a crucial role in monitoring government officials and policies. In this **"watchdog" role**, media organizations research and report on illegal practices or waste. Reports that **expose**, or reveal, wrongdoing or scandal can attract large audiences.

Throughout our history, the media have played this role and helped to protect the interests of the public. For example, the *Tampa Bay Tribune* published a series of reports on failing elementary schools in a Florida town. They reported that the local school board ignored the growing problems at the schools. The articles drew the attention of both local and national education officials.

acknowledge to publicly admit

watchdog role the role of keeping government honest by reporting on illegal practices or waste

expose to reveal

Public officials meet with reporters to announce plans and respond to events. In this way, they use the media to help them deliver messages to the public.

Analyzing For public officials, what are the pros and cons of an event like the one shown here?

UPI/Alamy Stock Photo

During wartime, reporters are sometimes allowed to travel with troops or other military units to cover the war. Here, journalists sit in the back of a Marine truck during the Iraq War.

Inferring What details in this photo suggest the dangers journalists faced during this assignment?

Media and National Security

Media are limited in their reporting on national security issues. *National security* refers to anything that threatens the safety of the nation or its people. The government can decide that some information is sensitive, or requires careful handling. It may classify the information, which keeps it secret by law. This kind of information cannot be shared with anyone outside a particular government agency, office, or group of officials.

In 2010 the website WikiLeaks provided thousands of classified U.S. documents to news media around the world. The government believed that the leaks had put Americans' lives in danger. Prosecutors found that prosecuting the act of publishing those documents would be difficult because of First Amendment protections. The First Amendment says that Congress cannot pass laws limiting the freedom of the press. However, they did prosecute an Army private who leaked many of the documents. She was convicted and sentenced to 35 years in prison.

The government also tries to shape the news. During the first part of the war in Iraq, some journalists traveled along with American troops going into battle. They reported on battles and on daily life of the troops. As a result, the public had information it would not otherwise have known. However, some critics said that this practice allowed the government to control news reporting.

✓ **CHECK FOR UNDERSTANDING**

1. **Identifying** How do the media influence public policy?

2. **Describing** How do mass media fulfill the watchdog role?

Protecting the Press

GUIDING QUESTION

What are the restrictions on freedom of the press?

The Framers understood that democracy needs a free flow of information and ideas. Citizens need information to understand public issues. They need that information to be free of government control. The Framers wanted the press to be independent. They tried to ensure that independence by adding the First Amendment to the Constitution.

The First Amendment prohibits Congress from making any law that would limit the freedom of the press. When it was written, the amendment applied to the only form of media in existence: print. Now this protection extends to radio, television, and the Internet as well.

Freedom Within Limits

Sometimes the media publish information that presents a government official in a poor light. The story might explain how a governor tried to hide information that was personally embarrassing or harmful. It might reveal that a member of Congress bought stock in a company just before voting on a bill that would affect the company's value, allowing the congressperson to profit. Members of the media have the right to do this under the First Amendment.

Because of the First Amendment, news media are free from prior restraint. **Prior restraint** refers to the act of stopping information from being known by blocking it from being published. Generally, the government cannot censor, or block publication, by the media in this way. Reporters and editors are free to decide what they will say. They cannot be prevented from publishing information because someone fears that it will be embarrassing or harmful.

Freedom of the press is not unlimited, though. As you have read, the government can keep some information secret when its release will endanger national security. National security refers to matters related to the defense of the country from threats or attacks. Also, the press is not free to publish false information that would hurt someone's reputation or unfairly influence how people view that person. Doing so is called libel. Anyone who believes that he or she has been harmed by a false written story can sue the publisher for libel.

Government officials rarely win libel lawsuits, however. The press has been protected from many libel prosecutions since the U.S. Supreme Court decided the case *New York Times Co.* v. *Sullivan* (1964). In that decision, the Court said that public officials must prove actual malice, or evil intent, to win a libel suit. The official must prove that the publisher either knew the material was false or carelessly ignored the truth. This standard protects press organizations that act responsibly from having to defend themselves against lawsuits with no basis.

The media also have some other protections. Gathering news may depend on getting facts from people who do not want to have their names made public. If people who give information to the press cannot be protected from punishment, they may refuse to come forward. Without their information, the press cannot serve its watchdog role of holding government and businesses accountable. The press and the government have fought many battles over reporters' right to keep their sources secret.

Most states have **shield laws**. These laws protect reporters from having to reveal their sources. However, there is no federal shield law.

---

prior restraint   the act of stopping information from being known by blocking it from being published

shield law   law that protects reporters from having to reveal their sources

There are many different media sources to choose from. For example, at this newsstand, a reader can choose from a variety of newspapers and magazines. This allows people to read the news from different locations in the country and world as well as from different viewpoints.

Cable networks such as Fox News are not subject to many FCC regulations.

Regulating the Media

Content regulations on print media are generally prohibited by the First Amendment. However, the federal government does have some power to regulate broadcast media. That is because the government controls the right to use the airwaves. The Federal Communications Commission (FCC) licenses the use of those airwaves to broadcasters. A **license** is a grant by the government of a right to engage in some activity. Congress decided that the purpose of organizing the airwaves is to better serve the public interest. As part of serving the public interest, the FCC requires that licensed broadcasters use a portion of their airtime to cover public issues. The FCC has also declared certain words objectionable and prohibited their use on the air.

Some FCC rules do not apply to cable television networks or satellite television or radio. These media do not have to obtain licenses to air their programming.

In the past, the FCC enforced a policy called the *fairness doctrine*. When a station aired opinion pieces or editorials, it was required to give airtime to those who disagreed so that viewers or listeners had more than one point of view. The FCC no longer enforces the fairness doctrine, however.

In addition, much of today's media would not be subject to the fairness doctrine, which applied only to broadcasters with licenses. It does not apply to cable or Internet sources. The end of the fairness doctrine—and the rise of non-broadcast media—has led to the existence of strongly partisan programming, or programming that favors a particular political party. Today, people can view and listen to news reports that are slanted to reflect their biases. This allows people to avoid hearing or seeing any opposing perspectives.

✓ **CHECK FOR UNDERSTANDING**

Identifying In what ways does the First Amendment protect the mass media?

LESSON ACTIVITIES

1. **Informative/Explanatory Writing** Research the circumstances that led to the *New York Times* v. *Sullivan* libel case. Write an essay to explain the case and its significance.

2. **Evaluating Arguments** With a small group, prepare and present a dialogue about journalists' need to keep their sources secret to protect them from retaliation, or revenge. Is protecting a source's identity covered by the First Amendment? Have the characters in the dialogue discuss why the law protects the press and why the law should or should not protect sources.

---

license a grant by the government of a right to engage in some activity

09
Analyzing Sources: Evaluating Media Influence

? COMPELLING QUESTION

Why should the public evaluate the media and its influence?

Plan Your Inquiry

DEVELOPING QUESTIONS

Think about the types of information and opinions that different forms of news media provide. Think about their credibility and accuracy. How might reporters, columnists, cartoonists, and others influence readers or viewers? Then read the Compelling Question for this lesson. What questions can you ask to help you answer this Compelling Question? Create a graphic organizer like the one below. Write these Supporting Questions in your graphic organizer.

Supporting Questions	Primary or Secondary Source	What the source tells me about the influence of the media on readers and viewers	Questions the source leaves unanswered
	A		
	B		
	C		
	D		
	E		
	F		

ANALYZING SOURCES

Next, examine the sources in this lesson. Analyze each source by answering the questions that follow it. How does each source help you answer each Supporting Question you created? What questions do you still have? Write these in your graphic organizer.

After you analyze the sources, you will:
- use the evidence from the sources,
- communicate your conclusions,
- and take informed action.

Background Information

Mass media includes newspapers, magazines, books, radio and television programs, and many websites on the Internet. Each media source chooses what information to present and how to deliver it. Each source typically has specific goals in mind. It may want to inform or to convince people to think in a certain way. It may want to spur people to action. Some media outlets are staffed by journalists who are trained to collect, write, and deliver the news. Others are staffed by people interested in advancing a point of view.

With so many sources of information available, how can ordinary people decide what to believe? How can they filter out facts from opinions? In this lesson, you will explore sources to learn how to think critically about information you read or hear.

People today have access to a variety of informational media across multiple television channels, streaming services, apps, and websites.

Code of Ethics for Journalists

Founded in 1909, the Society of Professional Journalists aims to help the public obtain the information it needs to make informed decisions. The organization also works to protect the First Amendment right of freedom of the press. This text comes from the society's Code of Ethics. A code of ethics sets standards of proper conduct.

PRIMARY SOURCE: DOCUMENT

> ### 66 Seek Truth and Report It
>
> Ethical journalism should be accurate and fair. Journalists should be honest and courageous in gathering, reporting and interpreting information. . . .
>
> - Take responsibility for the accuracy of their work. **Verify** information before releasing it. Use original sources whenever possible. . . .
> - Provide context [background information]. . . .
> - Never deliberately distort [twist] facts or context, including visual information. . . .
>
> **Minimize Harm**
>
> Ethical journalism treats sources, subjects, colleagues [other journalists] and members of the public as human beings deserving of respect. . . .
>
> - Balance the public's need for information against potential [possible] harm or discomfort. Pursuit of the news is not a license for **arrogance** or undue **intrusiveness**. . . .
> - Balance a suspect's right to a fair trial with the public's right to know. Consider the implications [possible effects] of identifying criminal suspects before they face legal charges. . . .
>
> **Act Independently**
>
> The highest and primary obligation [duty] of ethical journalism is to serve the public. . . .
>
> - Avoid **conflicts of interest,** real or perceived. . . .
> - Be wary [cautious] of sources offering information for favors or money; . . .
> - Distinguish news from advertising and shun [avoid] hybrids [combinations] that blur the lines between the two. . . .
>
> **Be Accountable and Transparent**
>
> Ethical journalism means taking responsibility for one's work and explaining one's decisions to the public. . . .
>
> - Acknowledge mistakes and correct them promptly and prominently [visibly]. . . . 99

— Society of Professional Journalists, Code of Ethics, 2014

---

verify to check the truth of

stereotype to make a general assumption about members of a group, particularly based on oversimplified or biased ideas

arrogance sense of superiority

intrusiveness interfering with people's privacy or personal business

conflict of interest the tension between a person's own benefit and official responsibilities

---

EXAMINE THE SOURCE

1. **Summarizing** Based on the source, what is ethical journalism?
2. **Evaluating** Why is "act independently" an important standard for journalists?

B

News and Media Bias

Journalists, like all people, have opinions based on their ideas, experiences, and values. They may present the news in ways that reflect their biases—their personal points of view. This article discusses another form of media bias based on what news the media present.

PRIMARY SOURCE: WEB ARTICLE

❝ There are hundreds of thousands of media outlets in the U.S. . . . These news outlets don't all take the same perspective [point of view] on any given issue. . . .

The notion [idea] of objective [unbiased] journalism—that media must report both sides of every issue in every story—barely existed until the late 1800s. It reached **full flower** only in the few **decades** [the 1950s to the 1980s] when broadcast television, limited to three major networks [ABC, CBS, and NBC], was the primary source of political information. . . .

If it bleeds, it leads

There is one form of actual media bias. Almost all media outlets need audiences in order to exist. Some can't survive financially without an audience; others want the prestige [status] that comes from attracting a big audience.

Thus, the media define as 'news' the kinds of stories that will attract an audience: those that feature drama, conflict, engaging [attention-getting] pictures and **immediacy**. That's what most people find interesting. They don't want to read a story headlined 'Dog bites man.' They want 'Man bites dog.'

The problem is that a focus on such stories crowds out what we need to know to protect our democracy, such as: How do the workings of American institutions benefit some groups and disadvantage [work against] others? In what ways do our major systems—education, health care, national defense and others—function [work] effectively or less effectively?

These analyses are vital [important] to us as citizens—if we fail to protect our democracy, our lives will be changed forever—but they aren't always fun to read. So they get covered much less than celebrity **scandals** or murder cases—which, while compelling [interesting], don't really affect our ability to sustain [keep] a democratic system. . . . ❞

—Marjorie Hershey, "Political bias in media doesn't threaten democracy—other, less visible biases do," *The Conversation*, Oct. 15, 2020

full flower having reached its peak
decade a ten-year period

immediacy a sense that something is current
scandal behavior that causes public outrage

EXAMINE THE SOURCE

1. **Analyzing Points of View** According to this source, what bias do most members of the media share?
2. **Identifying Themes** What effect does the author feel this bias has on journalism and on the public?

C

Yellow Journalism

In the late 1800s, competition for sales encouraged some newspapers to produce shocking headlines and stories to attract readers. This form of reporting is called *yellow journalism*. William Randolph Hearst used this approach in his *New York Journal*. Hearst's style of news coverage became important in 1898, when the USS *Maine*, an American warship, mysteriously exploded in the harbor of Havana, Cuba. Two days after the explosion, Hearst's newspaper had the front page shown here. The text excerpt discusses the rise of yellow journalism and what followed the explosion of the *Maine*.

PRIMARY SOURCE: NEWSPAPER

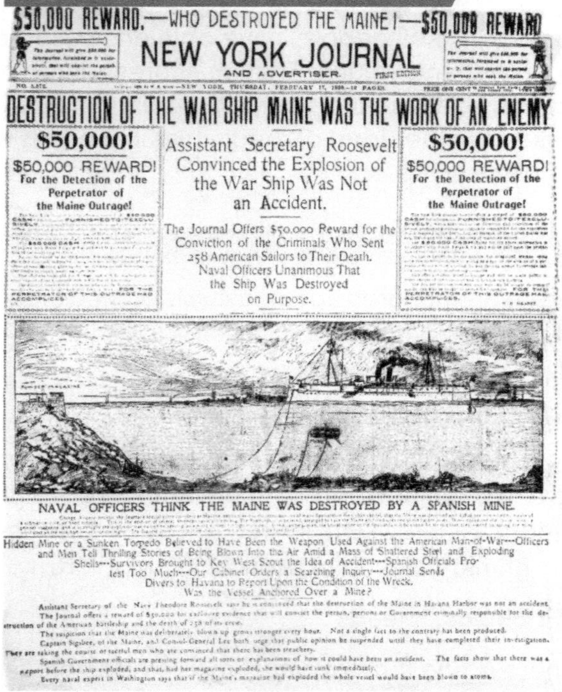

$50,000 REWARD.—WHO DESTROYED THE MAINE?—$50,000 REWARD

NEW YORK JOURNAL
AND ADVERTISER

DESTRUCTION OF THE WAR SHIP MAINE WAS THE WORK OF AN ENEMY

$50,000!
$50,000 REWARD!
For the Detection of the Perpetrator of the Maine Outrage!

Assistant Secretary Roosevelt Convinced the Explosion of the War Ship Was Not an Accident.

The Journal Offers $50,000 Reward for the Conviction of the Criminals Who Sent 258 American Sailors to Their Death. Naval Officers Unanimous That the Ship Was Destroyed on Purpose.

$50,000!
$50,000 REWARD!
For the Detection of the Perpetrator of the Maine Outrage!

NAVAL OFFICERS THINK THE MAINE WAS DESTROYED BY A SPANISH MINE.

Hidden Mine or a Sunken Torpedo Believed to Have Been the Weapon Used Against the American Man-of-War—Officers and Men Tell Thrilling Stories of Being Blown Into the Air Amid a Mass of Shattered Steel and Exploding Shells—Survivors Brought to Key West Scout the Idea of Accident—Spanish Officials Protest Too Much—Our Cabinet Orders a Searching Inquiry—Journal Sends Divers to Havana to Report Upon the Condition of the Wreck. Was the Vessel Anchored Over a Mine?

SECONDARY SOURCE: WEB ARTICLE

"The Spanish-American War is often referred to as the first 'media war.' During the 1890s, journalism that **sensationalized**—and sometimes even manufactured—dramatic events was a powerful force that helped propel [push] the United States into war with Spain. Led by newspaper owners William Randolph Hearst and Joseph Pulitzer, journalism of the 1890s used . . . a style that became known as yellow journalism. . . .

Yellow journals like the *New York Journal* and the *New York World* relied on sensationalist headlines to sell newspapers. William Randolph Hearst understood that a war with Cuba would not only sell his papers, but also move him into a position of national prominence. . . . [I]t was the sinking of the battleship *Maine* in Havana Harbor that gave Hearst his big story—war. After the sinking of the *Maine*, the Hearst newspapers, with no evidence, **unequivocally** blamed the Spanish, and soon U.S. public opinion demanded **intervention**.

Today, historians point to the Spanish-American War as the first press-driven war. Although it may be an exaggeration to claim that Hearst and the other yellow journalists started the war, it is fair to say that the press fueled the public's passion for war."

—"Yellow Journalism," PBS.org

sensationalize to portray or describe something in a way that makes it seem more shocking than it is

unequivocally done in a way that leaves no doubt

intervention the act of interfering in the affairs of another country, especially with armed force

EXAMINE THE SOURCE

1. **Identifying Bias** How do the headlines and stories on the front page of the newspaper answer the question posed in the line above the title of the paper?
2. **Explaining** According to the PBS article, how did the media influence public opinion in the lead-up to the Spanish-American War?

Balanced Journalism

Some news outlets reported the sinking of the *Maine* in a different way. *Harper's Weekly* was a weekly publication that had built its reputation during the American Civil War in the 1860s. It presented more balanced views of events and issues, including the explosion of the USS *Maine*. This excerpt is from a *Harper's* report on the *Maine*.

PRIMARY SOURCE: MAGAZINE ARTICLE

> ❝ [T]he fate of the *Maine* will continue an unsolved mystery for historians to wrangle [argue] over. Meanwhile all that we shall positively know is that the explosion occurred **forward**, and hence that the seamen rather than the officers were the sufferers; that not more than 26 of the men remained uninjured; 57 being wounded and 246 killed, and that two of the 24 officers are certainly lost. If the disaster were the result of design [a plan] and not of accident, it is considered probable that the blow would have been dealt the ship on the very spot where the explosion occurred—not because it would be more desirable to destroy the men than the officers, but because the **magazine** is always a preferable point of attack. ❞

— F.E. Leupp, "The Disaster to the Battle-Ship *Maine*," *Harper's Weekly*, February 26, 1898

forward toward the front of a ship

magazine storage area for gunpowder and explosives

EXAMINE THE SOURCE

1. **Contrasting** How do the tone and content of this excerpt differ from that of Hearst's headlines?

2. **Analyzing Perspectives** What purpose does the final sentence in the excerpt serve?

"Your News . . . [and] Mine"

The *New York Journal* shaped how its readers thought about events such as the explosion of the USS *Maine*. Similarly, some media outlets today present information in a biased way. That raises questions. What types of bias influence media outlets' reports? Are some sources less biased than others? How can people evaluate bias in reporting? Does consuming news from only one outlet provide a complete picture of events and issues? Does consuming news from more than one source help people make informed decisions? This cartoon from 2019 takes a look at some of these issues.

PRIMARY SOURCE: CARTOON

"Then we agree. 10 minutes of your news, then 10 minutes of mine."

EXAMINE THE SOURCE

1. **Interpreting** Why does the character in the cartoon talk about "your news" and "mine"?

2. **Drawing Conclusions** What does the cartoon suggest about consuming news from just one media outlet?

Understanding Bias

The News Literacy Project is a nonprofit group that focuses on educating people about how to use news media sources responsibly. One approach of the project is teaching people how to think about their own biases as well as those in the media.

PRIMARY SOURCE: WEBSITE

66 Our own perspectives, values and beliefs may lead us to assume that bias exists, especially if we have a strong opinion about the topic being reported on. This can result in confirmation bias (the tendency to quickly embrace [accept] information that affirms [proves] what we already think and feel) and to unfairly dismiss or criticize information that complicates [creates difficulties] or contradicts [goes against] those beliefs and perspectives. Because biases are baked into how we see and understand the world, we often fail to consider them when seeking or evaluating information. We may also perceive [see] bias only in reporting that disagrees with our beliefs or opinions. 99

—News Literacy Project

EXAMINE THE SOURCE

1. **Synthesizing** How does this excerpt relate to the ideas in Source E?
2. **Making Connections** What are some ways that people can challenge their biases when consuming news media?

Complete Your Inquiry

EVALUATE SOURCES AND USE EVIDENCE

Refer back to the Compelling Question and the Supporting Questions you developed at the beginning of the lesson.

1. **Analyzing** What are two questions that the sources raise for you about using the news media?
2. **Making Connections** What can you do to limit being influenced by biased media?
3. **Gathering Sources** Which sources helped you answer the Supporting Questions and the Compelling Question? Which sources, if any, challenged what you thought you knew when you first created your Supporting Questions? What information do you still need in order to answer your questions? What other viewpoints would you like to investigate? Where would you find that information?
4. **Evaluating Sources** Identify the sources that helped answer your Supporting Questions. How reliable is the source? How would you verify the reliability of the source?

COMMUNICATE CONCLUSIONS

5. **Collaborating** With one or two partners, take turns sharing your Supporting Questions and responses. Then, make a T-chart in which you identify positive and negative impacts that the news media can have on personal opinion. Share your completed chart with the class. Discuss how you and your fellow students can be responsible consumers of media.

TAKE INFORMED ACTION

Creating a Media Bias Handbook Work in a small group to develop a brief handbook of ways to detect bias in media news reports. Think about how media reports can use language, visual cues, and symbols to present a slanted or biased view of events, issues, or public officials. Use appropriate voice and tone when discussing. Provide examples of both biased and unbiased reports on the same story.

The News Literacy Project. "National News Literacy Week, Day 3: Understanding Bias." The News Literacy Project. January 29, 2020. https://newslit.org/news-literacy-week-2020/understanding-bias/.

ASSOCIATED PRESS

Types of Interest Groups	Ways Interest Groups Work
●	●
●	●
●	●
●	●

Interest Groups

GUIDING QUESTION

What are interest groups and what is their purpose?

Your congressperson in the U.S. House of Representatives may represent well over half a million people—that is the average for House members. You are only one person. How can you make your voice heard when that member of Congress is hearing from many others?

One way to **enhance**, or increase, your voice is to join with others who agree with you on an issue. When you join with others, you pool your resources and increase your influence. One way that people combine their voice with others is to form or join a type of organization known as an interest group

An interest group is a group of people who share a point of view and unite to **promote**, or work in favor of, their beliefs. Interest groups can be a powerful force to bring about change. The First Amendment guarantees Americans the right to assemble and to belong to interest groups. The right to petition the government—also protected by the First Amendment—makes it possible for those groups to meet with officials to promote their goals.

There are many different types of interest groups. Some groups are based on shared economic goals. For instance, the National Association of Manufacturers represents companies that produce goods.

enhance to improve or increase

promote to work in favor of

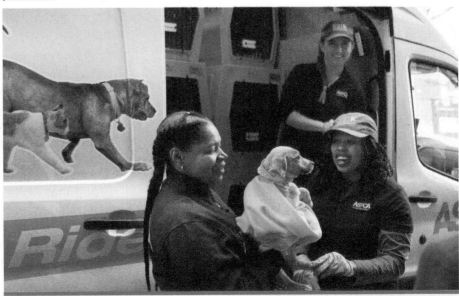

The ASPCA (American Society for the Prevention of Cruelty to Animals) is an interest group that rescues animals and encourages people to adopt them.

Total Campaign Contributions to Political Parties and Candidates by Interest Groups, 2020 Election

The chart shows the groups that gave the most money to all candidates and parties in the 2020 election.

Type of Group	Total Contributions (in millions)	Percentage Given to Democrats	Percentage Given to Republicans
Ideological or single-interest groups	$1,104	73%	27%
Finance, insurance, and real estate industry	$988	52%	48%
Business groups in an industry not otherwise listed	$567	53%	47%
Health industry	$451	63%	37%
Communications and electronics industry	$429	80%	19%
Lawyers and lobbyists	$354	77%	22%
Construction industry	$182	32%	67%
Energy and natural resources industries	$146	30%	70%
Agricultural industry	$142	32%	67%
Labor groups	$81	88%	12%
Transportation industry	$140	35%	65%
Defense industry	$44	44%	52%

Source: Data from Open Secrets, https://www.opensecrets.org/industries/index.php?ind=A&cycle=2020

ECONOMICS CONNECTION

1. **Identifying** Which of these groups promote business interests?
2. **Contrasting** How do the groups differ in which party and candidates they support?

Some organizations act for specific industries or specific types of businesses. The American Petroleum Institute, for example, represents the interests of companies in the oil and gas industry. The American Hospital Association represents the interests of hospitals and health care networks. Such groups try to influence legislation and regulation on issues that affect their industries.

Other interest groups are formed by workers. The American Federation of Labor and Congress of Industrial Organizations (AFL-CIO) is the largest of them. It is formed by many labor unions that have joined together. Unions try to improve wages, working conditions, and benefits for their members.

People who share similar characteristics may also join together to promote their interests. The National Association for the Advancement of Colored People (NAACP) works to improve the lives of African Americans. AARP represents the interests of older Americans. The National Organization for Women (NOW) works for equal rights for women.

Other interest groups focus on particular issues. The National Rifle Association (NRA) serves the interests of gun owners. The Brady Campaign to Prevent Gun Violence works to reduce the amount of gun violence in the country. **Public-interest groups** are organizations that support causes that affect the lives of Americans in general. Common Cause is a nonpartisan group that works to reform elections and campaign financing laws. A **nonpartisan** group has no ties to any political party and does not favor one party over another. Other public interest groups have varying goals. Some work to

public-interest group an organization that supports causes that affect the lives of Americans in general

nonpartisan a person or group that has no ties to a political party and does not favor one party over another

protect consumers, promote public health, protect the rights of children, or work for good government. Several public-interest groups work to protect natural resources. Examples are the Sierra Club and the National Wildlife Federation.

✓ CHECK FOR UNDERSTANDING

Identifying What are three types of interest groups?

Interest Groups at Work

GUIDING QUESTION

How do interest groups influence public policy?

Most interest groups try to influence the decisions of government officials and agencies. They work in four ways: being active in elections, participating in lawsuits, lobbying government officials, and trying to shape public opinion. Groups can use one or more of these approaches—and many do so.

Being Active in Elections

Many interest groups become involved in elections. They support candidates they see as favoring their interests and oppose those who they think do not support those interests. They can also work for or against a ballot measure that voters are considering in an upcoming election. For example, the Sierra Club backs candidates who favor laws to protect nature.

Lawyers for the NAACP—including future U.S. Supreme Court justice Thurgood Marshall in the center—celebrate their victory after the Court declared, in *Brown* v. *Board of Education*, that segregated schools were unconstitutional.

Bettmann/Getty Images

Interest groups spend money in elections through their political action committees (PACs). PACs collect money from group members. Then they donate money to candidates who support their positions on the issues they care about. PACs also buy ads on the Internet, television or radio, and billboards. They also send out mailings. These messages either support their candidate or criticize an opponent that they want to see defeated.

Working Through the Courts

Many interest groups **pursue** their policy goals by filing or supporting lawsuits. For instance, a group that supports workers might help a worker sue a company for forcing its employees to work in dangerous conditions without safety equipment. Such groups hope that a successful outcome in one case will influence other employers to fix similar unsafe conditions. The NAACP has used lawsuits to help end laws that treated African Americans unfairly and inhumanely.

Lawsuits can also bring attention to an issue and encourage Congress to act. For example, Lilly Ledbetter sued Goodyear Tire and Rubber for paying her unfairly because she was a woman. The U.S. Supreme Court ruled against her in 2007. It said she did not file her case soon enough. In response, Congress passed the Lilly Ledbetter Fair Pay Act in 2009. Different interest groups, like the American Bar Association (ABA), supported the law which extends the period for filing a pay discrimination lawsuit.

Directly Influencing Officials

Interest groups try to influence government officials to make government policy reflect their group's interest. The simplest way is by making donations to campaigns. Running for reelection is costly. Campaign finance laws require most interest groups to create PACs to give money to campaigns. Lawmakers who win reelection are likely to pay attention to the groups that helped them win.

The other key tool interest groups use to shape policy is lobbying. Lobbyists are representatives of an interest group who contact lawmakers or other government officials directly to influence their policy-making. Lobbyists are active at all levels of government—local, state, and national.

pursue to try to achieve

Successful lobbyists build relationships with government officials who have power and influence regarding their area of interest. Sometimes the most effective way to reach lawmakers is through their staff. As a result, lobbyists create good relationships with the people who work for elected officials as well as the lawmakers themselves.

Successful lobbyists understand how the government works. They also are skilled at making friends and speaking persuasively.

The most effective lobbyists supply lawmakers with information that lawmakers find useful—and that helps the lobbyists' cause. They suggest solutions to problems. They may provide witnesses who can testify to Congress in favor of their position. Sometimes they write drafts of bills for lawmakers to consider. The American Legislative Exchange Council (ALEC) is a lobbying group funded by large corporations. ALEC works with legislators to draft bills that benefit business. The group then passes these bills to state legislators across the country. Then, in turn, the legislators introduce those bills in their states. Over several years in the 2010s, at least 10,000 ALEC-produced bills were considered by legislatures.

While lobbyists supply information, that information can be biased in favor of the lobbyist's interest group. They must be careful in this area. A lobbyist who misrepresents the facts runs the risk of losing a legislator's trust and of losing access to that lawmaker. Of course, there are many lobbyists working for different special interest groups. If they want it, legislators may get information reflecting more than one perspective on proposed legislation.

The work of lobbyists does not end once a law is passed. Lobbyists also try to influence how laws are carried out by the executive branch. They do so by lobbying with agencies in that branch. To carry out the laws passed by Congress, executive agencies have to write rules. They turn general statements in the written law into specific rules that individuals and companies must follow. Lobbyists try to influence the wording of rules that affect the group or industry for which they work.

Shaping Public Opinion

All interest groups want to influence public opinion. They want to convince people that their cause is important and something that they should support. To get their message out, they may send information to people by email or through mail delivered to homes or businesses. They use paid advertisements on social media and in print media. They also hire social media specialists who actively post messages in favor of the group's interests and activities. Some public interest groups send volunteers to public locations. They meet with people to raise awareness for their cause, gather signatures for petitions, and have them sign letters to lawmakers. Interest groups also hold rallies and other public events to gain media coverage for their cause.

Effectiveness of Interest Groups

Several factors limit the effectiveness of interest groups. Different interest groups compete for influence. This prevents any single group from being able to control lawmakers and other public officials. Generally, a group with a large number of members will have members with a wider range of interests and beliefs. This diversity can make it difficult for a large national group to have

THE INTRICATE MECHANICS OF GOVERNMENT

PUBLIC ENTRANCE

LOBBYIST ENTRANCE

This political cartoon examines the influence of lobbyists.

Analyzing Points of View What is the cartoon's attitude toward lobbyists? How can you tell?

How Interest Groups and Individuals May Influence Congress

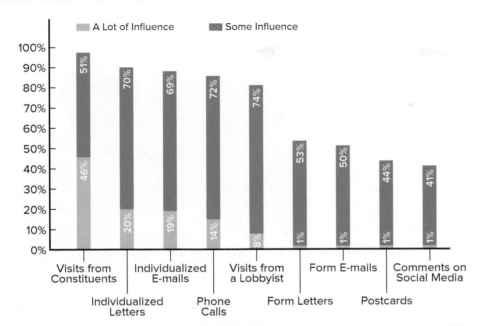

- A Lot of Influence
- Some Influence

Visits from Constituents: 46% / 51%
Individualized E-mails: 20% / 70%
Individualized Letters: 19% / 69%
Phone Calls: 14% / 72%
Visits from a Lobbyist: 8% / 74%
Form Letters: 1% / 53%
Form E-mails: 1% / 50%
Postcards: 1% / 44%
Comments on Social Media: 1% / 41%

Source: *Communicating with Congress: Perceptions of Citizen Advocacy on Capitol Hill,* The Partnership For A More Perfect Union at the Congressional Management

EXAMINE THE GRAPH

A survey of congressional staffers included these evaluations of how effective different methods of influence are on members of Congress.

Contrasting How much more or less effective are visits from constituents—the people whom a member of Congress represents—than visits from lobbyists?

broad policy goals. As a result, smaller interest groups or single-issue interest groups—those that unite people who have narrower aims—have been most effective in shaping policy. Large interest groups have many members, which gives them a large financial base. Still, most interest groups struggle to pay small staffs. In recent years, the greatest concern about the power of interest groups has been their financial contributions to political campaigns.

✓ **CHECK FOR UNDERSTANDING**

1. **Identifying** What tools do interest groups use to influence government officials?
2. **Understanding Supporting Details** How can an interest group use the courts to further its interests?

Regulating Interest Groups

GUIDING QUESTION

How does the government regulate interest groups?

Participation in interest groups is protected by the First Amendment. The First Amendment says that Congress shall make no laws that abridge the right to peaceably assemble or the right to petition the government. The courts have ruled that, under the Fourteenth Amendment, state governments must also respect those First Amendment rights.

Still, both the federal and state governments have laws that put some limits on what groups can do. Congress limits how much money PACs may contribute to candidates. Other laws govern lobbyists and their activities. For example, lobbyists must register with officials who then oversee the lobbyists' actions. Lobbyists must also say who hired them, how much they are paid, and how they spend money related to their work. These rules are meant to allow the public to know who is trying to influence lawmakers.

Federal and state laws also require former government officials to wait for a period of time before they can become lobbyists. The delay is meant to stop these former officials from using their relationships with current officials to benefit a group. Waiting periods can also prevent former officials from unfairly using inside information. However, this kind of law has not been successful. Many lawmakers simply wait until the waiting period is over and then become lobbyists. Because of their inside knowledge of the workings of government, they can be very helpful to an interest group.

Some people believe interest groups have too much say in government. They claim that special-interest groups gain power over elected officials by giving money to their campaigns. Many critics point to the example of Jack Abramoff. He was one of Washington's most powerful lobbyists. In 2006, Abramoff admitted that he corrupted government officials and stole millions of dollars from his lobbying clients. Some critics say that it is wrong for interest groups to have more influence than ordinary voters.

Some critics argue that all interest groups do not have equal access to government officials. Business groups have more money than groups that work for ordinary people, according to critics. Interest groups working for big business can donate more money to campaigns, making it easier to get meetings with government officials.

Other people defend interest groups. They say these groups help make known the wishes of large groups of people. In that way, they help make sure that the government responds to people's concerns. In this view, interest groups play a vital role in democracy by channeling the views of thousands—or even millions—of ordinary people in ways that those people could never achieve on their own.

Supporters of interest groups also say that these groups are an important part of a democracy. They provide a way for Americans to take an active role in government in a way they could not achieve if they were acting alone. By joining forces, ordinary people can convince the government to act on issues they care about.

People's opinions on interest groups may depend on what interest group is being discussed. Most small business owners might think that lobbying by the U.S. Chamber of Commerce is an important contribution to policy-making. At the same time, many small business owners would view a campaign by an interest group to raise the minimum wage as a problem.

✓ CHECK FOR UNDERSTANDING

Explaining Why did Congress decide that former government officials must wait before becoming lobbyists?

Many Americans think lobbyists have too much influence on government.

Inferring What problem does this person seem to be connecting to lobbyists?

LESSON ACTIVITIES

1. **Informative/Explanatory Writing** How can the government regulate lobbying? Do these regulations violate the First Amendment protections of freedom of speech and association? Write a brief, informative report that describes and explains lobbying regulations and the laws affecting them.

2. **Analyzing Information** With a partner, identify your member of Congress and research the PACs that contributed to your congressperson's most recent election campaign. Examine the representative's voting record on various issues. Prepare and deliver a brief presentation to your class. Summarize whether you think the representative's voting record reflects the campaign donations the representative received. Listen to other presentations to compare findings.

11

Reviewing Civic Participation

Summary

The People
- Exercise power by registering and voting
- Express their views to the government

Political Parties
- Work to win elections
- Link policy at different levels
- Monitor party in power when in minority
- Take part in a two-party system which is influenced by third parties

Mass Media
- Communicate news and opinion
- Operate for profit and need to attract audience
- Help shape public opinion and the public agenda
- Act as a watchdog due to protection by the First Amendment

Interest Groups
- Seek to promote the interests of groups of people with common goals
- Influence policy through campaign contributions, using the courts, directly influencing officials, shaping public opinion

The Government
- Created by and responsible to the people
- Holds elections to fill offices
- Influenced by parties, mass media, interest groups

adamkaz/Getty Images

Checking For Understanding

Answer the questions to see if you understood the topic content.

1. Identify each of the following terms and explain its significance to civic participation.

    A. third party
    B. direct primary
    C. plurality
    D. suffrage
    E. register
    F. polling place
    G. propaganda
    H. bias
    I. political action committee
    J. prior restraint

2. **Summarizing** How did the Democratic and Republican parties each form?

3. **Identifying** What are three of the functions of political parties?

4. **Identifying** Name four constitutional amendments that broadened voting rights and increased participation in the political process.

5. **Summarizing** What are the three steps a responsible citizen takes to participate in democracy by voting?

6. **Inferring** How does an initiative get placed on a state's ballot?

7. **Explaining** How do states determine who gets their electoral votes?

8. **Analyzing** How do interest groups influence public opinion?

9. **Evaluating** How does the mass media carry out their role as watchdogs of the government?

10. **Identifying** What are the four ways that interest groups monitor and influence government?

11. **Contrasting** How do the policy positions of the Republican and Democratic parties of today differ?

12. **Comparing and Contrasting** How are closed and open primaries alike and different?

13. **Summarizing** Why did Congress determine that the Voting Rights Act was necessary?

14. **Identifying Cause and Effect** Why is it important that citizens vote?

15. **Predicting** Suppose a mayor is running for reelection. An interest group airs a television ad featuring abandoned homes, streets filled with litter, and newspaper headlines about failing schools. How do you think undecided voters might respond to that ad?

16. **Explaining** How do political candidates receive the large sums of money they need to run a campaign?

17. **Synthesizing** Why are measures of public opinion needed for democracy?

18. **Explaining** How do the mass media influence public opinion?

19. **Summarizing** What restrictions are placed on freedom of the press?

20. **Comparing and Contrasting** In what way are lobbyists and PACs similar? How are they different?

NEED EXTRA HELP?

If You've Missed Question	1	2	3	4	5	6	7	8	9	10
Review Lesson	2, 3, 4, 6, 7, 8	2	3	4	4	6	6	7	8	10

If You've Missed Question	11	12	13	14	15	16	17	18	19	20
Review Lesson	2	3	4	4	6	6	7	7, 8	8	10

Apply What You Have Learned

Roosevelt, Franklin D. "Annual Message to Congress, January 3, 1938." The Public Papers and Addresses of Franklin D. Roosevelt. 1938 Volume, The Continuing Struggle for Liberalism: With a Special Introduction and Explanatory Notes by President Roosevelt [Book 1]. New York: Macmillan, 1941.

 ## Understanding Multiple Perspectives

Special interest groups represent specific points of view. Each group tries to advance its point of view—which can conflict with those of other groups.

ACTIVITY Comparing and Evaluating Special Interest Groups
Choose an issue that interests you. Identify at least three special interest groups active in that issue. Make sure you choose groups with different views on the issue. Prepare a graphic presentation that compares the three groups in these ways:

- Their position on the issue
- Their membership size (if available)
- Whether they have a political action committee (PAC) and, if so, how much it contributed in the most recent election and which candidates received contributions
- What they do to advance their point of view

In addition, write a brief evaluation of the three groups. Which group do you think is most effective in its efforts, and why do you think so? Cite evidence from your research to explain your reasoning.

 ## Building Citizenship

Voter turnout in the United States is quite low compared to other democracies. One reason is that individuals must take steps to register to vote and reregister if they move. Another is the declining influence of political parties, which makes their registration and get-out-the-vote campaigns less effective than in the past. Voter identification requirements might discourage some people from voting. Having elections on weekdays can make voting difficult for people who work.

ACTIVITY Creating a Presentation on Voter Turnout Over the years, many ideas to increase voter turnout have been proposed. Investigate several of those ideas. Then, make a slideshow or an oral presentation about some proposals for improving turnout. Identify the proposals you think would be most effective and those that you think would not have much effect. Be sure to explain your decisions.

 ## Writing an Argumentative Essay

President Franklin Roosevelt argued that the American people are the final authority on what the government can and cannot do:

66 The ultimate [final] rulers of our democracy are not a president and senators and congressmen and government officials, but the voters of this country. 99
— President Franklin Delano Roosevelt, speech at Marietta, Ohio, July 8, 1938

Some critics say that special interests control American government through lobbying and campaign contributions. Some say that one person's vote has little value when millions of ballots are cast.

ACTIVITY Writing About the Importance of Voting Write an essay of two or three paragraphs discussing your thoughts on the importance of voting. Think about the role played in American government by political parties, the media, and interest groups. Address Roosevelt's claim in light of those influences. How effectively does voting demonstrate people's power? When you are able to vote, what do you think your vote will mean for you and for the country?

D Making Connections to Today

The role of a free press and its importance was written into the U.S. Constitution in the 1700s. Thomas Jefferson, author of the Declaration of Independence and the third president of the United States, stressed the importance of the free press in a letter to a friend:

> ❝ The basis of our governments being the opinion of the people, the very first object should be to keep that right; and were it left to me to decide whether we should have a government without newspapers or newspapers without a government, I should not hesitate a moment to prefer the latter. But I should mean that every man should receive those papers. ❞
>
> — Thomas Jefferson to Edward Carrington (1787)

ACTIVITY **Writing About the Role of the Media** Think about Jefferson's words. Do you agree that the media in all its forms—print, television, radio, Internet, and social media—is vital to American democracy? Should the same freedoms that protect traditional news organizations extend to social media and the Internet? Why or why not? Write a response to Jefferson that states your position on the role of the media as it relates to democracy in the United States today. Explain to him how the media has changed and whether you think those changes have affected the way the media should be viewed.

E Building Citizenship

Elections are exciting civic events—and complex operations. People need to register to vote, learn about the candidates and their backgrounds and positions, find out when and how to vote, and then cast their ballots.

ACTIVITY **Simulating an Election** Take part in simulating an election. As a class, identify a recent local, state, or national election that you will simulate.

Among your classmates, pick some students to take the roles of the candidates in that election. They will have to learn about their candidate's background and positions on the issues. Choose a few members of the class as the board of elections. They will write the rules for registering and voting, which can be based on the rules for your state. They can create cards that the voters will use as identification cards. They should also prepare ballots.

The rest of the class should take part in a town hall event in which each student must ask each candidate one question. After the town hall, the voters should meet in small groups to discuss what they heard and who they support. In the period named as Election Day, voters—including the candidates—should show up at the polling place, present the identification cards created in order to receive a ballot, and cast their votes. The election board should count the votes, verify them to be accurate, and present the result. After the simulation, discuss as a class what you learned.

PHOTO: REUTERS/Alamy Stock Photo; TEXT: "From Thomas Jefferson to Edward Carrington, 16 January 1787," Founders Online, National Archives, https://founders.archives.gov/documents/Jefferson/01-11-02-0047; [Original source: The Papers of Thomas Jefferson, vol. 11, 1 January–6 August 1787, ed. Julian P. Boyd. Princeton: Princeton University Press, 1955, pp. 48–50.]

As the center of state government, capitol buildings are often grand and impressive. This photo shows the Capitol Complex in Tallahassee, Florida, with the Historic Capitol in front of the New Capitol.

State and Local Government

Sean Pavone/Alamy Stock Photo

Introducing State and Local Government

Governing Close to Home

Officials in state and local government make many decisions that affect citizens' everyday lives. They plan for services and safety. Parks, green spaces, schools, and roads are just some of the benefits residents enjoy as a result of the work of local government officials.

Bike Friendly Cities

Leaders in some cities are investing in bike trails to make their cities bike friendly. Bike riding benefits the health and well-being of community members and using bikes for transportation also helps the environment. Chattanooga, Tennessee, has more than 40 bikeshare stations throughout the city. This is one station along the Tennessee River. The public can rent a bike for commuting to work, running errands, or sightseeing. The city hopes their efforts will decrease traffic as well as air pollution.

» A city hall is the place where officials in a local government meet. City hall buildings can vary from being traditional to modern. This one in San Jose, California, has a transparent dome —a modern version of the traditional government building design. The rotunda, a circular building, serves as a public meeting space.

Parks as Public Services

Public parks are one of the many services that governments provide for communities. Park rangers lead tours about the park's wildlife, resources, and history. Here a ranger at Beulah State Park in Colorado teaches an outdoor class about biology.

» New Mexico Governor Michelle Lujan Grisham signs an education bill to increase spending on public schools. Governors are popularly elected and serve as the chief executive officers of the 50 states and five commonwealths and territories. Among their duties, governors implement state laws and oversee the state's executive branch.

Interesting Facts About State Constitutions

Every state is governed by its own constitution, and they are all different.

- The average length of a state constitution is about 39,000 words. This is much longer than the United States Constitution which is 7,591 words including amendments.

- The Alabama Constitution (pictured) is the longest with more than 380,000 words and more than 975 amendments.

- Massachusetts has the oldest state constitution. It took effect in 1780.

- Rhode Island's constitution is the newest. It was approved in 1986 and replaced the state's 1843 constitution.

Getting Ready to Learn About . . .
State and Local Government

Federalism at Work

When you wake up in the morning, you probably do not give much thought to how your government will affect your life today. Yet the government plays a major role in your day-to-day activities. It affects everything from the quality of the water that comes out of the faucet when you brush your teeth to the roads, sidewalks, and bike lanes you use on your way to school. It is not just one level of government that influences your life, either. It is several different levels of government, often working together to achieve similar goals.

The Framers established a system of federalism when they wrote the Constitution. *Federalism* means a system in which the national government holds certain powers, the state governments hold other powers, and some powers are shared between the two. In the United States, we also call the national government the "federal government."

For example, only the federal government can declare war. On the other hand, the power to conduct elections lies with the states. Both levels of government possess some powers, such as the power to collect taxes. State governments have sovereignty, or freedom from control by others. They can pass laws that affect the people

in their state, but they are not allowed to pass any laws that contradict, or go against, federal laws.

This division of powers between the federal government and state governments means that each often affects the other. One good example of this is American public schools. State governments have the power to establish education systems. Yet the federal government also plays a role. School districts across the 50 states receive money from the federal government. They use that money to serve their students. Federal money supports English language instruction, education for students with disabilities, teacher training, and programs for students from low-income families. In order to receive the money, schools have to follow certain national laws. For example, they must avoid discriminating against students because of gender or disabilities.

State Government

Every state constitution describes how the government for that state should be organized. These constitutions outline the areas where the state legislature can act and also limit what the government can do.

Just like the federal government, state governments are divided into three branches. The legislative branch makes the laws. Most states mirror the structure of the U.S. Congress and have a legislature with two houses. Both of these houses must pass a bill for it to become law. States also have an executive branch. The governor heads this branch and plays several roles that are similar to those of the president. States also have a judicial branch that contains the state's court system. Judges in state courts oversee trials or hear appeals from lower court decisions.

You may not always consider it, but state and local governing bodies affect your life in many ways. For example, education officials in your state's executive branch make decisions about what you learn in school. Your state's legislators pass laws concerning how many hours you can work when you are a teenager. The judges working in your state's courts make sure those laws—and many others—are applied correctly.

Sidewalks are an example of how local, state, and federal governments work together. Local governments build sidewalks, often with funding from the state and federal governments.

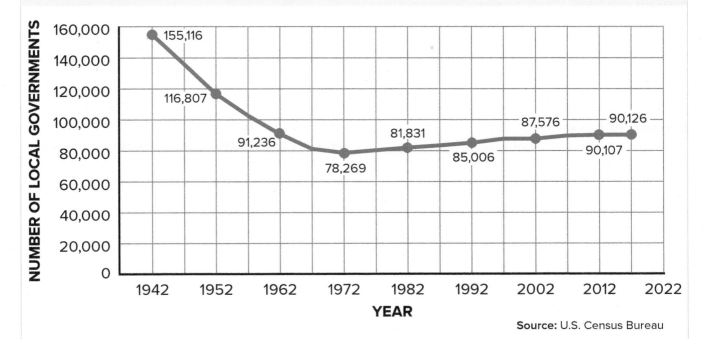

Total Local Governments in the United States, 1942–2017

The number of local governments in the United States declined from the 1940s to the 1960s as different governments began to combine services.

NUMBER OF LOCAL GOVERNMENTS

- 155,116
- 116,807
- 91,236
- 78,269
- 81,831
- 85,006
- 87,576
- 90,126
- 90,107

YEAR

Source: U.S. Census Bureau

HISTORY CONNECTION

Analyzing Describe the growth rate of local governments since 1972.

Local Government

The U.S. Constitution gives states the right to establish their own governments. Similarly, state constitutions establish forms of smaller, local governments. This category includes city, county, and town governments. These local governments serve the people of different communities within the state. They are the level of government closest to residents. They provide services tailored to the needs of the people in that community.

It is sometimes easier to notice the role of local government in your life than the actions of higher levels of government. When you take out the trash, the trucks that come to pick it up may be hired by the local government. This same government is supposed to ensure that the community parks you visit are clean and that there are enough police officers and firefighters to respond to emergency calls. Your local

government may have workers who regularly visit restaurants and other local businesses to make sure they are following health and safety laws.

Local governments can take a number of forms. The amount of power given to executives and legislators at the local level can vary. Some officials are elected, and others are appointed. All local governments are supposed to carry out laws that are meant to benefit their community—in the present *and* in the future. Local governments spend a large part of their time focusing on providing education, fighting crime, and maintaining local infrastructure, such as streets and parks. Doing this work requires planning. It also requires citizens to get involved. The people in the community need to speak their minds and let government decision makers know what they want. That is the surest way for people to have the kind of community they want to keep living in.

Looking Ahead

You will learn about state and local government. You will examine Compelling Questions and develop your own questions about state and local government in the Inquiry Activities. You can preview some of the key concepts that you will learn about by reviewing the infographic.

What Will You Learn?

In these lessons focused on state and local government, you will learn:

- the relationship between state governments and the federal government.
- the advantages and disadvantages of the federal system of government.
- the powers held by the state and federal governments.
- how state legislatures are organized and how they create laws.
- which services are provided by national, state, and local governments.
- the organization and duties of the state executive branch and its departments.
- the organization of state courts and selection methods of judges.
- how the powers and responsibilities of local governments are set by state constitutions.
- how local governments are organized and funded and how they make laws.
- what public policy is and how governments plan and apply public policy.

 COMPELLING QUESTIONS IN THE INQUIRY ACTIVITY LESSONS

- **How do laws on one issue vary at different levels of government?**
- **How do communities solve problems?**

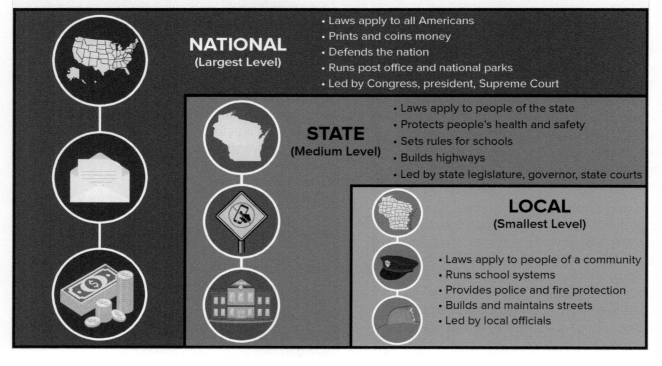

Comparing National, State, and Local Governments
State and local governments have different roles and functions than the federal government.

NATIONAL
(Largest Level)
- Laws apply to all Americans
- Prints and coins money
- Defends the nation
- Runs post office and national parks
- Led by Congress, president, Supreme Court

STATE
(Medium Level)
- Laws apply to people of the state
- Protects people's health and safety
- Sets rules for schools
- Builds highways
- Led by state legislature, governor, state courts

LOCAL
(Smallest Level)
- Laws apply to people of a community
- Runs school systems
- Provides police and fire protection
- Builds and maintains streets
- Led by local officials

The Federal System

READING STRATEGY

Analyzing Key Ideas and Details As you read, take notes in a chart such as this one to track your understanding of how constitutions affect the relationship between the federal and state governments.

Effect on State Governments	
U.S. Constitution	
State constitutions	

Federal, State, and Tribal Powers

GUIDING QUESTION

How does the federal system allow the national, state, and other governments to share power?

In the United States, major highways are marked with road signs that have a red, white, and blue shield and a number. This symbol shows that the road is an interstate highway. *Interstate* means "between states." Interstate highways connect major cities within and between different states. The federal government pays most of the cost to build these kinds of highways. Have you ever noticed that sometimes there is another sign next to the interstate highway sign? That sign might show the outline of a state with a number, which means that the road is a state highway. How can the same road be both a state and a federal highway? The answer lies in the United States' federal system of government.

States in the Constitution

Under the Articles of Confederation, the United States had been a loose union of states. The states had more power than the central government at that time. This often made it difficult to accomplish tasks for the whole nation. The Framers decided to change the system of government when they wrote the Constitution. They made the central government much stronger. The state governments, however, would continue to be important. This new structure gave both the central government and the state governments certain powers.

Both the federal and state governments have the power to build roads.

The final result was a federal system that divides powers between state and national governments. The Constitution limits the powers of states, but it also offers the states some protections. These protections can be seen in Article IV:

- Article IV, Section 1 says that each state must give "Full Faith and Credit" to the legal actions of each of the other states. For this reason, someone with a driver's license from one state can legally drive in any other state.

- Article IV, Section 2 requires each state to treat the citizens of other states equally. For example, states cannot give people from another state tougher punishment for a crime than their own citizens would get. This section also calls on states to turn over any person who enters their state while fleeing from law enforcement officers of another state.

- Article IV, Section 3 says that Congress can admit new states but guarantees each state's area. This section says that land cannot be taken from any state to make a new state without the approval of its legislature. It also says that two states cannot be joined into a new state unless they agree. Three states have been formed from land that belonged to another state—Kentucky in 1792, Maine in 1819, and West Virginia in 1863. The Virginia and Massachusetts legislatures agreed to let Kentucky and Maine gain statehood on their own. West Virginia split off from Virginia in 1863 without the approval of Virginia's legislature. That came during the Civil War, when Virginia was rebelling against the U.S. government. President Abraham Lincoln recognized the western counties that formed West Virginia as the true government of the area.

- Article IV, Section 4 promises each state a republican form of government. It also vows that the federal government will protect that government against an enemy attack or a revolt.

Sharing and Dividing Powers

Federalism is organized through the powers given to the federal government and those given to the state governments. The Constitution grants the federal government three kinds of power.

1. The *enumerated or expressed powers* are those powers found directly in the Constitution. For example, only the federal government may declare war on a foreign country.

2. *Implied powers* are not specifically given to the federal government in the Constitution. However, they can be inferred as federal powers based on the text. For instance, the Constitution names the president as the commander in chief of the armed forces. Therefore, the president has the implied power to send troops in response to a serious crisis.

3. *Inherent powers* are the kinds of powers a government has simply because it is a government. The authority to buy land from another country is an example of an inherent power.

Shared and Divided Powers of National and State Governments

The Constitution gives some powers to the federal government and reserves others for the states. Both levels of government also share some powers.

NATIONAL GOVERNMENT
- Coin money
- Maintain army and navy
- Declare war
- Regulate trade between states and with foreign nations
- Carry out all expressed powers

NATIONAL AND STATE GOVERNMENTS
- Establish courts
- Enforce laws
- Collect taxes
- Borrow money
- Provide for general welfare

STATE GOVERNMENTS
- Regulate trade within a state
- Protect public welfare and safety
- Conduct elections
- Establish local governments

EXAMINE THE DIAGRAM

1. **Analyzing** Which level of government runs elections?

2. **Speculating** Why do you think both levels of government have the power to collect taxes?

The power to establish courts is an example of a concurrent power. In Florida, the state Supreme Court has the final say about how state law and the state constitution are applied.

The Constitution gives states what are known as *reserved powers*. These powers are ones set aside, or reserved, for the states. They are not specifically listed. Instead, the Tenth Amendment explains that all powers not given to the federal government are reserved for the states. The power of a state to conduct elections is an example of a reserved power.

Some powers are held by both the national and state governments. These shared powers are called *concurrent powers*. The Constitution does not actually mention concurrent powers, but both levels of government need these powers in order to function. Such powers include the powers to set up courts and to create and enforce laws. They also include the power to tax.

Limits on State Power

The Constitution puts limits on the powers of both the national and state governments. For example, neither government can pass a law that punishes actions that took place before the law existed. The Constitution also puts some limits specifically on the powers of the states. For example, states cannot declare war, coin their own money, or impose taxes on imports from other countries or states. States also cannot make treaties with other countries. Only the federal government can enter into treaty agreements.

In addition, according to the Fourteenth Amendment, states cannot take away the rights of their citizens "without due process of law." Also,

states are required to give every citizen "equal protection of the laws." However, this was not always the case. When written, the Bill of Rights was focused on the federal government. For instance, the First Amendment says that Congress—not the states—cannot limit freedom of religion or speech. The Framers worried that a central government that was too strong could take away people's freedoms. They did not fear that state governments would limit rights and freedoms.

Yet, states did take away people's rights. For example, states in the South passed laws to limit the rights of African Americans. The Fourteenth Amendment gives courts a tool to stop states from making such laws. Over the years, the Supreme Court has ruled that most of the protections in the Bill of Rights apply to state governments as well as to Congress.

Another limit to state power comes from the supremacy clause. Article VI says that the Constitution, and all federal laws, "shall be the supreme Law of the Land." What happens if a state law **conflicts** with the Constitution or a federal law? If the state law is challenged in court, the U.S. Supreme Court can declare it unconstitutional.

conflict to disagree with

PHOTO: felixmizioznikov/Getty Images; TEXT: U.S. Constitution, Amendment XIV, Section 1, U.S. Constitution, Amendment V, US Constitution, Article VI

Working Together

The federal and state governments often work together. Each year the federal government gives billions of dollars to the states in **grants-in-aid**. This money is used to meet goals set by Congress. Grants might be for education, health care, or other purposes. Some grants come with specific instructions about what the states should do with the money. Others set goals but do not detail how to reach those goals or require that the money be spent in specific ways.

Occasionally conflicts arise between the states and the federal government. At times, Congress tells states to take certain actions without providing the funding to pay for those actions. State officials call these laws **unfunded mandates**. Many say these laws are unfair and violate the rights of state governments to govern themselves as they wish.

Sometimes states do not want to follow laws passed by Congress. For example, many states have resisted the Real ID Act, passed in 2005. This law required states to meet tough new ID standards for granting or renewing driver's licenses by 2023. Congress said these standards were needed for national security reasons. The law required people traveling by air to produce either a Real ID or another valid form of identification, such as a passport, before they would be allowed to fly. Within a few years of the law's passage, however, the legislatures of half the states formally protested the law. All states later agreed to put the law into action, but the COVID-19 pandemic made it more difficult for states to issue these IDs to all drivers. In 2021 the Department of Homeland Security extended the deadline for enforcement of the law to the spring of 2023.

State governments work with one another to achieve common goals. For example, Florida has an agreement with other states that makes it easier for people who have a teaching license in one state to get a Florida license. New Jersey and Pennsylvania have agreed not to charge income tax to people who work in one state but live in the other. Some states in the West have formed a group to design a common energy policy. During the COVID-19 pandemic, certain states formed agreements for how and when to lift stay-at-home orders or travel restrictions.

States also help one another through a legal process called *extradition*. In this process, a person charged with a crime who has fled to another state is returned to the state where the crime was committed. Extradition is needed because the accused must be tried in the jurisdiction where the crime was committed.

grant-in-aid money awarded to the states by the federal government

unfunded mandate requirement that state government do something required by the federal government without providing the money to pay for those actions

Some states work together on a lottery game to raise funds for their governments. This allows them to offer larger prizes, which attracts more people to the combined lottery and makes more money for each of the states.

There are hundreds of tribal governments across the United States. Shown here is the interior of the Tribal Administration Building for the Standing Rock Sioux in North Dakota.

Tribal Governments

More than half of the 50 states are home to tribal governments. Each of these governments serves a certain Native American nation. The federal government recognizes more than 500 tribal groups as sovereign, or self-governing, governments. These governments often have executive, legislative, and judicial branches, as the federal and state governments do. They can collect taxes, pass laws, and operate a tribal court system—separate from the U.S. government. At the same time, tribal governments cooperate with both the federal and state governments. This unique governmental arrangement allows Native American groups to protect their cultures, land, and rights.

✓ CHECK FOR UNDERSTANDING

1. **Identifying** Name two ways that the Constitution protects states and two ways it limits them.

2. **Explaining** How has the Fourteenth Amendment been used to limit what laws states can pass?

The State Constitutions

GUIDING QUESTION

What characteristics do all state governments share?

Think about what you know about states other than your own. When you visit or read about these states, you may notice some differences from your home state. Things like the climate and geography might be much different. What about the governments of those other states? How different are they from your state's government?

Similarities in State Constitutions

Each one of the 50 states has its own constitution. Every one of these documents explains the structure of the state's government. Like the U.S. Constitution, state constitutions organize government into three branches— the executive, the legislative, and the judicial. They also describe the powers of each branch. These powers are separated like they are in the federal government.

This gives each branch the ability to check the power of the other branches.

State constitutions also include a list of the specific rights guaranteed to citizens of the state. It is not surprising that states have recorded these rights. Lists such as these appeared in several state constitutions before the U.S. Constitution was written. In fact, James Madison drew on lists of rights in existing state constitutions when he drafted the Bill of Rights.

Another way state constitutions are similar is that they establish control over lower-level government. State constitutions usually include details about how local government should be organized within that state.

Differences Among State Constitutions

State constitutions differ in some ways. Massachusetts has the oldest constitution still in use. Its framework was written in 1780. Some states have had more than one constitution, replacing earlier versions.

The length of state constitutions varies from a little more than 8,000 words to well over 350,000. One reason why many state constitutions are so long is that they are often far more specific than the U.S. Constitution. For example, California's constitution includes a long list of the kinds of resources that cannot be taxed. These tax-free items include trees younger than four years old. When a large amount of specific information such as this is written into a state constitution, the result can be a very long document.

Some states' constitutions are longer than others because they have been amended many times over the years. Every time a state adds a new amendment to its constitution, the document gets longer. Alabama's state constitution has the most amendments—more than 975 of them. But nearly three-quarters of these amendments affect only one county in the state. In Rhode Island, the current constitution has only existed since 1986. This constitution has only been amended five times.

Some state constitutions allow for the creation of a special constitutional revision commission. The purpose of such a commission is to propose amendments. The Florida constitution requires a

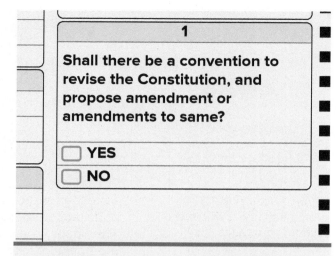

States differ in how they call a state constitutional convention to propose changes to the current constitution. In many states, such as Alaska, voters determine whether to hold such a convention.

commission review every 20 years to see if the constitution still meets the state's needs.

State constitutions reflect differences among the state governments. In each state, the state constitution is considered the supreme law within the state. That means no other laws in the state can go against it. At the same time, no state constitution can include elements that clash with the U.S. Constitution.

✓ CHECK FOR UNDERSTANDING

Comparing What do state constitutions have in common with each other and the U.S. Constitution?

LESSON ACTIVITIES

1. **Informative/Explanatory Writing** Think about what you have learned about the federal system. Write a short essay that explains the relationship between state governments and the federal government as defined in the U.S. Constitution. Use specific examples from the Constitution to describe this relationship.

2. **Interpreting Information** Work with a partner to identify three differences between your state's constitution and the U.S. Constitution. Then discuss why these differences might exist and what they tell you about the purpose of state government and the purpose of federal government.

State Legislative Branch

READING STRATEGY

Integrating Knowledge and Ideas Use a chart such as the one below to take notes as you read. Include information about who works in state legislatures, how they are organized, what they do, and how they pay for services.

State Legislatures	
Who works in legislatures	
How legislatures are organized	
What legislators do	
How legislatures pay for services	

How Legislatures Function

GUIDING QUESTION

What are the functions of state legislatures?

Every state has a legislative branch of government. The form of most state legislatures mirrors that of the federal government. Both federal and state legislatures are bicameral, meaning they have two houses. The upper house is called the senate. The lower house is usually called the house of representatives. Nebraska's legislature is the exception. It has a **unicameral** (YOO•nih•KAM•ruhl), or one-house, legislature.

Legislators and Leaders

Similar to the federal legislative branch, a state senate typically has fewer members than the lower house of the state legislature. Nebraska has the smallest legislature, with a total of only 49 senators. The largest legislature belongs to New Hampshire, with 424 members.

State senators serve four-year terms in two-thirds of the states. Terms in the other states are two years. House members generally serve for two years. The minimum age for state senators and representatives varies across states. All states require that legislators live in that state. Most also require legislators to be U.S. citizens.

Fifteen states limit how many terms a state senator or representative may serve. In several of these states, laws only limit how many consecutive terms a legislator may serve. A few states put limits on the total number of terms a legislator may serve.

unicameral having a one-house legislature

The New York State Capitol in Albany houses the state senate and state assembly.

Analyzing Visuals Describe the style and architecture of the New York State Capitol. Why do you think capitol buildings are often designed in this manner?

All states pay their legislators. Most states pay a *salary*, which is a set amount of pay per year, but a few pay lawmakers a daily rate while the legislature meets. Salaries range from New Hampshire's low of $100 per year to California's high of about $115,000 per year.

The amount of time a legislator works varies by state. In some states, such as California and New York, being a state senator or representative is considered a full-time job. These legislators typically have a staff to help them. In most other states, legislators work part-time in the government while also holding other jobs or having other sources of income. Legislative staff—and legislators' salaries—are therefore smaller.

As in the U.S. Congress, each house in a state legislature has a presiding officer. A presiding officer leads the chamber when it meets for business. In the lower chamber, members of the body choose that officer, who is typically called the speaker. In some states, the lieutenant governor heads the senate. Members of each party in each house choose someone to serve as their party's leader in that house. These members become the majority leader and minority leader.

They set the schedule for considering and debating the passage of bills.

Representation

State legislators represent districts that must have roughly the same populations. Those districts are based on information collected through the census done by the federal government. A *census* is a count of all the people living in the country. The government conducts a census every decade. The most recent census was in 2020. The year after the census, each state draws new district boundaries based on the new population numbers counted during the census. Those districts are used for the next 10 years, until the year after the next census. The task of working out the boundaries of legislative districts is called **redistricting** (ree•DIHS•trihkt•ihng).

In the past, many states often made little effort to draw new boundaries to reflect changes in population. As a result, urban districts often included far more people than rural districts. For example, in Alabama, one state senator from a city

redistricting the process of redrawing boundaries for legislative districts

Qualifications for Legislators

Congress and state legislatures all have certain age, residency, and citizenship requirements. These may vary at the state level.

	U.S. House of Representatives	U.S. Senate	State House of Representatives	State Senate
Age	At least 25 years old	At least 30 years old	Usually at least 21 years old, but can vary as young as 18 or as old as 25	Usually at least 21 or 25 years old, but can vary as young as 18 or as old as 30
Residency	Must be a resident of the state he or she represents	Must be a resident of the state he or she represents	Usually must be a resident of state and district, ranging from time of election to 5 years prior to election	Usually must be a resident of state, ranging from time of election to 7 years prior to election
Citizenship	Citizen for at least 7 years	Citizen for at least 9 years	Usually must be a citizen	Usually must be a citizen

EXAMINE THE CHART

Inferring The Constitution requires members of Congress to be U.S. citizens, but several states do not have a similar rule for their lawmakers. Why do you think these differences in qualifications exist?

State lawmakers, such as these California state senators, meet during legislative sessions to vote on bills. Each California state senator represents more than 930,000 residents.

represented more than 600,000 people. Another senator from a rural district represented fewer than 16,000. This huge difference gave rural citizens far more power than those living in cities. Having unfair district sizes like these is called **malapportionment** (ma·luh·PAWR·shuhn·muhnt).

The United States Supreme Court put an end to this practice. In the 1962 case *Baker* v. *Carr*, citizens in Tennessee's large cities asked that the state's legislative boundaries be redrawn to better reflect population shifts from rural areas to cities. The Court ruled that legislative districts within any state had to be roughly equal by population to that state's other districts. It resulted in the redrawing of legislative boundaries throughout the country. The goal was to try to ensure that each citizen in a state has an equal voice in government.

Redistricting can be a hotly debated topic. State legislatures are usually in charge of redrawing district borders. The political party with the majority may draw the lines to favor their members, a practice called *gerrymandering*. Some states have tried to stop this behavior. For example, Florida voters amended the state constitution in 2010 to prevent redistricting that helps a specific party or legislator. This change also offered more protection to underrepresented ethnic and racial groups. It prevents lawmakers

from purposefully drawing district lines that deny minorities a fair number of members. Although racial gerrymandering has been outlawed, gerrymandering is still a problem in many states, creating an advantage for the party already in power.

Legislatures at Work

Lawmakers meet during a legislative **session**. A session usually lasts a few months, though the members can agree to extend it. Sometimes legislatures meet in a special session. This is a meeting held for a specific purpose, such as addressing a crisis caused by a natural disaster. In most states, either the governor or the legislature can call these sessions. In some states, only the governor has this power.

State legislators do several jobs. They approve the people named by the governor to fill some state offices. They also work for the people of their district. For instance, they may help citizens by directing them to the correct state agency to solve a problem. They might contact the agency themselves to help the citizens.

The main job of state legislators is to make laws. The steps in this process are like those followed by Congress. Individual citizens, the governor, or legislators may suggest ideas for new laws. A lawmaker must introduce the bill.

---

malapportionment unequal representation in state legislatures

session a meeting of a legislative body to conduct its business

Then it goes to a committee that reviews the bill and may revise it. If the committee members approve the bill, it goes to the full chamber for discussion and a vote. If a majority votes to pass the bill, it goes to the other house. The same process—committee and then full vote—is repeated. Once both houses approve a final version of the bill, it goes to the governor to be signed.

The sessions of state legislatures are usually shorter than those of the U.S. Congress. That means state legislators have less time to get their work done. For this reason, many state legislatures have ways to help them get through all bills before the end of the session. Some states limit the number of bills that can be introduced in each session. Others set deadlines to keep bills moving along.

Citizen Power

Some state constitutions require the state legislature to ask voters to approve certain types of laws that it has passed. This is called a **legislative referendum**. For some states, this vote is necessary to approve borrowing money or raising taxes. In all states except Delaware, voters must approve changes to the state constitution.

In about half the states, citizens can petition for certain types of elections to be held. A *petition* is a written request for the government to act. If citizens dislike a law, they can petition for a **popular referendum** to be held. If enough registered voters sign the petition, the referendum is placed on the ballot. This tool allows voters to decide if they want to repeal a law to which some people object.

Initiatives are requests by citizens to make a new law. They also begin with petitions. If voters approve the proposals, they become law.

✓ CHECK FOR UNDERSTANDING

1. **Identifying** What is the main responsibility of state legislators?
2. **Comparing** Compare and contrast the lawmaking process at the state and national levels.

---

legislative referendum a vote called by a legislature to seek voter approval of a law

popular referendum a question placed on a ballot for voters to decide: usually to repeal an existing law

State Economic Issues

GUIDING QUESTION
What economic challenges do state legislatures face?

States have a difficult task. They must provide services but have limited funds. State officials must work with citizens and the state budget to make tough choices.

State Revenues and Spending

In every state except Vermont, state law requires that the state budget be balanced. This means that states cannot spend more money than they collect in revenue. **Revenue** is the income taken in by a government, mainly by collecting taxes from citizens and businesses. If the state's income falls short of what was expected, the governor or the state legislature must cut spending to balance the budget.

Unlike the states, the federal government can run a budget deficit. That is, it can spend more money than it collects in revenue. The federal government borrows money to make up the deficit. Most states cannot do so. States can borrow money for special projects by selling bonds. Bonds are money the state borrows to fund projects, such as building bridges and

---

revenue the income brought in by the government

Some states allow citizens to vote on statewide referendums that allow them to approve or repeal laws. Here, opponents of a Missouri law that affected labor unions watch as voting results come in.

Analyzing Visuals Based on this photo, how do these people feel about the results of this election?

State governments are responsible for maintaining their state parks, such as this one in Georgia.

maintaining roads. The money is repaid to investors with interest after a number of years.

All states impose taxes. Taxes supply most state revenue. The main source of most states' income is **property tax**. The tax is paid by property owners, based on the value of their property. Most states have a **sales tax**, ranging from a low of about 3 percent to a high of 7.25 percent. A 3 percent tax adds 30 cents to a product that costs $10.

Most states also have an **income tax**. Florida is one of only nine states that do not tax people's incomes. Some states have one tax rate for all income levels. Others use tax rates that increase as the amount of income increases.

States also get income from other sources. They charge fees for the licenses people must buy to marry, drive, and fish. They may also charge use fees, such as the toll, or fee, that a driver pays to travel on certain roads.

Most state spending goes to pay for services. These services include aid to local governments, benefits to people with economic disadvantages and disabilities, health care, education, and payroll for state workers. States have other

expenses as well, such as providing police protection, building and repairing roads, and maintaining state parks.

Budget Crunch

Balancing the budget becomes challenging for states when their income is less than what was expected. This was very **apparent**, or clear to see, in the first half of 2020, when the COVID-19 pandemic began. The pandemic caused serious problems for the U.S. economy. Some Americans stayed home because they were ordered to by state or local governments to stop the spread of COVID-19. Others had health concerns that made the virus even more deadly to them. This made it impossible to go out without risking their health, or even their life. Businesses such as hotels and theaters suffered and shut down or laid off employees. To lay off employees means to end workers' employment because there is not enough money to pay them. People shopped less. That meant state sales tax revenues fell.

The U.S. unemployment rate reached a record high of 14.8 percent in April of 2020. The unemployment rate is the percentage of people in the workforce who do not have a job. This was the highest rate recorded since the government began tracking this data in 1948. Because of so many job losses, state income tax revenues fell. State and local governments also began to lay off employees. As a result, many people could not meet their living expenses.

property tax a tax paid on property, which is usually land and the structures built on it

sales tax a tax paid on the purchase of certain goods and services

income tax a tax paid on the income that people earn from work or other sources

apparent clear to see

Average Change in Unemployment Rate by State, 2020

Unemployment increased across the country due to the COVID-19 pandemic, although some states were affected more than others. The map shows how much the unemployment rate went up during the year.

KEY
- 5.0% or higher
- 4.0–4.9%
- 3.0–3.9%
- 2.0–2.9%
- Less than 2.0%

SOURCE: Bureau of Labor Statistics

GEOGRAPHY CONNECTION

Patterns and Movement Name three states where unemployment increased the most in 2020.

State governments struggled to meet the needs of citizens hurt by job loss and other pandemic-related problems. Many states used emergency money supplied by the federal government to help citizens with everything from remote online learning to health care. Some of this federal money went to increase the payments states gave unemployed workers.

The national economy began to recover in the second half of 2020. By September 2021, 76 percent of the jobs lost earlier in the year had been recovered. Some states saw their economies recover faster than others. States whose economies relied on tourism, such as Hawaii and New York, were hit hard by the decline in travel during the pandemic. The economies of these states had a more difficult time recovering.

✓ CHECK FOR UNDERSTANDING

Making Connections Why are decisions about spending so difficult at the state-government level?

LESSON ACTIVITIES

1. **Narrative Writing** Think about what you have learned about the roles and responsibilities of state legislators. Use this information to write a journal entry describing one typical day in the life of a state senator.

2. **Using Multimedia** With a partner, visit the website of one member of the state legislature who represents your area. Find out what kind of services the legislator provides to the people of your area. Look at what committees they serve on and what issues interest them. Prepare a profile of the legislator that shows how they serve their district.

State Executive Branch

READING STRATEGY

Integrating Knowledge and Ideas As you read, take notes on the many roles of governors. Use a chart such as this one to record information.

Governors' Roles

The Governor

GUIDING QUESTION

What are the powers and duties of a governor?

Who comes to mind when you think about the leader of your state? Certainly, there are many people serving in important jobs in your state. However, you might first think of the governor, who is often one of the most visible state government officials. As head of your state's executive branch of government, the governor has to fill many important roles—often at the same time.

The Office of Governor

Every state has requirements that people must meet before they can run for governor. The first requirement sets a minimum age for candidates. In Ohio, Vermont, Washington, and Wisconsin, candidates for governor can be as young as 18 years old. In most states, however, candidates need to be at least 30 years old. This is younger than the requirement for U.S. presidents, who must be at least 35 years old. Other requirements for governors vary widely among the states.

In most states, governors must be residents of the states they govern. The length of time a person must have lived in the state varies from one state to another. A candidate for governor in Missouri or Oklahoma must have lived in that state for at least 10 years. In Rhode Island, a person is required to live in the state for only 30 days before running for governor. No state requires a governor to be a natural-born citizen, as is the case for president.

Florida Governor Ron DeSantis was the youngest governor in the country when he was elected at the age of 40 in 2018.

Most states limit a person to serving no more than two terms as governor. However, nearly a dozen states, including Wisconsin, have no term limit. Some states, such as Virginia, allow more than one term but do not allow the terms to be consecutive, or one after the other. In Virginia, someone who is governor for one term must sit out at least one term before being able to hold the office again. Most governors' terms are four years, although governors in New Hampshire and Vermont have two-year terms.

All states except Oregon allow the governor to be impeached. This happens when the governor is formally charged by the state legislature with wrongdoing. The governor can be removed from office by a vote of the legislature after it holds hearings about the charges. In most states, the process is similar to impeachment of the president. The lower house in the legislature votes to impeach. The upper house votes on whether to convict.

The Chief Executive

Much like the president, a governor has many roles. Each role comes with certain powers. Two of these roles have developed through tradition rather than by law. For instance, a governor's ceremonial role is based on tradition, not the state constitution. The same is true of the governor's role as state party leader. The other roles and duties are outlined in the state constitution.

A governor's main job, like that of the president, is to head the executive branch of government. In this role, the governor is responsible for making sure the laws of the state are carried out. State governments have many employees—about 4.4 million in total. These employees include professors in the states' universities, social workers, prison guards, state park rangers, and more. Other people, such as most teachers and police officers, work for local governments. Depending on the state, the governor may have responsibility for, and power over, many of these state and local government employees.

Also, just as the president commands the nation's armed forces, the governor is the head of the state's National Guard. This military force is made up of mostly part-time soldiers and is shared by the states and the federal government. A governor can activate a state's National Guard

The Roles of Governors

Governors serve many roles, often at the same time. Here, Hawaii Governor David Ige fulfills one of those roles as commander in chief of his state's National Guard.

Chief Executive
- Carries out state laws
- Prepares state budget
- Appoints other state officials

Commander in Chief
- Acts as head of the state's National Guard

Party Leader
- Leads his or her political party in the state

The Roles of Governors

Legislative Leader
- Proposes new legislation
- Approves or vetoes legislation

Ceremonial Leader
- Greets important leaders
- Represents the state in other regions

Judicial Leader
- Pardons, commutes, and paroles criminals
- Appoints judges

EXAMINE THE CHART

1. **Identifying** In which roles does the governor work with branches of government other than the executive branch?
2. **Comparing** Which role of a state governor is similar to the president's role in relation to Congress?

Party Control of State Governor and Legislature, 2021

In many states, the same political party controls both the legislature and the executive branch. In divided states, the governor belongs to a different political party than the majority party in the state legislature.

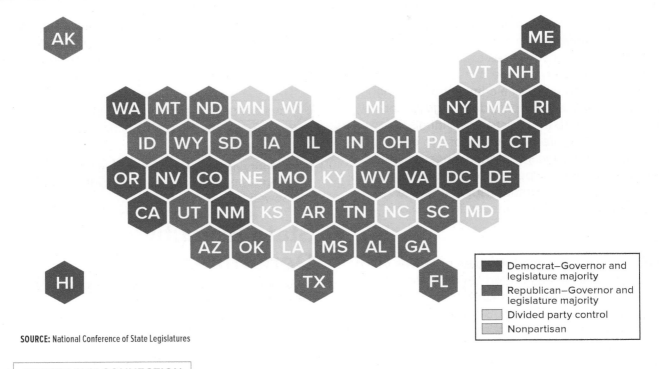

SOURCE: National Conference of State Legislatures

Legend:
- Democrat—Governor and legislature majority
- Republican—Governor and legislature majority
- Divided party control
- Nonpartisan

GEOGRAPHY CONNECTION

1. **Exploring Regions** In which parts of the country can you find the most state governments controlled by Democrats, and which parts have the most controlled by Republicans?

2. **Speculating** How might being in a divided state affect the work of a governor as legislative leader?

---

members during crises, such as when a region floods after a hurricane. Sometimes a president calls units from a state's National Guard into active duty. Then the president serves as their commander in chief.

Governors often have the power to name people to work in certain jobs in state offices. Usually these choices are not final until the state senate has confirmed, or approved, the governor's choice. However, governors do not have as much control over the people in their cabinets as presidents do. In most states, the governor can name someone to fill one of the state's seats in the U.S. Senate if it becomes vacant.

In most states, the governor also writes the state's annual budget. Typically, the legislature must approve the state budget before it goes into effect. In Virginia and Wyoming, the budget is *biennial*. This means it is submitted and then approved every two years.

Other Roles of the Governor

Governors have certain legislative duties as well. Like the president, they deliver an annual message to the legislature early each year. This "state of the state" message outlines the governor's goals to the state's legislature and its people. During the legislature's session, the governor sends bills that reflect those goals. Governors can also call a special session of the legislature to respond to a crisis.

Like presidents, all state governors have the power to veto bills. Unlike the president, most governors have a special veto power. They can issue a **line-item veto**. This means they can veto specific parts of a bill rather than the whole law if they disagree only with parts of it. Only six states do not allow the line-item veto.

line-item veto the power to reject only a specific part of a bill

They are Indiana, Nevada, New Hampshire, North Carolina, Rhode Island, and Vermont. The legislature can override either a line-item veto or a complete veto by voting to pass the bill again.

Governors have some judicial powers as well. They can appoint judges, though this power varies widely by state. For example, a Florida governor must work with a nominating commission to identify qualified candidates to be named judges. Governors can also change the sentence given to someone found guilty of a crime who is serving time in prison. Like the president, a governor may grant a pardon to a convicted individual. Additionally, a governor can choose to **commute**, or reduce, someone's sentence. These rulings can be made before any punishment has been served. Governors can also grant prisoners **parole** (puh•ROHL), or an early release from prison.

Next in Line

What happens if a governor dies or leaves office before their term has ended? In 45 states, the lieutenant governor is the **successor**, or next person in line. In the other 5 states, the secretary of state or president of the state senate becomes governor. In some states, candidates for governor and lieutenant governor run as a team. In other

---

commute to reduce a criminal's punishment

parole an early release from prison as long as the person meets certain conditions

successor the person who follows another in an office or position

---

states, they run separately and may even belong to different political parties. If a lieutenant governor from another party succeeds a governor, state policy may change.

The next person in line steps into the governor's position with some frequency. Between 2010 and 2021, governors were replaced 10 times in the United States. Often these replacements were necessary because a governor resigned to take a position in the federal government.

☑ **CHECK FOR UNDERSTANDING**

1. **Explaining** What is the governor's role in a state's legislative process?
2. **Identifying** Name an example of how another branch of government can check the governor's power.

State Executive Departments

GUIDING QUESTION

What is the role of the executives who head a state's administrative departments?

In the federal government, the executive branch has many departments and agencies. They serve a number of functions at the national level.

State governments also have many executive departments, agencies, and boards. Some are similar to those at the federal level, such as the departments of labor, justice, and agriculture.

Governors interact frequently with local government. Here, Massachusetts Governor Charlie Baker attends National Medal of Honor Day in 2021 with the acting mayor of Boston, Kim Janey.

Erin Clark/The Boston Globe/Getty Images

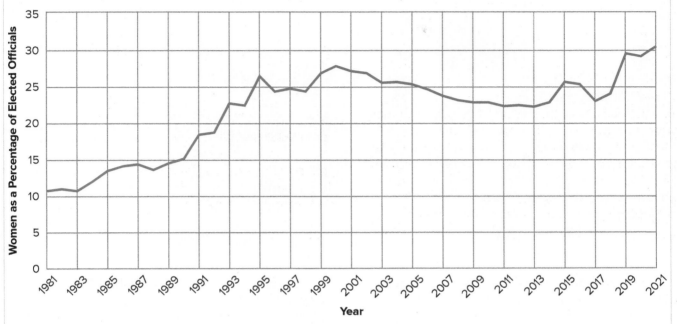

Women in Statewide Elective Executive Office, 1981–2021

The share of women holding statewide elective office in the states' executive branches has increased significantly over time.

Source: Center for American Women and Politics, Eagleton Institute of Politics, Rutgers University.

HISTORY CONNECTION

1. **Analyzing Visuals** What percentage of statewide offices were held by women in 2021?
2. **Comparing** How has the percentage of women holding statewide elective office changed from 1981 to 2021?

Others reflect the specific concerns of a state. For example, states have departments of public works and highways. Many states also have boards of welfare to help those in need.

Major Executive Officials

In the federal government, departments, agencies, and boards are headed by officials whom the president chooses and the Senate approves. Many state governments work differently. Voters elect the heads of many state departments. These officials get their jobs without the governor's involvement. That means they are independent of, and may choose not to work closely with, the governor.

Most states have five major executive officials. Each carries out important activities in the state. The titles of these officials differ from state to state.

- The secretary of state oversees elections in the state and sees that all laws are recorded and published. The secretary of state's office also keeps other kinds of official records.

- The attorney general is the state's chief lawyer. This official leads a team of lawyers who represent the state in legal matters. Sometimes the team represents the state in disputes with the federal government.

- The state treasurer manages and keeps track of the state government's revenues and spending.

- The state auditor reviews the actions of other parts of the state government to make sure that employees are working honestly and efficiently. The auditor's purpose is to ensure that tax dollars are not misused.

- The commissioner or superintendent of education is in charge of all the public schools in the state. This official works on such issues as the content students are supposed to learn in each grade.

State governments employ many people across different departments and agencies. This includes workers who protect wildlife, such as this wildlife biologist for the Wisconsin Department of Natural Resources helping a duck that was caught in a net.

In most states, voters elect the secretary of state, attorney general, and state treasurer. In about half the states, voters also elect the auditor. In other states, the auditor is chosen by one or both houses of the legislature or named by the governor. The head of education is elected in only about a third of the states. In the rest, this official is named by the governor or other state officials.

State Cabinets

Just as the president has a cabinet of advisers, so do governors. In most states, the heads of executive departments make up a governor's cabinet. The cabinet meets with the governor to give advice and share information. These officials from the different departments each bring special knowledge when discussing issues. The size of cabinets varies widely in different states, from only 3 in Florida to as many as 75 in New York. Some cabinets meet every week. Others meet only every one or two months.

Governors and cabinet members may work together on creating new policies and drafting new legislation. Meeting with cabinet members also gives governors a way to make sure that the department heads understand their goals. That way, they can communicate these goals to the employees within their departments.

Several states have established Children's Cabinets. These groups bring together state officials from agencies that work on issues that affect children and families. They also often include other state residents with connections to these issues. Children's Cabinets focus on ways to improve the lives of children across the state. Florida, Virginia, and Wisconsin are three states that have these special cabinets.

✓ CHECK FOR UNDERSTANDING

Determining Central Ideas What are the roles of state cabinets?

LESSON ACTIVITIES

1. **Informative/Explanatory Writing** Use a Venn diagram to compare and contrast the powers of the president and governors. Summarize your findings in three sentences that answer the question "How does the work of the president compare to that of state governors?"

2. **Interpreting Information** With two classmates, find three recent news articles that demonstrate how the governor of your state has been fulfilling one of the roles of the governor's office described in this lesson. Paraphrase your findings in a brief group oral presentation.

The Structure of State Courts

Analyzing Key Ideas and Details As you read, use a table such as this one to track information about different kinds of state courts at the lower and higher levels.

Level of Court	Type of Court	
	Trial	Appellate
Lower Level		
Name		
Types of Cases		
Higher Level		
Name		
Types of Cases		

GUIDING QUESTION

How is the state's judicial system organized?

If you regularly read or watch news reports, you probably hear about important court cases. Sometimes these news stories cover a decision by the U.S. Supreme Court. However, many of these cases are decided a lot closer to home. In fact, the vast majority of cases heard in the United States take place in state court systems. This is because state courts have the power to hear many different types of cases. Many of these cases include those that deal with state or local laws, or even the state constitution itself. Matters involving federal laws or the U.S. Constitution are mainly addressed in courts at the federal level.

Although each state has its own court system, all state court systems are organized in a similar manner. Every state has two sets of courts. These are known as lower courts and higher courts. At each of these levels, the courts hear cases that differ in how serious and complex they are.

Communities often built elaborate courthouses as a display of their civic pride. This example is the Lake Court House in Crown Point, Indiana, which was built in the late 1800s.

Lower Courts

The lower courts are trial courts. In a **trial court**, a judge or a jury listens to the evidence that is presented. Then the judge or jury reaches a verdict, or decision, in favor of one party to the case. Lower trial courts often have different names, such as *justice courts, municipal courts,* and *district courts.*

Lower-level courts may handle two types of cases. The first type is a criminal case. In a criminal case, a person is accused of committing a crime. Sometimes the accused person accepts the charge and pleads guilty. When this happens, the matter goes to a judge for sentencing. A *sentence* is the punishment someone must take for breaking the law. The judge chooses the sentence from a range of options set by law. If the accused does not plead guilty, the case goes to trial. When that happens, a jury or judge determines whether the person is guilty or innocent. Someone found guilty of a crime is then sentenced. Someone found not guilty is allowed to go free.

The lowest level of courts handles cases involving simple crimes, such as traffic violations

trial court type of court in which a judge or a jury listens to the evidence and reaches a verdict in favor of one party or another in the case

The neighbors who own the two properties shown in this photograph are engaged in a civil lawsuit. The owner of the land on the right built a garage blocking the view from the window on the home on the left.

Speculating Based on the photograph, which neighbor do you think might sue the other? Why?

or misdemeanors. **Misdemeanors** (MIHS•dih•MEE•nuhrz) are the least serious crimes, such as shoplifting and spraying graffiti. Usually, these crimes are punished by a fine or a short stay in a local jail rather than in a prison. Sometimes offenders are sentenced to probation, which is supervised time out of jail. Misdemeanor cases are often decided by a judge instead of a jury.

Lower-level courts also handle civil cases. In civil cases, two parties are involved in a dispute in which one claims to have been harmed in some way by the other. A *party* is any person, business, or organization. In a legal sense, "harm" does not always mean physical harm. In a civil case, harm can also mean breaking an agreement, violating someone's rights, or not paying money owed to someone. A civil case begins when a **plaintiff** files a lawsuit claiming to have been harmed in some way. The **defendant** is the party charged with causing the harm.

An example of a civil suit is a claim that a person suffered injuries caused by another driver in a traffic accident. Many civil cases involve *contracts*, or business agreements. Often in these cases, one party says that the other did not fulfill the promises they made in the contract. The civil cases heard in lower-level courts involve small sums of money.

Civil cases do not involve verdicts of guilt or innocence. Instead, the judge or jury rules in favor of either the plaintiff or the defendant. If the verdict is in favor of the plaintiff, the defendant may be told to pay the plaintiff a certain amount of money or take some other kind of action.

Higher Courts

The higher courts are the second level of state courts. Some higher-level state courts are trial courts. They handle more serious crimes called **felonies** (FEH•luh•neez). Some examples of felonies include assault, robbery, kidnapping, and murder. Trials in these courts can be decided either by juries or by judges. In a jury trial, the

misdemeanor the least serious type of crime

plaintiff the party in a civil case who claims to have been harmed

defendant the party in a civil case who is said to have caused the harm

felony a type of crime more serious than a misdemeanor

The rulings of state appellate courts often inspire a passionate response from affected groups. In this photo, protesters objected to the upholding of a labor law that unions did not support.

judge maintains order and decides questions of law. These are matters such as how to interpret the meaning of a law. The jury is made up of citizens who fulfill a responsibility of citizenship by serving on the jury. In a trial without a jury, the judge plays two roles. Judges must weigh questions of law while also considering the facts of the case. Under the U.S. Constitution, the accused person has the right to a jury trial but can choose to have a judge decide the case instead.

Higher trial courts also handle civil cases that are more serious than those heard in lower courts. They may involve large sums of money. Civil cases may also be decided either by a jury or by a judge.

The second kind of higher court is an **appellate** (uh•PEH•luht) **court**. They are also called *appeals courts*. An appeals court is involved when the party that lost a case in a lower court appeals the decision. To appeal means to ask a judge to review and reverse the earlier case. The party that appeals might claim that the lower court made legal errors that affected the outcome of the case. An appeal can also be made on a claim that the trial was conducted in an unfair way. The appellate court's task is to decide whether errors in applying the

appellate court type of court in which a party that lost a case in a lower court asks judges to review that decision and reverse it

law were made. An appellate court rarely reviews the facts of the case presented to the trial court.

In 41 states, there are two levels of appellate courts. The nine states that do not have two levels are generally states with small populations, such as Delaware and Montana. In these 41 states, appeals are made first to an intermediate appellate court. This court is often called the *court of appeals*. Usually a group of judges hears a case. It studies the information given by both sides and compares the case to past cases that are similar. Then the group agrees on a decision. It may decide to let the earlier court ruling stand, or it may choose to overturn it. The second level of appellate courts is the state supreme courts.

Courts in one state must decide cases based on the laws of their own state. They do not have to follow decisions that were made in another state's courts. However, a judge might look at the ruling from another state if that case was similar to the one the judge is considering.

State Supreme Court

The highest court in each state is the state supreme court. If a state has two levels of appellate courts, the higher level is the supreme court. Decisions made in the intermediate appellate courts are appealed by the losing party to the state supreme court. State supreme courts make final decisions, or rulings. They generally publish written explanations of their rulings.

The justices of the Mississippi Supreme Court hear arguments in a case heard in 2021.

These explanations do two things. First, they tell the parties involved in the case why the court decided what it did. Second, the written decisions guide judges in the state as they try other cases in the future. In most states, supreme courts take both civil and criminal cases. Oklahoma and Texas differ. They have two state supreme courts. One handles only civil appeals, and the other hears only criminal appeals.

The number of justices who sit on a state supreme court can vary. For example, the Florida state supreme court has seven justices. Five of the seven justices must be present to hear a case before that court. Four justices must agree for a decision to be reached. Alabama's state supreme court has nine justices.

State supreme courts are called "courts of last resort," but that is not entirely true. They do have the final word about what state law means and how to apply it. They also have the final word on questions that involve the meaning of the state constitution. However, someone who loses an appeal in the state supreme court may believe that the ruling violated their rights under the U.S.

Constitution. If so, that person can appeal the case to the U.S. Supreme Court. The U.S. Supreme Court may or may not choose to hear the case, however.

✓ CHECK FOR UNDERSTANDING

1. **Contrasting** How do state courts differ from federal courts in the matters that they consider?

2. **Contrasting** How do criminal cases differ from civil cases?

Staffing the Courts

GUIDING QUESTION

What are the usual methods for selecting judges?

What are the qualities a judge should have? Of course, a judge should understand the law. Judges also need to be able to hear cases without bias so they can decide fairly. Americans also expect judges to be independent. This independence helps them avoid any political pressure to decide cases a certain way.

Choosing Judges for Trial Courts

There are approximately 30,000 state court judges. They are chosen in various ways. Some judges are selected by governors, state legislators, the state supreme court, or city officials. Other judges are elected by voters. Some states use a combination of processes depending on whether it is a judge's first term or a later term. In this mixed approach, an elected official chooses judges for their first term on the bench. If a judge then seeks a new term, he or she has to stand for election by the people.

When judges are elected, the general public has the responsibility to research and choose judges wisely. In those cases, it falls to voters to identify who they think has the experience, knowledge, and character necessary to make a good judge.

The election systems differ. Some elections are nonpartisan, as in Wisconsin. This means that candidates do not identify the political party to which they belong. In other states, elections are partisan. In a partisan election, a candidate's political party is made known to voters.

The terms of office for judges also vary. Among the high-level trial judges, the term is usually from six to eight years. Some terms are as short as 4 years, and others are as long as 10 years.

Choosing Judges for Appellate Courts

In the appellate courts, about half of the states elect judges. In the other half, the governor chooses judges. In some of those states, the governor's appointments must be confirmed by the state legislature or another governmental body.

In 41 states, justices on the state supreme courts have terms lasting from 6 to 10 years. The rest have terms that are longer or shorter. Some states give longer terms to the chief justice than to the other justices on the supreme court. The chief justice is the head of the court. In other states, such as Missouri, all the justices on the court take turns serving as chief justice for two or three years each.

Once their term is done, judges have to be approved in some way to continue to serve on the bench. In 41 states, voters make this decision. Judges must stand in an election where people vote to keep them on the court or not. In the other states, either the governor or the state legislature decides whether or not to retain, or keep, the judges.

Federal judges have lifetime appointments. That means they stay on the bench until they retire or die. That is not the case for many state judges. About half of the states require that judges retire after they have reached a certain age. In most of these states, the retirement age ranges from 70 to 75. Other states do not require judges to retire at any particular age.

Like federal judges, state judges can be removed from office by impeachment. However, this process can take a long time. Most states also have special boards that have the authority to look into complaints about judges.

Judges who are elected often use campaign signs, just like other candidates for state offices.

Rogelio Solis/AP Images

Selection of State Supreme Court Justices

As this map shows, there are many ways that state supreme court justices are chosen for their first term. Methods are often different for deciding whether to allow a justice another term on the court.

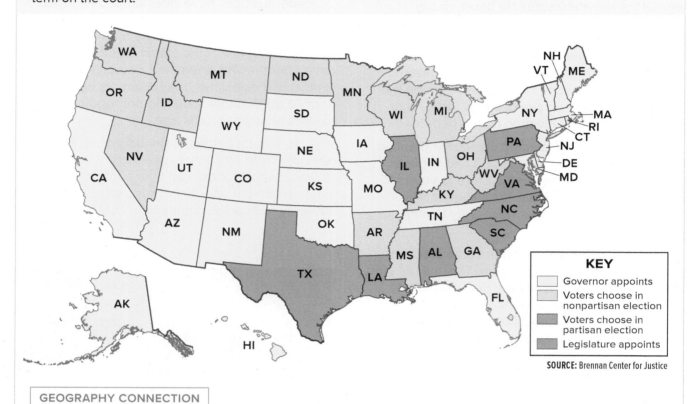

KEY

- Governor appoints
- Voters choose in nonpartisan election
- Voters choose in partisan election
- Legislature appoints

SOURCE: Brennan Center for Justice

GEOGRAPHY CONNECTION

1. **Patterns and Movement** What is the most popular method of selection?
2. **Patterns and Movement** What type of election is more common, partisan or nonpartisan?

If the board finds that a judge has acted improperly, it can make a recommendation to the state supreme court. The court has the power to **suspend** the judge while the matter is being investigated or to remove the judge from office.

✓ **CHECK FOR UNDERSTANDING**

Identifying In which type of court are the judges selected by many different methods?

suspend to stop an employee from working for a certain amount of time

LESSON ACTIVITIES

1. **Informative/Explanatory Writing** What is the general structure of a state court system? Describe the two broad levels of courts, the types of courts, and the kind of cases heard in each of those courts.

2. **Collaborating** Work with a partner to learn more about the types of cases heard in a lower-level trial court. Do research online to learn more about the types of cases these courts hear. Summarize your findings on a poster that you share with the class.

06

Analyzing Sources: Lawmaking in the Federal System

? COMPELLING QUESTION

How do laws on one issue vary at different levels of government?

Plan Your Inquiry

DEVELOPING QUESTIONS

Think about some of the different laws enacted by Congress, by your state legislature, and by local bodies in your county, town, or city. Consider the issues these laws deal with and the ways in which they relate or overlap. Then read the Compelling Question for this lesson. What questions can you ask to help you answer this Compelling Question? Create a graphic organizer like the one below. Write these Supporting Questions in your graphic organizer.

Supporting Questions	Primary or Secondary Source	What this source tells me about laws at a certain level of government	Questions the source leaves unanswered
	A		
	B		
	C		
	D		

ANALYZING SOURCES

Next, examine the sources in this lesson. Analyze each source by answering the questions that follow it. How does each source help you answer each Supporting Question you created? What questions do you still have? Write these in your graphic organizer.

After you analyze the sources, you will:
- use the evidence from the sources,
- communicate your conclusions,
- and take informed action.

Background Information

The United States has a federal system of government—meaning that different levels of government can share power but have their own powers. The Constitution delegates specific powers to the federal government and to the states. Federal laws apply to the whole nation. State and local laws apply to the people in their state or local jurisdiction. Many state and local issues are distinct from federal issues, such as laws for forming businesses and traffic laws. Some state and local issues do overlap with federal concerns. When that is the case, local and state law must be careful not to conflict with federal laws, including the Constitution.

Consider the sale and use of fireworks. Many people enjoy watching these displays, but fireworks can be dangerous. Each level of government enacts different laws to address issues such as public safety and the sale of fireworks.

Laws on a single issue can vary from one state to the next. Some states permit the sale of fireworks to consumers, while some states do not.

Federal Regulation of Fireworks

The Bureau of Alcohol, Tobacco, Firearms, and Explosives regulates only display fireworks. Federal departments and agencies publish their regulations so that individuals and businesses can know what they are—and be sure to follow them.

PRIMARY SOURCE: WEB ARTICLE

❝ **Display fireworks** are the large fireworks used in shows, generally under the supervision of a trained **pyrotechnician**. The regulations . . . require that any person engaging in the business of importing, manufacturing, dealing in, or otherwise receiving display fireworks must first obtain a Federal explosives license or permit from ATF for the specific activity.

Consumer fireworks are the small fireworks usually sold at stands around the Fourth of July holiday. ATF does not regulate the importation, distribution, or storage of completed consumer fireworks, but other federal, state, and local agencies do regulate these items to a varying degree. ❞

— "Fireworks Safety and Security," Bureau of Alcohol, Tobacco, Firearms, and Explosives

pyrotechnician person who specializes in the manufacture or use of fireworks

EXAMINE THE SOURCE

1. **Contrasting** How do the types of fireworks regulated differ? Why might ATF regulate one but not the other?

2. **Making Inferences** What requirements does ATF impose on the use of display fireworks? Why do you think that is?

Varying Laws

The Consumer Product Safety Commission (CPSC), a federal agency, determines which fireworks are safe for consumer use. State and local governments may add further restrictions.

EXAMINE THE SOURCE

1. **Analyzing Data** Which three colors indicate the most restrictive laws?

2. **Analyzing Maps** Why might officials in some states have a difficult time enforcing more restrictive laws?

SECONDARY SOURCE: MAP

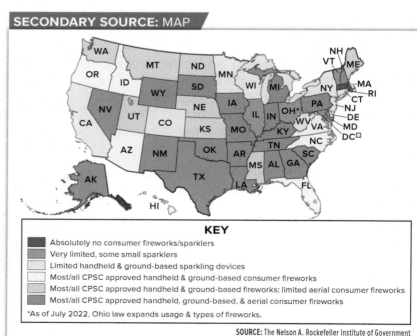

KEY

- Absolutely no consumer fireworks/sparklers
- Very limited, some small sparklers
- Limited handheld & ground-based sparkling devices
- Most/all CPSC approved handheld & ground-based consumer fireworks
- Most/all CPSC approved handheld & ground-based fireworks; limited aerial consumer fireworks
- Most/all CPSC approved handheld, ground-based, & aerial consumer fireworks

*As of July 2022, Ohio law expands usage & types of fireworks.

SOURCE: The Nelson A. Rockefeller Institute of Government

TEXT: Bureau of Alcohol, Tobacco, Firearms and Explosives. "Fireworks Safety and Security." June 14, 2021. https://www.atf.gov/explosives/fireworks-safety-and-security

Local Variations from State Law

States give some lawmaking powers to local governments. They also permit local government to "opt out" of some state programs and provisions. Proponents of local opt-out laws argue that having choice gives more control to local officials and citizens. Beginning in July 2022, the state of Ohio will allow adults to buy and set off fireworks on certain holidays. However, the new law (House Bill 172) allows for local communities to opt out, which University Heights, Ohio, is considering.

SECONDARY SOURCE: ARTICLE

66 As for University Heights, Vice Mayor Michele Weiss said, 'I just feel we're really a very **dense** city . . . , and it would be a real danger to residents if we allowed this.'

. . . [A] resident suggested that the city also ask its neighboring cities to join in such a ban.

'I like the idea that we should speak to other surrounding cities since we're so close to them,' Weiss said. 'You drive a minute in five directions (from University Heights) and you're in different cities.'

University Heights Fire Chief Robert Perko believes the city proposal is a good one. Perko said fireworks can be very dangerous when not handled by professionals. He said if HB 172 were permitted in the city, it would only serve to enhance (increase) the danger. . . .

Police Chief Dustin Rogers said that there has been an **uptick** in the number of fireworks-related complaints police have received in recent years. There were 20 such complaints in 2017, 14 in 2018 and 24 in 2019. The numbers increased to 58 in 2020 and 54 so far this year [2021].

Said Weiss, 'We're hopefully going to opt out (of HB 172) and create legislation that would be good for our city, in conjunction with updating some part of our zoning code, whichever way the law director . . . thinks it should be **fashioned**, to ensure that (high-powered) fireworks are not sold (in University Heights).' 99

— Jeff Piorkowski, "University Heights puts the fizzle on private, unregulated fireworks displays," Cleveland.com, November 17, 2021

dense crowded, with little space
uptick upward trend
fashion form or change

EXAMINE THE SOURCE

1. **Explaining** Why are officials in University Heights hoping to opt out of the new state fireworks law?

2. **Making Connections** If the communities around University Heights do not opt out of the fireworks law, what could happen?

Select State Laws

Most states allow the sale of some consumer-grade fireworks. Only a few prohibit the sale of all or most fireworks, including sparklers. Differences among the types of fireworks that are allowed vary greatly. Consumers must pay close attention to their state's regulations. Many people criticize the different state laws because people can easily cross state borders to obtain fireworks.

non-aerial not designed for use in the air

pyrotechnic relating to combustible substance

SECONDARY SOURCE: STATE LAWS

Select States' Fireworks Laws, 2021

State	Fireworks Permitted	Fireworks Prohibited	Age to Purchase
Connecticut	Hand-held and ground based sparkling devices that are non-explosive and **non-aerial**, and do not contain more than 100 grams of pyrotechnic composition per item.	All other consumer fireworks including multiple- tube sparkling devices that exceed 100 grams of total **pyrotechnic** composition. Novelty items are illegal.	16
Massachusetts	None	Firecrackers, torpedoes, skyrockets, flares, candles, bombs, sparklers, wheels, colored fire, fountains, mines, and serpents.	Does not apply
New York	Ground-based or handheld sparkling devices including cylindrical fountains, cone fountains, and wood sparklers/dipped sticks; party poppers, snappers.	Aerial consumer fireworks, firecrackers and chasers, skyrockets, roman candles, bombs, and metal wire sparklers.	18

Source: https://worldpopulationreview.com/state-rankings/fireworks-laws-by-state

---

EXAMINE THE SOURCE

1. **Synthesizing** Refer back to the map in Source B. Why might some people in Massachusetts be concerned about the laws in Connecticut?

2. **Contrasting** What other conditions regarding the sale of fireworks, besides the type, varies among the states listed?

Complete Your Inquiry

EVALUATE SOURCES AND USE EVIDENCE

Refer back to the Compelling Question and the Supporting Questions you developed at the beginning of the lesson.

1. **Drawing Conclusions** How do different state and local fireworks laws reflect economic interests?

2. **Making Connections** How do debates over the sale and use of consumer fireworks reveal a broader tension between individual freedoms and the common good, or general welfare?

3. **Gathering Sources** Which sources helped you answer the Supporting Questions and the Compelling Question? Which sources, if any, challenged what you thought you knew when you first created your Supporting Questions? What information do you still need in order to answer your questions? What other viewpoints would you like to investigate? Where would you find that information?

4. **Evaluating Sources** Identify the sources that helped answer your Supporting Questions. How reliable are the sources? How would you verify the reliability of the sources?

COMMUNICATE CONCLUSIONS

5. **Collaborating** In a group, discuss your Supporting Questions and write responses to each student's questions. Then take turns sharing your questions and answers. Choose a question from each group member that best helps answer the Compelling Question. Present those answers to the class.

TAKE INFORMED ACTION

Preparing a Guide to Government Laws In a group, select a teacher-approved issue that involves local, state, and federal laws. Investigate appropriate government and media websites to learn what laws at each level of government affect that issue. Are there current challenges to those laws or proposed laws? Use your research to make a mock website or a flyer to explain the differences in laws governing your issue.

How City Governments Are Created

READING STRATEGY

Integrating Knowledge and Ideas As you read about local governments, take notes on their forms in a chart such as this one.

Level of Local Government	Forms of Government
City or Municipal	
County	
Town, Township, Village	

GUIDING QUESTION

How are local governments created, funded, and organized?

The people of the United States live in many types of communities. About 82 percent of them live in cities or urban areas. These cities are run by local governments. Other people live in more rural areas where the local government may be a village, town, or county. In Louisiana, the equivalent of a county is called a "parish," and in Alaska, it is called a "borough." Local governments build the schools and sidewalks in a neighborhood. They are also responsible for providing police and fire departments to protect local communities.

Paying for Local Government

Local governments get the power to provide services from the state. State constitutions usually describe the powers and duties of local governments.

Higher levels of government pay for some of the services provided by local government. Grants from the state and federal governments make up about 35 percent of local governments' income. Local governments may also collect taxes. Across the United States, more than 30 percent of the money for local government comes from taxes on land and buildings. Other taxes, such as sales taxes and income taxes, make up about 10 percent of local budgets. The rest comes from fees for things such as parking on local streets and dog licenses and fines for traffic and other violations of local laws.

City governments make important decisions that affect local residents. For example, these governments usually have a planning department that decides which new construction projects should be allowed.

Becoming a City

A settled area usually becomes a town or city once it becomes **incorporated**. This means it is a local area with an organized government that provides services to residents. Such an area is officially called a *municipality*. Incorporation can happen in two ways. The people of an area can ask the state legislature for a **city charter**, which is like a constitution. The state grants the charter if the area meets certain standards, such as having the minimum number of people that meets state law. The charter describes the type of government the city will have. The charter also outlines the structure and powers of the officials in that government.

The second way to get incorporated is in those states that allow for home rule. This means that cities can write their own charters. Home rule allows cities to act with less interference from the state. Still, state laws do limit city governments' freedom of action. Just as states cannot pass laws that conflict with the U.S. Constitution, local governments cannot make laws that conflict with the state constitution.

✓ **CHECK FOR UNDERSTANDING**

Explaining What kinds of services do local governments provide?

incorporate to receive a state charter officially recognizing the government of a locality

city charter a document granting power to a local government

The people of a city can attend city council meetings, such as this one in Portland, Maine.

Analyzing Visuals Based on the photograph, how does the city council shown here allow for participation by the public?

Forms of City Government

GUIDING QUESTION

How do different forms of city government operate?

The governments of most cities in the United States fall into one of three categories: the mayor-council form, the council-manager form, and the commission form. Today, the mayor-council form of government is used by the largest American cities. The council-manager form is the second most popular form of city government and is used by about half of U.S. cities with populations over 100,000 people.

Council Forms

The mayor-council form of local government has a separation of powers, just as state and federal governments do. The elected mayor holds executive power, similar to a governor or the president. He or she oversees the running of various city departments and sometimes appoints people to head them. The city council is also elected and holds legislative power, like the state legislature or U.S. Congress. The city council passes city laws, which are usually called **ordinances**. The council also approves the city's budget.

Qualifications for mayor and council members vary across the country. The minimum age for most mayoral candidates is usually between 18 and 25 years. In most cities, mayoral candidates must also live in the city for a certain amount of time before and after the election. They serve terms of two or four years.

Most city councils have fewer than 10 members who usually serve four-year terms. Sometimes cities are divided into voting districts called *wards*, with the people in each ward electing someone to represent them on the city council. In other cities, council members are elected at-large. In an **at-large election**, council members are elected by voters in the entire city rather than in individual wards. Some cities mix these two systems, with some members chosen by wards and some elected at-large.

City council meetings are generally open to the public. This allows the people to hear,

ordinance a law, usually of a local government

at-large election an election for an area as a whole, such as an entire city

Forms of City Government

The two most common forms of city government are the mayor-council form and the council-manager form.

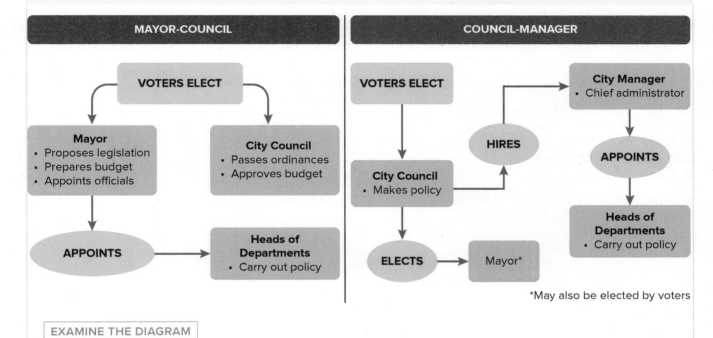

EXAMINE THE DIAGRAM

1. **Comparing** Who makes policy by passing laws in both forms of government?
2. **Making Generalizations** What different expectations do you think people living in a city would have of the council members they elect compared to the city manager who is appointed?

question, and comment on what their elected officials are discussing. Open meetings are an example of transparency of government institutions. *Transparency* refers to government processes that are not hidden from the public.

The council-manager form of government works differently in several ways. Council members in this form are elected, often through at-large elections. This local legislature then appoints a city manager. The city manager **administers** day-to-day affairs. City managers have careers working in city government and may move from one city to another when a local legislature hires them. For this job, cities typically hire people who have experience running a city or performing a similar job. Their work can include creating a budget and directing city departments. The city manager reports to the council, which has the power to dismiss the manager. In larger cities, a mayor with limited powers is also often elected by council members.

administer to manage

The Commission Form

The third form of city government is the commission form. In this form of government, the legislative and executive powers are combined. Very few cities use this form of government today.

In the commission form, the government is split into several separate departments, such as departments of health or police. The heads of these departments are called *commissioners* and they are elected by the city's voters. In their roles as department heads, commissioners have executive power. The commissioners also meet regularly as a group, called a *commission*, that passes laws and makes policy. One commissioner acts as chairperson and leads meetings, but the chair has no additional power.

One problem with the commission form of government is that there is no clear leader. As a result, local officials sometimes have difficulty setting and meeting goals. Commissioners might focus on their own department and not the city as a whole.

Some special districts are related to the management of water resources for a large area. This special district in Florida operates canals to assist with agriculture and oversees water supply and water quality for the area.

Most cities that used this form of government in the past have changed to one of the other two forms.

Other Units of Government

There are two other types of municipal governments. These are the special district and the metropolitan area.

A **special district** is a unit of government that is formed to handle a specific task. This government can include the areas of several towns or cities to manage the task for a large group of people affected by the same issue. A local school district is the most common example of a special district. A board or commission of elected or appointed members runs the district. Florida has more than 1,700 special districts that manage everything from healthcare units to controlling mosquitoes.

A metropolitan area is formed by a large city and its *suburbs*, or those communities near or around cities. A metropolitan area may also include smaller towns outside the suburbs but influenced by the city. These are very large regions—and are growing. Between 2010 and 2020, about 80 percent of metropolitan areas

grew in size and population. Growing metropolitan areas often face challenges. Traffic, pollution, and crime often increase. Conflicts may arise over how to use open land. These challenges can become worse if different governments try to address them separately. Therefore, communities in some metropolitan areas have decided to work together to face some of their challenges. They have created councils that bring together city and suburban officials. These councils make decisions that affect all the communities served by the council.

✓ CHECK FOR UNDERSTANDING

1. **Comparing** Explain how executive and legislative branches in local government are similar to those in state government.

2. **Making Connections** How are special districts and metropolitan areas alike?

County Government

GUIDING QUESTION

How is county government organized?

A **county** is another type of governed region. Counties are typically the largest unit into which

---

special district a unit of government that deals with a specific function, such as education, water supply, or transportation

county a type of government region that is normally the largest territorial and political subdivision of a state

the state is organized in terms of area and government authority. The U.S. Census Bureau recognizes more than 3,000 counties or similar divisions across the country. The first county in what is now the United States was formed in Virginia in 1634.

Connecticut and Rhode Island are the only states without counties. Texas has 254 counties. Delaware and Hawaii have only 3 each. Two states have a similar unit but use a different name. In Alaska, they are called *boroughs*. In Louisiana, they are known as *parishes*.

The size of county populations and the land area also varies. Some counties are very large. For example, more than 10 million people live in Los Angeles County, California. Loving County, Texas, however, has just over 60 residents.

County courthouses served as the center for county government services in the 1800s. Government records were stored at the courthouse, and trials took place there. The town that has the county courthouse is known as the *county* seat.

The Forms and Functions of County Government

County government has changed in recent decades. In some areas, cities now provide many services that counties once did.

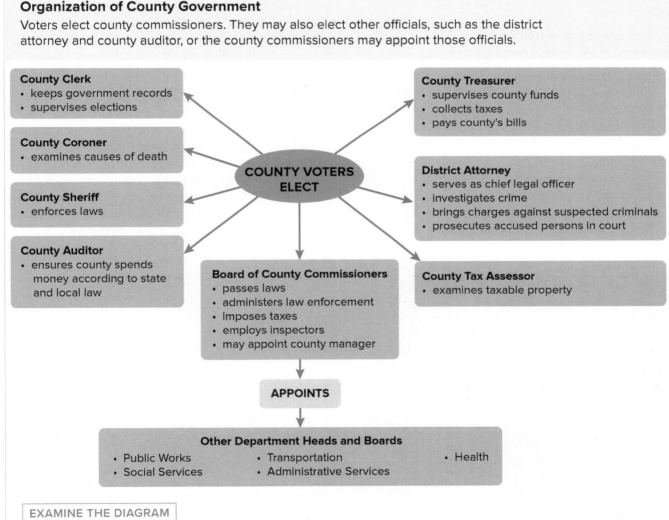

Organization of County Government

Voters elect county commissioners. They may also elect other officials, such as the district attorney and county auditor, or the county commissioners may appoint those officials.

County Clerk
- keeps government records
- supervises elections

County Coroner
- examines causes of death

County Sheriff
- enforces laws

County Auditor
- ensures county spends money according to state and local law

COUNTY VOTERS ELECT

County Treasurer
- supervises county funds
- collects taxes
- pays county's bills

District Attorney
- serves as chief legal officer
- investigates crime
- brings charges against suspected criminals
- prosecutes accused persons in court

Board of County Commissioners
- passes laws
- administers law enforcement
- imposes taxes
- employs inspectors
- may appoint county manager

County Tax Assessor
- examines taxable property

APPOINTS

Other Department Heads and Boards
- Public Works
- Social Services
- Transportation
- Administrative Services
- Health

EXAMINE THE DIAGRAM

1. **Identifying** Which officials have a role similar to the city council in a city government, and what is that role?

2. **Making Connections** Which official supervises the balance of power between the county government and state laws?

At the same time, many counties have taken on duties that city governments once handled. These duties range from providing sewer and water service to running mass transit systems and planning for new land use. State law can be strict in how much power is given to a county government. Generally, county governments decide on the county's budget, taxes, and land use.

Most counties are run by a board of elected officials called commissioners or supervisors. Typically, they have three to five members who serve four-year terms. Officials may or may not have previous government experience, and many hold other jobs outside the government. The board acts as the county's legislature and may also act as the executive. It passes ordinances, sets the county's budget for the year, and collects taxes.

The commission that runs a county's government can take one of three forms:

- **Strong commission:** In this form, the county board acts as both legislature and executive. Commissioners pass laws and carry them out. Other county officials, including department heads, help them carry out the functions of government.
- **Commission-manager:** In this form, the county board has only legislative power. Commissioners appoint a county manager. This job is similar to that of a city manager.

This manager carries out laws, appoints top officials, and manages county government.

- **Commission-elected executive:** The county board has only legislative power. Voters also elect a county executive, who has the same responsibilities as the county manager in the commission-manager form.

Sheriffs, Prosecutors, and More

Many other officials also play a role in county government. The number of officials needed to run county government has increased as counties have taken on more tasks.

Among these officials is the sheriff, or a county's chief officer for enforcing law. Sheriffs are elected officials who typically serve terms of two to four years. In Florida, the state constitution mandates that the state's 67 sheriffs serve four-year terms. The sheriff's department enforces court orders and runs the county jail. In some counties, the sheriff's department shares duties with one or more police departments.

Other county duties are handled by officials who may be appointed or elected. Bringing criminals to justice is the role of the district attorney (DA), called the *county prosecutor* in some counties. In most counties, the district attorney is elected by voters. The district attorney investigates crimes and brings charges against those suspected of breaking the law. The DA then works to prove in court that the accused persons are guilty.

A county sheriff responds to a crime scene with other local law enforcement officers and members of the U.S. Marshals Service.

The chart "Organization of County Government" describes other key county officials, including finance officers, the county clerk, and the coroner. These officials are often elected, but some counties appoint people to certain offices. Qualifications for these offices vary in terms of their work experience, time living in the county, and age.

✓ CHECK FOR UNDERSTANDING

Comparing How do the powers and responsibilities of county governments compare to those of state governments?

Towns, Townships, and Villages

GUIDING QUESTION
How are smaller local governments structured?

Counties are often divided into smaller political units that are smaller than cities. In New England, these are called **towns**. In the Midwest, they are called **townships**. The smallest unit of local government is villages. While all three receive their power to govern from the state, their relationship to county government can vary.

New England Town Meetings

Some New England towns are governed by town meetings. They are one of the oldest forms of democracy in the United States. Town meetings allow community members to speak out on local issues and take part in decision-making. In the original system, which started in the 1600s, citizens—rather than elected representatives—make the important decisions. This makes town meetings a form of direct democracy.

Town meetings are still important in some New England towns. Once a year, residents come to the meeting to discuss local ordinances, taxes, and budgets. The majority of registered voters who attend the meeting decide these issues during the meeting by voting. They determine how the town government will act in the year that follows. In between meetings, a group of officials called *selectmen* run the government, along with elected officials such as a treasurer.

town a political unit found in the New England states that is smaller than a city

township a subdivision of a county that has its own government

Voters in Stafford, Vermont, turn in their ballots at a town meeting. The citizens of Stafford and other New England towns have a long history of participation in local government.

However, governing some New England towns has become too complicated for direct democracy. In some of these towns, voters now elect what are known as town meeting representatives. These officials attend representative town meetings, voting on issues in the interest of those they represent. Other towns have replaced town meetings altogether with a town council that runs the local government.

Townships

Towns and township governments in New York, New Jersey, and Pennsylvania are similar to New England town governments. These local governments typically serve densely populated urban areas. This is different from the townships in states in the Midwest, such as Indiana, Kansas, Nebraska, and Ohio. Those governments provide services to more rural areas.

The use of the word *township* for a unit of government comes from another use of that word. As the United States expanded westward, the federal government **surveyed** the new land. Land was then organized into measured blocks known as *congressional townships,* or *survey townships.* When people settled in these areas, they used the name *township* for their local governments.

Many of these townships have borders that follow the original survey lines. In most townships, voters elect a small number of officials. They serve in a body known as a township committee, board of supervisors, or board of trustees.

survey to measure and examine

AP Images

In many Midwest townships, some roads are still laid out along the original township survey lines.

It has the power to make laws. It usually holds regular meetings that citizens may attend. That gives the people of the township a voice in their government.

Townships have become less important as cities and counties have taken over many township duties. Counties and townships may work together to provide local services.

Village Government

The **village** is the smallest unit of local government. Villages almost always lie within the borders of townships or counties, whose governments often handle their needs. However, sometimes a community may wish to govern itself more directly to have more control over issues that affect it. If the state grants permission, the community may form a village government.

The government of most villages is made up of a small board of elected trustees. This board can collect taxes and fund programs that benefit the community. This may include taking care of streets and schools. Residents of the village might also elect an experienced executive to help with administration. That official may be called *chief burgess* or *mayor*.

Becoming a village has many benefits for the people who live there. Local services may improve, and the community may become more appealing to new residents and businesses. However, having these benefits might require the residents of the village to pay higher taxes to support their local government and the services it provides.

✓ **CHECK FOR UNDERSTANDING**

1. **Describing** How have New England town governments changed over time?
2. **Identifying** Why do some communities choose to become villages?

LESSON ACTIVITIES

1. **Informative/Explanatory Writing** Write an essay that explains the structure of your local government. Focus on either your municipal or county government. Name the form and explain the structure. Also, identify your local government's executive and legislative leaders, when they were elected, and their terms of office. Research online to find the information you need and cite your sources.

2. **Analyzing Information** With a partner, discuss what you have learned about the lawmaking process at the local level. Then use prior knowledge and research to compare this process to the way laws are made at the state and national levels. Record your findings in a two-column chart that shows similarities and differences.

village the smallest unit of local government

C410

Alex Potemkin/Getty Images

How a Community Handles Issues

Analyzing Key Ideas and Details As you read, complete a graphic organizer such as the one shown to identify things that community leaders consider when making public policy decisions.

GUIDING QUESTION

How does public policy work to serve the needs of the community?

Community services are part of people's everyday lives. Every time we use water, attend school, visit a library, walk through a park, or drive on a road, we are using the services that communities provide to us.

Offering those services takes resources such as money and time. It also requires the efforts of responsible people and smart planning. Communities have to address a range of needs. How will they provide fire and emergency services? How will they dispose of garbage? Where will they get enough clean water?

People address some of these issues on their own. For instance, an individual might react to save or aid others in an emergency, and a family can purchase clean water from a company. Citizens also give their governments some of the responsibility to answer these questions. As citizens, we all have the power to influence our government. Does that seem like an impossible task for one person? Delaney Reynolds of Miami, Florida, did not think so. She has campaigned to help save the environment since she was 16. In 2017 she worked with the mayor of South Miami to draft a law called the Solar Mandate. This law requires residents who buy new homes or expand older homes to install solar panels to collect solar power for their energy needs.

Miami resident Delaney Reynolds is an example of how one person can influence public policy. Here she speaks about a lawsuit she and other young people filed against the Miami-Dade County government over its policies related to environmental change.

Public policy decisions are involved in changing or expanding an airport, such as the construction of a new terminal for Atlanta's main airport.

Analyzing Visuals How do the details of this photograph show the difficulty of adding to a human-made structure that already exists, such as an airport?

Solar panels create renewable energy without creating air pollution. It was the first such law to be passed in Florida.

Delaney Reynolds worked to change public policy. A public policy is the set of decisions and actions a government takes to solve problems in the community. All organizations, including governments and businesses, have policies. Most businesses, for example, set policies for how they want their workers to interact with customers.

In the same way, governments have a set of rules they follow when addressing problems or resolving issues in a community. A government's policies may involve the creation of laws and regulations. Government policies also involve decisions on spending money and the work of government employees. These policies should be designed to improve people's lives and safety. Public policy requires everyone to wear a seatbelt when riding in a car. Some policies encourage people to wear a helmet when riding a bicycle. Public policy determines what students are taught in school. Everyone is affected by the public policies created by federal, state, and local governments.

Public policy may address a specific issue. For example, the decision to build or not build a particular road or bridge is a public policy

decision. Public policy also deals with broader issues, such as health care and the environment.

Public Policy Origins

Ideas for public policy can come from many different places. Some begin with people inside the government. Ideas may be suggested by political parties, interest groups, or the media. Private citizens may contribute policy ideas, especially at the local level. As the example of Delaney Reynolds shows, even one person can have a direct effect on government policies.

Public policy works best when community members are active participants in the process. Most local governments allow the public to provide their views about the needs of their communities. Some officials do not wait for the public to come to them. Instead, they reach out to the public in a number of ways. They may visit gathering places in the community, such as restaurants, or talk with people at local fairs and festivals. They may send out surveys or call people at home to hear their views.

Addressing Local Problems

Every citizen who votes—whether for a candidate or on a public policy issue—influences the government. For that reason, voting is a responsibility that should be exercised. There can be limits to the effectiveness of voting, however. A citizen may be unhappy with an officeholder but an election in which the politician could be voted out of office may be far off. Also, it can be difficult and time-consuming to connect elections to a particular issue that may matter a lot to a voter. In addition, officeholders have to work on many issues at the same time. This can result in some issues getting less attention than some of the people they represent would like.

Sometimes an appeal to a government agency is a more effective way to resolve a problem. Government agencies take charge of specific parts of public policy. These are examples of federal agencies:

- The Environmental Protection Agency (EPA) focuses on protecting human health and the environment.
- The Department of Education works to promote student achievement by providing all children equal access to quality instruction.
- The Department of Commerce works to promote economic growth and opportunity.

Some government agencies have federal, state, and local offices. Each office addresses problems on its level. Other government agencies operate on the federal level but not locally. For example, the Department of Education enforces educational laws concerning privacy and civil rights, collects data on education, and coordinates federal assistance, such as student loans for

college students. The Department of Education does not create schools or colleges. Local-level authorities such as trustees and school boards shape education policy for their local communities.

Each public agency deals with certain areas of policy. Citizens can contact any public agency for help with issues in its area. A parent or teacher with a question about state education standards can contact their state's department of education. A question about school district policies would not be addressed to the state. The local school board would be the right group to contact about that issue.

✓ **CHECK FOR UNDERSTANDING**

1. **Analyzing** How does public policy serve the needs of the community?

2. **Identifying** Suppose you thought that a separate lane should be added for bicycle riders on major streets in your city. To whom would you talk: your representative in the U.S. House, someone in the state's Department of Transportation, or a city council member? Explain your answer.

Planning for the Future

GUIDING QUESTION

How do community leaders make public policy decisions?

Have you ever had to decide between two things you wanted to do? What did you have to think about before making a choice? You may have thought about the time each activity would take.

Many communities hold town hall–style meetings, such as this one in Hamtramck, Michigan, where citizens meet with local officeholders to discuss and learn about public policy.

You may have considered cost. In the same way, communities have to choose among actions to take. Community leaders make decisions that affect many people. Therefore, they have to make those decisions carefully.

People who make public policy should first think about the problem or issue they are trying to address. Why is it a problem? What is the best way to solve the problem or meet a need? They must also think about the future. They should think about what is most likely to happen as a result of their decisions. Then they can plan for these outcomes. Many local governments have groups called planning commissions to do this work. A **planning commission** studies and gives advice about future needs. Its goal is to prepare for and guide the community's future growth.

A planning commission may include many different people. Some may be business or community leaders. Others may be community members who have a particular interest in the future of their community. A planning commission may also invite **professionals**, people who have specialized education and skills, to advise its members. For instance, engineers and traffic experts may bring their skills to help design strategies for the community's infrastructure.

planning commission an advising group to a community

professional a worker with specialized education and skills

Short-Term and Long-Term Plans

Planning commissions are like other parts of local governments. They make both short-term and long-term plans. A **short-term plan** is a government policy that is meant to be done over the next few years. For example, agreeing to let a developer build an apartment building is a short-term plan. A **long-term plan** is meant to serve as a guide for the next 10 to 50 years. To make a long-term plan, a planning commission must make informed guesses about what a community will need in the future.

Suppose more people are moving into a community. This population growth may continue into the future. Having more people puts pressure on local resources. How will additional people affect the town's infrastructure—its roads, bridges, water, trash removal, and sewer systems?

Think about the impact of population growth on the local schools. As more people move to the community, will there be room for all the new children in the schools? Should the town build new additions on the schools? Or should it build a new school? Where will the town leaders get the money to implement the solution they choose?

short-term plan a government policy carried out over the course of a few years

long-term plan a government plan for policy that can span 10 to 50 years

Planning commissions seek comments and contributions from members of the community when they are planning for a city's future needs.

Scott Varley/Digital First Media/Torrance Daily Breeze/Getty Images

When a city's population increases, roads often become congested. Improved roadways are just one example of infrastructure improvements that communities need as they grow.

Priorities and Resources

To answer these questions, a community should consider priorities and resources. Priorities are the goals a community thinks are most important or urgent. A community has to decide what it values most in order to set its priorities. Suppose a developer wants to build a new high-rise office tower in town. The structure will bring new jobs, but it will also increase traffic. The community must decide: Is it more important to have a thriving business center or a peaceful place to live?

Communities are made of many people, who probably do not agree about everything. Therefore, communities need processes for making decisions. Sometimes that means that elected officials actually make decisions while citizens can express their opinions. In other cases, a number of citizens may actually make the decision to address an issue on their own. For example, if the problem is a daily traffic jam at a certain time of rush hour, the city government could try to solve it by providing more buses so that fewer people drive their own cars. Or many people could try to solve the problem by changing the time they drive home from work. Sometimes people disagree about whether a specific problem should be addressed by the government or not.

Decision-makers must begin by determining their goals, the priorities that are most important to a community's residents. Most communities'

priorities include public health, safety, education, and infrastructure. A community must identify its goals and rank them in order of importance. For example, suppose a town wants to attract new businesses, improve services, preserve open spaces, and improve its schools. The town government cannot do everything all at once, and some of these goals may not work together, so it begins by ranking these goals from most to least important. Citizens may disagree with the ranking and express their opinions.

They might also consider whether accomplishing one goal first could help them achieve other goals more quickly. For example, suppose a local government gets a large part of its revenue from sales taxes. It may decide that its top goal is to attract new businesses. New businesses give people jobs and spending money. When people have more money, they shop more. That means the government would gain more revenue from sales taxes. That revenue would allow town leaders to pursue their other goals. They could use some of that money to improve services or to maintain parks and playgrounds.

Once a community sets its priorities, it must identify its resources and decide how to use them. **Resources** are the money, people, and materials a community can use to reach its goals.

---

resource the money, people, or materials a community can use to reach its goals

Planners make models and drawings to present their ideas to the public for review and discussion.

Analyzing Visuals Why do you think planners would use models and drawings when they present their plans to the public?

Suppose, for example, that the town decides it wants to improve mass transit. How much money is needed to buy new buses? How much will it cost every year to pay bus drivers and to keep the buses running? The town will need to answer these questions. Then it will need to find ways to get the money required to meet those costs.

After priorities are set and resources are identified, a planning commission may be called upon to make specific decisions. The commission usually records these decisions in a **master plan**. This plan states a set of goals. It also explains the steps the government will take to meet those goals. The plan may also explain how the government will have to adapt to meet changing needs over time. If the local government accepts the plan, it becomes public policy. The government then is responsible for carrying out that policy.

✓ **CHECK FOR UNDERSTANDING**

1. **Speculating** What might be the advantage for a planning commission to create both short-term plans and long-term plans?
2. **Explaining** How could government leaders, business leaders, citizens, and professionals each contribute to the work of a planning commission?

LESSON ACTIVITIES

1. **Informative/Explanatory Writing** Suppose that you are a member of a planning commission creating a master plan for a city park. You want the park to provide enjoyment for those who visit, so there should be things for those visitors to do. You also want to ensure that the park retains its natural beauty. Describe in one or two paragraphs how those two goals could best be balanced. Compare your ideas with those of your classmates.

2. **Collaborating** Work with two classmates to research a recent or current issue of public policy in your city, town, or area. Create a written plan that:

   • clearly states the issue and its impact.

   • identifies a change in public policy that might resolve the issue.

   • describes a plan for bringing about that change in public policy.

   Your plan should specify which government agency, and at which level, should be contacted in an attempt to bring about change.

master plan a plan that states a set of goals and explains how the government will carry them out to meet changing needs over time

09

Analyzing Sources: Local Public Policy

? COMPELLING QUESTION

How do communities solve problems?

Plan Your Inquiry

Think about the public goods and services provided by local government as well as challenges faced by your community and others. Then read the Compelling Question for this lesson. What questions can you ask to help you answer this Compelling Question? Create a graphic organizer like the one below. Write these Supporting Questions in your graphic organizer.

Supporting Questions	Primary or Secondary Source	What this source tells me about the ways communities solve problems	Questions the source leaves unanswered
	A		
	B		
	C		
	D		
	E		

Next, examine the sources in this lesson. Analyze each source by answering the questions that follow it. How does each source help you answer each Supporting Question you created? What questions do you still have? Write these in your graphic organizer.

After you analyze the sources, you will:
- use the evidence from the sources,
- communicate your conclusions,
- and take informed action.

Background Information

The United States has thousands of rural and urban communities. They cover different areas, have populations of different sizes, and have different mixes of businesses and housing. These communities face many similar challenges, such as maintaining roads and bridges or building and running schools. They also have unique challenges, such as confronting wildfires, tornadoes, hurricanes, or blizzards.

These local governments provide the most direct services to people, such as fire and police protection, public libraries and schools, and waste management. They establish traffic laws that keep people safe and zoning laws that say how land in the community can be used. They also provide the most direct response in addressing other issues that arise in their communities.

Local governments meet the needs of their communities by making public policy. Public policy is how governments solve problems. Many people work in local government to help shape and carry out that policy. Many others participate by voting, calling and writing letters to officials, meeting with local officials, and attending meetings. There they make their voices heard—and contribute their ideas.

» Local governments typically provide fire departments that can be staffed by professionals or volunteers.

Art Phaneuf/Alamy Stock Photo

City Ordinance for Low-Income Housing

One issue that many towns and cities face is ensuring that people can find affordable housing. Market prices based on supply and demand often determine rents. This can make housing in some areas too expensive for people with limited income. Local governments must balance the needs of property owners, who earn money from rentals, with those of people who require homes. Some governments pay landlords to lower the rent for low-income persons. This is called subsidized housing. This newspaper article discusses the situation in an Ohio city.

PRIMARY SOURCE: ARTICLE

> 66 The **ordinance** approved by Council . . . is expected to affect thousands of rental units in the capitol city, opening up many neighborhoods that were previously off-limits. . . .
>
> A landlord found guilty of refusing to rent based on [the renter's] source of income would be guilty of a first-degree misdemeanor, punishable by up to 180 days in jail and a $1,000 fine, according to the city's website.
>
> The ordinance prohibits landlords from refusing to rent or making any distinctions or restrictions in the 'price, terms, conditions, fees, or privileges' based on the renter's sources of income. Landlords can't represent to a person that a dwelling is not available for inspection or rental if it in fact is, and if an operator requires that a prospective [possible] or current tenant must meet a certain threshold [beginning] level of income, any sources of income in the form of a rent **voucher** or subsidy [grant] must be included in the calculation. . . .
>
> Federal 'fair market rent' regulations limit a voucher user to units with rent under a calculated limit, often leading [voucher] holders to reside in impoverished [poor] neighborhoods. But finding a landlord that will accept a voucher 'can also be very difficult,' according to the American Civil Liberties Union of Ohio.
>
> 'Countless advertisements on Craigslist and in newspapers boldly declare 'No **Section 8.**' The tenant could pass an onslaught [large amount] of background and credit checks and still be denied simply based on their source of payment,' according to the ACLU website. 99

— Bill Bush, "Columbus Landlords could face jail if they deny Section 8 tenants a shot at housing," *The Columbus Dispatch,* March 9, 2021

---

ordinance a rule or law
voucher a paper that can be used as credit to pay for food or other goods

Section 8 government program for housing assistance to low-income families, the elderly, and the disabled

---

EXAMINE THE SOURCE

1. **Explaining** How does the city of Columbus try to ensure people can find affordable housing?
2. **Identifying** What problem does the author say people had faced in using Section 8 vouchers before the ordinance was passed?

Nonprofit Developer Approach to Low-Income Housing

Governments also work with nonprofit organizations to provide affordable housing. Nonprofits might operate their own housing units and accept housing vouchers that lower the total cost. Other nonprofits might receive grants or earn tax deductions to build units that they then rent for less money to low-income people. Homeport is a nonprofit organization that builds and renovates houses and other rental units in Columbus, Ohio, for people with low to moderate incomes. They rely on tax breaks and private donations and investment to fund their work.

PRIMARY SOURCE: INTERVIEW

❝ [T]he two primary **strategic** priorities of ours are number one, being able to . . . develop affordable housing, and to attempt to keep up with the market. . . . [S]econdly, and we feel very strongly about this, and it is . . . an equal strategic priority. And that is we have a laser focus on the clients that we serve. . . . [T]hey're living paycheck to paycheck, they do run into issues. . . .

So we spent a lot of time working with them on making sure number one, that the properties are in great shape, they're a great place to live, we'd all you know, be proud to live there.

Number two, we want to keep them housed. . . . [W]e help them not only through monetary means, but we also provide financial education services. . . . [A]n individual needs their car for work, the car breaks down, it's a large expense. And they literally make a decision to say, Do I pay for my car so I can get [to] work? Or do I pay the rent? And, and it's a very logical question. . . . [W]e would step in and help people that way, not only just with money, but then we would also want to . . . have them engaged in our financial education classes. So they're better prepared the next time if that happens. . . .

[T]he third element of that resident services would be linkages [connections] to services. . . . [W]e have **social workers** on our staff, who work directly with our individuals, with our clients, our residents, understand what the issue is, get them to the place the best place for them, and then follow back around with them to make sure they're being taken care of. ❞

— Bruce Luecke, Homeport President and CEO, Interview on Confluence Cast, November 2021

strategic skillfully planned

social worker a professional who helps others live and function to the best of their ability in their situations

---

EXAMINE THE SOURCE

1. **Summarizing** What three services does this nonprofit developer provide low- and moderate-income people?

2. **Inferring** How does a program like Homeport represent a community effort at problem-solving?

Privatizing Waste Hauling

Beginning in the late 1800s, local governments took on the responsibility of providing public sanitation in their communities. This has meant maintaining some manner of regular solid waste, or trash, removal and disposal. In recent years, however, waste management has grown more complex as populations have shifted and grown and as new rules for handling different kinds of waste have been issued. For example, many communities now offer recycling services. This article explores some related issues.

PRIMARY SOURCE: ARTICLE

" 'To be sure, waste management and pickup has become more and more costly, and complex, over the last two decades,' [government affairs and environmental attorney John] Fumero said. 'Residences and businesses generate increasingly diverse [varying] quantities and types of waste, which results in a wider variety of waste collection requirements and needs. Many municipalities have found they are able to respond to these needs in a more fiscally [financially] prudent [careful] and efficient manner through **outsourcing** waste collection.'

Indeed, the key **instigators** behind municipalities making the move to **privatize** waste pickup services vary, but the primary driving factor is cost. . . .

Kristin Kinder, waste manager at Ecova, said . . . the industry is seeing a few different models emerging. For example, some cities run their own infrastructure for hauling waste, some locations allow residents and businesses to contract with any waste hauler they prefer, and some cities contract with a professional hauling company or companies to collect all waste for them. . . .

Geoff Aardsma, vice president of client services at Enevo, a provider of waste and recycling services . . . said the main drawback of outsourcing waste collection to private hauling companies for the municipalities is that they lose some control. . . .

In addition to getting more value for the cost of waste collection through privatization, municipalities also benefit from a limited risk and cost control for significant expenditures [costs], such as maintenance for an aging **fleet**. 'Also, in facing the driver shortage of today's waste industry, cities have access to more consistency with personnel when outsourcing their collection services,' Aardsma said. "

— Maura Keller, "Privatization of Waste Hauling Expands Nationwide," *American Recycler News,* January 2018

outsource to hire an outside company to provide a service

instigator factor that causes a change

privatize to change from public to private control

fleet group of vehicles

EXAMINE THE SOURCE

1. **Explaining** What community problem does the source address? Why is it a potential problem for local government?

2. **Describing** What solution to this problem does the source describe? What are the benefits and drawbacks associated with that solution?

Keller, Maura. "Privatization of Waste Hauling Expands Nationwide." American Recycler News. January 2018. https://americanrecycler.com/8568759/index.php/news/waste-news/2846-privatization-of-waste-hauling-expands-nationwide.

Municipally Owned Trash Collection

In cities that use private waste collection services, city officials continue to monitor the effectiveness of service and cost as well as political advantages and disadvantages. After having hired private companies for trash collection, some cities are choosing to bring collection back under the control of local government. Port Angeles, Washington, is one such city.

Rosengren, Cole & Maria Rachal. "Roundup: How Cities are Bucking Privatization, Fighting Contamination Via Smartphones." WasteDive, March 26, 2021. https://www.wastedive.com/news/waste-roundup-port-angeles-memphis-recycling-contamination/597377/.

PRIMARY SOURCE: ARTICLE

❝ Almost 15 years into a 20-year arrangement with Waste Connections, the city of Port Angeles, Washington, moved to cancel its contract. . . . As soon as this fall, the city plans to take over operations of its transfer station, residential recycling collection routes, and other services – as well as negotiate new post-collection arrangements for processing and disposal.

This will mean filling 12 new full-time equivalent positions and possibly spending as much as $2.5 million on new equipment in the first year. Beyond these upfront costs, elected officials and staff described it as a way to ensure long-term rate stability for residents.

'I think it's becoming more and more difficult for **third parties** to compete when their labor costs are typically the same as ours and we don't have a **markup,**' said Thomas Hunter, director of public works and utilities. . . .

[There is a] common argument that private sector operations can be more cost-effective and efficient. While that may be the case at times, Port Angeles believes there's more to it.

'Sometimes it's politically easier to contract some of these things out. . . It sets your future for the next 5, 10, 15 years and kind of reduces the workload on continuing to strive for efficiency.' said Hunter. 'Just because we're a municipality doesn't mean that we can't be flexible, it doesn't mean that we can't act swiftly. It just means that we have to work a little bit harder than everybody else to do it.' ❞

— "Roundup: How cities are bucking privatization, fighting contamination via smartphones," Waste Dive, March 26, 2021

third party a group outside of the two primary persons or groups in a situation

markup increase in price

EXAMINE THE SOURCE

1. **Inferring** Why might a third party like a private waste collection service put a markup on their labor costs? Who pays that markup cost?

2. **Analyzing Perspectives** What arguments do elected officials in Port Angeles make about how changes to waste management will benefit the city?

E

Engaging the Community

After a disastrous public policy episode in 2001, the city of Longmont, Colorado, used a new approach to better engage its citizens. This report highlights how the city has reached out to groups of residents, who had not been involved in policymaking, to include them in problem solving.

PRIMARY SOURCE: REPORT

66 Longmont's population is 26 percent Latino, but this was not reflected in outreach results. The city began hosting **demographically** appropriate focus groups; reflecting the demographics of Longmont in age, gender, income, race and education level. The city also went to where people were to get input from those who might never attend a public hearing. Engagement efforts included helping bag food for needy families.
. . . After giving out the food, staff politely asked for interviews. Other staff engaged residents at the local Peruvian festival, a teen mom support group and various Longmont Area Chamber of Commerce events. . . .

Longmont serves a **multilingual** community, and supporting the large Spanish speaking population is particularly important. **Bilingual** employees are recognized with additional compensation [pay] for their fluency in the Spanish language (and in sign language). 99

—National Civic League: Civic Index, 4th edition, 2019

demographic relating to population characteristics or descriptions

multilingual having many languages

bilingual having two languages

EXAMINE THE SOURCE

1. **Identifying** What type of problem did Longmont have?
2. **Explaining** What solutions did city officials take to address the problem?

Complete Your Inquiry

EVALUATE SOURCES AND USE EVIDENCE

Refer back to the Compelling Question and the Supporting Questions you developed at the beginning of the lesson.

1. **Contrasting** What different approaches did Columbus take to addressing the affordable housing issue? What different opinions do people hold about municipal waste management?
2. **Synthesizing** How do the sources demonstrate that communities rely on a combination of public and private efforts to solve problems?
3. **Gathering Sources** Which sources helped you answer the Supporting Questions and the Compelling Question? Which sources, if any, challenged what you thought you knew when you first created your Supporting Questions? What information do you still need in order to answer your questions? What other viewpoints would you like to investigate? Where would you find that information?
4. **Evaluating Sources** Identify the sources that helped answer your Supporting Questions. How reliable are the sources? How would you verify the reliability of the sources?

COMMUNICATE CONCLUSIONS

5. **Collaborating** In a small group, take turns sharing your Supporting Questions and answers. Then, make a concept web to list problems that you think communities face. Brainstorm ways that local governments and citizens can address each issue. Share your ideas with the class.

TAKE INFORMED ACTION

Proposing a Community Solution With a partner, identify an economic, social, or environmental issue in your community. Use reliable sources to learn more about the causes and conditions of the problem and to identify potential solutions. Then, agree on one solution to develop as a proposal in which you argue for a set of public and private actions that can be taken to solve the problem. Include information to support your ideas and explain why you chose this solution. Present your proposal to the class.

National Civic League. Civic Index, 4th Edition. Denver, Colorado: National Civic League, 2019.

Education and Social Issues

How do public schools handle financial and social challenges?

READING STRATEGY

Integrating Knowledge and Ideas As you read, complete a graphic organizer such as the one shown by listing four educational and social issues that communities face.

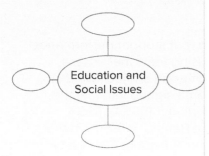

The U.S. Constitution outlines the powers and duties of the federal government. It does not mention education. The Tenth Amendment explains that all powers not given to the federal government are reserved to the states. Therefore, public education has generally been controlled by the states.

During colonial times, some local governments opened schools to educate children for free. By the late 1800s, free public schools had opened across most of the United States.

At first, local school districts decided how children would be taught and what they would learn. Today, in most states, local communities run elementary and secondary schools within rules set by state governments. The states establish standards that set out what students are expected to learn in each grade.

About 48 million students in the United States attend public schools, or take public school classes online. Close to 6 million more go to private schools. Fewer than 2 million children are homeschooled. Homeschooled students do not attend a public or private school. Instead, they are taught at home by their parents or guardians.

Millions of American students receive a free public education and transportation to and from school.

The Federal Government's Role

Although local districts have the greatest influence over public schools, the federal government also has an important role to play in education. The federal government provides schools with about seven percent of their funding. The federal government also requires schools to follow certain rules, such as how to meet the needs of students with disabilities.

The federal government has been involved with education for many years. The U.S. Department of Education is responsible for most federal funding and rules. The Department of Agriculture provides funding for school lunches. The Department of Health and Human Services runs the Head Start program. This program gives learning support to young children from low-income families to help prepare them for kindergarten. For college students, the federal government provides a variety of grants and loans.

People disagree about the federal government's increasing role in education. Some critics want to strengthen local control over schools. Some claim that by taking a greater role in education, the federal government is going beyond its constitutional authority.

Challenges: Financial and Social

Local communities pay about half of the costs for their schools. The rest of the money comes from states and the federal government. Local governments usually use property taxes to support education. If the homes and businesses in the town are worth more money, more taxes can be collected. As a result, the town will have more money to spend on schools. However, if a town's properties have lower values, it will collect fewer taxes. It will have less money to spend on schools.

Having more money to spend gives schools in wealthy areas an advantage. They can buy updated books, new computers, and other learning materials. Schools in poorer areas often lack the funds to buy the items they need or to replace older, outdated materials. The school buildings may be older and in poor condition and may lack heat or air conditioning. Students in low-income areas may not have access to after-school activities. In short, students in wealthy areas often have access to a better education.

Some schools have tried new approaches to raising the money they need. For example, some have tried teaming up with private companies. The companies put vending machines in the schools to sell soft drinks or snacks to students and teachers. In return, the companies give schools a share of the profits. Critics of this practice say this solution promotes products that are not healthy.

Schools are part of the larger community, and they face many of the same social and economic problems found in those communities. Difficult issues such as poverty, drug and alcohol use, racism, and crime affect many students. These issues can contribute to problems in the schools, such as low test scores, high dropout rates, crime, and violence.

Testing

Some experts believe that student performance can be improved by using tests that assess students' abilities in different subjects. In 2015 President Barack Obama signed into law the Every Student Succeeds Act (ESSA). ESSA replaced No Child Left Behind, a program that had been started under President George W. Bush. Like No Child Left Behind, ESSA requires that students take tests to show how well they have understood what they are being taught.

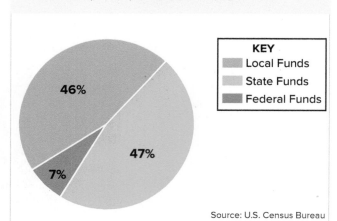

Sources of School Funding, 2020

School districts receive education funding from local, state, and federal sources.

KEY
- Local Funds
- State Funds
- Federal Funds

46%

47%

7%

Source: U.S. Census Bureau

ECONOMICS CONNECTION

1. **Analyzing** What is the largest source of school funding?

2. **Explaining** Based on this graph and your knowledge, why does the smallest amount of funding come from the source shown?

Many states try to assess how well students are learning by requiring them to take competency tests. This allows states to measure students' performance from one year to the next.

Under No Child Left Behind, states needed to fix schools that were struggling within a five-year period. Struggling schools were those with test scores that did not reach certain levels. If test scores did not show progress, the school could be shut down. Critics said that the act was unfair to schools in communities with less money. With low funding, they faced difficulties getting enough students to meet the test standards. ESSA also requires such schools to improve, but it does not say what the state must do if they do not.

ESSA made the testing process somewhat more flexible. One criticism of No Child Left Behind was that it did not adjust to each community's wants. So, while states still must test students, they now have choices. For example, they can have students take one large test each year or break it into several smaller tests.

Charter Schools and Vouchers

States are trying new approaches in educating students. Forty-five states, plus Washington, D.C., Puerto Rico, and Guam allow **charter schools** to be set up. These schools receive state funding. However, they do not have to meet some of the state regulations, or rules, for public schools.

Supporters of charter schools say that the schools are good because they offer alternatives, or other choices, for schooling. They believe that competition from charter schools encourages traditional public schools to find ways to improve their performance. Opponents say that charter schools drain resources away from traditional public schools. They also argue that charter schools are not accountable to the people who pay for them.

Some states give parents **tuition vouchers** to provide them with more choices for their children's education. Tuition vouchers are like coupons issued by the government to parents or guardians. They can use these vouchers to pay for their children to attend private schools. People who support tuition vouchers **appreciate**, or value, having more options in finding a school for their children. They believe that if schools must attract parents with vouchers, the schools will try to do a better job of educating all students.

Many people oppose the use of vouchers. Teachers' unions believe that vouchers draw money out of the public school system and put that money into private schools. They believe that taking money away from public schools is harmful, especially in poorer communities. Some people worry that private schools may not admit students fairly even if all students have vouchers.

Other people oppose vouchers because in some places they can be used at religious schools. These opponents think that using vouchers at religious schools violates the First Amendment. The Supreme Court, however, has ruled that it is constitutional to use vouchers for these schools if certain conditions are met. The funds must go directly to the parents or guardians, and not the schools, in order to be legal. Also, funding cannot be used to promote the religious goals of the school.

charter school a type of school that receives state funding but is excused from meeting some public school regulations

tuition voucher a certificate issued by the government providing money for education payments, allowing families the option of sending students to private schools

appreciate to value

Some school districts try to lower costs by hiring private companies to run the schools. School districts expect these companies to provide cost savings while maintaining the quality of education. Private companies make a profit for themselves.

✓ CHECK FOR UNDERSTANDING

1. **Explaining** How does the value of properties in a community affect school funding?
2. **Identifying** What is a charter school?

Crime and Social Problems

GUIDING QUESTION

What can governments do about crime and social problems?

The United States has more than 2 million citizens in prison. It has more prisoners than any other country in the world. It also has the largest percentage of its population in prison. Americans are more likely to commit serious crimes, including homicide, than people in other wealthy democratic countries.

Poverty and Crime

Across the United States, large cities usually have the highest crime rates. In these large cities, crime and poverty are often related. Well-paying, stable jobs may be difficult to find in densely populated urban centers. Many of the poorest people in inner cities have difficulty finding jobs at all. Some have substance abuse problems. These and other issues can result in poor inner-city residents being arrested and sent to prison more often than wealthier people who commit the same crimes.

Police Departments

Urban police are a major crime-fighting force in the nation. America's largest cities have more police officers than all the nation's other law enforcement units combined. In rural areas, more than 3,000 county sheriffs and deputies enforce the law. In addition, every state has a highway

Violent and Property Crime Rates, 2010–2019

Violent crimes include causing the death or injury of another person, physical attacks on another person, and robbery. Property crime means taking a person's belongings but without any attack, threats, or harm to the person.

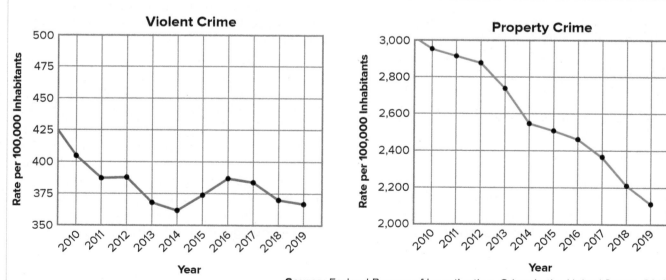

Source: Federal Bureau of Investigation, *Crime in the United States,* 2019.

HISTORY CONNECTION

Comparing and Contrasting Compare the trends in both graphs. In what way are they similar? In what way are they different?

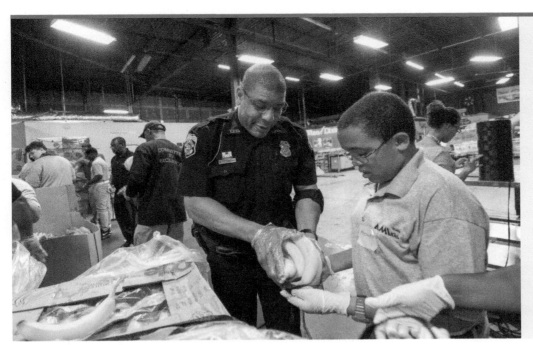

The practice of community policing has helped create better relations between officers and member of communities.

patrol or state police force. The main job of these agencies is to maintain highway safety, although they also play an important role in investigating crimes and capturing suspects.

Enforcing the law is the primary task of police departments. The best way for police to work in a community is when there is trust between officers and the community. When there is trust, people in the community feel comfortable around the police. They become more cooperative when the police investigate a crime. This can help make streets safer. However, some police officers have treated some people harshly or unfairly. Often the people treated in this way are members of underrepresented racial groups. Such actions weaken community trust. Some police actions have received a great deal of publicity. They have also led to criticism of how police are trained and how they do their jobs.

As a result, some communities have changed how police are allowed to arrest suspects. Some officers are now taught ways to de-escalate, or calm, tense situations without using force or violence. Some police departments are training officers to consider whether a suspect lives with mental illness or addiction. If a police officer thinks a person is mentally ill or using drugs, they may contact a mental health professional to help handle the situation. This approach can prevent a tragic outcome.

On average, crime rates in the United States have fallen in recent years. Some of this change may be a result of a type of police work called **community policing.** Under these programs, police play a visible and active role in neighborhoods. They walk or ride bicycles around the community and get to know the people who live there. These programs also encourage ordinary citizens to take part in neighborhood watch groups. Neighborhood watch members observe events in their neighborhoods. If they see something that concerns them, they report it to the police. The police then investigate the situation.

Social Programs

The government provides welfare programs to help people in need. These programs give financial assistance to Americans who are poor, sick, elderly, or have mental or physical disabilities. Figuring out the best way to help these people has been a long struggle for government officials. Critics of welfare claim that the people who receive help do not always deserve it. Those critics do not want to pay for welfare programs with tax money. Some say that helping people in need should be a role for charities, not the government. They also say people can become dependent on the help rather than taking charge of their own lives.

---

community policing local police force visibly keeping the peace and patrolling neighborhoods

Many communities offer job-training programs to help people gain the skills they need to find employment. These students are training for jobs in restaurants.

Supporters of welfare say that it is the only way many disabled individuals and low-income families can avoid hunger and homelessness. They argue that society has a duty to help those who face economic hardships.

The welfare debate has been going on for years. From 1935 to 1997, some people with children who had low incomes qualified for money that the federal government directly provided to them. In 1997 Congress changed the policy. It created a program called Temporary Assistance for Needy Families (TANF). Under this program, the federal government gives money to the states. The states use this money to give people financial support. Under TANF, each state decides who can receive benefits and how much money each person gets. State plans have to meet certain federal rules, however. For example, people can receive aid for only five years during their lives. States also have to provide education and job training programs to help people get off welfare.

The number of people on welfare fell after TANF became law. In 1995 about 14.2 million people received welfare payments. By the end of 2019, there were just over 2 million people receiving monthly payments. Supporters of TANF say that this reduction is a sign that the program is successful.

Opponents of the law say that TANF has failed to lift people out of poverty. They also argue that TANF's strict requirements mean that it reaches too few people in need.

1. **Identifying Cause and Effect** Why has community policing been successful?

2. **Citing Text Evidence** How does the government attempt to combat poverty through Temporary Assistance for Needy Families (TANF)?

LESSON ACTIVITIES

1. **Argumentative Writing** Most school districts get their funding from local property taxes, state funds, and the federal government. Review the "Sources of School Funding" graph in this lesson. Write a letter to the editor of a local newspaper expressing whether or not you think that the current balance of funding is right for the nation's schools. Should local schools be paid for with more local funds? Should the federal government pay a larger share of school budgets? Think about what you believe would be the best way to make sure students in every school receive good educational opportunities. Provide support for your opinion.

2. **Presenting** Work with two classmates to research a recent example of a proposal to change police behavior or processes. Create a presentation that does these three things:

   • explains what prompted calls for change.

   • describes specific actions taken to bring about change.

   • discusses the effects of those changes.

   Your presentation should be based on reliable sources and include specific examples.

REUTERS/Alamy Stock Photo

11

Reviewing State and Local Government

Summary

Federalism

- The federal system delegates some powers to the national government and reserves some for the states.
- The Constitution guarantees states a republican government and protection.
- The Constitution limits both state and federal power.
- The national and state governments often work together, with state governments working to meet goals set by Congress.

State Government

- Each state constitution structures the state's government into three branches. All state constitutions include a bill of rights.
- The governor leads the executive branch. All states except one have a bicameral legislature. Each state has a hierarchy of lower and higher courts.
- State actions are limited by the requirement to have a balanced budget.

West Virginia State Capitol

Local Government

- Local governments are established by the state government. Municipal governments are incorporated under a charter.
- Cities, counties, towns, townships, and villages all have local government. Other government units include special districts, metropolitan areas, and tribal governments.
- Local governments often have both executive and legislative officials. Some have only a commission, board, or council that passes and carries out laws.
- Local governments must balance many services and roles with limited resources.

Checking For Understanding

Answer the questions to see if you understood the topic content.

1. Identify each of the following terms and explain its significance to state and local government.

   A. unfunded mandate   E. county

   B. redistricting   F. long-term plan

   C. appellate court   G. tuition voucher

   D. ordinance   H. community policing

REVIEWING KEY FACTS

2. **Explaining** How is power assigned to different levels of government by the U.S. Constitution?

3. **Comparing** What are three things that every state constitution has in common?

4. **Explaining** How are state legislatures organized?

5. **Identifying** What are three jobs of state legislators?

6. **Summarizing** What are three judicial powers held by governors?

7. **Contrasting** What is the difference between trial courts and appellate courts?

8. **Explaining** How does a community become a city?

9. **Contrasting** How are the mayor-council and council-manager forms of local government different?

10. **Making Generalizations** Why is it important to local government that some community members serve on planning commissions?

11. **Explaining** What roles do federal, state, and local governments play in education?

CRITICAL THINKING

12. **Making Connections** How does the system of federalism limit government power?

13. **Drawing Conclusions** Why do you think the power to collect taxes is a concurrent power?

14. **Contrasting** How are the requirements for becoming a U.S. senator and a state senator different?

15. **Identifying Cause and Effect** Why do you think a line-item veto can be useful to a governor?

16. **Speculating** Why do you think the way state executive officials and judges are selected varies so much across the states?

17. **Evaluating** For city councils, do you think ward elections or at-large elections benefit the people of a city more? Why?

18. **Comparing** How is the commission-manager form of county government similar to the council-manager form of city government?

19. **Synthesizing** How might local government use technology to help get more involved in making public policy decisions to solve problems in the community?

20. **Explaining** How do the federal and state governments work together to combat poverty?

NEED EXTRA HELP?

If You've Missed Question	1	2	3	4	5	6	7	8	9	10
Review Lesson	2, 3, 5, 7, 8, 10	2	2	3	3	4	5	7	7	8

If You've Missed Question	11	12	13	14	15	16	17	18	19	20
Review Lesson	10	2	2, 7	3	4	4, 5	7	7	8	2

Apply What You Have Learned

A Making Connections

The power to make laws is a concurrent power that is shared by local, state, and national governments. This power to make laws may be similar, but each level of government has its own processes and procedures to make laws.

ACTIVITY **Comparing Local, State, and National Lawmaking Processes** Work with at least two other classmates to learn how laws are made at different levels of government. As a team, research the lawmaking process as it relates to your local (city or county) government, your state government, and the national government. Together, create three diagrams—one for each level of government—explaining the steps involved in that government's lawmaking process. Next, each member of your team should individually write an essay comparing the processes at all three levels of government.

B Understanding Multiple Perspectives

Education, crime, and social programs are major issues that local and state governments address. They are also issues that often generate debate among citizens living in those communities.

ACTIVITY **Evaluating Different Perspectives on a Public Policy** Identify a recent bill that was introduced in the state legislature. Find one that had both strong support and opposition and relates to education, crime, or social programs. Use a variety of sources, such as articles in local newspapers and online news reports, to find out why the legislation was proposed, arguments legislators made for or against it, and whether or not the bill became law. Find news stories or information from the websites of interest groups that explain why some people favored the bill and others opposed it. Then prepare a multimedia presentation that describes the purpose of the bill, explains the reasons people supported or opposed the law, and tells whether or not the bill passed.

» A protest over the elimination of a state scholarship program

C Geographic Reasoning

No matter where you live, your life is affected by multiple governments. This can include more than one local government, your state government, and the federal government. Some of these governments are confined to specific borders, while others provide services that stretch across communities or regions.

ACTIVITY **Creating an Annotated Map of Local Governments** Work with a partner to identify, locate, and investigate at least two, and if possible three, forms of local government that affect your life. Print out a map of your state and use different colors to mark the borders of your city or town, county, and any special districts. Then attach labels that explain the following about each government you have identified:

- when and how it was established
- what services it provides
- who receives those services
- its main sources of funding
- the names and offices of the officials who lead it
- how citizens can communicate with officials

» A county-operated mosquito control service

D Persuasive Writing

Local and state governments often have both chief executives and legislators with specific responsibilities or committee assignments. Citizens attempting to change public policy sometimes have to approach more than one person at more than one level of government to make their voices heard. Eleanor Roosevelt was First Lady from 1933 to 1945 while her husband Franklin was president. She reflected on the importance of learning about your government:

66 Our children should learn the general framework [structure] of their government and then they should know where they come in contact with the government, where it touches their daily lives and where their influence is exerted [placed] on the government. It must not be a distant thing, someone else's business, but they must see how every cog [part] in the wheel of a democracy is important and bears its share of responsibility for the smooth running of the entire machine. 99

— Eleanor Roosevelt, "The Responsibilities of Education for Citizenship," April 1933

ACTIVITY **Writing Letters to Suggest School Lessons on Government** Think about what Eleanor Roosevelt was trying to express about citizens and their government. Then write a one-page letter explaining what you think middle-school students need to know about their government. In your letter, suggest ways that both officials and government agencies could help students become more familiar with the role government plays in their life. Use the Roosevelt quotation to help support your arguments. Then identify at least two officials in local government and two officials in state government to whom to send your letter. Be sure to use appropriate voice and tone in your writing. Send each of the officials you selected a copy of your letter. Include information on how they can reply to you. Share any replies you receive with the class.

PHOTO: AP Images; TEXT: Roosevelt, Eleanor. "The Responsibilities of Education for Citizenship." The Ohio State University Bulletin 37, no. 3 (1932).

Police officers must follow certain procedures when arresting a suspect.

Understanding the Law

Law in the United States

Laws are essential to keep citizens and the community safe. There are different types of laws, both criminal and civil, created within the different levels of government. Just because an individual goes to court, does not mean they have committed a crime. People can go to civil court for several reasons including lawsuits, adoptions, or disputes between neighbors. In a criminal court, a judge or a jury of peers determines a guilty or not guilty verdict for the defendant.

Diagram of a Courtroom

A courtroom is a space where legal cases are presented and decisions are made. Each individual in a courtroom plays an important role in ensuring that a trial proceeds correctly and smoothly.

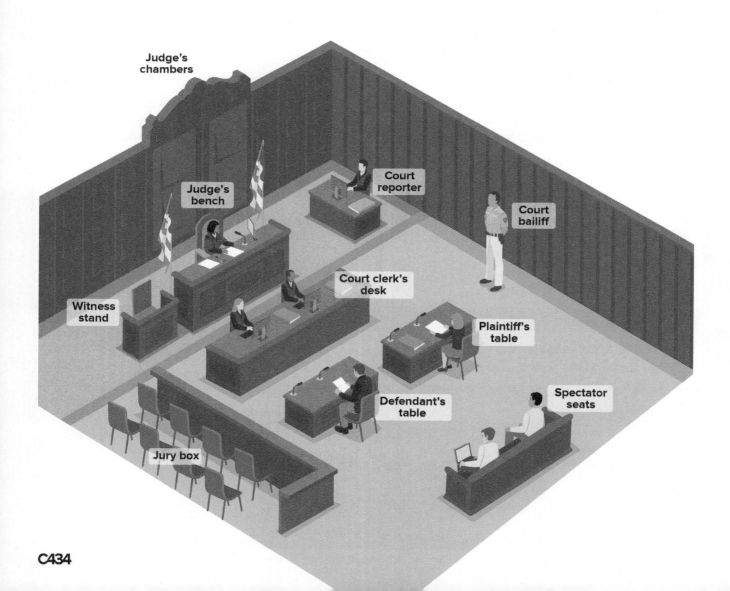

Judge's chambers

Court reporter

Court bailiff

Judge's bench

Witness stand

Court clerk's desk

Plaintiff's table

Defendant's table

Spectator seats

Jury box

Symbols of Justice

Lady Justice is a symbol commonly found in courthouses around the United States. Lady Justice is blindfolded to symbolize the unbiased nature of the justice system. In her right hand is a sword that represents the strength of enforcement and respect of laws. In her left hand are the scales of justice that represent the importance of weighing each side of the evidence before coming to a decision of guilty or not guilty.

> " I chose to be a lawyer and ultimately a judge because I find endless challenge in the complexities of the law. I firmly believe in the rule of law as the foundation for all of our basic rights. "
>
> — Supreme Court Justice Sonia Sotomayor, May 26, 2009

The Great Seal

The Great Seal of the United States appears on a number of buildings, objects, and documents within the national government. This includes United States District Courts in every state. The seal is present both inside and outside the courthouse, symbolizing peace with the olive branch and power with the thirteen arrows.

Getting Ready to Learn About . . . Understanding the Law

Breaking the Rules

One afternoon in a busy city, a teen calls a neighbor. She makes a rude joke, laughs, and quickly hangs up. Then she dials a different number to make another prank call. Across town, a young man sitting on a park bench eats a meal from a fast-food restaurant. When he finishes the meal, he leaves the wrapper and the cup that held his drink on the park bench and walks away. Outside the park, a young woman stands on a street corner at a red light. She is in a hurry, so she jaywalks, or crosses the street carelessly, instead of waiting for the light to turn green.

These three actions might seem very different, but they have one thing in common. They are all examples of breaking a law. What laws did these three people break? The teen who made prank calls committed harassment. The young man who left his trash littered. The young woman who jaywalked committed a traffic violation.

Those laws might not seem of great consequence, especially when compared to laws dealing with other offenses such as robbery and murder. However, all laws help to protect people and their communities. They protect people from being harassed, help keep the environment clean, and work to prevent traffic accidents.

What Are Laws?

Laws are rules that help our society function. They explain how people should treat each other and their surroundings. Laws create order and help a society run smoothly by making sure everyone has the same expectations about how people should behave.

For example, most towns have laws that set speed limits on public roads. Imagine what would happen if everyone decided to drive at any speed they wanted. The streets would be filled with vehicles that were going slowly, going fast, or going at some speed in between. Accidents would surely happen. Having speed limits means all drivers will know the rules of the road and what to expect.

Who Creates Laws?

The legislative branch of government makes the laws for a society. On the local level, that includes city councils or county boards. State legislatures make the laws for a state. The U.S. Congress makes the laws for the entire nation.

Littering is a minor, or less important, crime. However, it could still be subject to a punishment, such as requiring the offender to pay a fine.

Law and Justice in the United States

In the United States, different justice systems deal with government laws, private disputes, and crimes committed by juveniles.

Criminal Law System	Civil Law System	Juvenile Justice System
Deals with adults accused of breaking a law	Deals with disputes between individuals, organizations, or governments	Deals with juveniles accused of breaking a law

These laws help to govern how people do business, build homes, run schools, travel, and carry out many other activities. Laws range from minor rules, such as those that require people not to litter, to more serious ones, such as those that make murder a crime. They protect us by controlling the behavior of people in society.

Who Enforces the Law?

If you have ever seen a police officer giving a ticket to a driver, you have seen law enforcement in action. Such events are among the most obvious ways that citizens see public laws and regulations at work. The job of the police is to try to prevent crimes from taking place and to investigate them when they do occur. With minor offenses such as parking a car in an illegal spot, police can act immediately by giving out a ticket. With more serious crimes, they might have to look for clues, talk to witnesses, and gather evidence before they identify and arrest a suspect.

Local and state police work to enforce the laws of a community or the state. On the national level, the Federal Bureau of Investigation (FBI) is one of the units of the federal government that works to enforce the laws passed by Congress.

A person who has been accused of a crime enters the criminal justice system. This person may be arrested and may come in contact with prosecutors, judges, and juries. Just as citizens must follow the rules and not break the laws, the people in this system have rules they must follow. The U.S. Constitution provides safeguards that protect the rights of people going through this system. Police, prosecutors, judges, and juries all have to act according to due process. The Constitution put these protections in place to prevent the government from abusing its power and violating the rights of people.

What Happens When People Break the Law?

Someone found guilty of breaking the law faces some sort of punishment. The harshness of that punishment depends on what the person did. Someone who commits a lesser crime for the first time might be ordered to do community service, which means doing some kind of work to make the community a better place to live. Other people are fined, meaning they must pay the government a sum of money. For more serious crimes, those found guilty may spend time in prison. By punishing wrongdoers, the government hopes to convince other people to follow the law. This is one more way that the law is used as a tool to promote order in society.

Looking Ahead

You will learn about different types of laws in the United States. You will examine Compelling Questions and develop your own questions about the law in the Inquiry Activities. You can preview some of the key concepts that you will learn about by reviewing the infographic.

What Will You Learn?

In these lessons focused on understanding the legal system, you will learn:

- the sources of laws used in the American legal system.
- the types of laws and how they compare.
- how individual rights and the rights of the accused are protected in the United States.
- the significance of juries in the American legal system.
- the types of juries and how they are selected.
- what civil law is.
- the process followed in a civil case.
- the types of crimes that are subject to criminal laws.
- the differences and similarities of civil laws and criminal laws.
- the penalties for crimes and the procedures in criminal cases.
- the purpose and processes of the juvenile justice system.
- how the juvenile justice system differs from the adult system.

 COMPELLING QUESTIONS IN THE INQUIRY ACTIVITY LESSONS

- **How is equal justice for accused persons ensured in the American legal system?**
- **How should juveniles be treated in the criminal justice system?**

The American Legal System
Legislators pass laws on the local, state, and federal levels that apply to people in specific areas.

FEDERAL LAWS
apply to everyone throughout the United States.

STATE LAWS
apply to people who are citizens, residents, or visitors of a particular state.

LOCAL LAWS
apply to people who are citizens, residents, or visitors of a particular city, town, or municipality.

READING STRATEGY

Analyzing Key Ideas and Details As you read about early forms of law from ancient times, complete a graphic organizer such as the one shown here to note key details about each of the law codes presented.

Early Law	Key Details
Laws of Hammurabi	
Ten Commandments	
Justinian Code	

Why We Have Laws

GUIDING QUESTION

What is the purpose of laws?

Why do certain laws exist? For example, why do many communities create bicycle lanes on busy streets that cars are not allowed to use? Bicycle lanes help to protect cyclists from collisions with cars or other vehicles. This law works to prevent accidents and keep people from getting hurt. Laws not only keep us safe, but they also affect nearly everything we do—from how safe products are to where we vote.

Keeping the Peace

Laws are rules that help people get along and allow societies to function. People, organizations, and governments get along better when they have a set of rules and follow them. Societies create laws to make clear what actions they do and do not allow. They create a **code** that shapes the way people in a society behave. Laws set the rules for working out disagreements between citizens over money, property, and rights.

Laws also help keep the peace and address criminal acts when they occur. When people do commit a crime, the police and the courts enforce the law. The courts punish criminals both to make them pay for their crime and to discourage others from wrongdoing.

Every nation has laws. Not all laws are just, however. Sometimes laws deny some people rights they should have.

code an organized body of law

Many communities have set up bicycle lanes and created laws prohibiting cars from using those lanes.
Analyzing Visuals How does the bicycle lane protect the cyclist?

While serving as vice president of the United States, Spiro Agnew was charged with accepting bribes when he had been governor of Maryland, a criminal act. Agnew resigned as vice president.

The Rule of Law

The U.S. legal system is based on a concept known as the *rule of law*. This concept includes several important principles.

First, laws must apply to everyone in a society, even those who govern. Everyone must obey the law and be held accountable if they violate it, no matter how powerful the person. For example, it is illegal to steal money from a business. A thief who robs a gas station should face the same penalty as an executive who steals from a corporation.

Laws should be written in such a way that they are easy for most people to understand. Otherwise, people might break the law without knowing they are doing so. Of course, being ignorant of a law is not an excuse for breaking it. Still, if laws cannot be understood, people have no real opportunity to follow them. Also, no one should be punished for breaking a law unless it was a law at the time that that person committed the action in question. It is not fair to make an action illegal after someone has done it.

Laws must be enforced by public officials. Private citizens should not be taking the law into their own hands. Local, state, or federal officials should be the ones who catch possible criminals, try them fairly, and punish them only if they are guilty.

Some countries do not follow the rule of law. Their government leaders can break the law without fear of punishment. These leaders control the police and the courts. They know that their actions will not be challenged. People who do oppose them suffer. These leaders arrest those who protest their rule or journalists who report on abuses of power. They also make sure that the police and the courts leave their friends alone— even when those friends do illegal things. Life in a society without the rule of law is unfair, unequal, and unjust.

What Makes a Good Law?

The U.S. Constitution requires the rule of law. However, laws that meet this standard may not be wise and good. In a democracy, people may disagree about which laws are acceptable. People may feel that a specific law is too harsh or too weak or is just not a good idea. Democracy is a system for resolving disagreements about which laws are good.

Many people would agree that any law should be fair, reasonable, understandable, and enforceable. What do those terms mean when applied to laws?

A fair law gives equal treatment to all people who are in similar situations. For example, if a law says that people who live in one state can vote, while people who live in another state cannot, that law is not fair.

Good laws must be reasonable and must have reasonable punishments if they are broken. A law is reasonable if it makes sense to consider breaking that law a crime. Laws against driving too fast are reasonable because that behavior is dangerous. Laws against driving with the car windows open are not reasonable. In addition, the punishment must fit the crime. In some ancient cultures, crimes such as stealing or causing a public disturbance were punishable by death. Today we view that kind of punishment as harsh and unreasonable because it goes too far.

✓ CHECK FOR UNDERSTANDING

1. **Making Connections** How do laws help a society to function?
2. **Contrasting** What are the characteristics of a society that works under the rule of law and one that does not?

Development of the Legal System

GUIDING QUESTION

What early legal systems influenced the laws of the United States?

In the United States, the U.S. Constitution provides a set of laws for the entire nation. The Framers based their ideas on laws and traditions from earlier societies. Some of these concepts date back thousands of years.

Scholars believe that some form of law existed in even the earliest human societies. It is thought that prehistoric people had rules to follow, even though they were not written down. They were passed down orally. These rules helped early humans prevent conflict between members of the group. The rules also helped determine how to handle conflicts when they occurred.

This sculpture shows Hammurabi (standing) as he receives the blessing of Shamash, the god of justice. The laws of this Babylonian king were carved into this stone pillar below those two figures.

Analyzing Visuals Why do you think this scene is at the top of the monument? Why is it significant?

Laws of Hammurabi

Over time, people began to write down the laws for their societies. One written set of laws was developed in Babylonia, an ancient empire of the Middle East. The legal decisions of King Hammurabi (ha•muh•RAH•bee) were collected around 1760 B.C.E. This set of laws identified crimes in different **categories**, or groups of similar things. For example, some of these laws would fit into categories such as property law or family law.

In addition, the Laws of Hammurabi explained the punishments for violating these rules. Today we think of many of these punishments as far too harsh—or unreasonable.

❝ If fire break[s] out in a house, and some one . . . take[s] the property of the master of the house, he shall be thrown into that self-same fire. ❞

— Laws of Hammurabi, c. 1760 B.C.E.

Israelite Law

The Israelites lived in ancient times near the eastern coast of the Mediterranean Sea. Their written laws grew out of their religion, which later became Judaism. One source for their laws was the Ten Commandments. According to their holy book, the Hebrew Bible, a leader named Moses received these rules from God. The laws forbade such acts as murder and theft, which are still considered crimes today.

The Ten Commandments also emphasize justice and personal responsibility. For this reason, they have become an ethical influence on modern laws, including those of the United States. *Ethical* means "acting according to standards of right and wrong."

category a group of similar things

Justinian I (center) helped organize the laws of the vast Byzantine Empire over which he ruled.

Making Connections Why is it important for the United States to have a unified code of law?

Roman Law

Several laws that developed in Europe and North America had their beginnings in ancient Rome. The first code of Roman law was published in 450 B.C.E. The laws were known as the Twelve Tables because they were carved onto 12 bronze tablets. The tablets focused on different areas of justice, such as family law and laws about property.

The Romans built an empire, conquering other lands. They brought their laws to new areas they ruled. In this way, Rome's laws spread to other parts of Europe and to western Asia and northern Africa. As the empire grew and expanded, the Romans added new laws. Over time, the body of laws became very complex and difficult to follow.

In the early 500s C.E., Justinian I came to rule the eastern part of the Roman Empire. This area is also known as the Byzantine (BIH•zehn•teen) Empire. Justinian realized that Roman law had become very confusing. He ordered scholars to simplify the law. They reorganized the old collection of laws into a more orderly set of regulations, which was completed in 534 C.E. Called the Justinian Code, this collection of laws had influence beyond the Byzantine Empire. It also became part of the laws of the Roman Catholic Church. This church law, in turn, influenced laws outside the church.

Napoleonic Code

The Justinian Code eventually shaped the laws of many European countries, such as France. However, in 1804 the French emperor Napoleon Bonaparte decided to reform French law. This resulted in a unified law code that became known as the Napoleonic Code.

Like the ancient Romans, Napoleon conquered new territory. As he added lands, he brought his laws with him. In addition, many other places in Europe and South America based their laws on the Napoleonic Code. In fact, the laws of Louisiana are influenced by this code because France controlled that area for many years.

English Common Law

The most important influence on the American legal system is English law. English **common law** is not based on a legal code but on judges' decisions. The common law system involves judges analyzing a decision made by another judge. In this system judges use a previous case as a basis for their decision in a current case.

Common law first developed around 1100 C.E. Kings began to send judges into the countryside to hold trials to carry out the law. The judges reached their decisions using precedent, or rulings from similar cases from the past. Because the judges based their decisions on the same cases, the law became common to all regions.

The English blended Roman law and church law into the common law. English law included the basic principles of individual rights, such as the idea that someone suspected of committing a crime was innocent unless proven guilty.

Common law was the main source of laws in England for hundreds of years. Over time, the English Parliament became the country's lawmaking body. Even as Parliament played a larger role in the legal system, common law remained the foundation of English law.

Thousands of English settlers came to North America in the 1600s and 1700s and brought these traditions with them. The common law and ideas of individual rights became basic parts of U.S. law. They continue to influence the law in the United States today.

Natural Law

Underlying some of these legal systems was the idea of natural law. This is the idea that some laws are not created by society but are **inherently** part of being human. For example, according to natural law, every person has the right to live and not be injured or harmed by another.

The idea of natural law was discussed by ancient Greek philosophers, such as Aristotle. He wrote that there was a natural justice that could be applied in any society. In the 1100s C.E., a Christian thinker named Gratian said natural law was based on divine law, or the law established by God.

In the 1600s, a movement named the Enlightenment arose in Europe. Enlightenment thinkers tried to use reason to find basic truths about people and society. John Locke, who was one of these thinkers, argued in favor of natural law that is based on reason. Locke stated that all individuals are by nature equal. They have certain rights. They also have a duty to respect the rights of others.

Judge and legal scholar William Blackstone commented on English common law in the 1700s. His ideas influenced American laws.

> 66 The state of nature has a law of nature to govern it, which obliges [requires] every one: and reason, which is that law, teaches all mankind . . . that being all equal and independent, no one ought to harm another in his life, health, liberty, or possessions. 99

—John Locke, *Two Treatises of Government*

---

common law a system of law based on previous legal decisions

inherently present from birth

Thomas Jefferson drew on Locke's ideas when he wrote the Declaration of Independence. The concept of natural law strongly influenced the drafting of this document. Jefferson included the idea that everyone had the right to "life, liberty, and the pursuit of happiness." This phrase was based on Locke's belief that "life, liberty, and property" are natural rights.

✓ CHECK FOR UNDERSTANDING

1. **Making Connections** What are three legal systems that influenced the laws of the United States?
2. **Summarizing** According to John Locke, what is true based on natural law?

Types of Laws

GUIDING QUESTION

What types of law exist in the American legal system?

Many books, TV shows, and movies are about someone committing a crime, the police catching a suspect, and that person being put on trial. Crimes also get a lot of attention from TV news and newspapers. Crime is an important concern in our society. As a result, many laws relate to identifying and punishing criminal behavior. **Criminal laws** prohibit, or forbid, such acts as theft or drunk driving. Other kinds of laws deal with disputes between people (or groups of people) or between the government and its citizens. These are known as **civil laws**.

Criminal and civil laws directly affect all Americans. They help us enjoy a peaceful and orderly society.

Another branch of laws is called *public laws*. These laws set the rules for how the government is organized and how government officials act. Public laws also apply to people's interactions with the government.

Criminal Law

Criminal laws protect people and promote public safety. Crimes fall into two main categories based on how serious they are. Felonies are more serious crimes. They also carry more serious penalties for the criminal. Examples of felonies are murder or robbery. Misdemeanors are less serious crimes, such as shoplifting items of low value or threatening to hurt someone. Typically, misdemeanors carry a fine or a jail sentence of some months to a few years.

criminal law the body of laws that prohibits certain acts that are considered crimes

civil law the body of laws that relates to a dispute between people or groups of people or between people and the government

Vandalism is the crime of destroying property without permission, such as painting graffiti on a wall.

Analyzing Why do you think it is a crime to create graffiti?

PHOTO: vdbvsl/Alamy Stock Photo; TEXT: Constitutional Rights Foundation. "The Declaration of Independence and Natural Rights." 2008. https://www.crf-usa.org/foundations-of-our-constitution/natural-rights.html.

In addition to following the laws of the United States, members of the military must conform to another set of laws.

The most common type of crime involves harm to public or personal property. Stealing a bike, shoplifting, committing identity theft, and vandalism are all examples of property crimes. These kinds of crimes do not involve force or the threat of force against the victim. Crimes that hurt a person are called *violent crimes*.

Civil Law

Civil laws apply to disputes between people or groups. A civil case may be a disagreement over a broken contract. For example, suppose you have signed a lease to rent a storefront to open a bakery. In the contract, the property owner promised to provide a space that was in good condition. Then, after you come to the space to begin setting up your shop, you discover the plumbing does not work. You complain to the property owner, but he refuses to do anything about it. You ask the owner to give you back the payment that you made for the first month of rent, but he refuses to give the money back. To get your money back, you could take the property owner to court. To do so, you must file a **lawsuit**. This is a legal action to seek a remedy for harm that has been done. Lawsuits related to families, such as divorce, are also decided in civil courts.

Military Law

Military law is a set of laws that applies to the armed forces of the United States. It also applies to civilians who work for the military. Military laws concern acts such as disobeying or showing disrespect to superior officers, physically striking superior officers, and desertion. Desertion is leaving one's assigned post without permission.

People suspected of serious offenses of military law may end up at a **court-martial**, which conducts a military trial. In a court-martial, the lawyers and judges are all officers in the military.

Tribal Law

Several hundred Native American tribal groups have reservations in the United States in which they govern themselves. Most of these groups have their own tribal justice systems. Tribal courts hear a range of cases, and they can involve both Native Americans and non-Native Americans.

The power of a tribal court to hear civil cases that occur on a reservation is very broad. With criminal matters, though, they have less power. Tribal groups can choose which actions to make crimes.

lawsuit a legal action in which a person or group sues to collect damages for some harm they claim another has done to them

court-martial a court that tries members of the armed forces who are accused of crimes against military law

Statutes passed by state or local legislatures can affect many aspects of daily life.

They cannot impose punishments of more than one year in prison or a fine of more than $5,000. Tribal courts cannot prosecute people who are not Native Americans for crimes committed on the reservation. They also cannot prosecute Native Americans for a felony crime. These kinds of cases must be heard in federal court.

Constitutional and Statutory Law

Laws that govern our lives and protect our rights come from many sources. These include:

- the U.S. Constitution
- state constitutions
- statutes
- case law

The U.S. Constitution is the supreme, or highest, law of the nation. Although each state has its own constitution, no state government can create a law that conflicts with the U.S. Constitution.

Constitutional law relates to understanding the meaning of constitutions. In a constitutional

case, a court considers whether the actions of the government are allowed by the Constitution. Some cases involve weighing the power of the government against the rights of individual citizens.

Laws created by the legislative branch of government are known as **statutes**. They form the basis of **statutory law**. The U.S. Congress, state legislatures, and local legislatures write statutes. Statutes control our actions in different ways. They set rules people are familiar with, such as laws about obeying traffic signals or requiring young people to go to school. Statutes also provide rules that allow people to enjoy their rights, such as the right to a free public education.

Case Law

As in the common law, judicial precedent plays an important role in our justice system. Often, judges must decide how to apply a general statement in the law to a particular case before them. Their decisions carry the weight of law. The decisions become precedents, or examples. **Case law** is law that becomes established as a result of a judge's ruling.

✓ **CHECK FOR UNDERSTANDING**

1. **Contrasting** How do civil court cases differ from criminal court cases?

2. **Identifying** What document is the supreme law of the land in the United States?

LESSON ACTIVITIES

1. **Informative/Explanatory Writing** Write a short essay that describes the English system of common law and its influence on the laws of the United States.

2. **Collaborating** Working with three classmates, brainstorm examples of cases that could be heard in criminal court, civil court, military court, and tribal court. As a group, create an example of the type of case handled in each kind of court. Your group may need to do some additional research to find examples. Work together to make flash cards about the cases. On the front of a card name the kind of case. On the back, provide details about it, such as the kinds of decisions or punishments the court might reach. Use the flash cards to teach other groups about the issues handled in each of these courts.

---

constitutional law branch of law dealing with the formation, construction, and interpretation of constitutions

statutory law the body of laws created by a legislature

case law a law established by a judicial decision

Analyzing Key Ideas and Details As you read, complete a graphic organizer such as the one shown here to identify four elements that make a trial impartial based on the rights outlined in the Bill of Rights.

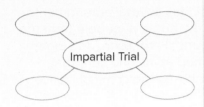

Impartial Trial

Basic Legal Rights

What basic legal rights are provided to all Americans?

If police officers in the United States want to look for clues in the home of someone they suspect of a crime, they cannot simply enter the property and start looking. First, they must ask a judge for permission. The judge then determines if taking this step meets the standards set by the law. If so, the judge agrees to the search. If not, the search is not allowed.

Why do the police have to follow this process? The U.S. Constitution protects Americans from unfair or unreasonable searches. The government has a duty to keep society safe. At the same time, authorities must recognize people's rights and not violate them. These rights are guaranteed by the U.S. Constitution. They prevent the government from abusing its power. The government must follow the rule of law and apply the law to all people equally.

Protections Against Unlawful Imprisonment

Article I Section 9 of the Constitution provides one of the most important protections, the writ of habeas corpus. *Habeas corpus* (HAY•bee•uhs KAWR•puhs) is a Latin phrase that roughly means "you should have the body." This phrase refers to the practice of bringing a prisoner—"the body"—before a judge.

In the United States, a prisoner has the right to ask for a court order known as a writ of habeas corpus. The writ requires the police to bring the prisoner before a judge and explain why they are holding the person.

Individuals arrested for a crime have specific rights that must be protected before they may be held in a prison or jail.

The judge then decides whether the government has a sound reason to hold the person. This practice protects people from being held in prison unjustly.

Article I of the Constitution also prevents two other abuses of power. Congress cannot issue bills of attainder or pass ex post facto laws. A bill of attainder is a law that declares someone or some group guilty. It usually mentions the person by name. This is unfair because the individual should be charged with a crime that applies to everyone. An ex post facto law allows a person to be punished for an action that was legal when it was done. Such a law is unfair because an individual should be able to know whether an action is legal or illegal before it is carried out.

Due Process Protections

The Fourteenth Amendment of the Constitution guarantees many rights to all people. It requires states to treat all people the same way under the law.

The Fourteenth Amendment also strengthens the right of due process. That right was first established by the Fifth Amendment. Due process means that the government must follow established and fair legal procedures. For example, a person accused of a crime has the right to be represented by an attorney. If the government denies that right, it has violated

In a criminal trial, a prosecutor represents the state and makes a case against the defendant to the jurors. A defense attorney represents the defendant and makes a case on behalf of his or her client. Both have a right to question witnesses, as shown in this court drawing.

the person's due process rights. Due process ensures that people retain their rights from questioning through arrest and trial.

✓ **CHECK FOR UNDERSTANDING**

Making Connections What might happen to a person accused of a crime without the ability to file a writ of habeas corpus?

The Rights of the Accused

GUIDING QUESTION

What legal protections does the U.S. Constitution offer someone who is accused of a crime?

The Bill of Rights includes several amendments aimed at protecting the rights of people from the government. The Fourth, Fifth, Sixth, and Eighth Amendments are aimed at making sure that people are treated fairly by the criminal justice system.

These rights are based on an important principle of U.S. law, the **presumption of innocence**. That means that a person is considered innocent unless proven guilty in a court of law.

This principle means that a defendant on trial does not need to prove that he or she did not commit the crime. Instead, the government must prove that the defendant is guilty. In addition, it must prove guilt beyond a reasonable doubt. The reason for this strict standard of proof is that the defendant's liberty is at stake. For the government to take away that liberty, it must provide convincing proof.

Fourth Amendment Rights

The Fourth Amendment protects citizens against "unreasonable searches and seizures." It gives Americans the right to be secure in their homes and property.

No police officer or other government agent can search your home or take your property without getting a judge to issue a **search warrant**.

---

presumption of innocence the idea that a person is considered innocent unless proven guilty in a court of law

search warrant a court order allowing law enforcement officers to search a suspect's home or business and take specific items as evidence

During the investigation of a crime, police must keep a careful record of any evidence they collect.

To obtain a warrant, the police must show the judge that there is probable cause that the person or the property was involved in a crime. The warrant limits police action during the search. It describes the place to be searched and exactly what objects may be seized, or taken.

The courts have determined that the Fourth Amendment provides another protection. If police find evidence of a crime through an illegal search, the evidence may not be used in court. This rule is the result of a 1961 Supreme Court decision in *Mapp* v. *Ohio*. The justices ruled that evidence obtained illegally must be excluded from, or kept out of, a trial in a state court. Such evidence had already been banned from a federal trial. This principle is known as the **exclusionary rule**.

This rule, however, does not prevent the arrest or trial or even the conviction of a suspect. It does mean that the conviction might be overturned by an appeals court. That can happen if the person was found guilty based on evidence that should have been excluded but was presented during the trial.

Fifth Amendment Rights

The Fifth Amendment provides additional protections for people. It protects individuals against self-incrimination, or saying anything that indicates they were involved in a crime.

The amendment states that no person can be forced "to be a witness against himself" in a criminal case. This means that individuals do not have to answer questions that might show they were involved in a crime.

Defense attorneys may suggest that their clients not testify during a trial to prevent them from saying anything that could indicate their guilt. An accused person cannot be forced to be a witness. In addition, the prosecutor is forbidden to remind the jury that the defendant refused to testify. Also, the judge instructs the jury not to draw any conclusions based on a defendant's decision not to testify.

In the past, police often pressured people to confess to a crime before they saw a lawyer or appeared in court. The Supreme Court addressed this practice with its ruling in *Miranda* v. *Arizona* in 1966. The Court said that the police must inform suspects of their right not to answer questions. The Court decision said that the Fifth Amendment protection against self-incrimination is "one of our nation's most cherished [treasured] principles."

The Court's *Miranda* decision requires police across the nation to take certain steps to protect a person's Fifth Amendment rights. Before they can question a person in their custody, police must now issue what is known as a **Miranda Warning**. The warning informs suspects that they have the right to remain silent, the right to a lawyer, and the right to avoid incriminating themselves.

The Fifth Amendment requires the government to bring a charge of a serious crime before a body called a grand jury. A grand jury is a group of 16 to 23 citizens who play an important role in our democracy. The grand jury members hear a prosecutor's evidence to decide whether or not the government has enough evidence to bring a suspect to trial. If so, the grand jury issues an indictment, which is a formal charge for a crime. An indictment simply states the grand jury's belief that the accused may have carried out a crime. A trial will decide if the accused is guilty or innocent. The requirement to go through a grand jury applies only to the federal government and not to the states.

exclusionary rule a rule that evidence gained by police in a way that violates the Fourth Amendment may not be used in a trial

Miranda Warning a list of rights that police must inform a person of before questioning the person, including the right to avoid self-incrimination and the right to a lawyer

PHOTO:felipe caparros cruz/Alamy Stock Photo; TEXT: (r)U.S. Constitution, Amendment V, (b) Miranda v. Arizona 384 U.S. 436 (1966)

"HOW DO YOU EXPECT ME TO CONCENTRATE WHEN YOU'RE READING ME MY RIGHTS ?"

A Miranda warning is meant to protect an individual's right against self-incrimination.
Analyzing Visuals In the cartoon, what is the police officer doing? Is the officer acting appropriately? Explain.

An accused person is in jeopardy, or at risk, of being found guilty and being sent to prison. Someone found innocent goes free. What if the government decides that it might get a guilty verdict from a different jury? Can it try the person again? The Fifth Amendment protects an accused person from **double jeopardy**. Someone tried for a crime and found not guilty cannot be tried for the same crime again.

Sixth Amendment Rights

The Sixth Amendment provides several important protections. It states that accused people have the right to know what they are being charged with. The government must reveal this so they can prepare to defend themselves. Accused people also have the right to question the witnesses who give evidence against them. In addition, they have the right to call witnesses in their defense. In fact, they can call on the power of the court to force people they want as witnesses to appear. The Sixth Amendment also gives the accused the right to be represented by an attorney, to have a trial by a jury, and to have a speedy and public trial.

Right to an Attorney A trial is a complicated process that requires an understanding of the law. Most people accused of a crime do not have the knowledge to defend themselves in a trial. They need a trained lawyer to ensure they get a fair trial. The Sixth Amendment provides this protection. It grants an accused person the right to counsel, which means the right to be represented by an attorney.

Many defendants cannot afford to hire a lawyer, however. In 1938 the U.S. Supreme Court ruled that an accused person had an absolute right to counsel when charged with a felony in federal court. If the accused could not afford a lawyer, the government had to provide one. In 1963 the Supreme Court extended this rule to the states when it decided *Gideon* v. *Wainwright*.

Trial by Jury The Sixth Amendment requires that anyone accused of a crime is told exactly what they are accused of. They also have the right to question witnesses or evidence in court. Both are part of the right to be tried by an impartial, or fair, jury.

Serving on a jury is an important civic duty. Being tried by a jury of one's peers is a treasured right claimed in England nearly 800 years ago. This right helps ensure that an accused person gets a fair trial. Serving on a jury is a way of protecting the rights of others living in the same community.

A jury is made up of people who know no one in the case and who have not already formed an opinion about it. These characteristics make jurors—the members of a jury—impartial. That is, they have not decided the outcome of the case in advance but will do so only after hearing all the evidence.

Juries serve in both state courts and federal courts. Jurors in state trials tend to live in or close to the area where the crime took place. Since federal trial courts cover a large area—as much as a whole state—members of a federal jury can live farther away from the site of the crime. Jurors in state courts hear a wider range of cases. Criminal cases can include robberies, lawsuits

double jeopardy putting someone on trial for a crime for which the person was previously found not guilty over traffic accidents, disputes over contracts, or child custody cases. Juries in federal cases hear cases involving federal laws. Federal criminal cases involve such matters as bringing drugs illegally into the country or using the U.S. Mail to commit fraud. *Fraud* means "cheating someone out of money or property."

Defendants can choose to waive, or give up, the right to a jury trial. In that case, a judge decides the verdict. Why would someone waive the right to a jury? One reason is that trials without a jury are faster and less expensive. In some cases, a defendant may think that a judge would be less harsh than a jury might be.

Speedy and Public Trial The Sixth Amendment also guarantees the right to a speedy and public trial. Without this, a defendant could be held in prison for a long period waiting for a trial.

Requiring that the trial be public prevents the government from trying people in secret.

The Constitution does not define *speedy*, so the government has set specific time limits for bringing a case to trial. If the trial does not take place soon enough, the case may be dismissed. Of course, defendants also want time for their attorney to prepare a strong defense. As a result, they sometimes waive their right to a speedy trial.

Eighth Amendment Rights

The Constitution also protects people after they have been convicted of a crime. The Eighth Amendment forbids "cruel and unusual punishments." This means that a punishment may not be out of proportion to the crime. For example, a 20-year prison sentence for painting graffiti on a wall would be extreme.

Constitutional Rights of the Accused

Different parts of the Constitution protect the rights of people in different ways.

Source	Rights
Article I	• requires government to respond to writ of habeas corpus • protects against bills of attainder • protects against ex post facto laws
Fourth Amendment	• protects against unreasonable searches and seizures
Fifth Amendment	• guarantees due process • protects against self-incrimination • protects against double jeopardy • provides for grand juries in the case of federal crimes
Sixth Amendment	• guarantees the right to counsel • guarantees the right to know the accusations • guarantees the right to a speedy public trial • guarantees the right to confront witnesses • guarantees the right to be tried by an impartial jury
Eighth Amendment	• forbids cruel and unusual punishments • prohibits excessive bail
Fourteenth Amendment	• requires the states to treat all people equally under the law • guarantees due process • guarantees equal protection of the laws

EXAMINE THE CHART

1. **Explaining** How does the Fifth Amendment protect defendants during jury trials?
2. **Analyzing** How does due process of law limit what the government can do when prosecuting a crime?

People who oppose the death penalty sometimes hold protests or other demonstrations to voice their opinion.

Many debates over the meaning of the Eighth Amendment involve the death penalty, or **capital punishment**. The death penalty was more common in the past than today. Today, many people believe that this punishment is too extreme. Critics also say that it is more often imposed on members of minority groups than on white people. The U.S. Supreme Court found this to be the case in the 1970s. In *Furman* v. *Georgia*, the Court said that African Americans and poor people were being sentenced to death unfairly. For a time, no executions were allowed anywhere in the United States. Gradually, a majority of states started using the death penalty again with new procedures to meet the Court's guidelines. Some states removed the death penalty from their law codes. By the early 2020s, nearly half of the states had outlawed the death penalty.

The Eighth Amendment also protects people from excessive **bail**. Bail is a sum of money paid by someone awaiting trial that allows their release from jail or prison until the trial date. The payment is made along with a promise to appear for the trial. When the defendant does appear for the trial, the money is returned. By preventing excessive bail, the Eighth Amendment can prevent people from being held for months before their case goes to trial.

✓ **CHECK FOR UNDERSTANDING**

1. **Identifying** Which amendment guarantees a defendant the right to counsel?
2. **Making Connections** Why do you think it is important for accused people to have public trials?

LESSON ACTIVITIES

1. **Informative/Explanatory Writing** Write one or two paragraphs explaining what due process means and why protecting due process rights is so important.

2. **Collaborating** Work in small groups to create a multimedia presentation on one of the amendments described in this lesson. Explain the rights that it has guaranteed to U.S. citizens and tell how it has affected procedures of the criminal justice system. Use digital media in the presentation, including at least three of the following: text, graphic, audio, visual, and interactive elements. Be sure your use of digital media adds to the viewers' understanding.

capital punishment the death penalty
bail a sum of money paid by someone awaiting trial that allows their release from jail until the trial date

04
Civil Law

READING STRATEGY

Analyzing Key Ideas and Details As you read, complete a graphic organizer such as this one to identify characteristics of civil law.

Type	Characteristics
Laws about contracts and property	
Laws about family issues	
Laws about personal injuries	

Types of Civil Law

GUIDING QUESTION

What is civil law?

When you think about the law, you may think about crimes and police. Criminal law involves the legal system seeking to punish someone who caused harm to society. There is another important branch of law, though—civil law. Civil law involves disagreements between two people or groups. Those who disagree—called *parties*—can be two people, one person and a company, two companies, or a person or a company and a government, or two governments such as state governments. Whoever the two parties are, the center of the dispute is that one party claims to have been harmed in some way by the other party.

Like criminal law, civil law can involve a court case. However, the kinds of cases are very different. A criminal case begins when a person is charged with a crime. During the trial, a representative of the state prosecutes the accused person. A civil case begins when an individual or a group files a lawsuit. In the legal system, to *file* means to "submit a formal document to the court." The party filing the lawsuit is the **plaintiff**. The party being sued is the **defendant**. Both sides typically hire an attorney to represent their position. Civil disputes involve such matters as disputes about property or family matters.

plaintiff the party that files a lawsuit

defendant the party that is being sued

In this photo, a lawyer for one party to a civil case presents the client's side of the dispute to the court using an illustration. Like criminal trials, civil trials feature lawyers for each side presenting their case and are presided over by a judge.

Laws About Contracts and Property

People enter into contracts every day. Renters sign agreements to rent an apartment. That agreement is a contract. Agreements with Internet service providers or cell phone companies are contracts too. People who take out a loan to buy a car sign a contract. The lender gives them money, which they agree to repay over a certain period of time.

A **contract** is an agreement between two or more parties to exchange something of value. The contract could be between two or more individuals, such as a few people who agree to join together to form a business. It can be between companies, such as a company providing computer equipment and services to a chain of stores. Contracts can also be between individuals and businesses, as is the case when people buy cell-phone plans. Contract law involves the duty all parties have to a contract to fulfill their promises.

Many contracts are formal, written documents. All contracts do not have to be written, though. For example, when you order a meal at restaurant, you are forming a contract. Each party promises the other something of value. The restaurant promises to make you a meal and serve it to you. You promise to pay for the food. This kind of contract is called an oral, or spoken, contract.

If a contract involves one party paying more than $500, it must be written for it to be enforced in court. Written contracts are often quite **complex** or have many parts. Because they are complex, people must read contracts carefully before signing them.

---

contract a set of promises between agreeing parties that is enforceable by law

complex having many parts

The construction of an office building involves many contracts with different companies. Once the building is completed, the owner will enter contracts with companies that rent office space.

Michael Doolittle/Alamy Stock Photo

In a contract, if one party does not do what was agreed upon, the other party can file a lawsuit. In that suit, the plaintiff makes a claim of injury or harm that resulted from the first party failing to follow the contract. For example, a store owner might sue a business that did not deliver merchandise that had been promised or that delivered the merchandise later than stated in the contract. A worker may sue an employer to receive a bonus payment that had been promised but not made.

Some contracts involve the buying and selling of homes, offices, farms, and other kinds of property. Others involve agreements about renting a property from the owner.

When property is sold, the seller must show papers that prove legal ownership of the property. Those papers make it clear that the person has the right to sell or transfer the property. Buyers will have those papers changed to show that they are now the legal owner. That way no one can challenge their right to the property.

Proper care for and use of property is another part of property law. For instance, laws require building owners who rent out offices to businesses to maintain the property and keep it in good shape. At the same time, the business that rents the space has a responsibility to treat the property well and not damage it.

Disagreements can occur between the two parties related to these responsibilities. For example, the owner of an apartment building may be responsible for providing working kitchen appliances along with the living space. If an appliance stops working, the owner has to pay to fix or replace it. If the renter damages it, however, the renter would be responsible for the repairs. Sometimes owners and renters disagree over how a problem started. In that case, one might sue the other to get the court to force them to take responsibility for the problem.

Laws About Family Issues

Civil law also includes family matters and issues. This type of law involves rules applied to relationships within a family. It focuses on matters such as birth, adoption, marriage, and death.

Divorce is a major area in family law. Many lawsuits relate to how to divide a home or other property that a divorcing couple owned together. Another common question in divorces is how the two people will share responsibility for raising any children they have.

Buying a home makes a person a property owner. It is a complex process, which gives the homeowner the right to sell the property later if desired.

When a family member dies, surviving family members sometimes disagree about how to divide the dead person's property. This may happen because the deceased family member did not leave a will. A **will** is a legal document that provides instructions about how to handle a person's money or property after death. These disputes can end up in court.

Laws About Personal Injuries

Picture a sidewalk covered with ice and snow after a massive storm. The sidewalk is slippery because the homeowner failed to shovel it in a timely manner. Now, suppose someone slips and falls on this sidewalk and twists an ankle or breaks an arm. The injured person could sue the homeowner to pay for any medical bills.

This example relates to the part of civil law called *personal injury* law. Personal injury involves wrongful actions that cause injury to another person or damage to a person's property. This kind of case is called a **tort**, which is a wrongful act or failure to act that results in injury or harm. The idea behind tort law is to provide relief to the person who suffered the loss and to have the person responsible for it bear the cost of that loss.

will a legal document that provides instructions about how to handle a person's money or property after death

tort a wrongful act, other than breaking a contract, for which an injured party has the right to sue

For example, a homeowner who fails to shovel a sidewalk likely does not intend for anyone to fall and hurt themselves. The idea is that the homeowner is responsible for the injury because of a failure to do something that a reasonable person would have done. Another example of a tort is if a company makes a product that does not work properly and causes harm, such as a heater that overheats and bursts into flames. In that case, the person who purchased the heater and suffered the injury can sue the company.

✓ CHECK FOR UNDERSTANDING

1. **Contrasting** How does civil law differ from criminal law?
2. **Identifying** In what way does personal injury law provide an opportunity for someone who suffers an injury to obtain justice?

Property owners may be found responsible for any harm or injury suffered by another person on their property if they did not do what a reasonable person would do to prevent an injury.

Explaining How is this homeowner protecting himself from this kind of problem?

The Legal Process in Civil Cases

GUIDING QUESTION
What legal procedures are followed in civil lawsuits?

A civil law case begins when the plaintiff's lawyer files a **complaint** with the court. A complaint is a formal notice to the defendant that the plaintiff has filed a lawsuit. It explains the harm or injury that the plaintiff has experienced and how the defendant is responsible for it.

A complaint may ask for a court order to require the defendant to do something, such as honor a contract and make good on what was promised. Often, it asks the court to order the defendant to pay the plaintiff a sum of money, known as **damages**. This sum compensates the plaintiff for the losses suffered.

For example, suppose that the Acme Company failed to deliver promised building supplies to a company named Home Builders. As a result, Home Builders lost sales when buyers cancelled their purchase agreements. Home Builders files a complaint against Acme over the business it lost. It could ask for damages such as Acme covering the cost of the lost business.

After receiving the complaint from Home Builders, the court issues a **summons** to the defendant, which is Acme. A summons is a court order that tells someone to appear in court at a particular day and time to face a complaint or charge.

Before the Trial

Acme responds to the summons by getting a lawyer to handle its defense. That lawyer files a written answer to the charges. In the next step, the lawyers on each side build their cases. They check the facts, question possible witnesses, and gather evidence to be used in a trial. This process is called *discovery*. During discovery, the two sides ask each other for certain kinds of

complaint a formal notice that a lawsuit has been brought

damages money ordered by a court to be paid for injuries or losses suffered

summons a notice directing someone to appear in court to answer a complaint or charge

Lisa Stokes/Getty Images

information. Each side is required to provide the requested documents. This helps make sure that the process is fair to both sides.

At any time, the two companies can reach an agreement to settle, or end, a lawsuit. This agreement is called a **settlement**. The defendant might agree to pay the plaintiff a sum of money—usually less than what the plaintiff has asked for—in return for the defendant dropping the lawsuit.

Most civil cases end in a settlement. Reaching a settlement can save the time and costs of a trial. Sometimes the parties settle after the trial begins but before it is concluded. One thing that defendants like about settlements is that the terms of a settlement are kept secret. The result of a trial, however, is a matter of public record.

The Trial

Suppose that Home Builders and Acme do not settle their case. Instead, it goes to trial. Generally, judges hear and decide civil cases, but either side can ask the court to call a jury. In either situation, the judge presides over the case, keeping order and making sure that both sides receive equal treatment.

In a civil trial, plaintiffs—in this example, Home Builders—present their evidence first. Then the defendant, Acme, offers its defense. Both sides can call the witnesses they want and present whatever documents they have as evidence. Lawyers for the party that called a witness question that person first. Then the lawyers for the other side ask any questions they have. After both sides have presented all their evidence, the lawyers take turns making closing statements, in which they summarize their case. Finally, the judge or jury delivers its verdict in favor of one of the parties.

After the verdict comes the decision on any damages. If the plaintiff—Home Builders—wins, the jury or the judge decides how much Acme, the defendant, must pay in damages. In some cases, the court awards **punitive** damages. This is additional money the defendant must pay as a punishment for bad conduct. If a defendant such as Acme wins, there are no damages.

settlement an agreement by the two parties to a lawsuit to settle the dispute without concluding the trial and having a verdict

punitive intended to provide punishment

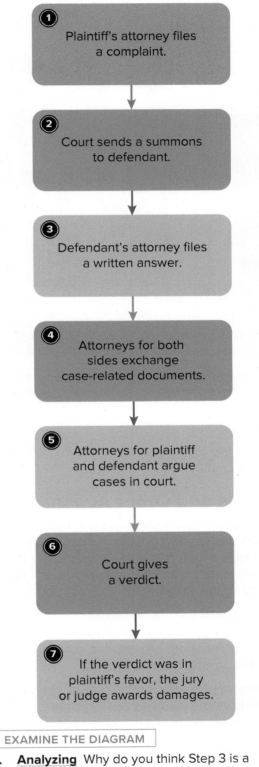

The Legal Process in Civil Cases

At any point in the process depicted here, the two parties can agree to settle the dispute.

1. Plaintiff's attorney files a complaint.
2. Court sends a summons to defendant.
3. Defendant's attorney files a written answer.
4. Attorneys for both sides exchange case-related documents.
5. Attorneys for plaintiff and defendant argue cases in court.
6. Court gives a verdict.
7. If the verdict was in plaintiff's favor, the jury or judge awards damages.

EXAMINE THE DIAGRAM

1. **Analyzing** Why do you think Step 3 is a necessary part of the process?
2. **Inferring** Which side do you think presents its case first in Step 5? Why do you think so?

Federal and state governments have appeals courts to review any errors that may have happened at the trial court. This courthouse is in Washington, D.C.

However, the judge may order the plaintiff to pay the court costs.

Appeals and Other Actions

The side that loses a civil case can appeal the decision to a higher court. In a civil case, either the plaintiff or defendant can appeal after losing. In a criminal case, only the defendant can appeal after losing the case.

The appeal cannot be based on the facts of the case. Appeals can only be made on the grounds of incorrect procedures at the trial or errors in applying the relevant law.

Sometimes a winning party must ask the court to become involved again. For instance, if the defendant does not pay damages that had been awarded, the plaintiff may ask the court for an order forcing the defendant to pay.

✓ **CHECK FOR UNDERSTANDING**

1. **Explaining** What are the advantages of reaching a settlement in a civil lawsuit?

2. **Analyzing** What are two examples of features of a civil trial that demonstrate the effort to provide each party in the dispute an equal chance to make its case?

LESSON ACTIVITIES

1. **Informative/Explanatory Writing** Write a brief paragraph that provides an example of a kind of dispute that may arise in each of the three areas of civil law described in this lesson. Do not repeat one of the examples given in the text.

2. **Collaborating** Work in small groups to create a brochure that explains the steps of a civil case that goes to trial. Your brochure should provide information for potential plaintiffs or defendants to help them understand the process from beginning to end.

Analyzing Key Ideas and Details As you read, complete a graphic organizer such as this one to identify facts about misdemeanors and felonies, including how they are the same and how they are different.

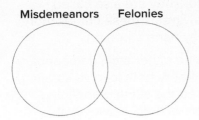

Misdemeanors   Felonies

Crime and Punishment

What does criminal law involve?

Civil law includes disagreements between people or organizations. Criminal law involves actions that a government defines as a crime. A **crime** is any act that breaks a criminal law. A good government defines only harmful acts as crimes. Some examples of crimes today are driving under the influence of alcohol, breaking into someone's home, and killing someone.

In an ideal society, people do not purposefully hurt each other or damage each other's property. If people break these rules, society can punish them. People who are found guilty of serious crimes can be sent to prison. The goal of punishment is to maintain order. First, the punishment may restore order by forcing a criminal to face consequences for committing a crime. Second, the punishment may warn others not to do the same thing that the punished person did.

Each state has a **penal** (PEE•nuhl) **code**. This document lists the state's criminal laws and identifies the proper punishment for each crime. The federal government has a penal code, too. Federal crimes include printing false U.S. currency and identity theft, among many other examples. Most crimes, though, break state laws. For that reason, most criminal cases are tried in state courts, and most prisoners are jailed in state prisons.

crime an act that breaks a law and causes harm to people or damage to property

penal code the written collection of criminal laws of a state or the nation

Some prisons offer programs to help inmates improve their lives and prepare to be contributing members of society after release.

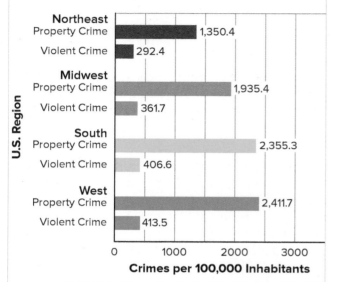

U.S. Crime Rates by Region, 2019

According to the Federal Bureau of Investigation, 7.7 million criminal offenses were reported in the United States in 2019. They fell into two main categories.

U.S. Region (vertical axis)

Northeast
- Property Crime: 1,350.4
- Violent Crime: 292.4

Midwest
- Property Crime: 1,935.4
- Violent Crime: 361.7

South
- Property Crime: 2,355.3
- Violent Crime: 406.6

West
- Property Crime: 2,411.7
- Violent Crime: 413.5

Crimes per 100,000 Inhabitants (0, 1000, 2000, 3000)

Source: Federal Bureau of Investigation, *Crime in the United States*, 2019.

EXAMINE THE GRAPH

1. **Analyzing Visuals** Which type of crime is more common in every region?
2. **Contrasting** According to the graph, which region of the country has the highest rates of both property crime and violent crime?

Types of Crime

Crimes can be divided into two broad categories based on the **severity**, or seriousness, of the offense. Minor crimes are **misdemeanors** (mihs•dih•MEE•nuhrz). Trespassing—entering or being on someone's property without permission—is a misdemeanor. Stealing something worth a small amount of money is also a misdemeanor. The punishments for misdemeanors are fines of a few hundred to a few thousand dollars or a year or so in jail.

A **felony** is a more serious crime. Examples are kidnapping and battery, which is purposefully having contact with someone in a way that harms the other person. Felonies are punishable by more than one year in prison.

Homicide—killing another person—is the most serious felony. There are various types of homicides. Involuntary manslaughter happens when someone kills another person without meaning to harm them. For example, a driver might hit and kill someone while speeding in a car. Voluntary manslaughter happens when someone intends to harm another person but not kill them, such as in a fight. A murder is killing another person when intending to do so.

Some crimes, such as theft, are property crimes. Others, such as battery and murder, are crimes against people. They are also called *violent crimes*. The law treats these crimes more seriously because they harm a person.

Some crimes can be either a misdemeanor or a felony. Theft and robbery both involve stealing, but they are not treated the same. Shoplifting something from a store is theft. However, it is more likely to be a misdemeanor. Taking something from a person by force or threat is robbery. That crime is almost always a felony.

Punishment for Crimes

Generally, more serious crimes result in harsher punishment. Shoplifting may be punished by a short jail term. Murder can result in life in prison or a death sentence, depending on state law.

Most criminal laws set minimum and maximum penalties for each type of crime. This gives a judge some leeway in determining the **sentence**, or punishment, for a particular case. For example, someone who commits a crime for the first time may be given a lighter sentence than someone who has committed a number of crimes in the past.

Some prisoners are **granted**, or allowed, parole. **Parole** is release from prison before a full sentence has been served. Someone who has been paroled must report to a parole officer. That official makes sure the person is behaving lawfully.

---

severity seriousness

misdemeanor a minor crime for which a person can be fined a small sum of money or jailed for a year or so

felony a more serious crime such as murder, rape, kidnapping, or robbery

---

sentence the punishment given to someone found guilty of committing a crime

grant to allow

parole release from prison before a full sentence has been served

The Purposes of Punishment

Prison sentences have several purposes. First, punishment may serve justice by punishing the offender for wrongdoing. Second, putting someone in prison can protect society by preventing that person from committing another crime. Third, punishment can warn other people not to break the law by showing that doing so has serious consequences. Finally, punishment can help criminals learn to act differently in the future. Some jails and prisons have counseling, education, and job-training programs. Prisoners can take part in these programs to gain skills that will help them become responsible members of society after they are released. A specific law that requires punishment may be unfair or ineffective, and in a democracy, people often disagree about appropriate punishments.

✓ **CHECK FOR UNDERSTANDING**

1. **Contrasting** How do felonies and misdemeanors differ in their nature and their punishments?
2. **Identifying** What are two purposes of punishing someone found guilty of committing a crime?

Criminal Case Procedures

GUIDING QUESTION

What are the legal procedures in a criminal law case?

The Bill of Rights protects a person suspected or accused of a crime at each step during a criminal case. To treat a suspect fairly, the government must follow the rules of due process.

Following due process includes the treatment an accused person receives during a trial. In a criminal case, the accused person is called the *defendant*. The government, which tries to prove the person's guilt, is the **prosecution**. In a civil case, the party being defended from the charge of causing harm is also called the *defendant*. The party that brings the lawsuit and charges that harm was committed is called the *plaintiff*.

Arrest and Booking

Criminal cases begin when police believe a crime has been committed. The police work to gather enough evidence linking a person or persons to the crime. If they have enough convincing evidence, a judge will issue an order called a warrant to authorize the arrest. Even at this early stage, police action is reviewed by the judicial branch.

When making the arrest, the police must follow the U.S. Supreme Court's rules about the Miranda Warning. They must tell accused persons of their right to remain silent and to have an attorney. Then the police take the suspect to a station for booking, or recording the arrest. Suspects are photographed and fingerprinted.

The Preliminary Hearing

After booking, the police bring the suspect before a judge to be charged. Lawyers appear at this stage. A prosecutor, who works for the government, must show the judge there is probable cause—a good reason—to believe the accused person has committed the crime. The judge explains the charges to the suspect. The defendant can have a lawyer present at this hearing.

With misdemeanors, the suspect pleads guilty or not guilty at the hearing. The judge sentences defendants who plead guilty or sets a trial date for those who plead not guilty.

With a felony, the suspect does not yet enter a plea. Instead, the judge either releases the suspect or instructs the police to continue to hold the person in custody. Sometimes, the judge requires the suspect to post bail in order to be released.

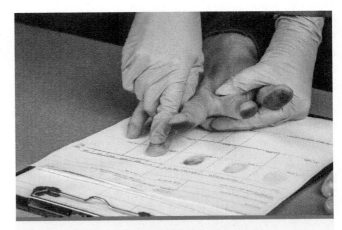

Police take the fingerprints of every person they arrest. Each person has a unique set of fingerprints that do not change during the person's lifetime.

---

prosecution the government acting in its role as the party who starts the legal proceedings against someone accused of a crime

Steps in a Criminal Case

The diagram shows all the steps that may take place with a criminal case. Many cases do not follow all these steps. With some, charges are dropped. In many cases, a plea bargain ends the case before reaching the final steps.

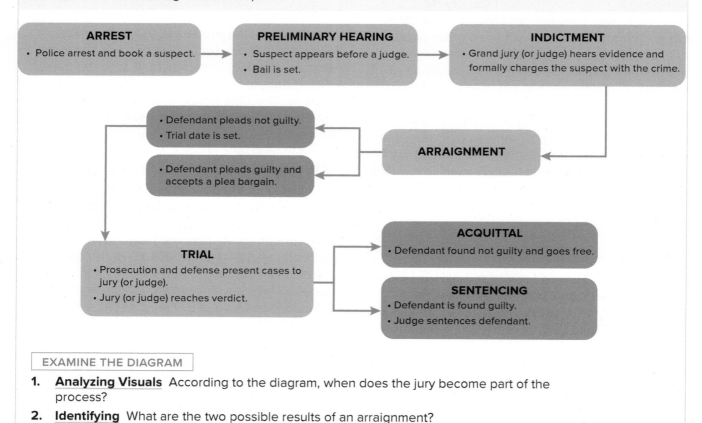

ARREST
- Police arrest and book a suspect.

PRELIMINARY HEARING
- Suspect appears before a judge.
- Bail is set.

INDICTMENT
- Grand jury (or judge) hears evidence and formally charges the suspect with the crime.

ARRAIGNMENT

- Defendant pleads not guilty.
- Trial date is set.

- Defendant pleads guilty and accepts a plea bargain.

TRIAL
- Prosecution and defense present cases to jury (or judge).
- Jury (or judge) reaches verdict.

ACQUITTAL
- Defendant found not guilty and goes free.

SENTENCING
- Defendant is found guilty.
- Judge sentences defendant.

EXAMINE THE DIAGRAM

1. **Analyzing Visuals** According to the diagram, when does the jury become part of the process?
2. **Identifying** What are the two possible results of an arraignment?

Indictment, Arraignment, and Plea

The next step in a felony case is to indict the accused, or formally charge the person with the crime. This step can be done either by a judge or a grand jury, depending on state law. If the judge or grand jury finds there is not enough evidence against the accused, they dismiss the case.

If the suspect is indicted, the next step is to arraign him or her. At this point, called the *arraignment*, someone accused of a felony enters a plea. As with a misdemeanor, a guilty plea results in sentencing. If the plea is not guilty, the judge sets a trial date.

The trial may never take place. Most criminal cases end through a **plea bargain**. In a plea bargain, a defendant agrees to plead guilty to a less serious crime in order to receive a lighter sentence. Plea bargaining saves the government the time and expense of a trial. If the two sides reach an agreement, the case ends there. Defendants generally receive a lighter sentence than they would if found guilty of the original charges.

The Trial

The Sixth Amendment guarantees a defendant the right to a trial by jury. Defendants can choose to waive that right, in which case the judge will determine whether they are guilty. That happens in most felony cases. When defendants do elect to have a jury, the first step in the trial is to choose jurors.

In many civil cases, juries can have as few as 6 members. For most felony trials, 12 jurors are chosen. The process begins by seating 12 people who have been called to jury duty.

plea bargain an agreement in which a defendant agrees to plead guilty to a less serious crime in order to receive a lighter sentence

The prosecution and defense lawyers get to question the possible jurors. They can ask the judge to dismiss any person they think might not judge the case fairly. Eventually, the needed number of jurors is chosen. Sometimes alternate jurors are also chosen. They take an oath to listen to all the evidence and judge the case fairly.

Next, the lawyers for each side make opening statements, with the prosecution going first. They use these statements to outline their cases. The next step is to present evidence, which again begins with the prosecution. Each side calls witnesses, who are sworn to tell the truth. The side that called a witness questions the person first. Then the other side has the opportunity to conduct a **cross-examination**. After those

cross-examination the questioning of a witness at a trial or hearing to check or discredit the witness's testimony

questions are done, the side that called the witness may ask the person follow-up questions.

After presenting their cases, the two sides make closing statements. The prosecution goes first, followed by the defense. Then the prosecution has a final opportunity to speak. The lawyers review the evidence they have presented and sum up the arguments they have given. They also point out the weaknesses they see in the other side's case. Next, the judge provides jurors with instructions about how to apply the law to make their decision.

The Verdict and Sentencing

Jurors then meet in private to discuss the evidence. They can meet for as long as necessary to reach a decision.

Jurors vote on whether or not to find the defendant guilty. Our legal system is based on the idea that a person is innocent unless proven guilty.

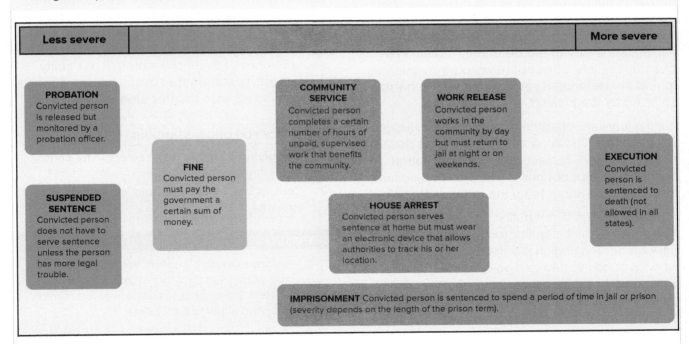

Sentencing Options

A variety of sentencing options are available for persons found guilty in a criminal trial, though all options are not available for all crimes or in all states.

Less severe		More severe

PROBATION Convicted person is released but monitored by a probation officer.

SUSPENDED SENTENCE Convicted person does not have to serve sentence unless the person has more legal trouble.

FINE Convicted person must pay the government a certain sum of money.

COMMUNITY SERVICE Convicted person completes a certain number of hours of unpaid, supervised work that benefits the community.

HOUSE ARREST Convicted person serves sentence at home but must wear an electronic device that allows authorities to track his or her location.

WORK RELEASE Convicted person works in the community by day but must return to jail at night or on weekends.

EXECUTION Convicted person is sentenced to death (not allowed in all states).

IMPRISONMENT Convicted person is sentenced to spend a period of time in jail or prison (severity depends on the length of the prison term).

EXAMINE THE CHART

1. **Analyzing Visuals** Which sentences do you think would be used for misdemeanors and which do you think would be used for felonies?

2. **Inferring** Would a judge be more likely to give a suspended sentence to someone who committed a crime for the first time or to someone with a criminal record? Why do you think so?

A sentence in a prison like this one is a possible punishment for committing a serious offense.

Analyzing Visuals How would you describe this prison?

In a criminal trial, the prosecution has the burden of proof. It must convince the jury of the defendant's guilt beyond a reasonable doubt.

With felonies, a guilty verdict must be unanimous—that is, all jurors must agree that the person is guilty. A verdict of not guilty does not mean the jury believes the person to be innocent. It only means that the prosecution failed to convince the jury of the defendant's guilt. In a civil trial the jury does not have to be unanimous to find the defendant responsible for the harm suffered by the plaintiff.

If a jury cannot agree on a verdict, the judge will declare a mistrial. A mistrial means no decision has been made. The accused person is found neither guilty nor not guilty. The prosecution must then decide whether to try the defendant again.

If the verdict is not guilty, the defendant goes free. If the verdict is guilty, the judge sets a court date for sentencing. In a civil case, a defendant who loses has to pay damages to the plaintiff who sued. In a criminal case, a defendant found guilty may be sent to jail. In some cases, judges may choose among other sentences.

Appealing the Verdict

A person who has been convicted of a crime has the right to appeal the verdict or the sentence. If the jury acquitted the defendant, the prosecution cannot appeal. That is one difference with a civil case. Either side that loses a civil case can appeal the decision.

The appeals court does not hear witnesses or listen to evidence about the facts of the case. The judges on the appeals court read briefs, or written documents, submitted by lawyers arguing whether or not the defendant's rights were violated or if the judge made errors during the trial. Their job is to determine if the trial was conducted in a fair way. For example, a judge could have allowed the jury to hear evidence that should not have been presented. If the guilty verdict was based on that evidence, the appeals court could reverse the decision.

✓ **CHECK FOR UNDERSTANDING**

1. **Identifying** How are juries selected for criminal felony trials, and why is their role important?

2. **Contrasting** How do criminal trials differ from appeals?

LESSON ACTIVITIES

1. **Informative/Explanatory Writing** Describe the process of a criminal trial, and point out at least three differences between a criminal trial and a trial in a civil case.

2. **Collaborating** Work in a small group to make a diagram showing the process of a criminal case from arrest to the appeal. Add notes to the diagram to explain how due process rights are involved in different stages. Cite specific amendments to the U.S. Constitution that are involved at each point.

06

Analyzing Supreme Court Cases: Rights of the Accused

 COMPELLING QUESTION

How is equal justice for accused persons ensured in the American legal system?

Plan Your Inquiry

DEVELOPING QUESTIONS

Think about the rights of the accused guaranteed in the Bill of Rights. What protections do the Fourth, Fifth, Sixth and Eighth Amendments provide? How have those rights been secured? Then read the Compelling Question for this lesson. What questions can help you answer this Compelling Question? Create a graphic organizer such as the one below. Write these Supporting Questions in your graphic organizer.

Supporting Questions	Primary Source or Secondary Source	What this source tells me about the rights of the accused	Questions the source leaves unanswered
	A		
	B		
	C		
	D		
	E		
	F		

ANALYZING SOURCES

Next, examine the sources in this lesson. Analyze each source by answering the questions that follow it. How does each source help you answer each Supporting Question you created? What questions do you still have? Write these in your graphic organizer.

After you analyze the sources, you will:
- use the evidence from the sources,
- communicate your conclusions,
- and take informed action.

Case Summaries

This lesson examines two Supreme Court cases dealing with the rights of those accused of committing a crime.

Gideon v. Wainwright In 1961 Clarence Earl Gideon was arrested and charged with breaking and entering a pool hall. When he appeared for trial, he asked the state of Florida to provide him with an attorney because he could not afford one. The judge denied his request. Gideon defended himself and was found guilty. He appealed the conviction and five-year prison sentence. He claimed that the judge's refusal to provide an attorney violated his Sixth Amendment rights. The Florida Supreme Court denied his appeal. He then filed with the U.S. Supreme Court, which agreed to hear the case.

Miranda v. Arizona In 1963 a woman identified Ernesto Miranda as the man who had kidnapped and assaulted her. Miranda was arrested. Police questioned him for two hours without an attorney being present. Miranda signed a written confession. He was convicted and sentenced to prison. His attorney challenged the verdict, arguing that Miranda had not been properly informed of his right to counsel during police questioning. The Arizona Supreme Court ruled against Miranda, but his case was appealed to the U.S. Supreme Court.

» Suspects being questioned by the police have the right to remain silent and the right to have an attorney present if they wish.

Opinion of the Court: *Gideon* v. *Wainwright*

The *Gideon* case came to the U.S. Supreme Court in the form of a handwritten appeal sent by Gideon from a Florida prison. In the 1930s, the U.S. Supreme Court had decided that the government had to provide an attorney to accused persons who could not afford one if they were charged with a federal crime. In 1942 a plaintiff named Betts argued that the same requirement should apply to those accused in state court. A divided Court ruled against Betts. In accepting Gideon's appeal, the Supreme Court asked lawyers to answer the question "Should this Court's holding in *Betts* v. *Brady* . . . be reconsidered?" The image shows the first page of Gideon's petition to the Supreme Court.

PRIMARY SOURCE: SUPREME COURT OPINION

66 The Sixth Amendment provides, 'In all criminal prosecutions, the accused shall enjoy the right . . . to have the Assistance of **Counsel** for his defence.' We have construed [interpreted] this to mean that, in federal courts, counsel must be provided for defendants unable to employ counsel unless the right is **competently** and intelligently waived [refused]. . . . Betts argued that this right is extended to indigent [poor] defendants in state courts by the Fourteenth Amendment. In response, the Court stated that, while the Sixth Amendment laid down 'no rule for the conduct of the States, the question recurs [repeats] whether the constraint [limitation] laid by the Amendment upon the national courts expresses a rule so fundamental and essential to a fair trial, and so, to **due process of law**, that it is made obligatory upon the States by the Fourteenth Amendment.' . . . [T]he Court concluded [in *Betts*] that 'appointment of counsel is not a fundamental right, essential to a fair trial.'

We accept . . . that a provision of the Bill of Rights which is 'fundamental and essential to a fair trial' is made obligatory upon the States by the Fourteenth Amendment. . . . [T]he Sixth Amendment's guarantee of counsel is . . . one of those fundamental rights. 99

— Justice Hugo Black, Opinion of the Court, *Gideon* v. *Wainwright*, 372 U.S. 335, 1963

---

counsel a lawyer

competently reflecting a sound mind

due process of law following established and fair legal procedures

---

EXAMINE THE SOURCE

1. **Explaining** Why does Justice Black reference the *Betts* ruling?
2. **Analyzing Perspectives** What did the Supreme Court decide in *Gideon*, and why?

PHOTO: National Archives and Records Administration (01073_2003_001_A); TEXT: Gideon v. Wainwright, 372 U.S. 335 (1963)

B

"The Legacy of *Gideon* v. *Wainwright*"

The Department of Justice oversees law enforcement across the nation. It tries to ensure that the criminal justice system provides fair and equal treatment to all persons who come in contact with that system. This article discusses issues related to the use of public defenders. These are the defense attorneys that governments provide to defendants who cannot afford to hire a lawyer.

SECONDARY SOURCE: WEB ARTICLE

66 Despite the significant progress that has been made over 50 years after the decision, the promise of *Gideon* remains unfulfilled. The quality of criminal defense services varies widely across states and localities. Many defenders struggle under excessive [heavy] caseloads and lack adequate funding and independence, making it impossible for them to meet their legal and **ethical** obligations to represent their clients effectively. . . .

The Justice Department is providing a number of tools and resources to help establish effective **indigent defense systems** across the nation. In 2010 the Department also launched the Office for Access to Justice—establishing a new, permanent office focused on enhancing access to criminal and civil legal services for those who cannot afford them. 99

— "The Legacy of *Gideon* v. *Wainwright*," U.S. Department of Justice website, 2018

ethical based on standards of how people ought to behave

indigent defense systems programs for providing public defenders for defendants who are poor

EXAMINE THE SOURCE

1. **Summarizing** Why does the article say that "the promise of *Gideon* remains unfulfilled"?
2. **Explaining** How is the Department of Justice working to fix the issues it sees with attaining the fair and equal treatment promised in *Gideon* v. *Wainwright*?

C

The Right to a Second Rate Lawyer

In this cartoon, the artist comments on the effectiveness of *Gideon* v. *Wainwright*.

PRIMARY SOURCE: POLITICAL CARTOON

"You have the right to legal representation, if you can't afford a lawyer, an inexperienced, second rate one will be appointed to you."

EXAMINE THE SOURCE

1. **Analyzing Perspectives** What does the cartoon suggest about the legacy of the *Gideon* v. *Wainwright* ruling?
2. **Making Connections** How is the cartoon related to the content of the web article?

Opinion of the Court: *Miranda* v. *Arizona*

The 1966 ruling in *Miranda* v. *Arizona* established rules that police officers must follow when interrogating, or questioning, persons suspected of having committed crimes. In particular, it requires officers to notify suspects of their rights under the Fifth and Sixth Amendments. The Fifth Amendment guarantees the right to not answer questions to prevent incriminating oneself. The Sixth Amendment guarantees the accused the right to an attorney, among other rights.

PRIMARY SOURCE: SUPREME COURT OPINION

66 That counsel is present when statements are taken from an individual during interrogation obviously enhances [improves] the **integrity** of the fact-finding processes in court. The presence of an attorney, and the warnings delivered to the individual, enable the defendant under otherwise compelling [forceful] circumstances to tell his story without fear, effectively, and in a way that eliminates the evils in the interrogation process. . . .

To summarize, we hold that when an individual is taken into **custody** or otherwise **deprived of** his freedom by the authorities in any significant way and is subjected to questioning, the privilege against **self-incrimination** is jeopardized [put at risk]. Procedural safeguards must be employed [used] to protect the privilege, and unless other fully effective means are adopted to notify the person of his right of silence and to assure that the exercise of the right will be scrupulously [strictly] honored, the following measures are required. He must be warned prior to any questioning that he has a right to remain silent, that anything he says can be used against him in a court of law, that he has the right to the presence of an attorney during the interrogation, and that if he cannot afford an attorney one will be appointed for him prior to any questioning if he so desires. Opportunity to exercise these rights must be afforded [given] to him throughout the interrogation. After such warnings have been given, and such opportunity afforded him, the individual may knowingly and intelligently waive [refuse] these rights and agree to answer questions or make a statement. But unless and until such warnings and waiver are demonstrated by the prosecution at trial, no evidence obtained as a result of interrogation can be used against him. 99

— Chief Justice Earl Warren, Opinion of the Court, *Miranda* v. *Arizona*, 384 U.S. 436, 1966

integrity being or believed to be honest and fair

custody control exercised by an authority, such as the police

deprived of had something taken away from

self-incrimination giving testimony likely to make oneself appear guilty of a crime

---

> EXAMINE THE SOURCE

1. **Making Connections** Which part of the warnings required under *Miranda* v. *Arizona* relate to the Fifth Amendment? Which to the Sixth?

2. **Identifying Cause and Effect** What might happen if these rights are not communicated to suspects before interrogation?

Dissenting Opinion: *Miranda* v. *Arizona*

While *Gideon* was a unanimous decision, *Miranda* was supported by only five justices. Four members of the Court disagreed with the majority. Justice Byron White wrote a dissenting opinion explaining his objections to the majority ruling. Two justices joined his opinion.

PRIMARY SOURCE: SUPREME COURT OPINION

❝ The obvious underpinning [basis] of the Court's decision is a deep-seated distrust of all confessions. As the Court declares that the accused may not be interrogated without counsel present, absent [without] a waiver of the right to counsel, and as the Court all but admonishes [warns] the lawyer to advise the accused to remain silent, the result adds up to a judicial judgment that evidence from the accused should not be used against him in any way, whether compelled [forced] or not. This is the not so subtle [faint] overtone [suggestion] of the opinion—that it is inherently [naturally] wrong for the police to gather evidence from the accused himself. And this is precisely the nub [point] of this dissent. I see nothing wrong or immoral, and certainly nothing unconstitutional, in the police's asking a suspect whom they have reasonable cause to arrest whether or not he killed his wife, or in confronting him with the evidence on which the arrest was based, at least where he has been plainly advised that he may remain completely silent. . . .

In some unknown number of cases, the Court's rule will return a . . . criminal to the streets and to the environment which produced him, to repeat his crime whenever it pleases him. As a consequence, there will not be a gain, but a loss, in human **dignity**. ❞

— Justice Byron White, Dissenting Opinion, *Miranda* v. *Arizona*, 384 U.S. 436, 1966

dignity being worthy of respect

> EXAMINE THE SOURCE

1. **Analyzing Perspectives** How does Justice White say this ruling will affect suspects? What does he suggest it concludes about police interrogations of suspects?

2. **Explaining** What does Justice White say will happen because of this ruling?

Protecting the Right to Counsel

As a senator from California in 2019, Kamala Harris introduced the Equal Defense Act in Congress. It was designed to boost resources for public defenders across the country, by offering a $250 million grant program and limiting the number of cases.

SECONDARY SOURCE: WEB ARTICLE

❝ A longtime prosecutor, Harris understands that a fully functional and adequately funded public defender's office is essential to the pursuit of justice and for ensuring safer communities and families. The promise of *Gideon* v. *Wainwright* . . . is meaningless without an adequately staffed office of dedicated attorneys to keep that promise.

Right now, New Orleans faces a public defense crisis. . . . The Orleans Public Defenders Office (OPD) handles 85 percent of criminal cases and . . . the OPD anticipates a $1.1 million deficit. . . . Firings and salary reductions could be next. In 2012, the OPD laid off attorneys because of a budget **shortfall**. In 2015 and 2016, budget shortfalls led public defenders to withdraw from cases — including that of a defendant charged with murder who has been waiting in jail for five years to go to trial and has had six different defense lawyers. . . .

Equal justice depends on adequate, **equitable** resources for public defenders. ❞

— Pamela Metzger, "Equal justice depends on properly funding public defenders," The Hill, May 22, 2019

---

shortfall failure to meet an expectation

equitable equally, fairly

EXAMINE THE SOURCE

1. **Drawing Conclusions** How might the rights of accused persons be affected by understaffed public defenders' offices?
2. **Inferring** In what ways could the Equal Defense Act help the OPD?

Complete Your Inquiry

EVALUATE SOURCES AND USE EVIDENCE

Refer back to the Compelling Question and the Supporting Questions you developed at the beginning of the lesson.

1. **Comparing and Contrasting** How are the rulings and the legal reasoning in *Gideon* v. *Wainwright* and *Miranda* v. *Arizona* similar and different?

2. **Making Connections** How do the secondary sources aid in your understanding of the cases in the inquiry?

3. **Gathering Sources** Which sources helped you answer the Supporting Questions and the Compelling Question? Which sources, if any, challenged what you thought you knew when you first created your Supporting Questions? What information do you still need in order to answer your questions? What other viewpoints would you like to investigate? Where would you find that information?

4. **Evaluating Sources** Identify the sources that helped answer your Supporting Questions. How reliable are the sources? How would you verify the reliability of the sources?

COMMUNICATE CONCLUSIONS

5. **Collaborating** Write a statement explaining whether these two cases "assure equal justice" for the accused. Share your ideas with one or two partners. Discuss how different individuals involved in the judicial process—police, accused persons, defense attorneys, and prosecuting attorneys—might view the two rulings. Would all of these individuals view the rights of the accused as equally important? Explain.

TAKE INFORMED ACTION

Informing People About Their Rights
With a partner, create a "test your knowledge" 5-question quiz on the protections the *Gideon* and *Miranda* decisions provide for accused persons. Your quiz should be multiple choice with one correct answer for each question and other realistic but incorrect answers. Be sure to provide the correct answers and a short explanation so others can learn. Post your quiz on your school website or have it published in the school newspaper for other students to take.

TEXT: Metzger, Pamela. "Equal Justice Depends on Properly Funding Public Defenders." The Hill. May 22, 2019. https://thehill.com/opinion/criminal-justice/444588-equal-justice-depends-on-property-funding-public-defenders?rl=1.

The Juvenile Justice System

READING STRATEGY

Analyzing Key Ideas and Details As you read, complete a chart such as this one to describe each type of hearing in the juvenile justice system.

Type of Hearing	Description
Detention	
Adjudication	
Disposition	

Juvenile Justice

GUIDING QUESTION

How has treatment of young criminal offenders changed?

Adults who commit crimes may have to pay a price. They may be fined or sent to prison for a period of time. What happens when a young person—a juvenile—commits a crime? Are they treated the same as adults? At one time, that was the case. They were not only treated the same as adults, but they were also placed in the same prisons as adults.

Beginnings of a Juvenile Justice System

In the mid-1800s, some people came to think that treating juveniles in this way was wrong. They believed that young people committed crimes because they had bad influences. They wanted to **reform**, or try to improve, the system of juvenile justice.

Reformers thought governments should establish special courts that would teach the young people right from wrong. By doing so, they would rehabilitate these young people. To **rehabilitate** (ree•uh•BIH•luh•tayt) someone is to help them achieve a healthful and productive way of life. The first juvenile court was set up in Cook County, Illinois, in 1899. The city of Chicago is in Cook County.

reform to attempt to improve something

rehabilitate to help someone reach a healthful and productive way of life

Many juvenile offenders sent to detention centers are placed in group sessions and given other kinds of help to try to lead them away from criminal activity in the future.

Changes to the System

Over time, new problems arose. By the 1960s, many people thought the juvenile justice system once again placed too much **emphasis**, or weight, on punishing children.

In 1967 the U.S. Supreme Court ruled that children should have many of the same rights of due process as adults. That year the Court ruled in a case called *In re Gault*. In it, the Supreme Court said that young offenders should have these rights:

- the right to know the charges they face
- the right to remain silent when questioned by authorities
- the right to have the advice of an attorney
- the right to cross-examine witnesses

In 1970 the Court made another important decision in the case *In re Winship*. It said that the government had to meet the same standard for juvenile cases that it had to meet for adults. That is, the government had to prove guilt beyond a reasonable doubt. Later, the Court ruled that imposing the death penalty on a youth violated the Eighth Amendment protection against cruel and unusual punishment.

The Supreme Court has allowed some exceptions to the guarantees found in the Constitution for accused persons when juveniles are involved. The Court ruled that neither public

emphasis weight or stress

Procedures for juvenile offenders take place in courtrooms separate from those for adult offenders, such as at this building in California.

trials nor jury trials are required in juvenile cases. The justices thought that keeping these trials secret protected the privacy of juvenile offenders.

By the 1990s, crime rates—including those for juveniles—rose. Many people called for more attention to law and order. As a result, state legislatures passed laws that set harsher penalties for both juveniles and adults. Some of these laws made it easier to try young offenders in adult courts.

Juvenile Justice Today

Each state has a special set of laws for handling **juvenile delinquents** (JOO•vuh•neye•uhl dee•LIHN•kwuhnts). That is the name given to young people who commit crimes. In most states, juvenile laws apply to those 18 or younger. In some, the cutoff age is 16. Those accused of a crime below that age are handled by the juvenile justice system. Those over that age are treated as adults.

Most states make an exception for juveniles charged with a serious felony, such as murder. Those individuals can be tried as an adult in most states. Still, young offenders who are found guilty must be placed apart from adult inmates when they are put in prison.

Juvenile Offenders

Some crimes that juveniles commit, such as shoplifting, are minor. Other crimes, however, are much more serious. Some young people commit armed robbery and even murder.

The justice system identifies two kinds of juvenile offenders. **Delinquent offenders** commit acts that would be crimes if committed by adults. Examples are robbery and assault. **Status offenders** commit acts that are crimes because of the youth's age. Examples are running away from home, not attending school, and breaking curfews. The justice system views status

juvenile delinquent a child or teenager who is determined to have committed a crime

delinquent offender a youth who has committed an offense that would be a crime if committed by an adult

status offender a youth who commits an act defined as an offense because of the youth's age

offenders as being beyond the control of their parents or guardians. For this reason, the court steps in to supervise them.

1. **Identifying** What due process rights has the Supreme Court recognized for juveniles within the justice system?
2. **Explaining** What are status offenders?

The Juvenile Court System

GUIDING QUESTION

What procedures are followed when a young person breaks the law?

Federal law does allow for federal courts to handle juvenile cases or to try juveniles as adults in some cases. Most juveniles are handled by the state juvenile court system.

Youths who have committed the most serious violent crimes are tried in adult courts. Most youth, however, have their cases handled by the separate juvenile justice system.

The juvenile justice system handles three types of cases—dependency cases, status offenses, and delinquency cases. Dependency cases are young people whose caregivers abuse them or fail to care for them. These youth are not criminal offenders but have come to the attention of the justice system. They are not treated as criminals but are given help. Typically, the juvenile court will remove these children from their homes and place them with other families or make some other arrangement.

Many status offenses are handled by agencies other than juvenile court. When courts do handle these cases, they generally put the youth on probation or place the youth in some setting outside the home. During probation, the youth is free for a period of time but must report to a probation officer. Federal law discourages states from holding these youth in detention centers.

Delinquency cases involve juveniles who commit crimes. They are more common than status offenses. In a recent year, juvenile courts saw more than 720,000 delinquency cases. That was eight times the number of status offenses.

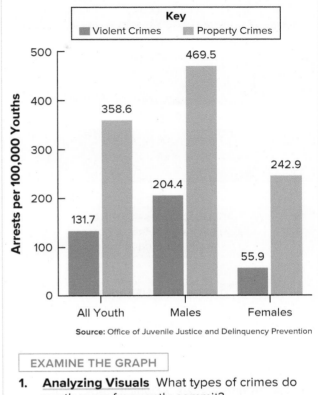

Youth Arrests, 2019
The government tracks the number of youths arrested for various crimes, from shoplifting to murder.

Source: Office of Juvenile Justice and Delinquency Prevention

EXAMINE THE GRAPH

1. **Analyzing Visuals** What types of crimes do youth more frequently commit?
2. **Calculating** How much more likely are male youths to be arrested than female youths?

The Intake Process

Cases involving juveniles are referred to the criminal justice system by the police or by others such as parents or school officials. If the youth committed a minor crime, the police may simply give the young person a warning and then release the youth to a parent or caregiver. If the youth needs drug treatment or counseling, they refer the youth to a social service agency.

Once a youth is in the juvenile court system, a social worker carries out a review called an *intake* to decide what to do. About 46 percent of cases are settled at this stage. Some are dismissed, and in some the young people are placed on probation. Around half of these youth are required to perform some other action such as doing community service or repaying someone for property taken or damaged.

The Process for Juvenile Cases

The process for juvenile cases is somewhat like that for adults.

ARREST
Juvenile is taken into custody.

↓

INTAKE
Social worker decides how the juvenile case should be handled.

↓

DETENTION HEARING
State shows there is good reason to believe the juvenile committed the offense.

↓

ADJUDICATION HEARING
Judge decides whether or not the youth is delinquent.

↓

DISPOSITION HEARING
Judge decides whether youth ruled delinquent is placed on probation, sent to a detention center, or treated in some other way.

EXAMINE THE CHART

1. **Analyzing Visuals** At which steps is a judge involved?
2. **Identifying** Who makes the initial decision about how the juvenile's case should be handled?

The Hearing Process

Youth who remain in the system after intake face up to three hearings. The **detention hearing** is like the preliminary hearing for adults. In this step, the state must show that there is probable cause to believe the young person committed the crime.

The **adjudication** (uh•joo•dih•KAY•shuhn) **hearing** is similar to a trial for an adult. Unlike a trial, however, it is not open to the public and

generally has no jury. At this hearing, an attorney for the state tries to prove that the youth committed the offense in question. The youth's attorney presents a defense. As in an adult trial, both sides call witnesses and question the other side's witnesses. The judge decides whether or not the youth is *delinquent*—similar to finding an adult to be guilty. Youth are found delinquent in just over half of these hearings.

Those found delinquent then have a **disposition hearing**. This step is similar to the sentencing hearing for adults. Nearly two-thirds of youth are placed on probation for a period of time. About a quarter of those found delinquent are sent to a detention facility. Most terms in these centers run from one to three years. If the youth completes the time in detention with no more trouble, the charges will be dropped and removed from the youth's record.

Sentences for the most serious crimes may be more severe, such as a lengthy prison term. However, in *Graham* v. *Florida* (2010), the Supreme Court ruled that juveniles cannot be given a life sentence without parole for any crime other than murder.

✓ **CHECK FOR UNDERSTANDING**

Comparing and Contrasting How are the hearing stages of the juvenile justice system similar to and different from the processes for adults?

LESSON ACTIVITIES

1. **Argumentative Writing** The U.S. Supreme Court has ruled that, unlike adults, juveniles can have a trial without a jury. Do you agree with the Court that this protects the privacy of the youth? Or do you think that this step denies them of a constitutional right? Write a brief essay taking a position for or against the Court's decision. Explain your reasons.

2. **Collaborating** Work in a small group to research programs in place in your community that aim to help juvenile offenders. Examples might include decision-making programs, drug counseling, or other approaches. Write a summary of what you find. Include some comments on how effective the programs seem to be.

---

detention hearing a juvenile court process in which the state must show there is probable cause to believe a young person committed a crime

adjudication hearing the procedure used to determine the facts in a juvenile case and to determine if the juvenile is guilty of committing a crime

disposition hearing the final settlement and sentencing in a juvenile case when the juvenile has been found guilty of committing a crime

08

Analyzing Sources: Juvenile Justice Sentences

? COMPELLING QUESTION

How should juveniles be treated in the criminal justice system?

Plan Your Inquiry

DEVELOPING QUESTIONS

Think about the process that juveniles accused of a crime go through. How is it similar to and different from that of the adult criminal justice system? Then read the Compelling Question for this lesson. What questions can you ask to help you answer this Compelling Question? Create a graphic organizer such as the one below. Write these Supporting Questions in your graphic organizer.

Supporting Questions	Primary Source or Secondary Source	What this source tells me about how juveniles are treated in the criminal justice system	Questions the source leaves unanswered
	A		
	B		
	C		
	D		
	E		

ANALYZING SOURCES

Next, examine the sources in this lesson. Analyze each source by answering the questions that follow it. How does each source help you answer each Supporting Question you created? What questions do you still have? Write these in your graphic organizer.

After you analyze the sources, you will:
- use the evidence from the sources,
- communicate your conclusions,
- and take informed action.

Background Information

In the early days of the United States, young people, or juveniles, accused of crimes were treated like adults. They faced the same processes and punishments. In the mid-1800s, that began to change. At that time, reformers questioned whether it was fair to treat children, whose lives were influenced by adults, in the same way as adults. They pushed for additional protections for juvenile suspects and defendants. Governments set up juvenile courts with their own processes.

Two different views competed over how to treat juveniles who were found responsible for committing crimes. Some thought young people should be taught to act in more socially acceptable ways. Others thought they should be punished for breaking the law.

The tension between rehabilitation and punishment continues to fuel debate over the juvenile justice system today. The impact of issues such as mental health, poverty, drug addiction, and abuse on juvenile behavior is also considered. New research into brain development in adolescents, or teens, also influences today's discussions about the proper response to juveniles who commit crimes.

» Today, all states have specific courts for juveniles, though states differ over the ages to which juvenile justice applies.

AP Images

Opinion of the Court: *In re Gault*

In 1964 a juvenile named Gerald Gault was arrested for a minor offense. Gault, aged 15, confessed in court to the crime without being given a lawyer or informed of his right to remain silent. He was found guilty and given a harsh sentence. Gault's mother appealed the case to the U.S. Supreme Court on the grounds that he had been denied due process. The Court agreed. Its decision extended several due process protections to juvenile cases.

PRIMARY SOURCE: SUPREME COURT OPINION

❝ Under our Constitution, the condition of being a boy does not justify a **kangaroo court**. The traditional ideas of Juvenile Court procedure, indeed, contemplated [considered] that time would be available and care would be used to establish precisely what the juvenile did and why he did it—was it a prank of adolescence or a brutal act threatening serious consequences to himself or society unless corrected? . . .

The essential difference between Gerald [Gault]'s case and a normal criminal case is that safeguards available to adults were discarded [thrown away] in Gerald's case. The **summary procedure** as well as the **long commitment** was possible because Gerald was 15 years of age instead of over 18.

If Gerald had been over 18, he would not have been subject to Juvenile Court proceedings. . . . [T]he maximum punishment would have been a fine of $5 to $50, or imprisonment in jail for not more than two months. Instead, he was committed to custody for a maximum of six years. If he had been over 18 . . . [t]he United States Constitution would guarantee him rights and protections with respect to arrest, search and seizure, and pretrial interrogation [questioning]. It would assure him of specific notice of the charges and adequate [enough] time . . . to prepare his defense. He would be entitled to clear advice that he could be represented by counsel. . . . So wide a gulf [gap] between the State's treatment of the adult and of the child requires a bridge sturdier than mere verbiage [words]. ❞

— Justice Abe Fortas, Opinion of the Court, *In re Gault*, 3847 U.S. 1, 1967

kangaroo court a court formed to convict someone already believed to be guilty

summary procedure a quicker process that omits certain steps, such as hearings, for resolving certain criminal matters

long commitment long sentence to prison

> EXAMINE THE SOURCE

1. **Interpreting** What reason does Justice Fortas give in the second paragraph for criticizing the way the juvenile court handled Gault's case?
2. **Analyzing Perspectives** Based on Justice Fortas's argument, what effect did the state court's actions have on Gault?

When Does Adulthood Begin?

The Marshall Project is a nonprofit news group that reports on the criminal justice system. This article discusses research about how the lack of brain maturity extends past the age of 18.

Schwartzapfel, Beth. "The Right Age to Die." The Marshall Project. August 12, 2018. https://www.themarshallproject.org/2018/08/12/the-right-age-to-die.

SECONDARY SOURCE: WEB ARTICLE

❝ The years between 18 and 21 are a sort of societal [social] **limbo period** when, in most states, you can smoke but not drink; make medical decisions for yourself but stay on your parents' health insurance policy; and try on a variety of identities and life experiences without anyone looking askance [showing disapproval].

With this in mind, Connecticut last year opened a dedicated [special] prison unit for young adults aged 18 to 25, and Vermont this year began allowing young adults up to age 21 to have all but the most serious cases tried in juvenile court.

When it comes to the most extreme punishments, the Supreme Court has ruled so far that 18 is a 'bright line.' If you're under 18 at the time of your crime, you can't be executed. You also can't be sentenced to life without parole without a hearing to consider your **maturity level**. But the high court has never extended those protections past age 18. . . .

But it wasn't until recently that scientists began to research what happens to the brain in late adolescence and young adulthood, says Laurence Steinberg, a professor of psychology at Temple University. . . .

And when they did, they found that those same youthful qualities seem to persist until the early- to mid-20s. In one recent study, Steinberg and his colleagues [coworkers] gave a series of tests to more than 5,000 children and young adults across 11 countries. They found that the impulse [urge] to chase thrills and look for immediate **gratification** peaks around age 19 and declines into the 20s. Steinberg describes this system of the brain like the gas pedal in a car. The 'brake' system—the ability to plan ahead and consider consequences—takes longer to catch up: it isn't generally fully mature until the 20s. ❞

— Beth Schwartzapfel, "The Right Age to Die," The Marshall Project, August 12, 2018

limbo period a state of being between two stages
maturity level degree to which one shows adult behavior
gratification satisfaction of desires

EXAMINE THE SOURCE

1. **Identifying** According to the source, what line has the U.S. Supreme Court drawn to divide young people from adults?
2. **Making Connections** What evidence in this report might officials in Connecticut and Vermont use to defend their policy changes?

Juvenile Life Without Parole

When sentenced to life without parole, an individual is likely going to spend the remainder of their life in prison. This sentence is usually given to those that have committed dangerous crimes. While it has been argued that juveniles should not receive a sentence like life without parole, some states still allow it.

SECONDARY SOURCE: MAP

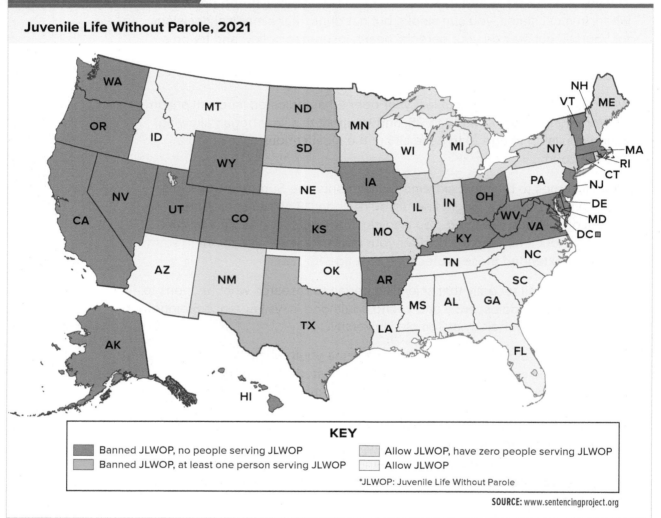

Juvenile Life Without Parole, 2021

KEY

- ◼ Banned JLWOP, no people serving JLWOP
- ◼ Banned JLWOP, at least one person serving JLWOP
- ◻ Allow JLWOP, have zero people serving JLWOP
- ◻ Allow JLWOP

*JLWOP: Juvenile Life Without Parole

SOURCE: www.sentencingproject.org

EXAMINE THE SOURCE

1. **Identifying** How many states have banned life without parole for juveniles? How many allow it?

2. **Inferring** What reasons might a state give for allowing or banning life without parole sentences for juveniles?

Opinion of the Court: *Jones* v. *Mississippi*

Convicted of murder at age 15, Brett Jones was given Mississippi's mandatory sentence of life without parole. Mandatory means "required." Soon after, the Supreme Court ruled that juveniles convicted of homicide, or murder, could be sentenced to life without parole only if it was not a mandatory sentence. Jones's case was reviewed by a state court, but he again received a sentence of life in prison without parole.

Jones appealed to the U.S. Supreme Court, arguing that this new sentence went against the Court's decision. He said that the Court's rules required the sentence court to sentence him to life without parole only if it had a hearing to consider the possibility that he could be reformed, or changed. The Court majority (6-3) denied his argument and upheld the sentence.

In his written opinion on this case, Justice Brett Kavanaugh explains how states may determine sentencing for juveniles convicted of murder.

PRIMARY SOURCE: SUPREME COURT OPINION

❝ As this case again demonstrates, any homicide, and particularly a homicide committed by an individual under 18, is a horrific [terrible] tragedy for all involved and for all affected. Determining the proper sentence in such a case raises profound [difficult] questions of morality and social policy. The States, not the federal courts, make those broad moral and policy judgments in the first instance when enacting [passing] their sentencing laws. And state sentencing judges and juries then determine the proper sentence in individual cases in light of the facts and circumstances of the offense, and the background of the offender. . . .

Importantly, . . . our holding today does not preclude [prevent] the States from imposing additional sentencing limits in cases involving defendants under 18 convicted of murder. States may categorically [without exception] prohibit life without parole for all offenders under 18. Or States may require sentencers to make extra factual findings before sentencing an offender under 18 to life without parole. Or States may direct sentencers to formally explain on the record why a life-without-parole sentence is appropriate notwithstanding [despite] the defendant's youth. ❞

— Justice Brett Kavanaugh, Opinion of the Court, *Jones* v. *Mississippi*, 2021

EXAMINE THE SOURCE

1. **Explaining** What government bodies have the proper authority to make sentencing decisions, according to the decision?

2. **Analyzing Perspectives** How does Justice Kavanaugh qualify the Court's ruling?

E

Sentencing Rates for Juvenile Delinquents

When considering sentences in juvenile cases, judges have the option to place teens in a residential facility or otherwise remove them from their homes. They may also put teens on probation or give other penalties, such as community service and fines. This graph shows the percentage of cases by type of offense that received specific sentences.

SECONDARY SOURCE: GRAPH

Sentences of Juvenile Cases Decided by a Judge, 2019

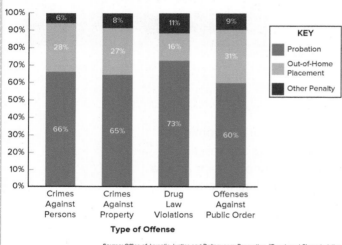

Source: Office of Juvenile Justice and Delinquency Prevention, "Trends and Characteristics of Delinquency Cases Handled in Juvenile Court, 2019"

EXAMINE THE SOURCE

1. **Contrasting** Which cases were most likely to result in probation, and which were more likely to lead to out-of-home placement?
2. **Analyzing** What do the overall probation rates suggest about sentences in the juvenile justice system?

Complete Your Inquiry

EVALUATE SOURCES AND USE EVIDENCE

Refer back to the Compelling Question and the Supporting Questions you developed at the beginning of the lesson.

1. **Comparing and Contrasting** How are the two Supreme Court rulings similar and different in their reasoning and outcomes for juveniles?
2. **Making Connections** Based on the sources, why do people think juveniles should be treated differently from adults by the justice system?
3. **Gathering Sources** Which sources helped you answer the Supporting Questions and the Compelling Question? Which sources, if any, challenged what you thought you knew when you first created your Supporting Questions? What information do you still need in order to answer your questions? What other viewpoints would you like to investigate? Where would you find that information?
4. **Evaluating Sources** Identify the sources that helped answer your Supporting Questions. How reliable are the sources? How would you verify the reliability of the sources?

COMMUNICATE CONCLUSIONS

5. **Collaborating** Individually, write a short response to the Compelling Question. Share your response with other students until you find at least two others with whom you roughly agree. Together, revise your ideas into one joint statement, using evidence from the sources as well as your own knowledge to support your position. Then, share your statement with the class.

TAKE INFORMED ACTION

Gathering Opinions About Juvenile Justice In a small group, use what you have learned in this lesson to create a questionnaire about how juveniles should be treated in the criminal justice system. Write 5-10 statements and have respondents rate them on a scale of 1-10 (1= Strongly Agree; 10= Strongly Disagree). Give your questionnaire to at least two distinct groups: classmates your age and adults. Analyze the results to see the range of responses. Then discuss the results as a class, keeping respondents' names anonymous.

Reviewing Understanding the Law

Summary

Sources and Types of Law	American Legal System	Court Systems
Basics of laws • Meant to maintain order, keep peace • Importance of rule of law: laws apply to all, are understandable, are enforced by officials • Good laws: fair, reasonable	**Basic legal rights** • Writ of habeas corpus, no bills of attainder, no ex post facto laws • Fourteenth Amendment; guarantees due process • Presumption of innocence	**Civil law** • About disputes between parties • Types: contract, property, family, personal injury • Based on complaint of injury or harm • A defendant found responsible may have to pay damages
Development of legal system • Hammurabi's laws • Israelite laws • Roman laws • Napoleonic Code • English common law • Natural law	EQUAL JUSTICE UNDER LAW	**Criminal law** • About harm done to society • Types of crimes: misdemeanors, felonies • Based on charge against accused person • A defendant found guilty may be sentenced to pay a fine, prison
Types of law • Criminal and civil • Military • Tribal • Constitutional, statutory (from legislature), and case (from judges)	**Bill of Rights protections** • Protection from unreasonable search and seizure • Protection from self-incrimination • Right to an attorney and a speedy trial by jury • Protection against cruel and unusual punishment	**Juvenile law** • Applies to youth under 16 or 18 years old • Types of cases: delinquent, status, neglected • Cases often sent out of the justice system to other services • A defendant found delinquent may be punished

Checking For Understanding

Answer the questions to see if you understood the topic content.

1. Identify each of the following terms.

    A. common law   F. defendant

    B. lawsuit   G. crime

    C. search warrant   H. plea bargain

    D. exclusionary rule I. delinquent offender

    E. plaintiff   J. status offender

2. **Explaining** Explain two of the four standards that must be met to make a law a good law.

3. **Identifying** How did Israelite law influence the U.S. legal system?

4. **Explaining** What are the sources of each of the following types of law: constitutional law, statutory law, and case law?

5. **Identifying Cause and Effect** Which Supreme Court decision protects people from being forced to speak to the police without an attorney present?

6. **Summarizing** What are three protections that accused people have under the Sixth Amendment?

7. **Identifying** What are three kinds of disputes that are handled in civil law?

8. **Explaining** What are the purposes of punishing someone convicted of committing a crime?

9. **Identifying** What is significant about the arraignment step in a criminal trial?

10. **Summarizing** How did the Supreme Court change the way the juvenile justice system worked in the 1960s and 1970s?

11. **Contrasting** What are two differences between the way criminal cases are handled for adults and juveniles?

12. **Making Connections** How do criminal laws show the importance of personal responsibility as an underlying idea of U.S. law?

13. **Contrasting** What are the main differences between civil law and criminal law?

14. **Explaining** Would a member of the armed forces who was accused of breaking a state law be tried in a court-martial or in a state criminal court? Explain your answer.

15. **Explaining** Why are juries so important to the U.S. legal system?

16. **Contrasting** Why are the due process protections that are given to those accused of crimes not given to defendants in civil lawsuits?

17. **Explaining** How do civil laws help keep order in society?

18. **Contrasting** What are the different roles of a grand jury and a trial jury?

19. **Contrasting** How do the procedures in a criminal trial differ from the procedures in an appeal?

20. **Analyzing** Why do such a large percentage of juvenile justice cases end with the youth being placed on probation or given community service rather than being sentenced to detention?

NEED EXTRA HELP?

If You've Missed Question	1	2	3	4	5	6	7	8	9	10
Review Lesson	2, 3, 4, 5, 7	2	2	2	3	3	4	5	5	7

If You've Missed Question	11	12	13	14	15	16	17	18	19	20
Review Lesson	7	2	2	2	3	3, 4	4	5	5	7

Apply What You Have Learned

A Understanding Multiple Perspectives

Opinions about how to handle juvenile offenders have changed over time. In the past, young people were prosecuted and punished in a manner similar to adult offenders. Reformers worked to change laws related to the juvenile justice system. Today, people still debate about the best approach to dealing with young people who have broken the law.

ACTIVITY **Evaluating Arguments** Conduct research online to find two or three different perspectives on prosecuting and sentencing juvenile offenders. Find at least two points of view on how to approach juvenile justice to ensure that young offenders are treated fairly and not punished harshly, but that also take into consideration the good of the community overall. Then create a presentation that summarizes all the perspectives you found and evaluates the strengths and weaknesses of each argument.

Mikael Karlsson/Alamy Stock Photo

B Building Citizenship

Many teens your age might not be familiar with the principles or processes of the U.S. legal system. They can be better citizens if they have a better understanding of these features of the community.

ACTIVITY **Making a Podcast on an Aspect of the Legal System** Think about one area of the U.S. legal system with which you think fellow middle school students should be more familiar. You might choose the importance of juries or the processes followed in civil, criminal, or juvenile courts. You might want to focus on the underlying principles of the legal system. Whatever topic you choose, work with a partner to write a three-minute podcast that presents clear, accurate information on your topic in a way that will interest middle school students. Then record your podcast, with you and your partner taking turns delivering parts of the podcast you wrote.

C Writing an Informative Paragraph

The Laws of Hammurabi were written in ancient Babylonia. They include rules and punishments related to family, farming, business, and other areas of ancient life. Read this excerpt from one of the laws:

> 66 *If any one steal cattle . . . , if it belong to a god or to the court, the thief shall pay thirtyfold therefor; if they belonged to a freed man of the king he shall pay tenfold; if the thief has nothing with which to pay he shall be put to death.* 99
> — Laws of Hammurabi, 1750 B.C.E.

ACTIVITY Analyzing the Laws of Hammurabi Write a paragraph to explain which crime the law describes and the punishment it indicates. Why do you think there was more than one punishment for this crime? Then explain how this section of the Laws of Hammurabi violates the individual rights we enjoy under the U.S. Constitution.

D Making Connections

Judges have some flexibility in issuing sentences for those found guilty of committing some crimes. Sentencing laws can change over time as public opinion shifts about what is a fair or reasonable approach to punishing offenders.

ACTIVITY Debating a Mandatory Sentencing Law
Imagine that the legislature of your state is considering a mandatory sentencing law. A mandatory sentence is a sentence that must be imposed in all cases. The bill would set a specific punishment for shoplifting, regardless of the circumstances of a particular case, including the value of the items taken and the age of the person committing the act. Work with a group of three other students to prepare a debate on this issue. First, conduct research online to learn more about mandatory sentencing. Then prepare a debate about this issue, with two students in the group supporting the change and two opposing it. Each team of two should prepare a one-minute statement to explain their viewpoint and a 30-second response to the arguments of the other side.

E Writing an Informative Essay

Laws are enforced through the civil, criminal, and juvenile court systems. Under the principles of the rule of law and equal justice for all, laws should be applied equally to everyone in a society in order to be fair.

ACTIVITY Writing About a Constitutional Amendment Write a three- or four-paragraph essay to explain how the U.S. Constitution was changed by the addition of amendments to apply the concept of rule of law and to make the laws fair for everyone. Identify one of the four amendments that address this issue and that have affected the criminal justice system. Explain the purpose of the amendment you have selected and why it was added to the Constitution. Then describe what resulted from this change. Consider also how decisions of the U.S. Supreme Court have applied those amendments over time.

PHOTO: Daxus/Getty Images; TEXT: King, L. W., Tr. The Code of Hammurabi. Eleventh Edition of the Encyclopedia Britannica, 1910-1911.

A doctor in the U.S. Army examines an Afghan child as part of a humanitarian visit to the child's village.

The United States and Foreign Affairs

GO ONLINE   Explore the Student Edition eBook and find interactive maps, charts, graphs, and tools.

Introducing The United States and Foreign Affairs

Working with the World

Not only does the U.S. government deal with issues that impact American citizens, but it also works with other countries around the world. The United States joins organizations, such as the United Nations, the World Trade Organization, and the North Atlantic Treaty Organization (NATO) to show its commitment to global issues. Additionally, diplomats can be sent to work and live in various countries to represent U.S. interests abroad.

U.S. Embassies

» The United States has embassy buildings around the world to represent American interests abroad. Regardless of which country an embassy building is located in, that building is considered part of the country that owns it. This means that an attack on a U.S. embassy in a foreign country is considered an attack on the United States. Shown here is the U.S. Embassy in London, England. This unique design embodies the ideals of the American government which include transparency, openness, and equality.

Top Environmental Issues Facing the World

- Air pollution
- Water pollution
- Global warming
- Overpopulation
- Waste disposal

- Loss of biodiversity
- Habitat loss
- Deforestation
- Ozone layer depletion
- Acid rain

Source: The Blue & Green Journey

» Greta Thunberg's sign reads "school strike for the climate."

> ❝ And yes, we do need hope, of course we do. But the one thing we need more than hope is action. Once we start to act, hope is everywhere. So instead of looking for hope, look for action. Then, and only then, hope will come. Today, we use 100 million barrels of oil every single day. There are no politics to change that. There are no rules to keep that oil in the ground. So we can't save the world by playing by the rules, because the rules have to be changed. Everything needs to change, and it has to start today. ❞

— Greta Thunberg, Swedish environmental activist, 2018

UN Sustainable Development Goals

In 2016 the UN General Assembly adopted the 2030 Agenda for Sustainable Development and challenged world leaders to meet the 17 Sustainable Development Goals shown here.

1 NO POVERTY
2 ZERO HUNGER
3 GOOD HEALTH AND WELL-BEING
4 QUALITY EDUCATION
5 GENDER EQUALITY
6 CLEAN WATER AND SANITATION
7 AFFORDABLE AND CLEAN ENERGY
8 DECENT WORK AND ECONOMIC GROWTH
9 INDUSTRY, INNOVATION AND INFRASTRUCTURE
10 REDUCED INEQUALITIES
11 SUSTAINABLE CITIES AND COMMUNITIES
12 RESPONSIBLE CONSUMPTION AND PRODUCTION
13 CLIMATE ACTION
14 LIFE BELOW WATER
15 LIFE ON LAND
16 PEACE, JUSTICE AND STRONG INSTITUTIONS
17 PARTNERSHIPS FOR THE GOALS

Getting Ready to Learn About . . .
The United States and Foreign Affairs

George Washington's Advice

When the United States gained independence, it was not a powerful country. To protect itself, it stayed out of conflicts with other countries. When Britain and France began a war in the 1790s, President George Washington kept the United States neutral. This means the nation did not join or support either side in the conflict. When Washington left office after two terms, he warned Americans to avoid foreign conflicts. He said, "It is our true policy to steer clear of permanent alliances." An *alliance* is an agreement among nations to defend each other if any of them are attacked.

Wars in Africa and Mexico

George Washington's message formed the basis for U.S. foreign policy for many years. The nation defended its ability to carry out trade, though, which prompted the Barbary Wars in the early 1800s. This was a brief fight against powers based in northern Africa. The U.S. Navy fought the Barbary states to ensure that American merchant ships could trade safely in the Mediterranean Sea.

In the 1800s, U.S. foreign policy focused on gaining territory and building trade. The United States fought many wars against Native Americans. The country signed treaties with France and Spain to add land west of the Mississippi River and to acquire Florida. In the 1840s, the nation fought a war against Mexico. In the treaty that followed, the United States gained land stretching from modern New Mexico west to California. The nation then reached all the way from the Atlantic Ocean to the Pacific Ocean.

More Overseas Involvement

Throughout the 1800s, the United States gradually became more involved overseas as it looked to increase trade. In the 1850s, the United States sent warships to Japan to pressure that nation to open its ports to U.S. trade. In the late 1890s, the United States annexed, or took control of, the Hawaiian Islands.

At around the same time, the United States fought in the Spanish-American War. As a result of winning this war, the country gained control of the Philippines, Puerto Rico, and Guam. The United States also established a military base on the island of Cuba that it still maintains. The Spanish-American War showed that the United States had become a major military power with significant interest in foreign affairs.

American Power Grows

In the early 1900s, President Theodore Roosevelt continued to increase U.S. involvement in other countries. The United States built the Panama Canal in Central America. This waterway connected the Atlantic and Pacific Oceans and shortened the time it took ships to travel from the eastern United States or Europe to Asia. This made trade and travel easier and helped the United States to become more of a naval power. Roosevelt also stated that the United States had the right to get involved in Latin American nations that seemed unstable.

World Wars in the 1900s

In 1914 war broke out in Europe. At first, the United States maintained a neutral stance. In 1917 the United States joined the war and fought alongside the Allied powers, which included the United Kingdom and France. The United States helped the Allies defeat Germany and Austria-Hungary. U.S. President Woodrow

Today, the United States often sends aid to help people in other countries suffering from the effects of war or natural disasters.

PHOTO: US Marines Photo/Alamy Stock Photo; TEXT: Washington, George. Washington's Farewell Address. New York, New York Public Library, 1935. pg. 105; 136. Courtesy of the Milstein Division of United States History, Local History & Genealogy; The New York Public Library, Astor, Lenox and Tilden Foundations.

U.S. Military Bases and Troop Levels, 2020

The United States has troops stationed on bases around the world.

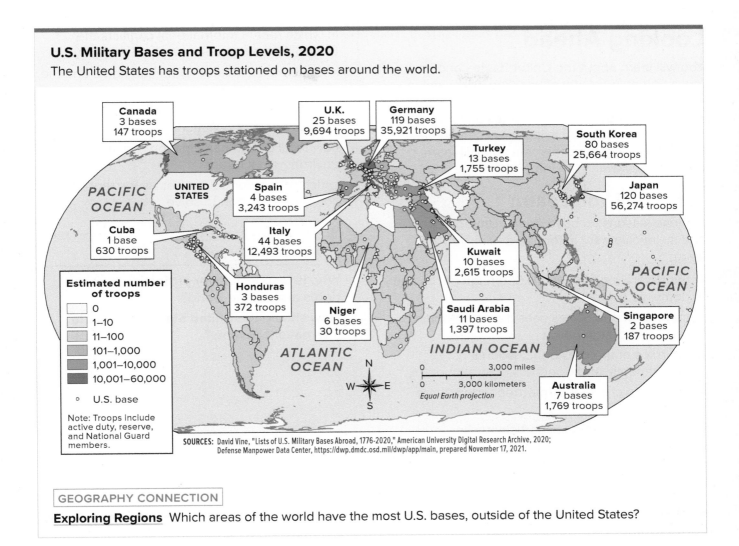

Canada
3 bases
147 troops

U.K.
25 bases
9,694 troops

Germany
119 bases
35,921 troops

South Korea
80 bases
25,664 troops

Turkey
13 bases
1,755 troops

Japan
120 bases
56,274 troops

Spain
4 bases
3,243 troops

Cuba
1 base
630 troops

Italy
44 bases
12,493 troops

Kuwait
10 bases
2,615 troops

Honduras
3 bases
372 troops

Niger
6 bases
30 troops

Saudi Arabia
11 bases
1,397 troops

Singapore
2 bases
187 troops

Australia
7 bases
1,769 troops

PACIFIC OCEAN · UNITED STATES · PACIFIC OCEAN · ATLANTIC OCEAN · INDIAN OCEAN

Estimated number of troops

- 0
- 1–10
- 11–100
- 101–1,000
- 1,001–10,000
- 10,001–60,000
- ○ U.S. base

Note: Troops include active duty, reserve, and National Guard members.

0   3,000 miles
0   3,000 kilometers
Equal Earth projection

SOURCES: David Vine, "Lists of U.S. Military Bases Abroad, 1776-2020," American University Digital Research Archive, 2020; Defense Manpower Data Center, https://dwp.dmdc.osd.mil/dwp/app/main, prepared November 17, 2021.

GEOGRAPHY CONNECTION

Exploring Regions Which areas of the world have the most U.S. bases, outside of the United States?

Wilson took an important role in the peace talks that followed the war.

In 1939 a second and even more costly global war began. Called World War II, it lasted until 1945. Once again, the United States did not immediately join the fighting but eventually played a major role in winning the war. The Soviet Union also contributed to this victory.

After the war, the United States and the Soviet Union became the world's two most powerful nations. The Soviet Union had a communist government and economic system. The United States was a democracy with a market economy. For decades, the two continued a tense and bitter rivalry for political influence around the world. This long period of tension and distrust was called the Cold War because the two nations never fought one another in a military action. However, the United States sent troops to stop the spread of communism in other countries. In 1991 the Soviet Union broke apart. Russia, the largest country to emerge from the former Soviet Union, moved away from communism. The Cold War was over, but relations between the United States and Russia remain strained.

The World in the 2000s

In the early 2000s, a new threat emerged. Terrorism became a major threat to global peace. After a terrorist attack on September 11, 2001, the United States fought wars in Afghanistan and Iraq. The United States is not engaged in any major wars today, but it still plays a major part in stopping terrorism and addressing other world problems.

Looking Ahead

You will learn about the United States and its involvement in foreign affairs. You will examine Compelling Questions and develop your own questions about the United States and foreign affairs in the Inquiry Activities. You can preview some of the key concepts that you will learn about by reviewing the infographic.

What Will You Learn?

In these lessons focused on the United States and its involvement in foreign affairs, you will learn:

- the difference between U.S. foreign policy and domestic policy.
- that the United States uses many methods to carry out foreign policy.
- the roles of the president, national departments, and Congress in foreign policy.
- how trade and global interdependence are related.
- how the United States participates in international organizations to solve common global problems.

- in which recent international conflicts the United States has been involved and why.
- about conflicts related to human rights and the spread of democracy and liberty.
- how the government protects the public from various forms of pollution.
- how local citizen participation can impact environmental issues.
- which of the world's current issues require cooperative action to solve.

 COMPELLING QUESTIONS IN THE INQUIRY ACTIVITY LESSONS

- **Who is responsible for protecting human rights around the world?**
- **How should the United States respond to international events?**

Official U.S. Foreign Policy Goals

The United States sets forth a number of official foreign policy goals for its dealings with countries around the world.

Protect national security

Promote trade

Promote U.S. economic interests

Ensure access to natural resources

Promote peace

Promote democracy

Support human rights

Provide humanitarian aid

Making Foreign Policy

READING STRATEGY

Analyzing Key Ideas and Details As you read, take notes about the different tools the United States uses to carry out its foreign policy.

Tool	Description
Treaties and executive agreements	
Diplomacy	
Foreign aid	
International trade	
Military force	
Espionage	

The President and Foreign Policy

GUIDING QUESTION

What are the goals of foreign policy?

Every nation has tools for dealing with other nations. How a nation uses these tools is its foreign policy. **Foreign policy** differs from **domestic policy**, which is how a nation deals with issues within its borders.

Presidents and Congress both influence foreign policy. These leaders try to achieve many goals in making the country's foreign policy. At times, these goals may stray from the official goals put forth by the government. For example, some foreign policy decisions are made to gain popularity with voters or to simply increase the power of the United States. However, leaders often point to four main foreign policy goals when they speak to American audiences and people overseas.

The first goal is national security. This refers to steps taken to protect the nation and its people. Without national security, the government cannot achieve any of its other goals. If the nation is under attack, the government needs to focus on defending its people. The government also sometimes acts to reduce or remove potential threats to its security.

foreign policy a nation's methods for dealing with other nations and world issues

domestic policy a nation's methods for dealing with issues within its borders

In their role as chief diplomat, presidents often meet with leaders all around the world. Here, President Barack Obama meets with Vietnamese President Tran Dai Quang in Hanoi, Vietnam, in 2016.

When presidents send troops into conflict, spending on the military usually goes up. This means more of the nation's financial resources are used to pay for war, leaving less money for other policy areas.

Analyzing Visuals What does this cartoon suggest is the impact of the Iraq War on spending on domestic policy, or the costs of running the country?

The Foreign Policy Team

Foreign policy decisions are complex and require more knowledge than one person could possibly have. Therefore, the president needs a team of experienced advisers to help make foreign-policy decisions. The National Security Advisor in the White House is the president's closest aide in this area. This official oversees the staff of experts on the National Security Council. Advisers also come from the State Department, the Department of Defense, and the office of the Director of National Intelligence.

Of course, the president makes the final decision on the policy. President Harry S. Truman noted,

> 66 No one who has not had the responsibility can really understand what it is like to be President, not even his closest aides. . . . [H]e is never allowed to forget that he is President. 99

—Harry S. Truman

The foreign policy team then must implement, or carry out, the president's policy.

Congress Versus the President

Under the U.S. Constitution, the president is commander in chief of the armed forces, but Congress has the power to declare war. Congress also decides how much money the armed forces receive. At times, the president and Congress have agreed on the use of military power. Sometimes, though, they have clashed over actions, goals, and priorities.

Congress has sometimes used its war powers to limit the president's use of the military. From the end of World War II to the early 1970s, presidents sent U.S. troops into conflict whenever they thought it necessary. Congress did little to check the president's power. Near the end of the Vietnam conflict, when public sentiment turned against that war, Congress passed a law to limit the president's ability to wage war. The situation changed again after the terrorist attacks of September 11, 2001. Once again, presidents committed U.S. troops without Congress declaring war, as President George W. Bush did in Afghanistan and Iraq in the early 2000s.

Congress also influences foreign policy in many other ways. Policies like providing money

The second foreign policy goal is to promote world peace. Peace among the world's nations helps keep the United States more secure.

A third goal of foreign policy is to build trade with other countries. The U.S. economy becomes stronger when its trade with other nations is strong. Trading with other nations builds and maintains markets for American products made by American workers. Trade also gives American consumers the opportunity to buy goods produced in other countries.

Finally, U.S. leaders sometimes act to promote democracy and human rights around the world. Both military and economic aid may be used to accomplish this goal.

Foreign and domestic policies are separate, but they do affect each other. When the United States makes a trade agreement with another nation, demand for American-made products may go up. That can help U.S. businesses and workers, although it could also cost some U.S. jobs. Going to war also affects domestic policy. It can create a need for more people in the armed forces and for U.S. factories to produce military supplies.

PHOTO: Ed Fischer/CartoonStock; TEXT: Truman, Harry S. The Memoirs of Harry S. Truman: A Reader's Edition. Edited by Raymond H. Geselbracht. Columbia, Missouri: University of Missouri Press, 2019.

or weapons to foreign governments require its approval. Sometimes Congress passes laws that affect foreign policy over the opposition of the president.

✓ CHECK FOR UNDERSTANDING

Making Connections How does trade with other countries connect to both U.S. foreign policy and domestic policy?

The Tools of Foreign Policy

GUIDING QUESTION

What are the tools the president uses to carry out U.S. foreign policy?

One factor that the president and Congress consider when they make foreign policy is the national interest. **National interest** is anything that benefits the country. Of course, people disagree about what benefits the country, and they may be concerned about other issues as well, such as the rights of people in foreign countries. The president and Congress carry out foreign policy by using several **methods**, or processes for doing things. These methods range from working with other countries to going to war with them.

Treaties and Executive Agreements

Nations sometimes sign *treaties*, or formal agreements among the governments of two or more countries. Some treaties concern defense. In 1949 the United States, Canada, and many Western European nations signed the North Atlantic Treaty. By signing this treaty, the nations agreed to defend any member that is attacked.

Under the Constitution, both the president and Congress play a role in making treaties. Presidents work out the details and sign treaties with foreign leaders. A treaty does not take effect until it is ratified by a two-thirds vote in the Senate.

Presidents do not need Senate approval to make an **executive agreement**. This is an agreement between the president and the leader of another country. These agreements often deal with such matters as trade or the armed forces of

national interest anything that benefits the country

method a process for doing something

executive agreement an agreement between the president and the leader of another country

the United States and other countries working together. Executive agreements are not as strong as treaties because they can be reversed by a later president.

Diplomacy

The U.S. government works closely with other governments. Much of this work is carried out by the roughly 190 ambassadors that the United States sends to other countries and the United Nations. Ambassadors are appointed by the president and confirmed by the Senate. Ambassadors are sent only to countries with governments whose right to exist is recognized, or accepted, by the United States. If the foreign policy team thinks the government of a certain country gained power illegally, the president could refuse to recognize it.

Foreign Aid

Another tool that the United States uses to carry out foreign policy is foreign aid. Foreign aid can include military help or humanitarian efforts. Humanitarian efforts include money, food or water, medical supplies, or help rebuilding after a natural disaster. After World War II, the United States provided money to countries in Western Europe so they could rebuild cities that were destroyed during the war. This effort was called the Marshall Plan. Other efforts include peacekeeping missions that aim to end violence and restore order in areas where there has been conflict.

Providing aid to other countries is an important foreign policy tool. In 2020 the United States donated medical supplies to Russia to help that nation during the COVID-19 pandemic.

Inferring What effect might foreign aid have on the way people in other countries view the United States?

PAVEL GOLOVKIN/POOL/AFP/Getty Images

Trade agreements have boosted trade between the United States and Mexico, resulting in heavy truck traffic crossing the countries' border.

International Trade

As noted, presidents can make agreements about trade with other nations. These agreements determine what products may be traded and describe the trade rules both countries must follow.

Sometimes presidents think that other countries have policies that threaten peace or security or abuse human rights. When that happens, they might take steps to punish the country. They might impose **trade sanctions**, which are barriers to trade. The hope is that the sanctions will cause enough economic pain to convince the country to act differently.

Sometimes the president declares a complete ban on trade with a country, called an **embargo**. The United States has had a trade embargo on Cuba since 1962. It imposed this embargo because of actions Cuba's Communist government took against American companies with operations there. Sometimes several nations join to stop trading with a **target** nation.

Congress also plays a role in making economic foreign policy. Congress sets tariffs, or taxes on goods that are bought from other countries. Congress must approve treaties that allow the United States to join trade groups.

Members of these groups agree to trade freely with one another. They include the United States-Mexico-Canada Agreement (USMCA) and the World Trade Organization (WTO).

Military Force

Sometimes foreign policy involves the use of force—or the threat to use force. The president's war powers are an important tool of foreign policy. In 2009 President Barack Obama increased U.S. troops in Afghanistan. In 2020 President Donald Trump ordered an air strike that killed a leading Iranian military commander.

Intelligence and Espionage

One way the United States stays alert to the threats that may be posed by other nations or by terrorist groups is by gathering intelligence, or valuable political or military information. The United States employs spies to gather such information. Equipment such as satellites and computer software can also be used to collect information. Should intelligence suggest a possible threat to the country, officials may use the gathered information to take action. Some intelligence is used by the military when fighting wars.

The United States also sometimes engages in **espionage**, or spying and other activities carried out to ensure national security. The government may send special agents to another country to seize terrorists. Sometimes the United States has agents working secretly to weaken a government that it sees as hostile.

✓ **CHECK FOR UNDERSTANDING**

1. **Contrasting** How are treaties and executive agreements different?
2. **Explaining** How is intelligence a useful tool of foreign policy?

LESSON ACTIVITIES

1. **Argumentative Writing** Do you think the president has too much power on matters related to using the armed forces? Write a brief essay in which you clearly state whether you believe the president or Congress should have more or less power. Give examples and reasons to support your answer.

2. **Presenting** Research a treaty or executive agreement signed by the United States in the past. Make a presentation to your class that describes why the treaty or agreement was signed and what it accomplished.

---

trade sanction an effort to punish another nation by creating barriers to trade

embargo a ban on trading with another nation

target selected person or thing to receive an action

espionage spying and other activities carried out to ensure national security

Global Interdependence and Issues

READING STRATEGY

Analyzing Key Ideas and Details As you read, use a graphic organizer such as the one shown to take notes about challenges rising from global interdependence.

Benefits of Global Interdependence	•
	•
	•
Drawbacks of Global Interdependence	•
	•
	•

Global Interdependence

GUIDING QUESTION

Why do nations depend upon one another?

Have you ever eaten pineapple? If you have, the fruit you ate was probably not grown in the United States but in another country. Most of the United States does not have a climate that is warm enough to grow pineapple plants. As a result, the United States must import pineapples, or buy them from another country where they grow.

Importing pineapples is an example of **global interdependence**. Global interdependence means that countries rely on one another for goods and services. Just as Americans import pineapples, people in other countries trade to obtain what they cannot or choose not to produce.

Trade involves more developed nations, such as the United States, and less developed nations, such as Jamaica. Generally, more developed nations buy raw materials and local products from less developed nations. Less developed nations tend to buy technology and medicine from more developed countries.

Global Trade

Nations have different resources. Those resources include raw materials, such as minerals or trees, and the skills of their people.

global interdependence the reliance of people and countries on one another for goods and services

A worker in Costa Rica places pineapples onto the back of a trailer. The pineapples will be shipped to another country.

Sources of Oil Imported into the United States

The United States imports a little less than half the oil it uses.

KEY
- 70–110 million barrels per year
- 110–300 million barrels per year
- More than 300 million barrels per year

SOURCE: U.S. Energy Information Administration

GEOGRAPHY CONNECTION

1. **Patterns and Movement** From which nation does the United States import the largest amount of oil?

2. **Exploring Place** What advantage might Canada and Mexico have over other countries in selling their oil to the United States?

A nation's resources give it a **comparative advantage** in producing certain goods. A nation has a comparative advantage when it can produce an item at a lower cost than other nations can. Nations usually produce the goods for which they have a comparative advantage. Then they trade what they produce for what they cannot produce, or at least what they cannot produce at a competitive price.

The United States produces raw materials such as soybeans, corn, and oil. It makes goods such as aircraft, auto parts, and medical equipment. The United States exports many of these products, selling them to nations that cannot produce the goods on their own. People in many countries also buy American entertainment products, such as movies, music, and video games. When it comes to exports, the United States has a comparative advantage in its resources and the skills of its workers.

However, the United States cannot produce everything it needs and must trade with other nations for some resources and products. For example, the United States uses almost 20 million barrels of oil per day. It does not produce enough to meet this need. As a result, it must import between 40 and 50 percent of the oil it uses. Canada, Mexico, Saudi Arabia, and Russia supply most of that oil.

Imported goods can benefit American businesses and workers. For example, workers build airplanes in Mobile, Alabama, and make cars in Talladega County, Alabama. To assemble these products, the workers depend on parts and supplies produced in other countries. Many of these supplies come into Alabama through the Port of Mobile. More than 150,000 workers have jobs at the port—another benefit to the state. However, when products are imported from other countries and sold in the United States, people in the United States who had previously made the same kind of product may lose their jobs.

Comparative advantage plays a role in nations' decisions about trade. For example, China has low manufacturing costs. Chinese goods can be sold at lower prices than the same goods made in other countries. As a result, people in other nations may choose to buy goods from China rather than from other nations. Electronics, textiles, plastics, furniture, and toys made in China are sold throughout the world.

Finally, natural resources play a role in global trade. The United States uses graphite, a form of carbon, to make steel and linings for brakes. However, the United States must import graphite from China, Mexico, Canada, and India.

Global Economic Cooperation

Nations often work together to make trading easier. Some sign free trade agreements. In these deals, nations agree to take away all barriers to

---

comparative advantage the ability to produce a good at a lower cost than other nations can produce it

trade with one another. The nations that belong to the European Union have such an agreement. Another example is the United States-Mexico-Canada Agreement (USMCA), which went into effect in 2020. That deal updated a trade agreement signed by those nations in the 1990s.

These agreements do not solve all trade-related problems. They do increase global interdependence.

✓ CHECK FOR UNDERSTANDING

Making Connections How does global interdependence benefit Americans?

Global Concerns

GUIDING QUESTION

What are some consequences of global interdependence?

Global interdependence has provided many benefits, such as increased trade, prosperity, and opportunities for some workers and businesses. However, these benefits are not shared equally around the world. Some workers are paid very poorly or must work long hours in dangerous conditions. The demand for lumber or farmland and the building of new factories has led to damage to the environment in some areas. These challenges have inspired some people around the world to work together to seek solutions. Many others, though, have shown little interest in addressing these issues.

Costs of Competition and Trade

Trade has increased global interdependence. It has also helped many parts of the world reach prosperity, or wealth. A greater amount of trade with fewer barriers usually results in consumers having more choices and lower prices.

Global trade does not just bring benefits. It can also cause problems. To save money, some U.S. companies have moved their factories to countries where workers are paid less. This can lead to job losses for American workers. Those workers may have trouble finding new jobs, especially jobs that pay as well as their former ones. They might have a difficult time learning new skills that would help them get another job. They could be forced to sell their homes and move to other parts of the country to find work.

Workers are not the only ones hurt when some companies move operations to another country. These actions also harm companies that stay in the United States and make the same products. They have a higher cost of doing business than do their relocated competitors. As a result, the companies that stay in the United States charge higher prices than the ones their competitors charge. That can result in lower sales, which may force them to cut costs by letting some workers go, or even to close.

Nations sometimes act to protect certain industries from imports produced in countries with cheaper labor. Governments may put up trade barriers, such as setting tariffs on imported goods. Tariffs add to the cost of imported goods, which helps companies in the country that imposes the tariffs. However, tariffs mean that consumers face higher prices for these goods.

Trade barriers can also lead to conflict with other nations. If Nation A puts tariffs on goods made in Nation B, Nation B might respond by putting tariffs on goods from Nation A. This can lead to a **trade war**, in which nations use tariffs to punish one another. The result is higher prices for everyone and fewer choices for consumers. Trade wars can also make it more difficult for a nation's economy to grow.

---

trade war economic conflict that occurs when one or more nations put up trade barriers to punish another nation for trade barriers it first erected against them

The closing of some factories, such as this steel mill, has been one cost of competition and trade. This can happen when American businesses are unsuccessful in competing against foreign companies.

More Developed and Less Developed Nations

The economies of nations do not develop at the same rate. Economists measure the size of a nation's economy using **gross domestic product (GDP)**. This is the value of all the goods and services a nation produces in one year. GDP does not show how well a nation uses its resources, however. A larger country is likely to have more resources and be able to produce more than a smaller country. To compare economies, economists use **per capita GDP**. This measure is found by dividing a nation's annual GDP by its population. The higher the per capita GDP, the more effective a nation is in using its resources.

More developed nations have high per capita GDPs. Their citizens are generally well-off and well educated. Their economies produce a variety of goods. Some of those goods use advanced technology, such as computers. They usually have political systems that are **stable**, or not subject to major changes, which makes it

gross domestic product (GDP) the value of all the goods and services produced in a nation in one year

per capita GDP a nation's annual GDP divided by its population, a measure of how effectively the nation uses its resources

more developed nation a nation with a high per capita GDP

stable not subject to major changes

Strong infrastructure such as the high-speed bullet train in Tokyo is one reason Japan is a more developed country.

Drawing Conclusions What kind of infrastructure is shown in this image, and how can that help a nation's economy?

easier for people to succeed economically. The United States, France, and Japan are examples of more developed countries.

Less developed nations have low per capita GDPs. Some of these countries lack natural resources, have limited infrastructure, do not have easy access to shipping routes, or have unskilled workers. Some have poor schools, which results in a lack of a skilled workforce. Some struggle with political unrest, which makes it difficult for people to do business. Many lack good sewage systems and clean water, which can lead to serious health problems.

Haiti is an example of a less developed nation. Haiti's exports of clothing are not enough to build a strong economy. Most of Haiti's people are poor and unskilled due to a history of slavery under French rule and foreign interference. Political unrest has also discouraged businesses from placing factories in Haiti. A series of natural disasters have caused even more problems. As a result, Haiti depends on aid from other nations.

The growth of world trade has affected nations differently. Generally, the more developed nations have grown richer. The gap between them and the less developed nations has not closed. Less developed nations are making some economic progress, but they are having trouble catching up. More developed countries and international groups have programs aimed at helping these countries build stronger economies.

Global Politics

The growth of world trade has led to political changes. Many countries in East Asia have larger economies than they did in the past. As a result, they have more influence in the world than before. European nations have become more unified. These changes have an impact on the role of the United States in world affairs. It needs to work with other nations to achieve its goals.

Nations have different views of what will make the world a better place. These differences can lead to disagreements. For example, China criticizes how the government of the United States handles domestic problems. At the same time, the United States condemns the way the Chinese government has treated some groups

less developed nation a nation with a low per capita GDP

Prisma by Dukas Presseagentur GmbH/Alamy Stock Photo

This photograph shows a section of the vast rainforest near the Amazon River in Brazil.

Analyzing Visuals
What environmental problem does the image show?

living in that country. Yet, both nations value the trade they have with one another. For that reason, they must find ways to cooperate.

Environmental Problems

In recent years, people have become more aware of the dangers to the world's environment. When industries in one country pollute, it can affect the air, water, and soil in neighboring countries. Burning fuels to make electricity and to power factories and cars sends harmful chemicals into the air. Trees and fish are harmed when rain carries these chemicals to the earth. Most climate scientists say that burning fossil fuels such as coal and oil is contributing to serious changes to Earth's climate. Temperatures are rising, and more intense storms are striking more often. Burning large amounts of fossil fuels can even affect the climate of the entire world.

Another problem is **deforestation**, which is the removal of trees from large areas. This can result in loss of habitat for animals as well as increased flooding and mud slides when heavy rains fall on an area that has been cleared. The removal of trees also leads to a greater buildup of carbon dioxide in the atmosphere since there are fewer trees to absorb this gas. This buildup is a leading cause of climate change.

deforestation the removal of trees over large areas

It is a huge challenge to solve these problems. Protecting forests may deprive poor farmers of land they need for growing crops. Switching to cleaner sources of energy can be costly. Leaders in many nations fear that taking steps to slow pollution will hurt their economic growth. They argue that their people will suffer if their economies are not allowed to improve.

People can reduce environmental damage through conservation. When conserving resources, people use them carefully and work to limit the harmful effects of human activity. For example, using less gasoline causes less air pollution. Recycling paper means fewer forests need to be cleared to meet the demand for paper products.

People disagree about the balance between protecting the environment and promoting economic growth. Some people argue that conservation increases costs for businesses. Others say that it will be much more costly to fix damage to the environment in the future rather than preventing that damage now.

Other Global Challenges

Other challenges arise from global interdependence. Immigrants often move to a new country to look for better jobs and living conditions. The vast majority of the U.S. population is descended from immigrants.

Refugees from Afghanistan arrive in the United States to begin new lives.

Sometimes people already living in a country worry about new people arriving from another country. They fear that the immigrants will take their jobs and increase demands for housing and services. Religious and ethnic differences between immigrants and people already living in the country can add to tensions. The people of an ethnic group share a common national, cultural, or racial background.

One controversy facing the United States is illegal immigration. Federal officials try to prevent people from entering the country illegally. They also have the power to force people to leave the country if they came illegally. Federal officials sometimes ask state and local law enforcement officials to help. Some cities disagree with the federal law and do not want to force people to leave. They have policies to prevent their police from helping the federal government. In response, some states have passed laws that prevent its cities from passing such policies.

In addition, famine, war, harsh treatment by governments, and natural disasters have driven millions of refugees from their homes. Refugees are people who have left their home to escape these dangers. They try to find shelter in another nation. Some are taken into people's homes and settle in a community. Many, though, live in camps and require help with food, clothing, and medical care. Many more people throughout the world lack basic necessities for life, such as food,

clean water, and health care. Meeting these challenges requires cooperation among nations.

Another challenge that comes from global interdependence is the threat of international **terrorism**. Terrorism involves acts or threats of violence to force people or governments to behave in a certain way. Plane flights make it easy for people to travel to other countries. Many countries, such as the United States, have security officials working in airports to try to stop any terrorists from entering the country. Government intelligence officials contribute to this effort.

✓ **CHECK FOR UNDERSTANDING**

1. **Understanding Supporting Details** Why do governments sometimes set trade barriers?

2. **Contrasting** How do the economies of less developed countries differ from those of more developed countries?

LESSON ACTIVITIES

1. **Informative/Explanatory Writing** Write an essay explaining the positive and negative effects of global interdependence. Explain how global interdependence affects the economy and the movement of people in both helpful and harmful ways.

2. **Using Multimedia** Conduct research on U.S. trade. Identify the leading imports into and exports from the country. Find out who the top U.S. trading partners are. Create a multimedia presentation that identifies these goods and the nations the United States trades with the most.

---

terrorism involves acts or threats of violence to force people or governments to behave in a certain way

The United States and International Organizations

READING STRATEGY

Analyzing Key Ideas and Details As you read, take notes about the work done by major governmental and nongovernmental organizations.

The Purpose of International Organizations

GUIDING QUESTION

What is the purpose of international organizations?

Thirteen tropical storms struck Vietnam and Cambodia in 2020. They caused devastating flooding and landslides that affected more than a million people. These two countries could not do everything needed to respond to the destruction themselves. Other nations sent food, water, medical supplies, and people to help.

Natural disasters are not the only concern that nations face. They also must address ongoing challenges that affect many nations, such as climate change, pollution, crime, and trade. No nation can fully address these issues by itself. Nations need to discuss the issues with one another to work on solutions. This work is done by **diplomats** who represent their countries' governments and meet to find actions that will satisfy all the countries taking part.

Nations have joined together to form different organizations so that they can work on issues on a continuing basis. Some of these organizations include countries from across the world.

diplomat a representative of a country's government who takes part in talks with representatives of other nations

Humanitarian workers distribute aid packages to help the people of Mozambique after strong tropical storms called cyclones struck the country.

Others are formed by nations in just one region. Other types of international organizations are not made up of governments but rather of private individuals committed to making the world a better place. They often carry out humanitarian work, such as disaster relief or public health efforts, or work to promote economic development.

✓ CHECK FOR UNDERSTANDING

Explaining Why do nations work together to address issues such as trade and pollution?

Governmental Organizations

GUIDING QUESTION

How do governmental organizations help people?

The organizations formed by nations working together are called *governmental organizations*. These organizations provide an opportunity for diplomats from member nations to meet regularly, discuss problems, and work on solutions. Sometimes they can reach agreements on issues important to multiple countries.

When nations join a governmental organization, they are required to support the organization's decisions and to follow its rules. One typical rule is that approval is needed from a certain number of member nations for another nation to join the organization. Also, members are generally required to contribute money to help fund the group's work.

Some governmental organizations are formed to carry out a single purpose. The World Trade Organization (WTO) works to promote trade and settle disputes about trade. The North Atlantic Treaty Organization (NATO) was created to help its member nations defend one another against military attack.

Other governmental organizations have broad objectives. The United Nations (UN), the largest governmental organization, has many goals. It promotes peace, fights disease, fights poverty, expands educational opportunities, protects cultural treasures, protects the environment, and works to improve health care.

Governmental organizations can make decisions that lead to major changes. For example, the European Union (EU) set up a common unit of money for most of its members, replacing the currencies of the individual nations. That currency, called the *euro*, is used by most members of the EU, which makes it easier for nations to trade.

The EU is an example of a regional organization. All its members are in Europe. The Organization of American States, which includes 35 nations in the Western Hemisphere, is also a regional group. It works to promote democracy, human rights, security, and economic development in the region. The African Union includes 55 African nations that work to address common issues.

Decisions made by large organizations can have a great effect, such as the adoption of the euro in the EU. However, these groups can face

Delegates from many countries listen to a speaker at the General Assembly of the United Nations.

UPI/Alamy Stock Photo

obstacles in achieving their goals. Most organizations cannot force member states to follow decisions made by the organization. In addition, the larger the group, the more difficult it is to get enough members to agree on a policy. Also, member nations with a lot of power can use that power to prevent the group from taking action. These groups can also fail to live up to their ideals and achieve their goals.

The United Nations

In 1945, at the end of World War II, 51 nations agreed to form the United Nations (UN). The UN was created to keep peace among nations and prevent another devastating war. More nations have joined the UN over the years, and the organization still carries out peacekeeping missions in locations around the world.

The General Assembly is the main forum for the UN's 193 member nations. It meets in New York City. The delegates of every member nation have the right to speak before the General Assembly. A smaller body called the Security Council meets to deal with immediate threats to world peace. The Security Council has five permanent members: the United States, Russia, the United Kingdom, France, and China. The General Assembly elects an additional 10 members to two-year terms on the Security Council. Each of the permanent members has the power to veto any action considered by the Security Council.

The UN has formed other units to address specific issues. For example, the United Nations Educational, Scientific and Cultural Organization (UNESCO) promotes science, education, and culture. It has protected and preserved world heritage sites, such as important historical and cultural locations. The United Nations Children's Fund (UNICEF) works to improve the lives of children around the world.

International Court of Justice

The International Court of Justice (ICJ), also called the World Court, is one of the major units of the United Nations. Its purpose is to settle legal disputes between member nations according to international law. The court has 15 judges who serve terms of nine years. These judges are elected by members of the General Assembly and the Security Council. The court hears disputes that member states agree to submit to it.

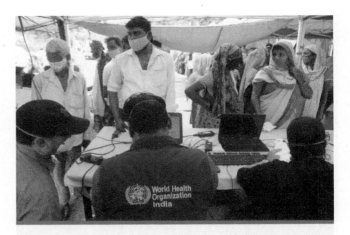

During the COVID-19 pandemic, the World Health Organization helped vaccinate people in India, focusing on those living below the poverty line.

World Health Organization

An important part of the UN is the World Health Organization (WHO). The WHO works in a variety of ways to improve the health of all people. It directs the UN's efforts to fight and prevent disease in nations around the world. One way the WHO promotes better health is by forming standards and guidelines for health-related measures. It also conducts research on public health issues.

The WHO has had success in ending smallpox and teaching people about the HIV virus. Both smallpox and the HIV virus can kill infected people. The WHO has also helped reduce the number of polio cases in the world by 99 percent. In Africa, the WHO has helped reduce the spread of a disease called river blindness. River blindness is caused by the bite of an infected blackfly. The disease had made some land too dangerous to farm, but reducing the threat of disease allowed farmers to use the land again.

The WHO has received criticism. Some critics have said the organization made some mistakes during the COVID-19 pandemic in 2020. They argued that the WHO was too slow to declare COVID-19 a public health emergency. Some believe that this delayed efforts to fight the disease before it became a pandemic.

North Atlantic Treaty Organization

The North Atlantic Treaty Organization (NATO) is a group of 30 nations in North America and Europe. Its main goals are to keep peace and defend all members in times of war.

Soldiers from the Netherlands served in Afghanistan as part of the NATO force.

NATO was formed in 1949 to protect countries in Western Europe from the Soviet Union. The United States is an important member of NATO.

Article V of NATO's charter states that if one ally is attacked, the other members must come to its defense. This principle has been put into use only once, after the United States was attacked by terrorists on September 11, 2001. The other members of NATO joined the United States in its fight against the groups in Afghanistan responsible for the attacks. Some NATO members also sent forces to fight in Iraq in 2003, but the organization did not decide as a whole to become involved. NATO also works with nonmember nations to help prevent conflict.

Like other international organizations, NATO is sometimes criticized. It uses military power in ways with which some people may disagree.

World Trade Organization

The World Trade Organization (WTO) was organized for the purpose of making it easier for nations to conduct trade. It promotes trade by encouraging member nations to remove trade barriers. The WTO also tries to resolve any trade disputes that may arise between countries. The WTO has about 160 members.

The WTO has received criticism. Some less developed nations say that the WTO favors more developed nations and the large businesses based in them. Some critics have argued that the WTO interferes with the sovereignty of its member nations. *Sovereignty* means "freedom from control by others." These critics believe the WTO makes it more difficult for nations to make the best decisions for their own people. Others argue that the focus of the WTO on trade and profit ignores concerns about the environment.

Peace Corps

The Peace Corps is a volunteer group run by the U.S. government. The government sends about 7,300 volunteers overseas to work in roughly 60 countries around the world. These citizens work on a variety of projects. Some work on public health issues, such as slowing the spread of HIV or helping people gain access to clean water. Other volunteers teach people ways to use modern technology and help them with local economic development.

The Peace Corps began in the 1960s when President John F. Kennedy encouraged young people to make a difference and support peace around the world. The original goal of the Peace Corps was to help Americans and the people of other nations understand one another.

✓ **CHECK FOR UNDERSTANDING**

1. **Explaining** Does the United States appear to have a powerful role within the United Nations? Explain.

2. **Determining Central Ideas** What is the purpose of Article V of NATO's charter?

Nongovernmental Organizations

GUIDING QUESTION

How do nongovernmental organizations help people?

Other international organizations exist to help people around the world. Instead of being linked to governments, these organizations are independent. Citizens form these groups to meet a need or to work for a cause. These groups are called **nongovernmental organizations (NGOs)**. Each NGO sets its own goals and rules. Those who lead them decide what actions they will take and where they will work.

Nongovernmental organizations usually depend heavily on private donations to raise the funds they need to do their work. NGOs hire staff people but also rely on volunteers. Many citizens of the United States work and volunteer for NGOs.

NGOs are not necessarily international. They may work in only one country and involve people from that country alone. In the United States, NGOs are often called "nonprofit organizations." However, some important NGOs are international.

nongovernmental organization (NGO) an organization that operates independently of any government body, usually through individual volunteer efforts and private donations

Peace Corps volunteers serve in countries around the world. This volunteer is teaching adults in Honduras.

Analyzing Visuals How might the work of this volunteer help promote the goal of the Peace Corps?

International NGOs often work closely with governmental organizations to carry out some activities. For example, some NGOs provide disaster relief after catastrophes, such as the tropical storms in Vietnam and Cambodia in 2020. NGOs sometimes collaborate with other organizations to address a specific problem that requires specialized knowledge or skills to resolve. For example, an anti-poverty NGO might work with a major insurance company to provide crop insurance to protect farmers against crop failures.

International Committee of the Red Cross

The International Committee of the Red Cross (ICRC) is an NGO. The ICRC gives aid to people who are suffering from the effects of war or natural disasters. The ICRC is based in Switzerland and unites the efforts of aid groups in countries around the world. In some countries these aid groups are called the Red Cross. In others, they are called the Red Crescent.

During a war, the ICRC tries to protect civilians and to make sure that prisoners of war are treated fairly. **Prisoners of war** are soldiers whom enemy forces capture during a conflict. The ICRC tries to locate persons who have become lost to family members because of conflict or disaster. It also brings food, clothing, and medicines to people in need in areas damaged by war.

The ICRC maintains a **neutral** position in conflicts. That is, it does not take sides in a war. Most nations do not interfere with its work because they respect the ICRC and its efforts to help people.

Doctors Without Borders

Doctors Without Borders, also known as *Médecins Sans Frontières* (MSF), sends doctors to war-torn areas to provide medical aid to people in need. It also works to prevent the spread of epidemics, or the widespread occurrence of an infectious disease. The group won a Nobel Peace Prize in 1999 for its work.

Doctors Without Borders has spoken out about the way nations and international organizations have ignored crises that have caused suffering.

prisoner of war a person captured by opposing forces during a conflict

neutral taking no side or part in a conflict or disagreement

International Nongovernmental Organizations

Groups have formed NGOs to serve many different needs.

NGO	AREA OF CONCERN
Amnesty International	Human rights
CARE International	Poverty, education, economic development, health
Cousteau Society	Environment
Doctors Without Borders	Health, disaster response/relief
Heifer International	Hunger, poverty, economic development
Hunger Project	Hunger
International Committee of the Red Cross	Human rights, public health, disaster response/relief
International Rescue Committee	Refugees, human rights, health education
MacArthur Foundation	Human rights, economic development, peace, education, environment
Nature Conservancy	Environment
Oxfam International	Poverty, hunger, human rights, economic development

EXAMINE THE CHART

1. **Identifying Themes** Which areas of concern are the focus of the most groups?
2. **Drawing Conclusions** Why do you think those areas have the largest number of NGOs working in them?

It also has pushed for improving medical treatments and the way they are given.

Other NGOs

There are many other NGOs that work to solve problems all over the world. Some focus on health, working to prevent disease or improve health care for those who need it. Others try to help people find ways to make a better living for themselves. Some work to promote economic development. These NGOs usually work in less developed nations. Some NGOs try to protect human rights. They tend to focus on nations with governments that rule in harsh or unfair ways. NGOs that focus on environmental problems work in locations all over the world.

✓ CHECK FOR UNDERSTANDING

1. **Contrasting** How are NGOs different from governmental organizations?
2. **Analyzing** How does being neutral help the International Committee of the Red Cross do its work?

LESSON ACTIVITIES

1. **Informative/Explanatory Writing** Learn more about one governmental organization to which the United States belongs. Conduct research using the organization's website to find information about its founding, its purpose, and at least two of its major successes, including the U.S. role in those activities. Write a short essay presenting your findings.

2. **Collaborating** Work with a partner on creating a poster to recruit volunteers to work for an NGO of your choice. Your poster should provide information about the purpose of the NGO, the projects that it works on, and the ways that volunteers can contribute to its efforts to make a better world. Visit the NGO's website to gather the information you need. Make your poster convincing and present your finished product to the class.

READING STRATEGY

Integrating Knowledge and Ideas As you read, make an outline listing the roles the United States plays in world affairs.

U.S. Roles in World Affairs

1.
2.
3.

Human Rights

GUIDING QUESTION

What are human rights?

People across the world share many needs and wants. People need food, water, and a clean place to live. They want to be safe and to be able to care for their families and live productive lives.

These shared desires lead to an understanding of basic human rights. A **human right** is a basic freedom that all people deserve to have simply because they are human. For example, there is a human right to be protected under the law and to have the freedom to think and speak as a person wishes. Some people have fought to secure these rights for themselves, as happened in the American Revolution. Other people work quietly to win these rights for themselves or for others.

Who is responsible for promoting human rights? Of course, *everyone* has a duty to avoid actions that violate or take away people's rights. But what should people do when governments in other countries violate their own people's human rights?

The Universal Declaration of Human Rights

The United Nations is an international organization formed in 1945 to maintain international peace and security. Soon after the United Nations was formed, its members adopted the Universal Declaration of Human Rights, or UDHR.

human right a basic freedom that all people should have simply because they are human

Former U.S. First Lady Eleanor Roosevelt led the group that wrote the Universal Declaration of Human Rights.

This document defines the human rights that all people should have. Something that is **universal** applies to all people everywhere.

Article 1 of the UDHR states that "All human beings are born free and equal in dignity and rights." They have "reason and conscience." This means people can think for themselves and judge what is right and wrong.

Article 2 says that all people should have human rights "without distinction of any kind, such as race, color, sex, language, religion, political or other opinion, national or social origin, property, birth or other status." The other rights in the UDHR are built upon these two basic statements.

These other rights include freedom from slavery and torture. The UDHR says people should be treated fairly by the justice system. It states that they should have the freedom to marry the partner of their choice. They should be free to own property, to move about as they choose, and to have a voice in their government. The UDHR also recognizes economic and social rights, such as equal pay for equal work and the right to a standard of living that is "adequate for health and well-being . . . including food, clothing, housing and medical care and necessary social services."

The rights listed in the UDHR have not always been upheld. People disagree about who has the responsibility to protect these rights for the people in each country. Most governments do not fully provide economic and social rights for all citizens. For instance, people debate whether the U.S. government has a responsibility to provide medical care for its own people.

Violations of Human Rights

Some governments show little respect for the human rights of their people. Many governments do not fully provide economic and social rights for all citizens. Some leaders maintain power through repression. **Repression** is preventing people from expressing themselves or living life as they wish. Many nations, such as China, Iran, and Saudi Arabia, deny people the rights to free speech and a free press. North Korea does not allow its people to leave the country or to criticize its leader.

---

universal applying to all people

repression preventing people from expressing themselves or from freely engaging in normal life

In some countries, governments treat particular ethnic or religious groups harshly and unfairly. For example, the U.S. secretary of state has said that China has put more than 1 million Uyghurs (WEE•goorz) in prison camps and has also tortured many of them. Uyghurs are a Muslim ethnic group that lives in China. The United States has accused China of genocide against the Uyghurs. **Genocide** is the attempt to kill all members of a particular national, ethnic, or religious group.

Protecting Human Rights

The U.S. government tries to promote human rights around the world. It protests when other governments deny their people basic human rights, as it has done with China. Sometimes it refuses to trade with those countries. In 2019 the United States gave about $34 billion in economic aid to other countries. This money provided humanitarian assistance, supported health care and democracy, and addressed other human needs.

---

genocide the attempt to kill all members of a particular national, ethnic, or religious group

The United States and other countries protest China's treatment of its Uyghur minority group. It is believed that the Chinese are holding more than a million Uyghurs in facilities such as the one shown here. The Chinese government says they use these facilities to teach job skills.

Analyzing Visuals What details in the photo suggest that the people in these facilities cannot move about freely?

PHOTO: GREG BAKER/AFP/Getty Images; TEXT: Universal Declaration of Human Rights. Adopted by the United Nations General Assembly, 10 December 1948.

Activists in the United Kingdom march in support of accepting refugees in their country.

The UN Human Rights Council issues reports aimed at convincing governments to respect people's rights. The UN Security Council can file charges against a government that it believes has violated its people's human rights. Another body of the UN, called the International Court of Justice (ICJ), will then hold a trial.

Many nongovernmental organizations (NGOs) also work to protect and support human rights. Amnesty International and Human Rights Watch both publish reports identifying countries that violate human rights. They also use publicity to try to pressure countries into changing unfair laws.

✓ CHECK FOR UNDERSTANDING

1. **Citing Text Evidence** What are three human rights all people should have according to the Universal Declaration of Human Rights?
2. **Identifying** In addition to the U.S. government, what organizations work to protect human rights?

Democracy, Liberty, and Conflict

GUIDING QUESTION

Why does conflict among nations occur?

In general, nations with democratic governments have respected human rights more than those led by authoritarian rulers. As more nations have become democratic, more people in the world have become free to live their lives as they wish.

The Growth of Democracy

In 1900 most people lived in countries where they had no voice in choosing their leaders. By the early 2000s, that situation changed. Today, about 60 percent of the world's nations are democracies.

The United States has often worked to spread democracy and freedom throughout the world. During World War I, President Woodrow Wilson said that he hoped the war would "make the world safe for democracy." During World War II, President Franklin D. Roosevelt said:

❝ Freedom means the supremacy of human rights everywhere. Our support goes to those who struggle to gain those rights or keep them. ❞

The United States and the Soviet Union became allies in World War II to defeat a common enemy. After the war, however, these allies split into two camps that had very different political and economic systems. The United States and most of Western Europe had democratic governments. They also had economies built on free markets. The Soviet Union and Eastern Europe practiced **communism**. In these countries, the Communist Party ran the government and the economy. People in these countries had little political or personal freedom.

The Cold War

These differences grew into a conflict called the Cold War. It lasted from the late 1940s to 1991. During the Cold War, the United States and the Soviet Union never directly fought each other. They did compete for influence around the world, however. The Soviet Union tried to take control of more nations. The United States and its allies tried to stop them. Sometimes the United States supported leaders who abused the human rights of their citizens because those leaders also opposed communism.

People in communist Eastern European countries moved against communist rule in the 1980s. While popular uprisings had been stopped by the Soviet Union in the 1950s and 1960s, the protests of the 1980s led to the collapse of the communist governments in many countries.

communism a one-party system of government based on the ideas of state ownership of property and government direction of the economy

New leaders pushed these countries toward democracy and market economies. In 1991 communism fell in the Soviet Union. That nation separated into 15 nations, one of which was Russia. The Cold War was over, but many of the countries of Eastern Europe continue to work towards true freedom.

Free and Not Free

While democracy advanced in the 1900s, many nations are not free. Governments in many parts of Africa, Asia, and South America still restrict the human rights of their people. Communist governments in North Korea, China, and Cuba deny their people basic human rights. These nations are not considered to be free.

Meanwhile, new threats to freedom have arisen in parts of the world. Terrorists have tried to force political change by using violence. Groups such as al Qaeda and ISIS have killed thousands of people around the world in their attempts to impose their beliefs on others.

✓ **CHECK FOR UNDERSTANDING**

1. **Explaining** What was the Cold War?
2. **Determining Central Ideas** How did the end of the Cold War affect the spread of democracy?

Communists built a wall dividing the city of Berlin, Germany, to prevent people in communist East Berlin from escaping to the noncommunist section of the city. The Berlin Wall became a symbol of the Cold War division of Europe.

Analyzing Visuals Which area shown in the photo was controlled by communists? Why do you think so?

Recent Conflicts

GUIDING QUESTION

Why has the United States engaged in conflict in recent years?

On September 11, 2001, members of al Qaeda hijacked four U.S. commercial jetliners and crashed them into buildings in New York City and near Washington, D.C. Almost 3,000 people died in those attacks. The United States responded in several ways.

Homeland Security

One response was to create the Department of Homeland Security in 2002. The Department of Homeland Security has three main goals: to prevent terrorist attacks in the United States, to reduce the threat of such attacks, and to help in the recovery from attacks or natural disasters. To do its work, the department has many powers. For instance, workers in the Transportation Security Administration, or TSA, check all plane passengers and their luggage for weapons and other dangerous or illegal items.

USA Patriot Act

Another response to the September 11 attacks was the Patriot Act of 2001. This law gave the government more power to gather information to help in the fight against terrorism. The government could search phone and financial records, listen to the phone conversations of suspected terrorists, and track Internet messages and voice mail recordings.

Many people felt that the Patriot Act went too far. They believed that the spying and mass data collection allowed by the act violated the Fourth Amendment right to freedom from unreasonable search and seizure. Although Congress made some changes to the law to address these concerns, some Americans still object to it.

The War in Afghanistan

The U.S. government also responded to the September 11 attacks with military force. Wars in Afghanistan and Iraq followed.

Al Qaeda trained terrorists in the country of Afghanistan. They were allowed to do so by the Taliban, a group that governed Afghanistan. In October 2001, the United States and its allies attacked Afghanistan. These forces quickly

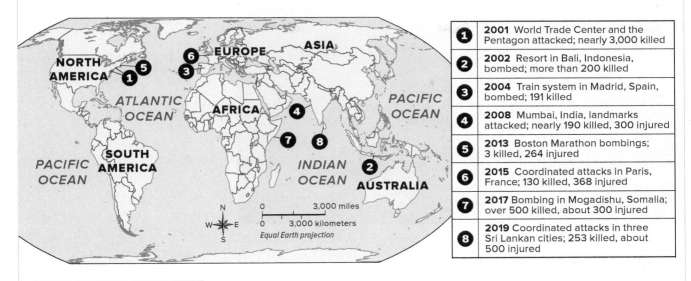

Major Terrorist Attacks, Early 2000s

Many nations have been the targets of terrorist attacks since the early 2000s.

1	**2001** World Trade Center and the Pentagon attacked; nearly 3,000 killed
2	**2002** Resort in Bali, Indonesia, bombed; more than 200 killed
3	**2004** Train system in Madrid, Spain, bombed; 191 killed
4	**2008** Mumbai, India, landmarks attacked; nearly 190 killed, 300 injured
5	**2013** Boston Marathon bombings; 3 killed, 264 injured
6	**2015** Coordinated attacks in Paris, France; 130 killed, 368 injured
7	**2017** Bombing in Mogadishu, Somalia; over 500 killed, about 300 injured
8	**2019** Coordinated attacks in three Sri Lankan cities; 253 killed, about 500 injured

GEOGRAPHY CONNECTION

1. **Global Interconnections** Which terrorist attack took the most lives?
2. **Patterns and Movement** Why do you think terrorists attack targets such as malls, landmarks, and train systems?

forced the Taliban out of power. However, they could not capture the leader of al Qaeda, Osama bin Laden.

In May 2011, U.S. forces located bin Laden in Pakistan. They raided his compound, and he was killed in the fighting. Meanwhile, fighting in Afghanistan continued. The Taliban grew strong again and began to challenge the new government in Afghanistan for control of the country. In 2020 President Donald Trump reached an agreement to withdraw U.S. troops. After President Joe Biden took office in early 2021, he completed the troop withdrawal. Taliban forces again took control of the government. The return of the Taliban raised concerns that it would once again rule harshly and allow terrorists to train there.

The War in Iraq

After September 11, President George W. Bush feared that Iraqi dictator Saddam Hussein might give terrorists weapons of mass destruction. A **weapon of mass destruction (WMD)** is a weapon that can kill or harm large numbers of people and

damage huge areas, such as entire cities. The United States and many of its allies believed that Iraq was a dangerous threat.

In early 2003, the United States and its allies joined to invade Iraq. These forces quickly defeated the Iraqi army. Saddam Hussein was captured, tried by Iraq's new government, and executed in 2006 for crimes against his people.

No WMDs were found in Iraq. Later research indicated that the administration's claims had been exaggerated. As a result, the U.S. government was criticized for the invasion.

U.S. troops stayed in Iraq in an attempt to build democracy and train that country's new army and police. Rebel groups battled U.S. forces with roadside bombs and surprise attacks. Conflicts among Iraq's ethnic and religious groups sometimes erupted into violence. By 2021 U.S. troops officially ended their military role in Iraq. However, about 2,000 troops stayed to serve as advisers to the government trying to rebuild the country.

weapon of mass destruction (WMD) a weapon that can kill or harm large numbers of people and damage a large area

These Iranian missile fragments were displayed in 2017 as proof that Iran was building up its weapons stockpile in violation of UN resolutions.

Foreign Policy Challenges Continue

The United States continues to face other global challenges. Iran began developing nuclear weapons. The United States **imposed** economic sanctions to try to shut down that weapons program. *Sanctions* are "steps meant to punish a country until it changes its actions."

The United States, China, France, Germany, Russia, and the United Kingdom worked together on the problem. In 2015 they signed an agreement with Iran called the Joint Comprehensive Plan of Action (JCPOA). Iran agreed to allow inspections to prove that it was not developing nuclear weapons. In exchange, the allies agreed to lift some economic sanctions. In 2018 President Trump cancelled the deal and put sanctions back in place. Iran began working on nuclear weapons again. After Joe Biden became president in 2021, he hoped to make a new agreement with Iran.

North Korea also worked to develop nuclear weapons and missiles to deliver them. The United States has used diplomacy to try to end this threat.

The United States also faced challenges with Russia. In 2014 Russian forces captured Crimea, a part of Ukraine. Russia also threatened other areas of Ukraine. In 2016 and 2020, Russia secretly worked to influence the presidential elections in the United States. The United States placed many sanctions on Russia as a result.

impose establish or force

Concerns over illegal immigration also challenged the United States. In the 2010s, many people fled poverty, corrupt governments, and violence in Mexico and Central America. President Trump ordered a larger wall to be built across the southern border of the United States to prevent people from entering the country illegally. He also made an agreement with Mexico to hold migrants from other countries in Mexico. President Biden tried to address the issues that caused people to flee other countries. The U.S. government aimed to provide economic aid to help those countries build stronger economies and more stable governments.

✓ CHECK FOR UNDERSTANDING

1. **Explaining** Why did the United States go to war in Afghanistan?

2. **Identifying** What are three tools of foreign policy the United States used to address the issues in Afghanistan, Iran, Russia, and Mexico and Central America?

LESSON ACTIVITIES

1. **Argumentative Writing** The United States has engaged in military actions all over the world. Do you believe the government is right to send the U.S. military to other areas? Or do you believe national defense should be limited to defending U.S. territory? Write three paragraphs to explain your opinion.

2. **Collaborating** Working with a partner, write a series of "breaking news" social media posts updating the information on the foreign policy issues discussed in the lesson. Compose at least four posts that explain key events.

DOD Photo/Alamy Stock Photo

06

Analyzing Sources: The United States and Human Rights Around the World

? COMPELLING QUESTION

Who is responsible for protecting human rights around the world?

Plan Your Inquiry

DEVELOPING QUESTIONS

Think about rights and freedoms that you consider essential for people in the United States. What obligation does the U.S. government have to promote or protect those rights for people in other parts of the world? Then read the Compelling Question for this lesson. What questions can you ask to help you answer this Compelling Question? Create a graphic organizer like the one below. Write these Supporting Questions in your graphic organizer.

Supporting Questions	Primary or Secondary Source	What this source tells me about the role of the United States in protecting human rights around the world	Questions the source leaves unanswered
	A		
	B		
	C		
	D		
	E		
	F		
	G		

ANALYZING SOURCES

Next, examine the sources in this lesson. Analyze each source by answering the questions that follow it. How does each source help you answer each Supporting Question you created? What questions do you still have? Write these in your graphic organizer.

After you analyze the sources, you will:

- use the evidence from the sources,
- communicate your conclusions,
- and take informed action.

Background Information

On December 10, 1948, more than 40 of the founding members of the United Nations (UN) approved the Universal Declaration of Human Rights (UDHR). This document defines the human rights that all people should have. It includes freedom of speech and religion, the right to a fair trial, and to equal treatment by the law. It also names access to adequate food, shelter, medical care, and education as human rights. Since then, the UDHR has inspired other international declarations intended to protect human rights. More than 190 countries have signed at least one of those declarations.

Still, human rights violations continue in many countries. People debate what to do when governments violate human rights. The United States says that promoting human rights is one goal of its foreign policy. Even so, it has struggled at times to uphold human rights within its borders. U.S. officials and citizens still express concern over human rights abuses.

In 2018 some people protested the U.S. policy of separating families trying to enter the country along the southern border. They viewed family separation as a violation of human rights.

Opinion of the Court: *Korematsu* v. *United States*

During World War II, the United States forced more than 100,000 Japanese Americans to live in internment camps. *Internment* means "to confine or imprison someone." Fred Korematsu refused to go to a camp and was convicted of violating a federal order. He appealed his conviction on the grounds that the order violated his rights. His appeal eventually went to the Supreme Court.

» Fred Korematsu, c. 1940

PRIMARY SOURCE: SUPREME COURT OPINION

❝ The **petitioner**, an American citizen of Japanese descent, was convicted . . . for remaining in San Leandro, California . . . contrary to Civilian Exclusion Order No. 34 . . . which directed that . . . all persons of Japanese ancestry should be excluded from that area. . . .

That order, issued after we were at war with Japan, declared that 'the successful prosecution of the war requires every possible protection against . . . **sabotage** to national defense. . . .'

[E]xclusion of those of Japanese origin was deemed necessary because of the presence of an unascertained [undetermined] number of disloyal members of the group, most of whom we have no doubt were loyal to this country. . . .

Compulsory [forced] exclusion of large groups of citizens from their homes . . . is inconsistent with [goes against] our basic governmental institutions. But when . . . our shores are threatened by hostile [enemy] forces, the power to protect must be commensurate [equal] with the threatened danger.

. . . Korematsu was not excluded from the Military Area because of hostility to him or his race. He was excluded because we are at war with the Japanese Empire. ❞

— Justice Hugo Black, Majority Opinion of the Court, *Korematsu* v. *United States*, 1944

petitioner person who brings a case to a court of law
sabotage purposely acting to damage or destroy property or equipment

---

EXAMINE THE SOURCE

1. **Summarizing** What reason does the opinion give for the internment of Japanese Americans?

2. **Evaluating** What do you think of the distinction Black makes in the final paragraph?

B

Apologizing to Japanese Americans

In 1988 Congress passed the Civil Liberties Act. This law stated that the internment of Japanese Americans during World War II was unjust. It promised to pay $20,000 to each person who had been interned or their descendants. The following is from the letter by President Bill Clinton that accompanied these payments.

PRIMARY SOURCE: LETTER

> "Over fifty years ago, the United States Government unjustly interned, evacuated, or relocated you and many other Japanese Americans. Today, on behalf of your fellow Americans, I offer a sincere apology to you for the actions that unfairly denied Japanese Americans and their families fundamental [basic] liberties during World War II.
>
> In passing the Civil Liberties Act of 1988, we acknowledged the wrongs of the past and offered **redress** to those who endured such grave [significant] injustice. **In retrospect**, we understand that the nation's actions were rooted deeply in racial prejudice, wartime **hysteria**, and a lack of political leadership. We must learn from the past and dedicate ourselves as a nation to renewing the spirit of equality and our love of freedom. Together, we can guarantee a future with liberty and justice for all. You and your family have my best wishes for the future."
>
> —President Bill Clinton, Letter of Apology to Japanese Americans, October 1, 1993

redress a remedy for a wrong

in retrospect looking back on the past

hysteria extreme behavior based on fear

EXAMINE THE SOURCE

1. **Analyzing Perspectives** How did the U.S. government's view of Japanese Americans differ from World War II to 1988, when the Civil Liberties Act was passed?
2. **Interpreting** What does Clinton suggest are the two purposes of the law in the second paragraph?

Clinton, William J. "Apology Letter to Japanese Internees, October 1, 1993." Children of the Camps: Historical Documents. PBS.org. 1999. http://www.pbs.org/childofcamp/history/clinton.html

"The Struggle for Human Rights"

Former First Lady Eleanor Roosevelt chaired the United Nations commission that wrote the Universal Declaration of Human Rights (UDHR). In this speech, Roosevelt discusses her view of human rights.

Roosevelt, Eleanor. "The Struggles for the Rights of Man." Sorbonne, Paris, September 28, 1948. https://erpapers.columbian.gwu.edu/struggle-human-rights-1948.

PRIMARY SOURCE: SPEECH

66 We must not be confused about what freedom is. Basic human rights are simple and easily understood: freedom of speech and a free press; freedom of religion and worship; freedom of assembly and the right of petition; the right of men to be secure in their homes and free from unreasonable search and seizure and from **arbitrary** arrest and punishment. . . .

Democracy, freedom, [and] human rights have come to have a definite meaning to the people of the world which we must not allow any nation to so change that they are made synonymous with [equal to] **suppression** and **dictatorship**. . . .

The future must see the broadening of human rights throughout the world. People who have glimpsed [seen] freedom will never be content [satisfied] until they have secured it for themselves. In a true sense, human rights are a fundamental [basic] object of law and government in a just society. Human rights exist to the degree that they are respected by people in relations with each other and by governments in relations with their citizens. 99

—Eleanor Roosevelt, "The Struggle for Human Rights," September 28, 1948

arbitrary random and unfair

suppression using force to stop or prevent certain behaviors

dictatorship form of government in which one leader or group of leaders exercises complete control over the state and the people

---

EXAMINE THE SOURCE

1. **Analyzing** How does the second paragraph explain why Roosevelt thought the UDHR was necessary?

2. **Interpreting** What point in favor of the UDHR does Roosevelt make in the final sentence?

The U.S. Record on Human Rights

In 1976 the United States, the Soviet Union, and many countries in Europe signed an agreement called the Helsinki Final Act that aimed to ensure human rights in those countries. Congress formed a commission to monitor how countries met the promises of the Helsinki Final Act. Missouri Congressman Emanuel Cleaver II served on that commission in 2020. In these remarks to the commission, Cleaver refers to the Black Lives Matter movement. This movement organized in response to repeated cases of discrimination toward African Americans.

PRIMARY SOURCE: TESTIMONY

66 When the United States signed the Helsinki Final Act, this country, along with 34 other nations, explicitly [openly] recognized respect for human rights as an essential [required] factor for the attainment [achieving] of peace, justice, and cooperation among nations. . . .

The United States has long been a champion of human rights and democracy in our foreign policy. . . . Our goal is always to encourage positive change and better implementation [enactment] of Helsinki commitments [promises]. Today we look inward as we examine the Black Lives Matter protests and related domestic **compliance** issues in the context of our . . . commitments and implications for U.S. foreign policy.

. . . If there is no respect for the rights of Americans to address wounds left open by centuries-old **systemic racism** we cannot achieve necessary healing, nor will we have the standing to advocate for [promote] fundamental freedoms abroad. We must practice what we preach. 99

—Representative Emanuel Cleaver II, in "Human Rights at Home: Implications for U.S. Leadership," July 2, 2020

compliance acting to meet a set standard

systemic racism widespread discrimination against African Americans

| EXAMINE THE SOURCE |

1. **Distinguishing Fact From Opinion** What opinion does Cleaver express in the second paragraph regarding the United States and human rights? Why?
2. **Analyzing Points of View** What does Cleaver suggest in the last sentence about the U.S. record on the human rights of African Americans?

+Cleaver II, Emanuel. In "Human Rights at Home: Implications for U.S. Leadership." Hearing Before the Commission on Security and Cooperation in Europe. 116th Congress, 2nd Session. July 2, 2020. Washington, DC: U.S. Government Publishing Office, 2021.

U.S. Department of State on Human Rights

Each year, the U.S. Department of State issues a review of human rights practices in countries around the world. In 2021 Secretary of State Antony Blinken reviewed issues and events of the previous year.

PRIMARY SOURCE: DOCUMENT

" Human rights are interdependent [connected], and the deprivation [denial] of one right can cause the broader fabric of a society to fray [weaken]. Despite potential [possible] risks to their health or threats of arrest or other repercussions [consequences], people around the world demanded that governments respect their human rights. . . . From Hong Kong to Belarus, from Nigeria to Venezuela, people assembled in the streets. They called for governmental protection of their human rights and fundamental [basic] freedoms, safeguards for free and fair elections, and an end to discrimination.

Too many people continued to suffer under brutal conditions in 2020. In China, government authorities committed **genocide** against **Uyghurs**, . . . and crimes against humanity including imprisonment, torture, . . . and persecution against Uyghurs and members of other religious and ethnic minority groups. . . . The war in Yemen has driven millions to extreme humanitarian need, preventing them from exercising many of their basic rights. . . .

In Nicaragua, the corrupt **Ortega regime** passed increasingly **repressive** laws that limit severely the ability of opposition political groups . . . and independent media to operate. Meanwhile in Cuba, government restrictions continued to suppress the freedoms of expression, **association**, religion or belief, and movement. . . .

These and other ongoing rights abuses cause untold damage well beyond the borders of any single country; unchecked human rights abuses anywhere can contribute to a sense of **impunity** everywhere. . . . Recognizing that there is work to be done at home, we are also striving [trying] to live up to our highest ideals and principles and are committed to working toward a fairer and more just society in the United States. We all have work to do, and we must use every tool available to foster a more peaceful and just world. "

— Secretary of State Antony J. Blinken, Preface to the "2020 Country Reports on Human Rights Practices," March 31, 2021

---

genocide the deliberate effort to kill all members of a particular group

Uyghur member of a minority ethnic group in China, most of whom are Muslims

Ortega regime government led by President Daniel Ortega

repressive tending to prevent people from expressing themselves or engaging freely in normal life

association right of people to gather freely in groups

impunity freedom from punishment

> **EXAMINE THE SOURCE**

1. **Identifying** What countries does the report name as violating human rights?
2. **Contrasting** How do the situations in China and Nicaragua and Cuba differ?

U.S. Department of State. Bureau of Democracy, Human Rights, and Labor. "2020 Country Reports on Human Rights Practices." U.S. Department of State. March 30, 2021. https://www.state.gov/reports/2020-country-reports-on-human-rights-practices/.

Helping Refugees

In 1951 members of the UN signed the Refugee Convention, a document that describes the rights of refugees. It also identifies the duty of nations to protect refugees and give them aid. This article examines the application of the convention's principles to the U.S.-led war in Afghanistan, which lasted from 2001 until 2021.

Linden-Retek, Paul. "Whose Suffering Matters?" Boston Review. September 22, 2021. https://bostonreview.net/articles/whose-suffering-matters/

SECONDARY SOURCE: MAGAZINE ARTICLE

" Honoring the Convention's promise today requires appraising [evaluating] the ethical [moral] vision—and ethical **dilemmas**—at its heart. What do we owe those who flee the risk of harm in Afghanistan—or disasters in Haiti, or civil strife in West Africa? What does answering this question in good faith demand of us? And what does it teach us about the role of refugee law in building a better world?

The Convention . . . [defines] refugee status and [specifies] protected categories of persecution due to reasons of race, religion, nationality, membership of a particular social group, or political opinion. . . .

The Convention . . . holds that no refugee, even those not yet **given formal status** by a state, can be returned to a place where they will be harmed. . . .

[T]he Convention harbors [includes] many structural tensions: between the **sovereignty** of states and the rights of individuals, between the specter [presence] of fear and threat and the promise of courage and commitment, between the calculation of benefits and costs and the **inviolability** of human personhood. . . .

[I]f the end of the war in Afghanistan should teach the United States and its allies **humility** about their conduct of foreign policy, one lesson ought to be the need to reflect more carefully on our claim to **humanitarianism**. How we justify our commitments to refugee protection matters deeply for how robust [strong] they are and how faithfully they respond to the needs of those who suffer. . . .

Consider first the most general moral claim for humanitarian protection of refugees: that we have a universal duty to rescue. This duty is owed . . . to all in need, when we are able to assist and it is not significantly costly to do so. . . . Who is to judge the quality of need, the ability to save, and the significance of the cost? From which particular perspective, and how? "

— Paul Linden-Retek, "Whose Suffering Matters?" *Boston Review,* September 22, 2021

---

dilemma a difficult problem

give formal status to officially recognize

sovereignty freedom from control by others

inviolability security from attack

humility feeling that one is not above making mistakes

humanitarianism promoting human welfare

EXAMINE THE SOURCE

1. **Identifying** What is one of the main principles of the Refugee Convention?
2. **Analyzing** What is the purpose of the paragraph about the tensions that the Convention includes? Include an example of these tensions.

Human Rights and China

The United States and China are important trade partners, and the United States depends on many Chinese imports. The following cartoon comments on the United States' relationship with China, which is complicated by China's unpopular stances on trade and human rights. The dragon is a traditional symbol for China, while Uncle Sam represents the United States.

PRIMARY SOURCE: POLITICAL CARTOON

EXAMINE THE SOURCE

1. **Inferring** How are China and the United States presented in this cartoon? Consider the sizes and positions of the two characters.

2. **Analyzing** What does the cartoon suggest about the U.S. threats to China over its human rights abuses? Why might that be?

Complete Your Inquiry

EVALUATE SOURCES AND USE EVIDENCE

Refer back to the Compelling Question and the Supporting Questions you developed at the beginning of the lesson.

1. **Making Connections** In Source E, Antony Blinken says the United States still has work to do on human rights. How do the other sources provide more context for that statement?

2. **Making Connections** How does Source E help you understand U.S. policy toward China as presented in Source G? What might Uncle Sam want the dragon to do?

3. **Gathering Sources** Which sources helped you answer the Supporting Questions and the Compelling Question? Which sources, if any, challenged what you thought you knew when you first created your Supporting Questions? What information do you still need in order to answer your questions? What other viewpoints would you like to investigate? Where would you find that information?

4. **Evaluating Sources** Identify the sources that helped answer your Supporting Questions. How reliable are the sources? How would you verify the reliability of the sources?

COMMUNICATE CONCLUSIONS

5. **Collaborating** In a group, record ideas about human rights in a large concept web. Summarize why human rights policy can be challenging, citing examples from the sources presented here. Share your group's ideas with the class. Then individually write a statement in response to the Compelling Question.

TAKE INFORMED ACTION

Writing a PSA on a Human Rights Crisis With a partner, identify from reliable news outlets a human rights issue in the world today that interests you. Read at least three sources to learn more about the causes of the crisis, the parties involved, how countries and organizations are responding, and possible solutions. Together, prepare a public service announcement (PSA) that summarizes the situation and explains whether you think the United States has any duty or reason to act in the situation.

Environmental Concerns

Analyzing Key Ideas and Details As you read, take notes on the types and sources of pollution that harm the environment.

Types of Pollution	Sources of Pollution

GUIDING QUESTION

Why is it important to protect and preserve the environment?

In the 1940s, the first modern insecticide became available. An *insecticide* is "a chemical substance that kills insects." Referred to by an abbreviation of its chemical name, DDT, it was very successful in killing the insects that caused terrible diseases such as malaria. DDT was widely used to control insects on farms, in schools, and in homes. It was sprayed widely over entire neighborhoods to kill mosquitoes. At the time, DDT was assumed to be safe for people, plants, and animals.

Rachel Carson, a biologist and science writer, recognized that DDT posed dangers to living things and their habitats. In 1962 she published a book titled *Silent Spring* that detailed how DDT caused cancer and other problems in humans and wildlife. Carson's book convinced the U.S. government to prohibit the use of DDT. The book also persuaded many people that the natural world needed protection.

What Is Environmentalism?

Rachel Carson helped people see the environment from a new perspective. So did NASA, America's space agency. When space travel began in the 1960s, astronauts saw Earth from a different viewpoint. In 1968 NASA released a photograph of Earth taken from outer space. The photograph showed Earth in a way few humans had ever seen it.

A U.S. astronaut orbiting the moon took this photograph of Earth in 1968.

Analyzing Visuals How does the point of view of this photograph differ from humans' normal point of view of planet Earth?

In the foreground of the photograph was the surface of the moon. Above it, Earth appeared small and vulnerable within a vast darkness. The photograph helped people understand that humans share a tiny planet in the vastness of space. Some people concluded that we needed to protect that planet. The photograph is credited by some for helping to start the environmental movement. **Environmentalism** is the movement concerned with protecting Earth's natural environment.

Until the 1970s, protecting the environment remained a low priority. Meanwhile, the human population grew, industry expanded, and pollution increased. **Pollution** is harmful substances that make the air, land, and water dirty and unsafe for living things. Congress took action in 1970. It created the Environmental Protection Agency (EPA) to set goals for protecting the environment. It also set standards to be met, such as maximum levels of polluting substances allowed in drinking water. That same year, Congress passed the Clean Air Act to reduce air pollution. Two years later, Congress passed the Clean Water Act to prevent pollution of fresh water. States also began to establish programs to improve air and water quality.

At the same time, some people joined groups that worked to protect wildlife and reduce pollution. Examples are the World Wildlife Fund and the Sierra Club. People also pressured governments to act to protect the environment.

Waste Disposal

One environmental problem is solid waste, or garbage. Each year, Americans produce about 290 million tons of solid waste. About half of that waste goes to **landfills,** or places set aside for storing waste. Although landfills keep waste separate from the rest of the environment, they can cause problems.

Landfills are filling up fast. That means people need to set aside more space to hold growing amounts of trash. It is difficult to find new landfill sites because no one wants to live near a garbage dump. Citizens' groups have blocked creation of many new landfill sites.

Another problem with landfills is that rainwater can soak through the garbage and seep down into the ground, where it can then pollute a community's water supplies. When harmful chemicals get into a water supply, the people and animals that drink or use it can become very sick.

More than 30 million tons of garbage is burned to make electricity. Building these power

---

environmentalism the movement concerned with protecting the natural environment

pollution materials or substances that damage the environment by poisoning the air, land, and water

landfill a place set aside for dumping garbage

Landfills are regulated to prevent harmful substances from seeping into the ground.

This teenager separates plastic bottles to recycle by placing them in a recycling bin outside of her home. Plastic bottles can be used to make new products including shoes and t-shirts.

plants is more costly than opening a landfill, however. Also, the burning releases **toxic**, or poisonous, smoke that causes air pollution. Waste-burning power plants need to have special equipment to remove these dangerous chemicals. This adds to the cost of building the power plants.

Recycling

Another way of reducing waste is by **recycling**. This means reusing old materials to make new ones. Around 70 million tons of garbage get recycled each year. Recyclable materials include paper, metal cans, plastic items such as bags, and plastic and glass bottles.

Another 25 million tons of garbage get composted. **Composting** involves allowing food waste to break down and rot into material that can be used as fertilizer. Fertilizer makes the soil healthier and better able to grow plants. Some towns have composting programs that collect this waste.

Paper is the material we throw away the most. For every 100 pounds (45 kg) of trash, about 31 pounds (14 kg) is paper. Paper can be recycled, which saves forests and reduces air and water pollution.

Recycling helps the environment in many ways. First, it means reusing materials instead of making new materials. Second, it reduces the amount of waste going into landfills. Third, it prevents buildup of stray amounts of waste.

The world's oceans have several large areas where plastics and other garbage have collected. One of them, called the Great Pacific Garbage Patch, floats in the Pacific Ocean between California and Hawaii. It has been estimated at approximately 618,000 square miles (1.6 million square kilometers). Most of the garbage is plastic. These masses of trash are dangerous to ocean life.

Conservation

Another approach to helping the environment is conservation. **Conservation** means preserving and protecting natural resources. A key concept in the conservation movement is sustainability. A **sustainable** process is one that does not reduce or spoil natural resources. For example, using oil and gas as energy sources is not sustainable because there is a limited amount of these resources, and people cannot make more of them.

There are many ways to promote conservation. Some stores charge a fee for using plastic bags. People who have reusable shopping bags do not have to pay this fee. Some communities require businesses to use less packaging for their products. People can conserve electricity by buying products that use less energy. The Energy Star program is an effort of EPA and the Department of Energy to provide people and companies with information on the energy efficiency of appliances, commercial equipment, and building materials. They can use this information before they buy these products. People can also conserve energy by turning off lights and faucets, driving less, or heating or cooling their homes less. Conservation is becoming a way of life for more and more Americans.

✓ **CHECK FOR UNDERSTANDING**

1. **Summarizing** What happens to the garbage that people produce?
2. **Speculating** Why is environmentalism a global necessity?

toxic poisonous, deadly, or damaging to living things

recycling reusing old materials instead of making new ones

composting allowing food and vegetable waste to decompose to make fertilizer

conservation preserving and protecting natural resources

sustainable referring to activities that do not waste or spoil natural resources

Factories and oil refineries, such as this one in Ohio, can release pollution into the air.

Protecting the Air, Water, and Land

GUIDING QUESTION

How do local governments control pollution and deal with waste?

How much pollution do you create? Much air, water, and land pollution comes from industrial sources. However, individuals can also cause pollution.

Pollution from Industry

Water pollution comes mostly from factories and large farming and mining operations. These industries produce many kinds of chemical waste. For many years, some factories, farms, and coal mines pumped this waste directly into rivers and streams. Others buried their waste, but once underground, the waste mixed with water below the land. The chemicals then **contaminated**, or polluted, the water. That dirty water then flowed into wells, lakes and rivers, and oceans. It made drinking water unhealthy and harmed plants, fish, birds, and other wildlife.

Factories that burn fuel for energy cause pollution too. Their smokestacks, or tall chimneys, release poisonous gases into the air. Some of these gases are unhealthy for humans and animals to breathe. They can harm people's lungs and cause cancer or other illnesses. These gases can also lead to water pollution. Some of those chemicals fall to Earth when it rains and pollute water supplies.

Farmers use fertilizers to make the soil produce more crops, and they use pesticides to kill insects. These products are made from powerful chemicals. They can pollute the air and water when they are blown by the wind and washed into the soil by rain. Many also remain on the fruits and vegetables sold in grocery stores. Additionally, huge "factory farms" that raise thousands of cows, pigs, and chickens for their meat or eggs produce large amounts of animal waste that pollutes the soil and water.

The energy industry is another source of pollution. The oil industry, for example, contributes significantly to air and water pollution. Oil refineries release harmful gases into the air as they turn crude oil into other products, such as gasoline. Oil is often transported by ship or offshore pipelines, which carries the risk of spills into the ocean. In late 2021, for example, an oil spill from a pipeline off the coast of California released about 25,000 gallons of oil into the Pacific Ocean.

Today, federal rules limit the amounts and kinds of waste factories, mines, and farms may release into the environment. However, those rules are not always fully enforced, and this type of pollution is still a serious problem.

Pollution from Individuals

Cars and trucks are the biggest source of air pollution in most cities. To reduce it, the federal government required oil companies to stop adding lead to the gasoline that fuels vehicles. Automakers had to redesign cars to work with unleaded gas. New laws also required them to make cars that used less gas per mile and to fit cars with devices that remove pollutants from

contaminate to pollute

exhaust. The federal government encouraged lower speed limits on interstate highways. Cars traveling slower get more miles per gallon, which means they burn less gas.

The less people drive, the less pollution they cause. Many cities provide bus, subway, or train services that people can use to travel to and from work or other destinations. People who use public transportation are responsible for less pollution than drivers. People can also reduce pollution by carpooling or sharing a ride.

Choosing to drive electric cars is one way individuals can reduce how much they pollute. Electric cars run on batteries. If the battery is charged using clean electricity, these cars produce almost no pollution. Hybrids are cars that use both battery power and gasoline power. They are more efficient than cars that run on gasoline only, but they do burn some gasoline.

Hazardous Waste

Hazardous waste is another danger. Perhaps the most serious form is radioactive waste from nuclear power plants. Some of this waste can harm living things for thousands of years. Congress passed a law in 1987 that would create a special underground storage facility for nuclear waste. Citizens' groups have objected to it, though, and it has not been built. Instead, this waste is being stored in 80 different places across the country. At least one is found in most states.

In the past, industry often disposed of toxic waste in the ocean. They put the waste in metal containers and enclosed them in concrete before dumping them. Congress passed laws to ban this practice in the 1970s and 1980s. Today, the only way to get rid of hazardous waste is by storing it at a specially designed disposal facility. However, those land disposal sites are filling up quickly.

Many household products such as paint, insecticides, motor oil, and batteries pose dangers to the environment. Many communities have set aside places to collect these products. They do so to make sure the products can be disposed of safely.

No matter how carefully hazardous waste is stored, it is never completely safe. Chemicals can leak into the soil and water and harm entire communities. A notable environmental disaster happened in Love Canal, a neighborhood in Niagara Falls, New York. Toxic waste buried underground for years leaked into the groundwater. People in the area developed serious health problems. The government had to move more than 900 families away from the community.

Grassroots Efforts and New Laws

By the 1960s, many Americans began seeking ways to become actively involved in protecting the environment. They joined groups such as the Sierra Club, the Audubon Society, and the Wilderness Society.

Electric cars recharge when connected to a charging station.

The Edith Green-Wendell Wyatt Federal Building in Portland, Oregon was renovated to be environmentally friendly. One way it does this is by using solar panels to convert sunlight directly into the energy that is needed to power the building. It is now one of the most energy efficient office buildings in the country.

Drawing Conclusions How can new approaches to designing and constructing buildings affect the environment?

These organizations work to protect the environment and conserve natural resources.

These groups have worked to convince communities and businesses to move toward sustainable development. This phrase refers to efforts that support economic growth while protecting the environment. City planners are trying to build more compact cities so that people do not need to travel far to work, school, and other locations. Local governments are setting aside more land for parks and open areas. Modern buildings use less energy to heat and cool them. For example, many have windows that keep out hot air in summer and cold air in winter. This leads to less energy use to cool or warm the building in those seasons. Tinted glass keeps out the sun's heat, reducing the need for air conditioning. These windows also prevent heated or cooled air from leaking out of the building.

Cities are beginning to replace their gasoline and diesel-powered vehicles and buses with cleaner alternatives powered by electricity or propane. For example, New York City plans to have all its school buses powered by electricity by 2035 and all city vehicles run on electric power by 2040.

The work of protecting the environment is large and complex. Governments, organizations, and individuals must work together to get the job done.

✓ **CHECK FOR UNDERSTANDING**

1. **Identifying** Which industries produce the most pollution? How is this pollution released into the environment?

2. **Explaining** What can individuals do to reduce the amount of pollution they produce?

LESSON ACTIVITIES

1. **Informative/Explanatory Writing** Write a short essay explaining at least four steps that individuals can take to conserve resources or reduce the amount of waste material or pollution they produce.

2. **Analyzing Information** Work with a partner to identify an environmental issue the United States faces now or has faced in the past. Create a leaflet explaining the issue and its causes and effects. Include information about what state or federal governments have done or are doing about the issue. Go online to find information and images for your leaflet.

Political and Social Issues

GUIDING QUESTION

What political and social issues must be solved by nations working together?

Today's world is more interdependent than ever before. People use goods made in other lands, eat food grown across the world, and use resources, such as oil, that are supplied by other countries. When a disaster strikes, people in one country may need aid from other countries to recover. Many problems in today's world cannot be solved by one country alone. They are considered global issues because they require many nations working together to solve them. Some of these issues involve political or social conditions. These include terrorism, refugees, and the status of women.

International Terrorism

Some extremist groups use terrorism to try to achieve political goals. Terrorism is the use of violence or the threat of violence against civilians to force people or governments to behave in a certain way. Before 1968, most terrorists attacked targets within their own country. These attacks are called *domestic terrorism*. Domestic terrorism still occurs. Over the past 50 years or so, however, international terrorism has become a serious problem. International terrorist groups recruit members from around the world and may attack anywhere.

Analyzing Key Ideas and Details As you read, take notes about global problems and related solutions in a chart such as the one shown.

Global Problem	Solutions
Terrorism	
Refugees	
Women's rights	
Food insecurity	
Environment	

A coordinated group of terrorists carried out suicide bombings that blew up this bus and three subway trains in London.

Inferring Why might terrorists target buses and subway trains?

To battle terrorists, the U.S. military has used drones to carry out limited, targeted attacks. Drones are controlled by a pilot located in a station that can be at a great distance from the drone's position. Here, workers load a missile onto a U.S. drone.

On September 11, 2001, international terrorists struck American soil, killing nearly 3,000 people. On that day, al Qaeda terrorists hijacked four commercial airliners. They crashed three planes into buildings: one into each of the two towers of the World Trade Center in New York City and one into the Pentagon in Washington, D.C. The fourth plane crashed in Pennsylvania. Since then, al Qaeda and other terrorist groups have struck many other countries. Some of these attacks have killed hundreds of people, often in crowded areas, and destroyed buildings and cultural treasures.

The United States and other countries have tried to stop terrorist attacks. They have identified individuals who were suspected of belonging to terrorist groups. When these countries see an opportunity, they have attacked known and suspected terrorists with force. For example, the United States has carried out military drone strikes against terrorists in different parts of the world. A drone is a remote-controlled, crewless aircraft carrying weapons.

These methods pose problems, though. Sometimes innocent civilians are killed or suffer injuries in these strikes. Killing civilians is a violation of international law. Drone strikes ordered by U.S. presidents in the early 2000s may have killed hundreds of civilians.

Refugees

A refugee is a person who is forced to leave a country because of war, violence, or natural disaster. The United Nations High Commissioner for Refugees (UNHCR) assists refugees around the world. As of 2021, UNHCR was monitoring more than 26 million refugees worldwide. Half of these refugees were children.

Syria has been devastated by a civil war since 2011. A civil war is a conflict between different groups within the same country. This long war has forced more than 13 million people to flee their homes. About half are living in another part of Syria. About half have fled to nearby countries. Many of them live in extreme poverty.

More than 5 million refugees have fled Venezuela in recent years. They have left because political unrest led to violence and harmed the country's ability to provide food, medicine, and basic services. Refugees from Venezuela now live throughout the Caribbean and Latin America.

In 2021 the United States ended its war against Afghanistan and withdrew its troops. The rapid takeover by the Taliban caused a crisis for many Afghan civilians, especially those who had helped U.S. troops. After the U.S. withdrawal, tens of thousands of people fled the country to escape the Taliban.

Some refugees are forced to live in temporary camps in other countries. In camps, people are **isolated**, unable to work at their jobs

---

isolated separate from other communities or groups

and provide for their families, and unable to take part in a community. Other refugees are housed in cities and towns where they can start to build new lives.

Since 1975, U.S. families and communities have accepted more than 3 million refugees from other countries. Before refugees are admitted to the country, they must go through a process meant to ensure that they would not **pose** a danger to the country. Then an agency must identify a place where they can live and start their new lives. The United States pledged to admit and resettle 125,000 refugees in 2022.

Women's Rights

Many countries around the world deny equal rights to women. Some nations deny women the right to an education. The United Nations estimates that more than 9 million girls living in Africa south of the Sahara will never attend school. This is about twice the estimated number of boys who will not be educated in that region. In south and west Asia, girls who do not receive an education outnumber boys by four to one. Worldwide, almost half of countries do not provide equal access to primary education to girls.

Unfair treatment of females takes other forms as well. In parts of the world, many women and girls do not have equal access to health care. Those who do have access often do not have the power to make their own medical decisions. In some cultures, women cannot legally have custody of their own children.

Women have more rights in the United States, but they have struggled against unfair treatment. Throughout much of the 1900s, many women did not work in jobs outside the home after they married. By 1980, a majority of American women had joined the workforce. However, women generally do not earn as much as men. Women's pay is about 77 percent of what men are paid for doing the same work. Pay is even less for women who are part of underrepresented ethnic groups. In addition, women are less likely than men to be promoted to leadership positions.

Many international organizations have launched efforts to ensure equal rights for women and girls. Members of the United Nations have joined agreements in support of women's rights. In 1960 more than 100 nations agreed they would not discriminate against women in education. In 1979 the UN approved a pledge to end all discrimination against women. However, all member nations have not signed this agreement. Some that did sign it have not followed it. Unfair treatment of women continues.

Congress has passed laws aimed at making conditions fairer for women. In 1963 it passed the Equal Pay Act. It was meant to ensure that women and men who did the same job for the same employer would receive equal pay. While women's wages have gone up since then, many still earn less than men for the same job. In the United States, equality in education has improved since 1972, when Congress passed a law called Title IX.

Malala Yousafzai, an activist from Pakistan, has worked since she was a teen to promote the right of girls to an education. She won a Nobel Peace Prize for her work.

pose to present

This law was meant to ensure that women had equal access to a college education.

✓ CHECK FOR UNDERSTANDING

1. **Explaining** Explain why progress on one of the three issues discussed in this section requires international cooperation.

2. **Predicting** What is the impact on a society's economy when women lack opportunities for education or work?

Natural Resource Issues

GUIDING QUESTION

What issues facing the world involve resource use and the environment?

Some global issues involve the availability or use of resources or caring for the environment. These issues also require the cooperation of many nations to address them.

Food Security

Food security is ready access to enough food for an active, healthy life for all people living in a household. Food insecurity is a lack of food security. More than 2 billion people around the world face food insecurity. That is, they struggle to get enough healthy food to eat.

About 10 percent of U.S. households experienced food insecurity in 2020. That is equal to about 38 million people, more than 6 million of whom were children. The federal government has created many programs to address food insecurity in the United States. The Supplemental Nutrition Assistance Program (SNAP) provides benefits to families to help them obtain enough food. Federal school breakfast and lunch programs ensure that students have the food they need to stay healthy and alert for their education.

food security ready access to enough food for an active, healthy life for all people living in a household

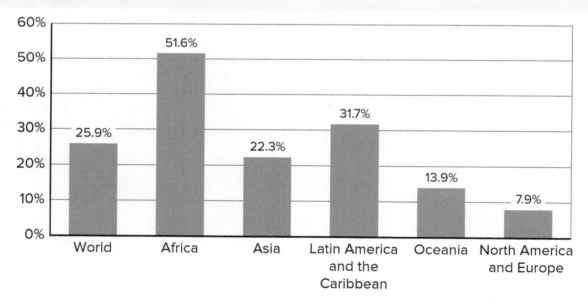

Percentage of People Who Experience Food Insecurity

The United Nations has estimated the percentage of people experiencing food insecurity in different regions of the world.

Source: Food and Agriculture Organization of the United Nations, *The State of Food Security and Nutrition in the World, 2020*

EXAMINE THE GRAPH

1. **Analyzing Visuals** Which region has the highest percentage of food insecurity?

2. **Analyzing Visuals** Which regions have the lowest amount of food insecurity?

Water is an important resource, and countries sometimes disagree over how to use the water in rivers that flows across borders. China plans to build a dam on the Brahmaputra River. The project might threaten the ability of India and Bangladesh to use water from this river, which flows through their countries.

Several factors contribute to food insecurity. The causes in some countries include wars, the lack of stable governments, natural disasters, and drought. Drought is the long-term lack of rain, which prevents people from growing enough food. The area of Africa south of the Sahara has several countries with major problems related to food security. In eastern and southern Africa, more than half of all people experience food insecurity. In the Western Hemisphere, Haiti has the worst food situation. Almost two-thirds of its people do not have enough food.

People who are food insecure must spend a large amount of time trying to find enough food to survive. They do not have the time or resources to start businesses that could create jobs and help produce the food their communities need. The economic development that could lift the community out of poverty cannot happen when people are working their hardest just to survive.

Global efforts to improve food security include humanitarian aid and help with economic development. Humanitarian aid in this case involves delivering food to areas where people are in great need. The World Food Programme is the United Nations agency dedicated to providing food aid to directly relieve hunger. The UN's Food and Agriculture Organization and International Fund for Agricultural Development work to help farmers produce food. The United States provides food through the U.S. Agency for International Development and the State Department. The World Bank provides loans, grants, and advice to help countries develop economically.

Some nongovernmental organizations (NGOs) also work in this area. For example, Oxfam provides emergency food aid. It also works to help countries overcome the poverty that prevents them from producing enough food for their people. The programs have helped some people, but the problem continues.

Issues With Water

Many countries also do not have enough clean water or sanitation facilities. More than 884 million people do not have access to safe drinking water. About a quarter of the world's population lacks access to basic sanitation, including safe disposal of garbage and human waste. Unsafe drinking water and lack of sanitation often lead to outbreaks of deadly diseases, such as cholera and typhoid.

Water is essential for life, and many important rivers flow across country borders. That means people in different countries need to agree on how to share the water—and on how to keep it clean. The Tigris and Euphrates Rivers begin in Turkey but flow eastward through Iraq into the Persian Gulf. The Tigris-Euphrates River basin also includes parts of Syria and Iran. A river basin is the entire area drained by a river and all the smaller rivers and streams that feed into it. All four countries need the waters of these rivers for drinking and for growing crops. Dams on the rivers are used to prevent floods in Syria and Iraq. But some dams are controlled by Turkey and Iran, who rely on them to provide electric power.

In the 1960s the four countries began to argue over who could use the water and how much they could use. When people living in the upper reaches of a river use water, the people living downstream have less. When people upriver allow chemicals to pollute the river, people downriver have a polluted water supply.

More recently the effects of environmental warming on the region have brought drought conditions. Drought in this region can cause farmland to turn to dust. Then people abandon farms and move to cities. Refugees fleeing political unrest have also increased the populations of cities.

Ban Ki-Moon, then UN secretary-general (second from left), and other United Nations officials at the Paris climate conference react after the signing of the Paris Agreement in 2015.

Inferring Why might these UN officials be celebrating the signing of the agreement?

With more people, cities have a greater need for water. As water becomes scarcer and the population continues to grow, conflicts over water rights may grow worse.

The Environment

Nature does not pay attention to national borders. The air and the water in oceans are **constantly** moving around the world. Scientists have found that the world's climate is changing. Climate change is a shift in the average weather conditions over many years. Scientists have shown that the world's average temperature has risen compared to what it was in the past. Warmer temperatures are having many effects. They are connected to stronger storms, severe droughts in some areas, heavy rains causing flooding in other areas, and huge wildfires. These issues can harm animal, plant, and human life. Burning fossil fuels such as coal, oil, and gas contributes to climate change. Burning these fuels releases substances called *greenhouse gases* into the air.

Countries must work together to protect the world. However, political disagreements can

---

constantly always

interfere with international cooperation. It is expensive to reduce pollution, for example switching from fossil fuels to renewable energy sources. Many American business leaders do not want to pay those high costs. The profits of some U.S. industries, such as oil and gas, depend on continued use of fossil fuels.

In 1997 more than 150 nations signed the Kyoto Protocol. This was an agreement to cut air pollution. The United States did not sign the treaty, because it said that the changes required by the agreement would be too expensive.

In December 2015, nearly 200 countries approved the Paris Agreement. The countries agreed to reduce the amount of greenhouse gases they produce. Wealthier countries also agreed to provide funds to help developing countries handle the costs of making needed changes.

In the years since the agreement was signed, many countries have not met the goals that they set. The United States signed the Paris Agreement, but in 2017, President Trump withdrew the country from the agreement. In 2021 President Biden's administration had the United States rejoin the Paris Agreement.

✓ **CHECK FOR UNDERSTANDING**

Making Connections How can climate change contribute to the problem of food insecurity?

LESSON ACTIVITIES

1. **Argumentative Writing** Choose one of the global issues discussed in the lesson and write an essay describing how you would like to see it addressed. Include a description of how it is currently being addressed and explain how your recommendations would improve the situation.

2. **Presenting** With a small group, choose one country and present a slideshow demonstrating how that country has responded to the five global issues discussed in the lesson: international terrorism, refugees, women's rights, food insecurity, and the environment. Research online to find information and images about your selected country.

09

Analyzing Sources: The United States and International Events

? COMPELLING QUESTION

How should the United States respond to international events?

Plan Your Inquiry

DEVELOPING QUESTIONS

Think about critical events, such as natural disasters and armed conflicts, that have occurred in the world in the recent past. Perhaps you heard or read about something that happened in another country on the news. How did the United States respond, if at all? Then read the Compelling Question for this lesson. What questions can you ask to help you answer this Compelling Question? Create a graphic organizer like the one below. Write these Supporting Questions in your graphic organizer.

Supporting Questions	Primary or Secondary Source	What this source tells me about the U.S. response to international events	Questions the source leaves unanswered
	A		
	B		
	C		
	D		
	E		

ANALYZING SOURCES

Next, examine the sources in this lesson. Analyze each source by answering the questions that follow it. How does each source help you answer each Supporting Question you created? What questions do you still have? Write these in your graphic organizer.

After you analyze the sources, you will:
- use the evidence from the sources,
- communicate your conclusions,
- and take informed action.

Background Information

In the United States, the federal government determines foreign policy, or how the nation interacts with other nations and international groups. Congress has the power to approve treaties and certain appointments, to determine what federal money can be spent, and to declare war. However, the executive branch largely oversees foreign policy decisions. Executive officials have several foreign policy tools that they use to respond to conditions and events around the world. They include diplomacy, treaties and other formal agreements, trade, foreign aid to respond to emergencies or countries facing economic difficulties, the use of military force, and intelligence gathering and the use of secret operations.

Presidents and their officials decide which tools to use for which events based on their broader foreign policy goals. They tend to define these goals in terms of three key interests—protecting national security, promoting world peace, and advancing international trade. Other goals include promoting democracy and protecting human rights.

Members of the U.S. armed forces and local volunteers unload food supplies sent by the United States to Haiti after a 2021 earthquake in that nation.

Using Economic Sanctions

The three countries mentioned in this article excerpt—Cuba, Iran, and North Korea—are ruled by authoritarian regimes. Iran and North Korea have also sought to develop nuclear weapons, which worries U.S. leaders. The Iranian hostage crisis occurred in 1979 and 1980 when Iranian students seized the U.S. embassy in Iran's capital. They held more than 50 Americans as captives for more than a year.

SECONDARY SOURCE: WEB ARTICLE

66 Economic sanctions are a way for large governments to exert [apply] their disapproval over one another. While wars are costly—both economically and politically—economic sanctions [penalties] tend to be somewhat less **tangible**, at least for the country doing the sanctioning. But for the country being sanctioned, the results can be enormous and long-lasting.

. . . [T]he U.S. sanctions [penalizes] countries that sponsor terrorism or perpetrate [commit] human rights violations on their people. . . . Here are some details on [three] of the longest-standing sanctioned nations.

Cuba . . . Since dictator [Fidel Castro] took power [in 1959], the U.S. has had **trade embargoes** in place as a punishment for impediments [barriers] to democratic rule. While Americans aren't generally allowed to trade or travel with Cuban interests, the close geographic proximity [nearness]—and large Cuban-American population [in the United States]—have ensured that a number of exemptions [exceptions] exist. . . .

Iran Following the Iranian Revolution of 1979, the Western-friendly **Shah** of Iran was deposed [overthrown] in favor of a **theocratic** government. The Iranian Hostage Crisis and other ensuing [following] events pushed the U.S. to levy [place] a trade embargo on the . . . nation. Sanctions continue with increasingly tenuous [weak] political relations, the sponsoring of terrorism [by Iran], and debates over the **enrichment of uranium**. . . .

North Korea North Korea is arguably the country most brutally affected by U.S. economic sanctions. North Korea's battles with the U.S. started in the 1950s with the United States' entry into the Korean War—a move designed to counter the USSR's [Soviet Union's] support for a unified, communist Korea. 99

— Jonas Elmerraji, "Countries Sanctioned by the U.S. and Why," *Investopedia*, June 30, 2021

tangible having clearly felt effects

trade embargo a ban on any trade with a country

Shah title used by the former monarchs of Iran

theocratic relating to a government controlled by a religious group and its beliefs

enrichment of uranium a process that makes nuclear fuel, which can be used to make nuclear energy or nuclear bombs, out of the mineral uranium

---

EXAMINE THE SOURCE

1. **Explaining** Why does the United States favor economic sanctions over military involvement in many instances?

2. **Drawing Conclusions** What can you conclude about Cuba, Iran, and North Korea? What other reasons might the United States have for sanctioning these countries?

U.S. Aid in Haiti

Haiti, an island nation in the Caribbean Sea, is among the poorest countries in the Western Hemisphere. On August 14, 2021, an earthquake struck Haiti. The disaster left more than 2,000 people dead and more than 12,000 injured. It also damaged or destroyed as many as 130,000 homes. The U.S. Agency for International Development (USAID) and the military's Joint Task Force-Haiti joined the relief effort.

PRIMARY SOURCE: INFOGRAPHIC

7.2 magnitude earthquake
Aug. 14, 2021

19 helicopters, 6 ships, and 8 transport aircraft

671 total missions (*DOD & U.S. Coast Guard*)

587,950 total pounds transported

FOOD

477 people assisted or rescued

Numbers reflect operations from Aug. 15 - Sept. 2, 2021

Source: U.S. Southern Command; Department of Defense

EXAMINE THE SOURCE

1. **Interpreting** What resources did the United States use to provide aid in Haiti?
2. **Speculating** What might conditions in Haiti have been like in the months following the earthquake without aid?

Military Force in Vietnam

The war in Vietnam erupted as part of the Cold War between the United States and the Soviet Union. During the Cold War, these two countries competed for influence in the world. Each worked to spread its political and economic ideas. Although the United States and the Soviet Union never engaged in direct military conflict, they did sometimes send troops to fight in other countries. The Soviet Union supported North Vietnam, while the United States backed South Vietnamese forces. U.S. troops fought in Vietnam from 1964 to 1973. Despite the years of military intervention, however, the United States was unable to prevent the spread of communism throughout Vietnam.

SECONDARY SOURCE: WEB ARTICLE

66 Before World War Two Vietnam had been part of the French Empire. . . .

After World War Two Ho Chi Minh captured **Hanoi** in 1945 and declared Vietnam independent. The French tried to take control again, but this was unpopular with the people. . . .

[T]he Treaty of Geneva agreed that the French would leave Vietnam and the country would be split . . . [in two] until elections could be held.

The elections were never held and the country remained divided:

North Vietnam was a **communist** republic led by Ho Chi Minh.

South Vietnam was a **capitalist** republic led by Ngo Dinh Diem. The Vietminh [members of a Communist nationalist movement] wanted to unite the country under communist leader Ho Chi Minh. . . .

War broke out between the North and South. . . .

The Domino Theory . . . was the belief that if one country fell to communism, it was likely that the neighbouring one would also fall—similar to a row of dominoes falling over. This had happened in Eastern Europe after 1945. China had become communist in 1949 and communists were in control of North Vietnam.

The USA was afraid that communism would spread to South Vietnam and then the rest of Asia. It decided to send money, supplies and military advisers to help the South Vietnamese Government.

. . . For the next ten years the USA's involvement increased. By 1968 over half a million American troops were in Vietnam and the war was costing $77 billion a year. 99

— "The Vietnam War," *BBC*, Bitesize

Hanoi capital city of Vietnam

communist describing an economic system in which the government controls most economic decisions

capitalist describing an economic system in which individuals own property and make economic decisions

EXAMINE THE SOURCE

1. **Summarizing** What actions did the United States take in Vietnam, and why?
2. **Inferring** How does U.S. involvement in Vietnam reflect core foreign policy goals?

U.S. Food Assistance in Somalia

Somalia, in East Africa, has experienced prolonged periods of drought and famine since 2006. Drought is a long period without normal amounts of rain, which can lead to loss of agricultural crops used for food. Famine is a long period of widespread hunger. Famine often follows a drought. Over the years, the United States has provided more than $3 billion in aid, largely through USAID (United States Agency for International Development). This agency provides humanitarian aid to nations and people in crisis. It aims to promote global stability by addressing needs related to poverty, health, education, hunger, water scarcity, and more.

PRIMARY SOURCE: AGENCY REPORT

66 Muna, a 31-year-old mother of eight, has seen her farm in Somalia grow, even as the country suffers from a severe drought and risk of famine. Muna . . . is expecting this season's harvest to be large enough to feed her family for up to six months with sorghum [a grain] and beans left over to sell at market.

Through a USAID-supported food assistance project, families like Muna's receive monthly **vouchers** for three months during the April-June rainy season, the length of time needed to plant and harvest a staple crop. USAID's **implementing** partner distributes vouchers worth a set amount to **beneficiaries** who then redeem [turn in] the vouchers for cash to purchase foods of their choice in local markets.

. . . To complement [go with] the vouchers . . . , farming households like Muna's receive a variety of high-performing seeds to grow nutritious foods . . . and other farming tools.

Muna now grows watermelon, onions, tomatoes, sorghum and beans, and for the first time she has been able to hire additional workers to help till [work] her farm. Before, Muna relied on relatives to help her provide food for her children, a common practice in Somali culture. Now, despite high food prices, the vouchers have enabled her to buy enough food for her family, which means she can also afford to pay her children's school fees.

'Without the program, I honestly do not know what I would have done to face the drought because the situation was bad,' Muna says. 'I want my children to have a good future, better than what my husband and I have endured [lived through]. I want them to get a quality education and good jobs so that they can help themselves and others.' 99

— USAID, "Critical Blend of Assistance Helps Somalis Avert Famine," July 2017

voucher a paper that can be used as credit to pay for food or other goods

implement to carry out or put into effect

beneficiary one who receives some form of aid

> ### EXAMINE THE SOURCE
>
> 1. **Summarizing** Based on the excerpt, what types of humanitarian aid does USAID provide?
> 2. **Making Connections** How do you think giving aid to Somalis advances U.S. foreign policy goals?

E

U.S. Role in World Affairs

Public opinion polls consistently show that most Americans believe the United States should participate, to some degree, in the global community. The CATO Institute reports that, since the 1980s, an average of 60 to 70 percent of Americans polled believe the United States should play "an active part" in international affairs. However, what people mean by "an active part" can vary greatly. Since the 1970s, the Chicago Council on Global Affairs has surveyed more than 2,000 U.S. adults to learn their opinions on foreign policy. The graph shows the results.

SECONDARY SOURCE: GRAPH

Americans' Opinions on U.S. Role in World Affairs

Do you think it will be best for the future of the country if we take an active part in world affairs or if we stay out of world affairs?

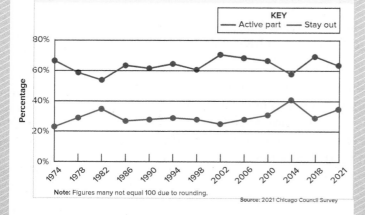

Note: Figures many not equal 100 due to rounding.

Source: 2021 Chicago Council Survey

EXAMINE THE SOURCE

1. **Analyzing** Since 2010, when did the largest majority of people think the United States should take an active part in world affairs, and when did the largest minority think the United States should stay out of world affairs?

2. **Making Generalizations** How would you describe the overall trend in public opinion on U.S. involvement in world affairs since the 1970s?

Complete Your Inquiry

EVALUATE SOURCES AND USE EVIDENCE

Refer back to the Compelling Question and the Supporting Questions you developed at the beginning of the lesson.

1. **Inferring** Consider the data in Source E. Why might Americans be more or less inclined to support the interventions described in the other sources at different times?

2. **Evaluating** How effective do U.S. foreign policy tools appear to be, given the information in the excerpts?

3. **Gathering Sources** Which sources helped you answer the Supporting Questions and the Compelling Question? Which sources, if any, challenged what you thought you knew when you first created your Supporting Questions? What information do you still need in order to answer your questions? What other viewpoints would you like to investigate? Where would you find that information?

4. **Evaluating Sources** Identify the sources that helped answer your Supporting Questions. How reliable are the sources? How would you verify the reliability of the sources?

COMMUNICATE CONCLUSIONS

5. **Collaborating** Working in a group, write your Supporting Questions on a sheet of paper. Pass the sheets around within your group and answer one another's questions. Then together, discuss your responses. Create a list of types of international events, then divide the list among your group members so that each of you individually writes a paragraph describing how the United States should respond to that type of international event.

TAKE INFORMED ACTION

Reporting on U.S. Involvement in World Affairs With a partner, research one of the foreign policy tools discussed in this lesson. Find two recent examples of the United States using that tool to influence world affairs. Prepare a poster or multimedia presentation to present your findings. Your presentation should evaluate the effectiveness of the U.S. foreign policy approach in both examples.

Reviewing The United States and Foreign Affairs

Summary

The president and Congress help set foreign policy.

Tools of foreign policy: treaties, executive agreements, diplomacy, aid, trade, military force, espionage

Interdependent world: nations connect by trade, economic cooperation

Global concerns: costs of competition, unequal development, global politics, environmental problems

Governmental organizations: United Nations and its units, NATO, World Trade Organization, Peace Corps

Nongovernmental organizations: Red Cross, Doctors Without Borders

The United States in the World

U.S. military involvement: Fighting in World War I and II

Competing with Soviet Union in Cold War

Recent wars in Afghanistan, Iraq

Environmental Issues:

Solid waste, landfills; Can address by recycling, conserving

Industrial pollution, individual pollution, hazardous waste; Addressed by laws, personal actions

Political and social issues: human rights, terrorism, refugees, women's rights

Resource issues: food insecurity, access to water, climate change

Checking For Understanding

Answer the questions to see if you understood the topic content.

1. Identify each of the following terms, and explain its significance to foreign affairs.

   A. foreign policy   **F.** repression

   B. espionage   **G.** environmentalism

   C. trade war   **H.** sustainable

   D. diplomat   **I.** food security

   E. human right   **J.** climate change

REVIEWING KEY FACTS

2. **Identifying** What four goals does the United States try to achieve in foreign policy?

3. **Explaining** How do trade sanctions and embargoes help the United States advance its national interest?

4. **Explaining** What are the benefits and drawbacks of free trade?

5. **Summarizing** What challenges do many refugees face?

6. **Identifying** What are three goals of the United Nations?

7. **Summarizing** Which governments or organizations work to promote human rights around the world?

8. **Identifying** What are three environmental challenges that the world faces?

9. **Explaining** What steps has Congress taken to try to protect the environment?

10. **Identifying** What are some ways that women are not treated equally in the United States and around the world?

CRITICAL THINKING

11. **Analyzing** Give an example of how domestic policy and foreign policy are related.

12. **Identifying Themes** What are some of the reasons why less developed countries have difficulty developing their economies?

13. **Summarizing** How have governments in the United States tried to address illegal immigration?

14. **Making Connections** How does the promise from NATO's members to defend other member nations if attacked help reduce the likelihood of an attack?

15. **Synthesizing** What criticisms does the World Trade Organization (WTO) face?

16. **Comparing and Contrasting** How does the United States at times fail to uphold human rights? How does the United States succeed at upholding such rights?

17. **Identifying Cause and Effect** What changes in the United States resulted from the September 11, 2001, terrorist attacks?

18. **Analyzing** How did Rachel Carson's work and NASA's missions to space contribute to environmentalism?

19. **Explaining** How do recycling and conservation protect the environment?

20. **Making Generalizations** Why would it cost more in the future to address climate change than it would if it is addressed now?

NEED EXTRA HELP?

If You've Missed Question	1	2	3	4	5	6	7	8	9	10
Review Lesson	2, 3, 4, 5, 7, 8	2	2	3	3, 5	4	4, 5	7, 8	7	8

If You've Missed Question	11	12	13	14	15	16	17	18	19	20
Review Lesson	2	3	3	4	4	5	5	7	7	8

Apply What You Have Learned

A Understanding Multiple Perspectives

One way the United States is involved globally is by working to advance human rights. This can become complicated when human rights violations occur in places where the United States has a strong economic interest. China has been accused of violating the rights of some of its people, but the United States depends on goods made in China. American companies, such as car manufacturers, send their products to China for sale.

ACTIVITY **Analyzing Different Perspectives on Trade and Human Rights** Conduct research to learn why some people support ending trade with nations that violate human rights. Find sources that argue in favor of trade with such nations. Consider the arguments on both sides and decide on your position. Write an argumentative essay that clearly states your view, gives strong evidence for your view, and reasons to support your position.

B Understanding Chronology

After World War I, President Woodrow Wilson wanted the United States to join an international organization called the League of Nations. The U.S. Senate rejected the treaty that called for U.S. membership in the League, however. At the time, many Americans did not want their country to be too involved in world affairs. Attitudes had changed by the end of World War II, and the United States helped form the United Nations, an organization in which it took a major role. Since then, the United States has joined many more international and regional organizations.

ACTIVITY **Creating a Time Line of International Participation** Research the organizations to which the United States belongs. Then create a time line that shows six to eight organizations the United States has joined since World War II. Include information such as when the United States joined each organization and a short explanation of the purpose of each organization.

Building Citizenship

There are many nongovernmental organizations (NGOs) that are active in various issues related to foreign policy. They do work in such areas as human rights, helping less developed countries develop economically, fighting world poverty, improving health care, protecting the rights of women and children, and protecting the environment.

ACTIVITY **Collecting Information on NGOs**

Focus on just one of these areas—or another issue that interests you. Identify three NGOs that are active in that field. Find out what kind of work they do and where each one is active. Learn how the NGOs do their work and what opportunities there are for people to volunteer to help or to provide needed funds. Create a fact sheet about each of the three organizations. Assemble your fact sheet with those of your classmates into a resource that interested students in your school can use to contribute to one or more of these groups.

 ## Making Connections

One of the most significant environmental concerns today is climate change. The United Nations has said that nations are not doing enough to limit the emissions that cause the planet to warm. There has been progress since the signing of the Paris climate agreement, but the UN says much more work needs to be done.

ACTIVITY **Creating a Slideshow Presentation on Climate Actions** Go online and research what countries and businesses are doing to reduce climate emissions. For example, you could look at the following actions:

- Actions by governments that encourage the use of clean energy, such as wind and solar power, to replace burning fossil fuels
- The evolving technology being used by automakers to build more electric or hybrid vehicles
- Automakers' plans for shifting to production of alternative energy vehicles
- The technology and methods being used by engineers and architects to create buildings that conserve energy
- Methods and technology used by private individuals to conserve energy

Make a slideshow presentation that highlights some of these actions.

What Is Economics?

Students stand in line to pay for back-to-school clothes. As consumers, they are part of the U.S. economy.

Royalty-free/Digital Vision/Getty Images

Introducing What Is Economics?

Economics: It's Everywhere!

An *economic system* produces the things people and countries need and want. Economics influences your life in many ways. It determines:

- Why you can't always get what you want

- What you buy—and *when* you buy it

- Which products are available to you—and how much they cost

- Why some jobs pay more than others

- Why some things cost more now than they did 10 years ago (and why other things cost less)

- Why some countries are richer than others

This cartoon shows how expectations about the future may affect your purchasing decisions today. That is economics at work.

Did You Know?

The word *economics* is derived from the Greek word *oikonomia*, meaning "management of the home." Were the Greeks referring to creating a budget and sticking to it? Perhaps. Today, however, *economics* refers to how we can learn to make the best choices to get what we want when we have limited resources, such as money or time.

Scarcity—The Basic Economic Problem

We have unlimited needs and wants, but only limited resources. This situation results in *scarcity*—limits or shortages—in resources or products. Even if everyone in the world were rich, there are not enough resources to satisfy all that we want. Scarcity forces people and societies to make choices.

Prices are a way to reduce the effects of scarcity. Consider what happens during the holiday season when parents are looking to buy the same "hot" toy for their children. Prices go sky-high. Only the people who can afford the high prices will get the toys.

1996
Tickle Me Elmo
The toy first sold for $28.99, but were resold for hundreds of dollars!

2006
Nintendo Wii
The Wii's introductory price was $249.99. When it was discontinued in 2013, it was priced at $99.99!

2016
Hatchimals
Initially priced at $60, but a market shortage resulted in some being sold on eBay for $1,200!

Rationing—Another Way to Deal With Scarcity

What if we're not talking about toys or games, but products necessary to life? How can an economic system distribute necessities fairly? Sometimes it must *ration*, or allow people to have a certain amount of something, using a system other than prices.

» During oil shortages in the 1970s, gas stations often ran out of gas before the end of the day. A system of rationing was introduced: If a license plate ended with an odd number, drivers could get gas only on odd-numbered days. Even-numbered license plates could get gas only on even-numbered days.

» Rationing is not just a thing of the past. Consider the pandemic of 2020 and the shortages that occurred. Stores had to ration toilet paper to keep supplies available.

Getting Ready to Learn About . . .
What Is Economics?

Economics Includes Goods and Services

Economics affects your life when you earn money or get birthday cash and then decide to spend it on something you need or want. You might buy *goods* such as clothes, food, electronics, or sports equipment. Or you might pay for *services* such as getting your hair styled or attending a concert.

Logs, a natural resource, have been cut, measured, and stacked onto rail cars for distribution and processing.

Economics Includes Resources

Resources make it possible for goods and services to get produced. Resources are at the heart of economics. What resources are shown in these photos? The logs are a *natural* resource. The engineer operating the train is a *human* resource. The machines—referred to as *capital* resources—are tools that create products. Some tools, such as hammers, paintbrushes, and sewing needles, are simple and have been in use for a long time. Other tools—such as robotics and computers—are much more complex machines. Risk-taking individuals who start a new business, introduce a new product, or improve a management technique are also resources—*entrepreneurs*.

Natural resources, human resources, capital resources, and entrepreneurs are called the *factors of production*. You will eventually be part of the human resources or entrepreneur categories—and perhaps both!

At this American auto factory, robotic machines do many of the production tasks. Workers are still needed, however, to run and maintain the machines and the assembly line.

» All of these images show a market.

Economics Includes Markets

When you want to *buy* a good or service, you need to find the people or companies who want to *sell* those goods and services. This happens in markets. A "market" can be a busy shopping mall, a single corner store, or a digital store online. Anywhere that buyers and sellers voluntarily exchange money for a product or a service is a market.

Economics Includes Making Choices

You make choices every day. Should you study another hour to get a better grade on the test? Or should you use that hour to play soccer or practice the violin? Or help get dinner ready? Or play a video game? You can't do everything in that ONE hour, so you have to make choices. The key is to make the BEST choice from all your alternatives. You can do that by considering the benefits and costs of each choice. Understanding the basics of economics will help you make better choices.

You aren't the only one who makes choices. Businesses and consumers do it all the time. For example, businesses have to think about the best locations for their stores and factories—near population centers, near resources, or in a virtual location online. Consumers make choices in how to get the goods and services they need and want.

Economics Includes Prices

Look again at the toys shown earlier, and the ways their prices changed. Prices let you know whether or not to buy something. Prices also let businesses know whether or not to produce something. The government does not set prices in the U.S. economy. Instead, prices vary because of the interaction of you—the consumer—and what you're willing to pay versus the amount that producers are willing to charge.

Demand and supply determine prices in a market economy.

Looking Ahead

Understanding the basics of economics will help you make better decisions. You will learn about scarcity and trade-offs, economic systems, how demand and supply affect prices, the circular flow of the U.S. economy, and how an economy can grow. You will examine Compelling Questions and develop your own questions in the Inquiry Activities.

What Will You Learn?

In these lessons about the basics of economics, you will learn:

- why we must make economic choices.
- the three basic questions societies and their economic systems answer.
- the effects of supply and demand on prices in economic markets.
- how prices aid consumers.
- how the circular flow of economic activity operates in the market system.
- how growth is promoted within an economy.

 COMPELLING QUESTIONS IN THE INQUIRY ACTIVITY LESSONS

- **Why do people need economic systems?**
- **How did changes in production impact the world?**

Julia buys a mower from a local store. The mower is a *good*.

Julia provides a *service* by mowing her neighbor's yard.

The neighbor withdraws money from the bank to pay Julia for her labor.

The gas station uses Julia's cash to pay employees and invest in more fuel.

Julia spends some of her pay on soda. The money returns to the soda company, which makes more product.

Julia purchases gas for her mower.

Julia puts some of her pay in the bank, which lends the money to businesses and individuals.

This man got a loan to start a business.

This diagram shows how everything is connected in an economy. You will learn more about these connections as well as where you fit into the American economy.

Scarcity and Economic Decisions

READING STRATEGY

Integrating Knowledge and Ideas As you read, fill out a graphic organizer comparing the four kinds of resources.

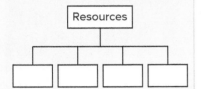

Our Wants and Resources

GUIDING QUESTION

What is scarcity, and how does it affect economic choices?

After an hour of shopping, Jayna found a dress she liked. Then, as she walked toward the cash register, a sweater caught her eye. It was her favorite color, and she liked it immediately. Jayna now had a problem. The sweater cost as much as the dress, and she did not have enough money to buy both. What should she do?

Jayna faced a common problem. She had to decide how to use her limited amount of money to satisfy her competing wants and needs. **Wants** are desires that people have that can be met by getting a product or a service. **Needs** are basic requirements for survival such as food, clothing, and shelter.

Sometimes a good or service can be both a want and a need. For example, the new dress could be both because it is clothing. If Jayna could live without it, however, it would be more of a want than a need.

Unlimited Wants

If Jayna is like the rest of us, her wants are not limited to just two items. If you think about all the things you want, the list is probably so long that we could say your wants are unlimited.

Wants fall into two groups. The first is **goods** and includes things we can touch or hold. The second is **services** and includes work that is done for us. Services include the health care provided by a doctor, the haircut by a hairstylist, or advice about money provided by a banker.

want desire for a good or a service

need basic requirement for survival

goods things we can touch or hold

services work that is done for us

A woman is signing for a package delivered to her home.

Analyzing Visuals What main good and main service do you see in the image?

Societies use many different resources for production. Land (top left) is a natural resource required for the production of crops such as corn. Workers in a lab (top right) are an example of labor, or human resources. Cranes (bottom left) are a capital resource. An entrepreneur (bottom right) designs a new clothing line for her business.

Making Connections Give an example of each type of resource necessary to create a pair of running shoes.

Limited Resources

If resources are limited, and if wants are unlimited, then we have to make choices. **Economics** is the study of how people choose to use their limited resources to satisfy their unlimited wants. **Resources** are all the things that can be used in making products or services that people need and want. Economists talk about four types of resources:

- *Natural resources* include a nation's land and all of the materials nature provides that can be used to make goods or services. Good soil for growing crops, trees for cutting lumber, and iron for making steel are natural resources.
- *Labor* includes workers and their abilities. The more workers a society has, the more it can produce. Workers' knowledge and skills are

important, too. The more workers know and the better their skills are, the higher the quality of goods and services they produce.

- *Capital*, which includes buildings and tools, is another type of resource. Businesses build factories to manufacture goods. Equipment such as computers can help work go more quickly. Trucks or trains are used to move goods around. Capital resources make work more productive.
- *Entrepreneurs* are a special resource. They are risk-taking individuals who start a new business, introduce a new product, or improve a method of making or doing something.

Economists refer to these four categories of resources as the **factors of production**. Each factor is necessary to produce goods and services.

---

economics study of how individuals and nations make choices about ways to use scarce resources to fulfil their needs and wants

resources things used to make goods or services

natural resources land and all the materials nature provides

labor workers and their abilities

capital factories, tools, and equipment that manufacture goods

entrepreneurs risk-taking individuals who start a new business, introduce a new product, or improve a method of making something

factors of production four categories of resources used to produce goods and services: natural resources, capital, labor, and entrepreneurs

Scarcity—The Basic Economic Problem

Jayna is not the only one who has the problem of satisfying her competing wants and needs. This is the type of economic problem that everyone—from individuals to businesses to cities, states, and countries—faces every day.

Scarcity occurs whenever we do not have enough resources to produce all of the things we would like to have. In fact, no country has all of the resources it needs, or would like to have. Because of this, *scarcity is the basic economic problem*. Economics is a social science that looks at how we go about dealing with this basic economic problem.

✓ CHECK FOR UNDERSTANDING

1. **Contrasting** Explain the difference between a want and a need.
2. **Identifying** What is the basic economic problem faced by people and nations alike?

Economic Decisions

GUIDING QUESTION

Why are trade-offs important in making economic decisions?

Have you ever had to make a choice between two things you really wanted to buy? If so, you have had some practice with economic decision making. Perhaps you had to choose between buying a video game and going to a movie with your friends. To make a good decision, you had to consider the benefits and the costs of each choice. In fact, you already think about many of your choices in the same way that economists do.

Trade-Offs

Making a **trade-off** is giving up one alternative good or service for another. If you choose to buy a pair of running shoes, you are exchanging your money for the opportunity to own the running shoes rather than something else that might cost the same amount.

A trade-off does not apply only to decisions involving money. For example, you might need to decide whether to go to a friend's party or study

for an important test. In this case, you would have to make a trade-off with your time. What will you give up—time with friends or studying time?

Businesses also make trade-offs. A company might have to decide whether to invest in research for new products or spend money on advertising to increase sales of existing products. Managers might need to choose whether to give big bonuses to a few workers or small raises to all workers.

Governments face trade-offs, too. If they spend money to build schools, they might not have enough money to build roads or pay for national defense.

When societies and civilizations understand that every decision involves a trade-off, they are better able to use scarce resources wisely. For example, early farmers faced declining crops as the soil became less healthy year after year. Then some farmers changed to a three-field rotating system. One field was left unplanted, and the other two fields alternated types of crops. The next year, a different field was unplanted. The trade-off for fewer crops overall was healthier soil and better harvests in the two planted fields.

Opportunity Costs

When faced with a trade-off, people eventually choose one **option**, or alternative, over all others. For example, you decide to buy a pair of running shoes and give up the chance to buy something else. Or, you choose to study and give up the opportunity to spend time with your friends.

When a city pays to build a new road or bridge like this one, the trade-off is a new school or park or anything else the money could have funded.

---

scarcity situation of not having enough resources to satisfy all of one's wants and needs

trade-off alternative you face when you decide to do one thing rather than another

option alternative, choice

Opportunity cost is the cost of the *next best* use of your money or time when you choose to do one thing rather than another. Economists use the term *opportunity cost* very specifically. The term is reserved only for the next-most-attractive alternative. Other options rejected earlier in the decision-making process are trade-offs but are not considered opportunity costs.

The choices made by businesses and societies also have opportunity costs. Suppose your city has narrowed its choices to spending money on park improvements or fixing city sidewalks. If it decides to spend money on the park, the opportunity cost would be the sidewalks that would not be fixed. If Congress votes to increase spending on preschools rather than on food programs, the opportunity cost is the support not given to the food programs.

Opportunity cost applies to all resources. Choosing to watch a television show one evening will not cost you any money. However, that choice has an opportunity cost. The cost is the time you

could have spent doing other things, such as listening to music or visiting your friends.

Businesses also face opportunity costs that do not involve money. For example, some companies may require employees to spend time learning new computer programs. The opportunity cost of that decision is the loss of the employees' work while they are being trained. Why would a company make such a decision? The company might believe the training will help workers be more productive in the long run. Good decisions involve weighing all possible options.

You might think you can avoid opportunity cost, but you really cannot. For example, suppose you want to watch television while you do your homework. You may think you can do both at the same time. However, you risk making careless mistakes while watching TV, or you may do your homework slower. In addition, you may miss some of the story in the TV show. There are costs to both activities when you try to do two things at once.

Opportunity costs will be different for everyone because people are different. If three people are asked to identify the opportunity cost of watching a single TV show, the first person may say it was the homework that could not be completed.

---

opportunity cost cost of the next best use of time or money when choosing to do one thing rather than another

A woman buys a plate at a yard sale. Opportunity costs are everywhere—even at yard sales.
Analyzing Visuals What is a possible opportunity cost for the woman who is buying the plate? Explain your answer.

David Sacks/Getty Images

The second might say the opportunity cost was the time missed talking to friends. The third may lose $20 that could have been earned mowing the lawn. Choosing to do something always has an opportunity cost, and that is why it's important to evaluate your alternatives.

Benefit-Cost Analysis

How can you make the best choices? Individuals, businesses, and governments often perform a benefit-cost analysis of alternative choices. **Benefit-cost analysis** divides the size of the benefit by the cost, and then selects the larger of the two. This type of analysis often helps businesses choose among two or more projects.

For example, suppose a business must choose between investments A and B. If project A is expected to generate $100 at a cost of $80, the benefit-cost ratio is 1.25. We get the number 1.25 by dividing $100 by $80. If project B is expected to generate $150, and if it costs $90, it will have a benefit-cost ratio of 1.67. The business would then choose the one with the higher benefit-cost number, or project B.

	Project A	Project B
Benefits:	$100	$150
Costs:	$80	$90
Benefits/Costs:	1.25	1.67

No decision-making strategy is perfect. But reasonable choices can be made if the short-term and long-term benefits and costs of competing projects are carefully evaluated. For example, suppose a choice must be made to fix an existing two-lane bridge or to build a new four-lane bridge. In the short term, it will cost less to repair the existing bridge, with the benefit of being repaired sooner than a new bridge would take to build. In the long term, building the new, wider bridge will cost more money but will benefit more drivers. People living near the bridge may want construction to be over quickly, so they will vote for repairing the existing bridge. Drivers who must wait in traffic to cross the smaller bridge may vote for funding the new wider bridge.

Finally, the decisions people face cannot always be evaluated in terms of money. Yet even those decisions can be analyzed with

benefit-cost analysis economic decision-making model that divides the total benefits by the total costs

benefit-cost analysis. For example, suppose you are deciding how long a nap to take. The benefit will be the greatest during the first hour of sleep, and then less and less. There would also be a cost: the opportunity cost of other things you could not do. The cost of the first hour of sleep would likely be small. But the longer you slept, the greater the cost would be. Even if you are not aware of it, benefit-cost analysis applies to almost everything we do. This is what it means to "think like an economist."

✓ **CHECK FOR UNDERSTANDING**

1. **Explaining** What is an opportunity cost in an economic decision?
2. **Analyzing** Why is it useful for individuals to do a benefit-cost analysis?

Societies and Economic Choices

GUIDING QUESTION

What determines how societies make economic choices?

Just as individuals and businesses make economic choices, so do entire countries. Scarcity is an economic problem in every nation. Will a society use its limited resources for education or for health care? Will a nation focus on helping businesses grow so they can create more jobs? Or will it spend money on training people for new jobs? Will it spend money on defense or on cleaning up the environment?

Three Basic Economic Questions

Scarcity of resources forces societies to make economic choices. These choices must answer three questions: WHAT goods and services will be produced? HOW will they be produced? FOR WHOM will they be produced?

Each country or society has to decide WHAT goods and services it will produce to meet its people's needs and wants. In making these decisions, societies consider their natural, human, and capital resources. A nation with plenty of land, fertile soil, and a long growing season is likely to use its land to grow crops. A country with large reserves of oil might decide to produce oil.

After deciding what to produce, entrepreneurs and other members of a society must decide HOW to produce these goods and services.

Choices All Societies Face

Societies must deal with the same economic problem of scarcity that individuals do.

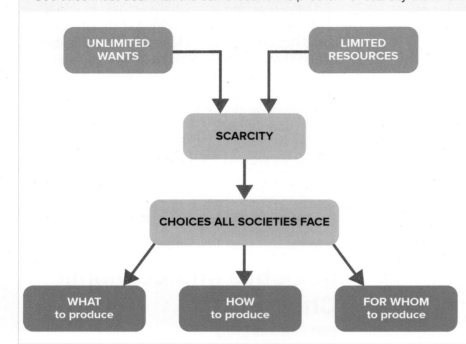

EXAMINE THE DIAGRAM

1. **Identifying** What are the three basic economic questions that societies face?

2. **Explaining** Why do societies have to make economic choices?

Should they encourage businesses to build factories for large-scale manufacturing of products such as automobiles or shoes? Or should they **promote**, or encourage, small businesses and individual craftwork instead?

After goods and services are produced, a society must decide WHO gets the goods and services. Societies have different ways of distributing goods. The choices they make for distributing goods affect how the goods are consumed. For example, should new housing units be reserved for low-income people, or should they be rented to anyone who can afford them? Should new cars be given to public officials, or should they be sold to the highest bidder? These are not easy questions to answer, but they are ones well-suited to benefit-cost analysis.

Values of a Society

The resources of a nation are not the only reason societies answer the three basic questions differently. What a society *values*, or thinks is most important, also has a big influence. Some societies value individual freedom the most. Others think that economic equality is most important.

promote to support or encourage

Different answers to the three basic questions help a society promote the ideas its people believe are most important. The key thing to remember is that all societies face the same three problems of deciding WHAT to produce, HOW to produce, and FOR WHOM to produce. In a separate lesson, you will learn about the various types of economic systems and how they answer the three basic economic questions.

✓ CHECK FOR UNDERSTANDING

1. **Summarizing** How do resources affect WHAT to produce?

2. **Explaining** What role do values play in answering the three basic economic questions?

LESSON ACTIVITIES

1. **Narrative Writing** Write a short story about a student your age who has to make an economic choice. In your story, reveal how plentiful wants conflict with scarce resources.

2. **Collaborating** With a partner, write and create a public service announcement video that explains the benefits of identifying opportunity costs when making decisions. Be sure to use appropriate voice and tone in your presentation.

03
Economic Systems

READING STRATEGY

Integrating Knowledge and Ideas As you read, complete a graphic organizer to identify features of different types of economic systems.

Traditional	Market	Command	Mixed

Traditional Economies

GUIDING QUESTION

What characteristics do traditional economies share?

Societies make economic choices or decisions in different ways. Each country has its own **economic system**, or way of producing and distributing the things people need and want. Economists organize economic systems into four general types: traditional, command, market, and mixed. The way a society answers the three basic economic questions—WHAT, HOW, and FOR WHOM to produce—determines its type of economic system. A country's economic system also relates to the resources it has (land, labor, capital, entrepreneurs) as well as its values and economic goals.

For centuries, most early societies organized their economic systems in what we now call traditional economies. In a **traditional economy**, the economic questions are answered on the basis of traditions and customs—or the way things have always been done. The WHAT to produce question is determined by tradition. If you were born into a family of farmers, for example, you would grow up to be a farmer. If your family always hunted, you would be a hunter. Tradition also determines the HOW to produce question. You would farm or hunt using the same tools your parents and grandparents did. The FOR WHOM to produce question is also answered by tradition. Hunters might keep the best portion of their kill and then share the rest evenly with other families. Farmers might provide crops to the elderly and children first—and then *barter*, or exchange, the rest of their crops for meat or fish from hunters and fishers.

economic system a nation's way of producing and distributing things its people want and need

traditional economy economic system in which the decisions of WHAT, HOW, and FOR WHOM to produce are based on traditions or customs

In the past, this Inuit boy would have learned the tools and techniques of hunting from his father and grandfather.

Analyzing Visuals What evidence identifies the Inuit as a former traditional economy?

Yvette Cardozo/Stockbyte/Getty Images

Traditional economies had advantages as well as disadvantages. The biggest advantage was less uncertainty about what to do. Everyone knew what was expected of them as they worked to take care of the community. Another advantage was that traditional economies used fewer resources than other types of economic systems. Their biggest disadvantage was they tended to discourage new ideas and were slow to adopt better ways of producing goods. Men and women stayed within their own economic roles.

Most traditional economies slowly changed over time. As they changed, some barter economies invented primitive forms of money. These monies included stones, brightly colored shells or beads, feathers from exotic birds, bundles of tea and tobacco, and eventually early gold and silver coins. The majority of traditional economies **evolved**, or progressed gradually, into ones with well-developed markets. Others with strong political or military leaders became economies based on rigid controls.

Traditional economies are rare today. Certain groups untouched by modern life in the Amazon rain forest or the mountainous regions of Papua New Guinea qualify as having traditional economies. Examples from the last century include the First Nations and Inuit societies of northern Canada and Alaska, and aboriginal peoples of Australia.

✓ **CHECK FOR UNDERSTANDING**

1. **Identifying** How are economic decisions determined in a traditional economy?
2. **Summarizing** What are some advantages and disadvantages of a traditional economy?

Command Economies

GUIDING QUESTION

Who makes the basic economic decisions in a command economy?

Over time, a few traditional economies with strong political or military leaders evolved into command economies. In a **command economy**, the government owns the majority of land, labor, and capital resources. Individuals and businesses do not have much say in how the economy works. Government planners *command* the actions that producers must follow. These powerful planners answer the basic economic questions. They decide WHAT to produce. For example, they decide whether the society will produce military tanks or consumer goods such as shoes.

---

evolve to progress or develop gradually

command economy economic system in which the government owns and directs the majority of a country's land, labor, and capital resources

A North Korean announcer reports on a military parade in Pyongyang, North Korea's capital.

Speculating What kinds of information do you think North Koreans are given on government-controlled programs?

Planners also decide HOW to produce these goods and FOR WHOM the goods and services will be produced. In theory, the government provides all housing, education, health care, and consumer products. In reality, much of the country's wealth goes to the leader or other high government officials.

Command economies are not very efficient. Workers are told where and how to work—and how many products to make. If planners mistake the amounts, people must go without goods and services. In addition, the pay for all workers—from factory workers to doctors—may be roughly similar. People do not get rewarded for working hard, so products are often low quality. And because of the vast number of decisions that central planners must make, command economies tend to grow slowly and inefficiently.

Central planning can provide advantages in rare instances. In times of emergency, planners can direct resources where they are needed most. For example, central planning helped the Soviet Union rapidly rebuild its economy after World War II. Planners shifted resources from farming and consumer goods to industrial factories. As a result, many Soviet people went for decades without decent housing, good food, and everyday products.

Modern examples of pure command economies are limited to a handful of dictatorships. North Korea is perhaps the leading example of a command economy where everything is either owned or controlled by the government. That includes businesses, electricity, transportation, housing, the Internet, and TV programs. Under Fidel Castro and his successors, the Cuban economy was another example of a command economy where consumer choices were limited.

Socialism

Another economy with command elements is socialism. **Socialism** is both an economic and political system in which the government owns some, but not all, of the factors of production. Under socialism, the government's goal is to serve the basic needs of all people, not just its leaders. Therefore, the government directs economic activity to provide transportation, education, jobs, and health care while allowing for some personal property. Sweden experimented briefly with socialism after World War II before it returned to being a market economy. Venezuela, under the direction of Hugo Chavez in 1999, was the most recent country to try socialism.

Communism

Communism is another version of a command economy that involves socialism. The goal of communism is to build a society run entirely by workers without any government involvement. Workers themselves would own all the resources and make all the economic decisions to improve society. Everyone would work to the best of their abilities, and use only the products they need. In this ideal society, no government would be necessary and could be removed.

There has never been a true communist economy. Modern communist leaders say that they must enforce a system of socialism to get ready for the eventual communist state. Meanwhile, they operate their political and economic system in such a way as to accumulate much of society's wealth for themselves. Today the term *communist* generally refers to a country's political system in which a ruling party has all the power. The citizens have limited democratic rights and freedoms.

✓ **CHECK FOR UNDERSTANDING**

1. **Identifying** What is the government's role in a command economy?

2. **Summarizing** What are the major problems with a command economy?

A sign in Cuba states "Young Communist's Union." Cuba has a command economy, but no country has a true communist economy.

---

socialism economy in which government owns some factors of production so it can distribute products and wages more evenly among its citizens; economic system with some command features

communism theoretical state where all property is publicly owned, and everyone works according to their abilities and is paid according to their needs

Dave Moyer

Market Economies

GUIDING QUESTION

What characteristics do market economies share?

Have you ever been to a flea market? You might see a person at one table selling used comic books. He can sell them because they are his to sell. You can choose to buy comic books from that seller, from another seller, or not at all. The seller sets the price of those comic books based on how much he thinks people will pay for them. If no one wants to buy his comic books at that price, he will probably lower the price.

In contrast, if many people are willing to pay that price, he may raise the price even more. Other tables at the flea market will have people selling different goods, which might be things they made by hand or used items they no longer want. The buying and selling in a flea market is an example of a free market economy.

Characteristics of a Market Economy

A **market** is where a buyer and a seller voluntarily exchange money for a good or service. It can be a busy shopping mall, a single corner store, or a digital store online.

In a **market economy**, individuals and businesses have the freedom to use their resources in ways they think best. This freedom helps answer the WHAT, HOW, and FOR WHOM to produce questions. For example, people can spend their money on the products they want most. This is like casting dollar "votes" for products and tells producers WHAT to produce.

Businesses are also free to find the best production methods when deciding HOW to produce. And the income that consumers earn and spend in the market determines the FOR WHOM to produce question.

Prices of goods and services also play an important role in the market economy. Prices are like signals. If the price of a good or service goes up, it is a signal to producers to make more. At the same time, it is a signal to buyers to think about buying less. Or, if the price of a good or service goes down, the opposite happens. It is a signal to producers to produce less, and it is a signal to buyers to buy more. In either case, the market will soon be operating at a new price established by both buyers and sellers.

In a market economy, individuals and businesses act in their own self-interest. No central authority makes their decisions. Instead, the market economy seems to run itself. Private individuals—not the government—own the factors of production. Because individuals own these factors, they have the power to decide how to use them.

The goal is to use limited productive resources to earn **profits**—money over and above the costs of making the product or service. As a result, entrepreneurs and businesses have the **incentive**, or motivation, to come up

market place where a buyer and a seller voluntarily exchange money for a good or service

market economy economic system in which individuals and businesses have the freedom to use their resources in ways they think best

profit money earned over and above the costs of making a product or service

incentive motivation

Price Signals in a Market Economy

In a market economy, a change in price signals a change in producer and consumer behavior.

When prices go UP ↑		When prices go DOWN ↓	
Consumers buy LESS ↓	Producers produce MORE ↑	Consumers buy MORE ↑	Producers produce LESS ↓

EXAMINE THE CHART

Identifying What event will signal producers to produce less?

One feature of a market economy is competition. These businesses, located close to one another, must compete for customers. Customers can compare prices, products, and service and make a choice.

Making Connections
Why is competition important to consumers?

with better products and efficient ways of producing them to earn higher profits.

Advantages and Disadvantages of a Market Economy

Market economies give people a lot of freedom. People are free to own property, control their own labor, and make their own economic decisions. Such freedom gives people who live in market economies a high level of satisfaction.

Another advantage of a market economy is the competition that occurs. Sellers compete with each other to attract the most buyers. Buyers compete with each other to find the best prices. Such competition leads to a huge variety of products and services for consumers. If a product can be imagined, it is likely to be produced in hopes that people will buy it. And because sellers must compete against other sellers, products are made with quality in mind.

Market economies do have some disadvantages. Although they enjoy a high degree of success, they usually do not grow at a steady rate. Instead, they go through periods of growth and decline. Although the periods of growth are much longer than the periods of decline, people can be hurt in the down times. For example, many people lose their jobs during down times.

Another problem is that businesses, driven by profit, might not give workers good working conditions or high wages. The profit motive can also result in harmful side effects of business activities, such as pollution.

Finally, a market economy does not provide for everyone. Some people may be too young, too old, or too sick to earn a living or to care for themselves. These people would have difficulty surviving in a pure market economy without help from family, government, or charity groups.

✓ **CHECK FOR UNDERSTANDING**

1. **Identifying** Who owns the factors of production in a market economy?

2. **Analyzing** What are the main advantages of a market economy?

Mixed Economies

GUIDING QUESTION

Why do most countries have a mixed economy?

Today most nations of the world have a **mixed market economy**, or an economic system that has elements of tradition, command, and markets that answer the WHAT, HOW, and FOR WHOM questions. A reason for mixed market economies is that nations tend to evolve, shedding some economic features and adding new ones.

mixed market economy economic system in which markets, government, *and* tradition each answer some of the WHAT, HOW, and FOR WHOM questions

Two factory workers wear hardhats, safety vests, and safety goggles. The U.S. government sets safety regulations such as these for businesses.

The United States economy is based on a market system with elements of command and tradition. Individuals and businesses can choose how to use their resources, and prices determine who will receive the goods and services produced. Businesses are usually free to compete for profit with limited interference from the government.

The U.S. economy is not a pure market economy because government has been asked to perform several important functions. It uses taxpayer money to provide some goods and services that competitive markets do not. These include highways, bridges, and airports. The government also provides a system of justice, national defense, and disaster relief.

The government helps markets function smoothly by making sure that sellers are honest and that buyers are protected. Although laws put some restrictions on business owners, people support these laws when they benefit society. The government makes rules for how workers are to be treated. It requires that a minimum wage be paid to most workers, and that workplaces are safe. In addition, the government requires workers to pay taxes on their income and on some of the things they own, such as cars, homes, and other property.

The American economy also has elements of a traditional economy. For example, many people often decide to work in the same job as a parent. Many people also take care of family members who are too old or too sick to care for themselves.

✓ **CHECK FOR UNDERSTANDING**

1. **Analyzing** What are signs that the United States does not have a pure market economy?

2. **Explaining** Why is the U.S. economy called a mixed market economy?

LESSON ACTIVITIES

1. **Argumentative Writing** Choose characteristics from at least two of the main economic systems. Write an essay explaining why these characteristics combined would make a better mixed system than one that was a pure traditional, command, or market system. Use examples and evidence to support your argument.

2. **Presenting** With a partner, think about the disadvantages of a traditional economy. Discuss what actions might be taken to boost economic growth without damaging the social structure on which the society survives. Use your ideas to create a multimedia presentation you might give to an elder member of the society. Show how his or her traditional economy combined with market forces could benefit the society.

Nitat Termmee/Getty Images

04

Analyzing Sources: Early Economic Systems

 COMPELLING QUESTION

Why do people need economic systems?

Plan Your Inquiry

DEVELOPING QUESTIONS

Think ahead a few years when you get your first steady job. In the U.S. free market system, you will work for wages or a salary, and then you'll use those earnings to buy what you need and want—either at a local store or online from anywhere in the world. Have you ever wondered how early people and civilizations obtained what they needed? Read the Compelling Question for this lesson. What questions can you ask to help you answer this Compelling Question? Create a graphic organizer like the one below. Write three Supporting Questions in the first column.

Supporting Questions	Source	What this source tells me about the economic system	Questions the source leaves unanswered
	A		
	B		
	C		
	D		
	E		

ANALYZING SOURCES

Next, read the introductory information for each source in this lesson. Then analyze each source by answering the questions that follow it. How does each source help you answer each Supporting Question you created? What questions do you still have? Write those in your graphic organizer.

After you analyze the sources, you will:
- use the evidence from the sources
- communicate your conclusions
- take informed action

Background Information

Four types of economic systems exist today: traditional, command, market, and mixed. They address the three basic economic questions of WHAT to produce, HOW to produce, and FOR WHOM to produce.

This Inquiry Lesson includes sources about earlier economic systems, including the barter system and early trade routes, manorialism, mercantilism, and the rise of capitalism. As you read and analyze the sources, think about the Compelling Question.

Merchants made long and difficult voyages along the Silk Road, which connected Asia, the Middle East, and Europe. Merchants traveled in caravans of pack animals such as camels to transport valuable goods.

The Barter System and Early Trade

A barter economy is a moneyless economy that relies on trade. Barter systems have existed since ancient times. The exchange of goods and services is difficult because the products some people have to offer are not always acceptable to others—or easy to divide for payment. For example, how could a farmer with a pail of milk obtain a pair of shoes if the cobbler wanted a basket of fish? It takes time to barter unless two people want exactly what the other has.

In their barter economies, many ancient societies used some form of commodity money—or "money" that has an alternate use as a product, such as clams or tobacco. The image below shows what an Aztec market scene might have looked like in Mexico in the 1400s. In Tenochtitlán and other large cities, Aztec merchants traded goods made by craftspeople. In exchange for the goods, the merchants obtained tropical feathers, cacao beans, animal skins, and gold—items they used as "money" to purchase other goods. When the Spanish arrived in the Americas in the early 1500s, they were astonished to find city markets considerably larger and better stocked than any markets in Spain.

SECONDARY SOURCE: ILLUSTRATION OF A MARKET

An artist has drawn an Aztec market scene. In the illustration, merchants exchange products for local "currency" in Mexico in the 1400s.

EXAMINE THE SOURCE

1. **Analyzing** What products are offered in the Aztec market?
2. **Drawing Conclusions** What appears to be the currency—or "money"—used for payment in this market?

The Silk Road

As trading became common, trade routes slowly formed between early societies. Possibly the most famous trade route in history is the Silk Road, which connected China to Europe.

SECONDARY SOURCE: ACADEMIC TEXT

❝ This framework of roads had its roots in the network of routes that started in Persia and along which **emissaries** with messages galloped throughout the empire in the 4th century B.C. However, in its final **configuration**, the Silk Road was officially opened in 130 B.C., when the Chinese emperor sent his ambassador Zhang Quian on a diplomatic mission in search of new allies. In addition to pacts, the ambassador returned with a new breed of horses and saddles and stirrups used by western warriors. This is the first example of the Silk Road's main function throughout history: the exchange of knowledge and technology.

The current view among historians is that the Silk Road—in service from its opening in 130 B.C. until the 14th century—was used by traders, religious, artists, fugitives and bandits, but above all by refugees and populations of emigrants or displaced persons. It is believed that it was precisely these groups of migrant populations who brought with them knowledge, tools, culture, products or crops (and with them possibly new techniques and irrigation systems). They fostered a cultural and technological "globalization" that was literally going to change the world.

On the **commercial** side, the Silk Road was a small-scale, local trade network, with goods passing from one merchant to another in the markets and exchange centres that lined the route. In both directions, food and animals, spices, materials, ceramics, handicrafts, jewellery and precious stones circulated. And although its name suggests otherwise, silk was not the main **commodity**. What's more, it never received this name during the almost 1,400 years that the Silk Road remained operational. The name was coined centuries later, in 1877, by the German geographer Ferdinand von Richthofen, because silk was the most valued and appreciated product among the nobles and dignitaries of the Roman Empire. ❞

— From "The Silk Road: The Route for Technological Exchange that Shaped the Modern World" by Miguel Barral, www.bbvaopenmind.com

emissaries agents
configuration arrangement
commercial business
commodity product

EXAMINE THE SOURCE

1. **Identifying** What products went back and forth along the Silk Road?
2. **Analyzing** How did products move from China to the nobles of the Roman Empire?

Barral, Miguel. "The Silk Road: The Route for Technological Exchange that Shaped the Modern World." BBVA OpenMind. August 29, 2019.

Manorialism

The manorial system arose in medieval Europe (800–1300 C.E.). A manor was an agricultural estate with a central castle or manor house. In exchange for the manor's protection, unfree serfs worked about three days a week farming the lord's share of land. Serfs paid rent by giving the lord a portion of every product they raised on separate pieces of land the rest of the week. Serfs also paid the lord for the use of the manor's common pasturelands, streams, ponds, and woodlands. Free peasants used the rest of the estate's land to grow food for themselves. Except for a few items such as salt and millstones, the manor provided everything. Most people rarely interacted with those outside of the manor.

Medieval lord and peasants

SECONDARY SOURCE: ILLUSTRATION OF A MANOR

Church
Village churches often had no benches. Villagers sat on the floor or brought stools from home.

Fields
In the spring, serfs planted crops such as summer wheat, barley, oats, peas, and beans. Crops planted in the fall included winter wheat and rye. Women often helped in the fields.

Castle
Castles were built in a variety of forms and were usually designed to fit the landscape.

Serf's Home
Serfs had little furniture. Tables were made from boards stretched across benches, and most peasants slept on straw mattresses on the floor.

EXAMINE THE SOURCE

1. **Analyzing** What obligations did lords and peasants fulfill on a manor?
2. **Summarizing** Summarize the manorial system in one to three words.

Mercantilism

From the 1500s to late 1700s, nation-states formed in western Europe. Market towns replaced manors as commercial hubs. Merchants in these towns paid taxes to the government. The taxes supported large armies that protected the nation and fought wars to gain colonies. In return, merchants expected the government to protect them from foreign competition. Thus, the economic system of mercantilism arose. The government increased the nation's wealth by controlling the products that came into and went out of the home country.

SECONDARY SOURCE: ACADEMIC TEXT

❝ These [mercantilist] policies took many forms. **Domestically**, governments would provide **capital** to new industries, **exempt** new industries from **guild** rules and taxes, establish monopolies over local and colonial markets, and grant titles and pensions to successful producers. In trade policy the government assisted local industry by imposing **tariffs**, **quotas**, and **prohibitions** on **imports** of goods that competed with local manufacturers. Governments also prohibited the **export** of tools and **capital equipment** and the emigration of skilled labor that would allow foreign countries, and even the colonies of the home country, to compete in the production of manufactured goods. At the same time, diplomats encouraged foreign manufacturers to move to the diplomats' own countries.

Shipping was particularly important during the mercantile period. With the growth of colonies and the shipment of gold from the New World into Spain and Portugal, control of the oceans was considered vital to national power. Because ships could be used for merchant or military purposes, the governments of the era developed strong merchant marines. . . .

During the mercantilist era it was often suggested, if not actually believed, that the principal benefit of foreign trade was the importation of gold and silver. . . . For nations almost constantly on the verge of war, draining one another of valuable gold and silver was thought to be almost as desirable as the direct benefits of trade. ❞

— From "Mercantilism" by Laura LaHaye, Library of Economics and Liberty

domestically at home, within the country

capital investment money

exempt free, to excuse

guild union, group of companies

tariffs taxes on imported products

quotas limits on imported products

prohibitions ban, to forbid

imports to bring products into a country from a foreign country

export to send or sell to another country

capital equipment machines that make products

EXAMINE THE SOURCE

1. **Inferring** Which segments in a country benefited most from mercantilism—producers, consumers, or government?

2. **Drawing Conclusions** How did mercantilism affect trade?

Capitalism

Adam Smith (1723–1790) is known as the father of economics. In 1776 he published *The Wealth of Nations*, an influential book that promoted free markets rather than markets regulated by governments under mercantilism. Smith also promoted capitalism—an economic system in which individuals privately own the factors of production and use them to make profits. Smith believed that society as a whole benefits when individuals pursue their own economic interests.

PRIMARY SOURCE: BOOK

> It is not from the **benevolence** of the butcher, the brewer, or the baker that we expect our dinner, but from their regard to their own interest. We address ourselves, not to their **humanity**, but to their self-love, and never talk to them of our own necessities, but of their advantages. . . .
>
> . . . [E]very individual . . . neither intends to promote the public interest, nor knows how much he is promoting it. . . . [H]e intends only his own gain, and he is in this, as in many other cases, led by an invisible hand to promote an end which was no part of his intention.

— From Adam Smith's *An Inquiry Into the Nature and Causes of the Wealth Of Nations.* Edinburgh: Thomas Nelson, 1827.

benevolence generosity
humanity kindness

EXAMINE THE SOURCE

1. **Analyzing** How does Smith describe a successful interaction between a buyer and seller?
2. **Inferring** According to Smith, what motivates people to work hard?

Complete Your Inquiry

EVALUATE SOURCES AND USE EVIDENCE

Refer back to the Compelling Question and the Supporting Questions you developed at the beginning of the lesson.

1. **Evaluating** Which of the sources affected your thinking the most? Why?
2. **Identifying Themes** What theme underlies all of the economic systems?
3. **Gathering Sources** Which sources helped you answer the Supporting Questions and Compelling Question? Which sources, if any, challenged what you thought you knew when you first created your Supporting Questions? What information do you still need in order to answer your questions? Where will you find that information?
4. **Evaluating Sources** Identify the sources that helped answer your Supporting Questions. How reliable is the source? How would you verify the reliability of the source?

COMMUNICATE CONCLUSIONS

5. **Collaborating** Work with a partner to create an illustrated time line of early economic systems and how they answered the basic economic questions. How do these sources provide insight into why economic systems developed and changed over time? Use the graphic organizer that you created at the beginning of the lesson to help you. Share your time line with the class.

TAKE INFORMED ACTION

Discussing How Piracy Affects Entrepreneurs Recall that a free market economy such as that promoted by Adam Smith and capitalism relies on profits as the incentive for entrepreneurs to take risks and create new products and services. Research the amount of money lost from pirated products, such as when individuals illegally download music or when countries illegally copy and sell DVDs. Discuss what actions, if any, you think American companies should take to stop piracy.

Smith, Adam. An Inquiry into the Nature and Causes of the Wealth of Nations. Edinburgh: Thomas Nelson, 1827.

Demand and Supply in a Market Economy

READING STRATEGY

Analyzing Key Ideas and Details As you read, complete a chart describing the factors that cause a change in quantity demanded and quantity supplied, as well as factors that cause a change in demand and supply.

Factors that Cause a ...	
Change in Quantity Demanded	Change in Quantity Supplied
Change in Demand	Change in Supply

Demand and Supply

GUIDING QUESTION

What are demand and supply?

The interaction of two forces—demand and supply—is key to the market economy. These forces result from the desires of two groups. **Consumers** are the people who *buy* goods and services. **Producers** are the people or businesses that *provide* goods and services. Let's take a look at the two forces of demand and supply.

Demand

In economics, **demand** is the amount of a good or service that people (consumers) are willing and able to buy at various prices during a given time period. Notice that this definition mentions four parts:

- *Amount*—Demand measures the quantity (or how much) of a good or service consumers are willing to buy over a range of possible prices. So the demand for a certain video game refers to the quantities that consumers would buy at prices such as $20, $40, and $60.
- *Willing to buy*—Consumers must be willing to buy a good or service or there is no demand.
- *Able to buy*—Consumers must have the ability to buy the good or service. Consumers who want a certain good but do not have the money to buy it do not affect the demand for that item.
- *Price*—The quantity that consumers are willing and able to buy is associated with a particular price, be it high or low.

consumer person who buys goods and services

producer person or business that provides goods and services

demand amount of a good or service consumers are willing and able to buy over a range of prices

A woman sells custom-made clothing to a mother and daughter.

Identifying Who is the consumer, and who is the producer?

As the price of a good or service goes up, consumers tend to demand fewer quantities. As the price goes down, they tend to demand larger quantities. Thus, price and quantity demanded have an *inverse*—or opposite—relationship (with price decreasing and quantity increasing—or the other way around). We will see that this inverse relationship can be expressed in a table and graph.

Graphing Demand

The quantity of a particular item that is demanded at each price can be shown in a **schedule**, or table. The information on a schedule can then be drawn as a line on a graph. The line on the graph is referred to as a *demand curve*.

Look at the **Demand Schedule and Graph for Fruit Smoothies**. In the schedule A, every price has a quantity demanded. For example, at a price of $9, the consumer will buy zero fruit smoothies.

If the price lowers to $6, however, the consumer will demand a quantity of 1 fruit smoothie. If the price is lowered further to $4, he or she will purchase 2. When the price reaches $2, the consumer will buy 4 fruit smoothies. This makes sense. The lower the price, the more quantities will be demanded. The higher the price, fewer amounts will be demanded.

Now look at the demand curve B. Notice how the prices and quantities from the schedule have been put into graph form. Each point on the demand curve shows the amount demanded at a particular price. As the price changes, the points move along the demand curve. At the price of $9, zero quantity is demanded. At $4, a quantity of 2 is demanded. How many quantities will be demanded at a price of $2? Trace the horizontal line that starts at $2. Notice that it connects with the point above the quantity of 4.

schedule table listing items or events

Demand Schedule and Graph for Fruit Smoothies

On economics graphs, prices are measured on the left side (called the *y-axis*), starting with $0 at the bottom and moving up to higher prices. Quantities are measured along the bottom of the graph, or *x-axis*. Notice how the quantity increases as you move from left to right on the bottom axis. Both the demand schedule and demand curve show that the quantity demanded changes as the price changes.

A Demand Schedule

Price	Quantity Demanded
$9	0
$6	1
$4	2
$3	3
$2	4

B Demand Curve

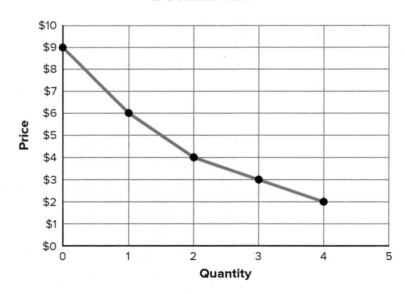

EXAMINE THE GRAPH

1. **Analyzing** What quantity of fruit smoothies will consumers demand at a price of $3?
2. **Explaining** What is the relationship between price and quantity demanded?

Supply Schedule and Graph for Fruit Smoothies

The supply schedule and the individual supply curve both show the quantity supplied at every possible price for a certain time period.

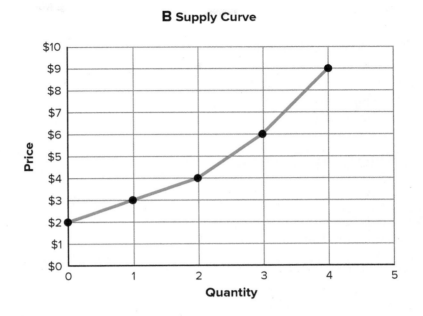

A Supply Schedule

Price	Quantity Supplied
$9	4
$6	3
$4	2
$3	1
$2	0

B Supply Curve

EXAMINE THE GRAPH

1. **Analyzing** What quantity of fruit smoothies are offered for sale at the price of $6?
2. **Explaining** What is the relationship between price and quantity supplied?

The demand curve slopes down to the right. At first glance, this may appear as if demand is decreasing from left to right. That is not the case. In fact, just the opposite is occurring. Notice the quantities along the bottom of the graph. The numbers increase from left to right. Thus, consumers demand more quantities when the price is low, and they tend to demand less (in this case, zero) when the price is high ($9).

Supply

Supply is the amount of a good or service that producers are willing and able to sell at various prices during a given time period. As the price of a good or service goes up, producers tend to supply larger quantities. As the price goes down, they tend to supply less. This happens because a high price is an **incentive**—a motivation or reward—for suppliers to produce more. Your incentive for studying hard is to earn the reward of a higher grade in class. The reward for producers to supply more quantities at a higher price is to make more **profit**—or the money a business receives for its products over and above what it cost to make the products. A low price is an incentive to produce less.

Graphing Supply

Quantity supplied—like quantity demanded—can also be shown two ways. See the **Supply Schedule and Graph for Fruit Smoothies**. The schedule A shows that at a price of $9, producers will offer 4 fruit smoothies for sale. At a price of $4, suppliers will offer only a quantity of 2. Suppliers will offer a quantity of zero at a price of $2.

The prices and quantities on the supply schedule have been copied over to the supply graph B. Each point on the supply curve shows

---

supply amount of a good or service that producers are willing and able to sell over a range of prices

incentive motivation or reward

profit money a business receives for its products over and above what it cost to make the products

the quantity supplied at a particular price. Notice how the supply curve slopes up when you read the graph from left to right. This shows that if the price goes up, the quantity supplied will go up too. As the price changes, the points move along the supply curve.

✓ CHECK FOR UNDERSTANDING

1. **Comparing** How is a high price an incentive for both consumers and producers?
2. **Contrasting** How does a demand curve differ from a supply curve?

Changes in Demand and Supply

GUIDING QUESTION

What factors affect demand and supply?

Factors Affecting Demand

You learned that when the price changes, the *quantity demanded* changes. This was shown along a single demand curve. The curve itself did not change, but the points (quantity demanded) along the curve changed according to the price change.

Sometimes, however, the entire curve moves because of a change in something *other than price*. When this happens, we say there is a change in *demand* (not quantity demanded).

Several factors affect demand, causing the entire demand curve to shift left or right. One factor that affects demand is the number of consumers. Look at the **Change in Demand for Video Games** graphs. If more consumers enter the market, they buy more of the product at each and every price. The demand curve shifts to the right as shown in the top graph. If consumers leave the market, then fewer people are available to buy the video games. This change causes the demand curve to move left, shown in the bottom graph.

Another factor that affects demand is a change in consumer income. If people earn more, they may buy more video games at each price. This causes demand to increase, and the demand curve moves to the right. In contrast, if people earn less, they do not buy as many games at every possible price. Then the demand curve shifts left.

A third factor that affects demand is a change in consumer *preferences*, or what people like or prefer. In summer, people want to be outside, so they may prefer to buy fewer video games at every price. This shifts the demand curve for video games to the left. In winter, consumers prefer indoor activities and would buy more video games at every price. This shifts the product's demand curve to the right.

Factors Affecting Supply

Sometimes the entire supply curve shifts because of a change in something *other than price*. When

A girl and her family eat shaved ice in front of an ice-cream truck. During warm weather months, demand increases for frozen treats. Because of this change in consumer preferences, people will buy more at every price.

Blend Images / Image Source

Change in Demand for Video Games

Many factors could affect demand for video games. The top graph shows demand expanding, or increasing. The bottom graph shows demand contracting, or decreasing.

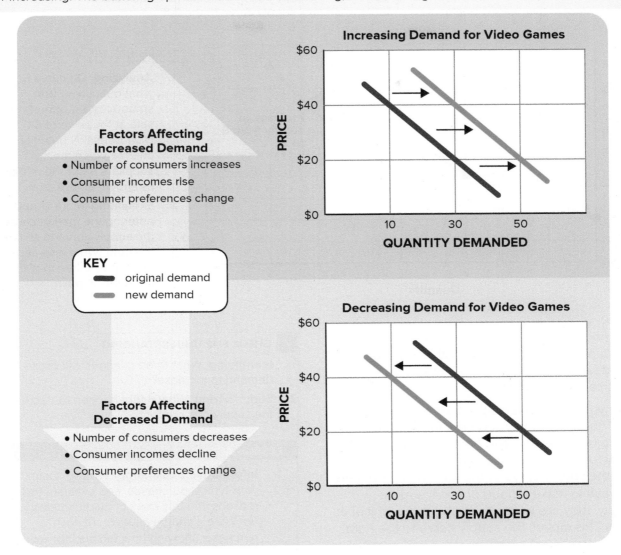

Factors Affecting Increased Demand
- Number of consumers increases
- Consumer incomes rise
- Consumer preferences change

KEY
- original demand
- new demand

Factors Affecting Decreased Demand
- Number of consumers decreases
- Consumer incomes decline
- Consumer preferences change

Increasing Demand for Video Games

Decreasing Demand for Video Games

EXAMINE THE GRAPHS

1. **Identifying Cause and Effect** What economic situation might cause consumers' incomes to go down, and what would happen to the video game demand curve?

2. **Analyzing Visuals** In the top graph, the original demand curve shows that at a price of $40, 10 video games are demanded. Then demand increased because of a change in consumer preferences. How many video games are now demanded at $40 as shown on the new demand curve?

this happens, we say there is a change in *supply* (not quantity supplied). Several factors affect supply, which shifts the entire curve left or right. The two key factors are the number of suppliers and the costs of production.

As the number of suppliers increases, more of an item is produced at all prices, and the supply

curve moves to the right. See the **Change in Supply for Fruit Smoothies** graph. The original supply curve **S** shows that at a price of $9, suppliers will offer 4 fruit smoothies for sale. At a price of $2, suppliers will offer a quantity of zero. But notice what happens when more suppliers enter the market. The new supply curve S_1 shows that more

Change in Supply for Fruit Smoothies

A change in supply means that producers will supply different quantities of a product at all prices. An increase in supply appears as a shift of the supply curve to the right. A decrease in supply (not shown here) appears as a shift of the original supply curve to the left.

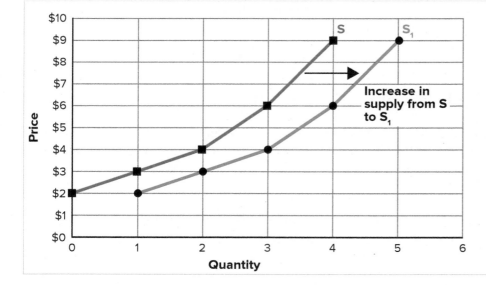

EXAMINE THE GRAPH

1. **Analyzing** On curve S, what quantity of fruit smoothies are offered for sale at the price of $4? How does this quantity change when more suppliers enter the market as shown on S₁?

2. **Explaining** More suppliers entering the market causes the supply curve to shift to the right. What else causes the supply curve to shift to the right? Explain.

fruit smoothies are produced at all prices. With more suppliers, now 5 fruit smoothies will be offered for sale at $9. And at $2, at least one fruit smoothie will be supplied.

Anything that affects the cost of production also influences supply. If producing a good or service becomes more expensive, producers supply less at every price in the market. This shifts the supply curve to the left. Or, if producers find ways to make a good or service more cheaply, they are willing to supply more of it at all prices. This moves the supply curve to the right.

New technology may drive down production costs. Computers, for example, make workers more efficient. A new manufacturing process can reduce waste. This cuts production costs. Lower costs of producing lead to more supply.

Finally, here's a tip that will help you remember the difference between a change in *quantity* demanded (or *quantity* supplied) versus a change in demand (or change in supply). *Only a change in price* can change quantity demanded or quantity supplied. Everything else affects either a change in demand or a change in supply.

✓ CHECK FOR UNDERSTANDING

1. **Identifying** What three changes will cause demand to increase?

2. **Summarizing** What might happen to decrease the supply of a product?

LESSON ACTIVITIES

1. **Informative/Explanatory Writing** Examine your typical purchases, and evaluate the reasons you buy them in the quantities you do. Write a short evaluation of each purchase, showing how factors, not including price, affect your demand.

2. **Collaborating** Work with a partner to identify one type of business in which the introduction of a new technology has greatly increased supply. Create a flyer or infographic describing and showing how the new technology lowered production costs and how that had an impact on supply.

06
Prices in a Market Economy

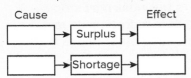
The Economic Role of Prices

GUIDING QUESTION

How do prices help consumers and businesses make economic decisions?

Price—the monetary value of a product—does much more than simply tell you how much you have to spend when you make a purchase. Prices help answer the three basic economic questions in a market economy. Prices also measure value. In addition, prices send signals to both consumers and producers.

Prices and the Economic Questions

In a market economy, prices help answer the three basic questions: WHAT to produce, HOW to produce, and FOR WHOM to produce. Prices help determine WHAT to produce by influencing the decisions of producers. If consumer demand for a product is high, demand drives up the price of that product. Businesses react by increasing production of that product to meet the demand and increase their profits. Or, if consumer demand for a product is low, the price of the product falls and businesses produce less of it. For example, why are no large-screen black-and-white televisions produced? The reason is that people will pay a higher price to see TV shows in color. To meet that demand, producers of large-screen TVs focus on making color TVs rather than black-and-white ones. This is how prices help answer the WHAT to produce question.

price the monetary value of a product

A consumer shopping for energy drinks checks prices on his mobile app.
Identifying Cause and Effect How do prices help producers figure out which products consumers are willing and able to buy?

FG Trade/E+/Getty Images

Prices also affect HOW goods and services are produced. For example, cars built by hand would be far too expensive. Instead, automakers use mass production to lower the price. This method lets them produce cars at a price consumers can afford to pay.

Prices also decide FOR WHOM goods and services are produced. Products are made for consumers who can and will buy them at a particular price.

Prices as Measures of Value

Every good and service in a market economy has a price. The price sets the value of each good or service on any particular day. Consumers and producers then use the prices to compare values of goods and services. If a T-shirt costs $10 and a pair of jeans costs $25, then a pair of jeans is worth two and a half T-shirts.

Prices for similar products may be different, however. This often happens when there are small but real differences in quality. It also happens when people *think* the differences are real when in fact they are not. For example, not all jeans have the same value for everyone. You or someone you know may prefer a certain brand or type of jeans. If a jeans company has good advertising, it may convince consumers to value its jeans more highly and pay more for them.

Prices as Signals

Prices send signals to consumers and producers. High prices are a signal for buyers to purchase less, and for producers to produce more. Low prices are a signal for buyers to purchase more, and for producers to produce less.

If consumers think an item is priced too high, some will not buy it. Suppose a bakery charges $5 for a bagel. If nearby bakeries charge less, some consumers will not buy the $5 bagel. This sends a signal to that bakery owner to lower the price.

Prices also serve as incentives to take other actions. If the price of a product goes up at one store, you may decide to shop for it at a different location, or purchase a similar but different item. **Likewise**, or similarly, a business may stop producing a low-price item to free up its land, labor, and capital to produce other things that can be sold for a higher price.

Rationing

What if we did not have prices? Without prices, another system must be used to decide who gets what. One method is **rationing**—a system in

likewise in the same way

rationing system of distributing goods and services without prices

THIS STORE IS PLEDGED TO CONFORM TO THE SUGAR REGULATIONS OF THE U.S. FOOD ADMINISTRATION

Your Sugar Ration is 2 lbs. per month

SUGAR 2 lbs.

SUGAR 1 lb. 1 oz.

SUGAR 11 oz.

AMERICA'S VOLUNTARY RATION ENGLAND'S COMPULSORY RATION

FRANCE'S COMPULSORY RATION

ITALY'S COMPULSORY RATION

We must confine our consumption of Sugar to not more than 2 lbs. per person per month in order to provide a restricted ration to England, France and Italy.

This store sign was a reminder for customers to bring their "ration cards" to purchase sugar. During World War I, the government rationed food, gasoline, nylon, tires, and many other items.

Shoppers buy fruit at a farmers market. Sellers at this farmers market—and in every other market—are competing against other sellers, so they keep their prices low enough to attract buyers.

which government decides everyone's "fair" share. Under such a system, people receive a ration coupon or ticket that allows the holder to obtain a limited amount of a product.

Rationing was used widely during World War I and World War II. Since then, rationing has occurred mainly after national disasters. During the 2020-2021 pandemic, for example, stores rationed basic items such as toilet paper and hand sanitizer. Instead of issuing ration coupons, however, stores generally *asked* consumers to personally limit purchases of these items—with mixed success.

✓ CHECK FOR UNDERSTANDING

1. **Explaining** How do prices help us make decisions?

2. **Analyzing** How do high prices serve as incentives for consumers and producers to take "other" actions?

How Prices Are Set

GUIDING QUESTION

How do shortages and surpluses help markets establish equilibrium prices?

As you've learned, markets are vital to the U.S. economy. A **market** is any place where buyers and sellers voluntarily exchange money for a good or service. Markets allow us to choose how we spend our money. In a market economy, buyers and sellers have exactly the opposite goals: buyers want to find good deals at low prices, and sellers hope for high prices and large profits. Neither can get exactly what they want, so some adjustment is necessary to reach a compromise. In this way, everyone who participates—including you!—has a hand in determining prices.

In addition, markets are efficient. To be efficient, markets for identical products must

market place or arrangement where a buyer and a seller voluntarily exchange money for a good or service

Market for Fruit Smoothies

Schedule A shows the quantity of fruit smoothies demanded and supplied at each price. When you plot this information on the graph B, you can see that the equilibrium price and equilibrium quantities occur where the two curves intersect—at $4.

A Demand and Supply Schedule

Price	Quantity Demanded	Quantity Supplied
$9	0	4
$6	1	3
$4	2	2
$3	3	1
$2	4	0

B Demand, Supply, and Equilibrium

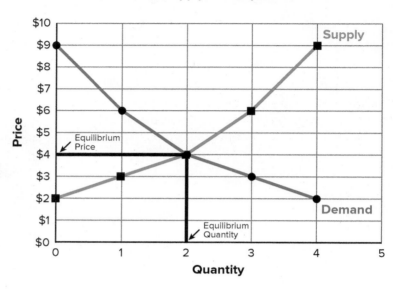

EXAMINE THE GRAPH

1. **Explaining** Why would a seller want to know the equilibrium price of a product?
2. **Analyzing** Why is the quantity demanded for fruit smoothies much lower at a price of $9 than the quantity supplied at that price?
3. **Speculating** What would cause the equilibrium price for fruit smoothies to go up?

have many competing buyers and sellers. This **competition**, or struggle among sellers to attract buyers, keeps a product's price at or near a certain level. This level is called the **equilibrium** (EE•kwuh•LIH•bree•uhm) **price**. Here, quantity demanded and quantity supplied are equal. If a market does not have a large number of buyers and sellers, then an exact equilibrium may not be reached. Instead, prices of identical products may be close but not always the same.

When markets operate freely, prices adjust gradually and automatically. Markets also help prevent the production of too many, or too few, goods and services.

Equilibrium

So, how does a market arrive at a compromise price that is "just about right" for both buyers and sellers? To see how this process works, we must put the demand and supply curves together to represent a market—see the **Market for Fruit Smoothies** graph. Note that the curves meet at one point. That point is the price the marketplace sets for the good or service. At this $4 equilibrium price, consumers want to buy the same amount of a good or service that producers are willing to offer. The **equilibrium quantity** at the equilibrium price is two. At the $4 equilibrium price, consumers want to buy a quantity of two fruit

---

competition efforts by different businesses to sell the same good or service

equilibrium price market price where quantity demanded and quantity supplied are equal

equilibrium quantity quantity of output supplied that is equal to the quantity demanded at the equilibrium price

smoothies, and producers want to supply a quantity of two.

Surplus

If the price were higher than the equilibrium price, producers would be willing to produce more. But consumers would not be willing or able to buy more. This would result in a **surplus**, in which the amount supplied by producers is greater than the amount demanded by consumers. A surplus tends to cause prices to fall.

For example, at a price of $6, three smoothies would be supplied but only one would be demanded. This would leave a surplus of two. And at a price of $9, there would be a surplus of four.

Shortage

If the price were lower than the equilibrium price, there would be a **shortage**. This occurs when the quantity demanded is greater than the quantity supplied. For example, at a price of $3, three smoothies would be demanded but only one supplied, leaving a shortage of two. And at a price of $2, there would be a shortage of four. A shortage will cause the price to rise. We often see this happen when a shortage of gasoline drives the price up.

Unless the government steps in to regulate prices, the forces applied by surpluses and shortages work to keep a price at or near its equilibrium level. Surpluses cause prices to go down, whereas shortages cause prices to go up. This process continues until there are no

surplus situation in which the amount of a good or service supplied by producers at a certain price is greater than the amount demanded by consumers

shortage situation in which the quantity of a good or service supplied at a certain price is less than the quantity demanded for it

A clearance sale is an example of a surplus.

Drawing Conclusions What must producers do to get rid of their surplus?

Demand and Supply for Oil

The price of crude oil is set by demand and supply. Crude oil is used to make gasoline, heating oil, jet fuel, and other products. Its price affects the whole economy.

Demand Schedule for Crude Oil	
Price Per Barrel	Quantity Demanded
$10	50
$20	40
$30	30
$40	20
$50	10

Supply Schedule for Crude Oil	
Price Per Barrel	Quantity Supplied
$10	10
$20	20
$30	30
$40	40
$50	50

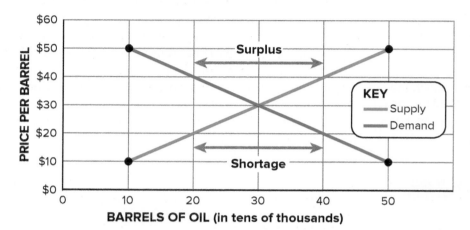

BARRELS OF OIL (in tens of thousands)

EXAMINE THE GRAPH

1. **Identifying** What is the equilibrium price of oil? At what quantity is this price reached?
2. **Analyzing** What would happen if the producer set the price at $50 per barrel?
3. **Analyzing** What would happen if the government set the price per barrel at $20?

surpluses or shortages, and an equilibrium price is reached.

Thus, a market finds its own price. Look at the graph **Demand and Supply for Oil** to see how surpluses and shortages work together in a large market to get to equilibrium.

✓ CHECK FOR UNDERSTANDING

1. **Explaining** How does competition help consumers?
2. **Identifying Cause and Effect** How do surpluses and shortages help establish an equilibrium price?

LESSON ACTIVITIES

1. **Informative/Explanatory Writing** Suppose you run a company that makes and sells skateboards. If the price of skateboards started to increase, would you choose to make more skateboards or fewer skateboards? In a paragraph, explain your decision.

2. **Collaborating** You and a partner have a new business selling cupcakes. You make 500 cupcakes a day. After a week of selling cupcakes for $4 each, you have a daily surplus of 100 cupcakes. You reduce the price to $3 and sell all the cupcakes daily, but customers would have bought 50 more a day at that price. Working together, discuss how to determine what the equilibrium price is for your product. Write a one-page report, including necessary graphs, explaining why you have settled on a particular price.

07

Economic Flow and Economic Growth

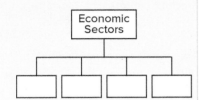

READING STRATEGY

Analyzing Key Ideas and Details As you read the lesson, complete a diagram like this identifying the four sectors of the economy.

Economic Sectors

The Circular Flow Model

GUIDING QUESTION

Why do resources, goods and services, and money flow in a circular pattern in a market system?

Economists like to use models to show how a country's economy works. A model is a graph or diagram used to explain something. Demand and supply curves are models. In this lesson we will study another one—the **circular flow model**. This model shows how resources, goods and services, and money flow between businesses and consumers. The model has a circular shape because its flows have no beginning or end. For example, someday you might have a job in a bookstore. Perhaps you use the income you earn to purchase a book. The bookstore uses that money to pay your wages, and so on. The money you earn circles back to the store and then back to you again. This is how the economy works.

circular flow model a model showing how goods, services, resources, and money flow among sectors and markets in the American economy

Circular Flow of Economic Activity

This simple model shows how the business and consumer sectors interact with the factor market and the product market.

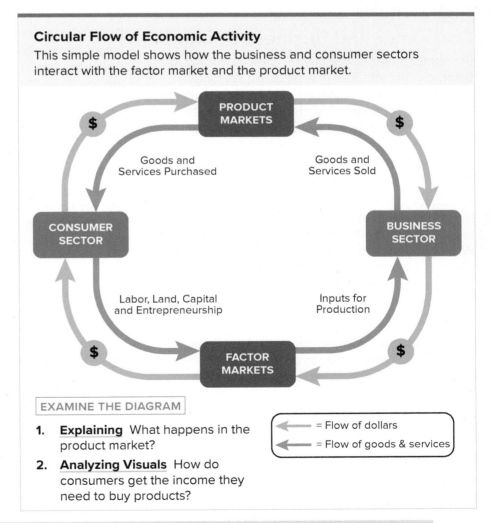

EXAMINE THE DIAGRAM

1. **Explaining** What happens in the product market?

2. **Analyzing Visuals** How do consumers get the income they need to buy products?

The circular flow model has four parts. Two parts are *markets* where buying and selling take place. Two parts are **sectors** that stand for the two main groups of participants in the markets—people and businesses. We will start by looking at the two markets.

The Factor and Product Markets

The first market is the **factor market**. This is where factors of production are bought and sold. When people go to work, they sell their *labor* in the factor market. *Natural resources* such as oil and timber are also sold in the factor market. *Capital resources* such as machines and tools are bought and sold in the factor market. *Entrepreneurs* organize and use the other three factors in their quest to make profits.

The **product market** is where producers sell their goods and services. Thus, the money individuals receive in the factor market returns to businesses in the product market when people buy products. You can think of this market as one big store where all products—both goods and services—are sold.

Consumer and Business Sectors

Economists think of the buyers in the economy as being divided into four groups called *sectors*. To keep the diagram simple, the circular flow model in this lesson has only two sectors: the *consumer sector* and the *business sector*. The two sectors not shown are the *government sector* and the *foreign sector*. After you learn how the first two sectors operate, the other sectors will be discussed.

Consumers take part in both the factor and the product markets. When consumers go to work, they sell their labor in the factor market. When they get paid, they take that money to the product market, where they buy goods and services. To earn more income, they return to the factor market and sell their labor again.

The business sector represents all the companies that produce goods and services. This sector is also active in both markets. Businesses sell goods and services in the product market where consumers spend their income. Businesses use the money they receive from these sales to buy land, labor, and capital in

When grocery shopping, this family is participating in the product market. The average American family spends 10 to 20 percent of its income on food.

Analyzing Visuals This family is acting as what sector of the economy?

the factor market. They then use these factors to make more things to sell in the product market.

The Circular Flow

If you look at the whole diagram, you see that the loop representing money flows in the clockwise direction. Starting with the consumer sector, money flows through the product market to the business sector. Money then flows through the factor market back to the consumer sector. The loop representing goods, services, and factors of production always flows in the opposite direction.

The key feature of the model is to show that money flows in one direction while the products and productive resources flow in the opposite direction. This is precisely what happens in real life. For example, suppose you earn some cash (in the factor market) by handing out advertising flyers for a new juice drink. With some of your earnings, you purchase a bottle of juice from a vending machine (in the product market). You put the money in, and the bottle comes out. The money and the product you buy flow in opposite directions. In addition, the money you put in will eventually return to the juice-making company. It will use the money to purchase more oranges, containers, and machines (in the factor market) to make more juice drinks to sell in the product market.

sector part or category distinct from other parts

factor market a market where productive resources (land, labor, capital) are bought and sold

product market a market where goods and services are bought and sold

The circular flow model also shows that markets link the consumer and business sectors. You probably will never set foot in the factory that makes some of your favorite products. However, you still interact with that factory when you buy its products.

Government and Foreign Sectors

The simplified circular flow model does not show the government and foreign sectors. Both of these sectors are important, but adding them to the model would make it more difficult to understand.

The *government sector* is made up of federal, state, and local government units. These units go to the product market to buy goods and services, just as people in the consumer sector do. Sometimes the government sells goods and services to earn income. For example, state universities charge tuition. If these charges are not enough to fund the universities, governments use taxes and borrowing to get the money needed to operate.

The *foreign sector* is made up of all the people and businesses in other countries. Foreign businesses buy raw materials in U.S. factor markets. They also sell their goods and services to consumers in U.S. product markets. In recent years, about 15 percent of the goods and services bought in the United States have come from foreign countries. Also, about 12 percent of the things we produce are sold outside the United States.

✓ CHECK FOR UNDERSTANDING

1. **Explaining** How do businesses and individuals participate in both the product market and the factor market in the U.S. economy?
2. **Making Connections** How does the circular flow diagram reflect the interdependence of the U.S. economy?

This F-16 Fighting Falcon costs roughly $30 million. The government is a big spender.

Making Connections How does the factor market connect the consumer and government sectors?

Promoting Economic Growth

GUIDING QUESTION

How can nations create and promote economic growth?

The United States has experienced mostly steady economic growth. **Economic growth** is the increase in a country's total output of goods and services over time. Government and business leaders work hard to promote economic growth. Why? Because when the economy grows, the nation's wealth increases. This also helps improve the **standard of living**, or quality of life of people living in a country.

A little over 100 years ago, a typical American could expect to live to age 53. Average income, in terms of today's dollars, was under $10,000 per year. Only 55 percent of homes had indoor plumbing, and only 25 percent had phones. No one had a TV, and cars were few. How did Americans, in just one century, manage to improve their standard of living so much? The answer is economic growth.

Two things are needed for economic growth. The first is additional resources. The second is increased productivity.

Additional Productive Resources

As you know, four factors of production are used to make goods and provide services. If a country were to run out of these factors, increasing production would be much more difficult and perhaps impossible. This would cause economic growth to slow or even to stop.

One key resource, land, is in limited supply. Only so much oil is under the ground, for example, and it may run out someday. There is only so much timber to be cut, so it is important to plant new trees regularly. When we make it our goal to save or preserve our trees, streams, and other natural resources, we are helping lay a foundation for future economic growth.

Economic growth also needs either a growing population or one that is becoming more productive. This takes us to the next requirement for growth—productivity.

economic growth the increase in a country's total output of goods and services over time

standard of living the material well-being of an individual, a group, or a nation as measured by how well needs and wants are satisfied

Increasing Productivity

Productivity is a measure of how efficiently businesses use the factors of production to create products. Suppose a factory that has always made 1,000 computers each week begins to make 1,100 a week with the same number of workers. In that case, its productivity has increased by 10 percent. Productivity is increasing when *more* products are made using the original amount of resources in the same amount of time. Productivity is decreasing if *fewer* products are created using the original amount of resources or more time.

Over the years, there have been two key changes in how products are made. These are specialization and the division of labor. Both improve productivity. **Specialization** occurs when people, businesses, or countries focus on the tasks that they can do best. For example, a region with a mild climate and fertile land will specialize in farming. A person who has good mechanical skills might specialize in car repair. By specializing, each becomes more efficient—or productive.

Specialization leads to another development that increases productivity: **division of labor**. This breaks down a job into separate, smaller tasks done by different workers. A worker who performs one task many times a day is likely to be more efficient than a worker who performs many different tasks in the same period. This improves productivity—which increases economic growth.

Businesses always strive to be more productive because their goal is to make more money. They may increase productivity in different ways. One way is to improve existing production methods or invent entirely new processes that do not use costly resources. The invention of the assembly line, for example, sped up production and changed manufacturing forever.

Businesses can also use new and better information technology. Computers originally let one person do the work that was once performed by several people. Now computers connect businesses and workers around the world and control robotics that manufacture products.

Productivity can also improve by using higher-quality factors of production. This is especially true of one factor: labor. When economists talk about the quality of labor, they use the term *human capital*. **Human capital** refers to the knowledge and skills workers can draw on to create products. How can we improve human capital? Three key

The automobile assembly line is a good example of the division of labor. Each worker stays in one place and performs a single task to assemble a car.

Drawing Conclusions How do you think the use of assembly lines in manufacturing affected the country's economic growth?

ways are education, training, and experience. As workers gain more of these, the quality of their work improves and they become more productive. As you know, greater productivity leads to economic growth and a higher standard of living.

✓ CHECK FOR UNDERSTANDING

1. **Explaining** What role does specialization play in the productivity of an economy?
2. **Synthesizing** How do people benefit from economic growth?

productivity the degree to which resources are being used efficiently to produce goods and services

specialization assignment of tasks to workers or factories that can perform them most efficiently

division of labor breaking down of a job into separate, smaller tasks to be performed individually

human capital people's knowledge and skills used to create products

LESSON ACTIVITIES

1. **Informative/Explanatory Writing** Research the ways in which the assembly line changed how Americans made cars. Write a report about your findings. In your report, include details on how these changes affected the price of automobiles.

2. **Presenting** With a partner, present information about a local business that answers these questions: What does the business sell in the product market? What does the business buy in the factor market? Where does the business get the money to make the purchases in the factor market?

08

Turning Point: The Industrial Revolution

  COMPELLING QUESTION

How did changes in production impact the world?

Plan Your Inquiry

DEVELOPING QUESTIONS

Two things are needed for economic growth: additional resources and increased productivity. The Industrial Revolution increased productivity drastically. Think about what life might have been like during the Industrial Revolution. Then read the Compelling Question for this lesson. What questions can you ask to help you answer this Compelling Question? Create a graphic organizer like the one below. Write three Supporting Questions in the first column.

Supporting Questions	Primary or Secondary Source	What the source tells me about the Industrial Revolution's impact on productivity and people's lives	Questions the source leaves unanswered
	A		
	B		
	C		
	D		
	E		

ANALYZING SOURCES

Next, examine the primary and secondary sources in this lesson. Analyze each source by answering the questions that follow it. How does each source help you answer each Supporting Question you created? What questions do you still have? Write these in your graphic organizer.

After you analyze the sources, you will:
- use the evidence from the sources
- communicate your conclusions
- take informed action

Background Information

Most economists use 1776 as the starting date of the Industrial Revolution. That year, James Watt introduced the first commercial steam engine. With the steam engine, mills no longer had to be located near rivers to power their huge water wheels and the creaking machinery inside. Instead, factory owners built their factories closer to their workers or their sources of raw materials. Powerful steam engines propelled trains that carried goods to cities and seaports where they were shipped vast distances. The use of the steam engine also meant that factories could be better organized to mass-produce goods of uniform quality.

Industrialism came at a cost, though. In the years that followed, people no longer lived in villages and made goods by hand in their homes. Instead, people flocked to cities that often became crowded with unhealthy living conditions. Working-class families, including children, worked long hours for low pay. Coal-burning factories belched smoke into the air, and many factory jobs were dangerous.

» Women spin wool into thread and yarn at home in the 1700s. Before the Industrial Revolution, many such "cottage industries" supported rural families.

First Industries

New inventions drove the Industrial Revolution and were often specific to one industry. The *spinning jenny* and *spinning mule* vastly increased the production of thread and yarn. The *power loom* industrialized the production of textiles, or fabrics. Factories were built to house these new machines, and new workers with diverse skills were required to operate the equipment.

The invention of the steam engine powered factory machines as well as steamships and locomotives. By the mid-1800s, trains pulled by steam-powered locomotives were faster and cheaper than any other kind of transportation. Railroads soon connected major cities across Europe and then in other nations, such as the United States. These new industries and faster modes of transportation fueled enormous economic growth.

SECONDARY SOURCE: ENGRAVING

This hand-colored woodcut shows a mill worker tending spinning mules in an industrial textile factory in the 1880s.

PRIMARY SOURCE: BOOK

" [The locomotive] has started into full life within our own time. The locomotive engine had for some years been employed in the **haulage** of coals; but it was not until the opening of the Liverpool and Manchester Railway in 1830, that the importance of the invention came to be acknowledged. The locomotive railway has since been everywhere adopted throughout Europe. In America, Canada, and the Colonies, it has opened up the boundless resources of the soil, bringing the country nearer to the towns, and the towns to the country. It has enhanced the **celerity** of time, and imparted a new series of conditions to every rank of life. "

— From *Men of Invention and Industry* by Samuel Smiles, 1895

haulage transportation of goods
celerity speed

EXAMINE THE SOURCES

1. **Contrasting** Contrast the engraving of the spinning mule with the image on the previous page of the women spinning thread at home. How did the spinning mule increase production of thread and yarn?
2. **Explaining** What does Samuel Smiles think are some benefits of the railway?

New Inventions

The Industrial Revolution also ushered in new inventions that changed people's daily lives. In 1856 Sir Henry Bessemer patented a new process for making high-quality steel efficiently and cheaply, known as the Bessemer process. Steel soon replaced iron to build lighter, smaller, and faster machines and engines. Steel was also used in buildings, railways, ships, and weapons.

Another important innovation was Alexander Graham Bell's telephone, which he invented in 1876. For the first time, telephones allowed people to speak to each other over long distances. Not everyone saw the telephone as an important invention at first, as Bell revealed in the interview excerpted here.

SECONDARY SOURCE: PAINTING

The Bessemer Converter allowed iron to be purified in large amounts so it could be processed into steel.

PRIMARY SOURCE: INTERVIEW

“ I always believed in a practical future for the telephone. But while I was experimenting on it some gentlemen who were paying the expenses of the experiments said to me, 'Mr. Bell, this is a very pretty scientific toy, but of no value practically. We wish you would not waste too much time on it.' ”

— From *Daily Evening Traveller,* September 1, 1880.

PHOTO: The History Emporium/Alamy Stock Photo; TEXT: "The Volta Prize of the French Academy Awarded to Prof. Alexander Graham Bell." Daily Evening Traveller, September 1, 1880. Alexander Graham Bell Family Papers, 1834-1974; Library of Congress, Manuscript Division.

EXAMINE THE SOURCES

1. **Drawing Conclusions** Based on the image of the Bessemer Converter, what workplace difficulties do you suppose iron workers faced?

2. **Inferring** Why do you think Bell's investors—the people paying for his experiments—thought the telephone had no practical value? Do you think their response was typical of new inventions? Explain.

3. **Speculating** In what ways do you think people's lives changed when they used a telephone for the first time?

New Methods of Production

Henry Ford became famous for new methods that increased productivity. He pioneered the assembly line for building vehicles in 1913. Between 1916 and 1917, he doubled his production from 500,000 to 1,000,000 cars a year.

PRIMARY SOURCE: AUTOBIOGRAPHY

66 A Ford car contains about five thousand parts—that is counting screws, nuts, and all. Some of the parts are fairly bulky and others are almost the size of watch parts. . . . The rapid press of production made it necessary to devise plans of production that would avoid having the workers falling over one another. . . .

The first step forward in assembly came when we began taking the work to the men instead of the men to the work. We now have two general principles in all operations—that a man shall never have to take more than one step, if possibly it can be avoided, and that no man need ever stoop over. . . .

In short, the result is this: by the aid of scientific study one man is now able to do somewhat more than four did only a comparatively few years ago. That line established the efficiency of the method and we now use it everywhere. The assembling of the motor, formerly done by one man, is now divided into eighty-four operations—those men do the work that three times their number formerly did. 99

— From *My Life and Work* by Henry Ford, 1922

PRIMARY SOURCE: PHOTOGRAPH

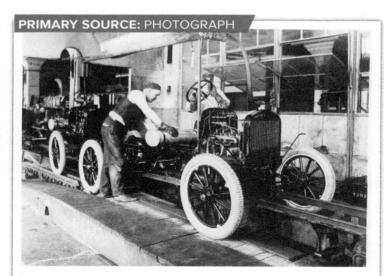

This image shows a motor vehicle on the assembly line at the Ford Motor Company in Detroit, Michigan, in the 1920s.

EXAMINE THE SOURCES

1. **Identifying Cause And Effect** What did Henry Ford do to increase the supply of vehicles?
2. **Determining Context** Ford credits his plant's increased productivity to "scientific study." How can you use context clues to determine the meaning of this term as used in this excerpt?

PHOTO: Library of Congress, Prints & Photographs Division, Detroit Publishing Company Collection, [LC-DIG-det-4a27966]; TEXT: Ford, Henry and Samuel Crowther. My Life and Work. Garden City, New York: Doubleday, Page, and Company, 1922.

Benefits of Industrialism

The assembly line and reduced transportation costs let manufacturers mass-produce goods of uniform quality quickly and with greater efficiency. Both supply and demand increased. A middle class emerged, and a consumer culture boomed. In the cities, department stores arose, made possible by steel and electricity. The stores sold a variety of new consumer goods—canned foods, ready-made clothing, clocks, bicycles, electric lights, and typewriters, for example—at affordable prices.

PRIMARY SOURCE: PHOTOGRAPH

Customers shop at Macy's Department Store in New York City around 1907. Electric signs on the building advertise other businesses.

EXAMINE THE SOURCES

1. **Analyzing** What evidence in the photo of Macy's Department Store shows the uses of steel and electricity?

2. **Inferring** What can you infer from the bicycle about daily life among the middle class?

Problems of Industrialization

One cost of industrialization was pollution. Another was that many young children had to work to help support their families.

PRIMARY SOURCE: PHOTOGRAPH

Pollution pours from Carnegie steel factories in Braddock, Pennsylvania, in 1905.

PRIMARY SOURCE: PHOTOGRAPH

Two boys work at a cotton mill in Macon, Georgia, in 1909.

EXAMINE THE SOURCES

1. **Making Connections** What kinds of health issues do you suppose the factories created for people living near them?

2. **Analyzing Points of View** Why do you think the photographer took the image of the young boys?

Complete Your Inquiry

EVALUATE SOURCES AND USE EVIDENCE

Refer back to the Compelling Question and the Supporting Questions you developed at the beginning of the lesson.

1. **Assessing** Which of the sources in this lesson do you find most striking or convincing? Why?

2. **Evaluating** Overall, what impression do these sources give you about the impact of the Industrial Revolution? Was it more positive or more negative? Explain.

3. **Gathering Sources** Which sources helped you answer the Supporting Questions and the Compelling Question? Which sources, if any, challenged what you thought you knew when you first created your Supporting Questions? What information do you still need in order to answer your questions? What other viewpoints would you like to investigate? Where would you find that information?

4. **Evaluating Sources** Identify the sources that helped answer your Supporting Questions. How reliable are the sources? How would you verify the reliability of the sources?

COMMUNICATE CONCLUSIONS

5. **Collaborating** Are the negative and positive impacts you learned about in this lesson just a thing of the past? In a small group, discuss how industrialism still causes problems today. Summarize your discussion and your group's conclusions and share them with the class.

TAKE INFORMED ACTION

Writing a Letter to a State Government Official Think about a problem caused by industrialism that still affects your state. Then write a letter—or work with classmates to write a group letter—to a state official, such as a state legislator or the governor. Let the official know what the problem is, why you think it is a problem, and what negative impacts it causes. Suggest some ways to improve the situation and ask the official to act on the problem. Be sure to include relevant evidence from your sources.

09

Reviewing What Is Economics?

Summary

Scarcity and Economic Decisions

Scarcity forces societies to make choices and trade-offs. A benefit-cost analysis can help individuals, businesses, and countries make the best choices.

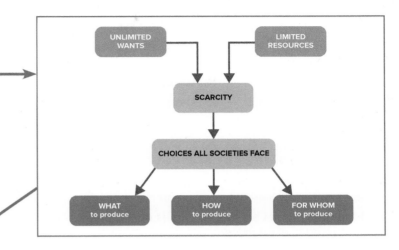

Economic Systems

The way a society answers the three basic economic questions—WHAT, HOW, and FOR WHOM to produce—determines its type of economic system. Economists organize economic systems into four general types: traditional, command, market, and mixed.

Demand, Supply, and Price in a Market Economy

Prices help answer the three basic economic questions in a market economy. The interaction of demand and supply determines price. The forces applied by surpluses and shortages work to keep a price at or near its equilibrium level.

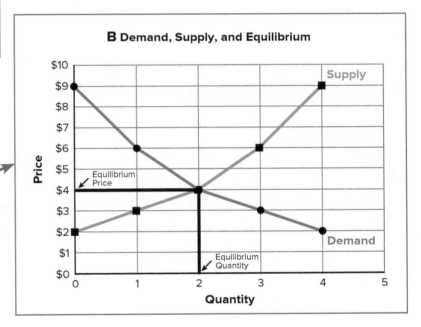

B Demand, Supply, and Equilibrium

Economic Flow and Economic Growth

The circular flow model shows how resources and products flow in one direction between businesses and consumers, while money flows in the opposite direction. Economic growth relies on additional resources and increased productivity.

Checking For Understanding

Answer the questions to see if you understood the topic content.

1. Define each of these terms:

    A. economics

    B. factors of production

    C. scarcity

    D. opportunity cost

    E. benefit-cost analysis

    F. economic system

    G. mixed market economy

    H. surplus

    I. shortage

    J. productivity

REVIEWING KEY FACTS

2. **Explaining** Why is scarcity considered the basic economic problem that people and nations face?

3. **Identifying** What are the four types of resources discussed in economics?

4. **Explaining** What does it mean when a company makes a trade-off?

5. **Identifying** In a command economy, who owns the factors of production?

6. **Explaining** How are economic decisions made in a command economy?

7. **Explaining** What determines the price of goods and services in a market economy?

8. **Summarizing** What are some disadvantages of a market economy?

9. **Explaining** What causes a change in the quantity demanded and the quantity supplied?

10. **Explaining** What most likely happens to the price of a product when the number of producers making it decreases?

11. **Explaining** If consumer demand for a product is high, what impact does that usually have on that product's price?

12. **Identifying** Which four sectors represent the buyers in the economy?

CRITICAL THINKING

13. **Synthesizing** Which type of resource is each of these an example of: delivery van, wind, bus driver, inventor of bar codes?

14. **Identifying Cause and Effect** How does competition affect the quantity and quality of goods and services in a market economy?

15. **Analyzing** What actions of the U.S. government indicate that our economic system is a mixed economy?

16. **Identifying Cause and Effect** A new technology drives down production costs. How will that affect the product's supply?

17. **Drawing Conclusions** There is a surplus of a new brand of cereal on the market. What will likely happen to the price of the cereal?

18. **Drawing Conclusions** How do both specialization and division of labor promote economic growth?

19. **Predicting** How can we ensure that we will have the natural resources needed for future economic growth?

20. **Summarizing** How do consumers take part in both the factor and the product markets?

NEED EXTRA HELP?

If You've Missed Question	1	2	3	4	5	6	7	8	9	10
Review Lesson	2, 3, 5, 6, 7	2	2	2	3	3	3	3	5	5

If You've Missed Question	11	12	13	14	15	16	17	18	19	20
Review Lesson	5	7	2	3	3	5	6	7	7	7

Apply What You Have Learned

Understanding Multiple Perspectives

Consider how economic systems influence societies when they answer the WHAT, HOW, and FOR WHOM to produce questions. Read these excerpts that provide two views of different economic systems.

ACTIVITY Comparing and Contrasting Perspectives on Economic Systems Write a brief essay answering these questions: What do the passages have in common? What economic goals does each passage present? What evidence do the authors provide to support their point of view?

> The State organizes, directs and controls the national economic activity according to a plan that guarantees the programmed development of the country, with the aim of strengthening the socialist system; satisfying the material and cultural needs of the society and its citizens with constant improvement; and promoting the development of the human being and his dignity, [and] the country's progress and security.
>
> In the preparation and execution of the programs of production and development, an active, conscious role is played by the workers in all branches of the economy, and of those in the other areas of social life.

— Article 16 from *Cuba's Constitution of 1976 with Amendments through 2002*

> Ultimately, the best evidence for free market capitalism is its performance compared to other economic systems. Free markets allowed Japan, an island with few natural resources, to recover from war and grow into the world's second-largest economy. Free markets allowed South Korea to make itself into one of the most technologically advanced societies in the world. Free markets turned small areas like Singapore and Hong Kong and Taiwan into global economic players. Today, the success of the world's largest economies comes from their embrace of free markets.
>
> Meanwhile, nations that have pursued other models have experienced devastating results. Soviet communism starved millions, bankrupted an empire, and collapsed as decisively as the Berlin Wall. Cuba, once known for its vast fields of cane, is now forced to ration sugar. And while Iran sits atop giant oil reserves, its people cannot put enough gasoline in their cars.
>
> The record is unmistakable: If you seek economic growth, if you seek opportunity, if you seek social justice and human dignity, the free market system is the way to go.

— President Bush Discusses Financial Markets and World Economy, November 13, 2008

Writing a Persuasive Argument

Consider why and how businesses make trade-offs.

ACTIVITY Writing a Report About an Economic Choice Suppose you are the marketing manager of a video game company. The creative team has two ideas for new video games. One game is for younger children and the other game is for teens.

They cost about the same amount to develop. Write a report to the company president explaining why the company can afford to invest in only one of these games, identifying the game you think is a better choice, and explaining why you think so. In your report, use economic ideas you have read about.

(l) Cuba's Constitution of 1976 with Amendments through 2002. Translated by Pam Falk, Milagros M. Gavilan and Anna I. Vellve Torras. ©Oxford University Press, Inc. Prepared for distribution on constituteproject.org with content generously provided by Oxford University Press.; (r) Bush George W. "President Bush Discusses Financial Markets and World Economy." The White House: President George W. Bush. National Archives and Records Administration, November 13, 2008. https://georgewbush-whitehouse.archives.gov/news/releases/2008/11/20081113-4.html.

Understanding Economic Concepts

The interaction of demand and supply is key to the market economy. When the price is low, consumers demand more quantities and producers tend to supply less. When the price is high, consumers tend to demand fewer quantities and producers supply more. Recall what affects demand for a product.

ACTIVITY **Applying Economic Concepts to a Graph** The graph shows a demand curve for a package of five trendy stickers. Explain what factors could produce the changes in demand that would move the demand curve to the left or to the right. Do any of the demand curves in the figure show a change in quantity demanded? Explain.

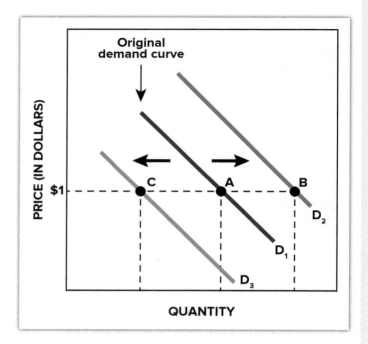

D Making Connections

Prices help answer the three basic economic questions in a market economy. Prices also measure value and send signals to both consumers and producers. Consumers can take advantage of competition to find the best price and save money.

ACTIVITY **Tracking Price Changes on a Chart and Graph** Identify a product or service that people buy regularly and that is widely sold either in your community or via the Internet. Research the price of the good or service at six businesses that offer it. Prepare a chart comparing the prices that different sellers have set for the good or service. Then make a graph showing how much a consumer can save in a year by buying the good or service at the lowest price. Share your findings with friends and family and your class.

TOPIC
12

Markets, Money, and Businesses

In the American free enterprise economy, people are free to start businesses, employ workers, and spend or save the profits.

01

Introducing Markets, Money, and Businesses

Based on Freedom

The U.S. economy is called a *FREE enterprise system* for a reason. It allows you the freedom to:

- Spend the money you earn on the products you like best

- Save or invest your money

- Choose your own job

- Start your own business if you don't want to work for someone else

- Produce goods and services that others will pay you for

- Get rewarded with *profits*—monetary rewards—for your own ideas and hard work

FOLKS, SURE THIS POCKETKNIFE IS A BETTER DEAL THAN ANY OTHER BECAUSE IT HAS A SCREWDRIVER, A LEATHER PUNCH, AND A PAIR OF SCISSORS...

...BUT THAT'S NOT ALL! IT ALSO CONTAINS A FLASHLIGHT, A MAGNETIC COMPASS, A CLOCK, A THERMOMETER AND AN ATTENTION-GETTING EMERGENCY WHISTLE!

80 - CALL NOW! 1-800-55

This cartoon shows an entrepreneur trying to convince customers that his product—a pocketknife—is unique and better than any other pocketknife. That is economics at work.

Did You Know?

The word *entrepreneur* is derived from the French word *entreprendre*, meaning "to undertake," and the English word *enterprise*, meaning "difficult or risky project that requires boldness and inventiveness." Today's entrepreneurs are exactly that: risk-taking individuals who start a new business, invent or introduce a new product, or improve a method of making something.

Entrepreneurs in America

Economic freedom allows entrepreneurs to create goods and services that will increase their chances for success. Here are a few famous historical entrepreneurs.

C. J. Walker,
Beauty Products Entrepreneur

» C. J. Walker was born Sarah Breedlove in 1867 to parents who were freed African Americans. She was poor and had little formal education but became one of the first female self-made millionaires in this country. With $1.50 in savings, Walker developed a line of beauty products for African American women. Her business earned $500,000 per year.

Walter Elias Disney,
The Walt Disney Company

» As a boy, Walt Disney loved to draw. In his early 20s, after his first film business failed, he moved to Hollywood to try again. There, Disney made a short cartoon with sound featuring a new character— Mickey Mouse. Disney and his staff then created full-length cartoons. Television provided a new outlet for his shows, and he opened Disneyland in 1954.

Levi Strauss,
Cofounder Levi's Jeans

» Levi Strauss migrated to America at age 18 to avoid Jewish discrimination in Germany. After gold was discovered in California, he traveled there to set up a store selling goods to miners. He and a tailor began making pants with rivets out of blue-dyed denim. Workers worldwide wanted the "Levi's," and Strauss & Co. made millions.

Getting Ready to Learn About . . . Markets, Money, and Businesses

Private Property

How hard would you work if you knew that anything you purchased could be taken away by someone else? Probably not as hard as you would work if you were certain that whatever you purchase is yours—and yours alone—to own.

The right to own private property is central to our democratic principles. The U.S. Constitution guarantees that no citizen will be deprived of "life, liberty, or property" without due process of law. Property ownership is also a vital part of the U.S. economy—also known as *free enterprise capitalism* (or simply referred to as *capitalism*). The ability to gain and keep private property gives citizens an incentive to work hard and save their money.

This young woman has used her hard-earned money to buy a TV. In a capitalist system, she owns her labor as well as anything she purchases from using her labor.

Labor

What job would you like to do when you enter the workforce? Key to a free enterprise economy is the freedom to choose your work. When your grandparents were young, about one-third of Americans worked in factories. They created products such as steel, food, clothing, automobiles, printed materials, and paper.

Today, far more Americans provide services instead of manufacturing goods. A service is work performed using special skills or knowledge that is of value to someone else. A hair stylist provides one kind of service. Other service industries include education, childcare, health care, food preparation, business consulting, beauty care, and social services. Whether in manufacturing goods or providing services, Americans perform a wide range of jobs in a variety of settings. They work for companies large and small, or in their own businesses.

A hairstylist performs a service as he works on his customer's hair at his salon.

Owning a Business

How would you like to wake up before dawn each morning, put in a full day of work making breads, pies, cakes, and cookies, and then work some more after the bakery has closed for the day? Owning a bakery—or any other small business—means hard work and long hours. Yet many Americans enjoy earning a living in this way. Still more dream of becoming business owners themselves.

Owning a business is one way to earn money. Like any other job, it has its risks and its rewards. Many people would rather work as someone else's employee. They may earn less, but they may also work fewer hours with less financial risk. They may also prefer having the freedom to move more easily from one job to another.

Owners of small businesses, such as this bakery owner, have much control over how they run their businesses. They also have many responsibilities.

Money

Money is a *medium of exchange,* which means money is what you give up to purchase a good or service. Money is also a way of assigning a value to a good or service. Suppose you were buying a ticket to a concert by one of your favorite singers. Which would probably get you a seat closer to the stage, the $75 or the $150 ticket? The higher-priced ticket should put you in a better location at the concert. By paying attention to the signals set by prices, we use money to measure value.

Perhaps you have earned some money—but not enough to purchase that large item you want. Where will you put the amount you have for now? You *could* stash it in a box under your bed. But the smart and safe move would be to save it in a financial institution such as a bank. To keep your money safe, the government insures your deposit against loss in case the bank fails.

Government Involvement

Government plays a role in our economy's health, but many people disagree on how big that role should be. Laws and rules regulate businesses to protect consumers. Government rules also help maintain healthy competition among businesses. With the right rules and regulations, our government hopes for a free market in which businesses and consumers feel comfortable and the national economy thrives.

The prices of goods and services, such as a gallon of gas, are given in dollars and cents.

Looking Ahead

In this topic, you will learn about capitalism and free enterprise, business organizations, the roles and responsibilities of businesses, employment and labor unions, money and financial institutions, government involvement in business, and income inequality. You will examine Compelling Questions and develop your own questions in the Inquiry Activities.

What Will You Learn?

In these lessons, you will learn:

- the features of free enterprise and capitalism.
- the characteristics, advantages, and disadvantages of sole proprietorships, partnerships, and corporations.
- how local businesses play a part in people's lives.
- who makes up the U.S. labor force, and why some workers organize into labor unions.
- the types of financial institutions and the services they provide.
- how the government helps maintain competition and regulates the economy.
- what leads to income inequality.

 COMPELLING QUESTIONS IN THE INQUIRY ACTIVITY LESSONS

- **What can be complicated about using money?**
- **Should we increase the minimum wage?**

Characteristics of Free Enterprise Capitalism

This diagram shows the characteristics of the U.S. economy. "Free enterprise capitalism" describes a market economy in which private citizens own the factors of production (land, labor, capital, entrepreneurship), and where businesses compete with little government interference.

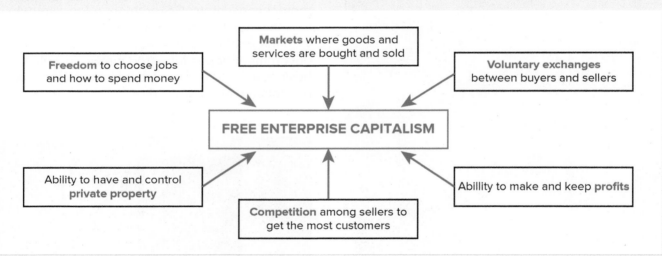

Freedom to choose jobs and how to spend money

Markets where goods and services are bought and sold

Voluntary exchanges between buyers and sellers

FREE ENTERPRISE CAPITALISM

Ability to have and control private property

Competition among sellers to get the most customers

Abillity to make and keep profits

02

Capitalism and Free Enterprise

READING STRATEGY

Integrating Knowledge and Ideas As you read the lesson, complete a web diagram by identifying the features of capitalism. Then provide an example of each feature.

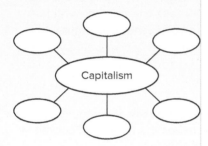

Capitalism in the United States

GUIDING QUESTION

What makes capitalism a successful economic system?

The American market economy is huge. It accounts for about one-seventh of all the economic activity in the world. How did the United States become such an economic powerhouse?

One answer is in the way in which American citizens go about satisfying their basic economic wants. People own the factors of production—the land, labor, capital, and their entrepreneurial efforts—needed to make goods and services. This kind of economic system is called capitalism. In **capitalism**, private citizens own and decide how to use the factors of production in order to satisfy their wants and needs. Our system is also called a free enterprise economy. In a **free enterprise system**, individuals and groups have the freedom to start, own, and manage businesses with little government interference.

Six unique features of the free enterprise system contribute to the economic health of the United States. These features are (1) economic freedom; (2) markets; (3) voluntary exchanges; (4) the profit motive; (5) competition; and (6) private property rights.

capitalism system in which private citizens own most, if not all, of the means of production and decide how to use them within legal limits

free enterprise economic system in which individuals and businesses are allowed to compete for profit with a minimum of government interference

Business partners prepare to open their store. Economic freedom allows entrepreneurs and businesses to choose the skills, markets, and goods and services that will increase their chances for success.

Identifying Cause and Effect How do you think the economy would be affected if people were not allowed to start their own businesses?

Economic Freedom

In the United States, economic freedom is the freedom to make our own economic decisions about the use of our land, labor, capital, and entrepreneurial efforts. As workers, Americans have the freedom to sell their labor. They can decide what jobs they will do and how to save, invest, and spend the money they earn. People are also free to become entrepreneurs and choose what type of goods or services to offer. They may also choose where to locate their business, whom they hire, and how they want to run the business.

These basic economic freedoms give the United States an important advantage over more restricted economies. These freedoms allow the marketplace to adapt quickly to changing economic conditions. As a result, the economy is more efficient and productive.

Markets

Markets are places where buyers and sellers exchange their goods and services. Two forces are at work in these exchanges: demand and supply. Who decides what is supplied and what is demanded? The buyers and sellers themselves—individuals and businesses—make these decisions. The government does not tell producers what to make or consumers what to purchase. Consumers demand products, and businesses supply them.

Because consumers can tell producers what they would like to have produced, consumers are sometimes thought of as the "king" of the market. **Consumer sovereignty** (SAH•vruhn•tee) is the term that describes the role the consumer plays. Think about it. When consumers spend, they are using their dollars to "vote" for the products they want most. This usually tells the market which products to produce, and in what quantities. Without these dollar votes, an economic system would not know which goods and services consumers prefer.

consumer sovereignty role of the consumer as ruler of the market that determines the types and quantities of goods and services produced

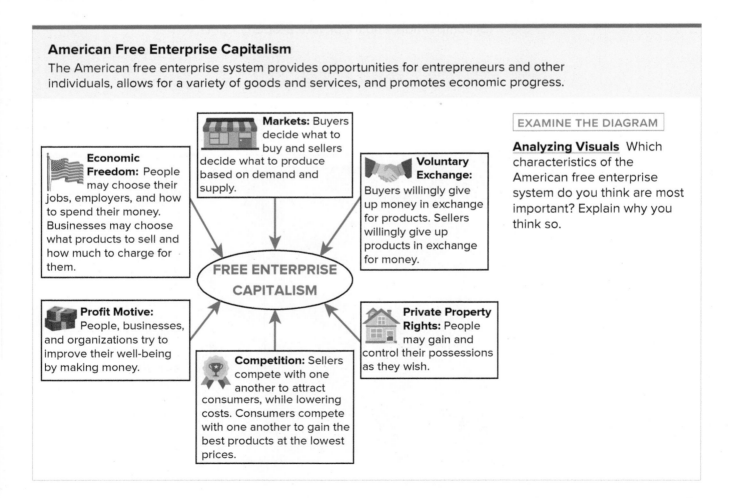

American Free Enterprise Capitalism

The American free enterprise system provides opportunities for entrepreneurs and other individuals, allows for a variety of goods and services, and promotes economic progress.

Markets: Buyers decide what to buy and sellers decide what to produce based on demand and supply.

Economic Freedom: People may choose their jobs, employers, and how to spend their money. Businesses may choose what products to sell and how much to charge for them.

Voluntary Exchange: Buyers willingly give up money in exchange for products. Sellers willingly give up products in exchange for money.

Profit Motive: People, businesses, and organizations try to improve their well-being by making money.

FREE ENTERPRISE CAPITALISM

Private Property Rights: People may gain and control their possessions as they wish.

Competition: Sellers compete with one another to attract consumers, while lowering costs. Consumers compete with one another to gain the best products at the lowest prices.

EXAMINE THE DIAGRAM

Analyzing Visuals Which characteristics of the American free enterprise system do you think are most important? Explain why you think so.

This consumer is shopping at a market on a laptop. A market is wherever a buyer and seller come together, whether in person or on online.

Markets are not perfect, though, because they cannot supply everything we need. Some types of goods, such as a system of justice, public defense, or an efficient highway network, are not easily bought and sold in markets. Still, markets are the best way to answer the WHAT to produce question. Markets establish the prices that help us make economic decisions. This is a major reason why our economic system needs only a limited role for government.

Voluntary Exchange

The activity that takes place in markets is **voluntary exchange**. Voluntary exchange is the act of buyers and sellers freely and willingly choosing to take part in marketplace transactions. These transactions are the buying and selling of goods, services, and the factors of production in exchange for money. In these exchanges, the buyer gives up money in exchange for a product. The seller gives up a product in exchange for money. When these exchanges take place voluntarily, or willingly, both the buyer and seller

are better off. If they did not benefit, the exchange would not have happened in the first place.

The Profit Motive

In a capitalist economy, people risk their savings by investing in new products and businesses. Investing is risky because the effort might not succeed. If it does, successful risk-taking results in making a profit. **Profit** is the amount of money left over from the sale of goods or services after all the costs of production have been paid. The **profit motive** is the driving force that encourages individuals and organizations to improve their material well-being. This is a major reason why capitalism is a successful economic system.

The profit motive pushes entrepreneurs to think of new or improved goods and services. It also leads them to imagine new and more productive ways of making and supplying those goods and services. The new things entrepreneurs do and the businesses they build help the American economy grow and prosper.

voluntary exchange the act of buyers and sellers freely and willingly engaging in market transactions

profit the money a business receives for its products or services over and above its costs

profit motive the driving force that encourages individuals and organizations to improve their material well-being

Without entrepreneurs, we would not have so many useful and interesting products such as computers, cell phones, Google maps, social media platforms, medicines and medical cures, and many other things that make life more comfortable or enjoyable. Think of the contributions made by entrepreneurs such as Elon Musk (inventor of PayPal, Tesla, and SpaceX rockets); Jack Ma (creator of Alibaba, the "Chinese Amazon"); Sundar Pichai (Google entrepreneur and Alphabet CEO), Beyoncé (singer-songwriter); and Caine Monroy (9-year-old founder of Caine's Arcade and YouTube star).

Competition

Starting a business does not ensure success. Businesses compete with one another. In fact, capitalism thrives on **competition**—the struggle among businesses with similar products to attract consumers. The most efficient producers sell goods at lower prices. Lower prices attract buyers. If other producers cannot improve their productivity or offer a better-quality product, they might be forced out of business. Competition leads to greater efficiency, higher-quality products, more satisfied customers, and more innovative products.

The Internet is just one innovation that has changed our lives. Consumers use the Internet to search for products, compare prices and features, and stream music or movies to their computers and tablets. Producers can sell their goods directly to buyers without having to put their products in stores. Schools can deliver entire curriculums to students when pandemics prevent them from going to the classroom. Businesses can hire more workers without having to provide for additional offices or more workspaces.

competition the struggle that goes on between buyers and sellers to get the best products at the lowest prices

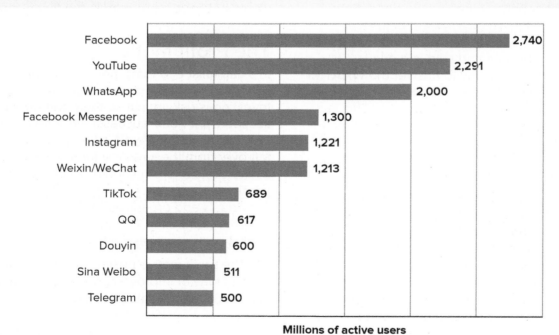

Most Popular Social Networks, 2021

Competition in a free enterprise system leads to a huge variety of choices, including among social media platforms.

Platform	Millions of active users
Facebook	2,740
YouTube	2,291
WhatsApp	2,000
Facebook Messenger	1,300
Instagram	1,221
Weixin/WeChat	1,213
TikTok	689
QQ	617
Douyin	600
Sina Weibo	511
Telegram	500

Millions of active users

Source: www.statista.com

EXAMINE THE GRAPH

1. **Analyzing Visuals** How many people actively used TikTok in 2021?
2. **Making Connections** What role does entrepreneurship have in a free enterprise system?

These shoppers willingly exchange money to purchase products. A voluntary exchange benefits both the buyer and the seller, or the exchange would not occur. In addition, private property rights give this seller the right to use her store property as she wishes.

Private Property Rights

Under capitalism, people and businesses have **private property rights**. This means they have the freedom to own and use their property as they wish. They can even choose to **dispose** of, or get rid of, that property. Property rights give Americans the incentive to work, save, and invest because we can keep any gains we earn. Private property has another important benefit: people tend to take better care of things they own.

✓ **CHECK FOR UNDERSTANDING**

1. **Explaining** Why do people risk their money to start businesses?
2. **Identifying** What are private property rights? How are you affected by them?

Origins of U.S. Capitalism

GUIDING QUESTION

How is the history of capitalism associated with the Founders?

In 1776 Adam Smith, a Scottish philosopher, published a book titled *The Wealth of Nations*. The book opposed the existing economic system of mercantilism. **Mercantilism** was the belief that government should control trade: increase the amount of goods a country exports (in exchange for gold and silver) and decrease the amount of goods imported. Smith argued that, instead, the best way for society to advance is for people to work for their own self-interest, or their own well-being. Because of this, Adam Smith is considered to be the father of economics.

Adam Smith understood that businesses want to earn a profit. That desire will lead them to make products that best meet people's needs and wants. In a similar fashion, people compete to sell their labor, and employers compete to purchase it. The result is an efficient use of resources and a stable society. Smith argued that all of this happens naturally, "as if by an invisible hand." In other words, market exchanges work best with little government interference.

From the writings of Smith and others came the idea of **laissez-faire economics**. *Laissez-faire* (LEH·SAY·FEHR), a French term, means "to let alone." According to this philosophy, government should not interfere in the marketplace. Instead, it should limit itself to those actions needed to **ensure**, or make certain, that competition takes place or in special cases where a market fails.

---

private property rights the freedom to own and use our property as we choose as long as we do not interfere with the rights of others

dispose get rid of

mercantilism economic system in which government promotes exports and restricts imports to increase the country's stock of gold and silver

laissez-faire economics belief that government should not interfere in the marketplace

ensure to make certain of an outcome

Shoppers purchase from sellers on Mulberry Street in New York City around 1900. Then, as now, the American economy was based on free enterprise. And just as voters in a democracy elect public servants, consumers in a free enterprise system use their dollars to "vote" for their choices of goods and services.

Drawing Conclusions Who or what is "let alone" in a laissez-faire system?

As time went on, economists began to use graphs and math to describe the way markets worked. Still, people never forgot that government was needed to solve some problems that markets could not solve. In fact, government was needed to *protect* markets so they could work efficiently, as Adam Smith thought they could.

Clearly, many of the country's Founders were influenced by *The Wealth of Nations*. James Madison read it, and Alexander Hamilton borrowed from it in his writings. Thomas Jefferson thought Smith's *Wealth of Nations* was the *best* book. The Founders would include Smith's idea of "limited government involvement" when they wrote the U.S. Constitution and Bill of Rights that narrowed the specific powers of government. They reasoned that a democracy, like a market economy, also works best when government power is limited.

✓ **CHECK FOR UNDERSTANDING**

1. **Explaining** What role did Adam Smith believe government should play in the marketplace?

2. **Making Connections** How did the writings of Adam Smith influence the economy of the United States?

LESSON ACTIVITIES

1. **Informative/Explanatory Writing** Adam Smith said that people work for their own self-interest. Write a paragraph describing this idea and whether you agree with it. Use examples of particular jobs to support your opinion.

2. **Collaborating** With a partner, write a public service announcement that explains the key features of capitalism and free enterprise in the U.S. economy.

03
Business Organization

Sole Proprietorships

GUIDING QUESTION

What are the advantages and disadvantages of a sole proprietorship?

Have you ever made money by mowing lawns or by babysitting? If you have, you had a small business. Every type of business organization is based on who owns the company and who provides the money to keep it running. Your lawnmowing or babysitting business probably took a simple form. In fact, you were probably the sole proprietor of a sole proprietorship!

A **sole proprietorship** (pruh•PRY•uh•tuhr•SHIP)—also simply called a proprietorship—is a business owned and operated by one person. All businesses in this form are small businesses. Usually they serve the area in which they are located. You see these businesses every day. Dry cleaners, auto repair shops, beauty shops, and local restaurants often take this form.

Sole proprietorships have several advantages. They are easy to organize, which is why they are the most common form of business organization. Sole proprietors are their own bosses. They decide what products or services they will sell. They decide what hours the business will be open. They make decisions without having to consult, or check with, other owners. As the only owner, a sole proprietor receives all the profits from the business.

sole proprietorship a business owned and operated by a single person

A bakery owner offers goods for sale at his store. Among sole proprietorships, the most popular types of businesses are professional, legal, and technical services; construction companies; and retailers—or stores and merchants.

Analyzing Visuals Which business type is shown in the photograph?

lightfieldstudios/123RF

Forms of Business Organization

Partnerships and proprietorships together account for more than 80 percent of all businesses but about one-third of total sales.

Number of Businesses

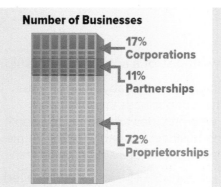

17% Corporations

11% Partnerships

72% Proprietorships

Sales

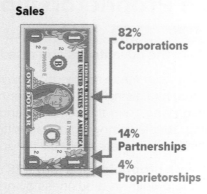

82% Corporations

14% Partnerships

4% Proprietorships

Source: IRS, Statistics of Income Division, 2020

EXAMINE THE DIAGRAM

1. **Analyzing Visuals** What percentage of all businesses are sole proprietorships? What percentage of businesses are partnerships?

2. **Inferring** Why do you think there is such a large difference between the number of proprietorships and their share of all sales?

Sole proprietorships also have some disadvantages. First, the owner may find it difficult to raise **financial capital**. This is the money needed to run or expand a business. Unless the business is run from the owner's home, the proprietor must buy or rent the place from which it operates. The owner might also have to buy equipment and supplies. If the business does not make enough money, the owner will have to use personal money to meet these costs.

Second, sole proprietors have no limits on their **liability** (LY•uh•BIH•luh•tee), or legal responsibility, for the business. This can be a problem if the business cannot pay its debts or loses a lawsuit. Then the owner's personal property—such as a home or car—may have to be sold to pay the business's debts. Third, sole proprietors might have trouble hiring skilled workers. Workers might prefer to take a job with a large company with better benefits, such as health insurance.

✓ CHECK FOR UNDERSTANDING

1. **Identifying** In a sole proprietorship, who receives all profits?

2. **Summarizing** What challenges and risks does the owner of a sole proprietorship face?

---

financial capital the money used to run or expand a business

liability the legal responsibility for something, such as an action or a debt

Partnerships

GUIDING QUESTION

What are the advantages and disadvantages of a partnership?

Suppose you are making so much money mowing lawns that you have little time for anything else. You could hire a helper. You have another option, too. You could find someone who could provide the extra help and use their own equipment in return for a share of the business. In this case, your business is no longer a sole proprietorship. It is now a **partnership**—a business that two or more people own and operate together.

As with your lawn-mowing business, partnerships sometimes start as sole proprietorships. In some cases, a single owner cannot raise enough money to expand the business. Or the owner may have enough financial capital but not have all the skills needed to run the business well. In either case, the owner may seek a partner with the money or skills that the business needs to grow.

How Partnerships Are Structured

A partnership is officially organized when two or more people sign a legal agreement called *articles of partnership*. This document states

---

partnership a business owned by two or more people

what role each partner will play in the business. It tells how much money each will contribute. It **clarifies**, or explains, how each partner will share in the profit or loss of the business. The document also states how each partner can be removed or how new partners can be added. Finally, it describes how the partnership can be ended if the partners decide to do so.

Three kinds of partnerships can be formed. The first is a *general partnership*. In this type, all partners are called general partners. They all own a share of the business, and each partner is responsible for its management and debts.

The second type is a *limited partnership*. In this form, some owners are limited partners, and some are general partners. Limited partners own a share of the business. However, they have no direct involvement in running or managing it. Instead, they usually just provide money the business needs to operate. The general partners run the business and are responsible for everything, including all debts.

The *limited liability partnership* (LLP) is the third and most common kind of partnership. It is popular because it protects all partners, even the general partners, if the business has a lot of debts. This makes the LLP a popular choice of doctors, lawyers, dentists, and most professional people. The initials *LLP* after a business's name show that it is a limited liability partnership.

Partnerships can be any size. They may have two partners, with no other employees. In other cases, a small firm of four or five partners may be just the right size for the market it serves. Other partnerships, such as major law or accounting firms, may have hundreds of partners providing services in many locations across the country.

Advantages of Partnerships

The biggest advantage that partnerships have over sole proprietorships is that they can raise more money to grow and hire more employees. A partnership has more than one owner, so it usually has more capital. Current partners can add new partners to provide additional funds. It is also easier for a partnership to borrow money from a bank.

Another advantage of partnerships is that each partner often brings special talents to the business. For example, one partner in an insurance agency may be good at selling policies to new customers. The other partner may be better at providing services to people who already have policies. This business will probably be more successful than if just one person owned and operated it.

Disadvantages of Partnerships

The main drawback of a general partnership is the same as that of a sole proprietorship. Each general partner has unlimited liability. He or she is fully responsible for all business debts.

What does this mean? Suppose that you are in a lawnmowing business with two other partners. Each of you had agreed to share one-third of the business profits and one-third of the losses. Now suppose that one of your partners buys an expensive new mower at the end of the season just as your business income drops. Or suppose that one of the business's customers gets hurt by your equipment, or the mower throws a stone through a car windshield. The business could be sued if neither the business nor your partners have enough money to cover the debt or the damages. You, as the remaining general partner, would have to pay 100 percent of the cost out of your personal funds!

✓ **CHECK FOR UNDERSTANDING**

1. **Identifying** What are three types of partnership?
2. **Comparing** How are a sole proprietorship and a general partnership alike regarding liability?

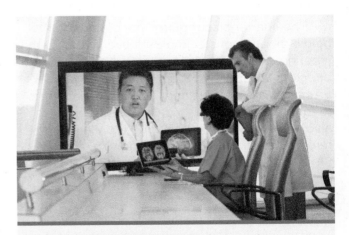

Three doctors consult about a patient's health. Doctors may be sued if patients think they were injured by the doctors' actions. For this reason, many medical practices are limited liability partnerships, or LLPs.

Drawing Conclusions What disadvantage of partnerships does this type of business solve?

clarify explain

Corporations

GUIDING QUESTION

How is a corporation structured, and what are its advantages and disadvantages?

The third major form of business is very different from either a sole proprietorship or a partnership. This third form is the corporation, the most complicated form of business. You can usually tell that a business is a corporation if the abbreviation *Inc.* follows the company's name. *Inc.* stands for "incorporated." Many corporations, such as Amazon and Apple, don't include the abbreviation in their name, however.

A **corporation** is a business owned by many people but is legally treated as though it were a single person. This makes the corporation separate from the people who own it. Under the law, a corporation has many of the rights and responsibilities that an individual has. Like a real person, a corporation can enter into contracts, sue and be sued, own property, and pays taxes.

How a Corporation is Organized

The state where the corporation is formed grants a **charter** to a group of investors. This permits the investors to sell ownership shares in the corporation. The ownership shares are called stock certificates, or **stocks** for short. Those who own the stocks are called stockholders or shareholders. This sale of stocks is how the corporation raises money to go into business.

The charter also requires the corporation to hold a meeting of stockholders every year. At this meeting, the stockholders elect a board of directors to represent them. The **board of directors** hires a president and other managers to run the company on a daily basis. The board also meets several times during the year to review the corporation's performance. Stockholders are not involved in the day-to-day operation of the company.

---

corporation type of business organization owned by many people but treated by law as though it were a person

charter state government document granting permission to organize a corporation

stocks shares of ownership in a corporation; same as stock certificates

board of directors the people elected by the shareholders of a corporation to act on their behalf

The Corporation's Advantages

The corporation has three main advantages. The biggest advantage is the ease of raising financial capital. It can raise huge amounts of money by selling stock. It can also borrow money by selling bonds, which are formal loan agreements between a borrower and a lender. It can then use that money to expand operations, open up businesses in new locations, or buy new equipment. It can also raise money to research new products. This ease of raising money is one reason why the corporation is the most common form of business for large companies.

The ease of raising money and favorable tax rates on corporate profits are why some corporations are so huge. The yearly sales of the biggest corporations are larger than the economies of most of the world's countries. For example, if Walmart were a country, it would be the twenty-third largest country in the world.

A second advantage of the corporation is limited liability. The corporation, not the owners, is responsible for its debts. The owners' property

General Motors (GM) is a major American corporation. Although it is headquartered in Detroit, Michigan, GM does business in more than 120 countries.

Identifying What document spells out how much stock a corporation can sell?

Corporate Structure

Every corporation has shareholders, a board of directors, a management team, and employees. The person who runs the business may be called the president, chief executive officer (CEO), or chief operating officer (COO).

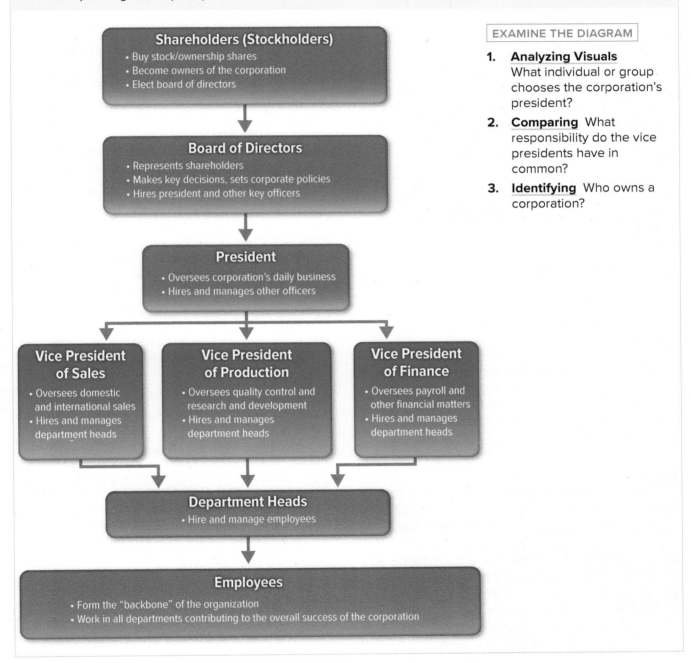

Shareholders (Stockholders)
- Buy stock/ownership shares
- Become owners of the corporation
- Elect board of directors

Board of Directors
- Represents shareholders
- Makes key decisions, sets corporate policies
- Hires president and other key officers

President
- Oversees corporation's daily business
- Hires and manages other officers

Vice President of Sales
- Oversees domestic and international sales
- Hires and manages department heads

Vice President of Production
- Oversees quality control and research and development
- Hires and manages department heads

Vice President of Finance
- Oversees payroll and other financial matters
- Hires and manages department heads

Department Heads
- Hire and manage employees

Employees
- Form the "backbone" of the organization
- Work in all departments contributing to the overall success of the corporation

EXAMINE THE DIAGRAM

1. **Analyzing Visuals** What individual or group chooses the corporation's president?

2. **Comparing** What responsibility do the vice presidents have in common?

3. **Identifying** Who owns a corporation?

cannot be touched to pay those debts. This advantage is important. Suppose some people want to try a risky business like building a nuclear power plant. They would first form a corporation because of its limited liability. If something were to go terribly wrong and the company were sued, the investors would be protected from losing their personal property to settle the case.

The third advantage is that ownership can easily be transferred. Proprietorships and partnerships may end when an owner resigns or dies. When a stockholder no longer wants to own part of a corporation, however, he or she simply sells the stock to someone else. Or, if a stockholder dies, his or her family receives the stock. This means that only the ownership changes, not the company or its name.

The Corporation's Disadvantages

Corporations also have some disadvantages. The government regulates them more than any other form of business. By law, corporations must make their financial records public. This means they have to release reports on expenses and profits on a regular basis. They must also hold a stockholders' meeting at least once a year.

Major corporations have millions of stockholders. If some are unhappy about the way the company is run, it is hard for them to unite and get managers to make changes. They can write a letter to the board or sell their shares and use the money for something else.

Other Business Forms

Corporations have been in the United States long before it was an independent nation. Jamestown, the first English settlement in the Americas, was founded in 1607 by the Virginia Company, a *joint-stock company* similar to today's corporation.

One type of business that has become very common in recent years is the **franchise** (FRAN•CHYZ). A franchise is a business in which the owner is the only seller of a product in a certain area. The owner pays a fee to the supplier for that right. The owner also gives that supplier a share of the profits. Fast-food restaurants and hotels are often franchises. Other popular franchises include Great Clips and Jiffy Lube.

To own a Wendy's franchise, a business owner has to buy the right to operate the restaurant and then pay a percentage of its monthly sales to the Wendy's corporation.

Speculating What might attract a person to buy a franchise like this one?

The franchise owner benefits because there is no competition from another nearby seller. The supplier also helps the franchise owner run the business. The biggest disadvantage is that the franchise owner does not have complete control over the business. The national company often has many rules the franchise owner must follow.

All the businesses you have read about so far have a common goal—to make a profit. However, there is another type of business called a **nonprofit organization**. These organizations provide goods and services without trying to make a profit. Many public hospitals and charitable organizations, such as foodbanks and the Red Cross, are nonprofit organizations.

Cooperatives, or co-ops, are another type of nonprofit organization. This is a business formed by people who want to benefits its members. Different kinds of co-ops exist. A consumer co-op buys goods in large amounts. Members then get those goods at low prices. Service co-ops provide members with services such as insurance or loans. Producer co-ops help members sell their products to large central markets where they can get better prices. Ocean Spray is a producer co-op that promotes the sale of cranberries.

✓ **CHECK FOR UNDERSTANDING**

1. **Explaining** How does a corporation raise financial capital?

2. **Analyzing** How does a cooperative work?

LESSON ACTIVITIES

1. **Argumentative Writing** If you owned a business, would you rather be a sole proprietor or a partner? Write a paragraph explaining why. Include evidence and examples to support your argument.

2. **Presenting** With a partner, select and research a specific nonprofit organization. Find a description of the organization, who its members are, who benefits from it and how, and the problems it faces. Create a multimedia presentation to present your findings to the class.

franchise company that has permission to sell the supplier's goods or services in a particular area in exchange for payment

nonprofit organization business that does not intend to make a profit for the goods and services it provides

Roles and Responsibilities of Businesses

READING STRATEGY

Integrating Knowledge and Ideas As you read this lesson, identify the responsibilities of businesses to their consumers and their employees.

Responsibilities of Businesses	
To Consumers	To Employees

Social Responsibilities of Businesses

GUIDING QUESTION

In what ways do businesses help their communities?

Does your school benefit, or gain, from help given by a business? That might seem like an unusual question, but businesses help schools in many ways. For example, do you play on a sports team? Does a local business sponsor that team? Has your school club ever held a car wash at the parking lot of a local business? Does a store in the area sell school supplies at a discount?

Businesses help their communities in many ways. Businesses play several important roles in society. As producers, they supply the food, clothing, and shelter we use to meet basic needs. They also produce many goods and services that make life more enjoyable and comfortable. Along with being producers, they also have a **social responsibility**. This is the obligation to pursue goals that benefit society as well as themselves.

social responsibility the obligation businesses have to pursue goals that benefit society as well as themselves

The Tide corporation has a truck that carries enough washers and dryers to do 300 loads of laundry a day. It sends the truck to areas hit by natural disasters to help provide clean clothes to people in distress.

Inferring How can this kind of action help a business?

Frederick Breedon/Getty Images

Have you ever eaten a White Castle hamburger? That fast-food chain was founded by a family named the Ingrams. The Ingrams have given more than $29 million to support education. They donate this money through the family's **foundation**, an institution created to promote the public good.

People who have enjoyed success in business, such as the Ingrams, can be very generous. Bill Gates, the founder of Microsoft Corporation, has given away some $50 billion. His foundation aids a wide variety of causes in the United States and around the world. For instance, his foundation **contributed**, or provided, $500 million to public schools. It also gave more than $250 million to fight diseases in Africa, Asia, and South America; and another $250 million to fight the COVID-19 pandemic.

In addition, many corporations have set up their own foundations. These groups give money to support causes they believe are important. The Walmart Foundation has given more than $40 million to help veterans returning to the workforce through job training and education.

Corporations give away about $20 billion each year. Some provide free goods or services.

For example, many drug companies give their products to people who need the medicines but cannot afford to pay for them. Apple and GAP give part of their profits to a fund that fights infectious diseases in 144 countries. GAP also donates millions of pieces of clothing to refugees. American Express has long been involved in helping disaster victims. The company gives money to relief agencies. These agencies use that money to provide food, clothing, and shelter for the victims. Another American Express program helps groups that are trying to preserve important historical sites or natural areas.

Donations do not come from just large American companies. About 75 percent of small companies also give money. Some support groups in their area. Others give to causes they believe in. You have seen examples of how some help schools. Some law firms or accountants provide free services to poor people or nonprofit groups.

✓ CHECK FOR UNDERSTANDING

1. **Explaining** What is social responsibility, and how do businesses show it?

2. **Identifying** What are some of the good causes that American companies have donated to?

---

foundation organization established by a company or an individual to provide money for a particular purpose, especially for charity or research

contribute to provide or give

In recent years, the Consumer Product Safety Commission has ordered the recall of many toys painted with dangerous lead paint. It has also recalled millions of riding toys because of a fire hazard.

Identifying Cause and Effect What incentives do businesses have to meet their responsibilities to consumers?

A report provides information about how a corporation is doing financially. Corporate managers must be transparent to stockholders about such information.

Other Business Responsibilities

GUIDING QUESTION

How do businesses carry out their responsibilities to their consumers, owners, and employees?

As they carry out their many activities, businesses have different responsibilities to the groups they interact with. Laws require firms to meet certain obligations. Business owners and managers may face serious problems or even legal action if they do not follow those laws. They also may suffer a loss of reputation, which might result in a loss of business.

Responsibilities to Consumers

Businesses have important responsibilities to their customers, the people who buy their goods and services. First, businesses must sell safe products that work properly. Services must be reliable. A new video game should run without flaws. An auto mechanic should change a car's oil correctly. Many companies guarantee their products and services for a period of time. They replace or redo those that do not work as they should. Second, businesses also have the responsibility to tell the truth in their advertising. Third, businesses should treat all customers fairly.

Responsibilities to Owners

Another responsibility is to the stockholders, who are the owners of the business. This is especially crucial for corporations. In this case, the people who own the company are not the same people who run it. To protect stockholders, corporations have to release financial reports regularly. Making this information public is called **transparency**. The information is published to give investors full and accurate information. People can analyze the facts before they choose to invest money in the company.

Sometimes the managers of a corporation are not honest in these reports. The government can then prosecute them for breaking the law. For example, the scandal involving the company Theranos showed the problems that arise when these reports are not truthful. The company raised hundreds of millions of dollars from investors. Theranos claimed that its miniature testing device could perform hundreds of laboratory tests by analyzing a single drop of blood. But its claims—and its financial statements—were false. When the company went out of business, investors lost all of their money.

Responsibilities to Employees

Finally, businesses have responsibilities to their workers. They are required to maintain a safe workplace. They must also treat all workers fairly and without discrimination. They cannot treat employees differently because of race, religion, gender, age, or disability. Doing so is against the law.

transparency the process of making business deals or conditions more visible to everyone

chormail/123RF

Google, the Internet company, has features in its offices to try to make the workplace enjoyable, comfortable, and healthy for employees. Workers can use company-provided bicycles and scooters to move from one building to another. Game rooms give employees a chance to relax and release tension from work.

Predicting How can a company benefit from taking these steps?

Companies cannot pay different wages to men and women who do the same work, for instance. Nor can they fire workers because they reach an older age. Such decisions must be based on the quality of the work the employees perform.

Many businesses try to help workers by providing benefits or services. For example, many companies help employees with the costs of trade school or college. Some pay for programs to help workers stop smoking, or provide childcare or fitness centers for workers. Others provide breakfast, lunch, and snacks at the office for their workers.

Health insurance is a benefit that many companies have traditionally given to their workers. However, as health insurance costs increased, many businesses grew worried about the cost of this benefit. Some stopped providing it. Others shifted more of the cost of this insurance to their workers. In 2010 Congress passed a law, the Affordable Care Act, requiring businesses to provide health insurance. Some parts of the law are designed to limit increases in the cost of health care and health insurance. The law also gives tax credits to small businesses when they buy health insurance. These limits and credits were meant to make the cost of the benefit easier to meet.

Helping workers in these ways benefits the employer as well as the worker. A worker who is in good health misses less work than one who is not. That worker also has more energy and can be more productive on the job. Benefits also make the worker happier and less likely to leave the job, which helps the employer maintain good workers.

✓ **CHECK FOR UNDERSTANDING**

1. **Explaining** Why is it important for corporations to publish financial information regularly?
2. **Summarizing** How does the government push businesses to act responsibly?

LESSON ACTIVITIES

1. **Argumentative Writing** A business has responsibilities to its customers, its employees, its owners, and its local community. Which of these responsibilities do you think is most important? Explain your point of view in a paragraph.

2. **Collaborating** The Equal Employment Opportunity Commission (EEOC) is a part of the federal government. Its job is to ensure that job applicants and workers are not discriminated against. Go to the EEOC website to learn its powers and how it works to uphold the law. With a partner, summarize what you find. Then write a public service announcement that explains your summary information.

Employment and Unions

Employment

GUIDING QUESTION

Who makes up the U.S. labor force, and how has it changed over time?

Every month, the Bureau of Labor Statistics conducts an important **survey**, or examination, that tells us who is working and who is not working in the United States. Specifically, this survey tells us about changes that might be happening to the nearly half of our population that makes up the civilian labor force. By definition, the **civilian labor force (CLF)** includes "all persons 16 years of age or over who are working or not working but are able and willing to work."

Some parts of our population are not part of the civilian labor force. This includes young students like yourselves who are not yet 16 years old, even if you work in a job after school. Nor does it include army, navy, or

survey examination, review

civilian labor force group made up of "all persons 16 years of age or over who are working or not working but are able and willing to work" and who are not in the military

Population and the Civilian Labor Force, 2020

The civilian labor force (CLF) includes both "Employed" and "Unemployed" people over age 16 who are willing and able to work—and are not in the military. In 2020, the total CLF was 160,808,000, and the number of unemployed was 13,025,000.

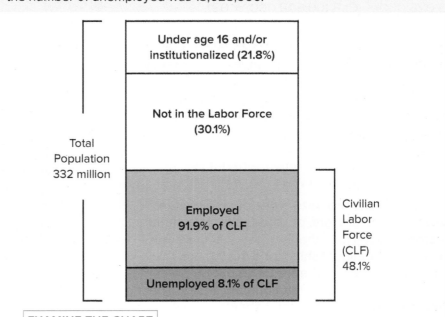

EXAMINE THE CHART

Contrasting What is the difference between those "Not in the Labor Force" and those who are "Unemployed"?

GO ONLINE Explore the Student Edition eBook and find interactive maps, charts, graphs, and tools.

E73

other armed services because the survey includes only "civilian" (nonmilitary) workers. Also, people confined to institutions such as hospitals or prisons are not part of the labor force.

Another major group includes people defined as "not in the labor force" because they choose not to work, even though they could. This group includes stay-at-home parents and retired workers. After all these groups are accounted for, we are left with the civilian labor force.

The **Population and the Civilian Labor Force, 2020** chart shows that 48.1 percent of our total population was in the civilian labor force. The chart also shows that the CLF has two parts. The first includes "employed" people. They made up 91.9 percent of the CLF who were working and had a job. The second category—the "unemployed"—amounted to 8.1 percent of the CLF and included those who did not have a job but were willing to work if they could find one. This is the category we are concerned about.

Unemployment Rate

The term *unemployment rate* is often in the news. The **unemployment rate** is the percentage of people in the CLF who are unemployed at any given time. We get this percentage by dividing the actual number of unemployed people by the size of the CLF. The unemployment rate in the chart is 8.1 percent, or (Number of unemployed 13,025,000) ÷ (CLF 160,808,000) = .081.

U.S. Employment Then and Now

In the past 50 years or so, changes have greatly affected the country's civilian labor force. One change is the kinds of jobs available, and thus a change in demand and supply for specific work skills. Some 50 years ago, for example, computer programmers were not in demand. Now they are. Another change is that unions are not as powerful as they once were.

Economists organize types of employment into four main sectors, or categories. The *primary sector* includes jobs that harvest or access raw materials. Farming, fishing, and mining are primary activities. In the 1850s, about 66 percent of Americans worked in the primary sector. The **Employment by Sector** chart shows that 1.4 percent worked in this sector in 2020.

unemployment rate percentage of people in the civilian labor force who are not working but are looking for jobs

The *secondary sector* includes jobs that change raw materials into finished products. Factory and construction workers perform secondary activities. In the 1970s, about 22 percent were employed in manufacturing jobs. That percentage dropped to 13 percent in 2020.

The *tertiary* [TUHR•shee•air•ee] *sector* is often called the "service sector." People in these jobs perform a service, such as restaurant work or shipping packages, but do not create a finished good. This was the largest sector in 2020.

The fourth, or *quaternary* [kwah•TUHR•nuh•ree] *sector*, is sometimes called the "knowledge sector." It includes specialized workers who provide information-based services, such as educators, doctors, and government officials.

✓ **CHECK FOR UNDERSTANDING**

1. **Identifying** What four groups does the Bureau of Labor Statistics divide the total population into?
2. **Identifying Cause and Effect** What caused the U.S. civilian labor force to change in the past 50 years?

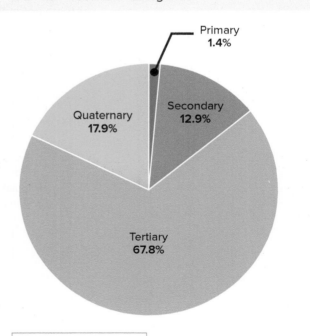

Employment by Sector, 2020
Economists organize types of employment into four main sectors or categories.

Primary 1.4%
Secondary 12.9%
Quaternary 17.9%
Tertiary 67.8%

EXAMINE THE CHART

Making Connections What four sectors do jobs get split into, and what is an example of a job found in each sector?

Types of Unions

Labor unions can be categorized as either trade (craft) unions or industrial unions.

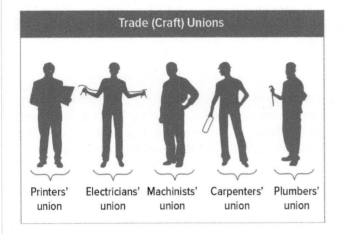

Trade (Craft) Unions

Printers' union · Electricians' union · Machinists' union · Carpenters' union · Plumbers' union

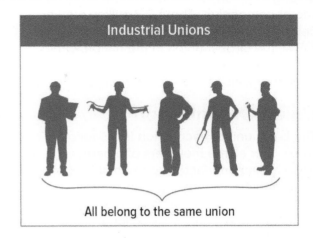

Industrial Unions

All belong to the same union

EXAMINE THE DIAGRAMS

Contrasting How does a trade union differ from an industrial union?

Organized Labor

GUIDING QUESTION

What is the role of organized labor in the U.S. economy?

The list below describes workers' rights that many take for granted in today's workplace:

- Weekends off from work
- The eight-hour work-day
- Safety measures at the workplace
- Paid vacation (or sick days)
- Days off for national holidays
- Extra pay for working overtime
- Minimum wage guarantee

Many of these rights came about because workers "organized" and demanded changes from employers. In other words, organized workers formed labor unions. A **labor union** is an organization of workers that seeks to improve its members' wages and working conditions.

Since 1970, the size of the labor force has nearly doubled. In those years, however, the number of workers belonging to labor unions has fallen. In the early 1970s, about one of every four workers belonged to a union. As of 2020, however, only one worker in ten was a union member. One reason for the decline in union membership is the shift from manufacturing jobs to service jobs. Also, many employers have kept their workplaces union-free.

Unions still play an important role in the United States, however. Workers in many industries belong to unions. Large numbers of coal miners, airline pilots, and truck drivers are union members, for example. Unions have also seen gains in the public sector, where teachers and government employees work.

Types of Unions

There are two types of unions. A union whose members all work at the same craft or trade is called a *trade union*. Examples are the unions formed by bakers or printers. A union that brings together workers from the same industry is called an *industrial union*. An industrial union might have electricians, carpenters, and laborers who work together to manufacture a product. An example is the United Auto Workers (UAW).

Unions have changed over time. In the past, they were formed mostly by industrial workers. Today, however, even actors and professional

labor union association of workers organized to improve wages and working conditions

athletes have unions. Another change is the increase of government workers who are union members. In fact, more government workers belong to unions than do workers for private sector companies. About 2.3 million workers belong to the National Education Association (NEA), the largest union in the nation. Other government workers, like police officers and firefighters, also have their own unions.

Union Organization

The basic unit of each union is the *local*. A local consists of all the members of a particular union who work in one factory, one company, or one geographic area. All of a union's locals together form the national union. This organization represents the locals on a national level.

Many national unions belong to the American Federation of Labor and Congress of Industrial Organizations (AFL-CIO). The AFL-CIO is the nation's largest federation (alliance or partnership of unions). It has about 12.7 million members. The next-largest federation is Change to Win, with about 4.5 million members.

Unions in the Workplace

Employees in a workplace cannot form a union unless most of them vote in favor of it. An agency of the federal government, the National Labor Relations Board (NLRB), makes sure these elections are carried out fairly and honestly.

A common way that unions organize a workplace is with a *union shop*. In these workplaces, companies can hire any person as an

Right-to-Work States

The map shows states with right-to-work laws. Right-to-work laws were made possible by a federal law passed in 1947.

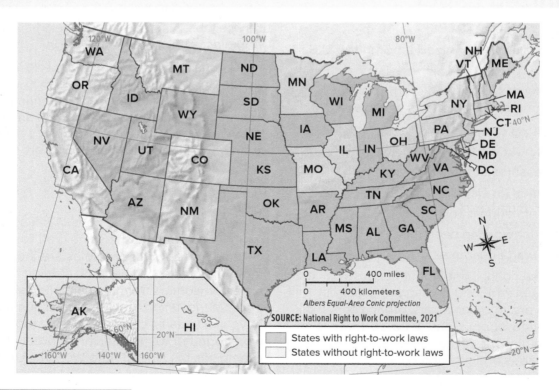

SOURCE: National Right to Work Committee, 2021

States with right-to-work laws
States without right-to-work laws

GEOGRAPHY CONNECTION

1. **Exploring Regions** In what regions of the country are right-to-work states mostly found?
2. **Patterns and Movement** Why do you think states pass right-to-work laws for companies located within their borders?

E76

employee. Once someone is hired, though, they must join the union shortly after starting to work.

Many companies do not like the union shop. In some states, companies have convinced state governments to outlaw these arrangements. Nearly half the states have **right-to-work laws**, which ban union shops.

Other states have what is called a *modified union shop*. In this situation, workers do not have to join a union. But if they do join, they must remain in the union as long as they hold their job. Some workplaces are *agency shops*. In an agency shop, workers who do not join the union still must pay a fee to the union for representing them.

✓ CHECK FOR UNDERSTANDING

1. **Contrasting** For what purposes do unions form?
2. **Summarizing** What role do unions play in the United States today?

Labor Negotiations

GUIDING QUESTION

How do labor and management negotiate?

When a company's workers have a union, the union and the company carry out **collective bargaining**. In this process, officials from the union and the company meet to discuss the workers' contract. The contract sets the terms for working at the company. These talks often focus on wages and benefits. Benefits include health insurance, sick days, and holidays. Contracts also cover rules for workers to follow and working conditions, such as breaks for meals during the workday.

With most contracts, the two sides reach an agreement during bargaining. Sometimes, though, negotiations break down. If that happens, unions and employers each have methods to pressure the other side to accept their position.

Union Tools

Labor unions have several tools to try to advance their cause. One method unions use is to call a **strike**. In a strike, all union members refuse to

---

right-to-work laws state laws forbidding unions from forcing workers to join

collective bargaining process by which unions and employers negotiate the conditions of employment

strike when workers deliberately stop working in order to force an employer to give in to their demands

These teachers demand increased funding for public education.

Analyzing Visuals What union tools are the teachers using in this photograph?

work. The idea is that without employees, one company—or all companies in the industry—will be forced to meet the union's demands. If they do not, the company or companies lose money every day that they refuse to work.

Striking workers usually stand in public view carrying signs stating that they are on strike. This tactic is called **picketing**. The goals are to embarrass the company and to build public support for the strike. Strikers also hope to discourage other workers from crossing the picket line to work at the company.

Another tool of labor is to put economic pressure on the company. For example, the union may ask people to boycott the company, or refuse to do business with it.

Strikes can cause problems for workers, too. They can drag on for months. If so, strikers may become discouraged. Some might want to go back to work. This can put pressure on the union to give in on some of its demands. Sometimes a strike will end without workers gaining anything they wanted. However, in most cases strikes are settled when the company and the union work out an agreement.

---

picketing a union tactic in which striking workers walk with signs that express their grievances

Employers' Tools

Employers also have ways to try to pressure unions. Their strongest tool is the **lockout**. In a lockout, the employer does not let workers enter the workplace. The employer hopes that the loss of income will force workers to accept company terms. During the lockout, the company often hires replacement workers so it can continue its business. That way, the locked-out workers suffer, but the company does not.

Companies may try to stop union actions by asking for an **injunction** (ihn•JUHNGK•shuhn). An injunction is a legal order from a court to prevent some activity. The company may ask the court to limit picketing or to prevent or stop a strike.

Outside Help

Unions may also seek injunctions. If issued against an employer, the injunction may order the employer not to lock out its workers. In certain industries considered important to the economy or national security, the government can seek an injunction. In 2002, for example, President George W. Bush asked for an injunction to end a lockout of dockworkers on the West Coast. He said keeping ports open was essential to military operations. A court order ended the lockout.

lockout when management closes a workplace to prevent union members from working

injunction a court order to stop some kind of action

A worker and his daughter rally against a company lockout. When unions oppose a wage cut, the company sometimes shuts down the plant or hires other workers until the union agrees to the cut.

Contrasting What is the difference between a lockout and a strike?

When the parties cannot agree on a contract, they have other options. First, they can try **mediation** (mee•dee•AY•shuhn). In this approach, they bring in a third party who tries to help them reach an agreement. They can also choose **arbitration** (ahr•buh•TRAY•shuhn), where a third party listens to both sides and decides how to settle the dispute. Both parties agree in advance to accept the third party's decision.

If a strike threatens the nation's welfare, the government can step in. Federal law allows the president to order a cooling-off period. During this time, the workers must return to work. Meanwhile, the union and the employer must try to reach an agreement. The cooling-off period lasts 80 days. If there is no agreement after that time, the workers have the right to go back on strike.

In an extreme situation, the government can temporarily take over a company or an industry. For example, in 1946 the government seized coal mines when a strike threatened to shut off the nation's coal supply.

✓ **CHECK FOR UNDERSTANDING**

1. **Identifying** What are the main areas of negotiation between unions and employers in reaching collective bargaining agreements?

2. **Comparing and Contrasting** Compare and contrast the terms *mediation* and *arbitration*.

LESSON ACTIVITIES

1. **Informative/Explanatory Writing** If you were an adult worker, would you join a labor union? Write a paragraph that explains the pros and cons of joining a union.

2. **Collaborating** A local union wants a pay raise and more paid time off. The company argues it cannot give a wage increase. In groups, assign yourselves three roles: union representative, business owner, and mediator. Each should write a paragraph explaining their position. Simulate a collective bargaining session. Write a new contract covering pay, benefits, and time off.

mediation situation in which union and company officials bring in a third party to try to help them reach an agreement

arbitration situation in which union and company officials submit the issues they cannot agree on to a neutral third party for a final decision

06

Money and Financial Institutions

READING STRATEGY

Analyzing Key Ideas and Details As you read, use a chart like the one shown to fill in details about each feature of money.

Money	
Feature	**Details**
Function	
Trait	
Form	

All About Money

GUIDING QUESTION

What gives money value?

Suppose you were selling a bicycle. Would you accept a four-ton stone in payment for it? You might if you lived on the Pacific island of Yap. For centuries, the people of Yap used huge stone disks as money. How could they do that? Money is anything that a group of people accepts as a means of exchange. A wide variety of things—from cheese to shells to dogs' teeth to gold and silver coins—have been used as money. People use money because it makes life easier for everyone.

Functions of Money

Money has three main functions. First, money serves as a *medium of exchange*. A **medium** is a means of doing something. People exchange, or trade, money for goods and services. If we did not have money, we would have to **barter**, or trade for something of equal worth. For example, a person might want to exchange running shoes for a pair of theater tickets. While this might sound like a simple task, the exchange might never take place. The person with the shoes may never find anybody willing to trade theater tickets for them.

Second, money is a *store of value*. This means that we can hold money as a form of wealth until we find something we want to buy with it. The person with the running shoes does not have to wait for someone willing to trade for them. Instead, the person can sell the shoes and hold the money until it is needed later.

medium a means of doing something

barter to trade a good or service for another good or service

Here, $100 bills are printed before being cut into separate bills. U.S. paper money is designed and printed by the Bureau of Engraving and Printing (BEP), which has operations in Washington, D.C., and Fort Worth, Texas. The BEP prints 26 million bills each day—worth about $974 million.

zefart/Shutterstock

Third, money serves as a *measure of value*. Money is like a measuring stick that can be used to assign value to a good or service. When somebody says that something costs $10, we know exactly what that means.

Characteristics of Money

For something to serve as money, it must have four characteristics:

- *Portable*. Money must be easy to carry around so people have it when they want to buy.
- *Divisible*. Money must be easy to divide into smaller amounts. That way it can be used for large and small purchases.
- *Durable*. Pieces of money should be hardy enough to stay in use for some time.
- *Limited Supply*. To be used as money, an object must be in limited supply. If money were easy to make, everyone would make it. The money would become worthless. That is why making fake money—or counterfeiting—is a crime.

Forms of Money

In the United States, money comes in three forms: coins, paper bills, and electronic money.

Coins are pieces of metal that are used as money. Examples of coins include pennies, nickels, dimes, quarters, and even some dollars. Our "paper" money is made out of high-quality cotton and linen. Coins and paper bills make up the **currency** of the United States.

Electronic money is money in the form of a computer entry at a bank or other financial institution. Electronic money does not exist in any physical form. An example would be the money you have in a checking or savings account. (Do not confuse credit cards with electronic money. A credit card is not money—it just gives the user permission to borrow.)

A new kind of money, according to some, is cryptocurrency. **Cryptocurrency** is electronic money not issued or managed by any country or central bank. Its value can fluctuate widely with

---

coin metallic form of money, such as a penny

currency money, both coins and paper bills

electronic money money in the form of a computer entry at a bank or other financial institution

cryptocurrency electronic money not issued or managed by any country or central bank

---

Features of U.S. Currency

Paper money has several special features that help prevent criminals from making counterfeit money.

Federal Reserve indicators
Microprinting
Portrait
Serial Number
Color-shifting ink
Security thread
Watermark

EXAMINE THE PHOTOS

1. **Analyzing Visuals** Which features shown will be useful for preventing counterfeiting?
2. **Inferring** Why would a government want to prevent counterfeiting?

These are symbols of Litecoin, Ethereum, and Bitcoin—three popular cryptocurrencies.

Speculating What characteristics must cryptocurrencies have before they are widely accepted as everyday money?

supply and demand. Bitcoin is perhaps the most popular cryptocurrency, and Ethereum is the second-most popular. Although gaining in popularity, none of the cryptocurrencies have achieved widespread adoption. This is due to none having all four required characteristics of money—portability, divisibility, durability, and limited supply.

✓ CHECK FOR UNDERSTANDING

1. **Explaining** What does it mean to barter? How does money make bartering unnecessary?
2. **Summarizing** What are three functions of money?

Financial Institutions

GUIDING QUESTION

What do financial institutions do?

The main function of financial institutions is to channel funds from savers to borrowers. When most people receive their pay, they put some money into a financial institution, such as a bank. The money that customers put into a financial institution is called a **deposit**. Businesses, too, deposit the money they receive from selling goods or services. Money is electronic when employers deposit workers' pay directly into workers' bank accounts. The funds in the employer's account go down, and the money in the workers' accounts goes up.

deposit the money that customers put into a financial institution

Taking Deposits

Banks have two main types of accounts—checking and savings. People use money deposited in a **checking account** to pay bills, buy goods and services, and meet other expenses. This is how checking accounts help money serve its function as a medium of exchange. People can withdraw their cash anytime by writing a check, using a debit card, or swiping a cell phone, which is why checking accounts are also called *demand deposit accounts*. Monthly banking fees for using checking accounts are almost always more than the interest paid on the checking deposits.

Deposits in a **savings account** help money serve its function as a store of value or wealth. Banks pay interest on savings accounts to encourage people to keep their money in the bank as long as possible. This allows banks to use some of the deposits to make loans. Savings accounts are usually free, deposits pay interest, and people can make limited but not frequent withdrawals.

A **certificate of deposit (CD)** is a loan you make to a bank, although it seems like a deposit.

checking account an account from which deposited money can be withdrawn at any time by writing a check, using a debit card, or swiping a cell phone; also known as demand deposit accounts

savings account an account that pays interest on deposits but allows only limited withdrawals

certificate of deposit (CD) a timed consumer loan to a bank that states the amount of the loan, maturity, and rate of interest being paid

This person is checking his bank accounts online. Customers often create multiple bank accounts so they can earn higher interest on savings and CDs.

Explaining What do people use checking accounts for?

You must leave the money in the bank for a fixed period, such as a year. Money taken out early faces a penalty in the form of a lower interest rate. The interest paid on CDs is higher than that paid on checking or savings accounts—another way that banks help money serve as a store of wealth.

Making Loans

After people deposit their funds, financial institutions put these deposits to work. Banks might keep some of each deposit in reserve, but the rest can be lent to individuals or businesses. People borrow to purchase a car or home, or pay college tuition. Businesses borrow to expand operations, make new products, or meet a payroll.

Banks charge interest on their loans. That is how they earn money. Banks also *pay* interest on deposits. So banks must be careful to charge a higher rate on loans they lend and pay a lower rate on interest to depositors. Before a loan is final, a lending officer at the bank and the borrower discuss the amount to be borrowed, the interest rate, and when the loan must be repaid.

Types of Financial Institutions

Consumers and businesses have several different financial institutions that can meet their needs. Two main types are commercial banks and credit unions.

Commercial banks offer the most financial services. They accept deposits, provide checking accounts, make loans, and offer other services such as safe deposit boxes where important documents and valuables can be kept. Commercial banks are the largest and most critical part of the financial system. Most businesses deal with commercial banks, and consumers can get loans if they have good credit ratings. Savings and loan associations (S&Ls) also offer many of the same services as commercial banks.

A **credit union** is a nonprofit cooperative that accepts deposits, makes loans, and provides financial services to its members. Credit unions are often formed by people who work in the same industry, work for the same company, or belong to the same labor union. Credit unions are cooperatives that their depositors, or members, own. Sometimes the only place a person can get a loan is from their credit union. Credit unions usually charge lower interest rates on loans, and they lend money only to members.

Regulating Financial Institutions

Because financial institutions are an essential part of our economic system, they must be financially sound and secure. To make sure this happens, several different state and federal agencies regulate or oversee the way they do business.

This regulation starts when they go into business. For example, a financial institution must first get a document called a *charter*. Individual states and the federal government grant charters, which are approvals to go into business. The government reviews the finances of the proposed institution to make sure it has enough money to succeed. Officials also examine the people who will run the business. They want to be sure they have the skills to use depositors' money wisely.

After the charter is issued, government officials watch to see how the financial institution is run. They try to make sure it stays in good financial condition and follows all relevant laws. These efforts protect the money depositors entrust to the institution and ensure that business operations are sound.

commercial bank a financial institution that offers the most banking services to individuals and businesses
credit union nonprofit service cooperative that accepts deposits, makes loans, and provides other financial services to its members

The money you deposit in a financial institution is safe for another reason—a federal **deposit insurance program** protects it. The Federal Deposit Insurance Corporation (FDIC) is the agency that protects deposits at commercial banks. The National Credit Union Share Insurance Fund (NCUSIF) is the agency that protects credit union deposits. Both programs cover deposits up to $250,000 for one person on all accounts within the same institution. Without these protections, our financial institutions would not be as safe for our deposits.

✓ CHECK FOR UNDERSTANDING

1. **Explaining** What is the role of financial institutions?
2. **Contrasting** How are savings accounts and certificates of deposit different?

How Banking Has Changed

GUIDING QUESTION

How has banking become safer, faster, and more efficient over the years?

Some form of banking has existed since civilization emerged in Mesopotamia around 8000 B.C.E. Temples acted as banks, often storing valuables for the wealthy and loaning seeds to local farmers. The Roman Empire extended loans to finance its empire-building. During medieval times, merchant banks minted coins and loaned money to finance trade on the Silk Road routes. Ever since our nation's founding, banking has also gone through many changes.

deposit insurance program government-backed program that protects bank deposits up to a certain amount if a financial institution fails

The Earliest Banks

States chartered most of the first banks. These banks even printed their own paper currency, which circulated as money. However, many of these banks were also unsound and often went bankrupt, or out of business. Early depositors in these banks usually lost all of their money because there was no form of banking insurance.

The strongest bank in our nation's early history got its charter from the federal government. This was the First Bank of the United States. It was chartered in 1791 to hold the government's money, make its payments, and lend to it during times of need. The bank had a charter for only 20 years. Then, during the War of 1812, the government discovered it had no place to borrow money. As a result, political leaders created the Second Bank of the United States, lasting from 1816 to 1836 when its charter ran out.

From the 1830s to the 1860s, states took over chartering and supervising privately owned banks. This control was inadequate, however, because banks continued to make loans by issuing their own paper currency. Again, private banks printed too many banknotes, leading to a greatly increased money supply and inflation. Demand arose for a uniform currency that was accepted anywhere without risk.

National Banks and the Federal Reserve System

In 1863 the Union government passed the National Bank Act to help bring order to the banking industry. This made it possible for banks to get a national charter, which were better funded than state banks. A government official called the Comptroller of the Currency regulated the national banks, which issued a uniform

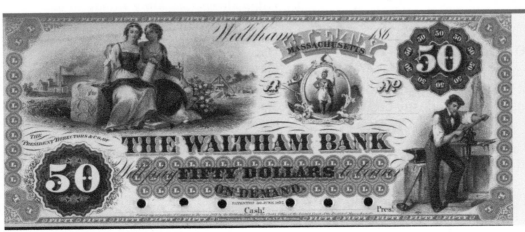

By 1860, more than 1,600 state banks issued their own paper currency, such as this one from Massachusetts.

Identifying Cause and Effect Why did the national government want to stop states from issuing their own currency?

currency backed by U.S. government bonds. National banks were safer than state banks but they did not have enough flexibility to deal with an economic downturn.

In 1913 Congress created the Federal Reserve System (Fed) to act as a central bank and oversee a new currency called Federal Reserve Notes. The Fed was a system of 12 regional banks designed to deal with economic problems in each of their districts. But the system was not perfect. Some of the 12 banks did not work together as planned. This problem made the Fed unable to take strong steps to end the Great Depression.

The Great Depression

During the Great Depression (1929–1933), many businesses failed. One out of four workers could not find a job. Panicky depositors all tried to withdraw their money from banks at the same time. This caused a crisis. Banks did not have enough cash on hand because they had loaned most of the money out. The crisis forced many banks to close their doors, which caused more panic, and then even more banks failed.

In response, President Franklin D. Roosevelt ordered all banks closed for four days. He assured people that banks would reopen after they had been checked by a government official and found to be healthy. Congress then passed the Banking Act of 1933. This law created the FDIC program and allowed the Fed to better oversee banks. Another law passed in 1935 gave the Fed even more powers to regulate banks. The Fed's Board of Governors (the main supervisory body of the Fed) also got more authority to regulate the 12 district banks. These reforms established the Fed as an effective **central bank**—a banker's bank that can lend to other banks in time of need and regulate the money supply.

Banks Since the Depression

The economy went through several difficult periods since the Great Depression of the 1930s. The first was the savings and loan industry crisis

---

central bank a banker's bank that can lend to other banks in time of need and can regulate the money supply

of the 1980s. The Great Recession of 2008–2009 was the second. The third was the COVID-19 downturn of 2020–2021. The FDIC, the Fed, and the federal government were responsible for successfully protecting customer deposits in banks during these periods.

The most significant banking regulations took place right after 2008 when banks were required to strengthen their reserves against losses. Banks were also required to pay more for their FDIC insurance, and laws limited risky loans that banks could issue. These changes increased costs and lowered profits for most banks. To reduce costs, free checking accounts disappeared, and many bank mergers took place. Other banks closed branch offices and moved many services online.

New Ways of Banking

New technology has introduced new forms of banking. Banking by cell phone, telephone, or automated teller machines (ATMs) lets people do their banking without setting a foot inside a commercial bank branch. Online banking allows people to use the Internet to check their balances and to see all transactions that have taken place. Many depositors have their bills paid automatically from their accounts. People can make purchases with a swipe of their cell phones rather than using a check or a credit card.

✓ **CHECK FOR UNDERSTANDING**

1. **Explaining** What problem was found with the national banks created under the National Bank Act?

2. **Identifying Cause and Effect** How did the changes after the Great Depression make the banking industry safer?

LESSON ACTIVITIES

1. **Informative/Explanatory Writing** Write a public service announcement (PSA) explaining why financial institutions are safe places for depositors to put their money. Make your PSA lively but informative.

2. **Using Multimedia** With a partner, create a multimedia presentation that explains the characteristics and functions of money in a way an elementary student would understand. Add visuals and music to support your explanations.

07

Analyzing Sources: A Cashless Society?

? COMPELLING QUESTION

What can be complicated about using money?

Plan Your Inquiry

DEVELOPING QUESTIONS

Read the Compelling Question for this lesson. What questions can you ask to help you answer this Compelling Question? Create a graphic organizer like the one below. Write three Supporting Questions in the first column.

Supporting Questions	Source	What this source tells me about the necessity of cash	Questions the source leaves unanswered
	A		
	B		
	C		
	D		
	E		

ANALYZING SOURCES

Next, read the introductory information for each source in this lesson. Then analyze each source by answering the questions that follow it. How does each source help you answer each Supporting Question you created? What questions do you still have? Write those in your graphic organizer.

After you analyze the sources, you will:
- use the evidence from the sources
- communicate your conclusions
- take informed action

Background Information

Money is a medium of exchange. That is, when you make a purchase, money is what you give up in order to get whatever you buy. In the country's early years, coins were the main form of money. Over time, paper money became far more common than coins as a medium of exchange. Today, however, many people carry neither paper money nor coins when they go shopping. Instead, many transactions occur electronically.

This Inquiry Lesson includes sources about the use of cash and noncash payments. As you read and analyze the sources, think about the Compelling Question.

» Do people need to carry cash anymore?

Skylines/Shutterstock

GO ONLINE Explore the Student Edition eBook and find interactive maps, charts, graphs, and tools.

E85

Electronic Transactions

Today consumers can make a purchase simply by swiping a plastic debit or credit card through a card reader, or by tapping or scanning a payment app on a cell phone. These devices are tied electronically to the nation's banking system.

PRIMARY SOURCE: PHOTOGRAPHS

A young woman purchases a book by using her credit card.

Cell phones with near-field communication (NFC) or radio frequency identification (RFID) technology allow customers to make "tap-and-go" purchases if the phone is held within a few inches of the point-of-sale terminal. These "contactless" payments became more popular in 2020 after COVID-19 struck.

EXAMINE THE SOURCE

1. **Analyzing** What must suppliers have available for electronic purchases to occur?

2. **Drawing Conclusions** How do electronic transactions fulfil the characteristic of money as a medium of exchange?

Online Shopping

People all over the world shop remotely online, and you can't do that with physical cash and coins. The table identifies the average *revenue*—or sales—created by an online shopper in the countries listed.

PRIMARY SOURCE: DATA

Country	Average Revenue Per Online Shopper
United States	$1,804
United Kingdom	$1,629
Sweden	$1,446
France	$1,228
Germany	$1,064
Japan	$968
Spain	$849
China	$626
Russia	$396
Brazil	$350

Source: "Online Shopping Statistics You Need to Know in 2021" by Coral Ouellette, January 2021.

EXAMINE THE SOURCE

1. **Evaluating** Are you surprised by any of the countries listed or the amounts of revenue shown? Why or why not?

2. **Analyzing** What information is missing that might help put this table's data in perspective?

Trends in Noncash Payments

Noncash payments include writing checks and using *debit cards* tied to a person's checking account. The amount a person can spend depends on how much money is in their checking account. Noncash payments also include *prepaid debit cards* not tied to a checking or savings account. An individual can load a certain amount of money onto a prepaid card—and that is the limit they can spend.

Credit cards are another type of noncash payments. Credit card companies offer loans, usually of a limited amount. If you purchase something using a credit card, the store is paid right away—and then you pay back the credit card company over time, with interest.

ACH transfers are yet another type of noncash payment. *ACH* stands for "Automated Clearing House." Computers process payments automatically from one financial institution to another. When you start a job, for example, the company you work for may pay your salary as a "direct deposit" instead of handing you a paper paycheck. In this situation, the ACH network automatically removes your pay from your employer's bank account and transfers it to your bank account.

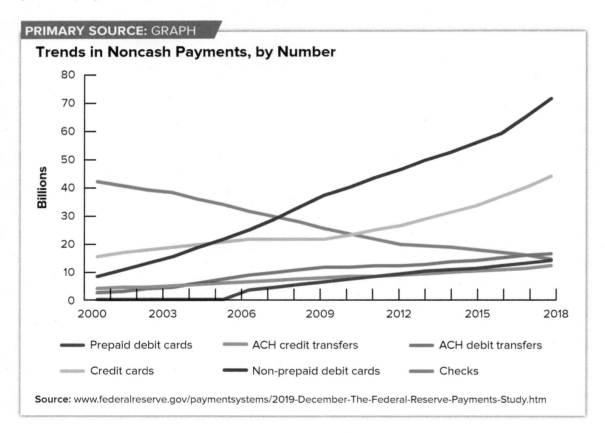

PRIMARY SOURCE: GRAPH

Trends in Noncash Payments, by Number

Legend:
— Prepaid debit cards — ACH credit transfers — ACH debit transfers
— Credit cards — Non-prepaid debit cards — Checks

Source: www.federalreserve.gov/paymentsystems/2019-December-The-Federal-Reserve-Payments-Study.htm

EXAMINE THE SOURCE

1. **Analyzing Visuals** According to the most recent data available in the graph shown, how are most payments made today?

2. **Speculating** The graph ends in 2018. What do you think happened to the trend for noncash payments after the COVID-19 pandemic occurred in 2020?

Pros of Using Credit

This article makes the case for using credit cards.

Fontinelle, Amy, "10 Reasons to Use Your Credit Card," Investopedia. May 17, 2021. https://www.investopedia.com/articles/pf/10/credit-card-debit-card.asp.

PRIMARY SOURCE: ARTICLE

66 Many of us use credit cards irresponsibly and end up in debt. However, contrary to popular belief, if you can use the plastic responsibly, you're actually much better off paying with a credit card than with a debit card and keeping cash transactions to a minimum. . . .

Paying with a credit card makes it easier to avoid losses from **fraud**. When your debit card is used by a thief, the money is missing from your account instantly. . . .

By contrast, when your credit card is used fraudulently, you aren't out any money—you just notify your credit card company of the fraud and don't pay for the **transactions** you didn't make while the credit card company resolves the matter. . . .

Certain purchases are difficult to make with a debit card. When you want to rent a car or stay in a hotel room, you'll almost certainly have an easier time if you have a credit card. . . .

Credit cards are best enjoyed by the disciplined, who can remain **cognizant** of their ability to pay the monthly bill (preferably in full) on or before the due date. 99

— From "10 Reasons to Use Your Credit Card" by Amy Fontinelle, Investopedia.com, 2021.

fraud illegal action, scam
transactions purchases, trades
cognizant aware

EXAMINE THE SOURCE

1. **Summarizing** In your own words, summarize the author's reasons to use credit cards instead of cash or debit cards.
2. **Drawing Conclusions** Why is it important to be disciplined when using a credit card?

Cash Is Still Here

In some countries, a large percentage of people still use cash for payments.

EXAMINE THE SOURCE

1. **Identifying** Which five countries shown on the graph have the highest percentage of *noncash* payments?

2. **Drawing Conclusions** Compare the cash payment percentages on this graph to the average revenue per online shopper shown in Source B. What are some conclusions you might draw about shoppers in Spain based on both sources?

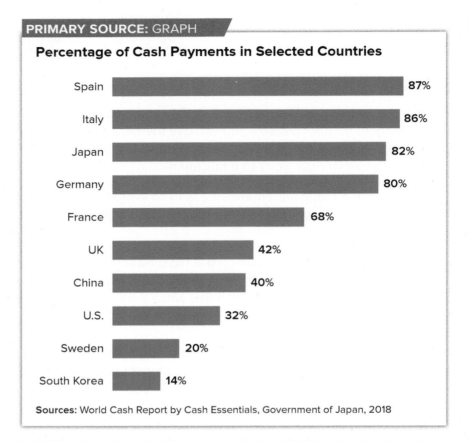

PRIMARY SOURCE: GRAPH

Percentage of Cash Payments in Selected Countries

Country	Percentage
Spain	87%
Italy	86%
Japan	82%
Germany	80%
France	68%
UK	42%
China	40%
U.S.	32%
Sweden	20%
South Korea	14%

Sources: World Cash Report by Cash Essentials, Government of Japan, 2018

Complete Your Inquiry

EVALUATE SOURCES AND USE EVIDENCE

Refer back to the Compelling Question and the Supporting Questions you developed at the beginning of the lesson.

1. **Identifying** Which of the sources affected you the most? Why?

2. **Evaluating** Overall, what impression do these sources give you about the importance of cash? Explain.

3. **Gathering Sources** Which sources helped you answer the Supporting Questions and Compelling Question? Which sources, if any, challenged what you thought you knew when you first created your Supporting Questions? What information do you still need in order to answer your questions? Where would you find that information?

4. **Evaluating Sources** Identify the sources that helped answer your Supporting Questions. How reliable is the source? How would you verify the reliability of the source?

COMMUNICATE CONCLUSIONS

5. **Collaborating** Work with a partner to create an infographic summarizing the various forms of noncash payments and their advantages and disadvantages. How do these sources provide insight into how noncash payments increased over time? Use the graphic organizer you created at the beginning of the lesson to help you. Share your infographic online.

TAKE INFORMED ACTION

Highlighting Smart Money Management
Research negative credit card experiences online. After reading about the situations, create a poster summarizing what NOT to do when students get their first credit card. Display the poster in the school for other students to read.

Government and Business

READING STRATEGY

Integrating Knowledge and Ideas As you read, identify ways the government's role in the economy benefits consumers.

Providing Public Goods

GUIDING QUESTION

What goods does government provide?

What products and services are available in your community without paying a fee? Do you walk on sidewalks or enjoy a local park? Do you have the protection of the police and the use of traffic signs? You do not have to pay for these things each time you use them. They are there for all to use. These products and services are different from those you pay for in stores and use for your own enjoyment.

Private and Public Goods

Businesses produce **private goods**, products that people must buy in order to use or own them. A person who does not pay for a private good is barred from owning or using it. In addition, private goods can be used by only one person. If you eat a meal, no one else can buy and eat it. Clothes, food, and cars are examples of private goods.

Unlike private goods, **public goods** can be consumed by more than one person. For example, your community's sidewalks are public goods. If you walk on a sidewalk, that does not prevent others from walking on it as well. Police protection and national defense are also public goods. A community—not just one person—enjoys the protection of the police.

private good economic good that, when consumed by one person, cannot be used by another

public good economic good that is used collectively, such as a highway and national defense

New York City's Central Park is a public good, meaning it can be "consumed" or used by more than one person.

GO ONLINE Explore the Student Edition eBook and find interactive maps, charts, graphs, and tools.

E91

Public goods are important to a number of people—even an entire community or nation. Yet businesses do not like to produce and sell them. Why is that? The reason is simple. It is difficult to charge everyone who might benefit from using public goods. For instance, how could someone figure out what to charge for your use of a sidewalk? Because it is hard to assign the costs, government takes on the responsibility for providing public goods. It pays for these goods through taxes and other fees it collects.

Externalities

Economic activities of all sorts produce side effects called **externalities** (ehk•stuhr•NAH•luh•teez). These are either positive or negative side effects of an action that impact an uninvolved third person.

Public goods often produce *positive* externalities. That is, there are benefits to everyone who uses those goods. Everyone—not just drivers—benefits from having good roads. Good roads make it faster and cheaper to transport goods. That means those goods can be sold at lower prices. As a result, all consumers benefit. A lower price is one positive externality that comes from having good roads.

Externalities can be *negative*, too. Negative externalities result when an action has harmful side effects. A car provides transportation, but its exhaust pollutes the air. Even people without cars may suffer from air pollution's harmful effects, such as breathing problems.

This airplane's flight path to the airport includes flying over a nearby highway and neighborhoods.

Speculating What positive and negative economic externalities might people living near the airport experience if the airport increases its number of flights?

Government's role is to encourage positive externalities and discourage negative ones. So the government provides public schooling because education leads to positive externalities. A well-educated workforce is more productive. To reduce pollution, the federal government has regulated car exhausts since the 1970s.

✓ **CHECK FOR UNDERSTANDING**

1. **Explaining** How does government pay for public goods?

2. **Making Connections** What is an externality? Provide an example of an externality, as well as its source, and identify it as positive or negative.

Maintaining Competition

GUIDING QUESTION

How does government encourage or increase competition among businesses?

Have you ever played the game Monopoly®? To win, a player tries to control all the properties in the game and bankrupt the other players. In other words, the winner becomes a monopoly. A **monopoly** (muh•NAH•pah•lee) is the exclusive control of a good or service. A *monopolist* is the one who has the monopoly.

Markets work best when large numbers of buyers and sellers participate. If a monopolist gains control of a market, it does not have to compete with other companies for buyers. As a result, it can charge a much higher price. Then consumers suffer because they are forced to pay a high price instead of being able to shop for a better one. To prevent this problem, a goal of the U.S. government has long been to encourage competition so that monopolies do not form.

Antitrust Laws

To protect competition, the government uses antitrust laws. A trust is a combination of businesses that threatens competition. The government's goal in passing **antitrust** (an•tee•TRUHST) **laws** is to control monopoly power and to preserve and promote competition.

---

externality economic side effect that affects an uninvolved third party

monopoly exclusive control of a good or service

antitrust law legislation to prevent monopolies from forming and to preserve and promote competition

In this political cartoon from 1904, artist Udo J. Keppler portrayed the Standard Oil Company as an octopus. The octopus "monopoly" has tentacles wrapped around the steel, copper, and shipping industries and the U.S. Capitol.

Explaining How do antitrust laws prevent monopoly behavior?

In 1890 the government passed its first antitrust law, the Sherman Antitrust Act. This law banned monopolies and other forms of business that prevent competition. In 1911 the government used the law to break up the Standard Oil Company because it had an oil monopoly. In the 1980s the government used the act to break up American Telephone and Telegraph (AT&T). This action ended a monopoly on phone service and created more competition.

In 1914 Congress passed the Clayton Antitrust Act. This law made the Sherman Act stronger and clearer. The Clayton Act banned a number of business practices that hurt competition. For example, a person could no longer be on the board of directors of two competing companies. The government legally took over some mergers.

Mergers

Sometimes two or more companies combine to form a single business. That joining is called a **merger** (MUHR•juhr). Some mergers threaten competition, which might lead to higher prices. In those cases, the government can use the Clayton Act to block the merger. The Federal Trade Commission (FTC) has the power to enforce this law. It looks at any merger that may violate antitrust laws. It also may take actions to **maintain**, or preserve, competition. In 2011, for example, AT&T proposed to merge with T-Mobile, a combination of the second- and fourth-largest wireless carriers in the country. The Justice Department argued that such a merger would lessen competition, so the merger was blocked.

merger a combination of two or more companies to form a single business

maintain to preserve

Natural Monopolies

At times it makes sense to let a single business produce a good or service. For example, it might be better to have one company, instead of two or three, build electric power lines for a city. In these cases, we have a **natural monopoly**. A single business produces and distributes a product better and more cheaply than several companies.

Natural monopolies have great power. They can choose to raise prices whenever they wish. For this reason, a government agency regulates, or closely watches, these companies. The agency usually has to approve any price increases or other changes in business activities.

Sometimes a local government can choose a different approach. It may become the owner of the natural monopoly instead. This is often the case with such services as water and sewers.

In recent years, many governments decided to put an end to certain natural monopolies by restoring competition. About half the states ended the monopoly of electric companies. This policy of ending regulation is called *deregulation*. The new approach has not always led to lower prices, though. Many states are now backing away from deregulation of natural monopolies.

✓ **CHECK FOR UNDERSTANDING**

1. **Summarizing** Why does government promote competition?

2. **Identifying Cause and Effect** Explain what a merger is. How can it lead to a monopoly?

natural monopoly a market situation in which the costs of production are minimized by having a single firm produce the product

Selected U.S. Government Regulatory Agencies

These are just a few of the federal government agencies that regulate businesses.

DEPARTMENT OR AGENCY	PURPOSE
Consumer Product Safety Commission (CPSC)	Protects the public from risks of serious injury or death from consumer products
Environmental Protection Agency (EPA)	Protects human health and the natural environment (air, water, and land)
Federal Trade Commission (FTC)	Promotes and protects consumer interests and competition in the marketplace
Food and Drug Administration (FDA)	Makes sure food, drugs, and cosmetics are truthfully labeled and safe for consumers
Occupational Safety and Health Administration (OSHA)	Makes sure workers have a safe and healthful workplace

EXAMINE THE CHART

Identifying Which regulatory agency has the power to make sure that competition exists in the marketplace?

Protecting Consumers

GUIDING QUESTION

How does government regulate business?

The government also plays a major role in protecting the health and safety of the public. The Food and Drug Administration (FDA) makes sure that foods, drugs, medical equipment, and cosmetics are safe. It also requires companies to tell the truth on product labels and in ads.

The Centers for Disease Control and Prevention (CDC) also tries to improve health. It checks air quality and distributes the flu vaccine, for example. The CDC helped develop and distribute the vaccine for the COVID-19 virus.

The goal of the Consumer Product Safety Commission (CPSC) is to protect consumers from injury. It oversees thousands of products, from toys to tools. The CPSC looks for problems in the design of a product that can create danger. If the CPSC finds a product unsafe, it issues a recall. A **recall** means the unsafe product is removed from stores. For those who bought the product, the manufacturer must change it to make it safe, offer a substitute, or return the customer's money.

The National Highway Traffic Safety Administration (NHTSA) also protects consumers. Between 2016 and 2019, the NHTSA recalled 67 million defective car airbags.

✓ CHECK FOR UNDERSTANDING

1. **Determining Central Ideas** How does government regulation protect the health and safety of consumers?

2. **Identifying** What is the role of the FDA?

LESSON ACTIVITIES

1. **Informative/Explanatory Writing** Identify a public good and a private good that you use regularly. Describe each good, and identify the characteristics that make the public good public and the private good private.

2. **Using Multimedia** Companies that make medicines must test their products before the FDA allows them to be sold. With a partner, research the FDA drug approval process for COVID-19 vaccines and create a slideshow that explains the steps.

recall government action that causes an unsafe product to be removed from consumer contact

09

Income Inequality

READING STRATEGY

Analyzing Key Ideas and Details As you read, identify factors that influence how much income people can earn.

Factors Affecting Income	
Factor	Details

Income Inequality

GUIDING QUESTION

What factors influence income?

The United States is often described as a wealthy country. However, not all Americans are rich. Some people have high incomes, but others are quite poor. Income levels vary for many reasons. Education level, family wealth, and discrimination each play a role.

Education

Education is a key to income. This is why the government wants Americans to graduate from high school and go on to higher learning. Every day, however, more than 7,000 students drop out of high school. The dropout rate hurts the nation's ability to compete economically. Without a high school diploma, people tend to receive lower wages and experience higher unemployment and imprisonment rates than graduates. To fix this problem, the government has been giving money to states and towns for dropout prevention programs since 2010. This federal program, known as High School Graduation Initiative, focuses its efforts on schools with the highest dropout rates.

The level of education a person **attains**, or achieves, has a great influence on their income. Education gives people the skills they need

attain to achieve

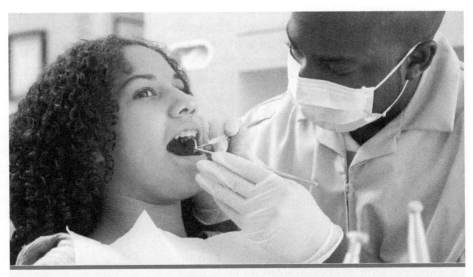

A dentist works on a young patient's teeth. Dentistry is one of the highest-paid occupations in the United States. To become a dentist, a person must first graduate from college and then attend a dental school for at least four years.

Drawing Conclusions What is the relationship between the education and skills of dentists and the amount they earn?

Lucidio Studio Inc./Getty Images

Weekly Earnings by Level of Education, 2020

Education increases human capital and helps people earn more money.

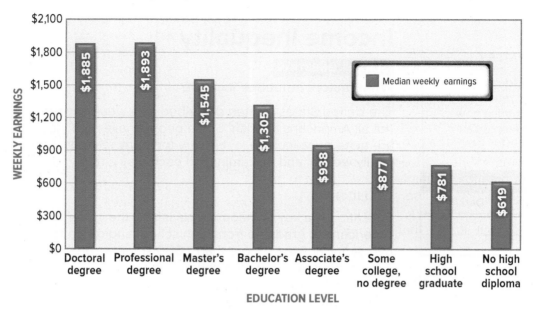

Source: Bureau of Labor Statistics, Current Population Survey.

EXAMINE THE GRAPH

1. **Calculating** What is the difference in earnings between a person with a Bachelor's degree and someone with an Associate's degree?
2. **Evaluating** Do you think a college degree is worth the expense? Why or why not?

to get higher-paying jobs. Look at the graph **Weekly Earnings by Level of Education**. Notice that a person with a bachelor's degree can earn nearly twice as much as a person with only a high school diploma. People with the most advanced degrees earn the most and have the lowest rates of unemployment.

For these reasons, the federal government encourages people to go to college. Some programs help students from low-income families and those with disabilities prepare for college. The government also offers low-cost loans and grants that help make college more affordable.

Family Wealth

People who are born into wealth have certain advantages. First, a person from a family with money has better access to education. As you just read, the more education a person has, the greater his or her **potential**, or possible, income.

Second, wealthy parents can often set their children up in family businesses where they can earn good incomes. Finally, such people usually leave their wealth to their children when they die.

Discrimination

Discrimination limits how much some people can earn. Unfair practices in hiring and promoting people hurt women and members of minority groups. Many of these people are prevented from getting top-paying jobs. For example, women generally earn less than men. In 2020, the American woman working full-time only earned about 81 percent of the American male working full-time.

Several important laws have been passed to end discrimination. These laws have closed the earnings gap between men and women, but some discrimination still exists.

- The *Equal Pay Act of 1963* requires that men and women be given equal pay for equal work. This means that jobs that have the same level of skill and responsibility must pay the same.

potential possible

- The *Civil Rights Act of 1964* bans discrimination based on gender, race, color, religion, and national origin.
- The *Equal Employment Opportunity Act of 1972* gave the government more power to enforce this law.
- The *Americans with Disabilities Act of 1990* gave job protection to people who have physical and mental disabilities.
- The *Lilly Ledbetter Fair Pay Act of 2009* allows workers who suffer unfair treatment because of their gender to sue employers.

The government has also encouraged companies to practice affirmative action. Such a policy is meant to increase the number of minorities and women at work. This effort helps to make up for past actions that held back people in these groups.

✓ **CHECK FOR UNDERSTANDING**

1. **Explaining** How does education affect income?
2. **Identifying** Which laws were the first to give protection to women and to those facing discrimination?

Poverty

GUIDING QUESTION

In what ways does government help those in poverty?

While many Americans are well off, many others are poor. In a recent year, more than 30 million people lived in poverty. This is about 10 percent of the total population in the United States, or about one person in 10. This means they did not earn enough income to pay for basic needs such as food, clothing, and shelter. Because tough economic times can easily add to these numbers, the country has enacted several poverty-fighting programs.

Welfare

To aid struggling families, the federal government provides welfare. **Welfare** is aid given to those in need in the form of money or necessities. The first welfare programs in the United States were established in the 1930s, during the Great Depression. President Franklin D. Roosevelt started these programs to help the millions of Americans who were facing tough economic times.

The government uses poverty guidelines to decide whether a person or family has too little money and therefore needs this help. These guidelines reflect the cost of enough food, clothing, and shelter to survive. The guidelines are updated each year.

Temporary Assistance for Needy Families (TANF) is one welfare program. The federal government provides the money. State governments distribute the funds. TANF began in 1996, replacing a program that was established in the 1930s. This new program set stricter rules for those eligible to take part in welfare programs. It also limited the amount of time during which a person can get benefits. These rules intend to encourage participants to find jobs quickly. In many states, TANF requires those who receive the benefit to work.

---

welfare aid given to the poor in the form of money or necessities

Temporary Assistance for Needy Families (TANF) welfare program paid for by the federal government and administered by the individual states

---

Poverty Guidelines for the 48 Contiguous States and Washington, D.C., 2021

The poverty guidelines are adjusted for different sized households. Those with incomes below the official poverty guidelines are eligible for certain federal programs.

Persons in Family/Household	Poverty Guideline
1	$12,880
2	$17,420
3	$21,960
4	$26,500
5	$31,040
6	$35,580
7	$40,120
8	$44,660

For families/households with more than 8 persons, add $4,540 for each additional person.

EXAMINE THE CHART

Calculating What must a family of four earn to stop being eligible for federal aid?

Programs like this are called **workfare** programs. Work activities often take the form of community service. Those getting the aid may be required to attend job training or education programs.

Another important welfare program is **Supplemental Nutrition Assistance Program (SNAP)**. It provides nutritional benefits to supplement the food budgets of needy families. Families wanting to apply for SNAP benefits must apply in the state where they currently live.

Unemployment Insurance

The government also pays some benefits to workers in special cases. One program is unemployment insurance. This program pays compensation to workers who become unemployed through no fault of their own. **Compensation** (KAHM·puhn·SAY·shuhn) is payment to make up for lost wages. If these workers cannot find new jobs, they are usually eligible for unemployment checks for a limited period of time. In addition, workers who are injured on the job may receive workers' compensation benefits, including lost wages and medical care.

Social Insurance Programs

Social Security, a Depression-era program designed to help people provide for their own retirement, is the largest and most powerful anti-poverty program in the United States. In a recent year, Social Security was responsible for keeping more than 27 million people out of poverty. Social Security is funded by a combined tax on workers and employers that amounts to 12.4 percent of a worker's income. This money is then transferred to retired Americans in the form of Social Security payments.

Two other programs are also important. The first is *Medicare*, a program for senior citizens regardless of income. It provides insurance to cover major hospital costs and other medical bills. The second is *Medicaid*, a joint federal-state medical insurance program for low-income persons.

workfare programs that require welfare recipients to exchange some of their labor for benefits

Supplemental Nutrition Assistance Program (SNAP) welfare program that provides nutritional benefits to supplement the food budgets of needy families

compensation payment to unemployed or injured workers to make up for lost wages

Social Security anti-poverty program that taxes working people and pays benefits to retirees

Laid-off workers carry their personal belongings out of the workplace. These workers are eligible for compensation.

Making Connections What is compensation? Under what circumstances does someone receive compensation?

Many people who receive payments from Social Security, Medicare, or Medicaid are already in poverty. But these programs are helpful because they ensure that the poorest members of society meet the basic human needs such as food, clothing, and shelter.

✓ **CHECK FOR UNDERSTANDING**

1. **Explaining** What is the purpose of poverty guidelines?

2. **Contrasting** How is workfare different from welfare?

LESSON ACTIVITIES

1. **Argumentative Writing** Suppose a friend of yours is planning to drop out of high school. Write an email using standard writing conventions and proper email etiquette to convince them to stay in school using what you have learned in this lesson.

2. **Collaborating** Which of the following goals do you think would be the most effective in reducing poverty: (1) provide a college education for everyone, (2) ensure living wages for all workers (wages about twice the minimum wage of $7.25 an hour), or (3) provide financial help and job-search assistance to the unemployed? Team up with two classmates, with each selecting one of the goals to research. Present your findings to each other, and decide which goal would be most effective.

Steve Debenport/E+/Getty Images

10

Multiple Perspectives: The Minimum Wage

 COMPELLING QUESTION

Should we increase the minimum wage?

Plan Your Inquiry

DEVELOPING QUESTIONS

Read the Compelling Question for this lesson. What questions can you ask to help you answer this Compelling Question? Create a graphic organizer like the one below. Write three Supporting Questions in the first column.

Supporting Questions	Source	What this source tells me about the minimum wage	Questions the source leaves unanswered
	A		
	B		
	C		
	D		
	E		

ANALYZING SOURCES

Next, read the introductory information for each source in this lesson. Then analyze each source by answering the questions that follow it. How does each source help you answer each Supporting Question you created? What questions do you still have? Write those in your graphic organizer.

After you analyze the sources, you will:
- use the evidence from the sources
- communicate your conclusions
- take informed action

Background Information

The minimum wage is the lowest hourly rate of pay that employers may pay their workers. This lower limit is set by law. Congress first set the minimum wage in 1938. At the time, the wage was 25 cents. Initially, the law applied only to those employees whose work was part of interstate commerce, or buying and selling products across state lines. Later, Congress changed the law and made it cover most workers. Congress has also raised the rate many times. The current national rate, $7.25, took effect in 2009. The minimum wage has been in place for more than 80 years. Still, the debate over it continues. Critics say the minimum wage discourages businesses from hiring workers. Supporters disagree.

This Inquiry Lesson includes sources about the minimum wage. As you read and analyze the sources, think about the Compelling Question.

Should Congress pass a higher minimum wage law?

Federal Minimum Wage Over Time

The federal minimum wage is the lowest legal wage that can be paid to most workers. As inflation and the cost of living increase, the government reevaluates and increases the minimum wage from time to time. This graph shows the increases in the actual minimum wage from 2000 until it reached its current level—$7.25—in 2009. The second line on the graph shows the minimum wage adjusted for inflation and the cost of living using the value of what the dollar was "worth" in 2009.

PRIMARY SOURCE: GRAPH

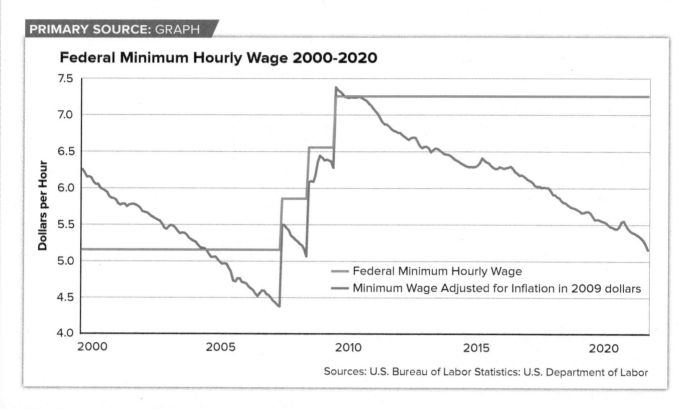

Sources: U.S. Bureau of Labor Statistics: U.S. Department of Labor

---

EXAMINE THE SOURCE

1. **Contrasting** What was the actual federal minimum wage in 2020? What was this wage worth in 2020 after being adjusted for inflation using 2009 prices?

2. **Analyzing** In what years did the inflation-adjusted purchasing power of the minimum wage fall below $7.25? In what years did the inflation-adjusted purchasing power of the minimum wage exceed the actual federal minimum wage?

State Minimum Wages

States can set their own minimum wage. For those states with no minimum wage, they must pay minimum-wage workers the federal minimum wage.

PRIMARY SOURCE: TABLE

State Minimum Wages Per Hour				
AL *None*	HI $10.10	MA $13.50	NM $10.50	SD $9.45
AK $10.34	ID $7.25	MI $9.65	NY $12.50	TN *None*
AZ $12.15	IL $11.00	MN $10.08	NC $7.25	TX $7.25
AR $11.00	IN $7.25	MS *None*	ND $7.25	UT $7.25
CA $13.00	IA $7.25	MO $10.30	OH $8.80	VT $11.75
CO $12.32	KS $7.25	MT $8.75	OK $7.25	VA $7.25
CT $12.00	KY $7.25	NE $9.00	OR $12.00	WA $13.69
DE $9.25	LA *None*	NV $9.00	PA $7.25	WV $8.75
FL $8.65	ME $12.15	NH $7.25	RI $11.50	WI $7.25
GA $7.25	MD $11.75	NJ $12.00	SC *None*	WY $7.25

Washington, D.C. $15.00
*As of May 1, 2021
Source: www.dol.gov/agencies/whd/minimum-wage/state

EXAMINE THE SOURCE

1. **Analyzing** Which state paid the highest state minimum wage in 2021?
2. **Drawing Conclusions** What wage do Alabama, Louisiana, Mississippi, South Carolina, and Tennessee pay their minimum-wage workers?
3. **Evaluating** The federal government has one minimum wage for the entire country, but the states' minimum wages differ based on the economic activity and cost of living in each state. Which minimum wage—federal or state—do you think makes more economic sense? Explain your answer.

Argument For a Higher Minimum Wage

Those in favor of increasing the minimum wage argue that it will help low-wage earners make ends meet and bring more people out of poverty.

PRIMARY SOURCE: WEBSITE

The benefits of gradually phasing in a $15 minimum wage by 2025 would be far-reaching, lifting pay for tens of millions of workers and helping reverse decades of growing pay inequality.

The Raise the Wage Act would have the following benefits:

- Gradually raising the federal minimum wage to $15 by 2025 would lift pay for 32 million workers—21% of the U.S. workforce.

- Affected workers who work year round would earn an extra $3,300 a year—enough to make a tremendous difference in the life of a cashier, home health aide, or fast-food worker who today struggles to get by on less than $25,000 a year.

- A majority (59%) of workers whose total family income is below the **poverty line** would receive a pay increase if the minimum wage were raised to $15 by 2025.

- A $15 minimum wage would begin to reverse decades of growing pay inequality between the most underpaid workers and workers receiving close to the **median** wage, particularly along gender and racial lines. For example, minimum wage increases in the late 1960s explained 20% of the decrease in the Black–white **earnings gap** in the years that followed, whereas failures to adequately increase the minimum wage after 1979 account for almost half of the increase in inequality between women at the middle and bottom of the wage distribution.

- A $15 minimum wage by 2025 would generate $107 billion in higher wages for workers and would also benefit communities across the country. Because underpaid workers spend much of their extra earnings, this **injection** of wages will help stimulate the economy and **spur** greater business activity and job growth.

  — From "Why the U.S. needs a $15 minimum wage," Economic Policy Institute Fact Sheet, 2021.

poverty line lowest level of income needed to buy necessities in life
median middle
earnings gap difference between the average pay between two different groups of people
injection addition
spur encourage

> **EXAMINE THE SOURCE**
>
> 1. **Identifying** What percentage of the U.S. workforce earns a minimum wage?
> 2. **Explaining** According to the writer, how would an increase in the minimum wage benefit communities?

D ———————————————————————— E103

Argument Against a Higher Minimum Wage

Those against increasing the minimum wage argue that raising the cost of labor hurts employment of low-wage workers as well as family income.

PRIMARY SOURCE: GOVERNMENT WEBSITE

66 The federal minimum wage of $7.25 per hour has not changed since 2009. Increasing it would raise the earnings and family income of most low-wage workers, lifting some families out of poverty—but it would cause other low-wage workers to become jobless, and their family income would fall. . . .

How would increasing the minimum wage affect employment? Raising the minimum wage would increase the cost of employing low-wage workers. As a result, some employers would employ fewer workers than they would have under a lower minimum wage. However, for certain workers or in certain circumstances, employment could increase.

Changes in employment would be seen in the number of jobless, not just unemployed, workers. Jobless workers include those who have dropped out of the labor force (for example, because they believe no jobs are available for them) as well as those who are searching for work. . . .

If workers lost their jobs because of a minimum-wage increase, how long would they stay jobless? At one extreme, an increase in the minimum wage could put a small group of workers out of work indefinitely, so that they never benefited from higher wages. At the other extreme, a large group of workers might shuffle regularly in and out of employment, experiencing joblessness for short spells but receiving higher wages during the weeks they were employed. . . .

How would increasing the minimum wage affect family income? By boosting the income of low-wage workers who had jobs, a higher minimum wage would raise their families' real income, lifting some of those families out of poverty. However, income would fall for some families because other workers would not be employed and because business owners would have to absorb at least some of the higher costs of labor. For those reasons, a minimum-wage increase would cause a net reduction in average family income. 99

— From "How Increasing the Federal Minimum Wage Could Affect Employment and Family Income," Congressional Budget Office, 2021.

| EXAMINE THE SOURCE |

1. **Analyzing Perspectives** According to the source, why would increasing the minimum wage result in a lower number of jobs available?

2. **Identifying Cause and Effect** How might increasing the minimum wage affect the length of unemployment and average family income, according to the source?

Congressional Budget Office. "How Increasing the Federal Minimum Wage Could Affect Employment and Family Income." Congressional Budget Office. April 5, 2021. https://www.cbo.gov/publication/55681.

Minimum Wage Workers

Many food service workers, especially those working in fast-food restaurants, start out earning the minimum wage.

PRIMARY SOURCE: PHOTOGRAPH

Employees picket to increase wages for fast-food workers.

EXAMINE THE SOURCE

Evaluating Most minimum wage jobs are considered "unskilled labor," meaning the jobs do not require a college education or specialized training. Do you think unskilled labor should be paid at a higher minimum wage? Why or why not?

Complete Your Inquiry

EVALUATE SOURCES AND USE EVIDENCE

Refer back to the Compelling Question and the Supporting Questions you developed at the beginning of the lesson.

1. **Identifying** Which of the sources affected you the most? Why?

2. **Evaluating** Overall, what impression do these sources give you about the importance of raising the minimum wage? Explain.

3. **Gathering Sources** Which sources helped you answer the Supporting Questions and Compelling Question? Which sources, if any, challenged what you thought you knew when you first created your Supporting Questions? What information do you still need in order to answer your questions? Where would you find that information?

4. **Evaluating Sources** Identify the sources that helped answer your Supporting Questions. How reliable is the source? How would you verify the reliability of the source?

COMMUNICATE CONCLUSIONS

5. **Collaborating** Work with a partner to create a storyboard or comic strip showing the advantages and disadvantages of raising the minimum wage. Include at least three frames. After discussing ideas, one of you might create the dialog between characters while the other creates the drawings. Share your storyboards or comic strips with the class.

TAKE INFORMED ACTION

Investigating Minimum Wage Jobs
Research the types of jobs in your community that pay minimum wage, or less than minimum wage if tips are included. Identify community problems that might be solved with an increase in the minimum wage. Also identify problems that might arise if the minimum wage were increased. Write a letter to your city mayor or city manager outlining your stance on the minimum wage.

11

Reviewing Markets, Money, and Businesses

Summary

Main Idea

In the U.S. *free enterprise capitalist economy,* private citizens own and decide how to use their land, labor, capital, and entrepreneurial skills—with little government interference. Six features contribute to our economic health: economic freedom, markets, voluntary exchanges, the profit motive, competition, and private property rights. The U.S. economy includes the following elements as well.

Supporting Detail

Businesses are organized in several ways. A *sole proprietorship* is owned and operated by one person. A *partnership* is owned and operated by two or more people. A *corporation* is owned by many people when they purchase stock in the business. LLPs and corporations have limited *liability.* Other business forms are *franchises* and *nonprofit organizations*—charities and cooperatives.

Supporting Detail

Businesses produce goods and services but also have social responsibilities. They also must sell safe products, treat workers fairly, and be *transparent* to stockholders.

Supporting Detail

The U.S. *civilian labor force* includes those who have a job and the unemployed who are looking for a job. Much of our labor force works in the service sector. In the past, *labor unions* fought for workers' rights, such as an eight-hour workday and pay for overtime. Fewer workers today are union members.

Supporting Detail

Income levels in the United States vary for many reasons, including level of education. Family wealth and discrimination also play a role. To aid struggling families, the government provides *welfare.*

Supporting Detail

When you work and earn money, you can spend it, invest it, or *deposit* it into a financial institution. These institutions channel funds from savers to borrowers—paying interest to savers, and charging interest to borrowers. The government regulates banks to protect deposits.

Supporting Detail

Businesses produce *private goods,* and the government provides *public goods,* such as public education. *Antitrust laws* maintain competition among businesses. The government also makes sure foods and drugs are safe.

Checking For Understanding

Answer the questions to see if you understood the topic content.

REVIEWING KEY TERMS

1. Define each of these terms:

    A. capitalism   **F.** transparency

    B. free enterprise   **G.** collective bargaining

    C. financial capital   **H.** currency

    D. liability   **I.** externality

    E. franchise   **J.** welfare

REVIEWING KEY FACTS

2. **Explaining** How does the limited government interference of capitalism contribute to a healthy economy?

3. **Identifying Cause and Effect** What happens if a sole proprietor cannot pay his or her business debts?

4. **Explaining** Why is it usually easier for a partnership to grow than it is for a sole proprietorship?

5. **Explaining** What is the role of a corporation's board of directors?

6. **Explaining** Why do companies create foundations?

7. **Speculating** How does a company's financial report help to protect potential investors?

8. **Identifying** What options exist for employers and unions when they cannot agree on a contract?

9. **Explaining** How do banks earn money?

10. **Explaining** How does the government pay for the public goods it provides?

11. **Explaining** What are the goals of antitrust laws?

CRITICAL THINKING

12. **Identifying Cause and Effect** How does the profit motive contribute to the economic growth of the United States?

13. **Inferring** In laissez-faire economics, what one government interference would be encouraged?

14. **Contrasting** How does a corporation's liability differ from that of sole proprietorships and partnerships?

15. **Inferring** Why do you think a business would organize as a nonprofit organization?

16. **Identifying Cause and Effect** How does an employer benefit by providing its employees with health insurance?

17. **Identifying Cause and Effect** How does a boycott put economic pressure on a company to meet the demands of the union?

18. **Making Connections** Why must money be limited in supply for it to have value?

19. **Comparing and Contrasting** How are a savings account and a checking account alike and different?

20. **Identifying Cause and Effect** How are consumers affected by a lack of competition in the marketplace?

NEED EXTRA HELP?

If You've Missed Question	1	2	3	4	5	6	7	8	9	10
Review Lesson	2, 3, 4, 5, 6, 8, 9	2	3	3	4	4	5	6	8

If You've Missed Question	11	12	13	14	15	16	17	18	19	20
Review Lesson	8	2	2	3	3	4	5	6	6	8

Apply What You Have Learned

 ## Understanding Multiple Perspectives

Although free enterprise limits government involvement in the economy, the U.S. economic system does include some government intervention. The government tries to ensure that businesses are competitive. The government also helps provide a safety net for those in poverty.

ACTIVITY **Comparing and Contrasting Viewpoints on Government Assistance** Read these excerpts that provide two views of government assistance to those who need it. Then write a brief essay answering these questions: How did President Johnson view the role of the federal government in combating poverty and aiding society? How did Benjamin Franklin believe poverty could be reduced? How might a speech like President Johnson's, delivered before Congress and televised live to the American people, influence government policy toward social programs?

❝ Let this session of Congress be known as the session which . . . declared all-out war on human poverty and unemployment in these United States; as the session which finally recognized the health needs of our older citizens; . . . and as the session which helped to build more homes, more schools, more libraries, and more hospitals than any single session of Congress in the history of our Republic. ❞

— President Lyndon B. Johnson, Annual Message to the Congress on the State of the Union, January 8, 1964

❝ I am for doing good to the poor, but I differ in opinion about the means. I think the best way of doing good to the poor, is not making them easy *in* poverty, but leading or driving them *out* of it. In my youth I travelled much, and I observed in different countries, that the more public provisions were made for the poor, the less they provided for themselves, and of course became poorer. And, on the contrary, the less was done for them, the more they did for themselves, and became richer. ❞

— Benjamin Franklin, "On the Price of Corn, and Management of the Poor" Printed in *The London Chronicle*, 1766.

 ## Writing an Informative Report

Many corporations have set up their own foundations. These groups give money to support causes they believe are important.

ACTIVITY **Writing About a Company's Charitable Giving** Research online a favorite store or a company whose products you would like to own someday. Go to the company's homepage and use search terms such as "philanthropy" or "foundation." Read about the causes the store donates to, and why. Then write a paragraph informing others about the company's giving practices.

C Understanding Economic Concepts

A market is a place where buyers and sellers exchange products and money. Markets are "capitalism in action."

ACTIVITY **Finding Evidence of a Market in a Photograph**
Study the photograph of a farmers' market. Identify in the photograph evidence of each of the following features of capitalism: economic freedom, markets, voluntary exchanges, the profit motive, competition, and private property rights.

D Making Connections

Have you ever heard of "Yankee ingenuity"? How about "American inventiveness"? Americans are famous for creating, inventing, and innovating in the U.S. free enterprise economy.

ACTIVITY **Creating a New Product** The entrepreneurial spirit runs deep in this country. Does it within you? Have you ever wanted to invent something? Here's your chance. A trick to inventing is to think of problems people face and then try to come up with a solution. Make a list of common problems and brainstorm solutions. When you come up with an invention, make a poster that advertises its features.

Government and the Economy

State and local governments, like the federal government, use taxpayer dollars to pay for many things. Taxes paid for the Main Street Bridge and this city park fountain in Jacksonville, Florida.

LawrenceSawyer/Getty Images

01

Introducing Government and the Economy

Signs of the Economy

Economists and government leaders want to know about the health of the economy. They look for signs that will answer questions such as:

- Are more or fewer people spending money at stores and restaurants?

- Is the economy getting better or worse?

- Are prices beginning to rise too fast?

- Is it more expensive or less expensive to get a loan from a bank?

- Are long lines of people waiting at the unemployment office because they've been laid off?

- Are people struggling to pay their bills?

- Is the government going to have a *deficit* (spend more than it receives)?

The government provides many goods and services to the public. Taxpayers must pay for those products. Today those taxpayers are your parents—but someday it will be you!

This cartoon shows—in an exaggerated way—the impact that taxes can have on a worker. Taxes of one kind or another have already taken half of the boy's pay.

Did You Know?

Taxes—and opinions about them—have been around as long as civilization.

- "In this world, nothing can be said to be certain, except death and taxes." –Benjamin Franklin, American Founder, 1789

- "Taxes are what we pay for civilized society." –Oliver Wendell Holmes, Jr., U.S. Supreme Court Justice, 1927

- "When there is an income tax, the just man will pay more and the unjust less on the same amount of income." –Plato, Athenian philosopher, in *The Republic*, 375 B.C.E.

TEXT: (t) Franklin, Benjamin. "To Jean Baptiste Le Roy, November 13, 1789." The Writings of Benjamin Franklin. Volume X: 1789-1790. New York: The Macmillan Company, 1907., (c) Supreme Court Of The United States. U.S. Reports: Compania De Tabacos v. Collector of Internal Revenue, 275 U.S. 87. Washington, DC: Government Printing Office, 1927, (b) Plato. The Republic. Translated by Benjamin Jowett. The Gutenberg Project, August 27, 2008. https://www.gutenberg.org/files/1497/1497-h/1497-h.htm.

What Taxes Pay For

No one likes paying taxes. But our lives would be very different if taxes didn't pay for public goods and services. Education, roads and bridges, national parks, and national defense are just a few things paid for with tax dollars.

» The federal government contributes some tax dollars to pay for public education. However, most funding for public schools comes from state and local taxes.

» Taxes pay for the National Park Service to maintain more than 400 national parks across the country. Two of the most famous include Everglades National Park in Florida and Yellowstone National Park in Wyoming, Idaho, and Montana. Visitors arrive to view Yellowstone's geyser named "Old Faithful."

» A Coast Guard helicopter crew practices a rescue. When people get in trouble at sea, they depend on the Coast Guard to come to their aid. In 2020, the Coast Guard received more than $12 billion from the federal government to fund its operations for the year. With these funds, the Coast Guard buys boats, helicopters, and other equipment. It also pays its highly skilled employees.

Getting Ready to Learn About . . . Government and the Economy

Why the Government Gets Involved

Americans have strong feelings about the role that government ought to play in our lives. Some people feel government does too much; others think it does too little. An important benefit of a democratic political system is that people can freely disagree about what the government should do—and then settle their disagreements peacefully. Yet there are times when people are forcefully reminded of the beneficial side of government involvement.

In 2008–2009, the economy experienced its worst *recession*, or economic downturn, since the Great Depression of the 1930s. Massive spending by the government prevented it from getting even worse.

In 2020, the country entered an even more difficult year. The rapid spread of the COVID-19 virus caused a partial shutdown of the U.S. economy. Millions of Americans and small businesses were hurt. But again, the government passed three spending bills totaling $5 trillion to aid states, families, and small businesses. As difficult as 2020 was, it would have been much worse without the government-provided economic stimulus.

During economic downturns, stores close and people become unemployed.

Measuring the Economy's Health

Everybody wants the economy to grow. Economic growth means businesses earn more profits, people have jobs, and incomes go up. With higher incomes, the government receives more in taxes, which helps the federal budget.

To see if the economy is growing, we like to look at real GDP. *Real Gross Domestic Product (GDP)* is the value of all final products produced in the country during a single year when measured with fixed base-year prices. If GDP increased this year over last year when fixed base prices are used, the economy's growth is real and not an illusion caused by rising prices—hence the term "real GDP."

Economists look at other measures too. They want to know how many people are employed and unemployed. They want to know if prices have changed since last year. They also want to know if stock prices are in a "bull market" or a "bear market." All of these measures help to tell us something about the economy's health.

A "bull market" is strong, like a bull, with stock prices going up. A "bear market" is mean, like a bear, with stock prices going down.

Where the Money Comes From

If you've ever created a budget, you understand that you need to figure out how much money is coming in. This amount tells you how much you can spend.

The federal government prepares a budget in a similar way. The budget has two parts—*revenue*, or money coming in, and *expenditures*, or money being spent. Much of the revenue coming in is from people paying individual income taxes. The more income people earn, the higher their taxes. Other taxes to fund programs such as Social Security are also taken from people's paychecks. In addition, corporations pay taxes on their profits.

The federal government shares some of the revenue it gets with state governments. But state and local governments collect their own taxes too.

Where the Money Goes

The revenue collected is then spent on an astonishing number of goods and services—many of which benefit you. As you learned earlier, taxes pay for education, highways, national defense, and national parks. Social Security payments go to the elderly. Unemployment benefits and welfare payments go to people who have been laid off and are looking for jobs.

Taxes are collected and then used to run the government and its programs.

Fixing the Economy

Have you ever purchased an item—only to find out later that its price had increased? An institution called the Federal Reserve System (the Fed) is in charge of *monetary policy*. Its goal is to manage the money supply as necessary to keep prices stable and keep economic activity strong.

A second policy—*fiscal policy*—is conducted by the government at the federal, state, and even local levels. It refers to how the government uses tax cuts and changes in spending to reach the economic goals of keeping people working, producing, and buying goods and services.

The federal government used fiscal policy when it pumped billions of dollars into the economy during the 2008–2009 Great Recession and the 2020 COVID recession. The government's tax cuts and increased spending led to record-setting *deficits*, or spending more than was collected in revenues. The economy would have been in much worse shape, however, without these policies.

The idea behind fiscal policy is simple. If the economy slows down or heats up too much, the government can help the economy become healthy again by adjusting taxes and spending. Spending is easy, but increasing taxes to pay for the spending is much more difficult.

Looking Ahead

In this topic, you will learn about GDP and other measurements of the economy, the Federal Reserve System and monetary policy, taxes, the federal budget, and fiscal policy. You will examine Compelling Questions and develop your own questions in the Inquiry Activities.

What Will You Learn?

In these lessons, you will learn:

- what GDP is and how it serves as a measure of our economy's health.
- the business cycle and its stages.
- how unemployment and inflation affect the economy.
- what makes up the Federal Reserve System and how the Fed influences the economy through its use of monetary policy.
- how and why governments create budgets.
- the sources of revenue and forms of expenditures for the federal, state, and local governments.
- how and why governments use fiscal policy to maintain growth and a stable economy.
- how the government used fiscal policy during the Great Recession of 2008–2009 and the COVID-19 recession of 2020.
- how deficits happen and why they turn into debt.

 COMPELLING QUESTIONS IN THE INQUIRY ACTIVITY LESSONS

- **Are tax rates fair?**
- **Should the U.S. government be required to balance its budget?**

Government and the Fed's Involvement in the Economy
In this topic, you will learn that Congress (upper left) and the Federal Reserve (upper right) get involved in the U.S. economy to promote economic growth and a higher GDP (bottom).

02
Gross Domestic Product

READING STRATEGY

Analyzing Key Ideas and Details As you read the lesson, complete a web diagram identifying the three types of GDP a country measures.

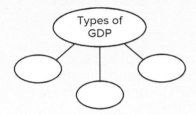

Why GDP Is Important

GUIDING QUESTION

Why is Gross Domestic Product important to a nation?

You can see the busy U.S. economy all around you. Farmers raise crops, and factories produce many kinds of goods. Employees stock goods on store shelves. Shoppers crowd the stores to buy those products. A **product** may be either a good or a service. Goods are something you can touch, such as bicycles, cell phones, books, pens, and clothes. Products also include services, or work done for someone. Vehicle repair, giving a haircut, and babysitting are examples of services. But did you ever wonder *how much* we produce every year?

GDP Measures Total Output

All this economic activity is reflected in **Gross Domestic Product (GDP)**. GDP is the total (gross) market value of all final products produced within a country's borders during a single year.

product anything that is produced; goods and services
Gross Domestic Product (GDP) total market value of all final goods and services produced in a country during a single year

This worker in a bicycle shop adds to the country's GDP. GDP provides two measures of a country's economy. It sums the total market value of all final *output* in a year, including new bicycles made in this country. It also sums the total *income* of the factors of production used to make those products, including this worker's wages. Output equals income in a given year.

Making Connections The word *domestic* comes from the Latin word *domus*, which means "home." How does this information help you better understand the meaning of *gross domestic product*?

Moxie Productions/Blend Images LLC

What is the GDP of the United States? In 2020, the annual output, or amount produced in the United States, was about $20 trillion. Twenty trillion dollars is a lot of output—$20,000,000,000,000 to be exact. This amount makes the United States the world's second-largest national economy. In fact, U.S. output is about one-seventh of all the goods and services produced in the world. In 2020 only China had a larger economy, with output worth about $24 trillion.

GDP Also Represents Income

Making goods and providing services create income for people in the economy. This is another reason why measuring GDP is important. Although measuring output is GDP's primary function, GDP also represents the nation's income. The workers who make a bicycle, for example, are paid for their labor. But *labor* is not the only factor of production that earns income when a bicycle is produced. So do the other factors of production. *Entrepreneurs*—those who formed the bicycle company and the person who opened a bicycle shop—earn income. Recall that *land* includes forests, soil, and mineral deposits. The natural resources that go into a bicycle—the metal used in the frame and the rubber used in the tires—must be paid for. As a result, this factor of production brings income to the companies that own those resources. The same is true of *capital*—the wrenches, machinery, buildings, and other tools used to make the bicycle. They, too, generate income for the companies and workers that make and sell these capital goods.

✓ CHECK FOR UNDERSTANDING

1. **Describing** What is Gross Domestic Product (GDP), and what does it represent?
2. **Explaining** Why does GDP represent income for all factors of production?

Measuring GDP

GUIDING QUESTION

Why is GDP difficult to measure?

Because so many different goods and services are produced during a year, measuring GDP is difficult. This is true for any economy, not just one the size of the U.S. economy. To calculate this and other measurements, the government uses thousands of highly skilled economists and government workers.

A simple example shows how economists could calculate the GDP of a nation. Suppose a tiny country has an economy that produces only two goods—watches and computers, and one service—concerts. The following table **Estimating Total Annual Output (GDP)** shows how the quantities of each product and their prices are summed to compute GDP.

Estimating Total Annual Output (GDP)			
	Quantity	× Price	= Value
Watches	10	$100	$1,000
Computers	10	$1,500	$15,000
Concerts	10	$200	$2,000
			GDP = $18,000

To find the GDP of this imaginary economy, we multiply the price of each product sold by the quantity produced. Then the three results are added. For this nation, the total amount of output, or GDP, would be $18,000 ($1,000 worth of watches, $15,000 worth of computers, and $2,000 worth of concert services).

A modern economy would have many more goods and services, of course, but the process of computing GDP would be about the same. The quantities of every final product times their price would be used to estimate their values, and GDP would be the sum of the values.

Economists do this sort of math to find the GDP of real countries. However, we need to know some additional information about GDP.

GDP Only Includes Final Products

Not all economic activities are included in GDP. GDP reflects only the market value, or prices, of final goods and services produced and sold. A *final* good or service is one that is sold to its final user. A bicycle sold to you is a final good. *Intermediate* goods are ones that go into making a final good. The parts used to make the bicycle—such as the tires, seat, and pedals—are intermediate goods. Intermediate goods are not counted in GDP because the final price of the bike already includes the value of those parts.

Products such as bicycles, clothing, and haircuts are called consumer goods and services. In other words, these are products we consume. Economists use the word *consume* to mean "use as a customer." But what about the final goods businesses use—such as machines or office supplies—to make consumer products? These are called producer goods. They are also known as investment goods or capital goods and are included in calculating GDP.

What GDP Does Not Include

GDP does not include every kind of activity in the economy. It includes only final goods and services produced and sold in the market. It does not include intermediate goods and services. GDP does not count services you do for yourself—such as mowing your lawn. The value of used—or secondhand—goods is also not counted. These products were already counted the year when they were first sold. Transferring them to a new owner creates no new production. Thus, buying a used good is not included a second time in the GDP.

Real GDP

Because of the way it is computed, GDP can appear to increase whenever prices go up. Say the price of concerts shown in the table **Estimating Total Annual Output (GDP)** increases from $200 to $225. After recomputing, GDP will appear to go up even though the number of concert tickets sold did not change. Therefore, to make accurate comparisons involving different years, GDP must be adjusted for price increases.

To do so, economists use a set of "constant" prices. They choose a year that serves as the basis of comparison for all other years. Suppose we compute GDP for several years in a row using only prices that existed in 2012. Then, any increases in GDP must be due to an increase in quantity and not an increase in prices. This measure is called **real GDP**, or GDP measured with a set of constant base-year prices. Real GDP removes the distortions caused by price changes.

You can think of real GDP as measuring output in an economy where prices do not change. This makes real GDP a better measure of an economy's performance over time because people's welfare ultimately depends on the quantities of products produced, not their prices.

---

real GDP GDP after adjustments for price changes

If a clothing manufacturer buys this colorful fabric to make shirts or dresses for customers to buy, the sale of fabric would not be counted in GDP. If an individual such as you purchases the fabric, however, the sale would be counted as a final good in GDP.

Explaining Why are intermediate goods not included in the measurement of GDP?

Real GDP 1950–2020 (in constant 2012 prices)

The U.S. economy expanded by 52% from 1960 to 1970, faster than any other decade in the graph.

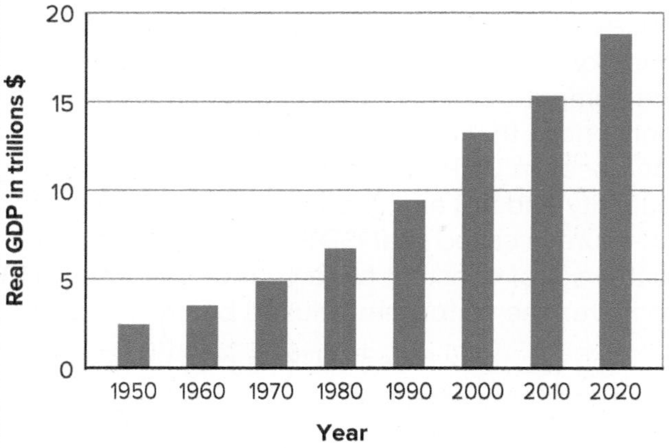

Source: Bureau of Economic Analysis

EXAMINE THE GRAPH

Calculating How would the 2020 GDP in the graph change if it were measured in current dollars instead of constant 2012 dollars?

For example, look at how real GDP for the United States appears in the graph **Real GDP 1950–2020 (in constant 2012 prices)**. The graph shows that the production of real goods and services has actually increased from 1950 to 2020. And none of the increase was due to higher prices. But if GDP is not measured in constant dollars, it is simply called GDP, or current-dollar GDP.

GDP Per Capita

GDP tells how large a country's economy is. But when we compare the output of countries that have different-sized populations, **GDP per capita** is a better measure. *Per capita* means "for each person." GDP per capita is calculated by dividing the country's GDP by its population. The result is the amount of output on a per-person basis. This makes it easier to compare the production of two countries.

The World Bank uses a different way of computing GDP for purposes of comparing two countries. Using its method, China has the world's largest GDP at $24 trillion, and the United States has the second-largest GDP at about $20 trillion. But China's population is much larger. To get a more realistic comparison of the two countries, we would divide China's GDP by its population to get a GDP per capita of about $18,200. If we divide the U.S. GDP by its population, we get a GDP per capita of $62,500. On a per capita basis, the U.S. GDP is more than three times larger than China's GDP; or ($62,500) ÷ ($18,200) = 3.43.

The Standard of Living

The **standard of living** is the quality of life of the people living in a country. GDP is not a measure of the standard of living. This is because GDP is an **aggregate**, or total, number. When we look at GDP, we do not know WHAT was produced, HOW it was produced, or FOR WHOM the production was intended. A country with a GDP that goes to a very few rich people might have a lower standard of living than a country of equal size that produces its goods and services for everyone.

How production takes place is also important. China has a very productive economy but is also a big polluter. If a country does not take steps to reduce its pollution, it could have a lower standard of living than another country.

✓ CHECK FOR UNDERSTANDING

1. **Contrasting** What is the difference between real GDP and GDP per capita?

2. **Analyzing** Why is GDP not necessarily an accurate measure of a nation's standard of living?

LESSON ACTIVITIES

1. **Informative/Explanatory Writing** Research online to find the top five countries based on current GDP, real GDP, and real GDP per capita. Write a short report that displays your findings in a chart and defines the three types of GDP.

2. **Collaborating** With a partner, create a poster illustrating items that are—and are not—counted in GDP. Add captions explaining why you categorized the products the way you did.

GDP per capita GDP on a per-person basis; GDP divided by the population

standard of living material well-being of an individual or a nation as measured by how well needs and wants are satisfied

aggregate total

Measuring the Economy

Economic Performance

Why is it important to measure an economy's performance?

When we want to measure the size of the economy, we look at GDP because it is our most comprehensive measure. But when we want to see if GDP is *growing*, we have to use real GDP.

Real GDP

As you recall, *real GDP* is measured with a set of constant base-year prices. Real GDP is useful because it removes the **distortions**, or misleading impressions, caused by price changes. This makes real GDP a better measure of economic growth over time.

Here's why: GDP is the total dollar value of all final goods and services produced by an economy in one year. But if a country has a bigger GDP in one year than it had in the year before, it does not necessarily mean that its economy grew. If the growth was caused only by an increase in prices and nothing else, the same amount of goods and services would only *appear* to be worth more. Because of this, rising prices can make increases in GDP misleading. To avoid this problem, we always use real GDP when comparing GDPs over time.

distortion misleading impression

The Business Cycle

Phases of economic recession and expansion shape the business cycle.

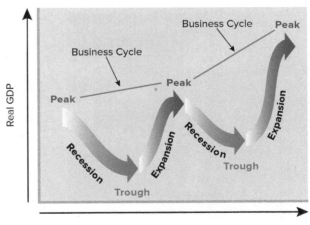

EXAMINE THE DIAGRAM

Analyzing Visuals What is the growing phase of the business cycle called? What happens in this phase?

Business Cycles

The U.S. economy does not grow at a steady rate. Instead, it goes through alternating periods of real economic decline and growth that we call the **business cycle**. Look at the diagram **The Business Cycle**. The diagram shows a simplified version of the economy. It is simplified because business cycles are not as smooth and regular in the real world.

Every business cycle has two distinct parts—a recession and an expansion. A **recession** (rih•SEH•shuhn) begins when real GDP declines after it reaches a *peak*. The recession ends when real GDP hits a *trough* and starts to go up again. Real GDP will then expand for a while, but eventually it will hit another peak and then start to go down.

A business cycle lasts from one peak to the next peak. This means that a business cycle contains one recession and one expansion. Most recessions are fairly short—lasting from about 6 to 18 months. Expansions tend to last longer. Most expansions since the end of World War II have lasted from 5 to 10 years. Economic growth will have taken place if the new peak is higher than the previous peak. Eventually, though, real GDP will start to decline again, marking the start of a new business cycle.

---

business cycle alternating periods of real economic decline and growth

recession period of declining economic activity lasting about six or more months

Unemployed men in Chicago line up outside a soup kitchen for free food during the Great Depression.

The Great Depression

A recession may turn into a depression if real GDP continues to go down rather than turning back up. A **depression** is a period of severe economic decline with rising unemployment and extreme economic hardships. The United States has had only one major depression. It started in 1929 and reached a trough in 1933. The drop in real GDP was so enormous that it took until 1939—a full ten years—for business activity to get back to the level where it had been in 1929. This is the longest period of no growth in U.S. history.

Most economists think that real GDP fell by almost half from 1929 to 1933. This was a time when one in four workers lost their jobs. About one-fourth of banks went out of business. Many stocks became worthless, and millions of people lost everything they had.

Fortunately, most economists think that something as serious as the Great Depression will not happen again. Laws were passed to prevent the kinds of actions that worsened the situation in the 1930s. We also better understand how the economy works and how to keep it healthy. For example, the government plays a bigger role in the economy today than it did in the 1930s. Because of this, the government is more likely to take steps to fix economic problems before they worsen.

✓ **CHECK FOR UNDERSTANDING**

1. **Identifying** What does a peak on a business cycle mean?
2. **Explaining** What is a recession, and what is a depression?

Recessions and Employment

GUIDING QUESTION

How do recessions affect employment?

Although most modern recessions were much less severe than the Great Depression of the 1930s, two recessions stand out. The first is the Great Recession of 2008–2009. The second is the COVID-19 recession of 2020. These recessions and others can be seen in the graph

---

depression state of the economy with high unemployment, severely depressed real GDP, and general economic hardship

U.S. Real GDP 1975–2021

The United States has experienced mainly economic expansion since 1975.

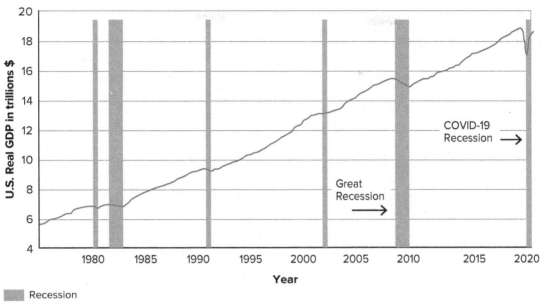

Source: Bureau of Economic Analysis

EXAMINE THE GRAPH

1. **Analyzing** What does a downward slope in the real GDP line show? What about an upward slope?
2. **Analyzing Visuals** How many recessions has the United States experienced since 1975?

U.S. Real GDP 1975–2021. The vertical shaded areas in the graph represent the times when the economy was in recession.

The Great Recession of 2008–2009

The Great Recession began in early 2008 and lasted for 18 months. It was the longest and deepest recession in the United States since the Great Depression of the 1930s. Real GDP declined by 4.5 percent during the 18 months of the Great Recession. Yet it took nearly four years for real GDP to get back to the previous high it had reached in 2008.

More than 8 million people lost their jobs during the Great Recession. This is more than the total number of people who live in Washington or Arizona today! Many of these people lost their homes and cars when they couldn't afford to make their monthly payments. Others were forced to use their retirement savings or went into debt just to cover everyday living expenses.

To prevent the economy from declining too much, the federal government passed two major stimulus programs totaling about $1.5 trillion in 2008. Some of the money was used to keep banks from going under. Some was used to help keep General Motors—the maker of Chevrolet, Buick, and Cadillac cars—in business. Other stimulus money went to unemployed people. Some of these expenditures were controversial, but the Great Recession would have been much worse without them.

Recessions and Unemployment

A key measure of how severe any recession can be is the **unemployment rate**. This is the percentage of people in the civilian labor force who are not working but are looking for jobs.

---

unemployment rate the percentage of people in the civilian labor force who are not working but are looking for jobs

In a normally healthy economy, the unemployment rate is low, usually around 4 percent. Because of a recession, however, the unemployment rate can easily double or triple.

Compare the civilian unemployment rates shown in the graph **U.S. Unemployment Rate 1975–2021** with the shaded areas that represent recessions. You can see that the unemployment rate goes up rapidly during or just before a recession begins. Sometimes the unemployment rate continues to go up after the recession has ended. This happens because businesses want to be sure that the economy is growing again before they hire more workers.

When real GDP declined 4.5 percent during the Great Recession, the unemployment rate more than doubled. It then took nearly 10 years for the unemployment rate to get back down to where it was before the recession started.

The COVID-19 Recession of 2020

After the Great Recession was over, the economy began an unprecedented expansion that lasted almost 11 years. Then, when the unemployment rate was at a record low of 3.5 percent in early February 2020, the COVID-19 virus struck. Many businesses and schools shut down to prevent the virus from spreading. The unemployment rate then quadrupled to a record high of 14.8 percent just two months later—the highest level since the Great Depression.

The government passed three stimulus bills totaling $5 trillion to aid states and the private sector. Part of the stimulus programs involved checks sent out to millions of Americans to restore some spending. This brought the unemployment rate back down from its record high, but did not restore it to the pre-recession low.

✓ **CHECK FOR UNDERSTANDING**

1. **Identifying** How long did the Great Recession last, and what happened to real GDP?
2. **Explaining** What action did the federal government take to prevent the COVID-19 recession of 2020 from getting worse?

U.S. Unemployment Rate 1975–2021

The graph shows changes in the unemployment rate from 1975 to 2021. Keep in mind that an upward movement of the unemployment rate line is bad because it means there are more unemployed workers.

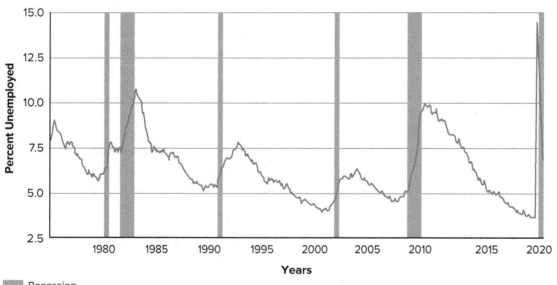

■ Recession

Source: Bureau of Labor Statistics

EXAMINE THE GRAPH

1. **Analyzing Visuals** How would you describe the unemployment rate from 2010 to 2019?
2. **Identifying Cause and Effect** Why does unemployment go up in a recession?

Changes in Prices, January 2021

The consumer price index (CPI) tracks how the prices of different goods most people buy can change over time. Ten of the 400 categories in the CPI are shown in the chart. The CPI is used to track inflation, or changes in the general level of prices in the economy.

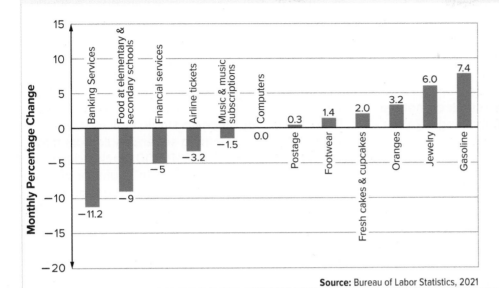

Source: Bureau of Labor Statistics, 2021

EXAMINE THE GRAPH

1. **Analyzing Visuals** What does each bar in the graph show?

2. **Calculating** Would consumers be more or less likely to buy jewelry in January 2021? Why?

Other Measures of Performance

GUIDING QUESTION

What are other signs of an economy's health?

Suppose someone asked you to describe your economic situation. Before answering, you might think about whether you get an allowance, have money to buy the clothes or music you want, or have money saved for a class trip. Adults think about their economic health in a similar way. Nations have economic health, too. To judge that health, economists look at specific *economic indicators*. These are signs that "indicate" how the economy is doing, such as the unemployment rate just discussed. Other key indicators are price stability, stock indexes, and a measurement called the Leading Economic Index®.

Price Stability

One sign of an economy's health is the general level of prices. If prices remain stable or steady, consumers and businesses can better plan for the future. This is especially important for people who are retired and live on a **fixed income**. A fixed income remains the same each month and does not have the potential to increase when prices go up.

When prices remain stable, money has the same purchasing power, or value. When prices go up, money loses some of its purchasing power. For example, suppose an ice-cream cone that costs a dollar doubles in price to two dollars. The higher price means that your dollar buys less. You need to spend twice as many dollars to buy the same ice-cream cone. As the chart **Changes in Prices, January 2021** shows, monthly percentage price changes are not always stable.

An increase in the price of one good does not affect purchasing power very much. If most prices rise, though, the situation is different. **Inflation** (ihn•FLAY•shuhn) is the name for a long-term increase in the general level of prices. Inflation hurts consumers and people on fixed incomes because it reduces everyone's purchasing power.

Every month the government tracks the prices of about 400 products consumers usually buy. Prices of these 400 products make up a measure called the *consumer price index* (CPI). Typically, the prices of some items in the CPI go up every month, and other prices go down. If the overall level of the CPI goes up, inflation is taking place.

fixed income an income that remains the same each month and does not have the potential to go up when prices are going up

inflation a long-term increase in the general level of prices

Of course, prices can go down as well as up. **Deflation** is the name for a prolonged decrease in the general level of prices. Deflation doesn't occur very often, but it did happen for 11 months during the Great Recession of 2008–2009. This had the opposite effect of inflation—it *increased* the purchasing power of everyone's money. But it also hurt sellers who received lower prices for the same products they usually sold.

Stock Indexes

Changes in the value of a single stock do not tell us much about the economy. But changes in *all* stock prices do. That tells us if investors have confidence in the economy.

Supply and demand determine the price of a company's stock. Supply is the number of shares people are willing to sell. Demand is the number of shares investors want to buy. Changes in a company's profits or the release of a new product can change the demand for a company's stock, and its price. A stock index consists of many stocks, so the change in the value of an index shows how the prices of all stocks are changing.

Two popular stock indexes are the Dow Jones Industrial Average (DJIA) and the Standard and Poor's (S&P) 500. The DJIA tracks the prices of 30 stocks. These include companies such as Coca-Cola, McDonald's, Walt Disney, and Walmart. The S&P 500 index tracks the total market value of 500 stocks.

When stock indexes go down, the stock market is called a "**bear market**." A bear market is a mean or "nasty" market (like a bear). Bear markets cause a drop in investors' wealth and can be a sign of an unhealthy economy.

This bull statue in New York City's financial district symbolizes hope for a strong stock market.

Identifying What do stock indexes measure?

If investors feel good about the economy and expect it to grow, they are more likely to buy stocks. These purchases will drive stock prices up. Rising prices mean rising stock indexes. A rising stock market fueled by confident investors is called a "**bull market**." Bull markets are strong (like a bull) and a good sign real GDP will grow.

The Leading Economic Index®

Another measure used to forecast changes in economic growth is the Leading Economic Index (LEI). This index combines several sets of data. The idea is that, since no single indicator works all of the time, combining several indicators may be more accurate. The S&P 500 stock index is in this index. Other data include the number of hours worked in manufacturing and the number of building permits issued in the previous month.

The index is called *leading* because it generally points to the direction in which real GDP is headed. For example, if the LEI goes down several months in a row, real GDP usually goes down a few months later. If the LEI goes up, real GDP usually goes up several months later. The Leading Economic Index, then, is a good tool for predicting the future of the economy.

✓ CHECK FOR UNDERSTANDING

1. **Explaining** What does inflation do to purchasing power? Why?

2. **Describing** How does the government keep track of inflation? Why does it do so?

LESSON ACTIVITIES

1. **Narrative Writing** Suppose you lived through a swing in the business cycle from recession to peak economic growth. Write a story contrasting life during a recession with life during a period of peak economic growth.

2. **Using Multimedia** With a partner, research images and music of the Great Depression. Prepare a slide show with audio that reveals how difficult life was during much of the 1930s. End the slide show with images of economic recovery in the United States.

deflation a prolonged decrease in the general level of prices

bear market period during which stock prices decline for a substantial period

bull market period during which stock prices steadily increase

04

The Federal Reserve System and Monetary Policy

READING STRATEGY

Analyzing Key Ideas and Details As you read the lesson, identify the functions of the Federal Reserve System.

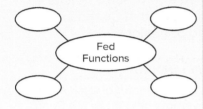

The Fed's Structure

GUIDING QUESTION

What is the structure of the Federal Reserve System?

In the early 1900s, the United States suffered several severe recessions. During these hard times, banks were unable to make new loans. This crisis hurt even the largest and strongest banks. As a result, most people thought conditions would be better if the nation had a central bank. A **central bank** is a bankers' bank that lends to other banks when times are difficult.

Although the country needed a central bank, the government did not have enough money to finance one. As a result, it decided to require all banks with a national charter to contribute funds to build the new central bank. In return, they would receive some stock in that central bank. The result was the 1913 creation of the Federal Reserve System, or "the Fed" as it is often called. This was the first true central bank for the United States.

Today, the Fed has several very important responsibilities. It manages our currency, regulates more than 5,000 commercial banks and savings institutions, serves as the government's bank, and conducts specific policies to keep the economy healthy and strong. To understand how it does all these things, we first need to see how the Fed is organized.

central bank a bankers' bank that lends money to other banks in difficult times

The Federal Reserve Building is located in Washington, D.C. The "Fed" is our nation's central bank.

Explaining What is the role of a central bank?

GO ONLINE Explore the Student Edition eBook and find interactive maps, charts, graphs, and tools.

E125

Glow Images

The Board of Governors

At the top of the Fed is a seven-member Board of Governors. Each member is nominated by the president and must be **confirmed**, or approved, by the Senate. The members serve staggered 14-year terms, so they are fairly free of influence from elected officials. This enables them to make decisions that are in the best interest of the economy. The Board typically meets every other week.

District Banks

The Federal Reserve System has 12 districts, each with a district bank. These banks are also called Federal Reserve Banks. Each bank carries out the Fed's policies and oversees banking within its district. Nine directors run each district bank. Any profits earned by these banks are paid to the U.S. Treasury.

The Federal Open Market Committee

The **Federal Open Market Committee (FOMC)** influences the whole economy by managing the money supply and thus affecting interest rates. The next section explains why and how the Fed makes changes to the money supply.

---

confirmed approved

Federal Open Market Committee (FOMC) powerful committee of the Fed that makes decisions affecting the economy by managing the money supply in order to affect interest rates

The Federal Reserve Bank of Chicago carries out Fed policy in District 7.

Advisory Councils

The Board of Governors receives advice from three advisory councils. One advises on consumer borrowing. The second advises on matters relating to the banking system. The third works with the Board of Governors on issues related to savings and loan institutions.

Member Institutions

The Federal Reserve System is more than just a bank. It is a true "system" that supervises more than 5,000 member institutions in all U.S. states and territories. The Fed also ensures that its members carry out the laws that Congress has passed regarding Fed operations.

✓ CHECK FOR UNDERSTANDING

1. **Speculating** How does the term of each member of the Board of Governors help make the Board independent of political influence?

2. **Making Connections** How are the parts of the Federal Reserve System related to one another?

What the Fed Does

GUIDING QUESTION

What are the functions of the Federal Reserve System?

The Fed has several important functions. One of these is conducting monetary policy. The Fed also regulates and supervises banks, maintains the currency, promotes consumer protection, and acts as the government's bank.

Conducting Monetary Policy

The Fed is in charge of conducting monetary policy. **Monetary policy** means managing the monetary base to affect the cost and availability of credit. The *monetary base* is the currency in circulation and the deposits that banks and other depository institutions have at the Fed. While this may sound complicated, think of it as a case of supply and demand that determines the interest rate—which is the price of borrowing money.

The two **Monetary Policy and Interest Rates** graphs show how this works. In panel A, the Fed expands the monetary base, shifting the money supply to the right.

---

monetary policy Fed's management of the money supply to affect the cost and availability of credit

The Federal Reserve System

The Federal Reserve System has a complex structure. Each part carries out specific functions.

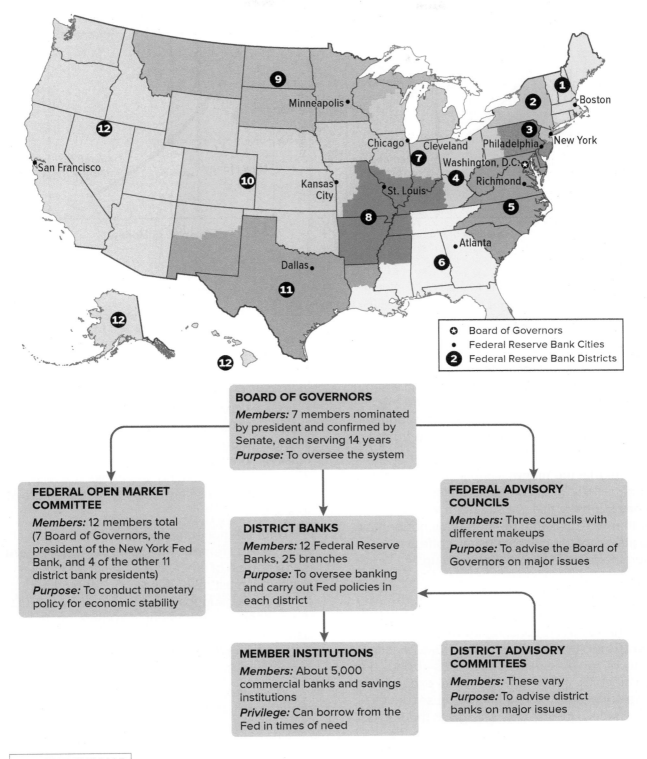

Map legend:
- ✪ Board of Governors
- • Federal Reserve Bank Cities
- ② Federal Reserve Bank Districts

Map cities: Minneapolis, Chicago, Cleveland, Philadelphia, New York, Boston, San Francisco, Kansas City, St. Louis, Washington, D.C., Richmond, Dallas, Atlanta

District numbers: 1, 2, 3, 4, 5, 6, 7, 8, 9, 10, 11, 12

BOARD OF GOVERNORS
Members: 7 members nominated by president and confirmed by Senate, each serving 14 years
Purpose: To oversee the system

FEDERAL OPEN MARKET COMMITTEE
Members: 12 members total (7 Board of Governors, the president of the New York Fed Bank, and 4 of the other 11 district bank presidents)
Purpose: To conduct monetary policy for economic stability

DISTRICT BANKS
Members: 12 Federal Reserve Banks, 25 branches
Purpose: To oversee banking and carry out Fed policies in each district

FEDERAL ADVISORY COUNCILS
Members: Three councils with different makeups
Purpose: To advise the Board of Governors on major issues

MEMBER INSTITUTIONS
Members: About 5,000 commercial banks and savings institutions
Privilege: Can borrow from the Fed in times of need

DISTRICT ADVISORY COMMITTEES
Members: These vary
Purpose: To advise district banks on major issues

EXAMINE THE MAP

1. **Exploring Regions** How many district banks are in the Fed? What are the roles of the district banks?

2. **Analyzing Visuals** Which component oversees the Federal Reserve System?

Monetary Policy and Interest Rates

The two graphs show the effects of the Fed's efforts to expand or contract the money supply.

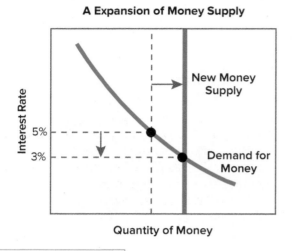

A Expansion of Money Supply

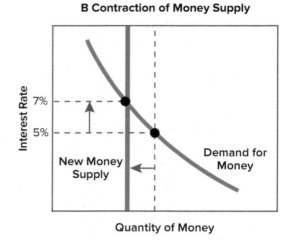

B Contraction of Money Supply

EXAMINE THE GRAPHS

1. **Analyzing Visuals** What happens to interest rates when the money supply expands?
2. **Explaining** Why might the Fed want to lower interest rates?

This lowers the interest rate to 3 percent from 5 percent. Panel B shows what happens when the Fed reduces the monetary base and the money supply contracts. This shifts the money supply to the left, and interest rates go from 5 percent to 7 percent.

Note that the money supply curve appears as a vertical line. This is because the size of the money supply is fixed at any point in time. Another reason is that the Fed does not behave like a for-profit firm, which usually offers more when the price of its product goes up.

Tools of Monetary Policy

The most important tool of monetary policy is open market operations. **Open market operations (OMO)** refers to the FOMC's action to buy or sell *government securities*—bonds and Treasury bills. If the FOMC wants to expand the monetary base, it buys government securities from financial institutions. This gives the banks money to be loaned to customers. With the money supply expanding, interest rates go down.

Businesses and people borrow more, which increases economic activity.

If the FOMC wants to *contract* the money supply, it sells some of the government securities it holds. To buy the securities, financial institutions must withdraw money and transfer it to the Fed. With less money to lend, the banks will raise interest rates, possibly causing economic growth to slow.

Another monetary policy tool is changing the reserve requirement. The **reserve requirement** is the portion of a new deposit that a financial institution must reserve and *cannot* lend out. For example, suppose someone deposits $100. If the reserve requirement is 20 percent, the bank must keep 20 percent of that $100—or $20—as a reserve. The bank can then lend the remaining $80.

When the Fed lowers the reserve requirement, all banks can loan more of their deposits. This *expands* the money supply, and interest rates go down. Lower interest rates help people who want to take vacations or buy things

---

open market operations (OMO) Fed's purchase or sale of U.S. government securities—bond notes and Treasury bills

reserve requirement percentage of a deposit that banks have to set aside as cash in their vaults or as deposits in their Federal Reserve district bank

such as cars and houses. In early 2020 during the COVID-19 recession, the Fed cut the reserve requirement to zero. This meant that banks could lend all the deposits customers made.

In contrast, raising the reserve requirement makes fewer reserves available to be loaned out, which *contracts* the money supply. This happens if the Fed thinks the money supply is getting too big, or that interest rates are too low.

A third way the Fed controls the money supply is by changing the discount rate. The **discount rate** is the interest rate the Fed charges on loans to member institutions when they borrow from the Fed. If the Fed wants to *expand* the money supply, it could lower the discount rate. The reduced rate might encourage banks to borrow from the Fed. Banks could then loan this borrowed money, and the money supply grows. If the Fed wants to *contract* the money supply, it raises the discount rate. A higher rate discourages borrowing.

A bank might also need to borrow money from the Fed's "discount" window if it faced a "liquidity crisis"—such as customers suddenly wanting to withdraw some or all of their deposits. If a bank had already loaned out all of its deposits, it would not have enough money on hand to give customers their withdrawals. But the

---

discount rate interest rate the Fed charges on its loans to financial institutions

bank could borrow from the Fed, the discount rate would be charged on the borrowed money, and depositors would get their withdrawals.

Regulating and Supervising Banks

The Fed writes other rules member banks must follow. These involve everything from ways that banks must report the reserve requirements to how they make loans to bank officers. The Fed also has the power to approve mergers between member banks. Many of the world's largest banks located in other countries have branch offices in the United States. The Fed is responsible for ensuring that all foreign bank branch offices that operate on U.S. soil follow all of our banking laws and regulations.

Maintaining the Currency

The Bureau of Engraving and Printing prints our "paper" money, which is really made of linen and cotton. After the new money is printed, it is sent to the Fed for safekeeping and distribution. It will not be counted as part of our money supply until it is released to commercial banks and other lending institutions.

The Fed is also responsible for pulling old money out of use. Whenever paper money becomes tattered and worn, it is sent to the Fed. The Fed exchanges the old bills for newer currency and destroys the worn-out currency.

A newspaper headline announces that the Fed will lower interest rates. This is front page news because people, businesses, and governments react to information from the Fed.

Consumers often pay for major purchases with borrowed money, or credit. When the Fed expands the money supply, interest rates go down, and the cost of borrowing money is lower. As a result, people like this father and daughter will be more likely to use credit to purchase big-ticket items, such as a car.

Making Connections What other action by the Fed protects the father and daughter purchasing the vehicle on credit?

Thus, the Fed plays a major role in keeping our currency in good condition.

Protecting Consumers

Based on laws passed by Congress, the Fed creates rules all lenders must follow. For example, the Fed designed most of the forms people have to sign when they take out a car loan. These forms require lenders to spell out the terms of the loan clearly. The Fed also writes rules that prevent lenders from using deceptive practices when making loans.

Acting as the Government's Bank

Finally, the Fed acts as the government's bank. Whenever people write a check to the U.S. Treasury to pay their taxes, those checks are sent to the Fed for deposit. The Fed also holds other money the government receives and keeps it until it is needed.

The government can write checks on these deposits whenever it needs to make a purchase or other payment. Any federal agency check, such as a monthly Social Security check, is taken out of an account at the Fed.

✓ **CHECK FOR UNDERSTANDING**

1. **Identifying** What is monetary policy?
2. **Explaining** What are two things the Fed can do to expand the money supply?

LESSON ACTIVITIES

1. **Informative/Explanatory Writing** Write an article for an online student resource that explains the functions of the Federal Reserve System and its role in the nation's economy.

2. **Collaborating** With a partner, make flashcards that give details about parts of the Fed. For example, one flashcard might state on the front: "There are 12 of these." The answer on the back of the card would be "District Banks, also called Federal Reserve Banks." After preparing 15 to 20 flashcards, challenge another pair of students to a quiz-off.

Financing the Government

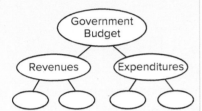

The Federal Budget Process

GUIDING QUESTION

How does the federal government prepare a budget?

Do you know how to make a personal budget? First, you figure out what your income is for a period, such as a month. Then, you estimate your savings and expenses for that month. Tally your regular expenses, such as weekly food costs. Account for occasional costs too—such as a birthday gift for a parent. If expenses are greater than income, you need to cut spending or find a way to earn more income. Another strategy is to borrow to cover overspending. Borrowing will lead to debt, however, and getting out of debt is often difficult.

The federal government also has a budget. It has two main parts—revenues and expenditures. **Revenue** is the money a government collects to fund its spending. The federal budget covers a period called a fiscal (FIHS•kuhl) year. A fiscal year is any 12 months chosen for keeping accounts. The **fiscal year** of the federal government begins October 1 and ends September 30 of the next year. For example, fiscal year 2022 began October 1, 2021, and ended September 30, 2022.

revenue money a government collects to fund its spending

fiscal year any 12-month period chosen for keeping accounts

The Federal Budget Process

Congress faces deadlines for acting on the budget. It is supposed to approve the budget resolution by April 15. It does not always meet this date, however.

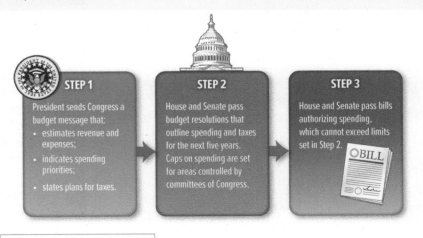

STEP 1

President sends Congress a budget message that:
- estimates revenue and expenses;
- indicates spending priorities;
- states plans for taxes.

STEP 2

House and Senate pass budget resolutions that outline spending and taxes for the next five years. Caps on spending are set for areas controlled by committees of Congress.

STEP 3

House and Senate pass bills authorizing spending, which cannot exceed limits set in Step 2.

BILL

EXAMINE THE DIAGRAM

1. **Making Connections** Why are tax revenue estimates included in the budget?

2. **Inferring** What relationship does the budget resolution have to the president's budget?

The Federal Budget Process diagram shows just the general steps in making a federal budget. This process is complex because of the size of the budget and the number of parties involved.

Steps in the Budget Process

The process starts when the president **transmits**, or sends, a budget message to Congress. This message states how much the president wants to spend on each federal program. This message must be sent no later than the first Monday in February.

Next, key members of Congress agree on a *budget resolution*. This is Congress's plan for revenue and spending on broad categories such as health. The budget has two different kinds of spending: mandatory (MAN•duh•TOHR•ee) and discretionary (dis•KREH•shuh•NEHR•ee). **Mandatory spending** is set by laws outside the budget process. One example is Social Security, which makes payments to retirees. Mandatory spending is generally fixed from year to year. **Discretionary spending** involves spending choices made and approved each year. It includes items such as national defense and highways. The amount of discretionary spending can differ from year to year.

Next, Congress must set spending on each program for the coming year. That process starts

---

transmit send

mandatory spending federal spending required by law that continues without the need for congressional approval each year

discretionary spending spending for federal programs that must receive approval each year

Americans obtain a Social Security number when they are born. Social Security falls under the "mandatory spending" category of the federal budget.

Explaining What is the difference between mandatory and discretionary spending?

---

when committees in the House write appropriations (uh•proh•pree•AY•shuhnz) bills. An **appropriations bill** gives official approval for the government to spend money. All appropriations bills start in the House of Representatives, but they must be approved by both the House and Senate. After the Senate and House pass each bill, it is sent to the president. The president can either sign it into law or veto it. If the bill is vetoed, Congress can rewrite the bill or override the veto.

Sometimes Congress does not pass the budget in time. When this happens, Congress approves a *continuing resolution*. This law sets spending for the coming year at the same level as the year before.

How the Budget Process Changed Over Time

When the federal government began, it had fewer sources of revenue and spent less than the government does today. The budget process was very informal, with little overall planning.

Over time, federal spending increased. As a result, the budget process had to be improved. Congress passed a law in 1921 that made the process more formal. For the first time, the president was required to send a budget to Congress each year. In 1974 Congress passed another law to improve the budget process. It required Congress to set up committees to focus on the budget. It also set up the Congressional Budget Office (CBO). That office has the job of estimating the cost of proposed legislation, tracking spending and revenue measures, and making reports to Congress.

The budget process still faces difficulties today, however. For example, members of Congress often add spending for pet projects to major bills. These add-ons can increase overall spending and often increase the category of discretionary or even mandatory expenditures.

✓ **CHECK FOR UNDERSTANDING**

1. **Comparing and Contrasting** How is making the federal budget similar to and different from making a personal budget?

2. **Analyzing** What kinds of choices are involved in making the federal budget?

---

appropriations bill legislation that sets spending on particular programs for the coming year

zimmytws/iStockphoto/Getty Images

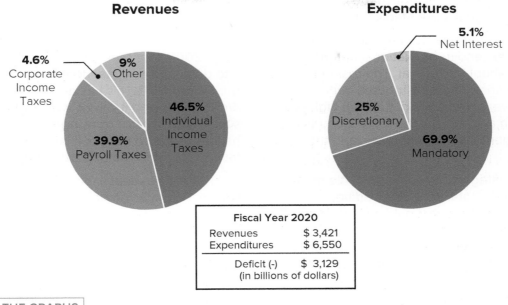

The Federal Budget, Fiscal Year 2020

Federal spending for Fiscal Year (FY) 2020 was much higher than revenues. This happened because the economy was in recession that year and there had been massive tax cuts.

Revenues

- 4.6% Corporate Income Taxes
- 9% Other
- 46.5% Individual Income Taxes
- 39.9% Payroll Taxes

Expenditures

- 5.1% Net Interest
- 25% Discretionary
- 69.9% Mandatory

Fiscal Year 2020	
Revenues	$ 3,421
Expenditures	$ 6,550
Deficit (-)	$ 3,129
(in billions of dollars)	

EXAMINE THE GRAPHS

1. **Analyzing Visuals** What are the two largest sources of revenue?
2. **Predicting** What happens to federal revenue when many people lose their jobs? Why?

Understanding the Federal Budget

GUIDING QUESTION

How does the federal budget reflect choices?

Federal Budget Revenues

The circle graph of **Federal Revenues** shows the individual income tax as the biggest source of federal revenue. This tax is paid by all people who earn income above a certain amount. The second-largest share of revenue is from payroll taxes. These are taken from workers' paychecks to fund social insurance programs such as Social Security and Medicare. Medicare provides some health care coverage for people age 65 and older. Finally, the third-largest source of revenue comes from the tax that corporations pay on their profits.

Taxes fall into three categories: progressive, proportional, and regressive. With a *progressive tax*, the tax rate goes up as income goes up. The federal income tax is a progressive tax. A *proportional tax* has a constant tax rate, regardless of income. The tax for Medicare is proportional because it is the same rate for all wage earners. A *regressive tax* takes a smaller percentage of your income as the amount you earn goes up. The sales tax is an example of a regressive tax.

Federal Budget Expenditures

The circle graph of **Federal Expenditures** shows mandatory and discretionary federal spending for Fiscal Year 2020. The mandatory part of federal spending is the largest category, accounting for almost 70 percent of all federal spending. Social Security (not shown) is the largest component of mandatory expenditures. Medicare, a federal health insurance program for senior citizens regardless of income, is the second-largest category. Expenditures for the Small Business Administration was third-largest. The COVID-19 recession pushed unemployment compensation expenditures into fourth place. Medicaid, a joint federal-state medical insurance program for low-income people, was the fifth-largest mandatory expenditure.

Collectively, mandatory expenditures are expected to increase as our population gets older and medical expenses continue to rise. Unemployment compensation expenditures will get smaller as the economy moves out of recession. And programs designed to help low-income Americans find better jobs and earn more secure incomes will reduce the demand for welfare-type programs like Medicaid.

Discretionary programs make up 25 percent of all federal expenditures. National defense accounts for about half of that. The rest of the discretionary spending is distributed over programs covering education, training, highway transportation and repairs, the federal courts and law enforcement, natural resources, and the environment.

The final category, amounting to little more than 5 percent of total federal spending, is *net interest*. This is the interest paid on the money the government has borrowed to cover its overspending. When the federal government borrows, it must pay interest on its debt, just like any consumer who takes out a loan. As government borrowing goes up, so does the interest owed. This category is expected to go up significantly if government borrowing continues and if interest rates rise.

Federal Budget Deficits

The **Federal Budget, Fiscal Year 2020** graph shows the federal budget situation in 2020.

An Amtrak train pulls out of a station in New Orleans. Funding for Amtrak, along with other public transportation systems, is a discretionary federal expenditure.

Identifying What other programs are included in discretionary expenditures?

With total revenues of $3,421 billion and total expenses of $6,550 billion, a *deficit*—or shortfall—of $3,129 billion remained. This was a staggering amount by any historical standard! In fact, the deficit for 2020 was almost as large as the total amount of money the government collected from all other sources that year.

The federal budget has had yearly deficits since 2001. Together, these annual deficits turned into debt, and our total debt is now larger than our annual GDP. This has not happened since World War II, and it will be a difficult problem to solve. Why? Even a growing economy will not have a balanced budget if current spending and taxing programs remain unchanged.

The federal debt is discussed more in a later lesson. For now, remember this: yearly deficits turn into total debt. And just like any consumer who takes out a loan, the government must pay interest on what it borrows. If people believe that reducing the deficit and debt are important, they must be willing to accept less from the federal government and pay more for the services they receive. Enacting necessary changes will require cooperation and courage by our elected leaders—soon. Solutions will be harder to achieve the longer they are delayed.

✓ CHECK FOR UNDERSTANDING

1. **Describing** What is a progressive tax? What is an example of a progressive tax?
2. **Explaining** Why does the government owe interest?

Budgeting for State and Local Governments

GUIDING QUESTION

How do state and local revenues and expenditures differ from those of the federal government?

State and local governments also prepare budgets. The governments of all states except Vermont cannot, by law, spend more than they receive in revenue. Local governments also have to limit spending so they do not exceed revenues.

State Governments

The **State and Local Government Revenue and Expenses** graphs are for all states combined. As you can see, the largest source of state income is

State and Local Government Revenue and Expenses

The federal government provides money to state governments. State governments, in turn, provide funds for local governments.

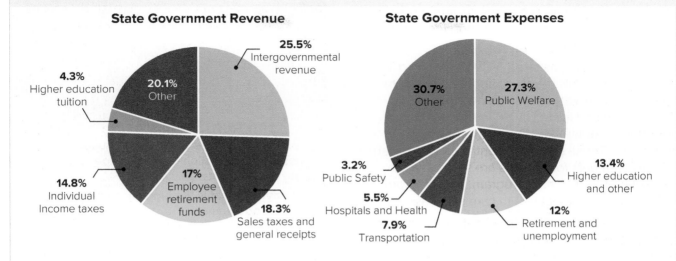

State Government Revenue

- 25.5% Intergovernmental revenue
- 20.1% Other
- 4.3% Higher education tuition
- 14.8% Individual Income taxes
- 17% Employee retirement funds
- 18.3% Sales taxes and general receipts

State Government Expenses

- 30.7% Other
- 27.3% Public Welfare
- 3.2% Public Safety
- 5.5% Hospitals and Health
- 7.9% Transportation
- 13.4% Higher education and other
- 12% Retirement and unemployment

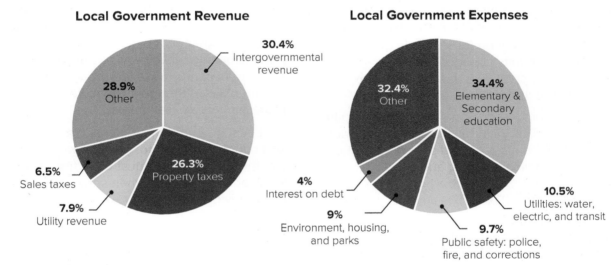

Local Government Revenue

- 30.4% Intergovernmental revenue
- 28.9% Other
- 6.5% Sales taxes
- 7.9% Utility revenue
- 26.3% Property taxes

Local Government Expenses

- 32.4% Other
- 34.4% Elementary & Secondary education
- 4% Interest on debt
- 9% Environment, housing, and parks
- 9.7% Public safety: police, fire, and corrections
- 10.5% Utilities: water, electric, and transit

EXAMINE THE GRAPHS

1. **Analyzing Visuals** What is one specific tax that local governments collect and state governments do not?

2. **Inferring** Which level of government—state or local—would be hurt more by an end to intergovernmental revenue? Why?

Intergovernmental revenue. These are funds that one level of government receives from another level of government. States receive this money from the federal government.

Sales taxes are the states' second-most-important source of revenue. A **sales tax** is paid when someone buys a good or service. All but five states have sales taxes. A 5 percent sales tax on clothing means that a person spending $100 on clothes pays another $5 in taxes. Sales taxes

can be regressive, meaning that they are a bigger burden on low-income than on high-income earners. As a result, many states do not tax essential goods such as food and medicine. Some states also declare sales tax holidays.

intergovernmental revenue funds that one level of government receives from another level of government

sales tax tax paid by consumers at the time they buy goods or services

During these periods, sales taxes on most products, including school supplies, are not taxed.

All but nine states have a personal or individual income tax. In some states this tax is proportional, with all taxpayers paying a flat rate. In others it is progressive, with high incomes taxed at higher rates.

The single biggest area of state spending is public welfare. This refers to programs meant to help those people with little money to maintain basic health and living conditions. Most of this spending is required by states' **entitlement programs**. These are called "entitlements" because the requirements for benefits are set by law. An example is the Medicaid program. This program helps poor people get health care services.

Education is another large category of state spending. Some of this spending goes to local governments to help fund buildings and operations at state colleges and universities. This spending helps **subsidize** (SUHB·suh·DYZ), or pay for, higher education for students going to the states' community colleges and state universities. This subsidy helps make higher education more affordable.

"Other" refers to additional state spending in all other areas. This includes insurance payments to retired state employees and spending in such areas as state police, prisons, and parks.

Local Governments

Like states, local governments must raise money. The biggest difference is that local governments rely heavily on property taxes. A **property tax** is a tax based on the value of land and property that people own. Generally, the higher the value of the property, the higher the property tax that is paid. Many states allow their local governments to charge sales taxes and collect income taxes as well. Fines for traffic and other violations, along with fees for permits and special services, also provide income for local governments.

Local governments provide many of the basic services on which citizens depend. Education is

---

entitlement program a government program that makes payments to people who meet certain requirements in order to help them meet minimum health, nutrition, and income needs

subsidize to aid or support a person, business, institution, or undertaking with money or tax breaks

property tax tax on the value of land and property that people own

A professor lectures to university students. Subsidizing education is a large expenditure for state governments.

Identifying What is the biggest spending area for state governments?

the largest portion of local spending. Water and electric utilities are the second-largest category of local spending. Police and fire protection are the third-largest part of local budgets. Professionals always provide police services. Volunteers can provide fire protection in small communities, although larger cities often have professionals as firefighters.

Local governments build and maintain city and county streets, too. In areas with harsh winter weather, city workers must clear the streets of snow and apply salt to melt snow and ice to make driving safe.

✓ CHECK FOR UNDERSTANDING

1. **Identifying** What is the largest local government expenditure?

2. **Explaining** What is intergovernmental revenue? How does it work?

LESSON ACTIVITIES

1. **Informative/Explanatory Writing** Write a paragraph explaining how the federal government prepares a budget and makes spending decisions. Include all steps through appropriations.

2. **Presenting** With a partner, use the Internet to find out how your state ranks among other states in terms of state sales taxes and individual income taxes. Then create a poster highlighting economic advantages of living in your state. Use the tax information—along with other economic statistics—to convince people to live in your state.

Shutterstock

06

Multiple Perspectives: Taxes

? COMPELLING QUESTION

Are tax rates fair?

Plan Your Inquiry

DEVELOPING QUESTIONS

Read the Compelling Question for this lesson. What questions can you ask to help you answer this Compelling Question? Create a graphic organizer like the one below. Write three Supporting Questions in the first column.

Supporting Questions	Source	What this source tells me about tax rates	Questions the source leaves unanswered
	A		
	B		
	C		
	D		
	E		

ANALYZING SOURCES

Next, read the introductory information for each source in this lesson. Then analyze each source by answering the questions that follow it. How does each source help you answer each Supporting Question you created? What questions do you still have? Write those in your graphic organizer.

After you analyze the sources, you will:
- use the evidence from the sources
- communicate your conclusions
- take informed action

Background Information

Taxes fall into three categories: progressive, proportional, and regressive. With a *progressive tax*, the tax rate goes up as income goes up. The federal income tax is a progressive tax. After you get a job and start earning wages or a salary, you will be required to give some of your paycheck to the federal and state and local governments. The more you earn, the more taxes you'll pay.

This Inquiry Lesson includes sources about tax rates. As you read and analyze the sources, think about the Compelling Question.

Is it fair to ask people to pay more in taxes than they already do?

Time Line of Top Federal Income Tax Rates

The percentage of income tax paid at the top bracket, or level, of wealth has changed over time.

PRIMARY SOURCE: ONLINE ARTICLE

❝ The tax law, like almost all laws, grows as lawmakers use it for **pork**, try to make it fairer, use it to stimulate a sector of the economy, or just want to raise revenue.

In 1913, the top tax bracket was 7 percent on all income over $500,000 ($11 million in today's dollars); and the lowest tax bracket was 1 percent.

World War I In order to finance U.S. participation in World War One, Congress passed the 1916 Revenue Act, and then the War Revenue Act of 1917. The highest income tax rate jumped from 15 percent in 1916 to 67 percent in 1917 to 77 percent in 1918. War is expensive. After the war, federal income tax rates took on the steam of the roaring 1920s, dropping to 25 percent from 1925 through 1931.

The Depression Congress raised taxes again in 1932 during the Great Depression from 25 percent to 63 percent on the top earners.

World War II As we mentioned earlier, war is expensive. In 1944, the top rate peaked at 94 percent on taxable income over $200,000 ($2.5 million in today's dollars). That's a high tax rate.

The 1950s, 1960s, and 1970s Over the next three decades, the top federal income tax rate remained high, never dipping below 70 percent.

The 1980s The Economic Recovery Tax Act of 1981 slashed the highest rate from 70 to 50 percent, and indexed the brackets for inflation. Then, the Tax Reform Act of 1986, claiming that it was a two-tiered flat tax, expanded the tax base and dropped the top rate to 28 percent for tax years beginning in 1988. . . .

The 1990s–2012 During the 1990s, the top rate jumped to 39.6 percent. However, the Economic Growth and Tax Relief and Reconciliation Act of 2001 dropped the highest income tax rate to 35 percent from 2003 to 2010. The Tax Relief, Unemployment Insurance Reauthorization, and Job Creation Act of 2010 maintained the 35 percent tax rate through 2012.

2013–2017 The American Taxpayer Relief Act of 2012 increased the highest income tax rate to 39.6 percent. The Patient Protection and Affordable Care Act added an additional 3.8 percent on to this making the maximum federal income tax rate 43.4 percent.

2018–2021 The highest income tax rate was lowered to 37 percent for tax years beginning in 2018. The additional 3.8 percent is still applicable, making the maximum federal income tax rate 40.8 percent. ❞

— From "History of Federal Income Tax Rates: 1913–2021," bradfordtaxinstitute.com

pork projects paid for with taxes that benefit only a local area or a pet (personal) project

---

EXAMINE THE SOURCE

1. **Identifying** When was the tax rate highest for the wealthy?
2. **Evaluating** What rate do you think is a fair rate for the wealthy to be taxed? Explain.

Income Before and After Taxes

The graph below includes four separate bar graphs—each dividing the U.S. population into *quintiles*, or fifths. The first graph on the left shows that the highest one-fifth—or 20% of Americans—earned, on average, more than $300,000 in 2017. The lowest quintile, or 20% of Americans, earned about $20,000.

The second set of bars shows the amount of "transfers" each quintile received. *Transfers* are cash payments and similar welfare benefits from federal, state, and local governments. They are designed to help individuals and families who have low income.

The third set of bars shows the amount of federal income tax each quintile paid in 2017.

The fourth set of bars shows the amount of income each quintile earned after *adding* in any transfer payments and *subtracting* the amount paid in federal income taxes.

PRIMARY SOURCE: GRAPH

Income Before and After Transfers and Taxes

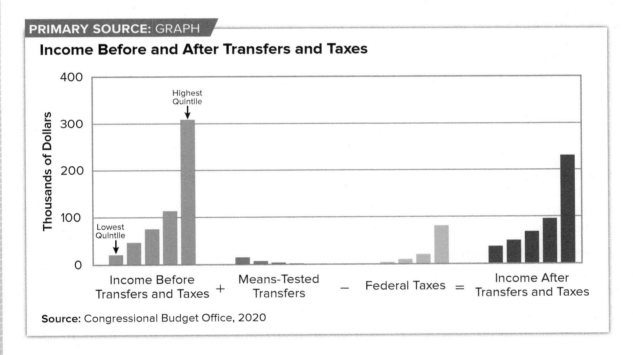

Source: Congressional Budget Office, 2020

EXAMINE THE SOURCE

1. **Speculating** Why are there essentially only four bars shown for "Means-Tested Transfers" and for "Federal Taxes"?

2. **Analyzing** About how much in federal taxes did the wealthy, or highest quintile, pay? What was their income after taxes were paid?

Wealth Tax

Some government leaders and economists have suggested taxing not only the *income* of the richest Americans, but also their *wealth*.

PRIMARY SOURCE: ONLINE ARTICLE

" Income is different from wealth. Income is what you earn from your labor each year as well as interest, dividends, capital gains, and rents (if you're lucky enough to have any). Wealth is the value of the things you own, such as stocks, bonds, houses, etc. The federal government taxes income, but generally doesn't tax wealth except when someone makes a profit on the sale of assets, such as a share of stock or a piece of property. The Federal Reserve estimates that the top 1% holds slightly more wealth (31.1%) than the entire bottom 90% of the population (29.9%), and their share has been rising over time.

Senator Elizabeth Warren's proposal would impose a 2% annual tax on households with a net worth of more than $50 million, and a 3% tax on every dollar of net worth over $1 billion. A family worth $60 million, for instance, would owe $200,000 in wealth tax on top of their income taxes. The developers of this tax, Emmanuel Saez and Gabriel Zucman of the University of California at Berkeley, estimate that 75,000 households—or about one out of 1,700—would pay the tax.

Advocates say a wealth tax would **dilute** the largest fortunes in the U.S. and restrain the emergence of a **plutocracy**. It could encourage the wealthy to **dissipate** their fortunes by spending the money, giving it to charity, or giving it to their children to avoid the tax. But even so it would still raise a lot of money. Saez and Zucman say Warren's tax would yield $2.75 trillion over 10 years. Critics . . . say that's a substantial overestimate.

Opponents say that a wealth tax could discourage or **penalize** the most successful entrepreneurs, not just old money. And they say these sorts of taxes are hard to administer—the **IRS** would have to value art collections and antiques, for instance—and would spur creative tax avoidance. "

— From "Who Are the Rich And How Might We Tax Them More?" by David Wessel, Brookings, 2019.

advocates those who are in favor of something

dilute reduce or weaken

plutocracy country or society governed by the wealthy

dissipate break up

opponents those who are against something

penalize punish

IRS Internal Revenue Service; institution that collects federal taxes

---

EXAMINE THE SOURCE

1. **Identifying** According to this source, what percentage of wealth does the top 1 percent of people hold in the United States?

2. **Summarizing** What reasons are given for advocating the wealth tax? What reasons are given for opposing the wealth tax?

TEXT: Wessel, David. "Who Are the Rich and How Might We Tax Them More?" Policy 2020. The Brookings Institute. October 19, 2020. https://www.brookings.edu/policy2020/votevital/who-are-the-rich-and-how-might-we-tax-them-more/.

The Rich Pay Enough

The article below makes the case that the rich already pay their fair share of taxes.

PRIMARY SOURCE: ONLINE ARTICLE AND CHART

> High-income Americans already pay the large majority of taxes, and the U.S. tax system is highly progressive when compared to those of other countries around the world.
>
> The latest government data show that in 2018, the top 1% of income earners—those who earned more than $540,000—earned 21% of all U.S. income while paying 40% of all federal income taxes. The top 10% earned 48% of the income and paid 71% of federal income taxes.

— From "In 1 Chart, How Much the Rich Pay in Taxes" by Adam Michel, www.heritage.org, 2021.

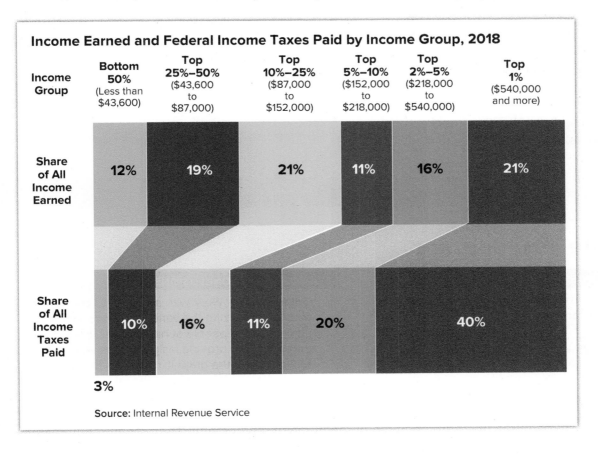

Income Earned and Federal Income Taxes Paid by Income Group, 2018

Income Group	Bottom 50% (Less than $43,600)	Top 25%–50% ($43,600 to $87,000)	Top 10%–25% ($87,000 to $152,000)	Top 5%–10% ($152,000 to $218,000)	Top 2%–5% ($218,000 to $540,000)	Top 1% ($540,000 and more)
Share of All Income Earned	12%	19%	21%	11%	16%	21%
Share of All Income Taxes Paid	3%	10%	16%	11%	20%	40%

Source: Internal Revenue Service

EXAMINE THE SOURCES

1. **Analyzing Visuals** According to the chart, what share of total taxes were paid by those with earnings of $87,000–$152,000?

2. **Evaluating** Do you agree with this source, that the wealthy already pay their fair share of taxes? Explain.

The Rich Should Pay More

Some people think raising tax rates for the wealthy is fair.

" Sometimes, the haggling and hemming and hawing over what to do about the debt overshadow a point that many Americans find obvious: It's simply a good, fair idea to tax the wealthy. They have **disproportionately** reaped the benefits of economic growth and the stock market in recent years, contributing to increasing inequality in the United States. The divide has become even more obvious during the Covid-19 pandemic, during which billionaires have managed to add heaps of dollars to their wealth even as millions of people were knocked on their heels. . . .

The chips of the economy are stacked in rich people's favor, and they're getting handed more chips constantly. So why not take a few chips away? "

— From "Seriously, Just Tax the Rich" by Emily Stewart, vox.com, 2021.

disproportionately excessively

EXAMINE THE SOURCE

Analyzing Why does this source believe it makes sense to increase taxes on the wealthy?

Complete Your Inquiry

EVALUATE SOURCES AND USE EVIDENCE

Refer back to the Compelling Question and the Supporting Questions you developed at the beginning of the lesson.

1. **Identifying** Which of the sources affected you the most? Why?

2. **Evaluating** Overall, what impression do these sources give you about paying taxes, and whether people pay enough? Explain.

3. **Gathering Sources** Which sources helped you answer the Supporting Questions and Compelling Question? Which sources, if any, challenged what you thought you knew when you first created your Supporting Questions? What information do you still need in order to answer your questions? Where would you find that information?

4. **Evaluating Sources** Identify the sources that helped answer your Supporting Questions. How reliable is the source? How would you verify the reliability of the source?

COMMUNICATE CONCLUSIONS

5. **Collaborating** Work with a partner to create a chart summarizing the various reasons for and against taxing people at higher rates. How do these sources provide insight on the various reasons? Use the graphic organizer that you created at the beginning of the lesson to help you. Share your chart with the class.

TAKE INFORMED ACTION

Writing an Editorial Take a side on the issue of whether people should pay higher taxes. Write an opinion paragraph—also known as an editorial—stating your position. Support your opinion logically by using evidence and details from the sources. Remember to analyze the validity of the sources for bias, and to cite—or give credit to—the sources you quote from. Work with your teacher to get your opinion published in the school paper or website or local newspaper.

TEXT: Stewart, Emily. "Seriously, Just Tax the Rich." Vox. May 18, 2021. https://www.vox.com/22432338/joe-biden-tax-plan.

07
Fiscal Policy

READING STRATEGY

Integrating Knowledge and Ideas As you read the lesson, complete a chart to identify the causes and effects of a federal deficit.

Causes ⟹ Federal Deficit ⟹ Effects

Managing the Economy

GUIDING QUESTION

How does the government try to influence the economy?

For much of U.S. history, the government had a limited economic role. It left most matters to consumers and businesses. In the 1930s, however, the government's economic role changed.

Franklin D. Roosevelt became president in 1933. The Great Depression had been going on for nearly four years, and millions were suffering. Roosevelt decided the nation could not wait any longer for

During the Great Depression, government programs hired workers to build roads, buildings, and dams (top left). Other workers were hired to record the histories of formerly enslaved women and men (top right), and to photograph the struggles of farm and migrant workers (bottom). Such programs were designed to stimulate the economy.

Analyzing Visuals What were two ways these government programs helped the country during the Depression?

(tl) Bettman/Getty Images, (tr) Library of Congress Manuscript Division [1610341], (b) USDA Photograph Archives

the economy to recover. Believing the government had to act, Roosevelt started new government programs that put people back to work. These programs paid people to build schools, post offices, bridges, parks, and more. These new programs helped the economy recover. Later, when America entered World War II, a stronger economy helped people provide supplies for the military.

Fiscal Policy

Government spending programs like those during the Great Depression are known as fiscal policy. **Fiscal policy** is the government's use of taxes and spending to stimulate the economy. The idea behind fiscal policy is simple: If the economy slows or enters a recession, the government can increase spending, reduce taxes, or do a combination of the two. Using fiscal policy to boost growth is called *stimulating* the economy.

By boosting spending, the government creates demand for goods and services. The extra spending helps convince producers to hire back workers they had laid off. Cutting taxes puts more money in people's pockets, which can also lead to increased demand. The government could also cut taxes that businesses pay. Lower taxes might encourage businesses to pay workers more or increase the production of goods and services.

Advantages of Fiscal Policy

Fiscal policy was used successfully several times since 1900. The first was during the Great Depression when the government spent billions to

fiscal policy government use of taxes and spending to stimulate the economy and reach economic goals

The U.S. Treasury sent stimulus checks to Americans during the COVID-19 recession. Stimulating the economy is a goal of fiscal policy.

reduce unemployment and stimulate production. This was followed by massive government spending on the military during World War II— spending that also stimulated economic growth. But when World War II ended, the country began to worry about falling back into depression. As a result, Congress passed the Employment Act of 1946, which set the three official economic goals. The three goals were to keep people working, to keep producing goods, and to keep consumers buying goods and services.

When the Great Recession of 2008–2009 struck, Congress passed two massive stimulus programs totaling about $1.5 trillion to prevent the situation from becoming worse. The government played a similar role during the COVID recession of 2020. By dramatically increasing spending, and by cutting taxes, the government helped restore demand for goods and services.

Without the massive government involvement during these periods, peoples' economic situation would have been much worse. Consequently, many people today feel that some government involvement is needed to improve their situation in life.

Problems with Fiscal Policy

Fiscal policy comes with problems, however. Even when politicians agree to pursue a stimulus program, they may disagree on how much to spend or which programs should be funded. For example, President Biden and the Democrats wanted to spend $1.9 trillion to stimulate the economy because of the COVID recession. But Republicans objected because they thought the proposed spending was too high. Disagreements like these are to be expected in a democracy, but not all sides can get what they want.

Fiscal policy can also be slow to take effect after a policy is approved. It may take months for the U.S. Treasury to print and mail stimulus checks to the right addresses. Other taxpayers may not receive the benefits of a tax break until they file their annual tax returns. By the time the money is spent, the state of the economy may have already improved.

Another problem is the difficulty of judging whether a stimulus bill is too big or too small. As mentioned above, about $1.5 trillion in stimulus spending was passed during the Great Recession. Yet the monthly unemployment rate took 10 years to fall back to its pre-recession low.

Unemployment insurance will help this laid-off worker pay bills while she looks for a new job. Unemployment insurance is an automatic stabilizer.

Economists agree that the recession would have been much worse without the stimulus bills, but they still did not know exactly how many jobs were saved.

Automatic Stabilizers

Because of problems that can occur with fiscal policy, economists like programs called **automatic stabilizers**. These are stabilization programs that do not need legislative approval to activate because of worsening economic conditions. In other words, programs already in place can automatically provide benefits without getting caught up in partisan congressional gridlock.

The most important automatic stabilizer is *unemployment insurance*. Think about how unemployment insurance works. In a recession, millions of people lose their jobs. After they are unemployed long enough, they are eligible to receive unemployment insurance payments. Using these insurance payments, unemployed workers can then pay their bills until they are rehired or find a new job.

Another automatic stabilizer is the progressive *income tax* system. When people work less or lose their jobs, they are taxed at a lower rate. This means they can keep a larger percentage of their income. Thus, lower tax rates partially **offset**, or counterbalance, the loss of income. When the economy recovers and they go back to work, they begin to make more money. Then, when they can better afford it, they are taxed at a higher rate. That, in turn, helps lower the deficit made worse by recessions.

Some people would like the individual income tax to be proportional instead of progressive. This may sound fair because a proportional tax requires everyone to pay the same percentage rate. But the individual income tax cannot work as an automatic stabilizer if it is proportional. This is a strong argument for maintaining a progressive income tax.

Automatic stabilizers prevent incomes from falling too far in hard times. They thus help offset periods of high unemployment that severely threaten economic growth. And when times are good, government spending falls and taxes rise.

✓ **CHECK FOR UNDERSTANDING**

1. **Identifying Cause and Effect** Under what conditions does the government use fiscal policy? Why?

2. **Explaining** What problems sometimes accompany fiscal policy?

automatic stabilizer program that works to preserve income without additional government action during economic downturns

offset to counterbalance

Budgets—Balanced or Unbalanced?

GUIDING QUESTION

What do governments do when the budget does not balance?

A **balanced budget** occurs when a government's annual revenues and spending equal each other. Most states *must* have a balanced budget. States can borrow money to invest in long-term projects but they cannot borrow to fund normal operating expenses or regular programs. States can also save money during the years in which they have a budget surplus. A **budget surplus** occurs when government collects more money than it spends. If revenues fall in another year, states can use the reserves they saved to balance the budget. Of course, they also have the option to cut spending.

The federal government is different. It is allowed to have a **budget deficit**, or spend more than it collects in revenues in a fiscal year. To make up the difference, the federal government borrows money by selling government securities: bonds, Treasury notes, and Treasury bills. A government bond is a contract in which the government promises to repay borrowed money with interest at a specific time in the future. Most government bonds are repaid in 10 to 30 years.

balanced budget annual budget in which expenditures equal revenues

budget surplus situation that occurs when a government collects more revenues than it spends

budget deficit situation that occurs when a government spends more than it collects in revenue

Savings bonds like these are a government security, or money borrowed from the purchaser of the bond that will be repaid with interest at some future date.

Treasury notes have shorter maturities and must be paid back in one to 10 years. Treasury bills, or T-bills, are short term obligations that must be repaid in one year or less.

Deficits Can Be Good or Bad

Deficit spending can be good if not abused. If the economy is in a recession, for example, then deficit spending can help stimulate economic growth again. In addition, deficit spending can be useful if it funds expensive infrastructure improvements. **Infrastructure** includes the highways, levees, bridges, power, water, sewage, and other public goods needed to support a population. Deficit spending for these projects might be justified because they have benefits for several generations. Deficit spending can also be justified if the deficits are repaid at some future time. But it is easier to spend money than to repay it. That is why deficit spending can be a problem.

Deficit spending by the federal government has several negative effects. First, deficits can turn into debt. The **federal debt** is money the government has borrowed and not yet paid back. The yearly interest payments on the federal debt strains the federal budget. More than 5 percent of the 2020 budget went to paying interest on the federal debt. If the government continues to borrow, or if interest rates go up, payments on the debt will go up, and the federal government will have less to spend on other programs.

More borrowing has another effect. People think of government securities as safe ways to invest money, so they are popular. The more money people invest in bonds, Treasury notes, or Treasury bills, the less they have to invest in private businesses. Businesses will have less money to increase productivity, which could cause slower economic growth.

Supply and demand could also drive up interest rates. If the federal government needs to borrow more funds, less money is left for other investors, so they must pay more to borrow. For example, if your parents take out a loan to buy a car, more government borrowing could result in the loan costing them more than it would otherwise.

infrastructure highways, levees, bridges, power, water, sewage, and other public goods needed to support a growing economy

federal debt money the government has borrowed and not yet paid back

Government Deficits Become Debt

A massive federal deficit during the COVID-19 recession of 2020 dramatically increased the federal deficit and the federal debt as a percentage of GDP.

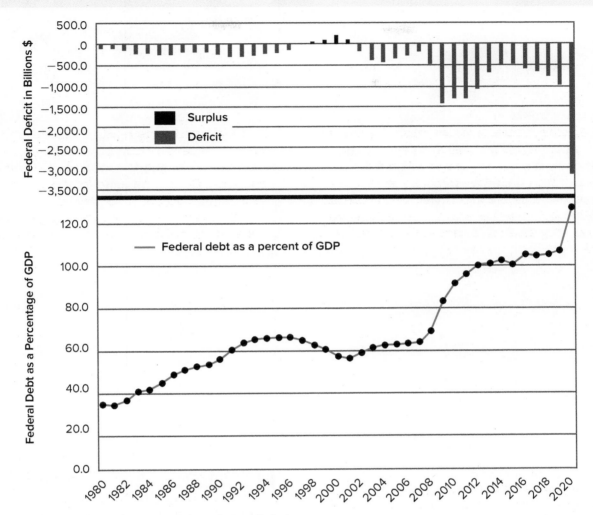

Source: White House, Office of Management and Budget

EXAMINE THE GRAPHS

1. **Analyzing Visuals** In which years did the federal government have a budget surplus?
2. **Inferring** How did the federal government respond, in terms of spending, to the recession that began in 2007 and worsened in 2008? How can you tell?
3. **Summarizing** For the most part, has the federal government had a balanced budget, a surplus, or a deficit over the last two decades?

Deficits Create Debt

Budget deficits create debt when the government borrows money. Each year that the federal government runs a deficit, its total debt goes up. If the federal government runs a surplus one year, it can use the extra money to pay down the debt. A budget surplus, then, can cause the federal debt to become smaller.

The government seldom runs a surplus that reduces the debt, however. The bar graph in **Government Deficits Become Debt** shows that the federal government has had only four budget surpluses in the last 40 years. The line graph in the same figure shows how those deficits have added to the total debt.

Some of the federal budget is used to fund education. This money may support programs for teachers and their students, such as this after-school technology club.

Making Connections How would cuts in spending on education affect you?

The size of our national debt is now larger than our annual GDP. This has not happened since the end of World War II. If people are concerned about the size of the debt, they must be willing to live with fewer government goods and services. Or they must be willing to pay higher taxes, which will help reduce the deficit. Economic growth alone will not be enough to enable the federal government to have a balanced budget. This is because the gap between annual spending and annual revenue collections has become too large.

✓ **CHECK FOR UNDERSTANDING**

1. **Analyzing** How are budget deficits related to debt?

2. **Contrasting** How does the federal government differ from state governments in its reaction to an unbalanced budget?

LESSON ACTIVITIES

1. **Argumentative Writing** As a member of Congress, you must consider a bill sent by the president cutting income taxes in the hope of stimulating the economy during a tough recession. Write a short speech for or against the president's plan. Give reasons for your position.

2. **Collaborating** When Congress works on a stimulus package, your local representative often attempts to get federal funding for programs in your area. With a partner, think of a local program or project that would benefit your community. Then create a presentation outlining your project idea and explaining why you think your community should get federal funding for it.

Multiple Perspectives: The Federal Debt

 COMPELLING QUESTION

Should the U.S. government be required to balance its budget?

Plan Your Inquiry

DEVELOPING QUESTIONS

Read the Compelling Question for this lesson. What questions can you ask to help you answer this Compelling Question? Create a graphic organizer like the one below. Write three Supporting Questions in the first column.

Supporting Questions	Source	What this source tells me about the federal debt	Questions the source leaves unanswered
	A		
	B		
	C		
	D		
	E		

ANALYZING SOURCES

Next, read the introductory information for each source in this lesson. Then analyze each source by answering the questions that follow it. How does each source help you answer each Supporting Question you created? What questions do you still have? Write those in your graphic organizer.

After you analyze the sources, you will:
- use the evidence from the sources
- communicate your conclusions
- take informed action

Background Information

The federal government is not required to have a balanced budget. Instead, it's allowed to have a *budget deficit*, or spend more than it collects in revenues in a fiscal year. To make up the difference, the federal government borrows money by selling bonds, Treasury notes, or Treasury bills. The government then has to pay back the borrowed amount with interest. Each year that the federal government runs a deficit, its total debt goes up.

This Inquiry Lesson includes sources about the federal debt and whether the country should have a balanced budget. As you read and analyze the sources, think about the Compelling Question.

State governments are required to balance their budgets. Should this be a rule for the federal government as well?

GO ONLINE Explore the Student Edition eBook and find interactive maps, charts, graphs, and tools.

E149

The Federal Deficit and Debt

The bar graph shows that the federal government has had budget deficits for the past twenty years. The line graph in the same figure shows how those deficits have added to the total debt. The size of our national debt is now larger than our annual GDP.

PRIMARY SOURCE: GRAPH

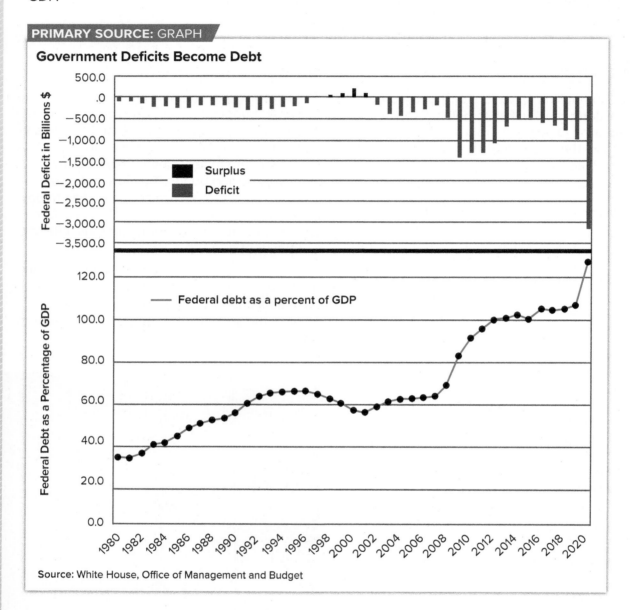

Government Deficits Become Debt

Source: White House, Office of Management and Budget

EXAMINE THE SOURCE

1. **Analyzing** What happened to the federal debt when the government had a budget surplus instead of a deficit?

2. **Drawing Conclusions** What can government leaders do if they are worried about the size of the federal debt?

National Debt—The Clock's Ticking

The national debt clock is located in New York City. It shows the accumulation of government deficits over the decades. Seymour Durst, an investor, created the first debt clock in 1989. President Franklin D. Roosevelt explains why the national debt is not something to worry about.

PRIMARY SOURCE: PHOTOGRAPH

The clock is constantly changing. During years when the deficit is low or there is a surplus, the clock runs backward. The debt was $22.48 trillion in 2019. It rose to $28 trillion by April 2021.

PRIMARY SOURCE: GOVERNMENT SPEECH

66 National income will be greater tomorrow than it is today because government has had the courage to borrow idle capital and put it and idle labor to work. . . . Our national debt after all is an internal debt owed not only by the Nation but to the Nation. If our children have to pay interest on it, they will pay that interest to themselves. A reasonable internal debt will not impoverish our children or put the Nation into bankruptcy. 99

— President Franklin D. Roosevelt, "Address Before the American Retail Federation, Washington, D.C." 1939.

EXAMINE THE SOURCES

1. **Speculating** Why do you suppose Durst created the clock?

2. **Calculating** According to the photo, what is the debt if divided by households in the United States?

3. **Analyzing Perspectives** Why was President Roosevelt not worried about deficit spending?

4. **Speculating** Do you think President Roosevelt would consider the current federal debt "reasonable"? Why or why not?

Balanced Budget Amendment

Regarding taxes, money, borrowing, and bankruptcy, the U.S. Constitution states in Article I, Section 8:

- The Congress shall have Power To lay and collect Taxes, Duties, Imposts and Excises, to pay the Debts and provide for the common Defence [Defense] and general Welfare of the United States; but all Duties, Imposts and Excises shall be uniform throughout the United States;

- To borrow Money on the credit of the United States; . . .

- To establish an uniform Rule of Naturalization, and uniform Laws on the subject of Bankruptcies throughout the United States;

- To coin Money, regulate the Value thereof, and of foreign Coin, and fix the Standard of Weights and Measures;

- To provide for the Punishment of counterfeiting the Securities and current Coin of the United States; . . .

Nowhere in the Constitution, however, does it state that the federal budget should be balanced. Some people would like to change that.

PRIMARY SOURCE: ARTICLE

❝ A balanced budget amendment would make it Constitutionally **mandatory** for the government to operate without a deficit in each fiscal year.

The primary benefit of such an amendment is that it would protect future generations against accumulated debt. In 1979, the national debt of the United States was $827 billion. In 2017, the national debt was $20.2 trillion. With the amendment, this debt could begin to be reined in to prevent fiscal irresponsibility.

The primary issue with a balanced budget amendment is that it would limit the tools available to the government during times of economic difficulty. Countering recessions or responding to a national emergency would require the costs be offset on other budget lines, which would likely limit the help people may need to simply survive. ❞

— From "12 Key Balanced Budget Amendment Pros and Cons" by Louise Gaille, vittana.org, 2018.

mandatory legally binding

EXAMINE THE SOURCE

1. **Analyzing Perspectives** What reasons does the source give for having a balanced budget amendment?

2. **Explaining** What is the primary issue against a balanced budget amendment, according to the source?

TEXT: (t) US Const. Article I, § 8. https://www.archives.gov/founding-docs/constitution-transcript#toc-section-8-. (b)Gaille, Louise. "12 Key Balanced Budget Amendment Pros and Cons." Vittana.org. February 1, 2018. https://vittana.org/12-key-balanced-budget-amendment-pros-and-cons.

Does the Debt Matter?

For decades, many people believed the huge federal debt would cause a collapse of the U.S. economy. That has not happened . . . yet. Even so, others suggest we might want to tackle the debt sooner rather than later.

PRIMARY SOURCE: ARTICLE

> ❝ As soon as it's reasonable to do so, we need to begin to repair the immense fiscal imbalance we have wrought. Post-pandemic, this suggests the need to make a commitment to fiscal responsibility—a pledge to take unpleasant but essential steps that politicians on all sides have paid lip service to but have rarely put into practice. Everything needs to be on the table—entitlement reforms, a restructuring of the tax code (including tax increases), changes to the federal budget process, etc.—to ensure that the United States can gradually bring the public debt down to more sustainable and safer levels. . . .
>
> The debt threatens our country's ability to prosper in the decades to come, but it probably will not bring on a sharp and sudden catastrophe. That means it poses a particularly difficult challenge for our politics. If the only way to motivate politicians and voters to take the debt seriously is to insist that we are on the edge of an **abyss**, we will almost certainly fail to address the challenge. Rather than scare ourselves senseless, we need to take responsibility for the future—and to treat Americans like serious adults who can understand what responsibility might mean.
>
> For decades, those warning that rising deficits and debt will lead to a sharp and catastrophic economic calamity were crying wolf. According to Aesop's fable, the villagers, tired of being tricked by the bored boy, started to ignore him. But that is not where the story ends. Eventually, the wolf did come. And things did not turn out well for the villagers when they ignored the boy then. ❞

— From "Does the Debt Matter?" by Peter Wehner and Ian Tufts, National Affairs, 2020.

abyss bottomless pit

EXAMINE THE SOURCE

1. **Summarizing** What actions does this source recommend taking to reduce the federal debt?

2. **Making Connections** How do the authors of this piece use a fable to get their point across?

TEXT: Wehner, Peter and Ian Tufts. "Does the Debt Matter?" National Affairs, No. 45, Fall 2020.

Money In, Money Out

The graph shows the ratio of each dollar of spending relative to each dollar of income by fiscal year.

EXAMINE THE SOURCE

1. **Analyzing Visuals** Of the years shown, which ones spent less than what was coming in?

2. **Speculating** What two years had the highest ratio of spending to income? What occurred during those years?

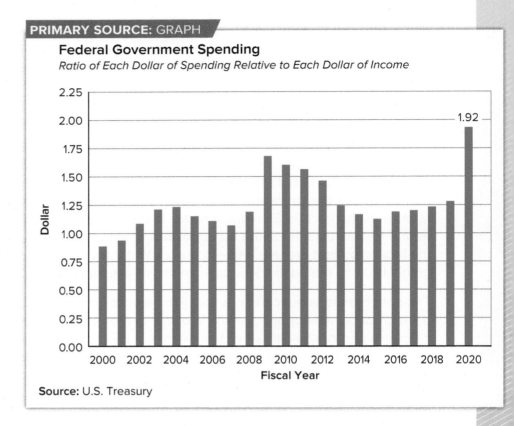

Federal Government Spending
Ratio of Each Dollar of Spending Relative to Each Dollar of Income

Source: U.S. Treasury

Complete Your Inquiry

EVALUATE SOURCES AND USE EVIDENCE

Refer back to the Compelling Question and the Supporting Questions you developed at the beginning of the lesson.

1. **Identifying** Which of the sources affected you the most? Why?

2. **Evaluating** Overall, what impression do these sources give you about the federal debt? Explain.

3. **Gathering Sources** Which sources helped you answer the Supporting Questions and Compelling Question? Which sources, if any, challenged what you thought you knew when you first created your Supporting Questions? What information do you still need in order to answer your questions? Where would you find that information?

4. **Evaluating Sources** Identify the sources that helped answer your Supporting Questions. How reliable is the source? How would you verify the reliability of the source?

COMMUNICATE CONCLUSIONS

5. **Collaborating** Work with a partner to create a short skit of a conversation between someone who wants a balanced budget and someone who does not think it is necessary. Include evidence from the sources in your dialog. Use the graphic organizer you created at the beginning of the lesson to help you. Share your skit with the class.

TAKE INFORMED ACTION

Writing a Letter to a Member of Congress Take a poll, or survey, of 10 adults, asking whether they believe the federal government should strive for a balanced budget, or whether it should consider passing a balanced-budget amendment. Write down their reasons for their opinion. Then write a letter to your representative or senator in Congress outlining your findings. Ask the lawmaker to reply with his or her opinion on a balanced budget.

Reviewing Government and the Economy

Summary

GDP

A major U.S. goal is to keep the economy strong. A strong economy provides a higher standard of living for Americans. The best way to measure the strength of the economy is by looking at the nation's *real Gross Domestic Product*—the total value of all final products produced in a country during a single year.

The Fed and Monetary Policy

The Federal Reserve System was set up to act as the country's *central bank*. The Fed uses *monetary policy* to keep the economy healthy and strong, and to maintain stable prices. The Fed also maintains the currency, regulates and supervises banks, promotes consumer protection, and acts as the government's bank.

Measuring the Economy

The U.S. economy does not grow at a steady rate. Instead, it goes through alternating periods of growth and decline known as the *business cycle*. Every business cycle has two distinct parts—a *recession* and an expansion.

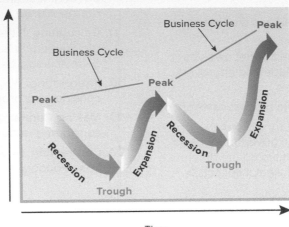

Financing the Government

Federal, state, and local governments prepare a budget every *fiscal year*. A budget is made up of two parts—*revenues* and *expenditures*. State and local budgets must balance, but the federal budget does not. The biggest source of federal revenue is the individual income tax. The largest federal expenditure is Social Security. If the government spends more than it receives in revenues, it runs a deficit—and *deficits* turn into *debt*.

Fiscal Policy

The government's goals are to keep people working, to keep producing goods, and to keep consumers buying goods and services. *Fiscal policy*—the government's use of taxes and spending—is used to achieve these goals. If the economy enters a recession, the government can increase spending, cut taxes, or a combination of the two.

Checking For Understanding

Answer the questions to see if you understood the topic content.

REVIEWING KEY TERMS

1. Define each of these terms:

   A. recession
   B. inflation
   C. bear market
   D. central bank
   E. monetary policy
   F. open market operations
   G. federal debt
   H. fiscal policy
   I. automatic stabilizer
   J. subsidize

REVIEWING KEY FACTS

2. **Explaining** How does real GDP differ from current GDP?

3. **Identifying** What economic indicators are used to judge an economy's health?

4. **Identifying** What name is given to a rising stock market fueled by investors optimistic about the economy's future?

5. **Identifying** By what name is the central bank of the United States known?

6. **Explaining** What three tools does the Fed use to control the money supply?

7. **Identifying** Which part of the budget involves spending choices that are made and approved each year?

8. **Identifying** What is the single biggest category of state spending?

9. **Explaining** When the federal government has a budget deficit, how does it make up the difference between what it spends and what it collects?

10. **Identifying** Which two automatic stabilizers are in place to preserve income when the economy slows?

11. **Identifying Cause and Effect** How does a budget deficit create debt for the federal government?

12. **Drawing Conclusions** What is the goal of a stimulus program?

CRITICAL THINKING

13. **Explaining** Why is real GDP per capita a better measure of comparing countries' economies than current GDP or real GDP?

14. **Predicting** If the Leading Economic Index goes up, what usually happens to the real GDP several months later?

15. **Identifying Cause and Effect** How does the Federal Open Market Committee (FOMC) affect the money supply when it buys and sells government bonds and Treasury bills?

16. **Drawing Conclusions** How does a lowered discount rate encourage financial institutions to borrow money from the Fed?

17. **Calculating** If the Fed has set the reserve requirement at 35 percent, how much of a $100 deposit would be available to lend out?

18. **Interpreting** Why is the federal income tax considered a progressive tax?

19. **Making Connections** Why are sales taxes considered regressive taxes?

20. **Contrasting** How does a budget surplus differ from a budget deficit?

NEED EXTRA HELP?

If You've Missed Question	1	2	3	4	5	6	7	8	9	10
Review Lesson	2, 3, 4, 5, 7	2	3	3	4	4	5	5	7	7

If You've Missed Question	11	12	13	14	15	16	17	18	19	20
Review Lesson	7	7	2	3	4	4	4	5	5	7

Apply What You Have Learned

A Understanding Multiple Perspectives

How involved should the federal government be in our economy?

ACTIVITY **Using Evidence in an Essay About Fiscal Policy** Read these excerpts that provide two opinions of government fiscal policy. Then use information in the excerpts to write a brief essay answering these questions: What are some benefits of fiscal policy? What are some drawbacks? What evidence from the lessons can you provide to support the two views?

❝ The great thing about fiscal policy is that it has a direct impact and doesn't require you to bind the hands of future policymakers. ❞

— Paul Krugman, "An Interview with Paul Krugman" in *The Washington Post,* 2012.

❝ Popular as Keynesian fiscal policy may be, many economists are skeptical that it works. They argue that fine-tuning the economy is a virtually impossible task, and that fiscal-stimulus programs are usually too small, and arrive too late, to make a difference. ❞

— James Surowiecki, "The Stimulus Strategy" in *The New Yorker,* 2008.

B Writing an Informative Report

Can a country's economy ever just shut down? Not really, but when government leaders cannot agree upon a national budget, selected shutdowns and closings can occur. In December 2018, parts of the federal government shut down until January. Many federal offices and departments closed. Museums and monuments run by the government were closed to visitors. Only federal workers who were essential to the country's safety, such as members of the armed forces, stayed on the job. At the root of this crisis was a disagreement between the president and members of Congress about how to spend the U.S. revenues. The budget crisis made Americans more aware of how complicated financing the government can be.

ACTIVITY **Writing About the Federal Budget** As the U.S. economy has expanded, both its revenues and expenditures have grown to amounts totaling trillions of dollars. As a result, the process for creating a federal budget has become more complex. Write a description of how the process for making the federal budget has changed since the early 1900s. Describe how the process works today.

Then prepare a family or personal budget. Assume a sum for monthly income. Include these "mandatory" expenses: housing, transportation, communication (phone and Internet). Also include "discretionary" expenses, such as leisure and recreation, or miscellaneous. Compare your income and spending categories to federal government budget allocations.

(t) Klein, Ezra, and Paul Krugman. "An Interview with Paul Krugman." The Washington Post. May 4, 2012. https://www.washingtonpost.com/blogs/ezra-klein/post/an-interview-with-paul-krugman/2012/05/04/gIQAR9xnIT_blog.html., (b) Surowiecki, James. "The Stimulus Strategy." The New Yorker. Condé Nast. February 17, 2008. https://www.newyorker.com/magazine/2008/02/25/the-stimulus-strategy.

Understanding Economic Concepts

The federal government is not required to have a balanced budget. Many people would like to see that change, however.

ACTIVITY **Apply Evidence in a Photograph to the Federal Budget** What do you see in this photograph? What natural occurrence might have caused this situation? Write a paragraph to explain how such an event might turn a national budget surplus into a budget deficit and, eventually, a debt. Discuss how the federal government responds to emergencies and disasters that strike states unexpectedly.

Houston, Texas 2017

Making Connections

Budgets are created at the national, state, and local levels. Budgets are also created at district levels, such as your school district.

ACTIVITY **Being an Active Citizen** Find out when your local school board will meet to discuss the school system's budget for the upcoming year. If possible, attend the meeting, listen to the discussion, and contribute your own ideas. Perhaps prepare a position on a school health-related issue, such as bullying prevention, Internet safety, or nutritional choices. Be sure to support your position with accurate health information. Then write a summary of the meeting. If you cannot attend, read a report of the meeting, and write a summary of it.

Currencies from all over the world are pictured here. These currencies are used to finance international trade.

The Global Economy

Ralf Siemieniec/Shutterstock.com

GO ONLINE   Explore the Student Edition eBook and find interactive maps, charts, graphs, and tools.

Introducing The Global Economy

Worldwide Connections

You might not realize it, but you are connected to the world. How so? You're connected by:

- The clothes you wear

- The foods you eat

- The cellphone you're using

- The games you play

- The Internet

- The sheets or blankets you're sleeping on

- And much more!

International trade gives you choices from around the world. Although some people would like to limit world trade, it's safe to say that it's here to stay.

This cartoon portrays the United States in the form of "Uncle Sam." He has built a wall to protect American industries from foreign competition. As you can see, however, there is also a drawback of blocking free trade: it prevents *American* firms from selling their products in international markets.

Did You Know?

Trading began in 6000 B.C.E. with the Mesopotamians in the earliest cultural hearths of human society. Ancient peoples used trade, or barter, to get such items as food, weapons, and spices.

Global Trade

Economies around the world rely on international trade. In the United States, businesses of all sizes influence trade with other countries. When countries rely heavily on one another, good trade rules and relations become vital. For countries that share borders, such as the United States with Canada and Mexico, the effects of trade are even more important.

» A small grocery store in New York City specializes in selling gourmet foods from France.

» People in London, England, buy DVDs of American movies filmed in Toronto, Canada.

» A farmer in Brazil harvests coffee beans to sell to a coffee store in Seattle, Washington.

» Halfway around the world, workers in an office in India answer service calls for the products of a company in Dallas, Texas.

Getting Ready to Learn About . . .
The Global Economy

Why Nations Trade

Individual nations do not always have the necessary resources to make the products their people need and want. To solve this problem of scarcity, nations trade with one another. They trade food, manufactured goods, services, and raw materials.

Nations *import*, or bring into the country, goods produced in other nations. They *export*, or sell to other nations, goods they produce. Trade between nations today is more extensive and important than ever.

When countries trade, they specialize in the things they can produce relatively better than other countries can. In other words, trade allows each country to focus on things it can make at a lower opportunity cost. This is called *comparative advantage*, and is the basis for international trade.

But while international trade is beneficial to almost everyone, it can be painful to some.

Companies that lose sales to lower-priced foreign-made goods often want to limit foreign trade. So do workers in those companies who may lose their jobs. Governments can help protect home industries with *tariffs*, or taxes on imports, which makes them more expensive than home products. Governments sometimes place *quotas*, or limits on the number of products that can come into their country. A third option is to give *subsidies*, or payments, to the home company so it doesn't raise its prices for home consumers.

Paying for Trade Goods

Most countries use their own currency, or money, to pay for the products they import. Currencies are bought and sold in markets, just like goods and services. As a result, the value of a currency, like the value of a good or service, can go up or down. The value of one currency in terms of another is called its *exchange rate*.

Evidence of international trade is hard to miss in the port of Barcelona, Spain. In this bird's-eye view, you can see colorful cargo containers stacked high as they wait to be loaded with massive cranes onto ships.

Global economic interconnections can be seen by this McDonald's restaurant in Bangkok, Thailand.

Economic Interdependence

Countries around the world rely upon one another for resources, goods, and services. Many of the products we use are made by *multinationals*, or corporations that have manufacturing operations in a number of different countries. This results in *economic interdependence*, and is the reason countries must cooperate when they trade. Over the decades, some countries have formed *trade blocs*, or alliances, to increase the benefits of international trade.

The European Union (EU) is the most famous trade bloc. Today the EU creates a free-trade zone that covers 27 European countries. Within this regional zone, goods, services, and workers can travel freely across national borders. The United States, Canada, and Mexico also merged to create the United States-Mexico-Canada Agreement (USMCA). This is also one of the world's largest free-trade areas.

The economic interdependence resulting from trade alliances provides benefits to almost everyone, but there are still problems. Jobs are often lost when multinational companies *outsource*, or move their factories to other countries with lower labor costs.

As mentioned earlier, protectionist policies such as tariffs, quotas, and subsidies are often used to help domestic industries that are threatened by free trade. These policies raise the prices of international goods to domestic consumers and encourage them to buy domestic products instead. These policies also weaken the potential gains from a country's comparative advantage.

Rich vs. Poor Countries

In *developed countries*, citizens experience a relatively high *standard of living*, or quality of life. In *developing countries*, average citizens go without plentiful food, medicine, and good housing. Developing countries face many challenges to economic growth. These include high population growth rates, few resources, little industry, war, disease, and corruption. Many countries are transitioning to a market-oriented economy to improve their standard of living. Others have stalled and are having difficulty making the transition.

Looking Ahead

In this topic, you will discover why nations trade. You will also learn information about trade balances, trade alliances, and issues with global trade. You will understand why some countries are wealthier than others, and how some countries are transitioning to market-based economies. You will examine a Compelling Question and develop your own questions in the Inquiry Activity.

What Will You Learn?

In these lessons, you will learn:

- why nations trade, and how this helps reduce the problem of scarcity.
- why some countries set up trade barriers to protect domestic jobs and businesses.
- how international trade relies on the ability to exchange foreign currencies.
- how a positive or negative balance of trade affects a nation's currency.
- how economies are globally interdependent.
- why trade agreements and international organizations are formed to facilitate trade among countries.
- about issues that have arisen because of economic interdependence.
- the difference between developed and developing countries.
- the obstacles developing countries must overcome to move toward a market economy.

 COMPELLING QUESTION IN THE INQUIRY ACTIVITY LESSON

- **How do we balance the needs of consumers and the needs of a sustainable planet?**

In this topic, you will learn how the world is interconnected through trade.

Travel mania/Shutterstock

Why Nations Trade

Effects of Trade Barriers

Trade Between Nations

GUIDING QUESTION

Why do nations trade with one another?

How is it that you can enjoy fresh summer fruit year-round? Why do Americans import cars from Japan or Korea when we can produce them here? Why is the United States the world's largest corn producer?

Individual nations do not always have the necessary resources to make the products their people need and want. To solve this problem of scarcity, nations trade with one another. Nations **import,** or bring into the country, goods produced in other nations. They **export,** or sell to other nations, goods they produce. The graph **Leading Exporters and Importers** shows that trillions of dollars' worth of products are exchanged by countries every year.

import to buy goods from another country

export to sell goods to other countries

Leading Exporters and Importers

The five leading export countries are also the five leading importers.

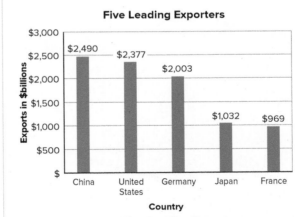

Five Leading Exporters

Exports in $billions

- China: $2,490
- United States: $2,377
- Germany: $2,003
- Japan: $1,032
- France: $969

Country

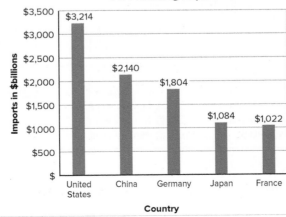

Five Leading Importers

Imports in $billions

- United States: $3,214
- China: $2,140
- Germany: $1,804
- Japan: $1,084
- France: $1,022

Country

EXAMINE THE GRAPHS

Analyzing Visuals
Which nation exports more than the United States?

Trade between nations today is more extensive than ever. The total value of exports globally is about $20 trillion per year. As the map **Export Partners: Selected Nations** shows, countries in widely different locations are closely tied to one another through international trade.

Comparative Advantage

As Adam Smith observed in 1776, nations trade for the same reasons people trade. It simply makes sense for people to focus on the things they can produce best and then exchange those products for the things other people can produce best.

However, even if we could produce something cheaper than anyone else could—a concept known as **absolute advantage**—we still would not have the time to produce all the things we need. The best use of our time is to make more of the things we produce best—and then trade them for other things we still need.

Thus, countries focus on their *comparative* advantage instead. **Comparative advantage** is the ability to produce something *relatively* more efficiently or cheaper—or at a relatively lower opportunity cost—than anyone else can. (Recall that opportunity cost is the value of the *next* best thing that is given up when choosing to do or produce one thing instead of another.)

The goods and services countries produce and sell in abundance are due to their comparative advantages. Brazil, for example, is the world's largest exporter of soybeans. China is the largest exporter of tea. Germany, a country about the size of Indiana, is the world's largest exporter of autos.

Trade increases specialization when everyone focuses on producing the products in

absolute advantage the ability to produce something cheaper than anyone else can.

comparative advantage a country's ability to produce a good relatively more efficiently than other countries can (or, a country's ability to produce a good at a lower opportunity cost than another country)

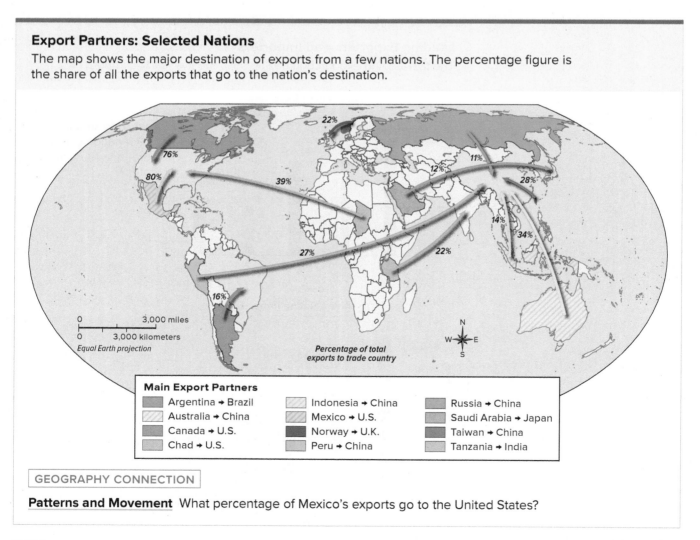

Export Partners: Selected Nations

The map shows the major destination of exports from a few nations. The percentage figure is the share of all the exports that go to the nation's destination.

Percentage of total exports to trade country

Main Export Partners
- Argentina → Brazil
- Australia → China
- Canada → U.S.
- Chad → U.S.
- Indonesia → China
- Mexico → U.S.
- Norway → U.K.
- Peru → China
- Russia → China
- Saudi Arabia → Japan
- Taiwan → China
- Tanzania → India

GEOGRAPHY CONNECTION

Patterns and Movement What percentage of Mexico's exports go to the United States?

Farmers harvest bananas in Ecuador. Ecuador's natural resources give it a comparative advantage in banana production.

which they have a comparative advantage. When people specialize, they produce the things they do best and exchange those products for what other people do best. States also specialize. For example, New York is a financial center for stocks and bonds, while vehicles are a major industry in Michigan. Texas is known for oil and cattle, while Florida and California are famous for citrus fruit.

Available Resources

A country's factors of production—its natural resources, labor, capital, and entrepreneurs—often determine its comparative advantage. For example, the climate and natural resources in Ecuador are excellent for growing bananas. It has a comparative advantage in producing bananas. It is also South America's largest exporter of bananas.

The United States is a major producer of gasoline. It has large petroleum reserves and specialized capital equipment needed to turn petroleum into gasoline. The United States has a comparative advantage in producing gasoline.

Because of these comparative advantages, Ecuador sells bananas to the United States, and the United States sells gasoline to Ecuador.

An economy with fewer resources can still specialize in a single export if it has a comparative advantage. These economies are known as single-resource economies. But to **rely**, or depend, on a single export makes a nation vulnerable to price changes in the marketplace. Diversified economies, which export a variety of products, are better able to respond to market changes.

✓ **CHECK FOR UNDERSTANDING**

1. **Contrasting** What is the difference between an import and an export?
2. **Explaining** What determines whether a country has a comparative advantage in producing a specific product?

Barriers to Trade

GUIDING QUESTION

How do trade barriers affect producers and consumers?

Home companies that lose sales to lower-priced foreign-made goods argue for **protectionism**—the use of tactics that make imported goods more expensive than domestic goods. Governments try to protect home industries and their jobs in three different ways: tariffs, import quotas, or subsidies. These policies can impact trade dramatically.

A **tariff** is a tax on imports. The goal is to make the price of imported goods higher than goods produced at home. Tariffs can give domestic industries some protection from foreign competition, but they raise prices for consumers. Tariffs should not be raised too high or last too long—or problems occur. When tariffs were widely used during the Great Depression, other countries struck back by putting high tariffs on U.S. goods. Everyone suffered. More recently, President Trump placed high tariffs on goods from major trading partners. These tariffs sparked a global *trade war* that caused other countries to put high tariffs on American goods. The result was that prices increased for consumers in all countries, and international trade was impacted.

rely to depend on

protectionism use of tactics that make imported goods more expensive than domestic goods

tariff tax on an imported good

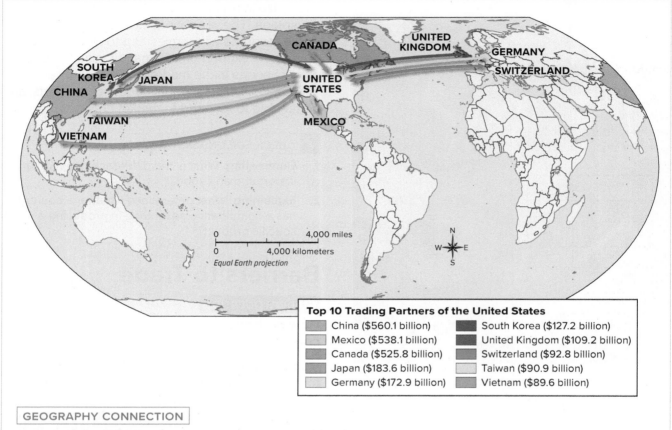

Top Ten Trading Partners of the United States, 2020

The map shows the United States at the center of a global trading system with its ten major partners.

Top 10 Trading Partners of the United States

China ($560.1 billion)	South Korea ($127.2 billion)
Mexico ($538.1 billion)	United Kingdom ($109.2 billion)
Canada ($525.8 billion)	Switzerland ($92.8 billion)
Japan ($183.6 billion)	Taiwan ($90.9 billion)
Germany ($172.9 billion)	Vietnam ($89.6 billion)

GEOGRAPHY CONNECTION

1. **Global Interconnections** Which country is the top trading partner of the United States?
2. **Spatial Thinking** What might be a reason the United States trades so much with Mexico and Canada?

Tariffs aren't the only barriers to trade. People may want a product so badly that higher prices do not stop them from buying it. In this case, a home country can block trade by using a quota. An import **quota** limits the amount of a particular good that enters the country.

Domestic firms can also ask for a subsidy. A **subsidy** is a payment or other benefit given by the government to help a domestic producer. A subsidy helps a producer offset some of its cost of production so it can choose to not raise its prices for the home market. Thus, the home product becomes more competitive with cheaper imported products.

quota limit on the amount of foreign goods imported into a country

subsidy payment or benefit given by the government to help a domestic producer keep prices low

✓ **CHECK FOR UNDERSTANDING**

1. **Explaining** Why do nations sometimes impose tariffs?
2. **Identifying Cause and Effect** How does protectionism harm consumers?

LESSON ACTIVITIES

1. **Argumentative Writing** Suppose you are an adviser to the president. Write a letter to persuade the president to lift or impose trade barriers. Cite specific reasons for your recommendation.

2. **Presenting** You must explain to a small country why it should engage in international trade. Prepare an outline for your speech that answers these questions: What should the country consider when deciding what to trade? How might trade benefit the country?

03

Exchange Rates and Trade Balances

READING STRATEGY

Analyzing Key Ideas and Details As you read the lesson, complete a graphic organizer like this one to describe the effects of trade deficits.

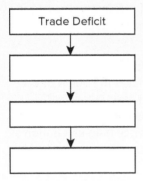

Exchange Rates

GUIDING QUESTION

How do exchange rates affect international trade?

Nations use their own **currency**—or system of money—to carry out trade with other countries. For example, when American companies trade with firms in Japan, they use the dollar ($). When Japanese companies trade with U.S. companies, they use their currency called the yen (¥). The domestic currencies used to finance foreign trade are called **foreign exchange**, whether they be dollars or yen. Supply and demand set the value of these currencies in relation to each other.

Currencies are bought and sold in foreign exchange markets, just like goods and services in other markets. As a result, the value of a currency, like the value of a good or service, can go up or down. The value of one currency in terms of another is called its **exchange rate**. For example, in the United States, the value of $1 might be ¥100. In Japan, the value of one ¥ is one U.S. penny, or one one-hundredth of a dollar.

currency system of money in general use in a country

foreign exchange the domestic currencies that are used to finance foreign trade

exchange rate the value of a nation's currency in relation to another nation's currency

Currency exchange rates are shown on a digital display board.

Suppose businesses in the United States want to import goods from Japan. Because Japanese firms want to be paid in their own currency, U.S. firms must sell dollars to buy yen. They can then use this yen to buy Japanese products. This action has two results. First, more dollars become available in foreign exchange markets where currencies are bought and sold. Second, the purchase of yen reduces the number of yen available for other countries to buy. The combination of the two pushes the value of the U.S. dollar down and the yen's value up. If this continues for too long, excessive imports can lower the value of the dollar.

The lower value of the dollar might not be completely bad. It will help companies in the United States increase their exports. The reason for this is simple. When a country's currency is less expensive, the prices of its goods are lower. That makes the goods in the United States more attractive to other countries. When companies in other countries buy these relatively cheaper American goods, they will have to buy U.S. dollars. This will push the value of the dollar back up again. And if a country continues to export more than it imports for too long—the value of its currency will rise.

If we want to know the value of the dollar in international markets, we have to look at the exchange rate of the dollar against several countries together. To do this, we look at a statistic called the *International Value of the U.S. Dollar*. This measure shows the dollar's value compared to a broad group of U.S. trading partner currencies. The broad dollar index graph—**International Value of the U.S. Dollar**—shows that the dollar's value has been relatively strong since the statistical measure was first used in 2006.

✓ CHECK FOR UNDERSTANDING

1. **Explaining** What determines the value of one currency in relation to another currency?

2. **Identifying Cause and Effect** How does a low value of a country's currency help its economy?

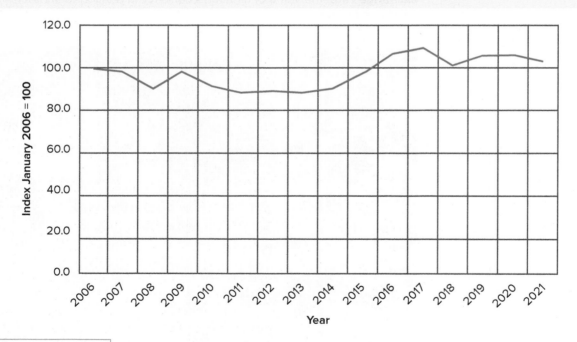

International Value of the U.S. Dollar
The forces of supply and demand help set the international value of the dollar.

EXAMINE THE GRAPH

1. **Analyzing Visuals** According to the graph, in what year was the value of the dollar highest?

2. **Inferring** In which years were U.S. exports least expensive for other countries to buy? What influence did this have on U.S. exports during those years?

Two cargo ships—one representing the United States and the other representing China—symbolize the desire of each country to increase exports to the other.

Balance of Trade

GUIDING QUESTION

How does a nation's trade balance affect its economy?

A country may sell a different amount of goods and services to another country than it buys from that country. The difference between the value of a nation's exports and the value of its imports is the **balance of trade**. That balance can be positive or negative.

Positive Balance of Trade

When the value of a nation's exports is greater than its imports, it has a positive balance of trade. For example, if a country's exports are worth $100 billion and its imports are worth $70 billion, the country has a positive trade balance of $30 billion.

A positive balance of trade is also called a *trade surplus*. A country with a trade surplus for a long time will find that the value of its currency goes up in international currency markets. This will eventually decrease the demand for the country's products because they have become more expensive.

Negative Balance of Trade

When a nation imports more than it exports, it has a negative balance of trade. Suppose a country exports $70 billion in goods and imports $100 billion. If so, it has a negative trade balance of $30 billion. This is called a *trade deficit*. If the country has a trade deficit for too long, it will find that the value of its currency will start to decline.

A large trade deficit with a single country—like the trade deficit the United States has with China—can also cause other problems. For example, it may cause job losses in American industries hurt by foreign competition. This situation usually gains the attention of politicians who often want to do something about it. That is why President Trump launched a trade war against China shortly after taking office. However, a deficit with one country is usually offset by surpluses with other countries. What counts is the overall trade balance, not the trade balance with a single country. This is why the dollar's international value, as shown in the graph **International Value of the U.S. Dollar**, has remained relatively strong despite significant trade deficits with China from 2006 to 2020.

balance of trade the difference between the value of a nation's exports and its imports

A Strong Dollar vs. a Weak Dollar

The diagram shows how trade imbalances tend to be self-correcting.

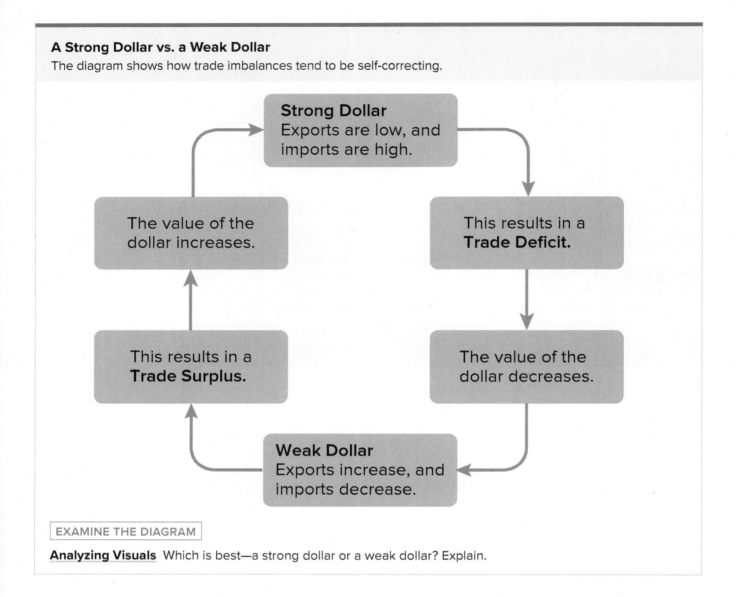

Strong Dollar
Exports are low, and imports are high.

This results in a **Trade Deficit.**

The value of the dollar decreases.

Weak Dollar
Exports increase, and imports decrease.

This results in a **Trade Surplus.**

The value of the dollar increases.

EXAMINE THE DIAGRAM

Analyzing Visuals Which is best—a strong dollar or a weak dollar? Explain.

There was a time when countries worried about their trade balances. The trade balance of the U.S. economy is a modest percentage of its GDP. But the imbalance is not a major concern because trade imbalances tend to be self-correcting. Trade imbalances slowly change the value of a country's currency in international markets, and these changes will usually work to correct the imbalance.

✓ CHECK FOR UNDERSTANDING

1. **Explaining** What is the balance of trade, and how does it go from negative to positive?

2. **Identifying Cause and Effect** How does a trade surplus affect the value of a nation's currency?

LESSON ACTIVITIES

1. **Argumentative Writing** You are listening to a political debate. One candidate complains about her opponent's support of a trade agreement that contributed to the weakening of the dollar. Write one or two paragraphs explaining why a weak dollar is or is not a problem.

2. **Using Multimedia** A group of entrepreneurs have asked you to explain how the international value of the dollar affects their businesses. Working with a partner, create a short multimedia presentation that explains the causes and effects of changes to the international value of the dollar.

04

Global Trade Alliances and Issues

READING STRATEGY

Analyzing Key Ideas and Details As you read the lesson, complete a graphic organizer to identify the functions or benefits of the trade agreements listed.

Trade Agreement	Functions/Benefits
GATT	
WTO	
EU	
NAFTA/USMCA	

Global and Regional Cooperation

GUIDING QUESTION

Why do nations depend on one another?

Look at the tags on the clothes you wear. Examine the labels on your headphones, laptop, stuffed animals, staplers, and any other products on your desk or in your room. You will find that workers in other countries made most of your possessions. Worldwide transportation, communication networks, and technology have supported international trade, which has made it possible for us to have an incredible variety of goods and services. International trade has also made for more economic interdependence than ever before. **Economic interdependence** means that we rely on others—and others rely on us—to provide for many of our wants and needs.

Economic interdependence is not an economic theory. It is a fact of life. Economic interdependence is due to the extensive global and regional cooperation that characterizes international trade. How did this come about? What are the implications? And is it possible that we have gone too far? These are important questions, but it helps if we first understand how we got to where we are today. It also helps to remember that nations trade for the same reason people trade: the value of the things we get in trade is more valuable to us than what we give up to get them.

economic interdependence the reliance of people and countries around the world on one another for goods and services

Bar codes and clothing tags specify the country where a product was made.

Making Connections What goods does your family regularly use that were produced in other countries? When you purchase one of these products, who profits from it?

GATT

Nations have a long history of trading with each other. But two world wars and the Great Depression of the 1930s severely damaged international trade. After World War II was over, countries faced two critical trade problems. First, the war had significantly disrupted trade between nations. Second, many tariffs that nearly doubled the prices of goods during the Great Depression were still in place.

Along with a small number of nations, the United States created the General Agreement on Tariffs and Trade (GATT). Founded in 1947, the GATT was a multilateral trade agreement designed to reduce tariffs—or taxes on traded goods—among its member nations. In a **multilateral agreement,** all parties agree to do the same thing at about the same time. For example, all nations might agree to reduce their tariffs on steel by 15 percent by a specific date.

The reduced tariffs worked, and more international trade took place. This encouraged the GATT countries to make more tariff reductions, which in turn led to more trade. Other countries also joined the GATT. As of the early 1990s, 120 countries had become members, with thousands of multilateral tariff reduction agreements between them.

Despite this success, the GATT had no way to ensure that all countries honored the tariff agreements. This led to the founding of the World Trade Organization (WTO) in 1995.

World Trade Organization (WTO)

The WTO functions like a world court where member countries can take complaints about tariff violations. The WTO brings countries together in front of a panel of nations to present their arguments. After countries have had a chance to register their complaints, they usually agree to settle their trade disputes. If they don't, the WTO will recommend a solution. If a country fails to follow final WTO recommendations after a dispute, its trading partners can seek compensation or impose their own trade sanctions. The WTO has no power to enforce its solution, however.

Today, with a membership of 164 countries, the WTO is the only international organization that tries to administer the global rules of trade. It oversees trade agreements, tries to settle trade disputes among its member nations, and it also helps developing countries negotiate successful trade agreements.

European Union (EU)

While GATT was working to reduce tariffs, some nations tried to reduce their tariff barriers even more by forming trade blocs. A **trade bloc** is a group of countries, usually located in a particular region, that cooperate to expand free trade.

---

multilateral agreement treaty in which multiple nations agree to give each other the same benefits

trade bloc group of countries, usually located in a particular region, that cooperate to expand free trade among one another

The World Trade Organization (WTO) headquarters are located in Geneva, Switzerland. The WTO deals with the global rules of trade.

154

WTO OMC

WORLD TRADE ORGANIZATION
ORGANISATION MONDIALE DU COMMERCE
ORGANIZACIÓN MUNDIAL DEL COMERCIO

Martin Good/Shutterstock

European Union

Since 1993, the EU has expanded its membership to include several Eastern European nations that were transitioning from a command economy structure to a market economy. The map shows other countries that want to become part of the EU.

Legend:
- Member
- Official Candidate
- Potential Candidate
- Non-member

Major Trade Bloc Comparisons	USMCA	EU*	U.S.
GDP (PPP), in billions	$24,893	$19,886	$20,525
GDP per capita	$43,786	$44,436	$62,530
Population, in millions	503.1	450.1	335.0
Labor Force, in millions	215.2	238.9	146.1

*2019 Data, Includes the UK

Source: CIA World Factbook, 2021

GEOGRAPHY CONNECTION

1. **Global Interconnections** Why do you think additional countries want to join the EU?

2. **Exploring Regions** How do the EU and USMCA compare in GDP and GDP per capita?

The European Union (EU) is the most famous trade bloc. The purpose of the EU was to **integrate**, or combine, the economies of its members. Politically, doing so would also help ensure that future wars on European soil would not happen. The effort was a great achievement, and the EU became a major success story. In 1993 the EU became the largest single unified market in the world in terms of population and GDP. As the map **European Union** shows, it continues to add members as certain requirements are met.

Today the EU creates a free-trade zone that covers 27 European countries. Within this regional zone, goods, services, and workers can travel freely across national borders. In addition, more than two-thirds of the EU nations share a common currency called the euro, making trade easier.

integrate combine

The United Kingdom was once a member but left the EU in 2020. Still, as the chart **Major Trade Bloc Comparisons** shows, the European Union rivals the United States-Mexico-Canada Agreement (USMCA), a trading bloc of which the United States is a member.

NAFTA and the USMCA

In 1994 the United States, Canada, and Mexico merged to create the North American Free Trade Agreement (NAFTA). The goal was to remove trade barriers and encourage economic growth among the three countries. Since then, trade among the three nations has more than tripled. This brought lower prices and a greater variety of goods to consumers and producers in all three countries. NAFTA was renamed the United States-Mexico-Canada Agreement (USMCA) in 2020 after President Trump secured changes to NAFTA's dairy, automobile, labor, and copyright laws.

Other nations have also created their own trading blocs. For example, the Andean Community is a trading bloc in South America between Colombia, Ecuador, Peru, and Bolivia. The Association of Southeast Asian Nations (ASEAN) was formed in Southeast Asia by ten nations in 1967 and has expanded recently to include other Asian countries. Despite these efforts, none have been as successful as the EU or the USMCA.

✓ **CHECK FOR UNDERSTANDING**

1. **Summarizing** What is economic interdependence?
2. **Explaining** How do trade blocs help member nations?

Global Issues in Trade

GUIDING QUESTION

What are some consequences of economic interdependence?

Increased specialization and trade make countries wealthier yet more interdependent. International trade also lowers costs for producers and consumers. Consider that many of the products we use are made by **multinationals**.

multinationals corporations that have manufacturing or service operations in several different countries

These are corporations that have manufacturing or service operations in several different countries. Apple, British Petroleum, Dell Technologies, General Motors, Nabisco, Mitsubishi, and Sony are examples of multinational corporations with worldwide economic importance.

Multinationals are important because they can move resources, goods, services, and financial capital across national borders. Multinationals are usually welcome because they bring new technologies and create new jobs in areas where jobs are needed. Multinationals also produce tax revenues for the host country, which helps that nation's economy.

Interdependence brings change, however, and change can be unwelcome or even harmful to certain groups. So who feels the pain, and should countries be concerned if international trade threatens their independence?

Factory workers assemble computers at a Dell factory in India. Dell Technologies is a multinational corporation with operations in 180 countries.

Workers in Detroit, Michigan, protest the outsourcing of auto jobs.

Free Trade Can Be Painful

Free trade provides benefits to almost everyone, but there are still problems. Workers—and sometimes even entire industries—are often threatened by free trade. In the United States, free trade has enabled companies to **outsource**, or move factories or business operations to other countries with lower labor costs. Many Americans consider outsourcing a problem because they fear losing their jobs to overseas workers. In the United States, for example, many automotive and steel factories have shut down, increasing unemployment in those industries. This happened because other nations were producing automobiles and steel relatively cheaper than U.S. factories.

Because the overall benefits of trade generally outweigh its costs, government policy can be used to limit the harms done by international trade without necessarily resorting to protectionism. For example, to offset the problems caused at home by outsourcing, the government can pay to retrain workers for other jobs. If a region is hard-hit by unemployment, the government can help people move to more prosperous locations. Retraining programs are expensive, however, and workers are often reluctant to leave the places where they have put down their roots.

There may never be a satisfactory way to resolve all the unemployment caused by international trade. As long as countries continue to specialize according to their comparative advantages, some workers will be displaced. Compensating these workers with other jobs might help heal the pain. Still, the overall positives of free trade—especially lower prices that consumers pay for goods and services—outweigh the negatives.

Loss of Independence

Free trade agreements can also threaten a country's independence. This is the major reason the United Kingdom left the European Union. The United Kingdom was worried that too many immigrant workers would be allowed to come in from other countries. It also worried that it could not control its own economic and trade policies because it had to follow EU laws and policies.

When President Trump was elected, he followed an "America First" policy for similar reasons. He thought too many immigrant workers would enter the country and work for lower wages, potentially displacing some of the American work force. He also thought international trade agreements under NAFTA

---

outsource to move factories to other countries with lower labor costs

Workers sew jeans at a garment factory in China. Many companies outsource their production to countries where labor costs are low, such as China.

Speculating Why do countries welcome multinationals into their borders?

threatened American independence, so he revised the treaty to make it the USMCA.

Some people believe multinationals also limit the power of governments. For example, some multinationals have been known to abuse their position and pay very low wages to workers or demand lower tax rates from the host country. They may also interfere with traditional ways of life and business customs in the countries where they do business. If government leaders voice disapproval, the multinational may threaten to move its operations to another country.

Yet close economic cooperation between nations also has a major political advantage—it reduces the threat of future military conflicts. Nations economically dependent upon one another will find it less appealing to start a war. For example, a war between any of the current European Union countries—such as France and Germany—is hard to imagine. Likewise, a military conflict between the United States and Canada or the United States and Japan is highly unlikely. The additional economic stability helps offset the threat to a nation's independence.

✓ CHECK FOR UNDERSTANDING

1. **Explaining** What are some reasons people and groups object to economic interdependence?

2. **Describing** What are the advantages and disadvantages of multinational corporations?

The Wealth of Nations

Analyzing Key Ideas and Details As you read the lesson, complete a graphic organizer identifying some of the obstacles developing countries face as they try to improve their economies.

Obstacles to Development

High-Income, Low-Income Countries

GUIDING QUESTION

How do we know that some countries are wealthier than others?

Are some countries wealthier than others? Does the type of economic system matter? These types of questions assess a country's standard of living. **Standard of living** is the quality of life measured by such things as having plentiful goods and services, high per capita incomes, and good health care. The countries with these features are often called **developed countries**. Their characteristics include:

- Strong industry due to investment in machines and factories
- Large service sector that includes shops and restaurants
- Strong *infrastructure*, such as highways, power, and sewers
- Public goods such as libraries, parks, and museums
- Private ownership of the factors of production
- Good institutions, such as courts and hospitals
- Low population growth rate

Countries without these characteristics are called **developing countries**. Their standard of living is lower than developed countries.

Income levels are often used to classify countries as "developed" or "developing." As the chart **Country Classification Levels** shows,

standard of living the material well-being of an individual or nation
developed country industrialized country with a high standard of living
developing country nonindustrial country with a low standard of living

Country Classification Levels
The chart classifies countries into two "Developed" categories and two "Developing" categories.

Country Classification	2021 Per Capita Income Levels	% of Global Population	% of Global GDP
Developed: High Income	$12,536 or more	17%	49%
Developed: Upper-middle Income	$4,046–$12,535	36%	34%
Developing: Lower-middle Income	$1,036–$4,045	40%	16%
Developing: Low Income	$1,035 or less	8%	Less than 1%

Source: World Bank, 2021

EXAMINE THE CHART

Analyzing Visuals Which category makes up the largest percentage of the global population? What percentage of GDP does it produce?

GDP Per Capita—Selected Countries

The map shows GDP per capita for a few nations in the world.

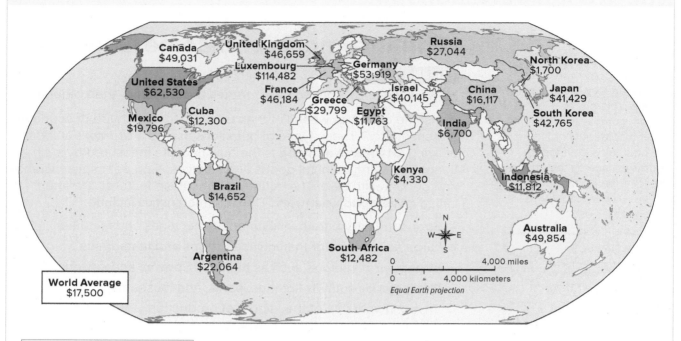

GEOGRAPHY CONNECTION

1. **Global Interconnections** Of the countries shown, where does the United States rank in GDP per capita?

2. **Patterns and Movement** Which country—North Korea or South Korea—do you think has a market economy? Why?

high-income countries account for about 17 percent of the global population. But they produce nearly half of the total world GDP.

Gross Domestic Product (GDP) per capita is one of the best indicators of living standards. Recall that GDP is the total market value of all final products produced within a country's borders during a single year. And *per capita* means "for each person." *GDP per capita* is calculated by dividing the country's GDP by its population. The result is the amount of output on a per-person basis. As the map **GDP Per Capita—Selected Countries** shows, per capita incomes range from $114,482 per person in Luxembourg, a tiny country with rich royalty, to North Korea, with an estimated $1,700 per person income. Other countries' per capita incomes may be higher or lower than the 23 countries shown.

So the answer to the earlier question is "yes," some countries *are* wealthier than others. And the gap between the wealthier and the poorer countries is getting wider every year. Why is this

happening, and can anything be done about it? Although many factors are involved, a country's economic system is one of the most important characteristics of high-income countries.

✓ CHECK FOR UNDERSTANDING

1. **Contrasting** What distinguishes developed countries from developing countries?

2. **Identifying** Which economic measurement is the best indicator of a country's standard of living?

Transitioning to a Market Economy

GUIDING QUESTION

What evidence shows that a market economy leads to the highest per capita incomes?

One way to see if market economies lead to the highest per capita incomes is to look at the alternatives—command economies. Command economies are not very efficient. People often face shortages of goods and services and products of low quality. When shortages occur, leaders usually provide for themselves first. The result is that government leaders have plentiful food, nice cars, and good houses, while average citizens often go without. In the past several decades, several command economies have begun transitioning to a market-based economy.

Transitioning Economies

Command economies have never performed as well as market/capitalist economies. As the map **GDP Per Capita—Selected Countries** shows, Cuba and North Korea—both of which have command economies—have some of the world's lowest GDPs per capita. Russia's GDP per capita was low when the Soviet Union collapsed around 1990. Russia's progress since then is partially due to its efforts to adopt some features of a market economy.

Russia's attempt to change its command economy to a market economy proved to be especially difficult. The biggest hurdle was privatization. **Privatization** is the process of changing state-owned businesses, factories, and farms into ones owned by private citizens. To do this, government-owned factories were converted into corporations with millions of shares of common stock. These shares were given directly to people or used as payment for factory wages. If done correctly, factory ownership would have been **transferred** to private citizens. But many of these ownership shares ended up in bureaucrats' pockets. This left the ownership of many important industries in the hands of a few high government officials.

Another difficulty was that people had to learn how to make decisions in an economy that had markets and prices. In the former Soviet command economy, people were told when and where to work. Wages were minimal but about equal, regardless of the work performed. The government provided some things for free, such as transportation, education, medicines, and some foods. People were able to have some of their needs satisfied even if they did not work, or work very hard. When converting to a market economy, however, people had to learn to work hard if they wanted to provide for their food, shelter, and clothing. This transition was difficult for many people to make.

Hungary and other former Soviet countries had some experience with black markets, which helped acquaint them with market economies. A **black market** is a market where illegal goods are bought and sold. This doesn't mean the goods are necessarily bad. Blue jeans were

privatization process of changing state-owned businesses, factories, and farms to ones owned by private citizens

transfer to shift or reassign

black market market where illegal goods are bought and sold

Russian women purchase shoes at a black market in the Soviet Union in the late 1980s.

Neil Proctor/Alamy Stock Photo

Comparing Economies

The United States has long enjoyed the benefits of having a market-oriented economy. Russia and China are making the transition. North Korea lags far behind with its command economy.

	North Korea	China	Russia	United States
GDP per capita	$1,700	$16,117	$27,044	$62,530
Real GDP	$40 billion	$22.5 trillion	$3.9 trillion	$20.5 trillion
Population	25,831,360	1,397,897,720	142,320,720	334,998,398
Labor Force (total)	14,000,000	774,710,000	69,923,000	146,128,000
Labor Force % in Agriculture % in Industry % in Services	37.0% 14.0% NA	27.7% 28.8% 43.5%	9.4% 27.6% 63.0%	0.7% 20.3% 79.0%
Exports	$222 million	$2.5 trillion	$551 billion	$2.3 trillion
Imports	$2.3 billion	$2.1 trillion	$367 billion	$3.2 trillion

Source: CIA World Factbook, 2021

EXAMINE THE CHART

1. **Comparing** In what area does China still lag well behind the United States?
2. **Analyzing Visuals** In what area of economic performance has China surpassed the success of the United States?

popular black-market goods in the Soviet Union because the government thought they were unnecessary and did not produce them.

Few of the former Soviet countries ever changed completely to market economies. Many kept some of their previous command features. This left them with a mixture of command, socialism, and market economies—known as a mixed economy. Today, Russia has a mixed economy with strong elements of a command economy, such as friends of high government officials owning significant properties and industries. At best, Russia and some of its former satellite countries *tried* to transition to capitalism, but stalled along the way.

China has been more successful at transitioning to a market economy. Starting in the late 1970s, China began adopting some features of a market economy. The result has been a dramatic rise in GDP and GDP per capita. China now has the world's largest economy when measured in terms of total real GDP produced. It also helps that it is one of the largest countries, which gives it one of the largest potential markets.

Yet some industries and markets are controlled by the government, and only one party—the Communist Party—controls the government. The government has been successful in propelling economic growth, but that success is not shared by most of the people. Whether entrepreneurs can flourish in a centrally controlled economy is yet to be seen.

Cultural Obstacles to Development

Command economies with few market structures are not the only obstacle to development. Cultural obstacles also hinder development. For example, some cultures place high value in having large families. This can lead to a high rate of population growth. When the population grows faster than GDP, GDP per capita declines. The result is that each person has a smaller share of what the economy produces. Therefore, countries with the highest rates of population growth often tend to have the lowest GDP per capita.

Countries with high rates of population growth face another difficulty. As more people are added to the population, more jobs need to be created for workers. A growing population will also need expanded services, such as transportation, health care, and education. Additionally, a high rate of population growth itself can result in poverty, or a rise in poverty.

Some cultures also hinder the ability of women to contribute to the economy. In Saudi Arabia and much of the Arab world, women are restricted to few occupations. Female education is limited. These women have few to no chances to help their country's economy to develop.

Political Obstacles to Development

War is a huge obstacle in some developing countries. Fighting claims lives and forces civilians to move away to safer areas. It also damages a nation's resources. Productivity slows and people face food, health care, and education shortages. As a result, warring countries have more difficulty investing in their economies.

Political corruption slows growth in many developing countries as well. Some leaders steal money that was meant to pay for economic development or other projects to help their people. Corrupt leaders base their economic decisions not on what is best for their country but on what is best for themselves. Some corruption often extends down to minor government officials who demand bribes for the smallest of favors.

Environmental Obstacles to Development

Diseases have crippled some developing countries. Malaria and dengue fever are mosquito-borne diseases found in tropical climates. Other diseases such as AIDS and COVID-19 have also been major problems in developing countries. These diseases affect the working population and can reduce the size of the labor force. All too frequently, young children and elderly parents are left behind to fend for themselves.

Even geography can be a problem for economic growth. Land-locked countries with no access to the sea may have difficulty getting goods to and from other countries. Many developing nations often lack the means to extract, use, and sell their resources.

Economic Obstacles to Development

Many developing countries have barriers to international trade. They do this because they want to protect domestic jobs and young industries. Trade barriers usually protect industries that are not efficient, however. Most economists think these barriers actually hold back the countries' ability to build their economies.

Developed countries have diversified economies, whereas less-developed countries may have single-resource economies. In a single-resource economy, a nation depends on a single export product for its economic growth. A failure of a crop, a decrease in the price of oil, or a similar problem with the one resource a country exports makes it difficult for a developing country to experience progress. In addition, focusing on only a single resource may lead to environmental problems, such as over-using the soil or polluting the water sources near mines.

Finally, many developing countries also face the problem of severe debt to developed nations.

A street in Syria lies in ruins after being bombed. In addition to the human toll, war destroys infrastructure necessary for development.

These students in India have benefited from the country's higher standard of living. India has overcome many obstacles to development by lowering trade barriers and investing in technology and infrastructure. As the industrial and service sectors have grown, the standard of living has improved as well.

Explaining How do trade barriers hurt development?

Many once borrowed large sums of money from wealthy nations to encourage economic growth. Much of that money was siphoned off by corruption, which slowed investment in capital resources and other development projects. The result was that economic growth was not fast enough to pay off those debts. Now the countries must use too much of their national income to pay off their debt.

Any one of these problems would be difficult for a nation to solve. Unfortunately, many developing nations have to deal with two or three of these problems at the same time. As a result, satisfactory economic progress has been difficult for them to achieve and the gap between the wealthy and the poorer countries gets wider every year.

The Wealth of Nations

In 1776, Adam Smith wrote that the wealth of a nation was its *people*, not its stock of gold and silver. The same thing is true today—but people also need an economic system that lets them grow and maximize their abilities. Economies with free markets generally do this successfully. The proof is that they have some of the highest per capita incomes in the world. These income levels are possible because free markets give people the opportunity to make decisions that are best for them, and ultimately best for the economy. Market economies are not perfect, but they are the best way to organize the billions of minor economic decisions that people make daily—decisions that ultimately determine our standard of living.

✓ **CHECK FOR UNDERSTANDING**

1. **Determining Central Ideas** What is the first step that a command economy must do before it can successfully become a market economy?

2. **Identifying Cause and Effect** In what two ways do high population growth rates hurt developing countries?

LESSON ACTIVITIES

1. **Informative/Explanatory Writing** Suppose you have friends who live in a country that is transitioning from a command economy to a market economy. Write a letter explaining to your friends how they need to adjust their thinking and work ethic in the new market economy. Include information about learning to make decisions on their own, taking initiative, interpreting prices, and fending for themselves in free markets.

2. **Presenting** With a partner, choose two developed countries and two developing countries. Find data on their GDP per capita, rate of population growth, type of government, type of economic system, and level of debt. Identify whether they are single-resource or diversified economies. You can find the data at the website for the CIA World Factbook, or you can consult another equally reliable source, such as the World Bank. Make a table to display your data. For the poorest-performing country you research, identify the obstacles to its development. Share your table and findings in a presentation to the class.

06
Analyzing Sources: Environmental Balance

 COMPELLING QUESTION

How do we balance the needs of consumers and the needs of a sustainable planet?

Plan Your Inquiry

DEVELOPING QUESTIONS

Read the Compelling Question for this lesson. What questions can you ask to help you answer this Compelling Question? Create a graphic organizer like the one below. Write three Supporting Questions in the first column.

Supporting Questions	Source	What this source tells me about environmental balance	Questions the source leaves unanswered
	A		
	B		
	C		
	D		
	E		

ANALYZING SOURCES

Next, read the introductory information for each source in this lesson. Then analyze each source by answering the questions that follow it. How does each source help you answer each Supporting Question you created? What questions do you still have? Write those in your graphic organizer.

After you analyze the sources, you will:
• use the evidence from the sources
• communicate your conclusions
• take informed action

Background Information

In recent years, people have become aware of dangers to the world's environment. Chemicals released by factories and vehicles pollute the air and water. *Deforestation*—the mass removal of trees—causes flooding, leads to mud slides, and lessens the amount of carbon dioxide that trees absorb. Plastic waste overflows landfills and finds its way into the oceans.

Some people have turned to conservation to reduce environmental damage. Conservation means carefully using resources and limiting the harmful effects of human activity. Points of view about conservation differ. Some people think conserving natural resources is less important than economic growth. They argue that limiting the ways that businesses operate drives up costs. Others claim that not conserving resources today will lead to greater future economic and environmental costs.

This Inquiry Lesson includes sources about finding that environmental balance. As you read and analyze the sources, think about the Compelling Question.

Trash litters the ocean. Modern life offers many comforts, but they can come at a cost to the environment.

A

Priority: Economic Growth?

Solving environmental problems is not easy. The process of switching to cleaner sources of energy can be costly. Protecting forests may deprive farmers of land they need to grow crops. Many developing nations fear that taking steps to curb pollution will slow their economic growth—growth they need in order to improve the lives of their people.

PRIMARY SOURCE: ONLINE ARTICLE

> “Developing countries currently cannot sustain themselves, let alone grow, without relying heavily on **fossil fuels**. Global warming typically takes a back seat to feeding, housing, and employing these countries' citizens. . . .
>
> Fossil fuels are still the cheapest, most reliable energy resources available. When a developing country wants to build a functional economic system and end **rampant** poverty, it turns to fossil fuels.
>
> India hopes to transition to renewable energy as its economy grows, but the investment needed to meet its renewable energy goals “is equivalent to . . . over ten times the country's annual spending on health and education.”
>
> Unless something changes, developing countries like India cannot fight climate change *and* provide for their citizens.”
>
> — From “Developing Countries Can't Afford Climate Change” by Tucker Davey, futureoflife.org, 2016.

fossil fuels fuels such as coal, gas, or petroleum that were formed long ago by the remains of living organisms

rampant widespread

EXAMINE THE SOURCE

1. **Identifying** Why do many developing countries rely on fossil fuels?
2. **Explaining** Why has India not transitioned to renewable energy sources?

Davey, Tucker. "Developing Countries Can't Afford Climate Change." Future of Life Institute. August 5, 2016. https://futureoflife.org/2016/08/05/developing-countries-cant-afford-climate-change.

Gaming and Energy

Conserving energy is one way to balance the needs of consumers and the planet. Here, an energy company offers tips on how gamers can help conserve energy.

Two teens in Texas play video games. One person is having more fun than the other, but both can help conserve energy.

PRIMARY SOURCE: ONLINE ARTICLE

❝ **Turn controllers off when not in use** Automatic shutdown functions can save power, but not all gaming consoles have them. Be proactive and turn off your console and its controllers when you're not using them to cut down on energy waste.

Unplug when you can Like many advanced electronics, gaming consoles can draw power even when turned off, which adds up over time. Unplugging them when not in use cuts game console energy consumption that's pure waste.

Avoid streaming on consoles The energy costs of streaming on game console systems can be considerable. Game consoles are not optimized for streaming like a streaming device such as an Apple TV or Roku. ❞

— From "How Much Energy Do Game Consoles Really Use?" by blog.constellation.com.

EXAMINE THE SOURCE

1. **Making Connections** Are you a gamer? Did you find these suggestions helpful? Explain.
2. **Speculating** In addition to gaming, what other home functions do you think require large amounts of energy?

PHOTO: Richard G. Bingham II/Alamy Stock Photo; TEXT:Constellation. "How Much Energy Do Gaming Consoles Really Use?" Blog. Constellation Energy Resources, LLC. April 29, 2020. https://blog.constellation.com/2020/04/29/energy-costs-of-gaming-consoles-and-gaming-pcs/

Pollution Tax

Economic incentives can help solve the global problem of pollution. Most economists argue that the best way to attack the problem is to attack the incentives that caused pollution in the first place.

SECONDARY SOURCE: TEXTBOOK

❝ Pollution does not occur on its own: it occurs because people and firms have an incentive to pollute. If that incentive can be removed, pollution will be reduced. For example, factories historically located along the banks of rivers so they could discharge their **refuse** into the moving waters. Factories that generated smoke and other air pollutants often were located farther from the water with tall smokestacks to send the pollutants long distances. Others tried to avoid the problem by digging pits on their property to bury their toxic wastes. In all three situations, factory owners were trying to lower production costs by using the environment as a giant waste-disposal system. . . .

A market-based approach [to reduce pollution] is to tax or charge firms in proportion to the amount of pollutants they release. Depending on the industry, the size of the tax would depend on the severity of the pollution and the quantity of toxic substances being released. A firm can then either pay the fees or take steps to reduce the pollution. . . . As long as it is cheaper to clean up the pollution than to pay the tax, individual firms will have the incentive to clean up and stop polluting.

An expanded version of pollution fees is the **EPA's** use of pollution permits— federal permits allowing public utilities to release specific amounts of **emissions** into the air—to reduce sulfur dioxide emissions at coal-burning electric utilities that contribute to the problem of **acid rain**.

Under this program, the EPA awards a limited number of permits to all utilities. . . . If the level of pollutants is still too high, the EPA can distribute fewer permits. A smaller number of permits will make each one worth more than before, which will again cause firms to redouble their efforts to reduce pollution. In the end, the market forces of supply and demand will provide the encouragement to reduce pollution. ❞

— From *Principles of Economics* by Gary Clayton, McGraw Hill, 2024.

refuse waste

EPA Environmental Protection Agency

emissions polluting gases

acid rain pollution in the form of rainwater mixed with sulfur dioxide to form a mild form of sulfuric acid

---

EXAMINE THE SOURCE

1. **Identifying Cause and Effect** Why do companies have an incentive to pollute? How can governments counteract this incentive?
2. **Making Connections** Why did the author call pollution fees a "market-based approach"?

Clayton, Gary E. Principles of Economics. Bothell, WA: McGraw Hill LLC, 2019.

Changing Views

The perception of energy use and economic progress has changed over time, as shown in this cartoon.

PRIMARY SOURCE: POLITICAL CARTOON

EXAMINE THE SOURCE

1. **Analyzing Visuals** The cartoonist is trying to convey a shift in the national conversation about the use of coal. In the first panel, why does the factory owner encourage the farmer to use coal?

2. **Speculating** Why have their positions reversed in the second panel?

Consuming Less

Another way to balance the needs of the planet is to use less.

Some 140 million tons of waste are emptied into U.S. landfills like this one every year.

EXAMINE THE SOURCE

Predicting What environmental problems might arise from too much trash?

Complete Your Inquiry

EVALUATE SOURCES AND USE EVIDENCE

Refer back to the Compelling Question and the Supporting Questions you developed at the beginning of the lesson.

1. **Identifying** Which of the sources affected you the most? Why?

2. **Evaluating** Overall, what impression do these sources give you about the importance of balancing environmental and human needs? Explain.

3. **Gathering Sources** Which sources helped you answer the Supporting Questions and Compelling Question? Which sources, if any, challenged what you thought you knew when you first created your Supporting Questions? What information do you still need in order to answer your questions? Where would you find that information?

4. **Evaluating Sources** Identify the sources that helped answer your Supporting Questions. How reliable is the source? How would you verify the reliability of the source?

COMMUNICATE CONCLUSIONS

5. **Collaborating** With a partner, conduct research about a renewable form of energy, including its advantages and disadvantages. Then debate whether you think this energy form will ever be economically viable. Each of you should give specific reasons for your opinions.

TAKE INFORMED ACTION

Writing an Editorial About Conservation
Governments, businesses, and people have different ideas on conservation, reuse, and/or recycling. Think about the views of each of these groups. Write a letter to the editor focused on one audience in which you take a position on one issue. Explain what conservation, reuse, and/or recycling efforts you think are important or are unnecessary, and why. Explain why you recommend those steps.

Reviewing The Global Economy

Summary

Why Nations Trade

Nations trade because of comparative advantage. Nations *import* goods produced in other countries. They *export* goods they produce. To protect home industries that lose sales to lower-priced imported goods, governments use trade barriers such as *tariffs*, *quotas*, or *subsidies*.

Trade Balances

The difference between the value of a nation's exports and the value of its imports is the *balance of trade*. That balance can be positive (trade surplus) or negative (trade deficit). Trade imbalances tend to be self-correcting over time. Currencies used to finance world trade are called *foreign exchange*.

Economic Interdependence

International trade has made for more *economic interdependence* than ever before. We rely on others—and others rely on us—to provide for our wants and needs.

Trade Alliances and Issues

International organizations such as the WTO oversee trade agreements and help settle trade disputes among member nations. Many countries form regional *trade blocs* to lower trade barriers and increase trade. Free trade can be painful for those who lose their jobs due to *outsourcing*, but overall, the net benefits of trade are positive even if countries lose some political independence.

The Wealth of Nations

Standard of living is the quality of life measured by plentiful goods and services and high per capita incomes. Countries with these features are *developed countries*. Countries without these features are *developing countries*. Many face obstacles such as high population growth rates, single-resource economies, low education and poor health care of citizens, corruption, and trade barriers.

Travel mania/Shutterstock

Checking For Understanding

Answer the questions to see if you understood the topic content.

1. Define each of these terms:

   A. import
   B. export
   C. comparative advantage
   D. protectionism
   E. tariff
   F. exchange rate
   G. balance of trade
   H. trade bloc
   I. outsource
   J. developing country

REVIEWING KEY FACTS

2. **Identifying Cause and Effect** Why do nations trade with one another?

3. **Explaining** What policies do governments use to restrict international trade and protect home industries?

4. **Identifying** When U.S. citizens travel to Japan, what type of currency will they receive in exchange for their U.S. dollars?

5. **Identifying** What does the exchange rate measure?

6. **Interpreting** What does it mean when a country has a positive balance of trade?

7. **Explaining** How do ongoing trade deficits hurt a country's economy?

8. **Identifying** What is the European Union?

9. **Contrasting** What is the difference between a developed country and a developing country?

10. **Explaining** What are black markets, and are they bad?

11. **Explaining** What happens when a developing country's population grows faster than the GDP?

12. **Contrasting** What challenges does a single-resource economy face that a diversified economy does not?

CRITICAL THINKING

13. **Inferring** How are comparative advantage and specialization related?

14. **Identifying Cause and Effect** What effect do trade barriers have on global interdependence?

15. **Drawing Conclusions** How does a country's ongoing balance of trade affect the value of its currency?

16. **Evaluating** Is a weak exchange rate for the U.S. dollar good or bad for the country?

17. **Summarizing** What roles do international trade organizations play in trade?

18. **Drawing Conclusions** Why do multinationals increase economic interdependence?

19. **Explaining** What is privatization and why have some governments used it?

20. **Summarizing** What are some obstacles to development that developing countries face?

NEED EXTRA HELP?

If You've Missed Question	1	2	3	4	5	6	7	8	9	10
Review Lesson	2, 3, 4, 5	2	2	3	3	3	3	4	5	5

If You've Missed Question	11	12	13	14	15	16	17	18	19	20
Review Lesson	5	5	2	2	3	3	4	4	5	5

Apply What You Have Learned

Understanding Multiple Perspectives

Should companies outsource their work force?

ACTIVITY **Using Sources to Write About Outsourcing** Read these excerpts that provide two opinions on outsourcing American jobs. Then write a brief essay answering these questions: What are some benefits of outsourcing? What are some drawbacks? What evidence from the lessons can you provide to support the two views?

66 The phenomenon of foreign outsourcing creates tangible benefits for the U.S. economy and American workers. Whatever negative impact it has had on specific firms and workers has been limited and is far outweighed by the benefits. 99

— Daniel Griswold, director of the Center for Trade Policy Studies at the Cato Institute.

66 One: How many more jobs must we lose before they become concerned about our middle class and our strength as a consumer market? Two: When will the U.S. have to quit borrowing foreign capital to buy foreign goods that support European and Asian economies while driving us deeper into debt? Three: What jobs will our currently 15 million unemployed workers fill, where and when? 99

— Lou Dobbs, former anchor and managing editor of Lou Dobbs Tonight, CNN.

Writing an Argument

The gains from trade help an economy to grow. The growth comes from three sources: more overseas customers for a country's exported goods and services, more resources to import that allow for more home production, and lower prices of goods and services that can increase savings for consumers. Yet while free markets and international trade can bring benefits, some people still object to trade when it harms home industries and their workers.

ACTIVITY **Writing About a Trade Policy for Athletic Shoes** Suppose you are in charge of trade policy for the United States. Would you recommend the country increase or decrease trade barriers on athletic shoes? Write a report making your recommendation and explaining why you want to increase or decrease specific trade barriers.

(l) Griswold, Daniel. "Why We Have Nothing to Fear from Foreign Outsourcing." Free Trade Bulletin No. 10. Cato Institute. March 30, 2004. https://www.cato.org/free-trade-bulletin/why-we-have-nothing-fear-foreign-outsourcing.,
(r) Dobbs, Lou. "Exporting America: False Choices." CNN Money. CNN. March 10, 2004. https://money.cnn.com/2004/03/09/commentary/dobbs/dobbs/

Understanding Economic Concepts

Recall that comparative advantage is the ability to produce something relatively more efficiently, or at a relatively lower opportunity cost, than another country can.

ACTIVITY **Creating a Chart Showing Comparative Advantage** Suppose that you and a partner are starting a lawn-mowing business. You will each contribute an equal amount of money to buy a mower, a trimmer, gas, and other materials. Work with your partner to list the tasks associated with your business in a table like the one shown here. Keep in mind that some of these tasks, such as asking a sibling or parent to drive you and the mower to the lawn site, will not be related to physically mowing. Revise your list after an extended time frame to use what you have learned about comparative advantage to divide the tasks.

Task	Time It Took	Opportunity Cost of Doing the Task

 Making Connections

Consider the following questions: Why is the economic health of all nations important in a global economy? In addition to the obvious economic benefits to companies and consumers, what social benefits arise from a healthy economy?

ACTIVITY **Being an Active Citizen** Identify and research one developing country that has used specialization to boost its economy. Prepare a short speech that explains the country's choices and describes the impact these choices have had on the country's GDP, employment, and wages. Also describe the impact that economic growth has had on the country's political and social stability. Deliver your speech to your classmates. As you speak, make eye contact with your audience and speak clearly.

APPENDIX

WORLD
POLITICAL

0   2,000 miles at Equator
0   2,000 kilometers at Equator
Equal Earth projection

Chukchi Sea
Beaufort Sea
Alaska (U.S.)
RUS.
Yukon R.
Anchorage
Bering Sea
Gulf of Alaska
Aleutian Islands
60°N
150°W
120°W
90°W
60°W
30°W

Great Bear Lake
Great Slave Lake
Hudson Bay
Baffin Bay
Baffin Is.
Greenland (Kalaallit Nunaat) (Den.)
Greenland Sea
ICELAND
Faroe Is. (Den.)
Nuuk
Reykjavík
UNITED KINGDOM
IRELAND
Dublin
London
FRANCE

CANADA
Calgary
Nelson R.
Lake Winnipeg
Great Lakes
Ottawa
Labrador Sea
Island of Newfoundland
Nova Scotia

Vancouver
Vancouver Island
Seattle
Missouri R.
Chicago
Toronto
Great Salt Lake
UNITED STATES
New York City
Washington, D.C.

San Francisco
Colorado R.
Ohio R.
Atlanta
Bermuda (U.K.)
NORTH ATLANTIC OCEAN

Los Angeles
Mississippi R.
Houston
Azores (Port.)
Madeira Islands (Port.)
PORTUGAL
SPAIN
Madrid
Lisbon
Rabat
MOROCCO

Rio Grande
30°N
Gulf of Mexico
Nassau
BAHAMAS
Canary Islands (Sp.)
Laayoune
Western Sahara (Morocco)

TROPIC OF CANCER
MEXICO
Port-au-Prince
DOMINICAN REP.
Santo Domingo
Puerto Rico (U.S.)
MAURITANIA
MALI

Hawaiian Islands (U.S.)
NORTH PACIFIC OCEAN
Guadalajara
Mexico City
Havana
CUBA
HAITI
ST. KITTS & NEVIS
ANTIGUA AND BARBUDA
Nouakchott
CAPE VERDE
SENEGAL

Revillagigedo Islands (Mex.)
GUATEMALA
JAMAICA
BELIZE
Caribbean Sea
ST. LUCIA
DOMINICA
Guadeloupe (Fr.)
Martinique (Fr.)
BARBADOS
Praia
GAMBIA
GUINEA-BISSAU

Clipperton Island (Fr.)
Guatemala
HONDURAS
EL SALVADOR
NICARAGUA
COSTA RICA
PANAMA
GRENADA
ST. VINCENT & THE GRENADINES
TRINIDAD & TOBAGO
Caracas
VENEZUELA
Georgetown
Paramaribo
GUYANA
French Guiana (Fr.)
SURINAME
GUINEA
SIERRA LEONE
BURKINA FASO
LIBERIA
CÔTE D'IVOIRE
GHANA

Medellín
Bogotá
COLOMBIA
Negro R.
Amazon R.
Niger R.

0°
EQUATOR
Galápagos Islands (Ecua.)
Quito
ECUADOR
Manaus
Madeira R.

KIRIBATI
Line Islands
PERU
Lima
BRAZIL
Recife
São Francisco R.
Ascension (U.K.)

American Samoa (U.S.)
Marquesas Islands (Fr.)
Tocantins R.
Salvador
St. Helena (U.K.)

Apia
SAMOA
Cook Islands (N.Z.)
French Polynesia (Fr.)
BOLIVIA
La Paz
Sucre
Brasília
SOUTH ATLANTIC OCEAN

TONGA
Nuku'alofa
PARAGUAY
Paraguay R.
Rio de Janeiro
São Paulo

TROPIC OF CAPRICORN
Pitcairn Islands (U.K.)
Easter Island (Chile)
Asunción
Porto Alegre

30°S
SOUTH PACIFIC OCEAN
Córdoba
Santiago
Buenos Aires
URUGUAY
Montevideo
Tristan da Cunha Group (U.K.)
PRIME MERIDIAN (MERIDIAN OF GREENWICH)

Chatham Islands (N.Z.)
CHILE
ARGENTINA

Falkland Islands (U.K.)
South Georgia (U.K.)
South Sandwich Islands (U.K.)

60°S
ANTARCTIC CIRCLE
Strait of Magellan
Tierra del Fuego
Scotia Sea

Drake Passage
Weddell Sea
30°W

150°W
Ross Sea
120°W
90°W
60°W
Berkner Is.

ARCTIC OCEAN

Svalbard (Nor.)
Norwegian Sea
Barents Sea
Novaya Zemlya
Kara Sea
Severnaya Zemlya
Laptev Sea
New Siberian Is.
East Siberian Sea

ARCTIC CIRCLE

R U S S I A

Oslo
St. Petersburg
Yekaterinburg
Omsk
Novosibirsk
Yakutsk
Lena R.

NORWAY
SWEDEN
FINLAND
DEN.
NETH.
GERMANY
BELG.
SWITZ.
ITALY
Rome
ALGIERS
TUNISIA
Tripoli

EST.
LATV.
LITH.
POLAND
BELARUS
Moscow
Kyiv (Kiev)
Paris
CZECHIA
AUST.
HUNG.
SLOV.
B.&H.
MONT.
ALB.
N. MAC.
GREECE

Samara
Nur-Sultan
KAZAKHSTAN
Aral Sea
Tashkent
Bishkek
Almaty
UZBEKISTAN
KYRGYZSTAN
TAJIKISTAN
Dushanbe
Ashgabat
TURKMENISTAN

MONGOLIA
Ulaanbaatar

Sea of Okhotsk
Kamchatka Peninsula
Bering Sea
Aleutian Is.

Harbin
Shenyang
Beijing
Tianjin
NORTH KOREA
P'yŏngyang
Seoul
SOUTH KOREA

Sapporo
Hokkaidō
Honshū
JAPAN
Osaka
Tokyo
Kyūshū

NORTH PACIFIC OCEAN

UKRAINE
MOLD.
ROMANIA
AZERBAIJAN
GEORGIA
ARMENIA
Black Sea
Ankara
TURKEY
CYPRUS
LEBANON
ISRAEL
SYRIA
IRAQ
Baghdad
JORDAN
Cairo
EGYPT

Caspian Sea
Tehran
IRAN
KUWAIT
BAHRAIN
QATAR
Riyadh
U.A.E.
Masqat
OMAN

Kābul
AFGHANISTAN
Islamabad
Lahore
PAKISTAN
Delhi
New Delhi
Karachi
Mumbai (Bombay)

Chengdu
CHINA
Huang He (Yellow R.)
Chang Jiang
Wuhan
Shanghai
Yangtze R.

Guangzhou
Hong Kong
Hainan

TAIPEI
TAIWAN
East China Sea
30°N

NEPAL
BHUTAN
Thimphu
Ganges R.
BANGLADESH
Dhaka
MYANMAR (BURMA)
Nay Pyi Taw
LAOS
Vientiane
THAILAND
Bangkok

Hanoi
VIETNAM
South China Sea
Luzon
Manila
PHILIPPINES
Mindanao

Philippine Sea
Northern Mariana Is. (U.S.)
Guam (U.S.)
MARSHALL ISLANDS

LIBYA
NIGER
CHAD
SUDAN
Khartoum
ERITREA
YEMEN
Sanaa
DJIBOUTI
Socotra (Yemen)
ETHIOPIA
SOMALIA
Mogadishu

SAUDI ARABIA
Red Sea
Nile R.
Arabian Sea
Hyderabad
INDIA
Bengaluru (Bangalore)
Chennai (Madras)
Kolkata (Calcutta)
Bay of Bengal

Phnom Penh
CAMBODIA
Ho Chi Minh City
BRUNEI
Kuala Lumpur
MALAYSIA
SINGAPORE
Borneo
Celebes

PALAU
FEDERATED STATES OF MICRONESIA
KIRIBATI
NAURU
TUVALU

NIAMEY
TOGO
BENIN
NIGERIA
Lagos
CAMEROON
EQ. GUINEA
GABON
SÃO TOMÉ & PRÍNCIPE
Cabinda (Angola)
Luanda
ANGOLA
CENTRAL AFRICAN REP.
Bangui
SOUTH SUDAN
Juba
DEM. REP. OF THE CONGO
Kinshasa
Brazzaville
CONGO

UGANDA
KENYA
Nairobi
RWANDA
BURUNDI
Dodoma
TANZANIA
Dar es Salaam
MALAWI
COMOROS
MOZAMBIQUE

SRI LANKA
Sri Jayewardenepura Kotte
Colombo
Male
MALDIVES

SEYCHELLES
Chagos Archipelago (U.K.)

INDIAN OCEAN

Cocos Islands (Australia)
Christmas Island (Australia)
Jakarta
Java
Surabaya
INDONESIA
New Guinea
PAPUA NEW GUINEA
Port Moresby
Dili
EAST TIMOR (TIMOR-LESTE)
Darwin
Arafura Sea

SOLOMON ISLANDS
Coral Sea
VANUATU
FIJI
New Caledonia (Fr.)

NAMIBIA
Windhoek
BOTSWANA
Gaborone
Johannesburg
Bloemfontein
Cape Town
SOUTH AFRICA
ZAMBIA
Lusaka
Harare
ZIMBABWE
MADAGASCAR
Antananarivo
Port Louis
MAURITIUS
Réunion (Fr.)
Tshwane (Pretoria)
Maputo
ESWATINI
LESOTHO

AUSTRALIA
Perth
Darling R.
Murray R.
Brisbane
Sydney
Canberra
Melbourne
Tasman Sea
North Island
Auckland
NEW ZEALAND
Wellington
South Island
Tasmania

SOUTH PACIFIC OCEAN
30°S

Crozet Islands (Fr.)
Kerguelen Islands (Fr.)
Prince Edward Islands (S. Af.)
Auckland Islands (N.Z.)

The Atlantic, Indian, and Pacific Oceans merge around Antarctica. Some define this as an ocean, calling it the Antarctic Ocean, Austral Ocean, or Southern Ocean. While most accept four oceans (including the Arctic Ocean), there is little international agreement on the name and extent of a fifth ocean.

SOUTHERN OCEAN

A N T A R C T I C A

30°E 60°E 90°E 120°E 150°E Ross Sea

60°S

ABBREVIATIONS

ALB.	ALBANIA
AUST.	AUSTRIA
B.&H.	BOSNIA & HERZEGOVINA
BELG.	BELGIUM
BULG.	BULGARIA
CRO.	CROATIA
DEM. REP. OF THE CONGO	DEMOCRATIC REPUBLIC OF THE CONGO
DEN.	DENMARK
EQ. GUINEA	EQUATORIAL GUINEA
EST.	ESTONIA
HUNG.	HUNGARY
KOS.	KOSOVO
LATV.	LATVIA
LITH.	LITHUANIA
MOLD.	MOLDOVA
MONT.	MONTENEGRO
NETH.	NETHERLANDS
N. MAC.	NORTH MACEDONIA
SERB.	SERBIA
SLO.	SLOVAKIA
SLOV.	SLOVENIA
SWITZ.	SWITZERLAND
U.A.E.	UNITED ARAB EMIRATES

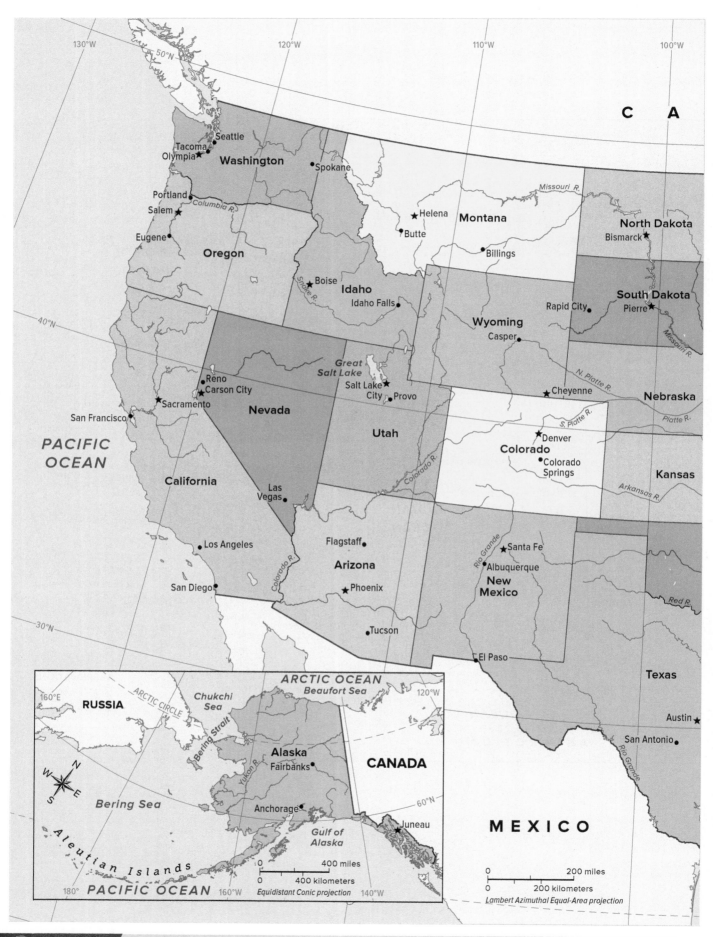

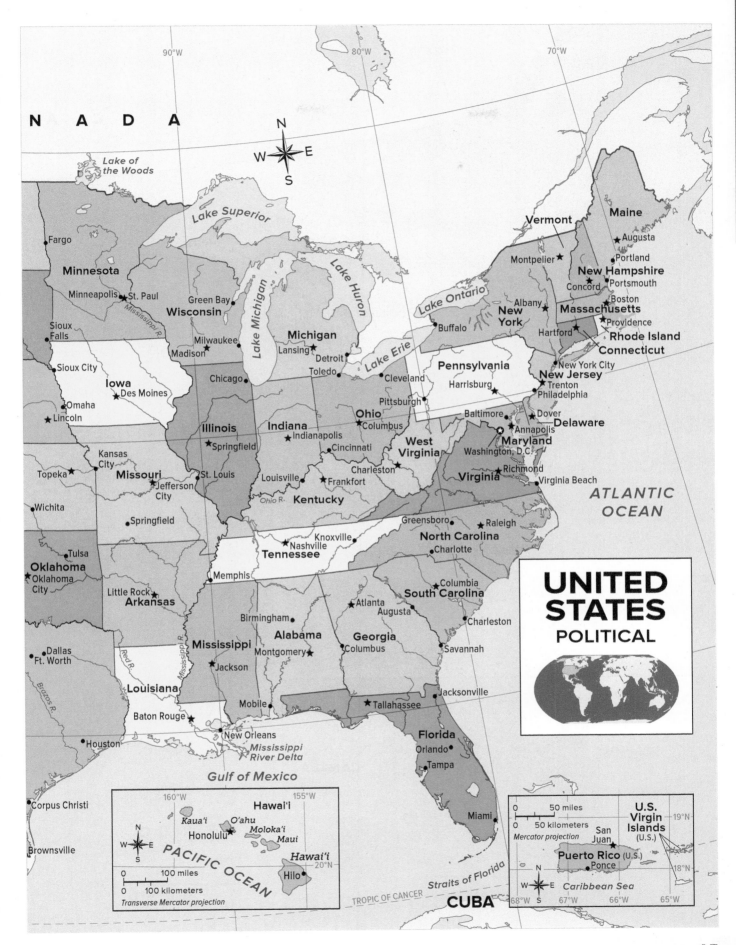

UNITED STATES POLITICAL

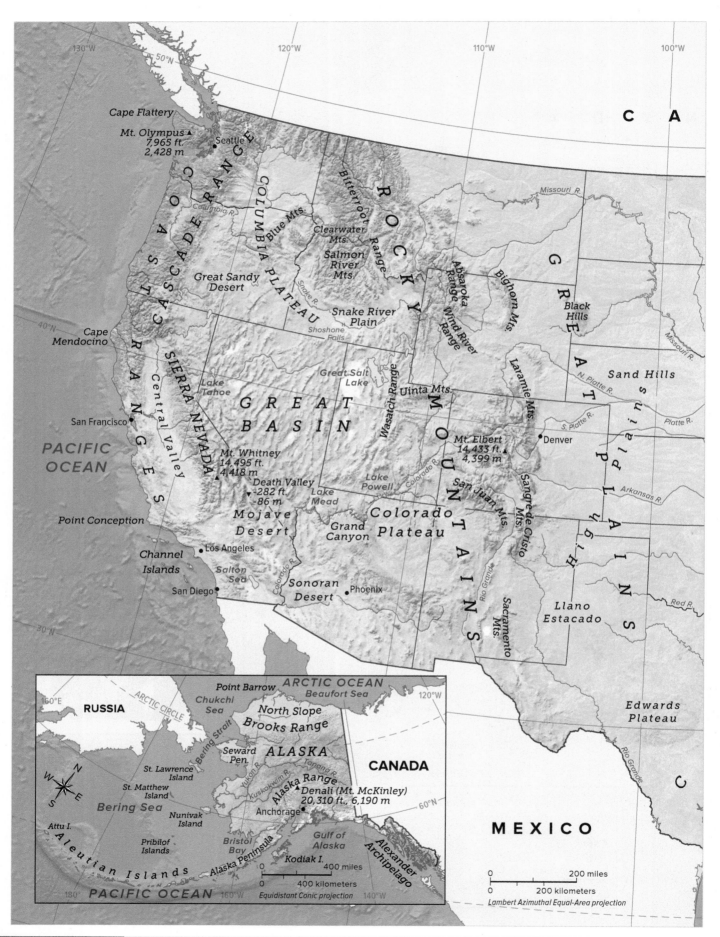

130°W   50°N   120°W   110°W   100°W

C A N A D A

Cape Flattery

Mt. Olympus ▲
7,965 ft.
2,428 m   Seattle

C O A S T

C A S C A D E   R A N G E

COLUMBIA PLATEAU

Bitterroot Range

R O C K Y

Columbia R.

Blue Mts.

Clearwater
Mts.

Salmon
River
Mts.

Great Sandy
Desert

Snake R.

Snake River
Plain

Shoshone
Falls

Absaroka
Range

Wind River
Range

Bighorn Mts.

Missouri R.

G
R
E
A
T

Black
Hills

Sand Hills

Missouri R.

40°N   Cape
Mendocino

R A N G E S

S I E R R A   N E V A D A

Central Valley

Lake
Tahoe

Great Salt
Lake

G R E A T
B A S I N

Wasatch Range

Uinta Mts.

Laramie Mts.

N. Platte R.

S. Platte R.

Platte R.

San Francisco

Mt. Whitney
14,495 ft.
4,418 m
▲

PACIFIC
OCEAN

Death Valley
▼ -282 ft.
-86 m

Lake
Mead

Lake
Powell

Colorado R.

M
O
U
N
T
A
I
N
S

Mt. Elbert
14,433 ft. ▲
4,399 m

Denver

H
i
g
h

P
l
a
i
n
s

Arkansas R.

Point Conception

Mojave
Desert

Grand
Canyon

Colorado
Plateau

San Juan Mts.

Sangre de Cristo Mts.

Channel
Islands

Los Angeles

Salton
Sea

Colorado R.

Sonoran
Desert

Phoenix

Rio Grande

Sacramento
Mts.

Llano
Estacado

Red R.

San Diego

30°N

MEXICO

Edwards
Plateau

Rio Grande

ARCTIC OCEAN

160°E   RUSSIA   Point Barrow   Beaufort Sea   120°W

ARCTIC CIRCLE

Chukchi
Sea

North Slope

Brooks Range

Bering Strait

Seward
Pen.

ALASKA

CANADA

St. Lawrence
Island

Yukon R.

Tanana R.

St. Matthew
Island

Kuskokwim R.

Alaska Range

Denali (Mt. McKinley)
20,310 ft., 6,190 m

Bering Sea

Nunivak
Island

Anchorage

60°N

N
W   E
S

Attu I.

Pribilof
Islands

Bristol
Bay

Kodiak I.

Gulf of
Alaska

Alexander
Archipelago

A l e u t i a n   I s l a n d s

Alaska Peninsula

0   400 miles
0   400 kilometers
Equidistant Conic projection

180°   160°W   PACIFIC OCEAN   140°W

0   200 miles
0   200 kilometers
Lambert Azimuthal Equal-Area projection

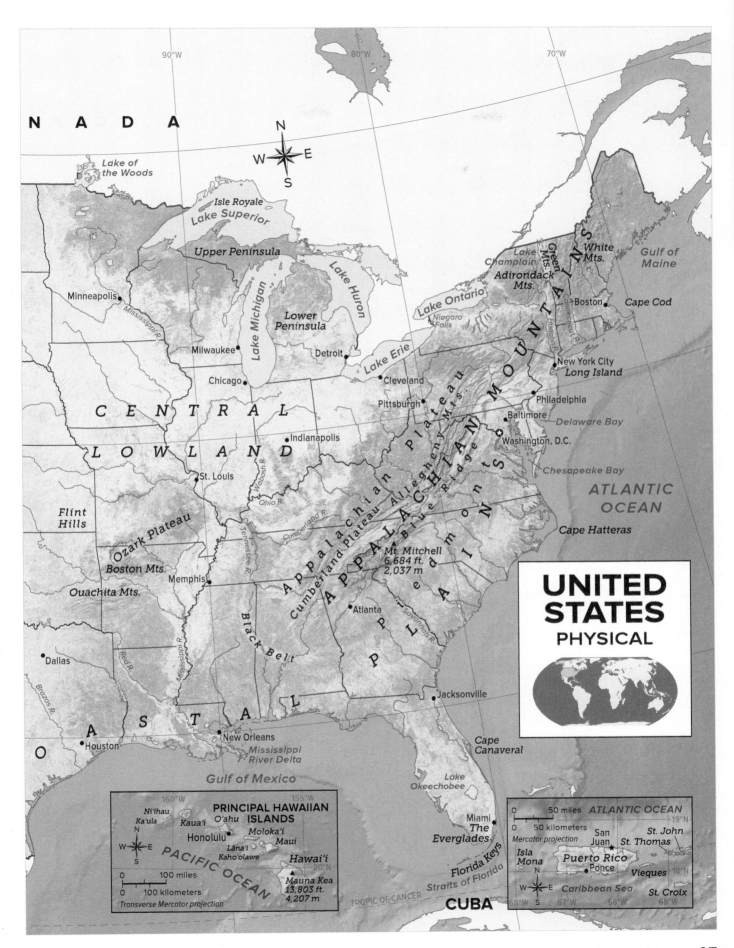

UNITED STATES PHYSICAL

CANADA

Lake of the Woods
Lake Superior
Isle Royale
Upper Peninsula
Lake Huron
Lake Michigan
Lower Peninsula
Minneapolis
Milwaukee
Chicago
Detroit
Lake Erie
Cleveland
Niagara Falls
Lake Ontario
Lake Champlain
Adirondack Mts.
Green Mts.
White Mts.
Gulf of Maine
Boston
Cape Cod
Hudson R.
Connecticut R.
New York City
Long Island
Philadelphia
Baltimore
Delaware Bay
Washington, D.C.
Chesapeake Bay
Pittsburgh
Allegheny Mts.
Appalachian Plateau
Blue Ridge
APPALACHIAN MOUNTAINS
Cumberland Plateau
Mississippi R.
CENTRAL LOWLAND
Indianapolis
St. Louis
Wabash R.
Ohio R.
Flint Hills
Ozark Plateau
Boston Mts.
Memphis
Cumberland R.
Tennessee R.
Ouachita Mts.
ATLANTIC OCEAN
Cape Hatteras
Mt. Mitchell 6,684 ft. 2,037 m
Piedmont
Atlanta
Savannah R.
Black Belt
Mississippi R.
Dallas
Red R.
Brazos R.
Houston
Jacksonville
COASTAL PLAINS
New Orleans
Mississippi River Delta
Gulf of Mexico
Cape Canaveral
Lake Okeechobee
Miami
The Everglades
Florida Keys
Straits of Florida
CUBA
TROPIC OF CANCER

90°W   80°W   70°W

PRINCIPAL HAWAIIAN ISLANDS
Niʻihau
Kaʻula
Kauaʻi
Oʻahu
Honolulu
Molokaʻi
Lānaʻi
Kahoʻolawe
Maui
Hawaiʻi
Mauna Kea 13,803 ft. 4,207 m
PACIFIC OCEAN
160°W   155°W
20°N
0   100 miles
0   100 kilometers
Transverse Mercator projection

0   50 miles   ATLANTIC OCEAN
0   50 kilometers
Mercator projection
19°N
Isla Mona
Puerto Rico
San Juan
Ponce
St. John
St. Thomas
Vieques
St. Croix
Caribbean Sea
18°N
68°W   67°W   66°W   65°W

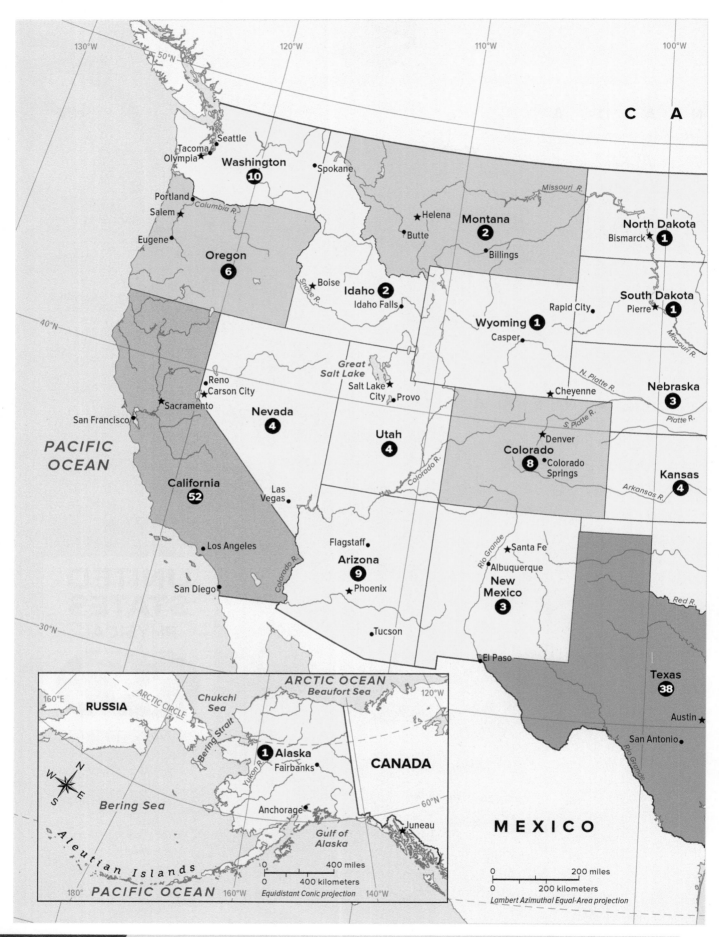

C A

PACIFIC
OCEAN

Seattle
Tacoma
Olympia ★
Washington
10
● Spokane

Portland
Salem ★
Columbia R.
Eugene

Oregon
6

Boise ★
Snake R.
Idaho **2**
Idaho Falls ●

★ Helena
Butte ●
Montana
2
● Billings

Missouri R.

North Dakota
Bismarck ★ **1**

Rapid City ●
Wyoming **1**
Casper ●

South Dakota
Pierre ★ **1**

Missouri R.

Reno ●
Carson City ●
Sacramento ★
San Francisco ●

Great
Salt Lake
Salt Lake ★
City ● Provo

★ Cheyenne

Nebraska
3

N. Platte R.

Platte R.

Nevada
4

Utah
4

Colorado R.

Denver ★
Colorado
8
● Colorado
Springs

S. Platte R.

Kansas
4

Arkansas R.

California
52

Las
Vegas ●

Los Angeles ●

San Diego ●

Flagstaff ●
Arizona
9
★ Phoenix

Colorado R.

Tucson ●

Rio Grande

★ Santa Fe
● Albuquerque
New
Mexico
3

El Paso ●

Red R.

Texas
38

Austin ★

San Antonio ●

Rio Grande

MEXICO

Alaska inset:

ARCTIC OCEAN
Beaufort Sea

RUSSIA
ARCTIC CIRCLE
Chukchi
Sea

Bering Strait

1 Alaska
Fairbanks ●

CANADA

N
W E
S

Bering Sea

Yukon R.

Anchorage ●

Juneau ★

Aleutian Islands

Gulf of
Alaska

PACIFIC OCEAN

160°E
180°
160°W
140°W
120°W
60°N

400 miles
400 kilometers
Equidistant Conic projection

0   200 miles
0   200 kilometers
Lambert Azimuthal Equal-Area projection

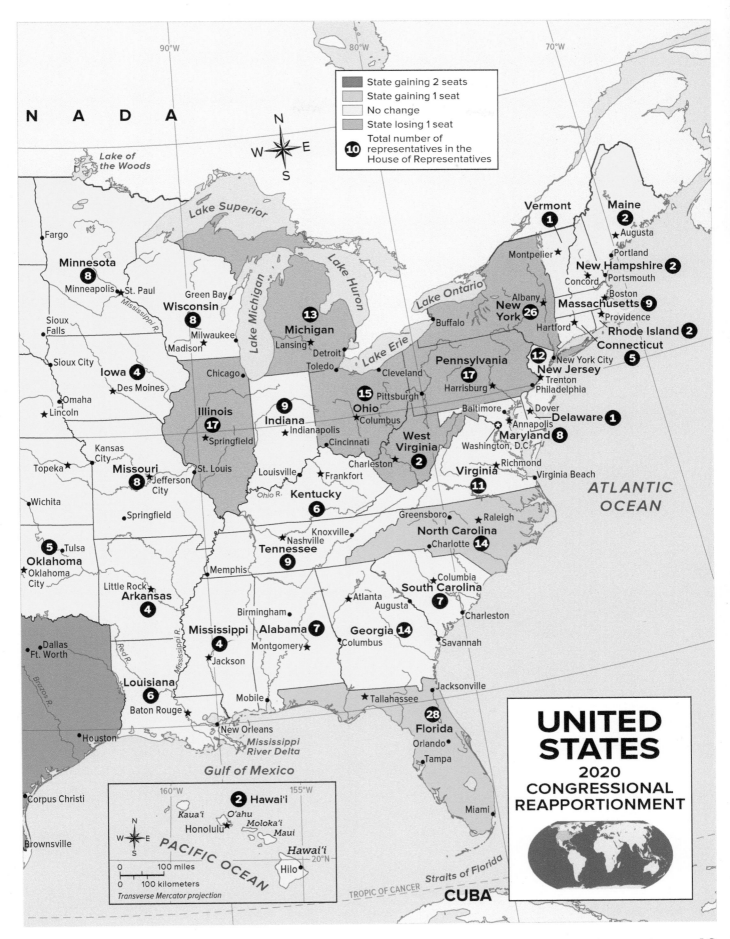

UNITED STATES
2020 CONGRESSIONAL REAPPORTIONMENT

Legend:
- State gaining 2 seats
- State gaining 1 seat
- No change
- State losing 1 seat
- ⑩ Total number of representatives in the House of Representatives

Civics Glossary/
Glosario de educación cívica

All vocabulary words are **boldfaced** and **highlighted in yellow** in your textbook.

A		ESPAÑOL
absentee ballot a type of ballot that allows voters to cast their votes without going to a polling place	(p. C325)	**voto en ausencia** *tipo de voto que permite que una persona vote sin tener que concurrir a los comicios*
accused a person officially charged with a crime	(p. C101)	**acusado** *persona culpada oficialmente por un delito*
acknowledge to publicly admit	(p. C349)	**reconocer** *admitir algo de forma pública*
acquit to find a defendant not guilty	(p. C166)	**absolver** *encontrar a un acusado no culpable*
active listening a way of listening that makes sure you are paying full attention to what another person is saying	(p. C290)	**escucha activa** *forma de escucha que asegura que se está prestando total atención a lo que dice otra persona*
adjudication hearing the procedure used to determine the facts in a juvenile case and to determine if the juvenile is guilty of committing a crime	(p. C476)	**audiencia de adjudicación** *procedimiento utilizado para determinar los hechos sucedidos en un caso de menores y determinar si el menor es culpable de cometer el crimen*
adjust to change	(p. C159)	**ajustar** *cambiar*
administer to manage	(p. C403)	**administrar** *dirigir*
alien a foreign-born resident of the United States who has not been naturalized	(p. C272)	**extranjero** *residente de Estados Unidos nacido en el extranjero que no ha sido nacionalizado*
alternative an option	(p. C67)	**alternativa** *opción*
ambassador an official representative of a country's government	(p. C202)	**embajador** *representante oficial del Gobierno de un país*
amendment any change to the Constitution	(p. C71)	**enmienda** *cualquier cambio a la Constitución*
amnesty a pardon for a group of people	(p. C203)	**amnistía** *indulto a un grupo de personas*
Anti-Federalist a person who opposed ratification of the Constitution	(p. C69)	**antifederalista** *persona que se opone a la ratificación de la Constitución*
apparent clear to see	(p. C385)	**evidente** *claro de ver*
appellate court type of court in which a party that lost a case in a lower court asks judges to review that decision and reverse it	(p. C395)	**tribunal de apelaciones** *tipo de tribunal en el que una parte que perdió un caso en un tribunal inferior pide a los jueces que revisen esa decisión y la revoquen*
appellate jurisdiction the authority of a court to hear a case appealed from a lower court	(p. C234)	**jurisdicción de apelaciones** *autoridad de un tribunal de escuchar un caso apelado por un tribunal inferior*
appreciate to value	(p. C425)	**apreciar** *valorar*
arbitrarily randomly, unreasonably	(p. C15)	**arbitrariamente** *al azar, irracionalmente*
arbitrary random and unfair	(p. C268)	**arbitrario** *aleatorio e injusto*
argument a statement of someone's position on an issue that is supported by reasoning and evidence	(p. C290)	**argumento** *declaración de la posición de una persona acerca de un tema que está respaldada por razonamiento y evidencia*

article one of seven main parts of the Constitution	(p. C71)	**artículo** *una de las siete divisiones principales de la Constitución*
Articles of Confederation the first constitution of the United States	(p. C62)	**Artículos de la Confederación** *primera Constitución de Estados Unidos*
at-large election an election for an area as a whole, such as an entire city	(p. C404)	**elección general** *elección para un área en su conjunto, como una ciudad entera*
authoritarian regime form of government in which one leader or group holds great power and is not accountable to the people	(p. C16)	**régimen autoritario** *forma de Gobierno en la cual un líder o grupo tiene un gran poder y no es responsable ante las personas*
authority power or influence over other people	(p. C33)	**autoridad** *poder o influencia sobre otras personas*

B		**ESPAÑOL**
bail a sum of money used as a security deposit to ensure that an accused person returns for the trial; a sum of money paid by someone awaiting trial that allows their release from jail until the trial date	(pp. C104, C452)	**fianza** *suma de dinero usada como depósito de seguridad para garantizar que un acusado regrese para el juicio; suma de dinero pagada por alguien que espera un juicio y que permite su liberación de la cárcel hasta la fecha de este*
ballot the official form provided to voters that they use to cast their votes	(p. C325)	**votación** *forma oficial dada a los votantes utilizada para que emitan sus votos*
benefit to be useful or profitable to	(p. C32)	**beneficioso** *ser útil o rentable*
bias a person's beliefs about another person or group that may not be based on facts and may affect the person's judgment	(p. C338)	**prejuicio** *creencia de una persona acerca de otra o de un grupo de personas que podría no estar sustentada en hechos, lo cual podría afectar su opinión*
bicameral having two separate lawmaking bodies called houses	(p. C61)	**bicameral** *tener dos organismos legislativos distintos llamados cámaras*
bill of attainder a law that punishes a person accused of a crime without a trial or a fair hearing in court	(p. C166)	**ley de intrusión** *ley que castiga a una persona acusada de cometer un crimen sin un juicio o una audiencia justa en un juzgado*
black codes laws from after the Civil War that kept African Americans from holding certain jobs, restricted their right to own property, and limited their rights in other ways	(p. C108)	**códigos negros** *leyes posteriores a la Guerra Civil que impedían a los afroamericanos obtener ciertos trabajos, restringían su derecho a la propiedad y limitaban sus derechos de otras formas*
boycott to refuse to purchase certain goods	(p. C34)	**boicotear** *rehusarse a comprar ciertos bienes*
brief a written document explaining the position of one side or the other in a case	(p. C250)	**declaración** *documento escrito que explica la posición de un lado u otro en un caso*

C		**ESPAÑOL**
cabinet group of presidential advisers that includes the heads of the executive departments	(p. C214)	**gabinete** *grupo de consejeros presidenciales que incluye a los jefes de los departamentos ejecutivos*
canvass meeting with voters to seek support for a candidate	(p. C338)	**sondeo** *reunión con los votantes que busca apoyo para un candidato*
capital punishment the death penalty	(p. C452)	**pena capital** *pena de muerte*

case law a law established by a judicial decision (p. C446)

jurisprudencia *ley establecida por decisión judicial*

caseload a judge's or court's workload of cases in a period of time (p. C250)

cantidad de casos *carga o número de casos de un juez o un juzgado en cierto periodo*

casework the work that a lawmaker does to help constituents solve a problem with a federal agency (p. C171)

trabajo social de casos *trabajo que un legislador hace para ayudar a los electores a solucionar un problema con una agencia federal*

cash crop a crop produced mainly for sale (p. C30)

cultivo comercial *cultivo producido principalmente para la venta*

category a group of similar things (p. C441)

categoría *grupo de cosas que son similares*

caucus a meeting of political party members held to conduct party business (p. C316)

caucus *reunión de los miembros de un partido político para llevar a cabo los asuntos de*

censorship the banning of printed materials or films due to alarming or offensive ideas (p. C92)

censura *prohibición de materiales impresos o películas debido a sus ideas alarmantes u ofensivas*

census a population count taken by the U.S. Census Bureau (p. C159)

censo *conteo de la población llevado a cabo por la Oficina del Censo de Estados Unidos*

charter school a type of school that receives state funding but is excused from meeting some public school regulations (p. C425)

escuelas financiadas por el Estado *tipo de escuela que recibe fondos del estado, pero está exenta de cumplir con algunas regulaciones de las escuelas públicas*

checks and balances a system in which each branch of government can check, or limit, the power of the other two branches (p. C80)

equilibrio de poderes *sistema en el que cada poder del Gobierno puede evaluar o limitar el poder de los otros dos poderes*

chief justice the leader of the U.S. Supreme Court who is also responsible for overseeing the whole federal judicial system (p. C240)

presidente de la Corte Suprema *líder de la Corte Suprema de Estados Unidos quien también es responsable de supervisar el sistema judicial federal en su totalidad*

citizen a member of a community of people who owe loyalty to a government and are entitled to its protection (p. C269)

ciudadano *miembro de una comunidad de personas que le deben lealtad a un Gobierno y tienen derecho a su protección*

citizenship the legal status of being a citizen, or official member of a nation, with certain rights and duties (p. C270)

ciudadanía *estado legal de ser un ciudadano o un miembro oficial de una nación, con ciertos derechos y deberes*

city charter a document granting power to a local government (p. C404)

carta de la ciudad *documento que garantiza el poder de un Gobierno local*

civic friendship a relationship based on appreciating others in the community and wishing them well (p. C288)

amistad cívica *relación basada en la apreciación de otros en la comunidad y desearles bien*

civics the study of how government works, and the rights and duties of citizens (p. C269)

educación cívica *estudio de la forma en que funcionan el Gobierno, y los derechos y deberes de los ciudadanos*

civil discourse reasoned conversation people use to discuss public issues (p. C287)

caso civil *asunto legal en el que una parte en una disputa afirma que ha sido perjudicada por la otra*

civil law the body of laws that relates to a dispute between people or groups of people or between people and the government (p. C444)

ley civil *cuerpo de leyes relacionadas con una disputa entre personas o grupos de personas, o entre las personas y el Gobierno*

civil liberty the freedom to participate in society and act without unfair interference from the government (p. C89)

libertad civil *autonomía de participar en la sociedad y actuar sin interferencia injusta del Gobierno*

civil rights the rights of full citizenship and equality under the law (p. C114)

derechos civiles *derechos de ciudadanía plena e igualdad ante la ley*

civil service system the processes used to hire government workers on the basis of open, competitive examinations and merit (p. C217)

sistema de servicio civil *procesos usados para contratar trabajadores del Gobierno sobre la base de concursos abiertos y méritos*

civilian person who is not serving in the armed forces (p. C215)

civil *persona que no sirve en las fuerzas armadas*

closed primary an election in which only the declared members of a political party are allowed to vote for that party's nominees (p. C318)

elecciones primarias cerradas *elección en la cual solo los miembros declarados de un partido político tienen permitido votar por los nominados de dicho partido*

cloture a procedure used in the Senate to limit debate on a bill and end or prevent a filibuster (p. C177)

clausura *procedimiento usado en el Senado para limitar el debate acerca de un proyecto de ley y finalizar o prevenir una táctica obstruccionista*

code an organized body of law (p. C439)

código *cuerpo organizado de ley*

common good the things that benefit all members of the community (p. C284)

bien común *cosas que benefician a todos los miembros de la comunidad*

common law a system of law based on previous legal decisions (p. C443)

ley común *sistema de ley basado en decisiones legales previas*

communism a one-party system of government based on the ideas of state ownership of property and government direction of the economy (p. C509)

comunismo *sistema de Gobierno de partido único basado en ideas de posesión estatal de la propiedad y dirección gubernamental de la economía*

community policing local police force visibly keeping the peace and patrolling neighborhoods (p. C427)

vigilancia policial comunitaria *fuerza de policía local que evidentemente mantiene la paz y patrulla los barrios*

commute to reduce a criminal's punishment (p. C390)

conmutar *reducir el castigo de un criminal*

comparative advantage the ability to produce a good at a lower cost than other nations can produce it (p. C496)

ventaja comparativa *habilidad de producir un bien a un precio más bajo del que otras naciones pueden producirlo*

complaint a formal notice that a lawsuit has been brought (p. C456)

denuncia *aviso formal de que un proceso legal ha sido iniciado*

complex having many parts (p. C454)

complejo *que tiene muchas partes*

composting allowing food and vegetable waste to decompose to make fertilizer (p. C523)

compostaje *permitir que desperdicios de comida y vegetales se descompongan para hacer fertilizante*

compromise an agreement in which disagreeing parties each get something they want but also give up something they want (p. C284)

compromiso *acuerdo en el que las partes en desacuerdo obtienen algo que quieren, pero también renuncian a algo*

concurrent jurisdiction authority of both state and federal courts to hear a case (p. C232)

jurisdicción concurrente *autoridad tanto del Estado como de las cortes federales de escuchar un caso*

concurrent powers powers shared by the state and federal governments (p. C81)

poderes concurrentes *poderes compartidos por el Estado y los Gobiernos federales*

concurring opinion a statement written by a justice who votes with the majority but reaches the same conclusion based on different legal reasoning (p. C253)

opinión concurrente *declaración escrita por un juez que vota con la mayoría, pero llega a la misma conclusión basado en un razonamiento legal diferente*

conduct to carry out (p. C111)

conducir *llevar a cabo*

confederal system a loose union of independent and sovereign states that give only a few powers to a central government (p. C12)

sistema confederado *unión flexible de estados independientes y soberanos que da pocos poderes a un Gobierno central*

confederation a group of individual state governments that unite for a common purpose (p. C62)

confederación grupo de Gobiernos estatales individuales que se unen por un propósito en común

confirm to verify (p. C106)

confirmar verificar

confirmation hearing set of meetings by the Senate Judiciary Committee to consider and vote on people nominated to be federal judges (p. C240)

audiencia de confirmación conjunto de reuniones del Comité Judicial del Senado para considerar y votar por las personas nominadas para ser jueces federales

conflict to disagree with (p. C377)

conflicto discrepancia

consensus the situation that exists when everyone in a group accepts a decision (p. C292)

consenso situación que tiene lugar cuando todos en un grupo aceptan una decisión

conservation preserving and protecting natural resources (p. C523)

conservación preservación y protección de los recursos naturales

constantly always (p. C532)

constantemente siempre

constituent a person represented by a government official (p. C159)

elector persona representada por un Gobierno oficial

constitution a detailed, written plan that establishes the rules for government (pp. C13, C61)

constitución plan escrito detallado que establece las reglas del Gobierno

Constitutional Convention meeting of delegates in 1787 that led to the writing of the U.S. Constitution (p. C66)

Convención Constitucional reunión de delegados en 1787 que dio paso a la escritura de la Constitución de Estados Unidos

constitutional government a government in which a constitution has authority to place clearly recognized limits on the powers of those who govern (p. C13)

Gobierno constitucional Gobierno en el que una constitución tiene autoridad de establecer límites claramente reconocidos sobre los poderes de aquellos que gobiernan

constitutional law branch of law dealing with the formation, construction, and interpretation of constitutions (p. C446)

ley constitucional rama de la ley que se encarga de la formación, construcción e interpretación de las constituciones

contaminate to pollute (p. C524)

contaminar polucionar

contract a set of promises between agreeing parties that is enforceable by law (p. C454)

contrato conjunto de promesas entre partes que están de acuerdo y que es ejecutable por ley

country a political community with a defined geographical area and organized government (p. C10)

país comunidad política con un área geográfica definida y un Gobierno organizado

county a type of government region that is normally the largest territorial and political subdivision of a state (p. C406)

condado tipo de Gobierno regional que por lo general es la subdivisión política y territorial más grande de un estado

court-martial a court that tries members of the armed forces who are accused of crimes against military law (p. C445)

corte marcial tribunal que juzga a miembros de las fuerzas armadas acusados de delitos contra la ley militar

crime an act that breaks a law and causes harm to people or damage to property (p. C459)

delito acto que infringe la ley y causa daños a personas o propiedad

criminal case legal matter concerning whether someone committed a crime (p. C230)

caso criminal asunto legal que busca determinar si alguien cometió un crimen

criminal law the body of laws that prohibits certain acts that are considered crimes (p. C444)

ley criminal cuerpo de leyes que prohíbe ciertos actos considerados crímenes

cross-examination the questioning of a witness at a trial or hearing to check or discredit the witness's testimony (p. C463)

contrainterrogatorio interrogatorio a un testigo de un juicio o audiencia que revisa o desacredita el testimonio del testigo

D		**ESPAÑOL**
damages money ordered by a court to be paid for injuries or losses suffered	(p. C456)	**indemnización** dinero que debe ser pagado como orden de un tribunal por lesiones o pérdidas
debate to discuss	(p. C288)	**debatir** discutir
defendant the party in a civil case who is said to have caused the harm; the party that is being sued	(pp. C394, C453)	**acusado** parte en un caso civil que se dice pudo haber causado el daño; parte que está siendo demandada
deforestation the removal of trees over large areas	(p. C499)	**deforestación** tala de árboles en áreas grandes
delegate representative to a meeting	(p. C36)	**delegado** representante en una reunión
delegated powers powers that the Constitution grants to the federal government	(p. C80)	**poderes delegados** poderes que la Constitución concede al Gobierno federal
delinquent offender a youth who has committed an offense that would be a crime if committed by an adult	(p. C472)	**infractor menor de edad** joven que ha cometido una ofensa que sería un crimen si fuera cometido por un adulto
democracy a government in which citizens hold the power to rule	(p. C17)	**democracia** Gobierno en el que los ciudadanos tienen el poder de gobernar
deny to take away	(p. C272)	**rechazar** quitar
despite in spite of	(p. C66)	**a pesar de** pese a
detention hearing a juvenile court process in which the state must show there is probable cause to believe a young person committed a crime	(p. C474)	**audiencia de detención** proceso de un tribunal juvenil en el que el Estado debe demostrar que hay causa probable para creer que una persona joven cometió un crimen
dictatorship form of government in which a leader or group of leaders exercises complete control over the state	(p. C16)	**dictadura** forma de Gobierno en que un líder o grupo de líderes ejerce control absoluto sobre el Estado
diplomat a representative of a country's government who takes part in talks with representatives of other nations	(p. C501)	**diplomático** representante del Gobierno de un país que participa en conversaciones con representantes de otras naciones
direct democracy a form of government in which the people vote firsthand	(p. C18)	**democracia directa** forma de Gobierno en que las personas votan de primera mano
direct primary an election in which voters choose candidates to represent a political party in a general election	(p. C317)	**elecciones primarias directas** elección en la que los votantes eligen candidatos para representar un partido político en una elección general
discrimination unfair treatment based on prejudice against a certain group	(p. C113)	**discriminación** trato injusto que se basa en prejuicios contra cierto grupo
disposition hearing the final settlement and sentencing in a juvenile case when the juvenile has been found guilty of committing a crime	(p. C474)	**audiencia de disposición** acuerdo y sentencia final en un caso de menores cuando el menor ha sido declarado culpable de cometer un delito
dissenter a person who opposes official or commonly held views	(p. C29)	**disidente** persona que se opone a opiniones oficiales o del común
dissenting opinion a statement written by a justice who disagrees with the majority opinion, and presents his or her opinion and legal reasoning	(p. C254)	**opinión disidente** declaración escrita por un juez que no está de acuerdo con la opinión de la mayoría y presenta su opinión y razonamiento legal
distinct separate and different	(p. C265)	**distinto** independiente y diferente
docket a court's calendar, showing the schedule of cases it is to hear	(p. C250)	**sumario de causas pendientes** calendario de un tribunal, presenta el horario de casos pendientes por audiencia

documented immigrant a foreign-born resident of the United States who is in the country legally (p. C273)

inmigrante documentado *residente de Estados Unidos nacido en el extranjero que se encuentra en el país legalmente*

domestic policy a nation's methods for dealing with issues within its borders (p. C491)

política interna *métodos de una nación para tratar problemas dentro de sus fronteras*

dominant in control (p. C311)

dominante *que tiene el control*

double jeopardy putting someone on trial for a crime for which the person was previously found not guilty (p. C450)

cosa juzgada *llevar a alguien a juicio por un delito por el cual la persona fue declarada no culpable previamente*

draft to write a rough or early version; to call for required military service (pp. C169, C253, C282)

esbozar *escribir una versión aproximada o temprana; llamar al servicio militar requerido*

dual court system a court system made up of both state and federal courts (p. C231)

sistema tribunal doble *sistema tribunal compuesto de tribunales tanto estatales como federales*

due process following established and fair legal procedures (p. C103)

debido proceso *seguimiento de los procedimientos legales establecidos y justos*

duty tax on an imported good; an action we are legally required to perform (pp. C34, C281)

obligación *impuesto a un bien importado; acción que se está obligado legalmente a realizar*

E	ESPAÑOL

early voting the process of casting a ballot in person during the allowed period prior to Election Day (p. C325)

voto anticipado *proceso de emitir un voto en persona durante el período permitido antes del día de las elecciones*

economy system for making choices about how to use scarce resources and distribute them to meet people's needs and wants (p. C30)

economía *sistema para tomar decisiones sobre cómo usar los recursos escasos y distribuirlos para satisfacer las necesidades y deseos de las personas*

elastic clause clause in Article I, Section 8 of the Constitution that gives Congress the right to make laws "necessary and proper" to carry out its expressed powers (p. C164)

cláusula flexible *cláusula del Artículo I, Sección 8 de la Constitución de Estados Unidos que le otorga al Congreso el derecho a hacer leyes "necesarias y convenientes" para llevar a cabo sus poderes expresos*

elector person appointed by their party to vote in presidential elections for president and vice president (p. C196)

elector *persona designada por su partido para votar en las elecciones presidenciales para presidente y vicepresidente*

Electoral College a group of people originally named by each state legislature, but now chosen by voters, to select the president and vice president (p. C68)

Colegio Electoral *grupo de personas originalmente nombradas por la legislatura de cada estado, pero ahora elegidos por los votantes, para seleccionar al presidente y al vicepresidente*

embargo a ban on trading with another nation (p. C494)

embargo *prohibición de comercializar con otra nación*

eminent domain the right of the government to take private property—usually land—for public use (p. C103)

dominio eminente *derecho del Gobierno de tomar propiedad privada, usualmente tierras, para uso público*

emphasis weight or stress (p. C472)

énfasis *peso o presión*

enhance to improve or increase (p. C359)

aumentar *mejorar o expandir*

environmentalism the movement concerned with protecting the natural environment (p. C522)

ambientalismo *movimiento que se preocupa por la protección del ambiente natural*

espionage spying and other activities carried out to ensure national security (p. C494)

espionaje *espiar y realizar otras actividades relacionadas con garantizar la seguridad nacional*

establish to found; to start something	(p. C28)	**establecer** *encontrar; empezar algo*
establishment clause a part of the First Amendment that does not allow Congress to establish an official state religion	(p. C90)	**cláusula de establecimiento** *parte de la Primera Enmienda que no permite al Congreso establecer una religión oficial del estado*
ethnic group a group of people who share a common national, cultural, or racial background	(p. C267)	**grupo étnico** *grupo de personas que comparten un origen nacional, cultural o racial*
ex post facto law a law that allows a person to be punished for an action that was not against the law when it was committed	(p. C166)	**cláusula ex post facto** *ley que permite que una persona sea castigada por una acción que no infringía la ley cuando esta fue cometida*
exclude to keep out	(p. C235)	**excluir** *mantener fuera*
exclusionary rule a rule that evidence gained by police in a way that violates the Fourth Amendment may not be used in a trial	(p. C449)	**regla de exclusión** *regla por la que la evidencia obtenida por la policía de manera que viole la Cuarta Enmienda no puede ser utilizada en un juicio*
exclusive jurisdiction sole authority to hear and decide a case	(p. C232)	**jurisdicción exclusiva** *única autoridad para escuchar y decidir un caso*
executive agreement an agreement between the president and the leader of another country	(p. C493)	**convenio ejecutivo** *acuerdo entre el presidente y el líder de otro país*
executive branch the branch of government that carries out laws	(p. C73)	**poder ejecutivo** *rama del Gobierno que ejecuta las leyes*
executive order a rule or command the president issues that has the force of law	(p. C203)	**decreto ley** *norma u orden que el presidente emite y que tiene fuerza de ley*
exploit to treat unfairly for someone else's gain	(p. C119)	**explotar** *tratar injustamente en beneficio de otra persona*
expose to reveal	(p. C349)	**exponer** *revelar*
expressed power power of the U.S. Congress that is specifically listed in the Constitution	(p. C163)	**poder expreso** *poder del Congreso de Estados Unidos listado específicamente en la Constitución*

F / ESPAÑOL

federal bureaucracy the agencies and employees of the federal government	(p. C215)	**burocracia federal** *agencias y empleados del Gobierno federal*
federalism a form of government in which power is divided between the federal, or national, government and the states	(p. C69)	**federalismo** *forma de Gobierno en la que el poder está dividido entre el Gobierno federal o nacional y los estados*
Federalist a supporter of the Constitution	(p. C69)	**federalista** *partidario de la Constitución*
Federalist Papers a series of essays written to defend the Constitution	(p. C69)	**El Federalista** *serie de ensayos escritos para defender la Constitución*
federal system a government that shares powers between national and state governments	(p. C12)	**sistema federal** *Gobierno que comparte poderes entre los Gobiernos nacional y estatal*
felony a type of crime such as murder or kidnapping, more serious than a misdemeanor	(pp. C394, C460)	**delito grave** *tipo de delito tal como un homicidio o un secuestro, más serio que un delito menor*
filibuster a tactic for defeating a bill in the Senate by talking or using other procedures until the bill's sponsor withdraws it	(p. C175)	**obstruccionismo** *táctica para frustrar un proyecto de ley en el Senado hablando o usando otros procedimientos hasta que el patrocinador del proyecto lo retire*

food security ready access to enough food for an active, healthy life for all people living in a household (p. C530)

seguridad alimentaria *fácil acceso a alimentos suficientes para una vida activa y saludable para todas las personas que viven en un hogar*

foreign policy a nation's methods for dealing with other nations and world issues (p. C491)

política exterior *métodos de una nación para tratar con otras naciones y problemas mundiales*

franking privilege the right of congresspeople to send job-related mail without paying postage (p. C169)

privilegio postal *derecho de los congresistas de enviar correo relacionado con su trabajo sin tener que pagar gastos de envío*

free exercise clause a part of the First Amendment that protects the freedom of individuals to observe and express their faith as they wish (p. C90)

cláusula de ejercicio libre *parte de la Primera Enmienda que protege la libertad de los individuos de mantener y profesar su fe como deseen*

free speech the right to say our opinions, in public or in private, without fear of being stopped or punished by the government for those ideas (p. C91)

libre expresión *derecho a expresar nuestras opiniones, en público o en privado, sin temor a ser detenido o castigado por el Gobierno debido a ellas*

fundamental basic (p. C315)

fundamental *básico*

G | ESPAÑOL

gender being male or female (p. C342)

género *ser hombre o mujer*

genocide the attempt to kill all members of a particular national, ethnic, or religious group (p. C508)

genocidio *intento de asesinar a todos los miembros de un grupo nacional, étnico o religioso en particular*

gerrymander an oddly shaped election district designed to increase the voting strength of a particular group (p. C159)

gerrymander *elección de distrito diseñada de forma extraña para aumentar la fuerza de voto de un grupo en particular*

global interdependence the reliance of people and countries on one another for goods and services (p. C495)

interdependencia global *dependencia de las personas y los países entre sí para obtener bienes y servicios*

government corporation a business owned and operated by the federal government to provide specific services (p. C216)

corporación gubernamental *negocio que el Gobierno federal posee y opera para proveer servicios específicos*

grand jury a group that hears evidence and decides whether to issue an indictment (p. C102)

gran jurado *grupo que escucha evidencia y decide si emitir una acusación o no*

grant to allow (p. C460)

conceder *permitir*

grant-in-aid money awarded to the states by the federal government (p. C377)

subvención *dinero que el Gobierno federal da a los estados*

grassroots movement a political movement that begins with the people (p. C319)

cabildeo de las bases *movimiento político que es iniciado por las personas*

Great Compromise an agreement providing a dual system of congressional representation (p. C67)

Gran Compromiso *acuerdo que proporciona un sistema dual de representación en el Congreso*

gross domestic product (GDP) the value of all the goods and services produced in a nation in one year (p. C498)

Producto Interno Bruto (PIB) *valor de todos los bienes y servicios producidos en una nación en un año*

H		ESPAÑOL
hate crime a violent act against a person because of a group they belong to	(p. C118)	**crimen de odio** *acto violento en contra de una persona por pertenecer a un grupo específico*
House of Representatives the lower house of Congress with representatives from each state, depending on population	(p. C158)	**Cámara de Representantes** *cámara baja del Congreso con representantes de cada estado, dependiendo de su población*
human right a basic freedom that all people should have simply because they are human	(p. C507)	**derecho humano** *libertad básica que todas las personas deberían tener por el simple hecho de ser humanos*

I		ESPAÑOL
ideology a strict idea about life and society	(p. C16)	**ideología** *idea estricta acerca de la vida y la sociedad*
immigrant an individual who moves permanently to a new country	(p. C265)	**inmigrante** *individuo que se muda permanentemente a un país nuevo*
immunity legal protection	(p. C169)	**inmunidad** *protección legal*
impact an effect	(p. C62)	**impacto** *efecto*
impeach to formally accuse a government official of misconduct in office	(p. C165)	**enjuiciar políticamente** *acusar formalmente a un Gobierno oficial de mala conducta en sus funciones*
implement to apply or enforce; to put into practice	(pp. C61, C201)	**implementar** *aplicar o hacer cumplir; poner en práctica*
implied power power of the U.S. Congress that is not specifically stated in the Constitution	(p. C164)	**poder implícito** *poder del Congreso de Estados unidos que no está establecido específicamente en la Constitución*
impose to establish or force	(p. C512)	**imponer** *establecer a la fuerza*
income tax a tax paid on the income that people earn from work or other sources	(p. C387)	**impuesto a la renta** *impuesto que se paga en correspondencia con el ingreso que las personas obtienen de su trabajo u otras fuentes*
incorporate to receive a state charter officially recognizing the government of a locality	(p. C404)	**incorporar** *recibir una carta estatal que reconoce oficialmente al Gobierno de una localidad*
indentured servant a worker who contracted with American colonists for paid passage, food, and shelter in return for labor	(p. C29)	**siervo por contrato** *trabajador que firmó un contrato con colonos americanos obteniendo pasaje, comida y alojamiento a cambio de mano de obra*
independent agency an executive agency that carries out certain activities and is not part of an executive department	(p. C216)	**agencia independiente** *agencia ejecutiva que lleva a cabo ciertas actividades y no es parte de un departamento ejecutivo*
indictment a document issued by a body called a grand jury that formally charges someone with a crime	(p. C102)	**acusación** *documento emitido por un organismo llamado gran jurado que culpa a alguien formalmente de cometer un delito*
influence to have an effect on	(p. C283)	**influenciar** *tener un efecto*
infrastructure the physical systems that allow a country, state, or region to function	(p. C8)	**infraestructura** *sistema físico que permite que un país, estado o región funcione*
inherently present from birth	(p. C443)	**inherentemente** *presente desde el nacimiento*
initiate to begin	(p. C236)	**iniciar** *comenzar*

English		Español
initiative process that lets voters propose new laws or amendments to the state constitution	(p. C336)	**iniciativa** *proceso que permite a los votantes proponer nuevas leyes o enmiendas a la constitución estatal*
institution a key practice, relationship, or organization in a society	(p. C268)	**institución** *una práctica, relación u organización clave en una sociedad*
interest group organization of people who share a point of view about an issue and unite to promote their beliefs	(p. C344)	**grupo de interés** *grupo organizado de personas que comparten un punto de vista acerca de un problema y que se unen para promover sus opiniones*
interpret to explain the meaning of	(p. C230)	**interpretar** *explicar el significado de algo*
isolated separate from other communities or groups	(p. C528)	**aislado** *diferente de otras comunidades o grupos*

J		ESPAÑOL
"Jim Crow" law Southern segregation law	(p. C113)	**Ley de Jim Crow** *ley de segregación racial*
joint resolution a resolution that is passed by both houses of Congress	(p. C174)	**resolución conjunta** *resolución que es aprobada por ambas cámaras del Congreso*
judicial branch the branch of government that interprets laws	(p. C73)	**poder judicial** *rama del Gobierno que interpreta las leyes*
judicial review the power of the Supreme Court to say whether any federal, state, or local law or government action goes against the Constitution	(p. C242)	**revisión judicial** *poder de la Corte Suprema de decidir si alguna ley federal, estatal o local, o alguna acción del Gobierno van en contra de la Constitución*
jurisdiction authority to hear and decide a case	(p. C231)	**jurisdicción** *autoridad de escuchar y tomar una decisión acerca de un caso*
juvenile delinquent a child or teenager who is determined to have committed a crime	(p. C472)	**delincuente menor de edad** *niño o adolescente, que, según se ha determinado, ha cometido un delito*

L		ESPAÑOL
landfill a place set aside for dumping garbage	(p. C522)	**vertedero** *lugar reservado para botar la basura*
law the set of rules and standards by which a society governs itself	(p. C19)	**ley** *conjunto de reglas y estándares por los que una sociedad se gobierna a sí misma*
lawsuit a legal action in which a person or group sues to collect damages for some harm they claim another has done to them	(p. C445)	**demanda** *acción legal que una persona o grupo de personas toma para cobrar por algún daño, que afirman, otro les ha hecho*
legislative branch the lawmaking branch of government	(p. C73)	**poder legislativo** *rama del Gobierno que hace las leyes*
legislative referendum a vote called by a legislature to seek voter approval of a law	(p. C384)	**referéndum legislativo** *votación convocada por una legislatura para buscar aprobación de los votantes de una ley*
legislature a group of people that makes laws	(p. C20)	**asamblea legislativa** *grupo de personas que crean las leyes*
less developed nation a nation with a low per capital GDP	(p. C498)	**nación en vía de desarrollo** *nación con un bajo PIB per cápita*
LGBTQ lesbian, gay, bisexual, transgender, and queer or questioning	(p. C120)	**LGBTQ** *lesbiana, gay, bisexual, transgénero y queer o en duda*

libel written untruths that are harmful to someone's reputation (p. C94)

libelo *mentira escrita que daña la reputación de alguien más*

liberty quality or state of being free (p. C33)

libertad *cualidad o estado de ser libre*

license a grant by the government of a right to engage in some activity (p. C352)

licencia *otorgamiento del Gobierno de un derecho para involucrarse en cierta actividad*

limited government the principle that a government can do only what the Constitution allows it to do (p. C78)

gobierno limitado *principio de que un Gobierno puede hacer solo lo que la Constitución le permita*

line-item veto the power to reject only a specific part of a bill (p. C389)

veto de partidas específicas *poder de rechazar solo una parte específica de una ley*

line of succession the order in which officials are expected to succeed, or come next, to an office (p. C199)

línea de sucesión *orden en que se espera que los funcionarios tengan éxito, o lleguen después, a un cargo*

litigant a party to a lawsuit (p. C237)

litigante *una de las partes en una demanda*

lobbyist representative of an interest group who contacts government officials to influence policy (p. C169)

cabildero *representante de un grupo de interés que contacta a los funcionarios de un Gobierno para influir en la política*

long-term plan a government plan for policy that can span 10 to 50 years (p. C414)

plan a largo plazo *plan gubernamental para la política que puede abarcar de 10 a 50 años*

M | ESPAÑOL

magistrate judge a federal judge who does much of a district court judge's routine work (p. C238)

juez magistrado *juez federal que hace gran parte de la rutina de trabajo de un juez de tribunal de distrito*

majority a number that is more than 50 percent of the total (p. C318)

mayoría *número que es más del 50 por ciento del total*

majority opinion the Court's statement of its decision in a case (p. C253)

opinión mayoritaria *declaración de la Corte de su decisión en un caso*

majority party in Congress, the political party whose members control each chamber (p. C160)

partido mayoritario *partido político cuyos miembros controlan cada cámara en el Congreso*

malapportionment unequal representation in state legislatures (p. C383)

mala distribución *representación desigual en las legislaturas del estado*

mass media methods of communication that reach large numbers of people (p. C343)

medios masivos de comunicación *métodos de comunicación que llegan a un gran número de personas*

master plan a plan that states a set of goals and explains how the government will carry them out to meet changing needs over time (p. C416)

plan maestro *plan que establece un conjunto de metas y explica la forma en que el Gobierno las alcanzará para suplir las necesidades que surjan con el tiempo*

merit system hiring people into government jobs on the basis of their qualifications (p. C218)

sistema de méritos *contratar personas en puestos gubernamentales con base en sus calificaciones*

method a process for doing something (p. C493)

método *proceso para hacer algo*

minority party in Congress, the political party that does not control either chamber (p. C160)

partido minoritario *partido político que no controla ninguna cámara en el Congreso*

Miranda Warning a list of rights that police must inform a person of before questioning the person, including the right to avoid self-incrimination and the right to a lawyer (p. C449)

derechos Miranda *lista de derechos que un policía debe informarle a una persona antes de interrogarla, incluyendo el derecho a no declararse culpable y a un abogado*

misdemeanor the least serious type of crime; a minor crime for which a person can be fined a small sum of money or jailed for a year or so	(pp. C394, C460)	**delito menor** *tipo menos serio de delito; delito menor por el que una persona puede ser multada con una pequeña suma de dinero o encarcelada por alrededor de un año*
monarchy form of government in which one person has great power	(p. C15)	**monarquía** *forma de Gobierno en la que una persona tiene un gran poder*
monitor to oversee	(p. C212)	**monitorear** *supervisar*
more developed nation a nation with a high per capita GDP	(p. C498)	**nación desarrollada** *nación con un alto PIB per cápita*

N	ESPAÑOL

nation a group of people united by common bonds of race, language, custom, or religion	(p. C10)	**nación** *grupo de personas unidas por lazos comunes de raza, lengua, costumbres o religión*
national committee representatives from the 50 state-party organizations who run a political party	(p. C316)	**comité nacional** *representantes de 50 organizaciones de partidos estatales que dirigen un partido político*
national interest anything that benefits the country	(p. C493)	**interés nacional** *cualquier cosa que beneficie a la nación*
national security involved with the protection of the nation and its people	(p. C212)	**seguridad nacional** *involucrados en la protección de la nación y su gente*
naturalization a legal process to obtain citizenship	(p. C270)	**naturalización** *proceso legal de obtener una ciudadanía*
natural rights freedoms people have simply because they are human beings, including the rights to life, liberty, and property	(p. C21)	**derechos naturales** *libertades que las personas tienen por el simple hecho de ser humanos, incluyendo los derechos a la vida, la libertad y la propiedad*
negotiate to work with other parties to come to an agreement on something	(p. C203)	**negociar** *trabajar con otras partes para llegar a un acuerdo en algo*
neutral taking no side or part in a conflict or disagreement	(p. C505)	**neutral** *no tomar parte o partido en un conflicto o discrepancia*
nongovernmental organization (NGO) an organization that operates independently of any government body, usually through individual volunteer efforts and private donations	(p. C505)	**organización no gubernamental (ONG)** *organización que opera independientemente de cualquier organismo de Gobierno, por lo general por medio de esfuerzos voluntarios individuales y donaciones privadas*
nonlegislative powers duty and responsibility Congress holds besides lawmaking	(p. C165)	**poderes no legislativos** *deberes y responsabilidades que tiene el Congreso además de legislar*
nonpartisan a person or group that has no ties to a political party and does not favor one party over another	(p. C360)	**imparcial** *persona o grupo que no tiene vínculos con un partido político y no favorece un partido sobre otro*
nonviolent resistance peaceful protest against laws believed to be unfair	(p. C116)	**resistencia no violenta** *protesta pacífica contra las leyes que se creen injustas*
Northwest Ordinance a 1787 law that set up a government for the Northwest Territory and a plan for admitting new states into the Union	(p. C62)	**Ordenanza del Noroeste** *ley de 1787 que estableció un Gobierno para el Territorio del Noroeste y un plan para admitir nuevos estados en la Unión*
nullify to cancel legally	(p. C242)	**anular** *cancelar legalmente*

O		ESPAÑOL
oligarchy a form of government in which a small group of people holds power	(p. C16)	**oligarquía** *forma de Gobierno en la que un grupo pequeño de personas tiene el poder*
open primary an election in which voters do not need to declare their party preference to vote	(p. C317)	**elecciones primarias abiertas** *elección en la que los votantes no necesitan declarar su preferencia de partido para votar*
opinion a detailed explanation of the legal thinking behind a court's decision in a case	(p. C236)	**opinión** *explicación detallada del pensamiento legal detrás de la decisión de un tribunal en un caso*
oral argument public session of the U.S. Supreme Court in which lawyers for each party discuss their view of the law and answer the justices' questions	(p. C251)	**alegato oral** *sesión pública de la Corte Suprema de los Estados Unidos donde los abogados de cada parte discuten su perspectiva de la ley y responden las preguntas del juez*
ordinance a law, usually of a city or country	(pp. C62, C404)	**ordenanza** *ley, por lo general de una ciudad o de un país*
Ordinance of 1785 a law that set up a plan for surveying western lands	(p. C62)	**Ordenanza de 1785** *ley que estableció un plan para inspeccionar tierras occidentales*
original jurisdiction the authority of a court to hear cases for the first time	(p. C233)	**jurisdicción original** *autoridad de una corte de escuchar casos por primera vez*
oversight the power to oversee the actions of another branch or agency	(p. C166)	**supervisión** *poder de monitorear las acciones de otra rama o agencia*

P		ESPAÑOL
pardon a declaration of forgiveness and freedom from punishment	(p. C202)	**indulto** *declaración de perdón y libertad de castigo*
parole an early release from prison as long as the person meets certain conditions	(pp. C390, C460)	**libertad condicional** *salida anticipada de prisión siempre que la persona cumpla con ciertas condiciones*
penal code the written collection of criminal laws of a state or the nation	(p. C459)	**código penal** *colección escrita de las leyes criminales de un Estado o nación*
per capita GDP a nation's annual GDP divided by its population, a measure of how effectively the nation uses its resources	(p. C498)	**PIB per cápita** *PIB anual de una nación dividido entre su población, medida de que tan efectivamente dicha nación hace uso de sus recursos*
persist to continue	(p. C323)	**persistir** *continuar*
petition formal request for the government to act	(p. C93)	**petición** *solicitud formal para que el Gobierno actúe*
plaintiff the party in a civil case who claims to have been harmed; the party that files a lawsuit	(pp. C394, C453)	**demandante** *parte en un caso civil que reclama haber sido dañada; parte que inicia una demanda judicial*
planning commission an advising group to a community	(p. C414)	**comisión de planificación** *grupo de asesoramiento a una comunidad*
plantation a large agricultural estate usually worked by people who live on the estate	(p. C31)	**plantación** *gran finca agrícola generalmente trabajada por personas que viven allí*
platform a series of statements expressing a party's principles, beliefs, and positions on issues	(p. C314)	**plataforma** *serie de declaraciones que expresan los principios, creencias y posiciones de un partido acerca de ciertas problemáticas*

plea bargain an agreement in which a defendant agrees to plead guilty to a less serious crime in order to receive a lighter sentence (p. C462)

declaración negociada *acuerdo en el cual un demandado acepta su culpabilidad de haber cometido un delito menor para recibir una sentencia más leve*

plurality the most votes among those running for an office, though it might not be more than half of all the votes (p. C318)

pluralidad *la mayor cantidad de votos entre los que se postulan para un cargo, aunque puede que no sea más de la mitad de todos los votos*

pocket veto president's power to kill a bill, if Congress is not in session, by not signing it for 10 days (p. C178)

veto indirecto *poder del presidente de acabar una ley, si el Congreso no está en sesión, al no firmarlo en los siguientes 10 días*

polarization the division of the public into groups with hardened and opposing political views (p. C289)

polarización *división del público en grupos con puntos de vista políticos endurecidos y opuestos*

political action committee (PAC) an organization set up by a corporation, labor union, or other special-interest group to support candidates by contributing money to their campaigns (p. C340)

comité de acción política (PAC) *organización establecida por una corporación, sindicato o grupo de interés especial para apoyar candidatos proporcionando dinero a sus campañas*

political appointee a person appointed to a federal position by the president (p. C217)

designado político *persona designada por el presidente a un cargo federal*

political party an organized group of voters with broad common interests and ideas about government who want to influence or control government decision making by electing the party's candidates to public offices (p. C309)

partido político *grupo organizado de votantes con amplios intereses e ideas en común acerca del Gobierno, quienes buscan influenciar o controlar sus decisiones mediante la elección de los candidatos de los partidos en cargos públicos*

political philosophy the study of how to distribute or limit public power to maintain human survival and improve quality of life (p. C14)

filosofía política *estudio de la forma en que se distribuye o limita el poder público para mantener la supervivencia humana y mejorar la calidad de vida*

polling place official place where people can vote in person on or before Election Day (p. C325)

lugar de votación *sitio oficial en que las personas pueden votar presencialmente el día de la elección o antes*

pollster a specialist whose job is to conduct polls (p. C345)

encuestador *especialista cuyo trabajo es realizar encuestas*

poll tax a sum of money required of voters before they are permitted to cast a ballot (p. C112)

voto censitario *suma de dinero solicitada a los votantes antes de que se les permita emitir su voto*

pollution materials or substances that damage the environment by poisoning the air, land, and water (p. C522)

contaminación *materiales o sustancias que dañan el ambiente al envenenar el aire, la tierra y el agua*

popular referendum a question placed on a ballot for voters to decide: usually to repeal an existing law (p. C384)

referéndum *pregunta puesta en un tarjetón para que los votantes decidan; por lo general, se usa para derogar una ley existente*

popular sovereignty the idea that power lies with the people (p. C78)

soberanía popular *idea de que el poder reside en el pueblo*

popular vote the votes cast by individual voters in a presidential election, as opposed to the electoral vote (p. C336)

voto popular *votos emitidos por votantes individuales en una elección presidencial, a diferencia del voto electoral*

pork-barrel project government project grant that primarily benefits a congressperson's home district or state (p. C171)

legislación por barril de cerdo *proyecto del Gobierno que concede beneficios principalmente al distrito o estado de origen de un congresista*

pose to present (p. C529)

plantear *presentar*

Preamble the opening section of the Constitution (p. C71)

preámbulo *sesión introductoria de la Constitución*

English	Spanish
precedent a judge's ruling that is used as the basis for a judicial decision in a later, similar case (p. C20)	**precedente** *decisión de un juez que se utiliza como base para una decisión judicial en un caso similar posterior*
presume to assume (p. C231)	**presumir** *asumir*
presumption of innocence the idea that a person is considered innocent unless proven guilty in a court of law (p. C448)	**presunción de inocencia** *idea de que una persona es considerada inocente a menos de que se pruebe su culpabilidad en un tribunal de ley*
primary election election to choose a party's candidates for each office in the general election (p. C335)	**elecciones primarias** *elección para elegir a los candidatos de un partido para cada cargo en la elección general*
principle a fundamental idea (p. C77)	**principio** *idea fundamental*
prior restraint the act of stopping information from being known by blocking it from being published (p. C351)	**censura previa** *acto de no permitir que se conozca información bloqueando su publicación*
priority ranking (p. C274)	**prioridad** *clasificación*
prisoner of war a person captured by opposing forces during a conflict (p. C505)	**prisionero de guerra** *persona capturada por fuerzas opuestas durante un conflicto*
probable cause a strong reason to think that a person or property was involved in a crime (p. C102)	**causa probable** *fuerte razón para pensar que una persona o propiedad estuvo involucrada en un delito*
proclamation an official, formal public announcement (p. C34)	**proclamación** *anuncio público formal y oficial*
professional a worker with specialized education and skills (p. C414)	**profesional** *trabajador con educación y habilidades especializadas*
promote to work in favor of (p. C359)	**promover** *trabajar a favor de algo*
propaganda messages that use biased or misleading ideas, information, or rumors to influence opinion (p. C338)	**propaganda** *mensajes que usan ideas o información sesgadas o erróneas, o rumores para influenciar la opinión de las personas*
property tax a tax paid on property, which is usually land and the structures built on it (p. C385)	**impuesto a la propiedad** *impuesto pagado en correspondencia con la propiedad, que generalmente abarca la tierra y las estructuras construidas sobre ella*
prosecution the government acting in its role as the party who starts the legal proceedings against someone accused of a crime (p. C461)	**enjuiciamiento** *acción del Gobierno como parte que inicia el proceso judicial contra alguien acusado de un delito*
provision specific part of a law (p. C242)	**cláusula** *parte específica de una ley*
public agenda the issues that government officials believe are most important (p. C347)	**agenda pública** *temas de mayor importancia para los funcionarios gubernamentales*
public opinion the ideas and attitudes that people hold about elected officials, candidates, government, and public issues (p. C341)	**opinión pública** *ideas y actitudes que las personas tienen acerca de funcionarios elegidos, candidatos, el Gobierno y asuntos públicos*
public opinion poll a survey that asks individuals' opinions about public issues or individuals who are holding or seeking office (p. C345)	**sondeo de opinión pública** *encuesta que pregunta la opinión de las personas sobre asuntos públicos o personas que ocupan o buscan un cargo*
public-interest group an organization that supports causes that affect the lives of Americans in general (p. C360)	**grupo de interés público** *organización que apoya causas que afectan las vidas de los estadounidenses en general*
public policy the decisions and actions a government takes to solve problems in the community (p. C9)	**política pública** *decisiones y acciones que toma un Gobierno para resolver problemas en la comunidad*

punitive intended to provide punishment	(p. C457)	**punitivo** *destinado a castigar*
pursue to try to achieve	(p. C361)	**perseguir** *tratar de alcanzar*

R	ESPAÑOL

racial profiling unfair treatment that occurs when police single out certain people as suspects because of their racial appearance	(p. C118)	**fichaje racial** *trato injusto que sucede cuando la policía señala a ciertas personas como sospechosas debido a su apariencia racial*
radical extreme	(p. C348)	**radical** *extremo*
random by chance	(p. C345)	**aleatorio** *al azar*
range variety	(p. C314)	**rango** *variedad*
recall a special election in which citizens can vote to remove an official from office before the term ends	(p. C336)	**referéndum de destitución** *elección especial en la que los ciudadanos pueden votar para destituir a un funcionario de su cargo antes de que termine su periodo*
recycling reusing old materials instead of making new ones	(p. C523)	**reciclar** *reusar materiales viejos en lugar de hacer nuevos*
redistricting the process of redrawing boundaries for legislative districts	(p. C384)	**reordenamiento** *proceso de redibujar límites para los distritos legislativos*
referendum a procedure by which citizens vote on state or local laws	(p. C336)	**referéndum** *procedimiento por el cual los ciudadanos votan por leyes estatales o locales*
reform to attempt to improve something	(p. C471)	**reforma** *intento de mejorar algo*
refugee someone who has left their home to escape danger, such as persecution by the government, war, or natural disaster	(p. C273)	**refugiado** *alguien que ha dejado su hogar para escapar del peligro, por ejemplo, de una persecución del Gobierno, guerra o desastre natural*
register to officially sign up to vote	(p. C324)	**registrarse** *inscribirse formalmente para votar*
regulate to manage or control	(p. C165)	**regular** *manejar o controlar*
regulatory commission independent agency created by Congress that can make rules concerning certain activities and punish organizations that break those rules	(p. C217)	**comisión reguladora** *agencia independiente creada por el Congreso que puede crear reglas concernientes a ciertas actividades y castigar organizaciones que las rompan*
rehabilitate to help someone reach a healthful and productive way of life	(p. C471)	**rehabilitar** *ayudar a alguien a llegar a un modo de vida saludable y productivo*
repeal to cancel a law	(p. C34)	**derogar** *cancelar una ley*
representative democracy a government in which citizens choose a smaller group to govern on their behalf	(p. C15)	**democracia representativa** *Gobierno en el que los ciudadanos eligen a un grupo pequeño para que gobiernen por ellos*
repression preventing people from expressing themselves or from freely engaging in normal life	(p. C508)	**represión** *prohibir que las personas se expresen o que tengan una vida normal*
reprieve an order to delay a person's punishment until a higher court can hear an appeal on the case	(p. C203)	**aplazamiento** *orden de posponer el castigo de una persona hasta que un tribunal más alto pueda hacer una audiencia y apelar el caso*
republic a representative democracy in which citizens choose their lawmakers	(p. C18)	**república** *democracia representativa en la que los ciudadanos eligen a sus legisladores*
republicanism commitment to a republican form of government in which citizens choose their lawmakers	(p. C15)	**republicanismo** *compromiso a una forma de Gobierno republicana en la que los ciudadanos eligen a sus legisladores*

reserved powers powers that the Constitution does not give to the federal government; powers set aside for the states	(p. C81)	**poderes reservados** *poderes que la Constitución no le da al Gobierno federal; poderes apartados para los estados*
resolve to settle a disagreement	(p. C282)	**resolver** *solucionar una discrepancia*
resource the money, people, or materials a community can use to reach its goals	(p. C415)	**recurso** *dinero, personas o materiales que una comunidad puede usar para lograr sus metas*
responsibility an obligation that we meet of our own free will	(p. C283)	**responsabilidad** *obligación con la que cumplimos por voluntad propia*
restrain to hold back	(p. C92)	**frenar** *contener*
retain to keep	(p. C105)	**retener** *conservar*
revenue the income brought in by the government	(p. C384)	**rentas públicas** *ingresos aportados por el Gobierno*
revise to improve	(p. C66)	**revisar** *mejorar*
rider a completely unrelated amendment added to a bill in the Senate	(p. C175)	**cláusula añadida** *enmienda completamente ajena agregada a un proyecto de ley en el Senado*
roll-call vote a voting method in the Senate in which members voice their votes in turn	(p. C178)	**votación nominal** *método de votación en el Senado en el que los miembros expresan su voto por turnos*
rule of law the principle that the law applies to everyone, even those who govern	(p. C79)	**imperio de la ley** *principio de que la ley aplica a todos, incluso a quienes gobiernan*
ruling an official decision by a judge or a court that settles a case and may also establish the meaning of a law	(p. C235)	**fallo** *decisión oficial de un juez o un tribunal que resuelve un caso y que podría establecer el significado de una ley*

S — ESPAÑOL

sales tax a tax paid on the purchase of certain goods and services	(p. C385)	**impuesto de venta** *impuesto pagado sobre la compra de ciertos bienes y servicios*
search warrant a court order allowing police to search a suspect's property and seize evidence	(pp. C102, C448)	**orden de registro** *orden de un tribunal que permite a la policía registrar la propiedad de un sospechoso y confiscar pruebas*
segregation the social separation of the races	(p. C113)	**segregación** *separación social de razas*
Senate the upper house of Congress, consisting of two representatives from each state	(p. C157)	**Senado** *la cámara más alta del Congreso, conformada por dos representantes de cada estado*
sentence the punishment given to someone found guilty of committing a crime	(p. C460)	**sentencia** *castigo impuesto a alguien que ha sido encontrado culpable de cometer un delito*
separation of powers the division of authority among the legislative, executive, and judicial branches	(p. C79)	**separación de poderes** *división de autoridad entre los poderes legislativo, ejecutivo y judicial*
session a meeting of a legislative body to conduct its business	(p. C383)	**sesión** *reunión de un organismo legislativo para llevar a cabo su propósito*
settlement an agreement by the two parties to a lawsuit to settle the dispute without concluding the trial and having a verdict	(p. C457)	**acuerdo** *convenio entre las dos partes de un juicio para resolver la disputa sin concluir el juicio y tener un veredicto*
severity seriousness	(p. C460)	**severidad** *seriedad*
Shays's Rebellion an uprising of Massachusetts farmers who did not want to lose their farms because of debt caused by heavy state taxes after the American Revolution	(p. C64)	**rebelión de Shays** *levantamiento de granjeros de Massachusetts que no querían perder sus granjas debido a la deuda causada por los altos impuestos estatales después de la Guerra de Independencia*

shield law law that protects reporters from having to reveal their sources	(p. C351)	**ley de protección de fuentes** *ley que protege a los reporteros de tener que revelar sus fuentes*
short-term plan a government policy carried out over the course of a few years	(p. C414)	**plan a corto plazo** *política del Gobierno llevada a cabo en el curso de unos pocos años*
slander spoken untruths that are harmful to someone's reputation	(p. C94)	**calumnia** *mentiras habladas que son dañinas para la reputación de alguien*
social contract an agreement among people in a society with their government	(p. C21)	**contrato social** *acuerdo entre las personas y la sociedad con el Gobierno*
special district a unit of government that deals with a specific function, such as education, water supply, or transportation	(p. C406)	**distrito especial** *unidad del Gobierno que tiene una función específica, tal como educación, abastecimiento de agua o transporte*
special-interest group an organization of people with some common interest that tries to influence government decisions	(p. C174)	**grupo especial de interés** *organización de personas con algunos intereses en común que intentan influenciar las decisiones del Gobierno*
specific definite	(p. C213)	**específico** *definido*
specifically for a particular purpose	(p. C339)	**específicamente** *para un propósito particular*
spoils system practice of filling government jobs by rewarding people for their political support	(p. C217)	**sistema de favoritismo** *practica de ocupar cargos gubernamentales recompensando a las personas por su apoyo político*
stable not subject to major changes	(p. C498)	**estable** *no sujeto a mayores cambios*
standing vote in Congress, when members stand to be counted for a vote on a bill	(p. C177)	**voto de pie** *cuando los miembros del Congreso se ponen de pie para que se cuente su voto en una ley*
stare decisis Latin for "let the thing stand"; the legal principle of using earlier judicial rulings as a basis for deciding cases	(p. C252)	**stare decisis** *en latín "estarse a lo decidido"; principio legal de utilizar sentencias judiciales anteriores como base para decidir casos*
state another word for country, or a smaller political unit, such as the fifty states of the United States, that is part of a larger country	(p. C10)	**estado** *otra palabra para país o una unidad política más pequeña, tal como los cincuenta estados de Estados Unidos, que es parte de un país más grande*
statistical numerical	(p. C345)	**estadístico** *numérico*
status offender a youth who commits an act defined as an offense because of the youth's age	(p. C472)	**delito por causa de estatus** *menor de edad que comete un acto definido como ofensa por su edad*
statute a law created by a legislative body	(p. C446)	**estatuto** *ley creada por un organismo legislativo*
statutory law the body of laws created by a legislature	(p. C446)	**ley reglamentaria** *cuerpo de leyes creadas por una legislatura*
submit to offer a bill for consideration; to put forward	(pp. C174, C243)	**entregar** *ofrecer una cuenta por consideración; postularse*
subpoena court order to appear in court or to produce evidence	(p. C238)	**citación** *orden de un tribunal de asistir a la corte o producir una evidencia*
subsequently later, following that	(p. C324)	**posteriormente** *más tarde, después de eso*
successor the person who follows another in an office or position	(p. C390)	**sucesor** *persona que le sigue a otra en un cargo o posición*
suffrage the right to vote	(pp. C110, C321)	**sufragio** *derecho a votar*

summons a notice directing someone to appear in court to answer a complaint or charge (p. C456)

citación aviso que ordena a alguien que comparezca ante el tribunal para responder a una queja o acusación

supremacy clause a clause stating that the Constitution and other laws and treaties made by the national government are "the supreme Law of the Land" (p. C82)

cláusula de supremacía clausula que establece que la Constitución y otras leyes y tratados hechas por el Gobierno nacional son "la ley suprema del país"

survey to measure and examine (p. C409)

encuestar medir y examinar

suspend to stop an employee from working for a certain amount of time (p. C398)

suspender impedir que un empleado trabaje durante cierto tiempo

sustainable referring to activities that do not waste or spoil natural resources (p. C523)

sostenible referente a actividades que no desperdician ni malgastan recursos naturales

symbolism the use of sounds or images that have strong positive or negative appeal (p. C338)

simbolismo uso de sonidos o imágenes que tienen un gran atractivo positivo o negativo

T	ESPAÑOL

target selected person or thing to receive an action (p. C494)

blanco persona o cosa seleccionada para recibir una acción

tenure the right to hold an office once a person is confirmed (p. C238)

permanencia derecho a permanecer en un cargo una vez una persona es confirmada para él

terrorism involves acts or threats of violence to force people or governments to behave in a certain way (p. C500)

terrorismo involucra actos o amenazas de violencia que fuerzan a las personas o los Gobiernos a comportarse de cierta forma

theocracy a form of government in which religious leaders rule the people (p. C16)

teocracia forma de Gobierno en la que líderes religiosos gobiernan a las personas

third party a political party that challenges the two main parties (p. C312)

tercer partido partido político que desafía a los dos partidos principales

Three-Fifths Compromise agreement providing that enslaved persons would count as three-fifths of other persons in determining representation in Congress (p. C68)

Compromiso de los tres quintos acuerdo que establece que las personas esclavizadas contarían como tres quintos de otras personas para determinar la representación en el Congreso

tolerance respecting and accepting others, regardless of their beliefs, practices, or differences (p. C284)

tolerancia respetar y aceptar a otros sin importar sus creencias, prácticas o diferencias

tort a wrongful act, other than breaking a contract, for which an injured party has the right to sue (p. C455)

agravio acto ilícito, distinto de la ruptura de un contrato, por el cual una parte lesionada tiene derecho a demandar

town a political unit found in the New England states that is smaller than a city (p. C409)

pueblo unidad política fundada en los estados de Nueva Inglaterra que son más pequeños que una ciudad

township a subdivision of a county that has its own government (p. C409)

municipio subdivisión de un país que tiene su propio Gobierno

toxic poisonous, deadly, or damaging to living things (p. C523)

tóxico venenoso, mortal o dañino para los seres vivos

trade sanction an effort to punish another nation by creating barriers to trade (p. C494)

sanción comercial esfuerzo de castigar a otra nación creando barreras para comerciar

trade war economic conflict that occurs when one or more nations put up trade barriers to punish another nation for trade barriers it first erected against them (p. C497)

guerra comercial conflicto económico que sucede cuando una o más naciones imponen barreras comerciales para castigar a otra nación por haber impuesto barreras primero contra ellos

treaty a formal agreement between the governments of two or more countries (p. C202)

tratado *acuerdo formal entre los Gobiernos de dos o más países*

trial court type of court in which a judge or a jury listens to the evidence and reaches a verdict in favor of one party or another in the case (p. C394)

juzgado *tipo de tribunal en el que un juez o jurado escucha evidencia y emite un veredicto a favor de una parte u otra en un caso*

tuition voucher a certificate issued by the government providing money for education payments, allowing families the option of sending students to private schools (p. C425)

vales educativos *certificado emitido por el Gobierno que proporciona dinero para pagos de educación, lo que permite a las familias considerar enviar a los estudiantes a escuelas privadas*

two-party system a system of government in which two major political parties compete for power (p. C309)

sistema bipartidista *sistema de Gobierno en el que dos grandes partidos políticos compiten por el poder*

U — ESPAÑOL

unanimous describing a decision with which everyone in the group agrees (p. C292)

unánime *decisión con la que todos en un grupo están de acuerdo*

undocumented immigrant a foreign-born resident of the United States who is not in the country legally (p. C273)

inmigrante indocumentado *residente de Estados Unidos nacido en el extranjero que no está en el país legalmente*

unfunded mandate requirement that state government do something required by the federal government without providing the money to pay for those actions (p. C377)

mandato infundado *requisito de que el Gobierno estatal haga algo requerido por el Gobierno federal sin proporcionar el dinero para pagar esas acciones*

unicameral having a one-house legislature (p. C381)

unicameral *poder legislativo que solo tiene una cámara*

unitary system a government in which the most important powers are held by the central or national government (p. C11)

sistema unitario *Gobierno en que los poderes más importantes son manejados por el Gobierno central o nacional*

unite to bring together (p. C267)

unir *juntar*

universal applying to all people (p. C508)

universal *que aplica a todas las personas*

V — ESPAÑOL

values the general principles or beliefs people use to make judgments and decisions (p. C267)

valores *principios generales o creencias que las personas usan para hacer juicios o tomar decisiones*

village the smallest unit of local government (p. C410)

aldea *la unidad más pequeña de un Gobierno local*

violate to go against (p. C10)

violar *ir en contra*

voice vote a voting method in which those in favor say "Aye" and those against say "No" (p. C177)

voto oral *método de voto en el que aquellos a favor dicen "Aye" y aquellos en contra dicen "No"*

volunteerism the practice of giving time and services to others without receiving payment (p. C285)

voluntariado *práctica de brindar tiempo y servicios a otros sin recibir pago*

voter turnout rate the percentage of eligible voters who actually vote (p. C328)

tasa de participación electoral *porcentaje de votantes elegibles que realmente votan*

CIVICS GLOSSARY

W	ESPAÑOL
watchdog role the role of keeping government honest by reporting on illegal practices or waste (p. C349)	**rol del organismo** *de control papel de mantener la honestidad del Gobierno informando sobre prácticas ilegales o desperdicio*
weapon of mass destruction (WMD) a weapon that can kill or harm large numbers of people and damage a large area (p. C511)	**arma de destrucción masiva (ADM)** *arma que puede matar o herir a un gran número de personas y dañar un área grande*
welfare the health, prosperity, and happiness of the members of a community (p. C284)	**bienestar** *salud, prosperidad y felicidad de los miembros de una comunidad*
will a legal document that provides instructions about how to handle a person's money or property after death (p. C455)	**testamento** *documento legal que brinda instrucciones acerca de la forma en que se maneja el dinero o propiedad de una persona después de su muerte*
winner-take-all a system in which the candidate who wins the popular vote in a state receives all of the state's electoral votes (p. C337)	**sistema en el que el ganador se lleva todo** *sistema en el que el candidato que gana el voto popular en un estado recibe todos los votos electorales de este*
writ of certiorari an order a higher court issues to a lower court to obtain the records of a particular case (p. C249)	**auto de avocación** *orden que un tribunal superior emite a un tribunal inferior para obtener los registros de un caso en particular*
writ of habeas corpus a court order that requires police to bring a prisoner to court to explain why they are holding the person (p. C166)	**solicitud de hábeas corpus** *orden de un tribunal que exige a la policía llevar a un prisionero a una corte para explicar por qué la están deteniendo*

Economics Glossary/ Glosario de economía

All vocabulary words are **boldfaced** and **highlighted in yellow** in your textbook.

A		ESPAÑOL
absolute advantage the ability to produce something cheaper than anyone else can	(p. E166)	**ventaja absoluta** *habilidad para producir algo más económico de lo que pueden los demás*
aggregate total	(p. E118)	**acumulado** *total*
antitrust law legislation to prevent monopolies from forming and to preserve and promote competition	(p. E92)	**ley antimonopolio** *legislación que evita la formación de monopolios y protege y promueve la competencia*
appropriations bill legislation that sets spending on particular programs for the coming year	(p. E132)	**ley de apropiaciones** *legislación que destina rubros presupuestales a programas específicos para el año siguiente*
arbitration situation in which union and company officials submit the issues they cannot agree on to a neutral third party for a final decision	(p. E78)	**arbitraje** *situación en la que representantes de sindicatos y compañías someten a un tercero neutral los asuntos que no pueden concertar para que este tome la decisión final*
attain to achieve	(p. E95)	**lograr** *conseguir*
automatic stabilizer program that works to preserve income without additional government action during economic downturns	(p. E145)	**estabilizador automático** *programa que trabaja para ajustar los ingresos, sin necesidad de acción gubernamental adicional, durante recesiones económicas*

B		ESPAÑOL
balance of trade the difference between the value of a nation's exports and its imports	(p. E171)	**balanza comercial** *diferencia entre el valor de las exportaciones e importaciones de un país*
balanced budget annual budget in which expenditures equal revenues	(p. E146)	**presupuesto equilibrado** *presupuesto anual en el que los gastos son iguales a los ingresos*
barter to trade a good or service for another good or service	(p. E79)	**trueque** *intercambio de un bien o servicio por otro bien o servicio*
bear market period during which stock prices decline for a substantial period	(p. E124)	**mercado bajista** *periodo durante el cual los precios de las acciones caen durante largo tiempo*
benefit-cost analysis economic decision-making model that divides the total benefits by the total costs	(p. E11)	**análisis costo-beneficio** *modelo de elección económica que divide los beneficios totales entre los costos totales*
black market market where illegal goods are bought and sold	(p. E181)	**mercado negro** *mercado en el que se venden y compran bienes ilegales*
board of directors the people elected by the shareholders of a corporation to act on their behalf	(p. E66)	**junta directiva** *personas elegidas por los accionistas de una corporación para que actúen en su nombre*
budget deficit situation that occurs when a government spends more than it collects in revenue	(p. E146)	**déficit presupuestario** *situación que se presenta cuando un Gobierno gasta más de lo que recibe por concepto de ingresos*

budget surplus situation that occurs when a government collects more revenues than it spends (p. E146)

superávit presupuestario *situación que se presenta cuando los ingresos de un Gobierno superan sus gastos*

bull market period during which stock prices steadily increase (p. E124)

mercado alcista *periodo durante el cual los precios de las acciones suben constantemente*

business cycle alternating periods of real economic decline and growth (p. E120)

ciclo económico *fluctuaciones periódicas de recesión y crecimiento económico reales*

C · ESPAÑOL

capital factories, tools, and equipment that manufacture goods or help work go more quickly (p. E8)

capital *fábricas, herramientas y equipos que producen bienes o agilizan el trabajo*

capitalism system in which private citizens own most, if not all, of the means of production and decide how to use them within legal limits (p. E57)

capitalismo *sistema en el que ciudadanos privados poseen la mayoría de los bienes de producción, si no todos, y deciden cómo utilizarlos dentro de los límites legales*

central bank a banker's bank that can lend to other banks in time of need and can regulate the money supply; a bankers' bank that lends money to other banks in difficult times (pp. E84, E125)

banco central *banco bancario que presta a otros bancos en épocas de necesidad y regula la oferta monetaria; banco bancario que presta dinero a otros bancos en épocas difíciles*

certificate of deposit (CD) a timed consumer loan to a bank that states the amount of the loan, maturity, and rate of interest being paid (p. E81)

certificado de depósito (CD) *crédito de consumo a término en el que consta el monto del préstamo, el vencimiento y la tasa de interés que se paga a un banco*

charter state government document granting permission to organize a corporation (p. E66)

acta constitutiva *documento gubernamental estatal que concede permiso para crear una corporación*

checking account an account from which deposited money can be withdrawn at any time by writing a check, using a debit card, or swiping a cell phone; also known as demand deposit accounts (p. E81)

cuenta corriente *cuenta de la cual se puede retirar en cualquier momento el dinero depositado escribiendo un cheque, utilizando una tarjeta débito o haciendo una transacción telefónica; se conoce también como cuenta de depósito a la vista*

circular flow model a model showing how goods, services, resources, and money flow among sectors and markets in the American economy (p. E37)

modelo de flujo circular *modelo que muestra cómo fluyen los bienes, servicios, recursos y el dinero en los sectores y mercados de la economía estadounidense*

civilian labor force group made up of "all persons 16 years of age or over who are working or not working but are able and willing to work" and who are not in the military (p. E73)

fuerza laboral civil *grupo conformado por "todas las personas de 16 años de edad o más que están trabajando o no están trabajando, pero que pueden y quieren trabajar" y no están en las fuerzas militares*

clarify explain (p. E65)

aclarar *explicar*

coin metallic form of money, such as a penny (p. E80)

moneda *dinero acuñado en metal, como un centavo*

collective bargaining process by which unions and employers negotiate the conditions of employment (p. E77)

negociación colectiva *mecanismo mediante el cual sindicalistas y empleadores negocian las condiciones de empleo*

command economy economic system in which the government owns and directs the majority of a country's land, labor, and capital resources (p. E14)

economía planificada *sistema económico en el que el Gobierno posee y controla la mayoría de las tierras, del trabajo y de los recursos de capital de un país*

commercial bank a financial institution that offers the most banking services to individuals and businesses (p. E82)

banco comercial *institución financiera que presta la mayoría de los servicios bancarios a individuos y empresas*

communism theoretical state where all property is publicly owned, and everyone works according to their abilities and is paid according to their needs	(p. E15)	**comunismo** *Estado teórico en el que toda propiedad es pública y las personas trabajan según sus habilidades y reciben un pago acorde con sus necesidades*	
comparative advantage a country's ability to produce a good relatively more efficiently than other countries can (or, a country's ability to produce a good at a lower opportunity cost than another country)	(p. E166)	**ventaja comparativa** *capacidad de un país para producir un bien de manera más eficiente que otros países (o capacidad de un país para producir un bien a menor costo de oportunidad que otro país)*	
compensation payment to unemployed or injured workers to make up for lost wages	(p. E98)	**indemnización** *pago que se hace a trabajadores desempleados o lesionados para compensar el salario perdido*	
competition efforts by different businesses to sell the same good or service; the struggle that goes on between buyers and sellers to get the best products at the lowest prices	(pp. E34, E60)	**competencia** *esfuerzo que hacen las distintas empresas para vender los mismos bienes y servicios; pugna entre compradores y vendedores por obtener los mejores productos al precio más bajo*	
confirmed approved	(p. E126)	**confirmado** *aprobado*	
consumer person who buys goods and services	(p. E25)	**consumidor** *persona que compra bienes y servicios*	
consumer sovereignty role of the consumer as ruler of the market that determines the types and quantities of goods and services produced	(p. E58)	**soberanía del consumidor** *rol del consumidor como gobernante del mercado que determina las clase y cantidades de los bienes y servicios producidos*	
contribute to provide or give	(p. E70)	**contribuir** *aportar, dar*	
corporation type of business organization owned by many people but treated by law as though it were a person	(p. E66)	**corporación** *tipo de empresa u organización de la que son dueñas muchas personas, pero que es considerada legamente como una sola entidad*	
credit union nonprofit service cooperative that accepts deposits, makes loans, and provides other financial services to its members	(p. E82)	**cooperativa de crédito** *servicio cooperativo sin ánimo de lucro que acepta depósitos, hace préstamos y presta otros servicios financieros a sus miembros*	
cryptocurrency electronic money not issued or managed by any country or central bank	(p. E80)	**criptomoneda** *dinero electrónico que no es emitido ni administrado por un país o banco central*	
currency money, both coins and paper bills; system of money in general use in a country	(pp. E80, E169)	**moneda** *dinero en moneda y en papel; sistema monetario en general que utiliza un país*	

D		**ESPAÑOL**	
deflation a prolonged decrease in the general level of prices	(p. E124)	**deflación** *disminución prolongada del nivel general de los precios*	
demand amount of a good or service that consumers are willing and able to buy over a range of prices	(p. E25)	**demanda** *cantidad de bienes y servicios que los consumidores quieren y pueden comprar entre un rango de precios*	
deposit the money that customers put into a financial institution	(p. E81)	**depósito** *dinero que consignan los consumidores en una institución financiera*	
deposit insurance program government-backed program that protects bank deposits up to a certain amount if a financial institution fails	(p. E83)	**programa de seguro de depósitos** *programa respaldado por el Gobierno que cubre los depósitos bancarios hasta un monto específico en caso de que una institución financiera quiebre*	
depression state of the economy with high unemployment, severely depressed real GDP, and general economic hardship	(p. E120)	**depresión** *estado de la economía caracterizado por una tasa de desempleo alta, una caída drástica del PIB real y recesión económica*	

English		Español
developed country country with a high standard of living, a high level of industrialization, and a high per capita income	(p. E179)	**país desarrollado** *país que tiene un nivel de vida alto, un nivel de industrialización y un ingreso per cápita altos*
developing country nonindustrial country with a low per capita income in which a large number of people have a low standard of living	(p. E179)	**país en desarrollo** *país no industrializado cuyo ingreso per cápita es bajo y en el que numerosas personas tienen un nivel de vida bajo*
discount rate interest rate the Fed charges on its loans to financial institutions	(p. E129)	**tasa de descuento** *tasa de interés que la Reserva Federal cobra por sus préstamos a instituciones financieras*
discretionary spending spending for federal programs that must receive approval each year	(p. E132)	**gasto discrecional** *gasto asignado a programas federales que debe aprobarse anualmente*
dispose get rid of	(p. E61)	**desechar** *descartar*
distortion misleading impression	(p. E119)	**distorsión** *impresión falsa*
division of labor the breaking down of a job into separate, smaller tasks to be performed individually	(p. E40)	**división del trabajo** *fragmentación de un trabajo en tareas pequeñas e independientes que se realizan individualmente*

E	ESPAÑOL

English		Español
economic growth the increase in a country's total output of goods and services over time	(p. E39)	**crecimiento económico** *aumento progresivo en la producción total de bienes y servicios de un país*
economic interdependence the reliance of people and countries around the world on one another for goods and services	(p. E173)	**interdependencia económica** *dependencia mundial mutua de personas y países para obtener bienes y servicios*
economic system a nation's way of producing and distributing things its people want and need	(p. E13)	**sistema económico** *modo en el que un país produce y distribuye cosas que su población desea y necesita*
economics study of how individuals and nations make choices about ways to use scarce resources to fulfill their needs and wants	(p. E8)	**economía** *estudio del modo en que individuos y naciones toman decisiones relacionadas con la utilización de recursos escasos para satisfacer sus necesidades y deseos*
electronic money money in the form of a computer entry at a bank or other financial institution	(p. E80)	**dinero electrónico** *dinero de un banco u otra institución financiera al que se accede por computadora*
ensure to make certain of an outcome	(p. E61)	**asegurar** *garantizar un resultado*
entitlement program a government program that makes payments to people who meet certain requirements in order to help them meet minimum health, nutrition, and income needs	(p. E136)	**programa de subsidios** *programa gubernamental que hace pagos a personas con requerimientos específicos para ayudarlas a satisfacer necesidades básicas en salud, nutrición e ingreso*
entrepreneurs risk-taking individuals who start a new business, introduce a new product, or improve a method of making something	(p. E8)	**emprendedores** *individuos que se arriesgan a crear una nueva empresa, introducir un producto nuevo o perfeccionar la manera de hacer algo*
equilibrium price market price where quantity demanded and quantity supplied are equal	(p. E34)	**precio de equilibrio** *precio en el mercado en el que la cantidad demandada es igual a la cantidad ofrecida*
equilibrium quantity quantity of output supplied that is equal to the quantity demanded at the equilibrium price	(p. E34)	**cantidad de equilibrio** *cantidad de producción ofrecida que es igual a la cantidad en demanda al precio de equilibrio*
evolve to progress or develop gradually	(p. E14)	**evolucionar** *progresar o desarrollarse gradualmente*
exchange rate the value of a nation's currency in relation to another nation's currency	(p. E169)	**tasa de cambio** *valor que tiene la moneda de un país en relación con la moneda de otro país*

export to sell goods to other countries	(p. E165)	**exportar** *vender bienes a otros países*
externality economic side effect that affects an uninvolved third party	(p. E92)	**externalidad** *efecto secundario económico que afecta a una tercera parte no implicada*

F | ESPAÑOL

factor market a market where productive resources (land, labor, capital) are bought and sold	(p. E38)	**mercado de factores** *mercado en el que los recursos productivos (tierra, trabajo, capital) se compran y venden*
factors of production four categories of resources used to produce goods and services: natural resources, capital, labor, and entrepreneurs	(p. E8)	**factores de producción** *cuatro categorías de recursos utilizados para producir bienes y servicios: recursos naturales, capital, trabajo y emprendedores*
federal debt money the government has borrowed and not yet paid back	(p. E146)	**deuda federal** *dinero que el Gobierno ha pedido en préstamo y no ha pagado aún*
Federal Open Market Committee (FOMC) powerful committee of the Fed that makes decisions affecting the economy by managing the money supply in order to affect interest rates	(p. E126)	**Comité Federal de Mercado Abierto (FOMC)** *poderoso comité de la Reserva Federal que toma decisiones de incidencia económica, como regular la oferta monetaria a fin de modificar las tasas de interés*
financial capital the money used to run or expand a business	(p. E64)	**capital financiero** *dinero utilizado para operar o expandir una empresa*
fiscal policy government use of taxes and spending to stimulate the economy and reach economic goals	(p. E144)	**política fiscal** *uso que hace el Gobierno de los impuestos y gastos para estimular la economía y alcanzar metas económicas*
fiscal year any 12-month period chosen for keeping accounts	(p. E131)	**año fiscal** *periodo de 12 meses fijado para llevar la contabilidad*
fixed income an income that remains the same each month and does not have the potential to go up when prices are going up	(p. E123)	**ingreso fijo** *ingreso que permanece igual mes a mes y no tiene el potencial de subir cuando los precios están en alza*
foreign exchange the domestic currencies that are used to finance foreign trade	(p. E169)	**divisas** *las monedas nacionales que se utilizan para financiar el comercio exterior*
foundation organization established by a company or an individual to provide money for a particular purpose, especially for charity or research	(p. E70)	**fundación** *organización establecida por una compañía o un individuo que suministra dinero para un propósito en particular, especialmente de carácter benéfico o investigativo*
franchise company that has permission to sell the supplier's goods or services in a particular area in exchange for payment	(p. E68)	**franquicia** *compañía autorizada para vender los bienes y servicios del proveedor en un lugar específico a cambio de un pago*
free enterprise economic system in which individuals and businesses are allowed to compete for profit with a minimum of government interference	(p. E57)	**libre empresa** *sistema económico en el que se permite a individuos y empresas competir por lucro con mínima intervención del Estado*

G | ESPAÑOL

GDP per capita GDP on a per-person basis; GDP divided by population	(p. E118)	**PIB per cápita** *PIB por persona; PIB dividido entre la población*
goods things we can touch or hold	(p. E7)	**bienes** *cosas que podemos tocar o asir*
Gross Domestic Product (GDP) total market value of all final goods and services produced in a country during a single year	(p. E115)	**producto interno bruto (PIB)** *valor total en el mercado del conjunto de los bienes y servicios producidos en un país durante un año*

ECONOMICS GLOSSARY

H | ESPAÑOL

human capital the sum of people's knowledge and skills that can be used to create products (p. E40)

capital humano *conjunto de conocimientos y habilidades de una persona que pueden utilizarse para producir productos*

I | ESPAÑOL

import to buy goods from another country (p. E165)

importar *comprar bienes a otro país*

incentive motivation or reward (pp. E16, E27)

incentivo *motivación o recompensa*

inflation a long-term increase in the general level of prices (p. E123)

inflación *aumento a largo plazo en el nivel general de precios*

infrastructure highways, levees, bridges, power, water, sewage, and other public goods needed to support a growing economy (p. E146)

infraestructura *carreteras, diques, puentes, energía, agua, alcantarillado y otros bienes públicos necesarios para sostener el crecimiento de la economía*

injunction a court order to stop some kind of action (p. E78)

medidas cautelares *orden emanada de un tribunal para impedir algún tipo de acción*

integrate combine (p. E175)

integrar *aunar*

intergovernmental revenue funds that one level of government receives from another level of government (p. E135)

ingreso intergubernamental *fondos que un nivel del Gobierno recibe de otro nivel del Gobierno*

L | ESPAÑOL

labor workers and their abilities (p. E8)

fuerza de trabajo *los trabajadores y sus habilidades*

labor union association of workers organized to improve wages and working conditions (p. E75)

sindicato *asociación de trabajadores organizados para mejorar los salarios y las condiciones laborales*

laissez-faire economics belief that government should not interfere in the marketplace (p. E61)

laissez faire *política económica según la cual el Gobierno no debe intervenir en el mercado*

liability the legal responsibility for something, such as an action or a debt (p. E64)

responsabilidad legal *obligación legal por algo, como una acción o una deuda*

likewise in the same way (p. E32)

igualmente *de la misma manera*

lockout when management closes a workplace to prevent union members from working (p. E78)

cierre patronal *cuando una empresa cierra el lugar de trabajo para impedir que los miembros del sindicato trabajen*

M | ESPAÑOL

maintain to preserve (p. E93)

mantener *conservar*

mandatory spending federal spending required by law that continues without the need for congressional approval each year (p. E132)

gasto obligatorio *gasto federal requerido por ley que continúa sin necesidad de que el Congreso lo apruebe cada año*

market place or arrangement where a buyer and a seller voluntarily exchange money for a good or service (pp. E16, E33)

mercado *lugar o sistema en el que compradores y vendedores intercambian voluntariamente dinero por bienes o servicios*

English		Español
market economy economic system in which individuals and businesses have the freedom to use their resources in ways they think best	(p. E16)	**economía de mercado** *sistema económico en el que individuos y empresas gozan de libertad para utilizar sus recursos de la manera que consideren más conveniente*
mediation situation in which union and company officials bring in a third party to try to help them reach an agreement	(p. E78)	**mediación** *situación en la que los representantes de un sindicato y una compañía recurren a una tercera parte para que los ayude a llegar a un acuerdo*
medium a means of doing something	(p. E79)	**medio** *recurso que permite hacer algo*
mercantilism economic system in which government controls the products that come into and go out of a country	(p. E61)	**mercantilismo** *sistema económico en el que el Gobierno controla los productos que ingresan al país y salen de él*
merger a combination of two or more companies to form a single business	(p. E93)	**fusión** *unión de una o más compañías para formar una sola empresa*
mixed market economy economic system in which markets, government, *and* tradition each answer some of the WHAT, HOW, and FOR WHOM questions	(p. E17)	**economía de mercado mixta** *sistema económico en el que los mercados, el Gobierno y la tradición responden cada cual algunas de las preguntas de QUÉ, CÓMO y PARA QUIÉN*
monetary policy Fed's management of the money supply to affect the cost and availability of credit	(p. E126)	**política monetaria** *control de la oferta monetaria, por parte de la Reserva Federal, que afecta el costo y la disponibilidad de crédito*
monopoly exclusive control of a good or service	(p. E92)	**monopolio** *control exclusivo de un bien o servicio*
multilateral agreement treaty in which multiple nations agree to give each other the same benefits	(p. E174)	**acuerdo multilateral** *tratado en el que múltiples países acuerdan concederse mutuamente los mismos beneficios*
multinationals corporations that have manufacturing or service operations in several different countries	(p. E176)	**multinacionales** *corporaciones que tienen operaciones industriales o de servicios en varios países*

N		ESPAÑOL
natural monopoly a market situation in which the costs of production are minimized by having a single firm produce the product	(p. E93)	**monopolio natural** *situación económica en la que los costos de producción se minimizan teniendo una sola firma que produzca el producto*
natural resources land and all of the materials nature provides that can be used to make goods or services	(p. E8)	**recursos naturales** *la tierra y todos los materiales proporcionados por la naturaleza que pueden utilizarse para producir bienes o servicios*
need basic requirement for survival	(p. E7)	**necesidad** *requisito básico para la supervivencia*
nonprofit organization business that does not intend to make a profit for the goods and services it provides	(p. E68)	**organización sin ánimo de lucro** *empresa que no se lucra de los bienes y servicios que suministra*

O		ESPAÑOL
offset to counterbalance	(p. E145)	**compensar** *contrapesar*
open market operations (OMO) Fed's purchase or sale of U.S. government securities—bond notes and Treasury bills	(p. E128)	**operaciones de mercado abierto (OMO)** *compra o venta, por parte de la Reserva Federal, de valores del Gobierno estadounidense (bonos y letras del Tesoro)*
opportunity cost cost of the *next* best use of time or money when choosing to do one thing rather than another	(p. E10)	**costo de oportunidad** *costo de la siguiente mejor alternativa de utilizar tiempo o dinero cuando se opta por hacer una cosa en lugar de otra*

ECONOMICS GLOSSARY

option alternative, choice	(p. E9)	**opción** *alternativa, elección*
outsource to move factories to other countries with lower labor costs	(p. E177)	**tercerizar** *trasladar fábricas a otros países a menor costo laboral*

P		ESPAÑOL
partnership a business owned by two or more people	(p. E64)	**sociedad** *agrupación comercial de la que son dueñas dos o más personas*
picketing a union tactic in which striking workers walk with signs that express their grievances	(p. E77)	**piquete** *táctica sindical en la que los huelguistas caminan portando pancartas con sus reclamaciones*
potential possible	(p. E96)	**potencial** *posible*
price the monetary value of a product	(p. E31)	**precio** *valor monetario de un producto*
private good economic good that, when consumed by one person, cannot be used by another	(p. E91)	**bien privado** *bien económico que, cuando es consumido por una persona, no puede ser utilizado por otra*
private property rights the freedom to own and use our property as we choose as long as we do not interfere with the rights of others	(p. E61)	**derechos de propiedad privada** *libertad para poseer y utilizar la propiedad como se quiera siempre y cuando no se interfiera con los derechos de los demás*
privatization process of changing from state-owned businesses, factories, and farms to ones owned by private citizens	(p. E181)	**privatización** *proceso de traspasar empresas, fábricas y granjas de propiedad del Estado al sector privado*
producer person or business that provides goods and services	(p. E25)	**productor** *persona o empresa que suministra bienes y servicios*
product anything that is produced; goods and services	(p. E115)	**producto** *todo lo que es producido; bienes y servicios*
product market a market where goods and services are bought and sold	(p. E38)	**mercado de productos** *mercado en el que se compran y venden bienes y servicios*
productivity the degree to which resources are being used efficiently to produce goods and services	(p. E40)	**productividad** *grado de utilización eficiente de los recursos para producir bienes y servicios*
profit money a business receives for its products over and above what it cost to make the products	(pp. E16, E27, E59)	**ganancia** *dinero que recibe una empresa por sus productos por encima de lo que cuesta producirlos*
profit motive the driving force that encourages individuals and organizations to improve their material well-being	(p. E59)	**ánimo de lucro** *fuerza impulsora que alienta a individuos y organizaciones a mejorar su bienestar material*
promote to support or encourage	(p. E12)	**promover** *apoyar o alentar*
property tax tax on the value of land and property that people own	(p. E136)	**impuesto al patrimonio** *impuesto sobre el valor de las tierras y propiedades que poseen las personas*
protectionism use of tactics that make imported goods more expensive than domestic goods	(p. E167)	**proteccionismo** *tácticas empleadas para hacer que los bienes importados sean más costosos que los bienes nacionales*
public good economic good that is used collectively, such as a highway and national defense	(p. E91)	**bien público** *bien económico que es utilizado colectivamente, como las carreteras y la defensa nacional*

Q		ESPAÑOL
quota limit on the amount of foreign goods imported into a country	(p. E168)	**cuota** *límite impuesto a los bienes extranjeros que importa un país*

R		ESPAÑOL
rationing system of distributing goods and services without prices	(p. E32)	**racionamiento** *sistema de distribución de bienes y servicios sin precios*
real GDP GDP after adjustments for price changes	(p. E117)	**PIB real** *PIB resultante de los ajustes a las fluctuaciones de los precios*
recall government action that causes an unsafe product to be removed from consumer contact	(p. E94)	**retiro** *acción gubernamental para evitar el acceso de los consumidores a productos peligrosos*
recession period of declining economic activity lasting about six or more months	(p. E120)	**recesión** *periodo de depresión de las actividades económicas que dura seis o más meses*
rely to depend on	(p. E167)	**depender** *necesitar de*
reserve requirement percentage of a deposit that banks have to set aside as cash in their vaults or as deposits in their Federal Reserve district bank	(p. E128)	**encaje bancario obligatorio** *porcentaje del depósito que los bancos deben reservar en efectivo en sus bóvedas o depositar en el banco de la Reserva Federal de su distrito*
resources things used to make goods or services: natural resources, capital, labor, entrepreneurs	(p. E8)	**recursos** *cosas que se utilizan para producir bienes y servicios: recursos naturales, capital, trabajo, empresarios*
revenue money a government collects to fund its spending	(p. E131)	**ingresos** *dinero recaudado por el Gobierno para financiar sus gastos*
right-to-work laws state laws forbidding unions from forcing workers to join	(p. E77)	**leyes de derecho al trabajo** *leyes estatales que les prohíben a los sindicatos que obliguen a los trabajadores a afiliarse a ellos*

S		ESPAÑOL
sales tax tax paid by consumers at the time they buy goods or services	(p. E135)	**impuesto a las ventas** *impuesto que pagan los consumidores cuando compran bienes o servicios*
savings account an account that pays interest on deposits but allows only limited withdraws	(p. E81)	**cuenta de ahorros** *cuenta en la que el dinero depositado genera intereses pero de la cual solo se pueden retirar montos limitados*
scarcity situation of not having enough resources to satisfy all of one's wants and needs	(p. E9)	**escasez** *situación en la que no hay suficientes recursos para satisfacer los propios deseos o necesidades*
schedule table listing items or events	(p. E26)	**calendario** *tabla en la que se listan asuntos o actividades*
sector part or category distinct from other parts	(p. E38)	**sector** *parte o categoría distinta de otra*
services work that is done for us	(p. E7)	**servicios** *trabajos que se hacen por nosotros*
shortage situation in which the quantity of a good or service supplied at a certain price is less than the quantity demanded for it	(p. E35)	**desabastecimiento** *situación en la que la cantidad de un bien o servicio ofrecido a cierto precio es menor que la cantidad demandada por él*
social responsibility the obligation businesses have to pursue goals that benefit society as well as themselves	(p. E69)	**responsabilidad social** *obligación que tienen las empresas de alcanzar metas que beneficien tanto a la sociedad como a ellas mismas*

ECONOMICS GLOSSARY

English		Español
Social Security anti-poverty program that taxes working people and pays benefits to retirees	(p. E98)	**Seguridad Social** *programa contra la pobreza que grava a los trabajadores y paga beneficios a los pensionados*
socialism economy in which government owns some factors of production so it can distribute products and wages more evenly among its citizens; a type of command economy	(p. E15)	**socialismo** *economía en la que el Gobierno posee algunos de los factores de producción para poder distribuir productos y salarios de manera más equitativa entre los ciudadanos; tipo de economía planificada*
sole proprietorship a business owned and operated by a single person	(p. E63)	**empresa unipersonal** *empresa que posee y opera una sola persona*
specialization when people, businesses, regions, and/or nations concentrate on goods and services that they can produce better than anyone else	(p. E40)	**especialización** *cuando personas, empresas, regiones o países se concentran en bienes y servicios que pueden producir mejor que otros*
standard of living the material well-being of an individual, a group, or a nation as measured by how well needs and wants are satisfied	(pp. E39, E118, E179)	**nivel de vida** *bienestar material de un individuo, grupo o país que se mide según lo bien que se satisfagan los deseos y las necesidades*
stocks shares of ownership in a corporation; same as stock certificates	(p. E66)	**acciones** *participaciones de propiedad en una corporación; lo mismo que certificados de acciones*
strike when workers deliberately stop working in order to force an employer to give in to their demands	(p. E77)	**huelga** *cuando los trabajadores dejan de trabajar deliberadamente para obligar al empleador a ceder a sus exigencias*
subsidize to aid or support a person, business, institution, or undertaking with money or tax breaks	(p. E136)	**subsidiar** *ayudar o subvencionar a una persona, un negocio, una institución o una empresa con dinero o mediante exenciones de impuestos*
subsidy payment or other benefit given by the government to help a domestic producer	(p. E168)	**subsidio** *dinero u otro auxilio dado por el Gobierno para ayudar a un productor nacional*
Supplemental Nutrition Assistance Program (SNAP) welfare program that provides nutritional benefits to supplement the food budgets of needy families	(p. E98)	**Programa de Asistencia Nutricional Suplementaria (SNAP)** *programa de asistencia social que proporciona auxilios nutricionales para complementar los presupuestos alimentarios de familias en situación de necesidad*
supply amount of a good or service that producers are willing and able to sell over a range of prices	(p. E27)	**oferta** *cantidad de un bien o servicio que los productos quieren y pueden vender a determinado precio*
surplus situation in which the amount of a good or service supplied by producers at a certain price is greater than the amount demanded by consumers	(p. E35)	**excedente** *situación en la que la cantidad de un bien o servicio ofrecido por los productores a determinado precio es mayor que la cantidad demandada por los consumidores*
survey examination, review	(p. E73)	**encuesta** *examen, sondeo*

T		**ESPAÑOL**
tariff tax on an imported good	(p. E167)	**arancel** *impuesto sobre bienes importados*
Temporary Assistance for Needy Families (TANF) welfare program paid for by the federal government and administered by the individual states	(p. E97)	**Ayuda Temporal para Familias Necesitadas (TANF)** *programa de asistencia social subvencionado por el Gobierno federal y administrado por cada estado*
trade bloc group of countries, usually located in a particular region, that cooperate to expand free trade among one another	(p. E174)	**bloque comercial** *grupo de países, ubicados por lo general en una misma región, que cooperan para ampliar entre sí el libre comercio*
trade-off alternative you face when you decide to do one thing rather than another	(p. E9)	**trade-off** *alternativa a la que te enfrentas cuando optas por hacer una cosa en vez de otra*

traditional economy economic system in which the decisions of WHAT, HOW, and FOR WHOM to produce are based on traditions or customs (p. E13)

economía tradicional *sistema económico en el que las decisiones de QUÉ, CÓMO y PARA QUIÉN producir se basan en tradiciones o costumbres*

transfer to shift or reassign (p. E181)

transferir *trasladar o reasignar*

transmit send (p. E132)

transmitir *hacer llegar*

transparency the process of making business deals or conditions more visible to everyone (p. E71)

transparencia *proceso de hacer más visibles para todos los tratos o condiciones comerciales*

U · ESPAÑOL

unemployment rate percentage of people in the civilian labor force who are not working but are looking for jobs (pp. E74, E121)

tasa de desempleo *porcentaje de personas de la fuerza laboral civil que no están trabajando pero están buscando empleo*

V · ESPAÑOL

voluntary exchange the act of buyers and sellers freely and willingly engaging in market transactions (p. E59)

intercambio voluntario *acción de compradores y vendedores que participan libre y voluntariamente en transacciones mercantiles*

W · ESPAÑOL

want desire for a good or a service (p. E7)

deseo *apetencia de un bien o servicio*

welfare aid given to the poor in the form of money or necessities (p. E97)

asistencia *ayuda dada a los pobres en forma de dinero o artículos de primera necesidad*

workfare programs that require welfare recipients to exchange some of their labor for benefits (p. E98)

workfare *programas en los que los beneficiarios de la asistencia social deben intercambiar parte de su trabajo por auxilios*

ECONOMICS GLOSSARY

Civics Index

Note: Italicized page numbers refer to illustrations. The following abbreviations are used in the index: *m* = map; *c* = chart; *p* = photograph or picture; *g* = graph; *ptg* = painting; *crt* = cartoon; *q* = quote.

D

CIVICS INDEX

Economics Index

Note: Italicized page numbers refer to illustrations. The following abbreviations are used in the index: *m* = map; *c* = chart; *p* = photograph or picture; *g* = graph; *ptg* = painting; *crt* = cartoon; *q* = quote.